Office XP for Law Firms

Ed Jones and Romena Benjamin

Hungry Minds™

Best-Selling Books • Digital Downloads • e-Books • Answer Networks • e-Newsletters • Branded Web Sites • e-Learning

New York, NY ✦ Cleveland, OH ✦ Indianapolis, IN

Office XP for Law Firms

Published by
Hungry Minds, Inc.
909 Third Avenue
New York, NY 10022
www.hungryminds.com

Library of Congress Control Number: 2002100189

ISBN: 0-7645-4913-8

Printed in the United States of America

10 9 8 7 6 5 4 3 2 1

1B/SV/QU/QX/IN

Distributed in the United States by Hungry Minds, Inc.

Distributed by CDG Books Canada Inc. for Canada; by Transworld Publishers Limited in the United Kingdom; by IDG Norge Books for Norway; by IDG Sweden Books for Sweden; by IDG Books Australia Publishing Corporation Pty. Ltd. for Australia and New Zealand; by TransQuest Publishers Pte Ltd. for Singapore, Malaysia, Thailand, Indonesia, and Hong Kong; by Gotop Information Inc. for Taiwan; by ICG Muse, Inc. for Japan; by Intersoft for South Africa; by Eyrolles for France; by International Thomson Publishing for Germany, Austria, and Switzerland; by Distribuidora Cuspide for Argentina; by LR International for Brazil; by Galileo Libros for Chile; by Ediciones ZETA S.C.R. Ltda. for Peru; by WS Computer Publishing Corporation, Inc., for the Philippines; by Contemporanea de Ediciones for Venezuela; by Express Computer Distributors for the Caribbean and West Indies; by Micronesia Media Distributor, Inc. for Micronesia; by Chips Computadoras S.A. de C.V. for Mexico; by Editorial Norma de Panama S.A. for Panama; by American Bookshops for Finland.

For general information on Hungry Minds' products and services please contact our Customer Care department within the U.S. at 800-762-2974, outside the U.S. at 317-572-3993 or fax 317-572-4002.

For sales inquiries and reseller information, including discounts, premium and bulk quantity sales, and foreign-language translations, please contact our Customer Care department at 800-434-3422, fax 317-572-4002 or write to Hungry Minds, Inc., Attn: Customer Care Department, 10475 Crosspoint Boulevard, Indianapolis, IN 46256.

For information on licensing foreign or domestic rights, please contact our Sub-Rights Customer Care department at 212-884-5000.

For information on using Hungry Minds' products and services in the classroom or for ordering examination copies, please contact our Educational Sales department at 800-434-2086 or fax 317-572-4005.

For press review copies, author interviews, or other publicity information, please contact our Public Relations department at 317-572-3168 or fax 317-572-4168.

For authorization to photocopy items for corporate, personal, or educational use, please contact Copyright Clearance Center, 222 Rosewood Drive, Danvers, MA 01923, or fax 978-750-4470.

Credits

Acquisitions Editor
Greg Croy

Project Editor
Susan Christophersen

Technical Editor
Lee Musick

Copy Editors
Susan Christophersen, Leah Cameron, Kyle Looper

Media Development Specialist
Angela Denny

Senior Permissions Editor
Carmen Krikorian

Media Development Manager
Laura Carpenter Van Winkle

Project Coordinator
Nancee Reeves

Cover Design
Anthony Bunyan

Proofreader
Kate Talbot

Indexers
Sharon Hilgenberg, Johnna VanHoose Dinse

Senior Vice President, Technical Publishing
Richard Swadley

Vice President and Publisher
Mary Bednarek

Editorial Managers
Kyle Looper, Ami Frank Sullivan

About the Author(s)

Ed Jones is the author of more than 30 books about database, spreadsheet, and word processing programs, among other technology topics. He has worked in the area of computer technology for the last 24 years and has worked primarily with law firms for the last 18 years. Presently, he is a Senior Program Analyst at Wilmer, Cutler & Pickering, a Washington, D.C.-based international law firm. Over the years, he has performed database development for law firms and government agencies and has worked as a technical editor on numerous computer books. He is a Microsoft Certified Professional in the areas of SQL Server Administration and SQL Server Database Implementation.

Romena Benjamin has worked in law firms in the Washington, D.C. area for the last 27 years. Her career started during the days of dedicated word processors (CPT, Vydec, NBI, Lanier No Problem, and the like). Her career in computers began when one law firm assigned her the responsibility of creating a training program complete with documentation for teaching the firm's lawyers and secretaries WordPerfect. The firm had one computer at that time. Since then, Romena has designed and managed training programs and prepared training materials at several other law firms, including Dow, Lohnes & Albertson and Wilmer, Cutler & Pickering. Romena is currently working as a Practice Specialist at Wilmer, Cutler & Pickering, leading a team of Practice Analysts who provide training and support to the administrative departments. She is a Microsoft MOUS Certified Expert in Word and Outlook.

Acknowledgements

As with any major work (and both authors can attest to the fact that this was a major work!), this book could not have reached your possession without the combined efforts of many, and the authors would like to take the opportunity to extend our sincere thanks.

To the Hungry Minds team: Our thanks to Greg Croy, who shared our vision for a Microsoft Office book aimed specifically at the legal environment. A heartfelt round of thanks to Susan Christophersen, whose outstanding efforts in the editorial process were instrumental in making this book a top-of-the-line product. Thanks also to Lee Musick for providing a thorough technical review, and thanks to everyone in the Production department for their invaluable collective assistance in bringing this book to market.

Individually, Ed Jones would like to thank one of my professors, the Hon. Judge William D. Missouri, Circuit Court of Prince George's County, Maryland, for helping me to absorb more about the law than I would have believed possible during a single semester; Ed Macnamara and the entire IT staff at WC&P, for their assorted suggestions and for helping provide a real-world view of technology issues at a law firm over the years; the folks at *Lizard Lounge*, for providing an escape zone when the simultaneous demands of work, legal studies, and Microsoft certifications all weigh in at the same time; best bud Rod McCoy, for a sounding board in my numerous goals and projects in life; Timothous M. Jones, for his support in all that I do; and the partners, associates, and entire support staff at Wilmer, Cutler & Pickering, for making this a truly special place to work (okay, so call me a little biased here!)

Individually, Romena Benjamin would first like to give praise and honor to God from whom all blessings flow! Thanks to Ed Jones for giving me this opportunity and who believed I could do this; and for his guidance, support, and understanding. To Greg Croy and Susan Christophersen, a heartfelt thank you for your acceptance of this project and, most of all, for your understanding and support for this first-time author during the hard times. A warm thank you to Joyce Gwadz and Linda Fritts, partners at Dow, Lohnes & Albertson, for taking the time to meet and for their contributions of sample worksheets that are included on the CD. Thanks also to Brent Hensley and Workshare Technology for allowing us to include a demo of Deltaview 7.0 on the CD. Thanks to my wonderful husband, Bradley Benjamin, who loves me unconditionally (thank God!); you are the joy of my life! Thanks to my mother-in-law, Josephine Benjamin, who ran our home, cooked all the meals, and helped with our children while the book was being written. To my sons, Jonathan and Christopher who gave me love and support and lots of hugs and kisses; you are my reason why! Thanks to my mother, Virginia Johnson, I owe you my life. Thanks to my nephew and niece, Robert and Acquenetta Thurston, and their children, Courtnie and Cameron Thurston, for your love and support. Thanks to Gaynell Mayo and Gail Williamson for their spiritual support and guidance.

Dedication

To all those lost, 9-11-2001. May we never forget.

Preface

Welcome to *Office XP for Law Firms*. For attorneys, law clerks, paralegals, legal secretaries, and other professionals who work within law firms and legal departments, this is your comprehensive guide to the major applications that comprise Microsoft Office XP: Word, Excel, PowerPoint, Access, and Outlook. Our goal with this book is to tell you everything you need to know about using the major Office applications within the legal environment. This book is first and foremost a comprehensive reference, but it also helps you learn by example. And as a guide for law firms and legal professionals, this book is packed with legal-specific tips and techniques to get the most out of the Office applications.

Although each chapter is an integral part of the book as a whole, each chapter can also stand on its own. You can read this book in any order you want, skipping from chapter to chapter and topic to topic. (This book's index is particularly thorough, so rely on the index to find the topics that interest you.)

Is This Book For You?

If you use (or will soon use) any of the components of Microsoft Office within the legal environment, this book is for you. As experienced knowledge workers at a leading multinational law firm for a number of years, we've seen the migration of law firms and legal departments to Microsoft Office as the standard for document creation, spreadsheets, presentations, and workgroup-sized databases. We're also familiar with the information-processing needs that are specific to the legal environment, and we've written this book to address those needs. As we describe shortly, this book is divided into parts, with each of the first five parts describing one of the major Office applications and the last part detailing how to use the Office applications to produce content for the law firm intranet. If you're an Office beginner, you can start with the first chapter in each section and work to the end. If you have some Office experience, you can skim through the chapters that cover topics you already know.

How This Book Is Organized

We've divided this book into six parts. The first five deal with the following applications, in this order: Word, Excel, PowerPoint, Access, and Outlook (the e-mail, contact, and time/tasks management application that's included with Office). The last part looks at the law firm intranet and shows how the various Office applications can be used to provide content for intranets in mid-size and large law firms or in legal departments within corporations and government agencies.

Part I: Word

Producing words in the form of briefs, depositions, memos, and interrogatories, to name a few, is a fact of life in the practice of law. Word helps you efficiently produce these documents, and this part tells you what Word can do for you. For those of you migrating from WordPerfect or another word processor to Word, Chapter 1 takes the thorns of document conversion out of your side and offers a systematic process to make the conversion go smoothly. Chapters 2 through 12 examine all the details involved in creating and formatting documents, handling numbering and outlines, working with styles and templates, creating legal forms, setting up your page layout and printing your documents, using Mail Merge, tracking revisions, and making repetitive tasks easier through the use of macros.

Part II: Excel

This part describes Office's spreadsheet application, Excel. In Chapters 13 through 18, you can learn to create and format workbooks, print your worksheets, create graphics and charts, build simple databases within Excel, and use Excel macros.

Part III: PowerPoint

This part tells you how to use PowerPoint to create great presentations. Chapters 19 through 22 show you how to design, save, and print presentations, how to use the automated features of PowerPoint to aid in producing your presentations, how to add charts and graphics, how to create speaker's notes and audience handouts, and how to package presentations for travel. This entire section is also packed with techniques that will help attorneys and legal personnel prepare presentations that can be used in the courtroom, at arbitration hearings, and at negotiation meetings.

Part IV: Access

This part tells you how to put Access, the database manager included with many versions of Office, to work within the legal environment. Chapters 23 through 34 teach the basics of Access: how to create databases and tables, how to add, edit, and work with your data, how to design queries, forms, and reports, and how to use Access macros. Chapter 28 discusses how you can use Access to develop simple to moderately complex custom applications that those who have little or no Access experience can use. Chapters 29-34 explain the six ready-to-use Access applications that were developed specifically for legal users and are included on the CD-ROM. (You'll find these six chapters, labeled Bonus Chapters, on the CD-ROM as well.)

Part V: Outlook

This part provides details about Outlook, the flexible e-mail client, contact manager, and time and tasks management application. Chapters 35 through 41 cover the many aspects of Outlook, including using e-mail, managing your contacts, using the Journal and Notes features, managing your time with the Calendar feature, and working with Outlook folders. The final chapter in this part, Chapter 41, provides an easy-to-follow introduction to creating custom legal forms using Outlook.

Part VI: Office XP and the Law Firm Intranet

In Chapters 42 and 43, you'll find details of how you can use the various features in Word, Excel, PowerPoint, and Access to create content that can be used on an intranet of a law firm or legal department.

Appendixes

Finally, we've included several appendixes that you are likely to find useful. Appendix A contains a listing of third-party software and Web sites of specific interest to the legal profession. Appendix B points you in the right direction for trying out the new speech recognition feature that works with all the Office XP applications. And Appendix C steers you through the contents of the CD-ROM that comes with this book.

Conventions Used in This Book

We've written a thick book: There's a lot to say about using Office in the legal environment! Therefore, we've used several devices to help you find your way. You'll see many Note-type boxes scattered throughout the text. These brief notes (which may also be labeled *Tip*, *Caution*, *Warning*, or *Cross-Reference*) highlight useful tips, alert you to critical information, warn you about problems, or tell you where to go for more useful information.

We also routinely use sidebars to highlight related information, give an example, or discuss an item in greater detail.

When we write command names, we use a convention that shows you the sequence of menu name and filename that you need to follow to execute the command. So, when we want you to execute the New command from the File menu, we write File ⇨ New. In case you prefer using the keyboard instead of the mouse, we also indicate the keyboard strokes, or hotkeys, to use for commands by underlining them. The hotkeys require holding down the Alt key while pressing the underlined letters. For example, the File ⇨ New command sequence indicates that you should hold down the Alt key, press F, and then press N. The shorthand way of writing keyboard combinations like this shows up in the book as Alt+F+N.

Finally, the action referred to as click and drag means to hold down the primary mouse key while moving the mouse.

Reach Out

We'd love to hear from you! Feel free to send the authors specific comments regarding the material in this book. We'll do our best to respond, although we can't guarantee individual replies to every inquiry. The best way to reach us is via e-mail:

For the Word and Excel sections of the book: `romenab@law.com`

For the PowerPoint, Access, and Outlook sections of the book: `edwardj@law.com`

Contents

Part I

Word

Chapter 1

The Ins and Outs of Document Conversion

In This Chapter

- To convert or not to convert
- Converting from WordPerfect
- Converting to and from prior Word versions
- Converting to WordPerfect
- Saving to other file formats
- Dealing with common document conversion problems

THE LEGAL INDUSTRY USES A VARIETY of tools and software in order to meet the needs of clients. With regards to document processing, more and more legal professionals are choosing the software that their clients are using. Why? Because it removes one of the variables that can greatly impact the collaboration process between clients and lawyers on documents. This chapter assists you in understanding the conversion issues, primarily between WordPerfect and Word, and provides guidance in your approach to these issues.

To Convert or Not to Convert

Individual practitioners and law offices alike are often faced with the issue of converting documents from one word-processing file format to another. There are many reasons for this. One reason is that some law offices that moved from one word-processing program to another decided not to convert archived documents on the old system when they made the switch. But in situations where these very cases either resurface or continue, some of these documents (or portions thereof) need to be used. The necessary documents have to be converted to the new word-processing software.

You might also consider converting to different word-processing software in your firm because you consistently share documents with your clients, who use a different word processor.

If you are working on a legal document in one file format — say, WordPerfect — and you are collaborating on the document with your client, who is working in a different file format, such as Word, you and your client will run into problems, usually one hour before the document has to be filed in a court or agency, or must be in the hands of your favorite courier, or needs to be filed electronically.

The process of editing a document first in one file format and then in another, and going back and forth repeatedly, is commonly referred to as *round-tripping*. This co-author has been involved in the document production stage as a legal secretary, as well as in the support stage while assisting others with resulting document problems. My best advice is, *don't do it!* The problems caused by sending a document back and forth between file formats are the best way to corrupt your document and lose your sanity at the 11th hour! A decision to operate in one file format should be made in the initial stages of document production. If necessary, the document should be converted, and everyone working in that document should work in the same file format from that point on.

If you have access to the file format in which the document originated, then you may be able to avoid converting altogether by working on the document in its native format. If you want to use only a portion of a document that originated in a different file format from the one that you use, you will likely be tempted to just cut and paste. When you use Edit ⇨ Paste (or the Paste icon on the Standard toolbar) to bring copied text into Word from a different file format, you are also introducing formatting or codes from the file format from which you are copying. The formatting can change the formatting in the Word document, and the codes, if not removed, can later cause the document to become corrupt. If you must cut and paste from one file format to another, you should *always* use one of the following techniques to avoid future problems with the document: the Keep Text Only option on the Paste Options menu (see Figure 1-1), which is accessible by an on-screen icon that appears immediately after pasting something in Word, or the Unformatted text option in the Paste Special dialog box. The Paste Special dialog box is accessed by choosing the Edit ⇨ Paste Special menus (see Figure 1-2). Using either of these techniques enables you to leave behind, at least in some cases, many of the legacy codes and formats found in the original document.

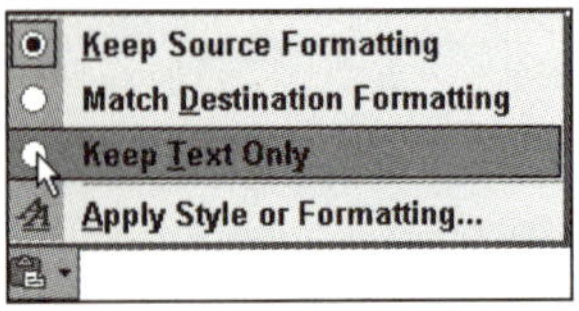

Figure 1-1: The Paste Options submenu

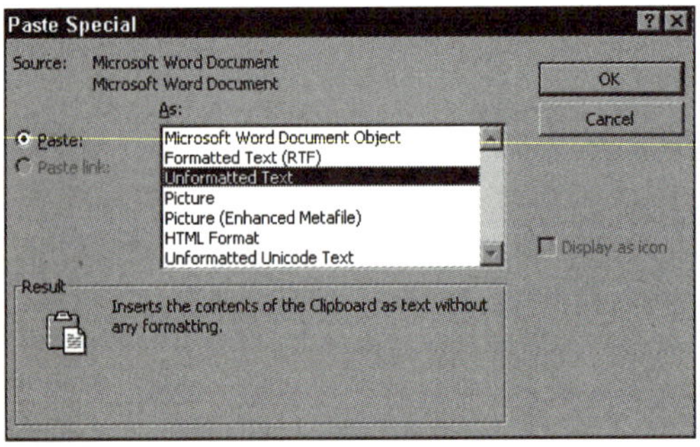

Figure 1-2: The Paste Special dialog box

You can choose File ⇨ Open to automatically convert into Word and open documents that originated in many different file types . Although this capability is a good thing, you should proceed with caution. Word allows you to directly open documents produced in different file formats, but you are, in many cases, also introducing formatting inherent in the source document, which can produce undesirable results (even corruption) in your document. We discuss some of these issues in the section of this chapter on converting WordPerfect documents to Word.

You can convert multiple documents simultaneously by using a batch conversion technique. To convert multiple files, follow these steps:

1. Move all the files to be converted to a single folder so that they are all in one location.
2. Choose File ⇨ New to open the New Document task pane. Click the General Templates hyperlink in the New From Template section of the task pane.
3. In the New dialog box that opens, click the Other Documents tab.
4. Double-click the Batch Conversion Wizard to open the Conversion Wizard dialog box; then click the Next button.
5. On the right side of the dialog box, click one of the following radio buttons as appropriate: Convert from Another Format to Word or Convert from Word to Another Format. In either case, click the drop-down list arrow under the option you have selected to choose the format to be converted. Then click the Next command button.
6. In the Folder Selection section, use the Browse button to navigate to the exact folder location of the file you are converting (Source); then click OK. Next, browse to the folder where you want to store the converted file (Destination), and click OK. Click the Next button.
7. The File Selection section of the Conversion Wizard appears. In the Available section, Word lists all the files it found in the folder you specified in Step 6 (which are of the file type you specified in Step 5). Double-click the names of the files you want to convert, to add them to the Convert section. If you add a file that you do not want to convert, double-click the name of the file in the Convert section to remove it. If you want to convert all the files listed, click the Select All button. You also can click the Remove All button to remove all the files added to the Convert box and then start over.
8. Click Finish to start the conversion process.

Converting from WordPerfect

When you are converting documents from WordPerfect to Word, you need to consider several aspects relating to the conversion process. Word automatically opens a WordPerfect document when you click File ⇨ Open menu and allows you to save that document into Word. However, the resulting file, though now open in Word, is still in many ways a WordPerfect document. The following sections discuss the changes you may need to make to a converted WordPerfect file.

Smoothing the way

The conversion process doesn't have to seem overwhelming or intimidating if you go about it methodically. The overall process (which we explain in detail) looks like this:

1. In Word, open the WordPerfect document you need to convert.
2. Set the Compatibility options.
3. Use File ⇨ Save As to save the document as a Word document.
4. Make sure that you have the Reveal Formatting task pane open.
5. Remove WordPerfect codes that remain in the document.
6. Deal with remaining formatting issues, such as restoring the fonts you lost in the conversion but want to use, and other issues.

The following sections explain each of these steps.

Setting the Compatibility options

Before clicking Save As to save a WordPerfect document to Word, you should check the compatibility options and change them from WordPerfect to Word. Until the compatibility options are changed, items such as footnotes and table rows may not behave correctly in Word because they are still using WordPerfect table row and footnote options. With the WordPerfect file that you plan to convert open, choose Tools ⇨ Options and click the Compatibility tab (see Figure 1-3). Click the arrow at the right of the Recommended Options For drop-down list to select the file format of the document you're about to convert. The options that Word recommends for that file type will automatically appear checked in the Options checklist. Figure 1-3 shows the compatibility options that Word recommends for converting a document from WordPerfect 6.*x*.

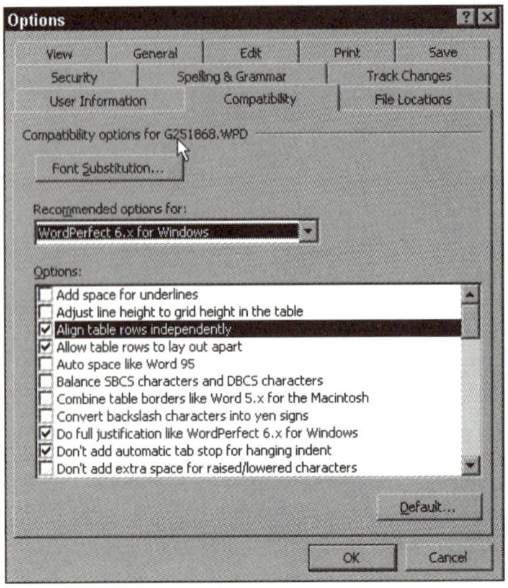

Figure 1-3: Setting the recommended compatibility options at the start saves work later.

Using Insert ⇨ File to convert a document

If you are trying to meet a deadline and you do not have time to convert a file using the techniques recommended here, click Insert ⇨ File to open the Insert File dialog box. Locate the WordPerfect file to be inserted and then click the Insert button to insert the WordPerfect file into a Word document. When you use this technique, the document automatically uses the Word 2002 Compatibility options so that it displays and prints correctly. You can then save the document as a Word 2002 file and work with it normally.

Using the Reveal Formatting task pane

We strongly recommend that you work with the Reveal Formatting task pane open when you're working with any converted file (see the discussion of this task pane in Chapter 2, "Understanding Word's Interface"). It is particularly important to use this task pane when working with a converted document or when you are cutting and pasting text from WordPerfect into a Word document. In the Reveal Formatting task pane, you can immediately identify formats such as character and paragraph formats applied using styles. You also can identify other formats that may have been applied without the use of styles, such as numbering or attributes such as underlining and boldface. Styles are discussed in detail in Chapter 4, "Creating Your Legal Document with Style." This formatting information is critical to know when you are trying to fix problems with paragraph numbering, and so on. Also, make sure to turn on the last two options in the Reveal Formatting task pane: Distinguish Style Source and Show All Formatting Marks.

Removing WordPerfect codes

If you use File ⇨ Open to open a WordPerfect file in Word after changing the compatibility options, you should also remove the WordPerfect codes. These codes would be needed only if the document were going to be converted back to WordPerfect again — which we strongly recommend against (see the "To Convert or Not to Convert" section early in this chapter). The two codes, in particular, that should be removed are the `{Advance}` and `{Private}` codes that can appear throughout the document. The appearance of these codes in a Word file immediately tells you that the document originated as a WordPerfect file. These codes can be removed one at a time or all simultaneously. To delete all these codes simultaneously, use these steps:

1. Select the WordPerfect code (including the braces before and after the code) that you want to remove; then copy it by choosing Edit ⇨ Copy, clicking the Copy icon on the Standard toolbar, or pressing Ctrl+C.
2. Choose Edit ⇨ Find.
3. In the Find and Replace dialog box that opens, click the Replace tab.
4. In the Find What text box of the Replace tab, press Ctrl+V to paste the WordPerfect code into that box. Leave the Replace With section of the Replace tab blank.
5. Click the Replace All command button to remove the WordPerfect code you selected from the document.

Substituting fonts

The fonts that were used in the WordPerfect document may no longer be available when it is converted to Word. If Word does not recognize the fonts in a WordPerfect file it is converting, the fonts in the converted file may not look the way you want them to look. To substitute fonts in the converted document for those that Word does not recognize, choose Tools ⇨ Options and click the Compatibility tab. Click the Font Substitution button to see a list of fonts that are not available in Word and a list of the fonts that Word is substituting for displaying and printing the document. The name of the original font as found in the WordPerfect document remains the same.

To select a font that is different from the one Word is recommending, click the font you want to change. Click the drop-down list beside the Substituted Font section of the dialog box and choose the font you want to use instead. If you want the names of the substitution fonts to display when working with the document, you will want to permanently replace the original fonts. Click the Convert

Permanently button in the lower portion of the dialog box for each substituted font that you want to convert permanently.

Applying paragraph formatting

Word provides two distinct methods of applying formatting. You can apply it directly (manually), paragraph by paragraph, by making use of the Format menu commands and the Formatting toolbar, or you can create styles. When a WordPerfect document is converted to Word, WordPerfect styles containing paragraph codes are converted to Word paragraph styles. However, if paragraphs were formatted manually in WordPerfect, the result may not be styled paragraphs in Word.

The Reveal Formatting task pane shows the formats that are included in styles or that are applied using the direct method. Figure 1-4 is an example of what you might see in the Reveal Formatting task pane when the insertion point is in a paragraph in which direct formatting was applied. Direct formats are applied and modified one by one. We recommend that you instead create a style containing the formats you want to apply to those paragraphs. To remove manual formatting from a paragraph so that you can create a style or eliminate the formatting altogether, select the paragraph, including the paragraph mark, and then press Ctrl+Q. All directly or manually applied paragraph formats are eliminated.

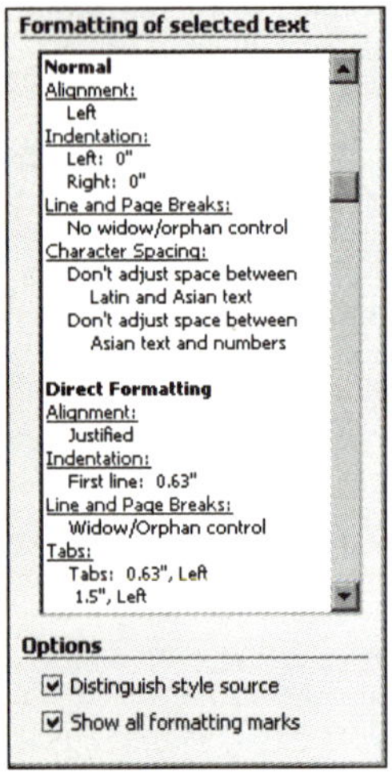

Figure 1-4: Formatting in a converted document displays in the Reveal Formatting task pane.

To easily create a paragraph style and apply it to all the paragraphs you want to receive the formats, follow these steps:

1. Select some text, or click in a paragraph that is formatted similarly to the way you want.
2. Click Format ⇨ Styles and Formatting to open the Styles and Formatting task pane.
3. Click the Select All button in the task pane. Word automatically selects all paragraphs in the document that are currently similarly formatted.
4. Click the New Style button, give the style a name (such as *Pldtxt* for body text used in a pleading) and choose a style type. Word has four types of styles: character, paragraph, table, and list. Character styles affect words, paragraph styles affect an entire paragraph, table styles are used in tables, and list styles are used to format lists.

5. Click the Format button and choose the format you want to modify from the submenu that appears. After you have completed making your modifications, click OK to close each of the open dialog boxes. The name of your new style appears in the Styles and Formatting task pane, and the text to which it will be applied is still highlighted. Click your new style name in the task pane, and the style you created is automatically applied to all the selected paragraphs.

Numbering paragraphs

In the original WordPerfect document, paragraph numbering would have been applied by inserting numbers using the Insert menu options or by using styles. During conversion, Word determines how to handle paragraph numbering depending on how it was originally applied in WordPerfect. If styles were used to apply numbering, then these styles translate into paragraph styles in Word and can be modified. If, however, numbering was applied using the Insert menu in WordPerfect, then this does not translate into automatic numbering in Word but rather numbering with no formatting attached. You can modify the numbering style with the following steps:

1. In the Reveal Formatting task pane, click the hyperlink for the numbering style you want to modify. Clicking the hyperlink opens the Style box shown in Figure 1-5.

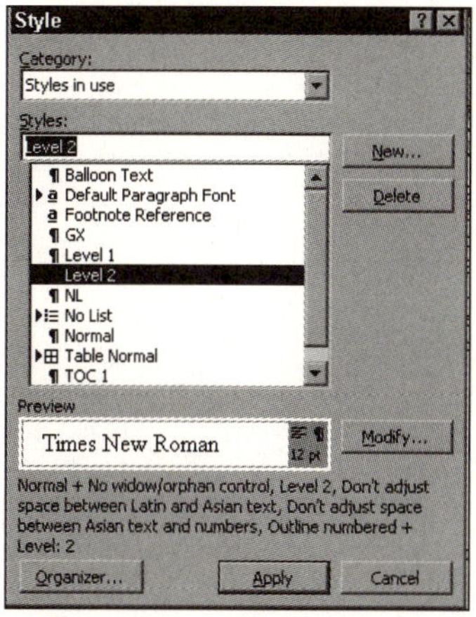

Figure 1-5: In the Style dialog box, select the style you want to modify.

2. Select the style you want to modify and click the Modify button. The Modify Style dialog box opens.
3. Click the Format button and choose Numbering from the submenu that appears (see Figure 1-6). (If you wanted to change the spacing, line or page breaks, and alignment of the numbered paragraphs, you would choose the Paragraph option from this submenu.) The Bullets and Numbering dialog box opens. This dialog box contains four tabs representing categories of bullets and numbering styles that you can apply (see Figure 1-7).
4. The numbering template in use is surrounded by a black border. Click the Customize button to open the Customize Numbering dialog box. Select the options that you want to set and then click OK.

CROSS-REFERENCE: See Chapter 6 for more about applying numbering.

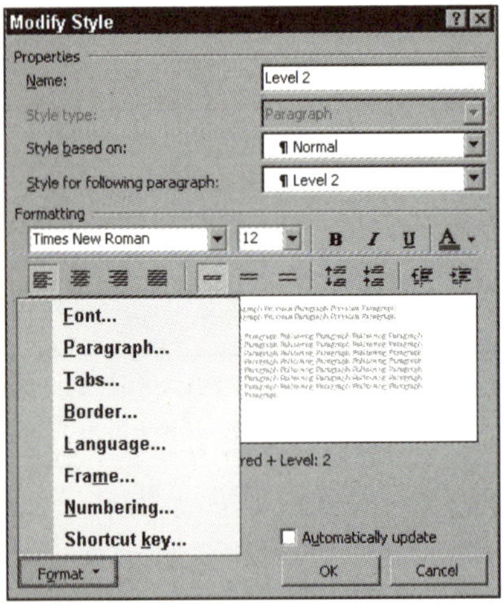

Figure 1-6: In the Modify Style dialog box, select the element that you want to modify from the submenu that appears.

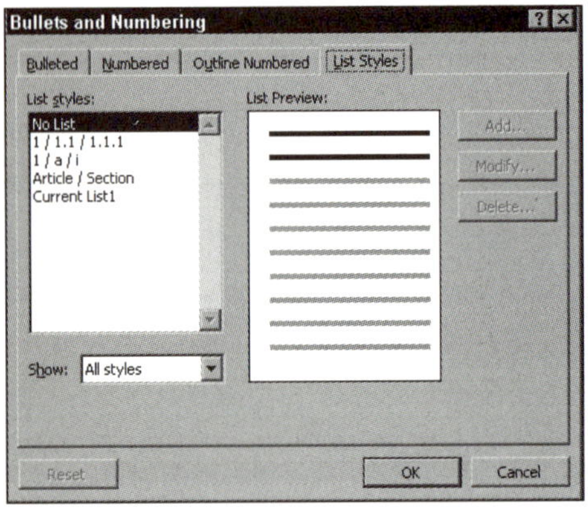

Figure 1-7: The Bullets and Numbering dialog box

Checking other format changes following conversion to Word

The preceding sections describe changes that may need to be made to a converted document, but the types of changes discussed so far are not the only items that you may need to change. Table 1-1 lists other features, important to legal professionals, that are supported or not supported when you convert to Word. Some changes have to be made because Word simply does not have a comparable feature to convert it to or because Word handles an item differently than WordPerfect.

Before you convert documents from WordPerfect to Word, you may want to take a look at the list of conversion issues found by using Word's Help feature. You can access Word's Help feature by clicking in the Ask a Question text box in the upper-right corner of the Word window or by choosing the Help ⇨ Microsoft Word Help menu. Type **Convert between Word and WordPerfect** to see a longer list of conversion issues.

Table 1-1
Supported and Unsupported WordPerfect Features in Word

WordPerfect Feature	***Supported in Word?***
Blank lines between paragraphs	Yes. Set the spacing before and after paragraphs by clicking Format ⇨ Paragraph and choosing the desired options.
Newspaper/parallel columns	Yes. Parallel columns are automatically converted to tables. Columns that were anchored to a particular page are changed to newspaper columns.
Pagination	Yes. Word applies section breaks at the point in the document where changes in page numbering occurs. To view page breaks, use the View ⇨ Normal menus. Remove or add section breaks as necessary.
Table of Contents and Table of Authorities codes	These items convert well. However, if updating the tables does not produce desired results, tables may need to be redefined and regenerated. These features are discussed in Chapter 6, "Formatting and Polishing Text."
Cross-References	No. Word does not recognize the Cross-Reference codes used by WordPerfect. Cross-references must be re-created by using Word's Insert ⇨ Reference ⇨ Cross-Reference options. This feature is discussed in Chapter 5, "Working with Outlines and Long Documents."
Footnotes	Yes. However, if a footnote style in WordPerfect does not exist in Word, footnotes may lose formatting.
Footnote references	Yes. However, you may lose styles, which means that the footnote number in the text and in the footnote itself may appear in the Normal style.
Header A/Header B, Footer A/Footer B	No. Word allows only one header or footer per section. Word inserts a section break for each header or footer change in the converted document. Unnecessary section breaks can be removed using the Edit ⇨ Find feature. Insert section breaks before creating a new header or footer in the document.
Redlining	Yes. This converts to Track Changes. Track Changes is discussed in Chapter 11, "Keeping Track of Changes."
Strikeout	Yes. Strikeout is converted to strikethrough, which is Word's name for the same feature. Text appears the same in both programs.
Line numbers	No. Line numbering must be reapplied. See Chapter 3, "Creating and Working with Documents," for details on applying line numbering.

Converting to and from Prior Word Versions

Although you may have made the switch to Word 2002, you will undoubtedly receive some legal documents created in earlier versions of Word from clients or co-counsel or as attachments to e-mail messages. If you are collaborating on documents with people who use earlier versions of Word, there are a few things to understand.

Opening and saving to Word 97 or Word 2000 file formats

If you need to open a Word 97 or Word 2000 document in Word 2002, you can do so without hesitation. You also can save a file back to its native format by clicking File ⇨ Save As and selecting the format you want to save the document in with the Save as Type option. One thing to keep in mind is that as a Word 2002 user, you may have used features in your document that may not be available in Word 97 or earlier versions. When saving, you can see a list of features in the document that Word will convert by following these steps:

1. Select Tools ⇨ Options and click the Save tab.
2. Check the Disable Features Introduced After box and choose the appropriate version of Word (see Figure 1-8).
3. Click OK to close the dialog box.

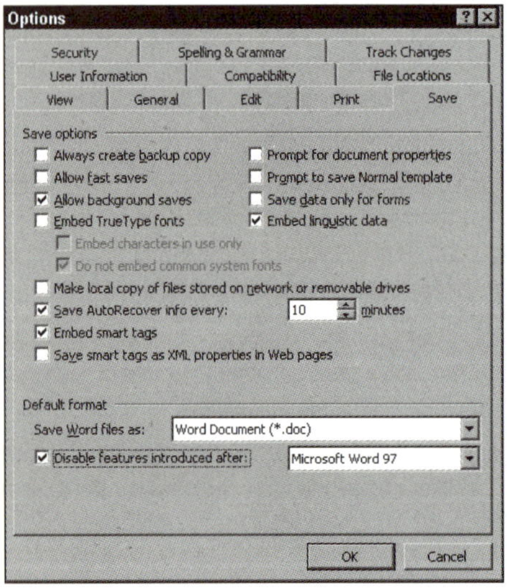

Figure 1-8: The Save tab of the Options dialog box

Opening and saving in Word 95, 6.0, 2.0, or earlier versions

Word 6.0 and Word 2.0 each use different file formats, and each file format is also different from Word 97 and Word 2000. You can open each of these file formats directly into Word 2002, and the formatting is preserved. Although a converter is not necessary to *open* these file formats in Word 2002, a converter is necessary when *saving* a Word 2002 document in one of these file formats. Word 2002 comes with a converter that allows you to choose Word 2x for Windows or Word 6.0/95 in the

Save as Type section of the Save As dialog box (click File ⇨Save As and then click the arrow next to the Save s Type box).

Converting to WordPerfect

There will likely come a time when you need to share a document with a client or co-counsel who is using WordPerfect. Word 2002 does come with converters that allow you to save a document in one of several WordPerfect file formats. Word comes with these WordPerfect converters:

- WordPerfect 5.0 (secondary file)
- WordPerfect 5.1 for DOS
- WordPerfect 5.1 or 5.2 (secondary file)
- WordPerfect 5.x for Windows
- WordPerfect 5.0 (*.doc)

If you need to share a Word 2002 document with someone who uses WordPerfect 6.1 for Windows, you can save the file as a WordPerfect 5.1 for DOS file that the intended recipient can then open in WordPerfect 6.1 for Windows.

It is important to know that certain changes may occur in documents converted from Word to WordPerfect. First, fonts available in WordPerfect are different from fonts available in Word. As a result, font appearance, size, or type of font found in the document may change after being converted to WordPerfect.

Other formatting, such as first-line indents, line spacing, and word spacing, will not be preserved in the same manner because WordPerfect and Word handle each of these formats differently. Changes may have to be made to the converted file in WordPerfect to solve these problem areas.

You may find that other elements in a converted WordPerfect file have changed as well. In particular, text included in text boxes in the Word document may be positioned differently inside a text box in WordPerfect. The text box converts fine, but the text may have moved within the text box. Graphics will usually convert, but any attributes applied to the graphics in the Word document may change after the document is converted to WordPerfect.

Saving to Other File Formats

In addition to the capability to save in various Word and WordPerfect file formats, Word 2002 also comes with the following converters, which display in the Save as Type section of the Save As dialog box:

- Web Page
- Web Archive
- Document Template
- Rich text format
- Plain text
- MS-DOS text with Layout
- Text with Layout
- Word 4.0 for Macintosh

- Word 5.0 for Macintosh
- Word 5.1 for Macintosh
- Word 97-2002 & 6.0/95
- Works 2000
- Works 4.0 for Windows

If the file format you want to save in is not on the Save as Type list in the Save As dialog box, you may need to install the converter. (Alternatively, you could also save the file in Rich Text format, which is recognized by many different programs.) To install a converter you do not currently have available, you will need to run the Office XP setup program — not to reinstall Word, but to add the specific converters you need.

Dealing with Common Document Conversion Problems

Following are some troubleshooting tips for handling issues that frequently arise during conversion from WordPerfect to Word.

Opening WordPerfect files containing graphics

One problem you may encounter when opening and converting WordPerfect documents is your computer "freezing" because the document contains a WordPerfect graphic file that Word does not understand. You might see an errorPage: 14
message indicating that the file appears to be corrupt and that conversion might be incomplete. If you have the WordPerfect program and the graphic files available to you, open the document in WordPerfect and remove the graphics. After you convert the file, reinsert the graphics in Word, using the Insert ⇨ Picture ⇨ From File menu options.

Cannot open a WordPerfect file

This is a common problem seen particularly when a WordPerfect file has arrived attached to an e-mail message. You double-click the attachment and are unable to open the file. Prior to WordPerfect 6.1, WordPerfect users were able to use any extension (except those used by other programs, of course) in the filename of the document. However, opening these files posed a challenge for Word because it simply could not recognize the file as a WordPerfect file. To solve this problem (assuming that the file is truly a WordPerfect file), simply rename the file with ***.wpd** as the file extension. Word can then open the file. Because you will not be able to double-click the file attachment to open it, you can rename the file when saving the attachment in your e-mail software.

Converted WordPerfect file appears corrupt

Try as we might, we cannot avoid being hit with some document corruption. Document corruption is when parts of a document contain a string of `^z` codes and text is missing before or after the code. Or junk appears in place of some of the text in a document. One workaround is to click Insert ⇨ File, as was mentioned earlier in this chapter, to bring the document into a more stable Word environment. Also, you can move everything to a new, uncorrupted document by following these steps:

1. Select everything in the document, except the final paragraph marker. The final paragraph marker contains many of the formatting codes used by Word. By not selecting the final paragraph marker, you leave behind some of the behind-the-scenes formatting that may be causing problems.

2. Open a new Word document.
3. Paste the text in the new document.
4. Save the new document, naming it as desired.
5. Delete the old document.

Summary

This chapter covered the main issues involved in converting other document formats to Word 2002, with special emphasis on WordPerfect conversion issues. This chapter discussed the following:

- Making the decision of whether to convert a document fully into Word. Also discussed was the issue of round-tripping, which we strongly urge you to avoid doing as much as possible.
- An overview of the WordPerfect-to-Word conversion process and a detailed breakdown of the issues to address and the Word features to use to minimize the work and potential problems.
- Other file formats that Word is capable of converting, as well as the possible need to install converters that weren't originally installed.
- Troubleshooting tips for common WordPerfect conversion issues.

The next chapter provides the basics of Word's interface so that you can quickly learn to make your way around in Word with ease.

Chapter 2

Understanding Word's Interface

In This Chapter

- Becoming acquainted with the Word window
- Using the toolbars, status bar, and scroll bars
- Viewing a document with Word's various viewing options
- Changing the default unit of measurement

WORD IS A WORD PROCESSING PROGRAM that you can use to create all your legal documents, such as correspondence (engagement letters, cover letters, law firm opinion letters) and legal briefs or pleadings (memos in support, memoranda of points and authorities) in whatever format the court you are filing in requires. In other words, you can safely choose Word as your word processor and know that it will meet all your legal document needs. This chapter introduces you to Word's interface and basic tools.

Getting Acquainted with Word 2002

When you first open Word 2002, a blank document named *Document1* displays on-screen in Print Layout view. (If your document doesn't appear in Print Layout view, feel free to change to that view so that you can follow along and identify the various elements of the screen. Just choose Print Layout from the View menu.) Above the Word window you will see the Menu bar and the Standard and Formatting toolbars. At the bottom of the Word window is the status bar and horizontal scroll bar; the vertical scroll bar appears at the right of the window. Also in Print Layout view are both the horizontal and vertical rulers. As with all the Office XP applications, you will also see one of the newest additions, the task pane. The elements you see when you open Word can be customized to meet the general document production needs of a particular law firm or for the individual legal professional. Figure 2-1 shows the elements of the Word window, detailed in the following list:

- **Print Layout view:** The Print Layout view is just one of the ways in which to view a document in the Word window. This view allows you to see how headers, footers, and other document elements will look when the document is printed.
- **Document window:** The wide-open area of the screen is where you add text or graphics. You can have more than one document showing at the same time on-screen by using the Window ⇨ Split command (see "Splitting a window" later in this chapter).
- **Insertion point:** The small vertical bar that you see blinking on-screen is the cursor, which indicates the insertion point for any text or other elements that you're working with.
- **Menu bar:** This bar is located at the top of the Word window. Beginning with File at the far left, the Menu bar consists of nine categories of menus containing Word's features. You select the menu you want to use by clicking the menu name and then clicking the desired option from

the next menu that drops down from the original one. Or if you prefer to use the keyboard, you can open a menu by holding down the Alt key and typing the letter that appears with an underline (such as File) in the menu name. Menus are totally customizable, as described later in this chapter.

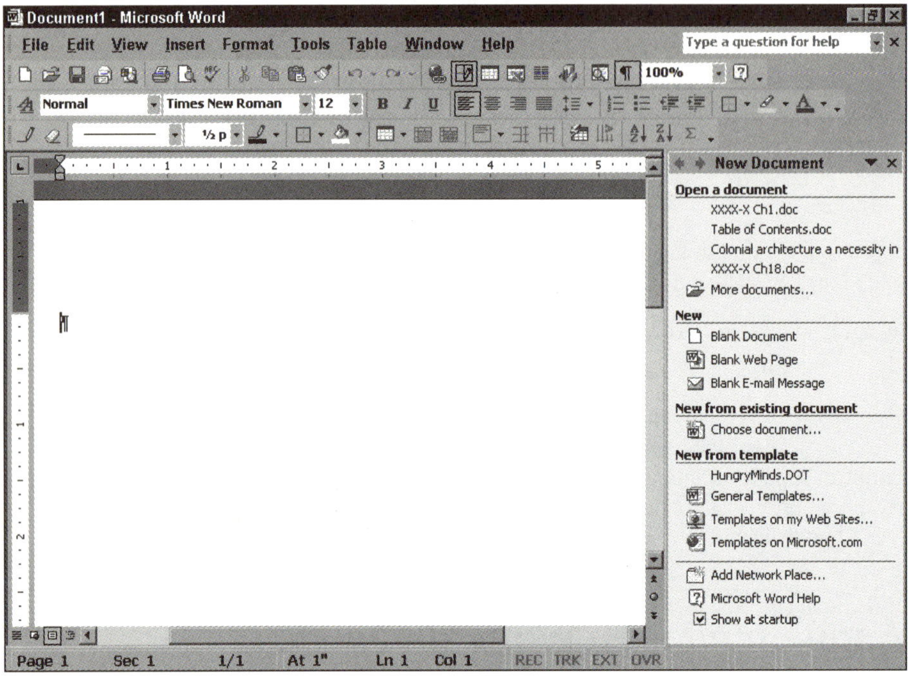

Figure 2-1: The elements of the Word window

- **Toolbars:** Toolbars appear below the Menu bar, and the Standard and Formatting toolbars are usually visible by default. Toolbars contain a variety of buttons that offer single-click access to commonly used features or dialog boxes in which additional options can be set. Word comes with a total of 18 toolbars, all of which can be viewed or removed from your view at will. You can customize the toolbars to include or remove desired buttons (see "Customizing toolbars" later in this chapter).
- **Status bar:** As its name suggests, the status bar gives you details about the current state of the Word document you have displayed on-screen. It shows, for example, the current page number, how many total pages the document contains, and other details. The status bar is located at the bottom of the Word window and is discussed in more detail later in the chapter.
- **Scroll bars:** You use the scroll bars to move around in the document vertically or horizontally. As you use the vertical scroll bars to move up or down through your document, you can see the page reference and major headings displayed in a pop-up box alongside the scroll bar. Another technique you can use to move through the document is to click the arrows at either end of the horizontal or vertical scroll bars.
- **Horizontal ruler:** This ruler enables you to view left and right margin settings, as well as tab and indent settings, for the *current* paragraph (the paragraph containing the the blinking cursor). You can change the margin and other settings by dragging or double-clicking on the ruler.

- **Vertical ruler:** You can use this ruler to change top and bottom margins and to change the row height of table rows. Double-clicking in the area of the Vertical ruler opens the Page Setup dialog box, in which you can set additional page options.
- **Task pane:** The task pane is a new addition to Word 2002 and can be quite helpful. For more information on how to use the task pane, refer to the section "Understanding the task pane" later in this chapter.
- **ScreenTips:** ScreenTips provide helpful information about a toolbar button, a description of an option in a dialog box, or an explanation of how to use a particular feature. ScreenTips appear automatically if you hover the mouse pointer directly over a particular button on the toolbar. In dialog boxes, you can display a ScreenTip about a particular option by clicking the question mark on the title bar of the dialog box and then clicking the option in question.

Until a document is saved in Word, it is unnamed and *Document1* appears in the title bar. Each time you create a new document during a session with Word, the document number increments by 1.

Using the status bar and scroll bars

The status bar and the horizontal and vertical scroll bars all display by default upon entering Word. These elements are most helpful for navigating around your document and for determining, well, the status of your document. If you do not see one of these elements, choose Tools ⇨ Options; then, in the Options dialog box that appears, click the View tab. In the Show section, check the elements that you want visible and uncheck the elements you want to remove from view. Figure 2-2 shows the View tab open, with check marks beside each of these and some other elements.

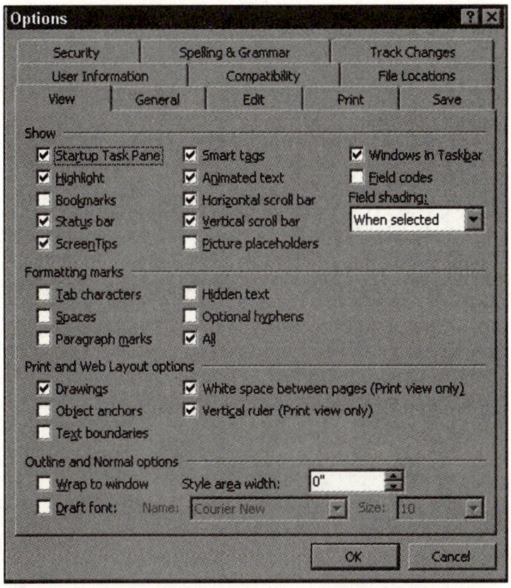

Figure 2-2: Use the View tab in the Options dialog box to control the display of the status bar and the scroll bars.

Using the Standard toolbar

The Standard toolbar is displayed by default in Word. It consists of commonly used commands. The exact tools that appear on the Standard toolbar, along with their order, can be modified automatically by Word as you use the program. Because there are so many tools that can appear, this "dynamic" behavior helps to make your toolbar appear less cluttered and complicated. The list that follows describes some of the more common tools that appear on the Standard toolbar; don't be concerned if you don't see all these tools or if you see different tools on your version of the Standard toolbar:

- **New Blank Document:** Click to create a new document
- **Open:** Click to display an existing document on-screen
- **Save:** Click to save your work in the document currently open
- **E-mail:** Sends the contents of the current document as the body of an e-mail message
- **Search:** Displays the Basic Search task pane so that you can find files, Web pages, and Outlook items
- **Print:** Prints the document that's currently displayed
- **Print Preview:** Shows how your printed document would look
- **Spelling and Grammar:** Checks the spelling and grammar of a selection or the entire document
- **Cut:** Removes the selected text or object from the document and stores it in the Clipboard
- **Copy:** Makes a copy of the selected text or object and places it in the Clipboard
- **Paste:** Places the contents of the Clipboard into the document at the location of the insertion point
- **Format Painter:** Copies the format of the selected text so that it can be applied to other text
- **Undo:** Undoes the effects of the previous edit
- **Redo:** Redoes an edit you previously undid
- **Insert Hyperlink:** Adds an active hyperlink to your document
- **Tables and Borders:** Displays the Tables and Borders toolbar
- **Insert Table:** Adds a table at the location of the insertion point
- **Show/Hide:** Displays or hides non-printing characters
- **Zoom:** Changes the magnification used to display the document
- **Microsoft Word Help:** Invokes Word's Help system

Figure 2-3 shows the Standard toolbar as it appears on a typical system. The tools on this toolbar correspond to those detailed in the preceding list. If you want to use any additional tools on the Standard toolbar (those that aren't displayed), you can click the Toolbar Options indicator at the right side of the Standard toolbar.

Figure 2-3: The Standard toolbar contains the buttons for standard functions such as creating a document, saving, printing, and so on.

Using the Formatting toolbar

The Formatting toolbar (see Figure 2-4) contains buttons and options for changing the formatting of the current paragraph. Formats added using buttons on this toolbar are either directly applied to the entire paragraph containing the insertion point or applied only to selected text. The types of formats you can apply using the default Formatting toolbar are as follows (listed here in the order of how they appear from left to right on the toolbar):

- **Style:** Applies the displayed style to the current paragraph.
- **Font and Font Size:** Changes the font style and point size of selected text. Selections are made from the drop-down list accessed by clicking the arrows beside each option.
- **Bold (B), Italic (I), and Underline (U):** Clicking one of these buttons applies the corresponding attribute to the selected text.
- **Alignment:** Clicking one of the four alignment buttons (Align Left, Center, Align Right, and Justify) changes the alignment of the paragraph that contains the cursor. Alignment changes affect the entire paragraph and take effect without your having to *select* (highlight) the text.
- **Numbering:** Adds numbering to the selected paragraphs.
- **Bullets:** Creates or removes a bulleted list from the current paragraph.
- **Decrease Indents:** Moves the selected paragraph to the previous tab stop.
- **Increase Indents:** Moves the selected paragraph to the next tab stop.
- **Borders:** Adds or removes borders around the selected text or object (such as a graphic).

Figure 2-4: The Formatting toolbar

As is the case with the Standard toolbar, Word doesn't display all the possible Formatting toolbar tools all the time. The tools displayed and the order in which they appear are automatically adjusted by Word, based on your usage pattern. To see all the tools available, click on the Toolbar Options indicator at the right side of the Formatting toolbar.

CAUTION: Although the Formatting toolbar buttons are easily accessible, using them to format your paragraphs is not the best method of applying formats in Word. Changing the formatting of individual elements can be time-consuming because you have to make them one at a time. You should include as many formats as possible in your styles (which we discuss in detail in Chapter 3).

Adding and removing toolbars

To add a toolbar to view on-screen, right-click over the toolbar area (or click View ⇨ Toolbars on the Menu bar). In the list that appears, click the name of the toolbar you want to use. Each time you add a toolbar to your view, it usually appears in the upper portion of the Word window, below the Standard and Formatting toolbars.

TIP: Adding too many toolbars at one time can reduce the amount of workspace available for your document, and the upper portion of your screen can become quite congested. To save on workspace, add toolbars to your view only as you need them, and remove them from view when you have completed your work.

You can make a toolbar available for use in the document window itself, where the toolbar's size can be reduced and its features are close at hand as you work. To drag a toolbar to the document window and to resize it, use the steps that follow.

1. Position the pointer over the faint gray vertical bar on the left side of the toolbar. If you are in the correct position, the pointer changes to a four-headed arrow.
2. Hold down the primary (left) mouse button and move the mouse to drag the toolbar to the desired location.
3. Drag the borders of the toolbar until it is the desired size.

If you have toolbars showing that you no longer need to use, consider removing these toolbars from your view by right-clicking over the toolbar area and clicking the name of the toolbar you want to remove from your view.

Customizing toolbars

You can modify existing toolbars to include your frequently used commands, and you can remove commands that you rarely use. For example, Word allows you to open multiple documents simultaneously. (All you need to do is open them; Word keeps track of all the documents and allows you to switch among them, using either the Window menu or the buttons on the Windows task bar.) If you frequently work with multiple documents open simultaneously, you can eliminate having to go into each document to close it if you use the Close All command. You can add the Close All command to the Standard toolbar (or to any toolbar, for that matter) to make it easier to close all open documents. The following sections detail the steps for adding and removing buttons to customize a toolbar.

Adding a button to a toolbar

To make changes to an existing toolbar, first add that toolbar to your view (see the preceding section). Next, right-click the toolbar area and choose Customize, which opens the Customize dialog box. To complete the process of adding a command button to an existing toolbar, follow these steps:

1. Right-click over the toolbar area, or click View ⇨ Toolbars on the Menu bar.
2. In the list that appears, click the name of the toolbar you want to use.
3. Right-click the toolbar area and choose Customize to open the Customize dialog box.
4. In the Customize dialog box, click the Commands tab and choose the category of commands you want to use.
5. From the Commands section, drag the desired button up to the target toolbar and into the exact position where you want it situated.

NOTE: If you return to your document after working with toolbars or other elements and find that your blinking cursor has gone away, simply click the mouse in the Word window. You can then pick up where you left off with your work.

Figure 2-5 shows the Close All button about to be placed on the Standard toolbar to appear to the right of the Save button, after the button has been dragged from the Customize dialog box. Note that a large, bold insertion point marks the spot on the toolbar where the new button is going (you'll see this more easily on your screen).

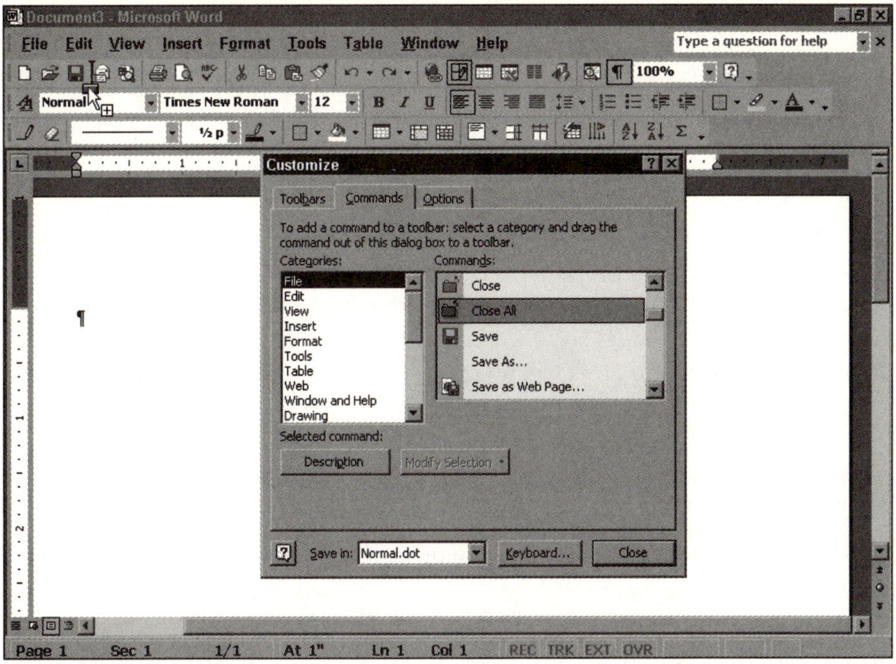

Figure 2-5: The Close All button was taken from the Customize dialog box and appears on the Standard toolbar.

Removing a button from a toolbar

If you want to remove a toolbar button, first make sure that the toolbar in question appears on-screen. Then follow these steps:

1. Make the toolbar you're removing the button from visible by right-clicking over the toolbar area or clicking View ⇨ Toolbars on the Menu bar. In the list that appears, click the name of the toolbar you want to use.
2. Right-click the toolbar area and choose Customize. (You will not actually use any of the options in the Customize dialog box to remove the button, but it must be open nonetheless.)
3. Click to drag the desired toolbar button down and off the toolbar. The button disappears.

There is an alternative method of removing a toolbar button — a method preferred by some people. (We'll let you choose which method you prefer. They both have the same result.)

1. Make the toolbar you're removing the button from visible by right-clicking over the toolbar area or clicking View ⇨ Toolbars on the Menu bar. In the list that appears, click the name of the toolbar you want to use.
2. Hold down the Alt key as you drag the desired button down and off the toolbar. The button disappears.

Customizing menus

Word does not limit your customization efforts to toolbars. You also can completely customize the menus used in Word. The steps you follow are very similar to the steps followed to customize toolbars. The following sections describe how you can edit Word's menus.

Adding your own menu

If you want, you can create your own menus. Many Word users do this so that they can keep their favorite menu commands in one place or to add their macros to a menu of their own making. To create your own top-level menu (one that appears right on the menu bar), follow these steps:

1. Choose the Customize option from the Tools menu, or right-click the menu bar and choose Customize. Word displays the Customize dialog box.
2. Make sure that the Commands tab is selected.
3. In the Categories list (left side of the dialog box), choose New Menu. This is the very last option in the list. The Commands list (right side of the dialog box) should change so that it has only a single option in it.
4. Choose the New Menu option from the Commands list and drag it to the position you want on the menu bar.

At this point, you have a new menu on the menu bar, called *New Menu*, and the Customize dialog box should still be open. You can rename your new menu by following these steps:

1. Right-click the menu you just added. Make sure that you right-click the actual menu, not anything in the Customize dialog box. Word displays a menu containing the properties of the menu item.
2. Click in the Name box and change the existing name (*New Menu*) to the name you want used.
3. If you want to define a shortcut key for the menu — one that you use in conjunction with the Alt key to invoke the menu from the keyboard — then simply place an ampersand (&) immediately before the letter you want used for the shortcut key. For instance, if the name of your new menu is *Romena* and you want the *R* to be the shortcut key, the name you type for the menu is **&Romena**.
4. Press Enter. Word updates the name of the menu.
5. Close the Customize dialog box.

Now you have a brand-new menu, but it doesn't do anything; there are no menu options available when you choose the menu. Read on to the next section to learn how to add menu items to an existing menu.

Adding a menu item

You can add menu items either to an existing Word menu or to a new menu that you create according to the steps in the previous section. To add items to a menu, follow these steps:

1. Choose the Customize option from the Tools menu, or right-click the menu bar and choose Customize. Word displays the Customize dialog box.
2. In the Customize dialog box, click the Commands tab and choose the category of commands you want to use
3. From the Commands section, drag the desired command up to the menu on which you want it to appear. Notice that as you move the mouse over the menu, Word displays the existing menu.
4. Drag the command down the menu and drop it at the position where you want it to appear. Word adds the command to the menu.

You can repeat Steps 2 through 4 for each additional item you want to add to a menu. If you want to rename a menu item, follow the same steps detailed in the previous section for renaming an entire menu. When you are done, close the Customize dialog box.

Removing a menu item

If you want to remove items from a menu, it is easily done:

1. Choose the Customize option from the Tools menu or right-click the menu bar and choose Customize. Word displays the Customize dialog box. (You will not actually use any of the options in the Customize dialog box to remove the button, but it must be open nonetheless.)
2. Click the menu containing the item you want to delete. (Click the actual menu, not anything in the Customize dialog box.) Word displays the menu. If the item to be deleted is on a submenu, make sure that you display that menu.
3. Click the menu item and drag it off the menu. As you do so, an *X* appears near the bottom of the mouse pointer.
4. Release the mouse pointer. The menu item is deleted.

Understanding the status bar

The status bar displays measurements that indicate the exact location of the insertion point in the on-screen document. Depending on the Word functions and features you are using, you will also see messages pertaining to what you are doing.

Double-clicking the left half of the status bar opens the Find and Replace dialog box and enables you to perform search or replace functions. You also can use this dialog box to go to (using the Go To tab) different locations in the document. In addition, several buttons appear grayed out on the status bar but can be turned on or off by double-clicking the corresponding button. These buttons enable the following features:

- **TRK (Track Changes):** When turned on, this displays editing marks that visually show the changes you make to the document (see Chapter 11, "Keeping Track of Revisions," for full details of this feature).
- **REC (Record Macro):** When turned on, Word records your keystrokes as macros, so you can replay them whenever you desire (see Chapter 12, "Working with Word Macros").
- **EXT (Extend Selection):** When turned on, this anchors the insertion point so that any movment extends the selection from that anchor to the new insertion point location (see Chapter 3, "Creating and Working with Documents").
- **OVR (Overtype):** This results in things you type replacing existing text: You "type over" existing text.

Using the scroll bars

The narrow shaded areas along the right side and at the bottom of the Word window are the scroll bars. Legal documents are often lengthy, and scroll bars are useful for moving around in and viewing different parts of the document. To move quickly to another portion of a document using the scroll bars, do one of the following:

- **Click the arrows at either end of the scroll bar.** On the vertical scroll bar at the right of the window, clicking an arrow moves the document display the direction you clicked, one line at a time. On the horizontal scroll bar at the bottom of the window, clicking an arrow moves the document display in the direction you clicked.

- **Drag the slider on the scroll bar in either direction.** The slider is the square-shaped element that moves between the arrow buttons at either end of the scroll bar. Dragging the slider up or down moves the on-screen display rapidly.
- **Click at any point within the scroll bar itself.** Clicking within the scroll bar moves the display a half page at a time. On the vertical scroll bar, clicking above the slider moves the display up; clicking under the slider moves it down. Likewise, on the horizontal slider, the left or right movement depends on where you click in relation to the slider's position.

NOTE: It is important to remember that the insertion point does not change location as you move through the document using the scroll bars. You are changing only the portion of the document visible within the work area.

One benefit of dragging the scroll bar is to see the ScreenTip that displays the page that has come into view and the first heading (albeit truncated) that appears on that page. If you use the arrow keys to view another area, you will not see the ScreenTip.

NOTE: Those four little buttons at the far left of the horizontal scroll bar are the View buttons, which you can click to easily choose among the types of views (such as Print Layout or Normal view). See "Choosing Your View of a Document" later in this chapter for a discussion of the various viewing options.

Understanding the task pane

The task pane is a new addition to Word 2002. It is a method to make commonly used commands available while you are working on your document.

There are several ways that you can display the task pane. The most direct method is to simply choose Task Pane from the View menu. When you do, Word displays the New Document task pane, as shown in Figure 2-6. The task pane is also automatically displayed when you select some other commands from Word's menus. For instance, the Styles and Formatting task pane is displayed if you choose Styles and Formatting from the Format menu.

Notice that there are controls at the top-right corner of the task pane. The *X* in the upper-right corner is used to close the task pane, exactly as the same control is used in a dialog box. The down-pointing arrow allows you to quickly select different task panes for Word to display. If you click the down arrow, you will see that eight different task panes are available.

You should consider the task pane as just another tool that Word provides for creating and editing your documents. If you don't like the pane, you can close it any time you desire. If you find it helpful, you can utilize it in any manner you see fit.

Figure 2-6: The New Document task pane contains commands related to creating new documents.

Choosing Your View of a Document

Six primary viewing options are available in Word. Table 2-1 lists each of the viewing options, along with a description of what you can see in a particular view.

Table 2-1
Document Views

Switch to This View	***What You Will See***
Normal	Page breaks appear as dotted lines. Document elements such as headers, footers, and some graphics are hidden from view. Useful when entering, editing, and formatting text.
Web Layout	Displays your document exactly as it will look when published on the Web.
Print Layout	Displays the document as it will look when printed. All elements — headers, footers, and graphics — are visible.
Outline	Use this view to focus on the organization of your legal document. You can collapse and expand sections, rearrange sections, and promote and demote section levels. Document elements are not visible.
Document Map	A useful tool for moving to different sections in the document. A separate pane appears on the left side of the document and lists all major headings in the document. The document appears on the right side of the window. Click the headings in the Document Map pane to quickly jump to that section of your document. The heading you clicked appears at the top of the screen, regardless of its physical location on that page.
Full Screen	The entire workspace is devoted to the document. The title bar, menu bar, and toolbars are hidden from view.

Changing your view of a document

You can change your view easily, using either of the following methods:

- Click the View menu to see a list of all the different views, and select the view you want from the list.
- Choose the Normal, Web Layout, Print Layout, or Outline view by clicking the appropriate button conveniently located on the left side of the horizontal scroll bar. Figure 2-7 shows the View buttons found at the bottom of the Word window.

Figure 2-7: Four viewing options are available on the left side of the horizontal scroll bar.

If you transitioned from WordPerfect to Word, you have undoubtedly wondered what happened to your reveal codes. WordPerfect's reveal codes feature is heralded by many users because it helps you easily identify formats within the document and make modifications to those formats. You've probably pressed the Alt+F3 key combination at least once in hopes of revealing or modifying document formats. Alas, nothing happens when you press Alt+F3 in Word.

In Word 2002, you can use the Reveal Formatting task pane to display formats in use in selected text or in the paragraph containing the insertion point. Word will even locate all text in a document that shares the same formatting, whether it was applied directly or was applied by using a style. After the text is selected, you can click a formatting hyperlink (such as Font) in the Reveal Formatting task pane to change that format in the selected text. Or you can switch to the Styles and Formatting task pane and create a style for the selected text, apply an existing style to the selected text, or modify a style already applied to the selected text. We anticipate that the Reveal Formatting task pane will have liberating effects in the legal community. In an age in which legal professionals prepare many of their own legal documents and for those who work in law firm word-processing departments, as well as secretaries who oftentimes are the recipients of documents containing a mix of formatting, the Reveal Formatting task pane is a welcome addition.

Using the Reveal Formatting task pane

To access the Reveal Formatting task pane to view or modify formats, you can use one of the following techniques:

- Click Format ⇨ Reveal Formatting.
- Click View ⇨ Task Pane.
- Select the text for which you want to reveal the formatting; then choose Help ⇨ What's This (or press Shift+F1) and click the selection to open the Reveal Formatting task pane.

Whichever technique you use, the task pane automatically opens on the right side of the Word window. If you used the What's This technique described previously, the Reveal Formatting task pane opens automatically. However, if you used the View ⇨ Task Pane technique, the task pane that opens may not contain the Reveal Formatting options but rather redisplay its previous contents. To display the Reveal Formatting task pane, click the black down-pointing arrow in the upper-right corner of the task pane and choose Reveal Formatting from the menu that appears. Figure 2-8 is an example of what you will see when you open the Reveal Formatting task pane.

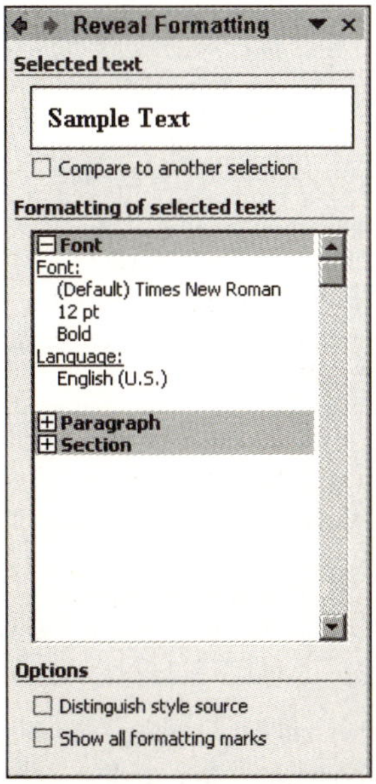

Figure 2-8: The Reveal Formatting task pane

In Figure 2-8, you can see the font in use in the selection below the Font hyperlink and the formats applied to the selected paragraph. However, the Section category is collapsed, as indicated by the plus symbol (+) in front of the category name. To expand a category to see the complete list of formats, click the plus symbol beside that category.

If you selected text before entering the Reveal Formatting task pane, you will see a portion of the text in the Selected Text section at the top of the task pane, and the formats you see are found in the selection only. If you did not select text but simply clicked in a paragraph, the word you clicked appears in the Selected Text section, but the formats you see are for the entire paragraph. When you aim the pointer at the Selected Text box, you will see an arrow that you can click to see additional options for formatting the selected text. Those additional options are as follows:

- **Select All Text with Similar Formatting:** Automatically highlights all text in the entire document that is formatted the same as the text you selected.
- **Apply Formatting of Surrounding Text:** Useful when you have pasted text containing different formats into your document. You can change the format to be consistent with the formatting around it.
- **Clear Formatting:** Removes all formatting from the selected text.

Below the Selected Text box is the Compare to Another Selection check box. Suppose that you have added text to a document originally prepared by your client and you want to make sure that the text you added is formatted the same as the text the client created. Using the Compare to Another Selection option, you can compare the formats of the text that you added with the formats found in the client document.

To compare formats of one section text with the formats of another section, follow these steps:

1. Select the text containing the formats you want to compare.
2. In the Reveal Formatting task pane, click the box beside Compare to Another Selection to place a check mark in it.
3. Select the text to which you are comparing formats.

After following these steps, the Formatting Differences section appears (see Figure 2-9). If Word found no differences between the two selections, you will see the message `No formatting differences`. If Word does find differences, you will see hyperlinks (blue, underlined text) for each category of format used in both selections. For instance, you may see Font, Paragraph, and Section hyperlinks. Below each format hyperlink, you will see the format found in the first selection, followed by an arrow (->) and then the different format found in the second selection.

When you are not comparing formats, below the Selected Text section you will see the Formatting of Selected Text section. In this section, just as with the Formatting Differences section discussed previously, you will see hyperlinks for each format category in use in the selected text. When the Reveal Formatting task pane is left open while you work, the contents of this section constantly change to include formats for text you are selecting or for the paragraph containing the insertion point.

TIP: If you want to see the formats in use in the entire document, open the Reveal Formatting task pane and click Edit ⇨ Select All (or press Ctrl+A) to select the entire document. Hyperlinks for all the format categories in use in that document are displayed.

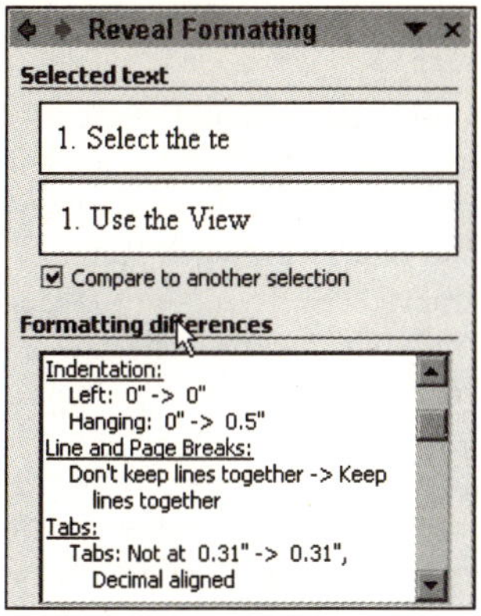

Figure 2-9: When comparing formats, differences are displayed in the Formatting Differences section.

You can make changes to the formats that are listed by clicking the appropriate hyperlink. Word automatically opens the dialog box for that format option, in which you can make changes to that particular format. For instance, if you want to change the font, click the Font hyperlink to open the Font dialog box and make the necessary font modifications.

The Options section of the Reveal Formatting task pane includes two additional formatting options. First, Distinguish Style Source, when checked, displays additional information detailing whether a style was used to apply the format or whether individual formats were applied using the Formatting toolbar or the Format menu. The Show All Formatting Marks is useful for when you want to see all the paragraph marks and spaces in your document.

Splitting a window

Another useful tool for viewing and working with a document is the Window ⇨ Split command. With this command, you can divide your screen into two separate windows containing the same document. Within each window, you can scroll around in the document and move back and forth between the windows, enabling you to view one part of the document in one window and another part in the other window. The insertion point moves in each window as well, enabling you to make changes to the text in either window. So, for example, you can use this feature to view text from a paragraph at the beginning of the document and cut and paste that text to appear at the end of the document instead.

To split your view of a document, follow these steps:

1. From the Menu bar, choose Window ⇨ Split. The horizontal line that appears will float until you "dock" it by moving your mouse to where you want to place it (you can make one window bigger than the other).
2. Click in either window to make that window the active one. To move to the other window, simply click in it.
3. When you want to remove the split, double-click the line separating the two windows, or choose Window ⇨ Remove Split.

Changing the Default Unit of Measurement

The default unit of measurement is used in displaying measurements on the horizontal and vertical rulers and is the measurement used to indicate the position of the insertion point in the document (the insertion point location is displayed on the status bar). Some of Word's text boxes also require that a measurement be inserted. For instance, the Style Area Width option, found on the View tab and accessed by clicking Tools ⇨ Options, requires that a measurement be entered specifying how wide you want the style area to be. (The style area can be displayed at the left of your document to indicate the styles in use in your document.) The default measurement used in Word is inches; the need may arise, however, for you to change the unit of measurement, particularly when working with legal documents originating in a European country, whose default unit of measurement may be centimeters. Word provides five different units of measurement options from which you can choose: Inches, Centimeters, Millimeters, Points, and Picas. You can change the default measurement at any time by following a few simple steps:

1. Choose Tools ⇨ Options and click the General tab.
2. In the Measure units section, click the drop-down list arrow and choose the desired measurement.
3. Click OK to apply the change.

TIP: When specifying a measurement in a dialog box, you can override the default unit of measurement by typing the number, followed by the unit of measurement you want. For instance, in the Page Setup dialog box (accessed by clicking File ⇨ Page Setup), you can create a custom paper size. If you are creating a paper size for printing in Europe, you will want to change your units of measurement to millimeters. You can do so without changing the default unit of measurement. Instead, in the Width and Height boxes on the Paper Size tab, type the values you want for the width and height of the paper, followed by **mm** to express that measurement in millimeters.

Summary

This chapter introduced you to the basic tools and features of Word. In this chapter, we discussed the following standard features:

- You'll find the nine categories of Word commands on the Menu bar, and you can customize these menus to suit your needs.
- The Standard and Formatting toolbars are visible by default, but many other toolbars exist that you can make visible; you also can add or remove buttons with any toolbar to customize them as desired.
- The scroll bars make moving to various locations in your document quick and easy, and the status bar reveals the location of your insertion point.
- You can make use of Word's various viewing options to suit the task at hand.
- The horizontal and vertical rulers indicate the width and height of your margins, and you can change the default unit of measurement, when necessary, to adapt your document to international variations.

The next chapter covers how to create new documents, open existing documents, and begin working with text.

Chapter 3

Creating and Working with Documents

In This Chapter

- Creating new documents and opening existing documents
- Moving and copying text
- Adding page breaks
- Using Find and Replace
- Using Word Count
- Using smart tags
- Adding page numbers and line numbers
- Inserting legal symbols
- Using AutoText
- Using document summaries
- Inserting bookmarks

THE TRUE MEASURE OF ANY WORD processor is the ease with which you can create and edit documents. It is relatively easy to come up with a word processor that lets you type and delete text; the proof of the program is in the tools provided to make creation and editing easier. Word provides a wide range of tools that you can use when working with documents. In this chapter, you examine many of those tools.

Creating Documents

Word offers three different techniques for you to use to create your legal documents:

- Click the New Blank Document button on the Standard toolbar. This action opens a blank document, with formats and settings based on Word's standard defaults.
- Choose File ⇨ New to open the New Document task pane. In the New Document task pane, you will see three sections containing hyperlinks to assist you in creating a new document. In the New section, you can create a blank document based on Word's defaults or a blank Web page with a split screen for the Document Map. Or you can create a blank e-mail message. In the New from Existing Document section, you can base your new document on an existing document that you select. Or in the New from Template section, you can select a predefined

template from those that ship with Word, you can access templates from your intranet, or you can go online and access document templates from the Microsoft Web site.

- If you prefer to use the keyboard to create a new document, press Ctrl+N to open a blank document based on Word's defaults.

Each time you enter Word to create a new document, the document is named *Document1,* and the name appears in the title bar. Each time you create a new document, the number in the name increases by 1.

Opening Existing Documents

You can use several techniques for opening existing documents in Word. By default, Word displays a list of the previous four documents you opened at the bottom of the File menu and as hyperlinks in the New Document task pane. Whether you use the File menu or the task pane, simply click the document name to open the document.

TIP: If you have worked with several documents and none of the filenames appear on the File menu or in the New Document task pane, you can easily correct that. You can decrease or increase the number of Word documents maintained on your recently used file list by choosing Tools ⇨ Options and selecting the General tab. If Word does not list any of your recently opened documents, chances are the Recently Used File List option is not checked at all. If this option is checked and you want to increase or decrease the number of documents Word lists, enter a number in the box beside the checked item, or use the spinner box to increase or decrease the number. When you have completed this process, click OK.

If the document you want to open is not one of the previous four you worked on and therefore does not appear in the New Document task pane or at the bottom of the File menu, you will need to use the Open dialog box to locate and open the document. You can use one of the following techniques to display the Open dialog box:

- In the New Document task pane, click the More Documents hyperlink.
- Click the Open button on the Standard toolbar.
- Choose File ⇨ Open.
- Press Ctrl+O (that's *O* for *Open*, not the number 0).

When the Open dialog box appears, you can specify the location of the file you want to use in the Look In section by navigating through the folders to the exact location of the file. In the Look In section, you can locate files on a disk, on the hard disk in your computer, or in a folder on a network. If you know the folder name(s) and filename of the document you want to use, you can type the complete path, including the filename in the File Name section of the dialog box. Here is an example of the way the path and filename might look:

F:\client folder\matter folder\filename.doc

If the document you want to open was created in an earlier version of Word, you will need to specify the file format in the Files of Type section. In addition to a number of file formats, you can open Word documents saved in versions 4.0–5.1 for the Macintosh, Word versions 6.0–Word 95, and Word files saved as Web pages or document templates. If you do not specify a different file type, Word assumes that you are opening a file created using Word 2002. This caveat applies only to Word documents, not to documents that Word may be able to translate from other word processors.

Moving and Copying Text

Any legal professional can testify to the fact that moving and copying text are the most common editing tasks performed on legal documents. Only a small difference exists between the two procedures. Unlike the Copy feature, Move is not an option on the Edit menu. Text to be moved is *cut* (deleted) from its current position and placed on the Windows Clipboard (a temporary storage area) until it is pasted in its new location. Text that is copied remains in its original location, and a copy is *pasted* in a new location. In both cases, cut items (deleted from their original location) or copied items reside on the Windows Clipboard until the Clipboard is cleared.

NOTE: The temporary storage area known as the *Windows Clipboard* has a very large capacity, limited only by the amount of memory in your system. The Clipboard maintains its contents until you store something else in the Clipboard. In other words, whatever you store in the Clipboard overwrites whatever was previously stored there.

Table 3-1 provides a quick reference for the basic commands for moving, copying, and pasting text (as well as the command for undoing what you've done, in case you change your mind).

Table 3-1
Commands for Moving, Copying, and Pasting Text

Command	***How to Do It***	***What It Does***
Cut	Choose Edit ⇨ Cut or press Ctrl+X.	Removes the text from its original location and stores it temporarily in the Clipboard.
Copy	Choose Edit ⇨Copy or press Ctrl+C.	Leaves the text in its original location and stores a copy of it temporarily in the Clipboard.
Paste	Choose Edit ⇨ Paste or press Ctrl+V.	Inserts the previously cut or copied text at the insertion point in the document.
Undo	Choose Edit ⇨ Undo or press Ctrl+ Z	Negates (undoes) the most recent action you took.

Selecting text

Before you can move, copy, or apply formatting, the text you want to work with must first be *selected* (highlighted). Table 3-2 lists a few ways text can be selected.

Table 3-2
Text Selection Techniques

Selection Technique	*Procedure*
Select a word.	Double-click the word.
Select a sentence.	Press Ctrl and click the sentence. The entire sentence, including the period and spaces after the period, is selected.
Select a paragraph.	Triple-click the paragraph to select the text, spaces, and the paragraph marker at the end.
Select all.	Choose Edit ⇨ Select All to select the entire document, or press Ctrl+A.
Drag.	Use the mouse to select text by holding the mouse button down and moving (dragging) it across the text to be selected.
Selection set.	Select the first block of text. Next, hold down the Ctrl key as you select the next block. Continue this procedure until all the desired blocks are selected. Figure 3-1 shows an example of multiple blocks of text that are selected.

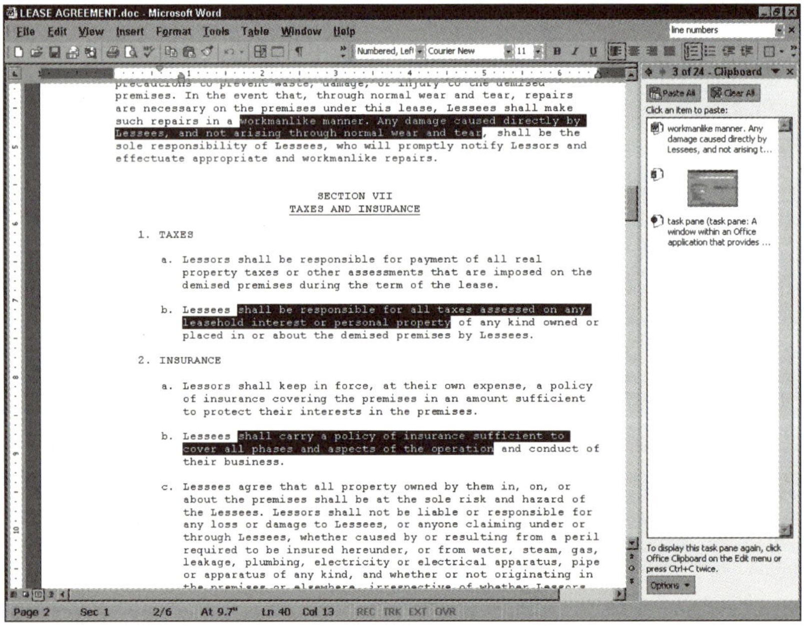

Figure 3-1: Noncontiguous blocks of text are selected and can be cut or copied as one unit.

You also can select text by using Word's Extend mode and the cursor-control keys. You use this mode by moving the insertion point to one end of the selection you want to make. Then you turn on Extend mode by pressing F8 or by double-clicking the letters *EXT* on the status bar. (When Extend mode is active, the letters *EXT* on the status bar appear in black.) Now, move the insertion point using the cursor-control keys. Notice that Word modifies the size of the selection as you move the insertion point. The result is a selection, just the size you want it.

Extend mode is turned off by either pressing the Esc key and then moving the insertion point or by taking some editing action, such as pressing the Delete key.

Controlling automatic selection options

Before selecting your text, you should consider the formatting of the text you plan to cut or copy and decide which of the following you want the pasted text to do:

- Look the same as it did in its original location
- Take on the formatting in use at its new location
- Have altogether different formatting

For instance, if you select an entire paragraph including — the paragraph mark at the end (the paragraph mark stores the formatting of that paragraph) — unless you specify otherwise, the pasted paragraph will be formatted as it was in its original location. If you do not include the paragraph mark at the end, the paragraph to be cut or copied will contain only character-based formatting, such as bold, underline, and so on. By default, Word includes the paragraph mark whenever an entire paragraph is selected. If you do not want the paragraph mark automatically included when selecting a paragraph, choose Tools ⇨ Options and click the Edit tab. Click the Use Smart Paragraph option in the Editing Options section to remove the check mark.

When you use the mouse to select text in your document, you do so by clicking at the start of your selection, holding down the mouse button, and moving the mouse to where you want the selection to end. By default, Word automatically selects entire words as you move the mouse from one word to another. If you don't want entire words automatically selected, choose Tools ⇨ Options and click the Edit tab. Make sure that the When Selecting Automatically Select Entire Word option is not selected. With this option unselected, Word makes no assumptions when selecting text and allows more precise control of text selections with the mouse.

Setting smart Cut and Paste options

In addition to the selection options described previously, there are additional settings that you can change to override Word's default Cut and Paste settings. We recommend that you review these settings and establish preferences before you begin to cut and paste. You can review the Cut and Paste settings by choosing Tools ⇨ Options, clicking the Edit tab, and then clicking the Settings button. The result is the Settings dialog box, as shown in Figure 3-2.

In most instances you should leave the default Cut and Paste options as they are shown in Figure 3-2. These defaults will satisfy most editors, but your firm may have special needs that dictate using different settings. The best way to discover what each of the options does is to click on the question mark button in the upper-right corner of the dialog box and click on the options in question. Make changes as you desire; then close the dialog box.

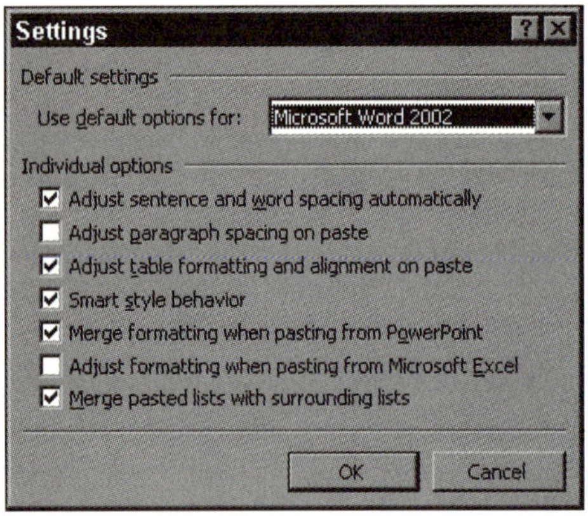

Figure 3-2: Control the automatic smart Cut and Paste options by changing these settings.

Moving text

To move text from one location to another, select the text to be moved, using one of the techniques listed previously in Table 3-2. Next, use one of the following techniques to cut the selected text:

- Choose Edit ⇨ Cut.
- Right-click the selection and choose Cut from the menu that appears.
- Click the Cut button (looks like scissors) on the Standard toolbar.
- Press Ctrl+X.

The cut text is removed from the current location and placed on the Clipboard. If the task pane is visible, you can click the drop-down list arrow on the task pane's title bar and select the Clipboard menu option to display the contents of the Clipboard. (To display the task pane if it is not visible, choose the View ⇨ Task Pane menu options.) After the desired text has been cut, place the insertion point in the exact location where you want to reposition the cut text. You can paste the cut text in its new location using one of the following techniques:

- Choose Edit ⇨ Paste.
- After positioning the insertion point in the target location, right-click over the insertion point and choose Paste from the menu that appears
- Click the Paste button (looks like a clipboard with a little piece of paper on one corner) on the Standard toolbar.
- In the Clipboard task pane, right-click over the text you are pasting and choose Paste from the menu that appears. (When your pointer is over the cut text in the Clipboard task pane, you also can click the drop-down list arrow to display the menu.)
- Press Ctrl+V.

Copying text

As mentioned earlier, the steps for copying text are very similar to moving text. First, select the text you want to copy. Next, choose one of the following techniques to copy the selected text:

- Choose Edit ⇨ Copy.
- Click the Copy button (looks like two document pages, one on top of the other) on the Standard toolbar.
- Right-click the selection and choose Copy from the menu that appears.
- Press Ctrl+C.

As was the case when moving text, copied text is placed on the Clipboard and can be viewed using the Clipboard task pane. To paste the copied text, use one of the same techniques you used to paste cut text:

- Choose Edit ⇨ Paste.
- After positioning the insertion point in the target location, right-click over the insertion point and choose Paste from the menu that appears.
- Click the Paste button on the Standard toolbar.
- In the Clipboard task pane, right-click over the text you are pasting and choose Paste from the menu that appears. (When your pointer is over the cut text in the Clipboard task pane, you also can click the drop-down list arrow to display the menu.)
- Press Ctrl+V.

Using Paste options

For years now, legal professionals have been warned about the problems created when they paste text from sources such as the Web and WordPerfect directly into their Word documents. Pasting text without regard to the format codes (seen and unseen) that travel with that text and ultimately get pasted into legal documents is dangerous because these extraneous codes and formats can wreak havoc on your Word document. And, of course, the problems always arise when you are in the final stages of editing and the deadline is fast approaching. The rule of thumb has always been to choose Edit ⇨ Paste Special and then choose the Unformatted Text option to paste the cut or copied text without any formatting. One reason that the warnings went unheeded is the several extra steps involved in using Paste Special. Another was that the user simply did not recognize the true value of using Paste Special or simply didn't remember to use it. Now, whenever you paste information into a document, you are immediately presented with a Paste Options floating menu that automatically appears below the pasted text, as shown in Figure 3-3. When you click the downward-pointing arrow at the right side of the floating menu, you are presented with a list of paste options based on the type of information you are pasting. For instance, if you are pasting text copied from another Word 2002 document, you will see a list of options similar to the ones described here.

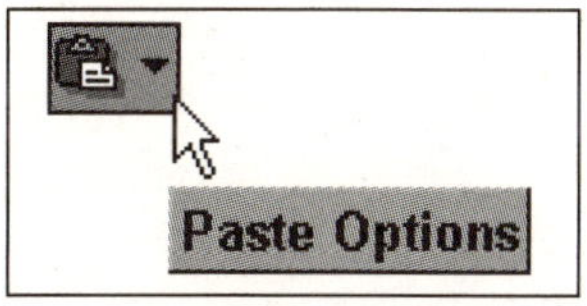

Figure 3-3: The Paste Options floating menu appears when pasting cut or copied text.

- **Keep Source Formatting:** The pasted text retains the formatting it had in its original location.
- **Use Destination Styles:** Pasted text loses its original formatting and assumes the formatting of styles used in its new location.

- **Match Destination Formatting:** Pasted text will lose its original formatting and be reformatted according to the formats in use in the new location.
- **Keep Text Only:** All original formatting of the pasted text will be removed and the text will be unaffected by formats or styles used in the new location.
- **Apply Style or Formatting:** This reselects the pasted text and opens the Styles and Formatting task pane, where you can choose the style you want to apply to the pasted text. Formats can also be cleared using the Style and Formatting task pane.

If, however, you are pasting an Excel worksheet into your Word document, the list of paste options changes to include such options as linking the data in the Word table back to the Excel worksheet, as shown in Figure 3-4. If you select this option, the table data is linked to the Excel worksheet so that whenever the data in the worksheet is modified, the data in the table is also updated. Word also recognizes when you have cut or copied a numbered list and presents you with paste options for continuing the numbering in the target location or for starting a new numbered list, another welcome addition for the legal community.

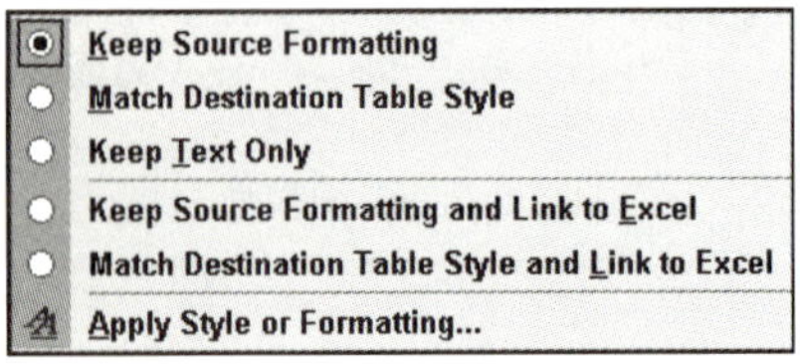

Figure 3-4: Paste options available when pasting Excel data into a Word document

Choosing an option from the Paste Options menu does not automatically close that menu. To close the Paste Options menu, press Esc. In addition, the Paste Options menu appears by default below the pasted information. If you do not want the Paste Options menu to appear at all, you can turn this feature off by choosing Tools ⇨ Options and selecting the Edit tab. Uncheck the Show Paste Options buttons in the Cut and Paste options section.

Using Paste Special

The Paste Special feature, accessed by choosing Edit ⇨ Paste Special, provides various options for pasting (see Figure 3-5). When you use this feature, you can insert or embed objects that you have stored on the Clipboard.

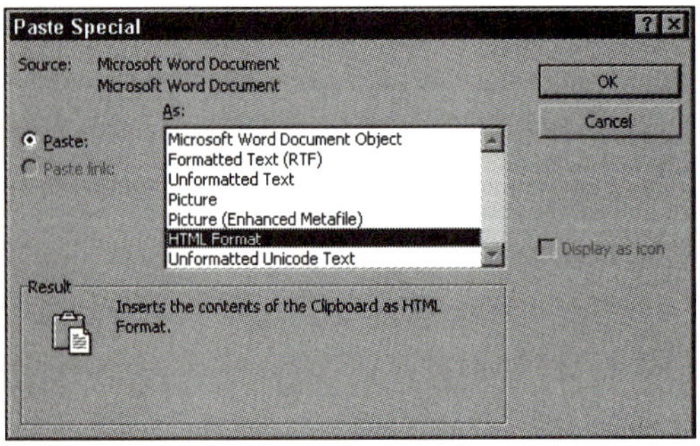

Figure 3-5: The Paste Special dialog box

Paste Special, as a menu option, has been around since the early days of Word. As described in the previous section, much of the reason for using Paste Special has been replaced by the Paste Options menu that appears when you actually paste something into your document.

So why would you choose to use Paste Special as opposed to the Paste Options menu? The answer is simple: You can use Paste Special to see your pasting options before doing the paste, whereas the Paste Options menu lists the ways in which you can convert information that has already been pasted. In either case, the options that are available will vary, based on the attributes of the data you are pasting in your document.

Cutting and copying text between two documents or file formats

Legal documents are often compiled by copying paragraphs that originated in a document provided by a client or from other sources, such as a legal research citation. Word allows you to cut and copy text between open documents and between different file formats. As mentioned previously, an Excel worksheet can be pasted into a Word document as a Word table. You also can cut and copy between open documents using the following steps:

1. Open both the source document and target document. Each document appears in its own window with a separate title bar, menus, and so on. You can use the Window menu to arrange the document windows so that you can see both the source document and target document simultaneously. If you do not want to see both documents at the same time, press Ctrl+F6 to easily move back and forth from one document window to the other. Or you can click Window on the Menu bar, which lists at the bottom the open documents. Click the document you want to display.
2. Choose among the Cut, Copy, and Paste options discussed earlier.

Word analyzes the source data and displays the pasted information in a comparable format that Word can understand. For example, when you paste an Excel worksheet into a Word document, Word converts the worksheet to a table format that it understands.

Adding Page Breaks

Unless you specify otherwise, Word automatically starts a new page when the current page is full. As you add or remove text, Word automatically adjusts the amount of text for each page and adjusts the page breaks. To change where Word automatically breaks the page, you can adjust the bottom margin in the Page Setup dialog box. To do so, choose File ⇨ Page Setup and click the Margins tab. The default bottom margin setting is 1", so Word automatically inserts a page break to make the text on that page stop before going over the 1" setting. When you work in Normal view, an automatic page break appears as a dotted line going straight across the page. In Print Layout or Full Screen view, an actual break occurs between pages so that you can see the bottom of the current page and the top of the next page, with blank space in between.

When your document consists of a cover page, a table of contents, and a certificate of service, you probably want each of these items to stand alone on separate pages without other text flowing onto the page. To accomplish this, you do not want to change the bottom margin for the entire document; rather, you simply want to end the current page sooner than Word will by default. In this case, you want to insert a manual page break. You can insert a manual page break in either of the following ways:

- Position the insertion point where you want to end the current page, and press Ctrl+Enter to automatically insert a manual page break

♦ Position the insertion point where you want to end the current page, and choose Insert ⇨ Break. In the Break dialog box that appears, choose Page Break in the Break Types section. Figure 3-6 shows the Break dialog box.

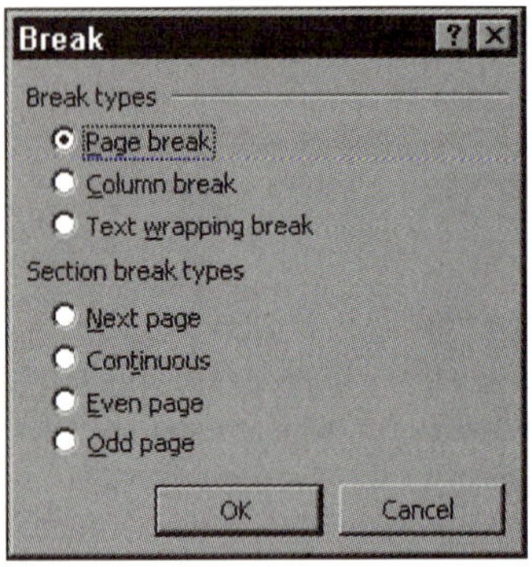

Figure 3-6: The Break dialog box

There are other things to take into consideration when working with page breaks. For instance, in the legal environment, it is never acceptable to begin a new page with the last line of a paragraph (a *widow*) or to end a page with the first line of a new paragraph (an *orphan*). These situations can be avoided by turning on widow/orphan control. To protect the first and last lines of paragraphs from page breaks, choose Format ⇨ Paragraph and then choose the Line and Page Breaks tab. Place a check beside the Widow/Orphan Control option.

Also unacceptable in the legal field is to end a page with a heading, with the associated text on the following page. To correct this situation, select the heading and check the Keep with Next option in the Paragraph dialog box. And last but not least, you also can keep a page break from being inserted in the middle of a paragraph by using the Keep Lines Together option. In the Reveal Formatting task pane, the Line and Page Breaks hyperlink is added to the Paragraph section. You can easily modify these options by clicking the hyperlink.

Although you certainly can make the types of changes described here on a paragraph-by-paragraph basis, a better approach is to define these (and other) types of paragraph attributes in a style and then apply the style to paragraphs throughout the document. Styles are a very powerful feature of Word and are discussed more fully in Chapter 4, "Creating Your Legal Document with Style."

Using Find and Replace

The Find feature locates specific terms in the current document. The Find feature not only can locate the words or phrases that you specify but also can have its search restricted to terms that appear in a certain case (such as all uppercase letters) or with certain character formatting (such as only items in bold type). The Replace feature can automatically replace the searched-for terms with the same terms but in a different character format. This section covers the various ways to find and replace both text and other items.

Finding text

Suppose that you want to search an agreement to find every occurrence of the word *tax* in order to review the surrounding text. Choose Edit ⇨ Find or press Ctrl+F. Type **tax** in the Find What section. If you have already searched for this term during the current editing session, you can select it from the drop-down list beside this option instead of having to retype it. After typing the search term, click the

Find Next button to move individually to each occurrence of the searched-for term. Word highlights each occurrence as it is found. If you do not set any other options, Word searches for every occurrence of the letters *tax*, regardless of whether they stand alone or are part of another word, and regardless of any other attributes of the letters (such as any formatting of them). For instance, Word will locate not only *tax* but also *taxes* or *tax* or *taxation* — literally every occurrence of the word.

You can direct Word to highlight all occurrences of the searched-for terms simultaneously and can specify where you want Word to look. By checking the Highlight All Items Found In option on the Find tab, you are asking Word to highlight all the terms simultaneously rather than one at a time. Below the Highlight All Items Found In option is a drop-down list in which you specify where you want Word to look for the terms: The choices available depend on how you have your document put together. For instance, you will always be able to choose Main Document, but you may be able to choose other parts of your document as well, such as Headers and Footers, Footnotes, Comments, or other special document elements. The choices available in the drop-down list are dependent on your document. If you select the Highlight All Items Found In check box, notice that the Find Next button becomes the Find All button.

Additional search options are available to help you narrow your search when you expand the Find and Replace dialog box. Before you expand the dialog box, it contains the More button, and the additional search options are not visible. To expand the dialog box in order to see the Search Options section, click the More button. The dialog box expands to reveal the search options, and the More button you clicked is now called Less. You can collapse the dialog box again by clicking the Less button. The search options described in the following sections can be selected (or deselected) based on the results you want.

Matching case

You can limit Word to finding every occurrence of a word(s) that is capitalized exactly as you type it by checking the Match Case option in the Find and Replace dialog box. If you type the search term in initial caps or in all caps and check the Match Case option, Word will locate the searched-for term only if it is capitalized the way you typed it.

Finding whole words only

To narrow a search even further, you can instruct Word to find whole words only by checking this option in the Find and Replace dialog box. With this option selected, Word will not locate *taxation* or *taxes* when searching for the word *tax*.

Using wildcards

Wildcards are useful when searching for part of a word and the part you are looking for may be at the beginning, in the middle, or at the end of the word. A *wildcard*, such as an asterisk, essentially is a placeholder for the information that you do not know. For instance, you may know that the term you are looking for (say, *tax*) appears at the end of the word, but you do not know what is in front of the word (it could be *pre-tax* or *post-tax*, for example). If you are not sure how many characters precede the word you are looking for, you can type the search criteria like this to match any number of characters:

***taxes**

In this example, Word finds the word *pre-tax* as well as *post-tax*. If you know that only a single character is in front of the term you are searching for, you can use the question mark (?) wildcard instead of the asterisk. You can find a complete list of available wildcards in Word's help system.

Using Sounds Like

Word can locate a word that sounds like the word you are looking for if you check the Sounds Like option in the Find and Replace dialog box. For instance, with this option activated, you can type the search term *principal*, and Word will locate both the word *principal* and the word *principle*.

Finding all word forms

If you select the Find All Word Forms option in the Find and Replace dialog box, Word will locate all the various word forms of your search term, whether past tense, plural, or other forms. For instance, if the search term is *tax* and the Find All Word Forms option is checked, Word will locate the words *tax*, *taxed*, and *taxes*.

You may wonder why this search option is necessary when you could find these variations of *tax* just by making sure that the Find Whole Words Only check box is not selected. If you choose the Find All Word Forms check box, Word assumes that you want to find only whole words. In fact, the Find Whole Words Only check box becomes inaccessible if you choose Find All Word Forms. With the option selected, Word finds *tax*, *taxes*, and *taxed*, but not words like *taxation* and *taxidermy*.

Setting the direction for your search

In the Search Options section, you also can specify the direction in which you want Word to search. The directional options available are as follows:

- **All:** Searches the entire document, regardless of the current location of the insertion point
- **Up:** Searches from the current location of the insertion point toward the beginning of the document
- **Down:** Searches from the current location of the insertion point toward the end of the document

To set the direction of the search, click the drop-down list arrow and select the desired direction.

Finding and replacing items other than text

In the Find section at the bottom of the Find tab (Edit ⇨ Find) and in the Replace section at the bottom of the Replace tab (Edit ⇨ Replace), you will find a Format button and a Special button. The Format button leads to formats that you can include in your search or that can be the sole focus of the search. You can look for a particular attribute such as boldface or a certain paragraph format. Say, for instance, that you want to look for every occurrence of the word *tax* that is underlined. To do so, you first enter **tax** in the Find What box. Then you click the Format button, followed by the Font button. In the Find Font dialog box that opens, click the down arrow in the Underline list box and choose the single underline style. Figure 3-7 shows the search term displayed in the Find What section and the selected format displayed below the search term.

When you have included formats in your search, the No Formatting command button in the Find section is active. (If you haven't included a format search, the button appears grayed out, indicating that it's inactive.) If you change your mind about including formats in the search, you can remove the format when you click this button.

Word also allows you to search for special characters by using the Special button on the Find or Replace tab. You can search for tabs, paragraph marks, nonbreaking spaces, and other special characters. To search for special characters, click the Special button, and select the special character you want to find from the menu that appears.

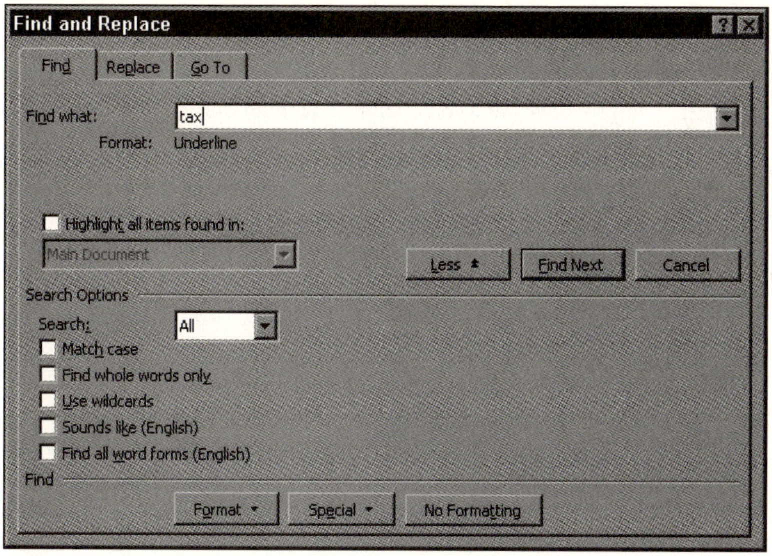

Figure 3-7: Formats included in the search display below the search term

Replacing text

If you want to replace the searched-for terms with different terms or formatting, click the Replace tab in the Find and Replace dialog box. Type the replacement terms in the Replace With section. All the techniques for narrowing the search or including formats described in previous sections are also available when replacing text.

Using Go To

The Find and Replace dialog box contains a Go To tab, which you use to specify an area of the document so that you can *go to*, or jump to that area. For instance, you can go directly to a particular page number by typing the number in the Enter Page Number section. Or you can choose from the list the document element you want to go to, such as a particular section or footnote. After you have relocated to the document element you selected, the Go To tab remains visible so that you can use the Previous and Next buttons to move to the next occurrence of the document element. When you are finished with the Go To feature, click Close to close the dialog box.

Using Word Count

Appeals documents and documents filed with the Supreme Court are usually governed by strict document production rules that dictate the number of words the filing can contain, and this is serious business. If the filing or pleading does not comply with the court's rules, the court can reject the filing altogether. Legal professionals can make use of the Word Count toolbar to ensure that they are following those rules. Word even counts characters with or without spaces, lines, pages, and paragraphs. To display the Word Count toolbar, right-click over the toolbar area and choose Word Count from the list of toolbars that appears. The Word Count toolbar initially appears as a floating toolbar in your document window. You can relocate the toolbar to the toolbar area above the document window by clicking and dragging the toolbar to the desired location.

Only two items exist on the Word Count toolbar. The first is the Word Count Statistics drop-down list; the second is the Recount button. The Word Count Statistics drop-down list (which initially displays the text `<Click Recount to view>`) is used to view different statistics calculated for your document. The statistics are meaningful only after you click the Recount button. If you want to make sure that the statistics displayed in the drop-down list are up-to-date, it is a good idea to get in the habit of clicking the Recount button.

In the majority of cases, the court's word count requirement also extends to text found in footnotes and endnotes, so these items must also be included in the total word count. To include footnotes and endnotes in your count, choose Tools ⇨ Word Count and check the Include Footnotes and Endnotes option in the Word Count dialog box. (You also can view the statistics for your legal document in this dialog box.)

Using Smart Tags

A tool that gives you access to another program without actually switching to that program is always of interest to busy professionals. Word's Smart Tags feature is just such a tool. Smart Tags recognize certain types of information and provides you with actions you can take that involve another program, right from within Word. With the initial installation of Word, six types of Smart Tag *recognizers* are available: Person Names, Dates, Times, Addresses, Places, and Telephone Numbers, in the default language you are using. Whenever Word recognizes one of these data types in your document, the data is marked with a dotted purple underline. When you move the mouse pointer over the tagged term, a Smart Tag symbol appears that lets you know Word has recognized the text you typed. You can find out the options available based on the data type by clicking the symbol. An Actions button appears near the data, with options for working with other programs. The type of data that Word recognizes depends on the options checked on the Smart Tags tab found within the Tools ⇨ AutoCorrect Options menus, as shown in Figure 3-8.

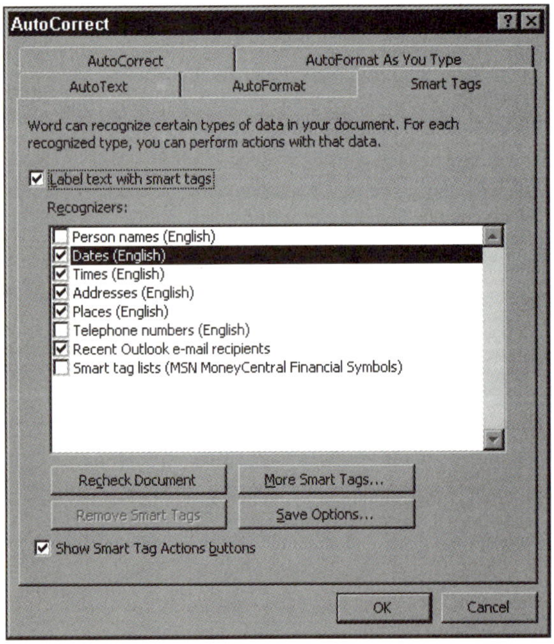

Figure 3-8: Word allows you to control what it should tag with Smart Tags.

Smart Tags gives you access to other programs without leaving Word. For instance, if you type a name in your document and the Person Names option is checked, a purple wavy line appears under that person's name. To see the actions you can take with the person's name, aim your mouse pointer at the item with the wavy blue line, and a Smart Tags Action box appears. You are then presented with options for adding that name to your Outlook Contacts list or even setting up a meeting with that individual. This saves you the trouble of switching to Outlook and then creating a meeting and having to switch back to Word. Smart Tags can be saved in your document for viewing on a different computer when sharing documents, or it can be viewed when saving a document on the Web.

The different actions available with a tagged term depend on the programs you have installed on your system. The example used in the previous paragraph cites how you could use Outlook with a person's tagged name, but the option to use Outlook would be available only if you have Outlook installed on your system and if the version of Outlook you have installed knows what to do with Smart Tags. (The version of Outlook provided with Office XP has this capability.) In the future, programs besides those in Office may be able to work with Smart Tags, and additional Smart Tags may be added to enable you to work with those programs. You can access additional Smart Tags by aiming your pointer at the text that contains the purple dotted underline and following these steps:

1. Choose Tools ⇨ AutoCorrect Options and click the Smart Tags tab.
2. Click the More Smart Tags option to be directed to Microsoft's Web site. Or from within your company's intranet, you can access the following Web address: `http://www.officesmarttags.com/`

Here you can view a list of Smart Tags created by Microsoft to use in your document.

Adding Page Numbers and Line Numbers

You can add page numbers at the top (header) of your legal documents, which is common for correspondence and memoranda, or at the bottom (footer) of your legal documents. You can add line numbers to the entire document or to a portion of the document. The first part of this section shows you how to add page numbers.

Inserting page numbers

To insert page numbers in your document, choose Insert ⇨ Page Numbers to open the Page Numbers dialog box. To specify where you want the page number to appear on the page, choose one of the options in the Position drop-down list box. To specify where you want the page number positioned within the margins of your document, choose one of the options in the Alignment drop-down list box. You can choose to position the page number on the left, center, or right side of the document within the margins, or if the document is going to be bound and you have specified a binding width, you can choose to place the page number inside or outside the binding width. In addition, most legal documents do not have a page number on the first page, so you will probably want to make sure that the Show Number on First Page option is not checked.

Word enables you to format your page numbers to follow a certain style of numbering (such as using Arabic or Roman numerals, or even alphabetical) and to include particular punctuation. To access these options, click Insert ⇨ Page Numbers and then click the Format button; doing so opens the Page Number Format dialog box. Most legal documents are numbered using the Arabic style surrounded by spaces and hyphens, and you can choose this format or other formats from the Number Format drop-down list box.

If your document includes appendices or indices, you may want the appendix or index number included as part of the page number. For instance, you may want Appendix A page numbers to be A-1, A-2, and so on. To include the appendix, index, or chapter number in the page number, check the Include Chapter Number box in the Page Number Format dialog box.

Also using the Page Number Format dialog box, you can specify the page number you want to begin with. For instance, if you want to continue the page numbering from the previous section, choose the Continue from Previous Section option. Or you can specify the page number you want to begin with by choosing the Start At option and typing the starting page number.

Page numbers can be viewed in the Print Layout view. To edit page numbers, you must edit the header or footer that contains the page number by choosing View ⇨ Header and Footer. If you are in a different view when choosing this menu option, Word automatically switches you to the Print Layout view, where the page numbers are visible. If the page number is in a header in the document, a separate section opens at the top of the document, and a rectangle appears within this section, surrounded by a dashed line. The word *Header* appears in the upper-left corner, and you can see the page number. (If the page number is contained in a footer, you will see a similar rectangle at the bottom of the page, with the word *Footer* instead.) In addition, a Header Footer dialog box opens, with options for changing the location, starting number, and so on. Figure 3-9 shows an example of a Header.

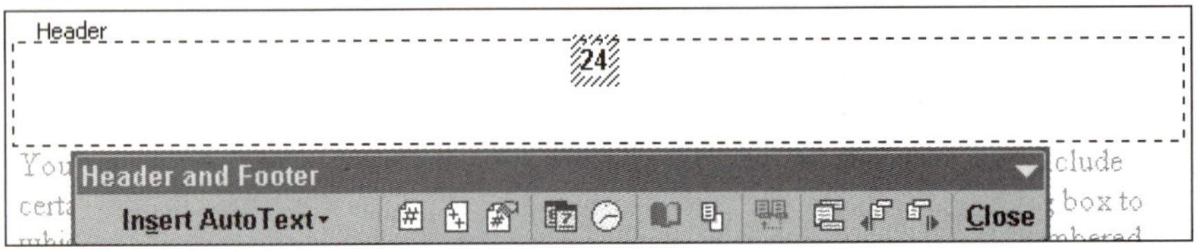

Figure 3-9: An example of a header containing a page number

The page number is located in a frame inside the header or footer. (Frames are predecessors to text boxes and have been available in Word for years and years. You can learn more about frames and text boxes through Word's Help system.) Click the number you are editing and you will see a box appear around the number. This is the frame. You will also notice that your insertion point is blinking inside the frame, indicating that you can now edit the number. Or you can add text, such as *Exhibit*, in front of the number. When you are finished making your edits, click Close to return to the document.

CROSS-REFERENCE: We discuss header and footer options in more detail in Chapter 6.

Inserting line numbers

Depending on the court receiving your filing, you may be required to include line numbers in your legal briefs and pleadings. To apply line numbers to your document, follow these steps:

1. Choose File ⇨ Page Setup and click the Layout tab.
2. In the bottom-left corner of the dialog box, click the Line Numbers option to open the Line Numbers dialog box.
3. In the Line Numbers dialog box, check the Add Line Numbering option to apply the numbering.

When line numbering is turned on, Word counts the lines on each page (except tables and items you can see only in Print Layout view, such as headers and footers, footnotes, and text boxes) and adds the line number beside each line. Line numbering is not applied to any extra space added before or after a paragraph. (You can format a paragraph with extra space before or after it, as you learn in Chapter 6, "Formatting and Polishing Text.") If you create a blank line by simply pressing the Enter key, then the blank line is counted with a line number. Line numbering can be applied to an entire document by selecting the whole document, or it can be applied to a particular section of the document. You'll find the options for controlling how your line numbering is applied in the Line Numbers dialog box.

If you want to start the line numbering at a number other than 1, which is the default, enter the desired beginning number in the Start At box. Another option you might want to change is the From Text box, which determines the amount of space there will be between the number and the text in the document body. The default measurement, Auto, places the number 1/4 inch away from the text. You can change this by entering a new measurement or using the spinner arrows to increase or decrease the measurement to the desired amount. You also can control whether to count every line, every other line, or another style by specifying a new interval in the Count By box. In the Numbering section, you can further control whether the line numbering starts over on each page (as is the case with most legal documents), whether it starts over with each new section, or whether it is continued from the previous page.

To remove line numbers, choose File ⇨ Page Setup and click the Layout tab. In the bottom-left corner of the dialog box, click the Line Numbers button to open the Line Numbers dialog box. Remove the check from the Add Line Numbering option.

Inserting Legal Symbols into Documents

The two legal symbols that legal professionals will want to include in briefs or pleadings are the paragraph symbol (¶) and the section symbol (§), which are commonly used in legal citations. You can insert these legal symbols (or other special characters) into your document by clicking Insert ⇨ Symbols. Click the Special Characters tab to see characters that are not available on your computer keyboard but can be inserted into your document. Figure 3-10 shows the Special Characters tab with the list of characters that can be inserted.

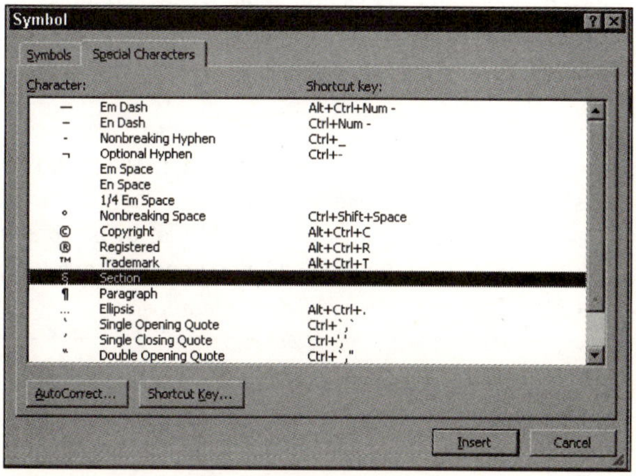

Figure 3-10: The Special Characters tab contains the section and paragraph symbols.

To insert a symbol, click to highlight the character; then click the Insert button. The symbol you selected is inserted at the location of the insertion point in your document. The dialog box remains open for you to insert another symbol if you like. When finished inserting the desired symbols, click the Close button.

The Special Characters tab contains a Shortcut Key button, which enables you to access some special characters using shortcut keys. Word does not include shortcut keys for the paragraph or section symbol, however. If you want to create shortcut keys for these (or other) symbols, you can do so by following these steps:

1. Click the Shortcut Key button on the Special Characters tab. Doing so opens the Customize Keyboard dialog box, shown in Figure 3-11. In the dialog box that opens, the highlighted symbol appears in the Commands section. If previous shortcut keys had been defined for this symbol, those keys would appear in the Current Keys section.

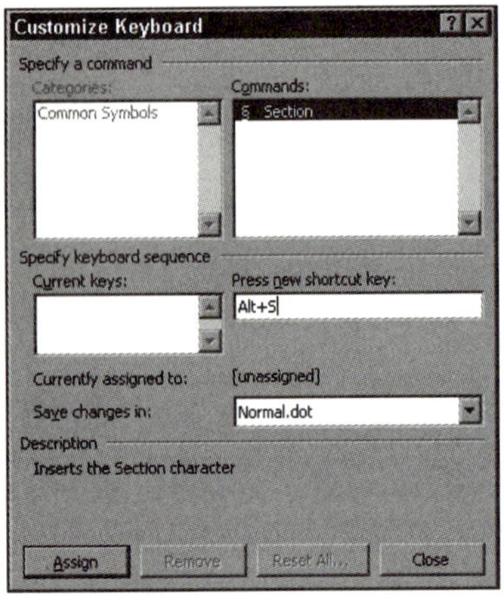

Figure 3-11: The Shortcut Key dialog box

2. Define the keys you want to use to access the highlighted symbol by entering them in the Press New Shortcut Key section. Simply press the combination of keys you want to use, and those keystrokes will display in this box. Figure 3-11 shows the Alt+S keys being assigned to the section symbol.

NOTE: If the keys you use are already in use, the Currently Assigned To area in this dialog box will show the name of the feature that is currently accessed using those keys. For instance, Ctrl+S is already assigned the function of saving a document, and you probably don't want to override that by assigning a new function to that key combination. However, you can choose to reassign existing shortcut keys — just remember that you will overwrite the original assignment.

---

3. Using the Save Changes In drop-down list, you can specify exactly where your shortcut key assignment should be saved. There are two general places where the assignment can be saved: with the current document or in a template. If you choose Normal.dot, then the assignment will be available for use with all documents you edit in Word. If you choose a different template, then the assignment will be available only to documents using that template. Finally, you can choose

the Document option if you want the keys available only when you are woking in the current document.

4. To complete assigning the shortcut key, click the Assign button. To use the keys to insert the special character in your document, just press the keys you assigned to the symbol, and the symbol is inserted.

Using AutoText

Legal documents often contain sensitive information that should be kept confidential to protect the client's rights, and some documents are covered by attorney-client disclosure rules. In light of these situations, you may want to include words such as *Attorney-Client Work Product* or *Privileged and Confidential*. If you find that you are frequently adding these words to your documents, you will appreciate the capability to store text as an AutoText entry and insert that text whenever you like. Instead of typing that text repeatedly, you can then just insert the predefined AutoText entry whenever you like.

You access the AutoText feature by clicking Insert ⇨ AutoText. A list of predefined AutoText entries will appear. To create your own entry, click the AutoText option in the list. Word should display the AutoCorrect dialog box, with the AutoText tab selected.

In the Enter AutoText Entries box, type the words you want as your entry and then click the Add button to add your entry to the list. After you have completed your entry, click the OK button. Word does not automatically insert the entry you created, as you might expect it would. The beauty of this feature is that you can insert your entry when you decide.

To insert an AutoText entry in your document, place your insertion point where you want the entry to go and then choose Insert ⇨ AutoText. In the list of AutoText entries that appears, select the desired AutoText entry.

Word also gives you the option of assigning an AutoText entry to a toolbar, which allows you to insert the AutoText entry by clicking that toolbar button. If you want to assign an AutoText entry to a toolbar, perform the following steps:

1. Right-click over the toolbar area and choose Customize from the submenu.
2. In the Customize dialog box, click the Commands tab (see Figure 3-12).

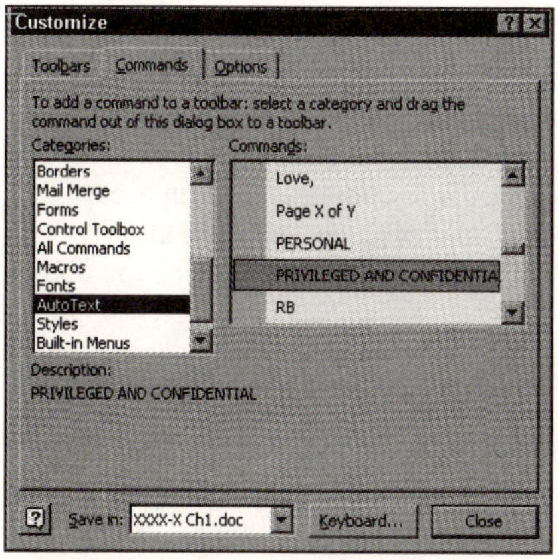

Figure 3-12: The Commands tab of the Customize dialog box

3. In the Categories section, scroll down to the AutoText entry. When you click this category, the adjacent box becomes the AutoText box, which displays the name of all AutoText entries that you have stored, as well as those that came with Word.
4. Click the name of the AutoText entry you want to assign to a button. The button appears shaded and is outlined with a black single line.
5. Drag the button to the toolbar to which you want to assign the AutoText button.
6. The name of the AutoText entry is used as the default name for the button, but you can change the name to whatever you want. With the Customize dialog box open, right-click the button you created; then click in the Name box of the menu that appears (see Figure 3-13). Make the desired changes to the wording and press Enter to automatically change the name on the button.

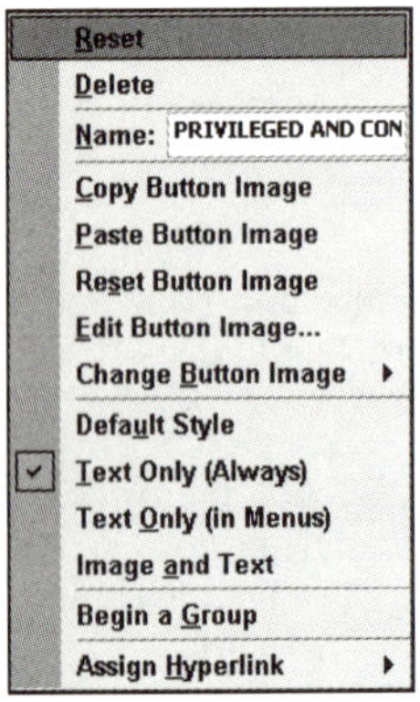

Figure 3-13: Modifications can be made to the AutoText button added to a toolbar.

Changes can be made to an AutoText entry at any time. Type the name of the AutoText entry and make the revisions. After making the revisions, select the entry and, in effect, redefine it by giving it the same name.

If you no longer need an AutoText entry, you can delete it by accessing the AutoText tab, selecting the entry you want to remove, and clicking the Delete command button.

Using Document Summaries

In many law offices, a document-management application controls where files are stored and provides techniques for retrieving those files common to a document-management environment. However, in case of the absence of a document management system, Word provides you with a document summary, or profile, that you can use to record information about the document. You can use this information as a way to search for desired documents. Document-management software almost always includes a profiling feature for your document, so if you have such software, using the one provided by Word would be redundant.

As noted previously, if the file you want is one of the last four that you worked on, it will be among the files listed near the bottom of the File menu. If you are using the New Document task pane, you can click More Documents to navigate to the location of the file. However, if you can't recall a filename, you can find the file by searching the document summaries. Choose File ⇨ Properties and click the Summary tab to view or edit the document summary. Figure 3-14 shows the Summary tab in the Properties dialog box.

The Properties dialog box contains a General tab, which gives information about the document's location, filename, size, and creation date and the last date the document was modified.

The Statistics tab of the Properties dialog box displays information similar to that provided by the Word Count feature, such as the number of words, lines, and so on. In addition, you can find out who saved the file most recently, how many revisions have been performed, and how much time has been spent editing the document.

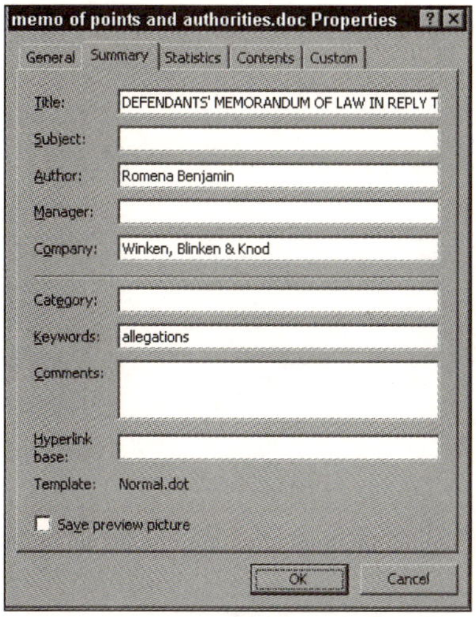

Figure 3-14: The Summary tab in the Properties dialog box

The Contents tab provides information about the pieces and parts that make up your document. A simple document will have only the document's title listed on the Contents tab, as well as any headings in the document (sort of like an outline). If the document contains data from other sources, such as an Excel workbook, then the Contents tab lists those parts as well.

On the Custom tab, you can assign values to a wide range of special document properties, or you can create custom properties that track information specific to your practice or law office. For instance, you may have a need to specify the partner ultimately responsible for each document. All you need to do is enter *Partner* in the Name box and the partner's name in the Value box; then click Add. The new custom property is listed at the bottom of the dialog box, along with its value.

If you fill in the fields of the Summary tab of the Properties dialog box for all your legal work, you can later find documents based on those fields. This is often helpful when you need to retrieve a document but cannot remember the filename. To search for a document based on the summary information, choose File ⇨ Open. From within the Open dialog box that appears, choose Tools ⇨ Search and click the Advanced tab in the Search dialog box that appears.

In the Property drop-down list of the Advanced tab (see Figure 3-15), specify where you want to search. For instance, if you want to search the document text or any properties of the document, you choose Text or Property in the drop-down list. You can then use the Condition drop-down list to specify how you want to match the specified property and then provide a value to be used in the comparison. When you have included all the necessary search criteria, click Add to add your criteria to the search. You can perform *and/or* searches by choosing the And andOr options and defining the next search. Remember to again click the Add button to include any new criteria in your search. In the

Other Search Options box, you can tell Word where to look for the file and the file format in which the file is saved.

When you are ready to perform the search, click the Search button in the middle of the Search dialog box. Files that meet the criteria you defined will appear listed in the Results section in the lower portion of the Search dialog box. Figure 3-15 is an example of how the results section looks after a search is performed.

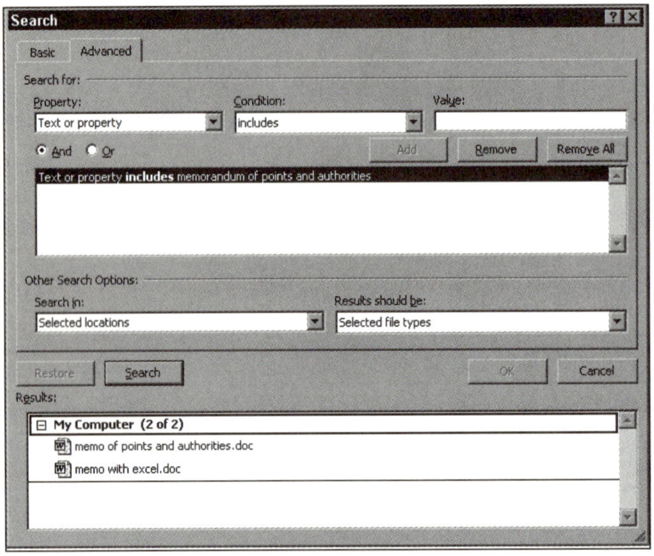

Figure 3-15: Search results are displayed in the lower portion of the Search dialog box.

Working with Bookmarks

You can insert bookmarks into your documents to mark a place in a document to which you want to return. In the event that you are reviewing a document on-screen and are interrupted, you can insert a bookmark in that location to return to it quickly. Another use for a bookmark is when you are reviewing the document and want to return to a specific location in order to change the language at a later time. Or if others are working on different parts of a document that are saved as separate files, you can insert bookmarks to mark the spot where each part is to be inserted.

Inserting bookmarks

To insert a bookmark, follow these steps:

1. Place the insert point at the location where you want the bookmark to appear and choose Insert ⇨ Bookmark.
2. In the Bookmark dialog box that opens, enter a name in the Bookmark Name box. The name you choose cannot contain spaces and must begin with a letter. The bookmark name can include numbers or the underscore.
3. In the Sort By section, specify how you want to organize the bookmarks you create in the dialog box. Bookmarks can be arranged alphabetically by choosing the name option or in chronological order by choosing the location option. If your bookmarks are hidden from view, you can display the bookmark names in the list by checking the Hidden Bookmarks option.

4. When you are finished creating the bookmark, click the Add button to both add it to the list of bookmarks and insert it into your document. Clicking the Add button also closes the dialog box.

If you selected text before you created the bookmark, the text you selected is surrounded by brackets after the bookmark is created. However, if you simply place the insertion point in the document where you want the bookmark to appear, the bookmark appears as an I-beam in the location of the insertion point. Figure 3-16 shows an example of both kinds of bookmarks.

> that they can state a claim, under [law], without pleading the alleged connection between their losses and a defendant. Finally, we show that plaintiffs have failed to salvage their claims under law.

Figure 3-16: Brackets surround text selected before creating the bookmark; an I-beam marks a bookmark created in a specific location.

If you cannot see your bookmarks at all, choose Tools ⇨ Options and click the View tab. Check the Bookmarks option in the Show section to see any bookmarks in your document.

To locate a bookmark in your document, choose Insert ⇨ Bookmark. In the Bookmark dialog box, select the name of the bookmark you want to locate and choose the Go To command. Word searches through the document and stops when the named bookmark is found.

Deleting bookmarks

If you no longer need a bookmark, it is a good idea to delete it. (No sense in letting unwanted bookmarks clutter up the landscape.) You can delete an existing bookmark by following these steps:

1. Choose Bookmark from the Insert menu. Word displays the Bookmark dialog box.
2. In the list of bookmarks, select the one you want to delete.
3. Click the Delete button. The bookmark is immediately deleted.

After you delete a bookmark, it is gone for good. If you change your mind, you will need to redefine the bookmark, using the steps detailed in the previous section.

Summary

This chapter has covered many of the fundamental aspects involved in creating and working with your documents in Word. As you continue to work in Word, most of the features covered here will soon seem like second nature to you. This chapter included how to

- Create new documents and open existing documents.
- Select, copy, cut, and paste text, set smart Cut and Paste options, and perform other essential text-editing functions.
- Use the Search and Replace features.
- Add page breaks and line and page numbers.
- Track your word count and other file properties.
- Insert legal and other symbols, AutoText, and bookmarks.

The following chapter details the use of templates and styles, which are formatting features whose advantages can't be overstated once you've become familiar with how they work.

Chapter 4

Creating Your Legal Documents with Style

In This Chapter

- Understanding the importance of styles
- Defining styles
- Understanding the Normal style
- Creating and applying styles
- Basing a new style on an existing style
- Copying styles to another document
- Renaming and replacing styles
- Assigning shortcut keys to styles
- Understanding the Styles and Formatting task pane
- Understanding Word's use of templates
- Using the Normal.dot template
- Applying templates
- Creating a template
- Basing a new template on an existing template

THE USE OF STYLE IS THE SINGLE MOST important formatting feature of Word for legal professionals to learn and understand when applying formats. You can spend hours preparing a document and getting it ready for submission to a court or agency and then, if you did not use styles to format the document, you can spend several more hours adjusting the formats. Applying styles enables you to spend more time on content and less on the appearance of the document. This chapter discusses what you need to know about creating and using styles.

Preparing to Create Your Legal Document

Much thought and time go into preparing legal documents and the legal arguments contained therein. Legal professionals who prepare their own documents often do not spend enough time thinking about how they want the document to look. This is generally because in many cases the formats they want to use in their document can actually be applied very easily, using the Format menu or the buttons that conveniently appear on the Formatting toolbar. The problem occurs when the formatting needs to change, because of a court or an agency requirement or because the author of the document decides to make changes. If styles were not used to format the document, then every place a format is directly applied, using the Formatting toolbar or menu, has to be revisited in order to effect a change. Not so with styles. Styles are groups of formats saved with a name that can be applied to sections of your document. This feature enables you to make changes that take effect immediately every place the style is used throughout the document.

We recommend that you take the time right from the start to think about how the document should look when it is finalized and create styles for formats that will be used consistently throughout the document. Word comes with many, many styles; it is to your advantage, however, to create custom styles with unique names that work for the types of documents you create. You also can save styles in a template that you can use every time you create an agreement, a pleading, or other legal documents.

Some of the format issues to consider before you begin to prepare your legal document are as follows:

- **Font:** What font style and size will you use throughout the document?
- **Paragraph formats:** What are the requirements for line spacing, indentation, and spacing before and after paragraphs (if necessary, consult court or agency requirements)?
- **Headers/footers:** What type of page numbering do you want in the document? Will the number be surrounded by spaces and dashes, and is there text that you want to appear consistently at the top or bottom of every page?
- **Footnote styles:** What font and font size are needed in the footnotes, and will the footnote number in the text and in the footnote use the same font attributes?
- **Headings:** How will each of the heading levels look? Will the text of all first-level headings be bold or underlined, for example, and how much space do you want before and after each heading level?

The decisions you make on these and other items are your ticket to creating styles to apply consistent formatting throughout the document. You can define a style containing the exact formats you want for every item in the preceding list. Then, when you are ready to prepare the document, you simply apply the style when you get to the section of text for which the style was created. You also can share these styles with others working on different sections of the document, to ensure uniformity throughout the various sections when they are combined.

Just as teams are assembled to talk about the content of a legal document, we recommend that similar teams be assembled to discuss the format of a legal document.

Defining Styles

After you have decided the formats a style should contain, create the style by choosing Format ⇨ Styles and Formatting from the menus to open the Styles and Formatting task pane. Choose New Style at the top of the pane to open the New Style dialog box (see Figure 4-1).

In this dialog box, give your new style a descriptive name, such as *Partner Name*, which could be a style used to format the names of your firm's partners. In the Style Type box, select the type of style you want. Styles can be created for paragraphs, characters, tables, or lists. Paragraph styles format an entire paragraph through the paragraph marker at the end. Character styles can be applied to words or phrases contained in the document. Table and list styles are applied to these document elements.

Also, rather than start from scratch for each new style, you can base the style you are creating on an existing style, such as one you've created previously or one that is available on one of the predefined Word templates. Select the style that you want to base the new one on, in the Style Based On drop-down list. If you prefer to create your style from scratch, you can choose No Style from the list. If you choose No Style, your style contains only Word's default formats until you add your own.

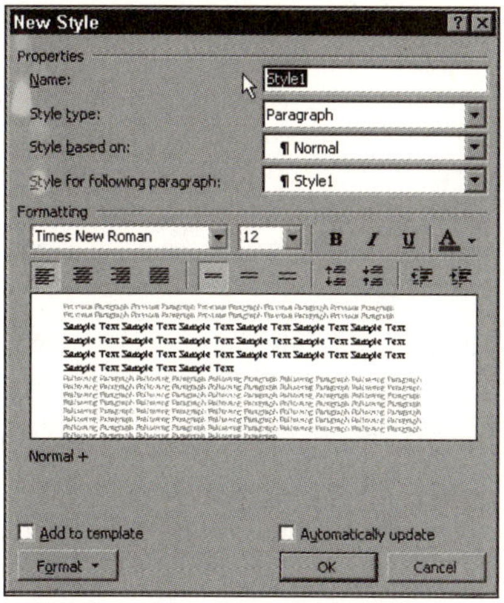

Figure 4-1: The New Style dialog box

Notice the Style for Following Paragraph drop-down list. This setting allows you to specify what paragraph style normally follows the one you are creating. This comes in handy when you are typing. For instance, say that you are typing along in a paragraph formatted with the Partner Name style. When you reach the end of the paragraph and press Enter, Word automatically changes the format of the new paragraph (the one following the one you just finished) to whatever style you specify here. The results are faster formatting and better construction of your documents.

In the Formatting section of the dialog box, you can change the alignment, apply a different font or style, and add other attributes that you want to include in your style. You will immediately see the impact these formats have on your text in the preview screen in the center of the dialog box. Below the preview screen, a list appears, showing all the formats you have added to the style.

To access formats that do not appear in the Formatting section, click the Format button at the bottom of the dialog box to display a list of additional formatting options (see Figure 4-2).

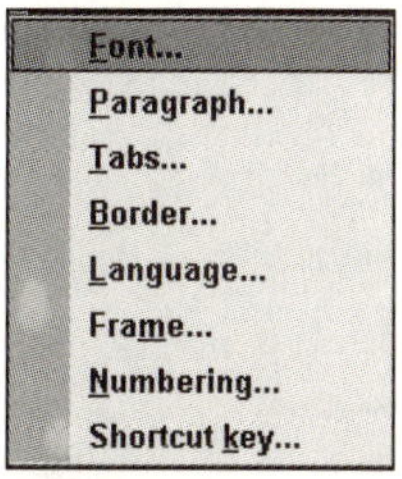

Figure 4-2: Access additional formatting options using the Format button

After you have created the style, you can make it available not only in the current document but also whenever you create a new document. To do so, check the Add to Template option in the New Style dialog box (refer to Figure 4-1). With this check box selected, Word adds the style you are creating to whatever template you are using for the current document. If you are using a specific template, then any other documents that use that template will also have access to this new style, and any new documents you base on the template will have access to the style. If you don't have a specific template attached to your document, then Word adds the new style to the default Normal.dot template. In this case, the style will be available to all Word documents in the future.

The final check box on the New Style dialog box is titled *Automatically Update*. You should carefully consider whether you want to select this option, because doing so can have far-reaching effects. If this option is selected and you later make explicit changes to a document paragraph that has this style applied to it, then those explicit changes are automatically applied to the style by Word. This means that any other paragraphs formatted with the style will also be updated. In most instances, this behavior is not desired by Word users. We would suggest not selecting this option unless you have a specific need to do so.

After you have completed defining the formats in your style, click OK. The style you create is saved in the document currently open.

Understanding the Normal Style

The Normal style is Word's default paragraph style, which is applied automatically to every paragraph in the documents you create, unless you specify a different style. The Normal style consists of Word's default font (Times New Roman, 12 point), language (U.S. English), left alignment, single-line spacing, and widow/orphan control formats. More important, many of the other styles that Word provides originate with (that is, are based on) formats contained in the Normal style. For example, another style that Word provides, called *Body Text* style, is based on the Normal style but has some differences. Figure 4-3 shows a ScreenTip displaying the formats used by the Body Text style. Note how Word specifies the format: Normal + Space After: 6 pt.

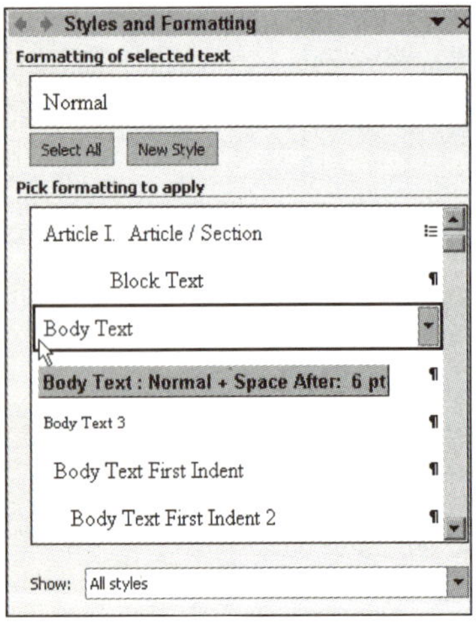

Figure 4-3: A style based on the Normal style

This description means that the Body Text style contains the same formats found in the Normal style, with the additional format to set the spacing after a paragraph. This also means that if you make changes to the Normal style, all the other styles that come with Word and are based on the Normal style are also affected by whatever changes you make. If your law office has decided to use a different default font for all legal documents, then you should modify the default font contained in the Normal style and save those changes to the Normal template (discussed later in this chapter) to change the font for all future documents.

Changing the default font in the Normal style is the only change we recommend making to the Normal style. For cases in which you want to change additional formats, your best move is to define a new style rather than make changes to the Normal style. As mentioned previously, any changes made to the Normal style are also applied to other Word styles based on Normal, such as the footnote style, for example.

You may also be surprised to know that if you modify formats in the Normal style and save the modified style to the default template, the formats applied using the Normal style in existing documents reflect the changes as well. You can control whether changes made to the Normal style affect all new and existing documents by choosing Tools ⇨ Templates and Add-Ins and then unchecking the Automatically Update Document Styles option (see Figure 4-4).

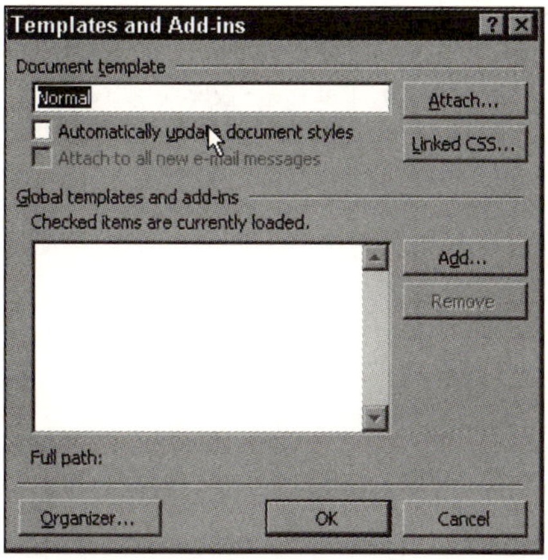

Figure 4-4: The Templates and Add-Ins dialog box

Because the Normal style contains reasonable formats for most legal documents and is automatically applied without any assistance from the legal professional, it is no wonder that many legal documents are based primarily on this style. However, the absence of custom-defined styles may make life difficult later if you make changes to the Normal style that are saved to the Normal template. These changes can affect formatting in your existing documents. So again, if you find that you need to change more than the default font, we strongly encourage you to define a new style containing all the desired custom formats.

Applying Styles

The Style drop-down list and the Styles and Formatting task pane are two ways in which you can apply styles. Whichever technique you use, you begin by identifying the text to receive the style. Then use one of the following methods.

To apply a style using the Style drop-down list, follow these steps:

1. When applying character styles, select the text to receive the style, or if you're applying a style to a paragraph, you can select the paragraph or simply locate the insertion point in the paragraph.
2. Select the style you want to apply from the Style drop-down list, which is the first control on the Formatting toolbar. When you click the arrow at the right side of the Style drop-down list, a list appears, displaying the names of the styles that are in use in the current document or are saved to

your Normal template. The list of style names you see changes when you are working in a different document containing different styles.

To apply a style using the Styles and Formatting task pane, follow these steps:

1. Choose Format ⇨ Styles and Formatting to open the Styles and Formatting task pane.
2. In the Pick Formatting to Apply section, select the style you want to apply.

   You will see the same list of style names as in the Style drop-down list. One benefit to using the Styles and Formatting task pane to apply styles is that paragraph styles are identified by the paragraph symbol (¶) displayed to the right of paragraph style names, and character styles are identified by the symbol "a" displayed to the right of character style names. The way the style name is formatted in the list is the way your text will be formatted when using that style. Another benefit of using the Styles and Formatting task pane is that if the mouse pointer is placed on a style name, a ScreenTip appears, displaying all the formats contained in that style. Figure 4-5 shows the identifying symbols displayed beside the style name, as well as a sample ScreenTip.

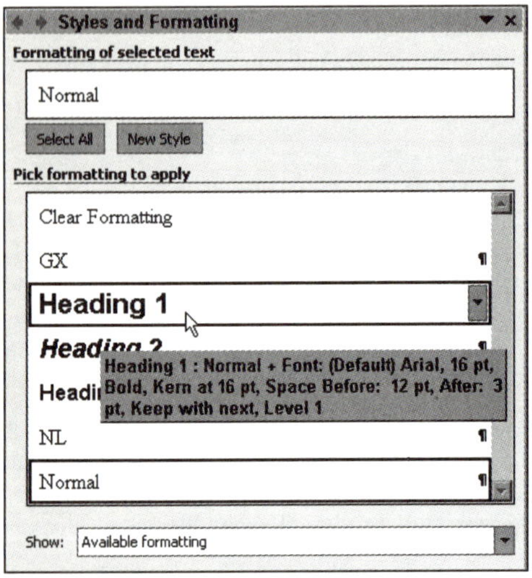

Figure 4-5: Symbols identifying style type (and a ScreenTip) display in this task pane.

In either case, when you use one of the techniques described in this section to apply your style, simply click the style name you want to use to apply that style to your text. Upcoming sections of this chapter discuss additional techniques for applying styles.

Basing a New Style on an Existing Style

As noted previously, Word comes with many styles, most of which are based on the Normal style. You also can define styles that are based on other styles. For instance, you may want to create a new heading style to format first-level headings. If you look in the Styles and Formatting task pane, you can see that the default Heading1 style includes many of the formats you want in your own first-level headings. Rather than reinvent the wheel, you can base your new style on the style containing the formats you want.

To base a new style on an existing style, follow these steps:

1. Choose Format ⇨ Styles and Formatting to open the Styles and Formatting task pane.
2. Click the New Style button to open the New Style dialog box.
3. In the Name text box, enter your new style's name and choose the style type from the Style Type drop-down list.
4. Click the arrow beside the Style Based On drop-down list and choose the style you're basing your new style on.

At this point, you can continue to define the style as you learned how to do earlier in this chapter. Use the options available through the Format button to define how you want the format to appear. When you are finished, click OK to save the style.

Figure 4-6 shows a new style, Brfhead1, being defined for first-level headings in a brief. The name chosen for the style is designed to identify what the style is used for. This style is based on the Heading1 style that comes with Word, and the formats seen in the rest of the dialog box initially contain formats for the Heading1 style. You can then modify or add formats to reflect how you want your level-1 headings to look in a brief.

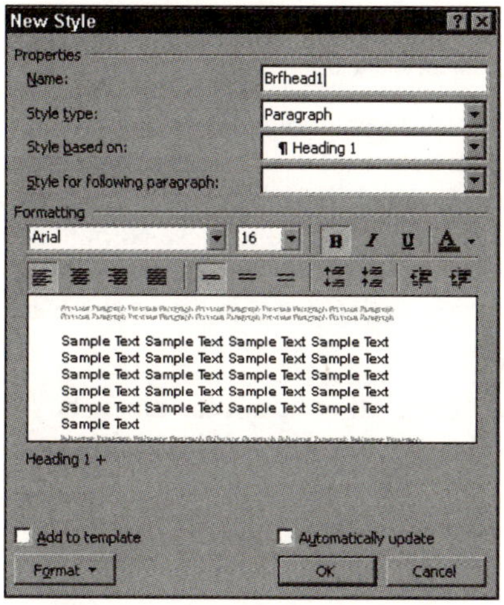

Figure 4-6: A new style to format headings is based on formats in the Heading1 style.

Copying Styles to Another Document

You may have several reasons for copying styles from one legal document to another. One reason is to be able to use styles contained in documents you have received from clients in the documents you create for that client. Or you have defined styles in one document that you want to use in another. You can copy styles from one document to another by using Word's Organizer tool. You start the Organizer by performing the following steps:

1. Choose Tools ⇨ Templates and Add-Ins.
2. In the Templates and Add-Ins dialog box, click the Organizer button to display the Organizer dialog box, as shown in Figure 4-7.
3. Click the Styles tab in the Organizer dialog box.

The Organizer allows you to transfer styles — among the other document elements represented by the different tabs — from one template or document to another. Notice in Figure 4-7 that the styles in two documents or templates are shown. On the left side of the dialog box are the styles in Document2; on the right side are the styles in the Normal.dot template.

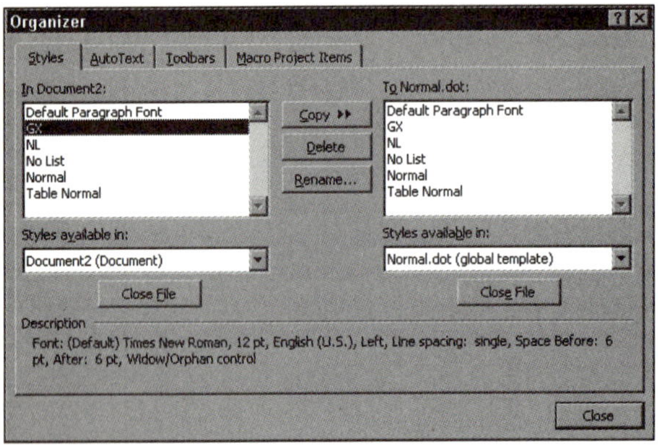

Figure 4-7: The Organizer is used for copying items from one template or document to another.

The idea behind the Organizer is that you display the styles in two different templates or documents and then transfer them from one to the other. For instance, say that you wanted to transfer styles from Document2 to a different template that you created previously and named *Pleadings.dot*. You need to have both Document2 and Pleadings.dot displayed in the Organizer, so you need to close Normal.dot. You do that by clicking the Close File button at the right side of the dialog box. Normal.dot is closed, and the Close File button changes to an Open File button. When you click Open File, you can locate and open the Pleadings.dot template.

With both Document2 and Pleadings.dot open, you can click a style in either side of the dialog box and copy it to the other side by clicking the Copy button. When you are through copying styles, you click the Close button at the bottom of the dialog box to dismiss the Organizer.

Renaming and Deleting Styles

You can rename a style by using one of the following techniques:

- Choose Format ⇨ Styles and Formatting. Right-click the style you want to rename and choose Modify from the submenu that appears. Make the desired changes to the style name in the Modify Style dialog box that opens.
- Choose Tools ⇨ Templates and Add-Ins, and click the Organizer button. Click the Styles tab and select the style name you want to change. Click the Rename button in the Organizer dialog box and type the new name in the Rename dialog box that appears.

To delete a style, click the desired style name on the Styles tab of the Organizer dialog box and then click the Delete button. You also can delete a style in the Styles and Formatting task pane by right-clicking the style name and choosing Delete from the submenu that appears.

NOTE: Word will not let you delete its predefined styles. You can delete only custom styles that you or others have created.

Assigning Shortcut Keys to Styles

Previously, we discussed two techniques for applying styles: using the Style drop-down list or using the Styles and Formatting task pane. Another technique you can use is to assign shortcut keys to your style. We discussed the benefit of using shortcut keys in the "Inserting Legal Symbols into Documents" section of Chapter 3, "Creating and Working with Documents." You can derive the same benefits when you use shortcut keys to apply your styles. You can assign shortcut keys to styles during the style-creation stage, or you can modify a style later to assign shortcut keys to it.

To assign shortcut keys to a style, perform the following steps:

1. Choose Format ⇨ Styles and Formatting. Right-click the style you want to assign shortcut keys to and choose Modify from the submenu that appears.
2. In the Modify Style dialog box that opens, click the Format button in the lower-left corner. Choose Shortcut Key from the submenu that appears. The Customize Keyboard dialog box opens.
3. In the Press New Shortcut Key section of the dialog box, press the combination of keys you want to use to apply your style. Remember to be careful not to reuse a key assignment in use by another feature (refer to "Inserting Legal Symbols into Documents" in Chapter 3).
4. Click the Assign button to complete the assignment.

Figure 4-8 shows that the keys assigned to the Brfhead1 style are Alt+B,1. This means that you hold down the Alt key and press B followed by 1 to apply the first-level heading style that you've defined as Brfhead1. This type of shortcut key assignment is very useful when creating a style for each level of heading in your document. With the base style name of *Brfhead* in the example, subsequent styles for successive levels of headings in the document can have the same root name. You cannot use the Alt+B,1 key combination to apply each one, however. Instead, you use Alt+B, 1 to apply the first-level heading, Alt+B,2 to apply the second-level heading, and so on.

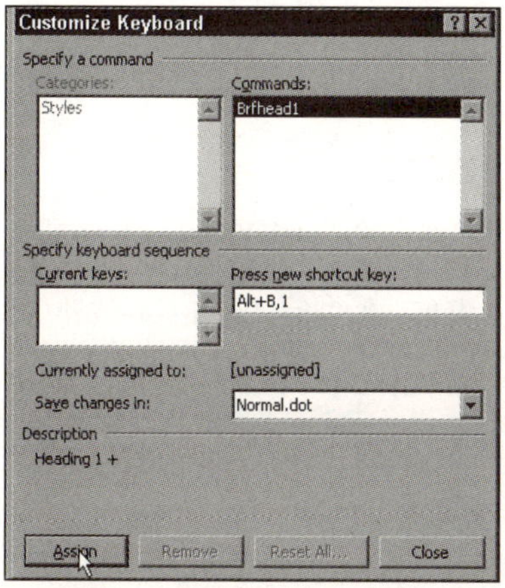

Figure 4-8: The Customize Keyboard dialog box

To apply a style that has shortcut keys assigned, do one of the following:

- **To apply a paragraph style:** Click in the paragraph and press the key combination assigned to the style.
- **To apply a character style:** Select the text and press the key combination assigned to the style.

Using the Styles and Formatting Task Pane

The previous sections have covered how to apply an existing style, create a new style, and modify and delete styles. This section discusses a few more options that are available in the Styles and Formatting task pane.

Replacing styles using Select All

The Formatting of Selected Text section contains a Select All button, which is useful for selecting all the text in your document that uses a specific style. All you have to do is select some text that uses a specific style or place the insertion point in a paragraph that uses the style you want to find. When you click Select All, Word automatically highlights all the text in the document that uses that style. After the text is highlighted, you can create a new style for the selected text or replace the style with a different style. This feature is helpful when, for example, you have received documents from outside sources and you want to apply styles throughout the document to replace the styles originally used. Using this technique, you don't have to worry about modifying or deleting the original style; instead, you can simply replace it consistently throughout.

Displaying styles

In the Pick Formatting to Apply section of the Styles and Formatting task pane, you have several options from which to choose to display the styles you want to show in this section. The options are as follows:

- **Available Formatting:** Displays all the formats available in the entire document
- **Formatting in Use:** Displays all the formats available in selected text or in the text containing the insertion point
- **Available Styles:** Displays all styles available in the entire document
- **Custom:** Lets you choose which styles to make visible

You can close the Styles and Formatting task pane at any time by clicking the *X* at the top of the pane.

Understanding Word's Use of Templates

If you want to carry your consistency of document design even further than character and paragraph formatting, you will want to make use of templates. *Templates* are saved files that contain a collection of styles for use when creating a specific type of document. For instance, a legal professional who wants to keep clients informed of rules or regulations that may affect their business or legal position may want to create a newsletter template to produce consistently formatted newsletters on a monthly basis. Or your office may want to produce letters formatted a certain way. Other examples are pleadings and briefs.

When you create a new document with the New command on the File menu, Word opens the New Document task pane. In the New from Template section, you can select a template from the list by clicking the template hyperlink, or you can click the General Templates hyperlink. The latter choice makes Word ask which template you want to use by displaying the available templates on several tabs in the Templates dialog box (see Figure 4-9).:

Templates that you create are stored in the default location for User templates and can be viewed by clicking Tools ⇨ Options ⇨ File Locations. Any new templates that you create appear on the General tab. If you click the OK button in this dialog box without making a selection, Word uses the default Normal template on which all documents are based unless another template is selected.

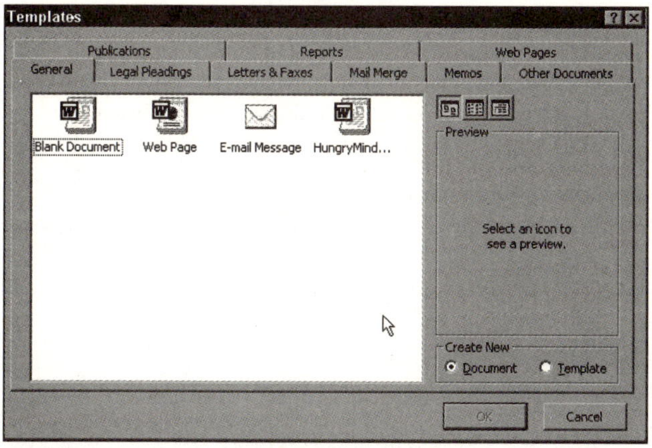

Figure 4-9: The General tab in the Templates dialog box

When you select a template from this dialog box, your new document takes on all the features belonging to that template — including any text stored in the template; any character, paragraph, and page layout formatting; any preset styles; and any new styles that you have added to the document. You also can store AutoText entries and keyboard, menu, or toolbar definitions in a template to make them available for use within a document.

You can use any of Word's predefined templates, or you can create and save your own templates. If you take the time to examine the templates provided with Word, you may find many that can be useful in your work. Word comes with several templates in the following categories, which you'll find on the tabs in the Templates dialog box:

- Publications
- Reports
- Mail Merge
- Letters and Faxes
- Legal Pleadings
- Memos
- Web Pages
- Other Documents

NOTE: The names and categories of templates available within Word depend on the options selected when you first installed Word.

Because a template is a document, you use the same procedure to create and save a template as you use for a document. Word lets you specify whether you want to create a document or a template when you use the General Templates hyperlink in the New Document task pane. At the lower-right corner of the Templates dialog box, simply click the Template radio button to make the new document a template; then click the OK button. When the new document appears on-screen, you can add whatever text, formatting, and styles that you want and then save the file with the Save command from the File menu.

You also can specify that a file be saved as a template after you have created it. For example, if you have created a boilerplate document and you want to store that document as a template, you can do so with the Save As command from the File menu. In the Save As dialog box, choose Document Template from the Save as Type list box. The file will be saved as a template with the .dot extension.

In the New Document task pane, you also can access templates on your Web site by clicking this hyperlink. If you want to use a template that is not found in any location heretofore mentioned, you can click the Templates on Microsoft.com hyperlink to search Microsoft's Web site for additional templates. Here you can find newsletter templates and other templates that may be useful.

Using the Normal.dot template

Some new users find Word's use of the same term *(Normal)* to identify both a style and template confusing. The Normal *style* refers to one particular style (available in all Word's default templates) that defines the character and paragraph formatting for the text. The Normal template, on the other hand, is a template file (saved as Normal.dot) that contains Word's default styles, along with the default keyboard, menu, and toolbar macro assignments. All styles and default keyboard, menu, and toolbar macro assignments that are saved to the Normal template are available for use from anywhere within Word.

Attaching templates

To put templates to work for you, you simply attach them to a document. When you create a new document based on a template (as described earlier in this chapter), the specified template is automatically attached to the new document. You can also attach a template to an existing document by following these steps:

1. Choose Templates and Add-Ins from the Tools menu. Word displays the Templates and Add-Ins dialog box.

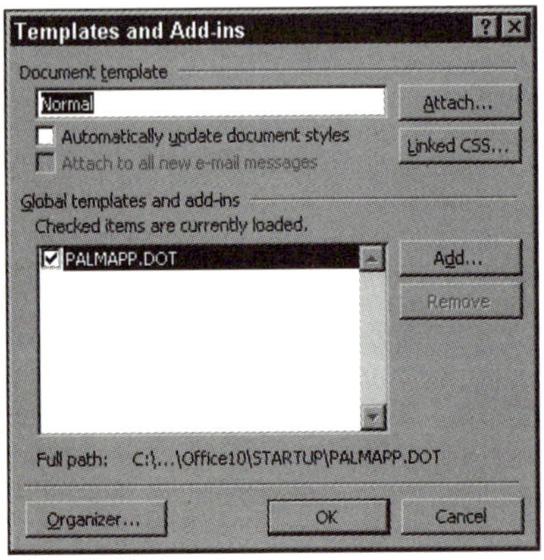

Figure 4-10: The Templates and Add-Ins dialog box

2. Click the Attach button. Word displays the Attach Template dialog box, which looks very much like a standard Open dialog box used elsewhere in Word.

3. Using the controls in the Attach Template dialog box, locate and select the template you want to attach to the document.
4. Click Open. The Attach Template dialog box closes and the template you selected is specified at the top of the Templates and Add-Ins dialog box.
5. If you want the styles within the template to override any identically named styles already within your document, select the Automatically Update Document Styles check box.
6. Click OK.

Creating templates

You can create a new template by performing the overall steps that follow:

1. Choose File ⇨New.
2. In the New Document task pane, click the General Templates hyperlink.
3. In the Templates dialog box that appears, click the Template radio button and then click the OK button.
4. Design your template as desired. Any text or graphics that you place in the template will be included in any new documents that you base on the template. In other words, the template can serve as a boilerplate for a new document.
5. When you are done making changes to your new template, choose File ⇨ Save.
6. In the File Name text box, enter a name for the template. By default, Word saves all template files to a folder named *Templates*.
7. Click the Save button to save the template.

Basing a new template on an existing template

You can use a simple variation of the steps in the preceding section to create a new template based on an existing template. In the Templates dialog box, click the Template radio button. Then, click the desired tab under which the existing template is stored, or choose the name of the template on which you want to base the new template. Click the OK button. When you save the template, be sure to save it under a different name than the original template.

NOTE: To modify an existing template, you simply open the template in a way similar to one of the ways you open a document, by choosing the File ⇨ Open command. In the dialog box that appears, select Document Template from the Files of Type list box. The list box then displays only those files with a .DOT extension. You can choose the desired template by name, or you can enter the name in the File Name text box. Make the desired changes to the template and save the template with the Save command from the File menu.

After the template is created, you can create new documents that are based on that template. The result will be a new document that already contains the formatting necessary for the type of pleading you're using it with.

Summary

This chapter covered how to create and use styles and templates to greatly increase your efficiency and reduce the tedium of making your documents adhere to requirements and look professional. In this chapter you learned how to

- Define new styles and use existing styles as a base for new ones.
- Copy styles to another document.
- Rename and replace existing styles.
- Work with the Styles and Formatting task pane.
- Use the Normal.dot template and attach existing templates to documents.
- Create new templates, as well as base a new template on an existing template.

The following chapter delves into the details of working with Word's outline feature to help you organize your documents.

Chapter 5

Working with Outlines and Long Documents

In This Chapter

- Understanding outlines
- Using Outline view
- Creating an outline
- Expanding and collapsing outline headings
- Promoting, demoting, and moving headings
- Applying numbering to outlines
- Printing outlines
- Adding cross-references

OUTLINING IS ONE OF THE WORD PROCESSING features legal professionals use the most. Using an outline feature allows legal professionals to give structure to legal documents they are preparing. In preparing to file or submit any legal document, usually the first step is to organize the document into major sections and subsections in an outline structure. As the preparation of the document progresses, details are added to the respective sections. Eventually, sections may need to be rearranged, added, or deleted. Word's outline feature provides the flexibility and clarity to organize and reorganize as needed.

Understanding Outlines

In Word, outlining is built in to a document. As you create a document, you can create an outline simultaneously. The only difference between a full document and an outline is the view that you use to examine the document. When you are in Outline view, you look at the document in the form of an outline, which is different from the other available views. Figure 5-1 shows a portion of a registration agreement document in Outline view.

Outlines consist of paragraphs formatted as heading styles and the associated text. Word provides nine predefined levels of heading styles, named *Heading 1* through *Heading 9*. Each heading style is preformatted to be aligned at the left margin or at a particular tab stop that reflects its place in the outline hierarchy. We recommend that you always use the default heading styles as a basis for creating new heading styles because the default style already contains formats to include that heading in a table of contents. For instance, Heading 1 is formatted to appear as a first-level heading, Heading 2 is formatted to appear as a second-level heading, and so on, when a table of contents is generated.

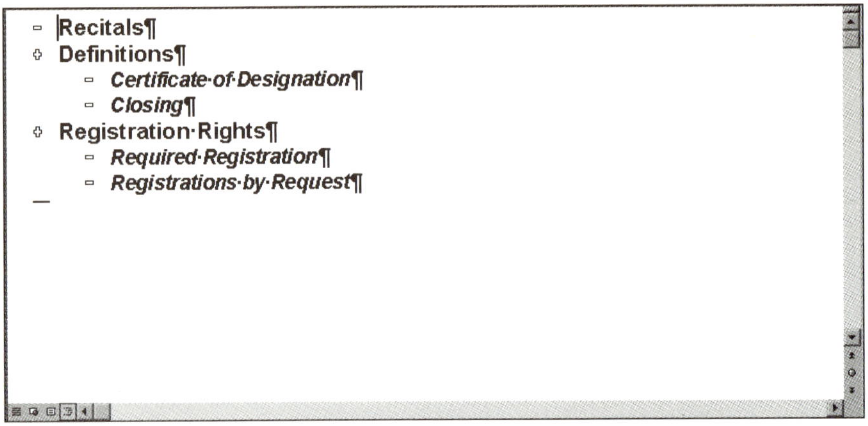

Figure 5-1: A sample document viewed in outline form

Body text is any text within an outline that has not been given a heading style. Word also uses the term *subtext* to refer to all headings and body text that appear below a particular heading.

When you are in Outline view, selecting text is basically the same as selecting text in other areas of Word. However, you should be aware of some differences. The most significant one is that you lose the capability to select a full paragraph with only part of another paragraph. If you use the mouse or keyboard methods to select past the boundary of a paragraph and into the following paragraph, the entire second paragraph becomes selected. As you drag the mouse across additional paragraphs, each paragraph becomes selected in its entirety. This feature makes editing more difficult in Outline view. (You can get around this by turning off Outline view while you do your editing.)

You can select a heading and all the subtext below it by double-clicking in the area just to the left of the heading (when you move the mouse pointer into the area where you can double-click, it points up and to the right) or by selecting the desired heading and subtext with a combination of the Shift and arrow keys.

Using Outline View

To work with a document in Outline view, choose View ⇨ Outline (or click the Outline view button on the left side of the Status bar at the bottom of the Word window). In Outline view, Word gives you additional tools to help structure the outline. A different toolbar, called the *Outlining toolbar*, automatically appears at the top of the screen when you choose the Outline command. Figure 5-2 shows the Outlining toolbar. In addition to the Outlining toolbar, small icons appear to the left of each paragraph.

Figure 5-2: The Outlining toolbar

A flexible feature of Word's outlining is that you can use it with a document at any time. You can create a document and later come back to it and structure the document in outline form, or you can create the document in outline form as you go along. You can add additional portions of a document, whether they are headings or body text, to your outline at any time.

You can change the structure of the outline by promoting a paragraph to a higher level or by demoting it to a lower level of importance. When changing the structure of an outline in Word, you generally select the desired paragraph and then click a button from the Outlining toolbar to change a feature of the outline. Table 5-1 explains the function of the Outlining toolbar's buttons.

Table 5-1
The Outlining Toolbar Buttons and Their Functions

Button	***Function***
Promote to Heading 1	Promotes a heading or body text to Level 1
Promote	Promotes a paragraph or body text to the next higher level
Outline Level	Reflects and controls the level of the heading selected
Demote	Demotes a heading to the next lower level
Demote to Body Text	Demotes a heading to body text
Move Up	Moves a heading or body text up to a new location in the outline
Move Down	Moves a heading or body text down to a new location in the outline
Expand	Reveals all text within a heading
Collapse	Hides a paragraph so that only the heading shows
Show Heading	Controls how many levels of the outline are displayed
Show First Line Only	When All is selected, shows just the first line of body text
Show Formatting	Shows or hides character formatting
Update TOC	Convenient tool for updating the table of contents following edits to headings
Go to TOC	Relocates insertion point to the table of contents
Master Document View	Switches to Master Document view
Collapse Subdocuments	Collapses subdocuments
Create Subdocument	Creates links in current document to a document created separately in Word
Remove Subdocument	Removes links to subdocuments
Insert Subdocuments	Inserts documents linked to current document
Merge Subdocument	Combines subdocuments
Split Subdocument	Separates subdocuments
Lock Document	Protects documents so that they cannot be changed

Keyboard users should note that there are keyboard shortcuts available for accessing the features on the Outlining toolbar. Table 5-2 summarizes the keyboard shortcuts.

TIP: Although Alt+Shift+5 on the numeric keypad is specified as the keyboard equivalent for converting headings to body text, laptop users should note that this keyboard combination does not work on many laptop keyboards because of the compromises made in designing laptop keyboards. These keyboards often give up the numeric keypad and combine all numbers with the character keys. If you are using a laptop and you plan on doing a lot of work with outlines, consider adding an external mouse so that you can use the Outlining toolbar. (For some people, the built-in mouse substitutes are difficult to use.)

Table 5-2
Keyboard Equivalents for the Outlining Toolbar

Keyboard Combination	***Function***
Alt+Shift+left arrow or tab	Promotes a paragraph
Alt+Shift+right arrow or Shift+tab	Demotes a paragraph
Ctrl+Shift+N	Demotes a paragraph to body text
Alt+Shift+up arrow	Moves a paragraph up
Alt+Shift+down arrow	Moves a paragraph down
Alt+Shift+plus sign	Expands body text
Alt+Shift+minus sign	Collapses body text under a heading
Alt+Shift+A	Displays all headings and body text
Slash (/ on numeric keypad)	Shows/hides character formatting
Alt+Shift+L	Toggles between showing all body text and just the first line
Alt+Shift+1 through Alt+Shift+9	Expands or collapses headings to specified levels (on numeric keypad) through level 8 or to show body text (level 9)

Creating an Outline

When creating a legal document, you can begin by creating the outline headings first and then filling in the body text, or you can create the headings and body text as you go along. The best practice to follow when creating a new outline is to decide what each heading should look like at the various levels of the outline. Then create customized heading styles (based on one of Word's heading styles) to apply to the appropriate levels of your outline. The following steps create an outline for an example purchase agreement:

1. To open a new document, choose File ⇨ New and click the Blank Document hyperlink in the New Document task pane that opens.

2. Choose View ⇨ Outline to switch to the Outline view.
3. Open the Styles and Formatting task pane by choosing Format ⇨ Styles and Formatting from the menus. (Or if you did not close the task pane after completing Step 1, click the arrow on the right side of the task pane's title bar and choose Styles and Formatting from the menu to switch to that task pane.)
4. Click the New Style button in the task pane and enter **PAHead1** to serve as the name of the style. This name will be the top-level heading for the purchase agreement outline.
5. Heading styles are paragraph formats, so select Paragraph as the style type.
6. Base the new style on the built-in Heading 1 style by choosing this style in the Style Based On drop-down list.
7. In this step, you decide the style that will be applied to the paragraph that follows the style you are creating. For this example, specify that the paragraph following your heading will be formatted as Body Text; to do so, choose that style in the Style for Following Paragraph drop-down list.
8. Click the Format button and choose the Paragraph option. Word displays the Paragraph dialog box. On the Indents and Spacing tab, change the alignment of the heading so that it is centered, with 6 points of spacing before and after the paragraph. On the Line and Page Breaks tab, make sure that the Widow/Orphan Control and the Keep with Next options are checked. These two options ensure that a page break does not split a heading paragraph and that the heading is not separated from the text that follows by a page break. (These settings are the defaults in the Word-provided heading styles.) Click OK to dismiss the Paragraph dialog box.
9. Make the style available in other documents besides the current document by checking Add to Template in the New Style dialog box. Click OK to complete creating the new style. The new style appears in the Styles and Formatting task pane.

This completes the process of creating a customized heading style for level 1 of the purchase agreement outline. You repeat Steps 1 through 9 to create a customized heading style for each successive level of the outline. To complete the example purchase agreement outline, use the preceding steps to create two more levels as follows. Name the second-level heading *PAHead2*, base it on Heading 2, and make it left-aligned, with 6 points of spacing before and after the paragraph and with a .5 indent. After clicking OK to dismiss the Paragraph dialog box (Step 8), click the Format button again to select the Font menu option and change the font to 12 points. Also, use the Underline Style drop-down list to indicate that this level has a single underline. Base the third-level heading, *PAHead3*, on Heading 3. Make the same changes you did for PAHead2, except indent the heading by 1" and make the font italic. Figure 5-3 shows how the three newly created styles appear in the Styles and Formatting task pane.

NOTE: Remember that you can assign shortcut keys to styles to make applying the styles easier (see Chapter 3).

Now that the customized styles have been created, the heading styles are applied as the outline is created, by using the techniques described in Chapter 4, "Creating Your Legal Document with Style." To apply the styles, click the style name in the Styles and Formatting task pane. Figure 5-4 shows the purchase agreement outline created with the new heading styles applied.

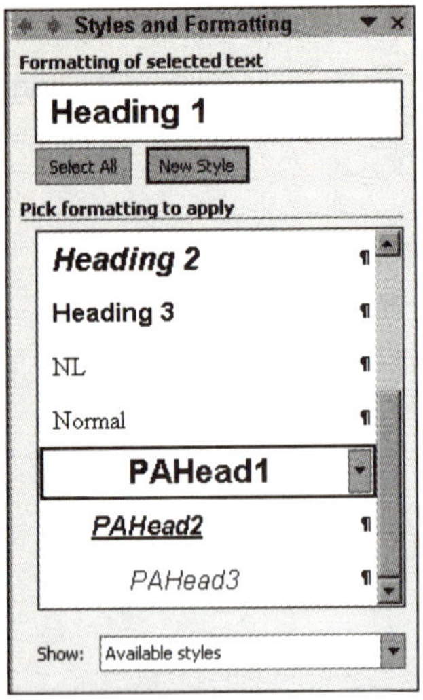

Figure 5-3: New heading styles appear in the Styles and Formatting task pane.

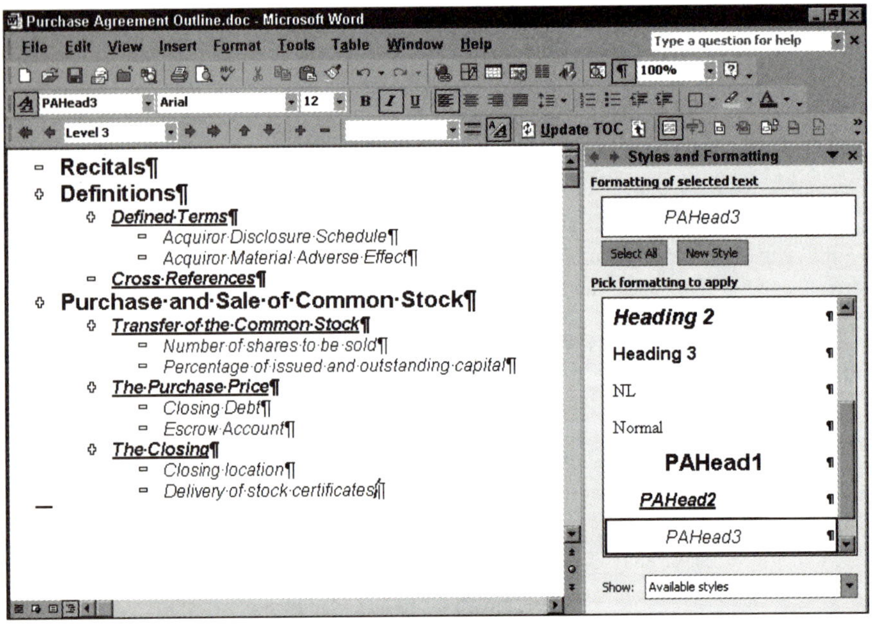

Figure 5-4: An outline created using customized heading styles

Next, you can begin adding body text to the various parts of the outline. Keep in mind that Word's flexibility means that you do not necessarily have to create your outlines in this same manner. You may choose to create headings and body text as you go along. To add some body text to the sample outline, perform the following steps:

1. Move the cursor to the end of the line of the heading under which you want to add some text; then press Enter to begin a new line. The format from the previous paragraph is carried forward to the new paragraph, as indicated by the fact that the icon aligns with the existing lines.

2. Click the Demote to Body Text button on the Outlining toolbar and begin typing the text. (We recommend that you apply a customized body text style.) The example shows a body text style called *PATXT*, which is formatted with a first-line indent of .5 and a different font from that used for the headings. Figure 5-5 shows body text that has been added after some of the headings in the purchase agreement.

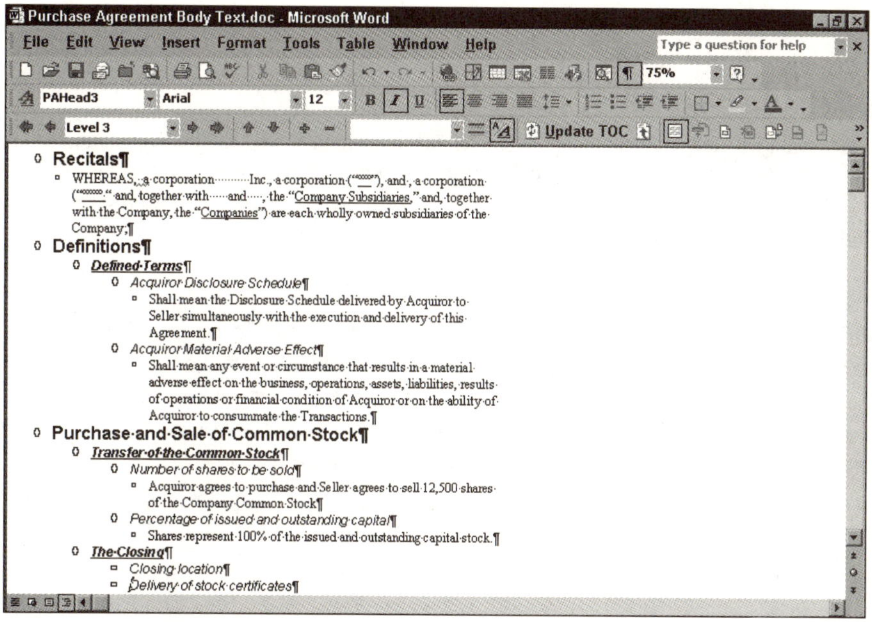

Figure 5-5: An example of body text in an outline

Expanding or Collapsing Outline Headings

It is very handy to be able to collapse an outline in order to focus on the primary elements of the outline without being distracted by the less important points or by the body text. An easy way to collapse an entire outline is to select from the Show Level drop-down list the level of the outline you want to view. Figure 5-6 shows the result of selecting Show Level 1 from the list. Only the paragraphs formatted with level-1 headings are visible; all other paragraphs are hidden from view (but not deleted).

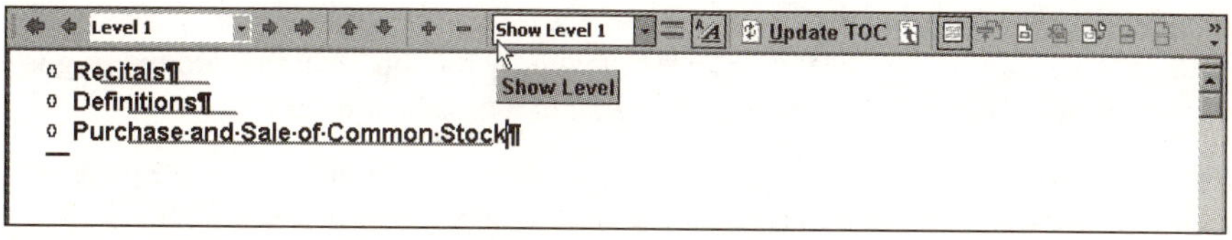

Figure 5-6: The outline is collapsed to show only level-1 headings.

You can collapse or expand an outline to include or remove from view any outline level in use in your document. However, to see all the headings and subheadings in an outline, including body text, choose Show All Levels from the Show Level drop-down list on the Outlining toolbar.

You also can individually collapse or expand each outline level, using the icons on the Outlining toolbar. To accomplish this, situate the insertion point within the level you are expanding or collapsing. Then click the icon on the Outlining toolbar containing a plus (+) symbol to expand that level, or click the icon containing the minus (–) symbol to collapse that level. Figure 5-7 shows the Expand and Collapse icons.

Figure 5-7: The Expand and Collapse icons

Promoting and Demoting Headings

If you find that you want a heading at a different hierarchical level than it was originally assigned, you can click anywhere in the heading and use the Promote and Demote buttons on the Outlining toolbar. It is important to note that the subheadings, however, are not promoted or demoted with the heading. (Word does promote or demote any associated body text with the heading.)

NOTE: The heading style associated with the promoted or demoted heading does not automatically change to reflect the heading's new level, unless you are using Word's built-in heading levels (Heading 1 through Heading 9). You must apply the appropriate style manually. If you have your custom styles set up correctly, the desired heading level will change to reflect the heading level associated with the style. Thus, it is often "cleaner" to simply use styles to set heading levels than it is to use the Promote and Demote tools.

To promote or demote subheadings, first select the subheadings and then click the Promote or Demote buttons as desired.

Moving Headings

In Outline view, you can easily move headings up or down in the outline. Moving a heading up means that you move it, along with any headings or text collapsed beneath it, closer to the beginning of the document. Similarly, moving a heading down moves it toward the end of the document. You can move headings by using the Move Up and Move Down buttons on the Outlining toolbar.

To move an individual heading up or down in the outline without moving its subheadings, click within the heading and then click the Move Up button or Move Down button. If subtext is not collapsed, it moves with the heading only if you have selected it with the heading. If you want to move a heading and its associated subheadings together to a new location in the outline, the best technique to use is to collapse that portion of the outline so that only the top level you are moving is visible and all subtext and subheadings move with the heading to a new location.

If the outline is expanded and you prefer to keep it that way, you can use another technique to select subtext and subheads in order to move them to a new location. To do so, follow these steps:

1. Aim the pointer at the plus (+) symbol on the left side of the heading you are moving until the pointer changes to a four-headed arrow.
2. Click the symbol to select all headings, body text, and subheadings in that portion of the outline (see Figure 5-8).
3. Click the Move Up button or Move Down button on the Outlining toolbar to relocate that portion of the outline. Or click to drag the selected portion of the outline to a new location in the

document. While dragging, you can see a faint gray horizontal line move along with you to indicate where your section of the outline will be relocated when you release the mouse button.

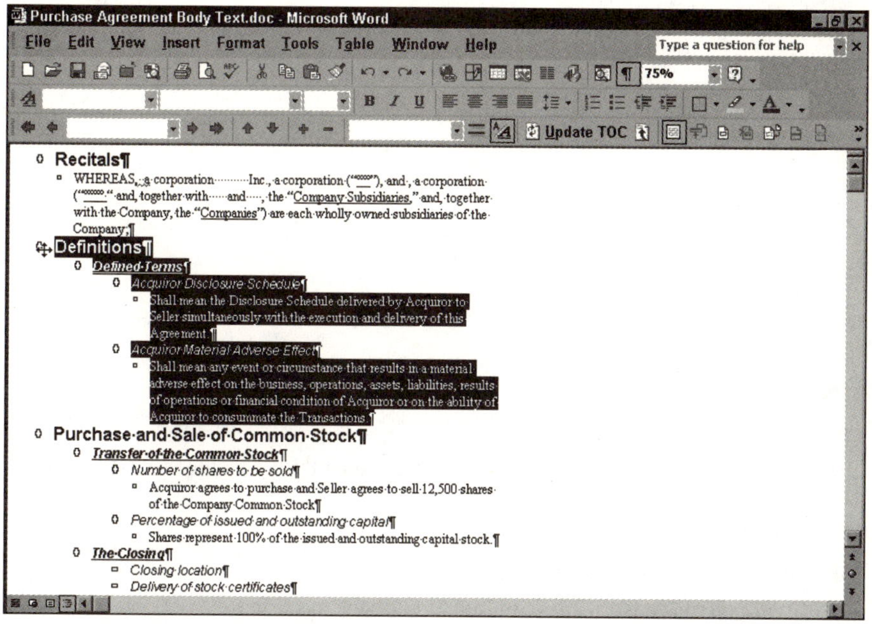

Figure 5-8: Click the outline symbol to select the outline level, along with subheadings and body text.

Applying Numbering to Headings

It is extremely rare to find headings in legal documents that are not numbered. If your document contains styled headings that you want to number, you can modify each heading style to include the automatic numbering. After automatic numbering is added to your headings, you can move, add, or delete numbered headings, and the numbering automatically adjusts following the change. If you used heading styles to format the headings as recommended at the beginning of this chapter, you easily can modify the heading styles to apply numbering to your headings. You also can apply numbering to customized headings that are not styled.

Adding numbering to styled headings

To modify heading styles to include numbering, follow these steps:

1. Select the heading style to be modified by placing the insertion point anywhere in a heading formatted with the style you want to change.
2. Choose Format ⇨ Styles to open the Styles and Formatting task pane. The name of the style applied to the selected heading appears at the top of the task pane. (If you do not preselect the heading containing the style before you open the task pane, you can select the style you want to modify after the task pane is opened.)
3. Click the drop-down list arrow beside the style you want to modify and choose Modify from the submenu that appears.
4. In the Modify Style dialog box, click the Format button in the lower-left corner and choose Numbering from the submenu that appears (see Figure 5-9).

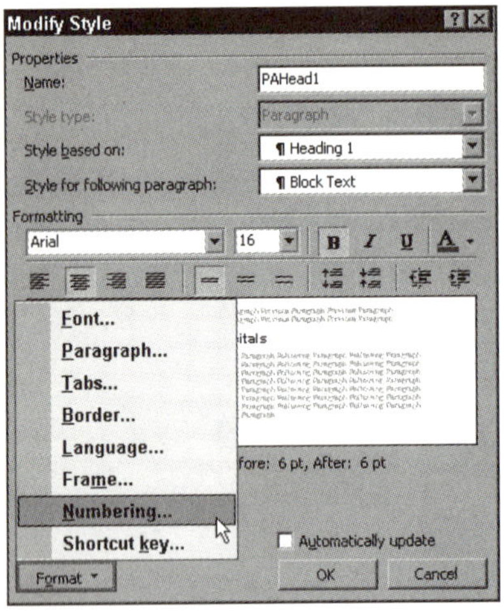

Figure 5-9: The Numbering option in the Modify Style dialog box

5. Choose a numbering scheme linked to a heading style from the Outline Numbered tab. You will know whether it is linked to a heading style if you see the word *Heading* in the preview pane for that numbering scheme.

6. Click the Customize button in the lower-right corner.

7. In the Customize Outline Numbered List dialog box that opens (see Figure 5-10), click 1 in the Level drop-down list and apply the formats you want for that level number.

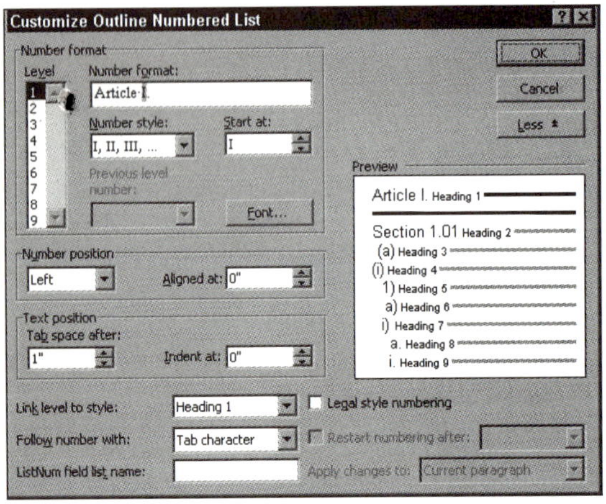

Figure 5-10: The Customize Outline Numbered List dialog box

8. Make sure that your style is linked to a heading style in the Link Level to Style drop-down list. If it is not linked to a heading style, click the arrow beside this option and select a heading style to which you want to link your customized style. If your style is not linked to a heading style, it may not be numbered or formatted in the manner you intended.

9. Click OK and then OK again to close all open dialog boxes.

These steps were used to add one of the outline numbered schemes (one linked to a heading style) to the three customized heading styles created in the example purchase agreement document. Figure 5-11 shows the results.

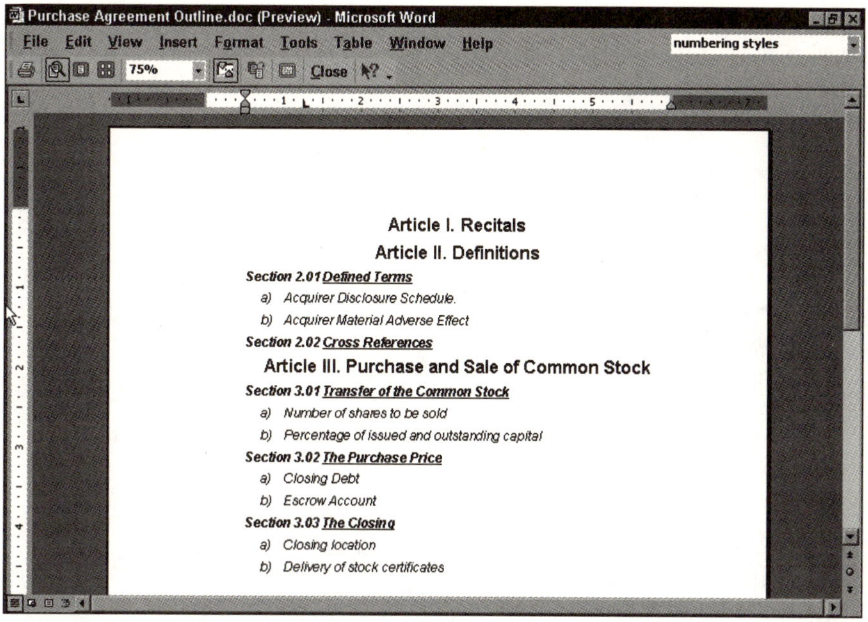

Figure 5-11: The results of adding numbering to the customized heading styles

The Modify Style dialog box contains four tabs representing numbering and bulleted schemes that you can apply in your document: Bulleted, Numbered, Outline Numbered, and List Styles. Many legal documents have headings whose numbering follows more of an outline scheme, so in the example purchase agreement document created in this chapter, we've applied the Outline Numbered scheme to the headings.

The Outline Numbered tab contains eight outline numbering schemes, one of which is None. When choosing a scheme, be aware that only four of the schemes are linked to heading styles. These are located along the bottom row. The remaining three schemes on the top row are not linked to heading styles. This is important to keep in mind because linking numbering to a heading style means that the paragraph format will include a defined outline level in the outline structure. For instance, the paragraph format for the built-in style Heading 1 includes the outline level-1 definition. Heading 2 is formatted as outline level 2, and Heading 3 as outline level 3, and so on through all nine levels of the built-in heading styles. When you apply numbering to these heading styles, each level of heading receives the next level number.

Suppose that you create a customized heading style that is not based on one of Word's built-in heading styles and is not formatted for an outline level. Before you apply numbering, you need to manually modify the paragraph format of your customized heading style to include an outline level by performing the following steps:

1. Select your customized heading style and then choose Format ⇨ Styles and Formatting to open the Styles and Formatting task pane. (Or open the Styles and Formatting task pane and then select the customized style to be modified from the list.)

2. In the task pane, click the drop-down list arrow beside the heading style you are modifying and choose Modify from the submenu that appears.
3. In the Modify Style dialog box, click the Format button in the lower-left corner and then choose Paragraph from the submenu that appears.
4. In the Paragraph dialog box that opens, click the Indents and Spacing tab (see Figure 5-12).

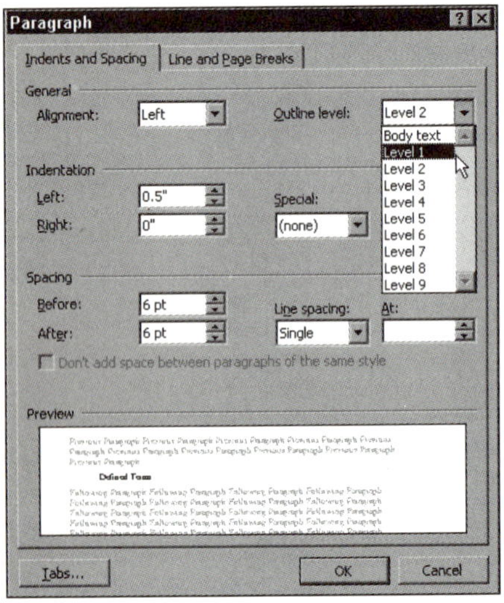

Figure 5-12: Use the Indents and Spacing tab of the Paragraph dialog box to choose the heading level.

5. Click the drop-down list arrow beside the Outline Level text box and choose the level you want to assign to that heading.
6. Click OK to close the Paragraph dialog box.

Repeat Steps 1–6 for each customized heading style that needs to be formatted for a particular outline level.

NOTE: After you have assigned an outline level to each of the customized heading styles, you may want to change the indentation of one or more of the levels. You can change the indentation of an outline level by clicking the Increase Indent and Decrease Indent buttons on the Formatting toolbar.

As you can see, it is a much simpler task to base your customized style on one of Word's built-in styles, which are already formatted for a specific level in the outline. After each customized heading style in your numbering scheme is modified to include an outline level, you can proceed with applying numbering, using the steps listed at the beginning of this section.

Adding numbering to headings that are not styled

Perhaps you have already typed the headings in your outline and formatted them the way you want without using styles. You can apply numbering to these headings as well without affecting the formatting of the heading. You will use steps similar to the ones for styled headings but less numerous. Follow these steps to apply numbering to headings that are not styled:

1. Place the insertion point in the heading you are numbering, or, in the case of an outline without body text, you can select all the headings in the document.
2. Choose Format ⇨ Bullets and Numbering.
3. In the Bullets and Numbering dialog box that appears, display the Outline Numbered tab and choose a numbering scheme that does not have the word *Heading* in any of its levels. These schemes are not linked to heading styles, so the outline level and indentation will remain the same.
4. Click the Customize button to modify the number format, style, position, text position, and other formats.
5. Click OK and then OK again to close the open dialog boxes.

Printing Outlines

Outlines print about the same as other documents, with one exception. In Outline view, outline levels can be collapsed so that they are hidden from view. If you want the outline levels to appear when the outline is printed, the collapsed levels will need to be expanded prior to printing. If you cannot see all the levels when viewing the outline on the screen, then you will not see all the levels on the printed copy. You can expand the outline to show all levels in a couple of ways. First, you can click the arrow beside the Show Levels list box on the Outlining toolbar and select Show All Levels. Or if you want only certain levels to appear on the printed copy, you can select from the same list box the number of levels you want to see. Choosing a level means that you can see all the levels that include and precede the level *you* selected. For instance, if you choose Level 3, you will see only headings formatted as Level 1, Level 2, and Level 3 in the outline. You also can change to the Normal or Print Layout view, which automatically expands the entire outline.

There may be times when you want to print only certain levels of the outline. In this case, you may want to collapse certain levels of the outline prior to printing.

Adding Cross-Referencing

Cross-referencing is frequently used in legal documents to direct the reader to another place in the document. Word allows you to create cross-references to eight different types of items, including paragraph numbering, footnotes, page numbers, bookmarks, and headings. Before creating the cross-reference, type any optional language you want to place before the actual reference, as in **see Article** or **see page**.

To insert a cross-reference in your document, place the insertion point after the optional language and in the exact location where you want the reference to appear. Then, follow these steps to create the cross-reference:

1. Choose Insert ⇨ Reference ⇨ Cross-reference.
2. In the Cross-Reference dialog box that appears (see Figure 5-13), choose the type of item you are referring to in the Reference Type drop-down list. Word provides eight reference types to choose from. After you have selected a reference type, all the items in the document that match that reference type are listed in the lower portion of the dialog box. If you choose Numbered Item as a reference type, then all the numbered items in the document appear in the dialog box. If you choose Footnote, then all the footnotes are listed. You may need to use the scroll bar to move down the list and locate the item you are referring to.

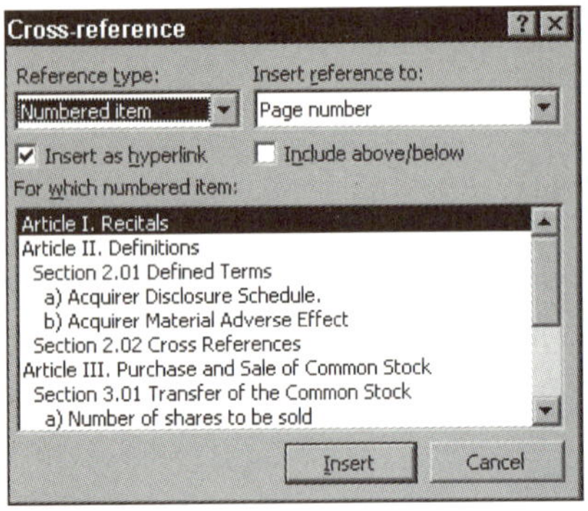

Figure 5-13: The Cross-Reference dialog box

3. Specify what you want to appear in the document as the reference in the Insert Reference To list box. The items in this list box dynamically change, based on the reference type selected in Step 2. For example, if the reference type selected is Numbered Item, then you can insert the page number, paragraph number, paragraph number (no context), paragraph number (full context), or paragraph text of the item in the document. If the reference type is Footnote, then you can insert the footnote number, the page number of the page containing the footnote, or the footnote number formatted as it is in the text. You also can choose above/below (for either of these reference types), which simply inserts the words *above* or *below,* based on the location of the item being referred to.

NOTE: Most of the options you will see in the Insert Reference list box are self-explanatory. However, if you are referring to a paragraph number, it may not be apparent when you should use Paragraph Number, Paragraph Number (no context), or Paragraph Number (full context).Choose Paragraph Number when you want the reference to include all the parent heading numbers leading up to and including the heading number of the current paragraph being referenced. For instance, if the heading number being referenced is at level 3 in the outline structure, the number that is inserted includes the level 1, 2, and 3 outline levels to produce a number similar to the following: I., A., 1. The Paragraph Number option shows the exact position of the paragraph you are referencing.

Choose Paragraph Number (no context) if you want only the paragraph number of the heading being referenced to be inserted without including the parent paragraph numbers. If you choose Paragraph Number (full context), the reference number that is inserted will indicate its position in the outline and display all parent levels.

---

4. Click the Insert as Hyperlink check box if you want to be able to jump to the referenced item from the reference itself. Click the Include Above/Below check box if you want Word to insert the words *above* or *below* after the reference that points to the location referenced relative to its position in the document.
5. Select the item to which you are referring in the For Which Numbered Item section of the dialog box.

6. Click the Insert button to insert the reference in your document. The dialog box remains open so that you can insert as many cross-references as you need.
7. After inserting all the cross-references you need, click Close to close the dialog box.

After you have created the reference, a field code containing the reference appears in the document at the insertion point. The number that is inserted is not a number that you type using the keyboard, but rather a field code that instructs Word as to the type of numbering you want. If you click Tools ⇨ Options and then click the View tab, you can choose one of the options in the Field Shading section so that field codes are shaded gray to easily distinguish them from text. The gray shading appears in Normal, Print Layout, or Outline view whenever the insertion point is within the reference.

NOTE: If you see a code similar to PAGEREF _Ref533604060 at the site of the reference, then you are not seeing the actual field code that Word inserts based on the selections that you have made in the dialog box. To make the page number, footnote number, or whatever applies appear at the reference site rather than the code appearing there, press Alt+F9. Or right-click over the reference and choose Toggle Field Codes from the submenu that appears (see Figure 5-14).

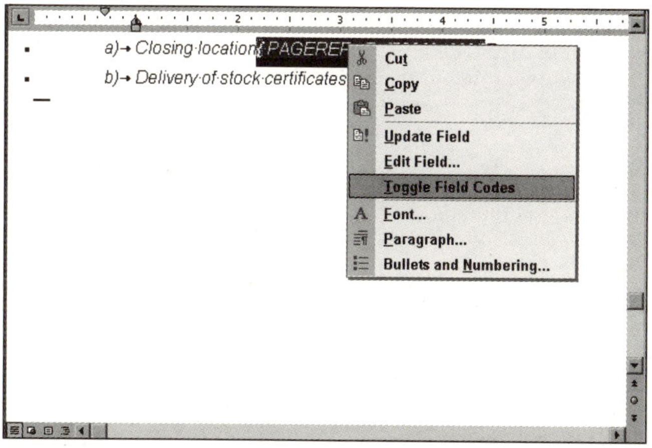

Figure 5-14: Choose Toggle Field Codes from the submenu to see cross-referencing results rather than the field code.

If you have clicked the Insert as Hyperlink check box, whenever the mouse pointer is directly over the reference, you will receive a helpful message (see Figure 5-15) that tells you how to jump to the location of the referenced item. To jump to the referenced item, press Ctrl and click the reference.

Figure 5-15: The Help prompt that instructs you how to jump to the item to which you are referring

Updating cross-references manually

Cross-references are inserted into a document using field codes, as you learned in the previous section. Field codes have many purposes in Word — they're not just for cross-references. When you first insert a cross-reference, Word updates the field code and displays the proper cross-reference. As you edit your document, the cross-references may move around and therefore be in need of updating.

Word does not automatically update fields, except at well-defined times. For instance, they are normally automatically updated when you print a document or when you use Print Preview. (See the following section for more information.) Fields are also automatically updated when you open a document.

You also can manually update your cross-references. For example, if you move a referenced heading to a different page, you need to make sure that the reference to that heading changes as well. To update a single reference, right-click the reference and choose Update Field from the submenu that appears. Or to update all references in the document after major edits, you may select the entire document and then use the Update Field option.

If you prefer to use the keyboard, select the cross-reference and press F9.

Updating cross-references automatically before printing

As mentioned in the previous section, cross-reference fields do not automatically update while you are editing a document. However, you can instruct Word to automatically update cross-references for you prior to printing. To instruct Word to always update cross-references for you before printing, choose Tools ⇨ Options and, in the Print dialog box that appears (see Figure 5-16), click the Print tab. In the Printing Options section, click the Update Fields check box.

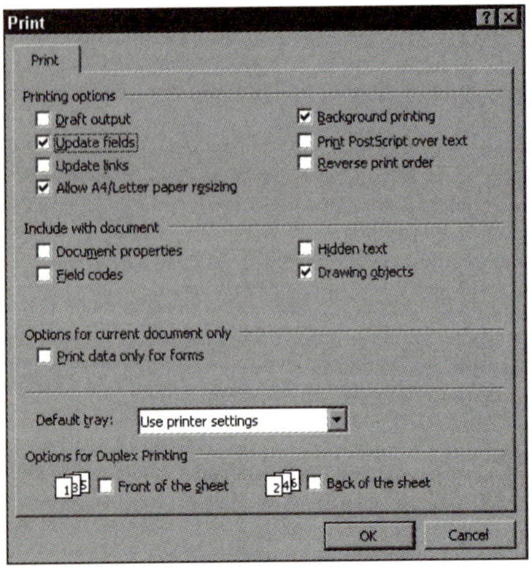

Figure 5-16: The Print tab of the Print dialog box

You also can access this print option by choosing File ⇨ Print and clicking the Options button in the lower-left corner of the dialog box. You will see the same dialog box as that shown in Figure 5-16.

Changing a reference type

If you want to change any element of the cross-reference, such as the reference type or the item you are referring to, simply select the cross-reference and choose Insert ⇨ Reference ⇨ Cross-Reference. Next, make the desired changes in the Cross-Reference dialog box.

Deleting a reference

You can delete a reference by selecting the reference (and the words *above* or *below*, if applicable) and pressing Delete.

Summary

This chapter covered Word's outlining tools, which help you build and clarify the structure of your documents. The chapter showed you how to

- Use the Outline view to create an outline.
- Expand, collapse, and move outline headings.
- Apply numbering to outlines.
- Print outlines.
- Add and work with cross-references.

The next chapter details the Word formatting features that help you buff and polish your documents to a fine shine.

Chapter 6

Formatting and Polishing Text

In This Chapter

- ♦ Creating both automatic and simple numbered lists
- ♦ Turning off and restarting numbering
- ♦ Customizing outline number formats
- ♦ Formatting margins, tabs, and line spacing
- ♦ Applying character, paragraph, and page formatting
- ♦ Applying section formatting
- ♦ Working with headers and footers
- ♦ Using spelling and grammar checking
- ♦ Setting up a legal dictionary
- ♦ Working with bullets
- ♦ Working with footnotes
- ♦ Generating tables of contents
- ♦ Generating tables of authorities

IN THE PRECEDING CHAPTER, YOU learned how to create an outline to add structure to your headings and apply numbering to those headings. In this chapter you'll see how to number a list of items both before and after the list is typed. This chapter also covers numerous other formatting features that can give your documents the professional appearance you require.

Creating and Working with Numbered Lists

Lists are used in a variety of ways by legal professionals, such as to itemize documents contained in a pleadings file or in a correspondence file. Word automatically adjusts the numbering when items are removed or added during editing. You can automatically number a list of items very easily; in fact, Word can recognize when you have begun a numbered list and will automatically continue numbering the list for you. For instance, if you type *1.* at the left margin, followed by a space and the necessary text, then when you press Enter, Word assumes that you want to continue the numbered list on the next line. Word automatically applies a list style that replaces the manually typed number with an automatic number and then inserts the next number (in the same number style) on the new line. In addition to inserting the number, the list style formats the inserted number.

The feature just described is an AutoCorrect feature within the category of AutoFormat as You Type. You activate this feature by choosing Tools ⇨ AutoCorrect Options and clicking the AutoFormat as You Type tab, shown in Figure 6-1. (You can also access these options by choosing Format ⇨

AutoFormat. In the AutoFormat dialog box that opens, click the Options button in the lower-left corner. In the AutoCorrect dialog box that opens, click the AutoFormat as You Type tab.) On this tab, you can check the Automatic Bulleted Lists option or the Automatic Numbered Lists options below the Apply as You Type section of the tab so that Word automatically continues list numbering for you.

NOTE: On the AutoFormat as You Type tab are several options that you can choose if you want Word to automatically handle those items for you. In the legal environment, however, thought should be given to the effect that implementing some of these options will have on your text.

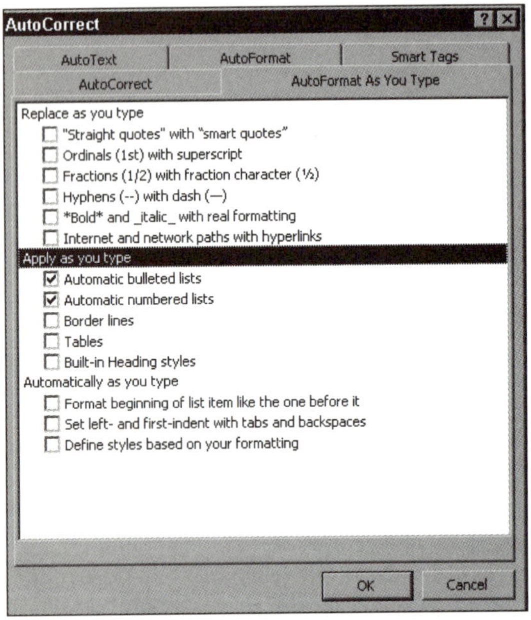

Figure 6-1: The AutoFormat as You Type tab of the AutoCorrect dialog box

As mentioned previously, when you activate these options, Word automatically applies the next bullet or number when you press Enter and automatically applies a list style to format the number. After you have typed the first number, typed the text, and pressed Enter, Word inserts the next number and applies a list style to that number and to the one you typed manually.

An AutoCorrect Options button appears the first time Word inserts an automatic number for you. (If you do not see the AutoCorrect Options button, choose Tools ⇨ AutoCorrect Options and click the AutoCorrect tab. Check the Show AutoCorrect Options Buttons check box.) When you click the arrow beside the AutoCorrect Options button, a submenu appears with the following options for you to select (or deselect) to override settings on the AutoFormat as You Type tab:

- **Undo Automatic Numbering:** Removes the automatic numbering that Word inserted on the new line and removes the list style that was automatically applied to the manually typed number in the previous line

- **Stop Automatically Creating Numbered Lists:** Turns off the automatic numbering feature on the AutoFormat as You Type tab for this and future documents
- **Control AutoCorrect Options:** Opens the AutoCorrect dialog box, in which you can check or uncheck options to apply

After you have made your selection from the submenu, press Esc to close the submenu button.

Creating simple numbered lists

You have just learned how to create numbered lists as you type by choosing the AutoFormat as You Type option. However, there are several other techniques you can use to create simple numbered lists. For instance, if you have already begun your list without numbers, you can apply one level of numbering after the list is typed by selecting the list and clicking the Numbering button on the Formatting toolbar.

You can also apply a single level of numbering to existing unnumbered lists by selecting the list and choosing Format ⇨ Bullets and Numbering. The Numbered tab contains seven numbering schemes to choose from; you can also customize those schemes as desired by clicking the Customize button in the lower-right corner of the dialog box that opens. Here you can change the font, number style, number position, text position, and starting number.

If you want to apply more than one level of numbering in your document, choose Format ⇨ Bullets and Numbering and then click the List Styles tab. Here you will find several list styles that come with Word that you can customize for up to nine levels of numbering using the Modify Style dialog box (see Figure 6-2). By clicking the arrow beside the Apply Formatting To option, you can customize the formats for each level of your list.

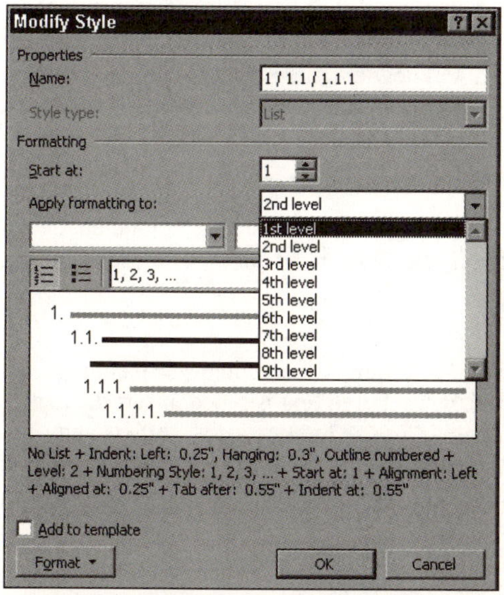

Figure 6-2: The Modify Style dialog box

In addition to changing the formats and numbering styles, you can change the indentation of the number you have inserted. You can also do this using the Modify Style dialog box, or you can place the insertion point on a numbered line whose indent you want to change. Next, click the Increase Indent button or Decrease Indent button on the Formatting toolbar. You can change the indentation one item at a time, or you can select the entire list before clicking the Increase Indent button or Decrease Indent button.

In the case of multilevel numbering, pressing either the Increase Indent or Decrease Indent button changes the number to the next level or to the previous level. For instance, pressing Enter after the text for item *2.* places a *3.* on the next line. Suppose, however, that you want the line to represent a new numbered list under the previous item (#2). All you need to do is press the Increase Indent button, and the number changes to a lowercase *a*, which is the next lower numbering level, with formatting for that level of numbering. When you want to return to the previous level, simply press the Decrease Indent button.

Turning off numbering

As you have learned, once you have begun automatic numbering of your lists, each time you press Enter, a new number is inserted into the document. You can turn off automatic numbering by pressing Enter to begin the next line and then pressing Backspace to remove the number just inserted.

If you applied numbering using the Format ⇨ Bullets and Numbering schemes, you can click the scheme you originally selected to remove the numbering scheme.

Restarting numbering

In case you need to start new numbering at any point, right-click the numbered item and choose Restart Numbering from the submenu that appears. The number automatically changes to *1.*

TIP: When you right-click over an automatic number, all numbers at that level that were automatically inserted will be highlighted in a light gray. (The number at the beginning of the line that you right-click over contains a slightly darker shade of gray.) This is helpful to know because the gray shading makes it easy to differentiate between numbers that were inserted automatically and those that were manually typed.

You can also choose Format ⇨ Bullets and Numbering. On the Numbered, Outline Numbered, and List Styles tabs, you will find a Restart Numbering option in the lower-right corner of those tabs.

Continuing numbered lists

Sometimes you will want to continue a numbering sequence after unnumbered items or paragraphs were typed. To continue the numbering sequence after the unnumbered text is typed, insert the next number using the Numbering button on the Formatting toolbar, or use the Format ⇨ Bullets and Numbering menus. Right-click over the number that is inserted and choose Continue Numbering from the submenu that appears (see Figure 6-3).

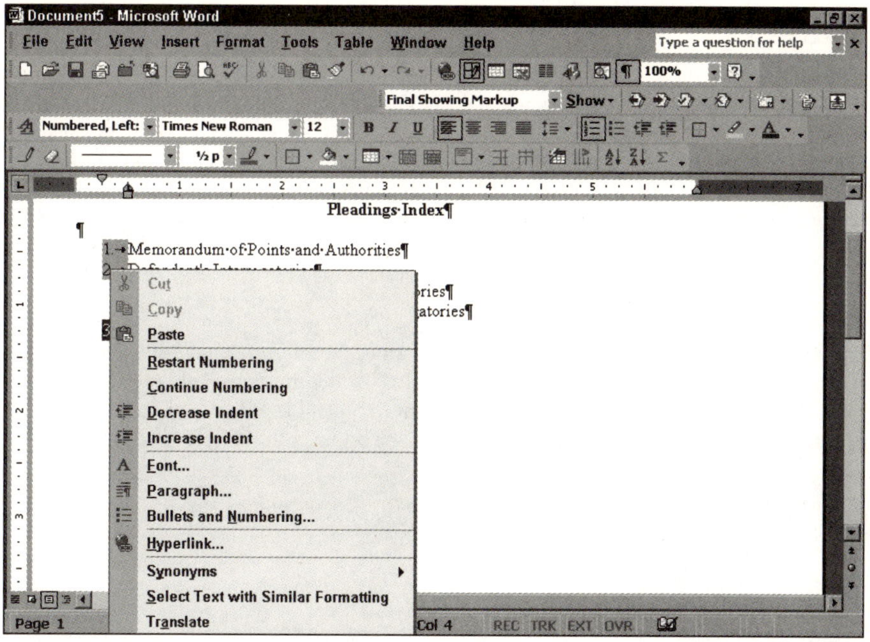

Figure 6-3: The submenu of options accessed by right-clicking over an automatic number

Customizing number formats

Number formats can be customized through the Bullets and Numbering dialog box. Each of the tabs available contains a Customize button. You can click the Customize button to change the number format for single-level numbering. When using multilevel numbering, you can click the Outline Numbered or List Styles tab and then click the Customize button to change number formats for each level of numbering in use in your document.

In the Customize dialog box, you can change the number, text position, and number style, among other things. In addition, you can add text and punctuation to your automatic numbering. To customize the number format, click before or after the number code in the Number format section of the Customize dialog box. Be careful not to delete the numbering field code, which is shaded gray. If you delete this field code, you cannot just type the number in. You have to cancel the dialog box and start over.

Formatting Margins, Tabs, and Line Spacing

The way that you set the margins, tabs, and line spacing will obviously affect your document's appearance. Margin changes affect the layout of the page, tab changes affect the appearance of paragraphs, and line spacing affects the amount of whitespace between lines of text and paragraphs. The changes made to these settings can be applied to the Normal.dot template or to any template you are using. Changes to each of these formats can also be made on the fly, if necessary. For instance, adjustments to margins and line spacing in particular may be necessary to make the text of your legal documents fit within a limited number of pages.

Changing margins

To change the margins in a document, you use the File ⇨ Page Setup command, which produces the Page Setup dialog box with its three tabs: Margins, Paper, and Layout. In the Margins tab (see Figure 6-4), you can enter a numeric value to determine the distance between the top of the page and the first printed line or between the bottom of the page and the last printed line. Word's default setting for these measurements is 1", which is typical for most legal documents. You can also enter a numeric value to determine the distance between the left edge of the paper and the left edge of the printed lines or between the right edge of the paper and the right edge of the printed lines. Word's default is 1.25", which is not the normal setting for most legal documents. Most law firms use 1" for each of these margin settings.

You can also enter a numeric value to determine the width of an optional *gutter*, an additional amount of whitespace that is allowed when a document is to be bound. This setting is useful when you are preparing a document such as a Supreme Court brief to be sent to a printer. After you enter the gutter measurement, you can specify whether the additional whitespace appears at the left or top of the page, depending on how it is bound.

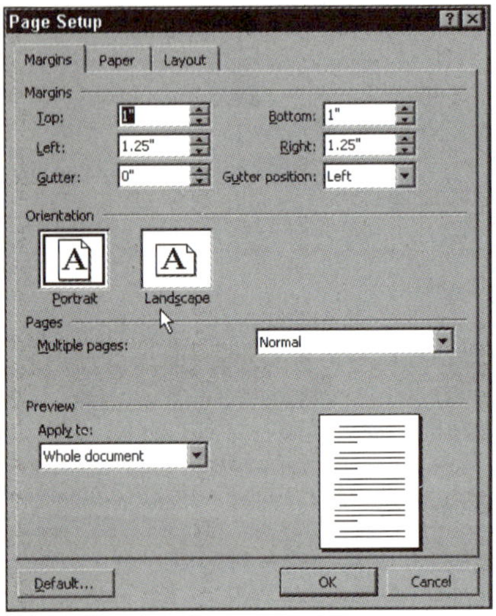

Figure 6-4: The Margins tab of the Page Setup dialog box

The Margins tab is also where you can set the orientation of the page to make it either Portrait or Landscape. You might need to change to Landscape if, for example, you have imported a table from Excel that is too wide for the page. When you change the orientation of a page, Word rotates your margins as well. For instance, if you had Portrait orientation set with a two-inch left margin, when you switch to Landscape orientation, the two-inch left margin will now be on the bottom margin because you rotated the page 90 degrees counterclockwise. Playing with the margins and orientation will make this clear. (It doesn't hurt to play around in this instance.)

In the Pages section of the Margins tab, you can specify how you want to lay out your page. For instance, you can use Mirror margins to control the outside and inside margins of odd- and even-numbered pages. If you were to place two pages side by side, as in a book, you would want the outside (left) margin of the page on the left to match the outside (right) margin of the page on the right. You would also want the right margin of the page on the left (inside) to match the left (inside) margin of the page on the right.

As its name implies, the 2 Pages per Sheet option lets you print two pages on the same side of a single sheet of paper. The layout of this page is determined by the orientation selected. That is, choosing Portrait causes one page to appear above the other on a page, whereas choosing the Landscape option causes each page to appear side by side.

You can also create a pamphlet or a booklet by choosing the Book Fold option in the Pages section of the Margins tab. When you use this option, Word assumes that you are printing on the front and back of a piece of paper. You can accomplish this by using a printer that has a duplex option, or you can manually duplex by choosing this option in the Print dialog box.

Working with tabs

In your legal documents, you might want to use tabs to indent headings or signature blocks for filings or letters. In Word, default tabs are predefined as left tabs and are preset to every 1/2 inch. There are four additional types of tabs that can be set: center, right, decimal, and bar. The type of tab you choose indicates precisely how the text is aligned with the tab. When you use a left tab, the left edge of the text aligns with the tab stop, and as you type, the text flows from left to right. With right tabs, the right edge of the text aligns with the tab stop and flows from right to left as you type. When you use centered tabs, the text centers at the tab stop. Decimal tabs are used when the decimal point in numbers must align with the tab stop. Finally, bar tabs are thin vertical bars that can be used to separate columns created by tabs within a document. Tabs can be set using the horizontal ruler or by choosing Format ⇨ Tabs to open the Tabs dialog box.

Setting custom tabs

One method for setting tabs is to use the mouse and the Tab button on the horizontal ruler. The Tab button is the square button on the far left of the ruler. To set tabs using this button, first click the Tab button on the ruler until you get the tab alignment that you want. (The symbol on the Tab button changes to reflect the type of tab. To identify the type of tab you've clicked, hold your mouse pointer over the button until a ToolTip appears.) When you have the type of tab you want to set, click just under or on the ruler at the desired measurement to set the tab. For example, to set a center tab at the 2-inch location on the ruler, first click the Tab button until the one for the center tab appears; then click just under or on the 2-inch marker on the ruler. To verify the position of the tab stop, choose Format ⇨ Tabs to see the tab you have set in the Tabs dialog box.

If the 2-inch tab stop is not in the exact position that you want, you can click the tab stop you just set and drag it to another position on the ruler. If dragging the tab does not produce the desired results, you can double-click the tab on the ruler to open the Tab dialog box, where you can enter a measurement in the Tab Stop Position section.

In the Tab dialog box, you can enter or clear tab stops. Enter the desired location for the tab stop in the Tab Stop Position section and then choose the type of tab that you want from the Alignment options. If you have additional tabs to set, click the Set button to set the tab and then go back to the Tab Stop Position box to enter the location for the next tab, again choosing the appropriate alignment. After you finish setting the tabs, click the OK button.

NOTE: Because tabs are paragraph formats, it is important to remember that tab settings are carried forward to each new paragraph you create. If you do not need the tabs in the next paragraph (or need to *not* have tabs there), you must remove them.

Moving and removing tabs

As with setting tabs, you can move tabs and clear (remove) them with the ruler and the mouse or with the Tabs command on the Format menu. To move a tab, simply click the tab and drag it to the desired location. To clear a tab, drag the tab up or down off the ruler.

The Tab dialog box displays all tab settings. To clear a specific tab, select the tab and press the Clear button. To clear all tabs, click the Clear All button.

Creating tab leaders

Leaders are characters placed automatically before a tab by Word. For instance, tab leaders are often used in a table of contents, where you see dots appear from the end of the text to a page number that is aligned with a tab stop.

To add tab leaders, set the tab as you normally would and then open the Tabs dialog box by choosing Format Tabs. In the list of tabs shown in the dialog box, choose the tab to which you should add a leader. Then, click the type of leader you want to use. Word offers three kinds of tab leaders: periods, hyphens, and underlines. After you select the desired type of leader, click OK to set the tab.

Adjusting line spacing

You can make line spacing adjustments to the amount of space between lines of text and before and after paragraphs. To change the line spacing between lines of text, use the Line Spacing button on the Formatting toolbar (see Figure 6-5). Because line spacing is a paragraph format, to change the line spacing, you can place the insertion point anywhere within the desired paragraph and then click the Line Spacing button. It is again important to be aware that this format carries forward to any new paragraphs you create right after the adjusted paragraph. In other words, if you format a paragraph as double-spaced, only that paragraph is affected. If you position the insertion point at the end of that paragraph and press Enter, then the newly created paragraph will also be double-spaced. No other paragraphs are affected.

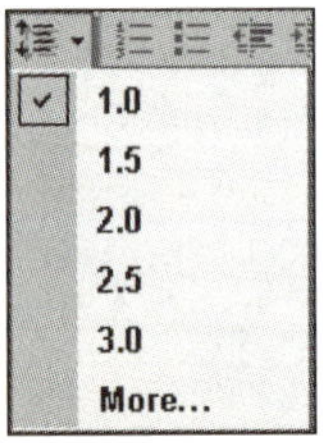

Figure 6-5: The Line Spacing button on the Formatting toolbar

You can also change line spacing and spacing before and after paragraphs by using the Format ⇨ Paragraph commands. The Paragraph dialog box appears, with the Indents and Spacing tab visible, as shown in Figure 6-6. Specify the amount of space you want to have preceding and following paragraphs in the Before and After text boxes. You can type any value that Word understands: inches (in.), centimeters (cm.), picas (pi.), points (pt.), or lines (li.) .

In the Line Spacing text box, specify the amount of spacing you want between lines of text. In the At text box to the right of the Line Spacing box, you can specify the kind of spacing that you desire: Single, Double, 1.5, At Least, Exactly, and Multiple. You can adjust the preset spacing of these options by clicking the arrows in the At box. The Exactly option makes the spacing exactly the specified amount. The At Least choice can be used to set the spacing to a specified amount or greater.

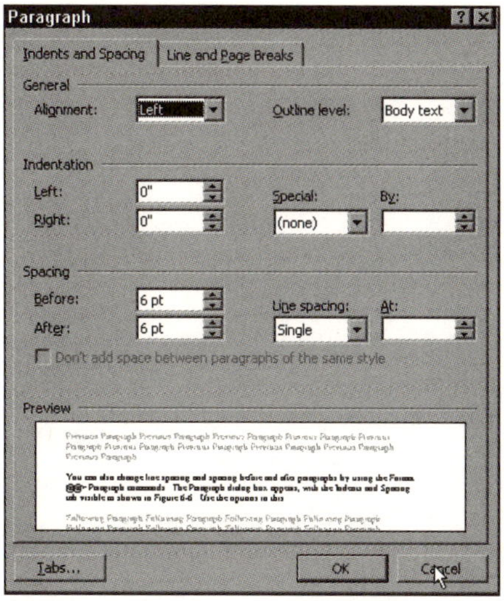

Figure 6-6: The Indents and Spacing tab in the Paragraph dialog box

Working with Character, Paragraph, and Page Formatting

Word provides formatting options for different levels of text, including characters, paragraphs, sections, and documents. We discuss section formatting later in this chapter. This section deals with some of the formats that are commonly applied to legal documents.

Applying character formatting

Character formats can be applied to as little as a single character or to more than one character without necessarily being applied to an entire paragraph. You can apply character formats after selecting text or to typed text after the format is selected. Some of the character formats that are commonly applied to legal documents are font changes or attributes such as bold, underline, and italic. One way to apply these formats is to first select the text and then specify the formatting you want to apply. Or you can click the buttons on the Formatting toolbar (see Figure 6-7).

Figure 6-7: The character formatting buttons on the Formatting toolbar

You can apply additional font attributes and character formats by choosing Format ⇨ Font (see Figure 6-8). In the Font dialog box that appears, you can choose formats such as double underlining, which is frequently used in tables under totals. Other formats used in legal documents, such as superscript and subscript, are also available in this dialog box.

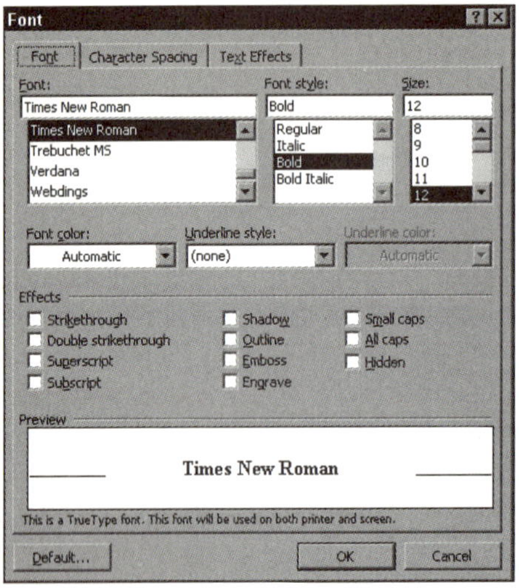

Figure 6-8: The Font dialog box

TIP: There is one character format that is useful when you want to redact certain text in a legal document before filing it with an agency or court. You can create a character style that contains the white font color that you can apply to selected text you want hidden on printouts. (Remember, you can define shortcut keys to make applying the style easier.) You can then change the font color in the style to Automatic to unredact text.

You can view character formats, whether applied directly or included in a style, in the Reveal Formatting task pane.

Using character formatting shortcuts

You can apply many character formats by using shortcut keys. The shortcut keys act as switches to turn the various Format commands on and off. Table 6-1 contains shortcut keys that you can use to apply character formatting.

Table 6-1

Shortcut Keys for Character Formatting

Format	***Shortcut Keys***
Bold	Ctrl+B
Italic	Ctrl+I
Underline	Ctrl+U
Word Underline	Ctrl+Shift+W
Double Underline	Ctrl+Shift+D

Format	***Shortcut Keys***
Subscript (H_2O)	Ctrl+Equal Sign
Superscript (X^2)	Ctrl+Shift+Plus Sign
Small Caps	Ctrl+Shift+K
All Caps	Ctrl+Shift+A
Change Case of Letters	Shift+F3
Hidden Text	Ctrl+Shift+H
Remove Formats	Ctrl+Spacebar or Ctrl+Z
Font	Ctrl+Shift+F
Symbol Font	Ctrl+Shift+Q
Point Size	Ctrl+Shift+P
Next Larger Size	Ctrl+Shift+>
Next Smaller Size	Ctrl+Shift+<
Up One Point	Ctrl+]
Down One Point	Ctrl+[

Identifying character formatting

Character formats are stored in the character itself. If the Formatting toolbar is used to apply formats such as bold, underline, and italic, the button used to apply the format will appear pushed in whenever the insertion point is in the text containing the format. The format can be removed by simply clicking the format button again. If it is not obvious which character format has been applied, you can select the text containing the format and then choose Format ⇨ Font. On the Font tab in the Font dialog box, you will see the character formats used in the selected text. Changes to the character formatting can be made within the dialog box.

You can also use the Reveal Formatting task pane to identify the character formats used in the text. To open this task pane, choose View ⇨ Task Pane. To change to the Reveal Formatting task pane if it does not appear automatically, click the down arrow on the task pane title bar and choose Reveal Formatting from the task pane that appears.

TIP: Another technique you can use to open the Reveal Formatting task pane is to choose the Help ⇨ What's This command, which attaches a question mark to the point. Click in the text containing the character formatting, and the Reveal Formatting task pane automatically opens.

Applying paragraph formatting

Word considers any amount of text that you enter between one paragraph mark and the next to be a single paragraph. If you want to see the paragraph marks in a document, press the Show/Hide button on the Standard toolbar (it is the button containing the paragraph symbol). As you can see from the example in Figure 6-9, paragraph marks appear at the end of each paragraph, where the user pressed the Enter key. Paragraphs can consist of a single line or many lines — it is entirely up to you.

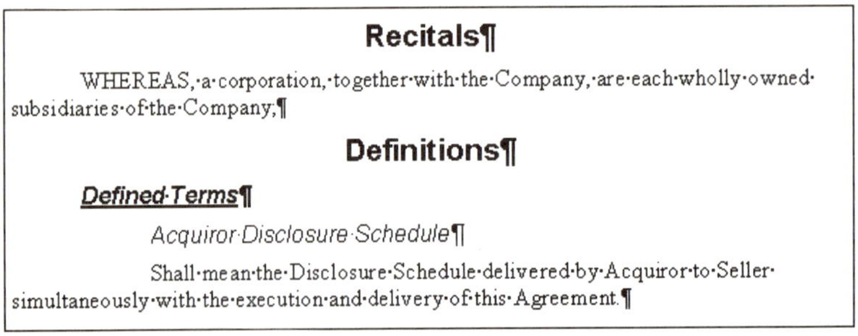
Recitals¶

WHEREAS,·a·corporation,·together·with·the·Company,·are·each·wholly·owned·subsidiaries·of·the·Company;¶

Definitions¶

Defined·Terms¶

Acquiror·Disclosure·Schedule¶

Shall·mean·the·Disclosure·Schedule·delivered·by·Acquiror·to·Seller·simultaneously·with·the·execution·and·delivery·of·this·Agreement.¶

Figure 6-9: Paragraph markers appear at the end of every paragraph.

Paragraph formats affect the entire paragraph through the paragraph marker at the end. When you press Enter after typing a paragraph, the formats in the current paragraph are automatically carried forward to the next paragraph until the formatting is changed. If you want to start a new line without beginning a new paragraph, you can press Shift+Enter to end the current line and begin a new line. This is considered a line break rather than a paragraph break. The line break symbol that is visible when Show/Hide is turned on can be seen in Figure 6-10.

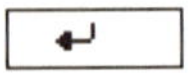

Figure 6-10: The line break symbol

The formats that can be applied to paragraphs affect alignment, indentation, line spacing, and page breaks. As with character formatting, you can apply paragraph formatting in different ways. You can use the paragraph formatting buttons on the Formatting toolbar to apply formats to your paragraphs (see Figure 6-11). Or you can choose Format ⇨ Paragraph to open the Paragraph dialog box.

Figure 6-11: The paragraph formats available on the Formatting toolbar

Aligning paragraphs

You can align text in four ways: left, centered, right, and justified. Left-aligned text is even on the left edge, centered text is situated evenly between the left and right margins, right-aligned text is even on the right edge, and justified text is even on both the left and right edge. Many legal documents today are left-aligned. However, a court or agency may require justification.

To change the alignment for the current paragraph, choose Format ⇨ Paragraphs. Click the Indents and Spacing tab that appears and select the desired alignment.

Indenting paragraphs

The Paragraph dialog box contains two tabs: Indents and Spacing, and Line and Page Breaks. When you want to indent paragraphs, you set the options in the Indentation section of the Indents and Spacing tab. In many legal documents, the first line of every paragraph is indented at .5", and some are indented 1". Instead of pressing Tab at the beginning of every new paragraph, you can specify that you want a first-line indent of .5", and the current paragraph and each subsequent new paragraph will have a first-line indent of .5".

Another type of indent that can be applied to paragraphs is a *hanging* indent, which means that the first line of the paragraph is not indented, but the subsequent lines are. This type of indent is used less frequently by law offices but can be useful when creating a bibliography.

To set one of these types of indents, select the type of indent you want in the Special section of the Indents and Spacing tab, specifying the amount of indent you want.

You can also indent an entire paragraph from the left or right margin (or both, in the case of an indented quote). To indent an entire paragraph, specify the amount of indent you want in the Left or Right text boxes.

See Figure 6-12 for an example of each type of indent just described.

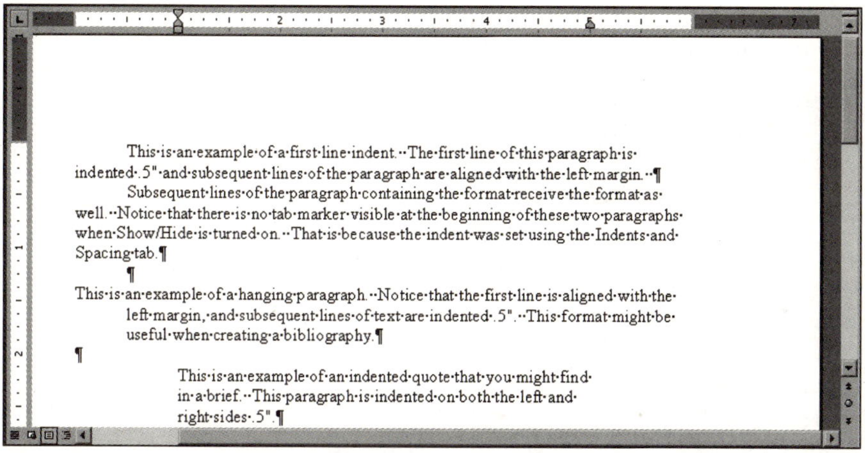

Figure 6-12: Examples of different types of paragraph indents

Indenting paragraphs using the horizontal ruler

You can also use the horizontal ruler to set left, right and first-line indents. When you change the values by using the Paragraph command, the triangle-shaped symbols on the ruler move accordingly. You can set the indentation by dragging the appropriate symbol on the ruler to the desired location. The left indent symbol is the square immediately below the two triangles. The hanging indent symbol is the lower of the two triangles (it points upward). The first line symbol is the top triangle, the one pointing downward.

Setting line and page break options

On the Lines and Page Breaks tab of the Paragraph dialog box, you will find options for controlling page breaks that can split paragraphs across pages or leave headings dangling. You can keep page breaks from splitting your paragraphs in inappropriate places by setting these options on the Line and Page Breaks tab. The following is a description of each option on this tab:

- **Widow/Orphan:** This prevents page breaks from leaving the first line of a paragraph at the bottom of a page and the last line of a paragraph at the top of a page.
- **Keep Lines Together:** This prevents a page break from being inserted in the middle of a paragraph.
- **Keep with Next:** The selected paragraph is not separated by a page break from the next paragraph. This is useful in keeping headings together with the text that follows the headings.

- **Page Break Before:** A page break is inserted before the current paragraph.
- **Suppress Line Numbers:** If line numbering is turned on, it is turned off for the current paragraph.
- **Don't Hyphenate:** If hyphenation is turned on (not common in law offices), it is turned off for the current paragraph.

Applying borders to paragraphs

Sometimes you might need to surround a paragraph with a border. Paragraph borders are sometimes used in financial documents filed with the Securities and Exchange Commission, for example. Borders are useful for emphasizing a particular portion of text. You can apply borders to paragraphs by choosing Format ⇨Borders and Shading (see Figure 6-13, which shows the dialog box that opens) or by clicking the Borders button on the Formatting toolbar.

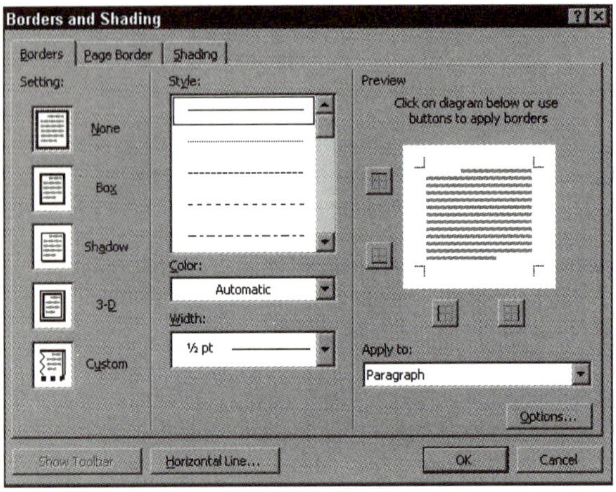

Figure 6-13: The Borders and Shading dialog box

Word offers several border styles. After you select the style of border that you wish to have for your paragraph, you still need to make a selection as to where you want the border to appear. You can pick one of the border settings from the left side of the dialog box, or you can select individual sides of your paragraph in the Preview area at the right side of the dialog box. Click the side of the paragraph that you want the border to appear on, or click one of the buttons that represent the different sides of the paragraph. The Preview area gives you a general idea of what the border will look like after it is applied to your paragraph.

You can change the color and the width of the line you use for the different borders in your document. To do so, click the down-pointing arrow in the Color section to see the color palette from which you can make a selection. For line width, click the Width text box to choose among the various line sizes.

The Shading tab of the Borders and Shading dialog box lets you add various kinds of shading to your text. The shading can range from a light gray to a solid black. Click the Custom radio button to select a shading and then select the desired level of shading from the list box. The color options in the Fill, Style, and Color sections of the Patterns area allow you to provide a background for the text that you are coloring and a style of pattern to the background color. The Preview area to the right will give you a general idea of how your choice will appear in your document.

Using Bullets and Numbering

The Formatting toolbar contains buttons that you can use to add numbering or bullets to your paragraphs. To apply numbering to a paragraph you have already typed, simply click in the paragraph and then click the Numbering button on the Formatting toolbar. If you are not satisfied with the amount of indentation that is used, click the Increase Indent and Decrease Indent buttons, also on the Formatting toolbar. Follow these same steps. Click anywhere in the paragraph and then click the Bullets button. Again, you can change the amount of indentation by clicking the Increase Indent and Decrease Indent buttons.

If you wish to change the style of numbering or punctuation that follows the number, choose Format ⇨ Bullets and Numbering. In the Bullets and Numbering dialog box on the Numbered tab (see Figure 6-14), click the style of numbering that you want. You can further customize the numbering style by clicking the Customize button and changing the number format, number style, number position, and text position as desired.

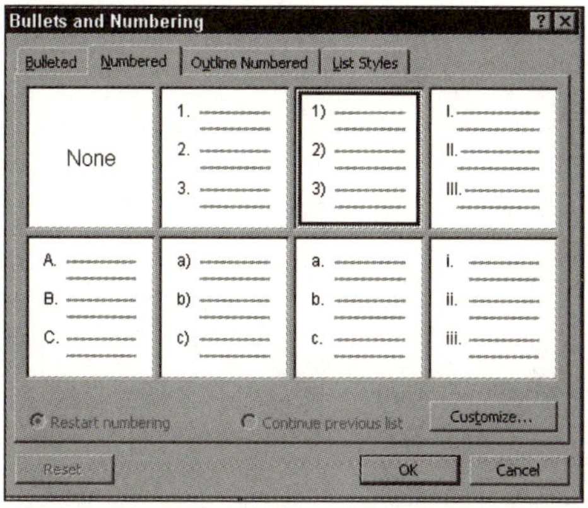

Figure 6-14: The Numbered tab of the Bullets and Numbering dialog box

The bullet character, bullet position, and text position can all be changed by choosing Format ⇨ Bullets and Numbering. Then click the Bulleted tab to display the options for these settings.

Stopping and continuing bullets or numbers

If you have used the Bullets button to apply numbering and you want the numbering to start over at the beginning in a new paragraph, choose Format ⇨ Bullets and Numbering. In the Bullets and Numbering dialog box, click Restart Numbering at the bottom of the box. For cases in which you are numbering a series of paragraphs but need to interrupt them with paragraphs that are not numbered, click the Continue the Previous List option when you're ready to continue the numbering again. You can find this option in the lower-right corner of the Bullets and Numbering dialog box.

Using Page Setup

In addition to setting margins, other options can be set to control the appearance of each page of your document. Several page-formatting options can be set by choosing File ⇨ Page Setup. In addition to the Margins tab, discussed previously, the Page Setup dialog box contains two more tabs: Paper and Layout.

The Paper tab has options for choosing a predefined paper size or specifying the height and width desired. When you have a printer with dual paper bins, you can also specify a paper source for the first page of a document (such as a letter that is printed on letterhead) and a paper source for subsequent pages of your letter. In the Apply To section of the dialog box, you can apply your settings to the entire document or from the insertion point onward.

On the Layout tab in the Page Setup dialog box (see Figure 6-15) are options laying out the text on each page. If you click the Section Start drop-down list, you will find options controlling how the text appears on each page. In the Headers and Footers section, you can indicate whether different headers and footers are used for odd and even pages or whether one appears only on the first page. In this section, you can also control the distance between the edge of the page and the header or footer by entering in a new value in the text boxes.

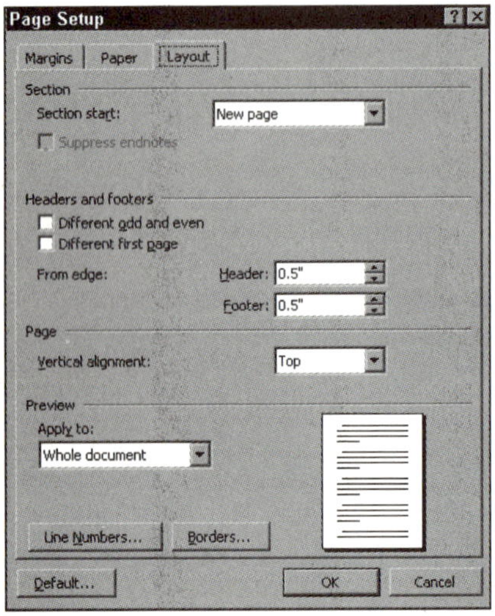

Figure 6-15: The Layout tab in the Page Setup dialog box

The Vertical Alignment option can be set to make the text appear where you want it on the page. Use this option if, for example, you want the text on a cover page to be centered in the middle of the page. Using this feature eliminates having to press Enter multiple times to move down to the center of the page before typing.

There are also two buttons in the Page Setup dialog box for adding line numbering required for documents filed in different jurisdictions, such as in the California courts.

CROSS-REFERENCE: To review how to apply line numbering, see Chapter 3.

Finally, in this dialog box you can add page borders. Clicking the Borders button opens the Borders and Shading dialog box, which contains the Page Borders tab. This is the same dialog box discussed previously in applying paragraph borders. The difference here is that the border is applied to the entire page rather than to a paragraph only.

Formatting Sections

Document *sections* can be defined as portions of text whose page margins, orientation, headers and footers, number of columns, and line and page numbering are different from the preceding text.

Section breaks are used to divide the document into sections and indicate that the current page formats are ending and that new page formats are about to begin. All formatting information is stored in the section break. If a section break is deleted, the text that appears before the section break loses its formatting and takes on the formatting options of the text that follows it. There is no limit to the number of sections you can define in a document, and there is no requirement that a document contain multiple sections. In fact, if page formatting does not change in the document, then section breaks are not needed and the entire document is just one section. Whether your document contains multiple sections is determined solely by the type of formatting you need in that document. Separate sections can be defined for different parts of a document. For instance, agreements and contracts usually consist of a cover page, a table of contents, and the body of the document. Such documents consist of three sections, each formatted differently from the preceding section.

A page can also be divided into sections. For instance, a page may begin with body text followed by a columnar chart, which in turn is followed by additional body text. In this scenario, a section break is inserted just before the columnar chart begins, and another section break is inserted before the next portion of body text. This page would thus consist of three sections and two section breaks.

Another example of when it is necessary to end the current section and begin another is a document that digests depositions of multiple deponents. Some legal professionals include the name of the person whose deposition they are digesting in a header on each page. This means that the header would change in the document every time the deponent changed. In order to end the current header and begin another, you would need to insert a section break after each deponent's section; then you would format the section following the section break with a different header.

To divide a document into sections, choose Insert ⇨ Break to display the Break dialog box (see Figure 6-16) and specify the kind of break you want. You will see two categories of break types —Page and Section.

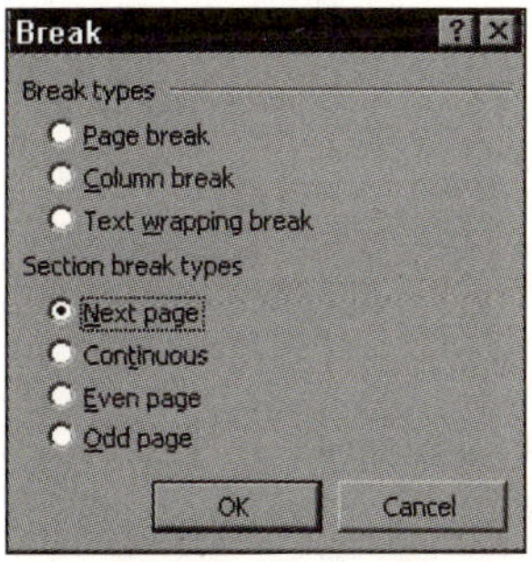

Figure 6-16: The Break dialog box

The following options appear in the Break Types section:

- **Page Break:** Ends the current page at the insertion point. Does not end the section.
- **Column Break:** Ends the current column and begins a new column.

NOTE: Page breaks and column breaks look similar in Print Layout view. Each is represented by dotted lines across the page with either the words *Page Break* or Column *Break* in the middle of the dots (but these do not appear in the printed document).

- **Text Wrapping Break:** Continues text after a graphic or image. A text wrapping break is represented by a symbol similar to the line break symbol discussed in the "Paragraph formatting" portion of this chapter. The difference is that a text wrapping break is preceded and followed by a vertical line.

The following options appear in the Section Break Types section of the Break dialog box:

- **Next Page:** Ends the current page and the current section.
- **Continuous:** Ends the section but not the page. The new section begins on the current page. This type of break is useful when inserting columnar charts between portions of text.
- **Even Page:** Ends the current section and begins another section on the next even-numbered page.
- **Odd Page:** Ends the current section and begins another section on the next odd-numbered page.

Working with Headers and Footers

If you wanted to include text or graphics at the top of the page (either on the first page only or on every page), you would want to create a header. For instance, you may want to include the words *Attorney-Client Work Product* or *Privileged and Confidential* at the top of every page. Likewise, if you want to include this information at the bottom of the page (again, either on the first page only or at the bottom of every page), you would create a footer. You can also include dates, times, and a document path and filename in a header or a footer. Also, including a page number in a header or footer is the preferred method for numbering pages in many law offices.

You can create headers and footers by choosing View ⇨ Header and Footer. Word switches to Page Layout view and the Header and Footer toolbar appears (see Figure 6-17).

Figure 6-17: The Header and Footer toolbar in Page Layout view

Creating sections and section headers and footers

Agreement documents frequently consist of a cover page that is not numbered, a table of contents that is numbered using lowercase Roman numerals (i, ii, and so on), and the body of the document, which uses Arabic numerals for page numbering but no number appearing on the first page. To define different headers for each section, your first step is to insert a Next Page section break after the cover page and table of contents, thus creating three separate sections in the document. You can now begin to define the headers for each section.

NOTE: Unlike WordPerfect, you cannot define two headers or two footers at a time. The way to define different headers or footers in a document is to divide the document into sections using section breaks and then formatting each section with its own header or footer.

The following steps take you through defining headers for each section in an agreement or contract. Remember, the first step is to insert Next Page section breaks to divide the document into multiple sections. Follow these steps after inserting the section breaks.

1. At the top of the cover page, choose View ⇨ Header and Footer. The Header and Footer toolbar appears. The area surrounded by a dashed border is where you type and format the text in your headers the same way as you normally type text in documents.
2. The cover page is not usually numbered, so click the Page Setup button on the Header and Footer toolbar. On the Layout tab, click the Different First Page check box, which indicates to Word that the first page of this section (the cover page) will have a different header than the following pages. When you click OK to dismiss the Page Setup dialog box, the words in the upper-left corner of the page's header area change to read *First Page Header -Section 1-*.
3. Without typing anything in the Header text box, click the Show Next button to move to the header at the top of section 2, which contains the table of contents. You will see the words *First Page Header -Section 2-* in the upper-left corner of the Header and Footer text box.
4. You will see the words *Same as Previous* in the upper-right corner of the header area. Word assumes that you want to use the same header in this section as was used in the previous section. To tell Word that you do not want the same header here (because you need a page number to appear on the first page of this section), click the Same as Previous button on the toolbar to turn that feature off.
5. Page numbers are usually centered in most legal documents, and you might want to surround the page numbers with spaces and dashes. To center the page number, click the Center button on the Formatting toolbar. You can also now type a dash followed by a space to further format the page number. (You aren't typing the page number itself because Word will supply that automatically.)
6. To number each page of the table of contents beginning with Roman numeral *i*, which is customary in legal documents, click the Format Page Number button on the toolbar.
7. In the Insert Page Number dialog box that opens (see Figure 6-18), choose lowercase Roman numerals from the Number Format section of the dialog box. You can also choose to include a chapter number as part of the page number.

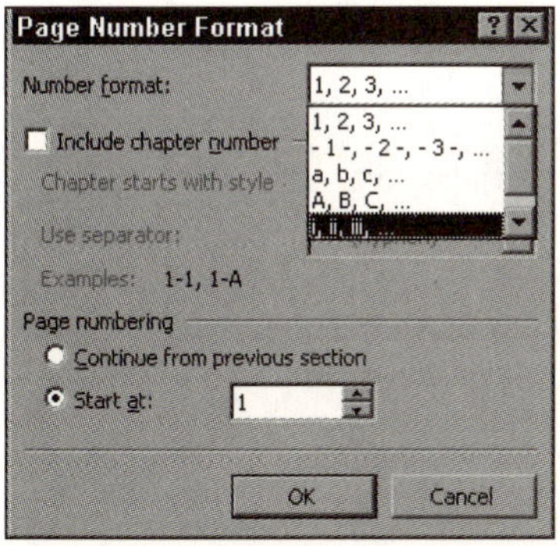

Figure 6-18: The Page Number Format dialog box

8. Choose Start At to specify the number *1* as the beginning number for your table of contents. Word uses the Arabic numbers by default in this text box. However, the online display and the printouts will reflect the style of numbering you have chosen. Click OK.

9. To insert a page number, click the Insert Page Number button on the toolbar. Follow the number with a space and then a dash.
10. Click the Show Next button to move to the top of section 3. You will see the words *First Page Header -section 3-* in the upper-left corner.
11. Click the Same as Previous button on the toolbar to turn that option off. In this section, the first page is not numbered, unlike the previous section, and the type of numbering used in this section is also different.
12. At the top of the first page of section 3, click the Page Setup button on the toolbar. As with the cover page, click the Different First Page option. Click OK.
13. Click the Show Next button on the toolbar to relocate to the top of the second page of section 3. Add the desired formatting in the Header and Footer text box, such as centering, dashes, and spaces.
14. Click the Format Page Number button to change the numbering format to Arabic. Also, change the Start At option to 2 because this is the second page in this section. Click OK.
15. Click the Insert Page Number button on the toolbar to insert the page number in the header. Add the desired formatting, such as spaces and dashes, after the number.

You can now close the Header and Footer toolbar. You can view your page numbering in Print Layout or by choosing File ⇨ Print Preview.

You can also enter the date and time as a header or footer in a document. To do so, click the Date and Time buttons on the Header and Footer toolbar. Remember, you can format any of these items in the same manner as you would regular text. In addition, there is an Insert AutoText button on the Header and Footer toolbar that you can use to insert AutoText items provided by Word or items you have customized.

Deleting headers and footers

Deleting a header or footer is a simple task. Choose View ⇨ Header and Footer and then select the text that you want to delete in the header or footer. Click the Show Next or Show Previous button on the toolbar to remove the preceding or next header or footer.

Positioning headers and footers

When you create headers and footers in a document, Word uses predefined styles that dictate how those headers and footers appear. For headers, Word uses the Header style; for footers, it uses the Footer style. These styles each have two tab stops defined in them. The first tab stop is centered between the left and right margins, and the other is positioned all the way at the right margin.

If you want to position information horizontally in your header or footer, the easiest way is to take advantage of these tab stops. Type the information you want at the left side of the header or footer, press the Tab key once to type the information you want centered, and then press Tab again to enter the information you want at the right side. If you want to change the horizontal alignment of information in the header or footer, just change the style associated with the header or footer, as described in Chapter 4, "Creating Your Legal Document with Style."

You can adjust the vertical position of the contents of the header or footer by clicking the Page Setup button on the Header and Footer toolbar. Then on the Layout tab, choose Top, Bottom, Center or Justified in the Vertical Alignment section.

You can also adjust the space between the header or footer and the top or bottom edge of the paper. Go to the header or footer that you want to adjust. Click the Page Setup button on the toolbar and adjust the measurements in the From Edge section of the Layout tab.

You can also adjust the space between the header or footer and the main document. Go to the header or footer that you want to adjust. Move your pointer to the vertical ruler at the left of your screen and point to the top or bottom margin boundary. The pointer becomes a double-headed arrow. If you want to reduce the space between the top of the document text and the header, simply drag the top margin boundary up or down. To adjust the space between the bottom of the document text and the footer, drag the bottom margin boundary up or down.

Using Spelling and Grammar Checking

You correct spelling errors in Word in the same manner as with other Microsoft applications. When you are ready to check spelling, choose Tools ⇨ Spelling and Grammar. From the insertion point forward, Word checks the spelling of each word against its *custom dictionary.* If it encounters a word that is not in its dictionary, it stops on that word and displays a Spelling and Grammar dialog box, which lists possible replacements for the misspelled word. You can replace the incorrect word with one from the list by highlighting the correct word and choosing Change, which changes the misspelled word this occurrence only, or you can choose Change All, which automatically replaces the misspelled word with the replacement word you selected during this spell check session. You can also choose the Ignore Once option (disregard the word this time) or Ignore All (disregard all the words on the current worksheet spelled this way during this spell check session only).

Adding words to a dictionary

Chances are at some point you will want to add words such as proper nouns to the custom dictionary provided by Word or to a dictionary you create with a more descriptive name. In either case, words added to a dictionary are no longer treated as misspelled words.

To add a word to a custom dictionary:

1. Choose Tools ⇨ Spelling and Grammar.
2. When Word stops on a word you want to add to the dictionary, click the Add to Dictionary button on the right side of the Spelling and Grammar dialog box.

To create your own dictionary:

1. Choose Tools ⇨ Spelling and Grammar. Word begins checking your document, displaying the Spelling and Grammar dialog box if it finds something to question
2. If Word is questioning the spelling of a word and you want to add that word to a dictionary you create, click the Options button in the lower-left corner of the dialog box. Word displays the Spelling & Grammar dialog box shown in Figure 6-19.
3. Click the Custom Dictionaries button. Word displays the Custom Dictionaries dialog box. This dialog box lists all the custom dictionaries on your system.
4. Click the New button. Word displays the Create Custom Dictionary dialog box.
5. In the File Name box, type a descriptive name for your new dictionary. It is not necessary for you to add the .DIC extension; Word does this for you.

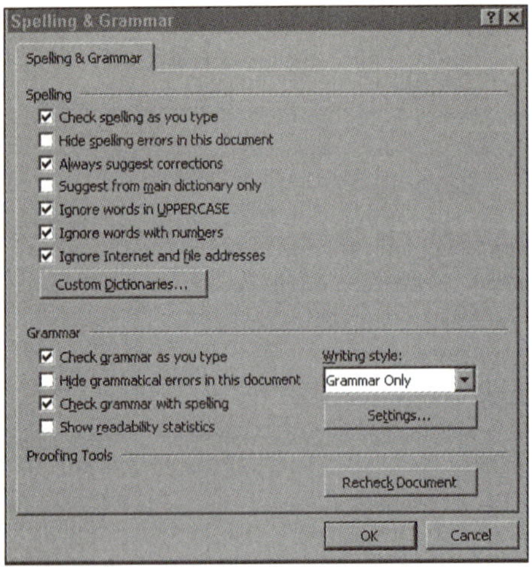

Figure 6-19: The Spelling & Grammar dialog box

6. Click Save. Word creates the dictionary you specified, closes the Create Custom Dictionary dialog box, and displays the newly created dictionary in the Custom Dictionaries dialog box.

NOTE: If you have more than one custom dictionary listed in the Custom Dictionaries dialog box, one of them will be designated as the default custom dictionary. This is the dictionary to which words are added when you choose to add words during a spelling check. (Otherwise, all custom dictionaries are treated the same.) You can change the default custom dictionary by selecting it and then clicking the Change Default button.

---

7. Click OK to dismiss the Custom Dictionaries dialog box.
8. Click OK to close the Spelling & Grammar dialog box.

After they're created, all custom dictionaries are available whenever you use Word. You can create as many dictionaries as your computer's memory allows. The CUSTOM.DIC and any dictionaries you create are not document-specific and are available whenever you check spelling.

TIP: If you inadvertently add a word to one of the custom dictionaries (such as adding a word that was misspelled), you can correct the spelling or remove the word altogether by selecting the dictionary in the Custom Dictionaries dialog box and clicking Modify. Word then shows you all the words in the custom dictionary. You can use the controls in the dialog box to add or delete words from the dictionary.

Using AutoCorrect

Another feature that exists in Microsoft programs is AutoCorrect, which automatically corrects words as you type. If you find that you consistently misspell a word in the same manner over and over, you can add the word to the AutoCorrect list so that the correctly spelled word automatically replaces the misspelled word as you type.

To add one of your commonly misspelled words to AutoCorrect, here are the steps:

1. Choose Tools ⇨ AutoCorrect.
2. On the AutoCorrect as You Type tab (see Figure 6-20), you can enter the word whose spelling you want automatically corrected in the Replace section; then enter the correct spelling of the word in the With section. Then click the Add button.

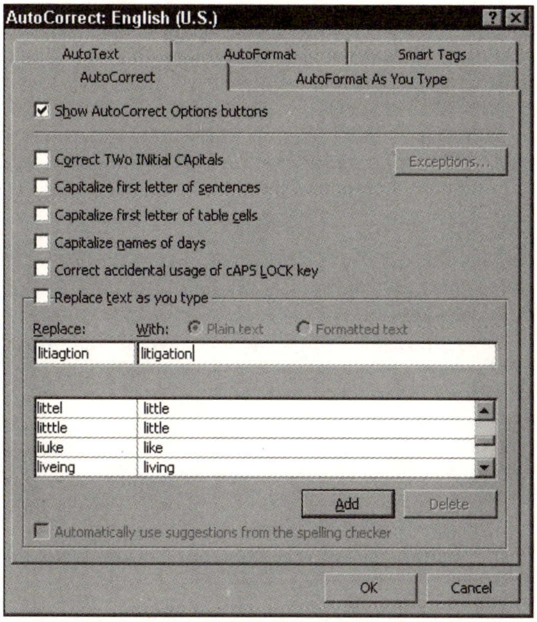

Figure 6-20: The AutoCorrect tab of the options in the AutoCorrect dialog box

If the Show AutoCorrect Options Buttons check box is checked, Word offers you a way out of automatically correcting misspelled words. For example, maybe you have a stubborn habit of typing *litiagtion* when you mean *litigation*. Fixing this through AutoCorrect means that whenever Word encounters your misspelling, it automatically corrects it. However, a blue rectangle appears under the corrected word, and when the mouse pointer is on the word, the AutoCorrect Options submenu appears and you have the following options:

- Change the corrected word back to its original spelling.
- Stop automatically correcting the word.
- Control AutoCorrect options by returning to the AutoCorrect tab.

We recommend that you customize the list of words on the AutoCorrect tab so that certain terms found in legal documents are not automatically corrected by Word. For example, AutoCorrect automatically changes "(c)" to the copyright symbol ©. As you know, "(c)" is commonly used to cite references in legal documents, and you would not want those changed to copyright symbols. To prevent such changes, you should customize the AutoCorrect list so that "(c)" is not automatically corrected.

Working with Footnotes

Legal professionals are probably the heaviest users of Word's Footnote feature. Footnotes are a standard document element for litigators and other legal professionals. Word's capability to display multiple portions of a document simultaneously makes adding footnotes to legal documents a simple matter. You can look at and work with the text of a footnote in a separate pane while the related portion of your document remains visible. There are four places you can position footnotes in Word: at the bottom of the page on which the reference occurs (which is typical for most legal documents), immediately below the reference, at the end of the section, or at the end of the document as a whole. When footnotes are placed at the end of a document, they are called *endnotes*.

The formatting of the footnote number in the text and in the footnote itself is controlled by the Footnote Reference style provided by Word, which formats the reference with the Default Paragraph Font plus superscript. The format of the text of the footnote is controlled by the Footnote Text style, which contains the formats found in the Normal style plus a change to a smaller font. You can change the formats of the footnote number and the footnote text by modifying these styles. Those of you who used WordPerfect were able to format the footnote reference in the text and the footnote itself so that it is a superscripted number that is underlined and followed by a slash. In Word, it would require a macro to create a footnote reference formatted this way. Many legal professionals have abandoned this type of format for the footnote reference and go instead with the default style that simply superscripts the number.

Inserting footnotes

To insert footnotes into your document, first position the insertion point in the document where you want the reference to appear in the text; then choose Insert ⇨ Reference ⇨ Footnote. The Footnote and Endnote dialog box that opens (see Figure 6-21) contains several options, which are briefly described below:

- **Location:** Footnotes can appear above the bottom margin or following the last line of text on the page. You can place all endnotes at the end of the document or at the end of the section.
- **Format:** You can change the style of numbering used for the footnote reference or choose a symbol to use instead, such as an asterisk. You can also choose from a variety of symbols to use as your footnote reference character. Here you can also specify the beginning footnote number, and the numbering can be continuous throughout the document or start over in each new section.
- **Apply Changes:** Changes made in this dialog box can be applied to the entire document, or for situations in which a document is divided into more than one section, changes can be applied only to the section containing the insertion point.

By default, Word first inserts the *footnote separator* (or *rule*, which just means a line) in the document and arranges the footnotes beneath the rule.

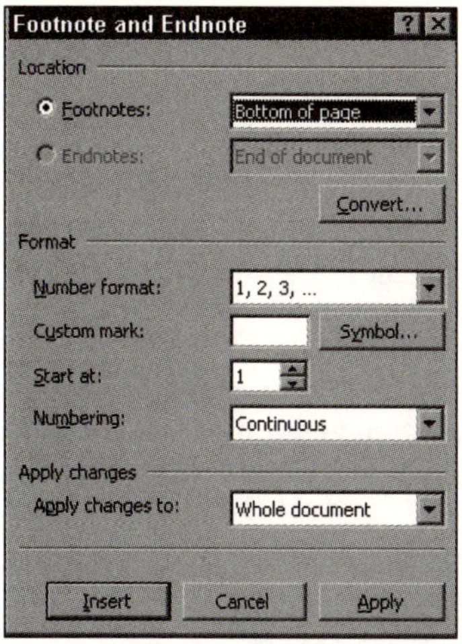

Figure 6-21: The Footnote and Endnote dialog box

Working with footnotes in different views

Footnotes are a valuable feature in Word, and you will undoubtedly work with them quite often. Exactly how you do that work depends on the view in which you are using Word. The following sections detail how you work with footnotes in Print Layout and Normal views.

Using footnotes in Print Layout view

When using the Print Layout view, footnotes appear at the bottom of the page as they will appear in the printed document. To move between footnotes contained in your document using this view, click the Select Browse Object button, which is situated between the blue Previous and Next arrows at the bottom of the vertical scroll bar. After clicking this button, choose the Browse by Footnote option (see Figure 6-22). Now, when you click the Previous and Next arrows on the vertical scroll bar, you can jump quickly between the footnote references in the text.

Figure 6-22: The Browse by Footnote option on the vertical scroll bar

To edit footnotes while working in the Print Layout view, do one of the following:

- Locate the footnote reference for the note you are editing by using the Use the Browse by Footnote option. You can also double-click the Status bar to open the Find and Replace dialog box and click the Go To tab. Next, type the footnote number you want to jump to.
- Double-click the footnote reference, which automatically moves the insertion point to the text of the footnote where you can make your edits.
- Choose View ⇨ Footnotes to move the insertion point to the area on the page containing the footnote text.

NOTE: When the pointer is over a footnote reference in the text, a ScreenTip box appears that expands to display the text of the footnote.

Using footnotes in Normal view

If you are working in Normal view, you will see only the footnote reference in the text, not the text of the footnote. To see the footnote text, choose View ⇨ Footnotes. A separate footnote pane opens in the bottom portion of the screen (see Figure 6-23). When the footnote pane is open, a split bar appears in the vertical scroll bar. You can use the mouse to drag the split bar up or down to change the size of the pane. At any time when you are working with footnotes, you can return to the main part of the document while leaving the footnote pane open. Press F6 (Next Pane). When you are finished typing or editing the footnote, you can drag the split bar to close the footnote pane, or click the Close button. You can see footnotes in your document only if you are in Page Layout view.

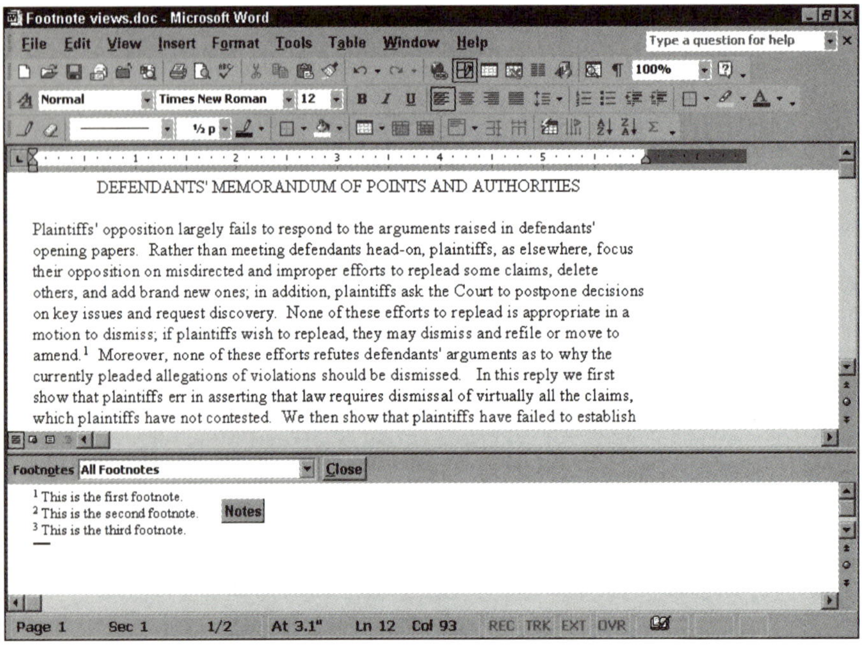

Figure 6-23: The Footnote pane

Continuing footnotes on a new page

It is not uncommon for litigation documents to contain 50 or more footnotes. Although footnote text starts on the page containing its footnote reference, many footnotes found in legal documents are so lengthy that the entire footnote cannot fit on the page and must be continued to a new page. Word automatically continues a footnote onto the next page if it cannot fit on the current page. However, the default *continuation separator* (the line that appears above the footnote) spans the width of the margins, unlike the default footnote separator, which is roughly a two-inch-long line. Also, you have to type the text you want Word to use as the footnote continuation notice. In some word processing programs, you can include a notice on the page the footnote is continued from, as well as on the page the footnote is continued to. In Word, you have to type the notice you want to appear; otherwise, none is included and the footnote simply continues. You can customize these options in the Normal view by choosing View ⇨ Footnotes. In the footnote pane that opens, click the Notes drop-down list to select the options you want to change.

Changing the length of the continuation separator line

You can change the length of the footnote continuation separator to match the length used for the footnote separator. While in Normal view, choose View ⇨ Footnotes and select the Footnote Separator option from the Notes drop-down list. Word hides the actual footnotes, instead showing the footnote separator in the footnotes pane. Select the separator line that appears below the drop-down list and press Ctrl+C to copy the line to the Clipboard. Next, choose the Footnote Continuation Separator option from the Notes drop-down list. Delete the line that appears and paste the line you just copied.

Specifying a footnote continuation notice

You can add specific continuation text that you want to use whenever footnotes are continued. This text appears below the footnote on the page it is continuing from but does not appear on the page on which the footnote continues. To add specific text to be used on the page from which a footnote continues, in Normal view choose View ⇨ Footnotes to open the footnote pane. Choose Footnote Continuation Notice from the Notes drop-down list and then type the desired text.

Moving and deleting footnotes

Footnotes are indicated by the reference marks in the document, so moving or deleting a footnote is as easy as moving or deleting the reference mark:

- **To move a footnote:** Select the reference mark within the document and move it to the desired new location.
- **To delete a footnote:** Select the reference mark and press Delete.

Whether you move or delete (or, for that matter, insert footnotes), Word automatically renumbers the footnotes accordingly.

Changing footnotes to endnotes

Changing all your footnotes (or just one footnote) to endnotes is easy. Activate the footnote pane by choosing the Footnotes command from the View menu. Select the footnotes that you want to convert to endnotes by moving the cursor to the beginning of each. Right-click in the footnote pane to open the shortcut menu containing the Note Options and Convert to Endnote submenu items. If you want to convert just the footnote on which you right-clicked, choose the Convert to Endnote option. To see the newly converted endnote, click the Notes drop-down list in the footnote pane and choose the All Endnotes option from the list.

If you want to convert all your footnotes to endnotes, right-click a footnote in the footnote pane. From the shortcut menu, choose Note Options to display the Footnote and Endnote dialog box. If you click the Convert button in the dialog box, Word gives you the option to change all your footnotes to endnotes.

NOTE: You can also use the Note Options choice from the shortcut menu to customize the number format, the starting number, and other options previously discussed.

Generating a Table of Contents

One powerful feature that Word provides is the capability to generate a table of contents quickly, based on the headings within a legal document. Legal professionals almost always create a table of contents for legal pleadings and transactional documents. As noted previously, Word's built-in heading styles include formatting for a table of contents. However, you can also change the default styles so that Word creates the table of contents based on your chosen styles, or you can build the table of contents by using TC fields, a special type of field that you insert into a document.

NOTE: Because the table of contents usually contains page numbering that is different from the main document, we recommend that you place a Next Page section break after the table of contents (if it is generated at the top of the document) or before the table of contents (if it appears at the end of the document).

If you want to generate a table of contents using standard heading styles, follow these steps:

1. Place the insertion point where you want to insert the table of contents.
2. Type the heading for the table of contents. Several lines down, right-align the word *Page*, which will appear above the page numbers associated with the heading.
3. Drop down a line or two and choose Insert ⇨ Reference ⇨ Index and Tables.
4. In the Index and Tables dialog box that opens (see Figure 6-24), click the Table of Contents tab.

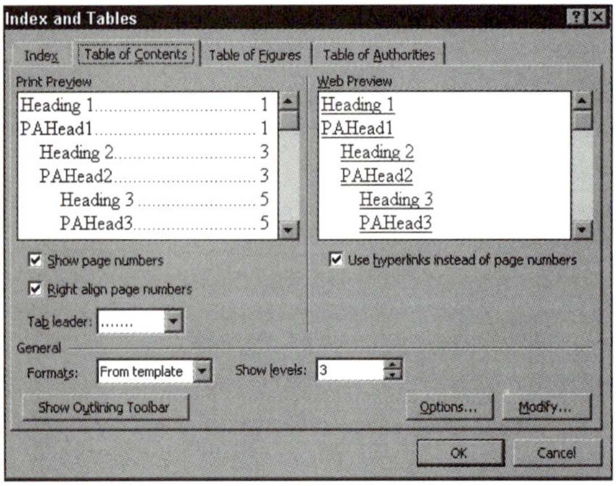

Figure 6-24: The Table of Contents tab of the Index and Tables dialog box

5. Select the number of heading levels you want to appear in your table of contents.
6. Select the format you would like to apply.
7. Click OK.

Word will assign the proper page numbers automatically. If you later change the contents of the document so that page numbers change, the table of contents will not be updated automatically. You must update the table of contents by right-clicking anywhere in the table (which displays a shortcut menu) and then choosing Update Field.

Creating a table of contents when manually marking headings

You can also generate a table of contents when your document includes nonstyled headings, by manually marking them. When you manually mark a heading, you are adding a field called *TC entries* (for *table of contents entries*) to your document. To mark headings for the table of contents, perform the following steps:

1. Select the heading you want to mark.
2. Press Alt+Shift+O to open the Mark Table of Contents Entry dialog box (see Figure 6-25). The selected text appears in the Entry section of the box. Because you can have more than one type of table in Word, each is assigned a one-letter identifier. For a table of contents, the identifier assigned is *C*.

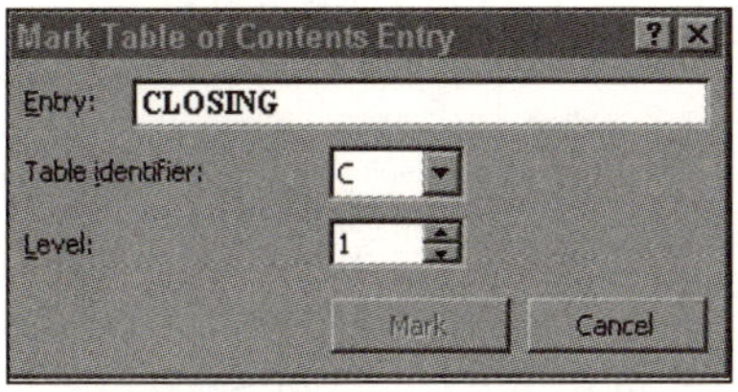

Figure 6-25: The Mark Table of Contents Entry dialog box

3. Select the level you want to assign to the heading you are marking. The level you select determines how that heading is indented in the table of contents.
4. Click the Mark button. The heading is marked with a TC entry field that looks similar to the following: The dialog box remains open, making it easier to move to the next heading that you want to manually mark.
5. When all marking is complete, click the Close button.

To generate a table of contents that includes styled and unstyled headings, perform the following steps:

1. Click the Show/Hide button on the Standard toolbar to make sure that Word's nonprinting characters are displayed.
2. Choose Insert ⇨ Reference ⇨ Index and Tables.
3. Click the Table of Contents tab.
4. Select the number of levels you want to appear in the table of contents.
5. Click the Options button to open the Table of Contents Options dialog box (see Figure 6-26).
6. If your document contains styled headings, the Styles check box is checked, and the heading styles used are listed.
7. To include manually marked headings, click the Table Entry Fields check box.
8. Click OK.
9. Click OK again to generate the table of contents.

When the table of contents is generated, all headings, styled and unstyled, are included.

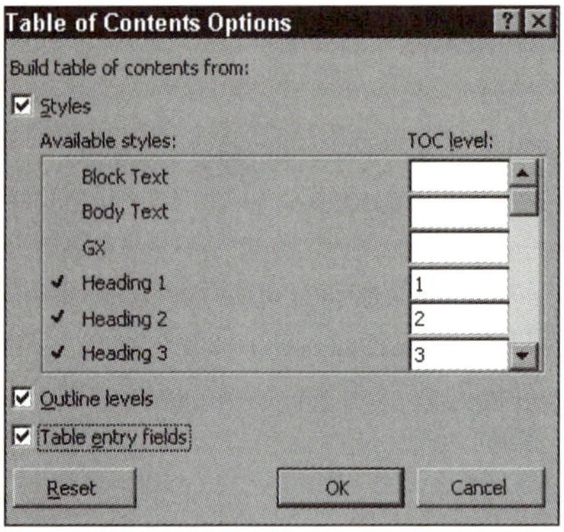

Figure 6-26: The Table of Contents Options dialog box

Viewing the table of contents

When using the Normal, Print Layout, or Outline views, the table of contents appears as regular text. However, if you click anywhere in the table of contents, it may appear shaded. This is because the Field Shading option on the View tab of the Tools dialog box is set to When Selected. This means that whenever you click a field, it becomes shaded automatically. You can set this option to Never or Always.

In Web Layout view, the headings appear as hyperlinks with the standard blue underlining. However, to jump automatically to one of the headings, you must press Ctrl before clicking the heading. If you do not press Ctrl before clicking a heading in the table of contents, your insertion point remains in the table of contents.

Although the hyperlinks are useful, you can remove hyperlinks from the table of contents. To remove hyperlinks, click anywhere in the table of contents and press Alt+F9. This reduces the table of contents to its field entry code, which resembles the following:

```
{ TOC \o."1-3" \f\h \z \u }
```

Remove the \h switch from the field and update the field. To restore the table of contents to show the headings, press Alt+F9.

Changing the table of contents format

You can change the format of your table of contents, including indents, by modifying the styles used to create the table of contents. To modify the styles, choose Insert ⇨ Reference ⇨ Index and Tables and then click the Table of Contents tab. Next, click the Options button to open the Style dialog box (see Figure 6-27).

The Style dialog box lists Word's built-in table of contents styles used for the formatting. Select the style you want to modify and then click the Modify button to open the Modify Style dialog box. Change the formats in the same way as described in Chapter 4.

Figure 6-27: The Style dialog box

Generating Tables of Authorities

To generate a table of authorities in Word, you must mark all full citations (Word calls these the *long form*) and abbreviated citations (*short form*) that are to be included. The long form of a citation includes the name of the case, the legal reference in which it is found, and any other information included as part of the citation. An example of the long form is *U.S. v. Winken,* Blinken & Knod, 138 U.S. 1540 F.2d 282 (2001). An example of the short form is *U.S. v. Winken*, Blinken & Knod. To mark citations for the table of authorities, perform the following steps:

1. Open the document containing the citations to be included in the table of authorities.
2. Choose Insert ⇨ Reference ⇨ Index and Tables from the menus and click the Table of Authorities tab (see Figure 6-28) in the Index and Tables dialog box that opens.

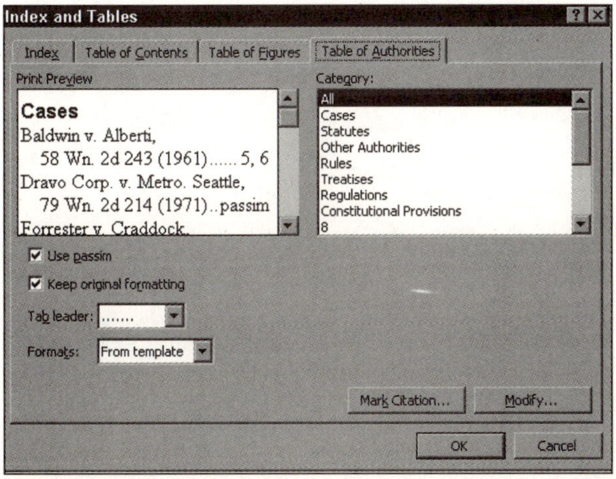

Figure 6-28: The Table of Authorities tab

3. Click the Mark Citation button. The Mark Citation dialog box appears.

4. Begin searching the document for the next long form or short form citation by clicking the Next Citation button so that Word locates the next citation in the document.
5. When Word finds the first citation, it places it in the Selected Text area of the dialog box.
6. In the Category section, select the appropriate category for the citation.
7. Modify as necessary the short form version of the citation in the Short Citation section.
8. Click the Mark button to mark the citation. You can also choose Mark All, which causes Word to mark every occurrence of that citation in the document. The Mark Citation dialog box remains open so that you can mark all citations in the document before closing the dialog box.

To generate a table of authorities, perform the following steps:

1. Create a new section for the table of authorities.
2. Type the heading you want to appear at the top of the table of authorities, followed by desired spacing.
3. At the insertion point, choose Insert ⇨ Reference ⇨ Index and Tables and click the Table of Authorities tab.
4. Set the desired options in the dialog box.
5. Click OK to generate the table of authorities and to close the dialog box.

Many legal professionals are using third-party software such as Full Authority by Lexis-Nexis. The main difference between the two programs is that, with Full Authority, citations contained in a document are automatically included in the table of authorities without going through the marking process.

Summary

This chapter has covered a lot of ground with respect to the Word features that will give your documents a professional shine. The topics in this chapter included the following:

- Automatic and simple numbered lists
- Margins, tabs, and line spacing
- Character, paragraph, page, and section formatting
- Headers and footers
- Spelling and grammar checking
- Creating a dictionary
- Footnotes
- Tables of contents
- Tables of authorities

In the next chapter, you'll learn how to work with Word's Print commands to make your documents look as good on paper as they do on-screen.

Chapter 7

Page Setup and Printing

In This Chapter

- ♦ Printing in the background
- ♦ Previewing documents
- ♦ Adjusting margins in Print Preview mode
- ♦ Performing multiple printings
- ♦ Changing the print orientation
- ♦ Changing the printer setup
- ♦ Printing envelopes

THIS CHAPTER DETAILS HOW YOU PRINT your documents and how you can preview them before printing. Keep in mind that your printer must be set up and ready before you can print documents — an obvious point, but many printer problems are traced to an incorrect printer setup or to a printer that was never turned on.

Printing in the Background

If you have just one printer connected to your computer (and you know that it works with other Windows applications), you can print a single copy of any document in Word with one simple action: clicking the Print button on the Standard toolbar. (The Print button is easy to find — it's the one that looks like a printer.) When you open any document and click the Print button, Word sends one copy of the document to the printer. As the document is processed by the built-in Windows Print Manager, the status bar in Word displays the progress of the printing process. Note that, by default, Word prints in the background and creates an image of the document on disk that can be sent to the printer when the printer is ready to receive data. So unless you're printing to a network laser printer that is the size of a compact car (one of those big, *fast* models), Word is likely to finish its part of the printing process long before your printer does.

If your system doesn't print in the background but rather waits until the printing is finished before it frees Word to do something else, you can change the system. Choose Tools ⇨ Options, click the Print tab, activate the Background Printing option, and click the OK button. Your system will print in the background.

Previewing Documents

The Print Preview command from the File menu (and the Print Preview button on the Standard toolbar) lets you see on your screen what a document will look like when you print it (see Figure 7-1). Print Preview saves trees: You don't waste paper printing draft copies before printing a final copy.

Print Preview shows footnotes, headers, footers, page numbers, multiple columns, and graphics. You can view more than one page at a time by clicking the Multiple Pages button on the Print Preview toolbar and selecting the number of pages that you want to see at one time. You can easily move between pages, but you cannot edit a document while in Print Preview mode.

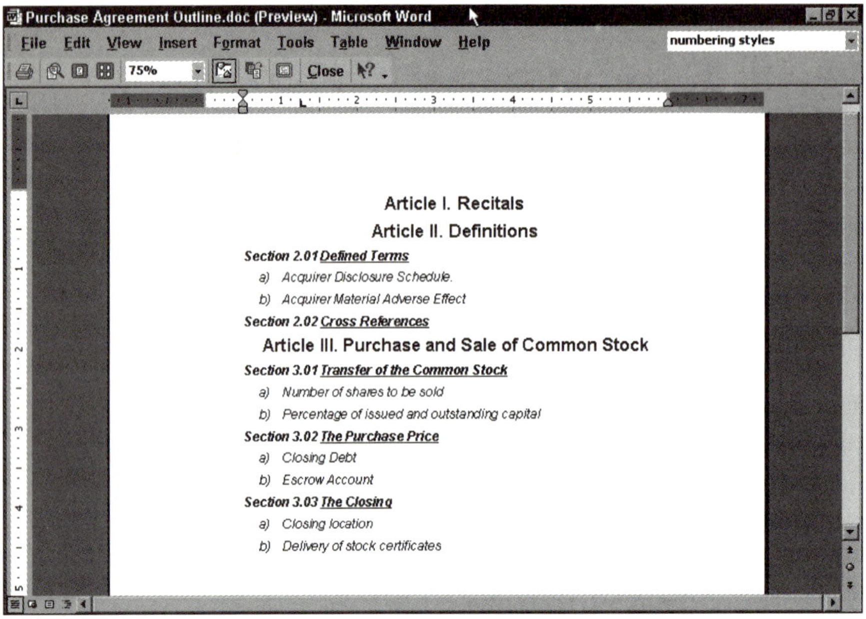

Figure 7-1: A document as it appears in the Print Preview window

Understanding the Print Preview toolbar

After entering Print Preview mode, the Print Preview toolbar appears (see Figure 7-2). It provides useful options when you are in Print Preview mode. Click the appropriate button to perform a task, as outlined in Table 7-1.

Figure 7-2: The Print Preview toolbar

Table 7-1
Print Preview Toolbar Buttons

Button	*Function*
Print	Prints the document.
Magnifier	Magnifies a certain section of your document that you may want to make larger.
One Page	Shows the current page in Print Preview mode.
Multiple Pages	Lets you see up to six pages at once on-screen. These pages appear so that you can see the layout of each page.

Button	***Function***
Zoom Control	Lets you control the distance at which you see the pages on the Print Preview window.
View Ruler	Lets you see a ruler for each of the pages that you have on-screen so that you can move the margins in Print Preview mode.
Shrink to Fit	Lets you shrink information so that it will all fit on one page. This feature helps you keep paragraphs together.
Full Screen	Lets you see your document in Full Screen mode.
Close	Returns you to Normal view.
Help	Provides online help for your printing questions.

A quick way out of Print Preview mode is to press the Esc key.

Adjusting margins and object locations

Although you cannot edit documents in Print Preview mode, you can make changes to some aspects of the document, such as the location of page margins, headers, and footers. You can easily make changes to page margins by displaying the ruler (choose View ⇨ Ruler). (Note that if you are in Full Page view, moving the mouse to the top of the screen brings the menu choices into view.) Select the text by clicking the Magnifier icon to change to the arrow. Next, click and drag to select the text you wish to highlight. Now, move the triangles on the ruler until the document takes on the appearance that you want. You also can use clicking and dragging techniques to move graphics in your document while you are in Print Preview mode.

If you inserted an object, such as a picture, into your document, you may want to frame it so that you can drag it to any location while you are in Print Preview. To frame the object while you are in Print Preview, first click the Magnifier button to turn off the magnifier. Then right-click the picture that you want to frame. Choose Format Picture from the shortcut menu. From the Format Picture dialog box, shown in Figure 7-3, choose the Colors and Lines tab. Choose the type of frame lines desired. When you do so, the frame appears around the picture.

If the text does not wrap around the frame, it means that text wrapping is not activated. Right-click the frame and choose Format Picture from the shortcut menu. Next, choose the Layout tab, as shown in Figure 7-4. Choose the type of wrapping style desired from the diagrams, and the text will then wrap accordingly.

If you click the Advanced button in the dialog box, you can then use the Distance from Text section of the Wrapping tab to control the distance of the text from the picture. This section of the tab will allow you to adjust the distance from all sides of the picture. Adjust the numbers in the top, bottom, left, and right sections of the Distance from Text section.

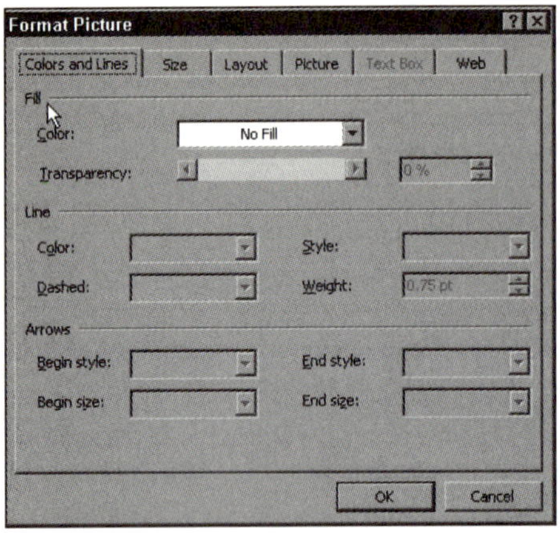

Figure 7-3: The Colors and Lines tab of the Format Picture dialog box

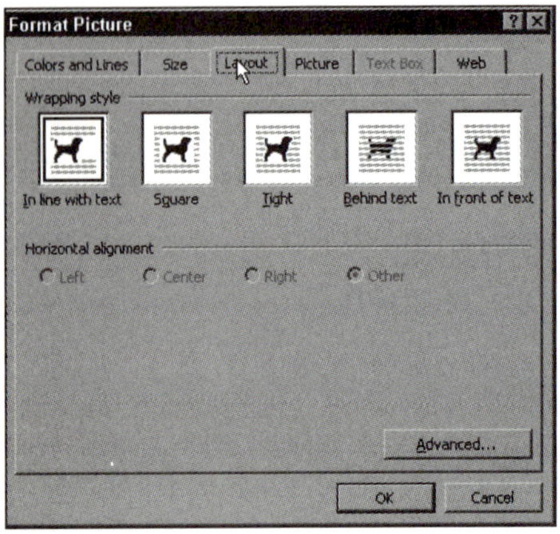

Figure 7-4: The Layout tab of the Format Picture dialog box

Printing a Document (and More)

Any word processor lets you print a document. But Word gives you more — you can print selected portions of a document, multiple copies of a document, and other information related to a document, such as summary information, annotations, AutoText entries, and style sheets. You can print documents by choosing File ⇨ Print. The Print dialog box appears, as shown in Figure 7-5.

The available options in the Print dialog box include

- **Printer:** The Name drop-down list box lets you choose the printer that you want to use by selecting it from the entries. After making a selection, Word provides you with the status and location of the printer on your system. If you don't see the printer that you want to use in the list box, you need to install it. Consult your Windows documentation for the steps.
- **Copies:** In the Copies area, you can enter the number of copies that you want printed in the Number of Copies drop-down list box (the default is 1). This area also lets you collate copies. When you check the Collate option for more than one copy of a document, Word prints all the

pages of each document before it goes on to the next set. If you do not check this option, Word prints all needed copies of page 1, followed by all copies of page 2, and so on.

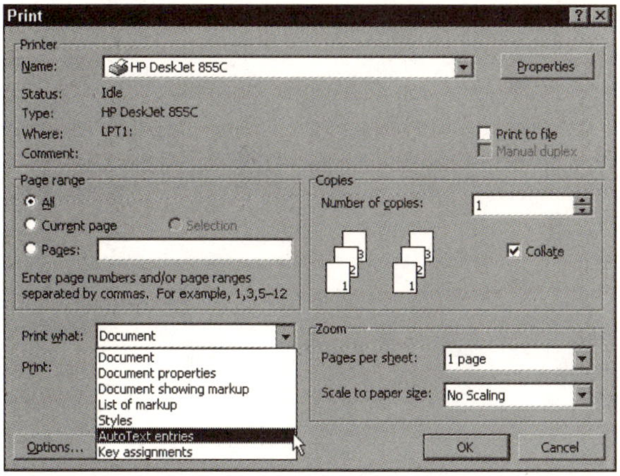

Figure 7-5: The Print dialog box

- **Page Range:** In the Page Range area, you can choose which portion of the document should be printed. Choose All to print the entire document, choose Selection to print a selection of text, choose Current Page to print just the current page, or choose Pages to print selected pages of a document. You can print a range of pages by separating the starting and ending pages with a hyphen. For example, entering **7-12** in the box tells Word to print pages 7 through 12 of the document. You also can separate numbers by commas to print individual pages. For example, entering **3,5,8,10-12** in the box tells Word to print pages 3, 5, 8, and 10 through 12.
- **Print:** In the Print list box, you can choose All Pages in Range to print all the pages in the chosen print range (as selected in the Page Range area of the dialog box). Or you can choose to print only the odd pages or only the even pages in the range.
- **Options:** Click the Options button to display additional options relating to printing (see the "Using the Print Options" section later in this chapter).
- **Properties:** The Properties button opens the Printer Properties dialog box. In this dialog box, you can set different options for your printer. The properties in this dialog box will be different for each printer.
- **Print What:** Use this box to choose what to print. You can print key assignments, summary information, annotations, AutoText entries, and other items related to your documents.

You can use the Print shortcut key combination (Ctrl+Shift+F12) rather than File ⇨ Print to open the Print dialog box and make your printing selections. You also can press Ctrl+P to activate the Print dialog box — a useful time-saver if you wish to print quickly.

After you have chosen your desired options in the Print dialog box, click the OK button to start printing.

Printing a portion of a document

You will encounter times when you want to print only a section of a document. You can choose between two methods to print a section of text. First, you can choose a starting and an ending page number to print and enter the page numbers in the Pages text box, located in the Page Range area of the Print dialog box. Word prints the starting and ending pages and all pages in between. Or you can first select a portion of text and then activate the Selection option in the Page Range area of the Print dialog box to print just that selection.

To print selected pages of a document, perform the following steps:

1. With the document open, choose File ⇨ Print.
2. In the Page Range area, click the Current Page radio button to print the current page. Or click the Pages radio button and enter the starting page number that you want to print. If you want to print consecutive page numbers, separate them with a hyphen. Nonconsecutive page numbers should be separated by a comma.
3. Click the OK button to begin printing.

To print a selection of text, perform the following steps.

1. Select the text that you want to print.
2. With the document open, choose File ⇨ Print.
3. Click the Selection radio button.
4. Click the OK button to print the selected text.

Printing more than documents

To print something other than the document itself, click the down arrow of the Print What drop-down list box in the Print dialog box to reveal the list of options that you can print (see Figure 7-6). Following are the available options:

- **Document:** Prints the document (the default)
- **Document Properties:** Prints the summary information for the document
- **Document Showing Markup:** Your document, with comments shown in place
- **List of Markup:** A list of comments, separate from the document
- **Styles:** Prints the style sheet for the document
- **AutoText Entries:** Prints the template AutoText entries
- **Key Assignments:** Prints the names of macros and the keys to which they are assigned

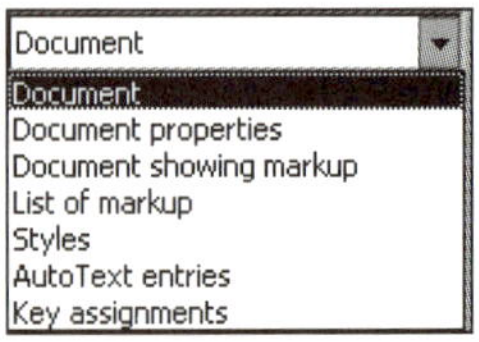

Figure 7-6: The Print What list box in the Print dialog box

You can print summary information or annotations simultaneously with the printing of the document. See the "Using the Print Options" section later in this chapter for more information on how to print these items simultaneously.

Printing in Landscape orientation

On occasion, you may want to print a document in Landscape orientation, which is particularly useful with very wide documents, such as those that contain a table of numbers or documents containing pictures. If your printer supports Landscape printing, you can easily print documents this way.

To print a document in Landscape orientation, follow these steps:

1. Choose File ⇨ Page Setup and click the Margins tab of the Page Setup dialog box.
2. In the Orientation area, click the Landscape radio button and then click the OK button.
3. Print the document by choosing File ⇨ Print. If there is no Landscape option in the Margins dialog box, then your printer does not support Landscape printing and you cannot print this way in Windows.

When you are finished printing in Landscape orientation, be sure to change your paper orientation back to normal (Portrait) mode. If you do not make the change, all successive printings will be in Landscape mode. To change back to Portrait mode, choose File ⇨ Page Setup and click the Margins tab. Then click the Portrait radio button in the Orientation area of the dialog box.

Using the Print Options

You can find additional printing options in the Print dialog box. These options enable you to include annotations or summary information with documents, to print in reverse order, and to print draft versions of documents. To use these options, choose File ⇨ Print and then click the Options button. Figure 7-7 shows the dialog box that appears. To choose any of the desired options, click the option, or press the Alt key plus the underlined letter of the option name.

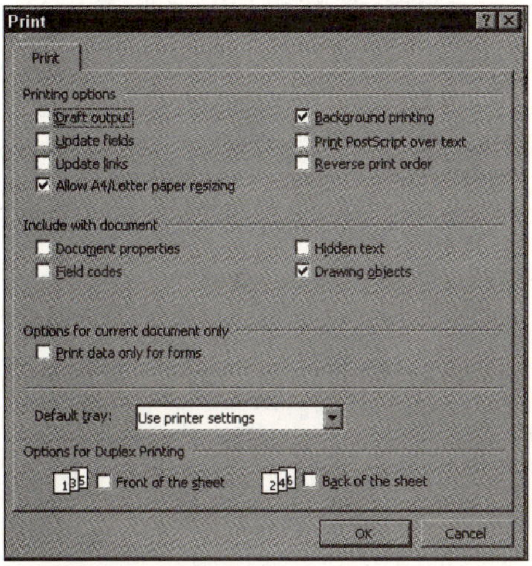

Figure 7-7: The Print tab options

The Print tab options include the following:

- **Draft Output:** When you choose the Draft Output option, Word prints a draft of your document. A *draft* is a document that is printed with minimal formatting. A document such as this has the character formatting removed, allowing you to print your documents faster.

- **Update Fields:** The Update Fields option makes Word update any fields that are in a document before it is printed.
- **Update Links:** When you choose the Update Links option, Word updates any fields that are in a document before it is printed.
- **Allow A4/Letter Paper Resizing:** This option tells Word to automatically resize the document to fit A4/European paper sizes.
- **Background Printing:** The Background Printing option lets you work in Word while you're printing. However, this option uses memory, so you may want to turn it off to speed up printing.
- **Print PostScript over Text:** If you are printing a document that contains Print field codes that, in turn, contain PostScript commands, this option controls whether those PostScript commands are printed in front of the text or behind the text.
- **Reverse Print Order:** The Reverse Print Order option causes the document to be printed last page first. This option is helpful with laser printers that are based on the first-generation Canon engine (such as the original Hewlett-Packard LaserJet). The design of such printers causes printed pages to come out face up, so a multiple-page document would be stacked with the last page on top (which is usually not where you want it). If you turn on the Reverse Print Order option, however, the print run starts with the last page and ends with the first page so that the printed document ends up in the proper order.
- **Include with Document:** Use the Include with Document options to specify which information should be included with the printed document. If you activate Summary Info, a summary information sheet is printed with the document. Click Field Codes to print field codes instead of the results of the fields. If you activate Annotations, Word prints the document and any annotations added to the document. Click Hidden Text to print the document and any text that you hid with the Hidden option from the Character dialog box. Also, you will see the Drawing Objects check box. This will print the drawing objects you may have included in your document.
- **Default Tray:** The Default Tray drop-down list box lets you select different paper feed bins (assuming that your printer allows feeding from different paper bins). Actual choices depend upon the printer you have installed. Typical choices are the following:
  - **Manual Paper Feed:** Choose this option to make the printer draw paper from its manual bin.
  - **Automatically Select:** Choose this option for automatic paper feed.
  - **Bin 1, Bin 2, Bin 3:** Choose Bin 1, 2, or 3 to draw paper from a specific bin.
  - **Mixed:** Choose Mixed to feed the first sheet from bin 1 and successive sheets from bin 2. Mixed feeding is a common technique with high-production office laser printers, which may have company letterhead stored in one bin and bond paper stored in another bin, for example. If the Default Tray option appears dimmed in your dialog box, then your printer does not support feeding from multiple paper bins. Print Manager contains the default setting for this option. If you wish to change it, click the arrow and choose one of the feeding options from the list.
  - **Options for Current Document Only:** This area applies the options that you select to the current document, but returns to the default options for the next print job. Print Data Only for Forms is used to print just the data for forms that may be in your documents.

Changing Your Printer Setup

Word provides access to the printer setup facility of Windows through File ⇨ Print. You can choose the default printer from among different printers. The Print dialog box lets you select a printer that is already installed under Windows in the Name list box; however, you cannot use this dialog box to choose a printer that is not yet installed under Windows. (See your Windows documentation if you need to add a new printer to your Windows configuration.)

If you have problems...

If you have difficulty printing or if the printer name in the dialog box doesn't match the printer that is connected to your computer, choose File ⇨ Print, and click the Name drop-down list box in the Printer field of the dialog box that appears. This opens the list of printers installed under Windows. Select the troublesome printer and then click the OK button. Try the Print command again. If the correct printer is selected and you still can't print, the problem is one of the following: the printer itself, the Windows setup on your system, or the lack of availability in Windows of the printer you wish to use.

If the printer you wish to use is not installed in Windows, try this: From the taskbar Start menu, choose Settings and then Printers. In the window that appears, double-click the Add Printers icon and follow the instructions from the Add Printer Wizard.

Word uses the Windows Print Manager to manage all printing. If you can't print from another Windows application (such as WordPad), you can't print from Word, either. If you can't print from Windows, refer to your Windows documentation or the *Microsoft Word for Windows Printer Guide* (supplied with your Word documentation). Also, be sure to check the obvious — make sure that the printer is properly connected, turned on, and online. If you still can't find the source of the problem, you can find many helpful troubleshooting tips in the *Printer Guide*.

Only one printer can use the same connection (printer port) at a time. If you change printers and the new printer is connected to the same printer port, you must use the Windows Control Panel to change the printer connection. To change the setting, choose Settings from the Start menu and then choose Control Panel. Double-click the Printers icon. Right-click the printer for which you want to change the port. Then choose Properties from the shortcut menu and select the Details tab (see Figure 7-8). In this tab, you can change the port for the printer. See your Windows documentation for more details. (Remember that the actual appearance of this dialog box depends upon the printer you're using.)

If you want only to change printers, you can do so from the Print dialog box if the printer is already installed in Windows. Choose File ⇨ Print. In the Print dialog box, click the arrow next to the Name drop-down list box to open the menu of available printers. Choose the printer that you want and then click the OK button to print the document. If you click the Properties button in the Print dialog box, you will see the printing options for the new printer. The properties displayed in the resulting dialog box can vary greatly, depending on the capabilities of the printer.

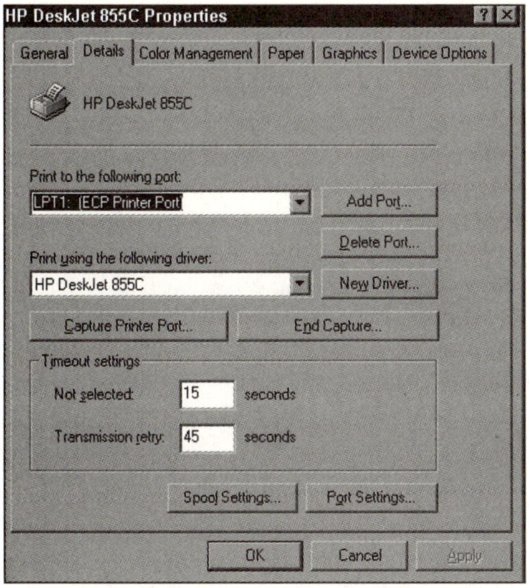

Figure 7-8: The Details tab of the printer Properties dialog box

If you are using a laser printer that employs font cartridges, you can select the fonts from a list box in the Print Setup dialog box. Refer to the *Microsoft Word for Windows Printer Guide* to determine the fonts that can be used with your particular laser printer.

Printing Envelopes

Word has an envelope-printing feature that makes printing envelopes a very simple matter if your printer is able to handle envelopes. Choose Tools ⇨ Letters and Mailings ⇨ Envelopes and Labels to open the Envelopes and Labels dialog box (see Figure 7-9). In this dialog box, you are provided with two text boxes, in which you can enter the delivery and return addresses. In the Return Address text box, Word enters, by default, your name and address as stored under the User Info tab of the Options dialog box. If you want to change the kind of envelope that you are printing, click the envelope in the Preview portion of the dialog box, or click the Options button to open the Envelope Options dialog box, shown in Figure 7-10.

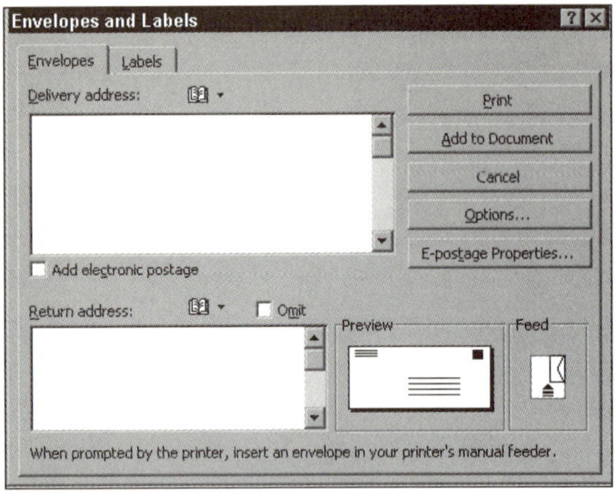

Figure 7-9: The Envelopes and Labels dialog box

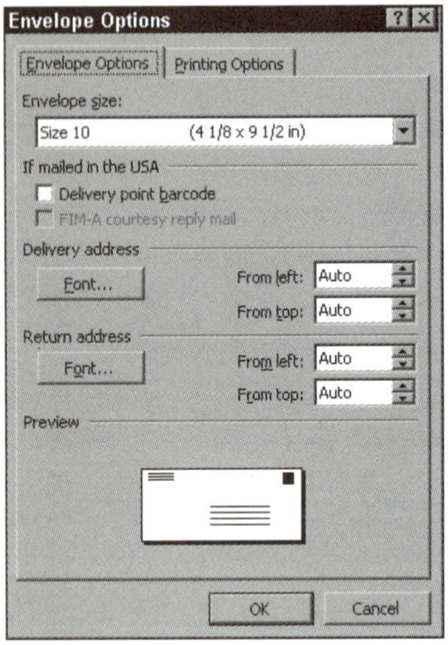

Figure 7-10: The Envelope Options dialog box

The Envelope Options dialog box contains two tabs. The Envelope Options tab lets you change the kind of envelope that you are printing, to add delivery point bar codes, to format the delivery and return addresses, and to control the positioning of the text on the envelope. The Printing Options tab of the Envelope Options dialog box lets you control the way envelopes are printed (see Figure 7-11). You can choose either a horizontal or a vertical feed method. You also can change the way envelopes are fed into your printer, whether you use a manual tractor, an upper or lower tray, and so on.

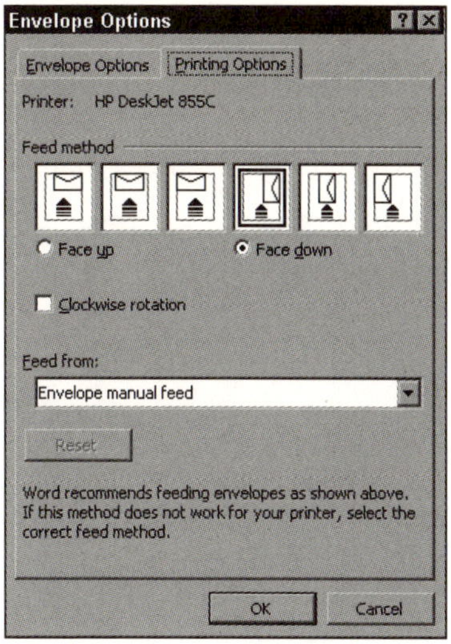

Figure 7-11: The Printing Options tab of the Envelope Options dialog box

After you have made all the necessary formatting changes and specified the size of the envelope that you want to print, you are ready to print the envelope. Just click the Print button in the Envelopes and Labels dialog box.

Summary

In this chapter, you learned how to examine the appearance of documents before you print them and how to print the documents in Word. We covered the following:

- Choosing File ⇨ Print Preview provides a useful way to see what a document will look like before it is printed.
- You can quickly print one copy of any document by clicking the Print button on the Standard toolbar.
- Using the options shown in the Print dialog box, you can print portions of the document, as well as other items (such as annotations, styles, macros, and keyboard assignments).

The next chapter takes the mystery out of working with tables so that you can work with Word's table feature with ease.

Chapter 8

Using Tables in Legal Documents

In This Chapter

- Understanding tables
- Creating tables
- Changing table structure
- Performing data entry within tables
- Formatting tables
- Converting text to tables
- Sorting within tables
- Nesting tables
- Performing simple calculations within tables

TABLES ARE COMMONLY USED IN LEGAL documents to summarize data, present financial statistics in appendixes or exhibits, contain headings for fax cover sheets, format memoranda, and sometimes to contain pleading captions. The table format is also useful for inputting data into a secondary file for merging with letters, labels, and envelopes. This chapter focuses on Word's Table feature.

Understanding Tables

The table layout consists of rows and columns that intersect to form boxes, or *cells*. By default, each cell is enclosed within borders consisting of single lines that are _ point thick. Tables usually contain at least two columns and rows. (You can use the Table feature to create a table with as little as one column and one row to form a box, but Word's Borders feature is better suited for this task.) The point at which a column intersects a row is called a *cell*, and each cell's location in the table is called a *cell address*. When you use Word's Merge feature (discussed in Chapter 10, "Word and Mail Merge"), you use the table structure to hold data to be merged with a form letter or forms such as envelopes or labels. Cells are considered fields, and rows are considered records.

You can type text, insert graphics, or create a table within a table (called *nesting* tables). You can have up to 63 columns in a table, and the only other limit to the size of your table is that a single cell cannot be larger than a page. You can resize columns and cells, and you can add rows, columns, and cells. As with many of Word's features, you can place a toolbar on-screen that contains the tools for specifically working with tables.

As mentioned previously, a table appears with borders surrounding the cells by default. These borders can be removed or modified, as desired. (How you do this is covered later in this chapter.) If you remove the borders, Word still displays gridlines that indicate the extent of the cells that make up your table. Gridlines do not print in your document; they are simply a visual aid for entering and editing text in tables. If you do not see the gridlines surrounding the tables that you create, choose Table ⇨ Show Gridlines to make the gridlines appear.

It is important to really take a look at how much information you plan to put into your table. The Tables feature is very flexible in that you can sort information, perform simple addition and subtraction, merge information with a form such as a letter, label, or envelope, and perform other functions. Tables are well suited for player's lists and for organizing financial data included in documents filed with the Securities and Exchange Commission. However, Summation or Access are better suited for litigation support because by design these programs can handle massive amounts of information and are easy to use. In addition, if you plan to include financial data for multiple subsidiaries of a client, you may need the power of Excel. Excel and Access are discussed later in this book. Although the Tables feature has some very simplistic database- or spreadsheet-like functionality, Access and Excel offer you far more advanced functionality when working with massive amounts of data.

Creating Tables

You can create a table by performing any of these steps:

- Choose Table ⇨ Insert ⇨ Table. The Insert Table dialog box opens (see Figure 8-1), in which you can specify a number of table properties as you create the table.

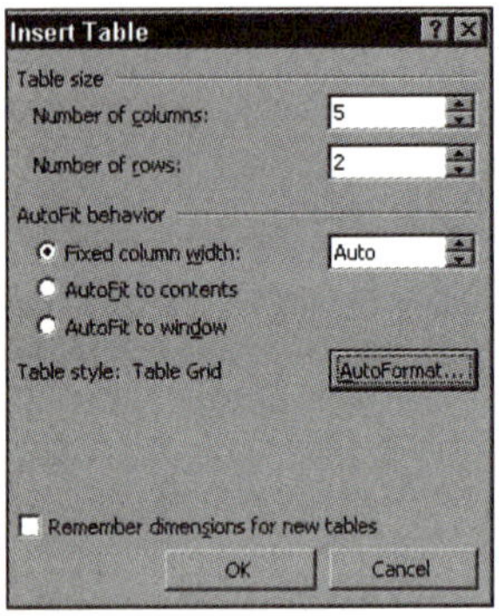

Figure 8-1: The Insert Table dialog box

- Click the Insert Table button on the Standard toolbar. On the grid that appears, drag the pointer down and across with the mouse until the number of columns and rows you want to start with in your table is shaded. The number of rows and columns your table will have is also shown when using this feature. The table is created in your document when you release the mouse button. You can change table properties and structure after the table is created.
- Click Table ⇨ Draw Table. The mouse pointer changes to a pencil, which you use to actually draw a customized table in your document. Some people find this technique difficult to master, and Word offers such flexibility in changing a table's structure and format that you may not need to use this feature very often. As with the previous techniques, table properties and structure can be changed after the table is created.

Whichever technique you use, except the Draw Table feature, Word creates a table using table styles that contain Word's table-formatting defaults, which you can modify. Figure 8-2 shows an example of a newly created table.

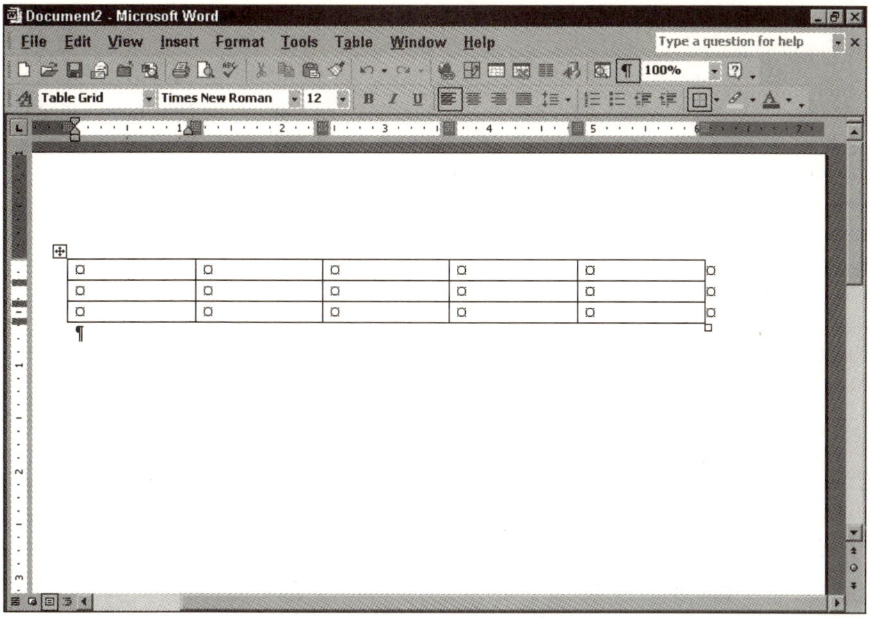

Figure 8-2: A table created with Word's default formatting

To move from cell to cell within a table, you can click the desired cell with the mouse, or you can use the Tab key (to move forward through cells) or the Shift+Tab combination (to move in reverse). Within a single cell, you use the same keys that you use to navigate in any type of Word text. Table 8-1 summarizes the keys that you use to navigate within a table.

Table 8-1
Navigation Keys to Use within Tables

Key	***Purpose***
Tab	Moves the cursor to the next cell in the table. If the cursor is in the last cell in the table, the Tab key adds a new row and moves the cursor to the first cell of the new row.
Shift+Tab	Moves the cursor to the preceding cell.
Alt+Home	Moves the cursor to the first cell in a row.
Alt+End	Moves the cursor to the last cell in a row.
Alt+PgUp	Moves the cursor to the top cell in a column.
Alt+PgDn	Moves the cursor to the bottom cell in a column.
Alt+NumLock+5	Selects the entire table.
Shift	Activates the eraser if you used the Draw Table feature, and you can then use the eraser to erase unwanted lines.
Arrow keys	Moves the cursor within the text in a cell and between cells. If the insertion point is at the edge of a table, you can use the arrow keys to move in or out of the table.

NOTE: One useful aspect of cells that may not be readily apparent is that you can have more than a single paragraph of text in a cell. At the end of any paragraph in a cell, you can press Return and keep right on typing. The cell expands vertically to accommodate the text. You can also format the paragraphs in a table just like paragraphs that are not in a table. For instance, you can format the paragraphs using indentation, alignment, line spacing, styles, and other attributes.

Changing Table Structure

By default, Word creates a very evenly spaced table. You can edit a table's structure in many ways after you have created it and added text. You can add or delete columns and rows, and you can merge the information from more than one cell. (If you are listing hundreds of documents, then Access or Excel would be better choices. You learn how to use Access and Excel in later chapters in this book.)

Inserting columns

Several ways are available to insert columns. One way is to click in the column that will follow the inserted column. Then choose Table ⇨ Insert ⇨ Columns to the Left (see Figure 8-3).

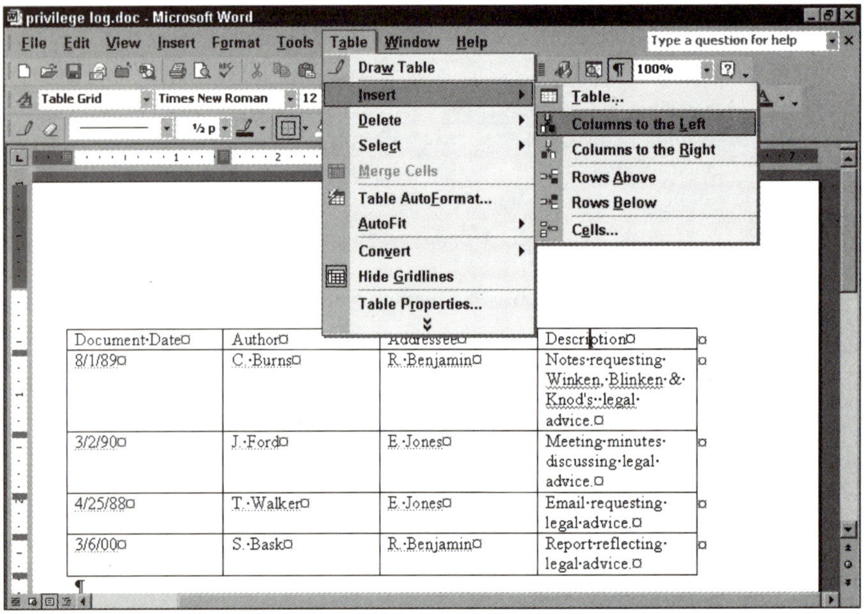

Figure 8-3: Choosing these menu options places the inserted column to the left of the column containing the insertion point.

You can also insert a column by selecting the column to the right of where the new column is to be inserted. Then position the pointer above the column. This causes the pointer to change to a downward-pointing black arrow. Click once to select the entire column, and then right-click and choose Insert Columns from the submenu that appears (see Figure 8-4).

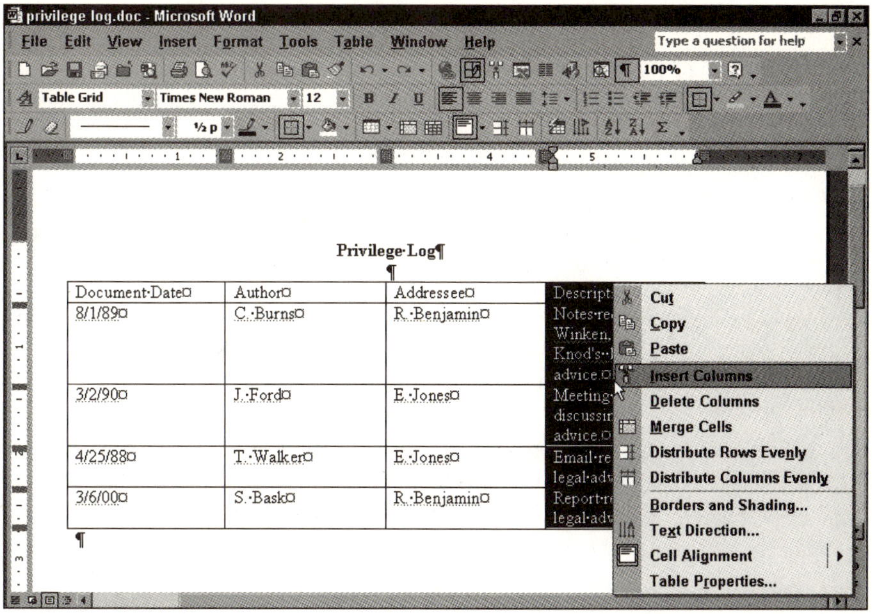

Figure 8-4: Use the Insert Columns option after selecting the column that will appear to the right of the adjacent column.

Each of the techniques just described for inserting columns enables you to insert a single column only. To insert multiple blank columns, you first need to select the number of columns in the table that you want to add, before using one of the techniques. Word will insert the same number of blank columns as you have selected.

Deleting columns

To delete a column, first select it and then right-click. Choose Delete Columns from the submenu that appears. To delete multiple columns, select the columns to be deleted, right-click, and choose Delete Columns from the submenu.

Inserting rows

Word's Table feature has the capability to sort information, so you don't need to insert rows for the purpose of ordering your data. However, you may sometimes need to insert rows in the middle of the table. The steps for inserting rows are similar to the steps for inserting columns. To insert rows, position the insertion point either in the row that will precede or the row that will follow the inserted row; then choose Table ⇨ Insert ⇨ Rows Above or Rows Below, as appropriate. A new blank row appears in the table. You can also select the row or rows (if you are inserting multiple rows) that will appear below the inserted row by positioning the mouse pointer in the margin of the row until it becomes a black arrow that points slightly upward. Then double-click to select the row. Next, right-click, and choose Insert Rows from the submenu that appears. The new rows will appear above the row containing the insertion point.

Deleting rows

To delete a row, click to drag across the row, and then right-click. Choose Delete Row from the submenu that appears. When deleting multiple rows, select all the rows to be deleted, and choose Delete Rows.

Expanding columns and rows

Rows expand vertically as you type to accommodate your data. If you want a wider column to better accommodate your data, you can make the adjustment by doing one of the following:

- Position the mouse pointer on the border of the column you are expanding. The mouse pointer changes to a double-headed black arrow. Drag the column border to the right.
- Double-click the column border. Word automatically adjusts the column width to accommodate the contents of the column.

If you want the column width to be a specific amount, select a single column by placing the insertion point in the column you are expanding, or select multiple columns by clicking and dragging across the desired number of columns. Then perform these steps to specify a certain measurement for the column width:

1. Choose Table ⇨ Table Properties.
2. In the Table Properties dialog box that opens, click the Column tab. Here you can specify an exact measurement for the column width (see Figure 8-5). The Preferred Width option may be checked and appear grayed-out, but you can enable the feature by double-clicking the check box. Then you can use the spinner buttons to go to a desired measurement, or you can type one in. Using the Measure In drop-down list, you can specify that you are entering the width either in Inches or in Percent, meaning a percentage of the entire table width.
3. Click OK to implement the change and close the dialog box. All selected columns will adhere to the change. You can undo the changes at any time.

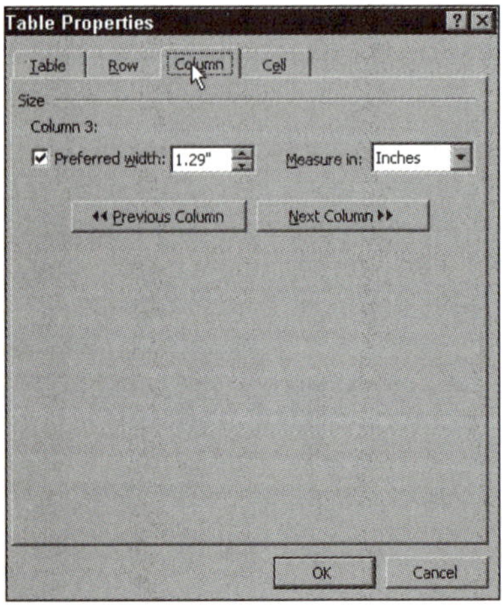

Figure 8-5: The Column tab of the Table Properties dialog box

You may also want to change the height of the rows if you are copying data from one table into another table. If you have not expanded column rows to be the same size as the structure the data is copied from, some lines of data may appear hidden, though they still exist. To change the height of a row, right-click in the row you are expanding, and choose Table Properties from the submenu that appears. In the Table Properties dialog box that opens, click the Row tab. Here you can specify an exact measurement for your row. Click OK to implement the change and close the dialog box.

You can change the height of a row by choosing Table ⇨ Table Properties and then clicking the Row tab (see Figure 8-6). After checking the box in the Size section and specifying the desired measurement, you can set additional options in the Row Height Is list box. Choosing the Exactly option causes Word to make the cell exactly the height you enter into the box. If you choose the At Least option, Word makes the row at least as tall as the value that you enter.

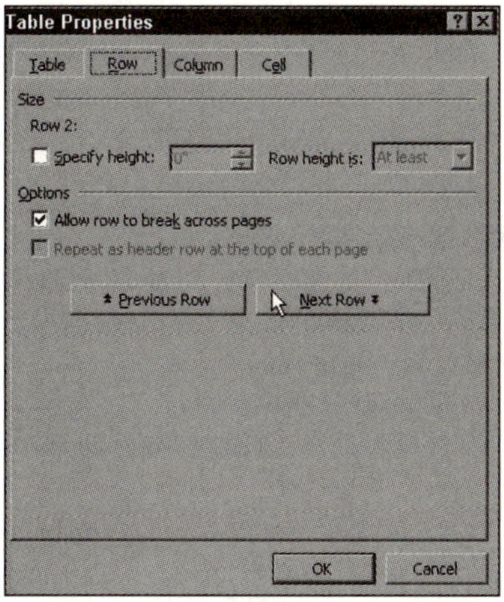

Figure 8-6: The Row tab of the Table Properties dialog box

When setting the row height, you may wonder whether you should choose Exactly or At Least. The answer is that it depends on the type of table you are creating. If you are creating a table that contains a small amount of information, then you can use the Exactly setting. This stops your table from increasing in vertical depth when someone changes font size or types too much information into a cell. This can, of course, work against you in tables that you want to contain more information.

This is where the At Least setting comes into play. If you specify row height using the At Least setting, you are effectively setting a minimum depth for the row. Word will expand the row height to accommodate the information in the row, but it won't decrease the row height beyond the value you specify.

Splitting rows across pages

Sometimes you may need the contents of a single row to be allowed to span more than one page. To make this possible, click Table ⇨ Table Properties, and click the Row tab. Check the Allow Row to Break across Pages option.

Creating header rows

Tables in legal documents often span more than one page, and you need the column headings to repeat on subsequent pages. To repeat column headings on each page of the table, select the rows you want Word to treat as your table headers. Choose Table ⇨ Table Properties, and make sure that the Row tab is selected. Check the Repeat as Header Row at the Top of Each Page option.

Merging cells

As noted previously, the characteristics of the cells in your table can be changed to meet your needs. For example, although a table's title normally sits outside and above the table, you may need to place subheadings within the table to identify subdivisions of its contents. You can use the Merge Cells feature to do this. To create a centered subheading, you can add a row anywhere within a table and then format it as a single cell to contain the heading text. To do so, follow these steps:

1. Click Table ⇨ Insert ⇨Rows Above to insert a new row.
2. Drag across all the cells in the new row to select them.
3. Right-click, and choose Merge Cells from the menu that appears. The individual cells join together to form a single cell.
4. You can then choose the center alignment and type the desired heading text. In Figure 8-7, the words *Defendants* is centered across the width of the table after cells were merged together.

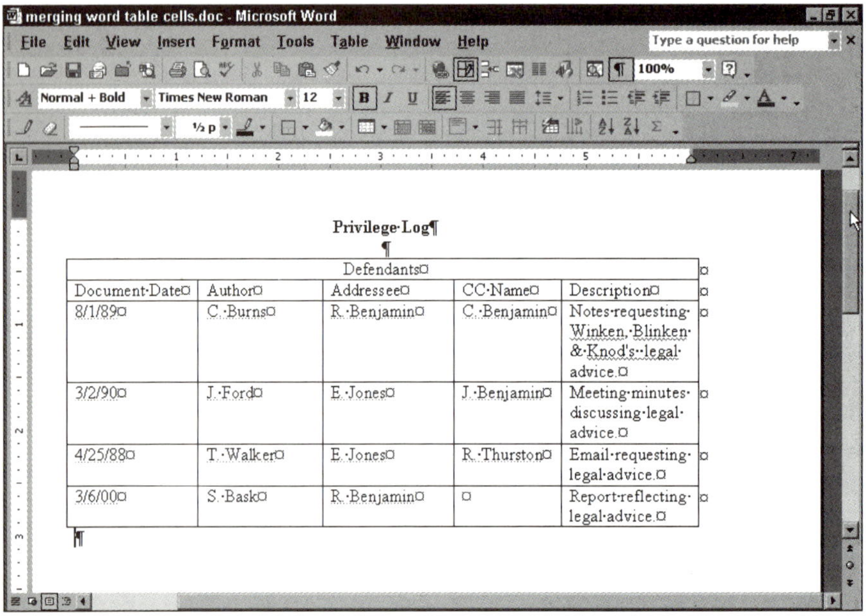

Figure 8-7: Cells are merged to form a single cell.

CAUTION: If you have merged cells in your table, deleting or adding columns is difficult. Try to be sure of the number of columns you will need in your table before merging cells.

Entering Data within Tables

Data entry within tables is not much different from data entry in a regular document. Word Tables can hold textual and numerical data, as well as graphics and other tables. There are a few things you should know about entering data. First, you can control the internal margins of all selected cells. To change cell margins, choose Table ⇨ Table Properties, and then click the Cell tab. In the lower-right corner, click the Options button to open the Cell Options dialog box (see Figure 8-8). Click to remove the check mark in the Same as the Whole Table check box. You can then specify different internal margins for all selected cells. If you check the Wrap Text option, Word breaks the line at the margin and wraps (continues) text to the next line, without changing the cell's width. If you check the Fit Text option, Word displays the text in smaller fonts as the amount of text you type increases.

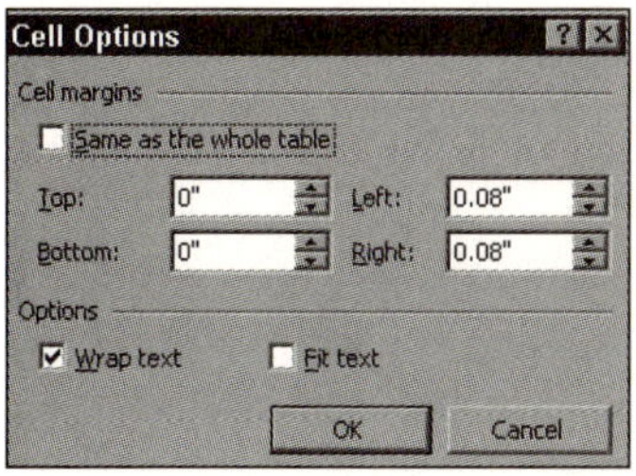

Figure 8-8: The Cell Options dialog box

You can also align table data horizontally or vertically as desired. You can use the alignment buttons on the Formatting toolbar to format text within a table, just as you do with text not in a table. You can also format the information in a cell by clicking Table ⇨ Table Properties and clicking the Cell tab. On the Cell tab, you can specify the vertical alignment (Top, Center, or Bottom) of your data.

You can format your data also just like regular text. Add attributes such as bold, underlining, and numbering as desired. You can also set tabs and indent table data. After you have set tabs in a table, actually inserting a tab is not intuitive. As mentioned earlier, pressing the Tab key moves the insertion point one cell to the right. To insert a tab in the cell contents, you need to press Ctrl+Tab. To indent table data, you can use the Decrease Indent or Increase Indent buttons on the Formatting toolbar, or you can drag the indent indicators on the horizontal ruler for the column containing the insertion point.

Formatting Tables

We have discussed how to change a table's internal structure, as well as row heights and column widths. But how do you change the dimensions of the table as a whole? Your initial table is created with the desired number of columns and rows and fills the page from the left to the right margin. Suppose, however, that you add or delete columns. Word does not readjust the table on the page to take up the full margin width. For example, Figure 8-9 shows a table with a column that has just been deleted, creating an imbalance on the page because there is more whitespace on the right side of the table than on the left. You can use Table ⇨ AutoFit ⇨ AutoFit to Window, as shown in the figure, to force this change. Figure 8-10 shows the more balanced-looking page that results.

Modifying table borders

Earlier in this chapter you learned a bit about table gridlines and borders. Gridlines are nothing but guides to where cells in a table end; they help you to see the structure of your table. Gridlines appear on-screen but are not printed. Borders, on the other hand, appear on-screen and are printed. Borders are added to a table by default when you create it. You can thereafter modify borders in any way desired. The only modification you can do with gridlines is to turn them off so that they are not displayed on the screen. (How you do this was covered at the beginning of this chapter.)

To remove borders from the table, choose Table ⇨ Table Properties. Click the Table tab, and then click the Borders and Shading button. On the Borders tab, click the None setting to remove all borders. You can use the other controls in the dialog box to modify table borders, as desired.

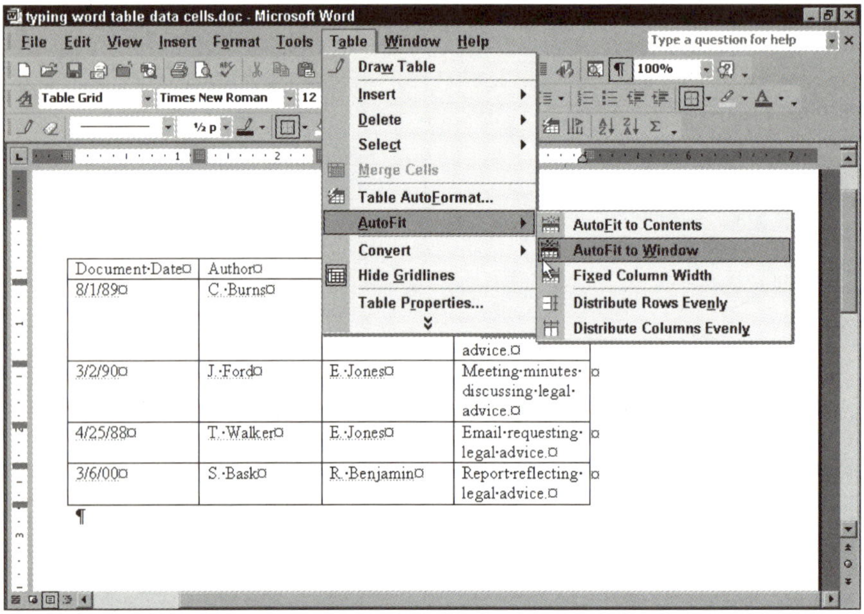

Figure 8-9: The AutoFit submenus

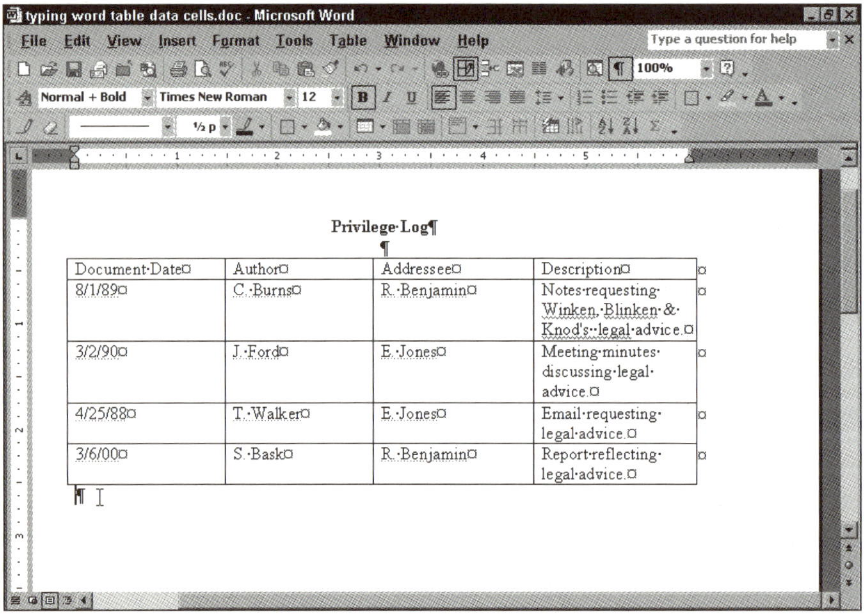

Figure 8-10: The AutoFit to Window option causes the table to fill more of the page horizontally.

Formatting table aspects

If you want a quick way to format an entire table, you can use the Table ⇨ Table AutoFormat menu to open the Table AutoFormat dialog box (see Figure 8-11).

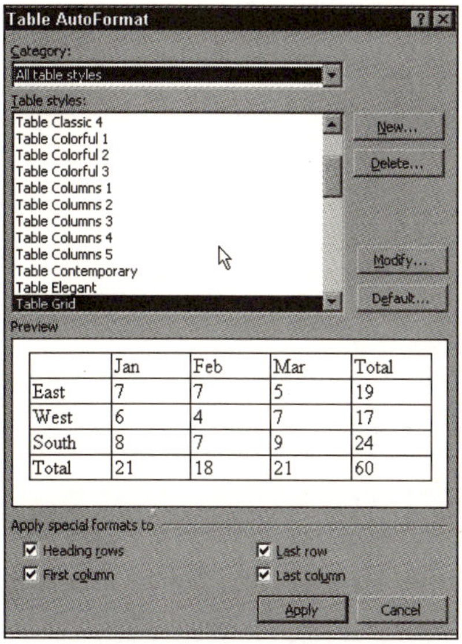

Figure 8-11: The Table AutoFormat dialog box

This dialog box contains a selection of various formats that you can apply to your table. Choose the format that you want to use, and select the areas to which you want to apply the format by clicking as many check boxes as you want. The Preview box lets you see what the table will look like after the formatting is done. When you are finished making your selections in the dialog box, click the OK button to apply the formatting to the table.

Converting Text to Tables

Before Word's Table feature came along, people typically set up tables by using tabs or indented paragraphs. Although this method works, it is very cumbersome and awkward. A table set up with tabs can be tricky to design when some cells in the table contain more than one line of text. You have to add all sorts of manual tabs to line up the information on-screen, and then you have no guarantees that the table will line up when you print it. Worse, any changes that you make to the table's text will also throw off the alignment of the tabs, so you have to constantly rework the table. Manually creating a table is more trouble than it is worth, but you may encounter tables formatted like this that you need to convert.

Word lets you convert any tabular tables into Word tables. To convert tabular text, choose Table ⇨ Convert ⇨ Text to Table. You can also use this feature to convert data in a comma-delimited format into a table form in Word. (Database programs often use comma-delimited formats to export information. See your database management software documentation for directions on creating comma-delimited files.) Text that is separated by tabs, by commas, or by paragraph marks can be converted into a table.

To convert text into a table, first select the text, and then choose Table ⇨ Convert ⇨ Text to Table. When the Convert Text to Table dialog box appears (see Figure 8-12), choose the Table Size, AutoFit

Behavior, and Table Style options that you want. Choose the Paragraphs, Tabs, or Commas option (as appropriate, based on the text to be converted) from the Separate Text At area of the dialog box.

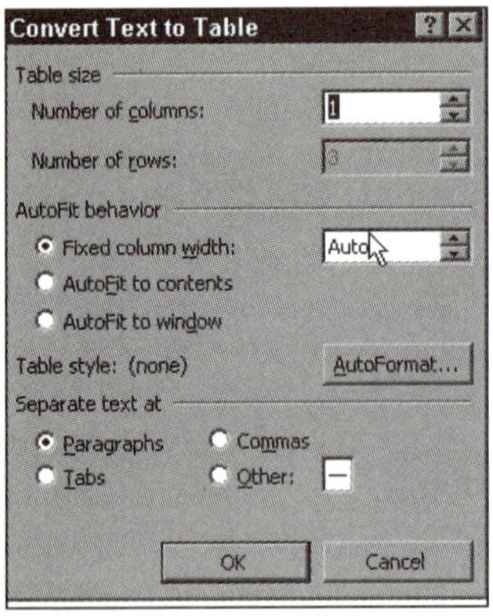

Figure 8-12: The Convert Text to Table dialog box

NOTE: When you specify the AutoFit Behavior options, you are choosing how Word determines column width for the new table. Fixed Column Width means that you can indicate the exact width of the columns (all columns will be the same width). AutoFit to Contents results in Word's analyzing the contents of the table and adjusting column width to best fit what is in the table. AutoFit to Window means that Word will cause the table to be as wide as the margins of the document allow or as wide as can be seen on the screen at one time, whichever width is narrower.

Performing Other Tasks in Tables

The following brief sections cover some miscellaneous tasks that you can do with tables in Word.

Sorting within tables

You may encounter times when you want to arrange a list of data (often within a table) in alphabetical or numerical order. You can use Word's Sort command for this task.

NOTE: The Sort command is not limited to use in tables. You can use the Sort command to sort any list of data, whether the information is in a table or in a simple list with paragraph marks separating the lines.

When Word sorts a list, it arranges the list entries in alphabetical, numerical, or chronological order. You can also choose whether to sort in ascending or descending order. Follow these steps to sort the data in a table:

1. Select the column, row, or cells in the table that you want to sort.
2. Choose Table ⇨ Sort. (If the selected information is not a table, the menu command is Sort Text instead of Sort.) The Sort dialog box appears, as shown in Figure 8-13.

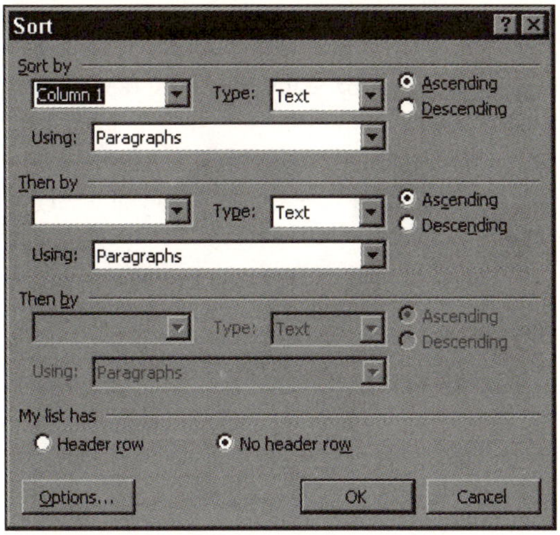

Figure 8-13: The Sort dialog box

3. If you have headings that you do not want sorted, click the Header Row radio button in the My List Has area at the bottom of the dialog box.
4. In the Sort By area at the top of the dialog box, use the first drop-down list to indicate what you want to sort by. In Figure 8-13, you see that the default choice is Column 1, meaning that Word will sort the rows of the table based on the contents of column 1.
5. In the Type drop-down list of the Sort By area, choose the Text, Number, or Date option, and then click either the Ascending or the Descending radio button.
6. In the Using drop-down list of the Sort By area, select what you want to sort by within the column specified in Step 4. Normally, you will not need to change this setting.
7. To optionally specify additional criteria for your sort, repeat Steps 4 through 6 as desired, using the two Then By areas.
8. Click the OK button to sort the data.

Nesting tables

Nesting a table means that it is created inside another table. This capability has not been around very long in Word, having been introduced in Word 2000. To create a nested table, follow these steps:

1. Position the insertion point in the cell of the main table where you want the new table placed.
2. Choose Table ⇨ Insert ⇨ Table.
3. Specify the number of columns and rows, and then click OK.

Performing Simple Math within Tables

You can perform simple mathematical operations, as well as some advanced functions, in your tables. (Excel is much better suited to such operations if you have a lot of data or complex mathematical functions to perform.)

The simplest function to perform is to sum a column or row of numbers. First, display the Tables and Borders toolbar (choose View ⇨ Toolbars ⇨ Tables and Borders). Then click in the cell where you want the result to appear (the cell should be to the right of or below the information you want to use in the operation). Click the AutoSum button on the Tables and Borders toolbar, and Word places the result automatically in the cell. Because numbers do not update automatically, you must repeat the process when the numbers on which the result is based change.

Word also allows you to perform other mathematical calculations on the data in your table. The general way that you do this is to, again, position the insertion pointer in the cell where you want to perform the calculation. Then choose Formula from the Table menu; Word displays the Formula dialog box, as shown in Figure 8-14.

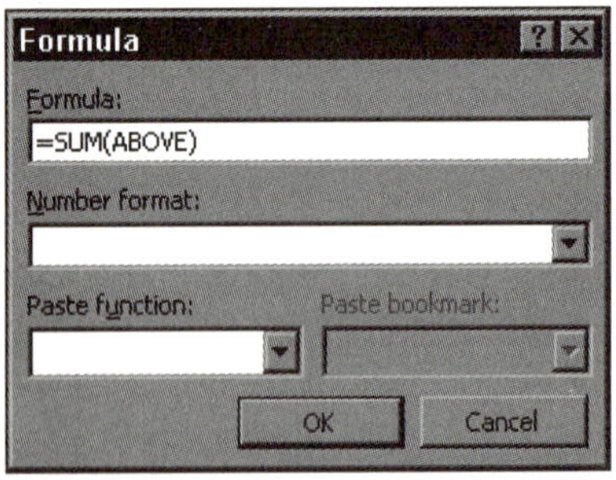

Figure 8-14: The Formula dialog box is used to perform operations on table data.

Word may suggest a formula in the Formula box; feel free to delete the formula — but leave the equal sign at the beginning of the formula. You can then use the Paste Function drop-down list to choose different operations you can use in your formula. For instance, you can average the values of a column by using a formula such as =AVERAGE(ABOVE). You can even use the Number Format drop-down list to choose different ways of displaying the result of the formula. When you are done with the formula, click OK to see your results.

Summary

Presenting information succinctly or efficiently through the use of tables is often not only desirable but also mandatory. This chapter showed you how to take advantage of Word's table feature. You saw how to

- Create tables
- Change a table's internal structure, as well as its overall appearance on a page
- Enter data into tables
- Format tables
- Convert text to tables
- Sort data within tables
- Nest tables
- Perform simple calculations within tables

The next chapter delves into creating forms. Although you'll want to use Access or Excel for your more complex forms, Word's capability for creating easy-to-use forms for everyday information exchange, such as requests for documents, is well worth using.

Chapter 9

Creating Legal Forms in Word

In This Chapter

- ♦ Understanding forms
- ♦ Creating a form
- ♦ Protecting the form
- ♦ Making a form available for use
- ♦ Understanding fields
- ♦ Using fields

IN ANY LAW FIRM OR LEGAL ENVIRONMENT, parts of the needed daily flow of information can be significantly aided through the use of forms. Forms can prove extremely useful in easing the creation of documents for back-end administrative needs such as personnel actions, secretarial-support requests, requests for documents from records management, library research requests, and the like. And although forms of various types can be created in different packages within Office — in Excel, Outlook, and Access — perhaps nowhere is the process of form creation and use as simple as it is with Word. The other Office suite products may offer more powerful capabilities associated with their overall use; for example, Excel forms can manage complex financial calculations, and Access forms support the permanent storage of data in a database. But for fill-in-the-blank type forms that must be filled out by users and passed elsewhere within the legal environment, Word forms suffice for many uses.

Understanding Forms

In Word, forms are nothing more than structured documents containing *fields* into which users can enter information. (Fields are explained in detail later in this chapter, in "Understanding Fields.") You create forms by typing the headings to identify your fields and then inserting fields that correspond to the headings into your document. You can insert text boxes to store text, check boxes indicating a yes or no choice, and list boxes with custom drop-down lists of items, tables, and graphics into your forms. Figure 9-1 shows an example of a completed form, ready to be filled in by a user.

Forms can be created, saved, and distributed as ordinary Word documents, but most forms are created as templates. When you create a form as a template, it can be easily selected by users from within the New Document task pane. In order for form templates to work correctly, you must *protect* the form using Word's Protect Document command (we give you the details on this later in the chapter). Protecting the form actually works to your advantage in any legal environment with multiple users because it prevents users from modifying the design of the form. Users can only enter information into the form's fields.

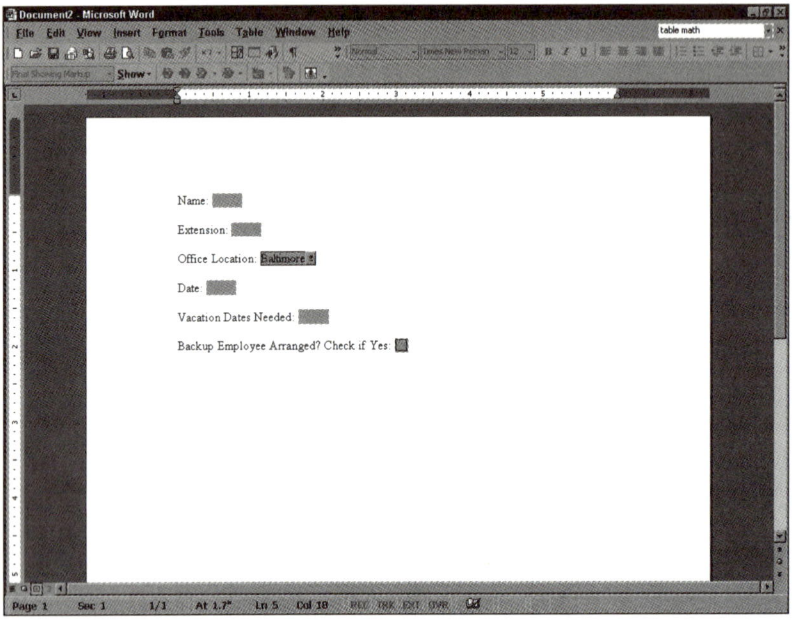

Figure 9-1: An example of a form in Word

After your form template is saved, other users can create new documents based on the form template. They can view and complete the form in Word or print the form and fill in the necessary information on paper. Forms can also be sent as attachments via e-mail, as can any Word document.

The process of creating forms is relatively simple, involving these basic steps: First, you create a template. Next, you design and lay out the form by typing your desired headings into the template. (In the example shown previously in Figure 9-1, the words *Name*, *Extension*, and *Office Location* are all headings.) You then add controls such as text boxes, check boxes, or drop-down list boxes at appropriate locations within the template. Next, you protect the form to make it operational (and to keep users from making changes to the form). Finally, you distribute the form to other users for general use.

Creating a Form

Because forms are essentially Word templates (or documents) that contain text as headings and various fields used to enter data, you begin the process of creating a form by creating a new template (or document). Assuming that you want to make the form readily accessible through the New Document task pane, you need to create the form as a template. Use the following steps to do this:

1. Choose File ⇨ New to display the New Document task pane.
2. In the task pane, click General Templates.
3. In the Templates dialog box that opens, click Blank Document.
4. Change the Create New option to Template; then click OK.
5. Choose File ⇨ Save As and enter a name for your template in the File Name list box.

After your template exists, you can type the headings that identify the information users will need to enter in your form, such as *Attorney Name*, *Case Number*, or *File Folder*. You also need to use the

Forms toolbar to insert the various types of fields into the template. If the Forms toolbar isn't currently visible, choose View ⇨ Toolbars and then select Forms from the next submenu that appears. The Forms toolbar contains ten buttons, as shown in Figure 9-2. Table 9-1 explains the purpose for each of the buttons, listed in the order they appear on the toolbar from left to right.

Figure 9-2: The Forms toolbar

Table 9-1
The Forms Toolbar Buttons

Button	***Purpose***
Text Form Field	Adds a text form field that can be used to enter text
Check Box Form Field	Adds a check box to indicate a yes/no choice
Drop-Down Form Field	Adds a drop-down list that provides the user with a list of available choices
Form Field Options	Shows the property settings for all form fields in a document
Draw Table	Displays the Tables and Borders toolbar, which can be used to draw a table within the document
Insert Table	Displays the Insert Table dialog box, which can be used to insert a table with a set number of rows and columns
Insert Frame	Inserts a frame into the document
Form Field Shading	Switches the gray shading of form fields on and off
Reset Form Fields	Resets field properties to the default settings
Protect Form	Protects the design of the form and makes the form ready for user input

Typically, you would place the insertion pointer to the right of each of your headings and then click the appropriate button in the Forms toolbar to insert the desired type of field. For example, to the right of a heading such as *Attorney Name:*, you would add a text field. To the right of a heading such as *Partner?*, you might add a check box field.

Inserting text form fields

When you need to provide space for users to type text (such as a person's name, a client name, or an address), you use text form fields. Text form fields can contain any combination of alphanumeric characters, so you can use them for storing words, dates, client or matter numbers, and the like.

First, type the heading that will ask the user for the desired information. Then, with the Forms toolbar visible (choose View ⇨ Toolbars and then click Forms, if necessary, to display it), click the Text Form Field button in the toolbar. When you do this, a text form field appears as a shaded box beside your heading. You can repeat this process for as many text form fields as are needed within your form.

After you add a text form field, you may want to change the default properties that determine how the field behaves when users are entering data into the field. You can do this by double-clicking the text form field to display the Text Form Field Options dialog box (see Figure 9-3).

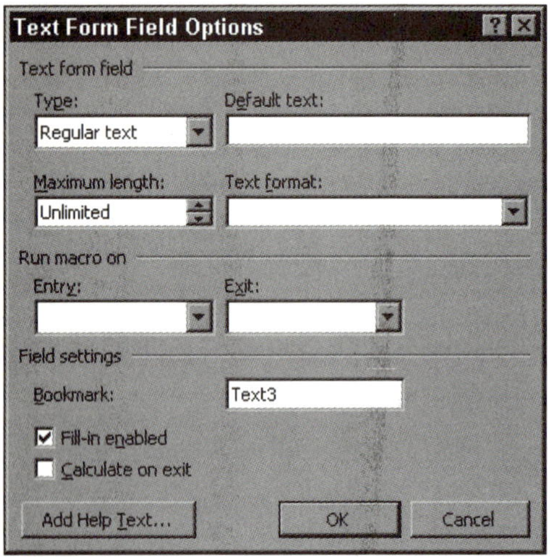

Figure 9-3: The Text Form Field Options dialog box

In the Type drop-down list, you can select one of the following:

- **Regular Text:** Allows the user to enter any characters
- **Number:** Limits entries to numeric values
- **Date:** Limits entries to a valid date
- **Current Date:** Causes the form to display the current date in the field
- **Current Time:** Causes the form to display the current time in the field
- **Calculation:** Allows you to enter an expression that performs a calculation when the form is used

The other options in the Text Form Field Options dialog box are as follows:

- **Default Text:** Specifies a default entry that appears in the field.
- **Maximum Length:** Limits the number of characters a user can enter in the field.
- **Text Format:** Controls the appearance of data entered into the field. The title and available options provided by this list box differ, depending on the selection you've made in the Type drop-down list. For example, if you chose Regular Text, the list box that appears here is called *Text Format* and offers options such as uppercase, lowercase, and first capital. If you chose Date in the Type drop-down list, the selection in the Format list box changes to Date Format, and offers various date-formatting choices.)

The Run Macro On options, which are shared among other field type property settings, are detailed later in this chapter in "Understanding the Run Macro options."

In the dialog box, enter or select any desired values and then click OK to put those values into effect for that text form field. You must repeat this process for each text form field whose properties you may wish to change.

Inserting check box form fields

When you want to add a check box to a form (which typically indicates a yes/no response to a particular question), you use a check box form field. For example, you might have a check box on a form indicating whether the form has been reviewed and approved by a partner within a law firm. The form could be e-mailed to a particular partner and that partner could check the box indicating his or her approval of the form.

To create a check box, first type a heading that will ask the user for the desired information. Then, with the Forms toolbar visible (choose View ⇨ Toolbars and click Forms, if necessary, to display it), click the Check Box Form Field button in the toolbar. When you do this, a check box form field appears as a shaded box beside your heading. You can repeat this process for any additional check box form fields needed within the form.

As with text form fields, you can change the default properties that determine the behavior of check box form fields. (Because these are check boxes, your options are, of course, far more limited than with text box form fields.) Double-click the check box form field to display the Check Box Form Field Options dialog box (see Figure 9-4).

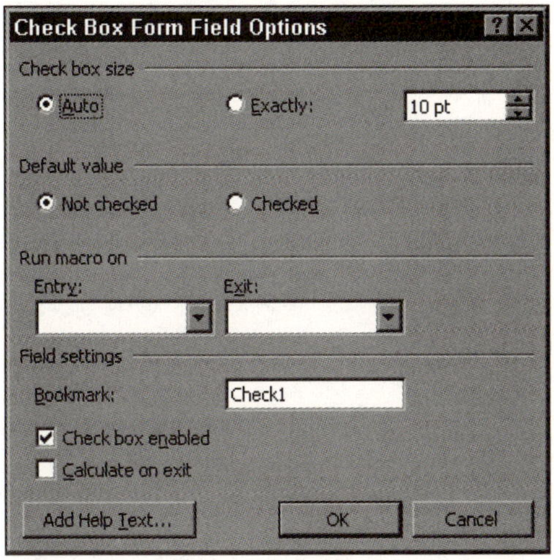

Figure 9-4: The Check Box Form Field Options dialog box

In the Check Box Size section, you can choose Auto (which automatically sizes the check box to match the font of the paragraph it is contained within), or you can choose Exactly, which lets you set a desired point size for the check box using the spinner box. In the Default Value section, you can choose whether the box should appear checked or unchecked by default when the user opens the form.

The Run Macro On options, which are shared among other field type property settings, are detailed later in the chapter in "Understanding the Run Macro options."

In the dialog box, enter or select any desired values and then click OK to put those values into effect for that check box form field. You can repeat this process for any additional check box form fields whose properties you may wish to change.

Inserting drop-down form fields

When you need to provide a list of possible choices for a user to select from (such as the name of a branch office), you use drop-down form fields. Drop-down form fields are ideal when you want to limit the user's entries to a predetermined list.

First, type a heading that will ask the user for the desired information. Then, with the Forms toolbar visible (choose View ⇨ Toolbars and then click Forms, if necessary, to display it), click the Drop-Down Form Field button in the toolbar. When you do this, a drop-down form field appears as a shaded box beside your heading. You can repeat this process for any additional drop-down form fields needed within the form.

When you add a drop-down form field, you need to specify the available choices that should appear in the drop-down list. You do this by double-clicking the drop-down form field to display the Drop-Down Form Field Options dialog box (see Figure 9-5).

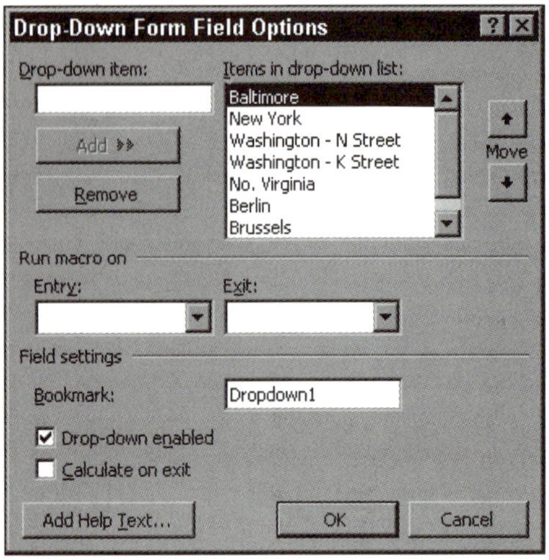

Figure 9-5: The Drop-Down Form Field Options dialog box

For each choice that you want to appear in your drop-down list, type the choice into the Drop-Down Item text box; then click the Add button to add that choice to your list of possible choices. For example, if you want a drop-down list of branch office names that include New York, Baltimore, and Washington, you type **New York** into the Drop-Down Item text box and click Add; then you type **Baltimore** into the Drop-Down Item text box and click Add, and so on.

After you've added your desired items, you can also change the order in which the items appear. To do so, select any item in the list and use the up- and down-arrow buttons to move the location of the item within the list. The order of the items in the list is the same as the order the user will see when the drop-down list is opened in the form. Also, note that with drop-down list form fields, the first item in the list always appears as the default choice within the form.

The Run Macro On options, which are shared among other field type property settings, are detailed under the following heading.

In the dialog box, enter your desired list choices, arrange the order if necessary, and click OK to put those values into effect for that drop-down form field.

Understanding the Run Macro options

With each of the common field types — text boxes, check boxes, and drop-down list boxes — you can use the Entry and Exit list boxes in the Run Macro On sections of the given dialog box to select a Word macro that should run, either when the user moves into the field (Entry) or when the user moves out of the field (Exit). You learn more about macros in Chapter 12, "Working with Word Macros." Any macros that you create can be associated with a field in your form.

The capability of associating macros with form fields lets you add simple programming capabilities to your form. For example, a macro could automatically print a form at the default printer when a user moves the cursor out of a particular field of a form. To use either the Entry or Exit option, you simply choose the desired macro name from the appropriate list box. If you want the macro to run when the user enters a field, choose the macro by name in the Entry list box. If you want the macro to run when the user leaves a field, choose the macro by name in the Exit list box.

Inserting tables and frames

You can also add tables and frames to a form. You do so by placing the insertion pointer at the desired location and clicking the Insert Table, Draw Table, or Insert Frame button in the Forms toolbar. Tables can be useful for forms in which you want users to be able to enter tabular data, such as a list of dependents' names and social security numbers. Frames prove useful when you want to insert an object, such as a graphic, and drag it to a particular location within a form. (Because graphics in forms are not a common legal application, this chapter does not spend additional time discussing the topic, but you can refer to the Microsoft Help screens for further details on using frames in forms.)

For tables, you click the Insert Table button or the Draw Table button in the Forms toolbar. You can then use the same techniques discussed in Chapter 8, "Using Tables in Legal Documents," to size your table as desired. When a document based on the form template containing the table is opened, the user can tab into the table and enter the desired information.

Protecting the Form

Before you can distribute a form to your users for general use, you must *protect* the form. As mentioned earlier, protecting a form serves two purposes: making the form operational and preventing users from making design modifications to the form. After a form template has been protected, users can open new documents based on that template. When users open the document, the form appears with the insertion pointer located within the first field. Users can then enter information into the form, using the Tab key or the mouse to navigate among the fields.

NOTE: Remember that a form will not operate until you take the step of protecting the form.

To protect a form, use the following steps:

1. With the form template open in Word, choose Tools ⇨ Protect Document from the menus. The Protect Document dialog box appears, as shown in Figure 9-6.
2. In the dialog box, click the Forms option.
3. If you want to add password protection to the form, enter a password in the Password text box. Remember that passwords are case-sensitive. (Optionally, you can choose to save the form without a password; however, keep in mind that if you do this, users could easily unprotect the form by choosing Tools ⇨ Unprotect Document. They can then modify your form.)

4. Click OK to save your settings. If you entered a password, you will be prompted to confirm that password.

Figure 9-6: The Protect Document dialog box

CAUTION: Be sure to keep a record of any passwords that you use. There is no way (short of some very advanced "hacker" skills) to determine a lost password for a document.

Putting a Form to Use

After the form has been protected, it is ready to be distributed to your users for general use. In a law firm or legal department of any size, you may want to store the form in a shared Workgroup Template directory on your firm or departmental server.

When a user opens a document based on a form template, the document appears, ready for use as a form, with the insertion pointer placed in the first field of the form. Users can navigate through the fields, using the Tab key to move forward or the Shift+Tab keys to move in reverse. Users can also use the mouse to click any field in the form and then enter data, check a box, or select from a list. When the insertion pointer is in a check box, keyboard users can use the spacebar to turn the check box on or off. Mouse users can simply click the mouse pointer at the check box to turn it on or off.

For list boxes, keyboard users can press the Alt+down-arrow key combination and then use the down- and up-arrow keys to navigate within the list, pressing Enter at the desired choice. Mouse users can simply click within the list. After they do so, the drop-down list opens, displaying all available choices, and users can click the desired selection.

Your users can view and complete the form in Word or print the form and fill in the necessary information on paper. Completed forms can also be sent as attachments via e-mail to the appropriate recipient or department within a firm for further processing.

These are all the basics that you need to know to create and use forms with Word. However, if your form needs grow more complex, you may find additional techniques behind the use of fields in Word forms (or within any Word document) to be useful. The portion of the chapter that follows provides a more in-depth discussion of the use of fields within Word documents.

Understanding Fields

In Word, a *field* is a special set of instructions that tells Word to insert certain information at a given location in a document. The basic difference between fields and normal text is that with fields, the computer provides the information for you. However, using fields does more than just save the effort of typing in the information. Fields are *dynamic* — they can change as circumstances change. You already may have used fields at various times in your work with Word; for example, when you insert the current date or page numbers in a document, you are inserting a certain kind of field.

Think of fields as special codes that you include in documents. The codes tell Word to insert information at the location where the codes appear. The codes can automatically update the text of your document, or you can tell Word to update the information produced by the fields only when you want it to. Typically, you will use fields to add text or graphics to a document, to update information that changes on a regular basis, and to perform calculations.

Word has dozens of types of fields. Some, such as page numbers and the current date, are simple to understand and use. Others are more complex and are beyond the scope of this book. But all fields can be inserted into a document and updated by using the same procedures explained in this chapter.

You can effectively work with fields after you understand the following: inserting fields in a document, viewing field codes, and updating fields so that they show the most current results, formatting fields, and moving between fields.

A field is made up of three parts: field characters, a field type, and instructions. Following is a date field:

```
{ Date \@ M/d/yy }
```

The *field characters* are the curly braces that enclose the field. The curly braces indicate the presence of a field in Word to the user. Inside the curly braces, you find the special code or instruction that tells Word what is to appear in this area. Note that although curly braces are used to indicate the presence of a field, you cannot insert a field in a document by typing curly braces. You must use a command or a key combination specifically designed to insert fields, such as the Insert ⇨ Field command.

The *field type* is the first word that appears after the left field character. In the preceding example, the word *Date* is the field type; this particular field type tells Word to insert the current date — based on the computer's clock — into the document.

The *instructions* follow the field type. Instructions are optional, depending on the field type, but most field types have instructions. The instructions tell Word exactly how the information specified by the field type will be displayed. In this example, `\@ M/d/yy` is an instruction that tells Word to display the current date in the American numeric format, with the month, day, and year separated by slashes. The contents of the instructions may appear somewhat cryptic, but you need not be concerned with what they mean because Word inserts the proper instructions for you automatically.

Inserting fields

Many Word commands automatically insert fields in your document. When you insert page numbers or a table of contents, for example, you are inserting fields to produce the page numbers or the table of contents. But when you want to manually insert fields into a document, you use a special command or key combination that is designed to insert fields, such as Insert ⇨ Field. Follow these steps to use the Field command to insert a field into your document:

1. After placing the insertion point where you want to insert the field, choose Insert ⇨ Field. The Field dialog box appears, as shown in Figure 9-7.
2. From the Categories list box, select the field category that you want to insert. The All category enables you to see all the fields in alphabetic order in the Field Names list box. You can use the scroll bars or the arrow keys to navigate among the possible field types.

3. From the Field Names list box, select the field that you want to insert. Just below the Field Names list, you see a description of whatever field you select.

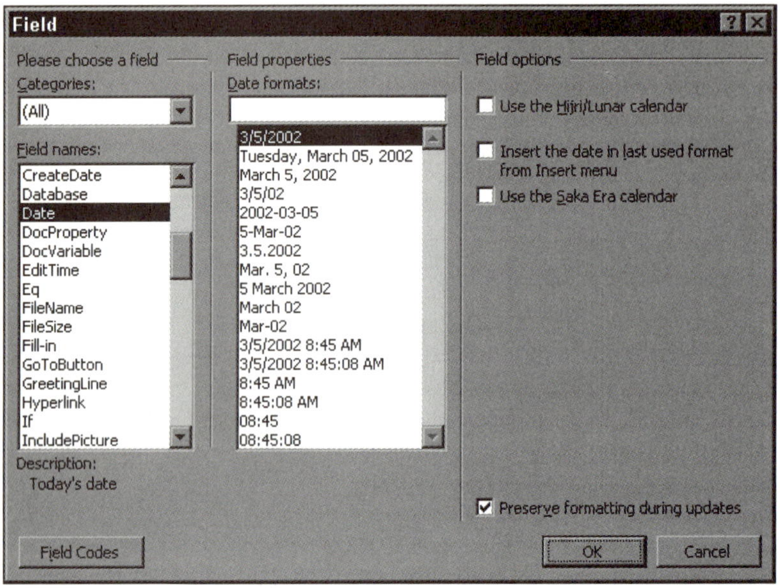

Figure 9-7: The Field dialog box

4. Word allows you to modify exactly how the field is interpreted. Click the Field Codes button and then click the Options button if you want to add *switches* (options that change certain characteristics of the field results, such as displaying characters as uppercase) or formatting to the field. When you click the Options button, the Field Options dialog box opens, as shown in Figure 9-8. To add switches or formatting, click the Add to Field button. If you change your mind and decide to remove the formatting or switches, click the Undo Add button.

5. Click the OK button to insert the field into the document.

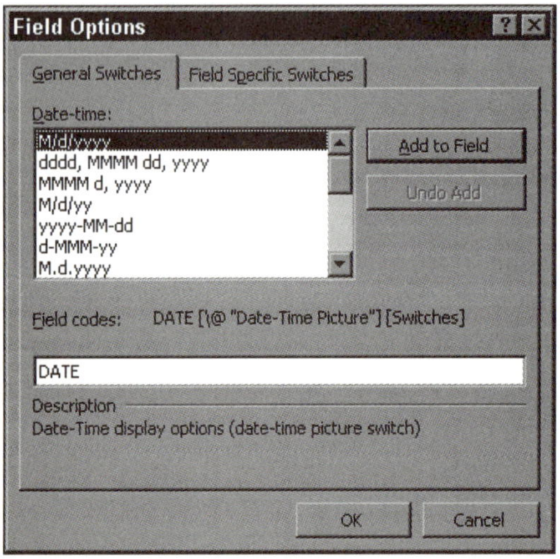

Figure 9-8: The Field Options dialog box

Word also provides an Insert Field shortcut key combination (Ctrl+F9). This shortcut inserts the field characters (curly braces) into the document, which enables you to type the field name and instructions manually. This method for entering fields is typically used by programmers who are familiar with the Visual Basic programming language that is built in to Word. Unless you are very familiar with field types and their instructions, you will probably find it much easier to add fields with Insert ⇨ Field.

Viewing field codes

By default, when you insert a field, you see the results of that field. For example, when you insert a date field, you see the current date. When you are editing documents, however, you may find it useful to see the actual field codes rather than the results. Field codes are how Word sees a field; they tell Word what to display and how to display it. Here's how to see field codes instead of field results:

1. Place the pointer in the field and right-click with the mouse. Word displays a shortcut menu.
2. Choose Toggle Field Codes to display the codes for the field. Perform the same steps if you want to hide the codes again.

Note that you can also view an individual field by using the Toggle Field shortcut key combination (Shift+F9). This shortcut switches between a field's results and its actual contents. Place the insertion point anywhere in the desired field and press Shift+F9.

TIP: If you are working with a large document that contains a number of fields, you may find it helpful to split the document into two panes (click Window ⇨ Split and then click the horizontal line that appears to place it where you want the pane to divide). You can then activate field codes in one pane by selecting the entire document and right-clicking to open the shortcut menu. From the shortcut menu, choose Toggle Field Codes.

Updating fields

You can update fields by selecting the text containing the field, right-clicking the text, and choosing Update Field from the shortcut menu that appears. Some fields, such as those used in page numbering, are automatically updated whenever you print or repaginate a document; others are not updated until you tell Word to update the fields.

To update fields in the entire document, select the entire document (Ctrl+A), and then right-click anywhere in the document. Choose Update Field from the shortcut menu that appears.

Moving between fields

To move to the next field, use F11 or Alt+F1. To move to a previous field in a document, use Shift+F11 or Alt+Shift+F1. If you're more comfortable with the mouse, just click the field that you want to move to.

Formatting fields

You can format the field results or the field codes, and you can add switches (which we explain shortly) to the field codes. To format the field when it displays its result, right-click the field and choose the desired formatting option from the shortcut menu. (Choose Font to format the fonts used or Paragraph to apply paragraph formatting.)

In some rare instances, you may want to actually format the field codes rather than the field results. (We're not sure why you would want to do this, but Word allows you to do it, nonetheless.) To format the field when it displays its code, perform the following steps:

1. Choose Tools ⇨ Options, click the View tab of the Options dialog box that appears, and check the Field Codes option. Then click OK. (If you just need to see the field codes for one field, place the insertion point in the field and right-click the field to open the shortcut menu. Then choose Toggle Field Codes.)
2. After the fields are displayed, right-click the field and choose the appropriate option (Font or Paragraph) from the shortcut menu. Fill in the options in the dialog box that appears to apply the desired formatting.

Adding switches to field codes so that you can format the fields is not a user-friendly process, to say the least. You can add switches to the field codes by typing them into the code. Switches are options that change certain characteristics of the field results, such as displaying characters as uppercase or converting numbers to roman numerals. For example, a simple `DATE` field looks like this:

```
{ DATE }
```

However, a field with the `DATE` code and a switch that tells Word how to display the date looks like this:

```
{ DATE \@ d-M-yy }
```

Table 9-2 lists some of the general switches and their functions.

Table 9-2
Commonly Used Switches

Switch	*Function*
* caps	Capitalizes the initial letter of each word in the result.
* firstcap	Capitalizes the initial letter of the first word in the result.
* lower	All letters in the result appear as lowercase.
* upper	All letters in the result appear as uppercase.
* arabic	Converts a number to Arabic (standard) format, overriding any default set elsewhere in Windows.
* dollartext	Spells out a number with two decimal places as words with initial capital letters, the word *and*, and the numbers that follow the decimal places (suitable for producing checks with currency amounts spelled out).
* roman	Converts a number to lowercase roman numerals.
* Roman	Converts a number to uppercase roman numerals.
\@ dddd, MMMM, d, yyyy	Displays a date as spelled out, as in *Wednesday, January 1, 2003.*
* mergeformat	Preserves manual formatting in the fields, such as character and paragraph formatting in text, and scaling and cropping dimensions in graphics.
* charformat	Applies the formatting on the first character of the field name to the entire field result.

Locking a field's contents

At times, you may want to prevent the results of a field from being updated. You can *lock* a field to prevent it from being updated until you unlock it. To lock a field, place the cursor anywhere in the desired field and press Ctrl+F11. To unlock the field, place the cursor anywhere in the field and press Ctrl+Shift+F11.

Summary

This chapter detailed how you can create forms that can be used by other Word users to easily record, print, and send structured data. It has also provided specifics on the use of fields within Word documents. In this chapter, you learned the following:

- You can create a form as a template that can be easily selected by users from within the New Document task pane.
- You design and lay out the form by typing any desired headings into the template.
- You add controls, such as text boxes, check boxes, or drop-down list boxes, at appropriate locations within the template.
- You must protect a form before it will be operational and usable by other users.
- Forms can be completed in Word and printed or be sent as e-mail attachments.
- You can insert and format fields for various purposes in forms, as well as any other Word document.

The next chapter shows you how to work with Word's Mail Merge feature, which is a valuable tool for creating mailing labels and other items that will go out to a large number of recipients.

Chapter 10

Word and Mail Merge

In This Chapter

- ♦ Automating large mailings with the Mail Merge Wizard
- ♦ Producing individual envelopes
- ♦ Producing individual labels

ONE WAY TO TAKE ADVANTAGE of the processing power of Word within the legal environment is to use Word's Mail Merge features to create personalized form letters. You can also create mailing labels and put together legal documents, firm brochures, and other items that must be sent to a large number of recipients. Mail merges let you print multiple copies of a document in which certain information (such as a name or address) changes for each document. The form letters that you receive from businesses are examples of mail merges at work.

Mail merges combine two kinds of documents: a *main document,* which contains the text that is identical for each printed copy, and a *data source,* which contains the text that is specific to each copy printed. The main document also contains fields that tell Word where to find the information that is stored in the data source. These fields are referred to as *merge fields.* As you type the main document, you can insert the fields at any desired location.

In the data source, you type the information that Word needs to fill in the fields inserted in the main document. For example, if your main document contains a Name field and an Address field, your data source should have names and addresses of all the people who should receive the letter.

Automating Large Mailings with the Mail Merge Wizard

Word's Mail Merge Wizard makes it easy to produce form letters, mass e-mails, envelopes, or labels. Just use these steps:

1. If you want to create a new document and enter text in the body of that document to serve as your main document, open a blank document now. If you have an existing document that you're using as your main document, open that document.
2. Choose Tools ⇨ Letters and Mailings ⇨ Mail Merge Wizard. The first of six Mail Merge panes appears within the task pane area, as shown in Figure 10-1.
3. In the task pane under Select Document Type, choose the type of output document that you want to create; then click Next: Starting Document at the bottom of the task pane to continue. (This example is indicating Letters as the type of document.) The second Mail Merge task pane appears, as shown in Figure 10-2.

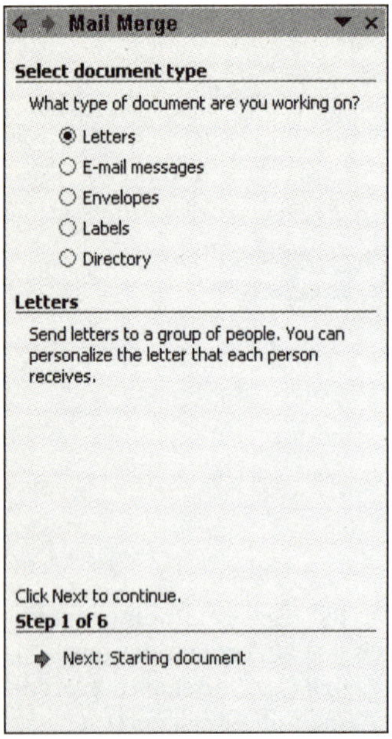

Figure 10-1: The Step 1 of 6 Mail Merge task pane

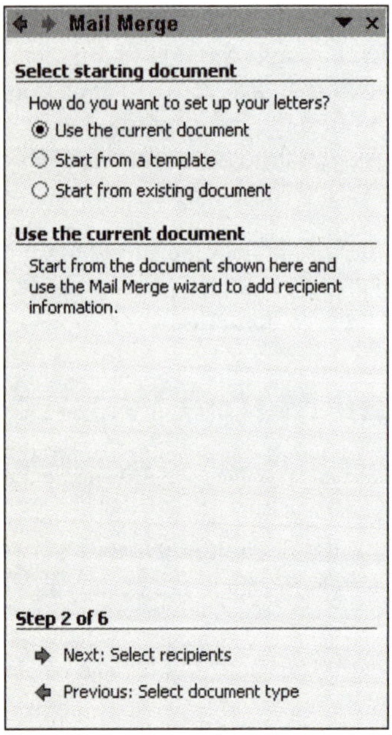

Figure 10-2: The Step 2 of 6 Mail Merge task pane

4. In the task pane under Select Starting Document, choose whether you want to use the current document, start from another existing document, or start from a document based on a template. Make your desired selection and then click Next: Select Recipients at the bottom of the task pane to continue. The third Mail Merge task pane appears, as shown in Figure 10-3.

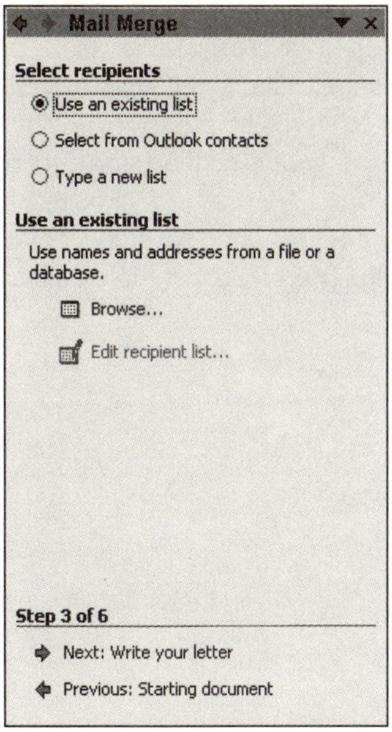

Figure 10-3: The Step 3 of 6 Mail Merge task pane

5. In the task pane under Select Recipients, choose what you want to use as the source of your mail merge data. Your options are the following:
   - **Use an Existing List:** This option lets you choose an existing database file containing the names and addresses that you want to merge. After making this selection, you can click the Browse button that appears, to locate and open the desired database file.
   - **Select from Outlook Contacts:** This option lets you use an Outlook Contacts folder as the source of the names and addresses. When you choose this option, you can then select the Choose Contacts Folder option that appears in the task pane to view and select the desired Outlook Contacts folder.
   - **Type a New List:** This option lets you type a list of names and addresses. When you select this option and then click Create in the task pane, a New Address List dialog box appears, as shown in Figure 10-4. You can enter the names and addresses using this dialog box, clicking New Entry after completing each entry to add another. When done, click the Close button (the X in the upper-right corner) in the dialog box, and the wizard will ask for a name and location to store the list. (Your list will be stored in a Microsoft Access database file, with the .MDB file extension.)

   If you choose to type a new list, Word stores your data in a Microsoft Access database file. This is different from previous versions of Word, in which information was stored in a different Word document. By using Access to store your information, you can add to it later using Access instead of Word. (For further information on adding information to an Access database, see Chapter 23, "About Databases and Tables.")

   The beauty of Word's Mail Merge feature is that you can pull information from a wide variety of sources. For instance, you can pull information from an Excel workbook or from an exisiting Access database. The idea is to make your data as accessible as possible and merge it into the format you need in order to accomplish the task at hand.

NOTE: If you use the Mail Merge Wizard to produce a set of envelopes or labels rather than form letters, the Step 2 of 6 Mail Merge task pane provides these options: Change Document Layout and Start from Existing Document. Choose Change Document Layout if you want to start with a custom layout for your envelopes or your labels. (You can then click the Envelope Options button or the Label Options button that appears and choose the desired layout options in the dialog box.) Alternatively, choose Start from Existing Document if you want to use an existing document designed for your envelope or label format. You can then choose the desired document in the list or click the More Files link to display an Open dialog box, in which you can navigate to a desired file.

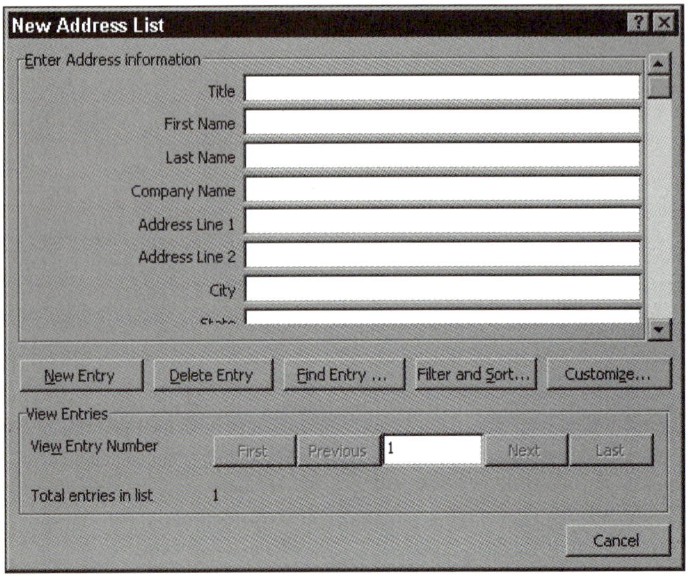

Figure 10-4: The New Address List dialog box

With this in mind, you should pick the data source that you want to use for your letters. In this example, we chose Type a New List and entered the address to which we wanted the letters sent. If you don't have data already existing in an Excel workbook or an Access database, this is probably the best choice for you as well. When you are done typing your list, Word returns to the third step in the Mail Merge Wizard (refer to Figure 10-3). The only difference is that the Use an Existing List option is now chosen and the task pane indicates the name of the Access database you used when saving the names you typed.

When you have finished specifying your data source, click Next: Write Your Letter at the bottom of the task pane to continue. The fourth Mail Merge task pane appears, as shown in Figure 10-5.

6. You can now enter or edit the document that will serve as the main document. You can type the text that will remain the same for each form letter, using the usual Word editing methods. To enter the appropriate *merge fields* (the data that changes for each form letter, such as the name, address, city, state, or postal code), you use the commands shown in the Step 4 of 6 Mail Merge task pane. The options available in the task pane vary, depending on the type of document you are creating. (You specified a document type back in the first step of the Mail Merge Wizard, remember?) Table 10-1 explains the commands available if you are creating a letter.

Figure 10-5: The Step 4 of 6 Mail Merge task pane

Table 10-1
The Step 4 of 6 Mail Merge Task Pane Commands

To Insert These Merge Fields	***Use This Task Pane Command***
A grouping of name and address fields, such as first and last names, address, city, state, and postal code	Address Block
A salutation block, such as *Dear Dr. Martin,*	Greeting Line
E-postage field, to print electronic postage	Electronic Postage
Postal Bar Code field	Postal Bar Code
Other unique merge fields from your data list, such as a firm name or company name	More Items

When done designing your main document, save your work with File ⇨ Save. Then click Next: Preview Your Letters at the bottom of the task pane. The next Mail Merge task pane appears, and a completed letter based on the first name and address in your list appears in the document window, similar to the example shown in Figure 10-6.

After this task pane appears, you can preview your form letters using the forward (>>) and reverse (<<) buttons shown in the task pane. You can also search for a particular recipient in the list of names and addresses by clicking the Find a Recipient link in the task pane and entering the search text into the Find Entry dialog box that appears. And you can modify the recipient list that's based on your chosen data source, if desired, by clicking the Edit Recipient List link in the task pane. When done previewing the results of the mail merge, click Next: Complete the Merge at the bottom of the task pane to continue. The last Mail Merge task pane appears, as shown in Figure 10-7.

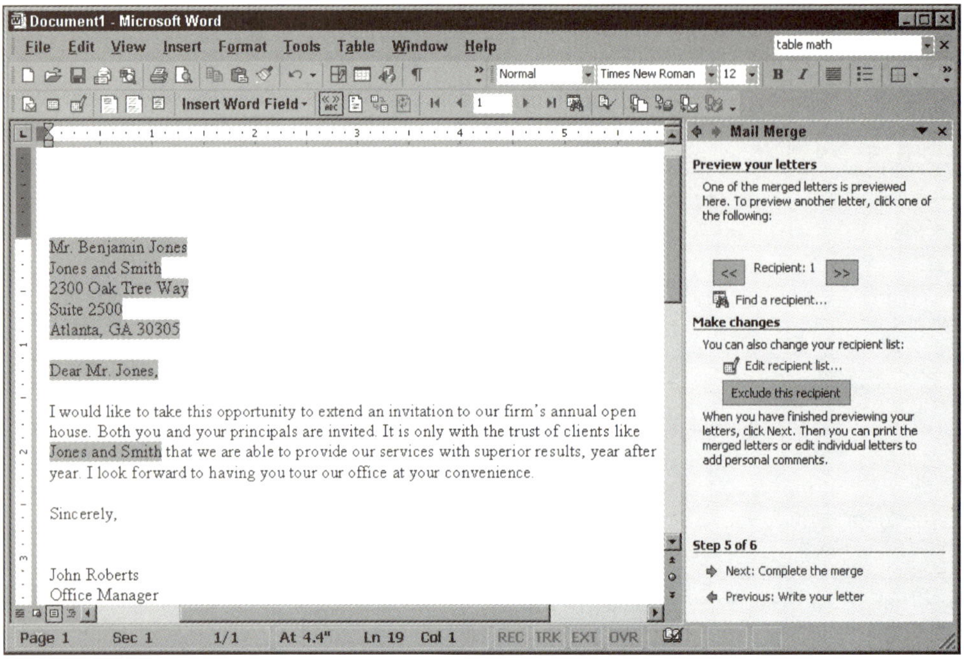

Figure 10-6: The Step 5 of 6 Mail Merge task pane, along with a preview letter

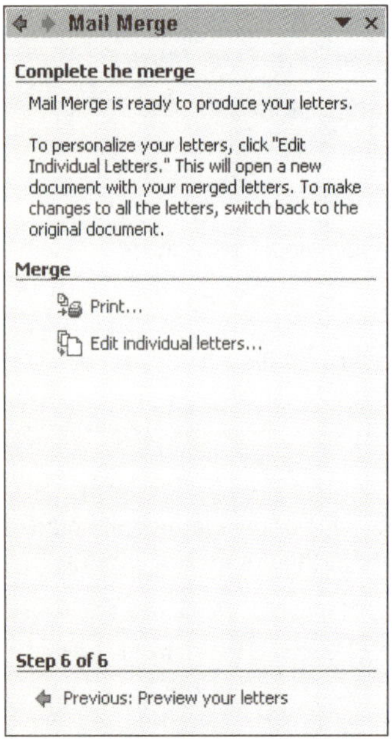

Figure 10-7: The Step 6 of 6 Mail Merge task pane

In the Merge area of the task pane, you can print your form letters immediately by clicking the Print command. Alternatively, you can choose to store all the completed letters in a single Word document by clicking the Edit Individual Letters link and then using the File ⇨ Save or File ⇨ Save As command.

TIP: Remember that at any step during the process of using the Mail Merge Wizard, you can use the Previous link at the bottom of the task pane to go back to a previous step and modify any desired options.

Producing Individual Envelopes

You can use the Envelopes and Labels menu command to print an individual envelope on demand. (If you need to print a series of envelopes for a list of addresses, you should use the Mail Merge Wizard, which is detailed earlier in this chapter.) To print a single envelope, use these steps:

1. Choose Tools ⇨ Letters and Mailings ⇨ Envelopes and Labels. In the Envelopes and Labels dialog box that appears, click the Envelopes tab (see Figure 10-8).

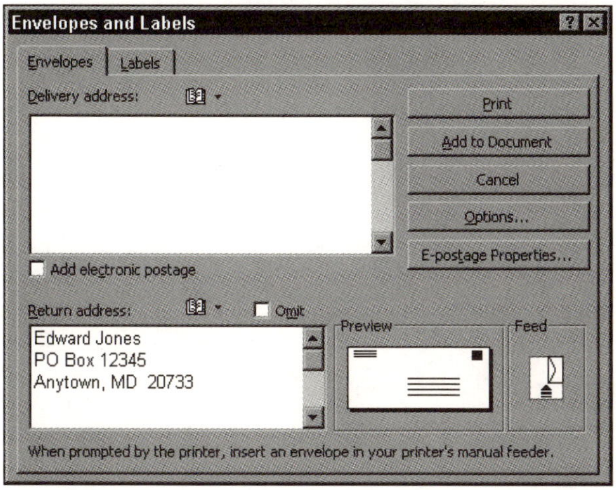

Figure 10-8: The Envelopes tab of the Envelopes and Labels dialog box

2. Type the recipient's name and address in the Delivery Address text box. (If you have a document already open and that document contains an address, it will automatically appear in the Delivery Address box, and you can edit it as needed.)
3. If you want to include a return address, type the return address into the Return Address text box. (If you've already specified a mailing address as part of Word's Setup under Tools ⇨ Options ⇨ User Information, that address will appear as a default return address.)
4. To change the default size or the layout of where the addresses appear, click the Options button on the Envelopes tab and choose the desired settings in the Envelope Options dialog box (see Figure 10-9).
5. To print the envelope, place the envelope in your printer and click the Print button in the Envelopes and Labels dialog box. (When inserting the envelope in your printer, you should orient the envelope so that it matches the orientation shown in the Feed portion of the Envelopes tab in the Envelopes and Labels dialog box.)

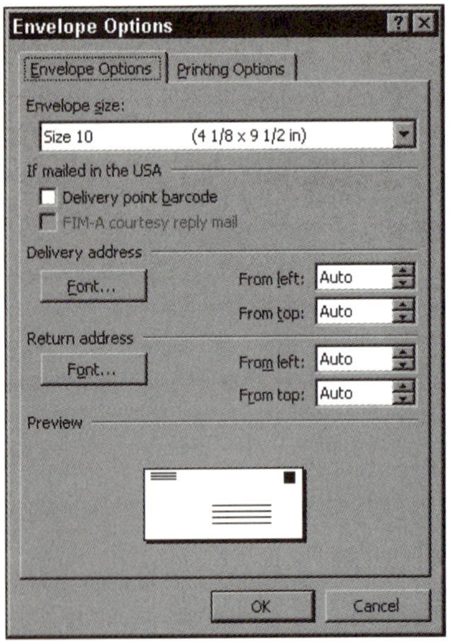

Figure 10-9: The Envelope Options dialog box

TIP: You can install e-postage software available from independent vendors and then have Word add your postage imprint directly to your envelopes or mailing labels by clicking the Add Electronic Postage option in the Envelopes and Labels dialog box.

Producing Individual Labels

You can use similar steps to print an individual label or a sheet of labels on demand, matching any of the popular Avery label sizes. To print a single label or label sheet, use these steps:

1. Choose Tools ⇨ Letters and Mailings ⇨ Envelopes and Labels. In the Envelopes and Labels dialog box that appears, click the Labels tab (see Figure 10-10).

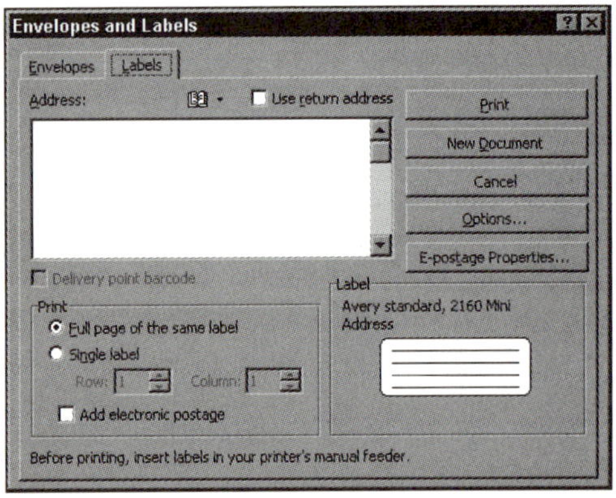

Figure 10-10: The Labels tab of the Envelopes and Labels dialog box

2. Type the desired address that should appear on the label in the Address box. Then, under Print, select Full Page of the Same Label (to print an entire label sheet using the same address repeatedly), or choose Single Label (to print a single label on the sheet).
3. The Label portion of the dialog box displays the type of label that Word will print. If you want to change this setting, click the Options button to display the Label Options dialog box (see Figure 10-11) and make your desired selections.

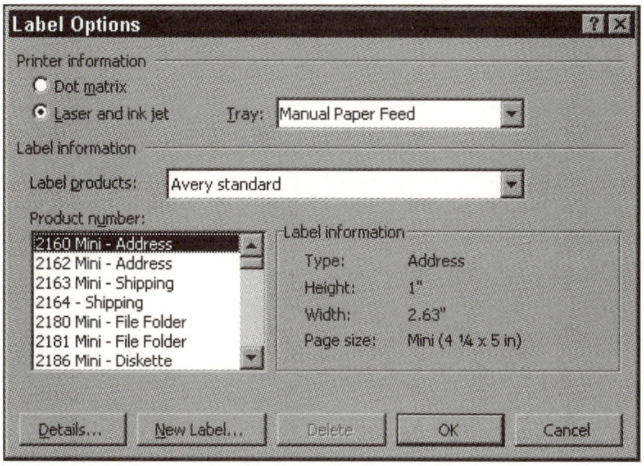

Figure 10-11: The Labels Options dialog box

4. After you have made your desired selections, click Print in the Envelopes and Labels dialog box to print your label.

Summary

This chapter has covered the ways in which you can generate form letters based on a list of names and addresses, a process also commonly known as *creating a mail merge*. In this chapter, you learned the following:

- A mail merge combines two kinds of documents: a main document, which contains the text that is identical for each printed copy, and a data source, which contains the text that is specific to each copy printed.
- You can use Word's Mail Merge Wizard to step through the process of creating a mail merge.
- You can base a mail merge on an existing database, a new list of names and addresses that you type, or an Outlook Contacts folder.
- You can use the Envelopes and Labels menu command to print an individual envelope, a label, or a sheet of labels on demand.

The next chapter details how to use Word's document control and document management features.

Chapter 11

Keeping Track of Revisions

In This Chapter

- Understanding the pros and cons of the Track Changes feature
- Using Track Changes
- Viewing tracked changes
- Printing tracked changes
- Adding comments
- Using versioning
- Protecting documents
- Using Word's document management features

WORD PROVIDES A BEVY OF TOOLS that you can use to facilitate the writing and editing of documents. You'll find these tools especially valuable when you work on documents in collaboration with others. This chapter introduces you to those tools: Track Changes, Comments, Versioning, and document management. Each tool has a specific purpose and can become an integral part of the way you use Word.

Understanding the Pros and Cons of Track Changes

Word's Track Changes feature, as its name implies, records changes made in a document. Before finalization, legal documents are often reviewed, edited, and commented on by the author, as well as others. By activating the Track Changes feature, you can keep track of every change made in the document, including the name of the editor and the date and time of each change. Changes are displayed in a color or an attribute that you select, and a vertical line appears in the margin of the document to indicate the location of the change. Word's Track Changes feature can also keep track of formatting changes made in the document. The changes made to the document do not become permanent until you accept them (using a specific Word command to do so) and save the document.

One difference between redlining a document and using the Track Changes feature is that the redlined document is usually a separate document that shows the differences between the original and a revised version of the original after the changes have already been implemented. When you use the Track Changes feature, all changes are recorded in the original document, and the person who has final responsibility for producing the final document gets to decide which changes are implemented, by either accepting the changes (one at a time or all at once) or rejecting the changes. When a change is accepted, the change is implemented in the document. When a change is rejected, the original text remains unchanged.

The obvious advantage of using the Track Changes feature is that it automatically keeps track of all changes made in the document. However, it is important to note that when Track Changes is active,

Word records all changes made in the document as part of the document. If all the changes are not accepted or rejected, it is possible for the recipient to see all the insertions and deletions that were made in the document. This is a critical point for legal professionals because this means that others could see confidential or proprietary information you thought that you had removed or changed.

Not remembering to accept or reject changes can also lead to problems when using programs such as CompareRite, which is also a redlining program that can stop working in a document in which Track Changes is used. CompareRite can stop working or never work to begin with in documents in which Track Changes is used — especially when all changes have not yet been accepted or rejected. We discuss document comparison programs in more detail near the end of this chapter. The following sections show you how to successfully use the Track Changes feature.

Using Track Changes

There are several ways to activate Track Changes to begin recording changes as they are made. You can use any of the following techniques:

- Double-click the TRK button on the status bar at the bottom of the Word window.
- Choose Tools ⇨ Track Changes.
- Click the Track Changes button on the Reviewing toolbar.
- Press Ctrl+Shift+E.

When Track Changes is enabled, the TRK button on the status bar is bold (it is dim when Track Changes is turned off). Once Track Change is enabled, the Reviewing toolbar (see Figure 11-1) automatically appears in the toolbar area. We discuss the options on the toolbar as the chapter continues.

Figure 11-1: The Reviewing toolbar

Specifying the changes you want to view

When using Track Changes, you can specify which changes you want to see on the screen. Track Changes will show you comments, insertions, deletions, and formatting changes. If more than one editor is working on the document, you can see changes made by all reviewers or a particular reviewer. Specify the changes you want to see by clicking the arrow for the Show drop-down menu on the Reviewing toolbar and choosing the desired options from the submenu that appears (see Figure 11-2).

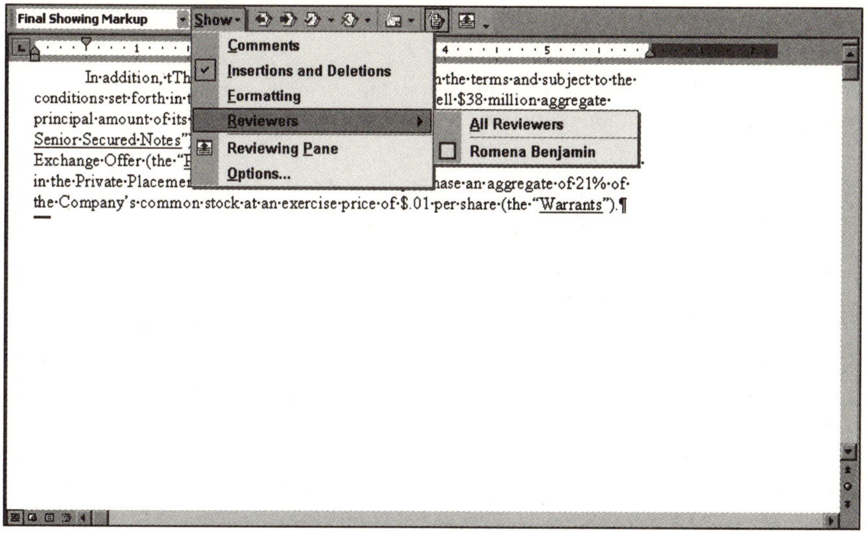

Figure 11-2: The Show options on the Reviewing toolbar

Changing the appearance of the changes

You have several options available for controlling what the changes look like when displayed in the text. These options are found on the Track Changes tab (see Figure 11-3), which can be accessed by clicking Tools ⇨ Options or by clicking the arrow for the Show drop-down menu on the Reviewing toolbar and choosing Options from the submenu that appears.

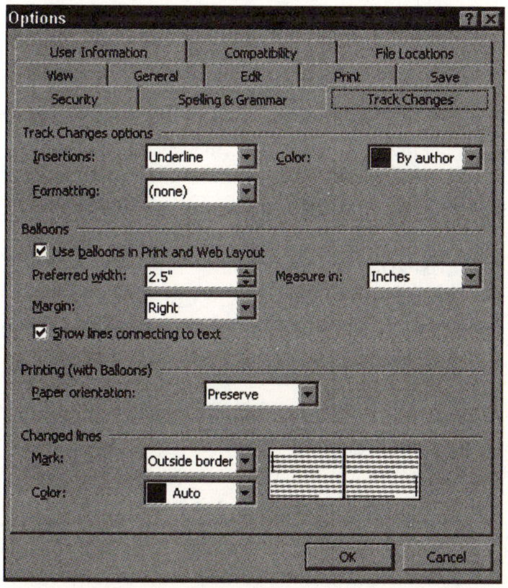

Figure 11-3: The Track Changes tab of the Options dialog box

The following briefly describes each section of the tab:

- **Insertions:** Assign an attribute such as Bold, Underline, or Double Underline. Any added text will then display with the attribute you chose.

- **Formatting:** If you choose to track changes made to formatting, you can assign an attribute to format changes.
- **Color:** Change the color used instead of or in addition to the attributes mentioned previously. You can assign a particular color to your changes, which is useful for differentiating the various editors of a document at a glance.
- **Balloons:** Balloons are bubbles of text that are primarily used for Word's Comment feature. They appear with a line extending from the balloon to the specific location in the document where the comment was inserted. (You learn more about comments later in this chapter.) Balloons are also used to show inserted text, if you instruct Word to display your original text showing the markup. In this section of the dialog box, you turn the balloons on or off when using Print Layout or Web Layout view. The default width of a balloon is 2.5 inches, which means that you may have to use the horizontal scroll bar or change the zoom percentage to be able to see the text and the balloon on-screen. Or you can change the width of the balloon in this section, as well as the measurement used. You can also change the balloon's margin location from Right to another location.
- **Printing (with Balloons):** You can print your document with the balloons showing, but you may find that the balloons get cut off the page. In this section, you can change the orientation in order to make everything fit. If you choose Auto, Word decides which orientation to print with.
- **Changed Lines:** By default, Word places a vertical line in the margin beside a changed line to make lines containing changes easier to see. In this section you can choose the particular border where you want the line to appear, or you can choose the None option to eliminate the line altogether. If you are using the Changed Lines indicator, you can have it displayed in a different color or keep the default color.

Accepting and rejecting changes

When finalizing a document in which Track Changes is used, it is important to accept or reject all changes made. If all changes are not disposed of one way or another, the changes can be seen by others who handle the document. All they have to do is turn Track Changes on and select a Display for Review option (to be discussed below). Any change not accepted or rejected can be viewed.

The Reviewing toolbar contains buttons that you can use to make it easy for you to move between changes, as well as accept and reject changes individually. You can also accept all changes or reject all changes simultaneously. The Previous and Next buttons allow you to move backward and forward, respectively, between the changes. When you click the Accept Change or Reject Change/Delete Comment buttons, a submenu of additional options appears, containing the options described in the following list:

- **Accept Change:** Implements the current change in the text.
- **Accept All Changes Shown:** Implements only those changes visible on the screen. Remember, you can control which changes are shown by using the Show drop-down menu on the Reviewing toolbar.
- **Accept All Changes in Document:** All changes are implemented, whether they are visible or hidden from view.

The following are the Reject options:

- **Reject Change/Delete Comment:** Removes the current change without implementing it and deletes the current comment

- **Reject All Changes Shown:** Removes all visible changes from the document without implementing them
- **Reject All Changes in Document:** Discards all changes, whether or not they are visible
- **Delete All Comments Shown:** Removes all comments that are visible
- **Delete All Comments in Document:** Discards all comments in the document, whether visible or hidden

Viewing Tracked Changes

You can view changes made when Track Changes is active in any view (Normal, Web Layout, Print Layout, or Outline). In Normal or Outline view, the changes are displayed differently from the way they are displayed in the Web Layout and Print Layout views. You can control how you want Word to display your changes by clicking the arrow for the Display for Review drop-down list (see Figure 11-4) and choosing the option you want. The following is a description of what you will see with each selection in the different views.

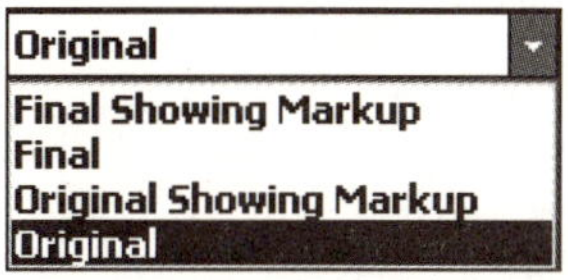

Figure 11-4: The Display for Review drop-down list, found on the Reviewing toolbar

- **Original:** This displays the document as it will look if the changes are rejected (see the example in Figure 11-5).

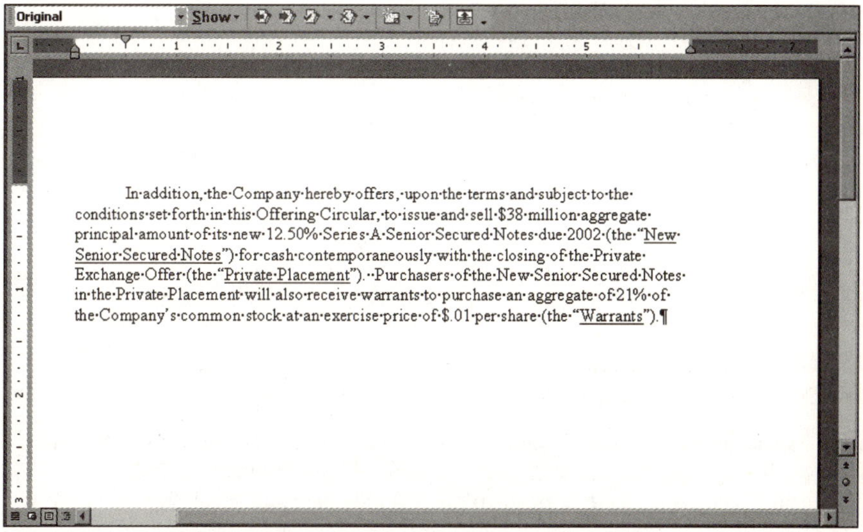

Figure 11-5: Revisions are not displayed when using the Original setting.

- **Original Showing Markup:** In the Normal and Outline views, the insertions and deletions appear in the text (see the example in Normal view in Figure 11-6). In Web Layout and Print Layout views, the deleted text appears in the document, and inserted text appears in a balloon to the right of the text (see the sample text in Web Layout view in Figure 11-7).

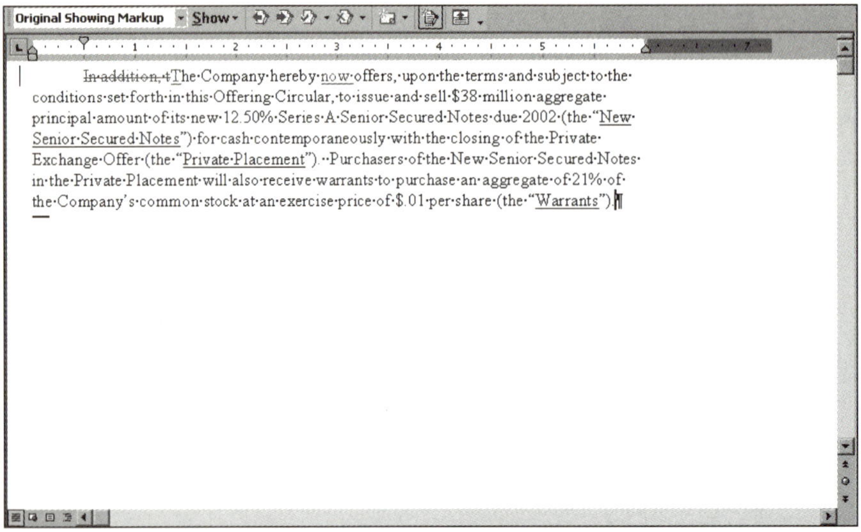

Figure 11-6: Sample text displayed as Original Showing Markup in Normal view

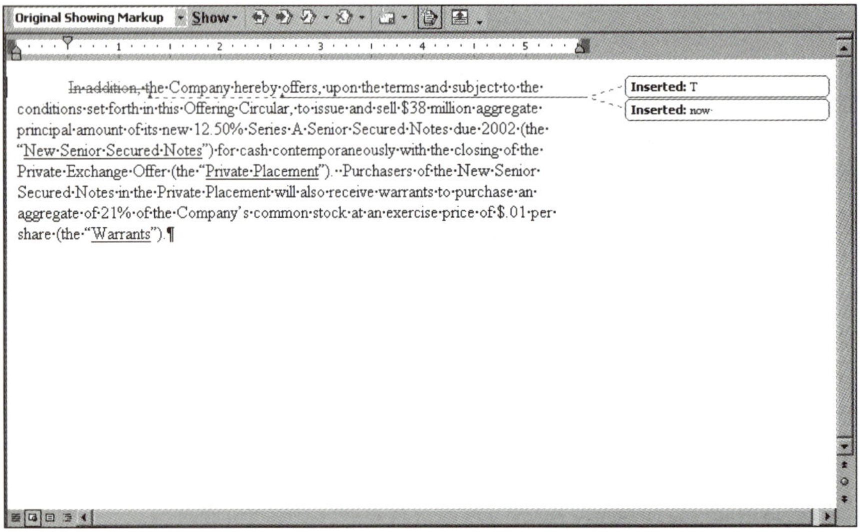

Figure 11-7: Sample text displayed as Original Showing Markup in Web Layout view

- **Final Showing Markup:** Normal and Outline views display changes the same as in Original Showing Markup. In Web Layout and Print Layout views, the deleted text displays in a balloon on the right side, and inserted material appears in the text (see the example in Figure 11-8).

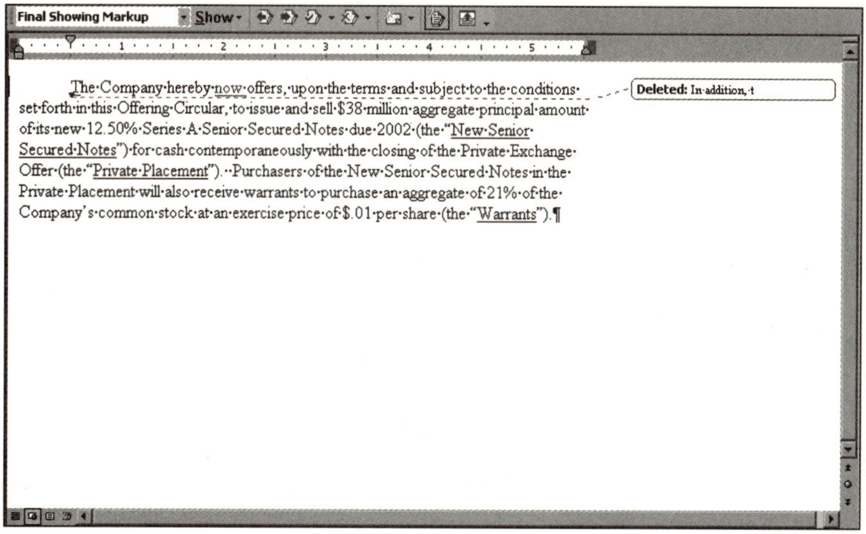

Figure 11-8: Sample text in Web Layout View using the Final Showing Markup option

- **Final:** This shows how the document will look if all the changes are implemented or accepted. Edits appear to take effect as you make them, but Word continues to track each change you make. Using this mode can be tricky. It is easy to forget that Track Changes is turned on, and if the changes are not accepted or rejected, you could make all your edits available to anyone who has access to the document.

You can also choose to view particulars about each change by choosing the Show drop-down menu on the Reviewing toolbar and selecting Reviewing Pane from the submenu that appears. When this option is selected, the document screen is split into two areas, with the document appearing in the upper portion and information about each change appearing in the lower portion. The information that displays is the category of change (insertion, deletion, and so forth), and the change itself is displayed. In addition, the reviewer's name appears, along with the date and time the change was made (see Figure 11-9). The Reviewing pane organizes the changes into sections, according to the part of the document where the change is made. For instance, edits made to a header or footer appear in the Header and Footer Changes section of the Reviewing pane.

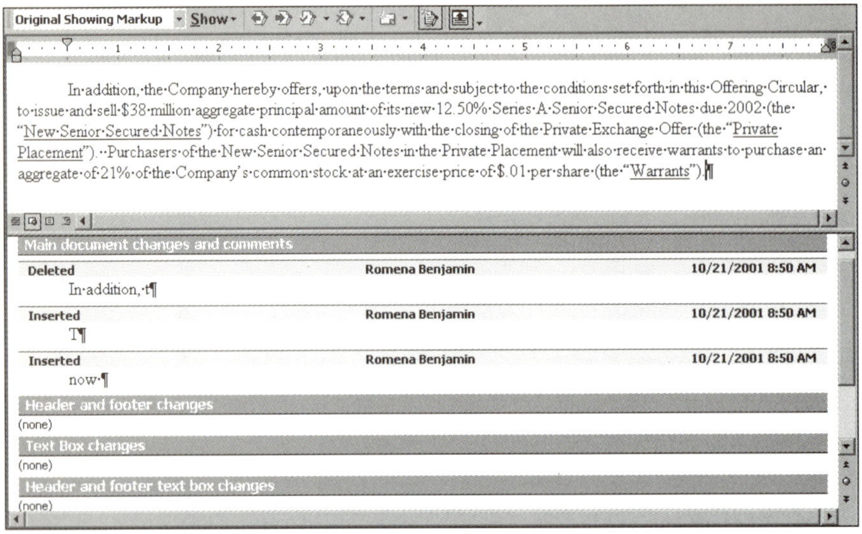

Figure 11-9: The Reviewing pane appears in the lower portion of the document window.

Printing Your Revised Document

You can print a marked-up copy of the document by clicking File ⇨ Print. Then, in the Print What section of the Print dialog box that opens (see Figure 11-10), choose Document Showing Markup and click OK. To see how the printed document will look before printing to a printer, choose File ⇨ Print Preview or change to Print Layout view. If you no longer want to print a marked-up copy of the document, you can change back to the Document setting in the Print What section of the Print dialog box.

You can also print a separate list of each change listed in the Reviewing pane by clicking File ⇨ Print. This time, in the Print What section of the Print dialog box that opens, choose List Markup. This option causes Word to print only the changes and not the rest of the document.

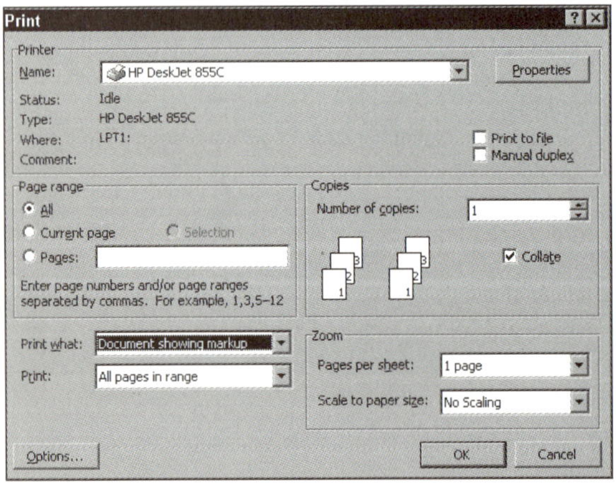

Figure 11-10: Choose your option for printing revisions in the Print What section of the Print dialog box.

Using the Comment Feature

Word's Comment feature gives you an efficient way to sprinkle notes throughout your document, both to yourself and to others who are collaborating on the document with you. Comments allow you to add notes of any length without disrupting the flow of the original text. This is a great feature during any collaborative writing or editing endeavor.

The following sections describe how you can work with comments in your documents.

Adding comments

Comments are a form of electronic note that you can embed in the text of your Word document. The Comment feature provides a useful and efficient collaboration tool for people working together on documents. Each comment includes the name of the person making the comment (actually, it's the name of the registered user of the Word program on a given computer).

To create a comment, place the insertion point at the desired location for the comment (or select the text on which you are commenting) and choose Insert ⇨ Comment. What happens next depends on the view in which you are using Word. If you are using Normal view, then Word displays a Comment pane at the bottom of the program window. If you are using Print Layout view or Web Layout view, then the active insertion point is automatically placed in the comment balloon beside the word *Comment*. There is also a bold line extending from the insertion point (or from the selected text) to the comment balloon. In either case, type the desired text for your comment (of any length). When you are finished writing the comment, press Enter. Figure 11-11 shows an example of a comment that has been added to a brief.

The text of the comment can be seen in its entirety in both Print Layout and Web Layout views. However, in the Normal and Outline views, a comment marker is located next to the text on which you commented so that you can know that a comment exists.

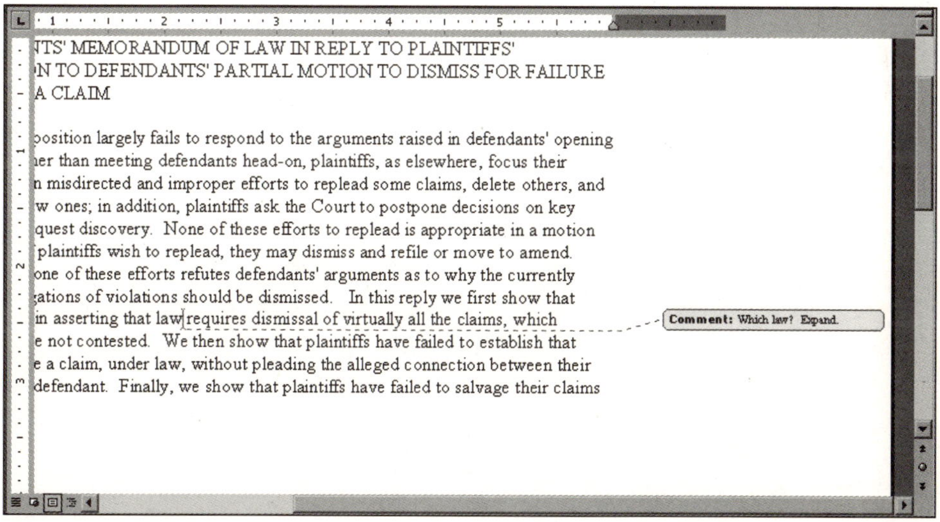

Figure 11-11: A comment added to a brief

Modifying comments

If your comments are not visible in the Print Layout view or Web Layout view, choose View ⇨ Markup to make the comments display. To edit the comment text, click in the comment balloon and make the desired modifications. When there are multiple comments on a page, you may want to see more than one at a time, and you can do so by adding the Reviewing toolbar to your view. Figure 11-12 shows the Reviewing toolbar, which contains the tools you can use to view all comments or to see a comment from a particular reviewer. These options are available through the Show drop-down menu on the Reviewing toolbar. To show the comments for a particular reviewer, choose Show ⇨ Reviewers, and choose the reviewer from the list that appears. You can easily move between multiple comments by using the Previous and Next buttons on the toolbar. The Reject Change/Delete Comment button on the toolbar gives you the option of deleting a comment.

Figure 11-12: The Reviewing toolbar

NOTE: Another way to locate comments is by using the Browse features located at the bottom of the horizontal scroll bar. If you click the button between the two double arrows, you can browse by comment. When this option is selected, you are able to move to the next or previous comments by clicking the double arrows. You can also double-click the status bar to open the Find dialog box. In this dialog box, you can select Comments in the Go to What section, or you can specify a particular reviewer in the Enter Reviewer's Name section.

The last button on the Reviewing toolbar opens the Reviewing pane at the bottom of your screen. Displayed there will be the full text of the comment, along with the author, date, and time the comment was created.

The Reviewing pane is particularly useful when your comment is inserted close to the end of a line and the full comment does not display on the screen. You can then click in this pane to review or modify the comment text. When you no longer need the Reviewing pane, you can remove it by clicking the Reviewing Pane button on the toolbar again. Figure 11-13 shows several comments listed in the Reviewing pane at the bottom of the screen.

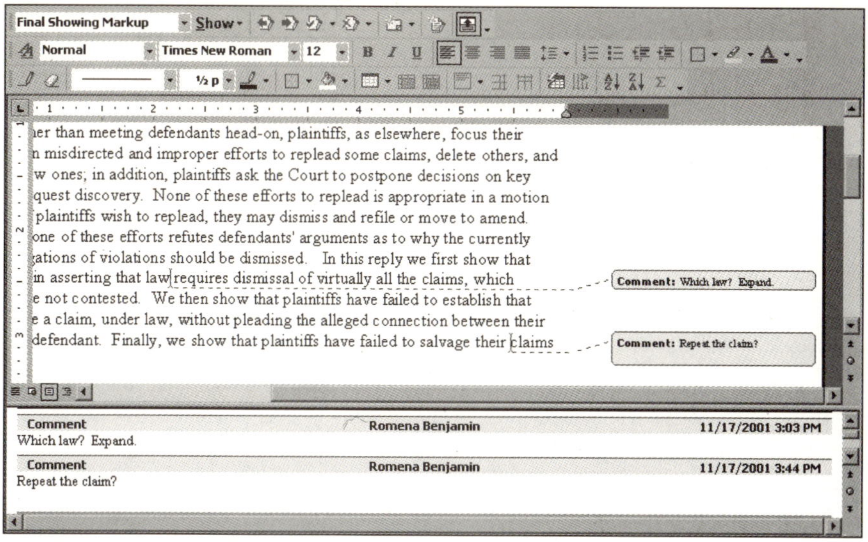

Figure 11-13: Use the Reviewing pane to easily view and modify multiple comments.

Protecting comments

You can protect comments from unwanted changes by making the document read-only or by requiring a password to be supplied before a document can be changed. To protect your comments, choose File ⇨ Save As. From within the Save As dialog box that opens, choose Tools ⇨ Security Options to display the dialog box shown in Figure 11-14. In the Security dialog box, type a password in the Password to Modify section. This is the password you want others to provide before they can modify the document. Or you can check the Read-Only Recommended option, which prevents others from modifying the document.

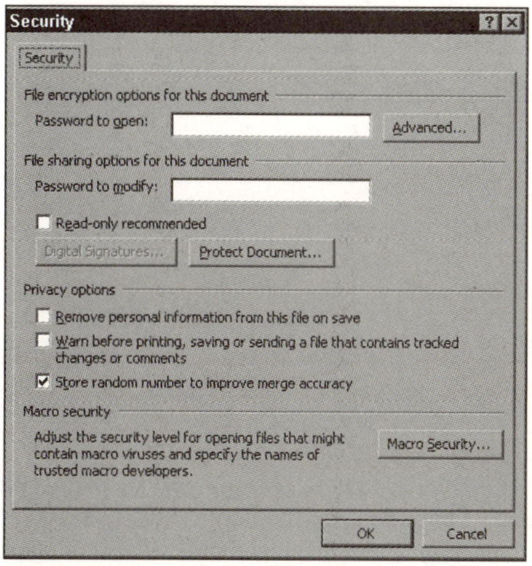

Figure 11-14: The Security dialog box

Understanding the Pros and Cons of Versioning

Many people like to create new “versions” of a document rather than overwrite an earlier version; this way, they can see how a document progressed to its current stage and can refer back to language used in earlier versions. The most common reason to keep various versions is to end up with documents that can be compared with one another to show the differences.

If you are using a document management system, this software has built-in version control that can create a new copy of the document saved with a different filename. With a document management system, it is not necessary to track versions using Word. However, if you are not using a document management system, you might find Word's Versioning feature useful.

NOTE: Word stores all versions of a document in a single file. If you want to be able to use a document comparison program (such as the ones described later in this chapter), you will need to use separate filenames for each version for those programs to work. To do so, choose File ⇨ Save As to manually save each version as a new document with its own filename.

Using Versioning

New versions of a document can be created manually by you or automatically by Word. To create a new version manually, open the original saved document and choose File ⇨ Versions. A dialog box opens with the name of the original file in the title bar (see the example in Figure 11-15). You can click the Save Now button in the New Versions section to create a new version of the document immediately, or you can check the Automatically Save a Version on Close option. When this option is checked, a new version is not created until you close the document. If you have previously created versions of the open document, each version is listed in the Existing Versions section of the dialog box.

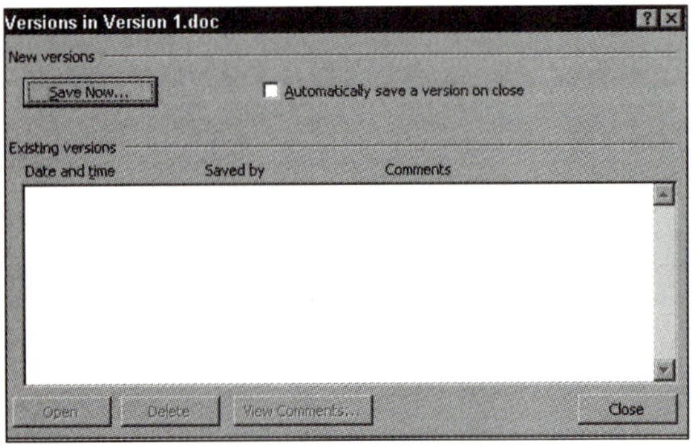

Figure 11-15: The Versions dialog box.

If you click the Save Now button, a Save Versions dialog box opens, in which you can type additional information about the new version you are creating. You don’t need to type the name of the author, date, or time the version is created because these items are already tracked for you and appear in the upper portion of the Save Versions dialog box.

If you want to open an earlier version of a document, choose File ⇨ Versions from the menus and highlight the version you want to open. Click the Open button to replace the current open version with the version you selected. You will need to repeat these steps for each version you want to open. Or click the Delete button to discard an existing version. If you want to view only the comments you typed in any version that exists, highlight the desired version and click the View Comments button.

Protecting Documents

If you are sharing a document with others and want to track any changes they make, you can force the Track Changes feature to stay on during any revisions. This is known as *protecting the document* for tracked changes. To protect a document to ensure that all changes are highlighted, choose Tools ⇨ Protect Document and then choose the Tracked Changes option in the Protect Document dialog box that opens (see Figure 11-16). When others open the document, Track Changes is automatically enabled and any changes made are recorded. To disable Track Changes, double-click TRK on the status bar, or choose Tools ⇨ Track Changes. Word also allows you to password-protect the document so that Track Changes cannot be turned off (except by you or anyone else who knows the password). However, as is the case with any password, you must remember it, or you will not be able to turn Track Changes off. You can also protect comments and forms from within the Protect Document dialog box.

Figure 11-16: The Protect Document dialog box

Merging Changes from Different Reviewers

It is not unusual for a document to be reviewed by many different people during the development process. For instance, this book you are reading was not just worked on by a single author, but by two authors and multiple editors. In the legal environment, you may need to have editors, paralegals, consultants, partners, clients, and a host of other people review a document.

For situations such as these, Word includes a feature that allows multiple reviewers to make changes in different copies of the same document and then later merge the copies back into a single document. To compare and merge documents, choose Tools ⇨ Compare and Merge Documents. The Compare and Merge Documents dialog box that opens looks similar to the File Open dialog box (see Figure 11-17). Here you navigate to the location of the file and then click the Merge button. If you click the drop-down list arrow beside the button, you can choose any of the following options: Merge, Merge into Current Document, or Merge into New Document. When the merge is completed, all differences are indicated in the familiar notation used by Word's Track Changes feature.

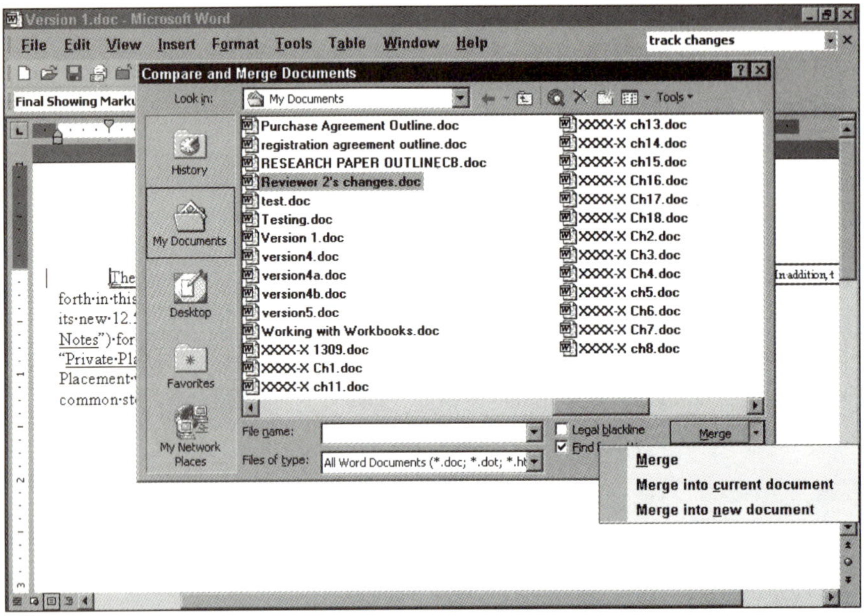

Figure 11-17: The Merge options available in the Compare and Merge Documents dialog box

Comparing changes in two separate documents

As mentioned earlier, many people like to keep earlier versions of a document in order to compare the original against revised versions of the document. However, you may also prefer to have the differences reported in a third document, leaving the original and revised versions intact. As noted previously, the Track Changes feature and the Versioning feature record changes in the document and do not create a third document automatically. If you want the document saved as a new document with a new filename, you have to do this manually, using the File ⇨ Save As command.

If you do not mind that the changes are recorded in the current document or if you are going to save the comparison document as a third document manually, then you may want to use Word's Compare feature.

NOTE: Microsoft actually recommends that Word's Compare feature be used only for very simple documents. Law offices, which typically work with documents containing complex formatting, are urged to use third-party document comparison programs such as the ones described in the following section of this chapter.

To do so, perform the following steps:

1. Open the original document, making sure to accept or reject all changes.
2. Choose Tools ⇨ Compare and Merge Documents.
3. When the Compare and Merge Documents dialog box opens, click the Legal Blackline option, which is beside the File Name text box.
4. Navigate to the location of the file you want to compare.

5. Click the Compare button in the lower-right corner.

6. If desired, choose File ⇨ Save As to save the document showing the changes as a separate document.

Using third-party comparison programs

Many legal professionals are accustomed to using Lexis-Nexis's CompareRite to automatically generate redlined documents. However, CompareRite can stall or not run at all when run against documents that contain complicated formatting. In addition, you may experience difficulty in running CompareRite against a Word document in which Track Changes was used. Usually, the problem is that not all of the changes were accepted or rejected in the document in which Track Changes was used and CompareRite produces inconsistent results. CompareRite can produce a third saved file showing the differences between the original and revised version. Also, many legal documents include tables, but CompareRite does not support tables.

DeltaView by Workshare Technologies, is another program. It is an off-the-shelf product that can compare two documents with complicated formatting, including changes to the structure of tables and auto-numbered paragraphs. DeltaView is very easy to set up and to use. One of its features includes a three-pane window view that displays the original document, the modified document, and the resulting comparison. DeltaView keeps all changes in a separate document, thus greatly simplifying the document. You will find an evaluation version of DeltaView on the CD that accompanies this book.

Summary

This chapter described the various features that Word provides for displaying and comparing editorial reviews of documents. In this chapter, you learned

- How to use the Track Changes feature to display revisions that you and others make to your documents
- How to print the tracked changes
- How to use Word's Comment feature
- How to create separate versions of a document
- How to protect your document so that others can't make changes that you don't know about
- How to use Word's Compare feature (and when not to)

The next and final chapter of this section of the book guides you through creating macros and putting them to use to make repetitive tasks easier.

Chapter 12

Working with Word Macros

In This Chapter

- ♦ Understanding macros
- ♦ Storing, creating, and running macros
- ♦ Deleting unwanted macros
- ♦ Understanding the Macro dialog box
- ♦ Using macros in an example
- ♦ Creating macros that run automatically
- ♦ Making macros secure

MACROS HAVE ALWAYS HAD a bad reputation. Macros were first made popular in DOS-based spreadsheet programs that you had to be a borderline programmer to use. Because things are no longer dismal from an ease-of-use point of view, you do not need to fear macros in Word. Macros are easy to create and can accomplish a great deal toward saving you time in your everyday work. In this chapter, you will learn what macros are and how to create them. You can then take a look at a step-by-step example that illustrates how you can use macros to automate your common tasks in Word.

Understanding Macros

Macros are recorded combinations of keystrokes and certain mouse actions. Macros can automate many of the tasks that you normally perform manually, keystroke by keystroke, within Word. In a macro, you can record a sequence of keyboard and mouse entries and link them to a single key combination, a menu option, or a toolbar button. Later, you can "play back" the recorded sequence by pressing the assigned key combination, clicking the toolbar button, or choosing the menu option. When the macro is played back, Word performs as though you had manually executed the operations contained within the macro. When your work involves highly repetitive tasks, such as producing daily reports or repeating certain formatting tasks, you can often save many keystrokes by creating a few macros.

At first glance, macros may seem similar to AutoText entries (see Chapter 3, "Creating and Working with Documents," for details on using AutoText), but significant differences exist. AutoText entries can reproduce text at any location in a document. Macros can do much more than simulate typing. Macros can perform menu and dialog box selections, something that you cannot do with AutoText entries. For example, if you routinely print two copies of a certain weekly report, you can create a macro that opens the document, chooses File ⇨ Print from the menus, and marks the dialog box options needed to send two copies of the report to the printer.

Word records your macros as instructions in the programming language used by the Microsoft Office applications: Visual Basic for Applications (or *VBA,* for short). Don't panic at the sound of the name (or the implication that you need to learn programming). You can create macros in Word without knowing an iota about Visual Basic for Applications. You can create macros in the following two ways in Word:

- You can record a series of keyboard and mouse actions, the most commonly used method. This method requires no knowledge of Word's programming language.
- You can type a macro directly into a VBA Editor window. This method enables you to accomplish some advanced tricks by means of VBA commands that you can't do by recording actions, but it requires you to "get your hands dirty," to some extent, with VBA.

Not only can you use a macro to combine a sequence of commands that you use regularly, but you also can use it to perform routine editing and formatting tasks faster. And you can create a macro to get to those well-buried Word features more quickly, such as the dialog box that you use to change printer options.

Macros are especially useful when you format documents. You may have to change a document's font and spacing, enter heading styles, change margins, and check spelling and grammar. If you make these changes regularly, create a macro so that you don't have to invoke the same commands over and over again. The following sections show you how to make your life easier with macros.

Alternatives to macros

After spending this much time touting the benefits of macros, you should know that sometimes a macro may not be the most effective solution to a specific need. Before you jump into the task of designing macros for any task that you handle often, consider whether another feature of Word can handle the task with less effort on your part. If you want to use a macro to apply many character or paragraph formatting options to selected text, consider using a style sheet instead. If you want to use a macro to type long, repetitive phrases, note that you can use AutoCorrect instead to designate an abbreviation of your choices to serve as the phrase. And if you are trying to use a macro to automate the process of filling out a form, you can use fields to make this task easier.

Storing Macros

Where you store macros depends on two things: the settings in the Template and Add-Ins dialog box (which appears when you choose Tools ⇨ Templates and Add-Ins) and whether you are using the default template (Normal.dot). If you are using the default template, macros are stored in Normal.dot. When you exit Word, you are asked whether you want to store the macros you've created during a session to the Normal.dot template; you can answer yes to store the macros or no to discard the macros.

When you choose Tools ⇨ Templates and Add-Ins, the Templates and Add-Ins dialog box appears, as shown in Figure 12-1.

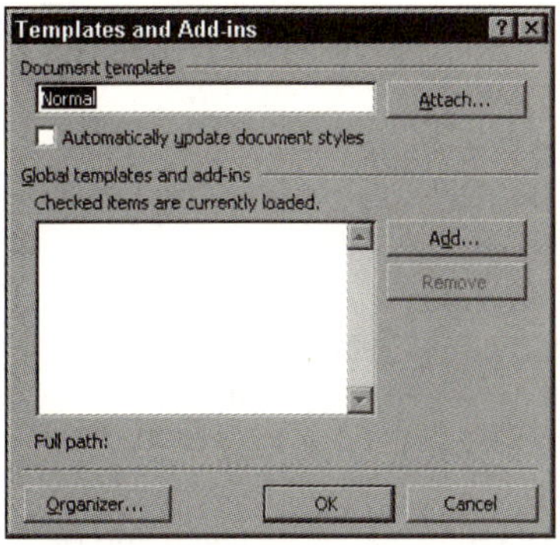

Figure 12-1: The Templates and Add-Ins dialog box

If you are using a template different from Normal.dot, the storage location for new macros depends on the settings in the Templates and Add-Ins dialog box. If you activate the check box for the template you are using, Word saves macros in that template. You can click the Add button to display all your templates and double-click any template to add it to the list in the Templates and Add-Ins dialog box. In addition to saving macros to templates that you've checked in the Templates and Add-Ins dialog box, on exit, Word will ask whether you want to save the new macros to the Normal.dot template file. All macros saved to Normal.dot are *global* in nature, which means that they are available from any document in Word.

Creating Macros

The easiest way to record a macro is to turn on Word's macro recorder by choosing Tools ⇨ Macro ⇨ Record New Macro and then following the steps in the dialog boxes that appear. You then perform the desired actions with your keyboard and mouse and tell Word to stop recording.

NOTE: You also can create macros manually by using Visual Basic for Applications, the programming language used with Word. Using Visual Basic for Applications to write and edit macros is beyond the scope of this chapter, but in short, you open a window into the VBA Editor and type macro instructions using VBA code. (You can learn more about Word and VBA programming in programmer's guides aimed at Word, such as Microsoft's *Office XP Developer's Guide*.)

TIP: The macro recorder is limited in an important way: You cannot record mouse actions within a document, such as selecting text with the mouse. If you try to use the mouse within a document, Word just beeps. You *can* use the mouse to select menu options and choose dialog box settings, however. If you want to select text as part of a macro, use the keyboard. (You can hold down the Shift key and use the arrow keys to select large amounts of text, and you can use the Ctrl+A key combination to select all text in a document.)

Preparing to create your macro

Before you record your macro, you need to make some decisions about how you will invoke (or, launch) your macro, in what kinds of documents you will use your macro, and so on. Keep the following points in mind:

- Give some thought to the overall workspace and how it should appear when the macro runs. You want to organize the workspace in the same manner as it should appear when the macro runs. For example, if you will use the macro in a blank document, you should have a blank document on-screen before you begin recording the macro.
- Think about all the steps you need to take to accomplish the task for which you are creating the macro. Write the steps down if this will help you remember them. You don't want to forget an important step as you are recording the macro (although if you do forget a step, you can stop recording, delete the macro, and start over).
- If you want the macro to apply to a selected piece of text, select the text before you begin to record the macro.
- Give the macro a name that reminds you of the macro's function. For example, if you have a bad habit of typing two periods at the end of a sentence and you want a macro that deletes the extra period, you can call the macro DELETE_PERIOD.
- Decide how you want to invoke your macro. You can assign a shortcut keystroke to your macro, place it in a menu on the Menu bar, or create a button for it in a toolbar (see Chapter 2. "Understanding Word's Interface," for details on customizing menus and toolbars).
- When you choose to assign a shortcut keystroke to a macro, you can use the Shift key, the Ctrl key, or a combination of the Ctrl and Shift keys with all letters, numbers, and function keys F2 through F12. (You cannot, however, use more than two letters in a key combination; for example, you could not assign a macro to Alt+P+Q+R.) Word also lets you use the Insert and Delete keys alone or with the Ctrl or Shift key. When you assign the keystroke, simply press it to execute the macro. For example, if you assign Ctrl+Alt+P to a macro that prints two copies of the document that's currently open and then you open a document and press Ctrl+Alt+P, the document prints twice.

CAUTION: It's not a good idea to assign a macro to the Insert or Delete key because doing so disables the normal editing function of these keys. Also, be aware that Word has several shortcut keys that have already been assigned to execute other functions. You can assign a macro to these preassigned keystrokes, but if you do, their preassigned function will be lost. For example, Ctrl+B makes typed or selected text appear in bold font. If you assign Ctrl+B to a macro, you will not be able to use that key combination to apply bold to any text. Don't worry about accidentally overwriting a keystroke, however, because Word tells you whether it's already assigned to another function.

Recording the macro

To record a macro, follow these steps:

1. Choose Tools ⇨ Macro ⇨ Record New Macro. In a moment, the Record Macro dialog box appears, as shown in Figure 12-2.

2. Change the default name that Word supplies for the macro to a new name you've chosen, and type that name in the Macro Name text box. (Macro names cannot contain spaces, commas, or periods.) Word creates a new macro, saves it in the Normal.dot template, and makes the macro available to all active templates unless you choose a different template in the Store Macro In list box.
3. If desired, add an optional description in the Description text box.

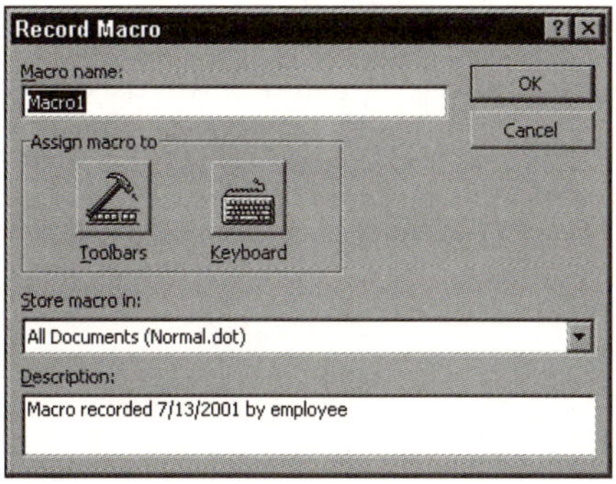

Figure 12-2: The Record Macro dialog box lets you assign a name for your macro and add it to a toolbar or a menu.

4. To assign the macro to a toolbar button or to a key combination, click the Toolbars button or the Keyboard button, as desired. (Which you use is up to you, and one isn't necessarily better than the other. People who aren't wild about the use of the mouse generally prefer keyboard shortcuts.)
5. After you choose how you want to activate the macro, the Customize dialog box appears.
6. If you choose to add the macro to a toolbar, click the Toolbars tab of the Customize dialog box (see Figure 12-3). Click the desired toolbar to make it visible if it isn't already. Then click the Commands tab and drag the name of the macro to the area on the toolbar where you want to place the button.

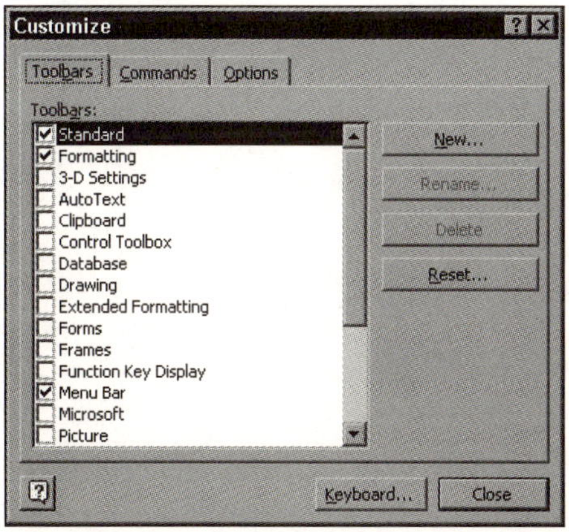

Figure 12-3: The Toolbars tab of the Customize dialog box

TIP: If you choose to assign your macro to a shortcut keystroke, the Customize Keyboard dialog box appears (see Figure 12-4). Click in the Press New Shortcut Key text box and press the keystroke combination that you want to assign to the macro.

7. When you have finished, click the Close button to implement the changes and start recording the macro.
8. The Macro Recorder toolbar appears (see Figure 12-5). This toolbar contains just two buttons: a Stop button (the one on the left) and a Pause button (the one on the right). Perform the steps that you want to record in the macro.
9. If you want to pause the recording of the macro while you carry out actions that you don't want recorded, click the Pause button. When you want to start recording again, click the Pause button again.

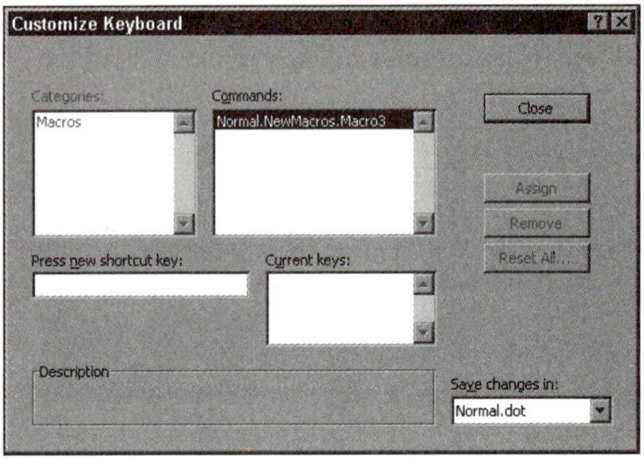

Figure 12-4: The Customize Keyboard dialog box

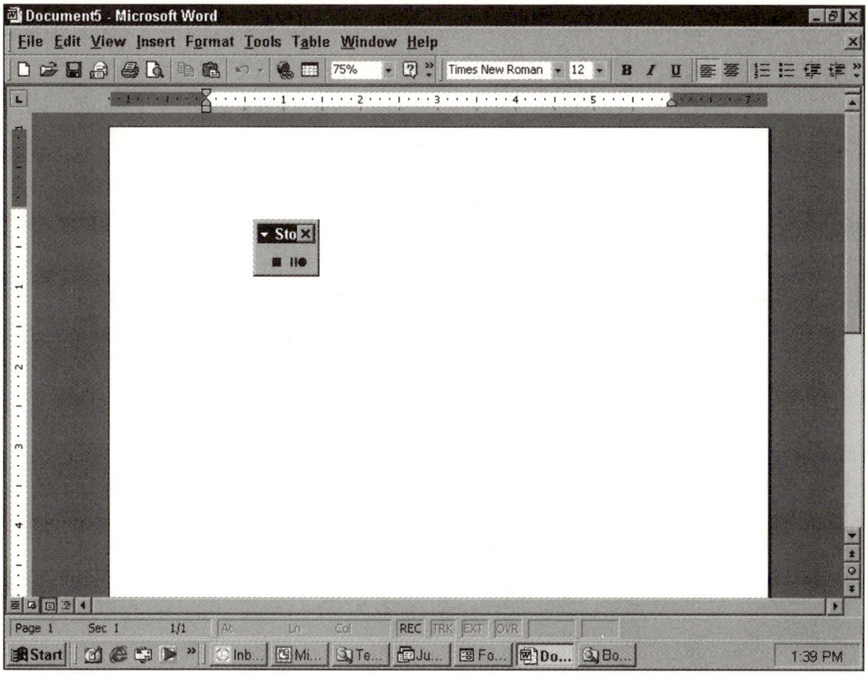

Figure 12-5: The Macro Recorder toolbar, with the Stop button on the left and the Pause button on the right

10. After you finish recording, click the Stop button on the Macro Recorder toolbar. (Alternatively, you can choose Tools ⇨ Stop Recording.)

Now you can activate the macro in the way that you chose in Step 4 — from the toolbar or by pressing the key combination. You can also choose Tools ⇨ Macros, as detailed in the following section.

What's recorded? What isn't?

Word's Macro Recorder doesn't actually record your *actions*; instead, it records the commands and the keystrokes that you enter. Remember that the Macro Recorder doesn't record mouse movements. If you want to create a macro that depends on selecting text, select the text by using the keyboard and not the mouse. Clicking the OK button in a dialog box — while you are recording a macro — records the state of every option in the tab that is visible in the dialog box. If you want to select options in another tab of the same dialog box, you must click OK to accept the options in the first tab and then re-open the dialog box. Click the new tab, select the options on it, and click OK to accept the options in the second tab. You do all these steps while you are recording the macro.

Running Macros

If you assigned your macro to a shortcut keystroke combination, a menu, or a toolbar, you can execute the macro by using the appropriate method. You also can run macros by choosing Tools ⇨ Macros. Follow these steps:

1. Choose Tools ⇨ Macro ⇨ Macros. The Macros dialog box appears, as shown in Figure 12-6.

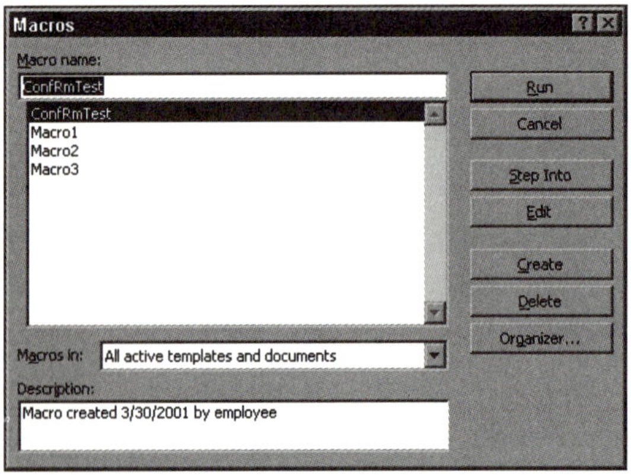

Figure 12-6: The Macros dialog box

2. Type the name of the macro in the Macro Name text box, or choose a macro from the list.
3. If the macro you want to execute isn't listed, Word may not be configured to run macros from all active templates. If the Macros In list box does not contain either All Active Templates and Documents or the name of the template in which you created the macro, select either of those values. This list box controls available macros based on the templates in which they were created.
4. Click the Run button. Word executes the chosen macro.

TIP: If you try to run a macro and you can't find it, chances are that your document is using a different template from the one to which your macro was originally saved.

Deleting Unwanted Macros

If you create a macro and later decide that you no longer need it, you can delete it. To delete a macro, choose Tools ⇨ Macros. In the Macros dialog box that appears, click the unwanted macro to select it; then click Delete. Finally, click Yes in the confirmation dialog box that appears, and the macro will be deleted.

Understanding the Macros Dialog Box

As noted previously, you enter the name of the desired macro in the Macro Name text box. After a name has been entered (or chosen from the list box), all the buttons at the right side of the dialog box are made available. Also, if you entered a description when you created the macro, the description appears in the Description text box at the bottom of the dialog box. The buttons in the dialog box perform the functions shown in Table 12-1.

Table 12-1
The Macros Dialog Box Buttons

Button	***Purpose***
Run	Runs the selected macro
Cancel	Closes the dialog box without running the macro
Step Into	Opens the selected macro in the VBA Editor and runs the macro one step at a time
Edit	Opens the selected macro in the VBA Editor, where you can edit the code
Create	Creates a macro by using the Visual Basic for Applications program code
Delete	Deletes the selected macro
Organizer	Displays the Organizer dialog box, which can be used to copy macros between templates

After you click the Organizer button in the Macros dialog box, you can use the Macros tab of the Organizer dialog box to copy macros from one template to another. This dialog box is very useful when you have created a macro in one template that you want to use in another template. Follow these steps to copy a macro from one template to another:

1. Choose Tools ⇨ Macro ⇨ Macros to bring up the Macros dialog box.
2. Click the Organizer button to bring up the Organizer dialog box, as shown in Figure 12-7. The Macro Project Items tab should be in the front of the dialog box.
3. You may need to close the open file. If so, click the Close File button on the left side of the dialog box. Then click the Open File button and choose the template in which you created the macro that you want to copy. On the right side of the dialog box, do these steps again: Click the Close File button, click the Open File button, and then choose the template to which you want to copy the macro.
4. The Copy button now appears active so that you can copy the macro to the other template. You also can rename the macro by clicking the Rename button and entering a new name in the Rename dialog box.

NOTE: Word stores your macros in the Normal.dot default template so that you can use them with every document. You can use the Organizer dialog box to sort out your macros by putting them into the templates in which you will use the macros most often.

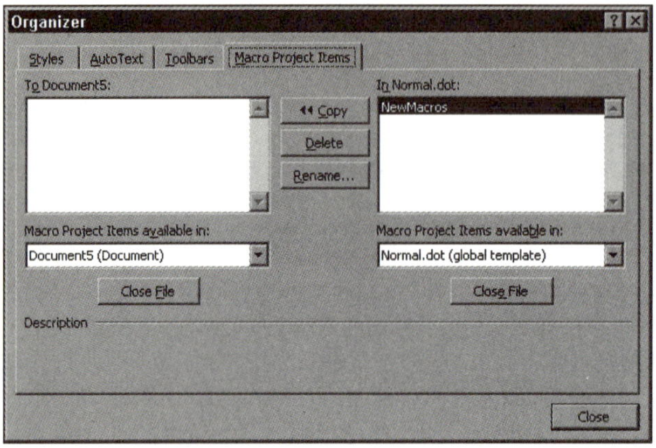

Figure 12-7: The Macro Project Items tab of the Organizer dialog box

Using Macros in an Example

To dispel any feelings that macros are intimidating, try your hand at creating the following sample macro. After following these steps to create the macro, you can then try one that will help you speed up other common operations at your office.

In this example, assume that you regularly switch to Print Layout view from Normal view so that you can see as much of your document as possible. You routinely choose View ⇨ Print Layout from the menus and then turn off the ruler. These steps are time-consuming if you do them a lot during a day, so you can save time by creating a macro to carry out the commands for you. To set the stage, first turn on your ruler, if it is not already on, by choosing the Ruler command from the View menu, and be sure that you are in Normal view. Now you can record the macro by following these steps:

1. Choose Tools ⇨ Macro ⇨ Record New Macro to bring up the Record Macro dialog box.
2. In the Macro Name text box, enter **PrintView** as the name for this macro.
3. Click the Keyboard button to assign a keyboard combination to the macro. The Customize Keyboard dialog box appears.
4. Because Word doesn't use Ctrl+period for anything, it makes a good shortcut key. Press Ctrl+period and then click the Assign button to assign this key combination to the PrintView macro.
5. Click the Close button to begin recording the macro.
6. Choose the Ruler command from the View menu to turn off the ruler.
7. Choose View ⇨ Print Layout to activate this view.
8. End the recording by clicking the Stop button (the one on the left) on the Macro Recorder toolbar.

To try out the macro, go back to the Normal view and redisplay the ruler. Then run the macro by pressing Ctrl+period. Word turns off the ruler and switches to Print Layout view. Now you can create a macro that switches it back!

Creating Macros That Run Automatically

You can give macros specific names that cause them to run automatically when you perform a certain action. For example, if you wanted a macro to run whenever you start Word, you would name that macro *AutoExec*. If you wanted a macro to run each time you open a new document, you would name that macro *AutoNew*. Table 12-2 lists the names that you can assign to macros to make them run when you perform the related action.

Table 12-2
Macros That Run Automatically on Their Related Actions

Macro Name	*Action That Triggers the Macro*
AutoExec	Runs when you start Word
AutoExit	Runs when you quit Word
AutoOpen	Runs when you choose File ⇨ Open
AutoNew	Runs when you choose File ⇨ New
AutoClose	Runs when you close the current document

You can have only one AutoExec macro for your copy of Word. However, you can have a different AutoOpen macro for each template. For example, a good use of an AutoOpen macro would be to activate a special toolbar that you need in that template, or to add a special message to the screen. Note that an AutoClose macro, which runs whenever you close a document, will also run whenever you exit Word before closing a Word document (because Word automatically closes documents when you attempt to quit Word).

TIP: An excellent use for an AutoOpen macro is one that automatically changes to your favorite subdirectory for your Word files. When you create this macro, name it *AutoOpen*, and while recording, use the usual selections in the Open dialog box from the File menu to switch to your favorite directory. After switching directories, click Stop to stop recording the macro. You could use an AutoClose macro to open another Word document, such as a listing of document summaries, to remind users to update that summary listing each time a particular document was edited.

Making Macros Secure

It seems that with many advantageous aspects of life come risks, and the same could be said to apply to the use of Word macros. Because Word macros make use of that powerful built-in programming language (Visual Basic for Applications), there are unsavory individuals at large who take pleasure in demonstrating their skills with that language by writing *macro viruses* that can do damage to your documents. Macro viruses operate like other software viruses, but they make use of Word's capability to run macros to perform their generally unwanted tasks. Fortunately, the macro security settings that are built in to Word can help protect computers at your office from macro viruses.

To set your macro security level, choose Tools ⇨ Macro ⇨ Security from the menus. Doing so displays the Security dialog box (see Figure 12-8).

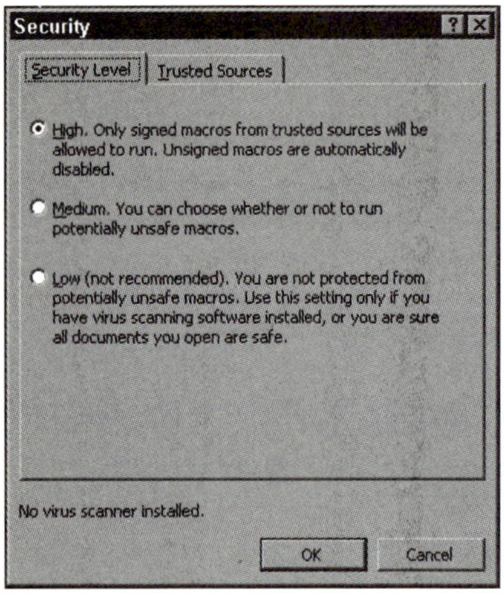

Figure 12-8: The Security dialog box is used to establish a desired level of macro security.

As shown in the dialog box, you can choose from one of three possible levels: High, Medium, and Low. If you choose High, only digitally signed macros from suppliers with a digital certificate (or macros that you yourself create on that same machine) will be able to run; all other macros will be automatically disabled. Choose Medium, and Word will display a warning before running any macro from an outside source that does not have a digital certificate. You can then click Enable Macro in the warning dialog box to let the macro run, or click Disable Macro in the dialog box to prevent the macro from running. Choose Low, and all macros will be enabled. (Note that the Low setting is *not* recommended by Microsoft, unless you have adequate virus protection software installed or you are certain that all documents that you open are safe.)

CAUTION: Although the Security option within Word can serve as a protection, it is *not* a substitute for a good antivirus software package. If, as with most legal environments, you exchange documents with clients, co-counsel, or other individuals or organizations outside your law firm or department, you should be protected with an up-to-date antivirus software package of your choosing.

Summary

In this chapter, you've learned the following about macros in Word:

- Macros are actually Visual Basic for Applications programs, but you don't need to know programming to create a macro. You can *record* a series of keystrokes and mouse actions as a macro.
- You can assign macros to toolbar buttons and key combinations.
- Some macros can be associated with starting Word, exiting Word, creating a file, opening a file, or closing a file. Such macros execute automatically when the event occurs.
- You can use the macro security setting within Word to determine the types of macros that will be permitted to run on your system.

This chapter completes the Word section of this book. The next section delves into the use of Excel, the powerful spreadsheet component of Microsoft Office.

Part II

Excel

Chapter 13

Working with Workbooks

In This Chapter

- Understanding workbooks
- Opening new and existing workbooks
- Navigating through worksheets
- Saving and closing workbooks
- Entering and editing data
- Copying and moving data
- Inserting and deleting cells, rows and columns
- Working with formulas
- Using functions
- Using Find and Replace
- Checking spelling
- Sharing workbooks with others at your firm
- Reviewing sample legal workbooks

MICROSOFT EXCEL IS A POWERFUL spreadsheet application that allows you to input text, numbers, and dates (collectively called *data*) into a file called a *workbook.* You can then analyze, sort, calculate, chart, graph, and apply statistical functions to that data. This chapter covers the basics of inputting and manipulating your data.

Legal Industry Uses

As a legal professional, you can find many uses for Excel in the practice of law. You can do virtually any type of data analysis you can think of — everything from totaling up a client's assets for a bankruptcy proceeding to doing a statistical analysis of DNA test results. The ways in which you can use Excel are entirely up to your imagination. Excel allows you to convert your data into charts and graphs for use as exhibits or appendices to your legal documents. You can also import your graphed or charted data into other Microsoft applications, such as PowerPoint, to make compelling and persuasive presentations to support your legal arguments. The workbooks you create with Excel can also be posted on the Web, or you can import data into Excel from the Web — both features are a great help when you need to share data with others or analyze the results of your online research.

- The corporate lawyer can provide company financial data as exhibits or appendices to governmental agency submissions or can include Excel files as part of court documentation.

- The personal injury lawyer can use Excel to calculate damages under different scenarios, and the domestic lawyer can easily calculate assets and liabilities of a client in preparation for a divorce settlement.
- The securities lawyer will find Excel useful for detailing company financials for the Securities and Exchange Commission.
- Banking lawyers and real estate lawyers will find that Excel's predefined functions for calculating loan payments and interest rates greatly help in using billable hours in ways other than performing calculations that Excel handles automatically.
- Administrative lawyers and those responsible for keeping track of billable hours or client bills will also find Excel useful.

Excel is useful not only to legal professionals but also to those in administrative departments who support the individual law practice or law firm. For instance, Human resource departments can use Excel for tracking leave balances and as staff timesheets. Law firm accounting departments can use Excel when preparing departmental budgets. Without a doubt, Excel is a powerful tool for the legal industry.

Working with Workbooks

A *workbook* is an Excel file that contains a collection of *worksheets,* which are the gridlike sheets of rows and columns that come to mind when you think of a spreadsheet application. The number of worksheets that a workbook can contain is limited only by the memory installed in your computer. Excel creates a blank workbook for you (named `Book1`) when you start Excel.

Creating or opening a workbook

After you start Excel, you can use the workbook that appears to do your work, create a new workbook from scratch, or base a new workbook on an existing workbook. Or you can simply open an existing workbook. The task pane, shown in Figure 13-1, can assist you with your file creation and retrieval needs. The task pane appears on the right side of the Excel window. If the task pane is not visible, you can choose File α New to open it.

The task pane features several sections that contain useful hyperlinks, which can be identified by their blue color. The following list explains some of the actions that you can accomplish using the task pane:

- **Create a new workbook:** To create a new, blank workbook, click the Blank Workbook hyperlink in the task pane.
- **Base a new workbook on an existing workbook:** To create a new workbook based on an existing workbook, click the Choose Workbook hyperlink to open the New from Existing Workbook dialog box, in which you can navigate to the workbook you want to use. After the workbook is open, a `1` appears at the end of the filename in the title bar to differentiate this new workbook from the workbook on which it is based.
- **Open an existing workbook:** If you simply want to open an existing workbook to make edits, you can click the hyperlinked name in the list that appears in the Open a Workbook section of the task pane. Your four most recently used workbooks appear here by default. If the workbook you want to use does not appear in the list, click the More Workbooks hyperlink to choose your workbook from the Open dialog box.

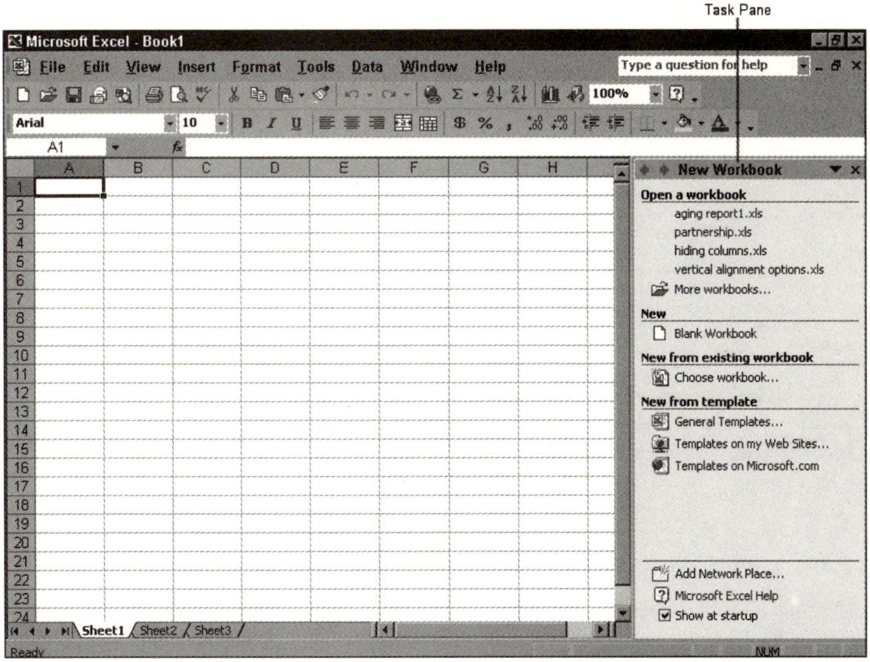

Figure 13-1: The Excel task pane

In the remaining sections of the task pane, you can create workbooks from templates available in Excel, on your Web site, or from the Microsoft Web site. If you want to close the task pane at any time, simply click the Close button (the X) in the upper-right corner of the task pane.

TIP: If you do not want to see the task pane each time you enter Excel, deselect the Show at Startup check box located at the bottom of the task pane.

Saving and closing a workbook

Workbooks and all worksheets contained therein reside only in your computer's memory until they are saved. If you do not save a workbook, it will be erased from memory when you exit Excel. When you are ready to save the workbook, choose File α Save or press Ctrl+S to open the Save As dialog box, shown in Figure 13-2. The first time a workbook file is saved, you choose where the file will reside, what the filename will be, and, if appropriate, in which file type your workbook will be saved. The selections you make initially are assumed at each subsequent save of your workbook. If you later want to save the workbook in a different location or in a different file format, choose File α Save As.

You name your workbook in the File Name drop-down list box. The workbook name you choose should be descriptive of the data contained in the workbook, and as with other Microsoft Windows programs, you are allowed to use spaces and some punctuation as part of the name. For instance, you cannot use slashes or colons in your filenames. If you try to use punctuation that Excel does not permit, when you try to save the file, you are informed that Excel can't use the name you provided.

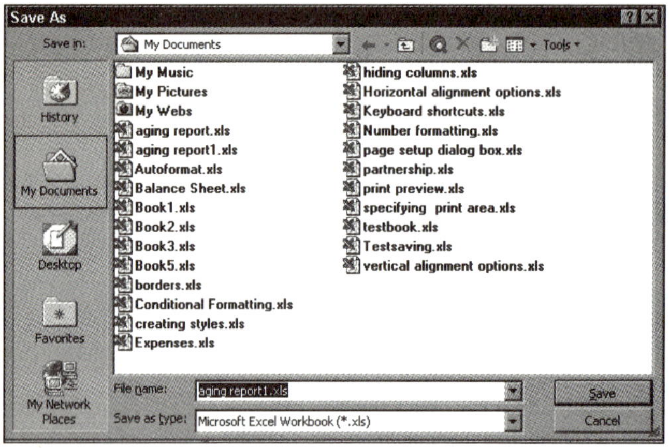

Figure 13-2: The Save As dialog box

When entering your filename, there is no need to type a period or an extension at the end of your filename because Excel automatically adds the period and the appropriate extension for you.

Unless otherwise specified, the workbook file is saved in the version of Excel you are currently using, in our case, Excel 2002. In the legal environment, many reasons exist for saving an Excel file in another format, for instance, if the client you are representing is using an earlier version of Excel or you plan to post your Excel workbook on the Web. If you want the workbook you are saving in a different file format, just click the arrow beside Save as Type and choose the desired file format from the list.

Choosing the default file location

When you enter the Save As dialog box, the Save In drop-down list box displays either your default file location (if this is the first time you are saving during this Excel session) or the last location you selected while saving (if you previously saved any workbooks during this Excel session). To pick a different location, click the down arrow beside the Save In drop-down list box and navigate to the new desired location.

One reason to change your default file location is to save your workbook in a shared network folder to make it available to others. If you want to change the default location for saving, follow these steps:

1. Choose Tools α Options to display the Options dialog box.
2. Click the General tab.
3. In the Default File Location text box, type the new location for saving.
4. Click OK.

Closing the workbook

After your workbook is safely saved, the best practice for closing your workbook is to use the File α Close command. An alternative to accessing this menu is to have a Close button on your toolbar. If you want to add a Close button to your toolbar, you can do so by customizing the toolbar. For information on customizing toolbars, see the section titled "Adding toolbar buttons" later in this chapter.

As you may know from using other Windows programs, you can also use the Close or Close Window controls in the upper-right corner of Excel's program window. Both of these controls look like a capital letter *X*; you can tell them apart by hovering the mouse pointer over the controls until you see a description of the tool. The Close control closes the current workbook and exits Excel. The Close Window control simply closes the current workbook; it is essentially the same as using the File ⇨ Close command.

Working in the Worksheet Window

The worksheet window consists of *cells* that can form up to 65,536 rows and 256 columns on each worksheet. A cell is formed at the intersection of a row and a column. Rows are numbered from 1 through 65,536 along the left side of the worksheet, and each column is named with a letter (A, B, C, and so on) along the top of the worksheet. Cells are identified by a *cell address,* which consists of the column letter and row number. A1, B25, and C80 are all examples of cell addresses. When you click a cell, its address appears in the Name box, which is located directly above the top-leftmost cell in the worksheet.

Changing the default number of worksheets

If you find that you often need more worksheets than Excel provides by default, you can increase the number of worksheets that each new workbook contains. For instance, if you frequently prepare weekly or monthly client billing sheets, you probably have a summary worksheet and a separate worksheet for each client or case.

You can control the number of worksheets each new workbook contains by choosing Tools α Options. In the Options dialog box that appears, click the General tab. From here, you can change the number of worksheets each new workbook contains. Figure 13-3 shows the General tab of the Options dialog box, where you can make this change. You change the number of entries in the Recently Used File List option.

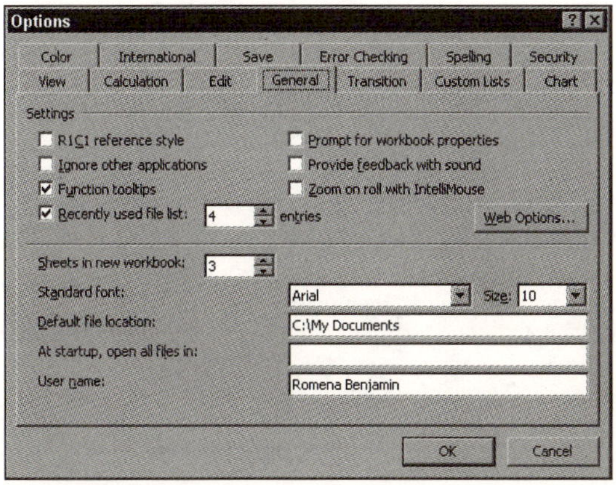

Figure 13-3: The General tab of the Options dialog box

Renaming worksheets

If you want to give your worksheets more descriptive names, you can do so by following these steps:

1. Right-click the tab of the worksheet to be renamed.
2. Choose Rename from the pop-up menu that appears.
3. Type the new name over the existing name and press Enter.

You can also choose Format α Sheet α Rename to change the name of a worksheet.

TIP: Excel 2002 even allows you to add color to your worksheet tabs for easier identification. If you want to add color to a worksheet tab, just right-click the tab and select the Tab color option to pick the desired color from the Format Tab Color dialog box.

NOTE: Renaming and changing the tab color of worksheets are just a couple of worksheet options you can control when you right-click the tab name. You can also insert additional worksheets and delete existing worksheets, as well as move, copy, or select all worksheets.

Inserting and removing worksheets

The only limitation in the number of worksheets a workbook can hold is your computer's virtual memory. Though each new workbook you create contains three worksheets (unless you have changed the default number of worksheets each workbook has), you can add or remove worksheets at will.

To insert a new worksheet, follow these steps:

1. Click the tab of the worksheet *before* which you want to insert the new worksheet.
2. Choose Insert α Worksheet.

The new worksheet is inserted before the active worksheet. New worksheets are always named using a default name determined by Excel, such as Sheet1, Sheet2, Sheet3, and so on. As you add additional worksheets, the number in the sheet name is increased by 1. You can rename the newly inserted worksheet to give it a more descriptive name. See the section titled "Renaming worksheets" earlier in this chapter for the steps to accomplish this task.

To remove unwanted worksheets, follow these steps:

1. Right-click over the worksheet tab that you want to delete. A pop-up menu appears.
2. Choose Delete to delete the worksheet.

Rearranging worksheets

If you want to rearrange the worksheets in a workbook, you can do so by simply dragging a worksheet to a new location. To move a worksheet to a different location, drag the worksheet tab to its new location. As soon as you begin dragging, a graphical representation of the worksheet appears at the tip of the pointer, and a downward arrow appears over the worksheet tabs, as shown in Figure 13-4. The worksheet is relocated to where the downward arrow is pointing.

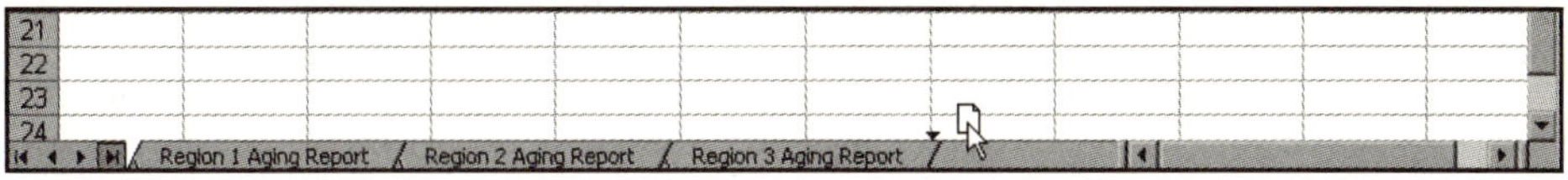

Figure 13-4: The worksheet that is being moved is attached to the pointer, and the downward-pointing arrow is used to position the worksheet in the desired location.

Moving to a different worksheet

You can choose among several techniques when you want to move to another worksheet in the workbook. The following list explains these techniques:

- Click the tab of the worksheet you want to access. This is the most intuitive method and will be available to you most of the time.
- If the worksheet tab that you want is not visible, right-click over the navigational arrows located in the lower-left corner of your worksheet window to pick the worksheet you want to access from a list of all worksheets. For example, in Figure 13-4, the `Region 1 Aging` worksheet is not visible. Figure 13-5 shows the menu that appears when you right-click over the navigational arrows.

You can also use the navigational arrows in the lower-left corner (shown in Figure 13-5) to scroll through the worksheet tabs. The left-pointing arrow with a vertical line on the left is used to move to the first worksheet in the workbook. The right-pointing arrow with the vertical line on the right is used to move to the last worksheet in the workbook. The right and left arrows without vertical lines are used to scroll left or right, one worksheet at a time.

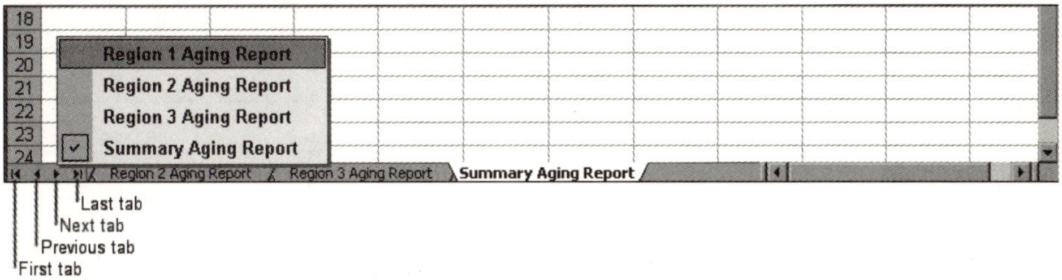

Figure 13-5: Right-click over the navigation arrows to view a list of worksheets, or use the tab navigation buttons to move from worksheet to worksheet.

Navigating within a worksheet

Several scroll bars are available to allow you to easily navigate within a worksheet. The vertical scroll bar on the right of the worksheet window is used to move up or down one row at a time. You can also drag the scroll box to move through multiple rows quickly. You can click the space just above or just below the scroll box when you want to move one window at a time.

TIP: If you are unable to see the horizontal or vertical scroll bars or if you want to hide them, choose Tools α Options and then click the View tab. Here you can select or deselect the horizontal scroll bar and vertical scroll bar Windows options.

The horizontal scroll bar moves the worksheet window to the left or right. This functionality is handy in situations in which all the columns are not visible in the window. You can use the arrows on the horizontal scroll bar to move to the left or right, one column at a time. Like the vertical scroll bar, you can move quickly through multiple columns by dragging the scroll box left or right. To move one window to the left or right, just click the space at the beginning or end of the horizontal scroll bar.

Navigating among cells

To select a cell into which you want to input data, you click a cell to activate it. The name of the cell appears in the Name box on the Formula bar. You can tell which cell is active because it is surrounded by a thick black border. As you add or edit data in your worksheet, you can move to different locations in the worksheet easily and quickly. You can press the Tab key to move to the adjacent horizontal cell to the right, and Shift+Tab moves you to the adjacent horizontal cell to the left. Table 13-1 provides a list of navigation commands that you can use to move from cell to cell using your keyboard.

Table 13-1
Keyboard Navigation Commands

Use This Key...	*...To Move*
Left arrow	One cell to the left
Right arrow	One cell to the right
Up arrow	Up one cell
Down arrow	Down one cell
PgUp	Up one screen
PgDn	Down one screen
Alt+PgUp	Left one screen
Alt+PgDn	Right one screen
Ctrl+Left arrow	Beginning of row or first cell containing data
Ctrl+Right arrow	End of row or last cell containing data
Ctrl+Home	Beginning of worksheet
Ctrl+End	Last row and column containing data

When working with large spreadsheets, you can jump to different locations by choosing Edit α Go To to open the Go To dialog box. In this dialog box, you can specify the cell address to which you want to move. After typing the cell address, click OK to close the dialog box and to relocate to the specified cell.

If you use the Go To feature more than once during any given Excel session, each cell that you go to is displayed in a list the next time you access that dialog box. The cell addresses displayed in the list include a dollar sign ($) before the column letter and before the row number and look like the following:

```
$A$1
```

The $ symbols make the cell address an absolute address. For more information on relative and absolute addresses, see the section titled "Understanding Relative and Absolute Addresses" later in this chapter.

You can revisit a cell by selecting the cell address in the list and clicking OK. Another technique for relocating to a different cell is by typing the cell address in the Name box directly above the top-leftmost cell in the window.

Selecting cells, columns, and rows

To use many of Excel's features, you first select the cells to be affected. After you click a single cell in the worksheet, that cell becomes the *active cell* and receives whatever data you type and any enhancements or attributes you apply. You also click a cell in order to make edits or to copy a cell's contents or to perform some other action, such as formatting. To perform any action on a single cell (or a group of cells), it must first be selected

The following list provides cell-selection techniques for multiple cells (also known as a *range* of cells). After selecting a range of cells, Excel places a bold border around all of the cells in the range, as shown in Figure 13-6.

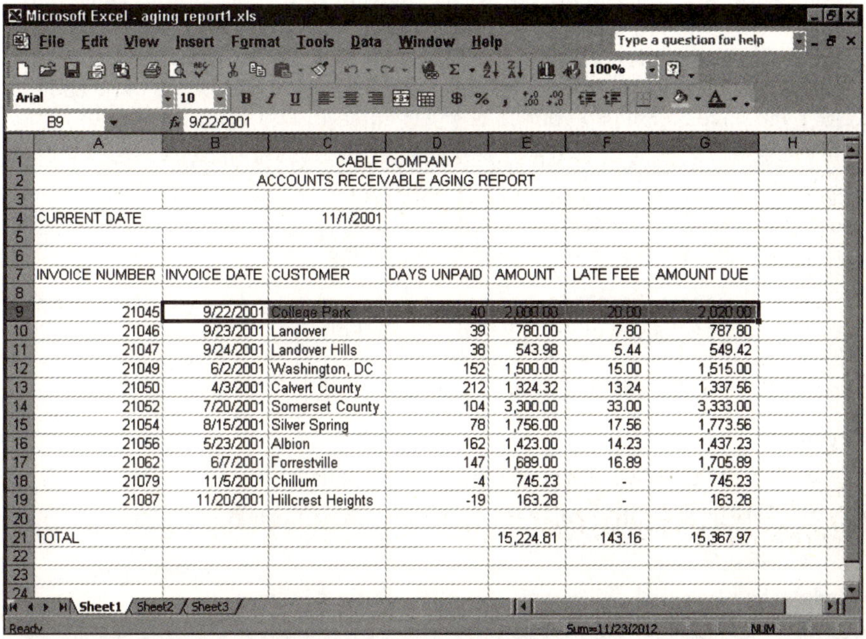

	A	B	C	D	E	F	G	H
1			CABLE COMPANY					
2			ACCOUNTS RECEIVABLE AGING REPORT					
3								
4	CURRENT DATE		11/1/2001					
5								
6								
7	INVOICE NUMBER	INVOICE DATE	CUSTOMER	DAYS UNPAID	AMOUNT	LATE FEE	AMOUNT DUE	
8								
9	21045	9/22/2001	College Park	40	2,000.00	20.00	2,020.00	
10	21046	9/23/2001	Landover	39	780.00	7.80	787.80	
11	21047	9/24/2001	Landover Hills	38	543.98	5.44	549.42	
12	21049	6/2/2001	Washington, DC	152	1,500.00	15.00	1,515.00	
13	21050	4/3/2001	Calvert County	212	1,324.32	13.24	1,337.56	
14	21052	7/20/2001	Somerset County	104	3,300.00	33.00	3,333.00	
15	21054	8/15/2001	Silver Spring	78	1,756.00	17.56	1,773.56	
16	21056	5/23/2001	Albion	162	1,423.00	14.23	1,437.23	
17	21062	6/7/2001	Forrestville	147	1,689.00	16.89	1,705.89	
18	21079	11/5/2001	Chillum	-4	745.23	-	745.23	
19	21087	11/20/2001	Hillcrest Heights	-19	163.28	-	163.28	
20								
21	TOTAL				15,224.81	143.16	15,367.97	
22								
23								
24								

Figure 13-6: A range of selected cells

- **Selecting adjacent cells:** If you want to select multiple adjacent cells, click the first cell, press Shift, and then click the last cell. This action selects the two cells that you click and every cell in between. All selected cells appear shaded except the first cell (which is nonetheless selected, as evidenced by the heavy border that surrounds it). You can also select adjacent cells by simply clicking in the first cell and dragging across the cells you want to select. All cells in the range are shaded except the first cell.
- **Selecting nonadjacent cells:** If you want to select cells that are not adjacent to one another, click the first cell, press Ctrl, and then click each additional cell that you want to select. Using

this technique, every cell is shaded except the last cell that you select (which is nonetheless selected).

- **Selecting columns:** You may want to add number formatting to an entire column of numbers. In this case, you can select the entire column by clicking the column letter.
- **Selecting rows:** If you want to select an entire row, just click the row number, and all cells in that row are selected.

Entering and Editing Data

You can type text, numbers or dates (called *values*), or formulas and functions into an Excel worksheet and easily format or edit that data. This section details how to type and edit data.

Typing text

Excel allows you to add text for any purpose. For instance, text is often used as row or column descriptors, as comments to point out important information about the data or calculations, or as a way of adding clarity to your worksheet. Text can be used for client names, billing addresses, or any of a thousand other purposes. You can use the usual command keys (Backspace, Delete, and so on) to modify your text. After you press Enter, your text is placed in the active cell. If you want to modify the text you just typed after pressing Enter, simply double-click the cell containing the text. Doing so places you in Edit mode. Next, use the arrow keys to position the insertion point and make your edits. After you have completed your edits, press Enter.

As you type, your data appears in the active cell and in the Formula bar (shown in Figure 13-7), and the Cancel and Enter buttons appear in the Formula bar (they look like a red *X* and a green check mark). You can press Enter or click the check to complete your entry and place the data in the active cell, or you can press Esc or click the *X* to cancel your typing.

The Formula bar displays all the text you have typed in a given cell up to 32,767 characters. A cell can only display 1,024 characters. As you add additional text, the Formula bar expands horizontally to display additional lines. When dealing with large amounts of text in a given cell, the Formula bar is a useful option. To use the Formula bar for making edits, follow these steps:

1. Click the cell you want to edit.
2. Click in the Formula bar where the cell's contents are fully displayed.
3. Use the arrows on your keyboard to position the insertion point in the text.
4. Add or remove desired text.
5. After you complete the edits, click the green check mark or press Enter.

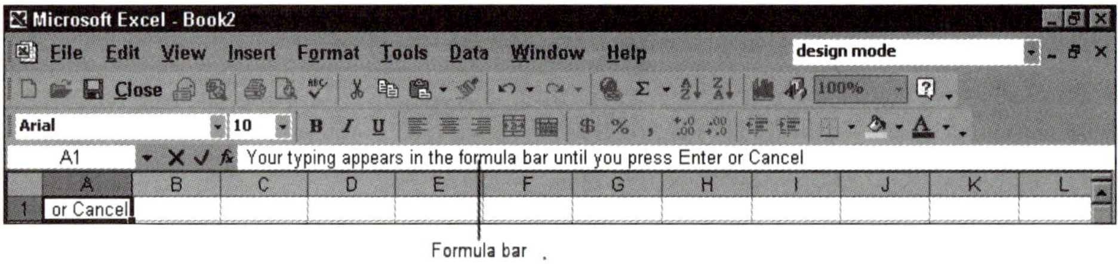

Figure 13-7: The Formula bar

The formatting of your text is based on Excel's defaults unless you specify otherwise. The default font style and size can be viewed by looking at the Formatting toolbar. For instance, in Figure 13-7, the Formatting toolbar shows that the text in the current cell is formatted using the Arial font style and that its size is 10 points. You can apply different formatting at any time by simply using the controls on the Formatting toolbar . You can also apply different formatting to a group of cells by first selecting those cells and then using the Formatting toolbar to change alignment, font size, and font style, to apply borders, and to increase or decrease indents.

The Format Cells dialog box allows you to make fine adjustments to the formatting of the text in your spreadsheet. To display the Format Cells dialog box, follow these steps:

1. Select the cell or cells that you want to format by using one of the methods we present in the section titled "Selecting cells, columns, and rows" earlier in this chapter. The formatting will apply to the selected cells
2. Choose Format α Cells to display the Format Cells dialog box.
3. Use options found on the various tabs of the Format Cells dialog box to customize formats for text. The following provides a brief overview of the purpose of each tab:
    - **Number:** After you first input data in a column, Excel makes an educated guess about what kind of data the column should contain and how you want it formatted. But Excel isn't always correct. This tab is where you can change the format of data displayed in a cell or cells. For example, you may want to display a date, a number with two decimal places, or just plain old text. If the data that you enter doesn't show up the way that you want it to, then you can define custom formats to meet your needs.
    - **Alignment:** On this tab, you can adjust the way in which data is aligned within a cell. The vertical alignment, particularly, is a setting that you may want to look at. This is set by default to vertically position text on the bottom of the cell. You can change the vertical alignment setting to have data appear at the top, at the bottom, or in the center of the cells. The alignment tab also allows you to specify what Excel should do with text if it is too wide to fit within a cell.
    - **Font:** This tab is used to specify the font, size, and attributes of text used to display the contents of a cell. Many of the controls on this tab are duplicated by tools on the Formatting toolbar.
    - **Border:** Excel allows you to place borders around the perimeter of a cell or even diagonally through a cell. This tab is where you specify the types of lines that should be used for cells.
    - **Patterns:** This tab is used to specify the color of a cell, as well as any patterns you want applied to the cell. These settings affect the cell itself, not the characters displayed in the cell. (Character color is specified on the Font tab.)
    - **Protection:** Excel allows you to "protect" information in a cell so that it cannot be changed. How you do this is covered later in this chapter in the section titled "Protecting Cells, Worksheets, and Workbooks."

If you are entering text into a cell, the settings on the Alignment tab should be of particular interest. It is not unusual for your text to be too wide to fit within a cell. If there is nothing in the cell to the right of the text, Excel allows the text to spill over into the adjacent cell or cells. If there is data in the cell to the right of the active cell, all of your text may not be visible, but instead appears truncated. Your text is not lost; it just cannot all be displayed.

Obviously, you can make a column wider to accommodate the width of your text. You do this by double-clicking the vertical line between the column heading of the column you are typing in and the column on the right. The settings in the Alignment tab, however, allow you to specify what Excel should do with text if it is too wide for a column. The Wrap Text check box, if selected, forces Excel to wrap text from one line to another until it all fits within the cell. The row height is affected by this option, as rows are resized so that the text can be displayed. The Shrink to Fit check box, if selected, causes Excel to compress the text in a cell so that all of it will fit within the allotted column width. The font size isn't changed; Excel simply makes each character narrower so that the text fits.

If you intend the text you type to be a heading for a particular worksheet, you may want this text centered across several columns. For this, you can choose Format α Cells, click the Alignment tab, and select the Merge Cells option.

You may also notice that the text you type automatically appears left-justified and is displayed on the bottom of the cell. These are Excel defaults, but you can change them. To change the alignment for your text, you can use the Align Left, Center, or Align Right button on the Formatting toolbar. Or you can make these and other types of formatting changes using the Format α Cells menu. To change the alignment or apply other formatting options, do the following:

1. Click the cell whose format you want to change.
2. Choose the Format α Cells menus.
3. Click the Alignment tab and make the desired changes to the options.

Using these steps, you can change the horizontal alignment or the vertical alignment.

TIP: You can make a formatting change to ensure that your text cells are always treated as text and not as numbers (even if the text cell does contain some numbers now or in the future). Choose Format α Cells and click the Number tab in the dialog box. Next, click the Text category that applies a format to the active cell. If there is a number in the cell when you apply the Text format, it is still treated as a number in calculations by Excel. If you enter a number in the cell after applying the Text format, it is not included in any calculations from that point forward (unless this format is removed).

Typing numbers

Numbers such as integers, decimals, and fractions can be typed in a variety of formats. Numbers appear right-aligned by default as they are typed. Table 13-2 provides categories from which to choose and a description of each.

Table 13-2
Number Types and Their Meanings

Category	*Description*
Number	Numbers appear right-aligned by default. You can control whether the number is formatted using commas, how many decimal places are displayed, and how negative numbers are formatted. The Currency and Accounting formats are recommended for monetary values.
Currency	Displays a monetary value. You control the number of decimal places, the negative

Category	***Description***
	number format, and the appropriate symbol for the type of currency being input. The Accounting format is recommended for the alignment of decimals.
Accounting	Decimals in currency are aligned, and you can control the number of decimal places.
Date	You choose a format from the predefined date formats provided by Excel.
Time	You choose from a list of predefined time formats.
Percentages	This format multiplies the cell value by 100 and displays the result with a percent symbol.
Fractions	You select the fraction format (halfs, quarters,and so on) and the number of digits.
Scientific	You can change the number of decimal places this number will hold.
Text	Cells are considered text cells unless otherwise specified. If the cell already contains a number, it is still used in calculations dependent on it. If you enter a value in the cell later, then the value is ignored in future calculations.
Special	Predefined zip code, phone number, and social security formats are available.
Custom	Design your own number formats based on one of the predefined formats that are available.

When you select a number format on the Number tab of the Format Cells dialog box, additional options appear on the right side of the dialog box. Only the options available for that format are displayed.

TIP: You can tell Excel which direction you want it to move when you press Enter. If, after you type the first number in a column, you press the down arrow, then Excel understands that you are heading downward. After you complete the second number, you can press Enter. Excel obediently moves the active cell to the cell below where you just typed. This technique works when typing across a row as well. After you fill the first cell, just press the right-arrow key. In subsequent cells, press Enter and you are automatically placed in the next cell on the right.

Entering, Modifying, and Auditing Formulas

Formulas perform calculations in a worksheet and are composed of cell references, operators, functions, and constant values. *Cell references* refer to the value of another cell; this cell can be from the active worksheet, a different worksheet, or a different workbook entirely. *Operators* are symbols that perform calculations or comparisons in your worksheet, such as + to add and – to subtract. Excel also provides an array of built-in functions for you to use to perform calculations on your worksheets without the need to manually construct the entire formula. These functions are discussed in the section titled "Using Functions." Finally, you can use constant values in your formulas. *Constant values* are simply numbers, such as 70 and 3.

Formulas always begin with an equal sign (=), which is then followed by the cell references, constant values, and functions that the formula will evaluate, as well as by the operators that tell the formula what to do with them. Because the real power of a spreadsheet is in its ability to refer to the value of other cells (which may in turn contain formulas themselves), cell references are used extensively.

To start a formula, click in the cell that will hold the result and then you type an equal sign. Typing the equal sign tells Excel you are typing a formula (or a function). After you enter the formula, the result of the formula replaces the formula that you typed. When you click the cell containing the result, the formula appears in the Formula bar. Without the equal sign Excel interprets what you type as data to be entered into the cell.

The fx button on the Formula bar leads you to an Insert Function dialog box for use when you do not know which function to use to achieve the desired result. We look more closely at functions in the section titled "Using Functions" later in this chapter.

TIP: You can display all formulas in a worksheet without selecting a particular cell. To view all formulas in a worksheet, press Ctrl+` (the key above the Tab key on the left side of the keyboard).

Using cell addresses and operators in formulas

Two of the most common elements used in creating formulas are cell addresses and operators. At their most basic, cell addresses consist of a column letter and a row number. When Excel sees a cell address in a formula, it replaces the address with the value contained by the cell at that address. Excel also allows you to specify cell ranges, which consist of two cell addresses separated by a specific operator, most often a colon. Ranges represent a group of cells that contain values you want to use in the formula.

In Figure 13-8, for example, the value displayed in cell G9 is the sum of cells E9 and F9 as displayed in the Formula bar. The equal sign (=) tells Excel that this is a formula, the cell references (E9 and F9) direct Excel to calculate the values in those cells, and the mathematical operator (the plus sign) tells Excel to add the values in each of those cells together. The formula looks like this:

```
=E9+F9
```

The above formula adds the contents of cell E9 to the contents of cell F9 (two adjacent cells), though you are not limited to referring to just two cells, nor do they have to reside close to one another. You can include in your formulas cell addresses from the current worksheet, from another worksheet in the same workbook, or to cells in another workbook altogether. You can also include many more cell references in your formula than were included in the above example. (As you will discover in the "Using Functions" section later in this chapter, Excel includes many functions that can save you time in entering formulas.)

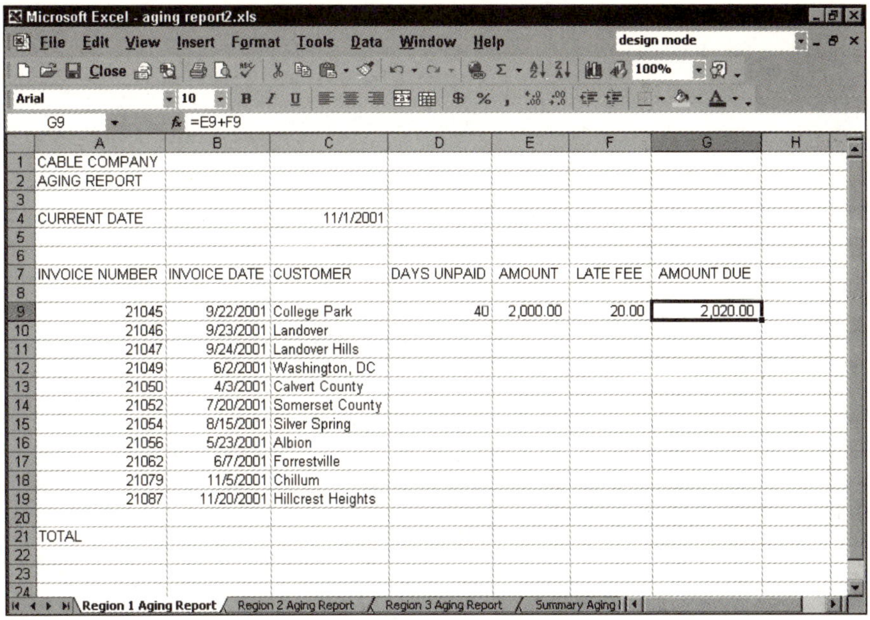

Figure 13-8: The contents of cells E9 and F9 are added together. The result appears in cell G9.

You can choose from three types of operators in your formulas — mathematical, logical, or range operators. Table 13-3 shows the symbol and a description of each type of operator

Table 13-3
Operators

Use These Symbols To...	*...Perform This Type of Function*
Mathematical Operators	
^	Exponentiate
*	Multiply
/	Divide
+	Add
–	Subtract
Logical Operators	
&	Concatenate
=	Equal to
<	Less than
<=	Less than or equal to
>	Greater than

continues

Table 13-3 continued

Use These Symbols To...	***...Perform This Type of Function***
>	Greater than or equal to
<>	Not equal to
Range Operators	
:	Indicates a range
,	Indicates the combining of two ranges
Space (press the spacebar)	Indicates the intersection of two ranges

You can also include parentheses in your formulas to tell Excel the order in which you want the calculation to be performed. For instance, if you want to add the values in two adjacent cells and then divide the result by 2, you would construct your formula as follows:

```
=(A5+B5)/2
```

Excel solves the part of the problem in parentheses before solving the portion outside the parentheses. When you do not use parentheses, Excel solves problems in the following order:

- Exponential calculations
- Multiplication and division (working from left to right)
- Addition and subtraction (working from left to right)

Consider the formula `=B12+C12/A10`. Excel first divides C12 by A10 and then adds the result to B12. To add the first two cells first and then divide, you would have to write it like this: `=(B12+C12)/A10`.

Formulas can contain up to 1,024 characters, including all cell references, all operators, and characters such as parentheses () or other symbols.

Typing cell references

You can choose from several techniques to include cell references in your formulas. Each technique is discussed below.

To type a formula manually, do the following:

1. Click the cell where the result will appear, making it the active cell.
2. Type the equal sign (=) followed by the cell reference `E9`.
3. Type the plus sign (+) as the operator, followed by the cell reference `F9`.

Selecting cell references

Rather than type a long string of cell references, you can select the cells for inclusion in your formula. You should consider this technique when your formulas include multiple cell references, to speed up typing time.

Here is an example where you might want to select the cell references instead of typing them:

```
=A1+B1+C1+D1+E1+F1+G1+H1
```

Here is how to select the cell references for inclusion in a formula:

1. Click the cell where you want the results to appear, making it the active cell.
2. Type the equal sign (=).
3. Click the first cell to be included in the formula (`A1` in our example). As soon as you click it, Excel places a moving dashed line around the cell and includes the cell reference in the Formula bar.
4. Type the desired operator. In our example, you would type the plus sign (+).
5. Click the next cell to be included in the formula. Excel places the cell reference after the operator you typed in Step 4.
6. Type the desired operator (another plus sign, in our example).
7. Repeat Steps 5 and 6 for each cell that you want to add.
8. After you type the last cell reference that you want to include in your formula, press Enter or click the check mark button on the Formula bar.

TIP: If you receive a `#Value` error message in the results cell, you may have forgotten to place operators between the cell references.

Copying formulas

After you create a formula, you can copy it from one cell to other cells in your worksheet. For example, if you were developing the worksheet shown in Figure 13-9, it makes sense to copy the formula from cell G9 to the cells in G10 through G19. Why? Because the same formula is used in each instance to calculate the amount due. To copy formulas to another cell in the current worksheet, perform these steps:

1. Right-click the cell containing the formula you want to copy, and select Copy from the menu that appears. Excel surrounds the copied cell with a moving dashed border.
2. Click the copied cell and drag down all the cells to receive the copy (or, if appropriate, across the desired number of cells). Excel shades all but the first cell in the selection and includes a thick bold border around all selected cells except the first cell, which still has the dashed border, as shown in Figure 13-9.
3. Press Enter to place the copied formula into the selected cells.

When copying formulas to adjacent cells, you may notice that the cell references refer to different rows or columns. This is because Excel changes the formula to refer to the context of where you are pasting the formula. This may sound a bit confusing, but think about it for a moment: The original formula in cell G9 is `=E9+F9`. When you copy the formula to cell G10, then Excel can figure out that you now want the formula to refer to E10 and F10. (You learn more about how Excel modifies copied cell references in the section titled "Understanding Relative and Absolute References.")

This is because the formula that is being copied directs Excel to calculate the values that are present in the cells to the left of the formula, which means whatever cell references are to the left of the cell containing the formula. If you copy this formula down, the instructions are the same but are applied to data on different rows. Excel automatically changes the cell references to reflect the formula's new location.

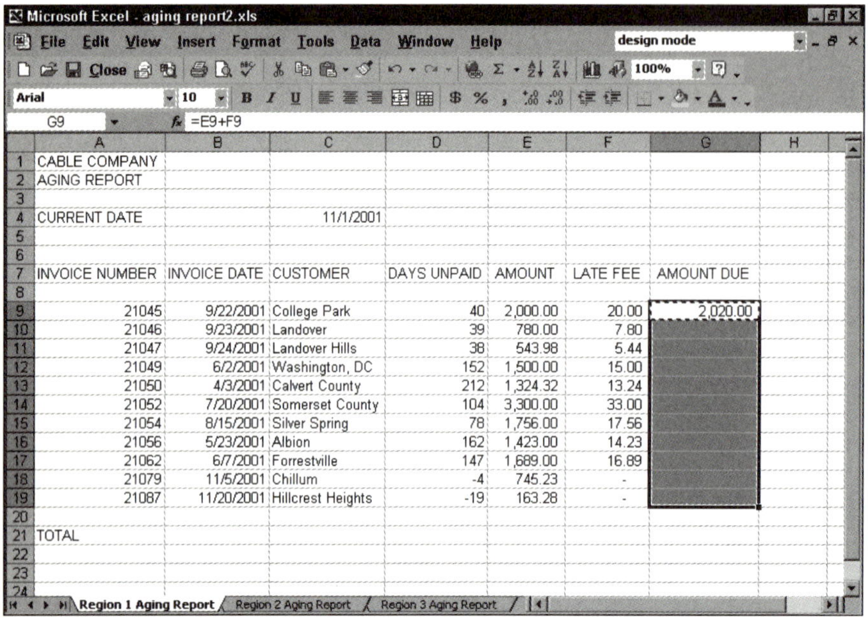

Figure 13-9: Copying the formulas from cell G9 to the shaded cells

To copy a formula down to a single cell or multiple cells below the cell containing the formula, perform these steps:

1. Click the cell containing the formula to make it the active cell.
2. A square black box called a *fill handle* appears in the lower-right corner of the active cell. As you hover the mouse pointer over the fill handle, the pointer changes to a black cross. Click, hold, and drag the fill handle down to select as many cells as you want to receive a copy of the formula. As you drag downward, the selected cells are surrounded by a gray border.
3. After you select the cell or range of cells to receive the copy of the formula, release the mouse button to drop a copy of the formula in each of the selected cells.

When dropping the copied formula into the selected cells, Excel gives you a choice of exactly what is pasted into those cells. You are presented with an Auto Fill Options submenu with three choices:

- **Copy cells:** The cells are copied, pure and simple.
- **Fill Formatting Only:** The formatting is copied, with nothing else.
- **Fill Without Formatting:** Only the contents of the cells are copied, without any formatting.

Understanding range names

A vertical or horizontal group of adjacent cells is considered to be a range of cells. A range of cells can be assigned a range name, and range names can be included in formulas. You can see the value of using a range name when you want to perform calculations on an entire column or row of values or on values that exist in numerous cells. Range names can also be used in formulas that include functions such as the `Sum` function. Which would you rather type? Look at the following example:

```
=A1+A2+A3+A4+A5+A6+A7+A8+A9+A10+A11+A12+A13
```

Or would you rather type

```
=Sum(capital_assets)
```

As you see in the above example, typing multiple cell addresses together with the appropriate operators can be a burdensome task if the values you plan to use in your formula exist in many cells. To ease the typing burden, you can assign range names to a row or column of numbers and include those range names in your formulas. One caveat to using range names is that they are always absolute, which is problematic if you plan to copy formulas to new cells in the worksheet. (See the next section for information on relative and absolute references.)

TIP: Range names cannot contain spaces. To use multiple words in range names, you can use the underscore character in place of spaces between the words.

You can also include column and row labels in your formulas. Suppose that column A contains first-quarter filing fees for a communications client and you have labeled that column *Filing Fees*. To make the column label automatically become *Filing_Fees*, you can turn on an option in Excel. To do so, choose Tools α Options and then click the Calculation tab. Select the Accept Labels in Formula option.

Understanding Relative and Absolute References

Earlier in this chapter you learned a little about how to put together cell addresses in a formula. For instance, the following includes two cell references, E9 and F9:

```
=E9+F9
```

As you will learn later in this chapter (see the section titled "Using Functions"), you can also use cell addresses in functions. The following is a simple example using the `SUM` function:

```
=SUM(G3:G9)
```

In both of these instances, the cell addresses are considered relative references. This simply means that Excel considers the address to be relative to the cell in which the formula or function is stored. This consideration by Excel becomes critical when copying or moving the formula or function to another cell. With relative references, Excel is free to modify the cell address to refer to the same relative position in the target cell.

To help understand this better, assume for a moment that the formula `=E9+F9` is stored in cell G9. Remember that Excel considers the cell addresses to be relative references. That means that Excel looks at the value two cells to the left of G9 and adds it to the value one cell to the left of G9. The result of the formula is then displayed in cell G9. If this formula is copied to another cell, perhaps to cell R13, then the same relative addresses are used, resulting in a formula of `=P13+Q13`, which are, respectively, two cells and one cell to the left of the target cell (R13).

The only time that Excel doesn't consider a cell address relative is when you add a dollar sign prefix to either the column or row designation in the address. For instance, consider the following formula:

```
=$E9+F$9
```

In the first cell address, the column (E) is designated as absolute, whereas in the second cell address the row (9) is considered absolute. If this formula were copied to cell R13, the result would be the following:

```
=$E13+Q$9
```

Notice that the column (E) and the row (9) were not changed by Excel when copying; they were treated as absolute and therefore are not subject to changing.

Understanding the difference between relative and absolute references is critical in Excel. Designating a portion of an address as absolute can help you make sure that your formulas work just as you intend, even when you copy or move them from one location to another.

Copying and Moving Data

Excel data can be moved or copied, and the steps to accomplish these tasks are similar. When you move or copy Excel data, Windows places the data on the Clipboard, from which you can paste it into a new location. Copied data remains in the original cell, while moved data is removed or *cut* from its original location. Data that is cut or moved can be pasted into the existing spreadsheet, to a different spreadsheet or workbook, or to a different application altogether.

Copying data

As with all Microsoft programs, you can choose from several techniques for copying data to the Clipboard. To copy data to the Windows Clipboard, click the cell to be copied and use one of the following techniques:

- Click the cell to be copied and press Ctrl+C.
- Click the cell to be copied and choose Edit α Copy.
- Click the cell to be copied and click the Copy button on the Standard toolbar.

Whichever technique you use, the result is the appearance of a moving dashed line that surrounds the cell you selected. This moving dashed line means that you can paste the material as many times as you like, as long as the moving dashed line surrounds the cell. To remove the moving dashed line, press Esc or select another group of cells. Assuming that the task pane is visible, you will also see the data you copied on the Clipboard in the task pane.

To retrieve copied data, click the target location for the copied data and use one of the following techniques to paste the data:

- Press Ctrl+V.
- Choose Edit α Paste.
- Click the Paste button on the Standard toolbar.

Another technique for copying is to use the drag-and-drop feature. There are two types of drag-and-drop editing in Excel: actually copying data and taking advantage of Excel's AutoFill feature. The availability of both options is controlled by the Allow Cell Drag and Drop check box that is available when you choose Tools ⇨ Options and then click the Edit tab.

You can use the drag-and-drop feature to copy cells in the following manner:

1. Select the cell you want to copy. A thick black border should appear around the cell.

2. Move the mouse pointer so that it is over the border. The mouse pointer changes to a four-headed arrow.
3. Hold down the Ctrl key as you click and drag the cell to a new location.

The other related feature for copying is referred to as *AutoFill*. To use AutoFill you click the fill handle in the lower-right corner of the cell you are copying and drag down to the cell below or to the cell on the right. When you release the mouse button, the data is copied to the selected cells.

When you have copied data, the status bar at the bottom of the Excel window displays a message to select the destination and press Enter or choose Paste.

Moving data

Your Excel data can be moved from one location to another for a better page layout, or as with copying, to another worksheet in the current workbook or to another workbook entirely.

As is the case with copying data, you can choose from several methods to move data around:

- **Keyboard:** Select the cell to cut, press Ctrl+X, select the cell in which to paste, and press Ctrl+V.
- **Menu:** Select the cell to cut, choose Edit α Cut, select the cell in which to paste, and choose Edit α Paste.
- **Toolbar:** Select the cell to cut, click the Cut button (it looks like scissors) on the Standard toolbar, select the cell in which to paste, and click the Paste button (it looks like a clipboard and scrap) from the Standard toolbar.

All cell contents are relocated to the new cell or cells. No other paste options are available when cutting and pasting moved data. For more information on paste options, see the following section.

You can also use Excel's drag-and-drop editing feature to move cells, as introduced in the previous section. The only difference is that you don't need to hold down the Ctrl key as you are dragging the cell — just drag it to where you want it!

CAUTION: Care should be taken when moving data, particularly if you have referred to the cell containing that data elsewhere in the worksheet. For instance, a formula may no longer produce the desired results if the values on which the formula was based have moved.

Pasting data with Paste options

When you copy a cell or multiple cells, you are copying the entire contents, including formatting, formulas, and the actual data. When you are ready to paste your data, you have a choice as to what is actually pasted in the new location. Excel gives you paste options for this added control, and these options are available by choosing Edit α Paste and clicking Paste Special or by right-clicking the target cell and choosing Paste Special. Additionally, when you are ready to paste the copied text, you can click the down-arrow just to the right of the Paste tool on the Standard toolbar. The options displayed are detailed in Table 13-4.

Table 13-4
Different Ways to Paste Information

Paste Option	*What It Does*
Formulas	Only the formulas are pasted.
Values	The actual data values as they exist in the cells are pasted.
No Borders	Everything in the source cell is pasted except the border.
Transpose	Rows becomes columns, and vice versa.
Paste Link	Pastes the copied data and makes a connection between the target cell and the source cell so that whenever one of these cells is edited, both cells receive the update.
Paste Special	Leads you to additional paste options.

TIP: If you do not see the Paste Options icon on the Standard toolbar, choose Tools α Options and click the Edit tab. Select the the Show Paste Options Button option.

Using Functions

Functions are predefined formulas that you can use to perform calculations in your worksheet. Hundreds of functions are organized into categories for your convenience. Functions consist of a function name, an open parenthesis, arguments specific to the function being used, and a close parenthesis. For instance, functions such as the `Sum` function are available to use when adding a column or row of numbers. In Figure 13-10 you can see in the Formula bar that the `Sum` function is used to produce the results in cell E21.

To use a function, you begin your formula as always with an equal sign (=) followed by the function name and an open parenthesis, followed by the required arguments, and ending with a close parenthesis. Not all functions require arguments, but many do. The information that is typed inside the parentheses is called an *argument,* and the arguments vary, depending on the function you are using. For instance, the function `Today()` is an example of a function that does not need an argument; the function name is followed by an open and close parenthesis:

```
=Today()
```

Entering this function into a cell returns the date for today. You can easily see why an argument is not necessary. However, if you want to enter a specific date (other than today's date) in a cell, you need to supply the arguments required by that function, separating each argument with a comma as shown in the following example:

```
=Date(year,month,day)
```

An argument is a variable (usually more than one) that is required by the function in order to return the values that you want. In the above example, the year, month, and day are all arguments or variables that the `Date` function requires in order to perform the calculations.

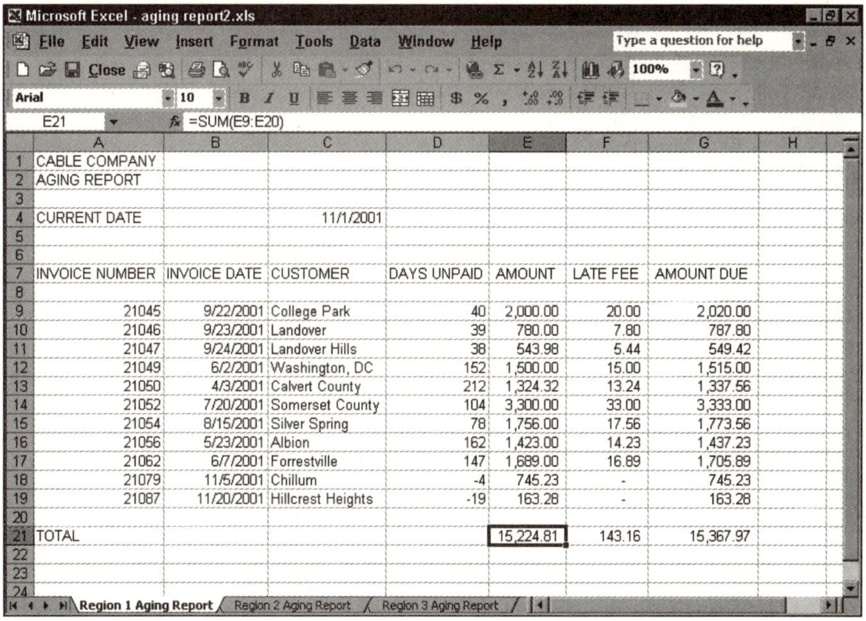

Figure 13-10: The Sum function is used in cell E21 to total all the values in column E.

Fortunately, you do not have to memorize the arguments needed for each function; you do not even need to memorize the list of available functions. You can explain what you are trying to do and let Excel search for and return a list of recommended built-in functions that you can use. Try to be as descriptive as possible so that Excel can recommend the best functions for your needs (you can, however, type as little as one word for your explanation). To let Excel make recommendations to you, click the fx (Paste Function) button on the Formula bar, which automatically places an equal sign in the formula and opens the Insert Function dialog box, shown in Figure 13-11.

Next, type your explanation and click Go. Excel returns a list of recommended functions you can use, based on your description of the problem you are trying to solve. For instance, Figure 13-11 shows the list of functions Excel recommends if you type *totals* as your description. In Figure 13-12, you notice that you receive a different list of recommended functions for the description *totals numbers*.

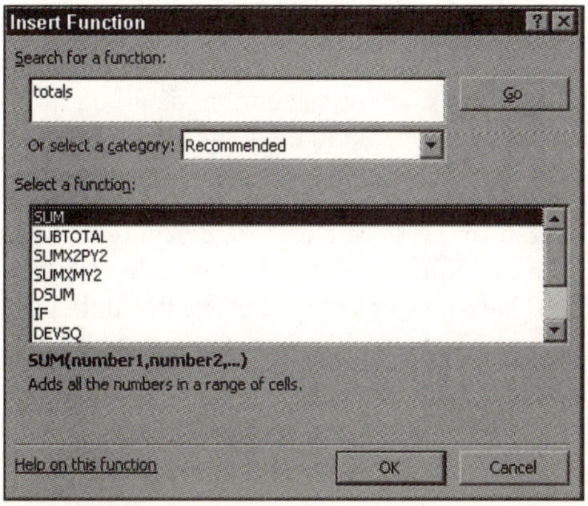

Figure 13-11: The Insert Function dialog box

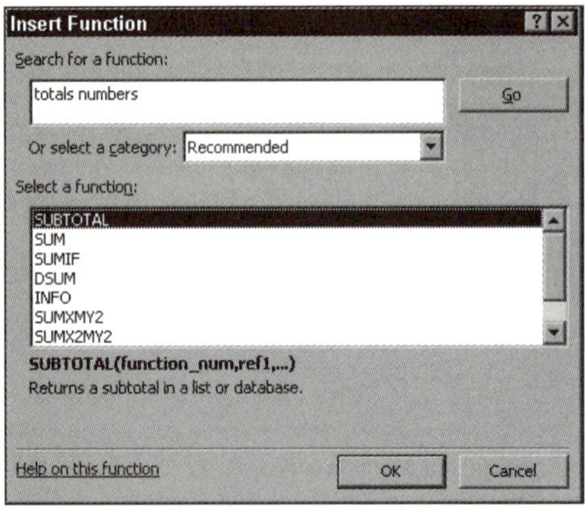

Figure 13-12: Excel can provide better results if you provide better search terms.

NOTE: Excel arranges its built-in functions into categories by data type, which makes it easy for you to locate the right function. The list of functions Excel recommends may comprise functions from different categories. However, you can specify the function category you want Excel to use when making its recommendations. For instance, if you want a function for finding an average, you will get different function recommendations when you click the Statistical and Financial categories. This is why it is important for you to be as descriptive as possible in the statement of the problem.

After you select a function in the Insert Function dialog box, Excel displays the function's *syntax,* which refers to the way that the formula should be typed, beginning with the function name followed by the required arguments. Excel also provides a description of the calculation to be performed. To select a function, double-click its name in the Select a Function window. Doing so opens the Function Arguments dialog box.

Excel displays fields for each argument required by the function at the top of the Function Arguments dialog box. In each of these fields, you type the appropriate value, cell reference(s), or text on which the function will do its work. As you type the values for each of the arguments, Excel immediately displays the result of both the function and the formula. As you view the results, you can edit the values at any time — in case you make a mistake. Beneath the arguments in the Function Arguments dialog box is a description of the function and each of its arguments. If you need more detail on the function you are about to use, click the Help on This Function link located in the lower-left corner of the dialog box to receive context-sensitive help.

Turning again to the Region 1 Aging worksheet, if the number of days a region is late paying its bill is 30 or more, we want to figure a 10-percent late fee in column F. You can use the `IF` function for this formula. First, click in cell F9, which will receive the result. Next, `=IF(` is typed in the Formula bar. Next, click the fx button (the Insert Function button) to open the Function Arguments dialog box. Here you can see more clearly where each value should appear in the argument. Figure 13-13 shows the Function Arguments dialog box with all the arguments completed.

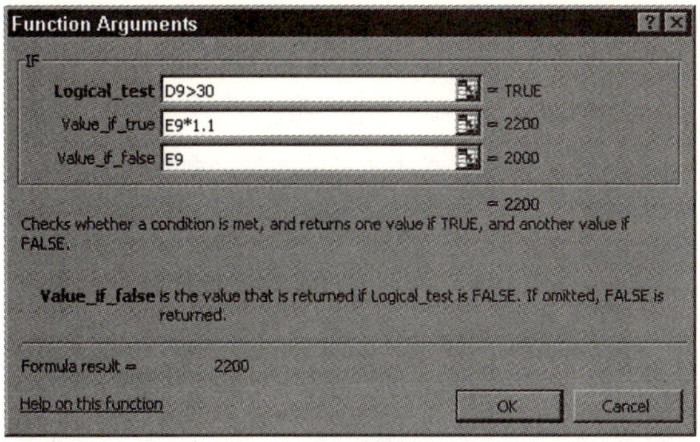

Figure 13-13: The Function Arguments dialog box with all arguments completed

---

TIP: If you commit errors while typing or selecting the values for the arguments, Excel displays an error in red to the right of the erroneous argument. As soon as the correction is made, the error message is replaced by the result. This is one of the reasons the Insert Function feature is so helpful.

Inserting and Deleting Cells, Rows, and Columns

You have been asked to provide data for the years '98, '99, and '00, and upon completion, you realize that you need to add another column of data for the year '97. This is easily accomplished by adding a new column to your spreadsheet. Or you finish your data entry, and you later learn you need to add a new row. At other times, you may find that you no longer need a column or row of data, and you then want to remove the unnecessary rows or columns. Again, this is easily accomplished.

Rows and columns can be added to or deleted from your spreadsheet at any time by following a few basic steps. Whenever you insert rows, Excel inserts the rows above the row containing the cell pointer. Whenever you insert columns, Excel inserts the new column to the left of the column containing the cell pointer. Conveniently, when deleting rows or columns, Excel closes the gaps left after the deletion.

Going back to the first example, we want to add a new column to the left of the '98 data (which is the first column). Click in the column containing the '98 data (in the example this would be column A). It is not necessary to select the entire column. Then choose Insert α Columns. A new column A appears immediately to the left of the column you first clicked. The old column A then becomes column B. Using this technique, you can insert one column at a time.

TIP: To insert more than one column or row at a time, you must select the same number of columns or rows you want to add; then choose Insert α Rows or Insert α Columns. You can also insert cells in your worksheet and control whether existing cells are shifted down or to the right. To do this, choose Insert α Cells. Then determine whether you want existing cells shifted down or to the right.

To delete a row or column, you must choose Edit α Delete; otherwise, you are deleting only the contents of the cells.

> **Do I cut, delete, or clear?**
>
> Cutting removes Excel data from the active cell and places it on the Windows Clipboard for pasting to a different location. You cut information by using the keyboard, menu, or toolbar options described in the section "Moving data." Delete is used for purposes of deleting the entire cell contents, including formats, formulas, and comments. You can delete single or multiple cells, rows, or columns by choosing Edit α Delete. Alternatively, you use the Clear feature when you want more control over exactly what is removed from your cells. For instance, you can clear everything from a cell (comments, contents, and formats), leaving an empty cell, by choosing Edit α Clear.

Protecting Cells, Worksheets, and Workbooks

In the legal industry, Excel data can be used to create exhibits, appendices, and other documentation on your client's behalf, and you often need to share this data with others in your firm. For this reason, we strongly encourage you to consider protecting your Excel data prior to sharing it with your colleagues. Inadvertent or unintentional changes made to the structure or contents of your workbook could result in lost billable time. Excel provides you with a number of options for protecting your data — including protecting the smallest element (a cell) to the largest (an entire workbook). In this section, we explore the protection options available to you.

Protecting cells

Excel allows you to protect the contents of your worksheet from modification. This is accomplished through a two-step process. First, you make sure that the cells you want protected are locked. Second, you instruct Excel to protect the worksheet. When this is done, information in the locked cells cannot be changed, overwritten, or deleted.

All the cells in a worksheet are locked by default, so you first need to unlock the cells. To unlock cells so that they can be edited after the worksheet is protected, follow these steps:

1. Click the worksheet tab that contains the cells you want unlocked.
2. Select the cells to be unlocked. To select multiple noncontiguous cells, hold down the Ctrl key as you click each cell.
3. Choose Format α Cells. The Format Cells dialog box appears.
4. Click the Protection tab.
5. Click to deselect the cell-locking option.

Now, to protect the worksheet and control the types of modifications that can be made, follow these steps:

1. Choose Tools α Protection and select Protect Sheet. The Protect Sheet dialog box appears, as shown in Figure 13-14.

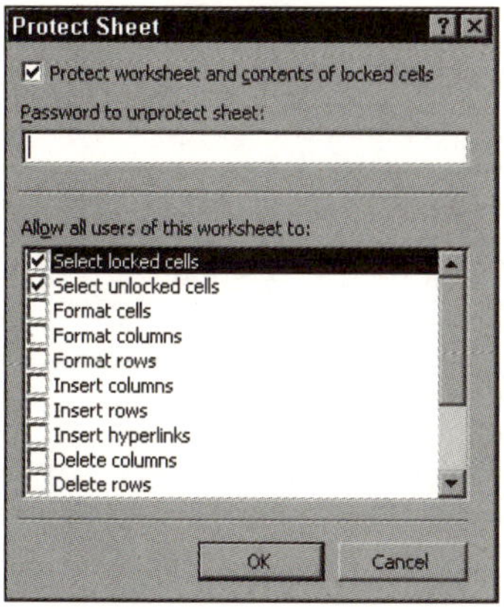

Figure 13-14: The Protect Sheet dialog box

2. You may want others to provide a password before they can unprotect a worksheet or make further changes to the types of protection applied; however, this is an optional feature.
3. Decide the type of modifications you will allow others to make. You can allow or disallow formatting, insertions, deletions, or changes to objects or scenarios. Placing a check in any of the boxes tells Excel that these are the types of changes you are allowing others to make to unlocked cells. Table 13-5 provides a list of available options.

Table 13-5
Permissions in a Locked Worksheet

Option	*What It Allows*
Select locked cells	Allows changes to the contents of locked cells.
Select unlocked cells	Allows changes to the contents of unlocked cells.
Format cells	Allows changes to alignment, number formats, text attributes, and border styles.
Format columns	Allows changes to column widths. Allows others to hide or unhide columns.
Format rows	Allows changes to row height. Allows others to hide or unhide rows.
Insert column	Allows insertion of columns in the worksheet.
Insert rows	Allows insertion of rows in the worksheet.
Insert hyperlinks	Allows insertion of hyperlinks to files or Web pages.
Delete columns	Allows deletion of the column structure and its contents.
Delete rows	Allows deletion of entire rows, including the structure and its contents.
Sort	Allows others to sort cell contents.

continues

Table 13-5 continued

Option	***What It Allows***
Use AutoFiller	Allows data to be extracted based on specific criteria.
Use PivotTable reports	Allows reports based on cells in the worksheet.
Edit objects	Allow users to make changes to objects on the worksheet.
Edit scenarios	Allow edits to be made to cells containing variable information.

NOTE: You can give access to unlocked cells without giving access to locked cells; but you cannot give access to locked cells without also giving access to unlocked cells.

Hiding and unhiding a worksheet

Excel allows you to specify whether a worksheet should be visible. You can *hide* a specific worksheet from view, effectively making it invisible. To hide a worksheet, follow these steps:

1. Click the tab of the worksheet you want to hide.
2. Choose Format α Sheet α Hide. The worksheet is hidden from view.

It is important to understand that hiding a worksheet is not enough to prevent unwanted changes. Unhiding the sheet is simple, unless the workbook is protected (as we show you in the next section). To unhide a previously hidden worksheet, just follow these steps:

1. Choose the Format α Sheet α Unhide. The Unhide Sheet dialog box opens.
2. Click the worksheet tab to be made visible and click OK.

Protecting a workbook

When you protect a workbook, you can prevent others from inserting, removing, unhiding, or renaming worksheets and from repositioning or resizing workbook windows. When you try to insert worksheets or unhide worksheets in a workbook that is protected, you will find these options are grayed out. In addition, the options for inserting, deleting, moving, copying, or renaming worksheets are also grayed out. The only way to access these options is to unprotect the workbook, which may require the use of a password if one was used when protecting it.

NOTE: Protecting your workbook alone does not prevent others from viewing the workbook or changing the contents or formulas. You will need to lock down cells and protect the worksheet for that kind of protection.

Using Find and Replace

Excel's Find and Replace features locate text or numbers and offer you several options to assist you in narrowing your search. You can access Find and Replace by choosing Edit α Find. The dialog box that opens displays the following options for narrowing your search (you may have to click the Options button to see the options).

- **What to search:** Choose worksheet or workbook
- **How to search:** Choose rows or columns
- **Where to look:** Locate the search string within cells containing formulas, comments, or values

---

TIP: You can limit your search to a range of cells by selecting the cells before you choose Edit α Find.

In addition to the listed options, you can specify that you only want to find your search string in cells formatted a certain way. Additionally, you can match the exact capitalization in your search criteria or match the cell contents exactly. All options are available whether you are finding or replacing.

To search for particular text, choose Edit α Find to open the Find and Replace dialog box. Click the Find tab to locate only; click the Replace tab to replace the found text with different text. In either case, click the Options button to expand the dialog box in order to access the additional options available for narrowing your search. Figure 13-15 shows the Find and Replace dialog box with the Replace tab selected and expanded to include available options.

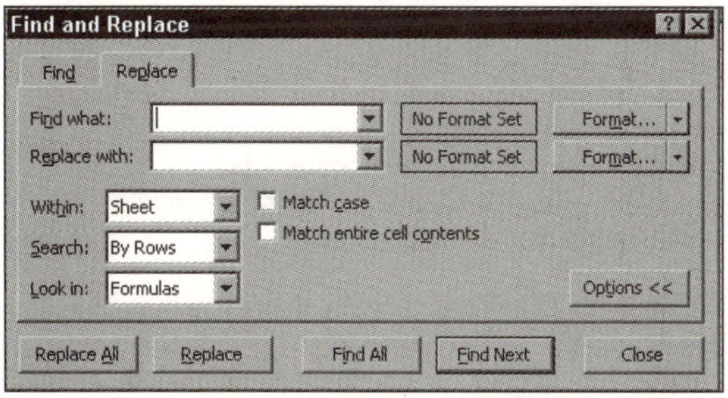

Figure 13-15: Click the Options button to reveal additional options for limiting your search.

To use Find or Replace, perform these steps:

1. Choose Edit α Find.
2. Click the Find tab to locate only; click the Replace tab to substitute different text or numbers.
3. Type your search criteria in the Find What box. If you are replacing data, type the replacement criteria in the Replace With box.
4. Specify a cell format by clicking the Format drop-down list on the right side of the dialog box. This leads you to the Find Format dialog box. You can specify any format that can be added to a cell or range of cells.

Excel allows you to include the question mark (?) and asterisk (*) wildcard characters at either the beginning or end of your search string (but not in the middle). Wildcard characters are helpful if what you are searching for is in a location other than the beginning of the cell. If you believe the search string is located in the middle of the cell, precede it with an asterisk. If you believe what you are trying to locate is not at the beginning of a cell, then place an asterisk in front of your search string. The asterisk takes the place of the cell contents that come before your search string. The asterisk is also helpful if what you are looking for was not typed consistently but you want to find all occurrences of it, regardless. For instance, if you want to find all occurrences of the word *Excel*, regardless of whether it is typed as *Excel XP*, *Excel 2002* or *Excel*, you would type your search string in the following manner:

```
Excel*
```

This tells Excel to look for all occurrences of Excel in the beginning of the cell, followed by an undetermined number of characters. If the search string is typed this way:

```
Excel?
```

Excel looks for all occurrences of the word *Excel* followed by at least one character. It will not, however, find occurrences of Excel that are followed by nothing.

After you specify the text to search for (and, if applicable, what to replace it with), the format you are looking for, and the options you want, you are ready to begin your search. Table 13-6 provides a description of the choices you have after the search string is located.

Table 13-6
Find and Replace Choices

Choices	*What Excel Does*
Find Choices	
Find Next	Finds the next occurrence of the search string. (Hold down the Shift key and click Find Next to see the previous occurrence.) After finding the last cell, clicking Find Next causes Excel to cycle back through all of the occurrences from the beginning.
Find All	Expands the Find and Replace dialog box to display the search results. Search results include the workbook and worksheet names, cell addresses (expressed as absolute), and values in which your search string was found. If the search string was located in a formula, the formula is also displayed.
Replace Choices	
Replace	Replaces the string you searched for with the replacement text. Moves to the next occurrence of the search string and waits for you to choose Replace or Replace All.
Replace All	Replaces automatically all occurrences of the search string with the replacement string.

When Excel has located the last occurrence of the search string a message displays, stating that no further occurrences have been found and displaying the total number of replacements made.

Checking Spelling

You correct spelling errors in Excel in the same manner as you would with other Microsoft applications. When you are ready to check your spelling, choose Tools α Spelling, and Excel checks the spelling from the active cell forward. Excel checks the spelling of each word, and if it encounters a word that is not in its dictionary, it stops on that word and displays a Spelling dialog box that presents you with several options for handling the misspelling.

In the Spelling dialog box, a list of possible replacements for the misspelled word appears. You can replace the incorrect word with one from the list by highlighting the correct word and clicking the Change button, which changes the misspelled word this time only, or you can click the Change All button to replace all occurrences of the misspelled word with the replacement word. You can also choose to Ignore Once (disregard the word this time) or to Ignore All (disregard all the words on the current worksheet spelled this way during this spell check session only).

As mentioned above, Excel checks the spelling from the active cell in the current worksheet forward. To specify a row(s) or column(s) to be checked, simply select all the rows and columns prior to using the spell feature. A single cell is spell checked by simply clicking that cell and choosing Tools α Spelling. Excel only checks the spelling of that cell's contents.

Adding words to a custom dictionary

Chances are, at some point you will want to add words such as proper nouns to the custom dictionary provided by Excel or to a dictionary you create with a more descriptive name. In either case, words added to a dictionary are no longer treated as misspelled words.

To add a word to a custom dictionary, follow these steps:

1. Choose Tools α Spelling.
2. When Excel stops on a word you want to add to the dictionary, click the Add to Dictionary button on the right side of the Spelling dialog box.

To create your own dictionary, follow these steps:

1. Choose Tools α Spelling.
2. When Excel stops on a word that you want to add to a dictionary you create, click the Options button in the lower-left corner of the Spelling dialog box to display the Options dialog box, shown in Figure 13-16.
3. Type a descriptive name for your new dictionary in the Add Words to Text box. It is not necessary for you to add the *.DIC extension. Excel does this for you.
4. Click OK.

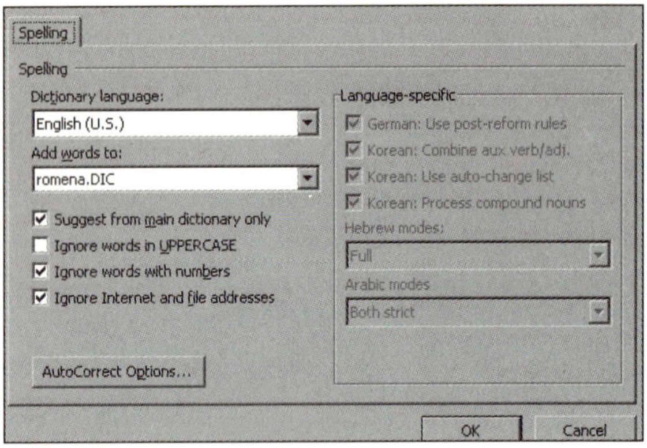

Figure 13-16: The Spelling dialog box

Once created, all custom dictionaries are available whenever you use Excel. You can create as many dictionaries as your computer's memory allows. The CUSTOM.DIC and any dictionaries you create are not worksheet-specific and are available whenever you check spelling. To specify which custom dictionary you want to use, click the arrow beside the Add Words To text box, highlight the name of the dictionary name, and click OK.

TIP: If you inadvertently add a word to one of the custom dictionaries or add a word that was misspelled, you can correct the spelling or remove the word altogether by editing the appropriate *.dic file. To locate the *.dic file, choose the Windows Search feature. You can use Notepad to edit any dictionaries you find.

TIP: You can also create a custom dictionary outside Excel. The only requirement is that the file is saved as a text file with a filename that includes the *.dic extension.

Setting AutoCorrect options

Another feature of Microsoft Office programs is AutoCorrect, which automatically corrects words as you type. If you find that you consistently misspell a word in the same manner over and over, you can add the word to the AutoCorrect list so that the correctly spelled word automatically replaces the misspelled word as you type.

To add a word to AutoCorrect during the spell check, follow these steps:

1. Choose Tools α Spelling.
2. When Excel stops on the misspelled word that you want to add to the AutoCorrect list, click the AutoCorrect button on the right side of the Spelling dialog box. Excel adds the word and then moves on to the next misspelled word.

The AutoCorrect feature provides several options for making corrections automatically and can be customized based on your individual preference. To access these options during spell check, perform these steps:

1. Choose Tools α Spelling. The Spelling dialog box opens.
2. Click the Options button to open the Options dialog box.
3. Click AutoCorrect Options in the lower-left corner of the Options dialog box.

Three tabs, representing categories of corrections that Excel can handle automatically for you, are visible in the AutoCorrect Options dialog box, shown in Figure 13-17. Excel's AutoCorrect options are similar to those found in Word, but there are a few differences, as follows:

- Only one option is available in Excel's AutoFormat as You Type tab: the option to replace as you type Internet and network paths with hyperlinks.
- Fewer data recognizers are available in Excel than in Word.
- Fewer smart tag recognizers are available in Excel than in Word.

Figure 13-18 shows the Smart Tags tab of the AutoCorrect dialog box. Enabling smart tags can be a nice feature, particularly if you share the workbook with others. If you want the person you share your workbook with to be able to see smart tags you create, you can turn the Smart Tags feature on by choosing the Label Data with Smart Tags check box. When users access your spreadsheet, they are able to view smart tags you create, regardless of whether they have the feature enabled.

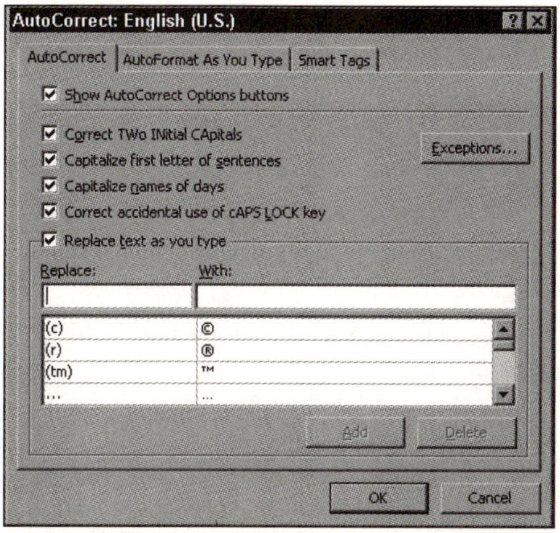

Figure 13-17: The AutoCorrect options in the AutoCorrect dialog box

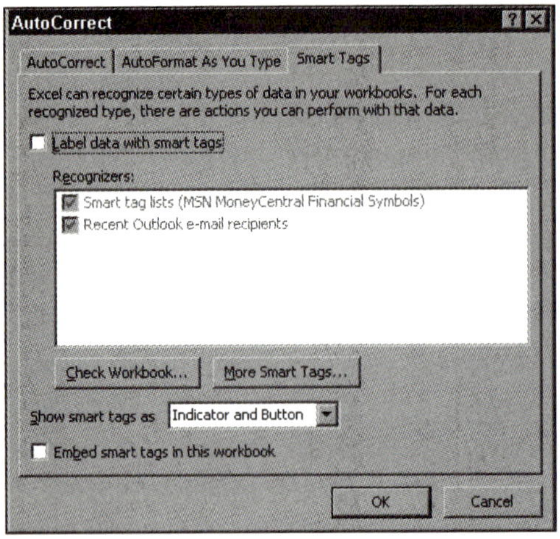

Figure 13-18: The smart tag options in the AutoCorrect dialog box

---

CROSS REFERENCE: For more on the Smart Tags feature, see Chapter 3, in the Word section.

NOTE: If you choose to have Excel automatically correct certain errors in typing for you, you may want to consider removing some that Excel provides from the list. For instance, since legal documents often include Rule numbers and citations that frequently contain *(c)*, chances are, you do not want that automatically changed to ©.

These are the same kinds of automatic corrections we discussed in the Word section of the book. Once again, legal professionals may prefer to handle the corrections themselves.

Sharing Your Legal Workbooks with Others

Legal professionals and those who assist them can collaborate on Excel workbooks if they are stored in a location on the network that can be accessed by each person. If you originally saved your workbook to a disk or to the hard drive, it must be resaved to the shared folder on the network before others can make edits. As the originator of the workbook that is being shared, you can allow multiple users to edit your workbooks while retaining control over which edits actually get made. After all edits are made by all users, you can decide later to use Excel's Merge feature to combine all of the changes into a single workbook, or you can use the Track Changes feature to accept or reject changes on an edit-by-edit basis.

To share your workbook with others, you can choose Tools α Share Workbook to allow users to make simultaneous changes and to set options for how often you want to see the changes, who can make them, and how you want conflicts resolved. The steps that follow show you how to do this.

NOTE: It is important to note that Excel provides you with some protection for your shared workbook. After a workbook is designated as *shared,* changes cannot be made to workbook and worksheet protection. If you have not taken steps to protect your data and workbook structure prior to sharing the workbook, the workbook is vulnerable to unintended and unwanted changes. Before sharing your workbook with colleagues, take a moment to reread the section "Protecting Cells, Worksheets, and Workbooks."

1. Open the workbook you want to share.
2. Choose Tools α Share Workbook. The Share Workbook dialog box opens, with two tabs —Editing and Advanced — shown in Figure 13-19.
3. Click the Editing tab and check the box labeled Allow Changes by More Than One User at the Same Time.
4. Click the Advanced tab and set the following options:
   - **Track Changes:** Choose whether to keep the change history and specify how long it should be kept.
   - **Update Changes:** Determine how often you want to see changes, and whether you see only your changes or the other users' changes as well.
   - **Conflicting Changes between Users:** This gives you the option of resolving conflicts in changes. When you are reviewing the workbook, Excel will give you an opportunity to resolve conflicts between a change you are about to make and a change that was already made. You get to decide which change actually takes place. If you select The Changes Being Saved Win setting, Excel will not notify you that you are about to override changes already made.
   - **Include in Personal View:** As owner or originator of the workbook, you can save any Page Setup and Print Preview print settings you have established, and they will be in effect each time you open the shared workbook.

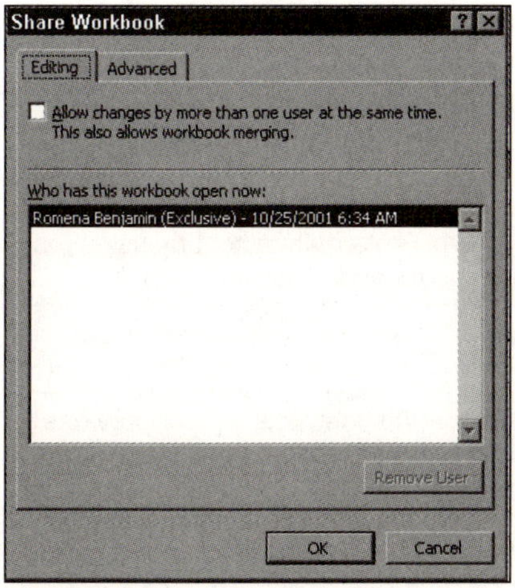

Figure 13-19: The Share Workbook dialog box

Customizing Toolbars and Menus

As with other Office applications, Excel allows you to easily customize the program's interface. The major program elements that are commonly customized are toolbars and menus. The following sections explain the types of customization you can do.

Adding toolbars and removing toolbars from view

Toolbars and menus can be customized in a variety of ways. You can customize a toolbar by adding it or removing it from view and by adding or removing buttons to it. You can also relocate toolbars to the top, bottom, and either side of the worksheet. The Standard and Formatting toolbars are usually open by default, and the menu bar is visible at the top of the Excel window. (The menu bar is a form of toolbar, except that it cannot be moved.) Several toolbars are available for your use in Excel. Table 13-7 lists each of the toolbars available in Excel.

Table 13-7
Excel Toolbars

Toolbar	*What You Can Do with It*
Borders	Buttons for drawing and erasing lines and for choosing a line style and a line color.
Chart	Buttons for choosing a chart style or chart type and applying formatting to charts.
Control Toolbox	Provides tools for use when creating forms. Text boxes and spin boxes can be added to your forms with the aid of these tools.
Drawing	Shapes, pictures, organizational charts, and more, can be added and formatted using these tools.
Exit Design Mode	Exits you from the design mode.
External Data	Provides tools for working with data that originated outside Excel.
Forms	Tools for creating and designing your forms.
Formula Auditing	Tools to help you find errors in formulas.
Picture	Tools provided for inserting, formatting, adding color, and rotating pictures. Buttons are also available for controlling the brightness and contrast.
PivotTable	Tools are available for creating a PivotTable manually or by using the Chart Wizard, which also enables you to display or hide details.
Protection	Provides buttons for use when protecting single cells, a worksheet, or an entire workbook.
Reviewing	When collaborating with others on a worksheet, this toolbar provides buttons for inserting and managing comments, creating Outlook tasks, and using Track Changes.
Task Pane	Opens a separate window on the right side of your Excel screen. Contains hyperlinks for opening existing workbooks and creating new workbooks. You can also create and manage network folders using this pane.

Toolbar	*What You Can Do with It*
Text to Speech	Tools for reading back to you data you have entered.
Visual Basic	Provides tools for designing automated routines using Visual Basic.
Watch Window	Provides tools for watching a formula and ultimate result taking shape even when all the cells are not visible. Useful for viewing formulas in selected cells or entire worksheets.
Web	Includes tools for adding data to the Web or using data from the Web.
Word Art	Create eye-catching wording in your worksheet using these tools.

To add toolbars or remove toolbars from view, follow these steps:

1. Right-click over the toolbar area, and a list of available toolbars appears. (Those toolbars that are already part of your view have a check in front of the name.)
2. Click the name of the toolbar you want to add to your view, or click a toolbar with a check to remove it from your view.

Adding toolbar buttons

You can customize your toolbars (including the menu bar) by adding additional commands. To add commands to a toolbar, follow these steps:

1. Add the toolbar you are customizing to your view.
2. Right-click over the toolbar area to display the list of available toolbars.
3. Choose Customize to open the Customize dialog box.
4. On the left side of the Customize dialog box is a list of categories of available commands. Select the category containing the command you want to add. Once a category is chosen, a list of available commands for that category displays on the right.
5. Drag the command to the toolbar you are customizing. This process automatically attaches the command button to the tip of your pointer, and a + symbol is attached to the bottom of the pointer. (An *X* replaces the + symbol if Excel thinks that you are placing the button in a prohibited area.) When the pointer is over the toolbar a bold I-beam indicates where the new command button will be placed. While the button is attached to your pointer, drag the button up to the target toolbar and to the desired location. After you have determined where the new button will reside, release the mouse button. Figure 13-20 shows that the Close button is added to the Standard toolbar between the Save and E-mail buttons.

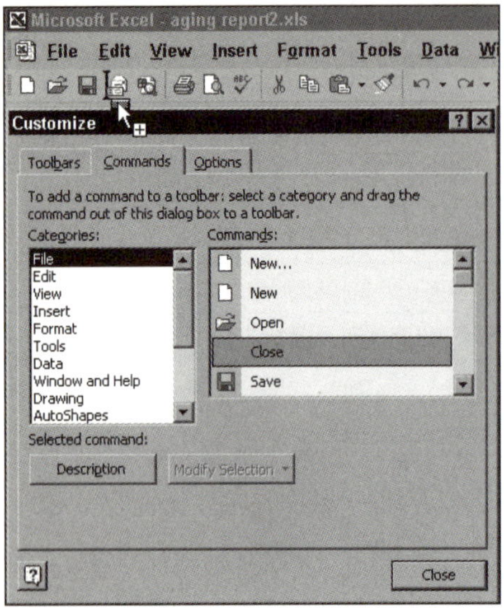

Figure 13-20: Drag the desired commands from the Customize dialog box up to the toolbar.

Removing toolbar buttons

You can easily remove a button from a toolbar after you open the Customize dialog box. First, add to your view the toolbar that you are customizing. (Choose View ⇨ Toolbars and then choose the toolbar to view.) As with adding toolbars, right-click over the toolbar area and choose Customize. This dialog box must be open to remove buttons from your toolbar, even though you do not actually use the dialog box to remove the button. Now, drag the button you want to remove down and off the toolbar.

Relocating toolbars

Toolbars (all except the menu bar) can be moved to the left, right, top, or bottom of your worksheet window. You can relocate a toolbar by aiming your pointer at the faint, gray vertical line that appears on the left side of the toolbar until the pointer changes to a four-way pointer. Next, drag the toolbar to the desired location.

Creating your own toolbar

Creating a customized toolbar that contains the features you use most often is easy. Here are the steps:

1. Right-click over the toolbar area.
2. Choose Customize.
3. Click the Toolbars tab and click New. Type the desired name for your new toolbar; then click OK. Your new toolbar appears in the list of toolbars with a check before it and in the worksheet area on the right.
4. Click the Commands tab.
5. Choose the category containing the commands you want to add.

6. Drag the command buttons to your new toolbar.
7. Close the Customize dialog box.
8. Click the title bar to drag your new toolbar to the desired location.

Customizing menus

The menu bar found at the top of the Excel window contains various categories of commands and features. You can add to or remove commands from the menu bar almost in the same manner as you did when customizing a toolbar. Instead of dragging the desired commands to the toolbar, drag the button up to the desired menu. Doing so opens so lets you situate the button in the exact location.

Sample Legal Workbooks

We have provided some examples of legal worksheets that may be useful in your practice. You can find the actual spreadsheets on the CD-ROM that accompanies this book.

- **Allocation of charges:** This worksheet is an allocation of charges on four projects to a client (see Figure 13-21). Projects A and B were joint projects with another client. The dollars are the fees and charges on the project for the respective month. YYYY was allocated 50 percent of the charges on projects A and B, and 100 percent on C and D. It's a very simple example, but the methodology can be used in more complicated situations.

  Replace the sample numbers given with your own. The Allocation column contains formulas for calculating the percentages of the Total column. The lower portion of the worksheet contains absolute references to the values found in the Allocation column. This worksheet was contributed by Joyce Gwadz, a partner with Dow, Lohnes & Albertson.

- **Section 1031 Calculations – Exchanges of Multiple Properties:** This is an example of the gain calculations necessary in a like-kind exchange of multiple properties under section 1031 of the Code. This worksheet was contributed by Linda Fritts, a partner with Dow, Lohnes & Albertson. This worksheet is intended to print on legal-sized paper, but a portion of the worksheet can be seen in Figure 13-22.

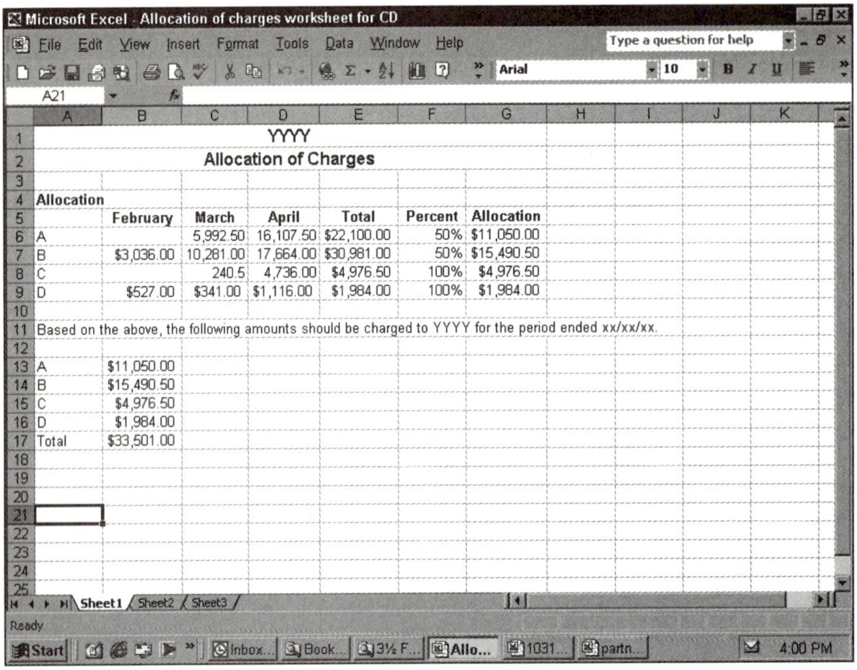

			YYYY			
		Allocation of Charges				
Allocation						
	February	March	April	Total	Percent	Allocation
A		5,992.50	16,107.50	$22,100.00	50%	$11,050.00
B	$3,036.00	10,281.00	17,664.00	$30,981.00	50%	$15,490.50
C		240.5	4,736.00	$4,976.50	100%	$4,976.50
D	$527.00	$341.00	$1,116.00	$1,984.00	100%	$1,984.00

Based on the above, the following amounts should be charged to YYYY for the period ended xx/xx/xx.

A	$11,050.00
B	$15,490.50
C	$4,976.50
D	$1,984.00
Total	$33,501.00

Figure 13-21: A portion of the Allocation of Charges worksheet

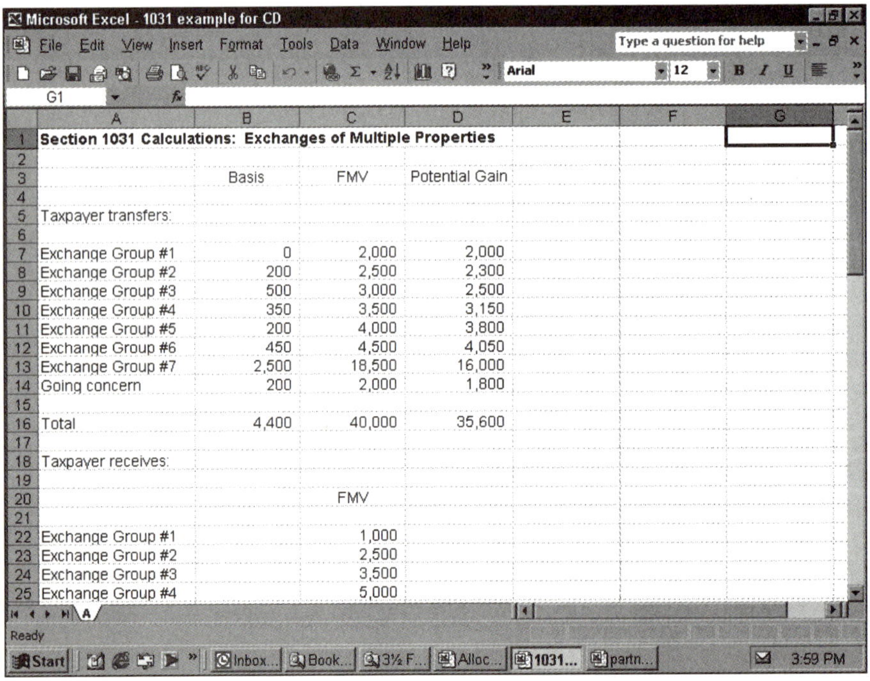

Section 1031 Calculations: Exchanges of Multiple Properties

	Basis	FMV	Potential Gain
Taxpayer transfers:			
Exchange Group #1	0	2,000	2,000
Exchange Group #2	200	2,500	2,300
Exchange Group #3	500	3,000	2,500
Exchange Group #4	350	3,500	3,150
Exchange Group #5	200	4,000	3,800
Exchange Group #6	450	4,500	4,050
Exchange Group #7	2,500	18,500	16,000
Going concern	200	2,000	1,800
Total	4,400	40,000	35,600
Taxpayer receives:			
		FMV	
Exchange Group #1		1,000	
Exchange Group #2		2,500	
Exchange Group #3		3,500	
Exchange Group #4		5,000	

Figure 13-22: A portion of the Section 1031 Calculations worksheet

Summary

This chapter provided a crash course in the basics of Excel. If you are already familiar with other Office applications, you probably breezed right through the techniques presented here. There are differences, however, as there should be for a program with Excel's focus. In this chapter you learned

- What workbooks are and how to use them
- How to navigate through a worksheet
- The proper ways to close and save a workbook
- Different ways you can enter and edit data
- How to move and copy data
- Ways to change the structure of workbooks by inserting and deleting cells, rows, and columns
- The power behind formulas and functions
- How to find and replace information in a worksheet
- How to use Excel's spell checker
- Easy ways to share workbooks with others at your firm

In the next chapter, you learn about formatting techniques that will help you improve the readability and effectiveness of your Excel worksheets.

Chapter 14

Formatting Workbooks

In This Chapter

- ♦ Changing row height and column width
- ♦ Changing alignment
- ♦ Using the Merge and Center feature
- ♦ Hiding columns, rows, and gridlines
- ♦ Applying styled font formats
- ♦ Applying borders, patterns, and colors
- ♦ Working with number, date, and time formats
- ♦ Using the AutoFormat feature
- ♦ Using conditional and custom formats

In a law office, content definitely takes precedence over appearance, but taking some time to work on the look of your spreadsheets can increase their readability and therefore their effectiveness. Adding formatting allows you to (a) differentiate parts of your spreadsheet, such as making row and column headings stand out from the data that they label, (b) direct the reader's attention to cells containing the results of calculations such as subtotals and grand totals, and (c) change the formatting of certain cells when particular conditions are met, by using Excel's conditional formatting feature.

This chapter covers techniques that you can employ to increase the understandability of your Excel worksheets through the application of a bit of judicious formatting.

Changing Row Height and Column Width

Row height and column width are two of the formatting features that you will use most often. *Row height* controls the distance between the top and bottom of the row. By default, Excel rows accommodate a row height for a font size of approximately 12 points. (A *point* is a typographical term that is approximately 1/72 of an inch. Thus, 12 points is approximately 1/6 of an inch.) As data is typed into a worksheet, Excel self-adjusts the row height to be tall enough to accommodate the largest point size of the font you are using in that row. *Column width,* the distance between the left and right borders of a particular column, is measured in characters. In addition, Excel adjusts the column width to accommodate numbers.

You can adjust the height of rows and columns for a variety of reasons. For example, you may want to

- ♦ Increase the row height of all the rows in a very large worksheet to add whitespace at the top of the row, thus making the worksheet easier to read.

- Increase the column width to accommodate a longer number. When you have a number that is too long for the cell, a #### error message is placed in that cell instead of the number you typed. If you increase the column width, the #### error message is replaced with the number you typed.
- As we explain in Chapter 13, "Working with Workbooks," when you exceed the width of a column and adjacent cells are blank, Excel spans your characters across several columns on the screen, when in reality your text is only in a single cell. So you may want to increase the column width so that it is more obvious that the text is in a single cell.

NOTE: Changes made to row height or column width affect every cell in the row or column.

You can choose from several techniques for changing the row height and column width measurements. You can type a measurement for a row or column to exert precise control, adjust the sizes by dragging your mouse, or adjust the size to fit existing content.

Adjusting row height and column width exactly

To change the row height to an exact measurement, follow these steps.

1. Highlight a single cell in the row that you want to adjust. To make this change on multiple rows, you click to select the row number and drag down the desired number of rows.
2. Choose Format α Row α Height to display the Row Height dialog box.
3. Type the desired measurement in points, from 0 to 409; then click OK. The change immediately takes effect, resulting in a taller row.

In a similar manner, you can change the column width to an exact measurement. Just follow these steps:

1. Click in a cell within the column that you want to change — as with row height, the entire column will be affected. (To change the width of multiple columns, click and drag across the column letters of all the columns you want to change.)
2. Choose Format α Column α Width to open the Column Width dialog box.
3. Type the exact measurement you want for your column(s). The measurement you enter represents the number of digits that can be viewed at the current default font size.

Adjusting row and column size with your mouse

Sometimes you don't know exactly how tall or wide you want your column to be, and "eyeballing" the size is easier. If you prefer to make row height or column width changes without specifying a particular measurement, you can do so by dragging your mouse. Here are some pointers:

- **Resize a row:** Click the line between the row numbers, hold the mouse button down, and drag up or down to resize a row.
- **Resize a column:** Click the line between the column letters, hold the mouse button down, and drag left or right to resize a column.

NOTE: As you change the row height or the column width by dragging the mouse, the measurement you achieve appears in a gray box above the mouse pointer as you drag.

Adjusting row and column size to fit content

If you want the column width to fit the cell contents in a single cell, double-click the line between the column you want to adjust and the adjacent column. Excel automatically adjusts the column width to accommodate the length of the cell contents. A similar technique can be used to change the row height of a *blank* row back to the default, which is 12.75.

NOTE: Another format, *text wrapping,* also has an effect on row height. Text wrapping allows text to wrap to a new line by doubling the height of the existing row. Although text wrapping is applied on a cell-by-cell basis, adding this format affects the entire row. Text wrapping occurs only within the cells to which it is applied. Text does not wrap within cells and ranges of cells that do not have the text wrapping option applied, even though space is sufficient for text wrapping to occur. For this reason, you often want to select an entire row or column before applying text wrapping to the cells. For more information on the text-wrapping feature, see "Wrapping text," later in this chapter.

Changing Alignment

If you want to change the vertical or horizontal positioning of your data within a cell or group of cells, you can change the alignment options for the cells. Data entered into a cell can be aligned between the cell borders (top, bottom, left, or right) in a variety of ways. Horizontal alignment controls how the data is positioned in the cell from the left to the right cell borders. Vertical alignment is the position of the data from the top cell border to the bottom cell border.

Horizontal alignment

The horizontal alignment type in use by default is General, meaning that unless otherwise specified, Excel applies the following defaults:

- **Text alignment:** Text is aligned on the left side of the cell.
- **Number alignment:** Numbers are right-aligned in the cell.
- **Error alignment:** Errors (such as the #### value that tells you that the column width needs to be increased) appear centered.

You can make changes to horizontal alignment by using several buttons on the Formatting toolbar, shown in Figure 14-1 and described in the following list:

- **Align Left**: Characters begin at the edge of the cell. This is the default alignment for text.
- **Center:** Characters are centered within the column width. This is useful for centering column headings.
- **Align Right:** This positions data against the right cell border. This is the default alignment for numbers.
- **Merge and Center:** This button enables you to distribute and center existing data across multiple rows, which is very useful when you want to give a spreadsheet a title.

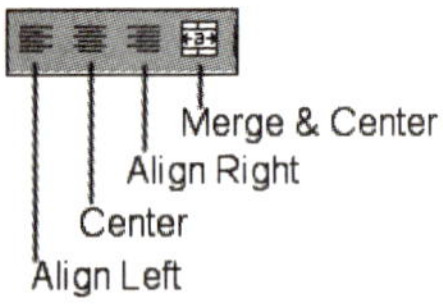

Figure 14-1: **The h**orizontal alignment choices available on the Formatting toolbar

Two additional alignment choices that come in handy are the Increase Indent and Decrease Indent buttons, shown in Figure 14-2. The Increase Indent button is useful when you want to show a hierarchy in your headings or subheadings. Increase Indent positions your data approximately one character away from the left margin each time that you click the button. The Decrease Indent button moves the data to the left one character at a time.

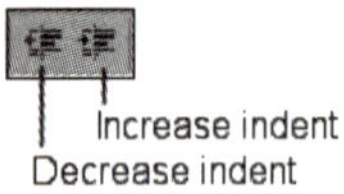

Figure 14-2: The Increase Indent and Decrease Indent buttons found on the Formatting toolbar

Figure 14-3 shows each of the horizontal alignment choices mentioned above.

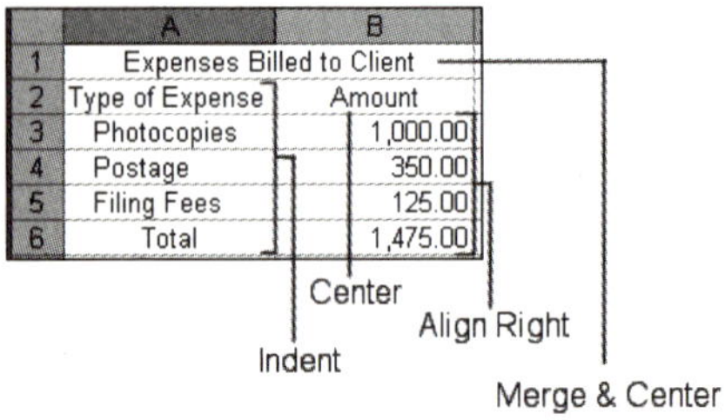

Figure 14-3: The horizontal alignment choices

When you revisit a cell in which you have changed the horizontal alignment, Excel places a border around the Formatting toolbar alignment button in use for that cell. For example, when you revisit a cell in which the Merge and Center alignment was used, a thin black border surrounds both the Merge and Center alignment buttons on the Formatting toolbar, shown in Figure 14-4. To remove an alignment option you have used, just select the cell or cells and click the alignment you want to remove.

Figure 14-4: A thin black border surrounds the Merge and Center buttons when a cell containing these formats is highlighted.

Additional horizontal alignment options are available when you choose Format α Cells to open the Format Cells dialog box. Below is a brief description of the horizontal alignment options not found on the Formatting toolbar. Figure 14-5 shows the drop-down list of horizontal alignment options available.

- ♦ **Fill:** Repeats data in a single cell or across selected cells.
- ♦ **Justify:** Multiline text is evenly aligned on the right, except for short last lines that are left-aligned.

- **Center across Selection:** This is an easy way to break up a lengthy string of text into multiple lines that are centered. If you use this option, you do not have to merge the cells before centering.
- **Distributed Indent:** Multiline data is indented a specific amount and evenly aligned on both sides. Short lines are centered. Cell height increases proportionately so that all text is visible.

NOTE: When using the Center across Selection option, the adjacent cells must be empty.

These horizontal alignment options can be applied to a single cell or to a cell range.

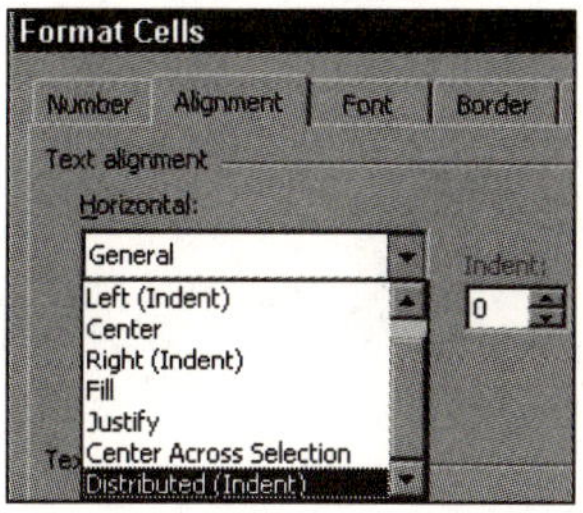

Figure 14-5: The horizontal alignment options

Vertical alignment

Vertical alignment is the position of data from the top to the bottom of a cell. The default vertical alignment is Bottom, which means that the data is closest to the bottom cell border. Other vertical alignment options include aligning the text in the center of the cell so that an equal amount of whitespace is placed above and below the data and aligning the text at the top of the cell, meaning that more whitespace is below the data. One reason you may want to change the vertical alignment from the default is to more evenly distribute the whitespace after increasing the row height. You may also want to change the vertical alignment for column headings so that they are more easily distinguishable from the data that they describe.

You can change the vertical alignment of a single cell or a cell range by first selecting the cells and then choosing Format α Cells. Figure 14-6 shows the effects of vertical alignment, and the following list explains each of the vertical alignment options:

- **Top:** Data is situated closest to the top of the cell.
- **Bottom (default alignment):** Data is situated closest to the bottom of the cell.
- **Center:** Data is situated in the middle of the cell.
- **Justify:** Multiple lines of data are evenly spread out between the top and bottom of the cell.
- **Distributed:** Multiple lines of data are evenly distributed between the top and bottom of the cell.

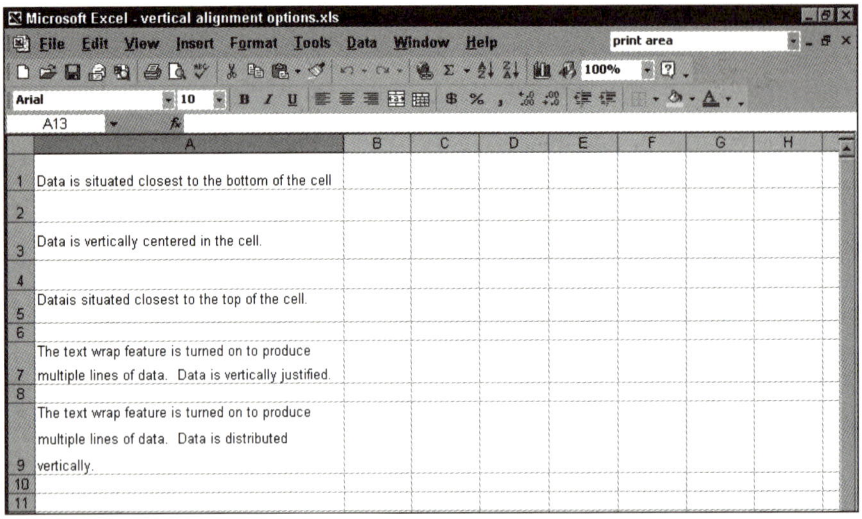

Figure 14-6: Sample data formatted with vertical alignment options

Wrapping text

Excel allows you to enter text into a cell just as easily as you can enter numbers and dates. Formatting text can be a problem, however. What should Excel do if the text you enter is too wide for the cell in which you enter it? By default, Excel allows the text to "spill over" into any adjacent cells that are empty. If those cells have information in them, however, Excel just displays the portion of your text that it can, but nothing more.

If you want to see all the text in a cell, you can use the Wrap Text formatting option. If you examine the Alignment tab of the Format Cells dialog box, you will see a check box labeled *Wrap Text.* If this check box is selected, then any text entered in the cell will not be truncated when the text is too wide for the cell. Instead, Excel will increase the height of the row and wrap the text to the next line in the cell. For instance, if it takes five lines to display the text in a cell, then Excel adjusts the row height so that all five lines can be displayed. Cell A9 in Figure 14-6 shows an example of text wrapping turned on in a cell.

Using Merge and Center

The Merge and Center feature is useful if you want to center headings or subheadings across several columns. In Figure 14-7, each year is centered across two columns. The year 1999 is centered across columns A and B, 2000 is centered across columns C and D, and the year 2001 is centered across columns E and F. You can use the Merge and Center feature before or after the data is typed. To merge and center data, follow these steps:

1. Click and drag across the columns you want merged to highlight them.
2. Click the Merge and Center button on the Formatting toolbar (refer to Figure 14-1).

When you select a range of cells, all cells in the selection are shaded except for the first cell. After using the Merge and Center option on selected cells, the shading disappears from all the cells, and the result is a single cell. Also, whenever you visit a cell that has been merged and centered, the name that appears in the Name box is the address of the first cell in the range that was merged.

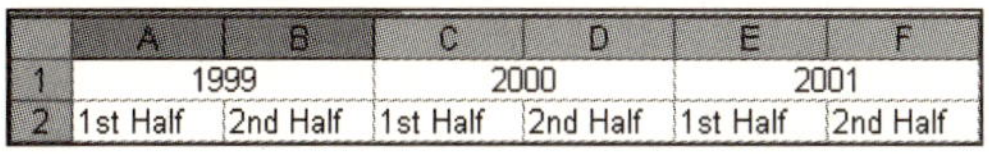

Figure 14-7: Examples of data that is merged and centered across columns

Hiding Columns, Rows, and Gridlines

The ability to hide columns and rows is useful to remove from view confidential information or information that you do not want changed when you share your workbooks with others. Columns or rows that are *hidden* are only removed from view; they still exist in the worksheet in the same location. To hide a single row or column, you must first select the rows or columns to be hidden. You can select contiguous rows and columns by clicking the row or column label and dragging left or right. Noncontiguous rows and columns can be selected by pressing Ctrl before clicking the row or column label.

After the rows or columns to be hidden are selected, right-click any part of the selection and choose Hide from the submenu that appears. After a row or column is hidden, the adjacent rows or columns move to fill the space left by the hidden element.

Hiding columns and rows

Suppose that your firm has been contracted to represent a magazine publisher. As part of the case, you need to pull together a list of advertisers in the magazine, as well as the sales people who handled the accounts. Your paralegal decides to produce a worksheet that lists advertisers, the salesperson that made a contact, contract start and stop dates, the date received, and the amount of revenue generated. You want to share the worksheet with others, but the revenue generated (column E) is not to be shared with others. You can hide the Revenue Generated column from view while sharing the remaining information. Figure 14-8 demonstrates first selecting column E and then choosing Hide from the submenu that appears. In Figure 14-9, you can see that column E is no longer visible on the worksheet. You will also notice that column F has moved to the left and now occupies the space formerly occupied by column E.

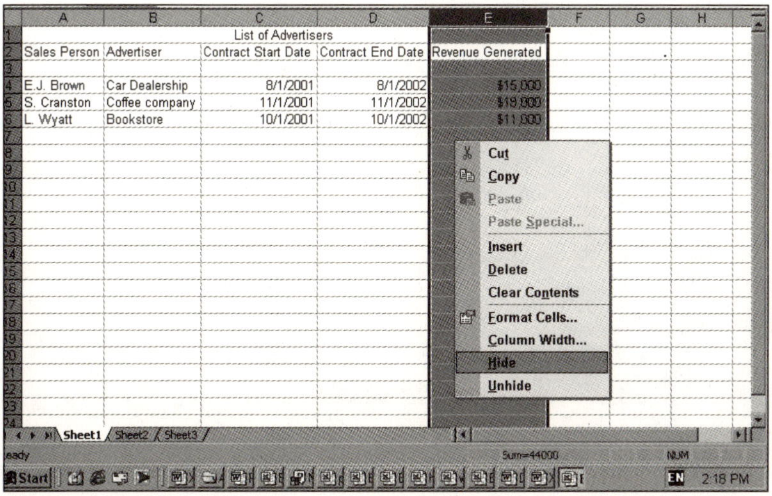

Figure 14-8: Select a column or columns and choose Hide from the submenu.

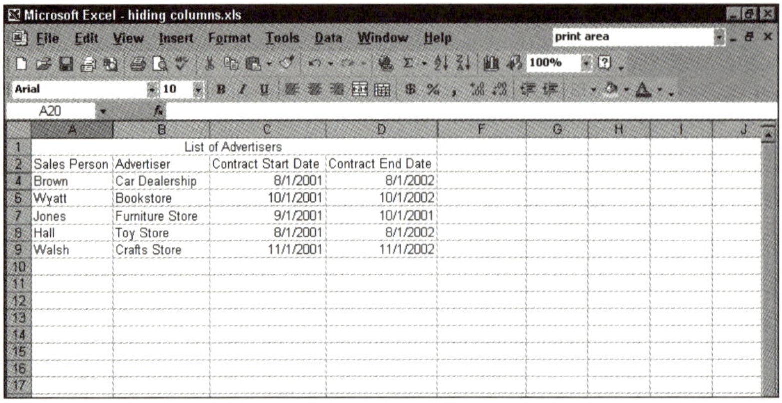

Figure 14-9: Column E is removed from view.

WARNING: Knowledgeable Excel users can unhide rows or columns if you have not protected the worksheet. If you do not want others to have the ability to unhide your rows or columns, you must first take the extra step of protecting the worksheet, described later in this chapter.

If you want to unhide columns, select the columns on both sides of the hidden column and right-click within the selection. Choose Unhide from the submenu that appears. To unhide column E in our example, we first selected columns D through F, as shown in Figure 14-10. Similarly, when unhiding rows, first select the row above and below the hidden row and right-click to choose Unhide from the submenu. (You can also double-click the row separators to unhide rows.) Once unhidden, rows and columns reappear in their original location.

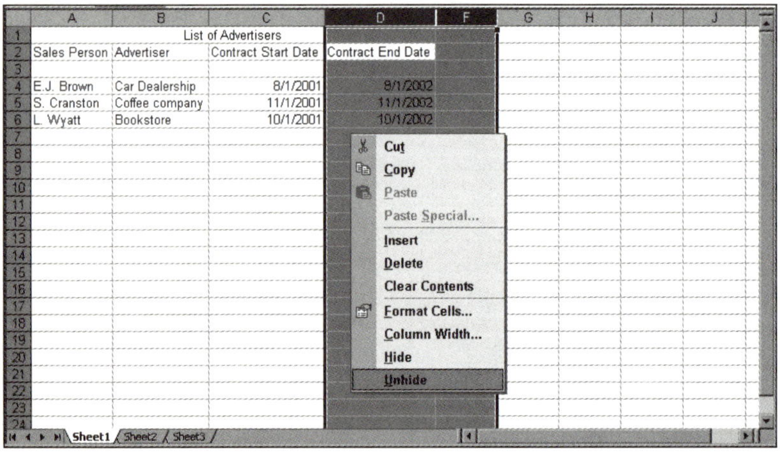

Figure 14-10: The columns before and after the hidden column are selected.

TIP: If you want to unhide all the hidden rows and columns in your worksheet, press Ctrl+A (Select All) to select the entire worksheet. Then right-click anywhere on the selection and select Unhide.

Another technique that you can use to hide columns is to drag the separator between the column labels (A, B, C, and so on) to the left until the column width measures 0. This technique, in effect, hides the column. In the case of hiding rows, you can drag the separator between the row numbers upward (1, 2, and so on) to hide the row above. When you are ready to unhide your columns, you may find that dragging the column separator to the right only widens the adjacent column and does not reveal the hidden column. To solve this problem, simply select the columns that border the hidden column on the left and right sides. Then double-click the column separator between the columns to reveal the hidden column. The technique is the same when unhiding rows. Select the rows that border the hidden row. Double-click the row separator to reveal the hidden rows.

Hiding and unhiding cell gridlines

Gridlines are frequently hidden on worksheets that contain charts or graphs. As you find out in more detail in Chapter 16, "Excel Graphics and Charts," you can create charts and graphs of your data using a variety of chart types. You can choose to place your charts on the same worksheet as the data, or you can chart your data separately on a different worksheet.

If you chart your data on a different worksheet, you may not want the worksheet gridlines to show. To eliminate the gridlines on a worksheet, follow these steps:

1. Click the Worksheet tab to select that worksheet. (Select multiple worksheets by pressing Ctrl before clicking the Worksheet tab.)
2. Choose Tools α Options to display the Options dialog box, shown in Figure 14-11.
3. Click the View tab.
4. Remove the check in the Gridlines check box located under Window Options.
5. Click OK to close the dialog box.

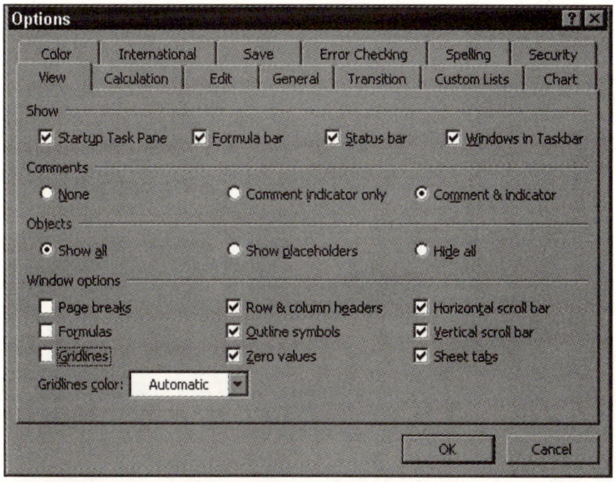

Figure 14-11: Viewing choices in the Options dialog box

To again view gridlines in your worksheets, click the Worksheet tab, choose Tools α Options, and choose the View tab. Place a check in the box beside Gridlines under Window Options.

Applying Style Formats

If you find that you frequently apply the same sets of formats to your cell contents (for example, a currency number type with two decimal places, left-aligned, and Times New Roman font at 12 points), you may want to consider creating a single style that contains all these formats. Your specific formatting preferences for text and numbers can be grouped together and named to form a *style* of formatting, which can then be applied to your cell contents — whether in individual cells or in a range of cells. You also benefit from the ability to change that formatting quickly throughout the entire worksheet by simply changing the definition of a style that is applied to multiple cells (the cells will immediately change to reflect the new style definition).

Like Word, Excel automatically uses a style named *Normal* that contains Excel's default formats for worksheet cells. If you want to view the formats contained in the Normal style, choose Format α Style to open the Style dialog box. Scroll in the Style Name box until you find the word `Normal` in the Style Name drop-down list; the formats included in the Normal style appear under Style Includes. Unless modifications have been made, Figure 14-12 shows the default formats that are included in the Normal style.

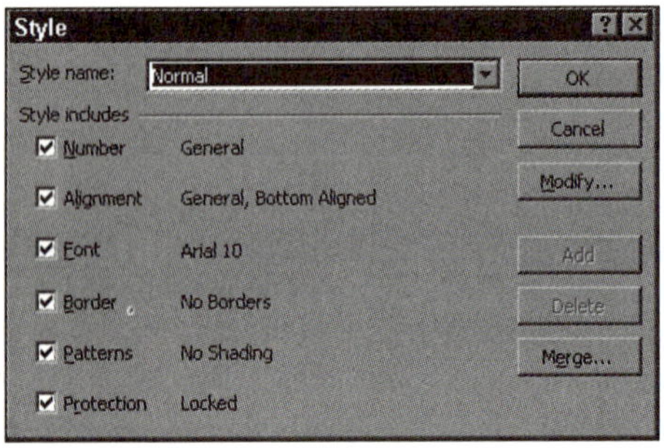

Figure 14-12: The default Normal definition

Besides Normal, Excel predefines some additional styles for your use. If you click the arrow beside the Style Name drop-down list, you will see the full list of available styles. Following is a description of the predefined styles that Excel provides:

- **Comma:** Formats a number with commas and aligns on two decimal places
- **Comma [0]:** Formats a number with commas and does not display decimal places
- **Currency:** Formats a number with the default currency symbol (dollar sign) and includes two decimal places
- **Currency [0]:** Formats a number with the default currency symbol and does not include decimal places
- **Percent:** Formats a number with the percent symbol

While a complete list of built-in styles can be viewed in the Style dialog box, it is not necessary to access this box each time you want to apply one of these styles. To apply the Comma, Currency, or Percent style, simply select the cells you want to format and click the appropriate icon on the Formatting toolbar, shown in Figure 14-13. (The Comma [0] and Currency [0] styles are similar formats to the first two except they do not include decimal alignment.)

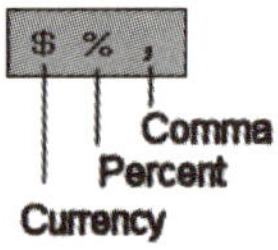

Figure 14-13: The Currency, Percent, and Comma style icons on the Formatting toolbar

Creating a custom style

If a cell contains attributes that you want to use in other cells, you can select that cell and create a *style by example.* To create a style by example, follow these steps:

1. Apply formatting to a particular cell. For example, you might apply a larger font size, boldface, and underline to cells that you want to use as column headings.
2. Choose Format α Style to open the Style dialog box.
3. Type a descriptive name for your style, such as **Heading**.
4. You can access additional attributes that you can add, remove, or change by clicking the Modify button to open the Format Cells dialog box. Click OK to close the dialog box after making your changes.
5. Click OK to close the Style dialog box.

Applying a custom style

Creating a custom style does not make much sense unless you intend to apply the style to cells or ranges of cells. This section explains how to apply your styles.

To apply a custom style, follow these steps:

1. Select the cell or range of cells to be formatted.
2. Choose Format α Style to open the Style dialog box.
3. Click the arrow beside the Style Name box and select the style to be used.
4. Click OK to close the Style dialog box.

Modifying a style

You derive the real benefit of using style formats in your worksheets when you want to modify the formatting of the cells based on a style. You can change the formatting of all cells based on a particular style by changing the style's definition. Changing a style definition provides two significant benefits: It saves you from having to change the formatting of the styles a cell at a time, and it ensures that the cells are all formatted in exactly the same way.

To modify a style, follow these steps:

1. Select a cell that contains the style that you want to modify.
2. Choose Format α Style. The name of the style you are modifying appears in the Style Name drop-down list.
3. Click the Modify button to open the Format Cells dialog box. In this dialog box, you can make adjustments to the number format, alignment, font, protection, borders, and patterns.
4. Make your desired changes and then click OK to close the Format Cells dialog box.
5. Click OK to close the Style dialog box. Each cell in which the style is in use will conform to the changes made.

CAUTION: Excel automatically applies the formatting that you specify to the active cell, and the Undo feature does not undo the formatting, so be sure that you select a cell in which you want the formatting to apply before changing style definitions. To remove an unintended format, choose Format α Cells and choose another style.

Deleting a style

If you find that you no longer need a style that you created, you can delete it. Just follow these steps:

1. Choose Format α Style to open the Style dialog box.
2. Select the style to be deleted from the Style Name list.
3. Click the Delete button.

CAUTION: It is not a good idea to delete any of the predefined styles; doing so means that you lose the Currency, Comma, or Percent styles provided by Excel. If you delete one of these predefined styles, you then have to apply those formats manually, using options in the Format α Cells dialog box.

Applying Borders and Shading

The Borders and Shading feature of Excel allows you to add lines and boxes to your worksheets to break up your worksheet into chunks, thus enhancing understandability of your spreadsheets. Borders allow you to box, underline, or separate columns to your liking. Shading allows you to use gradient patterns to call attention to sections of your spreadsheet. The following sections show you how to use these formatting features.

Changing borders

Varying the color, thickness, or style of cell borders is a useful method of drawing the reader's attention to certain areas of the worksheet — whether on screen or in a printout. Take a look at the example in Figure 14-14. Rows 4 and 12 contain important regional information that is difficult to make out. Figure 14-15 shows the same example with a thick black border around the regional headings, making them stand out.

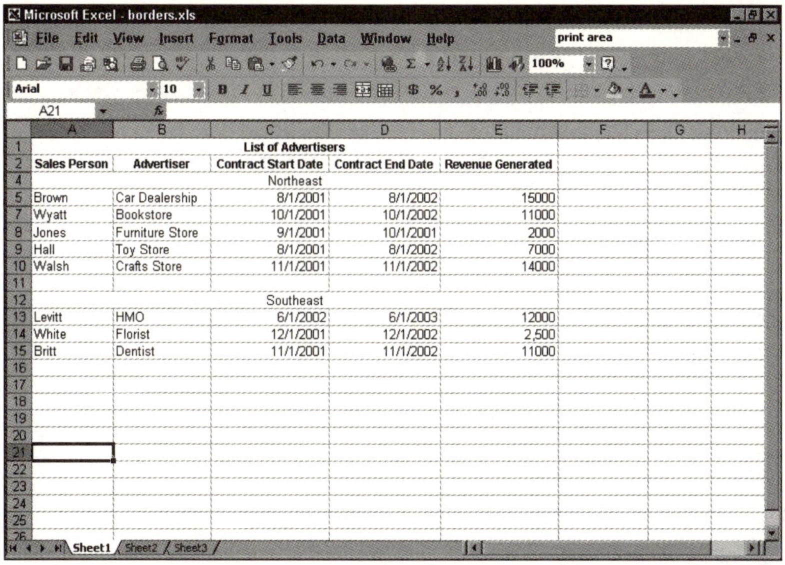

Figure 14-14: The regional headings are not distinctive.

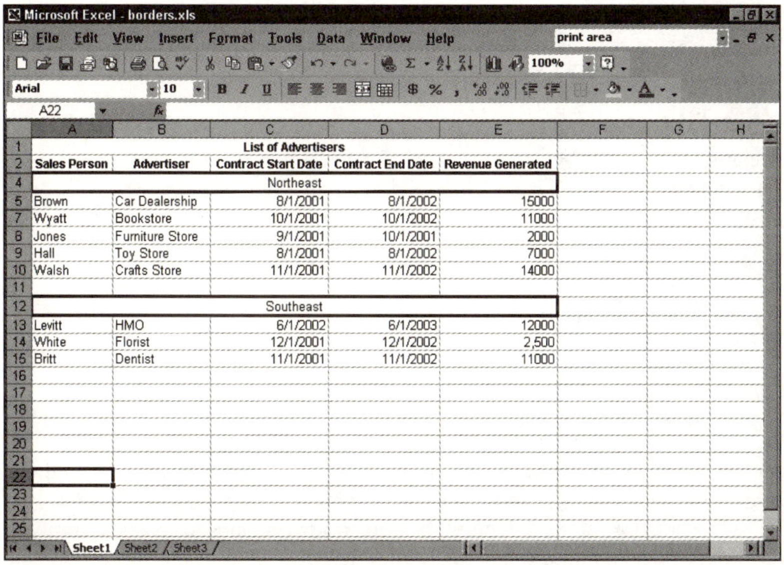

Figure 14-15: Black borders make the regions stand out!

Applying borders to a cell or range of cells is easy. Just follow these steps:

1. Select the cell or cells to which you want to apply a border.
2. Right-click over your selection and select Format Cells from the context-sensitive menu. The Format Cells dialog box appears.
3. Click the Border tab of the Format Cells dialog box, shown in Figure 14-16.

4. Select the type of line you want from the Style list. You can also select a color for the line in the Color box (if you don't change this, the color is black).
5. You can select on which sides of the cell you want the border to fall, in one of three ways:
   - **Choose a preset button.** The choices are None, Outline, and Inside. None removes borders if they have previously been set. Outline puts a border around the outside of the selected cells. Inside, which is disabled unless multiple cells are selected, creates a grid effect in which every side of every selected cell is bordered. The preview diagram displays the effect of the selection.
   - **Click border buttons.** The border buttons allow you to choose which sides of the cell range you want to border. The images on the buttons give you a handy graphical cue as to what the borders will look like after selection. As you click the buttons, the preview diagram displays the effect of the selection.
   - **Click the borders in the preview diagram.** You can toggle the selection of borders on or off by clicking the side of the cell that you want to toggle on or off in the preview diagram (the word `Text` is in the middle of it, as shown in Figure 14-16).
6. Click OK to apply the borders.

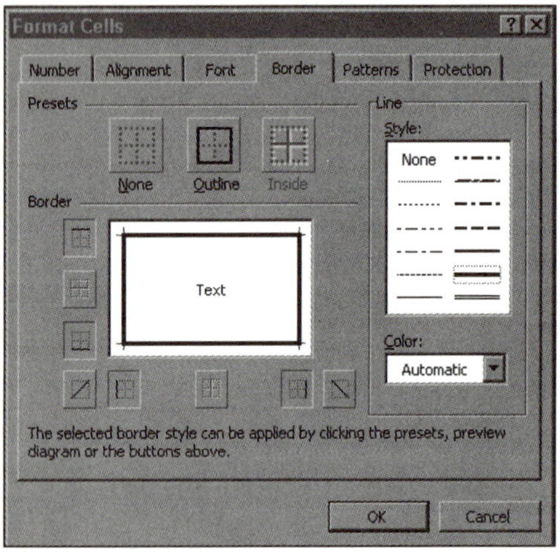

Figure 14-16: Applying borders in the Format Cells dialog box

Another technique that you can use to apply borders is to click the Borders icon that appears on the Formatting toolbar. On the drop-down list shown in Figure 14-17, you will find the same border buttons as are available in the Borders tab. After selecting the cells that you want to format, simply click the arrow beside the Borders icon and then select the border that you want to use.

TIP: To remove a border from selected cells, click No Border in the Borders drop-down list or click the Borders tab.

Figure 14-17: The drop-down list of options on the Borders icon on the Formatting toolbar

Applying fill and shading

You can add background colors (fill) and patterns (shading) to selected cells. To apply a fill color to a cell or range of cells, follow these steps:

1. Select the cells to receive the fill.
2. Select the fill color selection by clicking the Fill Color button's drop-down arrow (the Fill Color button looks like a paint can — refer to Figure 14-17) to pick from the color palette. You can skip this step if the color that you want appears on the button.
3. Click the Fill Color button to apply the color to the cell range.

To apply shading to a cell or range of cells, follow these steps:

1. Select the cells to receive the shading.
2. Choose Format α Cells and then click the Patterns tab.
3. Select a different background color or a specific percentage of gray shading to fill the selected cells. Using this technique, you can also choose one of the predefined crosshatch or stripe patterns that are available to fill the selected cells, by clicking the Pattern drop-down list, as shown in Figure 14-18.

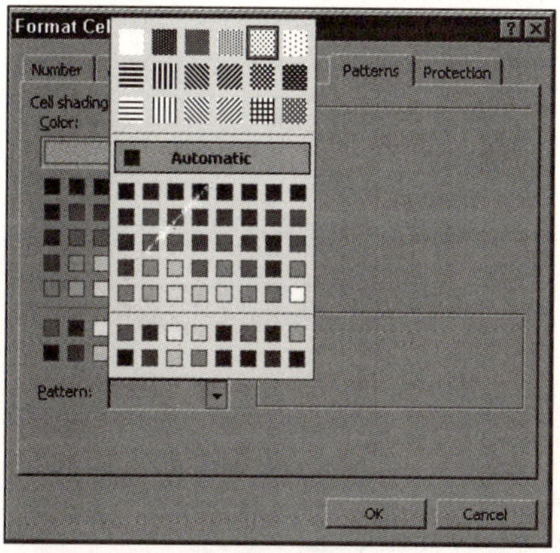

Figure 14-18: Available pattern selections

Working with Number, Date, and Time Formats

In addition to having the ability to format text and cells, you can select formatting options for numbers, dates, and times. Excel offers many options for adjusting the appearance of numbers, dates, and times. For instance, if you are preparing a balance sheet to report assets and liabilities for an international client, you may want to use the correct currency and currency symbol in use for the client's geographical location. As an example, you may want to use the Belgian franc and the symbol associated with that type of currency. Or when you type a date, you want it to display in the same date format that your client uses. Preferred number, date, and time formats can be added after the data is typed or to empty worksheet cells.

Number formats

Number formats are organized into categories. You select the categories by choosing Format α Cells and clicking the Number tab in the Format Cells dialog box. After you select a category, additional options appear. If you have selected cells prior to accessing the Number tab, the sample box displays how the data in the cell will appear after the format is applied. Table 14-1 describes each category.

Table 14-1
Number Categories Used in Excel

Number Categories	*Description of Formats*
General	The number appears just as you type it. This is the default setting.
Number	Numbers can be formatted with a specified number of digits to the right of the decimal point. This format also includes an option for including commas and allows you to specify how negative numbers are displayed.
Currency	This category formats the number for a monetary value and allows you to choose a specific currency symbol. You can also specify the number of decimal places displayed and the format for negative numbers. Numbers are aligned on the currency symbols.
Accounting	Numbers align on the currency symbol.
Date	Seventeen date formats are available. Excel works with Date values as serial numbers representing the number of days from January 1, 1900, but you can display the date as a long date, short date, and month only, as well as other formats.
Time	Nine time formats are available. Excel internally stores times as a numeric extension of the date format. You can display times in a variety of formats, including 24-hour notation, AM/PM notation, and with or without seconds.
Percentage	Value is multiplied by 100 and displayed with a percent symbol. Decimal places can be included.
Fraction	The type of fraction displayed can be formatted to include 1, 2, or 3 digits, such as 1/2, 11/12, or 111/112.
Scientific	A number can be displayed in scientific notation, for example, 1.23E+03. The number of decimal places can be selected.
Text	Text is displayed as entered and appears left-aligned.
Special	Predefined formats are available for zip code, zip code plus 4 digits, phone number, and social security number.
Custom	You can create custom number, date, and time formats using codes when predefined formats are not enough. Custom formats are saved with the workbook.

If you want to apply a number format, follow these steps:

1. Select the cells to be formatted. Selected cells can be empty or already contain numbers that you want to format.
2. Choose Format α Cells and click the Number tab.
3. Select a category and set the options for the number format you want.
4. Click OK.

Date formats

When you enter a date into Excel, it tries to display that date using the default format for your computer system. For instance, you can type a date such as *September 2, 2001,* and it may appear in the worksheet as *2-Sep-01* (which is a date format commonly used outside the United States). This is because Excel is using a *d-mmm-yy* format by default. The *d* represents the day of the week and is at the beginning of the format, followed by a dash and then the first three letters of the month (*mmm*), followed by another dash and a two-digit year.

The formats that Excel provides cannot be changed, but you can create a custom date format that meets your needs. To create a custom date format, follow these steps:

1. Select the cell or cells to receive the date format.
2. Choose Format α Cells and click the Number tab.
3. Click the Custom category.
4. In the Type text box, enter the codes and any spaces and characters you want included in the new date format. If the selected cells contain data, the results of what you type are displayed.
5. Click OK to close the dialog box and apply the new format to selected cells.

Time formats

You can apply predefined or customized time formats to your spreadsheets. An additional formatting option, Locale, is available when choosing the Date category to use predefined date formats. When a locale is selected from this list, the date code in the Type text box reflects the time format commonly used for the specified locale. If you are creating a customized time format, you can type the codes in the format you want to use for a particular locale.

To apply a time format, follow these steps:

1. Select the cell or cells to receive the date format.
2. Choose Format α Cells and click the Number tab.
3. Select the Time category.
4. Select a predefined time display.
5. Click OK to apply the format.

To create a custom time format, follow these steps:

1. Select the cell or cells to receive the date format.
2. Choose Format α Cells and click the Number tab.
3. Select the Custom category.

4. In the Type text box, enter the codes and any spaces and characters you want included in the new date format. If the selected cells contain data, the results of what you type are displayed.
5. Click OK to close the dialog box and apply the new format to selected cells.

Using AutoFormat

Adjusting column widths, changing alignment, and adding borders to a worksheet can sometimes require more time than you have. Luckily, Excel provides some good formatting choices for you that you can apply with the click of a mouse. In this section, we show you how to apply a collection of formats to the entire worksheet automatically by using the AutoFormat feature.

To apply AutoFormat, follow these steps:

1. Select a range of cells or the entire worksheet.
2. Choose Format α AutoFormat to open the AutoFormat dialog box, shown in Figure 14-19. Here you will find tables with sample formatting applied. Only six tables are displayed at a time, but you can scroll through the entire set of samples.
3. Select the format that meets your needs and click OK.

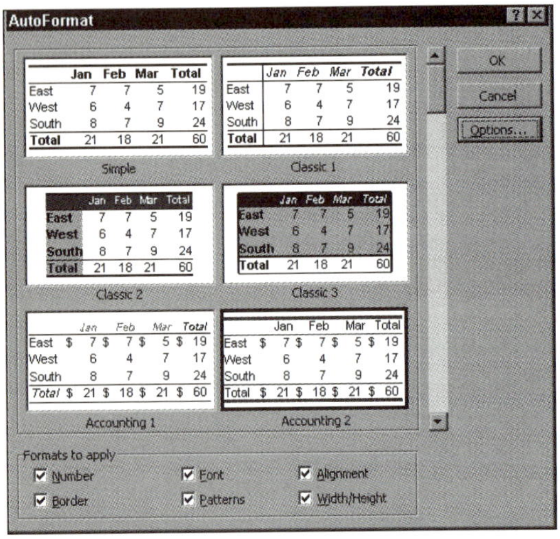

Figure 14-19: The AutoFormat dialog box

TIP: Selecting a table sample does not mean that you are stuck with all of the formats contained in that sample. In the bottom section of the AutoFormat dialog box, you can find formatting options that you can select or deselect. In other words, you can select the formats in a particular sample that you want and deselect the formats you do not want.

Using Conditional Formats

As the name implies, *conditional* formatting is applied to cells only if certain conditions are met. An example would be changing the background of a number only if the cell value is less than or greater than a certain number. In this way, you can draw attention to the value.

The first step in using the conditional formatting tool is to think about which cells may contain the values you are looking for and then select all those cells. After the cells containing the desired values are selected, follow these steps to apply conditional formatting:

1. Choose Format α Conditional Formatting to open the Conditional Formatting dialog box, shown in Figure 14-20.
2. In the Condition 1 section of the dialog box, select Cell Value Is to apply conditional formatting based on specific values. You can also apply conditional formatting to a cell containing a specific formula.
3. If you are specifying a value, you can select an operator that you want to use. If you are specifying a formula, type the exact formula you want.
4. Click the Format button to open the Format Cells dialog box in order to specify a font, border, or pattern to be added to those cells that meet your conditions. A preview of the result of applying the formatting can be seen in the Conditional Formatting dialog box.
5. You can specify multiple criteria by clicking the Add button to establish a second set of conditions.
6. After the format has been determined, click OK to close the Format Cells dialog box; click OK again to close the Conditional Formatting dialog box and apply the formats.

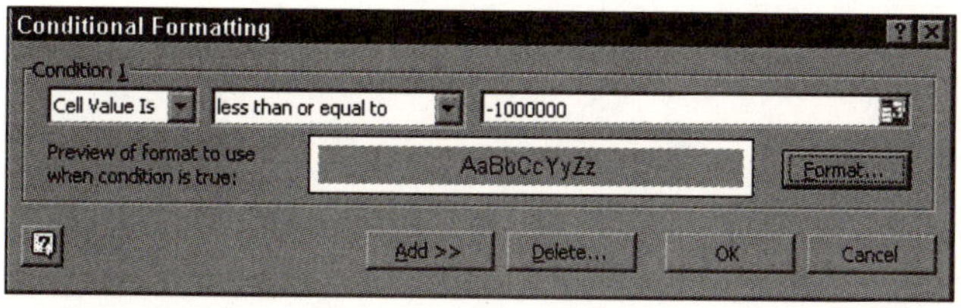

Figure 14-20: Setting conditions in the Conditional Formatting dialog box

For example, in Figure 14-21, the conditional format has been set to highlight cells that are less than or equal to 100,000.

If you have received a workbook from outside sources, it may not be immediately apparent whether conditional formatting was used in the worksheet. However, performing the following steps will enable you to determine which cells have been selected for conditional formatting:

1. Choose Edit α Go To to open the Go To dialog box.
2. Click Special in the lower-left corner to open the Go To Special dialog box.
3. Select Conditional formats.
4. Ensure that All is selected as the Data Validation option.
5. Click OK.

All the cells that were selected for conditional formatting are again selected. To determine the conditions that were established before the formatting was added, follow these steps:

1. Choose Edit α Go To to open the Go To Special dialog box.
2. Select Conditional formats to reselect cells that were selected when the formats were applied.
3. Choose Format α Conditional Formatting to view the conditions that were established.
4. Click the Format button to see the formatting that was applied.

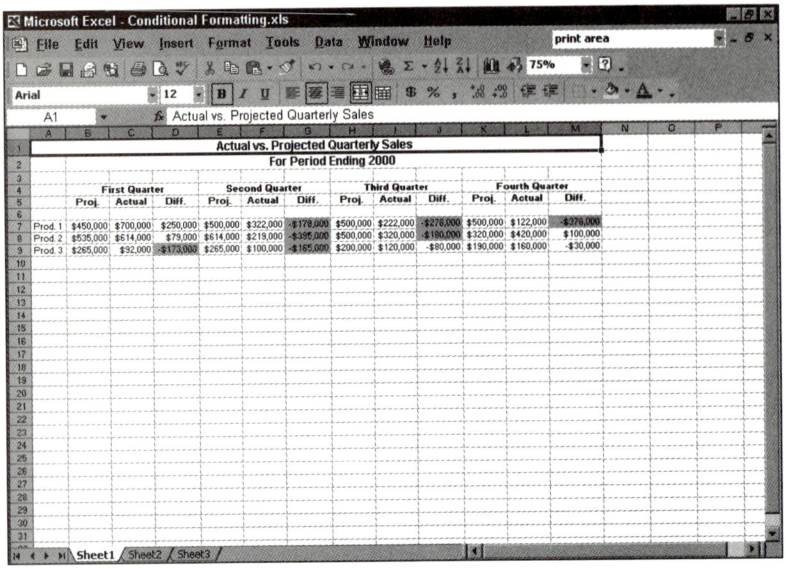

Figure 14-21: Formatting has been added to all cells that contain the values specified in the Conditional Formatting dialog box.

TIP: You can also remove conditional formats by first using the Go To Special options to select cells that were included when the conditional formats were applied. Next, choose the Format α Conditional Formatting menus to see the conditions that were set. Click the Delete button to remove the formats that were applied.

Summary

Excel provides a variety of ways you can format the data in a worksheet. Through judicious use of the formatting tools provided by Excel, your data can appear just the way you want it. This chapter has introduced you to Excel's formatting tools, and you have learned how to apply them to your own data. This chapter covered the following:

- Adjusting row height and column width and aligning text within a cell
- Merging cells and centering the information in them
- Hiding columns, rows, and gridlines
- Excel's use of styles
- Adding borders, patterns, and colors to cells
- Understanding number, date, and time formats
- Applying Excel's AutoFormat feature
- How conditional and custom formats work

In the next chapter, you learn how to produce some real output: how to print your worksheets just as you want them.

Chapter 15

Printing Worksheets

In This Chapter

- Selecting data to print
- Specifying a print range
- Previewing a print job
- Setting aspects of printing
- Changing printer properties
- Choosing network printers

AFTER YOU HAVE CREATED YOUR worksheets and applied the desired formatting, you are ready to print. Excel offers options for specifying what you want to print and the way that the printed pages will appear. In this chapter, you find out what the options are and how to use them.

Selecting What to Print

Excel gives you flexibility over whether you print a single worksheet, multiple selected worksheets, or an entire workbook. To print an entire workbook, follow these steps:

1. Choose File ⇨ Print to open the Print dialog box, shown in Figure 15-1.
2. In the Print What section, select Entire Workbook.

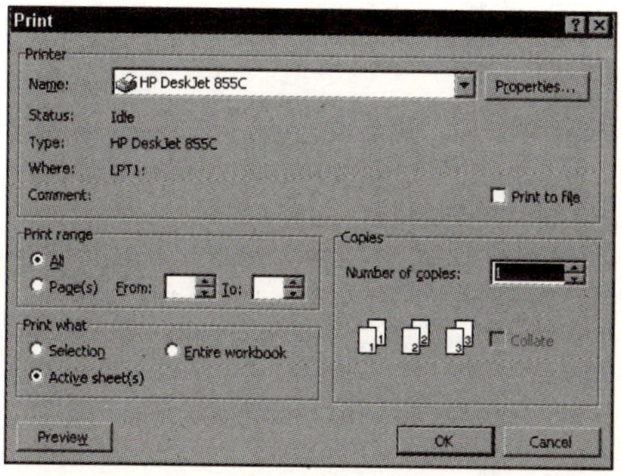

Figure 15-1: Print options available in the Print dialog box

If you want to print several worksheets, follow these steps:

1. Press Ctrl and then click the tab of each worksheet that you want to print,
2. Choose File ⇨ Print to open the Print dialog box.

3. In the Print What section, choose Active Sheet(s).

Specifying a Print Range

Excel allows you to print not only entire worksheets but also portions of worksheets. If you want to print a specific range of cells rather than the entire workbook or selected worksheets, follow these steps:

1. Drag to select the range of cells that you want to print.
2. Choose File ⇨ Print.
3. Select the Selection option in the Print What panel.

When you want to select noncontiguous cells to print, press Ctrl before clicking each cell. It is important to note, however, that although contiguous cells print on one page, noncontiguous cells print on separate pages, regardless of whether the selected cells are located in the same row or column.

Specifying a print area

By default, Excel prints the entire selected worksheet. However, you may only want to print a certain area of a worksheet. Printing part of a worksheet can be useful if the worksheet contains both details and summary information. You may only want to print the summary information without the details. Excel provides you with the Print Area option to allow you to choose the area to print exactly.

The difference between specifying a print area and simply selecting the cells you want to print is that after defining a print area, the print area is saved as part of the worksheet and is available for reprinting at any time. To specify a print area, follow these steps:

1. Select the cells you want to specify as the print area.
2. Choose File ⇨ Print Area ⇨ Set Print Area, which places a dashed border around the selected cells. While the cells are selected, the words *Print_Area* appear in the Name box.

Another technique you can use to specify a print area is as follows:

1. Choose File ⇨ Page Setup and click the Sheet tab shown in Figure 15-2.
2. Select the cell range. You can do this in one of two ways:
   - **Type the range:** Type the cell range that you want to define as the print area in the Print Area text box.
   - **Select the range:** Click the Collapse Dialog button on the right side of the Print Area text box to collapse the Page Setup dialog box and reveal the worksheet window (see Figure 15-3). In this view, you can select the range of cells you want defined as the print area. If necessary, you can drag the Print Area text box so that you can see all the cells you want to include. After you select the cell range, a moving dashed border appears around the selected cells and the absolute cell references appear in the Page Setup - Print Area text box. Press Enter to expand the Page Setup dialog box.
3. Click Print and then click OK to produce a printed copy of the defined print area.

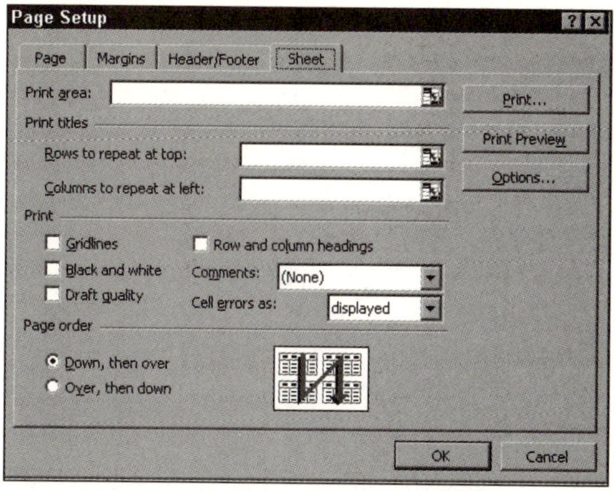

Figure 15-2: The Sheet tab of the Page Setup dialog box

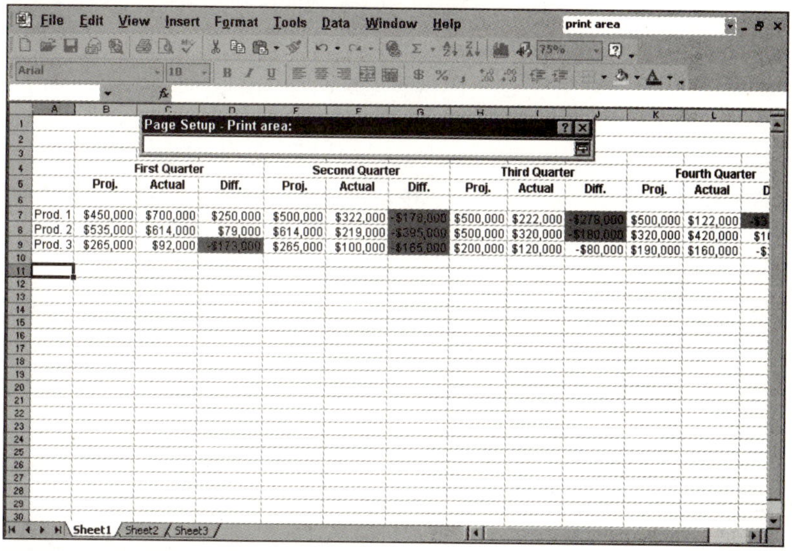

Figure 15-3: The collapsed Print Area text box

If you want to reprint a previously defined print area, follow these steps:

1. Open the worksheet in which the print area is defined.
2. Click the arrow beside the name list box and select Print_Area from the list that appears. Your predefined print area is selected, as shown in Figure 15-4.
3. Choose File ⇨ Print and then click OK to print.

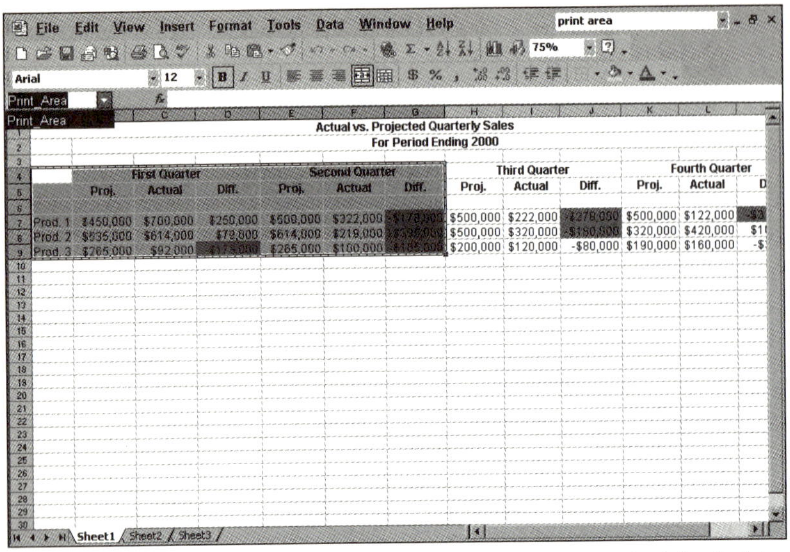

Figure 15-4: Selecting Print_Area from the name drop-down list reselects the defined print area.

TIP: If you want to define multiple print areas in a given worksheet, you are responsible for giving each print area that you define a different name in the name list. You can do so by renaming the first area *Print_Area1* and simply increment the number for each subsequent print area you define.

Clearing a print area

If you no longer need a defined print area, it can easily be cleared from the worksheet. To clear a print area from your worksheet, follow these steps:

1. Select the print area you want to clear in the name list.
2. Choose the File ⇨ Print Area ⇨ Clear Area menus to clear the definition. If only one print area was defined, the dashed border is removed from the selected range of cells.

Previewing a Print Job

It is very common to want to see what the printed copy will look like before you actually print to a printer. In Print Preview, you can see the effects of any formatting you have added or any other changes you have made before printing. Print Preview enables you to see how the entire worksheet (or any specified print areas) will look. You can access the Print Preview option by opening the worksheet you want to preview and by using one of the following techniques:

- Choose File ⇨ Print Preview.
- Choose File ⇨ Page Setup and click the Print Preview button.
- Choose File ⇨ Print and click the Preview button in the Print dialog box.
- Click the Print Preview button on the Standard toolbar.

Whichever technique you use to access the preview option, the active worksheet (or defined print area) appears magnified in the Print Preview window. Figure 15-5 displays the quarterly sales worksheet in Print Preview in the magnified mode.

Figure 15-5: A quarterly sales worksheet appears magnified in the Print Preview window.

Upon entering Print Preview, you discover that the worksheet is greatly reduced in size and may be difficult to read. In Print Preview mode, the pointer assumes a double role. As a magnifying glass, one click enlarges the worksheet to a full-screen view and changes its orientation to Landscape. Figure 15-6 is an example of what the full-screen view looks like. Another click returns the worksheet window to the magnified view.

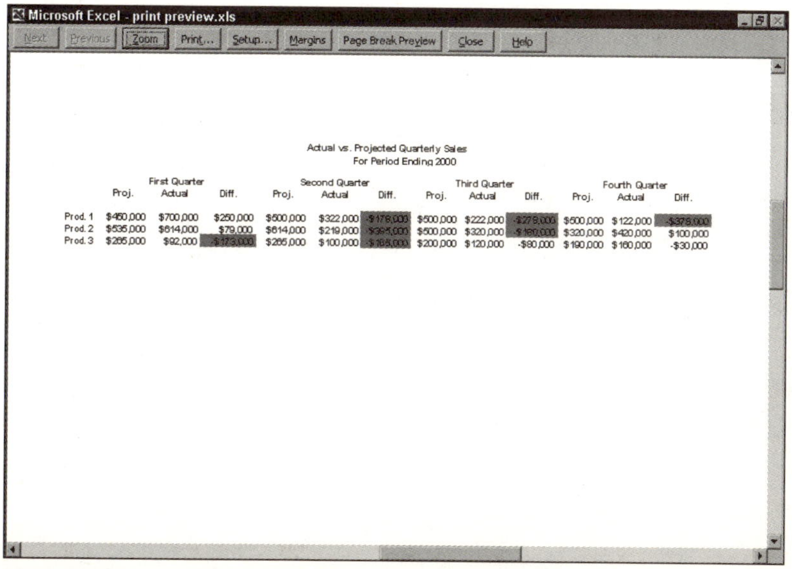

Figure 15-6: An example of the full-screen view in Print Preview

If the active workbook contains more than one worksheet, you may want to preview a worksheet other than the one that is displayed. For your convenience, Excel provides you with a separate Print Preview toolbar that contains options for controlling what you see in the Print Preview window, as well as options for controlling how the worksheet is viewed. Figure 15-7 shows the Print Preview toolbar.

Figure 15-7: The Print Preview toolbar

Table 15-1 describes each of the commands on the Print Preview toolbar.

Table 15-1
The Print Preview Toolbar Commands

Command	*What It Does*
Next	Displays the next worksheet in the workbook.
Previous	Displays the previously viewed worksheet.
Zoom	Toggles between full-page view and magnified view. The end result is the same as if you click the mouse while in Print Preview mode.
Print	Opens the Print dialog box for setting print options and printing.
Setup	Opens the Page Setup dialog box for setting page, margin, sheet, and header/footer options.
Margins	Displays page margins, as well as the margins for each column.
Page Break Preview	Large worksheets could span several pages. Use this tool to add or delete page breaks or move where the page breaks occur.
Close	Closes Print Preview and returns you to the Normal view.
Help	Describes each of the commands on the Print Preview toolbar.

Setting Aspects of Printing

Excel provides a variety of ways in which you can enhance the appearance of your worksheet. In the Page Setup dialog box, you can find many options for controlling how the worksheet looks on the printed page. To access the Page Setup dialog box, you can choose File ⇨ Page Setup, or if you are in the Print Preview window, you can click the Setup button on the Print Preview toolbar.

In Figure 15-8, you can see the four tabs in the Page Setup dialog box that represent categories of options that you can set to control how the printed page will look. The four categories of options are Page, Margins, Header/Footer, and Sheet. Table 15-2 describes the options that are available for each category in the Page Setup dialog box.

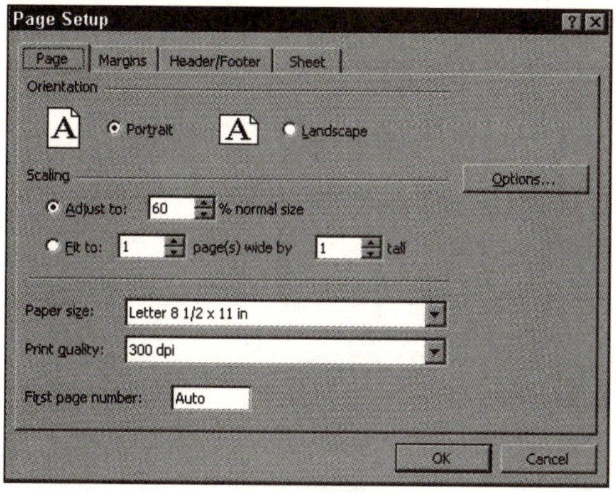

Figure 15-8: The Page Setup dialog box

Table 15-2
The Page Setup Options by Category

Page Setup Category	***Used To...***
Page	Set options for orientation, scaling, paper size, or print quality, or set a starting page number. Changes affect the entire page.
Margins	Adjust page margins, control how far the header/footer prints from the top or bottom of the worksheet or the distance from the data to the header or footer. This is also where you can center the worksheet horizontally or vertically on the print page.
Header/Footer	Choose from a list of built-in headers and footers that include elements such as dates and page numbers in a default format. Or use the Custom Header or Custom Footer buttons to include the elements and the desired formats you prefer.
Sheet	Select a specific area for printing; include row and column labels on multipage worksheets; print the gridlines, row (1, 2, 3,), and column (A, B, C, etc.) labels, comments, and cell errors; and specify the order in which you want the data on multipage worksheets to print and how the pages are numbered. The effect of these choices can be seen in the sample picture beside this option.

After you set all desired options for the way you want the worksheet to look on the printed page, you can review your changes by using the Print Preview button that appears on each tab except the Margins tab. On this tab is a sample box that displays the results of the margin changes you make.

TIP: If you are unclear about a particular option, click the What's This question mark in the right corner of the Page Setup title bar. Next, click in the area of the option to receive context-sensitive help about that option.

Setting page options

This section and those following show you the effects of setting available options on the worksheet's appearance. (Because we show the results in Print Preview mode, we increased the font size for the entire worksheet to 14 points.) First, take a look at the effect of landscape orientation that is derived from choosing File ⇨ Page Setup and selecting the Landscape option on the Page tab. Viewing the results in Print Preview mode provides the results shown in Figure 15-9.

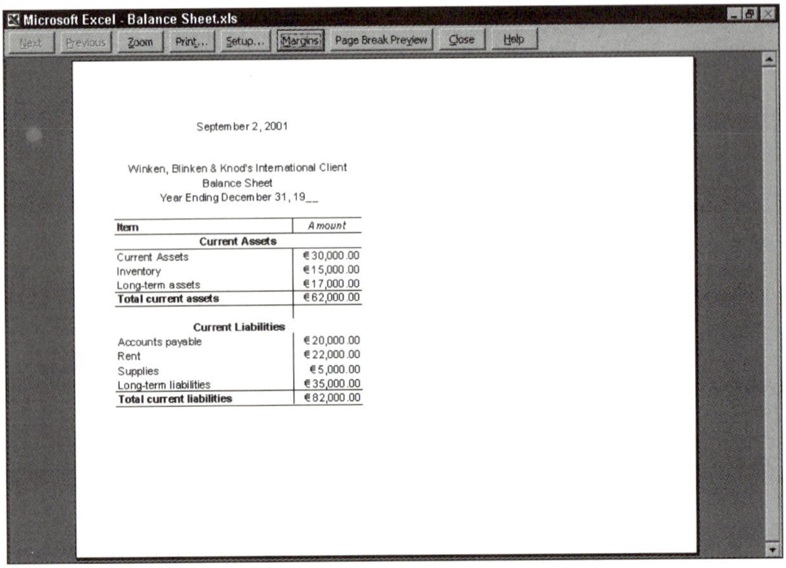

Figure 15-9: The results of changing the page orientation to Landscape

Setting margin options

When the orientation is changed to landscape, the worksheet appears situated closer to the left margin, but the appearance is generally better when the spreadsheet is centered between the left and right margins. To center the spreadsheet on the printed page, click the Setup button on the Print Preview toolbar to open the Page Setup dialog box. Use the Center on Page option found on the Margins tab to center the worksheet horizontally on the page. Figure 15-10 shows the Margins tab, with the results of this change appearing in the sample picture. View the magnified results of choosing this option as displayed in the Print Preview window in Figure 15-11.

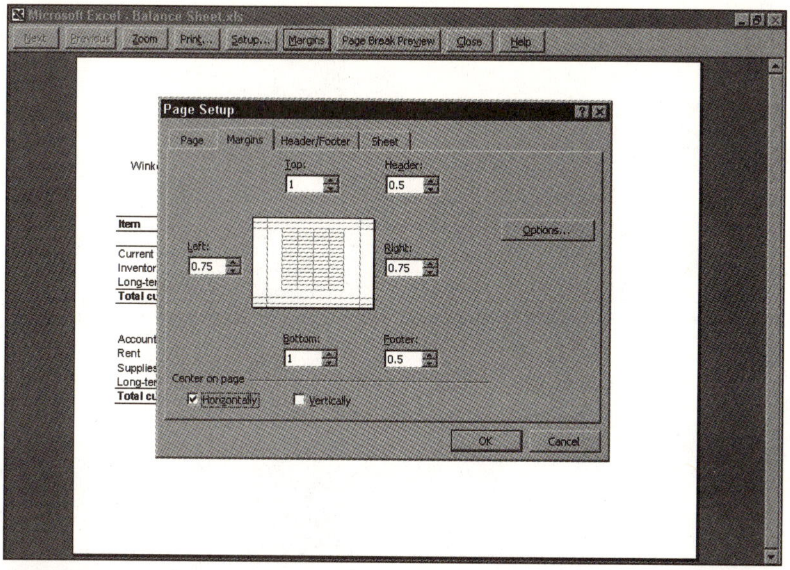

Figure 15-10: The Center on Page option set to Horizontally on the Margins tab in the Print Preview window

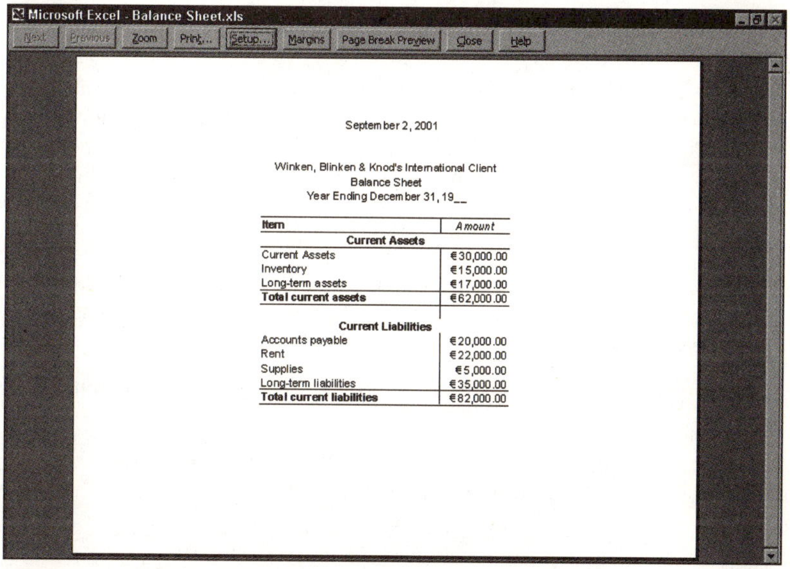

Figure 15-11: The effects of centering the worksheet horizontally on the page

Setting header and footer options

Suppose that you want to create a custom header that prints the name of your law firm in bold in the left corner. To do so, follow these steps:

1. Click the Setup button in Print Preview mode to open the Page Setup dialog box.
2. Click the Header/Footer tab.
3. Click the Custom Header button to open the Header dialog box, shown in Figure 15-12.

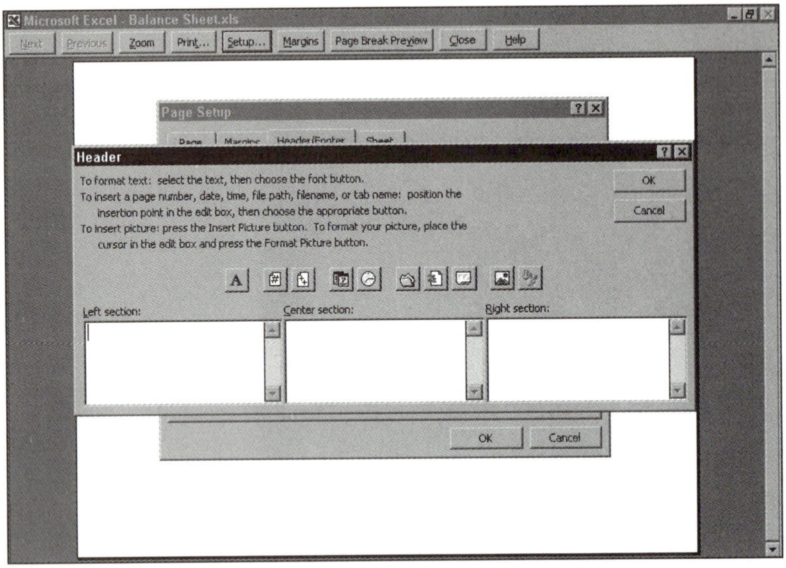

Figure 15-12: The Header dialog box

4. Select the edit box that corresponds to the area in which you want to insert header information. Your choices are the left section, center section, and right section.
5. Click the toolbar buttons in the Header dialog box to insert different types of elements into the edit boxes provided. The date, time, path and filename, filename only, text, and page numbers can all be inserted. In addition to the elements themselves, you can include spaces, symbols, and punctuation with the element. You can also select the text you type in order to change the font, font style, or font size and you can apply special effects such as superscript, subscript, and strikethrough to the selected text.

An example of a header for a law firm would be the firm name on the left side of the page, the page number to print in the center of the page, and the words *Attorney-Client Work Product* to print in bold on the right side of the page. To create this custom header, follow these steps:

1. Click in the left section and type your firm name. In the example, we typed **Winken, Blinken & Knod**.
2. Select the text that you just typed and click the Text button (the button with the capital *A*) to open the Font dialog box. Select the bold font style and then click OK.
3. Click in the center section and click the number sign on the picture toolbar to insert a page number code. In the example, we also included dashes and spaces around the page-numbering code.
4. Click in the right section and type **Attorney-Client Work Product**.
5. Select the text `Attorney-Client Work Product` and click the Text button to open the Font dialog box. Change the font style to bold. Figure 15-13 displays the example information inserted into the edit boxes.
6. Click OK to close the Header dialog box. Figure 15-14 shows the worksheet in Preview mode after the header is applied.

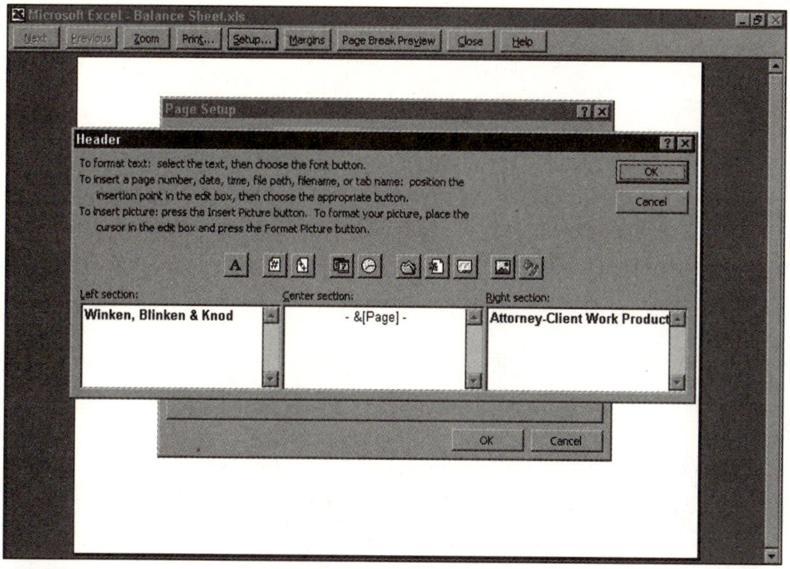

Figure 15-13: The Header dialog box displaying the custom header we created

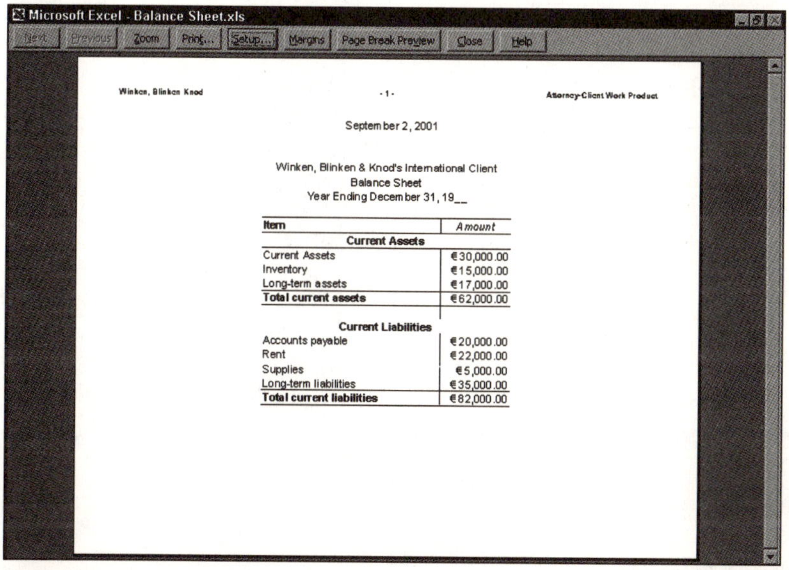

Figure 15-14: The custom header is applied to the balance sheet worksheet as displayed in Preview mode.

Setting sheet options

On the Sheet tab, you can elect to print the gridlines, row numbers, and column letters on the printed balance sheet. Figure 15-15 shows the Sheet tab with these options selected. Figure 15-16 shows the worksheet in Print Preview mode displaying the gridlines and row and column headings.

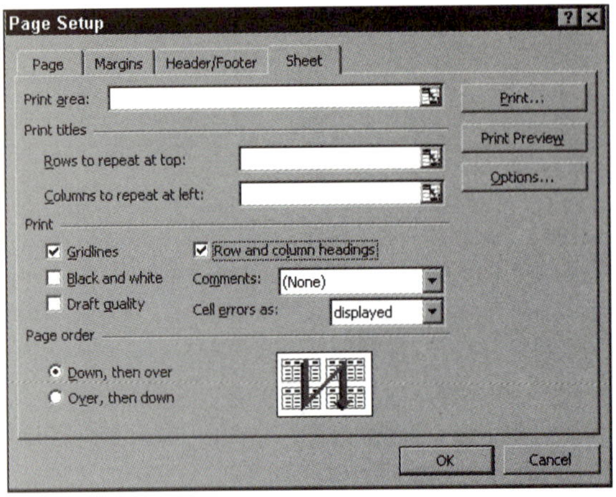

Figure 15-15: The print gridlines and row and column headings options are checked on the Sheet tab.

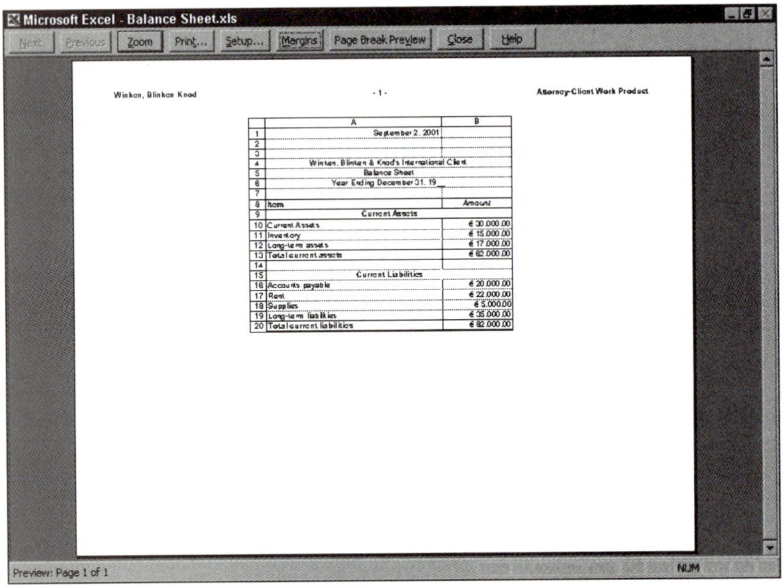

Figure 15-16: The balance sheet displayed in Print Preview mode now displays the gridlines and row and column headings.

Repeating rows at the top

Often, worksheet printouts span more than one printed page. In such cases, you often want the headings to appear on pages subsequent to the first page. The Sheet tab is useful for specifying the row headings or column headings that you want to appear on every page of the printed worksheet. Select the Rows to Repeat at Top option, and you can type the cell range that you want to repeat at the top of each page of the worksheet.

If you don't want to type the cell range, you can click the Collapse Dialog Box button. Doing so allows you to select the rows on the worksheet that you want to repeat on each page. Figure 15-17 shows the collapsed Rows to Repeat at Top option and also shows that a dashed line (which is moving in real life) surrounds the row that is selected.

After selecting the row(s) to repeat at the top, press Enter to return to the Sheet tab. The selected cell range appears in the text box. Use similar techniques for repeating columns on the left of the printed worksheet. The only difference is that the Columns to Repeat at Left option is selected instead of the Rows to Repeat at Top option.

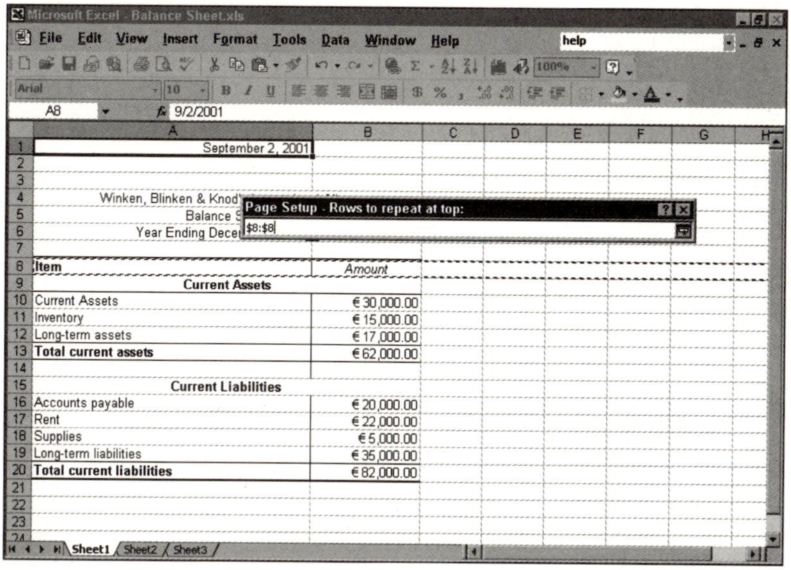

Figure 15-17: The absolute cell reference of the selected cell range appears in the Rows to Repeat at Top text box and will print on each page of the worksheet.

Changing Printer Properties

When you are ready to print, choose File ⇨ Print or click the Print button on the Standard toolbar to open the Print dialog box. The Print dialog box displays the selected printer's name and type and provides options for specifying how much to print and what to print. In addition to these options, the Properties button allows you to access the properties dialog box, shown in Figure 15-18.

The properties you can change are paper, device options, and graphics. Only properties that can be changed in the currently selected printer are available. For example, the currently selected printer in Figure 15-18 is an HP DeskJet 855C. This type of printer holds a single paper tray, as evidenced by the list of options under the Paper Source option, shown in Figure 15-19. If the currently selected printer was a printer that holds more than one paper tray, then the Paper Source option on the Paper tab would likely include bin numbers from which to choose.

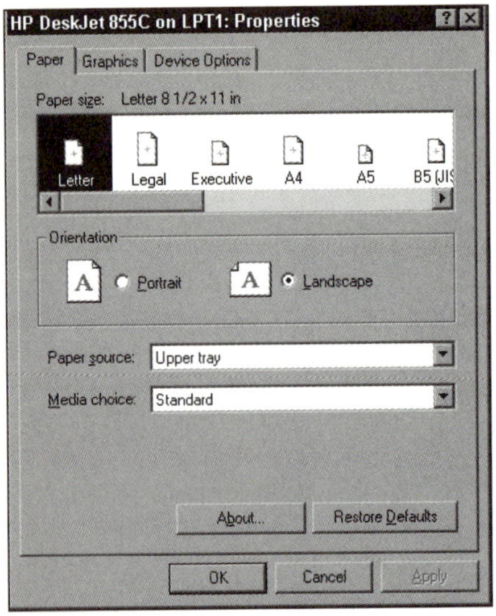

Figure 15-18: The printer properties dialog box

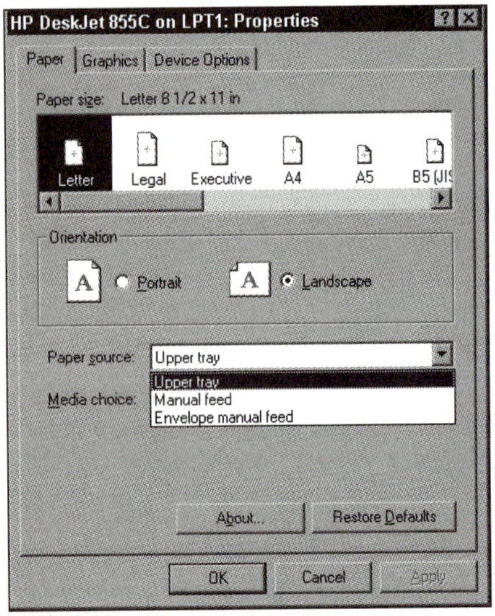

Figure 15-19: The list of options available under Paper Source changes, depending on the type of printer that is selected.

Choosing Printers

When you are ready to print, you can direct your output to a local printer (a printer cabled to your computer) or in a network environment to a network printer. When you print by choosing File ⇨ Print, in the Print dialog box, you can view the available printers in the Name drop-down list. The name of the default printer appears in the Name list. To change from the default printer to a different printer, follow these steps:

1. Choose File ⇨ Print to open the Print dialog box.

2. Click the arrow beside the Name drop-down list to see a list of your available printers.
3. Select a different printer from the list.
4. Click OK to print.

If you want to print to a printer not yet available to you, do the following:

1. Choose Start ⇨ Settings ⇨ Printers and double-click the Add Printer icon to start the Add Printer Wizard.
2. Click Next to move to the starting point to set up a new printer.
3. In the next wizard screen (see Figure 15-20), choose local if the printer is connected to your computer or choose network if the printer is attached to a local or wide area network.
4. Click the Next button.

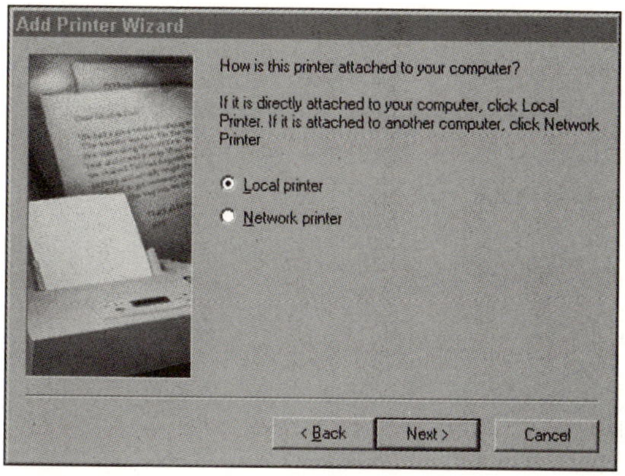

Figure 15-20: In the Printer Wizard, you can add a local printer or a network printer.

5. Choose the printer. This step is different, depending on whether you are adding a local printer or a network printer as follows:
   - **Local Printer:** Specify the manufacturer name and type.
   - **Network Printer:** Specify the network path or queue name in the text box provided (shown in Figure 15-21) or click the Browse command to navigate to the path where the printer is located. You can also indicate whether you plan to print MS-DOS–based applications using the printer you are adding.
6. Click Next.
7. When adding a local printer, you are asked to specify the printer's port, as shown in Figure 15-22. Select the appropriate port and click Next.
8. The name of the printer appears in this wizard screen. You can change the name of the printer to include the user name, the printer location, or other descriptive information. Here you can also specify whether you want to set this printer as the default. Whether or not it is selected as the default, the printer you have added is available to use at any time.
9. In the last wizard screen, you are asked whether or not you want to print a test page. It is always a good idea to perform a test print just to confirm that you have chosen the right printer port. If you have chosen a port other than the one the printer is connected to, the test page will not print. Whether or not you choose to perform a test print, click Finish.

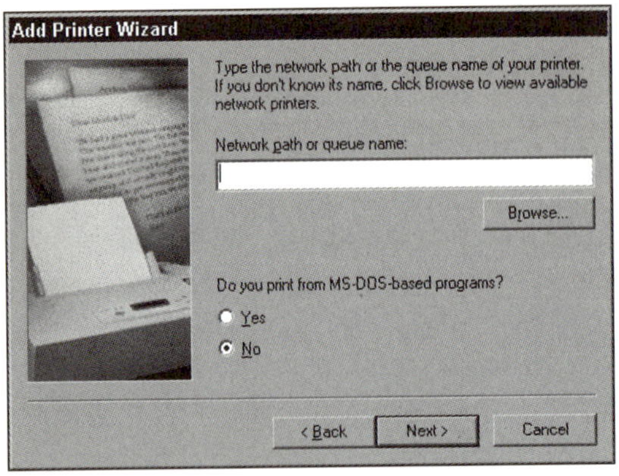

Figure 15-21: The path name or queue name of the network printer you are adding is required.

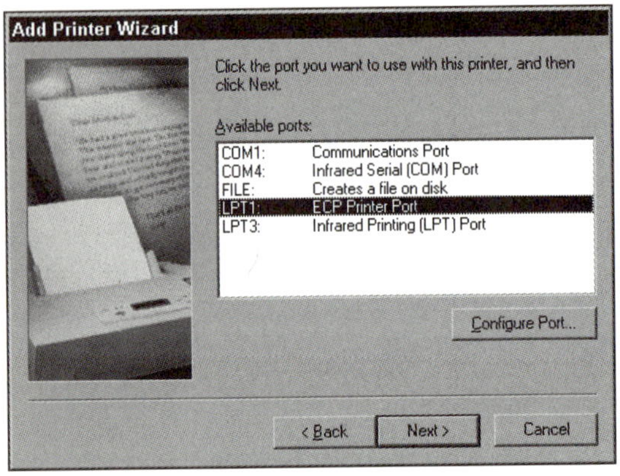

Figure 15-22: Specify the specific port on the computer where the printer is connected.

You can confirm that the printer is added by choosing Start ⇨ Settings ⇨ Printers to see the name of the printer you have added.

Summary

This chapter covered how to work with the Excel printing options. You learned how to do the following:

- Select data to print and specify a print range.
- Preview what you plan to print.
- Set Page Setup options.
- Change printer properties.
- Choose network printers.

The next chapter shows you how to represent your worksheet data in a compelling way through the use of graphs and charts.

Chapter 16

Excel Graphics and Charts

In This Chapter

- ♦ Excel charting overview
- ♦ Creating charts with the Chart Wizard
- ♦ Printing and saving charts
- ♦ Formatting chart objects
- ♦ Changing plotting methods
- ♦ Inserting graphic objects and files

CHAPTER 14, "FORMATTING WORKBOOKS," shows you how to adjust the formatting in your worksheets to enhance readability and to add clarity. In this chapter, you find out how to graphically represent the worksheet data that you so carefully formatted. Using Excel's tools to depict your data with charts and graphic elements can help you to persuade or to drive home a point when you need to make a presentation to either a client or a jury. Because pictures are worth a thousand words, data that you depict in this visual way can make for compelling evidence.

Excel Charting Described

A *chart* is a collection of facts set up in a visual format such as a diagram, table, or graph. Excel's easy-to-use Chart feature is a tool that helps you turn worksheet data into various visual formats, or types of charts. You can create charts based on a built-in collection of standard and custom chart types. Some chart types available in Excel and commonly used by law offices are bar charts, pie charts, and area charts. Excel will also handle more esoteric charts that are not commonly used in law offices, such as scatter plots and radar charts.

Excel can automatically create a chart for you when you select the values and the corresponding column headings that you want to chart and press F11. Or you can make all the decisions (about the chart type, chart labels, headings, how the data is plotted, and so on) by stepping through a series of dialog boxes in the Chart Wizard. But whatever charting method you choose, you need to prepare your worksheet data and have a good idea of what you want your chart to show. The following bullets describe activities and decisions that are essential for creating useful charts with Excel:

- ♦ **Organizing your data:** In order to have data to chart, your worksheet should contain categories (like column headings) to identify the data and values (in cells under the column headings). You select these column headings and values to tell Excel what data to include in your chart.
- ♦ **Choosing the right chart type:** Excel offers a variety of chart types, and each type depicts your data with a different emphasis. For example, a *pie chart* displays the contribution of each value to a total, whereas a *line chart* shows a trend over time or across categories. You can look through the chart types in the Chart Wizard and decide which type best depicts your data.

- **Positioning your chart:** Excel lets you position your charts within the worksheets that contain the charted data or on separate *chart sheets* that appear as separate sheets in your workbook. Like worksheets, the number of charts that a workbook can hold is limited only by your computer's virtual memory.

REMEMBER: Excel does a good job of keeping your charts up-to-date. When Excel creates a chart, it forms a link between the data values selected and the chart. This link ensures that if the data in the worksheet changes, the chart automatically changes as well.

Recognizing chart terms and elements is important for understanding how to use Excel's Chart feature and apply charting options. The following bullet list defines some common charting terms, and Figure 16-1 shows the corresponding chart elements.

- **Category axis:** The chart axis (such as the *x* axis in a column or line chart) that delineates the data categories
- **Category axis labels:** The labels displayed for each category shown on the category axis
- **Chart title:** A descriptive name chosen for the chart
- **Chart area:** The area that encompasses the chart and all its headings and labels
- **Data labels:** Headings displayed next to the data markers representing data series elements
- **Data marker:** A symbol representing a data series element, such as a column in a chart, a point on a line graph, or a pictorial representation of the type of data being charted
- **Data series:** A set of values selected for representation in a chart
- **Gridlines:** Evenly spaced horizontal or vertical lines that flow through a chart's plot area
- **Legend:** The key that relates the data marker (the column, point, pie slice, and so on) to the data series that it represents
- **Plot area:** The chart area containing the data markers, which represent the selected data series' values
- **Tick marks:** Points along a chart axis that marks uniform division of values on the value axis or categories on the category axis
- **Value axis:** The chart axis (such as the *y* axis in a column or line chart) that delineates the values (dates, numbers, and so on) of the data series
- **Value axis labels:** The labels shown for each value depicted by a tick mark on the value axis

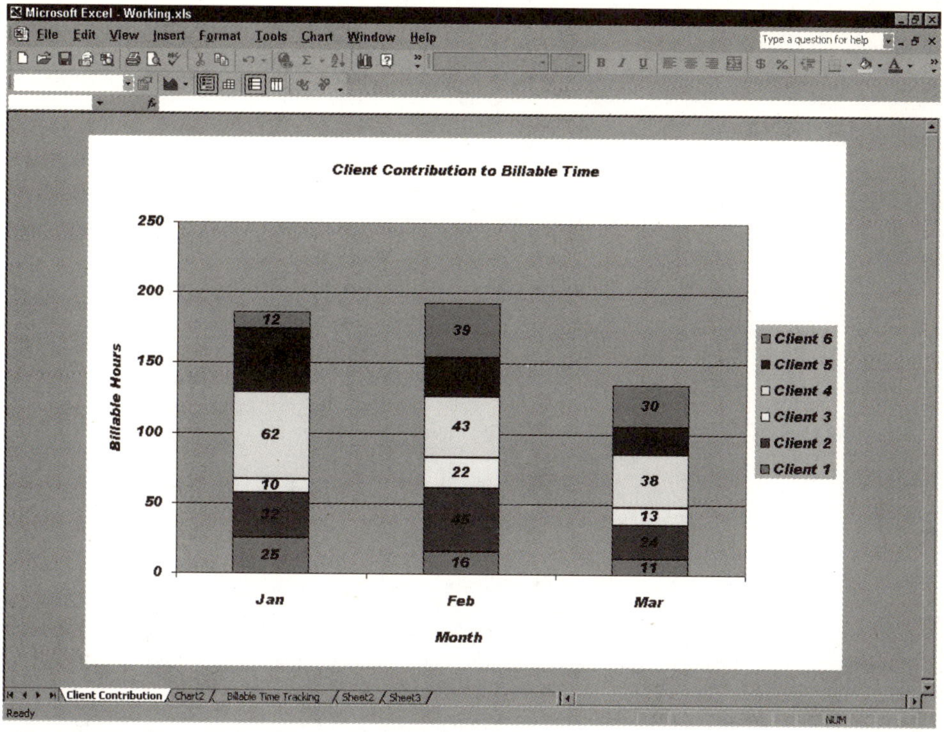

Figure 16-1: Know your chart elements and what Excel calls them.

Charting the Simple Way

If you have a simple range of data to chart, Excel can make the chart creation process simple. You select the source range of data on your worksheet and press F11, and the program does the rest. That is, Excel makes all the decisions about what kind of chart to make, what labels to add, and where to place the final creation. When you take this easy route, Excel creates a column chart based on your selected worksheet cells and places it on a chart sheet named *Chart1*. (The first chart you create in a workbook goes on the Chart 1 sheet. For each additional chart you create in this way, Excel adds another chart sheet and increments the number in the chart sheet name.)

Figure 16-2 shows the source range of categories and data that you need to select so that, when you press F11, Excel produces the simple column chart shown in Figure 16-3. Excel plots the data series (represented by the columns), puts labels on the category and value axes, and creates a legend.

TIP: When selecting the source data range for your chart, you can click and drag in the worksheet to select adjacent cells, or you can press and hold the Ctrl key while selecting nonadjacent cells to include in the data range.

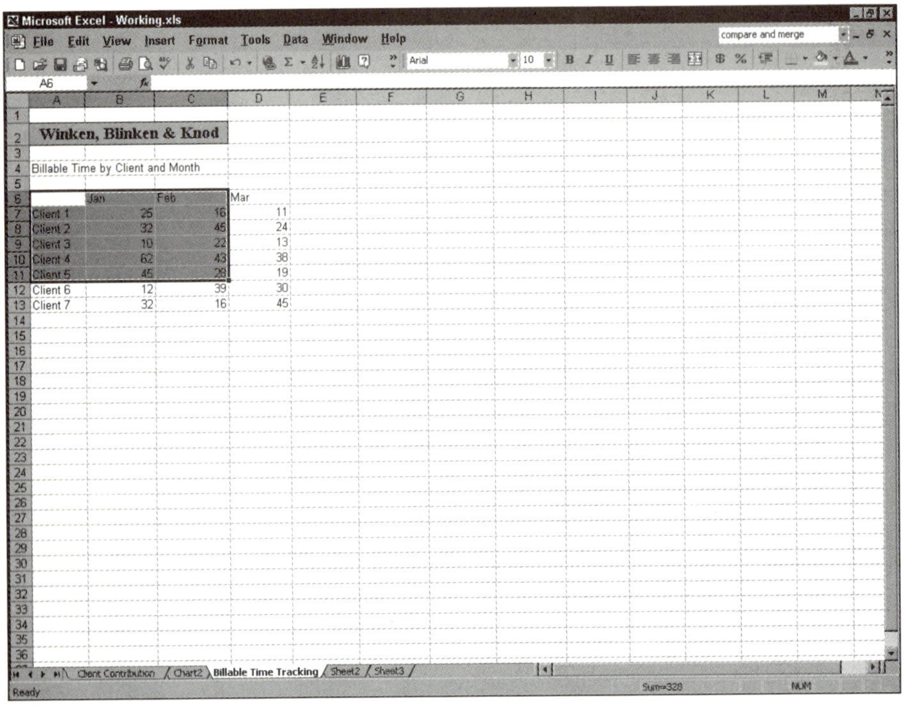

Figure 16-2: The source data in the Billable Time by Client and Month worksheet

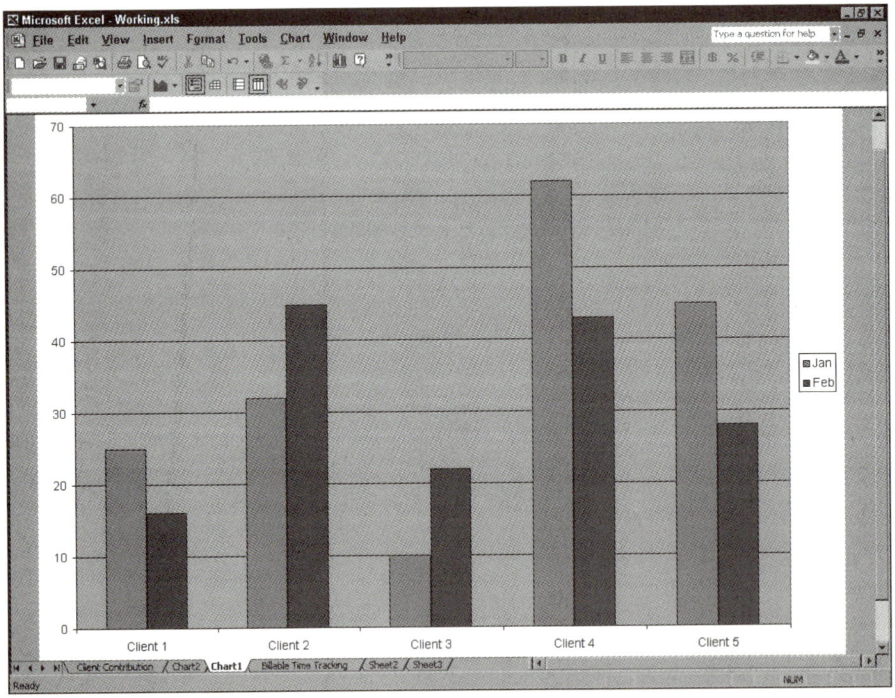

Figure 16-3: Excel creates a column chart on the chart sheet based on the selected data.

Using Excel's Chart Wizard

Excel's Chart Wizard leads you through the step-by-step process of creating a chart that you can place directly on the worksheet containing your source data or on a separate chart sheet. You are not required to select the data range to chart before you enter the Chart Wizard because you can select (and also modify) the data range from within the wizard. However, if you choose to select the data range beforehand, you can select any combination of adjacent or nonadjacent cells.

TIP: When you are ready to select the data range you want to chart, try to include the row or column headings that describe the data and, in situations where the worksheet contains totals, include either the totals or the lists of numbers that add up to the totals. Following these simple guidelines will make charting easer and allow you to make fewer changes to achieve your desired result.

You initiate the Chart Wizard by clicking the Chart Wizard tool on the Standard toolbar or by choosing Insert ⇨ Chart. The Chart Wizard involves four distinct steps. Table 16-1 describes the four-step sequence that you follow when you are creating a chart by using the Chart Wizard.

Table 16-1
Chart Creation Steps in the Chart Wizard

Chart Wizard Steps	*What You Need to Do*
Step 1 of 4 – Chart Type	Click the Standard Types tab to choose a chart type and subtype from a list of popular types or click the Custom Types tab to choose from a list of less common chart types.
Step 2 of 4 – Chart Source Data	If you did not select the data range to chart before entering the Chart Wizard, use this step to specify the data range on the Data Range tab or the series on the Series tab. You can also specify category (*x*) axis labels at this time.
Step 3 of 4 – Chart Options	Choose the desired charting options from the options arranged on six category tabs: Titles, Axis, Gridlines, Legend, Data Labels, and Data Table.
Step 4 of 4 – Chart Location	Specify whether you want Excel to create the chart on a separate chart sheet or embed the chart in the worksheet containing the source data.

The Chart Wizard provides choices and a preview of the chart you're constructing at each step. To get the Chart Wizard started, choose Insert ⇨ Chart from the Excel main menu. After completing Chart Wizard Steps 1–3, you click Next to move on. At Step 4, you click Finish. The following sections look more closely at each step in the Chart Wizard.

Step 1: Choosing a chart type

Step 1 of the Chart Wizard's creation process leads you through choosing a chart type. In the Chart Type dialog box, you find two tabs — Standard Types and Custom Types. On the left of the Standard Types tab, shown in Figure 16-4, you find a list of 14 commonly used chart types. As you click a chart type, a group of two or more associated subtypes (variations of the chart type you selected) displays on the right. Alternatively, you can click the Custom Types tab to choose a more elaborate chart type from a list of 20 provided there.

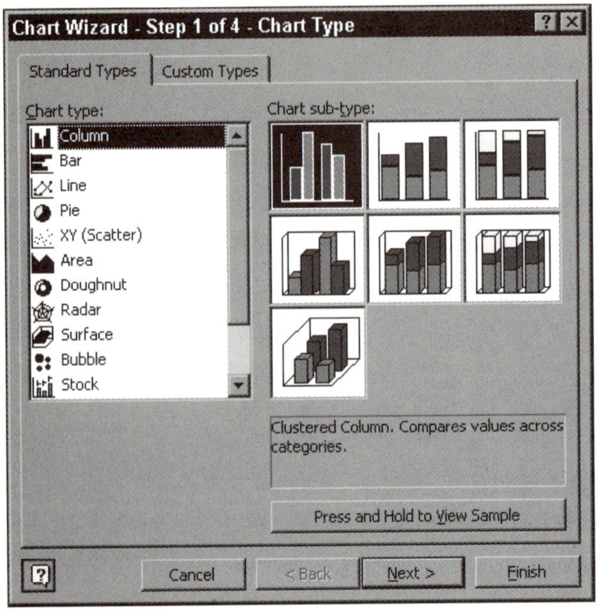

Figure 16-4: Choose a chart type from Excel's built-in standard or custom types.

TIP: Take care to choose the appropriate chart type for the kind of information you want to show. For example, a column chart compares values across categories and is appropriate for depicting billable hours by client if you want to see how your billable time is divided among your clients. However, you can use a pie chart to depict this same data if you want to show how each client's billable hours contribute to the whole of your monthly billable activities. Alternatively, a line chart may be more appropriate when you want to show billable activity trends over time.

If you selected the source data range prior to entering the Chart Wizard, you can select the desired chart type (and subtype) and preview your chart before actually applying the chart type. To see a sample of your charted data before making a commitment, click (and hold) the Press and Hold to View Sample button and see your chart preview in the Sample box that appears on the right. When you are satisfied with your choice of chart type, click Next to move to Chart Wizard – Step 2 of 4 – Chart Source Data.

Step 2: Specifying the chart source data

This dialog box of the Chart Wizard – Step 2 of 4 – Chart Source Data is where you specify the data range to be plotted from your worksheet and identify the series to be shown. This dialog box contains two tabs: Data Range and Series. ***Note***: If you selected the data range and series prior to entering the Chart Wizard, then you see the information already entered on this tab and may be done with this step. You can also use this step to change the data range and series, if necessary.

Identifying the data range

On the Data Range tab of the Chart Source Data dialog box, shown in Figure 16-5, you can specify the *data range* (the collection of worksheet cells containing the values and labels to be plotted) by either of the following methods:

- **Selecting the data range directly on the worksheet:** If you did not select the data range prior to entering the Chart Wizard, you can click and drag in the worksheet to collapse the Chart Source Data dialog box and select the desired range. This method is easiest and most likely to ensure that you chart the values that you want.
- **Entering the cell range values in the Data Range text box:** Notice that Excel uses absolute references for the cell composing the data range so that the references do not change even if the values in those cells change.

Also, select the appropriate option button to specify whether the data series should fall in columns or rows. The selection you make — Rows or Columns — is up to you and will affect the way your final chart looks. If you are unsure of which to choose, first click Rows and then Columns, and select the option that results in your data appearing the way you want it to appear. Figure 16-5 shows the selected data range in the Data Range text box and shows Rows selected for the Series In option.

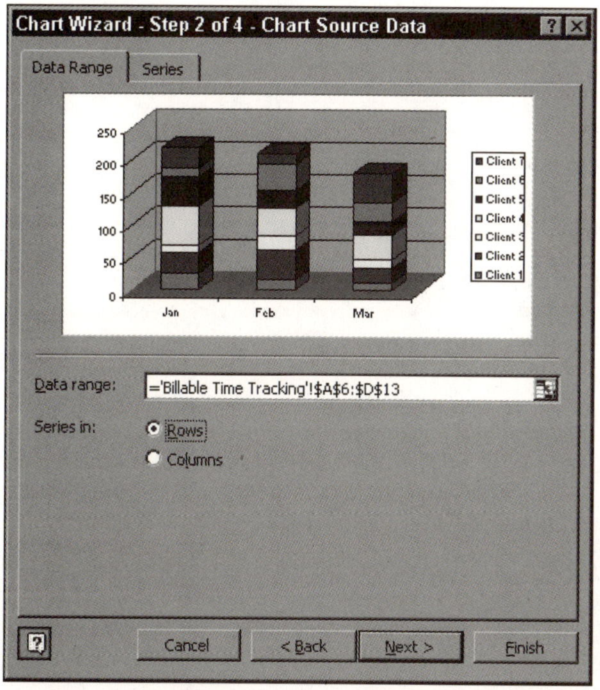

Figure 16-5: The Data Range tab in the Chart Source Data dialog box

Identifying the series

On the Series tab, you identify the elements of your data series — that is, you specify which cells contain the actual values to be charted and which cells contain the labels associated with those values. Again, this information may already be present if you select the data range before entering the Chart Wizard or from the Data Range tab. If the data range selected does not encompass the cells containing the labels, Excel shows default names for the series, such as *Series 1* and *Series 2*.

If you have series labels that aren't included in the original data range, follow these steps to add them on the Chart Source Data dialog box Series tab:

1. Click the default name in the Series list box to select that series. Excel highlights the default name, as shown for Series 1 in Figure 16-6.
2. Click in the Name text box.
3. Select the worksheet cell containing the label for that series or type a descriptive series name in the Name text box. Excel replaces the default series name with the label from the worksheet or with the name you type.

If you have more than one series to name, you must name them one at a time.

To add a new series to your chart, follow these steps:

1. Click the Add button under the Series list box. Excel adds a default series name in the list box and selects that series.
2. Click in the Name text box.
3. Select the worksheet cell containing the series label from the worksheet or type a descriptive series name.
4. Click in the Values text box.
5. Click and drag to select the worksheet cells that contain the series values. Excel adds the new series to your chart.

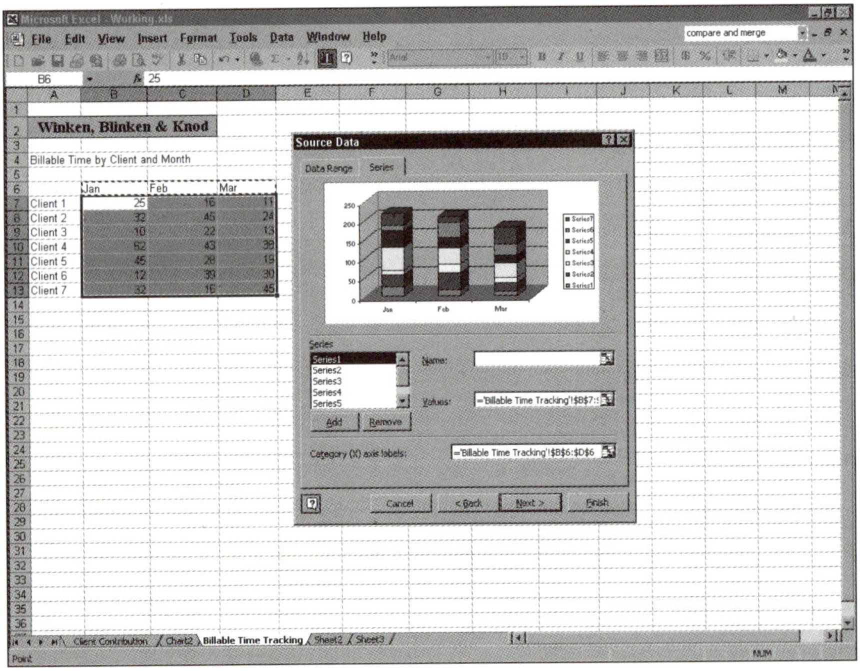

Figure 16-6: The Series tab now includes the data range to be used as category axis labels.

Also, you can select the labels to be used on the category axis from the Series tab. Click in the Category (X) Axis Labels text box and click and drag in the worksheet to select the cells that contain the category axis labels. Excel surrounds the selected cells with a moving dashed border (until you press Enter) and places the corresponding data range in the Category Axis (X) Labels text box.

Step 3: Selecting chart options

In the Chart Wizard – Step 3 of 4 – Chart Options dialog box, you find six tabs, each of which represents a category of options that you can apply to a chart. These options allow you to control the visual formatting and labeling of your chart. Table 16-2 lists the tabs in the Chart Options dialog box and describes the presentation options available on each tab.

Table 16-2
Setting Options in the Chart Wizard

Chart Options Tabs	***What You Do There***
Titles	Type titles for the chart and for the category and value axes in the appropriate text boxes.
Axes	Select check boxes and option buttons to display or remove value labels (on the value axis) and category labels (on the category axis).
Gridlines	Select check boxes to display or remove major or minor gridlines on the category and value axes.
Legend	Select the check box to display the legend and control its placement in the chart area by selecting the appropriate option button.
Data Labels	Select option buttons to include the data values or category names in the chart area. If you want to include the series identifiers, select the check box to place a legend key next to the respective data labels.
Data Table	Select check boxes to include a table with the values and related legend keys for each data series in the chart area.

Including a chart title is usually a good idea because it helps you and anyone referencing the chart to quickly identify the contents. The other chart presentation options that you decide to use depend on how you intend to use the chart, the level of detail required, what you want the chart to highlight about your data, and so on.

The chart in Figure 16-7 shows titles for the chart and both axes, major gridlines for the value (Z) axis, a legend positioned on the right, and data value labels.

Step 4: Picking a location for the chart

In the final dialog box of the Chart Wizard – Step 4 of 4 – Chart Location, you see two option buttons that govern the placement of your chart:

- **As New Sheet:** Select this option button if you want to place your chart on a separate chart sheet. Notice that Excel provides a text box next to this option button where you can type any name you like (up to 31 characters long) for the new chart sheet. Placing a chart on a separate chart sheet is a good idea when you don't need to have both the worksheet data and the chart visible at the same time.
- **As Object In:** Select this option button to embed your chart in the worksheet containing the chart's source data or in any other worksheet in the workbook. The list box next to this option

button shows the worksheet containing the source data as the default for placing your chart. To choose a different worksheet, click the down arrow on the list box and choose the worksheet name from the drop-down list. When you make a chart an embedded object, you may discover that Excel automatically adjusts the axis labeling and spacing between tick marks to attain a chart size that is appropriate for the worksheet.

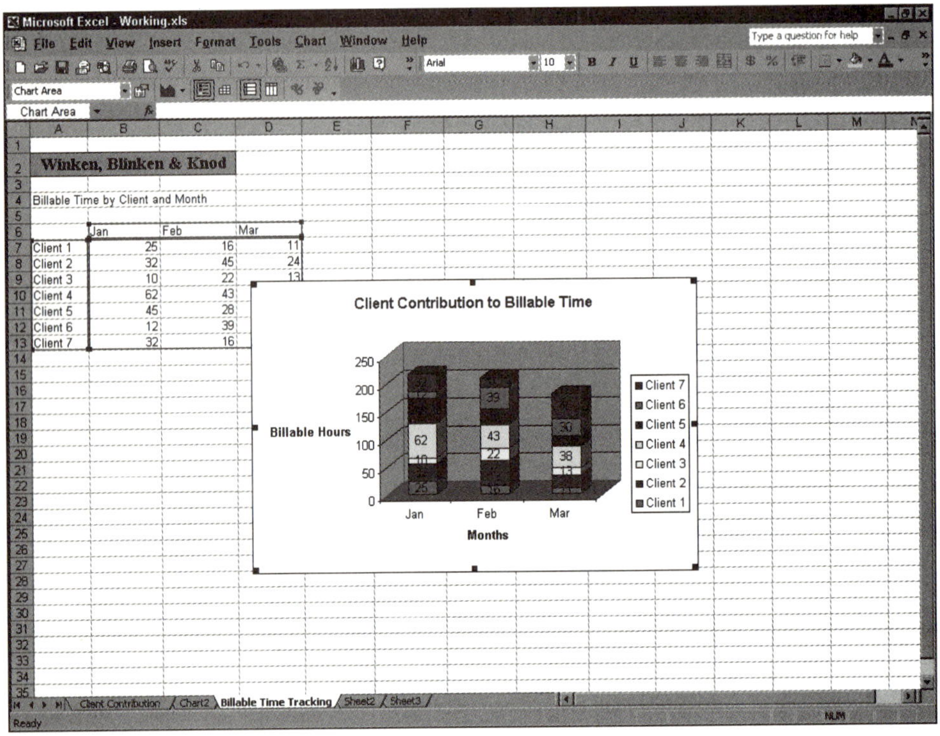

Figure 16-7: A chart with descriptive titles

Because an embedded chart is a picture, you can move it around on the worksheet or resize it to fit in a different area. If you want to move a chart around on the worksheet, click in the chart area to select the entire chart and hold down the left mouse button while you drag it to a new location. Notice that, when you click in the chart area, a thin, black border with sizing handles appears around the chart (refer to Figure 16-7). Also notice that, after you click in the chart area, the words *Chart Area* appear in the Name box (the same text box that shows you which worksheet cell is selected).

Changing the Chart You Just Created

The preceding two sections present two ways to make Excel charts. Whether you create a simple chart by pressing F11 or follow the step-by-step method of the Chart Wizard, you may need to make changes to your chart later.

When you use the simple F11 method, you cannot set many desirable options until after the chart is created. If you want to make changes to the chart, right-click in the chart area and choose from the pop-up menu that appears. Among the options on this menu, you find the following choices: Chart Type, Source Data, Chart Options, and Location. You probably recognize these choices as the steps from the Chart Wizard (refer to Table 16-2), and clicking these options brings up the same dialog boxes that lead you through creating a chart with the wizard. You can freely change any of the chart options — including titles, data ranges, and chart location — by choosing from the pop-up menu and setting options in the resulting dialog box.

Saving and Printing Charts

Whether you create a chart on a separate chart sheet or as an embedded chart, Excel saves the chart as part of the workbook file. To save the workbook for the first time, you can choose File ⇨ Save from the Excel main menu. If you add charts to a workbook and want to give the workbook file a different name or change the file type or workbook location, choose File ⇨ Save As from the Excel main menu. Refer to Chapter 13, "Working with Workbooks," for more information on saving workbook files.

In Chapter 15, "Printing Worksheets," we show you how to preview your worksheet data and how to make changes to its appearance on the printed page. In the following sections, we tell you about the additional options available when printing worksheets that contain embedded charts or chart sheets.

Printing an embedded chart on a separate page

If you want to print an embedded chart on a separate page, click to select the chart area and choose File ⇨ Page Setup from the Excel main menu. In the Page Setup dialog box that appears, you find the following tabs that help you control the printing options for your chart:

- **Page:** On this tab, you find options to control the orientation, scaling, paper size, and numbering.
- **Margins:** Use the options on this tab to control page margins and placement of headers and footers.
- **Header/Footer:** Create custom headers and footers for your printed pages on this tab.
- **Chart:** This tab appears in place of the Sheet tab when you select a chart before choosing File ⇨ Page Setup. The Chart tab contains additional options for controlling the printed chart size (Use Full Page, Scale to Fit Page, or Custom) and the printing quality (Draft Quality or Print in Black and White).

After you set the desired options on these tabs, you can click Print Preview to see what the chart will look like when printed. When you are satisfied with your chart's appearance and are ready to print, click Print and work your way through the Print dialog box.

Printing a chart sheet

When printing a chart sheet, you have the same options available as you have when printing an embedded chart. A chart sheet automatically prints on a separate page. You can set print options (in the Page Setup dialog box) by choosing File ⇨ Page Setup or by displaying the chart in print preview mode and choosing Setup from the Print Preview toolbar.

Formatting and Clearing Chart Objects

Excel gives you several ways to format your charts — whether you created the charts on separate chart sheets or as embedded charts on your worksheet. You can format either type of chart according to your preferences by first selecting the chart objects and then applying the formats. A *chart object* refers to any individual item that makes up the chart, including the Chart Title, Value or Category Axis, and Legend.

Following are three ways to select the chart object that you want to format:

- With your chart sheet or embedded chart showing, right-click the chart object you want to format. This method selects the chart object and opens a pop-up menu containing options for formatting or clearing the formats for that chart object. Figure 16-8 shows the pop-up menu that appears after you right-click the Chart Title object.

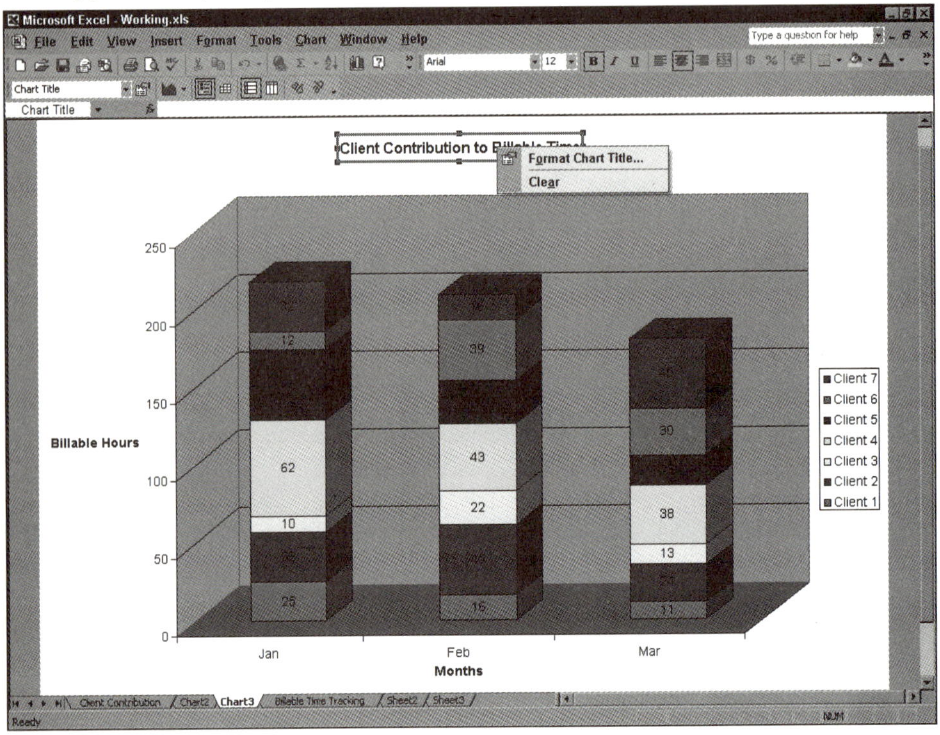

Figure 16-8: Right-click a chart object, and a formatting pop-up menu appears.

- With the Chart toolbar and selected chart showing, choose the chart object that you want to format from the toolbar's drop-down list of chart objects. The Chart Objects drop-down list shows all chart objects used in the active chart.
- With your chart sheet or embedded chart showing, click anywhere within the plot area or chart area to select a chart object. You can then use the arrow keys to move the selection to a different chart object.

Whichever technique you use to select a chart object, the formatting choices available depend on the chart object you select. Table 16-3 lists the formatting elements that you can apply to several of the more common chart objects.

Table 16-3
Chart Object Formatting Elements

Select This Chart Object	*Apply These Formatting Elements*
Chart Area	Patterns and font
Plot Area	Patterns
Axis (Value or Category)	Patterns, scale, font, number, and alignment
Legend	Patterns, font, and placement
Axis Title (Value or Category)	Patterns, font, and alignment
Chart Title	Patterns, font, and alignment
Data Series	Patterns, axis, Y error bars; data labels, series order, and shape. Formatting elements available change, depending on the type of chart selected.

TIP: Keep in mind that you may be able to change the formatting for elements of several chart objects at once. For example, you can change the desired font for all text in the chart by selecting the entire chart area, right-clicking, choosing Format Chart Area, and making your changes on the Font tab of the dialog box that appears.

Removing, or clearing, objects from your chart is simple. If you want to remove any object from your chart, right-click over the chart object and choose Clear from the pop-up menu that appears. Also, you can actually remove any chart object without accessing a menu or toolbar; simply click to select the object you want to remove and press Delete.

WARNING: Be careful when using the Clear feature from the formatting pop-up menus. If you choose Clear after right-clicking the Chart Area, you find that your entire chart disappears.

Changing Source Data and Plotting Methods

In addition to applying formatting defaults to your chart objects, Excel also applies defaults for plotting your data. And just as you can change formatting defaults (see the preceding section), you can use options from the chart object pop-up menus or from the Tools menu to change your source data and how it is plotted. The following subsections lead you through adding source data and changing a few of Excel's default plotting methods.

Adding a new data series

Even after you create and format a chart, you can return later and add a new data series by following these steps:

1. Click and drag in the worksheet to select the new source data range with the values and headings that you want to add to the chart.
2. Choose Edit ⇨ Copy to copy the selected data.
3. Click the chart you want to receive the copied data and choose Edit ⇨ Paste.

Excel adds the headings from the new source data to the legend and reflects the data values on the category or value axis, as appropriate.

TIP: If your chart plots more than one data series, the chart is easier to understand when you include data labels for the multiple categories, values, or series. To include data labels, right-click over the data marker in the chart and choose Format Data Series from the pop-up menu that appears. In the resulting Format Data Series dialog box, click the Data Labels tab and select the type of data label you want to include in the chart. The types of data labels available will depend on the type of chart you are creating.

Changing data series order

By default, Excel plots your data series from the highest amount to the lowest. You can reverse this decision and have your data plotted from the lowest amount to the highest. To change the order in which the categories or values are plotted in your chart, follow these steps:

1. Right-click over the value or category axis and choose Format ⇨ Axis from the submenu that appears. The Format Axis dialog box appears.
2. Click the Scale tab. Figure 16-9 shows the Format Axis dialog box with the Scale tab that appears when you right-click over the category axis.

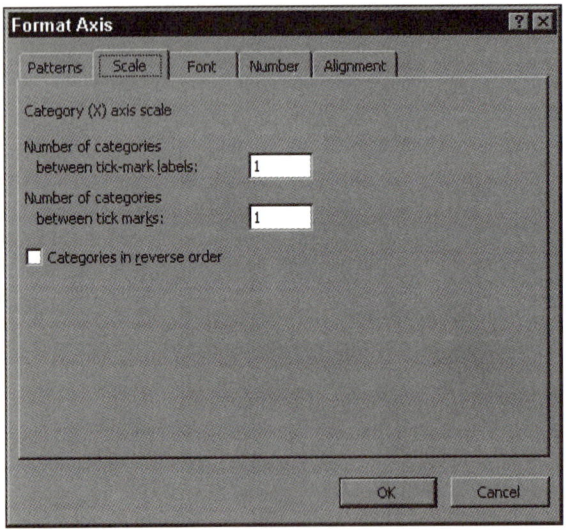

Figure 16-9: Click the right option on the Scale tab to reverse the category order.

3. Click to select the Categories in Reverse Order check box to change the order of categories along the category axis. If you want to change the order of values on the value axis, make sure that you right-click over the value axis in Step 1. Then select the Values in Reverse Order check box on the resulting Format Axis dialog box Scale tab.
4. Click OK to close the dialog box and apply the change to your chart.

Plotting empty cells

You may have situations in which your chart's source data range includes empty worksheet cells. You can specify how you want empty cells plotted by choosing the Tools ⇨ Options menu. In the resulting Options dialog box, click the Chart tab and choose one of the following options to handle your empty cells:

- **Not Plotted (leave gaps):** Lets you ignore empty cells, but results in a break in the series.
- **Zero:** Assigns a zero value to the empty cells.
- **Interpolated:** Calculates a value for the empty cells based on the value of the data that resides on either side. (This option applies to certain types of charts, such as scatter and line charts.)

Plotting hidden data

Suppose that you create a chart based on a data series visible in your worksheet. However, for reasons of confidentiality, you later hide the rows or columns containing cells that make up the chart's data series. When you go back to the chart, you find that the data in the hidden cells no longer shows up in the chart. This situation occurs because, by default, Excel plots only the data in visible cells. But you can change this default. To ensure that all cells (whether visible or hidden) within the source data range show up in the chart, choose Tools ⇨ Options from Excel's main menu, click the Chart tab in the resulting Options dialog box, and *deselect* (remove the check mark from) the option Plot Visible Cells Only.

Reworking and Relinking Charts

After you create a chart, you are not stuck with the options that you selected while creating it. Any time you want, you can change the chart's characteristics, including chart type, source data, chart options, and chart location. (You may recognize these characteristics as the Chart Wizard's four main steps, as presented in the earlier section "Using Excel's Chart Wizard.")

To access the dialog boxes that let you modify your chart's characteristics, try one of these techniques:

- Select the chart that you want to modify, choose Chart from the Excel main menu, and choose the desired menu option (Chart Type, Source Data, Chart Options, or Chart Location).
- Right-click over the chart area and choose the desired option from the pop-up menu that appears.

After the requested dialog box appears, make your chart modifications and click OK or Cancel to apply the changes.

You can make other modifications by using the Chart toolbar; if the Chart toolbar is not visible on-screen, choose View ⇨ Toolbar and select Chart from the submenu. The Chart toolbar gives you a drop-down list of your chart objects and several buttons that let you control your chart's characteristics. For example, to change your chart type to one of the other chart types provided by Excel, select the chart (either embedded or on a separate chart sheet) and choose a type from the Chart

Type drop-down on the toolbar. If you want to add a data table to your chart, click the Data Table button on the toolbar. The Chart toolbar offers additional options for formatting the legend, titles, axes, and other chart objects.

Earlier, we told you that chart values are linked to worksheet data. That is, if the values in the data range on the worksheet change, so do the values in the chart. You can also link text labels in the chart back to the worksheet so that the chart labels change with the labels on the worksheet.

After the chart is completed, you can set up the link between chart labels and worksheet labels by following these steps:

1. Click to select the label that you want to link back to the worksheet.
2. Type an equal sign (=) in the Formula bar.
3. Click the worksheet tab that contains the worksheet labels you want linked. (If you are working with an embedded chart, skip to Step 4.)
4. Click to select the cell containing the label to be linked.
5. Press Enter.

Inserting Graphics in Your Worksheets and Charts

Legal professionals routinely prepare documentation, filings, and submissions on behalf of their clients. In many instances, the submissions appear on law firm letterhead or other stationery. But sometimes legal documents are prepared using the client's logo or company name. These situations used to be handled by having the client provide stationery (with the company's logo, fonts, and other style elements) that the law office would use to prepare the documents. However, with the technology that exists today, law firms can scan the image of a company logo or other artwork, convert the scanned image into a graphic file, and insert the file into a worksheet, chart sheet, or embedded chart. Scanned images are only one type of graphic that you can include in your Excel worksheets and charts. Excel accepts graphics objects from a variety of sources and in a variety of formats. The following list gives an overview:

- **Formats accepted:** Common graphic file types (and related file extensions) that Excel recognizes include Joint Photographic Experts Group (.jpg), Microsoft Windows bitmap (.bmp, .rle, .dib), Graphics Interchange Format (.gif), and Windows Metafile (.wmf). **Note that,** to ensure that you are using one of the graphic file formats that Excel can recognize, you can review the complete list of graphic file types Excel uses by accessing the Help feature. If you have a graphic file type that you do not see in this list, you may need to use one of Excel's filters to convert your graphic file to a format that Excel understands. The Microsoft Office Web site offers help with accessing and using Excel's filters.
- **Microsoft as a graphics source:** One convenient source of Excel-friendly graphics is the Microsoft Clip Art Gallery, which ships with Office XP. Choose Insert ⇨ Picture ⇨ Clip Art from the Excel main menu to open the Insert ClipArt dialog box and locate a suitable graphic.
- **Drawing your own:** You can draw graphic objects yourself by using Excel's Drawing toolbar. If you do not see the Drawing toolbar in the Excel window, right-click over the toolbar area at the top of your window and select Drawing from the toolbar list that appears. Among the tools located on the Drawing toolbar is an AutoShapes button that you click to access an AutoShapes submenu. On this submenu, you find a variety of graphic objects to draw, including basic shapes, block arrows, connectors, and lines. You can create a graphic object using any of these AutoShapes and then use the resulting object as you would an already made graphic file, such as a picture or Clip Art.

You can insert graphic objects into Excel worksheets, chart sheets, or embedded charts, and the graphic objects you insert can consist of pictures or text. You can place these graphic objects into headers or footers or on top of (like layering) the worksheet or chart. Using graphic objects can add interesting visual appeal (such as Clip Art pictures to illustrate the data being charted) or explanatory information (such as text boxes created by using the Drawing toolbar) to your charts. Consider inserting graphic objects into a chart's data markers as the *fill color* (like the color of the column in a column chart) or as the data marker itself. As with other chart objects, you can later move, resize, reformat, or delete the graphic objects or pictures that you place in your worksheet, chart sheet, or embedded chart.

Summary

Many people use Excel primarily for crunching numbers, but in some situations a picture is worth a thousand words. Excel allows you to create amazing charts based on the data in a worksheet or to add different types of graphics, as needed. In this chapter you learned the following:

- How Excel creates charts
- How to put the Chart Wizard to work
- How to print charts and save them to disk
- How to change the way Excel displays objects in a chart
- How Excel can plot your data
- How to insert graphic objects and files

In the next chapter you learn how to use the database functions available in Excel.

Chapter 17

Excel Databases

In This Chapter

- ♦ Understanding databases
- ♦ Creating a database
- ♦ Adding, editing, and deleting data
- ♦ Searching for data
- ♦ Using AutoFilter
- ♦ Deciding on Excel or Access for your database project

IN THE LEGAL ENVIRONMENT, REQUESTS for information are often time sensitive and time dependent; there's not much time between when the questions are asked and when the answers must be given. A properly designed database gives you enormous power to provide timely answers because it places vital information at your fingertips. This chapter demonstrates this feature by creating a sample database of names, addresses, and other necessary information about all the parties in a class action suit. When the Class Action Claimants database is created and ready, the chapter demonstrates how to add, edit, sort, and filter records according to the information contained in the database.

Understanding Databases

A *database* is a collection of related information about a specific subject. When well designed, the structure of a database can make your business information much more easily useful. You can generate many types of reports and diversify the types of inquiries you make. In addition, the data included in Excel databases can be merged with letters or labels, simplifying the process of mass mailing. Databases are usually designed and created to handle large amounts of data and often replace a paper-based system. Rolodexes, phone books, and document indexes are examples of paper-based databases. Although databases are designed to hold large amounts of information, the proper organization and structure of that data make it easily accessible and readily available in a short period of time.

To be an effective tool, a database must contain information about something specific — for example, documents, clients, or the parties involved in a case. A player's contact list might contain contact information for all the lawyers and opposing counsel involved in a case. In addition, information contained in a database must be consistently organized — and customarily a database uses categories (structured as rows and columns) to make the data coherent and easy to locate. Each row in a database is a *record*; each column is a *field*. As the subunits of records, fields contain the individual items of information in the database. *Field names* — descriptive labels put at the tops of columns to identify fields — should correspond to the types of information held in each field. (An Excel field can hold numbers, text, dates, or other information.)

A practical example helps to illustrate the relationship between records and fields: If you're creating a contact list, the body of information about each contact is a *record* made up of several smaller pieces of information — the *fields*. Each field — for example, first name, last name, business address, city, state, or ZIP Code — holds a separate piece of information. Taken together, the columns and rows of data form the *list* (which is another term for the database itself). The resulting database structure looks like the one shown in Table 17-1.

Table 17-1
A Sample Contact Database

First Name	***Last Name***	***Address***	***City***	***State***	***ZIP***
John	Doe	1005 Highway Lane	Anywhere	USA	12345
Mary	Doe	2445 S Street, NW	Washington	DC	20037

In Table 17-1, each row is a new record; each column is a field within the record. Notice that each record has the same number of fields — proper data entry depends on that consistency.

Creating a database takes careful thought and planning. The best way to start designing a database is on paper. Think about the information you want to get out of the database and write it down. Weed out unnecessary information; you don't want to turn your database into a junkyard. When you have a list of the essentials, you're ready for several more vital areas of consideration:

- **What information do you want to track?** Figuring out the answer to this question tells you what fields to include. When deciding what to track, think about how you plan to use the data once it is included in the database — for example, do you plan to sort the data alphabetically? filter the data by certain criteria? generate labels? run queries on the data?
- **Who else will use the database and what do they need from it?** Consult with others who may need to use the database; find out what kinds of reports they may want to generate.
- **What are the most useful field names?** Each field name should be unique and descriptive of the information contained in that field. If you separate the pieces of information you plan to work with by putting them in different fields, they are easier to find and handle later. For example, if you intend to merge the names in the database with a letter or labels, consider creating separate fields for the last name and first name.

Sometimes the way an Excel database works can help you decide what goes in each field. For example, a few more steps (and a bit more time) go into sorting records by last name if the last names are included in the same fields as the first names. Creating separate fields for last and first names can make the records easier to sort — as an added bonus, the names become easier to retrieve and use accurately (especially in the inside addresses and salutations of personalized business letters).

The Class Action Claimants example given here uses eight fields: last name, first name, address, city, state, ZIP Code, phone number, and amount each claimant is entitled to receive. First name and last name occupy separate fields to make the list easier to alphabetize by last name. Why so many fields? Simple: You may need access to any of those specific details. Well-defined specifics are easier to locate if each one occupies its own field.

When you have worked out the design and the desired details for your Excel database, you're in a much better position to start building it. That process is the subject of the next section.

Creating a Database

You can begin your database by entering a heading to identify the list, skipping a row to separate the heading from the data. Then type your field names on a new row, entering one field name into each column of the worksheet (beginning with Column A).

CAUTION: After you have begun to type the field names, be careful not to leave any blank columns or rows between the field names and the data itself. If there are blank columns or rows between the data, you will not achieve the desired results when sorting, filtering, alphabetizing, and so on.

Field names can contain uppercase and lowercase letters and spaces. Adding formatting to the row of field names — for example, shading or a different font — helps you easily distinguish the field names from the actual data they identify.

CAUTION: Don't add formatting to the data itself. Normally, such a measure is unnecessary at best and confusing at worst.

Figure 17-1 shows the completed Class Action Claimants database. Notice that after the database portion of the worksheet begins, no blank columns or rows are included.

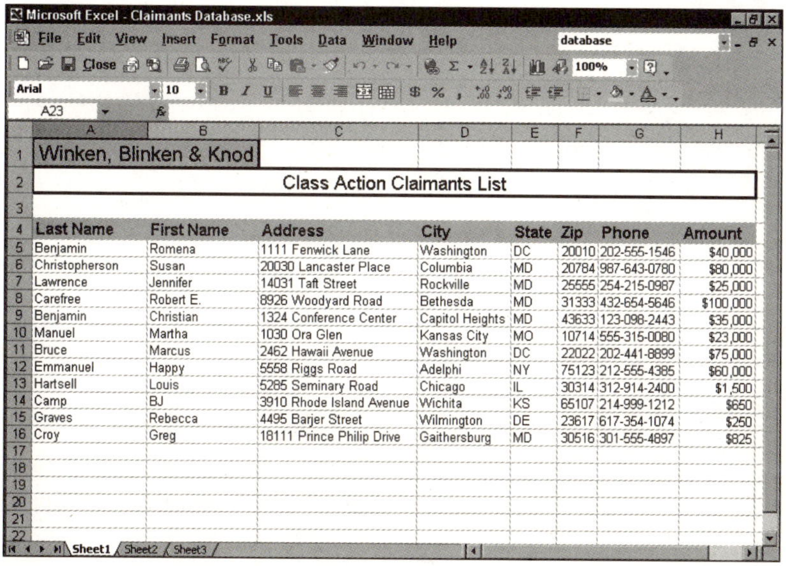

Last Name	First Name	Address	City	State	Zip	Phone	Amount
Benjamin	Romena	1111 Fenwick Lane	Washington	DC	20010	202-555-1546	$40,000
Christopherson	Susan	20030 Lancaster Place	Columbia	MD	20784	987-643-0780	$80,000
Lawrence	Jennifer	14031 Taft Street	Rockville	MD	25555	254-215-0987	$25,000
Carefree	Robert E.	8926 Woodyard Road	Bethesda	MD	31333	432-654-5646	$100,000
Benjamin	Christian	1324 Conference Center	Capitol Heights	MD	43633	123-098-2443	$35,000
Manuel	Martha	1030 Ora Glen	Kansas City	MO	10714	555-315-0080	$23,000
Bruce	Marcus	2462 Hawaii Avenue	Washington	DC	22022	202-441-8899	$75,000
Emmanuel	Happy	5558 Riggs Road	Adelphi	NY	75123	212-555-4385	$60,000
Hartsell	Louis	5285 Seminary Road	Chicago	IL	30314	312-914-2400	$1,500
Camp	BJ	3910 Rhode Island Avenue	Wichita	KS	65107	214-999-1212	$650
Graves	Rebecca	4495 Barjer Street	Wilmington	DE	23617	617-354-1074	$250
Croy	Greg	18111 Prince Philip Drive	Gaithersburg	MD	30516	301-555-4897	$825

Figure 17-1: The Class Action Claimants database

You can put data into your worksheet in one of two ways:

- **Manual input:** Type the data directly into the worksheet rows and columns.
- **Semiautomatic input:** Use a data form to place data in the worksheet.

Using a data form is particularly helpful if you have a lot of data to input across many columns; you can focus easily on only the record you're entering. You can also use a data form to edit records — or even eliminate them from your database.

To create a data form, you have only two steps to follow:

1. Select any cell in an existing database (or you can select a cell containing a field name if you have not yet begun to enter data).
2. Choose Data ⇨ Form. A dialog box named Sheet1 appears, showing all the field names in the order in which they should be typed.

If you selected a field name and the data has not yet been typed, the dialog box offers blanks beside the field names so that you can use the form to begin entering your data. If you selected a cell that contains actual data, the dialog box opens to the first actual record in the database. The result looks similar to Figure 17-2.

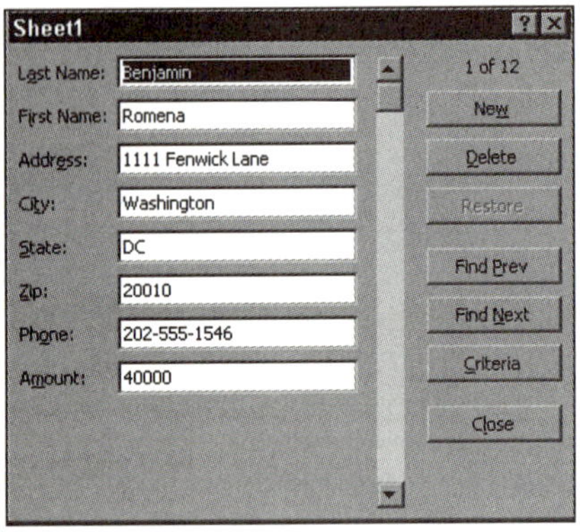

Figure 17-2: A form dialog box named *Sheet1* contains either a blank record or a record in the database.

To add a new record using the data form, follow these steps:

1. Click the New command button.
2. Type the information for each field name, using the Tab key to move to the next field.
3. When all the information is typed for a particular record, press Enter. Doing so places the completed record on the worksheet and takes you to a new blank form, in which you can type the next record.

TIP: If you inadvertently press Enter before you finish typing in the data for a record, use the Find Prev command button to return to the incomplete record.

Adding, Editing, and Deleting Data

When you type your data directly into a worksheet, navigation is simple:

- To go to the next record, move to the first blank row that follows the data you just input.
- To move from one field to the next, press the Tab key.
- To move to the next blank row after you enter data into the last column in the current row, press Enter.
- To get a new blank record, click the New command button in the data form.

Editing the contents of a field is the same as editing the contents of any worksheet cell in Excel. Simply click the field once; then edit the contents in the formula bar at the top of the worksheet. If you want to delete an entire record, simply click the row number to select the entire row, and then right-click to choose Delete from the submenu that appears (or choose Edit ⇨ Delete).

You can use the data form to locate the record you want to edit or delete; simply follow these steps:

1. Click either the Find Prev or Find Next command button. When the record you want is displayed in the data form, click in the field you want to edit. Then make the desired changes.
2. When you have finished editing the record, press Enter to put the changes into the worksheet (or use either the Find Prev or Find Next button to locate the next record you want to edit).

TIP: If you decide you don't want to finalize the changes you've made, click the Restore button before completing Step 3. Excel backs you out of the changes.

If you want to delete a record using the data form, locate the record you want to delete and then click Delete. A warning box appears (shown in Figure 17-3), telling you that the displayed record will be deleted permanently. Click OK or Cancel, as appropriate. If you click OK, you cannot use Restore to get the deleted record back.

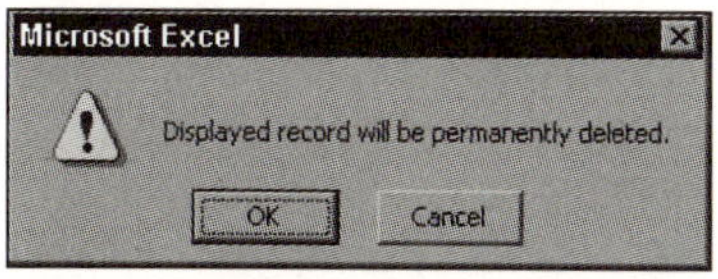

Figure 17-3: Excel warns you that the displayed record will be permanently deleted.

Searching for Data

If you're not using a data form to locate data in your database, normally you can locate any data in your worksheet by choosing Edit ⇨ Find, typing in the piece of information you're looking for, and then choosing Find Next. You can also use Edit ⇨ Find to replace data in your worksheet. If your database is small or medium-size, these techniques should be sufficient. (Note, however, that you'll see not only the data you're looking for but also all the other information in the worksheet.)

After your database reaches a certain size, however, finding a record by using the Find Prev and Find Next buttons is just too slow. In such a case, you can use a data form to search for records. The procedure for doing so looks like this:

1. Click the Criteria command button. A blank form appears.
2. Using a field name that you know exists in the record, type in the field name of the information you want to find. (In Figure 17-4, for example, the name *Camp* is the criterion typed in the `Last Name` field.)
3. Click the Find Next button. Excel searches through all the records to find the field that matches the one you typed. When the search is complete, Excel displays the desired record, placing its record number in the upper-right corner of the dialog box.

TIP: If multiple records meet your criteria, you can use both the Find Next and Find Prev buttons to move through all the records that meet your criteria.

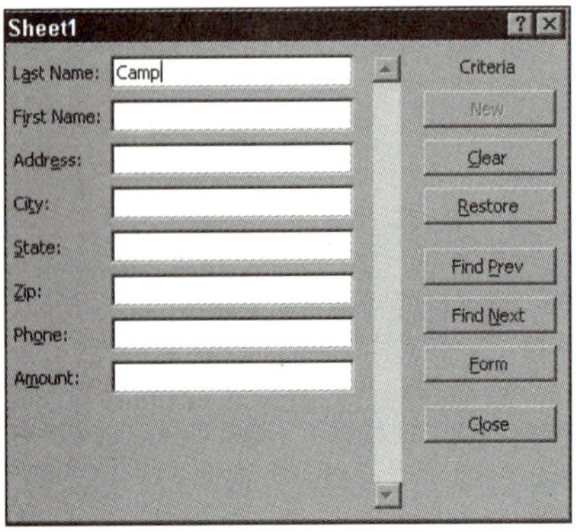

Figure 17-4: The Criteria data form

When you want to locate another record, click the Criteria button again and type in the criteria for the next record you want to find. If you make a mistake while entering the criteria, simply click the Clear button to return to a blank form so that you can start over.

CAUTION: If you don't click the Criteria button before you type the information you're looking for, Excel assumes you're editing the data — and will place your changes in the record when you press Enter.

Sorting Data

Sorting is a handy Excel capability that can rearrange data in a single worksheet or in the entire database. There are generally two items that must be specified when sorting — the field to be sorted and whether the data is sorted in an ascending or descending order. If you choose ascending, data is arranged alphabetically from A to Z, numbers from lowest to highest, and dates from first to last. When you specify descending, data is sorted from highest to lowest.

You can perform up to three levels of sorting — helpful if more than one record contains the same information in the field you decided to sort. Such multilevel sorting is for breaking ties. If you simply want to rearrange a single field, click anywhere in the field and then click either the Sort Ascending or the Sort Descending button (on the Standard toolbar, shown in Figure 17-5). The Sort Ascending button has a down arrow, indicating lowest-to-highest sort order; the Sort Descending button has an up arrow, indicating highest-to-lowest sort order.

Figure 17-5: The arrows on the Sort Ascending and Sort Descending buttons indicate the sort order.

WARNING: When you use the Sort feature, never select an entire column before you start the sort. If you do, Excel displays a warning box letting you know that only the information in the selected column will be sorted, but the data in the associated columns will not. Once sorted, a selected column is (in effect) disconnected from the adjacent columns — which makes the database no longer accurate.

Figure 17-6 shows the warning that Excel provides if someone has selected a column and chosen one of the Sort buttons. At this point, you can either expand the selection to include adjacent columns or continue sorting the selected column — just keep in mind that the accuracy of the database may be at stake.

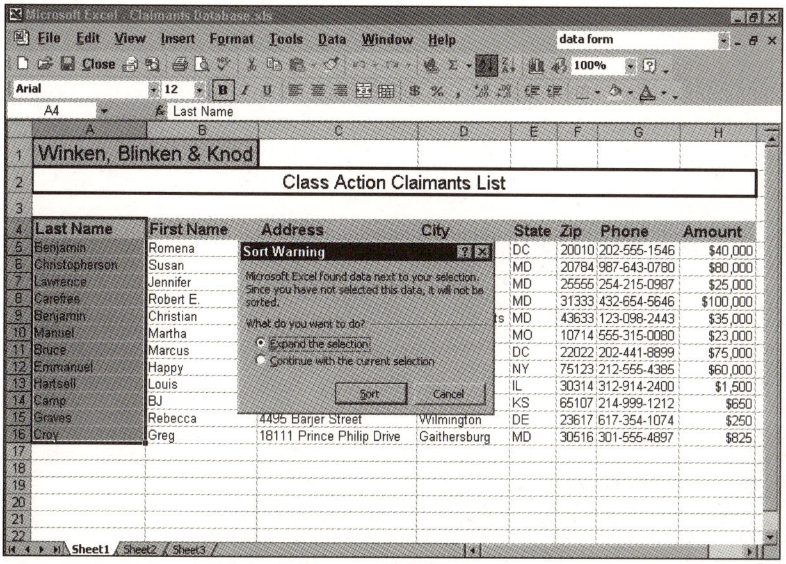

Figure 17-6: A warning box displays if only a single field is selected for sorting.

In the Class Action Claimants example, instead of selecting an entire column, we simply clicked one cell in the column and chose the Sort Ascending button. Figure 17-7 shows the results of sorting the Last Name column this way.

Notice that Figure 17-7 shows two claimants with the last name *Benjamin*, appropriately placed at the top of the list but not arranged alphabetically. To correct this situation, a multilevel sort is the appropriate tool for putting the two Benjamins in alphabetical order.

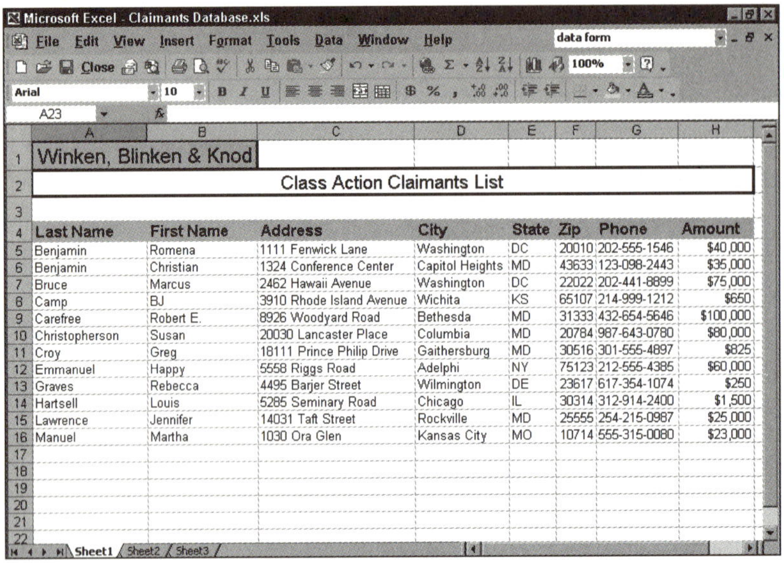

Figure 17-7: The Last Name field, sorted alphabetically

If you want to perform a multilevel sort, here are the steps to take:

1. Click any cell that already contains data.
2. Select the Data ⇨ Sort menus. If the active cell is blank, you receive the error message displayed in Figure 17-8 (in which case, click OK and then repeat Step 1).

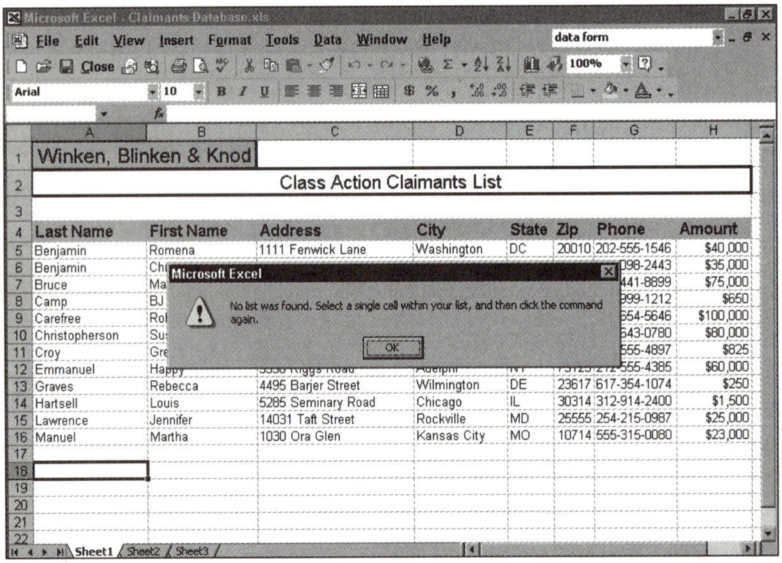

Figure 17-8: The error message that appears if you're trying to sort a blank field.

3. When you complete Steps 1 and 2, the Sort dialog box appears and the entire database is automatically selected. In the Sort dialog box you can specify which field you want to sort by choosing the field name from the Sort By drop-down list, which contains a list of all the field

names used in the database. Then, in the case of a tie, you can specify a second field to sort by choosing that field name in the Then By drop-down list. Excel enables you to sort up to three fields at one time. In our example, we tell Excel to sort by the `Last Name` field and then by the `First Name` field (see Figure 17-9). Notice that the Sort dialog box shows the Header Row option as selected. Choose this option when you have a header row (such as the column headings and the field names) so that this row is not sorted but remains above the database.

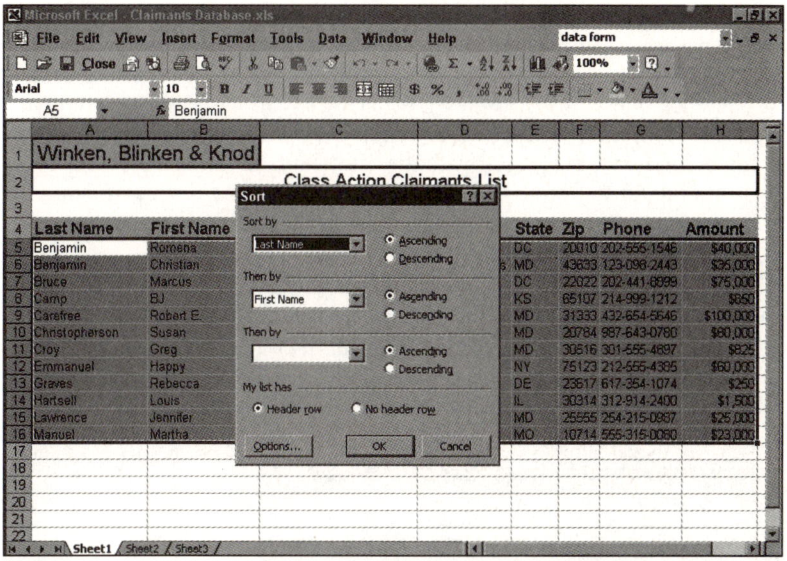

Figure 17-9: Specify the fields to sort by choosing the field names from the drop-down lists.

In Figure 17-10 you can see that all the last names are alphabetized — and although two last names are the same, their respective first names are also alphabetized.

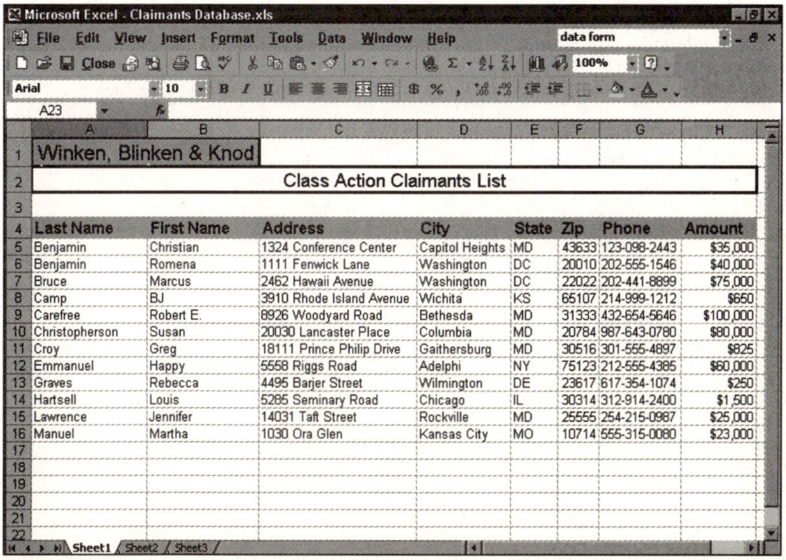

Last Name	First Name	Address	City	State	Zip	Phone	Amount
Benjamin	Christian	1324 Conference Center	Capitol Heights	MD	43633	123-098-2443	$35,000
Benjamin	Romena	1111 Fenwick Lane	Washington	DC	20010	202-555-1546	$40,000
Bruce	Marcus	2462 Hawaii Avenue	Washington	DC	22022	202-441-8899	$75,000
Camp	BJ	3910 Rhode Island Avenue	Wichita	KS	65107	214-999-1212	$650
Carefree	Robert E.	8926 Woodyard Road	Bethesda	MD	31333	432-654-5646	$100,000
Christopherson	Susan	20030 Lancaster Place	Columbia	MD	20784	987-643-0780	$80,000
Croy	Greg	18111 Prince Philip Drive	Gaithersburg	MD	30516	301-555-4897	$825
Emmanuel	Happy	5558 Riggs Road	Adelphi	NY	75123	212-555-4385	$60,000
Graves	Rebecca	4495 Barjer Street	Wilmington	DE	23617	617-354-1074	$250
Hartsell	Louis	5285 Seminary Road	Chicago	IL	30314	312-914-2400	$1,500
Lawrence	Jennifer	14031 Taft Street	Rockville	MD	25555	254-215-0987	$25,000
Manuel	Martha	1030 Ora Glen	Kansas City	MO	10714	555-315-0080	$23,000

Figure 17-10: The two *Benjamins* are now in alphabetical order.

Using AutoFilter

AutoFilter is a way to see only the records that meet certain criteria. For instance, in our example, each of our claimants will receive a specified amount of money at settlement. Suppose we want to see all the records that contain the name *Camp* in the Last Name field. To do so, you could choose Data ⇨ Form ⇨ Criteria or use the AutoFilter command.

As with sorting, you begin by clicking any cell containing data. Then select the Data ⇨ Filter ⇨ AutoFilter menus. Drop-down list arrows are added at the end of each field name. This option is a toggle; if you no longer need the drop-down list arrows, you can remove them by choosing Data ⇨ Filter ⇨ AutoFilter. When you click one of the drop-down list arrows, you see a list of all data in that field. Simply select the data you want to see. Doing so removes all the records from view (but does not delete them), leaving behind only the record with the selected data. In Figure 17-11, for example, we selected `Camp` from the `Last Name` field; Figure 17-12 shows the results of using AutoFilter to select that same record.

To return to the complete database, click the drop-down list arrow and choose All.

Suppose you want to see only those records that contain monetary amounts greater than or equal to $100,000. In this case, you would need to choose Custom from the drop-down list to open the Custom AutoFilter dialog box, where you can choose from a list of operators to use and specify the criteria you're looking for. In the sample, the Show Rows Where section specifies that we want to see all records where the Amount is greater than or equal to $100,000 (which was also selected from the list).

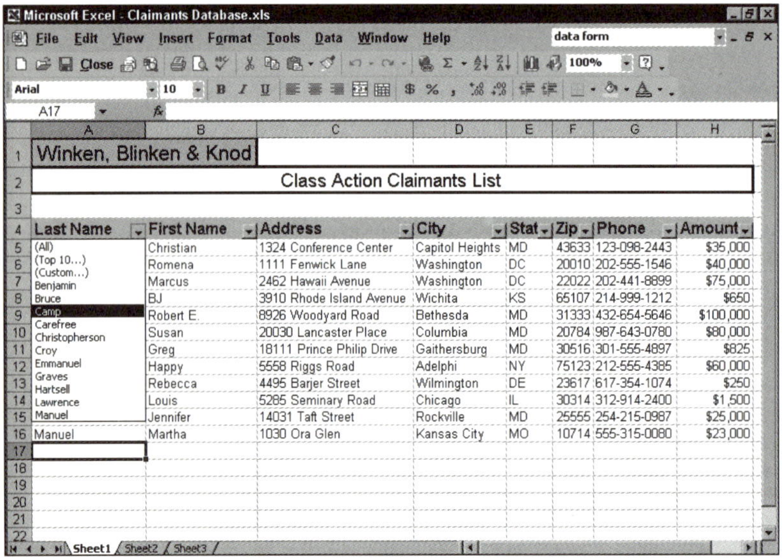

Figure 17-11: Select the desired record by choosing the particular data from the appropriate field.

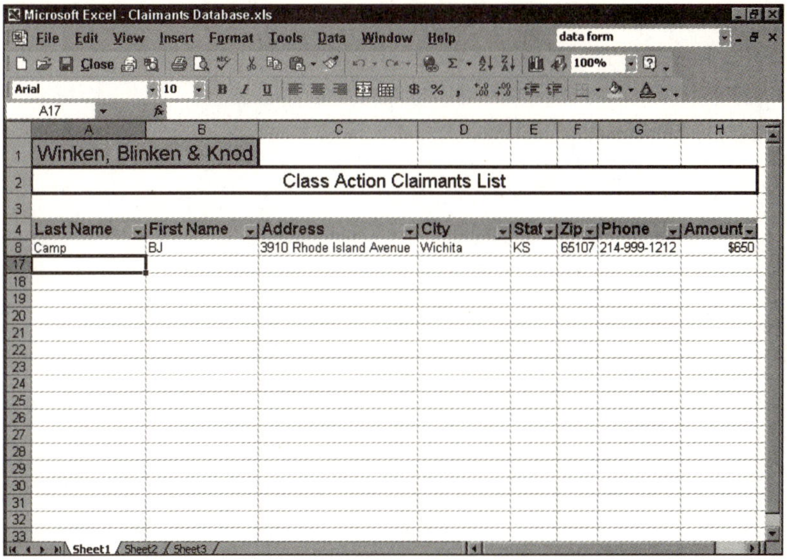

Figure 17-12: When you use AutoFilter, all records except the record containing the selected item are removed from view (but not deleted).

Notice that Excel uses the Amount field in the dialog box because it corresponds to the drop-down arrow we selected. Figure 17-13 is the Custom AutoFilter dialog box in which we made these selections; Figure 17-14 shows the results.

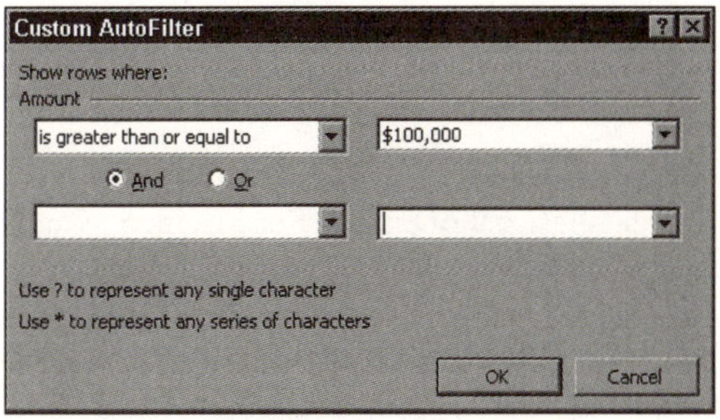

Figure 17-13: The Custom AutoFilter dialog box

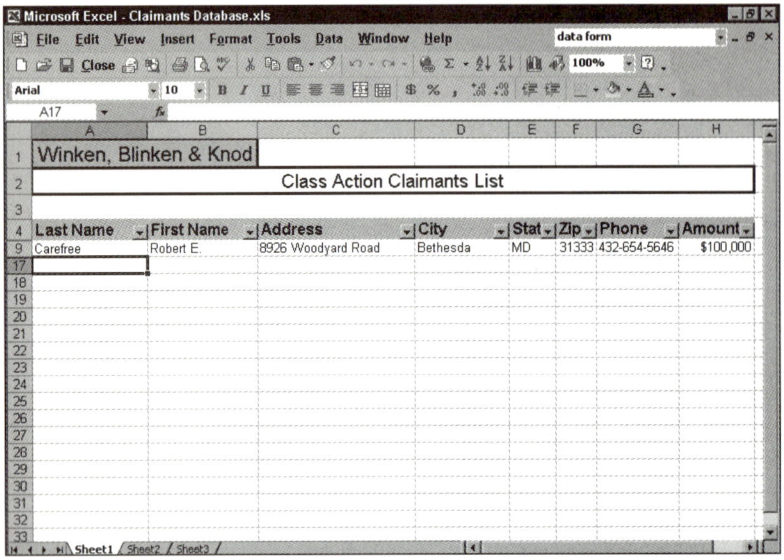

Figure 17-14: Only the records containing amounts greater than or equal to $100,000 are visible.

Deciding Whether Excel or Access Is Best for Your Database Project

A *relational database* is the most powerful type; it can create links to other databases, whether internal or external. Although both Excel and Access can run queries on data that exists in external databases, only Access can link to more than one database at a time. This is truly the power of a relational database.

By contrast, Excel produces a *flat-file database* — perfectly serviceable for small, self-contained database projects but unable to cross-reference multiple databases at one time. For instance, Excel can access an external client name list, an external client number list, and a billing attorney list, but it must do so one at a time. It cannot access them all at the same time. Thus, any query you run or report you generate can't gather and present all three pieces of information simultaneously. The real power of Access is that it can handle this extra degree of complexity. As long as there is a single field of information common to all three databases, Access can respond to a query or generate a report using information from all three databases.

Accordingly, you have one more dimension to add to the database planning mentioned at the beginning of this chapter: Consider whether the data you want to include in your reports and queries should be contained in a single database or multiple databases. If multiple databases seem likely, consider using Access instead of Excel.

Summary

Excel can be a great tool for keeping track of limited amounts of information and building small databases. In this chapter you have learned the ins and outs of how this works. Specifically, you have learned the following:

- What a database is
- How to put a database together
- How to use the tools for adding, editing, and deleting data
- How to search for data
- How the AutoFilter feature can help
- How to determine whether Excel or Access is best for your database project

In the next chapter you are introduced to a powerful feature of Excel: macros. You will learn how to automate many of the tasks you need to do on a regular basis.

Chapter 18

Excel Macros

In This Chapter

- Getting started with macros
- Assigning macros to toolbar buttons
- Running macros
- Making macros available globally
- Changing macro options
- Renaming a macro
- Deleting macros

SUPPOSE THAT EVERY TIME you begin a worksheet for client billing, you include your law firm's name in the upper-left corner. And maybe you also like to apply borders and shading, change the font size, and add attributes such as bolding. These tasks are not difficult to do manually, and you do not mind performing the steps every now and then. But if you routinely perform these steps each time you create a new client billing worksheet, you will undoubtedly start to look for ways to automate the process. Using Excel macros can help you automate the process and eliminate having to repeat routine steps. This chapter explores how you can make your life easier (while getting more work done) by creating and working with macros.

In this chapter, we introduce you to the wonderful world of Excel macros. In reality, macros can be a complex and overwhelming topic. The wonderful thing about Excel macros, however, is that you don't have to be overwhelmed — you can learn how to perform common, mundane tasks using macros, without the need to get too deep. If you would like more information about macros than is included here, you should refer to one of the many books available for Excel macro programming, such as *Excel 2002 Power Programming with VBA,* by John Walkenbach (published by Hungry Minds Inc.).

Getting Started with Macros

In Excel, *macros* are named routines containing a sequence of commands that perform a particular Excel task. You can create your own macros to perform a series of tasks that you routinely do, assign your macro to a keyboard shortcut or toolbar button, and then activate your macro by pressing the shortcut keys or clicking the button. In effect, activating a macro allows you to do a series of Excel tasks with one command.

The simplest way to create a macro is to let Excel record your routine program tasks (keystrokes, menu selections, options set, and so on). When you finish with your routine, tell Excel to stop recording and save the sequence as a macro. Your macro is then available to replay your recorded tasks later.

Before you begin creating your macro, you need to think through the tasks that you want to repeat and make decisions about when and how to activate the macro. One decision you can make concerns the positioning of the repeated tasks within your worksheet.

In Chapter 13, "Working with Workbooks," you learn about absolute and relative addressing when it comes to cell references. When creating a macro, you also need to be concerned about this issue. If you instruct Excel to record your macro using absolute references, then it will always work on exactly the same cells, over and over again. For instance, if you record a simple macro that makes the text in the current cell bold and you record it while cell A7 is selected, then the next time you run the macro, only the contents of cell A7 will be affected. If, instead, you want the macro to affect whatever cell you happen to have selected when you run it, then you want Excel to do the recording using relative references. When you do this, all commands are recorded as if they are executed relative to the position at which the macro will later be executed.

If you want the macro to work on cells that are relative to a starting point, you must click the Relative Reference button on the macro toolbar. This toolbar becomes visible when you actually start the recording process, as you will shortly see. To ensure that the macro works on specific cells (that is, in an *absolute* position, rather than relative to a starting point), deselect the Relative Reference button.

TIP: When recording a macro, you can change between relative and absolute reference positions at any time during the process by clicking the Relative Reference button.

Another item that you should think about in advance is where you want to store your macro. The place you select has a direct bearing on the accessibility of your macro in the future. In general, there are three places in which a macro can be stored:

- **The personal macro workbook.** This is a special workbook that is loaded automatically each time you start Excel. It is hidden, which means that you can't see it, but the macros it contains are available for use at any time. The bottom line is that if you store a macro in the personal macro workbook, it is available in all other workbooks you may be using.
- **The current workbook.** If you store a macro in the current workbook, it is available only when you have the workbook open. This is a natural place to store specialized macros that only have meaning for a specific set of data.
- **A new workbook.** When you are recording a macro, you can instruct Excel to store the macro in a brand new workbook. Excel obediently opens a new workbook and stores the macro there. The macro will only be available when that new workbook is open in the future.

After you know how you want to record the macro (absolute or relative) and where you want to store it, you are ready to actually do the recording. To record and save an Excel macro, follow these steps:

1. Choose Tools ⇨ Macro ⇨ Record New Macro. The Record Macro dialog box appears and offers the selections and options you need to name, describe, and position your macro for replay.
2. In the Record Macro dialog box, type a descriptive name for your macro. Make sure that your macro name has no embedded spaces. For this example, we named the macro *Firmname*, as shown in Figure 18-1.

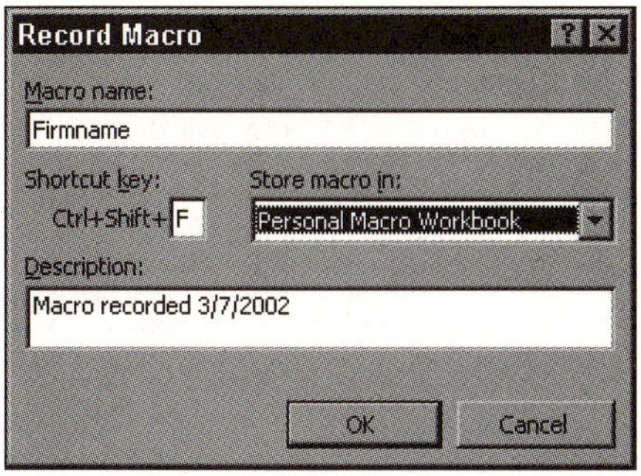

Figure 18-1: Information in the Record Macro dialog box is specific to the macro you are creating.

3. If you want to assign your macro to a keyboard shortcut, type your letter of choice into the Shortcut Key text box. After choosing your letter, the shortcut shows up in the dialog box as Ctrl+ your letter (if you used lowercase) or Ctrl+Shift+ your letter (if you used uppercase). In this example, we assign our macro to the shortcut key Ctrl+Shift+F.
4. Using the Store Macro In drop-down list, specify where you want this recorded macro to be stored. You have three options, as described earlier in this section.
5. Type an optional description for your macro in the Description text box. The text box contains default information, as shown in Figure 18-2, and changing this is not required.
6. After you complete typing and selecting in the Record Macro dialog box, click OK to close the dialog box. You are returned to the worksheet where you can create the macro by performing the steps that you want the macro to include. You see the word `Recording` in the status bar, and a floating macro toolbar containing two buttons (Stop Recording and Relative Reference) appears, as shown in Figure 18-2.
7. Perform the Excel tasks that you want included in your macro. For this example, we typed our firm name, *Winken, Blinken & Knod*, and formatted it the way we wanted it to look. For the macro in Figure 18-2, we recorded the name of the firm and formatted it as follows:
   - Merge and center the firm name across columns A–C.
   - Change the font to 14 point and add bold.
   - Apply a thick outline border to the cells containing the text.
   - Add shading to the cells.
8. After you finish the Excel tasks for your macro, click the Stop Recording button on the macro toolbar or choose Tools ⇨ Macro ⇨ Stop Recording to turn off the macro recorder.

NOTE: When assigning your macro to shortcut keys, remember to select a key combination that is not already in use by other Excel commands.

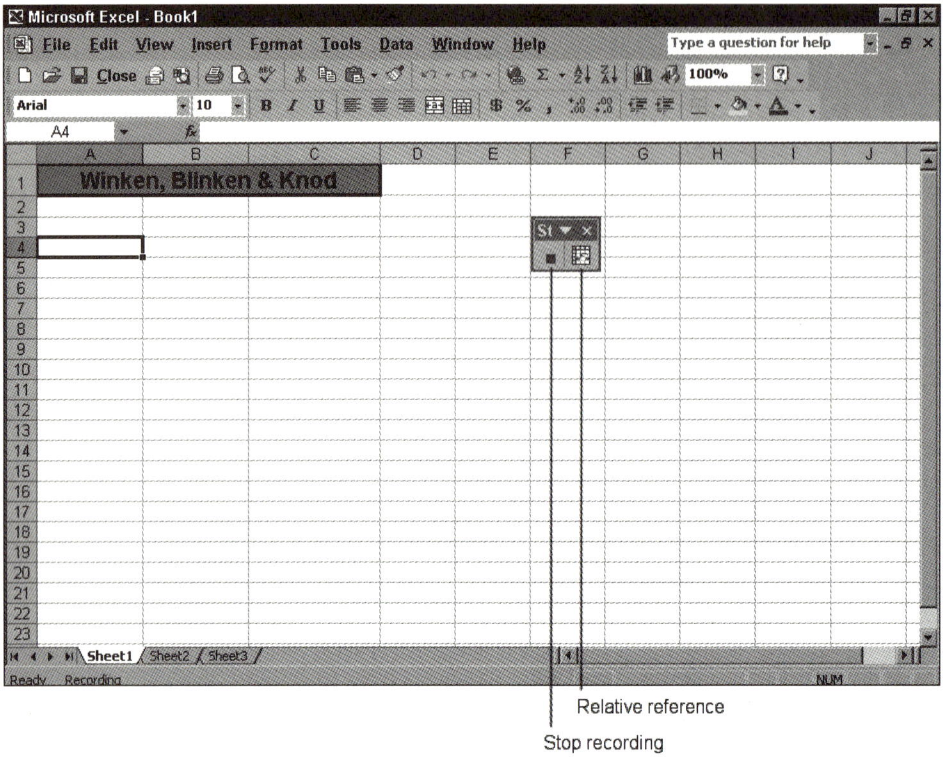

Figure 18-2: When recording a macro, the macro toolbar appears, and the word `Recording` shows up in the status bar.

Assigning a Macro to a Toolbar Button

A good way to make your frequently used Excel macros easily accessible is to assign the macros to toolbar buttons. After you do so, you simply click the appropriate toolbar button to activate the macro, which then performs its prerecorded tasks. You can add a macro button to any toolbar that is showing in the Excel window. If a toolbar that you want to customize is not visible, add it to your view by right-clicking over the toolbar area and choosing the toolbar name from the pop-up menu that appears. To customize a toolbar by adding a macro button, follow these steps:

1. Right-click over the toolbar that you want to contain the macro button, and choose Customize from the pop-up menu that appears. The Customize dialog box opens.
2. In the Customize dialog box, click the Commands tab and choose Macros from the Categories list.
3. From the Commands list, click and drag the Custom button (a smiley face icon by default) to the desired location on the toolbar, as shown in Figure 18-3. The button appears where you place it on the toolbar.

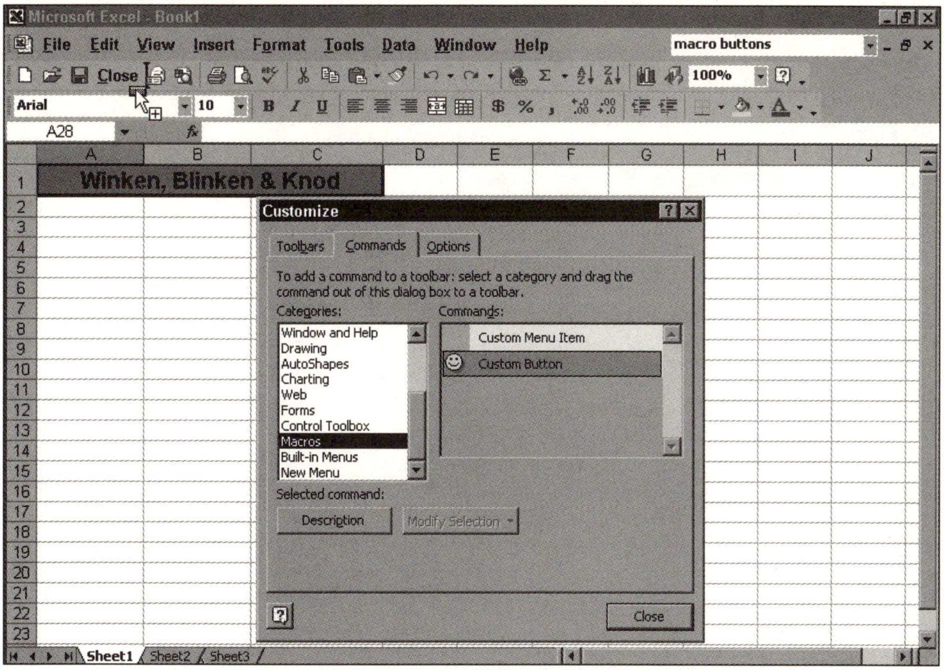

Figure 18-3: Click and drag the Custom button (a smiley face by default) to the desired location on your toolbar.

4. With the new button selected, click the Modify Selection button in the Customize dialog box.
5. In the pop-up menu that appears, choose Name, and following the ampersand (&), highlight and replace the words `Custom Button` by typing a descriptive name for your macro. In our example, we name the button `Firmname`.
6. Choose Change Button Image to select a different picture for your macro button; Figure 18-4 shows the choices. Or you can choose Edit Button Image to design your own picture in the Button Editor.
7. From the Modify Selection pop-up menu, choose an option to control what is displayed on your macro button. Your choices are
   - Default Style, which displays only the button image
   - Text Only (Always), which displays only the macro name
   - Text Only (in Menus), which displays only the button image (with no text)
   - Image and Text, which displays the macro name and the image you chose
8. Choose Assign Macro to open the Assign Macro dialog box.
9. Select the name of the macro you are assigning to the toolbar button from the list of macro names and click OK.
10. Close the Customize dialog box.

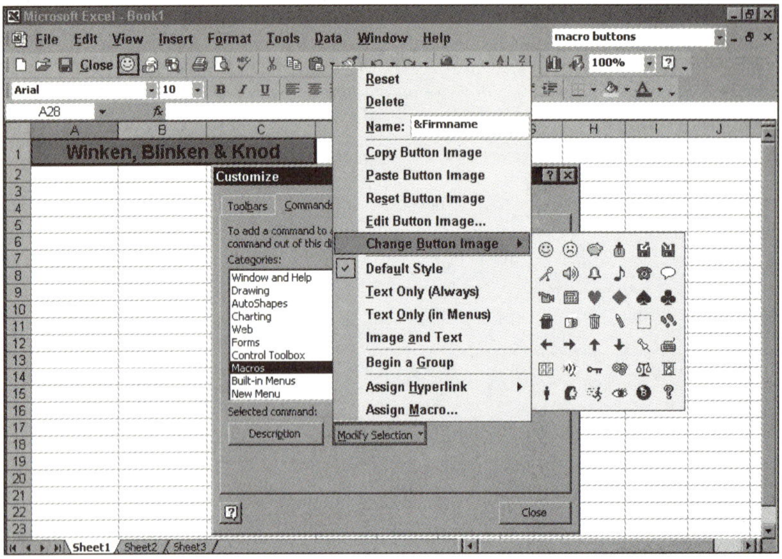

Figure 18-4: Replace the default smiley face with a new image for your macro button.

Your macro is now assigned to a toolbar button and ready for action with a single click. Figure 18-5 shows how the sample Firmname macro button looks on the Standard toolbar. When the mouse pointer is over the button, the macro name appears.

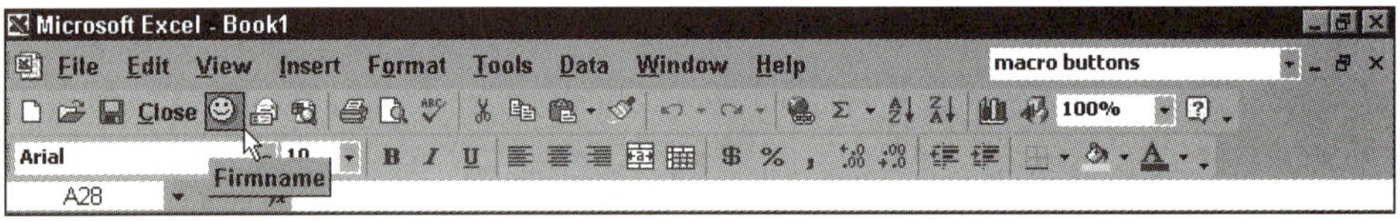

Figure 18-5: The Firmname macro button appears on the Standard toolbar.

Creating a Macro Button Directly on a Worksheet

In addition to placing a macro button on a toolbar, Excel allows you to create a macro button directly on a worksheet. By appearing on the worksheet itself, a macro button offers a highly visible reminder to run the macro. Suppose that your law firm keeps a spreadsheet database — perhaps a list of claimants for a class action lawsuit — that is updated frequently with rows added at the end. To keep this database accessible, you may need to regularly sort it, and you probably want to create a macro to do so.

Before you can place a macro button on your worksheet, you first create the macro that you want to run with the button. You can create the macro by recording it (see the earlier section "Getting Started with Macros"), and make sure to store the macro in the workbook where you want the button to appear. When you are ready to add the macro button to your worksheet, make sure to add the Forms toolbar to your view and follow these steps:

1. Drag the Button button from the Forms toolbar to a blank area on the worksheet. The new button appears with a border (which you can click and drag to reposition the button), resizing handles (which you can use to change the button's size), and a default name (usually *Button 1*).

2. In the Assign Macro dialog box that opens, click the name of the macro you are assigning to the button and then click OK.
3. While the resizing handles are present around the button, click in the macro name and type a more descriptive name for your button. In this example, we name the button *Sort list*.
4. Right-click over the button borders to open the Format Control dialog box, shown in Figure 18-6. Make the desired selections from this dialog box to change font size or style or to otherwise format the macro button.
5. Click in another area of the worksheet to finish. Your macro button is now in plain view and easy to access from the worksheet.

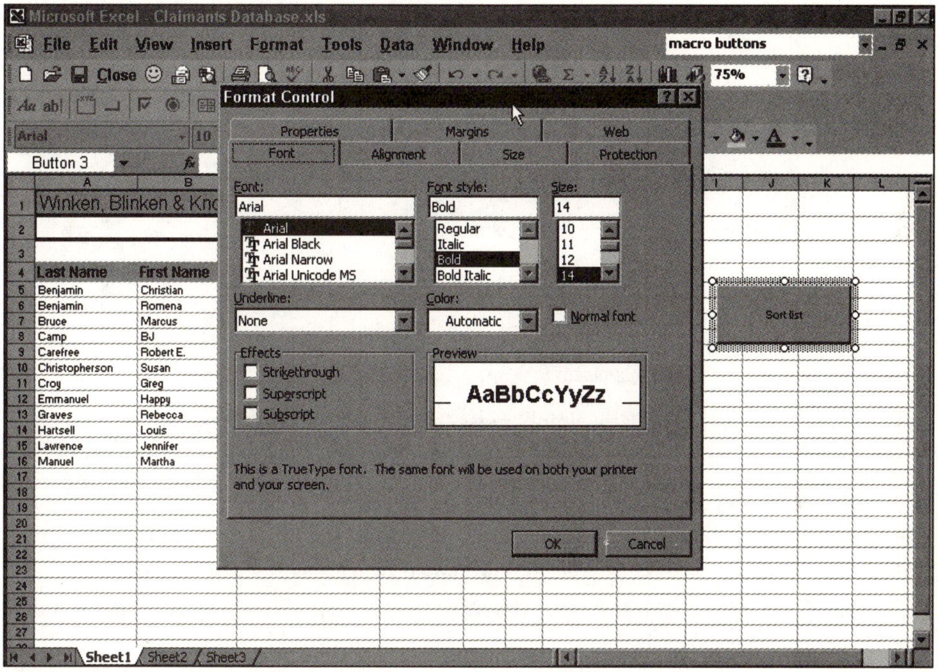

Figure 18-6: Use the Format Control dialog box to format a macro button for your worksheet.

Running a Macro

After you create, store, and make your macros accessible, running them is the easy part. First, you must open the workbook and choose the appropriate worksheet. When you are ready to run your macro, you have several options available:

- To use the menus, choose Tools ⇨ Macro ⇨ Macros to open the Macro dialog box, shown in Figure 18-7. In this dialog box, click the name of the macro you want to run and choose Run, or simply double-click the name.

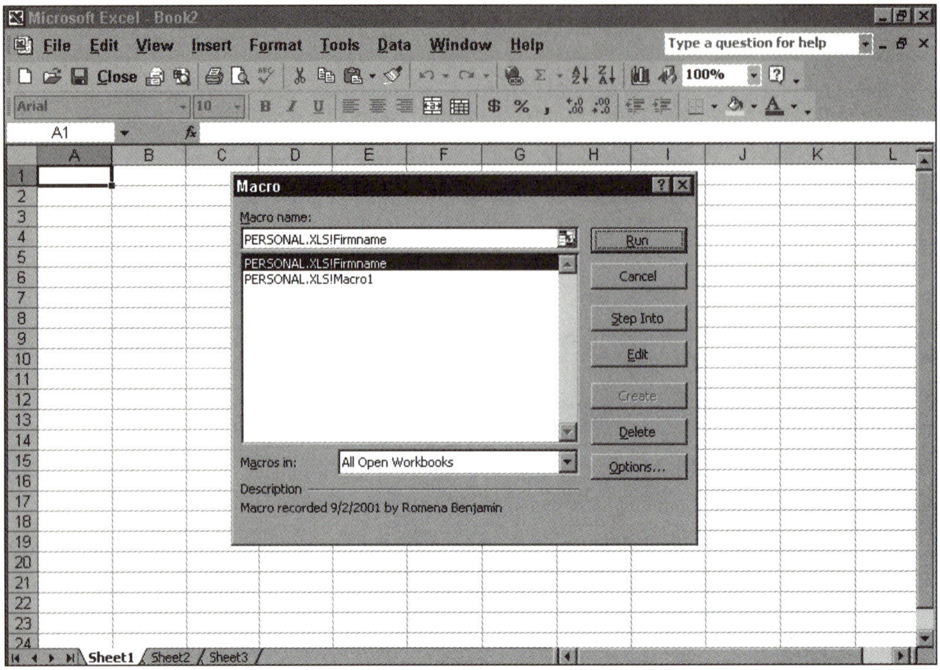

Figure 18-7: Use the Macro dialog box to run your macro.

- To use shortcuts keys to run a macro, simply press the shortcut keys at the appropriate place on the worksheet where you want the macro to run. Before you can run your macro with shortcut keys, you must assign these keys to your macro when you create it (see the earlier section "Getting Started with Macros") or when changing macro options on an already created macro (see the section "Changing Macro Options"). In our example, we assigned the shortcut Ctrl+Shift+F to run the macro that creates the formatted firm name in the active worksheet.
- To use a toolbar or worksheet button to run a macro, simply click the button in either location, and the macro runs automatically.

Making a Macro Available Globally

When you create a new macro, you can specify where you want the macro stored through the Record Macro dialog box, as noted in the earlier section "Getting Started with Macros." You determine where to store the macro based on when you want the macro to be available. If you want the macro to be available for use with any Excel workbook, store your macro in the personal macro workbook. When you do, Excel automatically adds the name of your personal macro workbook to the beginning of your macro name and thereby identifies the location of the stored macro. For example, our macro name *Firmname* becomes *PERSONAL.XLS!Firmname*.

Excel stores the personal macro workbook — named *Personal.xls* by default — in the following location:

```
C:\WINDOWS\APPLICATION DATA\MICROSOFT\EXCEL\XLSTART
```

WARNING: Removing the Personal.xls file (also known as the *personal macro workbook*) from its default location means that the personal macro workbook does not open automatically when you start Excel and any macros you have stored there will no longer be available.

Changing Macro Options

After you initially create and store your macro, you may later decide to make a few changes. By accessing the Macro Options dialog box, you can change the shortcut keys used to run your macro, or you can add, edit, or remove the description. The macro Options button is available in the Macro dialog box that appears when you are running a macro from the menus. (Press Alt+F8 to quickly display the Macro dialog box.) Click the Options button to access the Macro Options dialog box, shown in Figure 18-8.

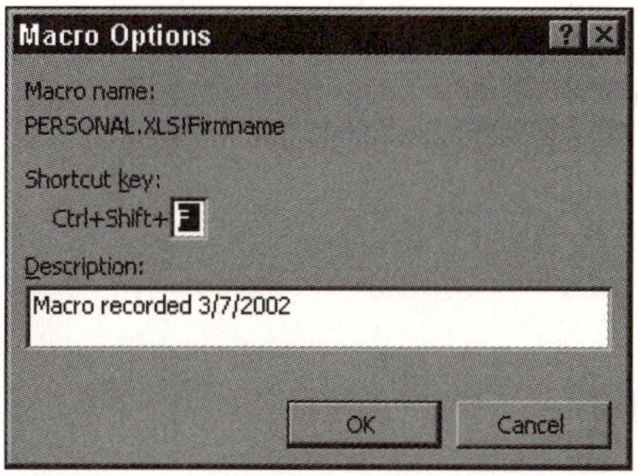

Figure 18-8: The Macro Options dialog box

If you want to change the shortcut keys used to run a macro, simply click the Shortcut Key text box and press the keys you want to use. If the shortcut keys you press were used in another macro, Excel returns an error message directing you to select different keys. However, Excel returns an error only if the shortcut keys were used in another macro. That is, if you use shortcut keys already assigned to an Excel command, you do not receive an error message, and these shortcuts are overwritten. For example, if you choose Ctrl+A to run a macro, you will no longer be able to use Ctrl+A to select the entire worksheet.

In addition to changing shortcut keys, you can type a description for your macro, edit the existing macro description, or remove the macro description altogether by clicking the Description text box and making the desired changes.

Renaming a Macro

At some point, you may need to rename an Excel macro that you previously created. This is relatively easy to do; Excel does not force you to keep the macro name the same at all times.

Exactly how you rename a macro depends on where you stored it. If you stored it in a workbook, the macro name is easy to change. If you stored it as part of your personal macro workbook, then a macro takes a bit more effort to change. If you stored your macro in the personal macro workbook, you must first unhide the workbook so that you can make changes. You do this by choosing Window ⇨ Unhide. Excel displays the Unhide dialog box, shown in Figure 18-9.

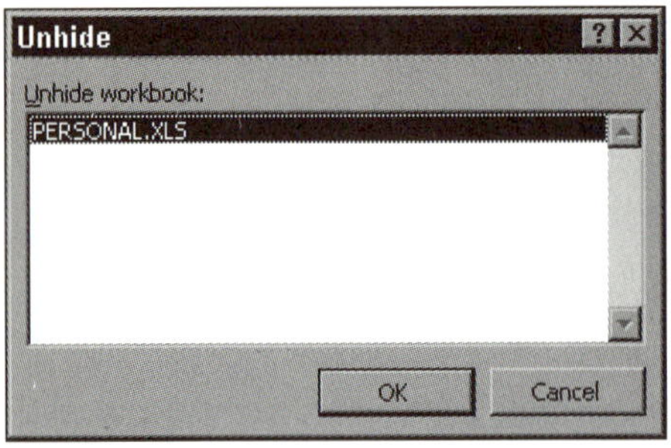

Figure 18-9: The Unhide dialog box is used to choose the worksheet that Excel should make visible.

Because the Personal.xls worksheet is already selected in the dialog box, simply click OK. Excel unhides the worksheet and displays it. You are now ready to rename your macro, just as if you were doing so with one stored in a regular workbook. Follow these steps:

1. Choose Tools ⇨ Macro ⇨ Macros, or press Alt+F8. Excel displays the Macro dialog box.
2. In the list of available macros, select the one you want to rename. For instance, if you want to rename your Firmname macro, you would choose Firmname from the list of macros.
3. Click the Edit button. Excel displays the Visual Basic Editor, showing all the code in the Firmname macro, shown in Figure 18-10.

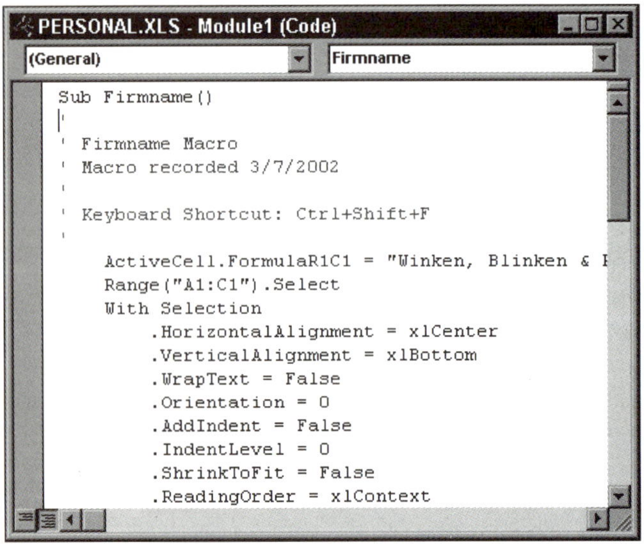

Figure 18-10: The Visual Basic Editor shows the coding behind a macro.

4. The line at the beginning of the macro code (beginning with `Sub`) defines the start of the macro. It also defines the macro's name. If you want to change the name of the macro, simply change this one line. In this case, you could replace the word *Firmname* with another name, such as *SetFirm*. Make sure that you don't change anything else in the macro, unless you want to modify how the macro does its work.
5. Choose File ⇨ Close and return to Microsoft Excel.

If you had to unhide the Personal.xls workbook earlier, you need to rehide it now. Do so by making sure that Personal.xls is displayed and then choosing Window ⇨ Hide.

Deleting a Macro

Alas, some macros are destined for a short life. If you have a macro that has outlived its usefulness, you can rather easily toss it aside so that it no longer clutters up your workbook. If you want to delete a macro, follow these steps:

1. Choose Tools ⇨ Macro ⇨ Macros, or press Alt+F8. Excel displays the Macro dialog box.

NOTE: If the macro you want to delete is in the Personal.xls workbook, you must unhide the workbook before you can make any deletions and must rehide it when done. The process for doing this is discussed in the previous section.

---

2. In the list of available macros, select the one you want to delete.
3. Click the Delete button. Excel displays a dialog box asking you to confirm that you really want to delete the macro. (This is a good idea because you cannot "undo" a deletion.)
4. Click OK. The macro is deleted.

Summary

You have learned quite a bit about how to record and use macros in this chapter. Specifically, you learned the following:

- How to start recording and saving macros
- How to assign macros to toolbar buttons
- How to run a macro once it is saved
- Why saving a macro in Personal.xls is a good idea
- How to edit macro options
- How to rename a macro
- How to get rid of macros you no longer need

This chapter has barely scratched the surface of macros. The macro language used in Excel is a variation of the popular Visual Basic programming language. Because of this, you can do many, many tasks using macros. How to take full advantage of the macro environment is beyond the scope of this chapter and this book. For more information on macros, refer to a good Excel macro programming title.

Part III

PowerPoint

Chapter 19

The Legal Essentials of PowerPoint

In This Chapter

- PowerPoint on trial, in a dozen easy steps
- Understanding the presentation window
- Using the views of PowerPoint
- Working with shortcuts and the Task Pane
- Using the toolbars
- Getting help
- Three choices for creating a PowerPoint presentation
- Using the AutoContent wizard
- Creating a new presentation with a design template
- Creating a blank presentation
- Opening an existing presentation
- Saving a presentation
- Creating a new presentation based on an existing presentation
- Creating the basic bulleted list
- Working with text
- Working with slides
- Working with objects
- Using clip art
- Inserting photographs and graphic images in slides
- Inserting a slide into a legal brief

POWERPOINT IS MICROSOFT'S POPULAR presentation graphics program. Within the legal environment, you can use PowerPoint to create attention-grabbing slides with ease, to collaborate with workgroup members on your presentations, and to share your presentations with clients, co-counsel, or the public via your firm's Web site.

Communicating facts, issues, ideas, and concepts is vitally important in the practice of law, and PowerPoint helps you to accomplish such tasks by providing a comprehensive set of tools to make your presentations look professional. Whether a presentation is needed for in-house use, for displaying to a group of clients, as part of a mediation or arbitration hearing, or before a jury during trial, you can use PowerPoint to produce the presentations you need to get your points across to your audience.

In the courtroom, you can use bullet lists that serve to highlight your opening statements and closing arguments. You can present slides that contain photographs, diagrams, or scanned correspondence admitted as evidence for a trial. Inside a law firm, you can use presentations to outline facts and issues regarding a particular case to a team of attorneys and paralegals. From an administrative standpoint, numerous departments within a large law firm or organization — including human resources, accounting, and the IT staff — can use PowerPoint for a variety of targeted presentations. You can even save PowerPoint presentations as Web pages and upload the files to a Web server for viewing by co-workers or clients using standard Web browsers.

PowerPoint on Trial, in a Dozen Easy Steps

The usefulness of PowerPoint within the legal environment can be illustrated with a short hands-on exercise, even if you've never used the program before. Here is the hypothetical situation. (Incidentally, this hypothetical case is loosely modeled after an actual case brought before the United States Court of Appeals, 1st Circuit — the law students among readers can research case 97-1949, if you'd like the full particulars.) You are an attorney on a team representing a plaintiff — a widow of a deceased victim of an automobile accident. The deceased (who had a history of heart problems) was traveling on company business, driving alone, when he suffered a major heart attack. The car he was driving left the road, went down a 15-foot embankment, and struck a tree with significant force. On the medical report, the coroner listed the cause of death as "motor vehicle accident, precipitated by acute coronary insufficiency."

The employer of the deceased provided an accidental death insurance policy issued by a major insurance company. The insurance company has contested the benefits claim made by the plaintiff, arguing that the cause of death was the coronary failure and not the vehicle accident. In your closing arguments, you have a critical need to sum up the facts of the case before a jury. Knowing that virtually any opening or closing statement can be aided through the use of an effective, concise bullet list, you decide to create one using PowerPoint. Start PowerPoint, and try the following twelve steps to get an idea of the capability of PowerPoint to get your concepts, ideas, and arguments across to a critical audience:

1. From the menus, choose View ⇨ Task Pane. (The Task Pane is an area at the right side of the screen where common tasks are performed; it may already be visible, but if it isn't, this step will display the Task Pane.)
2. From the menus, choose File ⇨ New (or press Ctrl+N). (This will ensure that the New Presentation pane appears in the Task Pane.)
3. In the Task Pane, under New, click Blank Presentation.
4. Under Slide Layout in the Task Pane, click the Title and Text box, which looks like this:

5. In the new slide that appears in the center of the screen, click in the box that reads Click to Add Title, and type the heading **The Facts**.

6. Click in the box that reads Click to Add Text and type the following, pressing Enter after each line:

   John Doe was a 55-year old male

   Recent history of heart problems

   Driving alone at night

   Car struck a tree at high rate of speed

   Cause of death: motor vehicle ACCIDENT, precipitated by coronary failure

   Policy terms clearly state coverage for accidental death

7. From the menus, choose Format ⇨ Slide Design to show the Slide Design pane in the Task Pane area at the right.
8. Scroll down in the Apply a Design Template area of the Task Pane and click an attractive style of slide to apply it to your presentation.
9. Choose Insert ⇨ New Slide (or press Ctrl+M) to add another slide to the presentation.
10. Click in the box that reads Click to Add Title and type the heading **In Summary**.
11. Click in the box that reads Click to Add Text and type the text **Under the law, our client deserves full compensation as promised by the terms of the policy.**
12. From the menus, choose View ⇨ Slide Show (or just press the F5 key) to view the first slide and then press the spacebar to advance to the second slide.

That's an example of PowerPoint, quite useful in one of the most important legal settings you may encounter — standing before a jury. (You can press Esc to exit the presentation and choose File ⇨ Close from the menus; there's no need to save this presentation as it will not be referenced elsewhere in this book.) Normally, you would use to save your presentation. You typically would insert additional slides, as needed, to emphasize all the points that you wanted to cover.

TIP: While showing a presentation, you can use the spacebar or PgUp key to advance to the next slide, and use the Backspace or PgDn key to move back to a slide that was shown previously. See Chapter 23, "About Databases and Tables," for more details about presenting your presentation.

This chapter covers the basics that you need to know to create and display a presentation, whether doing so before a jury, in front of a group of clients, or for co-workers. The successive chapters in this section of the book provide additional details to help you further refine your presentations, to present those presentations, and to accomplish tasks within PowerPoint that go beyond the basics of everyday use.

Understanding the Presentation Window

The PowerPoint presentation window is where you can create and arrange slides in your presentation. Creating and arranging slides constitutes the bulk of the work that you will do in PowerPoint. Hence, familiarizing yourself with all the capabilities of the PowerPoint presentation window is important to helping you function effectively within the program. Even if you've used recent versions of PowerPoint, you'll find that the interface in PowerPoint 2002 has changed significantly in comparison to earlier versions.

Figure 19-1 shows the presentation window in PowerPoint while in Normal view. (Other views of PowerPoint are explained shortly.)

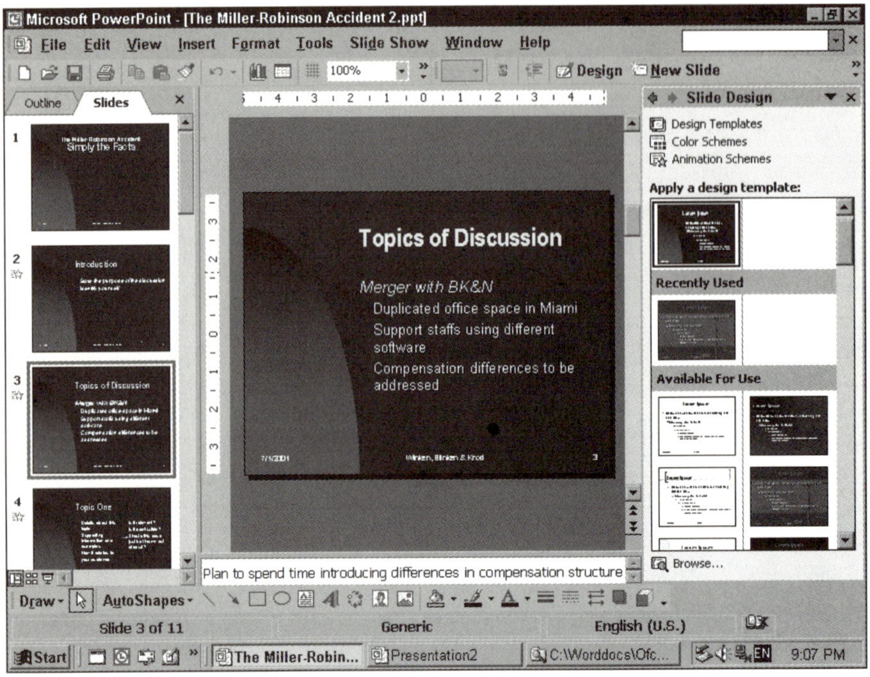

Figure 19-1: The presentation window in PowerPoint's Normal view can be used for a variety of tasks related to preparing slides of your presentation.

When in Normal view, the center of the presentation window displays the slide that you are currently developing as part of a PowerPoint presentation. To the left of this area are two tabs labeled *Outline* and *Slides*, respectively. (If these tabs do not appear on your machine, you can choose View ⇨ Normal to display the tabs.) The right side of the window contains the Task Pane, which is an integral feature of all Office XP applications. At the top of the screen are the menus and the default toolbar used by PowerPoint, and an additional toolbar appears by default at the bottom of the screen. (If the Task Pane is not visible, you can choose View ⇨ Task Pane to display it.)

The text box that is directly beneath the area where a slide appears when in Normal view is called the *Notes pane*. This feature provides an area where you can easily add notes about your slides as you create and work with them. Later, you can print the notes separately for your personal use or for distribution to the audience during a presentation.

Also new to this version of PowerPoint is the Office Assistant's Ask a Question box at the right side of the menu bar. You can click in the text box, type a search term about a topic you need help with, and press Enter. A Help menu containing various options relevant to your topic then appears.

At the lower-left corner of the presentation window are view buttons that enable you to switch among different views in the PowerPoint presentation window. The view buttons include Normal View, Slide Sorter View, and Slide Show View; these views are explained shortly. (You can also change views by choosing the appropriate commands from the View menu.)

At the left side of the window, you can click the Outline tab to show your slides in outline form. Here, you can edit content and move headings, topics, and other information by clicking and dragging (how you do this is detailed later in this chapter). You can use the Outline tab to view the title and body text of a group of your slides simultaneously.

In this same area, you can click the Slides tab to view smaller representations of the slides in your presentation. You can click any image to cause that slide to appear in the center of the presentation window.

Using the Views of PowerPoint

As you are working within PowerPoint, you can work with slides in one of three main views: Normal view, Slide Sorter view, and Slide Show view. (A fourth view, Print Preview, shows your slides in grayscale if your default printer is a monochrome printer and in color if your default printer is a color printer. A fifth view, Notes Page view, is useful for adding notes to slides and is detailed further in Chapter 23.)

Normal view

Figure 19-1, shown at the start of this chapter, shows a typical PowerPoint slide in Normal view. In Normal view, you can edit the contents of a slide, add notes to a slide using the Notes pane, and perform various common tasks using the Task Pane. By default, a single slide occupies most of the display area in Normal view; however, you can increase the size of the Task Pane or the Outline and Slides tabs (or all of these) by dragging the edges of these areas. Doing so correspondingly reduces the available area for viewing the current slide.

Slide Sorter view

As you are working on a presentation, you may need to see the general arrangement of most or all of your slides. You will often want to select a particular slide from within a group of slides to move the slide to a different location in the presentation. The Slide Sorter view can be used for these types of tasks. When you click the Slide Sorter view button at the lower left or choose View ⇨ Slide Sorter from the menus, PowerPoint switches to Slide Sorter view. An example of Slide Sorter view is shown in Figure 19-2.

If you have a large presentation with a number of slides, you can use the vertical scroll bar to bring additional slides into view.

Slide Show view

At any point, you can click the Slide Show button at the lower left (below the Outline and Slide tabs) to run the slide show after you have completed creating the slides. (You can do the same by choosing View ⇨ Slide Show or by pressing F5.) When you do this, you enter PowerPoint's Slide Show view (note that the presentation will begin on whichever slide you are positioned in Slide Sorter view or in Normal view). In Slide Show view, each slide fills the screen (see Figure 19-3), and you can press the spacebar to advance to the next slide. When done, press the Esc key to return to the presentation window. In PowerPoint, you can also present your slides as a timed presentation (how you do this is detailed in Chapter 22, "Producing Presentations").

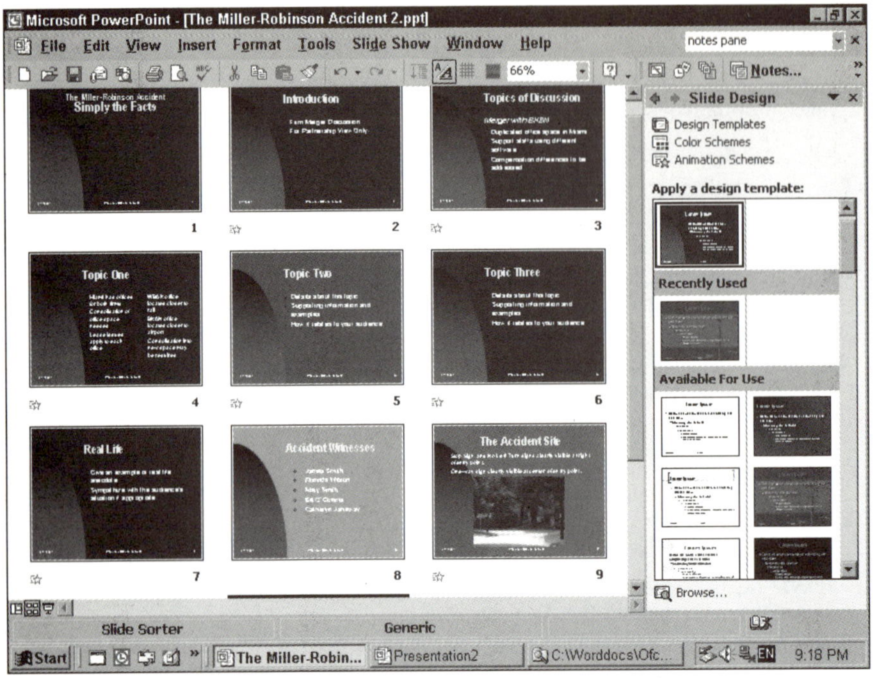

Figure 19-2: In Slide Sorter view, you can see multiple slides contained within your presentation.

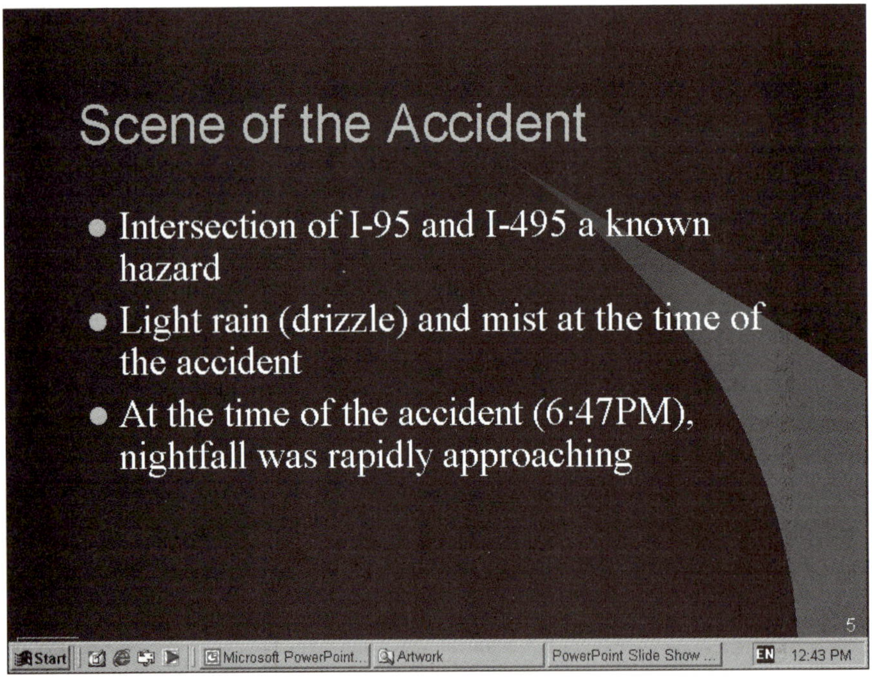

Figure 19-3: Slide Show view is used to actually present the presentation, in electronic (on-screen) format.

Print Preview

In this version of PowerPoint, you can also use a new feature, Print Preview, to see your slides, in grayscale if your default printer is a monochrome printer or in color if your default printer is a color printer. At any time while working on a presentation, you can choose File ⇨ Print Preview to switch to this view of PowerPoint.

TIP: If you find that much of your work in PowerPoint makes use of the same view, you can specify that PowerPoint should always use that view when the program initially starts. To do this, choose Tools ⇨ Options and click the View tab in the dialog box that appears. In the list box shown at the bottom of the tab, select the view you use most often.

Working with Shortcuts and the Task Pane

As with other Office XP programs, PowerPoint offers shortcut menus, shortcut buttons, and the Task Pane to make creating your presentations as easy as possible.

Using the shortcut menus

PowerPoint provides shortcut menus that you can use to perform different commands without having to use the pull-down menus. Shortcut menus can save lots of time. To activate any of the shortcut menus, move the pointer to the object that you want the command to act on and then right-click. Figure 19-4 shows a shortcut menu in PowerPoint. Throughout this book, many Office tasks are illustrated through the use of shortcut menus.

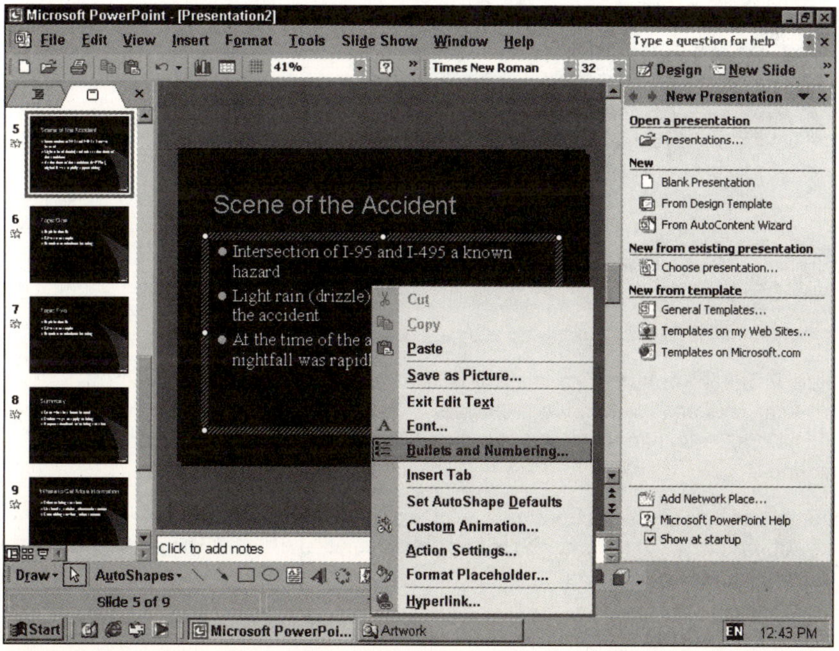

Figure 19-4: A shortcut menu in the PowerPoint window

Using the Task Pane views

PowerPoint offers a number of views in the Task Pane area. You can use these views, depending on what tasks you want to accomplish at a particular time. To open a menu of the available views, click the downward-pointing triangle at the top right of the Task Pane.

When you choose New Presentation from the Task Pane menu, you can click any of the options shown in the Task Pane to create a new PowerPoint presentation. You can create a new presentation using the AutoContent Wizard (detailed shortly), by using an existing template provided with PowerPoint (or stored at the Microsoft Web site if you are connected to the Internet), or by effectively starting from scratch (with the blank presentation option).

When the Slide Layout view is displayed within the Task Pane, you can click any of the layouts shown to apply various text and content layouts to a slide that you are working with. Figure 19-5 shows the Slide Layout view of the Task Pane.

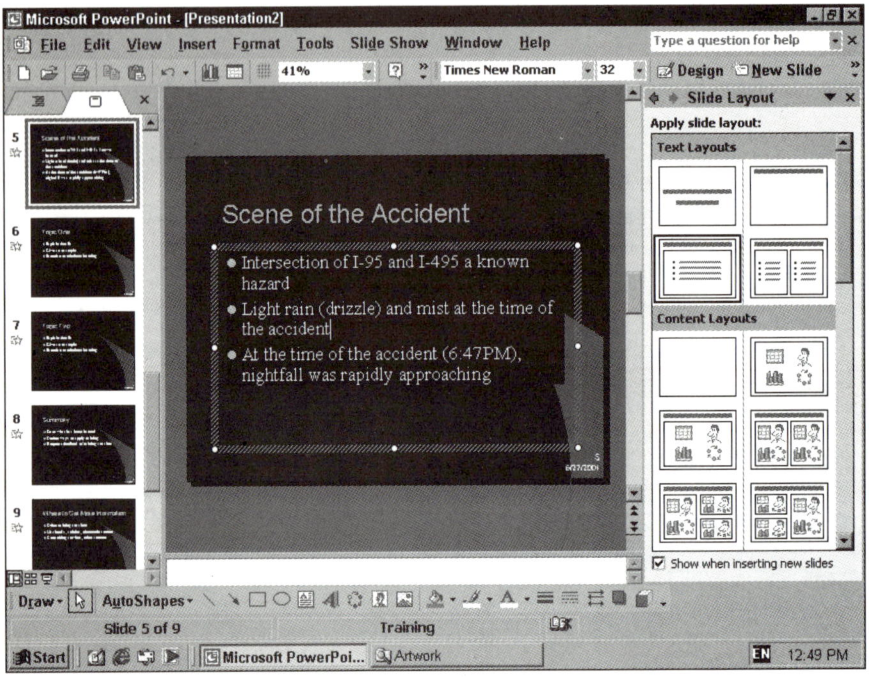

Figure 19-5: The Slide Layout view of the Task Pane is used to apply a particular layout to a given slide.

When the Slide Design/Design Templates view is displayed within the Task Pane, various preformatted designed templates are available for your use. You can click any of these templates in the Task Pane, and the colors, style, and formatting used by the template will be applied to all the slides in your presentation.

You can use the remaining Task Pane menu options — Color Scheme, Slide Transition, Animation Schemes, and Custom Animation — to modify slides or produce special effects. The use of these options is detailed in later chapters of this section of the book.

Using the Toolbars

When you launch PowerPoint and begin creating a presentation, four toolbars are normally visible by default: the Standard toolbar, the Formatting toolbar, the Drawing toolbar, and the Task Pane. If you (or someone else using your computer) have used PowerPoint previously and changed the settings of the toolbars, these may not be visible because PowerPoint remembers the last-used toolbar settings upon startup. You can choose View ⇨ Toolbars and select Standard, Formatting, Drawing, and Task Pane, as needed, to display (or hide) any of these commonly used toolbars.

Use the Standard toolbar to open presentations and to save, print, and insert objects such as tables and charts. Use the Formatting toolbar to perform tasks related to formatting, such as applying different fonts and styles and changing the indentation of the presentation. Use the Drawing toolbar, located by default at the bottom of the screen, to perform tasks related to controlling the appearance of shapes. You can draw shapes, rotate them, and control different aspects of their appearance on-screen.

You can activate the other toolbars that are available in PowerPoint by choosing the Toolbars command from the View menu and then selecting the toolbars from the list in the Toolbars menu. Alternatively, right-click the toolbar area of the screen and then select the toolbars that you want from the shortcut menu that appears.

In PowerPoint 2002, as in PowerPoint 2000, the Standard and Formatting toolbars share the same line, and most buttons of the Standard toolbar aren't visible. You can access the hidden buttons by clicking the downward-pointing triangle on the toolbar to open a pop-up menu of the hidden buttons, as shown here.

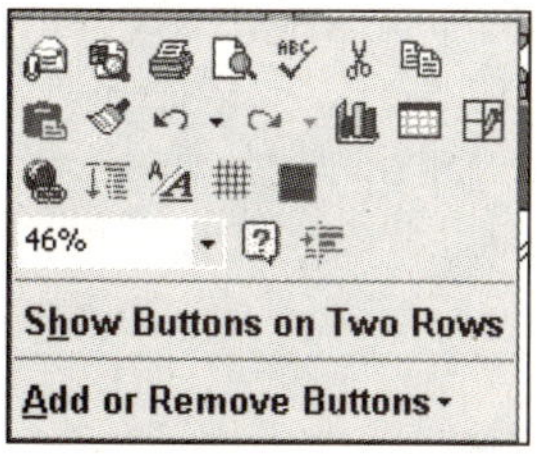

If you prefer to see all the toolbar buttons, you can choose to display both toolbars on separate lines. (Of course, doing so reduces the available remaining screen space by a small amount.) Choose Tools ⇨ Customize, click the Options tab in the dialog box that appears, click the Show Standard and Formatting Toolbars on Two Rows check box, and click Close.

Getting Help

As with all Office applications, help is readily available when you need it. In addition to using the Ask a Question text box mentioned earlier, you can press F1 at any point in time to display a help window with three tabs: Contents, Answer Wizard, and Index. (If you use the Help feature in any recent Microsoft product, the help screen will be familiar to you.) You can double-click any topic shown in the Contents tab and then click any subtopic to see a help window about that subtopic. The Answer Wizard works just like the Ask a Question text box: Click the Answer Wizard tab, type a question in the text box that appears, and click Search to see a list of matching topics; then double-click a desired topic for more information. The Index tab lets you type a keyword and see all topics in an alphabetical index matching that keyword. You can then double-click a topic and see a help screen for that particular topic.

While we're on the subject of help, you should know about a feature of PowerPoint called *Detect and Repair*, which happens to be located on the Help menu. If PowerPoint ever starts behaving strangely and you suspect that the program may have developed an internal problem, choose Help ⇨ Detect and Repair from the menus. In the dialog box that appears, choose whether you want to keep any Office shortcuts you've created and whether you want to discard any custom settings and restore the default settings of PowerPoint. Select your desired options and click Start. The Detect and Repair feature will proceed to fix any errors found in your PowerPoint program files. Note that this option checks all program files associated with PowerPoint, so it may take some time to complete.

Where are my menu options?

If you've upgraded to PowerPoint 2002 from PowerPoint 97 or earlier, you should know about a special feature of all Office XP programs that Microsoft calls *adaptive menus*. When you open a menu, the entire menu does not initially appear; instead, the menu containing your most commonly used options appears. If you hold the menu open for a moment without making a selection, it opens further to reveal all the available menu options. As you use PowerPoint, the initial choices on the menus will change to reflect the options that you use most often (hence the name *adaptive menus*). If you find the behavior of adaptive menus to be annoying, you can turn them off. To do so, choose Tools ⇨ Customize. On the Options tab of the dialog box that appears, click the Always Show Full Menus check box and click Close. From this point on, full menus will always appear.

Three Choices for Creating a PowerPoint Presentation

PowerPoint provides you with three different options for creating a presentation. Before you start a new presentation, you should decide which method is most appropriate. Your choices are the following:

- **With the AutoContent Wizard:** Like all wizards in Microsoft Office, the AutoContent Wizard asks a series of questions and produces an end product (in this case, a presentation) based on your answers to those questions. In the legal environment, the AutoContent Wizard will likely be the method that offers the most useful assistance while meeting your specific needs. When you create a presentation with the AutoContent Wizard, your presentation takes on a standard yet attractive look, and default content (which you can modify) is added automatically.
- **From a design template:** When you choose to base a new presentation on a design template, you get an attractive design of colors, fonts, and styles applied to all the slides in your presentation. However, no sample content of any kind is provided. A design template is basically a preformatted presentation that doesn't contain any slides. As you add slides, PowerPoint applies the color scheme and the overall layout for formatting to the slides that you add. Hence, the design template choice may be your best option when you need to produce a

presentation containing content that does not match any of the options provided by the AutoContent wizard.

- **From a blank presentation:** This is the option to use if you desire full control over all aspects of the design of your presentation. In effect, you are starting from scratch, with a single blank slide with no colors or special formatting applied. (If you want anything more complex than a series of simple bulleted lists, this may not be the best approach for beginners.)

Using the AutoContent Wizard

PowerPoint's AutoContent Wizard helps you define both the appearance and the contents of your presentation. It offers ready-made content for common business tasks, such as recommending a strategy, selling your ideas, motivating a team, or communicating bad news. In case you need to create a legal-specific presentation that matches none of the available options, the wizard offers a "generic" choice. To use the AutoContent wizard, perform these steps:

1. Choose File ⇨ New, and in the Task Pane, click From AutoContent Wizard. This activates the AutoContent Wizard, and you can click Next to proceed.
2. The second dialog box asks you to choose the type of presentation you want to give. You have choices divided into several categories. Clicking the button corresponding to the category makes all the choices for that category appear. The default is All, which shows all the listings from all the categories.
3. You use the third dialog box to choose the presentation output options. Under the type of output selection, select the way you will be presenting your slides. You can choose from On-screen Presentation, Web Presentation, Black and White Overheads, Color Overheads, or 35 mm Slides, as detailed in the following paragraphs. After you have made your selection, click Next to go to the fourth dialog box of the AutoContent Wizard.

   These are your presentation options in more detail:

   - **On-Screen Presentation:** Use this option when you want to use a computer and attached monitor or projection system to present your presentation to an audience.
   - **Web Presentation:** Use this option when you plan to give the presentation files to a Webmaster who will install them on a Web server for viewing on an intranet or on the Internet
   - **Black and White Overheads:** Use this option when you plan to produce black-and-white transparencies that will be used with an overhead projector. (You can purchase transparencies at most office supply stores and load them into your printer.)
   - **Color Overheads:** Use this option when you plan to produce color transparencies that will be used with an overhead projector. (You can purchase transparencies at most office supply stores and load them into your printer.)
   - **35mm Slides:** Use this option when you plan to send your presentation to a photo processing shop to have 35mm slides made. (If you work at a very large law firm or organization, check with your audio-visual department; your firm may have the needed equipment on site.)
4. You use the fourth dialog box of the AutoContent Wizard to set up your title slide. The wizard also allows space for any additional information that you wish to add to the title slide of the presentation. After you have finished making your desired entries, click Next to go to the final dialog box of the AutoContent Wizard.

5. At the final AutoContent Wizard dialog box, click the Finish button. PowerPoint then creates the presentation using the responses that you provided to the wizard. In the Outline tab at the left, you see the text (the content) that was added by the wizard for each slide within the presentation. Figure 19-6 shows the result of using the AutoContent wizard to produce a presentation based on the Recommending a Strategy option. (In the figure, the fourth slide in the presentation has been selected in the Outline tab and is visible in the preview portion of the screen.)

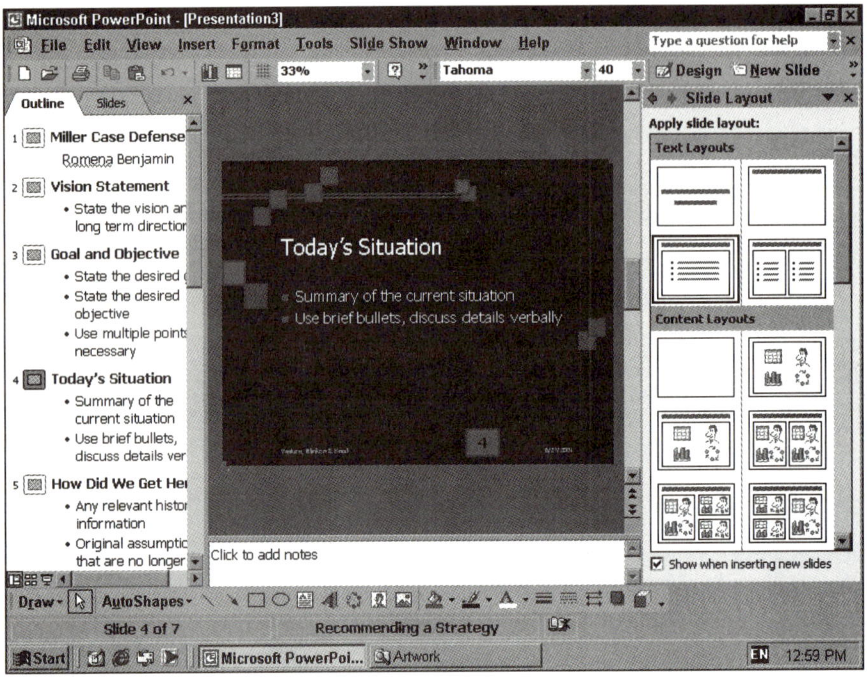

Figure 19-6: The results of the use of the AutoContent Wizard

After the presentation appears, you can replace the boilerplate text with your own text. To do this, just select a line of boilerplate text and begin typing; your typing will replace the preceding entry. You'll find additional details on text editing in the section "Working with Text," later in this chapter.

TIP: If you use the AutoContent Wizard and want to change the style of the slides at a later time, choose Format ⇨ Slide Design and click a desired design template in the Task Pane. Your new design will then be applied to all the slides within your presentation. (Optionally, you can click the down arrow of the template to apply the design to selected slides.)

NOTE: Chapter 22 provides more details on ways to present your finished presentation, but you don't have to flip over so many pages just to find out how to see the results. Choose View ⇨ Slide Show (or press F5) to display the presentation, and press the spacebar to advance to each successive slide. When done viewing your work, press the Esc key to get back to the presentation window (and, if you're satisfied, remember to save your work with File ⇨ Save).

Creating a New Presentation with a Design Template

If you want to bypass the ready-made content that's provided by the AutoContent Wizard, you can opt for creating a new presentation using a design template. You won't get any ready-made content, but you will get an attractive style and color design of your choice for all the slides within the presentation. This can be a useful approach when you just need a series of classic bullet-list slides for an arbitration hearing or for a trial.

To create a new presentation using a design template, choose File ⇨ New and click From Design Template in the Task Pane. You can then scroll down in the list of available templates and click a desired template to apply it to the presentation.

NOTE: You might select a design template that hasn't been installed as part of your Office XP installation. If this happens, PowerPoint asks whether you want to install the feature. If you click Yes, you are prompted to insert your Office XP installation CD or connect to a network drive containing the installation files. If you have disk space to spare, you can avoid messages like this by rerunning Office Setup and installing all options.

You add more slides to the presentation by choosing Insert ⇨ New Slide or by clicking the New Slide button in the toolbar (or by pressing Ctrl+M). You have to add your content to the slides manually; to do this, see the section "Working with Text," later in this chapter.

TIP: Microsoft Publisher shares some formatting style and color combinations with PowerPoint. (In PowerPoint, these combinations are called *design templates*, whereas Publisher calls them *design sets*.) For example, the Artsy, Blends, Capsules, Strategic, and Soaring design templates in PowerPoint can also be found in Microsoft Publisher. This common use of formatting and color schemes can prove helpful to solo practitioners and small firms that use Microsoft Publisher to produce marketing brochures or firm newsletters. If you are designing a PowerPoint presentation that will be viewed by clients, you can choose a design template that is the same as a design set you use for your brochures or newsletters created in Publisher. This feature gives your firm a consistent look for both your PowerPoint presentation and the printed materials you create using Publisher.

Creating a Blank Presentation

If you want to go completely on your own, you can start with a blank presentation. A blank presentation contains a single, blank slide with no colors or styles of formatting applied. To create a blank presentation, use these steps:

1. Choose File ⇨ New from the menus.
2. In the Task Pane, choose Blank Presentation.
3. In the Slide Layout view within the Task Pane, select a slide layout to apply to the slide.
4. Enter your desired content, using the techniques outlined in the section "Working with Text," later in this chapter.

5. Add slides to the presentation as needed, using the New Slide button on the Standard toolbar or the Insert ⇨ New Slide command.

Presentation content hints

With any approach to creating a presentation, you should keep some overall design recommendations in mind. These are not specific to PowerPoint; rather, they apply to any on-screen presentation of main points that will be viewed by an audience. Try to stick with what is called the *six-by-six rule*, which states a limit (if possible) of six words per line and a maximum of six lines of text per slide. Make sure that each slide highlights a single overall concept or theme. Use a serif font, such as Times New Roman, for a legal or professional audience; if your audience is a more casual one (such as co-workers at a law firm), you can use a sans serif font such as Arial or Tahoma. Avoid more than two different fonts on any given slide, and if you apply background colors, use colors that contrast well when viewed against your text.

Opening an Existing Presentation

To open an existing presentation, choose File ⇨ Open to display the Open dialog box. Navigate to the desired PowerPoint presentation and click Open in the dialog box to open the presentation.

Saving a Presentation

You save a presentation in PowerPoint the same way that you save a file in other Microsoft programs: Choose File ⇨ Save or click the Save button in the Standard toolbar. If you have not saved the presentation before, the Save As dialog box opens, where you are prompted to enter a name for the presentation. If you have already given the presentation a name, it is saved under that name.

You also can perform other tasks in the Save As dialog box. You can change the name of a presentation by entering a new name in the File Name text box. You can save files as earlier versions of PowerPoint or as Web pages by selecting the desired file type from the Save as Type list box and then clicking the Save button to save the file. When you have completed your work in PowerPoint and you want to exit, choose File ⇨ Exit.

Creating a New Presentation Based on an Existing Presentation

"Don't re-invent the wheel" is a popular saying. If someone at your firm or organization has already created a PowerPoint presentation for a need that is similar to yours, you can easily create a new presentation based on that existing presentation. Technically, you could copy and rename the presentation file and then open it in PowerPoint, but menu options exist to make the process even easier. Just use these three steps:

1. In the Task Pane drop-down menu, choose New Presentation to display the New Presentation pane of the Task Pane.
2. Under New from Existing Presentation, click Choose Presentation.
3. In the dialog box that appears, navigate to and select the existing presentation; then click Create New.

The existing presentation appears with a new default name (such as *Presentation1*, *Presentation2*, and so on). You can modify the presentation to suit your needs and then click File ⇨ Save As to save it under a desired filename.

Creating the Basic Bullet List

For many attorneys, the basic bullet list is the most commonly used type of slide in a PowerPoint presentation. (Figure 19-3, shown earlier in this chapter, offers an example of the basic bulleted list.) You can easily create this type of slide using the Title and Text layout in the Slide Layout pane of the Task Pane. Use these steps to quickly create a basic bullet list:

1. At the desired location within your presentation, choose Insert ⇨ New Slide.
2. In the Slide Layout pane of the Task Pane area, under Apply Slide Layout, click the Title and Text layout.
3. In the slide, click in the Click to Add Title area and type the desired text for your title.
4. In the Click to Add Text area, click and type the desired points of your bullet list, pressing Enter after each item.
5. Open the drop-down menu at the top of the Task Pane and choose Slide Design/Design Templates from the menu that appears.
6. In the Task Pane, click a desired template to apply its colors and formatting to your slide.
7. Repeat Steps 1 through 4 for each additional bullet list needed in your presentation.
8. Save your work by choosing File ⇨ Save.

Working with Text

As you work with presentations created using a design template or a blank presentation, you will need to insert your own desired text as content. Even when you use the AutoContent Wizard, you will likely need to edit the ready-made content provided by the wizard to suit your needs. This section shows you the basics of adding and editing text in your slides.

To replace existing text, you must first select the text. If you want to insert new text, click to place the insertion pointer at the desired entry point; then start typing. You can edit directly in the slide in Normal view, or you can use the Outline tab. Both methods are discussed in the paragraphs that follow. With either method, you can use the keys shown in the following table to navigate within the text of a slide and to move or copy text from one location to another.

Key	*Effect*
Home	Move to the start of a line.
End	Move to the end of a line.
Ctrl+left arrow	Move one word to the left.
Ctrl+right arrow	Move one word to the right.
Ctrl+C	Copy.
Ctrl+V	Paste.
Ctrl+X	Cut.

CROSS-REFERENCE: After you've entered your text into the slides of your presentation, you can check spelling at any time by pressing the F7 key or by choosing Tools ⇨ Spelling. For more on the subject of spelling correction, see Chapter 20.

Editing on the Outline Tab

The Outline tab is excellent for editing text and enables you to see the overall content of the entire presentation. Click the Outline tab at the left (if the tabs are not visible, choose View ⇨ Normal, or click the Normal View button in the status bar to display the tabs). You can edit text on the tab by simply clicking it and moving the cursor to the area that you want to change. Use the Delete key to remove characters to the right of the cursor and use the Backspace key to delete characters to the left of the cursor.

When you select text in PowerPoint, the program selects whole words. If you want to select individual characters, choose Tools ⇨ Options. In the Options dialog box, choose the Edit tab. Next, uncheck the When Selecting, Automatically Select Entire Word option and click OK.

TIP: Readability studies indicate that most people have an easier time reading text that consists of a normal mix of initial caps and lowercase letters than text that consists entirely of uppercase letters. Unless you need all uppercase letters to emphasize a point, it is probably best to stick with normal capitalization for the text contained within your slides.

Editing a slide directly

You can edit text directly on the slide that appears in the center of the presentation window when you are in Normal view. You can edit text by clicking the text to select it or by clicking in the space where you want the cursor to appear and then making the desired changes.

You can add additional bulleted topics underneath existing topics created by the wizards. To do so, place the insertion pointer at the end of a topic and press Enter.

Creating subordinate points

Often with bullet lists, you need to include *subordinate points*, which are items in the list that are indented underneath a higher-priority item. As an example, the following list of bullet points are all at the same level:

- John Doe was a 55-year old male
- Recent history of heart problems
- Driving alone at night
- Car struck a tree at high rate of speed

By comparison, the following list of bullet points contains two items that are subordinate points underneath the second bullet:

- John Doe was a 55-year old male
- Recent history of heart problems
  - a. Mild stroke at age 54
  - b. Irregular heart rhythm detected during 1998 physical
- Driving alone at night
- Car struck a tree at high rate of speed

You can easily create subordinate points within the text of a PowerPoint slide by performing the following steps:

1. Click anywhere within the text of the bullet point that is to be made a subordinate of another point.
2. Click the Increase Indent button on the Formatting toolbar. (If the button is not visible on the toolbar, click the downward-pointing triangle on the Formatting toolbar to open a menu of available buttons and then click the Increase Indent button. After you use the button, PowerPoint adds it to the Formatting toolbar.)
3. If you want to add another subordinate point at the same level, move the insertion pointer to the end of the current line, press Enter and type the text for the new subordinate bullet point.

Creating a text box

When you want to add additional text to a slide, you must first create a text box that will contain the text. You can add a text box using these steps:

1. If you want to place the text box within a new slide, insert the new slide into the presentation by choosing Insert ⇨ New Slide (or pressing Ctrl+M).
2. Click the Text Box tool in the Drawing toolbar, or choose Insert ⇨ Text Box from the menus.
3. Click the slide where you want the text box to appear.
4. Type the text that is to appear within the text box. As you type, the text box will expand to accommodate the text that you enter.
5. When you finish entering the text, click anywhere outside the text box.
6. If desired, click the text box to display its selection handles and then drag the handles to resize the text box.

7. To change the font or font size, select the text within the text box and choose Format ⇨ Font to display a Font dialog box, within which you can apply a desired font or font size.

Changing text alignment

By default, text that you add in a text box is set flush left against the edge of the text box. When you need to change the alignment of the text, perform these steps:

1. Click anywhere inside the paragraph you wish to realign.
2. From the menus, choose Format ⇨ Alignment.
3. From the submenu that appears, choose Align Left, Center, Align Right, or Justify to align the text as desired.

TIP: There are alignment keyboard shortcuts in PowerPoint for those who regularly work with a lot of text in their slides. You can select text in a text box and then use a control key combination in place of the dialog box options. Use Ctrl+L for left alignment, Ctrl+E for centering, or Ctrl+R for right alignment.

Changing the line spacing

If you enter a number of lines of text in a text box, you may wish to change the line spacing of the text. By default, PowerPoint uses single spacing for multiple lines in a text box. Perform these steps to change the line spacing:

1. Click anywhere inside the paragraph that you want to change, or select all the paragraphs to be changed.
2. From the menus, choose Format ⇨ Line Spacing. The Line Spacing dialog box appears, as shown in Figure 19-7.

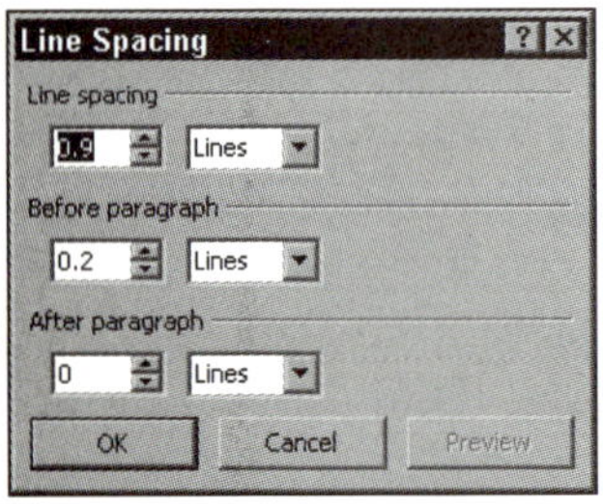

Figure 19-7: The Line Spacing dialog box is used to change the line spacing of a paragraph of text.

3. Use the spinner boxes (click the up or down arrow) under Line Spacing to change the amount of line spacing as desired.
4. Use the spinner boxes under Before Paragraph and After Paragraph to increase or decrease the amount of space that appears before or after a paragraph. (You also can click inside the text portion of the spinner boxes and type your desired value.)
5. Click OK.

TIP: Assuming that you are using Microsoft Word as your word processor, you can get an easy-to-print, at-a-glance idea of the text content of your presentation by choosing File ⇨ Send to Microsoft Word. Select Outline Only in the dialog box that appears; then click OK to open an outline version of the presentation in Word. You can then print the presentation and examine the printout to be sure that you've covered all your important topics. For more on using this feature, see Chapter 23.

Formatting text automatically

If you type more text than a text box can accommodate (or if you copy a large amount of text into a text box that is too small to contain all the text), PowerPoint does not expand the text box to hold the text. Instead, PowerPoint applies automatic text formatting, reducing the font size and expanding the text box until the text fits into the text box. By default, PowerPoint uses the AutoFit Body Text to Placeholder option. If you would rather not use this type of automatic text formatting, from the menus choose Tools ⇨ AutoCorrect Options, click the AutoFormat as You Type tab in the dialog box that appears, turn off the AutoFit Body Text to Placeholder option, and then click OK.

Working with Slides

You can use the Slides tab to do most of your work with slides. The Slides tab lets you see each slide much as it will appear in your presentation. It also lets you move between the slides in your presentations and click and drag to move the slide within your presentation. Note that you can expand the width of the Slides tab to allow you to more clearly see your slides. To do so, place the pointer at the right edge of the tab until the pointer changes shape to a double-headed arrow; then drag the border to a desired size. This action correspondingly reduces the size of the center portion of the presentation window. Figure 19-8 shows a presentation window with an expanded Slides tab.

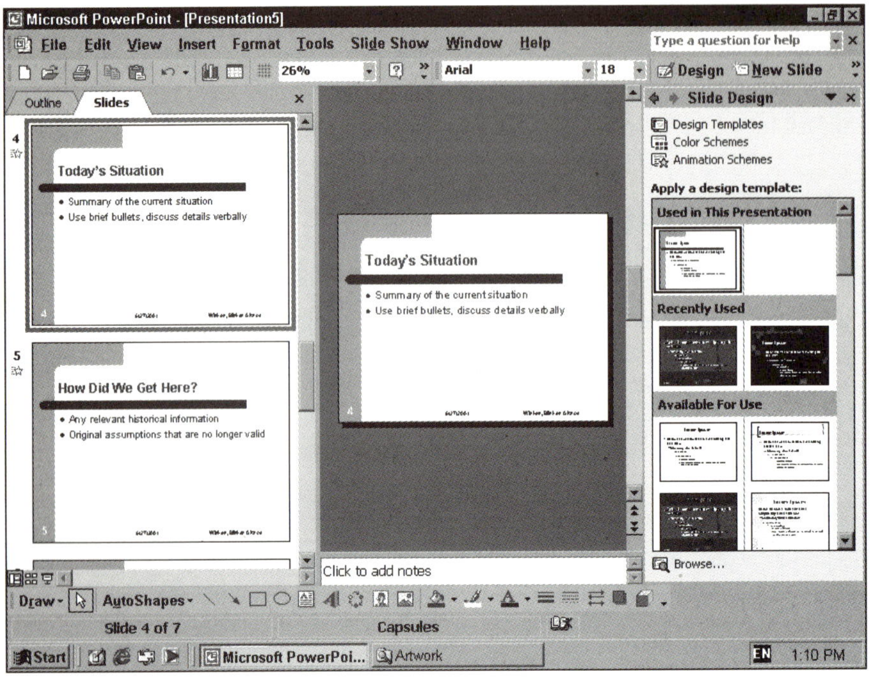

Figure 19-8: A presentation window with an expanded Slides tab

Moving between slides

When you have more than one slide in a presentation (and if you have only a single slide, why bother with a presentation?), you must be able to move easily among the slides so that you can quickly work on any of the slides. You can drag the scroll bar in the Slides tab up or down until the slide that you want to view or edit appears. Then you can click that slide to display it in the center of the presentation window (depending on the speed of your hardware, there may be a brief delay before the chosen slide appears in the center of the presentation window). Alternatively, you can switch to Slide Sorter view (choose View ⇨ Slide Sorter) and locate the desired slide, using the vertical scroll bar if necessary.

When less is more...

Resist the temptation to get carried away when it comes to working with text in PowerPoint slides, particularly with bullet lists. One of the most common design errors committed by attorneys and paralegals working with PowerPoint involves using too much text for a single point or on a single slide. Attorneys, by nature, are accustomed to creating documents containing lots of words, but you should resist the temptation to treat PowerPoint as if it were a word processor. With a bullet list, you are creating a series of statements, and each statement is designed to convey a single thought. Strip unnecessary words such as *a*, *an*, and *the*, and keep your statements concise and to the point.

Inserting slides

As you build your presentation in PowerPoint, you naturally will need to make changes to the presentation by inserting, deleting, and copying slides. Follow these steps to add a slide to a presentation:

1. On the Slides tab or in Slide Sorter view, choose the slide after which you want the new slide to appear.
2. Choose Insert ⇨ New Slide.

If you want to change the new slide's layout, follow these steps:

1. In the Task Pane, choose Slide Layout from the drop-down menu at the top of the Task Pane to display the available slide layouts.
2. Click a desired layout to apply it to the slide.

Deleting slides

Deleting a slide is relatively simple and can be performed in any view except Slide Show. Navigate to the slide and choose Edit ⇨ Delete Slide to remove the slide. If you delete a slide by accident, choose Edit ⇨ Undo Delete Slide, or click the Undo button on the Standard toolbar to bring back the slide.

Copying and moving slides

You can copy slides in PowerPoint just as you copy items in other Windows programs, by using the Copy and Paste commands from the Edit menu. You can copy a slide by performing the following steps:

1. On the Slides tab or in Slide Sorter view, click the slide that you want to copy.
2. Choose Edit ⇨ Copy.
3. Move to the slide after which you want to place the copied slide.
4. Choose Edit ⇨ Paste.

Rearranging slides

From time to time, you will need to change the order in which the slides appear in your presentation. You can easily do this by dragging slides around on the Slides tab or in Slide Sorter view. Follow these steps to rearrange the order of your slides:

1. On the Slides tab or in Slide Sorter view, click the slide that you want to move.
2. Drag the slide up or down within the Slides tab to a new location, or drag the slide to a new location within Slide Sorter view. As you drag the slide, its new location is indicated by a thin line. When you release the mouse button, the slide appears at the line location.

Using the black slide

In older versions of PowerPoint, a common design technique was to place a black or neutral color slide with no information at the end of the presentation. This was done to avoid ending the presentation on a screen that also displayed the PowerPoint menus and toolbars. It's not necessary to do this in PowerPoint 2002 because the program displays a black slide at the end of a presentation automatically. You may still want to use this trick between existing slides if you plan to be talking for a while at some point and don't want the audience to be distracted by a slide remaining on the screen. For courtroom presentations, you may want to use a black slide as the first slide in the presentation; this avoids having information visible to the jury before you are ready to speak. Just insert a new slide where desired, using the techniques discussed, right-click the slide and choose Background, set the color to black or to a neutral color in the dialog box that appears, and click Apply.

Working with Objects

In PowerPoint, the basic component that you use to create a slide is an object. An *object* can be the box where you enter text, a picture brought in from another source, or a shape that you draw using various options of the Drawing toolbar. You can have a variety of objects on a slide.

Selecting objects

To select the object that you want to work with, click it. Then you can add text to it and change its orientation, shape, color, or pattern. You also can select multiple objects within a slide by holding down the Ctrl key as you select the objects. To deselect an object, simply hold down the Ctrl key and click the object again.

Moving and copying objects

As you work on a presentation, you may often have to move your objects around. To move the objects, follow these steps:

1. In the slide (in the center of the presentation window when in Normal view), select the object(s) that you want to move or copy.
2. Choose Edit ⇨ Cut to move the object to a new location via the Clipboard; choose Edit ⇨ Copy to copy it.
3. Move to the location within the presentation where you wish to insert the object.
4. Choose Edit ⇨ Paste to place the Clipboard information onto the slide.

Sometimes you may find that you need to remove an object from a slide. To remove an object, select it and press the Delete key, or choose Edit ⇨ Clear.

Cropping pictures and graphs

In your quest to give your presentation a refined look, you may find it necessary to crop either pictures or graphic images that you add to a presentation. *Cropping* is the trimming of an object to remove elements that you do not want from the image. Follow these steps to crop a graphic image:

1. Right-click the object and choose Show Picture Toolbar from the menu that appears.
2. Click the Crop button in the toolbar.
3. Place the mouse pointer over a selection handle. If you want to crop two sides simultaneously, you need to use a corner handle. If you want to crop only one side, use a top or bottom handle. Figure 19-9 shows an image that has been cropped along the bottom edge. Click and drag to do the cropping. (The border handles will disappear after you click off the graphic.)

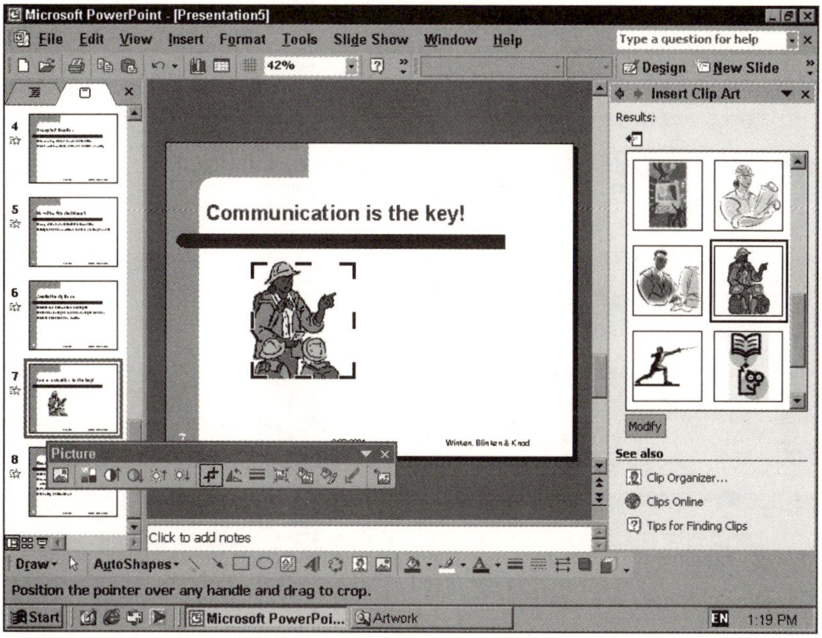

Figure 19-9: A graphic image cropped within a PowerPoint slide

Aligning objects

Giving objects the same sort of alignment is best. The following figures show before and after views of some objects on a slide in PowerPoint. As you can see, the slide with aligned objects (Figure 19-11) has a better appearance than the one in which the objects are not aligned (Figure 19-10). Aligned objects make your objects appear more organized than those that are not aligned.

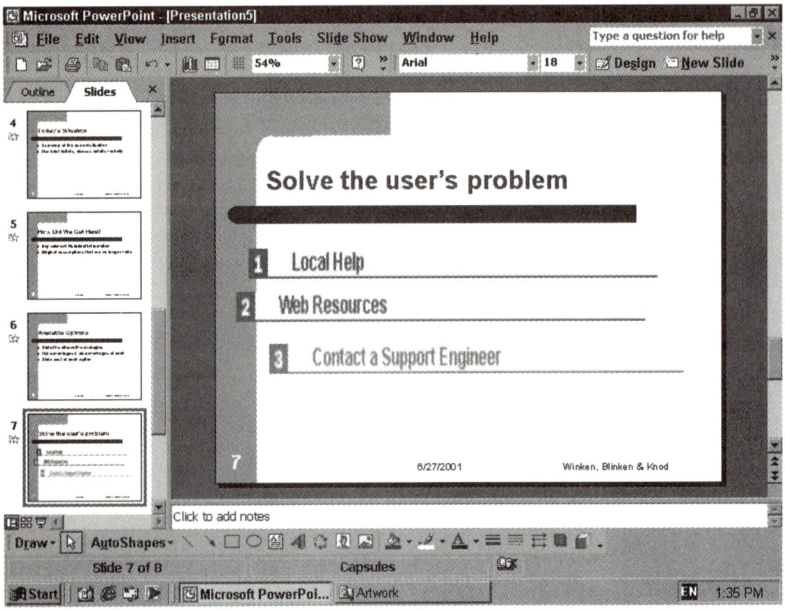

Figure 19-10: Objects on a slide, before alignment

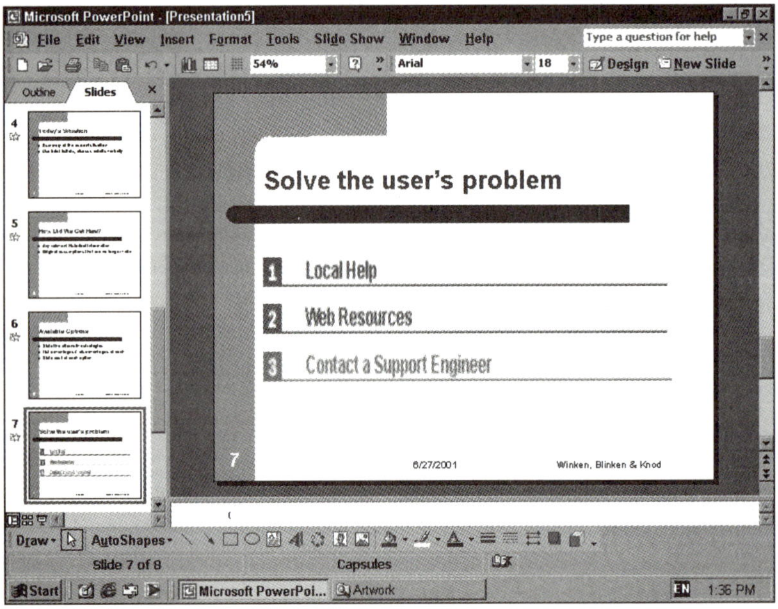

Figure 19-11: Objects on a slide, after alignment

The Align command enables you to choose the method of alignment that you want to use. You can select objects and then align them, or you can use the rulers available in the PowerPoint window. PowerPoint is equipped with a reference system for aligning objects on slides. The system uses a grid and guides. The invisible grid covers the slide, with twelve grid lines per inch and five lines per centimeter. When objects are drawn, their corners align on the nearest intersection of the grid, which is how PowerPoint helps you to align objects.

The guides that PowerPoint provides are two rulers: one horizontal and one vertical. When the corners or center of an object (whichever is closer) is close to the guide, it snaps to the guide, which is how you align the object. You can even align a group of objects.

To align objects, follow these steps:

1. Select the objects that you want to align.
2. Choose Draw ⇨ Align or Distribute from the Drawing toolbar and then choose the alignment that you want from the submenu that appears. You can choose from Align Left, Align Center, Align Right, Align Top, Align Middle, and Align Bottom. You can also space a group of objects evenly apart by choosing Distribute Horizontally or Distribute Vertically from the same menu.

Using Clip Art

PowerPoint comes with an assortment of clip art, which can prove useful in creating presentations that will be used primarily within your firm or organization or for presentations made to clients. (Most types of clip art do *not* have the professional appearance that you need for courtroom purposes.) The clip art comes in many different categories. To access the ClipArt gallery, perform the following steps:

1. Choose Insert ⇨ Picture ⇨ Clip Art. (If you have never used this feature before, you may see a message about the Clip Art Gallery being organized, and you can click Now to proceed.) In a moment, the Task Pane changes to reveal the ClipArt Gallery pane.
2. In the Search Text box, enter a search term that describes the clip art you would like to insert and then click the Search button. For example, if you want to insert clip art of a person, you could type the term *people* into the Search Text box.
3. In a moment, the results of your search will appear as a selection of images in the Task Pane. Click the desired image, and PowerPoint inserts it at the insertion point.

Inserting Photographs and Graphic Images in Slides

For many presentations that are used during arbitration sessions or during a trial, photographs are needed as part of a presentation. Photographs can be scanned from conventionally developed prints, or they can be downloaded directly from a digital camera. If you lack access to a digital camera or a scanner, you can have a conventional photograph scanned and saved to disk at a commercial copy shop. If you need to include a large number of photos, you can have a local film-processing shop place a series of photos or the contents of an entire roll of exposed film onto a CD as graphic images. If you use this approach, be sure to request .JPG type image files from the film or copy shop; this type of file takes up less disk space and can be imported easily into PowerPoint while maintaining good image quality. You should also request to have any scanned photos scanned at a resolution of at least 300 dpi, or dots per inch, and not the coarser resolution setting of 72 dpi, which will result in very grainy images.

After the photograph exists in the form of a file, you can insert the photograph into a PowerPoint slide. You can use the same technique to insert a graphic image created in another Windows program. As an example, Figure 19-12 shows a photograph inserted into a PowerPoint slide.

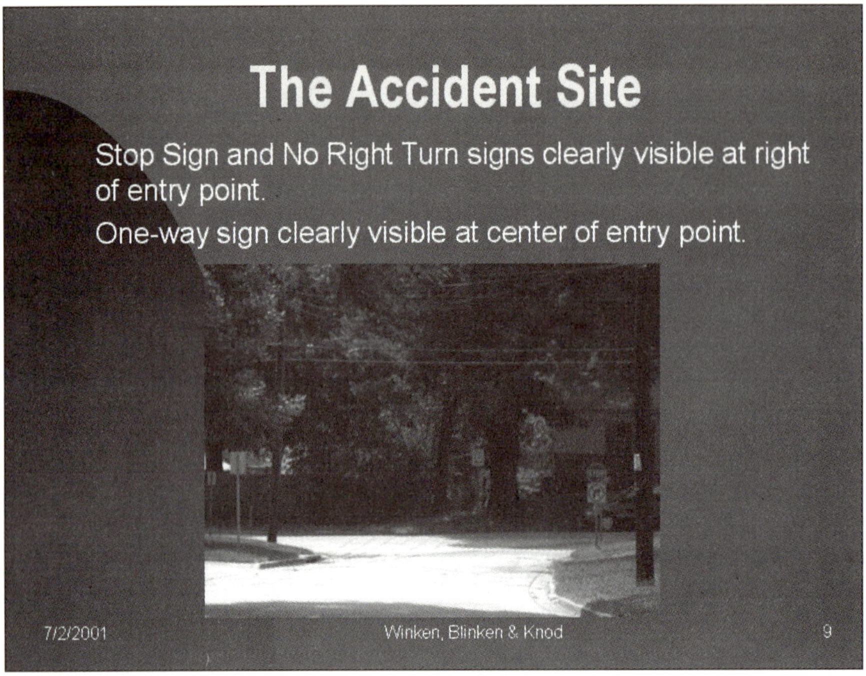

Figure 19-12: A photograph inserted into a PowerPoint slide

PowerPoint can insert photographs that have been stored as files using a number of common graphics file formats, including the three most commonly used: Joint Picture Experts Group (.JPG or .JPEG files), Graphical Interchange Format (.GIF files), and Windows Bitmap (.BMP files). In addition to these, you can import any of these types:

- Enhanced Metafile (.EMF)
- Portable Network Graphics (.PNG)
- Windows Metafile (.WMF)
- Tagged Image File Format (.TIFF)

Additionally, if your digital camera cannot save an image file in a format that is compatible with PowerPoint, you can usually use the Edit ⇨ Copy and Edit ⇨ Paste commands to copy the image from your camera's software into the PowerPoint slide. (See the sidebar for details.)

My camera doesn't save files in any of the formats you list!

Many digital cameras save image files using proprietary file formats that may be recognized only by the software that is provided with the camera. Even in these cases, you can usually utilize the photographs taken with your digital camera by making use of your digital camera software and the Edit ⇨ Copy and Edit ⇨ Paste commands that are common to virtually all commercial Windows programs. If your digital camera software cannot save files in a format that PowerPoint can recognize, you can try these steps instead:

1. Start the software program that is provided with your digital camera and use the appropriate commands to view the desired image stored within the camera.

2. Using your camera's software, select the image (the Edit menu may have a Select All command or a Select Image command that lets you do this; refer to your camera documentation for details).

3. Choose Edit ⇨ Copy from the menus of your camera's software package. (If there is no Edit ⇨ Copy command, consult your camera documentation to determine how to copy the image to the Windows Clipboard.)

4. Switch to PowerPoint and select the slide where the image should appear.

5. Choose Edit ⇨ Paste to insert the photograph into the slide.

After the photo has been inserted, you can use the corner sizing handles to resize it as desired. Be warned that if you copy and paste photos using the preceding techniques and then resize them with any handles other than the corner handles, you may affect the aspect ratio of the photo in ways you hadn't planned. For example, if you change the height while leaving the width alone, the result will be a picture that appears distorted by being too short or too tall. Use the corner handles, or right-click the photo and choose Format Picture from the shortcut menu that appears; then click the Size tab in the Format Picture dialog box. You can then make sure that the Lock Aspect Ratio check box is turned on. You can change the value in the Height box or the Width box, and the other corresponding value (Width or Height) will change accordingly. This prevents distortion as you resize a photograph. (Note that using the Windows Clipboard means that you are resigned to the resolution of the image as it comes from the source.)

To insert a photograph that has been saved to a file into a slide, use the following steps:

1. On the Slides tab, select the slide on which the photo should appear.
2. From the menus, choose Insert ⇨ Picture ⇨ From File. The Insert Picture dialog box appears.
3. In the dialog box, navigate to the file that you wish to use. As you select graphic files in the list box, you can see a preview of each file at the right side of the dialog box. (If the preview does not appear, click the View button at the top of the dialog box until the preview appears.)
4. With the desired file selected, click Insert to place the photograph or image onto the slide.

If the image is too large or too small, you can right-click the photo, choose Format Picture from the shortcut menu that appears and click the Size tab in the Format Picture dialog box. Make sure that the Lock Aspect Ratio check box is turned on (see the Caution that follows) and change the value in the Height box or in the Width box to resize the photo as desired.

CAUTION: If you want to resize a photo by selecting and dragging one of the sizing handles, *don't* be tempted to use any of the handles on the middle sides, center top, or center bottom of the photo. Use only the corner handles to resize the photo. If you use a handle other than a corner handle, you will distort the photo by changing its *aspect ratio* (the ratio of width to height). The corner handles can resize a photo while maintaining its proper aspect ratio. (Or you can use the Format Picture dialog box, as described previously, to change the size of the photo.)

Whether you use the Insert ⇨ Picture command or the Edit @> Paste command along with your camera software, you can use a number of features of PowerPoint to enhance the photo after you have inserted it into the slide. With the photo selected, choose View ⇨ Toolbars and select Picture from the submenu that appears, to display the Picture toolbar (see Figure 19-13).

Figure 19-13: The Picture toolbar

You can often improve the appearance of photos by adjusting the brightness, contrast, or both. Use the buttons on the Picture toolbar to do this, or you can right-click the picture, choose Format Picture from the shortcut menu that appears, and click the Picture tab in the dialog box (see Figure 19-14).

You can use the Brightness and Contrast sliders on this tab to adjust the brightness or contrast of the photo for optimal viewing. As you make your adjustments, you can click the Preview button at the lower-right corner of the dialog box to see the effects of your adjustments on the photo. (You may need to drag the dialog box to one side so that you can view the photo.) When you're done making adjustments, click OK and save your changes to the presentation with File ⇨ Save.

You also can *crop* a photo, effectively trimming part of one or more sides. To do this, right-click the photo, choose Show Picture Toolbar from the menu that appears, and click the Crop button in the toolbar. Place the mouse pointer over a selection handle and drag the handle to crop the photo. (If you want to crop two sides simultaneously, you need to use a corner handle. If you want to crop only one side, use a top or bottom handle.)

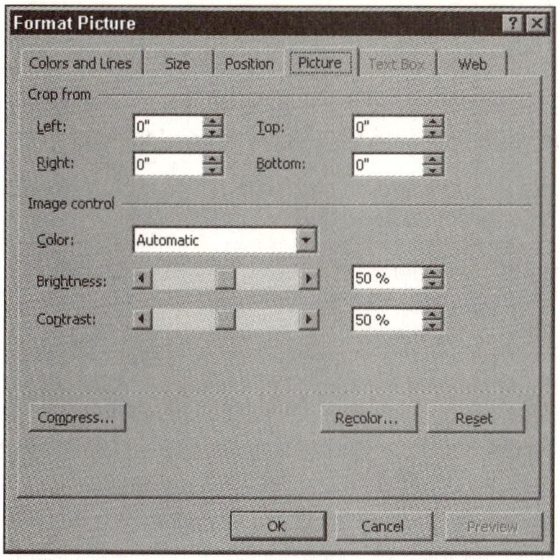

Figure 19-14: The Picture tab of the Format Picture dialog box

Table 19-1 describes the purpose of the buttons within the Picture toolbar.

Table 19-1
The Picture Toolbar Buttons

Button	*Purpose*
Insert Picture	Displays the Insert Picture dialog box, which you can use to insert a picture or graphic file into a slide
Color	Lets you choose Automatic, Grayscale, Black and White, or Washout as options affecting the colors of the picture
More Contrast	Increases the contrast of the picture
Less Contrast	Decreases the contrast of the picture
More Brightness	Increases the brightness of the picture
Less Brightness	Decreases the brightness of the picture
Crop	Adds crop handles to the picture, which you can then drag to crop the image as desired
Rotate Left	Rotates the picture 90 degrees left (you can click the button repeatedly to achieve additional rotation, if desired)
Line Style	Lets you apply a rule line border to the picture
Compress Picture	Compresses the image so that it does not cause a large increase in the file size of your presentation (using this feature may result in some loss of resolution in the picture)
Recolor Image	Lets you change the hues used by the picture

Button	Purpose
Format Picture	Displays a Format Picture dialog box, which contains additional options to control the size, position, brightness, and contrast of the picture
Set Transparent Color	Lets you change a solid color in the picture to a transparent color
Reset Picture	Resets all settings (contrast, brightness, size, cropping, and others) to the original settings of the picture

CAUTION: If you crop a photo that you plan to use as part of a presentation in a courtroom, you risk the possibility of an objection raised by opposing counsel, assuming that the uncropped photo was originally submitted as an exhibit. Opposing counsel may claim that the photo you are presenting as part of the presentation does not match the photo originally submitted by your team as evidence. If cropping the photo is an important part of your trial presentation, you may want to show two slides — one slide with the complete photo, followed by a second slide with the cropped version.

Inserting a Slide into a Legal Brief

At times, you may want to use the contents of a PowerPoint slide within a legal brief or other memoranda that you are writing using Microsoft Word. Although you could print the slide and manually insert the printed page into the printed pages of your brief or memoranda, there's an easier way. Here's all you need to do:

1. In PowerPoint, in Slide Sorter view, select the desired slide.
2. From the menus, choose Edit ⇨ Copy.
3. Open the desired document within Microsoft Word and place the insertion pointer where you want to add the slide.
4. From the Word menus, choose Edit ⇨ Paste. A graphic of your slide will appear within the Word document.

If you're using a word processor other than Microsoft Word (we could ask *why*, but we'll resist the temptation!), you can try the preceding steps. These steps will work in many Windows word processors. If the preceding steps don't work in your word processor, you can use the following (and somewhat more complex) process:

1. In PowerPoint, in Slide Sorter view, select the desired slide.
2. From the menus, choose File ⇨ Save As.
3. In the Save As dialog box, change Save as Type to GIF Graphics Interchange Format (*.gif).
4. Enter a filename in the File Name box and click Save.
5. In the dialog box that appears next, click Current Slide Only.

6. In your word processor, use the appropriate picture or graphics import command to import the image you saved in Steps 2 through 4. (See your word processor's documentation for details.)

Summary

This chapter described many techniques that you can use in the everyday use of PowerPoint. With these skills, you can build presentations, enter the text that you want, and choose a desired slide layout. This chapter covered the following areas:

- Creating a basic presentation using the classic bullet list style of slide
- Using convenient shortcut menus, which simplify your work in PowerPoint by providing fast access to various options
- Using the Task Pane, a new feature of PowerPoint 2002, to perform common tasks
- Using wizards and built-in templates to make the task of creating a presentation less time-consuming
- Inserting text into your presentations and editing that text
- Moving and copying objects and inserting clip art.
- Inserting pictures into a PowerPoint slide and changing the appearance of those pictures to increase the clarity of the slide

The next chapter covers ways that you can enhance your presentations in PowerPoint.

Chapter 20

Polishing a Presentation

In This Chapter

- Working with slide layouts
- Using the Slide Master
- Working with lists and columns
- Changing the look of text
- Checking your spelling
- Using find and replace
- Adding comments to a slide
- Adding a summary slide
- Drawing lines and shapes
- Creating special effects with WordArt
- Displaying text documents and diagrams with annotations
- Adding data from Excel worksheets to a presentation
- Inserting tables in slides
- Adding multimedia to presentations
- Adding animations

POWERPOINT PROVIDES A WIDE assortment of tools for you to use to give any presentation a more professional look. To help you along, PowerPoint provides various layouts to better meet a particular purpose. You can use columns, bullet lists, and tables to focus a viewers' attention on a specific group of facts or issues. You can add comments that assist you or others during the review phase, and you can insert scanned images that can prove useful for trial purposes. If you want to make extensive use of *multimedia* in a presentation, you can add sound, video clips, and audio tracks from recorded CDs. This chapter covers these techniques for enhancing the appearance of your presentation in various ways.

Working with Slide Layouts

In PowerPoint, the term *layout* refers to precisely how your objects — bullet headings, text, images, clip art, tables, and others — are arranged on a slide. Consider, for example, Figures 20-1 and 20-2. Figure 20-1 shows a Title and Text slide layout as it appears in the Slide Layout pane of the Task Pane. For most applications, this layout is the most typically used slide layout in a PowerPoint presentation. A slide that uses this layout contains a title at the top of the slide and bulleted text headings underneath.

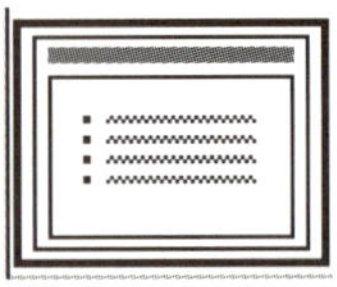

Figure 20-1: A Title and Text slide layout contains title and bulleted text.

By comparison, Figure 20-2 shows a Title, Content, and Text slide layout as it appears in the Slide Layout pane of the Task Pane. A slide that uses this particular layout contains a title at the top, a placeholder for content (such as a photograph, clip art image, or numeric graph) at the left, and bulleted text headings at the right.

Figure 20-2: A Title, Content, and Text slide layout contains title, content, and bulleted text.

Although you can lay out any slide manually by starting with a blank slide and inserting text and objects from scratch, the AutoLayout feature of PowerPoint can save you time. It speeds the process of slide design by providing you with a collection of ready-to-use layouts for different purposes. You can use these layouts with new slides that you add to a presentation or with existing slides.

Whenever you add a new slide to a presentation (by clicking the New Slide button in the toolbar, or choosing Insert ⇨ New Slide, or pressing Ctrl+M), the Slide Layout pane appears in the Task Pane area. Figure 20-3 shows the Slide Layout pane; in the figure, the pane has been intentionally widened to show more available slide layouts. (You can widen the pane by placing the pointer at the left edge, where the pointer changes shape to a double-headed arrow; then you drag to the desired width.)

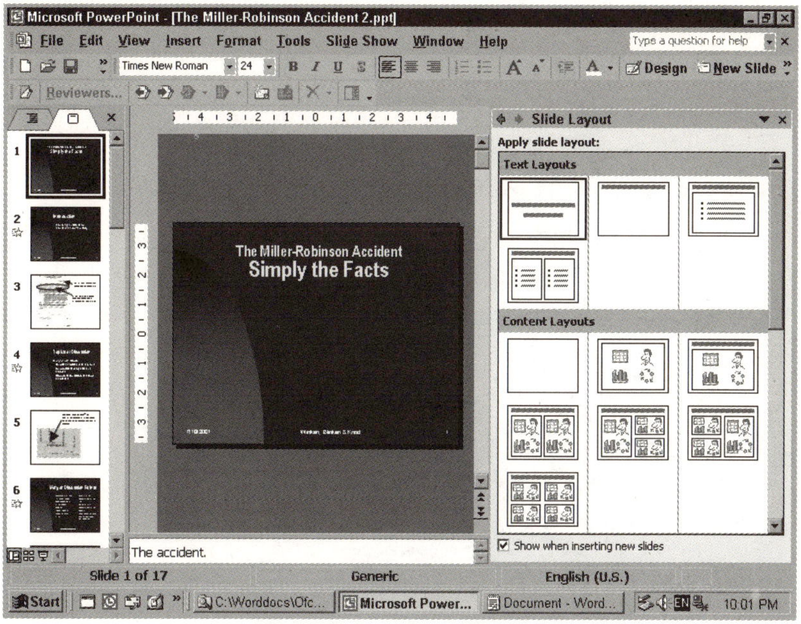

Figure 20-3: The Slide Layout pane visible in the Task Pane area

The various layouts are quite useful when you're adding new slides to your presentations or you want to change the appearance of existing slides. After you add the slide, click the desired layout in the Slide Layout pane to apply that layout to the new slide.

To change the layout of an existing slide, first click the desired slide either on the Outline tab or while in Slide Sorter view. Then choose View ⇨ Task Pane to display the Task Pane (if it isn't already visible), choose Slide Layout from the drop-down menu in the Task Pane, and select the desired layout in the Task Pane to apply it to the slide.

When preparing a presentation for arbitration or a trial, don't underestimate the importance of choosing a slide layout that will best accommodate the thoughts or concepts you are trying to present. For example, if you need rather lengthy bulleted points, you may want to utilize a Title and Text slide layout, as illustrated in Figure 20-4.

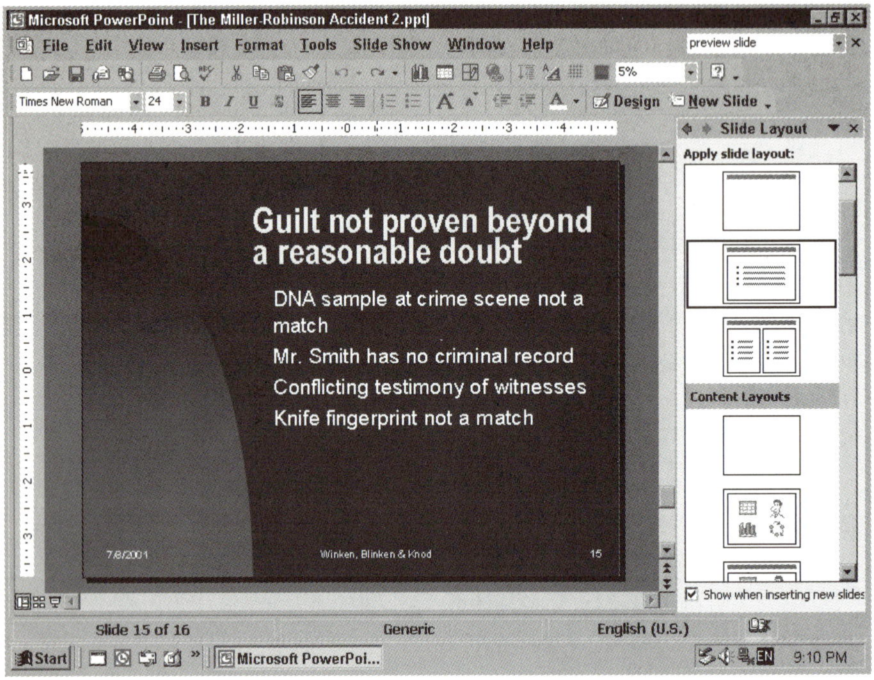

Figure 20-4: A Title and Text slide layout prepared for a trial presentation

On the other hand, if you have a larger number of shorter bulleted points that you want the audience to take in at a single glance, you may be better served with a Title and 2-Column Text slide layout, as illustrated in Figure 20-5.

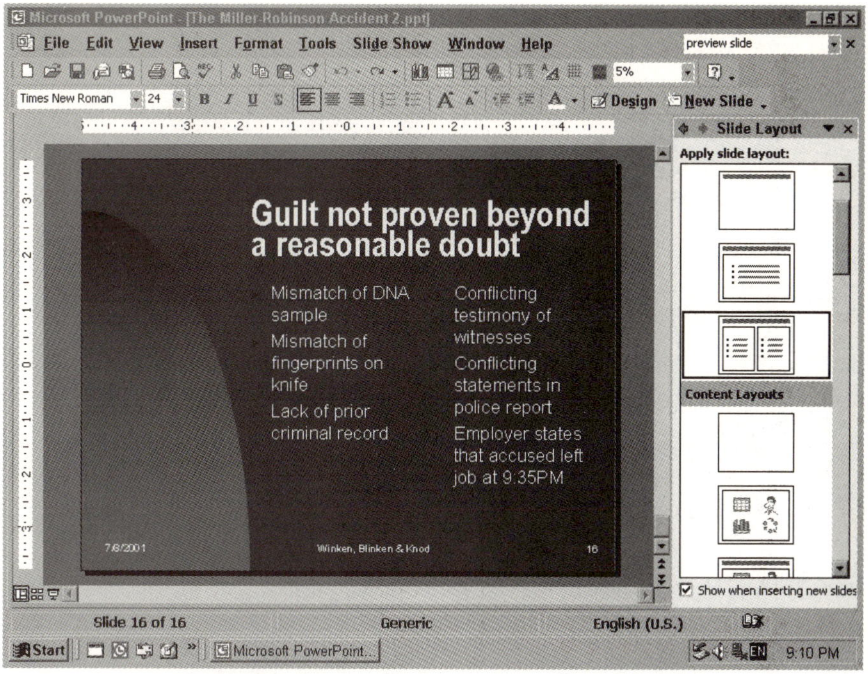

Figure 20-5: A Title and 2-Column Text slide layout prepared for a trial presentation

Using the Slide Master

Use the Slide Master to control the overall appearance and layout of each slide in a presentation. Editing with the Slide Master is very useful whenever you want to change all the slides in your presentation and not just one. You can even add graphics or other layouts to the Slide Master, and they will automatically show up in all the slides in that presentation. Make all the changes that you want on the Slide Master, and these new formats are applied to all the slides in your presentation.

TIP: As long-time Information Systems pros within the legal environment, we've often seen attorneys and paralegals perform the tedious task of adding the *very same* information (such as a case name or the current date) over and over to every slide in a presentation that contains dozens of slides. There's no need to put yourself through this kind of torture! With the Slide Master, you can add your information once. It then appears throughout the presentation.

The Slide Master contains two important elements: a title area and an object area. The formatting in the title area is specific to the title of each slide in your presentation. The title area tells PowerPoint the font size, style, and color to use for the text. The object area contains the formatting for the remaining text on the slide. The object area also sets up specifications for bullet lists, which include the indents for each of the lists, the font styles, and the size of the fonts. Figure 20-6 shows the Slide Master.

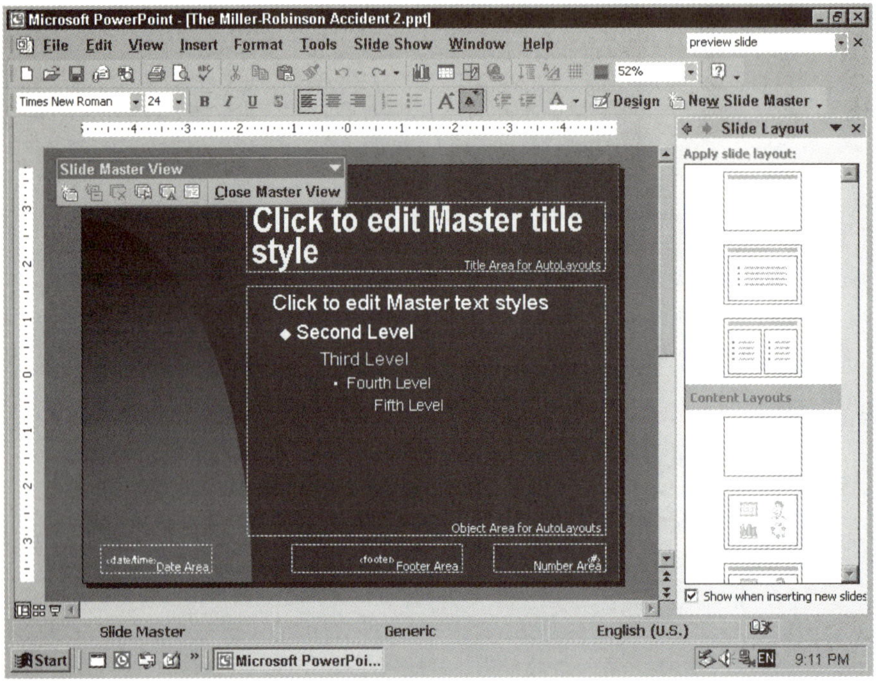

Figure 20-6: The Slide Master controls the appearance and formatting of all slides within a presentation.

Along with the usual text formats and object setups, you can use the Slide Master to include borders, page numbers, logos, clip art, and many other elements on the slides of your presentation. Perform the following steps to work with the Slide Master:

1. Open the desired presentation and choose View ⇨ Master ⇨ Slide Master. The Slide Master appears.
2. You now can make any adjustment that you want to the Slide Master. To bring up a shortcut menu of available formatting options, right-click the desired area within the slide. You can change the Master Layout dialog box or the Background dialog box. You also can change the color schemes used by your slides, as described in the paragraphs that follow.
3. When you have finished making desired adjustments to the Slide Master, return to a particular slide by choosing the Normal or Slide Sorter commands of the View menu, or by clicking the Normal View or Slide Sorter View buttons at the lower-left corner of the PowerPoint window.

If you want to change the colors used by all the slides in your presentation, you can easily do so by changing the colors of the Slide Master. With the Slide Master visible, choose Format ⇨ Slide Design so that the Slide Design pane appears in the Task Pane area. Next, click the Color Schemes link in the Task Pane. You will see a group of coordinated color schemes in the Task Pane. Click the desired color scheme to apply it to the Slide Master (and thus to all the slides in your presentation).

If none of the available color schemes suits your fancy, you can edit the color scheme. To do so, click the Edit Color Schemes link at the bottom of the Task Pane, and the Edit Color Scheme dialog box appears.

In the Scheme Colors area of the Custom tab, click the box whose color you want to change and then click the Change Color button. A Color dialog box appears, appropriate to the box you selected. For example, if you select the Fills box, the dialog box is titled *Fill Color*, whereas if you select the Accent box, the dialog box is titled *Accent Color*.

On the Standard tab, click any color that suits your fancy. In the unlikely event that these choices are not sufficient to your tastes, use the Custom tab. Click anywhere in the Colors box to choose a color, or enter a numeric value in the Red, Green, and Blue spinner boxes to create a custom color based on a mix of the primary colors of light. When you're done, click OK to close the Color dialog box; then click Apply in the Edit Color Scheme dialog box to apply your choice to the appropriate part of your color scheme.

You can repeat this color-choosing process for any item in the color scheme. When you finish, return to Normal View or to Slide Sorter view, and the new colors (and any other changes you have made to the Slide Master) will be applied to every slide in your presentation.

CAUTION: After making a change to the background color used by the Slide Master, be sure to view every slide in your presentation and check for readability. You will want to ensure that a change in background color for the entire presentation does not make some aspect of a particular slide hard to read.

After you apply the editing in the Slide Master to all your slides, you can still edit and change individual slides in whatever way you want. You can even change the headings or the formatting of an individual slide while retaining the formatting within the Slide Master for the remaining slides. If you don't like the formatting that you have done to a slide, however, and you want to return that individual slide to the same formatting as used by the Slide Master, simply reapply the Slide Master formatting. Follow these steps:

1. Move to the slide to which you want to reapply the Slide Master formatting.
2. Choose Format ⇨ Slide Layout. The Slide Layout pane appears in the Task Pane, with the current layout selected.
3. Right-click the selected layout and choose Reapply Layout. The slide now contains the formatting of the Slide Master.

Working with Lists and Columns

When you create your presentations, columns and bullet lists become important parts of your slides because you use them often. Putting columns and bullet lists into your slides is easy with PowerPoint.

You can use indents to create bullet lists. You can also use this technique for objects (shapes that you can add). Refer back to Figure 20-4 for an example of a bullet list in PowerPoint.

Perform the following steps to create a bullet list:

1. After opening a presentation, switch to Normal view and click the New Slide toolbar button (or choose Insert ⇨ New Slide, or press Ctrl+M). In the Slide Layout pane within the Task Pane area, choose Title and Text or Title and 2-Column Text, depending on whether you want one or two columns.
2. Choose View ⇨ Ruler so that the PowerPoint ruler is displayed on-screen.

3. Click the Click to Add Text placeholder and enter a series of topics of your choosing, pressing the Enter key after each topic.
4. After entering your topics, drag the bottom indent marker within the horizontal ruler to the right. You will notice that the bottom marker moves the text farther away from the bullets, and the top marker moves the bullets. You can use these indent markers to set the indentations where desired.

You also can change the appearance of the bullet characters or use numbering or letters in place of the bullets. To do so, perform these steps:

1. In the Outline tab, select the item or items whose bullets you want to change. (Remember, you can select multiple items by holding the Shift key as you click each item.)
2. Choose Format ⇨ Bullets and Numbering to open the Bullets and Numbering dialog box.
3. On the Bulleted tab of the dialog box, choose a style and desired color for the bullets and click OK.
4. If you prefer to use numbering (or letters) in place of the bullets, click the Numbered tab of the dialog box and choose a desired numbering style and color.

Columns can be useful when dealing with slides that contain moderate amounts of text, as opposed to short, bulleted points. Most people have an easier time reading shorter lines of text, and columns provide an effective and consistent way to keep your lines of text at a reasonable length. If you have a large amount of textual information to get across in your presentation, you can take advantage of columns to make the information easier to comprehend. Figure 20-7 shows an example of columns of text placed in a slide.

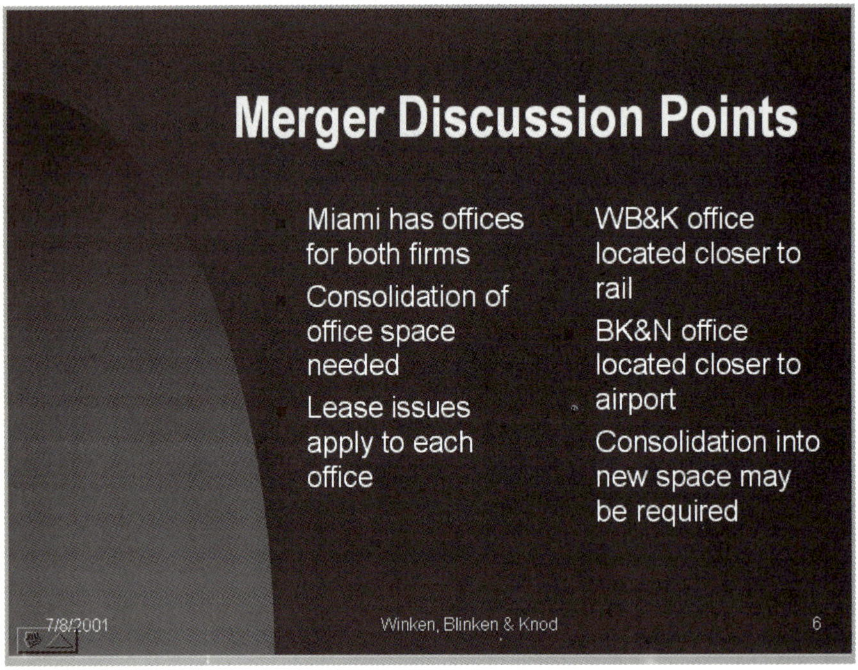

Figure 20-7: An example of columns of text displayed within a PowerPoint slide

TIP: If your columns of text span multiple rows, consider inserting a table into the slide instead of using columns. The topic of inserting tables into slides is detailed later in this chapter.

You can add columns to a slide by performing the following steps:

1. Before entering your text, choose the Slide Layout view in the Task Pane and select Title and 2-Column Text as the desired layout for the slide.
2. Next, right-click Bullet in the column text box. From the shortcut menu that appears, choose Bullets and Numbering.
3. When the Bullets and Numbering dialog box appears, choose None and click OK. Doing so removes the bullet and lets you enter columnar text.

If you want to create columns of bullet lists, however, you can use one of the slide layouts from the Slide Layout pane in the Task Pane area. To apply it, choose the Slide Layout view within the Task Pane and select the 2-Column Text choice. By default, this is a bullet list. Enter the text you want and press Enter at the end of each line to move to the next bullet.

Remember that you can perform any of these changes on the Slide Master if you want them to apply to all your slides in the presentation.

Changing the Look of Text

Although PowerPoint presentations can contain various objects that include text, images, clip art, photographs, and even sound and video, most slides that you create are likely to be based primarily or entirely on text. As part of effective design, you need to know how to design and arrange text for maximum impact. In the preceding chapter, you learned basic ways of inputting text. Topics within this section further detail various ways in which you can work with the text in a presentation.

Formatting text with the Font dialog box and the Formatting toolbar

When you want to change the typeface, size, style, or color of your text, use the Font dialog box. In PowerPoint (as in Word), the word *font* refers to a family of text having the same typeface, such as Courier or Times New Roman. You can take any given font and apply different styles — such as bold, italic, or underlining— to that font. And you can change the size of the font: the smaller or larger the size, the smaller or larger the letters. In PowerPoint, you use the Font dialog box or the Formatting toolbar to change the appearance of your text. To use the Font dialog box to format your text, perform these steps:

1. In the slide, click and drag as needed to select the desired text. (You can do this in the slide itself or in the Outline tab.)
2. From the menus, choose Format ⇨ Font (or right-click the selection and choose Font) to display the Font dialog box.
3. In the Font list, select a desired font.
4. In the Font Style list, select any desired style for the font (or select Regular to remove a previously applied style).
5. In the Size list, select the desired size, or type the size value directly into the box.

6. In the Effects portion of the dialog box, select any desired special effect that you want to apply to the selection.
7. If you want to use a different color, click the arrow button at the right of the Color list, and choose a desired color for the font.
8. Click OK in the dialog box to apply the changes to the text.

NOTE: If you change font colors for text on a slide, remember to consider the effects of contrasting background colors. Some text colors may prove difficult to read when contrasted against a background color used by a particular design template or color scheme.

Optionally, you can use the Formatting toolbar, shown in Figure 20-8, to format your text. If you don't see the Formatting toolbar, choose View ⇨ Toolbars and then choose Formatting from the menu that appears.

Figure 20-8: The Formatting toolbar

Use these steps to format text using the Formatting toolbar:

1. Select the desired text within the slide or in the Outline tab.
2. To change fonts, open the Font drop-down list and select the desired font.
3. To change the font size, open the Font Size drop-down list and select the desired size, or type the size value directly into the box. (If you just want to make the font slightly larger or smaller, use the Increase Font Size and Decrease Font Size buttons on the toolbar.)
4. To add a desired style or special effect, click the appropriate toolbar button.

If you are viewing the Standard and Formatting toolbars on the same row, you also can use the shortcut menu, accessible from the Formatting toolbar, to change the appearance of your text. Select the text that you want to change and click the downward-pointing triangle on the Formatting toolbar to open a menu of formatting options.

With text selected, click a button in this menu to apply bold, italic, underlining, shadow, or color. If you click a formatting button before you begin to type, the formatting is applied to all the text that you type, until you click the button again.

TIP: If you don't like having some buttons of the Formatting toolbar hidden, choose Show Buttons on Two Rows from the shortcut menu accessible from the Formatting toolbar to display the Standard and Formatting toolbars on separate rows.

Adding shadowing, superscripts, or subscripts to text

Note that you can select text and apply *shadowing* to add a special emphasis to the text. Shadowing adds a drop shadow behind the text. To add shadowing to text, select the desired text and click the Shadow button in the formatting options shortcut menu described previously.

You also can apply superscript (^{superscript}) and subscript ($_{\text{subscript}}$) to text in your slides. From the menus, choose Format ⇨ Font. In the Effects area of the Font dialog box, you will see the two check boxes for these options. After you click one of the options, enter a percentage by which to offset the text in the Offset box and click OK.

TIP: When preparing a presentation for use in the courtroom, color can be a valuable asset in helping to draw the attention of the jury to key facts or issues on a given slide. For example, you might choose red letters for an important statement that appears within a bullet list of statements.

Checking Your Spelling

PowerPoint includes the spell-checking capability that is built in to all Microsoft Office products. You can save yourself from possibly embarrassing blunders in the slides of a presentation by checking its spelling *before* you make your presentation to an audience. You also can add words to a custom dictionary used by the spelling checker to handle specialized words that you use often (such as legal terms).

When PowerPoint checks spelling, it checks the entire presentation, including all your slides, notes, and handout pages, and the Slide Master. To check the spelling in your presentation, choose Tools ⇨ Spelling, or click the Spelling button on the Standard toolbar, or press F7. PowerPoint checks the spelling in the presentation. If it finds what it thinks is a misspelled word, you'll see the Spelling dialog box.

When PowerPoint finds a misspelling, it tries to provide a number of options for a correct spelling of the word in the Suggestions list box. In the Change To text box, enter the correct spelling, or click one of the suggested spellings in the Suggestions list box, which adds that spelling to the Change To box. You can then click the Change button to make the change and to proceed to the next misspelling (if any exists).

The Ignore button lets you leave a word as is, and the Close button stops the entire spell checking operation at that point. Clicking Ignore All tells PowerPoint to ignore all suspected misspellings of the same term; Change All tells PowerPoint to change all misspellings to the entry that you accept in the Change To box. The Add button lets you add a word to the selected custom dictionary, which is named *Custom.DIC* by default. (For details on creating and changing custom dictionaries, see Chapter 6, "Formatting and Polishing Text.")

TIP: You can also check your spelling as you enter text if you've activated the Check Spelling as You Type option in PowerPoint. Choose Tools ⇨ Options, click the Spelling and Style tab in the dialog box that appears, click the Check Spelling as You Type option, and click OK.

With Check Spelling activated, any words that PowerPoint thinks are misspelled will appear with a wavy red line underneath as you type them. You can right-click any word that appears with a wavy red line underneath it to display a shortcut menu that includes suggestions for the correct spelling, along with Ignore All, Add to Dictionary, and Spelling options. Choose a suggestion from the menu to apply that correction to the word. Or choose Ignore All to ignore all occurrences of the word, choose Add to Dictionary to add the word to the default custom dictionary, or choose Spelling to display the Spelling dialog box, in which you can access any of the options detailed previously.

Using Find and Replace

Useful features that PowerPoint has borrowed from the word processing world are Edit ⇨ Find and Edit ⇨ Replace. As do their counterparts in Microsoft Word, these commands search for text and optionally replace that text with other text. To search for a word or a phrase in a presentation, perform the following steps:

1. Choose Edit ⇨ Find or press Ctrl+F. You will see the Find dialog box.
2. In the Find What text box, enter your search term.
3. If you want your search to be case-sensitive, click the Match Case check box.
4. Click the Find Whole words only check box if you want the search to find only complete words. If you leave this option turned off, PowerPoint will find text where either part or all of the phrase matches the search term.
5. Click the Find Next button to find the first occurrence of the search term.

After you have entered the parameters for a search in the Find dialog box, you can repeatedly click the Find Next button to continue searching for the same text.

Use the Replace command of the Edit menu to search for a word or phrase and replace it with other text. The process is similar to Edit ⇨ Find, with the additional step of specifying replacement text. Here are the steps:

1. Choose Edit ⇨ Replace or press Ctrl+H. You will see the Replace dialog box.
2. In the Find What text box, enter your search term.
3. In the Replace With text box, type the replacement text.
4. If you want your search to be case-sensitive, click the Match Case check box.
5. Click the Find Whole Words Only check box if you want to search to find only complete words. If you leave this option turned off, PowerPoint will replace text where either part or all of the phrase matches the search term.
6. Click the Replace All button if you want to find and replace all occurrences of the search term with your new term. Or click Find Next to find the next match in your presentation, and after examining it, click the Replace button to replace just that match. When you're done making your replacements, click Close.

NOTE: Clicking Edit ⇨ Undo (or pressing Ctrl+Z) rolls back the effects of a replace operation.

Adding Comments to a Slide

If you plan to share your presentation with co-workers, or send a presentation to other members of a team or to co-counsel for review, you might want to add comments to a slide. Figure 20-9 shows a slide containing a comment.

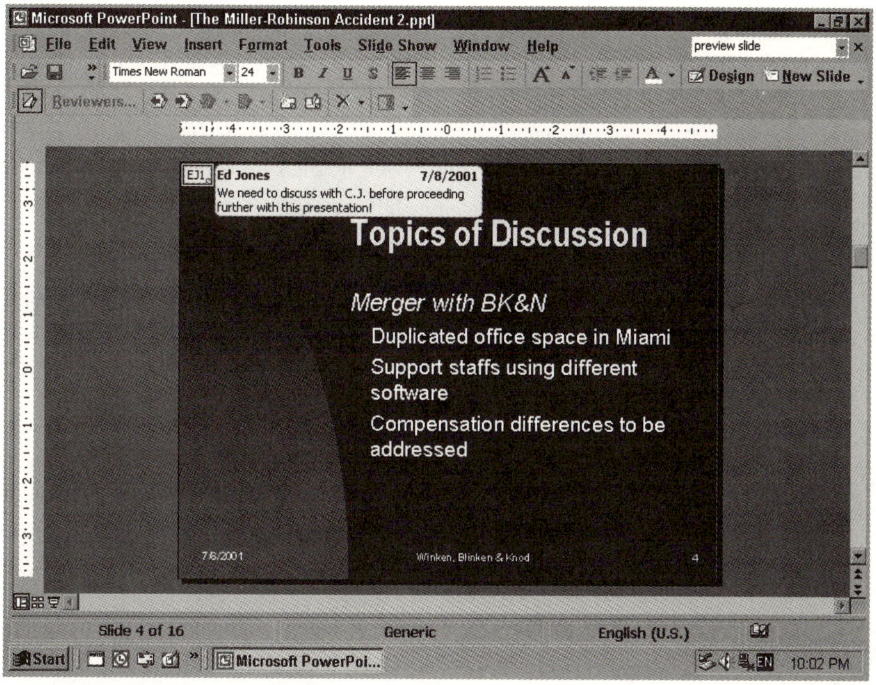

Figure 20-9: An example of a comment placed on a slide

Comments differ from notes in that comments appear within a balloon over part of the slide, depending on the setting of the View ⇨ Markup command. Notes, on the other hand, appear as text on the Notes page and in the Notes pane when in Normal view. When you want to provide notes that the audience can read from printed copies of Notes pages, use notes. When you want to include editorial comments that other reviewers of the presentation can see *before* it gets shown to an audience, use comments.

To add a comment to a slide, use these steps:

1. In Normal view, choose Insert ⇨ Comment. You'll see a comment box containing a flashing insertion pointer, your name, and the current date.
2. Type the desired comment.
3. To change the reviewer name that normally appears at the top of a comment, choose Tools ⇨ Options, click the General tab in the dialog box that appears, edit the contents of the Name box, and click OK.
4. After you finish typing the comment, click anywhere outside the comment box to close the box.

The comment appears on a slide as long as the View ⇨ Markup option is activated. View ⇨ Markup is a toggle, so you can choose it repeatedly to alternate showing or hiding comments.

To edit or delete a comment, use View ⇨ Markup to display the comment (if needed). Right-click the icon for the comment and choose Edit Comment from the shortcut menu (to edit an existing comment), or choose Delete Comment from the menu to delete the comment.

Adding a Summary Slide

You can use a summary slide in your presentation to summarize the main points made by all slides or by a selected group of slides. When created, a summary slide automatically takes the titles from a selected group of slides and uses these titles as bulleted points. Use the following steps to create a summary slide:

1. In the Outline tab, select the slides that are to be summarized by the summary slide.
2. Click the Summary slide button on the Outlining toolbar. (If the Outlining toolbar isn't visible, choose View ⇨ Toolbars and then choose Outlining to display it.) When you click the Summary slide button, a summary slide appears before the first slide in the group you selected. (If you selected a large number of slides, the summary slide may be created as more than a single slide.)
3. Change the title and bulleted text of the summary slide as desired.
4. If desired, move the summary slide to a different location.

Drawing Lines and Shapes

Although PowerPoint is not a graphic design software program, it does provide a basic set of tools that you can use for drawing lines and shapes that can appear within your slides. PowerPoint provides a drawing toolbar that you can use to draw various lines and shapes and to manipulate those shapes. Choose View ⇨ Toolbars and then select Drawing to display the Drawing toolbar. (Or right-click any toolbar to display a shortcut menu and then choose Drawing from the shortcut menu.) When the Drawing toolbar appears, you can move it as you would move any toolbar, by clicking any blank area of the toolbar and dragging it to a desired location.

Drawing a line or simple shape

To draw a line, arrow, rectangle, circle, or oval, use these same general steps:

1. Click the button on the drawing toolbar that corresponds to the shape you want to draw. For example, to draw a line, click the Line button.
2. Move the mouse pointer to where you want one end of the line or one edge of the shape to appear. (If you're drawing an arrow, move the pointer to the location where you want to place the end of the arrow *without* the arrowhead.)
3. Click and drag to where the opposite end of the line or shape should appear; then release the mouse button.
4. If you use the preceding steps to add a rectangle, circle, or oval, the shape appears with moving and sizing handles attached. You can then drag any of the corner handles to change the size of the rectangle or the shape of the circle or oval, and you can drag the green handle to rotate the object.

TIP: In some cases, you may want to have two shapes occupy part of the same area of a slide, and you may specifically want one shape to partially overlap the other. To change whether one shape that overlaps another appears above or beneath the other shape, right-click the shape, choose Order, and choose Bring to Front or Send to Back.

Working with AutoShapes

When you want to add more complex shapes to a slide, doing so can be quite tedious with the basic drawing shapes. For this reason, PowerPoint has many predefined complex shapes, called *AutoShapes*, available. These shapes include block arrows, flowcharts, stars, banners, and action buttons. To draw a shape using the AutoShapes feature, follow these steps:

1. Click the AutoShapes button in the Drawing toolbar to reveal a menu of overall types of shapes.
2. Choose the type of shape that you want to add to your presentation. You will see a submenu containing an assortment of your chosen type of shape. As an example, Figure 20-10 shows the available block arrows.

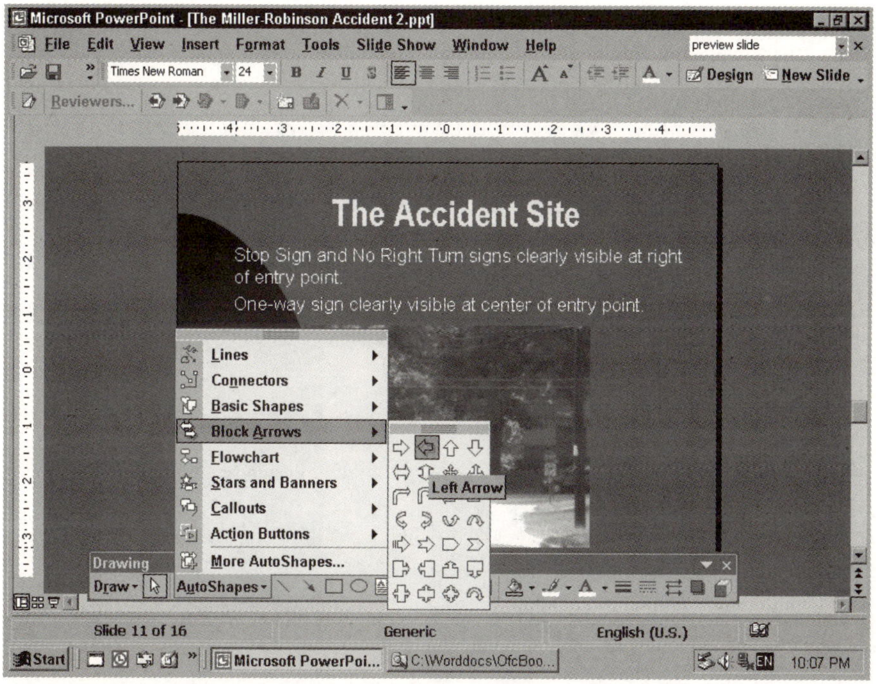

Figure 20-10: The Block Arrow shapes available from the AutoShapes menu

3. Make your choice from the submenu and move to the area of the presentation where you want to add the shape.
4. Click to add the chosen shape to the slide. You can then drag any of the corner handles to change the size of the shape, and you can drag the green handle to rotate the shape. Some AutoShapes also contain a yellow handle, which you can drag to change various appearance aspects of the particular shape.

If desired, you can change the color of the shape by right-clicking the shape, choosing Format AutoShape from the shortcut menu that appears, and changing the color in the Fill Color list box of the dialog box that opens.

TIP: With both ordinary shapes and AutoShapes, you can add shadowing and 3-D effects. To do so, first select the desired shape. Then in the Drawing toolbar, click the Shadow Style button and choose a desired shadow effect from the submenu, or click the 3-D Style button and choose a desired 3-D effect from the submenu.

CROSS-REFERENCE: At first glance, shapes and drawings may not seem to be useful PowerPoint techniques for law firms, but they can be important aids when preparing *relationship charts* for use in the courtroom. For details, see Chapter 21.

Adding text to a shape

You can add text to a shape such as a rectangle, oval, or block arrow. This feature can be particularly useful when you want to annotate a slide. For example, you might want to add a rectangle containing some text, along with an arrow pointing from the rectangle to an object on a photograph. Figure 20-11 shows this use of shapes on a slide to annotate a photograph.

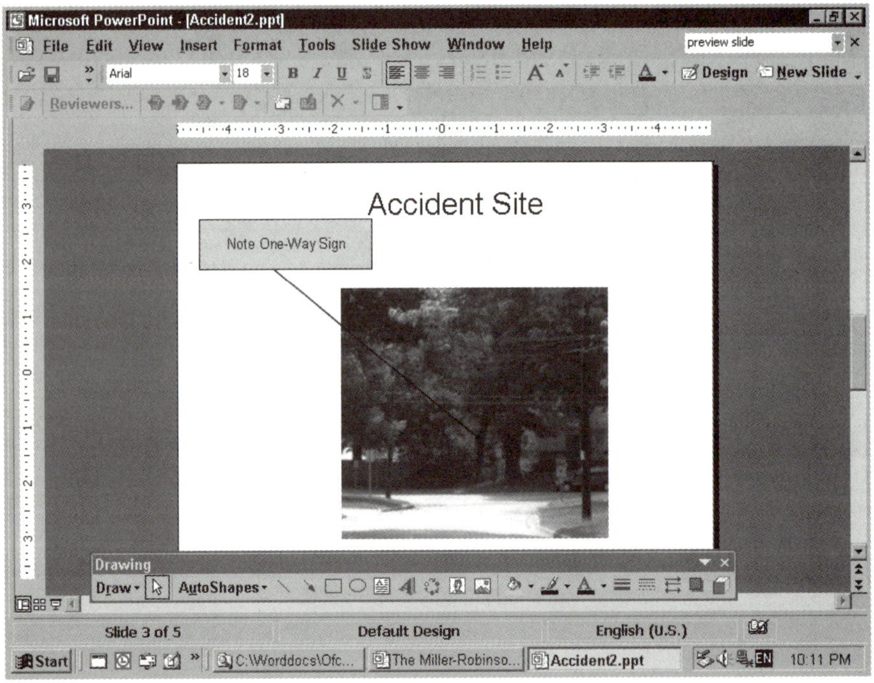

Figure 20-11: A slide with an annotation emphasizing a portion of a photograph

You might be tempted to add text to a shape by typing the text into a text box and placing the text box over the shape. However, the advantage of typing text directly into the shape is that if you move the shape, the text moves when it. Use these steps to insert text into a shape:

1. Click the shape in which you want to place your text.
2. Type the text. As you type, the text appears in a single line within the shape.
3. From the menus, choose Format ⇨ AutoShape.
4. Click the Text Box tab in the dialog box that opens (see Figure 20-12).

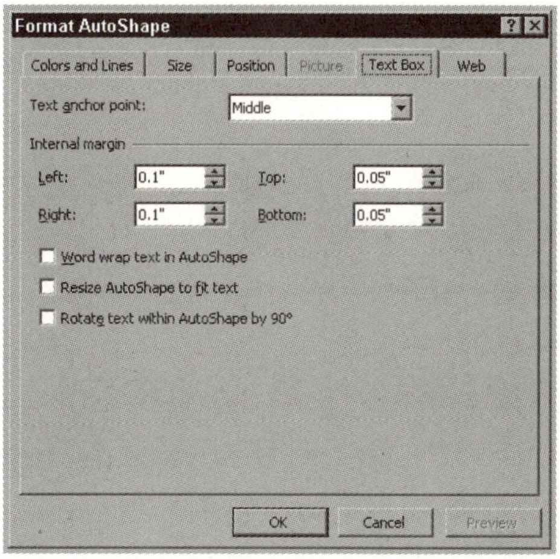

Figure 20-12: The Text Box tab of the Format AutoShape dialog box

5. In the Text Anchor Point drop-down list, choose a desired position for the text in relation to the shape.
6. In the Internal Margin area, set the margins for all four sides of the shape to control how much white space remains between the edges of the shape and the text.
7. If desired, click the check boxes for any of the options:
   - **Word Wrap Text in AutoShape:** Wraps text to a second line if the text is wider than the shape.
   - **Resize AuoShape to Fit Text:** Makes the shape larger or smaller so that the text fits precisely within the margins you specify in the Internal Margin area.
   - **Rotate Text within AutoShape by 90 Degrees:** Rotates the text by ninety degrees inside the shape.
8. Click OK to save your changes.

Creating Special Effects with WordArt

Another means of enhancing a presentation is by using WordArt, a program in Office that lets you make text take on a variety of shapes. The following steps show how to use WordArt to give your text any of the available appearances:

1. Place the Insertion Pointer where you wish to place WordArt and choose Insert ⇨ Picture ⇨ WordArt from the menus.
2. In the WordArt Gallery dialog box that appears, choose a desired style and click OK. The Edit WordArt Text dialog box appears.
3. Enter your text in the text box.

4. Choose a font and size; then click OK.

When you click OK, the text is inserted into the slide, as a WordArt object. Figure 20-13 shows an example of WordArt used in a slide.

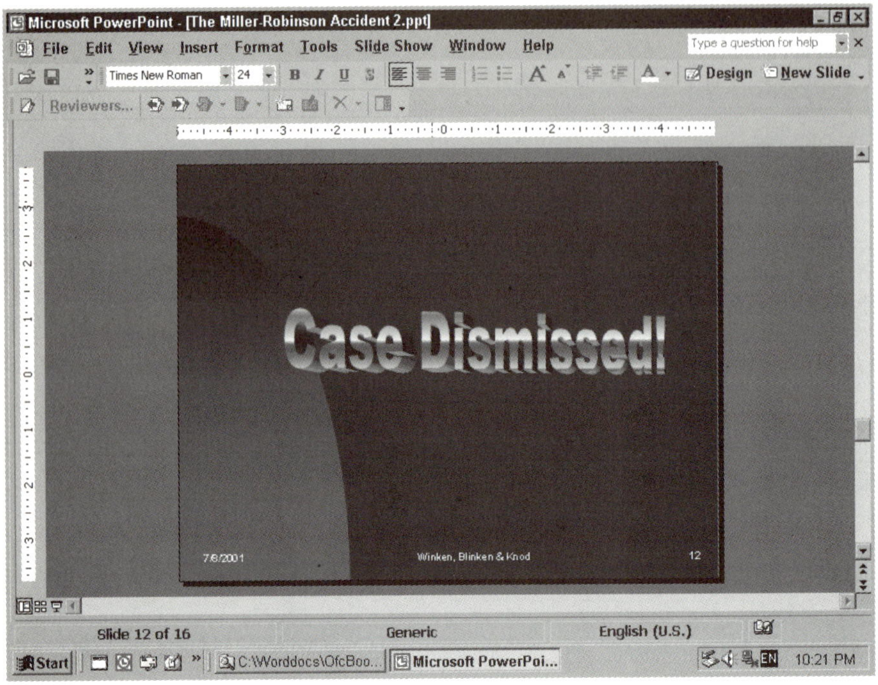

Figure 20-13: WordArt placed within a slide of a presentation

You can make changes to the object using the WordArt toolbar that appears near the bottom of the slide window. Table 20-1 explains the menu options that are available on the WordArt toolbar.

Table 20-1
The WordArt Toolbar Options

Button	*Purpose*
Insert WordArt	Inserts a WordArt object at the current location within a slide.
Edit WordArt Text	Redisplays the Edit WordArt Text dialog box, which you can use to edit the text of a WordArt object.
WordArt Gallery	Allows you to choose a style for the WordArt you are inserting. If you want to change the WordArt text after you have inserted it into the slide, double-click the text to activate the text box and to make changes to it.
Format WordArt	Allows you to change the color, fill, size, and rotation for the WordArt.
WordArt Shape	Applies a shape to the text according to your selection from a dialog box of available shapes.
WordArt Same Letter Heights	Changes all the WordArt letters to the same height.

continues

Table 20-1 continued

Button	***Purpose***
WordArt Vertical Text	Changes the WordArt text from a horizontal to a vertical appearance.
WordArt Alignment	Allows you to choose an alignment for the WordArt you have inserted in your slide.
WordArt Character Spacing	Opens a Spacing between Characters shortcut menu that lets you adjust the spacing between the characters.

If you use WordArt often, you may want to set it as one of your active toolbars. You can do this by choosing Tools ⇨ Customize. On the Toolbars tab of the dialog box that appears, click the check box for WordArt. Doing so activates the WordArt toolbar, which then appears as an active toolbar each time you start PowerPoint. Next, simply dock the toolbar where desired on the screen, and it will be there for your use during each of your PowerPoint sessions.

Displaying Text Documents and Diagrams with Annotations

During a hearing or a trial, you often encounter the need to refer to the text of a document or a diagram (such as a street map or a floor plan) admitted as an exhibit. As any trial attorney is well aware, passing out copies of text documents or diagrams to a judge and jury can be a time-consuming process. Attempting to keep every member of the jury focused on a particular portion of an exhibited document (distributed as photocopies) can present a challenge of its own. PowerPoint can help you overcome these drawbacks. Rather than distribute multiple copies of a document or a diagram, you can scan the document or diagram and place the scanned image onto a slide in a presentation. You can then *annotate* the scanned image by adding text boxes with your explanatory comments and lines with arrows that point to important aspects of the image. Figure 20-14 shows a slide that uses this approach to annotate a text document. Figure 20-15 shows a slide that uses a similar approach to annotate a diagram, in this case a street map.

Use the following steps 1–15 to create a slide like these:

1. Scan the needed document or diagram. (When saving the file using your scanner software, you may want to use the .JPG file format where possible, because it results in relatively small files with good clarity. See your scanner documentation for details.)
2. In your PowerPoint presentation, create a new, blank slide at the desired location by choosing Insert ⇨ New Slide (or pressing Ctrl+M).
3. In the Slide Layout pane of the Task Pane, click the Blank content layout.
4. Right-click any blank area of the slide and choose Background from the shortcut menu that appears.
5. In the Background dialog box that appears, change the color to white, click the Omit Background Graphics from Master check box and then click Apply. This action results in a blank slide with a white background.
6. Choose Insert ⇨ Picture ⇨ From File.
7. In the Insert Picture dialog box that appears, navigate to the file containing the scan of your document or diagram and click Insert.

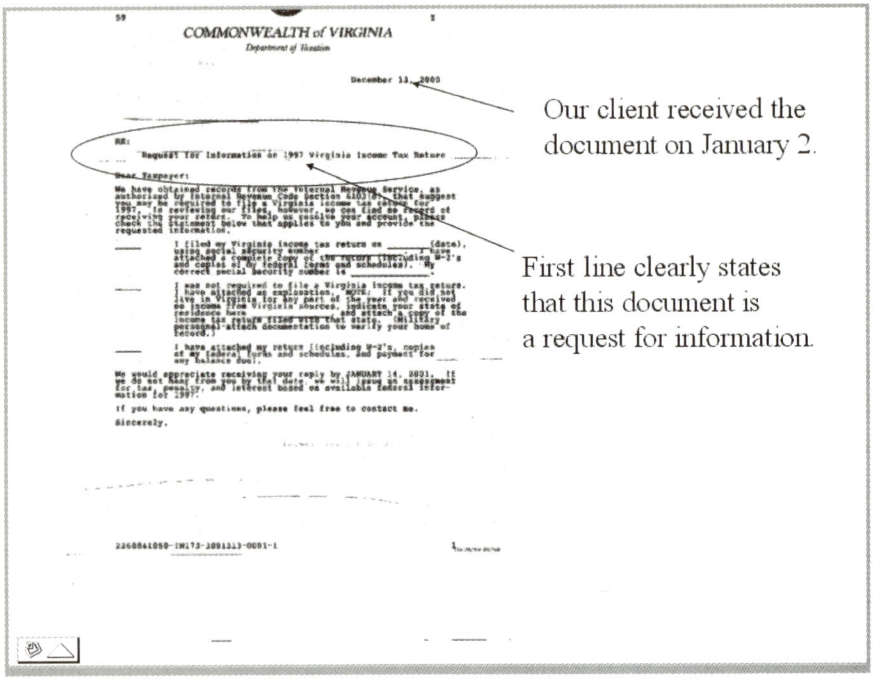

Figure 20-14: An example of a text document scanned into a slide, with annotations added

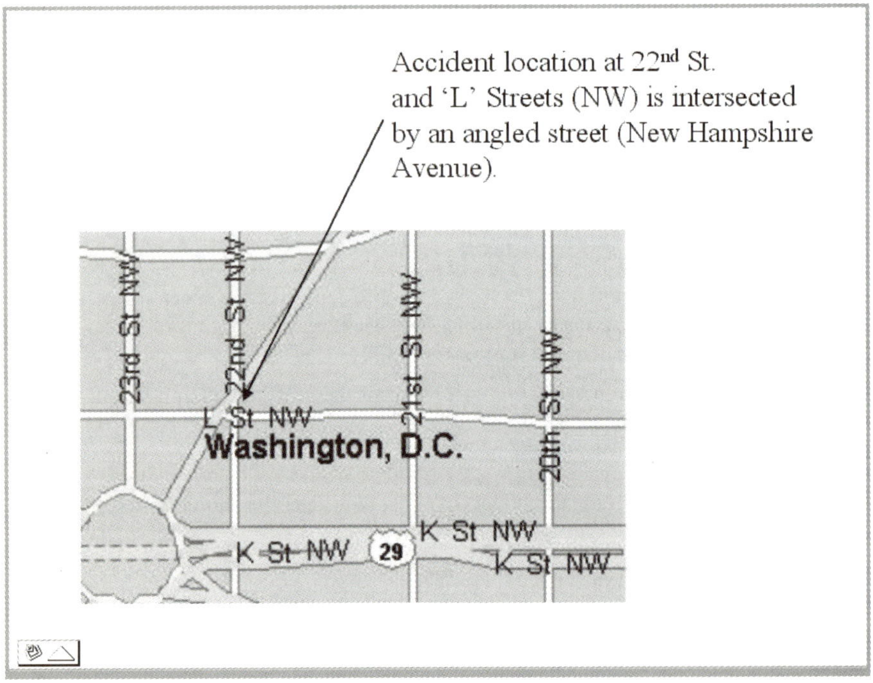

Figure 20-15: A street map scanned into a slide, with an annotation added

8. Using the moving and sizing techniques described in Chapter 19, size the image to fill the slide and place it where desired. (For example, you may want to place the image at the left side of the slide and place your annotations at the right side of the slide.)
9. Choose View ⇨ Toolbars and then choose Drawing to display the Drawing toolbar (which you will use shortly).
10. Choose Insert ⇨ Text Box, click in the slide where you want to add an annotation and type the text of your annotation.
11. Select the text, right-click, choose Font, and ensure that your font color is set to black.
12. Click the arrow tool in the Drawing toolbar.
13. To create an arrow, click near the text of your annotation and drag to the area of the scanned image that you want to emphasize.
14. Right-click the arrow, choose Format AutoShape, and set the color to black (or to a different color if desired). You also can change the thickness of the line and the style of arrowhead. When done, click OK.
15. Repeat Steps 10 through 14 for each annotation that you want to add to the slide.

You may want to experiment with other features of the Drawing toolbar to further enhance your slide and help get your point across to your audience. For example, you could use rectangles or ovals around significant paragraphs of a scanned text document and draw arrows from text boxes to those rectangles or ovals. (The example shown previously in Figure 20-14 uses an oval to highlight a statement in this manner.) If you place a rectangle or oval over a scanned image, you will need to remove the fill color so that the rectangle or oval appears as transparent. (Right-click the shape, choose Format AutoShape, and set the color to No Fill and the Line color to black.)

TIP: If you want to draw the attention of the audience to a particular area during an on-screen presentation, use the Pen feature to draw or "scribble" on a slide, using the mouse. While presenting the presentation, press Ctrl+P to change the mouse pointer to the shape of a pen. You can then click and drag to draw on the slide. Your scribblings made in this manner aren't permanent; when you move off the slide, the markings are removed. You also can change the pen color during the presentation. To do this, right-click the slide, choose Pointer Options ⇨ Pen Color, and select a desired pen color from the submenu that appears.

Adding Data from Excel Worksheets to a Presentation

Another useful feature of PowerPoint is its capability to copy existing information from an Excel worksheet in a PowerPoint slide. This feature can save you significant amounts of time because you don't have to retype the information. Figure 20-16 shows an example of data copied from an Excel worksheet that appears as a table in a PowerPoint slide.

Follow these steps to insert data from an Excel worksheet into a PowerPoint slide:

1. In Excel, open the worksheet containing the information that you want to insert into your presentation.
2. Select the information by using the standard selection methods. Remember that you need to select just the area of the worksheet you wish to paste on the slide; doing so lets you size your

insertion to fit. If you don't do this, the resulting table of information in PowerPoint will appear to flow off the slide.

3. Click the Copy button on the Standard toolbar (or choose Edit ⇨ Copy, or press Ctrl+C).
4. Switch to PowerPoint and select the slide on which you want to place the information.
5. Click the Paste button on the Standard toolbar (or choose Edit ⇨ Paste, or press Ctrl+V).
6. Size the resulting table as desired.
7. To change the fonts for the table, select the data and then right-click the selection, choose Font, and make the desired changes in the Font dialog box that appears.

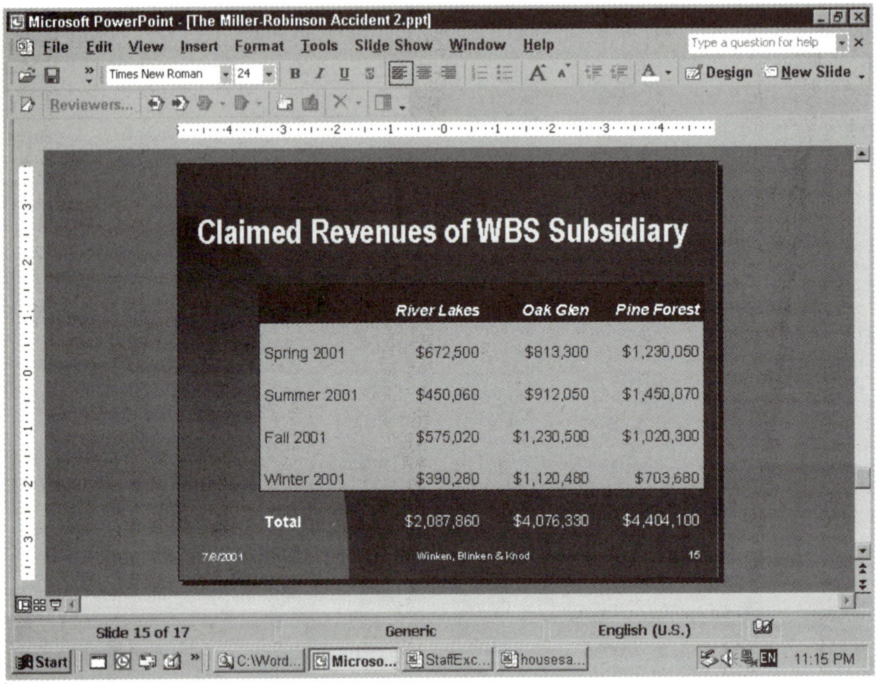

Figure 20-16: An Excel worksheet placed within a slide of a presentation

Inserting Tables into Slides

Tables of information can also be added to PowerPoint slides. Tables can be used when you need to display columnar information that spans multiple rows, and they are easy to add to slides. Figure 20-17 shows an example of a table placed into a PowerPoint slide.

Use the following steps when you need to add a table to a slide:

1. Select the desired slide where the table should appear.
2. From the menus, choose Insert ⇨ Table to display the Insert Table dialog box.
3. Enter the number of rows and columns that you want for the table and click OK. A table is then inserted onto the slide.

4. Enter the desired text in the cells of the table, or click within the desired cells and use the Edit ⇨ Paste (Ctrl+V) command to add graphics copied from other sources. As you enter text, you can use the Tab key to move between the cells, or you can click in any desired cell.

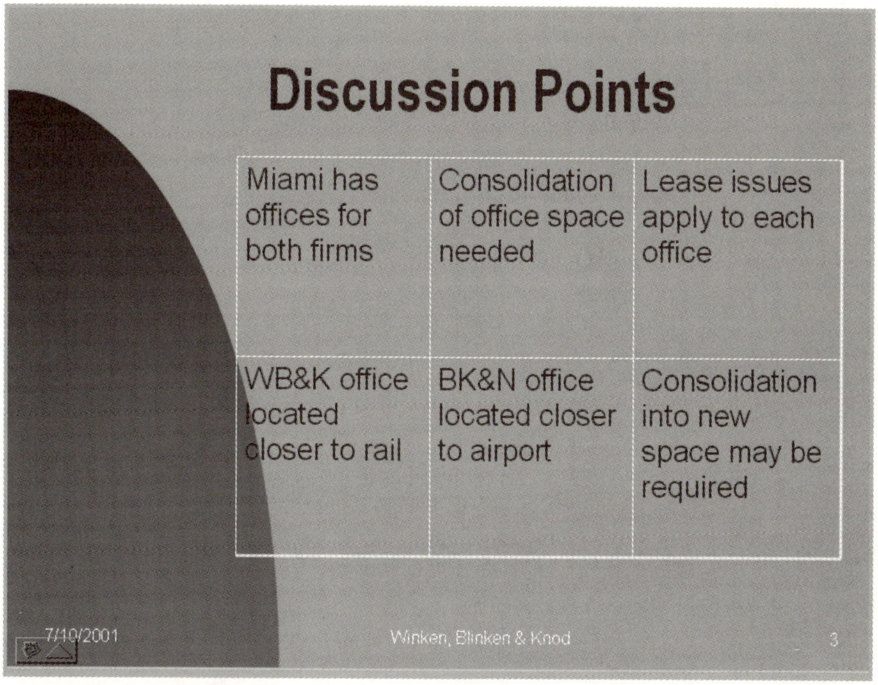

Figure 20-17: A table placed within a slide of a presentation

Adding Multimedia to a Presentation

You can add multimedia, in the form of sound clips or video clips, to a PowerPoint presentation. Although at first glance this might seem to present attention-drawing possibilities for a presentation, be careful not to overuse such effects. Too much in terms of sound effects or unnecessary video can distract your audience and actually draw attention away from the important aspects of your presentation. Having said that, in instances where you need multimedia capabilities, PowerPoint provides these for your use.

Adding sound or video clips to a slide

Sound clips are typically stored using one of three popular formats: as .WAV files (often called *wave* files), .MP3 files, or .MID files (often called *midi* files). A small collection of sample files is provided with the media gallery collection that comes with PowerPoint, and you can find sound files at many Internet Web sites.

PowerPoint can play "movies," or desktop video files, in a number of formats. These include .AVI, .MLV, .MOV, .MP2, .MPA, .MPG or .MPEG, and .QT. You can insert one or more video clips into a single slide. As with sound, you can let PowerPoint play the video automatically when the slide appears during a presentation, or you can have the video play when you click a frame containing the video in the slide.

To add sound or a video clip to a slide, use these steps:

1. Choose Insert ⇨ Movies and Sounds and then choose one of the following:
   - **Sound from Clip Organizer:** Uses one of the sample sounds provided with Office
   - **Sound from File:** Uses a sound file stored on disk or on your network
   - **Movie from Clip Organizer:** Uses one of the sample video clips provided with Office
   - **Movie from File:** Uses a video file stored on disk or on your network
2. If you choose the Clip Organizer, locate the desired sound or video clip in the Task Pane and double-click it. If you choose Sound from File or Movie from File, navigate to the desired file in the Insert dialog box that appears, select the file, and click OK. The Insert Sound dialog box and the Insert Movie dialog box are virtually identical except for the heading that appears in the title bar of the dialog box.
3. After you click OK, another dialog box appears, asking whether you want the sound or movie to play automatically in the slide show. If you want the sound or movie to play as soon as the slide appears, click Yes. If you want the sound or movie to play only when you click an icon or on a frame containing a movie, click No.
4. When you make a Yes or No selection in the dialog box, a sound icon or a frame containing the first scene in a movie appears on the slide. You can size the icon as desired and move it to the location you want on your slide. Figure 20-18 shows a sound icon on a slide.

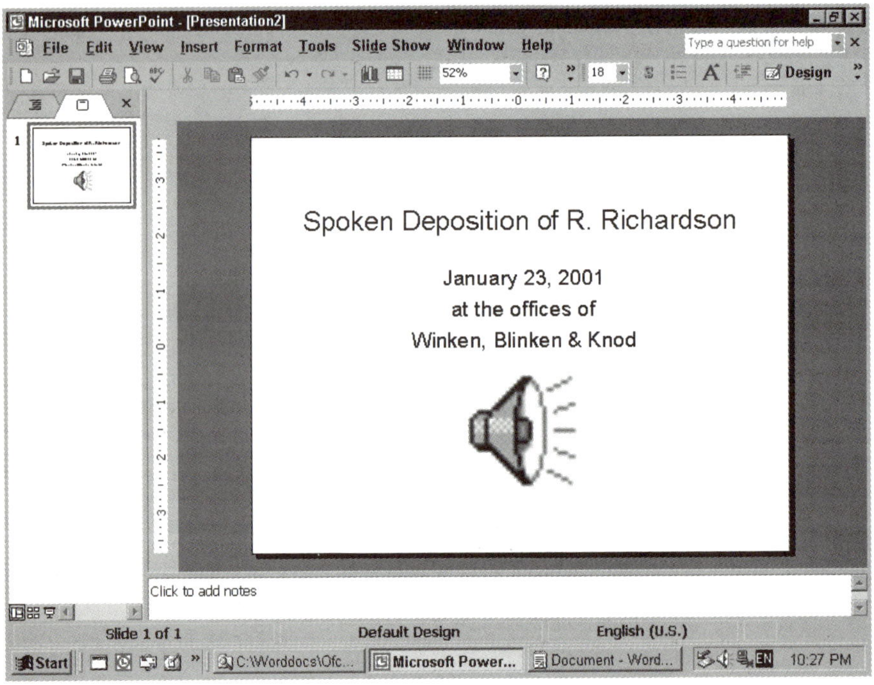

Figure 20-18: A sound placed on a PowerPoint slide

By default, a sound that you add plays just once. You can force the sound to play repeatedly by right-clicking the sound icon in the slide and choosing Edit Sound Object from the shortcut menu that appears. When the Sound Options dialog box appears, click the Loop until Stopped check box and click OK. When the sound is played in Slide Show view, it will repeat until you move to a different slide or exit the slide show.

In a similar fashion, a movie that you add to a slide plays just once by default. You can force the movie to play repeatedly, if desired; you also can force the movie to rewind after it plays. To do so, right-click the movie icon in the slide and choose Edit Movie Object from the shortcut menu that appears. The Movie Options dialog box appears.

In this dialog box, you can activate either of two options: Loop Until Stopped (to repeat the movie until you move to a different slide or exit the slide show), or Rewind Movie When Done Playing (to return the movie to the initial frame when it completes playing). Click either check box and then click OK.

NOTE: By default, PowerPoint links sound and video files that are larger than 100 KB to a presentation, rather then embed them internally. If you use sound or video and you plan to manually copy the presentation to another computer to present your presentation, be sure to copy the associated sound or video files to the same folder that contains the presentation on the computer you will use to show the presentation.

Playing CD audio tracks

You can play audio tracks from a CD as part of a PowerPoint presentation. You can play an entire audio track or just a portion of the track. (Of course, this assumes that a CD-ROM drive is present on your computer. If you're traveling with a laptop that uses an external CD-ROM drive, you'll need to connect the external drive.) Use these steps to play all or part of a CD audio track with a slide:

1. From the menus, choose Insert ⇨ Movies and Sounds and then choose Play CD Audio Track. The Movie and Sound Options dialog box appears, with more options than appear in the dialog box for inserting video clips.
2. Click the Loop Until Stopped option if you want the track to play repeatedly until you move to another slide or until you stop the slide show.
3. In the Play CD Audio Track portion of the dialog box, choose a starting track and an ending track. (To play all or part of a single track, choose the same track number in both Track spinner boxes.)
4. If you want to play just a portion of a track, enter starting and ending times, in minutes and seconds, in the At boxes.
5. Click OK. Another dialog box appears, asking whether you want the audio track to play automatically in the slide show. If you want the audio track to play as soon as the slide appears, click Yes. If you want the audio track to play only when you click a sound icon, click No.
6. When you make a Yes or No selection in the dialog box, a sound icon appears on the slide. You can size the icon as desired and move it to a desired location on your slide. When viewing the slide in Slide Show view, click the icon to play the audio track (assuming that you did not set it to play automatically).

Adding Animations

For a special effect when the slide appears, you can add animations. For example, you might want to have bulleted items fade in one by one or have the slide slowly fade in or fade out. PowerPoint offers literally dozens of predefined animation effects. And in case these predefined effects don't offer a sufficient array of choices, you can define custom animations.

Animations fall into two categories: *transitions*, which apply to the way that a slide appears, and *effects*, which are applied to individual parts of a slide (such as each bullet in a bullet list). In the Animation Schemes pane of the Task Pane, you can choose from a number of predefined animations that control the transitions and effects of a slide in a variety of ways. Follow these steps to apply an animation effect to a slide:

1. In Normal view or in Slide Sorter view, select the slide for which you want to apply an animation.
2. From the menus, choose Slide Show ⇨ Animation Schemes. A series of available animation schemes appears within a list box in the Task Pane, as shown in Figure 20-19. The available schemes are grouped under Subtle, Moderate, and Exciting categories. If you hold the mouse stationary over any scheme, a pop-up help window appears with details about the transition and effects provided by that scheme.

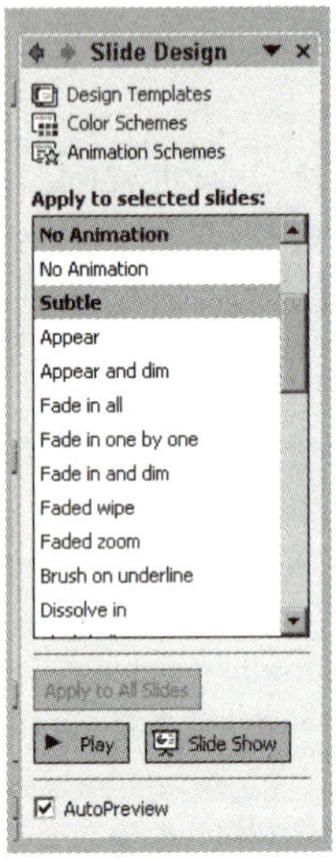

Figure 20-19: The animation schemes as shown in the Task Pane

3. Click a desired effect in the list to apply it to the selected slide. (If you want to remove a previously applied animation, click the No Animation choice in the Task Pane.)
4. To apply the effect to all the slides in your presentation, click the Apply to All Slides button near the bottom of the Task Pane.

Using animation to highlight points during a trial

In the courtroom, you may want to introduce the points on a bullet list one by one as you speak about each point before a jury. A number of animation schemes will work for this, but two of our favorite suggestions for this use appear under the Subtle category: Fade in One by One and Wipe. Select a slide and then select either of these effects in the Animation Schemes pane of the Task Pane. When the slide appears during your presentation, you will need to repeatedly click the mouse (or press the spacebar or PgDn key) to display the title, followed by each bulleted point in succession.

TIP: You can preview the effects of an animation without switching to Slide Show view. Click the Play button at the bottom of the Animation Schemes pane in the Task Pane to preview the animations used for the selected slide.

Using custom animations

The predefined animations offered in the Animation Schemes pane will suffice for most animations desired by most users of PowerPoint. If you want to exercise more control over the slide's animation, you can resort to using the Custom Animations pane in the Task Pane. Here are the steps to do so:

1. In Normal view or in Slide Sorter view, display the slide for which you want to apply the custom animation.
2. Choose Slide Show ⇨ Custom Animation to display the Custom Animation pane in the Task Pane.
3. In the slide, select the object to which you want to apply the custom animation.
4. Under Add Effect, select a desired effect from the menus. You can choose from Entrance, Emphasis, Exit, and Motion Paths; each option provides a submenu of available choices of special effects. Depending on your selection, additional options will appear in the remainder of the Task Pane, and you can use these options to customize the animation effects as desired.

Don't overdo it...

As with sound and video, keep in mind that it's possible to overdo it with slide animations. In particular, if you are creating a presentation for use in the courtroom, it is usually best to err on the conservative side rather than risk adding effects that overpower a judge or jury. Remember that the important point of your presentation is the message you are trying to convey, not the special effects.

Summary

In this chapter, you learned about a variety of techniques that can be used to enhance your presentations. You learned the following:

- You can use the Slide Layout pane to apply a particular layout to one or more selected slides.
- The Slide Master can control the overall appearance and layout of every slide in a presentation.
- You can add columns, bullet lists, and tables to slides.
- You can format text, change the colors of text, and check spelling in a presentation.
- You can use the Drawing toolbar to add lines and shapes to a slide.
- You can insert scanned documents or diagrams into slides and add annotations by adding text boxes and arrows.
- You can copy data from an Excel worksheet into a presentation.
- You can add multimedia, such as sound or video clips, to a presentation.

- You can add animations to a slide to determine how a slide appears or how bulleted items on a slide appear.

The chapter that follows covers how to create various types of charts, including relationship charts for courtroom use, in PowerPoint.

Chapter 21

Creating Charts in PowerPoint

In This Chapter

- The chart types of PowerPoint
- Inserting charts
- Editing charts
- Enhancing a chart's appearance
- Changing the appearance of 3D charts
- Creating relationship charts for the courtroom
- Creating organization charts

AMONG POWERPOINT'S STRONG features is its capability to create charts that can be included in presentations that are needed within the legal environment. Charts in PowerPoint can be based on numeric data that you enter into a spreadsheet-like window called a *datasheet*. These charts are generated by Microsoft Graph, a Windows mini-application included with many Microsoft applications (including Word and Access). Additionally, you can create a type of chart known as a *relationship chart*. This chart is not necessarily based on numbers but instead illustrates relationships between facts and a conclusion, or between individuals and events. You create these types of charts with the aid of shapes available from the Drawing toolbar.

Figure 21-1 shows an example of a typical number-based chart in a PowerPoint presentation. (Note that charts are sometimes referred to as *graphs*; in fact, Microsoft uses the terms interchangeably.) Each chart is made up of a series of *markers*, which represent the data that you enter in the datasheet. The appearance of the markers varies according to what type of chart you decide to insert in your presentation. In a bar chart, the markers appear as a series of horizontal bars. In a column chart, they resemble a series of vertical columns. Line charts use markers that look like a series of thin lines. In pie charts, the markers are the wedges of the pie, and doughnut charts use markers that appear as slices of the doughnut.

With the exceptions of pie charts and doughnut charts, all number-based charts use at least two axes: a horizontal axis (also known as the *category axis*) and a vertical axis (also known as the *value axis*). With three-dimensional charts, you also have a third axis, called the *series axis*.

In addition to the markers aligned along the axes, charts can contain titles and *legends* (which serve to identify the categories indicated by the various markers). Microsoft Graph, running from within PowerPoint, lets you customize any of these items in your charts.

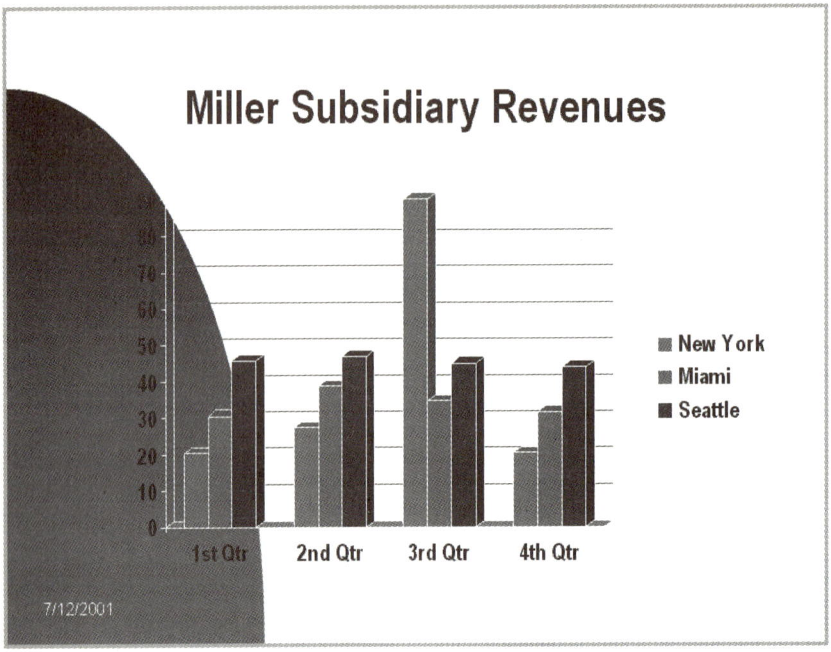

Figure 21-1: A typical chart

The Chart Types of PowerPoint

Microsoft Graph, the program used to insert charts in PowerPoint, provides area, bar, column, line, pie, doughnut, radar, XY scatter, surface, bubble, stock, cylinder, cone, and pyramid charts. Each chart type has optional subtypes. The following descriptions identify the various chart types:

- *Area charts* show the significance of change during a given time period. The top line of the chart totals the individual series, so area charts make it visually apparent how each individual series contributes to the overall picture. Area charts emphasize the magnitude of change as opposed to the rate of change. (If you want to emphasize the rate of change, use line charts instead.)
- *Bar charts* use horizontal bars to show distinct figures at a specified time. Each horizontal bar in the chart shows a specific amount of change from the base value used in the chart. Bar charts visually emphasize different values, arranged vertically.
- *Column charts* are very much like bar charts, using columns to show distinct figures over a time period. The difference is that column charts are oriented horizontally, with the columns running up or down from a base value used in the chart. When you want to show numeric values across a passage of time in the chart, column charts usually work well.
- *Line charts* are perfect for showing trends in data over a period of time. Like area charts, line charts show the significance of change, but line charts emphasize the rate instead of the magnitude of change.
- *Pie charts* show relationships between the pieces of a picture. They also can show a relationship between a piece of the picture and the entire picture. You can use a pie chart to display only one series of data at a time because each piece of a pie chart represents part of a total series. If you

have a large number of series to plot, however, you are probably better off with a column chart because a pie crowded with slices is hard to interpret.

- *Doughnut charts* show relationships between pieces of a picture, as do pie charts. The difference is that the doughnut chart has a hollow center.
- *Radar charts* show the changes or frequencies of a data series in relation to a central point and to each other. (Every category has an axis value that radiates from a center point. Lines connect all data in the same series.) Radar charts can be difficult to interpret unless you're accustomed to working with them.
- *XY scatter charts* show relationships between different points of data to compare trends across uneven time periods or to show patterns as a set of x and y coordinates. These charts are commonly used to plot scientific data.
- *Surface charts* show trends in values across two dimensions in a continuous curve.
- *Bubble charts* compare sets of three values. In appearance, these are similar to scatter charts, with the third value interpreted by the size of the bubbles.
- *Stock charts* are also known as *open-hi-lo-close* charts. They are used to display the day-to-day values of stocks, commodities, or other financial market data. Stock charts require series containing four values to plot the four points (open, high, low, and close).
- *Cylinder charts* are column charts with the columns appearing as cylindrical shapes.
- *Cone charts* are column charts with the columns appearing as cone shapes.
- *Pyramid charts* are column charts with the columns appearing as pyramid shapes.

Charts in Excel or in PowerPoint?

You can create charts in PowerPoint using Microsoft Graph and the techniques detailed in this chapter, or you can create charts in Excel using the techniques detailed in Chapter 16. Because Excel charts can be selected, copied, and pasted into a PowerPoint presentation, you have two ways of creating charts in PowerPoint. So, where should you create your charts?

If you don't mind the added complexities of a spreadsheet (maybe you're already an accomplished Excel user), you're probably better off creating your charts in Excel and then pasting them into PowerPoint. Why? Because Excel's charting capabilities exceed those of Microsoft Graph, and Excel has Chart Wizards that help you quickly design the precise kind of chart that you need. Also, you can take advantage of Excel's capability to perform calculations on the data that's used as the basis of the chart. In contrast, the Microsoft Graph Datasheet window won't let you add 2 and 2, much less perform any complex calculations. On the other hand, if you're not an Excel user and have no desire to become one, stick with Microsoft Graph within PowerPoint.

Inserting Charts

PowerPoint includes a mini-application, Microsoft Graph, that helps you create charts. Microsoft Graph displays a Datasheet window, in which you can enter the numeric data that will serve as the chart's basis. (If the Datasheet window does not appear, choose View ⇨ Datasheet, or click the View Datasheet button in the Microsoft Graph toolbar to display it.) After you enter your data, Microsoft Graph translates the data into professional-looking charts.

The nice thing about Microsoft Graph is that it lets you create your chart right in PowerPoint. Here's how to insert a chart on a PowerPoint slide:

1. Choose Insert ⇨ Chart, or click the Insert Chart button on the Standard toolbar. A column chart appears in your presentation (this is the default type, but you can easily change it), and a Datasheet window appears atop the chart, as shown in Figure 21-2. Also, note that the menus and toolbar change to reflect the fact that Microsoft Graph is active within PowerPoint.

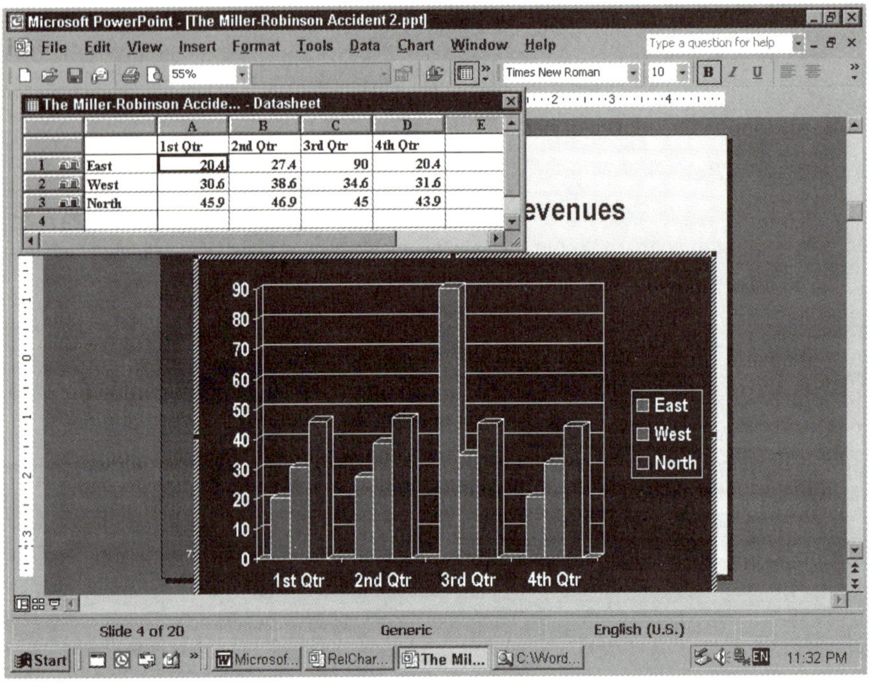

Figure 21-2: The default column chart and Datasheet window

2. Enter your data directly into the Datasheet window. (You'll find more details on this in "Entering and editing data in the Datasheet window.")
3. Choose Chart ⇨ Chart Type to select the type of chart that you want. After selecting the chart type you want, click OK. (You also can right-click the chart and choose Chart Type from the shortcut menu that appears.)
4. Open the Chart menu and choose Chart Options to use the various options to add titles, axes, gridlines, legends, data labels, and data tables. The Chart Options dialog box contains the following options:
   - **Titles:** Displays chart title fields, which you can use to add titles to the chart or its axes.

- **Axes:** Enables you to show or hide axes in the chart.
- **Gridlines:** Gives you the option to show or hide major and minor gridlines along any of the chart axes.
- **Legend:** Enables you to add legends to your chart.
- **Data Labels:** Adds data labels to a data series or to all data points in the chart.
- **Data Table:** Enables you to show or hide a data table for your chart.

5. When you're done refining the chart, click anywhere outside it. The chart will appear inside your presentation and the menus and toolbars will revert back to those of PowerPoint.

If you later want to make more changes to the chart's design, you can double-click the chart to switch back to the Microsoft Graph menus and toolbar.

TIP: You can move and size your completed chart as you would any other object in a presentation, either by dragging it to the desired location or by dragging its size handles.

Entering and editing data in the Datasheet window

To enter data in the Datasheet window, just move to the desired cell and type the data. You'll also want to enter the names for each data series into the leftmost column and enter the labels for each category into the top row. (The default data that appears in the Datasheet window gives you a model that you can follow when you enter your own data.) When you enter text in the top row and the leftmost column, Microsoft Graph assigns that text as category names and legend names in the resulting chart.

For example, with the data provided in the Datasheet window shown in Figure 21-3, the text labels in the leftmost column of the datasheet — New York, Washington, and Miami — are automatically used for the legend that accompanies the chart. The headings that are entered in the top row of the datasheet — 1st, 2nd, 3rd, and 4th Qtr — appear as labels for the markers in the chart.

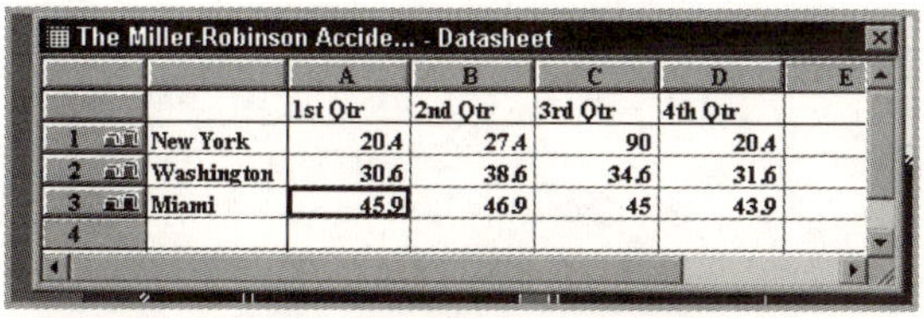
The Miller-Robinson Accide... - Datasheet

		A	B	C	D	E
		1st Qtr	2nd Qtr	3rd Qtr	4th Qtr	
1	New York	20.4	27.4	90	20.4	
2	Washington	30.6	38.6	34.6	31.6	
3	Miami	45.9	46.9	45	43.9	
4						

Figure 21-3: The Datasheet window

Navigate within the Datasheet window with either the mouse or the arrow keys. You can widen the columns if they're too narrow to display the numbers that you enter. Do this in one of three ways: by dragging the column's right edge with the mouse, by clicking in any cell in the column that you want to widen, or by choosing Format ⇨ Column Width and then entering a width for the column.

When typing numeric data into cells, you can include dollar signs in front of the numbers to cause them to appear as currency values. When you do this, Microsoft Graph automatically includes the dollar sign with the values in the value axis in the chart. To apply a specific format by selecting a cell or group of cells in the datasheet, open the Format menu and choose Number. In the Number Format dialog box that appears, choose a desired number format and then click OK.

After the chart exists on a slide, you can bring up the Datasheet window at any time by double-clicking the chart to make it active and choosing View ⇨ Datasheet.

Inserting blank cells in the Datasheet window

If you need to insert blank cells into a datasheet that contains an existing set of values, select the row, the column, or the group of cells where you want to insert new cells, and choose Insert ⇨ Cells. If you've selected an entire row, Microsoft Graph inserts a new row above the current row; if you've selected an entire column, Microsoft Graph inserts a column at the left of the current column.

If you've selected a group of cells, an Insert dialog box appears, containing four options: Shift Cells Right, Shift Cells Down, Entire Row, or Entire Column. Select the desired option (to determine whether your insertion pushes existing cells down, to the right, or adds an entire new row or column) and click OK to insert the cells.

Editing Charts

Changing circumstances may require the figures used to create a chart to change. When this happens, you'll need to make adjustments to the chart's datasheet. At times you may also want to edit a chart for the sake of altering a presentation.

If you wish to update figures used when you created a chart, choose View ⇨ Datasheet and then make the necessary changes in the datasheet (using the customary methods of editing).

Excel users may prefer Excel charts

If you're familiar with Excel, you may prefer using Excel's worksheet and charting techniques for producing charts to use in your PowerPoint presentations.

To add an existing Excel chart to a PowerPoint presentation, go into Excel, select the chart, and choose Edit ⇨ Copy. Switch to PowerPoint, move to the slide where you want to insert the chart, and choose Edit ⇨ Paste. The Excel chart appears in the slide, and you can move and size it to your liking, using the usual Windows moving and sizing techniques.

To add a new Excel chart to a PowerPoint presentation, go into PowerPoint and move to the slide where you want to place the chart. Next, choose Insert ⇨ Object and then choose Microsoft Excel Chart from the list of objects to insert. PowerPoint then inserts a default Excel chart on the PowerPoint slide, and Excel menus become active within PowerPoint. You can then use Excel techniques (detailed in the Excel section of this book) to manipulate the data that produces the chart and to change the chart's appearance.

Changing the data series

In some cases, you may want to swap the data series for a chart. For example, you might want to do this if you had set up a chart to show the total billable hours over three months for branches of a large law firm with offices in different cities and you had wanted the columns to symbolize each branch — but instead, the columns represent the months. Swapping the data series would fix that.

You do this by choosing either Data ⇨ Series in Rows or Data ⇨ Series in Columns. To see an example of the effects of the selection of data series, take a look at Figure 21-4, which shows a data series arranged by rows. In contrast, note the same data shown in Figure 21-5. Here the data in the datasheet is arranged by columns in the resulting graph.

You also can change the actual display of the information. Do this using the shortcut menu that appears when you right-click the bars, columns, lines, or pie slices of the chart. This shortcut menu contains commands related to changes in the display of the chart information. The shortcut menu includes the following commands:

- **Format Data Series:** This command lets you add labels or change the color of the data series. When you choose this option, the Format Data Series dialog box appears, with the Patterns tab visible. Using the *Patterns tab*, you can add a border to the data series by setting the options in the Border portion of the dialog box. You can vary the border's style, color, and weight (or thickness) by selecting what you want in the Style, Color, and Weight list boxes.

  In the Area portion of the Patterns tab, you can change the color of the data series to your liking. You can select a color or click the Automatic option, which applies the Windows default. Choosing None makes the marker invisible. Turning on the Invert If Negative option in the dialog box reverses the foreground and background colors for a marker if the value is negative.

  The *Shape tab* of the dialog box lets you choose a 3-D shape for the selected data series.

  The *Data Labels tab* of this dialog box lets you determine whether labels appear beside the markers to the data series. You also can have a legend appear next to the label; do this by clicking the corresponding check box.

  The *Options tab* of this dialog box lets you change the appearance-related options of gap width, gap depth, and chart depth. As you change these options, you see the effects on the sample chart in the dialog box. Make your desired selections and click OK. The options are as follows:

- **Chart Type:** This command of the shortcut menu lets you change the chart type. When you choose this option from the menu, the Chart Type dialog box appears. The options for this dialog box are discussed in the next section.

- **Add Trendline:** This option adds trendlines to area, bar, column, line, and scatter charts.

- **Clear:** This command removes a data series, the actual markers related to that series of numbers.

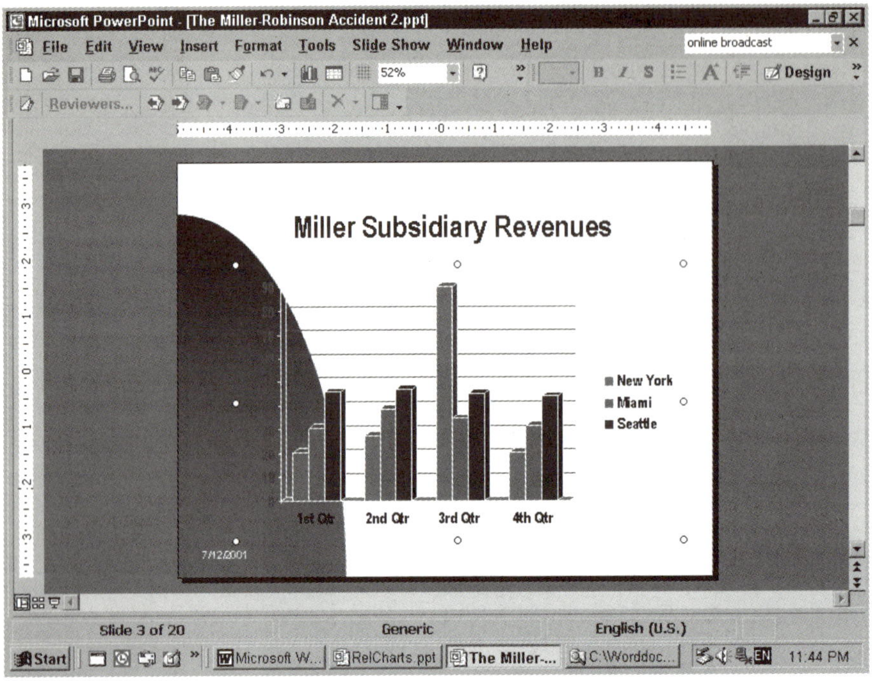

Figure 21-4: A data series arranged by rows

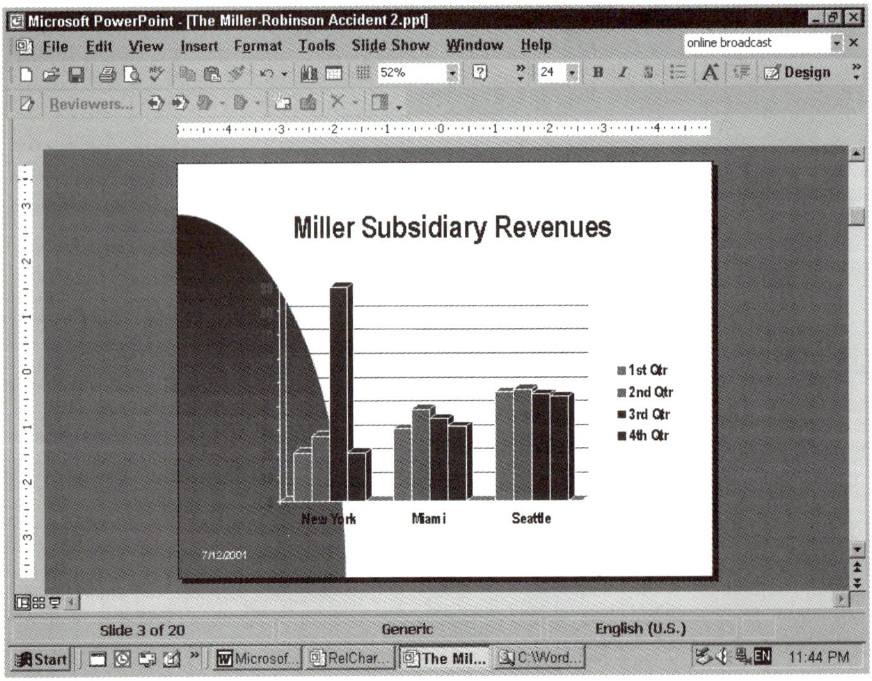

Figure 21-5: A data series arranged by columns

Changing the chart type

After creating a chart, you can experiment to be sure that you've selected the type that best represents your data. Microsoft Graph provides a range of chart types that you can view with a few mouse clicks; Table 21-1 lists them.

Table 21-1
PowerPoint Chart Types

Two-Dimensional Charts	*Three-Dimensional Charts*
Column	3-D Column
Bar	3-D Bar
Line	3-D Line
Pie	3-D Pie
Area	3-D Area
Doughnut	3-D Surface
Radar	3-D Bubble
Scatter	3-D Cylinder
Area	3-D Cone
Bubble	3-D Pyramid
Stock	
Cylinder	
Cone	
Pyramid	
Surface	

You can select chart types using different methods. The fastest of these is to click the down arrow button on the Standard toolbar to display the available toolbar buttons; then click the Chart Type button. Doing so gives you a drop-down list of chart types. Select the chart you like, and the values will be applied to it.

The other methods of changing the chart type are to choose Chart Type from the Chart menu or right-click the chart and choose Chart Type from the shortcut menu. The Chart Type dialog box then appears.

When you select a chart type, you also can click the Custom Types tab in the Chart Type dialog box to use built-in custom chart types or user-defined chart types. The Custom Types tab contains many combinations of formatting, such as exploded pie charts, floating bars, and other chart types that can be very useful for specialized chart needs. You can select any custom chart type in the list at the left side of the tab to view a sample and explanation of that type in the right side of the tab.

Enhancing a Chart's Appearance

You can do several things to enhance the appearance of a chart. A few are simple, such as changes to fonts and colors. Others, however, are a little more involved, such as adding text boxes. All can make a difference in the appearance of a slide containing a chart.

Changing fonts

You easily can change the fonts used for text anywhere in your chart. This includes fonts used for titles, legends, or axes.

To change the fonts, right-click the text for the item you wish to change. For example, if you want to change the fonts used for a legend, right-click the legend. From the shortcut menu that appears, choose either the Format Axis or the Format Legend option. Depending on which you select, you will see either the Format Axis dialog box or the Format Legend dialog box. Both contain the same two tabs (we discuss the additional tabs shortly): Patterns, for making pattern changes to the chart, and Font, for making font changes to the chart.

Within the Font tab, you'll see your options for setting the fonts used by the selected item. Choose a font, font style, and font size. You also can select underlining, color, and background and activate special effects such as strikethrough, superscript, and subscript. Under the Patterns tab, you can change various options that control the style and color of the background pattern for the object. .

If you chose Format Legend from the shortcut menu, a Placement tab appears in the dialog box, along with the Patterns and Font tabs. You can use the options shown on the Placement tab to indicate where in the chart the legend appears. You can place legends at the bottom, corner, top, right side, or left side of the chart.

When you're done making your desired selections, click OK in the dialog box to put them into effect.

Changing chart colors

Creating and changing color schemes is another effective way to improve your chart's appearance. Color schemes are sets of colors that are designed to be used as main colors for presentations and to ensure that the presentations have a professional look.

Each presentation that you open in PowerPoint has a default color scheme, but as you work with the program more and more, you may want to create your own color schemes. Chapter 20, "Polishing a Presentation," discusses in detail what's involved in doing this for an entire presentation. This section focuses on changing chart colors. .

Changing the colors of your chart is relatively simple, thanks to shortcut menus:

1. After choosing a chart and setting it up on your slide, double-click the chart to make it active for edits and then right-click the bar or section of the chart that you want to change. This action opens the shortcut menu.
2. From the shortcut menu, choose Format Data Series. The Format Data Series dialog box opens, with the Patterns Tab visible. This tab of the dialog box lets you change the colors for the series and the border settings, selecting from a range of line styles.
3. To change the color of the particular section of the chart that you want to change, move to the Area portion of the Patterns tab and then click the color that you want. You also can change the fill effects by clicking the Fill Effects button and then choosing an option from the Fill Effects dialog box that appears. When done, click OK to accept the changes.

> **Looks aren't everything, but...**
>
> As you work with fonts, colors, and other appearance-related aspects of a chart, remember the principles of good design by using fonts and colors wisely. It's easy to get carried away with fonts and colors and produce a chart that is so visually "busy" that it distracts the viewer. You should rarely need more than two and never more than three fonts in the same chart. You'll probably need more colors because each set of markers typically uses its own color — but, again, be judicious. Stick with complementary colors. PowerPoint does this automatically, but if you customize the colors, avoid clashing combinations such as bright pink against lime green. (Some designers argue strongly against using these two colors anywhere, anytime!) Keep colors elsewhere in the chart to a minimum. Before committing the chart to your presentation, step back and give it a critical, overall review for visual clarity and organization. Better charts in your presentations make for better overall presentations.

Adding titles

You might find adding titles to your charts useful. For one thing, titles help an audience understand what a chart means, and they help you quickly find values that you want to point out when giving your presentation.

To add titles to a chart area, right-click the area to open the shortcut menu and choose Chart Options. Next, choose the Titles tab of the Chart Options dialog box. .

The Titles tab lets you add a title either to your entire chart or to just one of the available axes. To enter the titles, click in the text boxes and type the titles that you want.

You also can format the text on a chart after the text has been entered. To do this, double-click the text and choose the patterns, fonts, or text alignment desired from the Format dialog box.

Changing axes

You can modify the axes used by your charts to emphasize the points that you're trying to get across. You can change the line style, the font of the axes' text, the scale used by the numbers, and the alignment.

To change any of these formats, select one of the axes by clicking it. Next, choose Format ⇨ Selected Axis, right-click the axis, and choose Format Axis. Another method is to double-click the selected axis. Either way opens the Format Axis dialog box, containing various tabs and options. Table 21-2 describes what you can accomplish with each of these tabs.

Table 21-2
Tabs of the Format Axis Dialog Box

Tab	*Purpose*
Patterns	Change axis formatting or choose tick mark types, both major and minor. (Tick marks are the evenly spaced horizontal or vertical marks that appear along the axis of a graph.)
Scale	Control the scale settings for axis values. Also set logarithmic scales, reverse the order of the values, and set the Floor XY Plane (the floor of the chart) at a value other than zero.
Font	Change font settings for the axis.
Number	Control the number formats for the numbers used for the axis.
Alignment	Control the alignment of text used in the axis.

Changing borders

You also can change a chart by changing its borders. To do this, right-click outside the chart itself but inside the container for the chart; then choose Format Chart Area from the shortcut menu. The Format Chart Area dialog box appears. This dialog box has two tabs, Patterns and Font. Make the changes that you want within these tabs and then click OK. .

Changing the Appearance of 3-D Charts

Three-dimensional (3-D) charts are a popular variation of basic charts. Creating 3-D charts is simple in PowerPoint: When you choose Chart ⇨ Chart Type, the Chart Type dialog box that appears gives you the option of selecting a 2-D or a 3-D chart.

If you use 3-D charts often, it's good to know about the flexibility that Microsoft Graph offers for changing various aspects of appearance of 3-D charts. You can change the elevation, rotation, and perspective used for the chart with the following steps:

1. Double-click the 3-D chart to activate it and then choose Chart ⇨ 3-D View. (Alternatively, you can right-click the area of the chart and select 3-D View from the shortcut menu that appears.) The 3-D View dialog box (see Figure 21-6) appears. As you change the settings in this dialog box, the picture of a chart near the center of the dialog box reflects your changes.
2. To change the chart's elevation, click the up arrow or down arrow buttons above *Elevation*, or enter a value in the Elevation text box.
3. To change the chart's rotation, click the left or right rotation buttons, or enter a value in the Rotation text box.
4. To change the chart's perspective, if Right Angle Axes is not activated, click the up arrow or down arrow buttons that appear above *Perspective*, or enter a value in the Perspective text box.

The 3-D View dialog box also contains options for AutoScaling, Right Angle Axes, and Height % of Base:

- **Right Angle Axes:** This option, when activated (indicated by a check mark appearing in the check box), sets the chart's axes at right angles independent of what you set the rotation or elevation to. (If you want to see the axes in perspective, you must turn off this option.)
- **Auto Scaling:** If Right Angle Axes is activated, this option is enabled. The AutoScaling option scales 3-D charts so that they are closer in size to 2-D charts.
- **Height % of Base:** This option controls the height of the value axis and walls of the chart, relative to the length of the category axis (the base of the chart). For example, if you enter *300%* in this box, the chart's height becomes three times the length of the base.

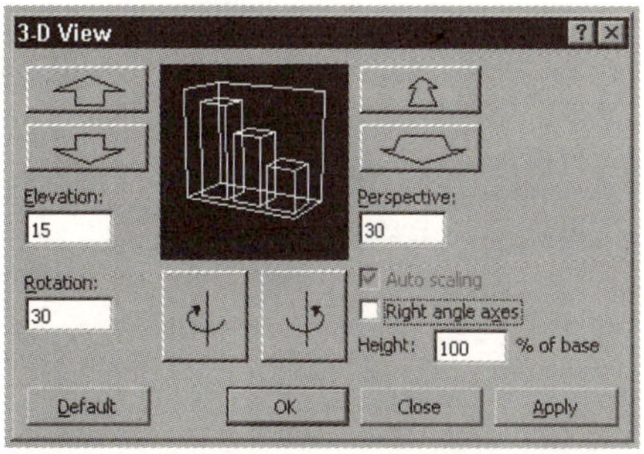

Figure 21-6: The 3-D View dialog box

Without closing the dialog box, you can see how your changes will affect your chart in PowerPoint by clicking the Apply button. When you finish making your changes, click the OK button. You can use the Default button to undo your changes and return the settings to their defaults.

3-D charts can lie (or at least greatly mislead)

With 3-D charts, it's easy to get carried away with changing the various viewing angles by modifying the chart's elevation and perspective. Get *too* carried away and you can wind up with a chart that's so hard to interpret, it becomes meaningless. Get even slightly carried away and you can produce charts that distort the meaning of the underlying numbers.

For example, changing the elevation so that a chart is viewed from a high angle tends to overemphasize growth; presenting the chart as viewed from a low angle tends to minimize growth. (Could that be why many advertisements in business and financial magazines use 3-D charts viewed at high angles?)

Be aware of the effects that such changes can have on your charts, and use them only when you intend to obtain such distorted results.

Creating Relationship Charts for the Courtroom

Relationship charts can prove useful in illustrating a connection between individuals, between an individual's actions and an event, or between facts and a conclusion. You also can use relationship charts to illustrate how a process works or how a sequence of events occurred in the past. Relationship charts can serve as an ideal aid in presenting a complex argument to a jury: Even the most experienced trial attorney can face a challenge when detailing complex interpersonal or event-based relationships purely by means of the spoken word. Relationship charts are not your typical kind of PowerPoint chart; rather, they are diagrams containing shapes and text that illustrate the desired relationship. You can create relationship charts using the AutoShapes option of the Drawing toolbar.

The common types of relationship charts used in the courtroom include the "Step 1, Step 2, Step 3, Conclusion" chart and the "All paths reach the same conclusion" chart. The "Step 1, Step 2, Step 3, Conclusion" chart illustrates a sequence of events or facts that lead to a final conclusion. Figure 21-7 shows an example of this type of chart.

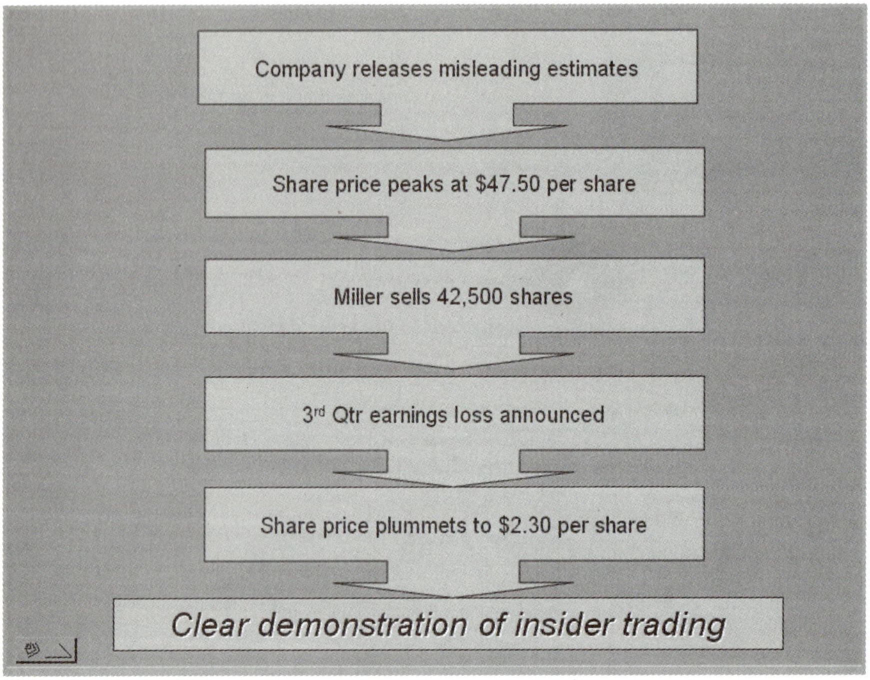

Figure 21-7: A "Step 1, Step 2, Step 3, Conclusion" type of relationship chart

By comparison, an example of the "All paths reach the same conclusion" type of relationship chart is shown in Figure 21-8.

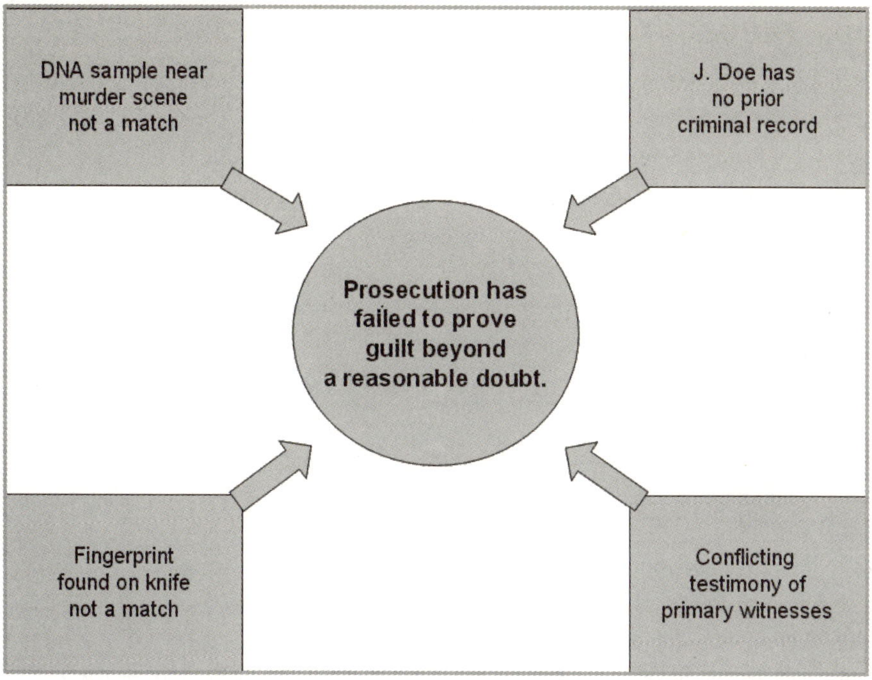

Figure 21-8: An "All paths reach the same conclusion" type of relationship chart

Creating the "Step 1, Step 2, Step 3, Conclusion" chart

You can create a "Step 1, Step 2, Step 3, Conclusion" relationship chart using the following steps:

1. Create a blank slide using a Blank layout.
2. Choose View ⇨ Toolbars and then choose Drawing to display the Drawing toolbar.
3. On the Drawing toolbar, choose AutoShapes ⇨ Block Arrows and select the rightmost arrow on the sixth row (called *Down Arrow Callout*).
4. Near the top of the slide, click and drag to create a rectangle with an arrow pointing downward for your first step. Size the rectangle to a sufficient size to hold your desired text for the step.
5. Choose Edit ⇨ Copy; then choose Edit ⇨ Paste to create another rectangle, and drag it under the first.
6. Choose Edit ⇨ Paste as many times as are necessary to create rectangles for all additional steps needed in the relationship, dragging each new step beneath the prior step.
7. Click the Rectangle tool in the Drawing toolbar; then click and drag to create a rectangle for your conclusion.
8. Size the rectangle as needed to accommodate the text of your conclusion, and place it underneath the rectangle-with-arrow you created for the final step in the relationship.
9. Click in each shape and type the text of your steps and conclusion.
10. Save your work with File ⇨ Save (or press Ctrl+S).

Creating the "All paths reach the same conclusion" chart

You can create this type of chart using the following steps:

1. Create a blank slide using a Blank layout
2. Choose View ⇨ Toolbars; then choose Drawing to display the Drawing toolbar.
3. Use the Rectangle tool to add rectangles near the corners or the edge of the slide for all the outlying facts in the relationship.
4. Click inside the rectangles and type the text of your facts.
5. Use the Circle tool to place a circle or oval in the center of the slide.
6. Click within the circle or oval and type the text of your conclusion.
7. On the Drawing toolbar, choose AutoShapes ⇨ Block Arrows and select the first arrow from the first row.
8. Click in a blank area of the slide near a rectangle to place the arrow on the slide.
9. Choose Edit ⇨ Copy; then choose Edit ⇨ Paste and drag the new arrow to another blank area of the slide near a rectangle.
10. Choose Edit ⇨ Paste as many times as are needed to add the number of arrows that you need; then drag each arrow to a blank space near a rectangle.
11. Drag each arrow near one of the rectangles containing your facts.
12. Use the green sizing handle to rotate the arrow, and use a white handle to drag the arrow, as needed, so that it points from the rectangle containing your fact toward the conclusion. (Note that you can hold the Shift key down while dragging the arrow, which will apply the rotation in 15-degree increments.)
13. Repeat Steps 11 and 12 for each arrow.
14. Save your work with File ⇨ Save.

TIP: Of all the types of charts that you can use during a trial, relationship charts are the type that most often result in objections from opposing counsel. This is to be expected because relationship charts are argumentative by design — they help you argue a specific conclusion (usually one that opposing counsel does not want the jury or judge to reach). Keep this in mind as you prepare relationship charts for use at a hearing or trial. Keep your points clear, concise, and above all, *defensible*.

Creating Organization Charts

Organization charts are useful in a presentation for showing the hierarchy of an organization. Although you can manually create such a chart by drawing lines and adding shapes to a slide, PowerPoint provides an Organization Chart toolbar and a set of predefined shapes that greatly simplify the process. Figure 21-9 shows an example of an organization chart created in PowerPoint.

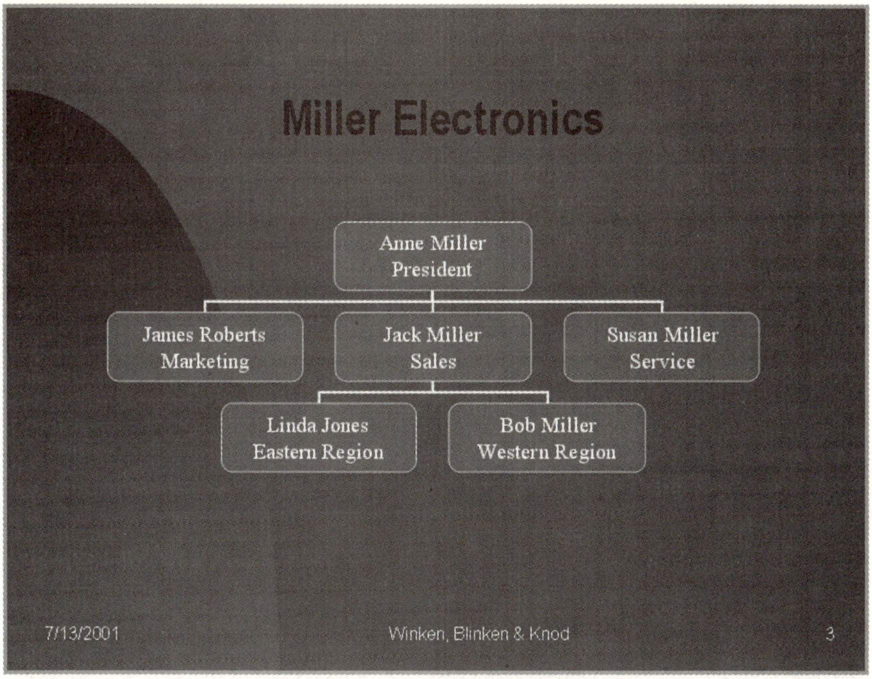

Figure 21-9: You quickly can create organization charts in PowerPoint using the Insert Diagram or Organization Chart button on the Drawing toolbar.

Use the following steps to create an organization chart:

1. On the Drawing toolbar, click the Insert Diagram or Organization Chart button (it's the button containing a circle composed of arrows).
2. In the dialog box that opens, click the Organization Chart diagram and then click OK.
3. A simple organization chart appears within the slide. You can click inside each box and type the name of a member of your organization. You can press Enter after the name and type a title if you wish to add a title underneath the person's name.
4. Add boxes to the chart as needed. On the Organization Chart toolbar that appears, open the Insert Shape menu to reveal choices for adding boxes for the different members of an organization. Each of the options lets you add boxes at a different level on the chart. Select a box in the chart representing a member of the organization; then choose the menu option that corresponds to the level of organization member that you want to add. You can add Subordinates (these are placed directly beneath the existing member), Coworkers (these are placed on the same organizational line as the existing member), or Assistants (these are placed below and to the side of the existing member).
5. After creating your chart, you may want to edit it. To do this, click in the box containing the name or entry that you want to change and then make the desired changes.
6. To change the size of the fonts used in the boxes, select one or more boxes (you can multiple-select by holding the Shift key as you click each box). Then choose Format ⇨ Font from the menus. Make the desired changes in the Font dialog box that appears.

7. To save the changes to the presentation, click anywhere outside the chart and choose File ⇨ Save.

After the chart is placed in PowerPoint, you can size it to your liking by selecting the object and sizing the border handles as desired.

Summary

This chapter showed you the different options for using charts in your PowerPoint presentations. The following topics were covered:

- ♦ You can add a numeric chart to any slide of a presentation either by choosing Insert ⇨ Chart or by clicking the Insert Chart button on the Standard toolbar.
- ♦ When you add a numeric chart, a Datasheet window appears, where you can enter the numeric information that serves as the chart's basis.
- ♦ After adding a chart to a presentation, you can double-click the chart and then choose Chart ⇨ Chart Type to change the chart's type.
- ♦ You can right-click any object in a chart and then choose Format from the shortcut menu that appears,to display a dialog box that lets you change the appearance of the selected object.
- ♦ You can use the AutoShapes menu of the Drawing toolbar to create relationship charts that illustrate a connection between individuals, between an individual's actions and an event, or between facts and a conclusion.
- ♦ In addition to conventional charts, you can create organization charts in PowerPoint.

The chapter that follows provides strategies and techniques for presenting presentations, printing all or parts of a presentation, collaborating with co-workers on a presentation, and producing presentation files that can be uploaded to an intranet or Internet Web site.

Chapter 22

Producing Presentations

In This Chapter

- Choosing a method of presentation
- Printing presentations
- Changing the timings for a slide show
- Adding speaker's notes and audience handouts to a presentation
- Adding spoken narration to a presentation
- Creating custom slide shows
- Saving a presentation as a Web page
- Using the PowerPoint viewer
- Using the Pack & Go Wizard
- Using the Send To command

AFTER YOU HAVE CREATED all the slides, you will want to prepare your work for presentation. This chapter covers the methods that you can use to produce your work, including printing presentations, creating slide shows, producing Web pages for use on the Internet or an intranet, using the Send To command to collaborate with co-workers, co-counsel, or clients, and creating speaker's notes and audience handouts.

Choosing a Method of Giving Your Presentation

PowerPoint offers a variety of ways to present your finished presentation to your audience. The most popular method is to present the presentation as an on-screen slide show, which typically is done using a laptop computer that is connected to a large-screen monitor or a projection system. Another method is to print the slides onto overhead transparencies or onto paper printouts that can be sent to a graphics shop or photo shop for conversion to 35mm slides. A third option is to save the presentation as a Web page for presentation via the Internet or on your firm's intranet. When you choose this approach, PowerPoint creates a series of HTML files and graphic files that can be uploaded by the Webmaster of a Web site. Because the on-screen presentation is by far the most popular method, this chapter examines that method in detail first, followed by the options for printing a presentation and for saving a presentation as Web pages.

Choosing a type of on-screen presentation

Even when you decide to present your presentation as an on-screen presentation, you still need to decide on a presentation format. You have three possible options in this area:

- **Presented by a speaker:** This is the most commonly used method. You have full control over when your slides appear, you can skip a slide or back up to a previously seen slide to highlight a point, and you can end the presentation at any given time. This is the type of presentation you would use in a courtroom.
- **Viewed by an individual:** This type of on-screen presentation lets someone else view the presentation. This is the approach you will typically use when you want to share a presentation with co-workers in other offices or with clients by e-mailing the presentation.
- **Browsed at a kiosk:** This type of presentation runs continuously, restarting at the first slide after the last line has been viewed. Such a presentation runs unattended, typically at a professional convention or trade show of some sort. (At large law firms, this type of presentation could also be used by internal departments. For example, a human resources department could use such a presentation to outline changes in the firm's health care policies to the support staff.)

When you have a choice of screens

In some instances, you may not have a choice when it comes to what projection equipment will be connected to your computer for an on-screen presentation. But some high-tech courtrooms and well-equipped law firms may offer you a choice of a large-screen monitor or a projection system. If you get to choose, which is best? The answer, as you might expect, is that there is no correct answer. It depends on the audience and your location, and both systems have their drawbacks. Large-screen monitors are brighter and sharper than projection systems. But in rooms containing windows, they can suffer from glare on the glass surface and can be difficult to see with large audiences, because it's rare to find monitors larger than 36 diagonal inches. Projection systems, on the other hand, accommodate larger audiences because of the larger screen sizes. But the resulting image on projection screens tends to be not as bright or as sharp as with glass monitors, and projection screens can be difficult to view from an angle.

A new option gaining in popularity (particularly if you need to bring your own equipment) is the stand-alone LCD monitor. These use the same display technology as do laptop computers. The resulting image is bright and sharp, and LCD monitors are lightweight compared to conventional (glass screen) monitors. Disadvantages include their relatively small size and high cost: a 21-inch monitor is about as big as it gets in this area, and costs can easily run upwards of $3,000 at the time of this writing.

Before running the slide show, you should change the options in the Set Up Show dialog box, if needed, to reflect the choice you want to use. Follow these steps:

1. Choose Slide Show ⇨ Set Up Show to reveal the Set Up Show dialog box (see Figure 22-1).

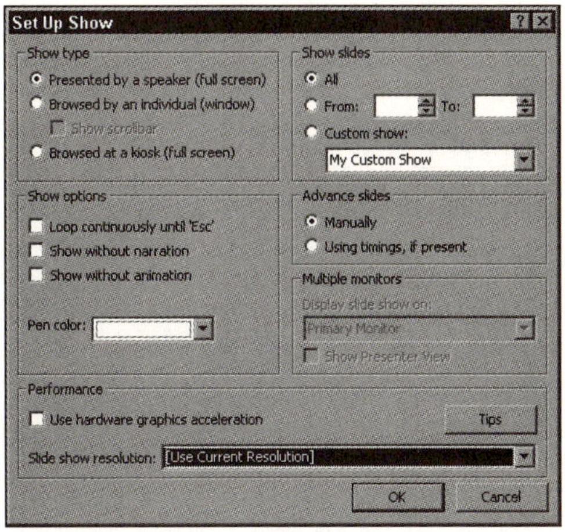

Figure 22-1: Use the Set Up Show dialog box to set up the type of on-screen presentation desired.

2. In the Show Type portion of the dialog box, choose your desired type of on-screen presentation: Presented by a Speaker (Full Screen), Browsed by an Individual (Window), or Browsed at a Kiosk (Full Screen). If you choose Browsed by an Individual (Full Screen), you can activate an option for including a scroll bar in the presentation that lets the person viewing the presentation navigate within it.
3. In the Show Slides portion of the dialog box, leave the default of All selected to present all the slides in the presentation, or select a range of slides to be shown. If the presentation contains any custom shows made up of selected slides, you can choose a desired custom show by name. (Creating custom slide shows is detailed later in this chapter.)
4. In the Advance Slides portion of the dialog box, indicate whether you want to advance your slides manually or by using timings, if you have added them. (You can add slide timings using the rehearse timings feature detailed in the section "Using the rehearse timings feature to time a presentation" later in this chapter.)
5. When you finish choosing your desired options, click OK and then choose File ⇨ Save to save the presentation with your current options selected. You can then proceed to give your presentation by choosing View ⇨ Slide Show or by pressing F5.

Learning the important keyboard shortcuts

When making a presentation to an audience, you'll want to know how to move around within the presentation. Experienced attorneys who use PowerPoint as a litigation aid will tell you that standing before a jury is no time to appear confused about how to return to a previously viewed slide. If you don't remember any other keys, remember the spacebar (to advance a slide at a time) and the Backspace key (to back up a slide at a time). Table 22-1 shows a more detailed list of keys you may find helpful when making your presentation.

Table 22-1
Useful Keyboard Shortcuts for Showing a Presentation

Key	*Used For*
Begin slide show in Slide Show mode.	F5 key
Move forward by one slide.	Spacebar or PgDn or down arrow key or left mouse button
Move backward by one slide.	Backspace or PgUp key or up arrow key
Toggle screen to black at any time.	B key
Change mouse pointer to a pen that lets you draw on the screen with the mouse.	Ctrl+P keys
Terminate slide show.	Esc key

Printing Presentations

PowerPoint lets you print slides, outlines, speaker's notes, and audience handouts. These items all can be printed on overhead transparencies or on paper. Slides can also be saved to a file or shipped to an outside graphics shop to create film slides in 35mm format. The printing process is much the same, regardless of whether you are printing outlines, notes, or handouts: You open the presentation, identify what you want printed, specify the range of slides to be printed, and choose the number of copies.

Plan for what can go wrong

When creating a presentation for use in a courtroom, you never want to be wholly dependent on technology. Things can and do go wrong: Hard drives crash, projection systems fail, and laptops are stolen from airport check-in areas on a daily basis. *Always* have a backup plan. You can print your slides as overhead transparencies and carry a set of these as an inexpensive backup. If the presentation is a critically important one, consider carrying extra hardware (such as a backup laptop computer) just in case.

Setting up your slides for printing

Before you print your presentation, you need to open it and set it up for printing. Follow these steps:

1. Choose File ⇨ Page Setup to open the Page Setup dialog box.
2. Select the desired size for the slides. Keep in mind that by default, PowerPoint is set up to create and print slides in Landscape orientation. Also remember that by default, the slides are set up to print 10 inches wide by 7.5 inches tall and printing begins with the first slide. Use the Slides Sized For list box to change the page settings to any of the following:

- **On-Screen Show:** This option sets the width at 10 inches and the height at 7.5 inches with Landscape orientation.
- **Letter Paper (8.5 x 11 inches):** This option sets the width at 10 inches and the height at 7.5 inches with Landscape orientation. These measurements cause the slides to fill the page. Choose this option when you want to print on paper and fill the entire page.
- **Ledger Paper (11 x 17 inches):** This option sets the width at 13.32 inches and the height at 9.99 inches. Your printer must support the use of 11-by-17-inch paper.
- **A3 Paper (297 x 420 mm):** This option sets the width at 14 inches and the height at 10.5 inches. The slides then fill A3 (European size) paper.
- **A4 Paper (210 x 297 mm):** This option sets the width at 10.83 inches and the height at 7.5 inches with Landscape orientation. The slides then fill A4 (European size) paper.
- **B4 Paper (250 x 353 mm):** This option sets the width at 11.84 inches and the height at 8.88 inches. The slides then fill B4 (ISO Standard size) paper.
- **B5 Paper (176 x 250 mm):** This option sets the width at 7.84 inches and the height at 5.88 inches. The slides then fill B5 (ISO Standard size) paper.
- **35mm Slides:** This option sets the width at 11.25 inches and the height at 7.5 inches. These measurements allow the contents to fill the slide area in Landscape orientation, ideal for reduction to a 35mm slide.
- **Overhead:** Use this option when you want to create transparencies. It makes slides fill the transparencies, making them easier to see when they are placed on an overhead projector.
- **Banner:** Use this option to change the layout of your slides to a banner layout. This is both for printing and an on-screen presentation.
- **Custom:** This option lets you set dimensions of your own choosing, either by entering values in the Width and Height boxes or by clicking the up and down arrows to enter the desired value.

3. In the Orientation portion of the dialog box, choose the desired orientation (Portrait or Landscape). Keep in mind that you can separately set the orientation for your speaker's notes, handouts, and outlines.
4. If you want to use a starting number other than 1 for your slides, enter the desired number in the Number Slides From list box.
5. Click OK.

TIP: If the use of 35mm slides along with a slide projector will work best for your situation, a number of commercial firms can convert your PowerPoint presentation directly to 35mm slides. One well-known company is Genigraphics (`www.genigraphics.com`). You can send a PowerPoint presentation to the company by e-mail or on a disk and receive 35mm slides by overnight courier service the next business day. See the company's Web site for additional information.

Printing parts of your presentation

After your printing dimensions have been set by means of the Page Setup dialog box options, choose File ⇨ Print to open the Print dialog box.

In this dialog box, choose what parts of the presentation you want to print. In the Print Range area, choose All to print all slides, or choose Current Slide to print just the slide that is currently visible in Normal view or selected in Slide Sorter view. In the Number of Copies box, you can enter the number of copies that you want, and you can turn on the Collate option if you want multiple copies to come out in collated order.

Use the Print What list box to tell PowerPoint exactly which parts of your presentation you want to print. The choices that you have from the Print What list box include the following:

- **Slides:** This option prints your slides on paper or on overhead transparencies.
- **Handouts:** You can print audience handouts that contain one, two, three, four, six, or nine slides per page. One or two slides per page is a good choice for a large image with great detail. Use three or four slides per page if you want to leave a reasonable amount of space for the audience to write notes. If you want to provide a presentation outline with the most information on each page of the audience handout, use six or nine slides per page.
- **Notes Pages:** This option prints the speaker's notes pages that correspond to the slides that you decide to print.
- **Outline View:** This option prints the outline that appears in the Outline tab.

In the dialog box you can also specify the number of copies that you want to print, along with the range of slides or notes. If any slides in the presentation have been hidden (by choosing Slide Show ⇨ Hide Slide), the Print Hidden Slides check box becomes available in the Print dialog box, and you can click it to tell PowerPoint to include hidden slides in the printout. In the Color/Grayscale list box, you can choose Grayscale or Pure Black and White to optimize the printing of color slides when printed on a conventional (noncolor) printer. The Grayscale option causes colors to be printed in shades of gray. The Pure Black and White option is used to print the slides in black and white while printing on a color printer; this will change all the shades of gray to either black or white. (This option is useful only if you have a color printer and, for some reason, you don't want the presentation in color.)

The Frame Slides option frames the printouts so that they best fit transparencies when they are reduced, and the Scale to Fit Paper option scales the printout to the paper that you have loaded in the printer. Choose your desired printing options in the dialog box and then click OK.

Getting the results you want

Don't be in a rush to print by clicking the Print button on the Standard toolbar or by immediately clicking the OK button in the Print dialog box to accept the defaults, which you do in many Windows applications. Because PowerPoint has so many options for what you can print and how you can print it, you may not get what you want by fast clicking. Think of the Print dialog box and the Slide Setup dialog box as working in combination to give you exactly what you want. Be sure that you set the options correctly before you start printing.

If you activate the Print to File check box after you choose the other desired options and click OK, a Print to File dialog box appears, in which you can enter a filename. When you enter a name and click OK, PowerPoint writes the file as an encapsulated print file that can be used at a later time (you can select the file in Explorer or in My Computer and print it). Things can get tricky with this option, however, so you may want to avoid using it.

Changing the Timings for a Slide Show

Slide shows are the primary strength of PowerPoint, and you can create professional-looking slide shows without a great deal of hassle. You can create a slide show by accepting PowerPoint's defaults and then choosing the Slide Show command from the View menu (or by just pressing F5). The slide show will then begin, and you can use the left mouse button or the spacebar to advance to each successive slide. If you wish to change the default settings (such as the time settings between each of the slides) and any transition effects you wish to add to the presentation slide, you first need to go to Slide Sorter view. In Slide Sorter view, you need to do the following to change the timing or other settings of the slide presentation:

1. Select the slide you want to set timings or effects for. Click the Slide Transitions button on the toolbar, or choose Slide Show ⇨ Slide Transition. This action opens the Slide Transitions pane in the Task Pane, as shown in Figure 22-2.

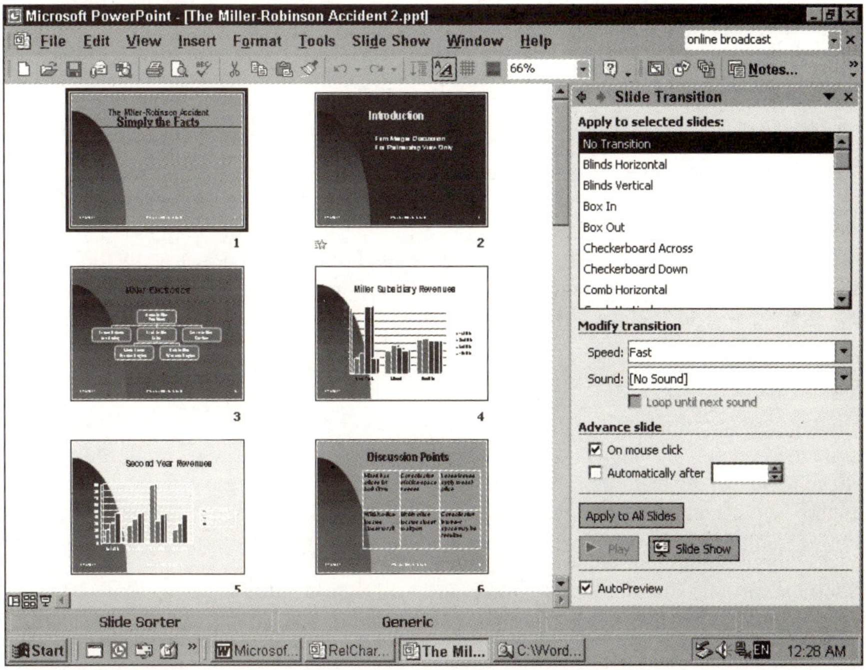

Figure 22-2: The Slide Transitions pane, as shown in the Task Pane area

2. From the Apply to Selected Slides list box of the Task Pane, choose the effects you want for the slide. (As you click each option, you see the effect on the selected slide.)

3. Move on to the Advance Slide section to set your timings, or choose the mouse (or the spacebar) as the signal to move to the next slide. In the Advance Slide area of the Task Pane, choose On Mouse Click if you want to move to the next slide manually during the show, or choose Automatically After if you want the slide to advance automatically at a timed interval and then enter the number of seconds that should elapse until the next slide in the spinner box.

4. In the Modify Transition area of the Task Pane, in the Sound list box, you can add one of the default sounds shown in the list as you move to the next slide, or you can choose Other Sound to open a file dialog box that lets you select a sound file to be played when moving to the next slide. Keep in mind that all the effects you set are for the slide or slides you currently have selected in Slide Sorter view, unless you click the Apply to All Slides button at the bottom of the Task Pane.
5. Move through your presentation, setting the desired effects for each slide if you wish to vary the effects for each of the slides.

When in Slide Sorter view, the toolbar contains a Hide Slide button, a Rehearse Timings button, a Summary Slide button, and a Notes button (in addition to the Transition button, discussed previously, that displays the Slide Transition pane in the Task Pane). Use the Hide Slide button to hide slides in a show. Use the Rehearse Timings button to set and rehearse the timings for both an individual slide and the entire slide show. The Summary Slide button is used to create a slide that will give you a summary of your presentation, as discussed in Chapter 20, "Polishing a Presentation." The Notes button displays a Notes dialog box that lets you add speaker's notes to a selected slide. You will find this toolbar to be useful in quickly assigning settings to each of your slides for a slide show.

When you are finished choosing the various options in the dialog box, click Slide Show to run the presentation.

Using the rehearse timings feature to time a presentation

If you want to set your own timings for a slide show based on your spoken narration, choose the Rehearse Timings option of the Slide Show menu. Advance the slides using the PgDn key or by pressing the spacebar while dictating your accompanying narration in "practice" mode. As you advance each slide, PowerPoint keeps track of the time that you take to advance from one slide to another. After you complete your narration, switch to Slide Sorter view. Underneath each slide you will see the time that you have used to discuss for that slide.

Creating continuously running slide shows

If you want slides that are set for timed intervals to run continuously until the Esc key is pressed (a great option for unattended displays, such as those you see running at kiosks at legal technology conferences), you need to set up the timings for a slide or a group of slides (to govern the amount of time a slide stays on the screen), and you need to set an option that tells PowerPoint to restart the show at the beginning when it ends. Use the following steps to make a presentation run continuously:

1. On the Slides tab in Normal view or in Slide Sorter view, select the slide or slides that you want to set the timing for. (You can select multiple slides by pressing the Ctrl key as you click each slide.)
2. From the menus, choose Slide Show ⇨ Slide Transition.
3. In the Task Pane, under Advance Slide, click the Automatically After check box and enter the number of seconds you want the slide to appear on the screen.
4. Choose Slide Show ⇨ Set Up Show from the menus. In the dialog box that appears, click the Loop Continuously Until 'Esc' check box.
5. In the Advance slides portion of the dialog box, make sure that the Using Timings, If Present option is activated.
6. Click OK and save your changes to the presentation using File ⇨ Save.

After you start the show in Slide Show view, the slides will advance automatically according to the timings you established in Step 3. When the slide show reaches the final slide, after the timed interval elapses, it will start again at the first slide.

Giving slide shows with polish

Giving a good presentation isn't entirely a matter of mastering PowerPoint technique. Most of what creates a presentation that captivates (rather than enslaves) your audience falls under the more general heading of "tips for better presentations."

Always, always, always, *always* (did we say that enough?) test your presentation on the hardware that you plan to use, *before* the audience starts taking their seats. No matter how well things worked back in the office, there's no guarantee that the hardware you're using at a client's office or a hearing or trial site is correctly set up or will behave as well as the hardware at your office. And always have a backup plan to deal with a possible hardware failure.

Try not to spend too much time on a single slide. If a slide stays on-screen for five minutes or more, rethink your content. Believe it or not, five minutes is a long time when a speaker drones — and this has put many an audience to sleep. The audience stays with you if you break up big chunks of information into two or three separate slides.

As you verbally emphasize points, you can use the mouse pointer as an on-screen pointer. (A commercial laser pointer is nicer but also costs a lot more than the mouse that's already installed on your computer.)

Hiding and unhiding slides

The capability to hide or unhide slides is another useful PowerPoint feature. You may want to give similar presentations to different groups but modify the content to fit each group. For example, you might want to present a budget to various managers within a large law firm. It might make sense to show detailed financial data to, say, the Accounting and Client Administration managers, but more general numbers to the Human Resources, Secretarial, and Facilities managers. PowerPoint lets you use one presentation for both groups — but you hide slides so that they do not appear for one group, and you unhide the slides so that they do appear for the other group. To hide a slide, perform the following steps:

1. Display the slide that you want to hide. In Slide Sorter view, you can select more than one slide by holding down the Ctrl key while you click each slide that you want to hide.
2. Choose Slide Show ⇨ Hide Slide. (If you are in Slide Sorter view, you can also click the Hide Slide button in the toolbar.) When you do this, the slide's number is marked with a line through it. During the slide show, the slide will not appear.

The menu option is a toggle, so you can unhide a hidden slide by selecting the slide in Slide Sorter view and choosing Slide Show ⇨ Hide Slide. Or you can simply click the Hide Slide toolbar button again.

Adding Speakers Notes and Audience Handouts to a Presentation

In PowerPoint, you can add two items to your presentation that help improve the presentation: speaker's notes and audience handouts. Each of the slides has a companion notes page that includes a small version of the slide and room for typed notes. You can print the notes and use them to recall the points that you want to make for each slide. (Notes that appear on these pages are the same ones as any notes typed into the Notes pane while in Normal view.) You can also print audience handouts. Audience handouts make it easy for the audience to follow your presentation and give the audience members something to take with them after the presentation is over. The handouts can contain one, two, three, four, six, or nine slides per page.

To create speaker's notes for a presentation, perform the following steps:

1. Select the slide to which you want to add a notes page. Choose View ⇨ Notes Page to enter the Notes Page view of PowerPoint. In this view, a notes page appears beneath the slide, as shown in Figure 22-3.

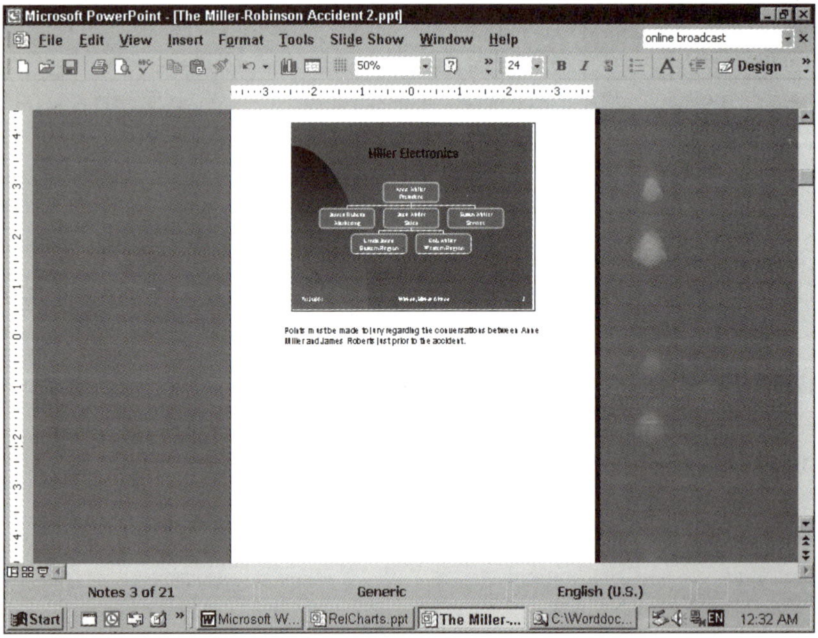

Figure 22-3: A typical notes page

2. At this size, you will have difficulty reading the notes that you add to the notes page. Use the zoom control on the Standard toolbar to increase the size of the notes page to 75 or 100 percent (see Figure 22-4).

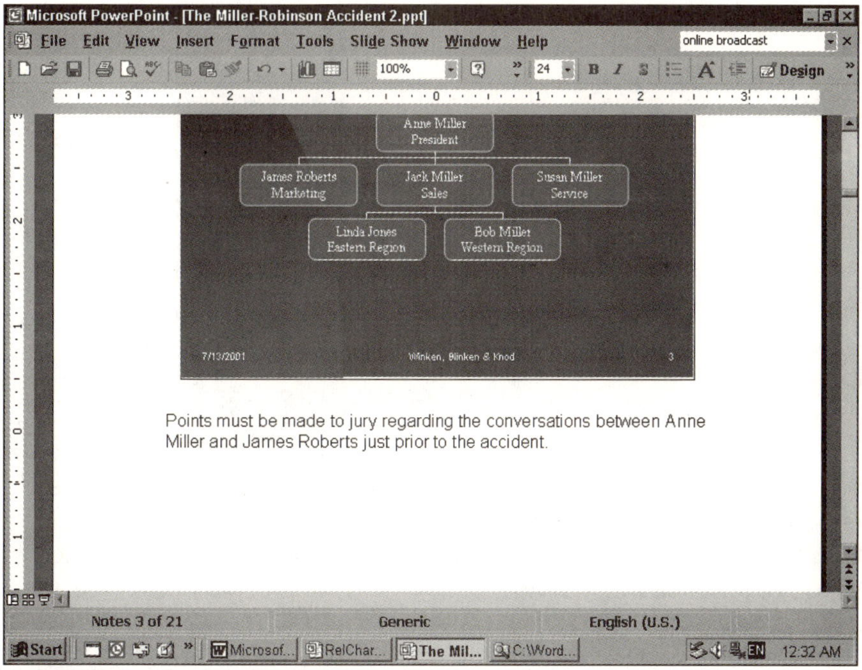

Figure 22-4: The notes page magnified to 100 percent

3. To enter the notes, click the box provided for notes and type your entry. After you have added speaker's notes to a presentation, you can print the notes by using the steps outlined in "Printing parts of your presentation" earlier in this chapter.

It's generally easier to see the text that you type in the notes box if you change the default magnification. From the Zoom Control list box on the Standard toolbar, choose a magnification of 75 percent or larger.

You also can control the overall appearance of your audience handouts by performing the following steps:

1. Choose View ⇨ Master ⇨ Handout Master. The areas outlined by means of dotted lines represent where your slides will appear, depending on whether you've selected one, two, three, four, six, or nine slides per page. To select the number of slides you want to appear per page, choose File ⇨ Print and specify the number in the Print What list box of the Print dialog box.
2. Choose Insert ⇨ Text Box; then click and drag in a desired blank area inside the Handout Master to the desired size. You can then type the desired text. Figure 22-5 shows an example of this approach.

You can add the date and time or page numbers to text boxes in your handouts. To do so, place the insertion point where you want the text inside the text box, open the Insert menu, and choose the Date and Time or Page Number command. Then select the format that you want in the dialog box that appears.

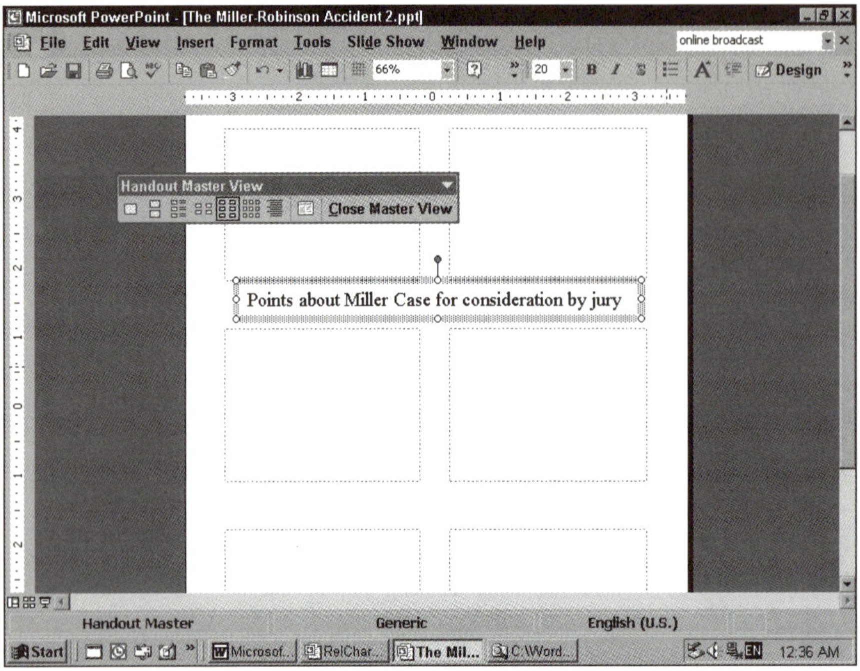

Figure 22-5: Adding a text box and text to the Handout Master

Notes and handout pages have masters, too

In PowerPoint, both notes pages and handout pages have masters, so you can use them in the same manner that you use the Slide Master. When you change the appearance of an aspect of the Notes Master, for example, the change is reflected in every notes page of the presentation. Likewise, any change in the Handout Master is reflected in every handout page of a presentation. You can take advantage of this design trait by placing information on the masters that should appear on every notes page or handout page.

Adding Spoken Narration to a Presentation

You can record spoken narration that runs along with an entire presentation. Although this feature is commonly used with self-running shows at trade shows, attorneys may find it helpful for a very different reason. You can use this feature to share strategy for a particular case with a given client or with co-counsel located in another city. You could create the presentation, narrate it in your own voice and then e-mail the presentation to the client or co-counsel. (Before doing this, check to make sure that the client or co-counsel has a computer with sound capabilities.) Another possible use for this feature would be to illustrate to potential new clients how your law firm would handle a particular matter. Such a presentation could run unattended on a machine located in a conference room or a reception area.

To use the Record Narration feature of PowerPoint, your computer will need to be equipped with a sound card, a microphone, and speakers. Assuming that the hardware supports this feature, you can use the following steps to add narration to a presentation:

1. Choose Slide Show ⇨ Record Narration. The Record Narration dialog box appears, showing the available disk space and the maximum recording time in minutes. (This available recording time varies, depending on the level of sound quality you choose; Step 3 details how to change the level of sound quality.)
2. Click the Set Microphone Level button and follow the directions in the Microphone Setup Wizard that appears, to ensure that your microphone is working properly.
3. Click Change Quality to display the Sound Selection dialog box. In this dialog box, change the level of sound quality if desired and then click OK. You can choose CD quality (best sound but uses the most disk space), radio quality (good sound and makes moderate use of disk space), or telephone quality (fair sound and uses minimal amounts of disk space).
4. Click OK in the dialog box and begin recording your narration for each slide. As you complete each slide's narration, use the mouse (or the spacebar) to move from one slide to the next.
5. If you need to pause the narration, right-click anywhere within the current slide and choose Pause Narration from the menu that appears. When you're ready to continue, right-click within the slide and choose Resume Narration.
6. After you display the last slide, the End of Slide Show screen appears. Click the mouse (or press the spacebar) once more and you will see a dialog box asking whether you want to save the slide timings for each slide along with the narrations.
7. Click Save if you want to include the slide timings with the narrations, or click Don't Save to save only the narrations. (If you want an unattended slide show with the slides matching your narration, you must click Save.)

After saving the slide show, you can run it at any time, and the narration plays automatically.

CAUTION: Narration that you add to a slide show overrides any other sounds, such as slide transition sounds or .WAV files that you have inserted into slides as sound clips. If other sounds are needed as part of your presentation, your only option is to mix those sounds with the narration track that feeds into your microphone. You could play the required sounds using another device (such as another computer, an audio CD player, or a cassette tape recorder) connected to a speaker and place the speaker near your microphone as you dictate the narration. Or you could mix the sounds and your narration using an audio mixer and feed the mixer output into your computer's microphone jack (a topic that's, admittedly, *way* beyond the scope of this book).

Creating Custom Slide Shows

PowerPoint offers you the flexibility of custom slide shows. These are basically variations of the same presentation. When using a custom slide show, you are able to give the same presentation to different departments of a large law firm, for example. Create custom shows by performing the following steps.

1. From the Slide Show menu, choose Custom Shows. You then see the Custom Shows dialog box.
2. Choose the New button. Doing so activates the Define Custom Show dialog box.
3. Select the slides that you want included in the Slides in Presentation area of the dialog box; click Add to add each desired slide or slides. (Remember that if you wish to select multiple slides, hold the Ctrl key while clicking.)
4. Using the arrows beside the Slides in Custom Show box, move the slides up or down to appear in the order that you want.
5. Give the custom slide show a name, click OK, and click Close.

After you've created a custom slide show, you can show it at any time by opening the presentation, choosing Slide Show ⇨ Custom Shows, selecting the custom show by name in the Custom Shows dialog box, and clicking Show.

This feature can really come in handy when making on-the-fly adjustments to a presentation, something that many presenters do. It also provides you with a way to make a presentation more adaptable to the circumstances. What began as multiple presentations on the same topic but directed at different audiences with some slides in common can now become one presentation with several ways of running it.

TIP: To see a preview of a custom show, select the name of the show in the Custom Shows dialog box and then click Show.

Saving a Presentation as a Web Page

Yet another way to present your publication is on a Web site, either on your law firm's internal intranet or on the Internet. You can use the Save as Web Page command in PowerPoint to save an entire presentation as a series of HTML files, and a Webmaster can then upload those HTML files to an intranet or Internet site. Follow these steps to save a presentation as HTML files for publication on the Web:

1. Open the presentation that you want to save as a series of Web pages.
2. Choose File ⇨ Save as Web Page. The Save As dialog box appears, with the Save as Type list box automatically set to Web Page.
3. Navigate to the desired folder where the main HTML file and all associated files should be saved; then enter a name for the file in the File Name text box.
4. Click Change Title if you want to change the page title that appears when the presentation is viewed on the Web. Click Save.

TIP: If you are preparing a presentation for use on a Web site, you can see how the slide show will look on the site by choosing File ⇨ Web Page Preview. When you do this, the slide show opens within Microsoft Internet Explorer, as shown in Figure 22-6. Click the links at the left side of the browser window to show an appropriate slide in the remainder of the browser window.

PowerPoint creates a series of HTML files and saves them, along with all necessary graphics and animations, in the specified folder. You can then upload these files to the Web server that hosts your intranet or Internet Web site.

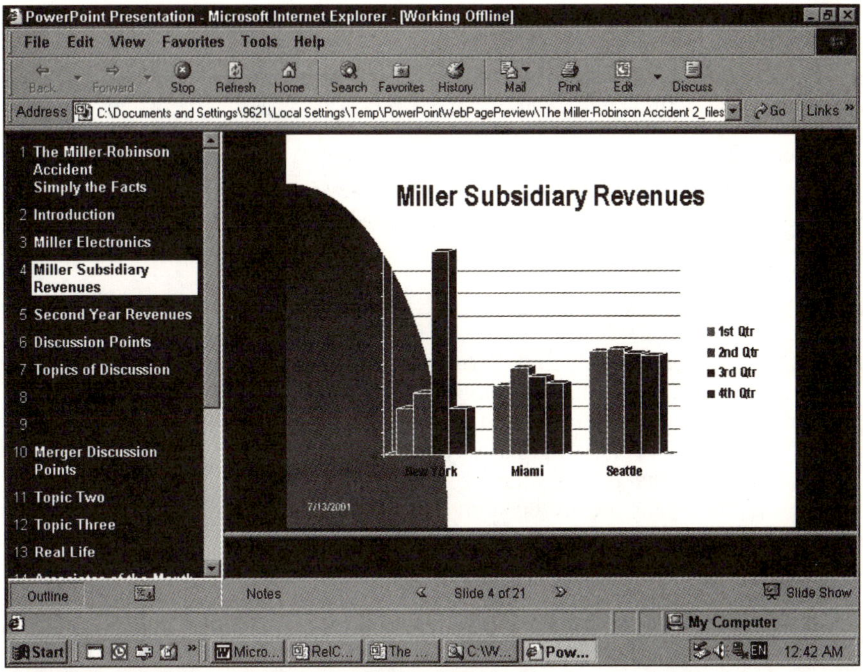

Figure 22-6: The Web Page Preview command lets you see how a presentation will appear when viewed in a Web browser.

CAUTION: When you create a presentation for display on a Web site, keep in mind that different browsers may display certain features of your presentation differently. PowerPoint presentations that are saved as Web pages are optimized for display within Microsoft Internet Explorer. Graphics and animations, in particular, may be rendered differently in another browser (such as Netscape Navigator). If the presentation is being uploaded to your law firm's public Web site, you may want to check the presentation using both Internet Explorer and Netscape Navigator before settling on a final design.

Using the PowerPoint Viewer

Microsoft also provides, free of charge, a separate program called the *PowerPoint Viewer* that is useful when you want to view a presentation with another computer that does not have PowerPoint installed. The PowerPoint Viewer provides the software needed to load and view any presentation created in PowerPoint. You can also use the Pack & Go Wizard in PowerPoint to package any presentation onto one or more floppy disks (see the next section). Then all you need to give your presentation at a site lacking PowerPoint is the PowerPoint Viewer program and the disks containing your presentation.

Microsoft freely gives permission for the PowerPoint Viewer program to be installed on any Windows-based computer. The PowerPoint Viewer program does not provide an operational copy of PowerPoint. The Viewer only lets you view presentations. You must download the PowerPoint Viewer from Microsoft's Web site.

To install the PowerPoint Viewer, go to the Microsoft Office Web site (`www.microsoft.com/office`), follow the links to PowerPoint and then to Downloads, and click the Converters and Viewers link. Follow the instructions that appear for installing the Viewer.

After the installation is complete, you can run the PowerPoint Viewer on a computer by opening the Start menu, choosing Programs, and then choosing PowerPoint Viewer. The Viewer displays an Open dialog box that asks for the name of the PowerPoint presentation that you want to view. Find the desired presentation in the folder it is stored in, select it, and click Open to run the presentation.

Using the Pack & Go Wizard

You can use the Pack & Go command from the File menu to create a packaged presentation on one or more disks. This menu command launches the Pack & Go Wizard, which then steps you through the process of packaging a presentation and saving it to as many disks as are needed. You can then carry the disks from site to site and give the presentation on any computer that has either PowerPoint or the PowerPoint Viewer installed. (Note that if both your site and the destination site have access to e-mail, it will probably be easier to e-mail the presentation as an attachment. How to do so is detailed in the section that follows.)

All this wizard stuff! Why can't I just copy the presentation file to the other computer?

Actually, you probably can, assuming that the file will fit on a single disk. The Pack & Go Wizard makes life easier if the file is too large for a single disk or if you're not comfortable with moving files around to package a presentation and install it on another system. If you're perfectly comfortable with using Windows Explorer, My Computer, or (horrors!) DOS commands to copy files from place to place, you can always just copy the presentation file onto a disk and then from that disk to the other system (again assuming that it will fit on a single disk) and open it in PowerPoint or in the PowerPoint Viewer. Keep in mind that if your presentation has any OLE objects in it (such as portions of Word documents or sound or video files larger than 100 KB), it's probably a wise idea to use the Pack & Go Wizard because the wizard automatically includes any linked files. You, on the other hand, may very well leave them at the New York office and discover that they are missing when you are standing before a jury in Omaha. Using the Pack & Go Wizard prevents you from forgetting those needed files for your big presentation.

To package a presentation for use elsewhere, perform the following steps:

1. Choose File ⇨ Pack & Go to display the first Pack & Go Wizard dialog box. This dialog box explains the purpose of the wizard but in other respects is pretty useless. Click the Next button.
2. In the next dialog box of the wizard, you can choose to package the presentation that is currently open, or you can click the Other Presentations option, click Browse, and choose another presentation from the dialog box that appears. Make your desired selections and then click the Next button.
3. The next dialog box asks which drive you want to use to store the presentation. Select the desired drive and enter a path if needed; then click Next.
4. The next dialog box asks whether you want to include any linked files (such as a Word document that may be pasted into your presentation or sound or video clips that may be in your presentation). Click any desired options and then click the Next button.
5. The last dialog box asks whether you wish to include the PowerPoint Viewer for a computer that does not have Power Point installed. Make sure that there is a blank disk in the drive that you selected earlier. If any additional disks are needed, PowerPoint asks you to insert one when it needs one. When the process is complete, you are returned to whatever view of PowerPoint you were in when you started the wizard.

To install the presentation on another machine, insert the first disk created by the wizard into the drive and choose the Run command from the Windows Start menu. In the Run dialog box that appears, browse the disk drive, find and select the program called *PNG Setup*, and click Open to run that program. When you run the program, it displays a Pack & Go Wizard dialog box that asks you for a destination folder in which to store the presentation. Enter a folder name and then click OK. (If you enter a new folder name, the program asks you for confirmation before creating the folder.)

If the program needs to read more than one disk, the program asks for the additional disks as it needs them. When the installation is complete, you can view the presentation by opening it in PowerPoint or by using the PowerPoint Viewer (described in the preceding section).

Using the Send To Command

One other common option that you have for "producing" your presentation is the Send To command of the File menu. With this command, you can send the presentation to another person on a network. If your system is configured to send e-mail to others (such as through the use of Microsoft Outlook and a Microsoft Exchange server on your firm's network), you can collaborate with co-workers, co-counsel, or clients by sending your PowerPoint presentations via e-mail for review.

CAUTION: Before sending a presentation to co-counsel or to clients, you may want to remove any personal information, such as the author name, reviewer names, and file properties (Last Saved By, for example). To remove this information, choose Tools ⇨ Options and click the Security tab. Under Privacy Options, click the Remove Personal Information from This File on Save check box, click OK, and save your presentation.

In addition to sending a presentation for review, you also can send a presentation as an attachment. You can send a presentation for review if you are using Outlook 2002 or any other 32-bit e-mail program that is compatible with the Messaging Application Programming Interface (MAPI) and if your network is using a Microsoft Exchange server or another type of network server. You can send a presentation as an attachment as long as your e-mail system supports MAPI and the recipient can receive an attachment through his or her e-mail system.

Sending a presentation as an attachment

To send a presentation as an attachment, follow these steps:

1. Open the presentation that you want to send.
2. From the menus, choose File ⇨ Send To ⇨ Mail Recipient (as Attachment).
3. In the To and CC boxes of the dialog box that appears, enter the recipient names (if on your internal mail system) or Internet mail addresses (if located outside your network).
4. Click Send.

Sending a presentation for review

To send a presentation for review if you are using Outlook as your e-mail program and Exchange server as your firm's network mail server, follow these steps:

1. Open the presentation that you want to send.
2. From the menus, choose File ⇨ Send To ⇨ Mail Recipient (for Review).
3. In the To and CC boxes of the dialog box that appears, enter the recipient names (if on your internal mail system) or Internet mail addresses (if located outside your network).
4. Click Send.

If you are using an e-mail program other than the Outlook or if you are using a network server other than Microsoft Exchange, follow these steps:

1. Choose File ⇨ Save As.
2. In the File Name box, rename the presentation. In the Save as Type list box, choose Presentation for Review.
3. Click Save.
4. Use your particular e-mail program to send each reviewer a copy of the saved file as an attachment. Or if you want to use a network server other than Microsoft Exchange, save the presentation to a shared folder on a network server. You will then need to notify your reviewers to review the copy of the presentation that you have stored on the server.

Sending a presentation to Microsoft Word

Assuming that Microsoft Word is installed on your machine (after all, you are using the Office suite, or why would you be reading this book?), you also can send a PowerPoint presentation directly into a Word document. To do this, open the presentation and choose File ⇨ Send to ⇨ Microsoft Word. The Send to Microsoft Word dialog box appears, as shown in Figure 22-7.

Choose the desired page layout in Word (Notes Next to Slides, Blank Lines Next to Slides, Notes Below Slides, Blank Lines Below Slides, or Outline Only). Next, choose whether you want the presentation embedded in your Word document (by choosing Paste) or linked to the Word document (by choosing Paste Link). If you paste the presentation, it becomes a part of the Word document, and the Word document increases in size by a corresponding amount. If you use the Paste Link option, Word maintains a link to the PowerPoint presentation, and the Word document does not increase significantly in size. However, you must keep the PowerPoint presentation saved in the original folder on the same machine from which you run Microsoft Word.

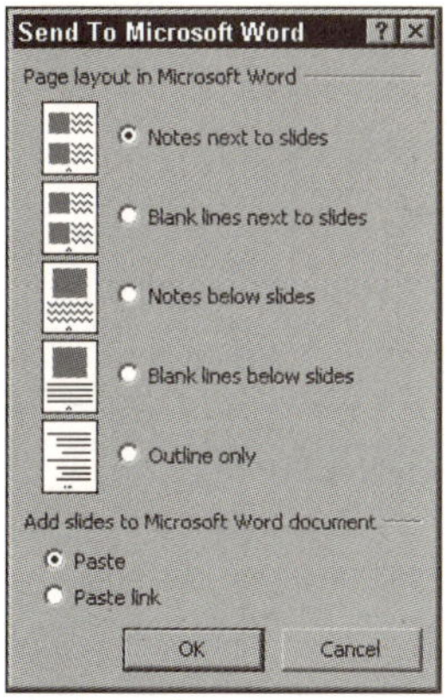

Figure 22-7: Send a presentation directly to a Word document.

When you finish choosing the desired options in the dialog box, click OK. Microsoft Word launches automatically (if it isn't running already), and a new Word document containing the presentation is created. (Each slide is pasted into a separate page of the Word document, so if you have a large presentation, this may take a few moments.) Figure 22-8 shows an example of a Word document that contains a PowerPoint presentation; this was created using the Send to Microsoft Word feature of PowerPoint.

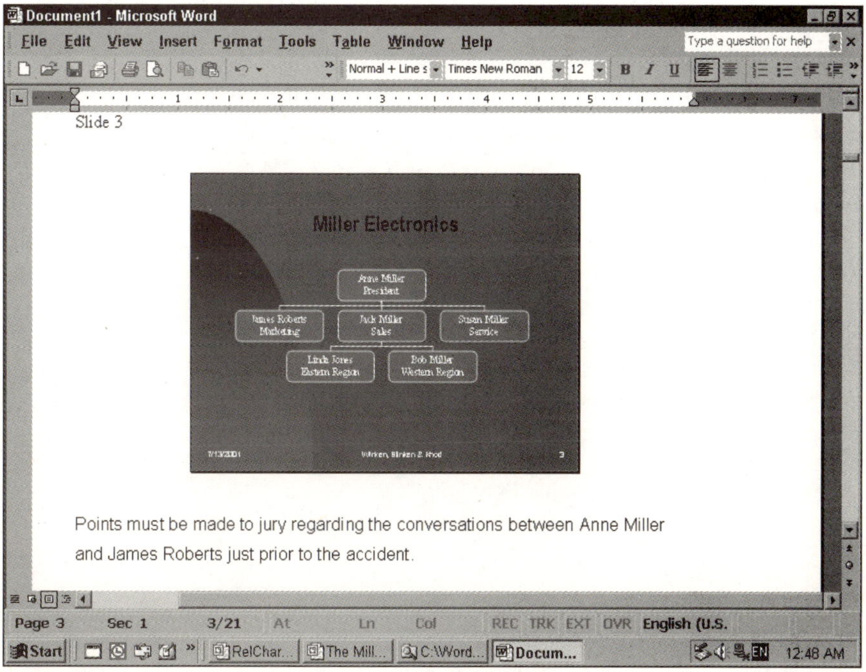

Figure 22-8: A Word document containing a PowerPoint presentation

Sending a presentation to an Exchange Public Folder

If your firm uses Microsoft Exchange as its mail server and you have been granted permission to save information in public folders, you can send a PowerPoint presentation directly to a public folder. (Check with your firm's Exchange Server administrator to determine whether you have permission to store documents in public folders.) To send a presentation to a public folder, perform these steps:

1. Open or create the presentation that you want to send.
2. From the menus, choose File ⇨ Send To ⇨ Exchange Folder.
3. If prompted for a profile name, choose your normal e-mail profile name in the list box and click OK.
4. In the Send to Exchange Folder dialog box that appears, navigate to the desired public folder.
5. Click OK.

After you've stored a PowerPoint presentation in an Exchange public folder, co-workers who have permission to access that folder can open the folder in Outlook and double-click the presentation by name. Assuming that PowerPoint is installed on the co-workers' computers, PowerPoint will start and the presentation will appear.

Summary

As demonstrated in this chapter, producing your work in PowerPoint is not an incredibly involved process. This chapter showed you how to print presentations and use different methods to customize your on-screen slide presentations. The chapter covered the following points:

- You can print presentation slides by choosing File ⇨ Print, but you should first set up your presentation for the type of printing that you want. Choose File ⇨ Page Setup and then select the desired options in the Page Setup dialog box.
- You can change the options for your on-screen slide shows by choosing Slide Show ⇨ Set Up Show and selecting the desired options from the Set Up Show dialog box.
- You can add speaker's notes or audience handouts to presentations. You can print these items separately for distribution to the speaker or the audience.
- You can use File ⇨ Pack & Go to launch a wizard that lets you package a presentation to run on any computer.
- You can choose File ⇨ Save as Web Page to save a presentation as a series of HTML files that can be uploaded to the Internet or to an intranet.
- You can collaborate with others by sending presentations via e-mail, as attachments, or for review.

In the chapters that follow, you'll learn ways to put Access, the database management component of Microsoft Office, to work within the legal environment.

Part IV

Access

Chapter 23

About Databases and Tables

In This Chapter

- ♦ Understanding databases
- ♦ Starting Access
- ♦ Understanding Access file formats
- ♦ Understanding the Database window and the desktop
- ♦ Exiting Access
- ♦ Creating tables
- ♦ Setting field properties
- ♦ Adding and editing data
- ♦ Printing a table
- ♦ Finding data
- ♦ Changing the appearance of a table
- ♦ Adding indexes
- ♦ Establishing relationships between tables
- ♦ Using external data in Access
- ♦ Compacting and repairing a database
- ♦ Using the Upsizing Wizard

THIS CHAPTER INTRODUCES THE USE of Microsoft Access to legal professionals. At law firms and within the corporate legal environment, you can use Access for many case-related needs (such as for litigation-support databases), as well as for other general law firm administrative needs (such as law firm marketing and personnel tracking). Although database tasks can, by nature, be more complex than working with tasks in Microsoft Word or Excel, on an overall basis Access is easy to use. Access is also powerful — you can use it for simple or complex database-related tasks at any size law firm.

Understanding Databases

In computer terminology, a *database* is any collection of related information grouped together. Often, when defining the concept of a database, it helps to compare computerized databases to the noncomputerized variety, such as filing cabinets of information or a box of 3-by-5 cards containing names and addresses. A random collection of information technically is not a database; what makes the information a database is that the data is arranged in some type of logical order. With computers, information is routinely arranged and stored in the form of tables, with rows and columns in each table. One or more tables containing the data in an organized manner is considered to be a database.

Access takes this common analogy further by adding the tools that you use to manage the data — such as queries, forms, and reports — to the database.

Collecting data in tables

Access stores your data in the form of *tables*, which are collections of data arranged in rows of records and columns of fields. This arrangement, commonly used by spreadsheets, also is used by virtually every Windows database manager on the market. Each row of the table contains one *record*, or one complete set of information, such as a person in a table of employees or a specific phone call in a listing of phone calls to clients. Each column in the table contains a separate *field*, or type of information, such as the first name of an attorney or the date of the phone call. Figure 23-1 shows a simple client list using a columnar name-and-address format applied to a table in Access.

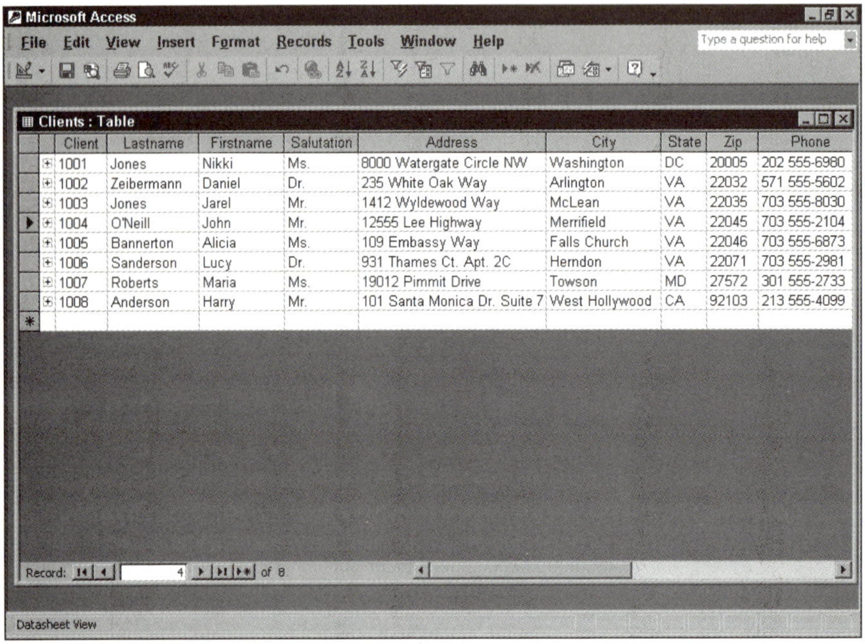

Figure 23-1: A mailing list stored as a table

Recalling data using queries

After your data has been stored in the form of tables, you can obtain specific subsets of that data by using queries. The word *query* literally means "to ask," and Access queries provide a way of asking about your data. You can use queries to find a specific record (such as that of a trial witness named Mary Smith), to print mailing labels for all persons living in a certain ZIP or postal code, or to display all employees who haven't had a performance review in 12 months.

Queries let you display and work with selected data from up to 16 tables at a time. (Queries can be based on other queries; therefore, in the unlikely event that you need to work with more than 16 tables simultaneously, there are ways to do so in Access.) When you design your query, you identify which records should be included in the results of the query and which fields should be included. You can specify *criteria*, which determine what records appear in the query. The results of your queries can be used by the forms and reports you create. Access also lets you create *action queries*, which can be used to quickly modify or delete large amounts of data stored in tables.

Displaying data in forms

In Access, you use *forms* to display the data that's stored in your tables. You can think of forms as being computerized equivalents of the paper-based forms that are so familiar to businesses. Forms routinely are used for adding new data to a table and for editing or displaying existing data, usually in a one-record-at-a-time format. Using the Form Wizards provided with Access, you can quickly create many variations of forms, or you can use the custom form design capabilities in Access to manually create any type of form desired. Forms can be designed to work with data that comes from more than one table at a time. In Figure 23-2, the form shown is based on a relationship between multiple tables, displaying one table of clients, along with all the details of phone calls placed to each client. (Chapter 25, "Working with Forms," details the design and use of forms.)

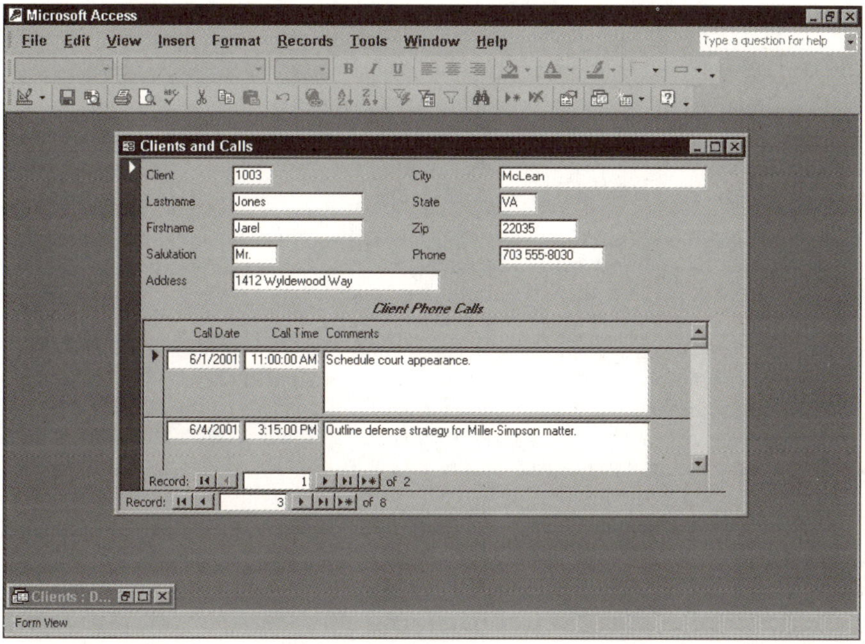

Figure 23-2: In Access, a form based on multiple tables lets you view relational data at a glance.

Printing data using reports

Often, the desired result of any database is to provide information in the form of *reports*, and Access is no slouch in this area. You can print reports from tables or from queries in virtually any desired format. As with forms, you can design reports manually, or you can use the Report Wizards to help you quickly design reports. Reports can contain graphics stored in Windows OLE (Object Linking and Embedding) fields or graphics as decorative items stored in bitmap files by programs such as Windows Paint.

CROSS-REFERENCE: Chapter 26 details the design and use of reports.

Automating tasks with macros

In many other programmable database managers, you design complete applications by writing hundreds of lines of program code to accomplish specialized tasks. In Access, you can use *macros*, which are groups of instructions, to replace the hundreds of lines of program code required by similar products. When you run the macro, Access carries out the list of instructions, following the sequence of steps determined by the design of the macro.

As an example, perhaps you routinely open two forms and a certain report and usually work with these throughout your day. You can create a macro that automatically opens the desired forms and reports and places them on your screen in the desired locations. As another example, if you run a query and export the results of that query to an Excel spreadsheet on a weekly basis, you can create a macro that handles this task.

CROSS-REFERENCE: Chapter 27 provides details about Access macros.

Performing special tasks with modules

In those rare cases in which programming is necessary, you can write *modules*. Modules are collections of program code written using VBA (Visual Basic for Applications), the programming language that is built in to Access. VBA is the programming language that is included with all the Microsoft Office applications (Word, Excel, Access, and PowerPoint). You can use modules to extend the functionality of Access, performing specialized tasks that cannot easily be performed (if at all) without the use of VBA. One common use of VBA is to provide automated exchange of data between Access and other Windows applications. Another common use of VBA is to perform tasks at the operating-system level (such as writing data in a special format directly to a disk file). This book does not detail the use of VBA and programming in Access, but you can consider additional resources (such as books dedicated to Access programming) if you care to delve into this area of Access's capabilities.

Starting Access

On the Windows desktop, double-click the Microsoft Access icon, or, using the Windows taskbar, click Start ⇨ Programs ⇨ Microsoft Access. Access loads, and in a moment you see the Access program window. This main window in Access is the *desktop*, or the working surface where you manipulate your various Access objects (such as tables and forms). At the right side of the window, the Task Pane appears. (If you don't see the Task Pane, choose View ⇨ Toolbars ⇨ Task Pane to display it.)

The Task Pane, which appears in all Office XP applications, lets you perform common tasks. In the case of Access, you can use the Task Pane to open existing databases, create new blank databases, and create new databases based on existing files or templates. (In previous versions of Access, the templates are referred to as the *Database Wizards*.).

When you want to create a new database within Access, you can use either of the following approaches:

- **Database Wizard option:** In the Task Pane, under New from Template, click General Templates and, in the dialog box that appears, click Databases. Then click one of the available templates and click OK to start the Database Wizard. You can use this wizard to step through the process of creating a database using predesigned tables supplied by Microsoft. The Database

Wizard asks a series of questions about the type of database you want to create, and based on your responses, creates a database, complete with tables, forms, and reports. (Unfortunately, all these predesigned databases are designed for business tasks that are not among those commonly encountered in the legal environment; hence, the Database Wizards aren't covered in any detail in this book.)

- **Blank Database option:** Alternatively, under New in the Task Pane, you can select the Blank Database option to create an empty database. When you do this, a File New Database dialog box appears, asking for a name and location for the new database. Navigate to the desired drive or folder, enter a filename in the File Name dialog box, and click Create. Access creates a database under the name you specified on your hard drive or network drive.

Understanding Access File Formats

Access 2002 lets you work with either of two Access file formats when creating and using databases: the newer Access 2002 file format or the older Access 2000 file format. The newer format supports certain features that are specific to Access 2002, including faster data access and better database processing for large databases. However, not all users at a law firm may be using Access 2002, or you may need to share databases with law firm clients who do not have Access 2002. If some users or clients are using Access 2000 and others are using Access 2002, you should use the Access 2000 file format. By default, Access 2002 uses the older (Access 2000) file format for creating new databases, unless you change this setting.

To choose the desired file format that Access will always use when creating new databases, choose Tools ⇨ Options from the menus and click the Advanced tab in the Options dialog box that appears. Under Default File Format, select Access 2002 or Access 2000, as desired. Then click OK to have the changes take effect for all databases that you create from this point onward. Note that when using Access 2002, you can tell which file format is used by a database from the description that appears at the top of the Database window.

Using the Database Window and the Desktop

After you open an existing database in Access (or immediately after you create a new database), you see the Database window, shown in Figure 23-3. In this figure, the Database window shows the objects in the Northwind sample database that's provided with Access. By default, the Tables tab appears selected, and you see a list of all the tables in the database. You can click any of the remaining tabs to see the other objects in the database; for example, clicking the Reports tab displays all reports in the database.

As illustrated in Figure 23-3, Access displays a menu bar and a toolbar (near the top of the window). The menu options and the toolbar buttons vary, depending on where you are in Access and depending on what objects you are working with at a given time. For that reason, various menu and toolbar options are explained as they are needed throughout this book. The Database window is visible (unless you have hidden it with the Window ⇨ Hide menu option). In addition, you see any objects of the type currently selected by the tabs in the Database window. Any objects that you have already opened also appear as separate objects on the screen. Using standard Windows techniques, you can move and size these windows as desired.

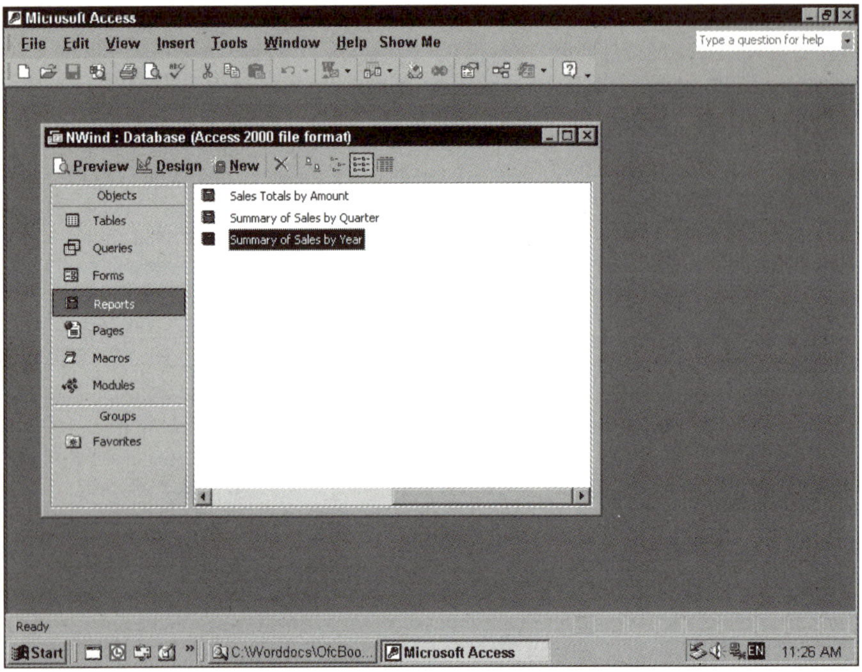

Figure 23-3: The Database window contains tabs at the far left that, when clicked, display their respective Access objects.

Exiting Access

When you are done with Access, you can exit the program by choosing File ⇨ Exit. (If the Database window is the only open window, you can also press Alt+F4 to exit Access.) Be sure to always exit Access in this manner. Never exit Access, or any other Windows application, by simply turning off the computer while you are still in Access. Doing so can damage a database.

Creating Tables

In Access, you can create new tables using a number of different methods. You can make use of the Table Wizards. The *Table Wizards* are automated helpers that walk you through the process of table creation and suggest ready-made structures for your tables. The Table Wizards do a good job if you need to create tables for common business tasks outside the legal environment, such as managing inventory or keeping track of customers. However, the needs of law firms and legal departments are not met by any of the tables created with the aid of the Table Wizards. Hence, we skip coverage of the Table Wizards and assume that you prefer to manually create your tables. By manually creating your tables, you gain needed control over the table creation process.

Creating new tables

In Access, it's a simple process to manually create new tables. When you want to create a table, just perform the following steps:

1. Click the Tables tab at the left side of the Database window.

2. Click the New button in the Database window. In a moment, the New Table dialog box appears.

3. Choose Design View from the list of available choices; then click OK.

After you perform these steps, you see the Table Design window (shown in Figure 23-4). Access assigns the table a sequential name (such as *Table1*, *Table2*, and so on), and that name appears at the top of the window until you save the table under its own name. As you design the table, you specify the field names and the types of fields that are to be used in the new table, using the columns within the Table Design window.

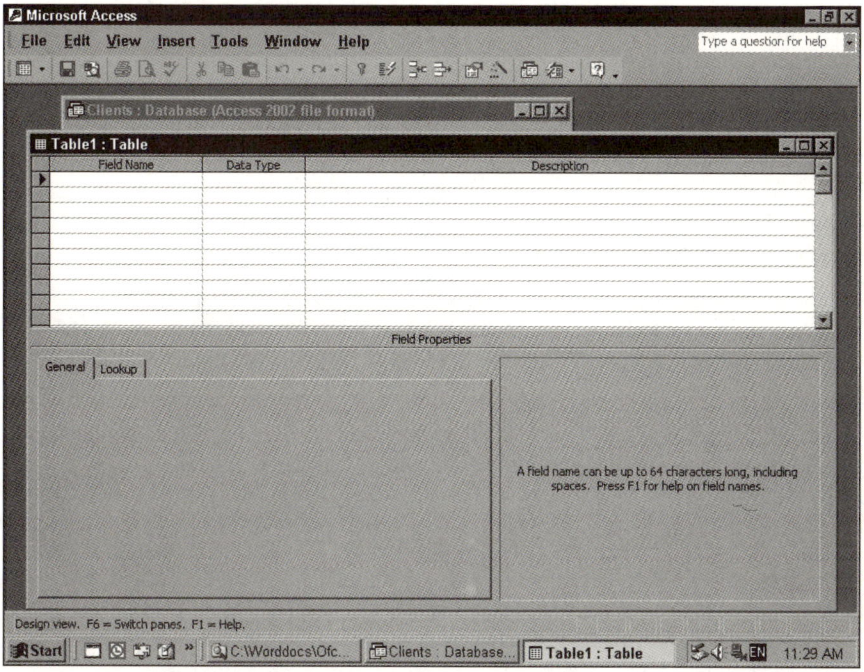

Figure 23-4: The Table Design window contains columns for the field names, data types, and descriptions.

Access lets you examine tables using either of two possible views: Design view or Datasheet view. In *Design view*, you create or modify the design, or structure, of the table. Using Design view, you can name your fields, specify the types of data that each field should contain (such as text, dates, or currency), and specify any optional rules that will control data entry as users enter data into your tables.

The second view, and the one you more commonly use after your tables exist, is referred to as *Datasheet view*. After a table exists in an Access database, you can use Datasheet view to add and edit records in the table or to delete records from the table. (Note that you can also add and edit data in tables using forms, a topic that Chapter 25 covers in detail.)

To open a table that already exists in Design view, first click the table name in the Database window to select it. Next, click the Design button within the Database window to open a Table Design window for the table. (Alternately, you can right-click the desired table in the Database window and then choose Design from the shortcut menu that appears.)

Three columns appear within the upper portion of the Table Design window: Field Name, Data Type, and Description. In the Field Name column, you enter the desired name for a field. Your field names can be up to 64 characters in length, and you can use letters, numbers, spaces, and punctuation marks in them. Because Access permits the use of spaces within field names, you can be descriptive with your field names. For example, a name such as *Date of Deposition* would likely make more sense to other users at your firm than a field name such as *DepoDate*.

TIP: Keeping your field names short is a good idea. Access uses your field names as default field labels in forms and as default column headings in reports. If you give your fields long names, your report design, in particular, may become a nightmare because Access creates overly wide columns to accommodate the field names.

Selecting the data types

After you enter the field name, press Tab to move the insertion pointer into the Data Type column of the Table Design window. Here, you select a type for the data that will be stored in the field. Access defaults to a data type of Text unless you specify otherwise. To change the data type, click the arrow at the right side of the Data Type column to open a drop-down list of data types.

Access offers you a choice of nine data types, as well as a choice called the *Lookup Wizard*. The Lookup Wizard helps you define a field that will obtain its value by looking up the contents of another field in a different table. Here are the different field types that you can use in your Access tables:

- **Text:** Stores any combination of characters, such as client names, case names, and opposing counsel names and addresses. Text fields can include letters, numbers, punctuation marks, blank spaces, and special symbols. Text fields can contain up to 255 characters, and Access defaults to a length of 50 characters. (To change this length, click in the Field Size box in the General tab at the bottom of the window and change the default to the value you want.) Numbers that you do not intend to perform calculations on (such as Client or Matter ID codes, ZIP codes, or telephone numbers) should be stored using Text fields. When you need to store very large amounts of text (more than 255 characters), use a Memo field.
- **Memo:** Stores large amounts of text (such as entire paragraphs). Memo fields can store up to 65,535 characters. Typical uses for memo fields include deposition transcripts, portions of legal briefs, medical transcripts, and employee evaluations. If you plan to store the text of entire Microsoft Word documents, consider the use of an OLE Object field instead; see the sidebar "Whether to use a Memo field or an OLE Object field," later in this section.)
- **Number:** Stores numeric values other than currency. You can enter fractional values with decimals, and you can enter negative values by preceding the value with a minus sign or by enclosing it in parentheses. Number fields are typically used for any noncurrency values that must be calculated. If you don't have to perform calculations on the number (as with Client/Matter ID codes, postal codes, or phone numbers), store it in a text field instead.
- **Date/Time:** Stores dates or times. Although you can store dates or times in a text field, using a date/time field has advantages. Validation of proper dates and times is automatic (you can't get away with storing a date such as 13/42/2002 or a time such as 25:87 p.m.), and you can perform calculations based on the entries in date/time fields for tasks such as adding a number of days to a date already stored in the field. Access can handle dates with years ranging from 100 A.D. to 9999 A.D. (see the note at the end of this section, however).
- **Currency:** Stores numeric amounts used specifically for currency. Access automatically adds a fixed number of digits to the right of the decimal point to prevent rounding errors that may occur if you use number fields for this task. (Note that if you calculate amounts based on the

contents of currency fields, Access may, on occasion, store more than the usual two decimal places.)

- **AutoNumber:** Automatically increments a numeric value in the field for each record that you add. Hence, the first record receives a value of 1, the next record receives a value of 2, and so on. (In versions of Access prior to Access 97, these fields are called *counter fields.*) AutoNumber fields are often used as primary keys in tables that are related to other tables, because they are always unique for each record. Keep in mind that after records are added, the values stored in AutoNumber fields cannot be changed.
- **Yes/No:** Stores logical (yes or no) values. During data entry, the fields can contain true or false, yes or no, on or off, or the numeric values of zero (0) for no, or –1 for yes.
- **OLE Object:** Contains OLE data. *OLE data* is data that is stored in other Windows applications that support OLE (Object Linking and Embedding). OLE data may include sound clips, video clips, or parts or all of a Word document or Excel spreadsheet. See the sidebar "Whether to use a Memo field or an OLE Object field," later in this section.
- **Hyperlink:** Stores a combination of text and numbers that serves as a *hyperlink address*, a path to a document or Web page. A hyperlink address can be a URL (an address to an Internet or intranet Web site) or an address to a file on your firm's local area network.
- **Lookup Wizard:** Although this item appears in the list of available field types, it is not actually a type of field. Instead, it enables you to restrict the field so that it can accept only data based on a list of values from a field in another table. For example, if you want to add a field to your current table to store the names of U.S. states, you can create another table that has a State field and enter a record containing the two-letter code for every acceptable state in that table. Then if you use the Lookup Wizard to create a field in the current table based on a lookup of the State field in the other table, users of the current table are able to enter only values that match the two-letter codes in the other table.

NOTE: With date fields, Access makes certain assumptions if the year portion of a date is entered using two-digit entries. If the year value is between 00 and 29, Access assumes the date to be a twenty-first century date. If the year value is between 30 and 99, Access assumes the date to be a twentieth century date. For the majority of uses, these rules will work out (at least for the immediate future). If for some reason the storage of dates in your particular database doesn't always work with these assumptions, you need to use all four characters of the year during data entry so that the year will be properly stored.

Adding a description

After entering a field name and choosing a field type, you can enter an optional description in the Description column of the Table Design window. (This description is limited to 64 characters in length.) Whatever entry you make in the Description column appears in the status bar during the data entry and editing process, whenever the insertion pointer is in that field of a table.

After entering any desired description for the field, press Tab again, and the insertion pointer moves to the next field. You can continue the process of entering names and data types for your fields, as necessary. As an example of a table design, Figure 23-5 shows the Cases table of the Case Management database (detailed in Chapter 29) while in Design view.

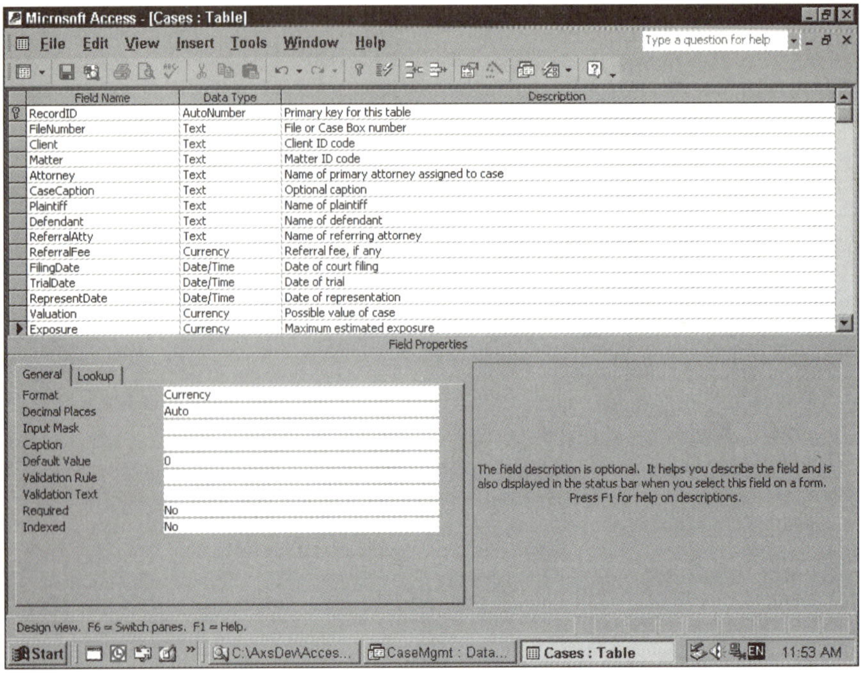

Figure 23-5: The Cases table of the Case Management database, shown in Design view

Whether to use a Memo field or an OLE Object field

If you're thinking of using a memo field to store the entire text of word processing documents, you may want to consider whether you should use an OLE Object field instead. Memo fields tend to work well when you have several sentences of text, perhaps making up a few paragraphs. OLE Object fields usually work well when you have large amounts of text, such as multiple-page documents, stored in a Windows word processor. Assuming that you are using Microsoft Word, you can use Edit ⇨ Copy within Word and Edit ⇨ Paste in Access to insert documents into OLE Object fields within a table. Remember that if you copy lengthy Microsoft Word documents into OLE Object fields of a table, your Access database can quickly consume large portions of disk space as you add records. Also keep in mind that you *cannot* perform searches on the contents of OLE Object fields, so if you want to search your text, you need to resort to memo fields instead.

Adding a primary key

When you are designing a table, Access lets you designate one or more fields to serve as a primary key. *Primary keys* are unique fields in records that provide Access with a method of identifying every record in a table. Primary keys are quite useful (so useful that if you try to save a new table design without specifying a primary key, Access displays a dialog box suggesting that you add one). Primary keys speed performance and also make the addition of relationships between tables possible (a topic that is covered later in this chapter in the section "Establishing Relationships between Tables").

By default, Access displays table data with the primary key listed first. You always want to use data that can never be duplicated in more than one record for a primary key. Common choices for primary keys include client ID codes, matter ID codes, social security numbers, and invoice numbers. It's inappropriate to use a field such as Last Name as a primary key because you would not be able to add two records with the same last name.

Also, keep in mind that sometimes it makes sense to use a combination of fields as the primary key. For example, in a table that tracks weekly timesheets submitted by attorneys, a combination of an attorney ID field and a week ending field may be an appropriate primary key because no single attorney would submit two timesheets for the same work week. You establish a primary key using these steps:

1. While in Design view for the table, choose the field or fields that you want to use as the primary key in the Table Design window. To choose one field, click the row selector for that field (at the far left). To choose more than one field, select the first desired field, hold down the Ctrl key, and click the row selector for each additional field that you want to use.
2. Choose Edit ⇨ Primary Key, or click the Primary Key button in the toolbar (it's the one containing a picture of a key). Access displays a primary key indicator at the left of the fields you've chosen.

NOTE: Because Access displays by default the table's data with the primary key listed first, you may want to designate a primary key (if possible) for fields that you want to appear in a certain order (assuming that the fields contain data that is unique for each record), even when you don't need a primary key for your table. You may notice that when you save the design of a new table, Access always suggests the use of a primary key if one does not exist. Although primary keys are not required, they do speed the performance of Access in sorts, queries, and other common database operations. (A primary key is required when you want to create a default relationship between tables.) Timekeeper IDs, document numbers, client ID numbers, and matter ID numbers are commonly used as primary keys in legal applications. If a table that you are creating does not appear to need a primary key, you can define a field as an AutoNumber field, name it *Record number* or *Record ID*, and let that field serve as the primary key. As data is added, Access automatically assigns the proper values to that field.

Rearranging and deleting fields

If you decide to make changes to the design of a table, you can easily do so within Access. You can move fields around within a table, change the names of fields, add new fields, and delete any fields that are not needed. To change a field, just click in the field where you want to make the change; then make the necessary changes, using the Delete or Backspace keys to remove existing characters.

To move a field to another location within the table, first select the field by clicking the Field Selector to the left of the field name. When you do this, the entire field becomes highlighted. Then click the Field Selector again, hold the mouse button down, and drag the field to the desired location.

If you want to delete a field that is no longer needed, first select the field by clicking the Field Selector. Then press the Delete, key or choose Edit ⇨ Delete Rows from the menus. (Alternatively, you can right-click within a field and choose Delete Rows from the shortcut menu that appears.)

To insert a new field at a specific position in the table, click within any row of the table and choose Insert ⇨ Rows. (Alternatively, you can right-click within a field and choose Insert Rows from the shortcut menu that appears.) A new blank field appears above the existing row, and you can set the field name and type as you would for any field.

Saving the table

When you complete the design for a new table, you must save the table structure before you can add data to the table. To save a table, perform these steps:

1. From the menus, choose File ⇨ Close, or double-click the Control menu icon (it's at the upper-left corner of the Table window). In a moment, you will see the save reminder dialog box. Click Yes and the Save As dialog box appears.
2. Type the desired name for the table. (You can use any names up to 64 characters in length for your tables. You *cannot* use periods, exclamation points, brackets, or leading blanks within table names.
3. Click OK. If you did not define a primary key for the table, Access presents a dialog box asking whether you want to add one now.

If you choose Yes and no AutoNumber field exists in the table, Access creates an AutoNumber field, calls it `ID`, and makes that field a primary key. (If an AutoNumber field already exists, Access assigns a primary key designation to the existing field.) If you click No, Access saves the table structure without a primary key.

After the table is saved, it appears by name in the Database window. You can view the table using Datasheet view and you can add, edit, or delete records, as described in "Adding and Editing Data in a Table," later in this chapter.

Setting Field Properties

During the table design process, you may also want to set field properties for the table. *Field properties* are settings for the individual fields that enable you to control how the data is stored or displayed in the table. For example, if you have a text field that will store social security numbers, you may want to change the field size from the default of 50 characters to something more reasonable (such as 11, for nine numerals and two hyphens). For a number field, you might want to specify the desired number of decimal places. You also can use the Field Property settings to enter validation rules. *Validation rules* are used to identify conditions that entries must meet before the data will be accepted.

In the lower half of the Table Design window, you see the Field Properties area of the dialog box. You can specify the properties for each field of the table in this portion of the Table Design window. Ignoring this area of the window during the table design process is easy because Access doesn't require you to make any changes to it, but assigning field properties can aid you in controlling how users are allowed to enter data into the new table and how users can view the data. As you click anywhere in a specific field (in the upper half of the window), the field properties for that field appear in the lower half of the window, as shown in Figure 23-6.

You can set any of the field properties by performing these steps:

1. While in the Table Design window for the table, click anywhere in the row for a field whose properties you want to set.
2. In the Field Properties portion of the Table Design window (refer back to Figure 23-6), click the General tab and click within the desired property.
3. If an arrow appears to the right of the property, click the arrow to open a list box and choose an option; otherwise, enter the desired setting. Table 23-1 lists the field properties used in Access.

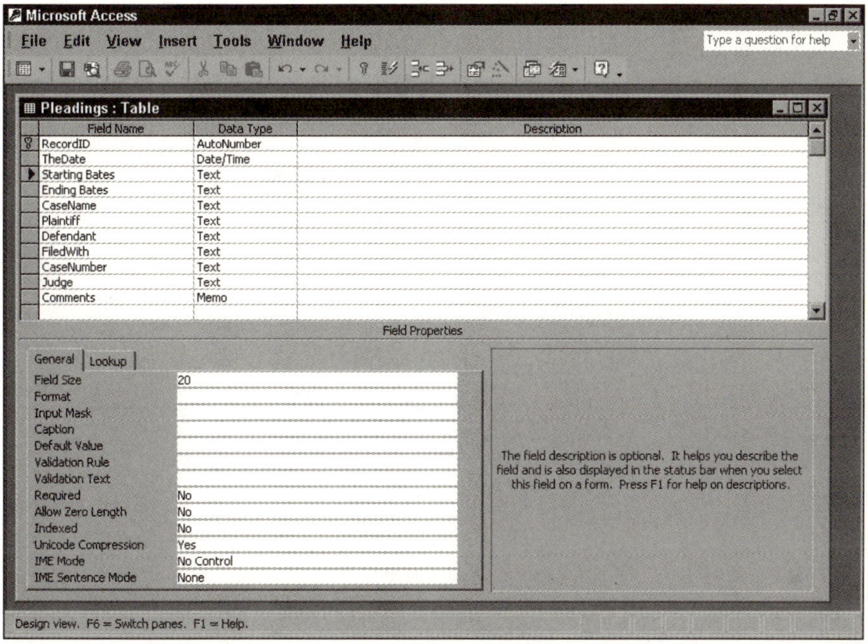

Figure 23-6: The Field properties for the Starting Bates field are shown in this example of a Table Design window.

Table 23-1
The Field Properties Used in Access

Property Name	***Use***
Field Size	Specifies the maximum length of a text field or limits the allowable values in a number field.
New Values	Used only with AutoNumber fields. Determines whether values automatically entered in the field are created in sequential order (the default) or as random values.
Format	Sets a desired format for displaying text, numbers, dates, and times. You can choose from a list of predefined formats, or you can create a custom format using valid formatting symbols.
Decimal Places	Sets the number of places that appear to the right of the decimal point.
Input Mask	Sets a pattern that data entered in the field must match. You can use predefined masks, or you can design your own.

continues

Table 23-1 continued

Property Name	***Use***
Caption	Sets a default field label that appears as the field name in forms and reports.
Default Value	Specifies a default value that automatically appears in a field when new records are added.
Validation Rule	An expression that defines a data entry rule that the data must meet before it will be accepted.
Validation Text	Specifies message text that appears if data is entered that does not meet the rule specified under Validation Rule.
Required	Determines whether an entry in the field is required for any record added to the table.
Allow Zero Length	Determines whether zero-length (empty) strings are allowed in any record added to the table.
Indexed	Names a single-field index added to speed searches.

After you make all desired additions or changes to a table's design, remember that you can save it by choosing File ⇨ Close from the menus or by double-clicking the Table icon at the upper-left corner of the Table Design window. When a dialog box appears, asking whether you want to save the changes to the table structure, click Yes and enter a name for the table, if prompted.

TIP: If you are not sure about what to enter as a property when entering property settings for field types, you can easily obtain help with these settings. Click anywhere within the property in the lower portion of the window and press F1. A help window appears with a detailed explanation of the settings.

Adding and Editing Data in a Table

You can add and edit data in an Access table using Datasheet view. In *Datasheet view*, the table has a row-and-column format (similar to that of an Excel worksheet), and you can type data directly into the datasheet of the table. When viewed using Datasheet view, every table in Access contains a blank record, which appears at the bottom of the datasheet (see Figure 23-7). In Figure 23-7, the empty row containing an asterisk at the far left is the blank record.

When you open a new table in Datasheet view, the table contains just one blank row. As soon as you begin entering data, a new blank record appears directly beneath the existing record. You can move from one field to the next by pressing the Tab key or the Enter key. Pressing Tab at the end of the last field in the table moves you to the next blank record, and you can continue the process of data entry.

When entering data, keep in mind that there are some fields you cannot edit in Access. You cannot edit any of the following types of fields:

- **AutoNumber fields:** Access automatically increments and stores values in AutoNumber fields. After the record exists, Access does not let you change the value.

- ♦ **Locked fields:** When a field's Enabled property is set to No or its Locked property is set to Yes, you cannot edit the contents of the field.
- ♦ **Fields in certain types of queries:** You cannot edit some fields in queries that establish relationships between more than one table, and you cannot edit totals in some queries.
- ♦ **Calculated fields:** Because calculated fields do not exist as a separate field (but are displayed as a calculation based on one or more fields), you can't edit these fields.

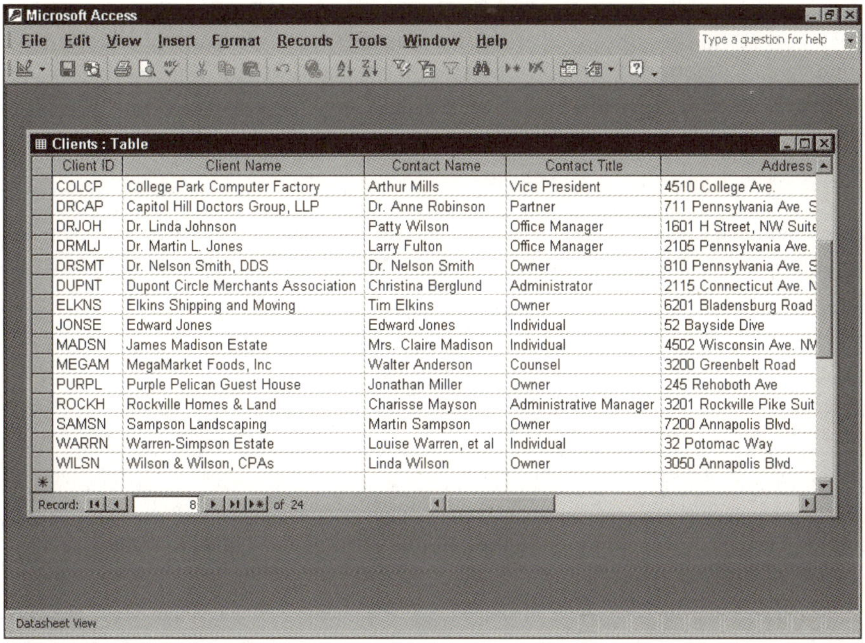

Figure 23-7: Datasheet view for a table

Working with memo fields

You can enter data in memo fields by typing it directly into the field, but it is often difficult or impossible to view all of the data simultaneously. One easy way around this problem is to open the Zoom box for the memo field, using the Zoom key combination (Shift+F2). Place the insertion pointer anywhere in the memo field and then press Shift+F2. When you do this, a Zoom box into the memo field opens.

In the text box of the Zoom dialog box, type the entry (or make changes to any existing entry in the field). When you're done, you can click OK to close the Zoom dialog box and then return to viewing or editing data in Datasheet view.

Adding data to OLE Object fields

As mentioned earlier in the chapter, you can specify OLE Object as a field type in an Access table. OLE Object fields store OLE data, such as word processing documents, spreadsheets, and sound or video clips. When you need to insert OLE data into an OLE Object field, follow these steps:

1. In the Windows application that contains the data you want to insert in the Access field, select the desired data.

2. Choose Edit ⇨ Copy.
3. In Access, place the insertion pointer in the OLE Object field of the desired record and choose Edit ⇨ Paste. A copy of the data appears in the field.

Editing and deleting records

To edit data in Datasheet view, place the insertion pointer at the location where you want to make the desired changes and make your needed corrections, using the Backspace or Delete keys as needed. To delete a record, place the insertion pointer anywhere in the unwanted record and then choose Edit ⇨ Delete Record from the menus. Remember that in Access, after you confirm the deletion, the deletion is permanent. After you delete a record, there's no way to get it back (short of reentering the entire record from scratch).

Printing a Table

At times, you may want to print a table directly from Datasheet view. (The printout will resemble the table's layout when in Datasheet view; if you want a more precise design, you can create a report.)

CROSS-REFERENCE: Chapter 26 details the techniques for creating a report.

To print a table from Datasheet view, use these steps:

1. Open the desired table in Datasheet view.
2. If you want to print a select group of records, sort the table so that the records appear in one continuous group. Then select the group of records by clicking and dragging along the record selectors at the left edge of the table.
3. From the menus, choose File ⇨ Print. The Print dialog box appears.
4. To print all the records, click OK. To print a select group of records, turn on the Selected Records option and then click OK.

Finding Data

As your tables grow in size, you need a way to search for specific records. An easy way to do this is with the Edit ⇨ Find command. (You can also search for a specific group of records, using a query.)

CROSS-REFERENCE: See Chapter 24 for details about queries.

Use these steps to search for a record while in Datasheet view:

1. Click anywhere within the field that you want to search.
2. From the menus, choose Edit ⇨ Find (or press Ctrl+F).
3. In the Find and Replace dialog box that appears, enter the text you want to search for in the Find What box.
4. Make sure that the Look In box is set to the name of the field that you want to search.
5. In the Match box, choose one of the following:

- **Any Part of Field:** To search for any part of the string
- **Whole Field:** To find a record only when the entire field's contents match the search term
- **Start of Field:** To start a search from the beginning of the field

6. To find the first occurrence of the search term, click the Find Next button. You can use the same button on successive searches to find additional occurrences of the same search term.

Changing the Appearance of a Table

If you do a significant amount of work with your tables in Datasheet view, you will probably want to change the appearance of the data to suit your preferences. You can change the width of columns, change the height of rows, hide columns, move columns to new locations, and even change the fonts used to view the data.

- **To change a column's width:** Place the insertion pointer over the right edge of the top of the column until it changes into a double-headed arrow. Click and drag the column to the desired width.
- **To change the row height:** Place the insertion pointer at the left edge of the table between any two record selectors until it changes into a double-headed vertical arrow. Click and drag the row to the desired height.
- **To move a column to a different location:** First, select the column you want to move by clicking its field selector at the top of the column. Then click the column and drag it to its new location.
- **To hide or show a column:** Click the column's field selector (at the top of the column) to select it and then choose Format ⇨ Hide Columns from the menus. (To show a column that was hidden earlier, choose Format ⇨ Unhide Column and select the column that you want to show in the dialog box that appears.)
- **To change the fonts used to display the data:** Choose Format ⇨ Font from the menus. In the dialog box that appears, select the desired font, font style, and size; then click OK.

Adding Indexes

Previously we mentioned the use of primary keys as a means of ordering records in your tables. Additionally, you can add indexes to any of the fields in a table. An *index* provides a way for Access to internally order the records of your table. This speeds performance when you need to do searches and generate reports with the records arranged in a certain order. (Note that you cannot index on Yes/No, OLE Object, or memo fields.) You can add an index by performing the following steps.

1. Open the desired table in Design view and click anywhere within the field that you want to index.
2. At the bottom of the window, click the General tab (if it isn't already visible).
3. In the Index Properties box at the bottom of the window, click the arrow to open the list and choose Yes (Duplicates OK) or Yes (No Duplicates). If you choose Yes (Duplicates OK), you allow the existence of more than one record with the same data in this field. Choosing Yes (No Duplicates) prohibits multiple records with the same value in the field.

If you want to add an index based on more than one field, the procedure is a little different. You need to perform these steps:

1. Open the desired table in Design view.
2. Click anywhere in the field where you want to add the index.
3. Click the Indexes button in the toolbar, or choose View ⇨ Indexes to open the Indexes dialog box, shown in Figure 23-8.
4. In the Index Name column, enter a name for the index.
5. Click in the Field Name column, choose the first field that you want to use as the basis of the index from the list box, and then choose Ascending or Descending (your choice) in the Sort Order column.
6. In successive rows of the window, repeat steps 4 and 5 for each additional field on which you want to base the index.

As an example, the multiple index shown in Figure 23-8 and titled *Date and Source* is based on a combination of the Date of Document and Source fields. When creating indexes based on multiple fields, remember that the name for the multiple-field index should be included only in the row of the first field that you choose. (Until Access encounters a row containing a different index name, it treats all rows in the Index dialog box as belonging to the same index.)

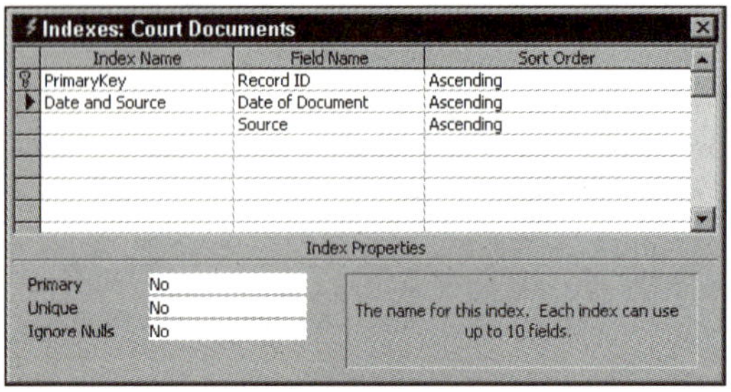

Figure 23-8: A multiple index based on date of document and source fields

Establishing Relationships between Tables

One of the most powerful features of Access is the capability to establish relationships among multiple tables. You can establish relationships in Access with the Tools ⇨ Relationships command. After you establish relationships in Access, the relationship is automatically used to link fields in the queries, forms, and reports that you create. Although you're not required to establish relationships between tables, this feature saves you time and ensures proper end results when you are designing complex forms and reports.

Another advantage of establishing relationships among tables is that you can use *referential integrity*, a feature that requires relationships between tables. Referential integrity is a feature that Access uses to automatically protect data against certain changes or deletions that would break the links between records in related tables. For example, if you have a table of clients and a related table of all phone calls made to those clients, the referential integrity feature of Access would prevent you from adding a phone call for a client who does not exist. (For more on relationships, see the sidebar "Understanding relationships between tables," near the end of this chapter.)

You can view the relationships that you establish at the database level in the Relationships window, which you open by choosing Tools ⇨ Relationships from the Tools menu. Figure 23-9 shows an example of the Relationships window. In this example, the Relationships window is based on the Firm Marketing Database described in Chapter 31.

You establish relationships at the table level by performing the following 10 steps (continued after the sidebar):

1. With the tables visible in the Database window, choose Tools ⇨ Relationships (or right-click the Tables button of the Database window and choose Relationships from the shortcut menu). The Relationships window appears. If you are establishing the relationship for the first time, the window opens to the Show Table dialog box.

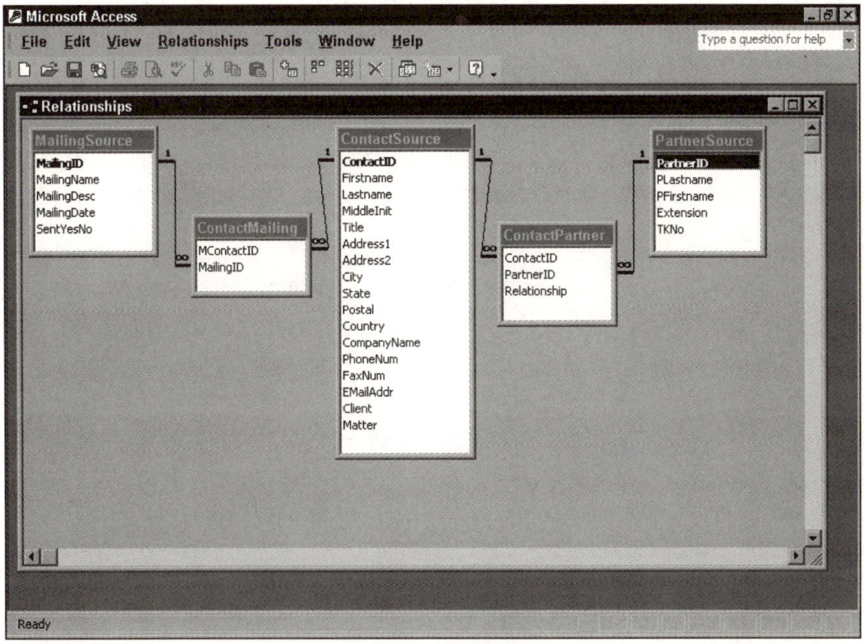

Figure 23-9: The Relationships window used by the Firm Marketing Database (described in Chapter 31)

2. Click the Tables tab to view the tables in the database, or click the Queries tab to view the queries in the database. To view tables and queries simultaneously, click the Both tab. Select the table or query that you want to use as a part of the relationship and click Add to add the table or query to the Relationships window.
3. Repeat Step 2 for each table or query you want to add to the window and then click Close. (In the case of this example, each table — first the Calls table and then the Clients table — is selected and the Add button is used to add the table to the Relationships window.) The order in which you add the tables or queries does not matter, as long as you add all the tables or queries needed for the relationship.
4. To create the links between tables that form the relationship, drag the field(s) you want to use for the link from the primary table or query to the matching field(s) of the related table or query. (In most relationships, the primary key of the first table or query is related to a similar field of the second table or query.) After you drag and drop the field, the Edit Relationships dialog box appears.
5. If needed, you can change the selected fields that Access suggests in the Edit Relationships dialog box. (Access usually suggests the best possible relationship, based on which field in one

table or query matches a field in the other table or query, but sometimes its best guess is not what you prefer to use.)

Understanding relationships between tables

If you plan on working with related data in Access, you should be familiar with the various types of relationships that you can establish between tables. PC-based database managers support three types of relationships: *one-to-one, one-to-many,* and *many-to-many*. The names represent the number of records in the first, or *parent*, table that are related to the number of records in the second, or *child*, table.

One-to-one

When a field in one record (and only one record) of a table relates to a field in one record (and only one record) in another table, you have a *one-to-one* relationship. For example, a personnel database may contain two tables, with one table having an employee social security number and a corresponding last name, first name, address, and phone number for each employee. The other table might also have an employee social security number and a corresponding department, supervisor name, and salary for each employee. The tables could be linked by the social security number, which would be unique for each employee. Because one record in the table of employee names and addresses would be linked to only one record in the table of employee departments and salaries, the relationship between the tables would be considered to be a one-to-one relationship.

One-to-many

The most common type of relationship you will have between your tables is known as a *one-to-many* relationship. In such a case, one record in a table can be related to one or more records in another table. A common, legal-specific example involves a table of client names and addresses and a corresponding table of phone calls made to those clients. Any single client can have one or more phone calls placed to that client, so in the database you could track this information with a table of clients and a related table of phone calls. In the example described, one record in the clients table could be related to any number of records in the phone calls table. However, each record in the phone calls table would be related to one (and only one) client in the clients table. Hence, the name *one-to-many relationship*.

Many-to-many

Finally, a less common type of relationship (but one that you sometimes need) is the many-to-many relationship. With this relationship, many records in one table can be related to many records in another table. A common example involves the tracking of students assigned to training classes. Any single class can be related to a group of students, and any single student can be related to a group of classes. Access does not directly support the creation of a many-to-many relationship, but you can indirectly support a many-to-many relationship by combining two one-to-many relationships, with the table on the "one" side of both relationships serving as a common table. The Firm Marketing Database, supplied on the CD-ROM and described in Chapter 31, makes use of a many-to-many relationship between a law firms' outside contacts and the attorneys within the firm. Because any attorney can have multiple contacts and any single contact can be connected with more than one attorney inside a law firm, a many-to-many relationship was needed for the design of this database.

When to establish relationships and which type to use

If you are just starting to work with relational databases, two of the hardest concepts to grasp firmly are when you should use relationships and how you should structure them. No hard-and-fast rules exist to answer these questions, but thinking about how your data needs to appear in forms and reports supported by your relational queries can be helpful. Typically, an indication that relationships between tables are needed is evident when you find yourself duplicating data repeatedly. For example, entering the same case number or the same deposition name again and again in a table of records is a good indication that the table's data might better exist within two tables, with a common field used to establish a relationship between the tables.

NOTE: Fields that you use to establish a relationship do not have to have the same name, but they must have the same field type (with the exception of AutoNumber fields, which you can relate to Number fields).

6. If you want to use referential integrity, click the Enforce Referential Integrity check box. When the box is turned on, you can also use the options shown below it if you want.
7. When the Cascade Update Related Fields option is on, changes made to the linking field in the first table or query are automatically updated in the fields of a related table or query containing the same data. When the Cascade Delete Related Records option is on, the deletion of records in the first table or query automatically deletes associated records in the linked table or query.
8. If the default relationship type that Access suggests is not what you want, choose the desired type of relationship (One-to-One or One-to Many) by clicking the Join Type button. When you do this, the Join Properties dialog box appears. Select a desired type of join and then click OK to close the Join Properties dialog box. (When you close it, the Edit Relationships dialog box is still visible.) In most cases, you will use a one-to-many relationship.

CROSS-REFERENCE: See the sidebar "Understanding relationships between tables" for help with types of relationships.

9. Click the Create button in the Edit Relationships dialog box to create the relationship. When you do so, the Edit Relationships dialog box closes and a join line appears between the two tables in the Relationships window. Refer to Figure 23-9 for examples of this line. Note the tiny symbols (a number *1* and an infinity symbol) beside the linking field in the field lists. Those symbols refer to the relationship type established, with *1* meaning *one* and the infinity symbol meaning *many*.
10. Repeat Steps 1–8 for every relationship that you want to add between tables. When you're finished, close the Relationships window. When Access asks whether you want to save the changes to the relationship, click Yes.

NOTE: You can edit existing relationships by opening the Relationships window as described earlier and then double-clicking any line between two tables. This action opens the Edit Relationships dialog box, where you can make design changes. To delete a relationship, click the line connecting the tables and press Delete.

Using External Data in Access

It's pretty common these days to have to deal with data that exists in a wide variety of formats. The data you want may be stored in spreadsheet form or in a file format used by another database manager, such as Corel Paradox. Access provides unusual flexibility because it not only can import data from a variety of sources but also can link to tables in other file formats. This powerful feature enables Access to work with data in its native format. (Microsoft originally chose the name *Access* to emphasize the product's flexibility in dealing with different types of data.)

When you want to use Access to use data stored in other file formats, you have two choices. First, you can *import* the data into an Access database where Access stores it in an Access table in its own format. Or you can *link* to the table stored in the different file format and work with the data without changing its file format. (In some older versions of Access, the process of linking to another table is called *attaching*.)

There are some tasks that you cannot perform on linked tables. You cannot make changes to the table's structure, nor can you add primary keys to a linked table. You cannot establish any rules for referential integrity, and you also cannot create relationships between multiple tables, although you can get around this limitation by designing relational queries. In addition, there are limitations as far as data entry, editing, and deletions are concerned, depending on the type of file you are linked to. These limitations are further detailed in the paragraphs that follow.

- **Linking text files:** With text files, Access lets you link to delimited or to fixed-width text. You can't edit existing records in the linked text file, nor can you delete existing records. Access does, however, let you add new records to the linked table.
- **Linking Excel spreadsheets:** When you link to an Excel spreadsheet, Access lets you add new records or edit existing data. However, you cannot perform deletions of records.
- **Linking dBASE and Paradox tables or Microsoft Outlook/Exchange data:** With linked dBASE or Paradox tables, Outlook .PST files, and Exchange data, you have full add/edit/delete capabilities. You can also select a corresponding dBASE index file when you establish the link. If you link to a dBASE III file, you can select a corresponding NDX file as the index file during the linking process. Linking to a dBASE IV or a dBASE V file allows you to choose MDX files as indexes. (Note that with linked Exchange data, although you can edit or delete records, this is *not* usually a good idea on the Exchange side unless you know what you are doing. If in doubt, check with your firm's Exchange Server administrator before attempting to use Access to make changes to data stored on an Exchange Server.)
- **Linking XML and HTML Files:** You can link to XML and HTML files (typically, these are stored on a firm or organization intranet). When you link to an HTML file, Access gives you the option of using the first row of the file as field names in the linked tables. With XML files, Access uses the XML tags to establish default field names in the linked tables. Linked XML/HTML files are the most restrictive of all linked files: you can only view the data. Access does not support any additions, edits, or deletions to a linked HTML file.

Importing and linking files

When you need to use data that's stored in another format in an Access database, you can import the data, or you can link to the external file. You import or link external data to an Access database by performing these steps:

1. Make sure that the Database window is the active window. To import data, choose File ⇨ Get External Data ⇨ Import. To link data, choose File ⇨ Get External Data ⇨ Link Tables.
2. In the Files of Type list box, choose the data source. (Your options include files stored in other Access databases, text files, Excel files, Microsoft Exchange or Outlook (.PST) files, HTML files, Paradox files, dBASE files, Lotus 1-2-3 files, XML documents, and data files supported by ODBC drivers.)
3. Use the Look In list box and the Up One Level button in the dialog box to locate the file you want to import; then click the file to select it.
4. Click the Import button (or if you are linking, the Link button). Access imports the file or establishes a link to the file. When you import files from a foreign file format, a dialog box for the Import Wizard appears, and you can follow the directions in the dialog box to determine which rows and columns of the foreign file you want to import.

TIP: If you import data on a regular basis, you can combine the techniques in this section with those detailed in Chapter 27 to create macros that import data. In macros, you can add macro actions that are specifically designed to import (or export) data. These actions include the Transfer Database, Transfer Spreadsheet, and Transfer Text actions.

Deciding whether to import or link

Because Access offers both methods, when making use of external data, you may quickly face a decision as to whether you should import the data or link to existing tables stored in some other data format. In general, if you are going to work with the data exclusively in Access, importing the data makes sense. Access can work most effectively with data that is in its own format. Another advantage to importing (in addition to speed) is that you don't face the limitations with imported data that you do with linked data. After you import the data into native Access format, the tables containing the data are no different from Access tables that you create from scratch. You can change their structure (something you cannot do with linked tables) and you can take advantage of the full range of field properties, such as validation rules and default values.

On the other hand, when you need to share data with existing applications that use the other database file formats (such as dBASE or Paradox), linking is the way to go. Linking also saves disk space when compared to importing if you are going to maintain the file in its original format elsewhere. Table 23-2 summarizes the important differences between importing and linking.

Table 23-2

The Differences between Importing and Linking

Imported Table	*Linked Table*
Data is copied directly into an Access table.	Data is linked to the Access table.
Access responds faster in adding, editing, and retrieving data.	Access runs more slowly when working with the data than it would if the data was imported.
You can make changes to table structure and add primary keys.	You cannot change table structure or add primary keys. In some cases, edits to the data are not allowed (as with HTML and XML data).
Referential integrity can be implemented and enforced from Access.	Referential integrity cannot be implemented from within Access (although it may be possible, using the software that created the original data).
Relationships can be established at the table level with the Tools ⇨ Relationships command.	Relationships cannot be established at the table level (but you can get around this by creating relational queries).
Results in overall increase in disk space, if table is maintained in original format elsewhere.	Results in virtually no increase in the amount of disk space used.

CAUTION: If you choose to link to an existing table stored in another file format, moving the file to another drive or directory after the link has been established confuses Access. After the file has been moved and you attempt to open the database containing the linked file, Access displays a dialog box complaining that the file could not be found. If this happens, you must delete the linked table in the Database window (because it is only a link to the file, you are not deleting the actual data); then you must re-link to the data at its new location.

Compacting and Repairing a Database

As you make regular use of a database, the database file may require maintenance from time to time. As large numbers of records are deleted, Access databases should be compacted from time to time, or the database will grow unnecessarily large in size. Also, Access databases can occasionally become partially damaged because of hardware failures or system crashes in the midst of operations. When this happens, you can repair the database.

In versions of Access prior to Access 2000, compacting and repairing are individual processes. Menu options are provided to compact a database or to repair a database. Also, you have to close the database before you can compact it or repair it. Access 2002 (and its immediate predecessor, Access 2000) improves on this process by combining what were two operations into a single operation. You can use a single menu option to compact and repair a database at the same time. Also, there is no need to close the database before performing a compact and repair operation. You can use a single menu option to perform the compact and repair process.

If an Access database is in need of repair, it displays a dialog box stating that fact when you try to open the database. You can answer Yes to the prompt that asks whether you want to repair the database by performing the compact and repair operation.

To compact a database at any given time, open the database that is in need of compacting and choose Tools ⇨ Database Utilities ⇨ Compact and Repair Database. The Database window disappears, and Access performs the compact and repair process, compacting the database and validating the internal indexes for proper operation. The amount of time this process requires varies greatly, depending on the size of the database. When it is done, the Database window reappears.

NOTE: In a multiple-user environment, before you can compact and repair a database, it must be open in single-user mode. In other words, all other network users must be out of the database before you can perform the compact and repair process.

Using the Upsizing Wizard

Like many businesses with mountains of data, law firms and large corporate legal departments often stress programs such as Access to their limits when faced with any task that requires the storage of massive amounts of information and multiple users. Although Access is an excellent product, it does have its limits. For example, if you are using an Access database to track documents for a large litigation matter and you have more than 50,000 records and two dozen paralegals keying in and editing records on a daily basis, you likely have already encountered these limits. You may find that the database "locks up" too often, that you must compact and repair the database on an ongoing basis, and that multiple users regularly encounter situations in which one user's process of making edits temporarily prevents other users from getting to the data. In this case, it isn't the size of the database as much as the number of simultaneous users that is causing your problems. (Chances are that the same 50,000-plus record database could be used day in and day out by one or two users and you would experience no problems.)

In theory, an Access database can be shared by up to 255 simultaneous users. But a practical reality is generally very different than those theoretical limits. The number of simultaneous users you can have without experiencing problems varies, depending on a number of factors, including the speed of your network, the users' computers, and the ratio of changes to records (additions and edits) as opposed to read-only operations (such as running queries and producing reports). How many simultaneous users are too many? The number is open to wide debate even among expert Access developers. Some warn of problems with Access databases used by ten people simultaneously, whereas others claim success and minimal problems with more than a hundred simultaneous users. Much depends on how your group of users makes use of the database. If no one (or only one person) is adding and editing records and all the other users are running queries or printing reports, Access can get much closer to that theoretical maximum of 255 users. But the general consensus among a wide swath of Access experts is that with routine adding and editing of records, you can run into problems when you move beyond the range of 10 to 20 simultaneous users.

If you are running the industrial-strength database known as Microsoft SQL Server (versions 6.5, 7.0, or 2000), you can move your Access data from an Access database into what is known as a *client/server* environment, in which the tables containing the data reside on the SQL Server and the forms and reports that you use remain within the Access database. Microsoft SQL Server is designed to handle massive amounts of data and thousands of users, and SQL Server databases do not experience the corruption problems that Access databases regularly encounter when being edited by many users. The Upsizing Wizard is a feature of Access that lets you easily copy data from an existing Access database to a SQL Server running on your network. Note that although the Upsizing Wizard works with SQL Server versions 6.5, 7.0, and 2000, if your server is running version 6.5, Service Pack 5 must be installed on the server before the Upsizing Wizard can be used.

CAUTION: Before using the Upsizing Wizard, it is *vital* that you talk to the SQL Server administrator at your firm or organization (or to whomever is responsible for maintaining your SQL Server). The Upsizing Wizard has the power to make major modifications to an existing SQL Server, and these modifications could cause serious performance problems with other programs that are using the SQL Server (such as your time-and-billing software). Before moving any Access database onto an existing SQL Server, someone should take the time to make sure that sufficient space exists on the SQL Server, that proper maintenance procedures are in place, and that the database design for the Access tables is a sound design to begin with.

After you have discussed the issue of moving your data to SQL Server with the appropriate person in your organization, you can perform the following steps to make use of the Upsizing Wizard:

1. Log on to the network that has the SQL Server available.
2. Start Access and open the database containing the tables that you want to move to SQL Server.
3. From the menus, choose Tools ⇨ Database Utilities ⇨ Upsizing Wizard. In a moment, the first dialog box of the Upsizing Wizard appears.

4. Choose Use Existing Database if you want to place the Access tables into a database that already exists on the SQL Server, or choose Create New Database to create a new database on the SQL Server. Then click Next. (Unless you are intimately familiar with the design of an existing database on your SQL Server, we don't recommend the first option because it could result in unwanted changes to an existing SQL Server database.) After you make your choices, the second dialog box of the Upsizing Wizard appears.
5. In this dialog box, enter the name assigned to your SQL Server, the Login ID and password for the SQL Server, and a name you want to assign to the new database that will be created on the SQL Server (or if you chose Existing, the name of the existing database on the SQL Server). In a moment, the third dialog box of the Upsizing Wizard appears.
6. Under Available Tables, double-click the tables that you want to move to your SQL Server, and the tables will appear in the Export to SQL Server list box at the right side of the dialog box. When you're done choosing tables, click Next to display the fourth dialog box of the Upsizing Wizard.
7. Here you can decide what attributes of the tables, in addition to your table data, you want to move to SQL Server. You can choose to move indexes, validation rules, defaults, and table relationships. If you choose to include table relationships, you must also decide whether to use DRI or triggers on the SQL Server (ask your SQL Server administrator for details on which choice you should make; it's a topic far too technical for discussion in this book). You can also choose whether to create *timestamp fields*, which are a type of field used by SQL Server, to the new tables. Also, you can choose whether to move the data from Access (the default) or to only create the table structures with no data. Make your desired selections and then click Next to display the fifth dialog box of the Upsizing Wizard.
8. Here you can decide whether to create a new Access 2002 Application Data Project (ADP) file that will be connected to the new SQL Server tables, whether to link the new SQL Server tables to the existing Access database, or whether to just copy the data over to SQL Server while making no changes on the Access side. Make your desired selections and then click Next to display the final dialog box of the Upsizing Wizard.
9. You can choose to open the new Access Application Data Project (.ADP) file or keep the existing Access file format database (.MDB) file open. Make your desired selection and click Next.

Access proceeds to create the tables on your SQL Server and transfer the data. This process may take some time, depending on the amount of data that is stored in your Access tables. When the process is finished, Access displays an Upsizing Wizard Report that shows the status of the process, including whether tables and indexes were copied to SQL Server and whether modifications were made to the existing Access database or a new client/server (.ADP) Access Data Project file was created. Figure 23-10 shows an example of the Upsizing Wizard Report.

By its very nature (of dealing with moving Access data to SQL Server, a rather technically complex product), the Upsizing Wizard deals with concepts — such as Access Data Projects, timestamp fields, and triggers for enforcing referential integrity — that are beyond the scope of this book. You can find more information on these subjects in more technical books that deal specifically with Access or with SQL Server. Two examples you may want to consider are *The Access 2002 Bible* by Cary N. Prague, Michael R. Irwin, and Jennifer Reardon and *SQL Server Developer's Guide* by Joseph J. Bambara and Paul R. Allen. Both can be found at your local bookstore or can be ordered through the Hungry Minds, Inc. Web site at `www.hungryminds.com`.

Also keep in mind that the availability of the Upsizing Wizard (not to mention an available SQL Server with free disk space) is *not* necessarily a panacea for performance problems you may be experiencing with a large Access database that's being used by dozens of users. If the database is poorly designed to begin with, you will see problems no matter what platform the data resides on. This isn't a book about the rigors of proper database design, but you should be aware that database design does have a major effect on performance with large databases, whether the data is stored in Microsoft Access or on a Microsoft SQL Server.

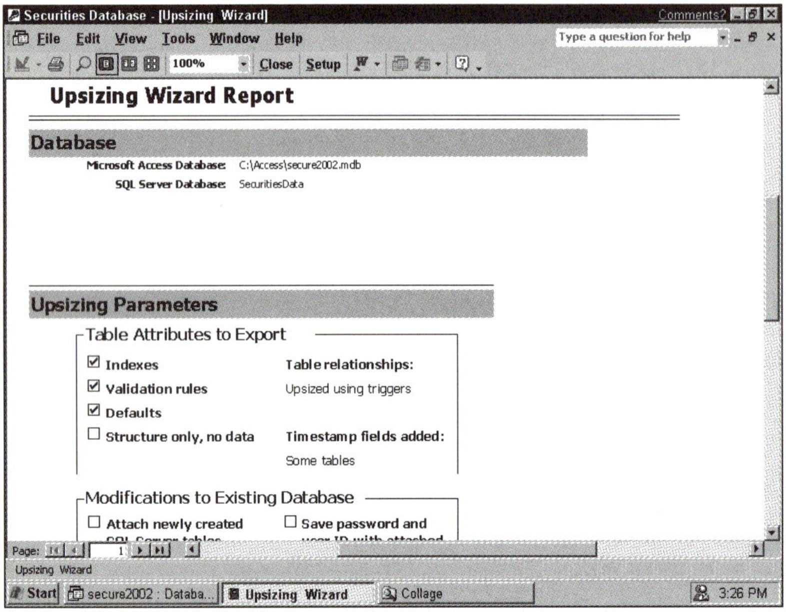

Figure 23-10: The Upsizing Wizard Report created at the end of the upsizing process

Summary

In this chapter, you learned about the core objects of Microsoft Access — tables, queries, forms, and reports — and you learned how to create new databases, which can be likened to containers that hold your tables, queries, forms, and reports. You learned how to

- Create tables, choosing field names, appropriate data types, descriptions, and field properties.
- Add primary keys to speed performance and support the use of relationships between tables.
- Add and edit data in a table, search for data, and change the appearance of a table.
- Add indexes to a table to facilitate fast retrievals and sorts of data.
- Establish relationships at the table level and use referential integrity, which requires relationships between tables to work.
- Use data stored in other file formats by importing and linking tables.
- Compact databases to conserve disk space and repair damaged databases.
- Use the Upsizing Wizard to move Access data to a Microsoft SQL Server database.

In the chapter that follows, you learn how you can obtain specific data from your tables by designing queries that retrieve the precise data needed by your forms and reports.

Chapter 24

Working with Queries

In This Chapter

- ♦ Understanding Access queries
- ♦ Creating queries
- ♦ Using criteria in queries
- ♦ Saving queries
- ♦ Printing queries
- ♦ Using queries to draw relationships
- ♦ Using parameter queries
- ♦ Using action queries
- ♦ Creating crosstab queries
- ♦ Using queries in forms and reports

IN THE PRECEDING CHAPTER, you learned how you can create tables, the foundation of data storage, in Access. You learned how to open and edit tables in Datasheet view, how to organize your tables by means of primary keys, how to search for data, and how to establish relationships between tables. In this chapter, you can learn how to put an important feature of Access queries to use in your legal applications. Access uses a technology known as *graphical query by example* to let you graphically describe the data that you want to retrieve. *Queries* are the Access objects that you use to obtain the precise data that you need from your tables and to supply that data to your forms and reports. The query by example technology built in to Access allows you to design queries by dragging objects around within a Query Design window.

Understanding Access Queries

Access offers two overall types of queries: *select queries* and *action queries*. Select queries select specific subsets of data, extract those subsets, and provide the results in the form of a visible dynaset or as a source of data for an Access form or a report. Action queries perform some sort of modification to a table. There are four types of action queries: *make-table, append, update,* and *delete*. Make-table queries create new tables containing the data extracted by the query. Append queries add selected records to an existing table, and update queries make global updates to records in a table. Finally, delete queries delete all records meeting the query's criteria. Most of the queries that you create as you use Access are likely to be select queries. Figure 24-1 shows an example of a query's design and of the results produced by the query.

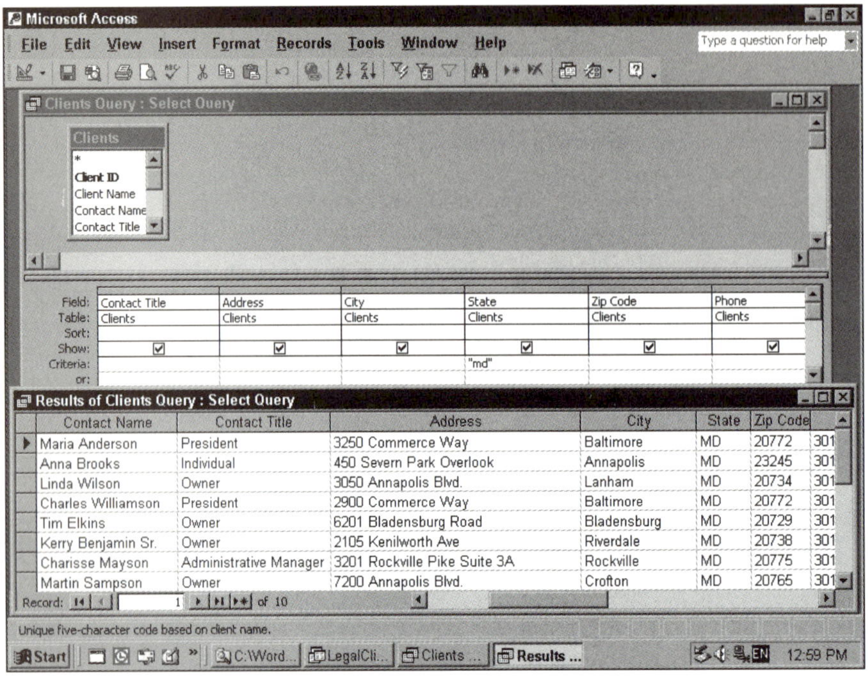

Figure 24-1: An example of a query's design and the results of the query

Some query types that are occasionally mentioned separately include *crosstab queries* and *parameter queries*. Crosstab queries are a specialized form of select query. Crosstab queries summarize data, presenting the data in a row-and-column arrangement similar to a spreadsheet. Parameter queries are also a specialized form of select query and allow users to enter different parameters used by the query into dialog boxes each time that the query runs. These types of queries are detailed at various locations in this chapter.

Queries as a data source

Many users of older PC-based database products are accustomed to using query by example as a way to generate ad hoc listings of data that meets a certain criteria. However, it is important to realize that in Access, queries can do much more than this. Access queries can be saved as a part of your database, and in their saved form, you can use them as a source of data for forms and reports. This feature of Access can save you significant amounts of time when you must develop complex database applications for use within the legal environment. Consider an example: Perhaps you are using a database that contains a large listing of depositions and you need a report that shows all depositions of a particular party. Using Access, you could create a query that retrieves all the depositions for that party and then save the design of the query. You could then base a report on that particular query. If you later changed the query's design to retrieve all the depositions for a different party, the report when reprinted would automatically contain the depositions for that new party.

By designing a form or report to make use of a query as the data source, you enable the form (or report) to automatically retrieve the most up-to-date data, based on the query. To specify a query as the data source for a form or a report, select the query by name in the New Form or New Report dialog box that appears when you create the form or report. (If the form or report already exists and you want to change it to use a particular query as a data source, change the Record Source property of the form or report to the name of the query. You can find details on how you can do this in Chapter 25 (for forms) or Chapter 26 (for reports).

Creating Queries

Access lets you create queries using various methods. You can create queries manually or use a feature known as the *Query Wizards*. The Query Wizards are designed to help you quickly create queries for special tasks, such as displaying duplicate records, finding records that lack matching records in another table, or creating numeric crosstabs. However, for typical applications within the legal environment, you need to design your own queries manually. This may sound challenging but is actually a fairly straightforward process. From the Queries tab of the Database window, you click New to open a new query. You then add the fields you want included in the query to the query design. In the Sort row, you specify any sorting conditions for the data. Finally, in the Criteria row, you enter expressions to ask any questions about the data so that the records you desire are retrieved by the query.

After you have finished designing the query, you can save it as a part of the database. At a later time, you can run the query to retrieve your desired data. To create a new query manually, use these steps:

1. In the Database Window, click the Queries tab.
2. Click New. In a moment, the New Query dialog box appears (see Figure 24-2).

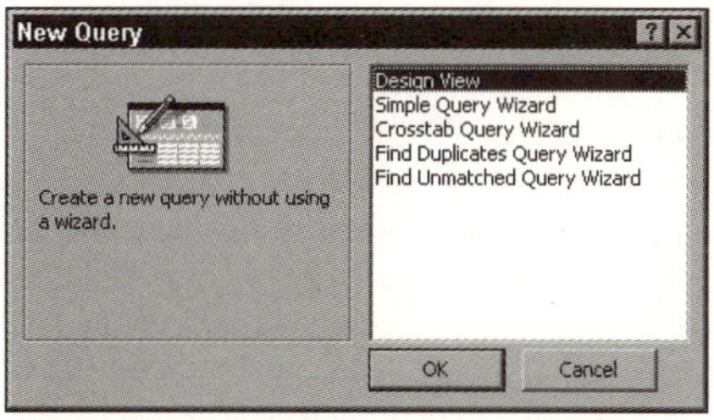

Figure 24-2: The New Query dialog box lets you select the type of query you wish to create.

3. In the dialog box, choose Design View and click OK. A new query appears in a window, and the Show Table dialog box appears above the window, as shown in Figure 24-3.

After you open a design window into a new query, you can perform many different operations as part of the design process. You can add tables to the query, add fields from the tables that you've added to the query, specify the criteria that the query uses, choose a sort order for the query, hide fields, run the query, save the query, and print the query's results. The following sections explain these operations in detail.

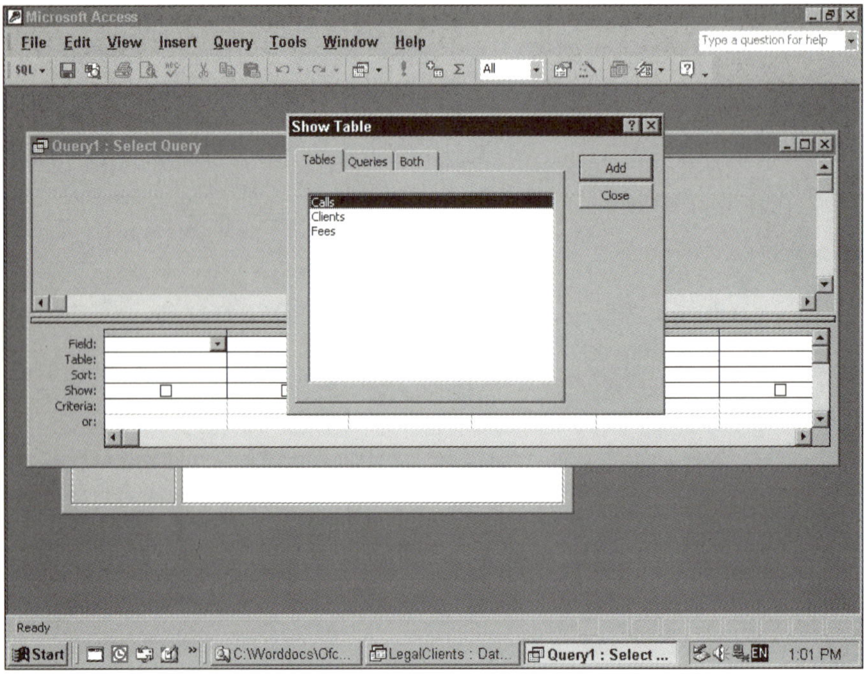

Figure 24-3: The Show Table dialog box displays existing tables and queries in the current database.

Adding tables to queries

After you have opened a Query window, the first step in the design process is to add the table or tables that provide the data you want to search. In the Show Table dialog box (refer to Figure 24-3), click the Tables tab and then click the table (or tables) that you want to use as the data source for the query. Alternatively, you can base a query on an existing query; if you want to do this, click the Queries tab and then click the existing query that you want to use as the source of data.

Queries can be based on a single table or an existing query, or they can be relational (based on more than one table or query). When you base queries on more than one table, you may need to designate the common field that links the tables (or queries) by dragging the common field from one table's list box to the other. (If you establish relationships between tables during the table design process, the link in a query will appear automatically.) When you are building a relational query, you select a table or query in the Show Table dialog box and click the Add button for every table or query that you want to add as a data source. After you have finished adding the desired tables or existing queries to the query's design, you can click Close to close the Show Table dialog box. (Relational queries are discussed in more detail at the end of the chapter.)

NOTE: If you close the Show Table dialog box and then decide that you want to add another table or existing query to the query's design, you can click the Show Table button in the toolbar or choose Query ⇨ Show Table to redisplay the Show Table dialog box.

After you close the Show Table dialog box, you have a full screen view of the Query Design window.

The Query Design window is divided into two parts. The upper portion contains the list boxes for all the tables or queries that you have added as the basis of the query. Figure 24-4 shows an example of this window. (In this example, a single table, Clients, has been added to the query design.) The lower portion contains the query grid. The *query grid* is where you specify the fields that you want to include, the criteria that control which records appear in the query, and the sorting order (if any) that you want to use to affect the query's results.

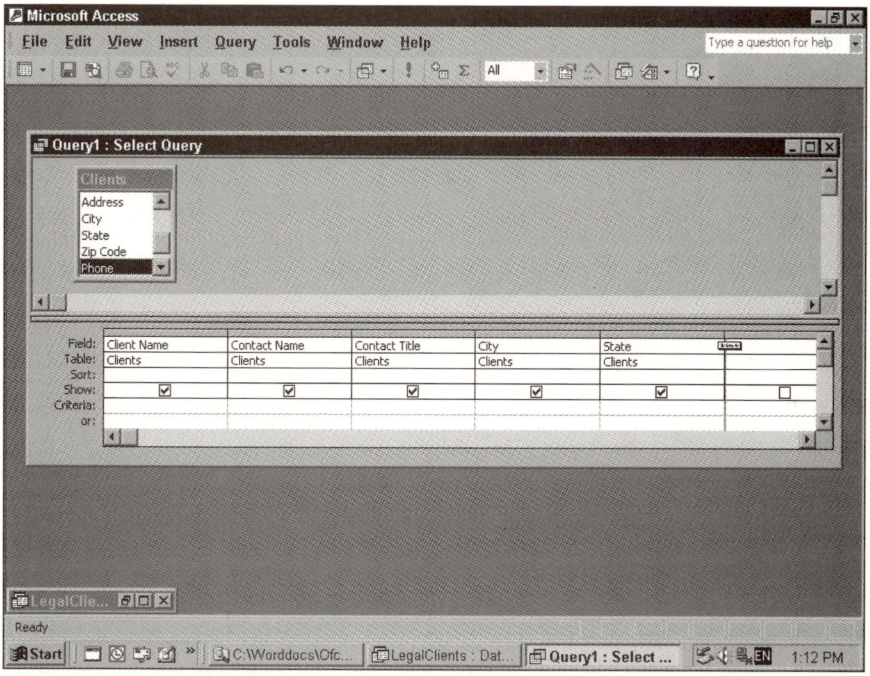

Figure 24-4: The Query Design window with the Clients table added

Adding fields to queries

After you have chosen the source of the data for the query, you tell Access which fields need to be included in the results of the query. The most commonly used method of adding fields to the query is to click and drag each desired field from the Field List to the next empty cell of the Field row in the query grid.

As an example, you might want to create a query using a table within a simple database used for tracking client names and addresses. If you wanted to create a query using the Client Name, Contact Name, Contact Title, City, State, and Phone fields from the table, you would do this by dragging each of these fields into the Field row of the query grid. Figure 24-5 shows an example based on this scenario.

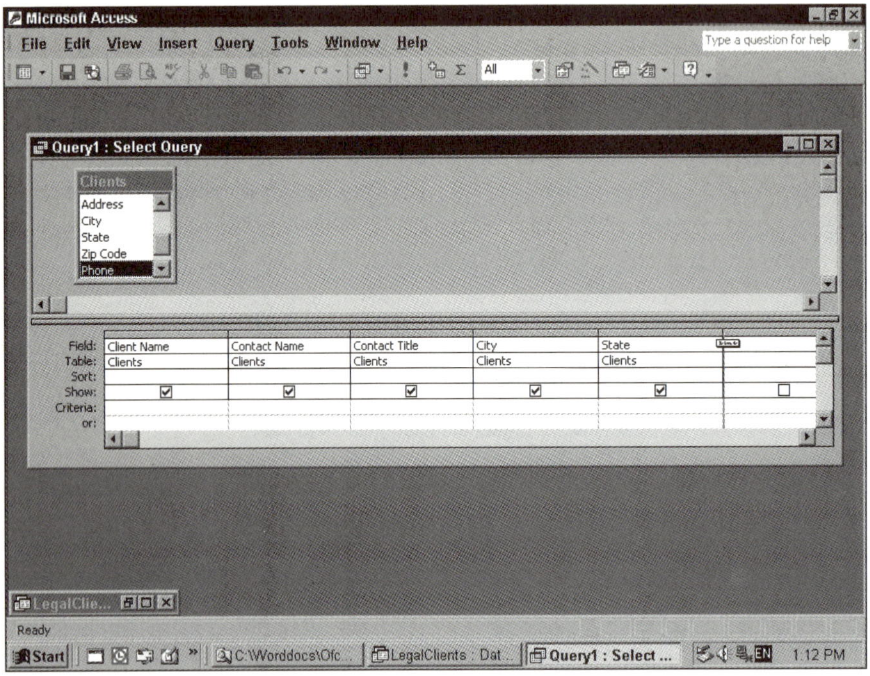

Figure 24-5: You add fields to the query by dragging them from the Field List to the Field row of the query grid.

Alternatively, you can double-click any field in the Field List to add it to the next blank column in the Field row of the query grid.

TIP: If you want to quickly add all the fields in the Field List to a query's design, double-click the title bar at the top of the Field List to highlight all the fields. Then click and drag any of the highlighted fields to the first empty cell in the Field row of the query grid. The fields will move as a group.

Rearranging, inserting, and deleting fields

As you are working with a query, you can rearrange the fields in the query grid and add new fields or remove existing fields. To move a field, click the field selector (the narrow bar directly above the field name) to highlight the entire column. Then click the selector again and drag the column to the desired position in the grid. To insert a field, click within the Field List to select the field that you wish to insert and then drag that field to the desired column within the query grid. As you do this, existing fields are moved to the right to accommodate the new field. To delete an unwanted field, click the field selector in the query grid to select the unwanted field, and press the Delete key.

Specifying sorting and selection criteria

The last step in designing the query is to specify how the data should be sorted and what criteria (or selection rules) should be used to retrieve the necessary data. To specify a sort order, use the following steps:

1. Select the field that Access should assign the highest priority to when ordering the records. As an example, if you are querying a table of clients, you may want to see the records in order of client number or client name.
2. Click in the Sort row for the field that you want Access to assign the highest priority for the sort. Then, from the drop-down list, choose the desired sort order (ascending or descending).
3. If you are sorting based on multiple fields, repeat the preceding steps for each additional field that you want to sort. (When you are sorting based on more than one field, the field of highest priority must be the leftmost field in the query grid. If needed, you can click and drag columns to different locations in the grid so that the highest-priority field for the sort is the leftmost field.)

To specify a selection criteria that determines which records should be retrieved, use these steps:

1. Click in the Criteria row inside the field that you want to use to retrieve the needed information.
2. Enter the selection criteria in the column. If you want to retrieve all records where a given field contains a certain value (such as a date or a numeric value), enter that value. If you want to retrieve all records matching a certain text string, such as a City field equal to "Washington", enter that text string. Figure 24-6 shows an example of the use of criteria in a query grid.
3. Repeat Step 2 for all additional fields where you need to specify selection criteria.

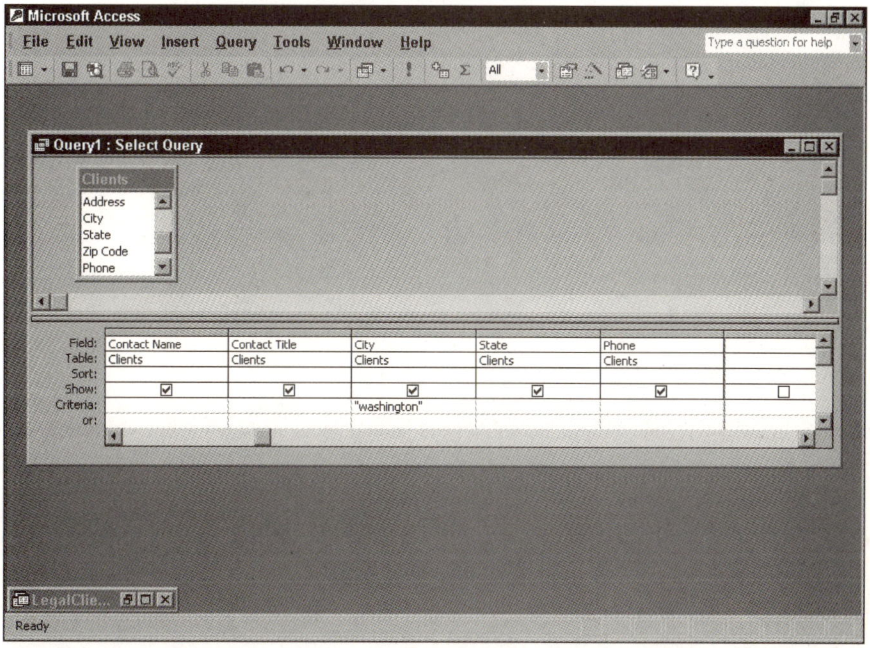

Figure 24-6: This query's selection criteria will select all records containing "Washington" in the City field.

Running queries

After you have performed all the preceding steps, you can run the query by choosing Query ⇨ Run from the menus or by clicking the Run button in the toolbar. Using either method, the desired data appears in a dynaset similar to the example shown in Figure 24-7.

TIP: If you select the Datasheet View button in the toolbar, you get a preview of what will be selected with no actions being taken if you are using an action query. This can be a useful technique for visually testing the results of an action query before performing the action. For more on action queries, see "Using Action Queries," later in the chapter.

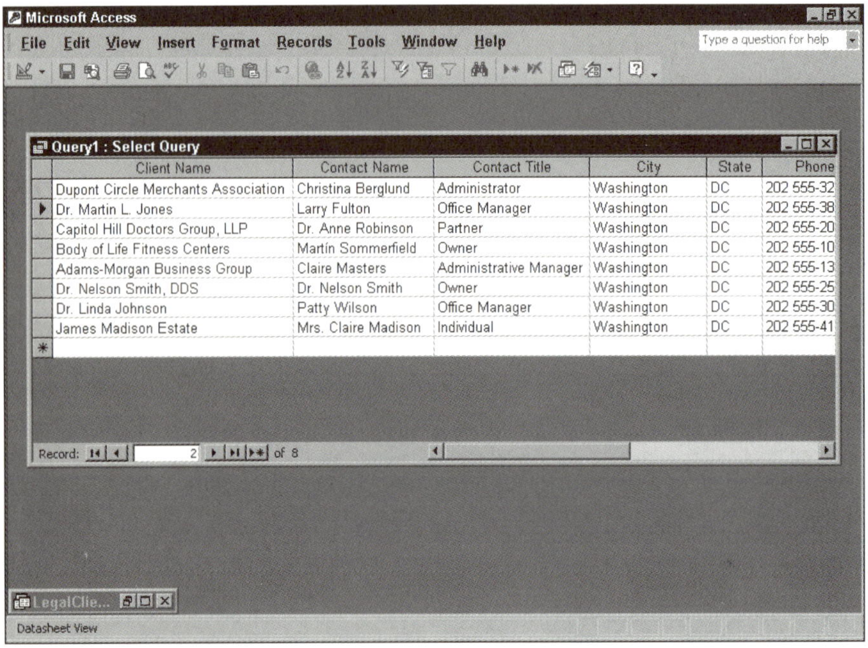

Figure 24-7: A response to a typical query is called a *dynaset*. In appearance, a dynaset resembles a table in Datasheet view.

Using Criteria in Queries

The real power behind the effective use of queries in Access lies in properly designing your criteria expressions in order to retrieve the precise data you need. With queries and criteria, actual examples best demonstrate the effective use of criteria. Hence, this portion of the chapter illustrates how you can design various select queries using the Legal Clients sample database provided in the `Legal-specific databases and files/Access/Databases` folder of the CD-ROM packaged with this book. (If you want to follow these examples, you need to copy the database file, Legal Clients.MDB, from the CD-ROM onto your hard drive.) Open the Legal Clients example database and try these steps to demonstrate the use of criteria in Access queries:

1. Click the Queries tab in the Database window; then click New.
2. Choose Design View in the list box and click OK. In the Show Tables dialog box that appears over the new Query window, click Clients, then Add, and then Close. The resultant query contains the Field List for the Clients table.
3. Double-click the title bar at the top of the Field List to highlight all the fields; then click and drag any of the highlighted fields to the Field row of the query grid, underneath the first empty column. This causes all fields in the Fields List to be added to the query grid (see Figure 24-8).

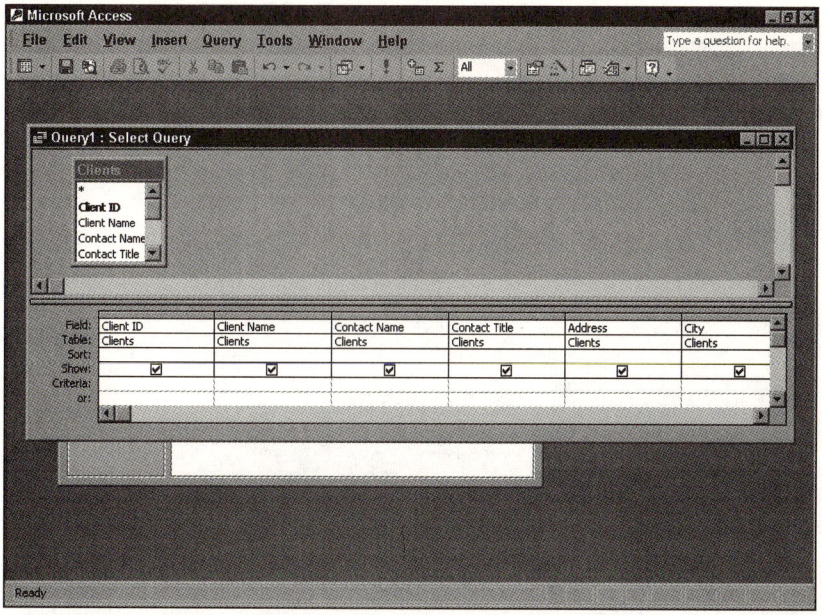

Figure 24-8: The appearance of a query in Design view with all fields added to the Customers query

4. For this example, you want to see all clients in Maryland, so use the horizontal scroll bar to scroll the query grid until the State field comes into view. Then click in the State field within the Criteria row and type **md**. (If you move out of the field, Access will automatically surround the entry with quotation marks, indicating that it is a text value.) Note that by default, entries in criteria fields of an Access query are *not* case-sensitive.
5. Click the Run button in the toolbar, or choose Query ⇨ Run from the menus. The dynaset that appears shows the records for those clients based in Maryland (see Figure 24-9).
6. Choose View ⇨ Design View to switch back from the dynaset to Design view for the query.

If you needed to see all records meeting a certain criteria in two or more fields, you would simply enter the desired criteria in each field of the query grid. For example, to see all clients based in Arlington, Virginia, you would perform these steps:

1. In the Criteria row inside the Country field, replace the entry of "md" with **va**.
2. Click in the City field within the Criteria row and enter **Arlington**.
3. Click the Run button in the toolbar, or choose Query ⇨ Run from the menus. The dynaset that appears when you do so shows the records for those clients based in Arlington, Virginia (see Figure 24-10).
4. Choose View ⇨ Design View to switch back from the dynaset to Design view for the query.

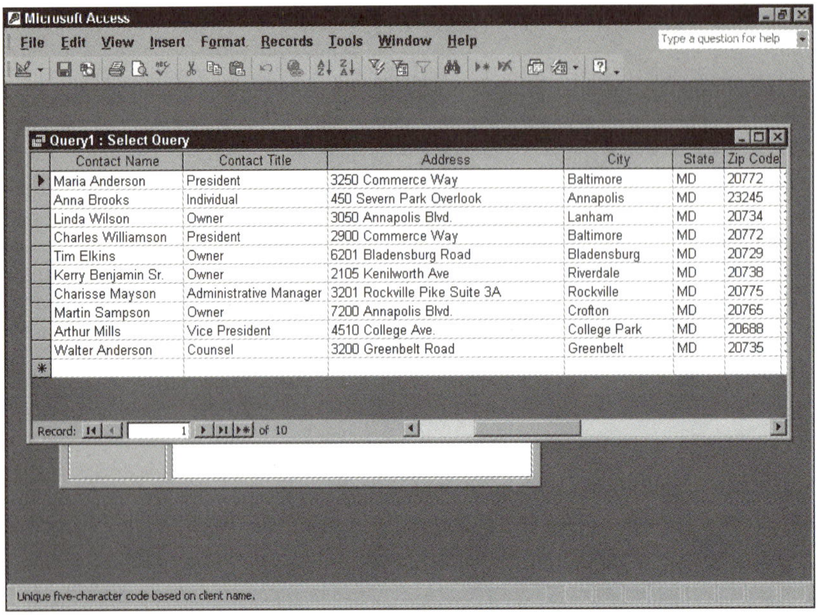

Figure 24-9: The results of a query containing a text criteria of "MD", meaning all clients based in Maryland

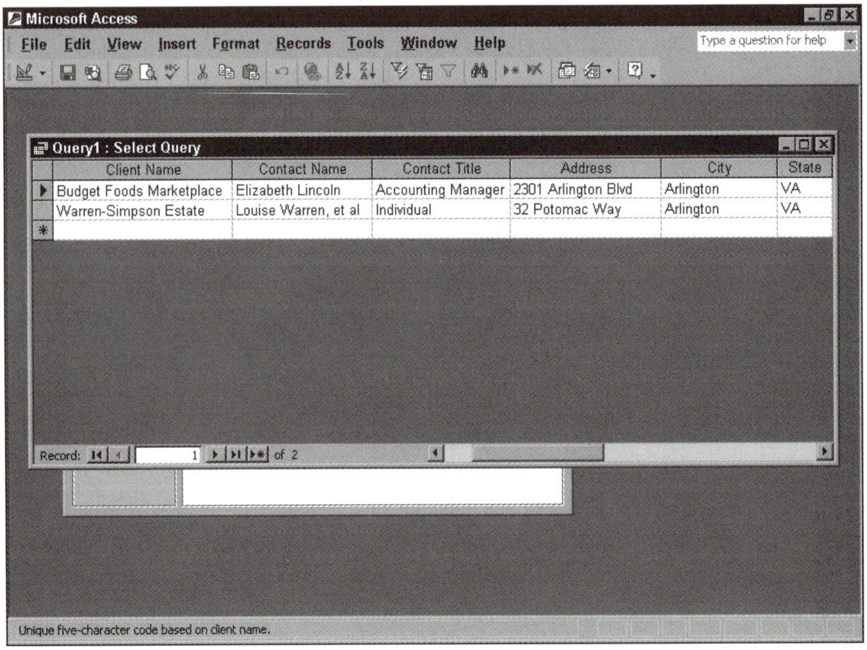

Figure 24-10: The results of a query for clients based in Arlington, Virginia

When you enter criteria into the Criteria row of a query grid, you are entering expressions that define conditions the data must meet before it will be included in the results of the query. As an example, entering *San Diego* in a Criteria row underneath a City column would cause Access to retrieve only those records containing the words *San Diego* in the City field of a table. If a table of records documenting the hours spent on a case by a group of paralegals contained an Hours Worked field, you could enter *>=10 and <=100* in a Criteria row underneath the Hours Worked column of a query to cause Access to retrieve only those records with amounts between ten and one hundred hours in the Hours Worked field of the table.

When you need to specify more than one condition for a query, you can do so using either of two methods. You can enter the desired conditions in multiple columns of the query grid, or you can include OR statements as part of the expressions that you enter. For example, in a table of employees for a law firm with multiple branches in different cities, you could enter *Johnson* in the Criteria row underneath the Last Name column, and you could enter *New York* in the Criteria row underneath the City column. This would cause Access to retrieve all records containing the name *Johnson* in the Last Name field and *New York* in the City field of the underlying table. Alternatively, you could enter *San Diego* in the first criteria row underneath the City column and *San Francisco* in the second criteria row underneath the City column. This would cause Access to retrieve records with either the phrase *San Diego* or *San Francisco* in the City field of the underlying table.

The secret to effective design of select queries involves constructing your expressions properly to obtain the data that you need. Although the examples cited in this chapter have been relatively simple, you can use operators to build very complex expressions for your query criteria. Operators that are commonly used include the math operators (such as >, <, >=, <=, <>) and the logical operators (such as AND, OR, and NOT). Table 24-1 provides examples of typical criteria that are commonly used in creating queries.

Table 24-1
Examples of Criteria Used in Typical Queries

Field	***Criteria Expression***	***Results of Criteria***
City	"Dallas"	Retrieves records containing *Dallas* in the City field
City	"Dallas" or "Houston"	Retrieves records containing *Dallas* or *Houston* in the City field
City	NOT "Chicago"	Retrieves records containing any entry except *Chicago* in the City field
Last Name	Like "G*"	Retrieves records containing last names that begin with the letter *G*
Last Name	Like "[A-M]*"	Retrieves records containing last names that begin with any letters from *A* to *M*
Last Name	Like "Th*"	Retrieves records containing last names that begin with the letters *Th*
Salary	< = 12.50	Retrieves records containing amounts of 12.50 or less in the Salary field
Salary	Between 15.00 and 20.00	Retrieves records containing amounts from 15.00 to 20.00 in the Salary field
Hire Date	<= Date( ) – 60	Retrieves records containing entries in the Hire Date field which are 60 days old or more
Deposition Date	Year([Deposition Date]) = 2001	Retrieves records containing entries in the Deposition Date field during calendar year 2001

Building queries based on OR criteria

Until now, the examples provided in this chapter have described queries that retrieve records based on one criteria "AND" another criteria being true. Because both criteria must be true, the type of criteria used is known as *AND logic*. Another type of criteria that you will often need is referred to as *OR logic*. In this case, the records are retrieved if one criteria "OR" another criteria evaluates as true. Here's a real-world example, again using the Clients table in the Legal Clients sample database. Assuming that you need to retrieve all records for clients based in Washington or Baltimore, using such OR logic in Access is a simple matter. You add the additional criteria on multiple lines below the first criteria, using as many lines as are needed. As an example, consider the query shown in Figure 24-11.

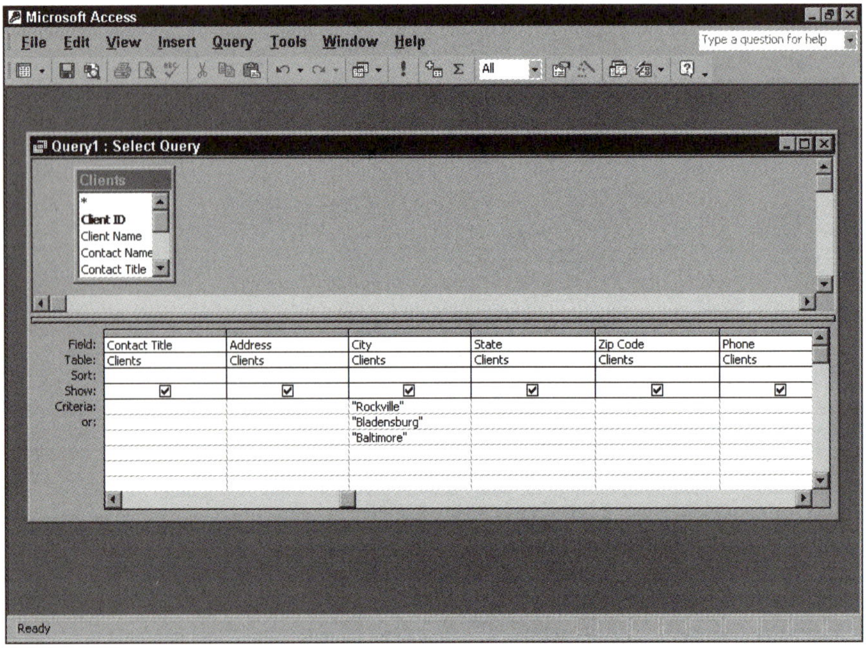

Figure 24-11: An example of a query using OR logic to select records in which the City field contains *Rockville, Bladensburg,* or *Baltimore.*

In this example, expressions have been entered in three Criteria rows underneath the City field. Because the entries are *Rockville*, *Bladensburg*, and *Baltimore*, the query will retrieve only those records in which the entries in the City field are *Rockville*, *Bladensburg*, or *Baltimore*.

Combining AND and OR criteria

Often, you will find it necessary to mix the use of AND and OR criteria in the same query to achieve the desired results. Again, using the Legal Clients sample database as a basis for an example, you might need a listing of all clients for whom the Contact Title field contains "Individual", located in either Maryland or D.C. (the District of Columbia). To retrieve this data, you would enter **MD** and **DC** in separate criteria rows underneath the State field, and you would enter **Individual** in these same rows underneath the Contact Title field. The design of this query is shown in the example in Figure 24-12.

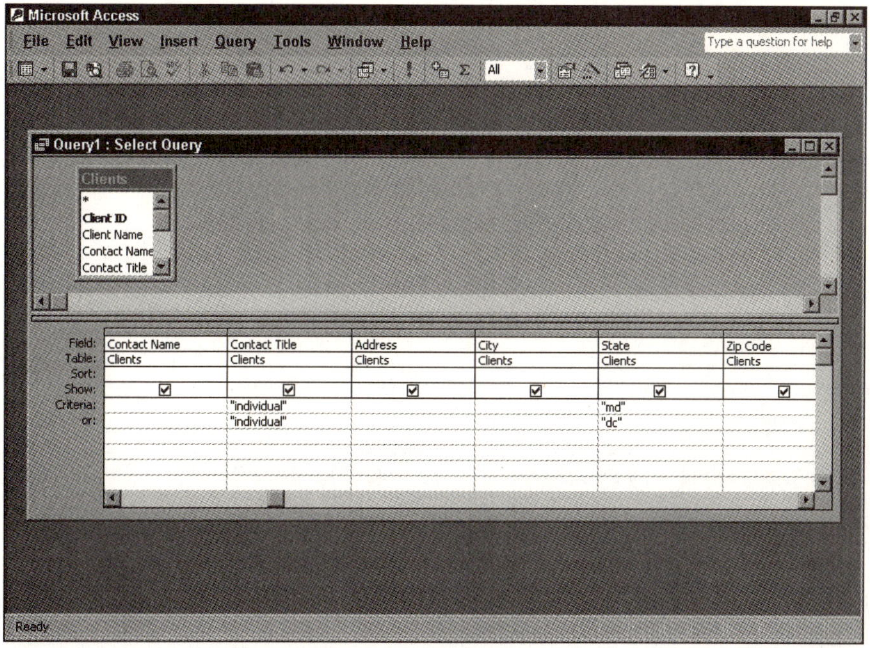

Figure 24-12: A query using a combination of AND and OR logic

One important point to note in the case of this example is that the expression "Individual" has been placed in both Criteria rows of the query grid. This is required in order to obtain all individual clients based in Maryland or the District of Columbia. If the "Individual" criteria were omitted from the second row, the query would interpret this as all individual clients based in Maryland or all clients based in the District of Columbia.

Available query symbols and operators

When constructing the expressions needed for your criteria entries, you can use any of the symbols and operators shown in Table 24-2. You can combine these symbols within your expressions to select records based on a variety of numeric conditions, ranges, and pattern matches.

Table 24-2
Valid Query Operators

Symbol	*Means*	*Example*
=	equals	= Jones
>	greater than	> 8.50
<	less than	< 200
>=	greater than or equal to	>= 6/30/99
<=	less than or equal to	<= 12.50
<>	not equal to	<> Chicago

continues

Table 24-2 continued

Symbol	**Means**	**Example**
between	between two values, including the values	between 8 and 19
in	within a set of values	in (USA Mexico Canada)
is null	field contains no data	is null
is not null	field contains data	is not null
like	used for pattern matching	like Mor*
and	both expressions are true	>6/30/99 and <12/31/99
or	either expression is true	USA or CANADA
not	expression is not true	not Mor*
?	pattern matching for any one character	=(202) 555-????
*	pattern matching for any characters	Mor*

The asterisk and question mark symbols are commonly used for *pattern matching* in cases when you need to retrieve records where a text entry in a field matches a given pattern. As the table indicates, the asterisk denotes any number of characters and the question mark denotes a single character. As an example, for a date field, you might enter the expression

```
LIKE * / * / 99
```

to retrieve records where entries in the date field match any dates during the year 1999. In a text field containing last names, you might use the expression

```
LIKE "M*"
```

to query a last name field for names that might include *Morris*, *Merrick*, and *Murphy*.

TIP: In legal applications that require a full text search, the asterisk symbol is commonly used to search for text that is contained somewhere within a field. To do a full text search, you include an asterisk both before and after the desired search text. As an example, perhaps you need a listing from a table of documents for a case, but you want to see only records in which the Summary field (which happens to be a memo field containing large amounts of text) contains the word *mortgage*. In the Summary field of the query grid, in the Criteria row, you would enter an expression like ***mortgage*** to retrieve the desired records. You can use this technique with memo fields whenever you need to locate a text string that appears somewhere in the contents of the field.

Querying for today's date

You also can query a date field for records matching the current date (according to the computer's system clock). To do this, use the date function in Access, which is `DATE()`. As an example, if you were to enter the following expression:

```
date( )
```

in the criteria cell for a date field, the resulting query would display all records with an entry in the field that matches the current date.

You also can include calculations based on the current date in the design of your queries containing date fields. As an example, this expression could be utilized in a query containing a date field:

```
between #3/20/2001# and date( )
```

As a result, the query would retrieve all records with a date between March 20, 2001, and the current date. Alternatively, you could design a query to display all records containing a date entry within the past 30 days with an expression like the following:

```
between date( ) and date( ) - 30
```

Entering expressions

Access is quite flexible in how you enter text-based expressions. You can enter text with or without quotation marks, precede the text with an equal symbol, or omit the equal symbol. (When you move the insertion point out of the field that contains the text expression, Access automatically encloses the text with quotation marks.) Hence, you can enter any of these expressions into a text field, and Access interprets them all the same way:

```
London

"London"

=London

="London"
```

When you have fields that contain number or currency values, you can use math operators in expressions to obtain the desired data. Expressions such as `=20.00` and `between 5 and 12` are typical types of expressions that you can enter as *numeric criteria*.

For fields that contain date values, you can also use math operators to specify date-based criteria in your expressions. You can enter dates in any acceptable date format. Access is also very flexible when it comes to how you enter dates. In Access, any of the following entries are acceptable within a date/time field in a Criteria row of a query grid:

```
Jun 23 99

#6/23/99#

6/23/99

23-Jun-99
```

Surrounding dates with the # symbol dates is optional; if you don't add the symbols, Access inserts them automatically when you move the insertion point out of the Criteria row.

You can enter logical (yes/no) values as Yes or No, True or False, and On or Off or as numeric values of -1 (meaning yes) and 0 (meaning no).

Using the IS NULL operator

Access offers a special operator, IS NULL, which can be used whenever you need to retrieve a set of records that contain no data in a field. (Note that this is not the same as simply leaving a field in the query grid empty. An empty field in the query grid tells Access that it does not matter what is in that field in a given record.) The term IS NULL indicates that the field must be empty before the record will appear in the resulting dynaset. Access also offers an opposite expression, Is Not Null, that can be used to indicate that the field must contain some kind of data.

Using the NOT operator

You can use the NOT operator to select records that are missing data in a particular field. For example, you could enter an expression such as *not Chicago* in a criteria cell for the City field of a query to retrieve any records with any entry in the field except the word *Chicago*. You could enter an expression such as `not 120.00` in an Hourly Rate field to find all records with an Hourly Rate other than 120.00.

Omitting fields from the results

You also can hide any fields that you don't want to see in the query's results. You hide fields by turning off the Show check box in the appropriate field's column. By default, the Show check box is turned on when you add a field to the query.

This option is useful when you need to include fields in queries for criteria or sorting purposes but you don't want the contents of the field to appear in the query's results. For example, you may want a query to retrieve all records for clients in a certain city. You need to include the City field so that you can define the selection criteria, but you do not need to view the City name in the resulting dynaset because the query results contain records with the same city.

Adding calculated fields to queries

Access lets you add calculated fields to a query in addition to those fields that are already part of a table's design. You can add calculated fields to queries and then place those fields in forms and reports you design that are based on the query. Typically, calculated fields are based on number, currency, or date fields, but they can also be based on concatenations of text.

You create a calculated field within a query by entering the expression that will perform the calculation in an empty cell in the Field row. You can precede the expression with a name and a colon; if you do so, that name will be used for the field name in the query's dynaset. If you omit a name and colon, Access names the field *ExprN*, where *N* is a numeric value starting with 1 for the first calculated field used and incrementing by 1 for each calculated field in the query.

As an example, if a query contained fields for Billing Rate and for Hours Billed, you could create a calculated field for total cost by entering an expression like this one in an empty cell of the Field row:

```
TotalCost:[Billing Rate]*[Hours Billed]
```

When the query ran, Access would multiply each of the values in the Billing Rate field by the corresponding values in the Hours Billed field to produce the new values, which would be displayed in the TotalCost field. Table 24-3 shows some examples of expressions that could be used to create calculated fields within a query.

Another common use for calculated fields in queries is to *concatenate*, or combine, text strings. To do this, include the concatenation operator (&) as a part of the expression. When you do this, you must include double quotation marks surrounding spaces and punctuation that you want to include within the overall expression, as shown in the example that follows. As an example, you could create a calculated field in a query that would combine the Last Name, First Name, and Middle Initial fields into a single name, using an expression like the following:

```
[First Name] & " " & [Middle Initial] & ". " & [Last Name]
```

Table 24-3
Typical Calculation Expressions Used within Queries

Expression	*Results*
[Salary] * 1.06	The salary plus 6 percent
NewSalary:[Salary] * 1.1	The salary plus 10 percent, to be displayed in a field labeled *NewSalary*
Due Date:[Filing Date]+60	A date 60 days from the date stored in the Filing Date field, to be displayed in a field labeled *Due Date*
Name:[Firstname] & " " & [Lastname]	The values in the Firstname and Lastname fields, separated by a space and displayed in a field labeled *Name*

Saving Queries

You save queries for later use with the same techniques used to save objects elsewhere in Access. While the Query Design window is active, choose File ⇨ Save (or click the Save button in the toolbar). You also can press Ctrl+F4 to close the Query Design window and answer Yes in the dialog box that appears, asking whether you want to save the query. If you are saving the query for the first time, a dialog box prompts you for the name of the query, as shown in Figure 24-13. Enter the desired name in the dialog box and click OK to save it.

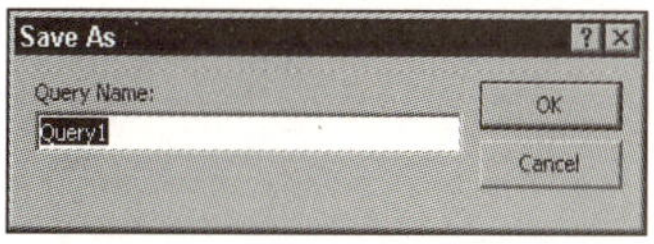

Figure 24-13: The dialog box that appears when you save a query

CAUTION: Queries and tables *cannot* share the same name in Access. The database engine that operates within Access considers tables and queries to be the same type of object (basically, a reference to a set of data). If you try to give a query the same name as an existing table, Access will present a dialog box asking whether you wish to replace the existing table with the new query. If you click Yes, the existing table gets overwritten by the query.

Printing Queries

To print a query's results, run the query to view the resulting dynaset and choose File ⇨ Print (or click the Print button in the toolbar). In the Print dialog box that appears, make your desired selections and click OK. This method gives you a simple columnar report with a layout resembling the layout of the dynaset. If you want a fancier layout, you need to save the query and create a report that uses the query as a data source. You also can print a query from the Database window by clicking the desired query to select it and then clicking the Print button in the toolbar, or by choosing File ⇨ Print, or by right-clicking the query in the Database window and choosing Print from the shortcut menu that appears.

Using Queries to Draw Relationships

As the preceding chapter mentioned, you can draw relationships between tables using either of two methods. One way (described in Chapter 23, "About Databases and Queries") is to use the Tools ⇨ Relationships command to create the relationships at the table level. The other approach involves creating a *relational query*. A relational query is similar in overall design to a nonrelational query; the only significant difference is that you add more than one table to the query and you establish a link between the tables (by dragging a field in one Field List to a related field in another Field List). Here are the steps you can use to create a relational query:

1. In the Database window, click the Queries tab; then click New.
2. In the New Query window that appears, click Design View; then click OK. This causes a new Query window to appear, with the Show Table dialog box above it.
3. In the Show Table dialog box, add each table needed by the relational query to the query design by selecting each table and clicking Add (or by double-clicking the table).
4. Create the relational link needed between the tables by dragging the common field from one Field List to another. As you do this, join lines appear between the common fields in the tables. (If you previously established relationships at the database level using the Tools ⇨ Relationships command, Access will add the join lines automatically.)
5. Add the necessary fields to the query, using the same techniques you would use to design any query.
6. Add any needed sorting and selection criteria to the query's design.
7. Save and run the query.

As an example, Figure 24-14 shows a relational query based on two tables, with a join line established between the Client ID fields of both tables. Fields have been added to the query from both tables, and Figure 24-15 shows the results when the query is run.

Notes about relational queries

As you work with relational queries, keep in mind that limitations exist for editing the data in the resulting dynaset. One of the longtime claims to fame of Access is that it lets you edit data in the resulting dynaset of a query and reflects the changes in the underlying tables. This feature usually works with relational queries as well, but some limitations apply. While editing records within a relational query, you cannot edit primary key fields on one side of the relationship when you've established referential integrity at the database level and included the key field as part of the relationship. (Typically, you can update all fields on the *many* side of the relationship in a one-to-many query.) You also cannot edit a primary key if referential integrity has been established at the database level and the field is part of the relationship, unless the Cascade Update Related Fields check box has been turned on. For more specifics on defining referential integrity at the database level, see Chapter 23.

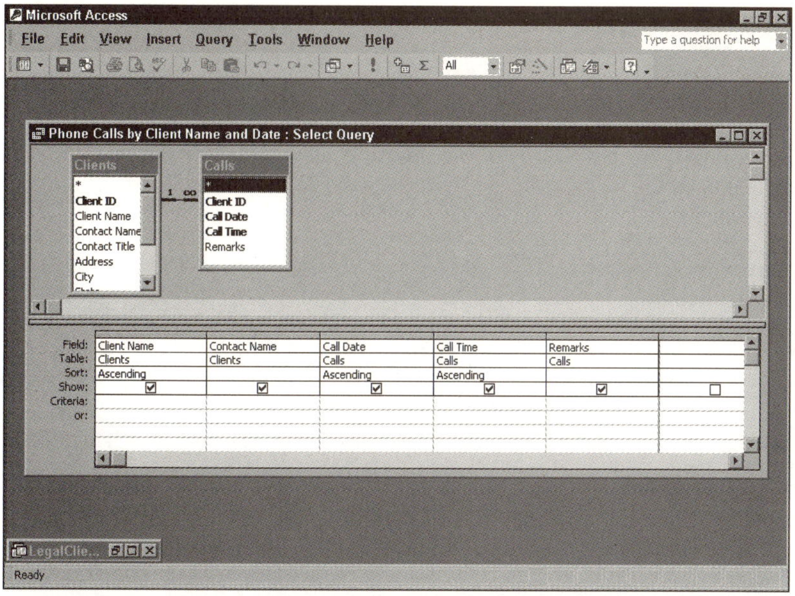

Figure 24-14: A query based on multiple tables is also known as a *relational* query. Note the join line between the common field of the tables (in this case, the Client ID field).

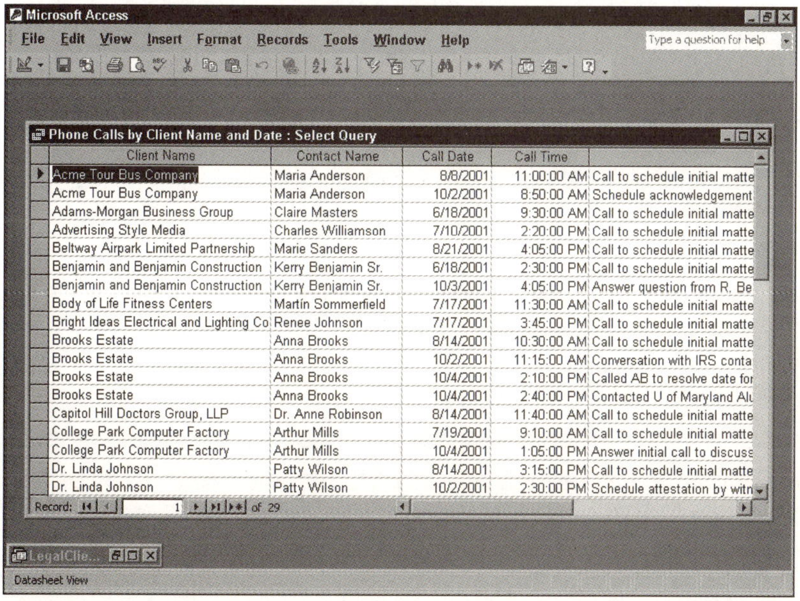

Figure 24-15: The results of the relational query show the names of clients and the phone calls made to each client.

If Access adds a join line that you don't want, you can easily delete it. To delete the unwanted line, click it to select it and then press the Delete key. If you want to remove a table that you've added to a query's design, just click anywhere within the Field List for the table and press the Delete key.

A note about missing joins

If you omit a join line in an Access table, the resulting dynaset is incorrect and displays erroneously large amounts of data. The reason is that when a join line is left out of a query, Access joins every record in one table with every record in the other table. The result is something called a *Cartesian product*, or a cross product of the two tables. For example, omitting a join for a query containing two tables (each having 200 records) produces a dynaset with 40,000 records, of which 39,800 of the records are absolutely meaningless.

Using Parameter Queries

If you find that you use the same query repeatedly, with a different criterion in a criteria cell each time you run the query, you will likely find parameter queries to be significant time savers. A parameter query asks for the needed criteria every time it runs. For example, you can design a query to provide a list of trial dates for a specific period of time; every time the query runs, Access asks the user for a starting and an ending date, and the query uses those dates to establish a range of acceptable records. You can change existing queries into parameter queries by adding parameters to the existing query designs, as outlined in the following steps. You can create parameter queries by performing these steps:

1. Create the select query using the query design techniques outlined previously in "Creating Queries."
2. In the Criteria cells below the fields that you want to use as parameters, enter the text of the parameter, enclosed within square brackets. For example, if you want a parameter in a Date of Document field to ask for a date when the query runs, you can enter an expression such as *[Enter the date of the document:]* in the Date of Document column of the Criteria row. If you want a parameter in a number field to ask for a minimum and a maximum amount, you can use an expression such as *between [Enter minimum amount:] and [Enter maximum amount:]* in the number column of the Criteria row.
3. Save the query by choosing File ⇨ Save, or by pressing Ctrl+F4 and answering Yes in the dialog box that appears.

For an example of a parameter query, consider the query design shown in Figure 24-16. The parameter query's design includes a parameter for a range of dates for client calls. (In the figure, the Call Date column was widened to show the text of the complete parameter.)

After entering a starting date, another dialog box appears, asking for the ending date. After you supply these values, Access uses them as the query criteria to produce the query results.

TIP: In the legal environment, parameter queries can prove highly useful as the data source for reports that are produced on a regular basis. See Chapter 26 for details on how to change the record source of a report to make use of a parameter query.

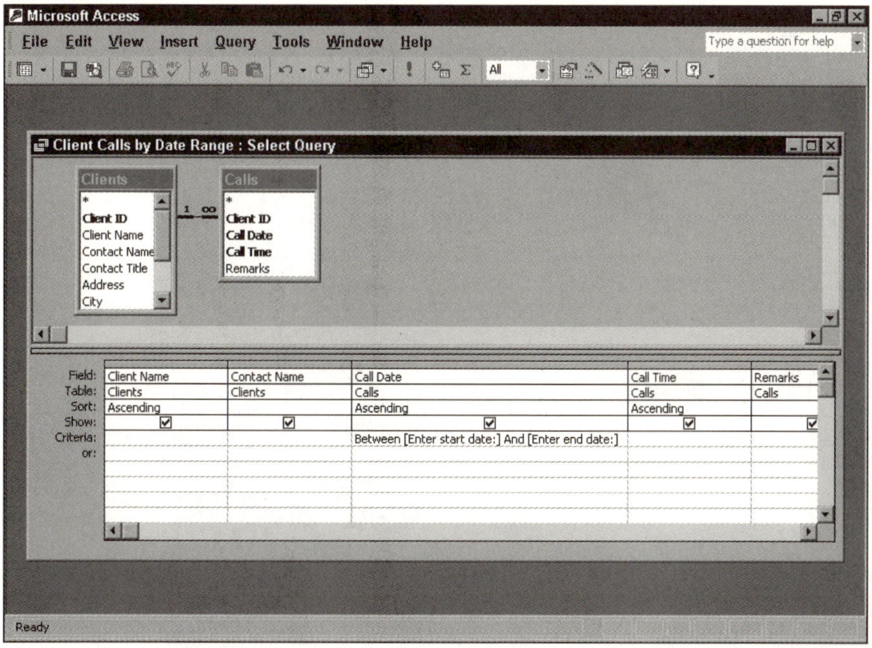

Figure 24-16: A parameter query for the client calls contains a parameter in the Call Date criteria cell.

When the query runs, it produces the Enter Parameter Value dialog box (see Figure 24-17).

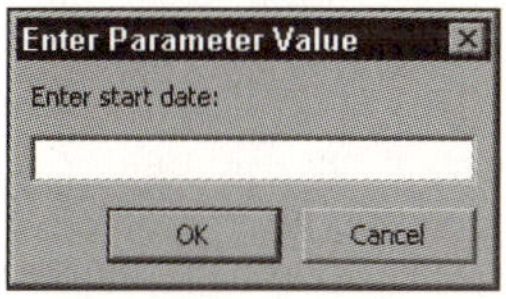

Figure 24-17: The Enter Parameter Value dialog box presented when a parameter query is run

Using Action Queries

Whereas select queries retrieve and display data in the form of a dynaset, action queries perform some type of action on the data it retrieves. In Access, action queries are created in the same manner as select queries. You begin the design process by creating a select query that will get the desired data. You then convert the select query to an action query by clicking the appropriate toolbar button or by opening the Query menu and choosing the appropriate type of action query, as discussed in the sections that follow.

As with select queries, action queries are visible after you click the Queries tab in the Database window (as are all queries). You can visually differentiate action queries from other queries by the exclamation point that appears to the left of the query when you view it in the Database window. Figure 24-18 shows action queries contained in the Database window.

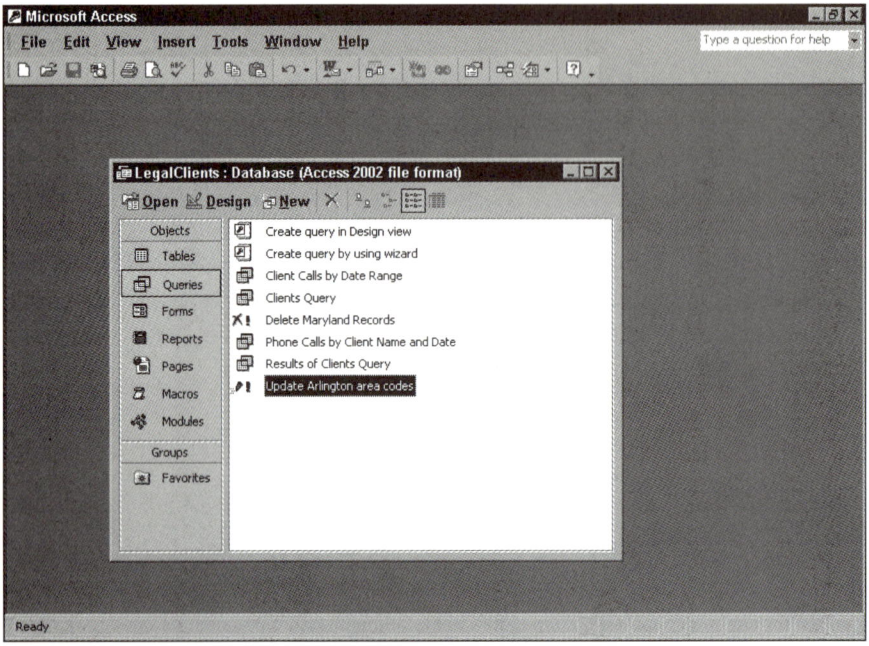

Figure 24-18: The action queries listed in the Database window contain an exclamation mark at the left of each query name.

Here are some practical uses for action queries. Action queries are handy in Access applications for any of the following tasks:

- **Deleting or archiving records:** A common task when working with large, transaction-based systems (such as the tracking of all faxes sent from a large law firm) is deleting groups of records or moving groups of records to an archive file. You can design action queries to delete groups of records or to copy groups of records to another table and then delete them from the first table.
- **Handling batch updates:** If a large group of clients in a table of firm clients is assigned to a certain attorney and then that attorney leaves the firm, you won't want to manually re-enter a new attorney name for each affected client record. You can design and run an update query to handle the changes in a single step.
- **Handling complex, changing reporting needs:** Another task is to make global or batch updates to a subset of data. You may have a half-dozen reports based on a complex query that uses data that changes monthly. Every time you want to run one or more reports, you must run the query first, which can be time-consuming because the underlying tables contain thousands of records. To save time, you can create a make-table query, which runs on a monthly basis, to create a new table that has the specific data that the original query normally produces. You can then base all reports on the new table produced by the make-table query.

As discussed at the beginning of this chapter, Access lets you create four types of action queries: *make-table queries*, which create new tables based on the results of the query; *append queries*, which add records to existing tables; *update queries*, which change the data in existing tables, and *delete queries*, which delete the records selected as a result of the query.

Creating and using make-table queries

You use make-table queries in Access to create new tables from the results of another query. All records selected by the original query are added to the new table created by the make-table query. Make-table queries are commonly used for creating backups or archives of data, for providing a source of data for time-based reports, or for exporting selected data to files in foreign file formats. To create a make-table query, you perform these steps:

1. Create the select query that will retrieve the records you want to copy to the new table, using the query design techniques outlined previously in "Creating Queries." You can test the query to ensure that it provides the desired results by clicking the Datasheet button in the toolbar.
2. With the select query open in Design view, choose Query ⇨ Make-Table Query, or click the arrow beside the Query Type button on the toolbar and choose Make Table Query from the menu that opens. After you perform this task, you see the Make Table dialog box, shown in Figure 24-19.

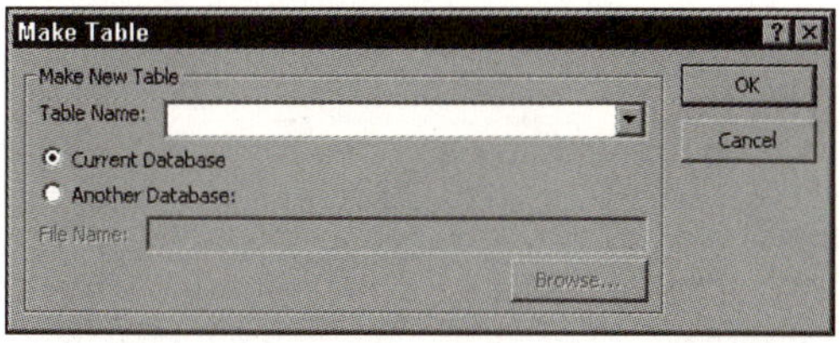

Figure 24-19: The Make Table dialog box for the make-table query

3. In the Table Name text box, type the name for the new table, or click the down arrow at the right and choose a table name from the list (if you want to overwrite an existing table). To append the data to another table in a different database, click the Another Database option button and enter the filename for the other database in the File Name list box.
4. After you choose the desired options, click OK. The title of the query changes to Make Table Query, indicating that the query's design has changed from a select query to a make-table query.
5. Run the make-table query by choosing Query ⇨ Run or by clicking the Run button on the toolbar. Access displays a confirmation dialog box indicating how many records will be added to the new table. Click OK, and the query runs and adds the records to the new table.

NOTE: When you create a new table using a make-table query, Access does not transfer any field properties or primary key field designations to the new table. You need to re-create any desired primary key field designations or custom field properties after the new table has been created.

Creating and using append queries

You can use append queries to append data from an existing table to another table. Append queries can copy data to other tables in the same database or to tables in different Access databases. (By default, the data is appended to tables in the same database.) The tables do not need identical structures, but the field types between the tables must match. You can create and run an append query by performing the following steps:

1. Create the select query that will retrieve the records you want to copy to the new table, using the query design techniques outlined previously in "Creating Queries." You can test the query to verify that it provides the desired results by clicking the Datasheet button in the toolbar.

2. With the query still open in Design view, choose Query ⇨ Append Query, or click the arrow beside the Query Type button in the toolbar and choose Append Query from the menu that opens. After you do this, you see the Append dialog box, nearly identical in appearance to the Make Table dialog box (refer to Figure 24-19). (The dialog box is titled *Append* rather than *Make Table* in this case, but all other options in the dialog box are identical to the options that appear when you create a make-table query.)
3. In the Table Name text box, type the name for the table to which you want to append the data, or click the down arrow at the right and choose the table name from the list. To append the data to another table in a different database, click the Another Database button and enter a filename for the other database in the File Name list box.
4. After you choose the desired options, click OK. The title of the query changes to Append Query, indicating that the query's design has changed from a select query to an append query.
5. Run the query by choosing Query ⇨ Run or by clicking the Run button on the toolbar. Access displays a confirmation dialog box indicating the number of records Access will add to the end of the existing table. Click OK, and the query runs and adds the records to the new table.

TIP: If you use append queries to add data to another table that contains an AutoNumber field, you can keep the value in the AutoNumber field from the original table, or you can force Access to add new AutoNumber values for all records that it adds to the destination table. To keep the AutoNumber values the same as those stored in the original table, include the AutoNumber field in the query grid when you design the append query. To force Access to add new AutoNumber values, omit the AutoNumber field from the query grid when you design the append query.

Creating and using update queries

Update queries are action queries that update (or make specific changes to) all records that meet the criteria specified by the query. Update queries are very useful when you need to make global, or *batch*, updates to a subset of data. For example, you may need to change the area codes of phone numbers for all records with a certain city name. You can use the following steps to create an update query:

1. Create the select query that will retrieve the records you want to update in the table, using the query design techniques outlined earlier. You can test the query to confirm that it provides the desired results by clicking the Datasheet button in the toolbar.
2. With the query still open in Design view, choose Query ⇨ Update Query, or click the arrow beside the Query Type button in the toolbar and choose Update Query from the menu that opens. After you perform this task, the title of the query changes to *Update Query*. Also, Access adds a new row to the query design grid, called *Update To*, as shown in Figure 24-20.
3. Click in the Update To row underneath the field that you want to update; then enter the expression that determines how the data will be updated. For example, if your query contains a Fee Amount field with currency amounts and you want to increase every entry in the field by 15 percent, you can enter an expression such as *[Fee Amount] * 1.15* to get the desired results. Figure 24-21 shows an example of such an expression used to increase the amount in the Fee Amount field of the Fees table.

4. Run the query by choosing Query ⇨ Run or by clicking the Run button on the toolbar. You see a confirmation dialog box telling you how many records the query will update. When you click OK, Access runs the query and updates the data in the table.

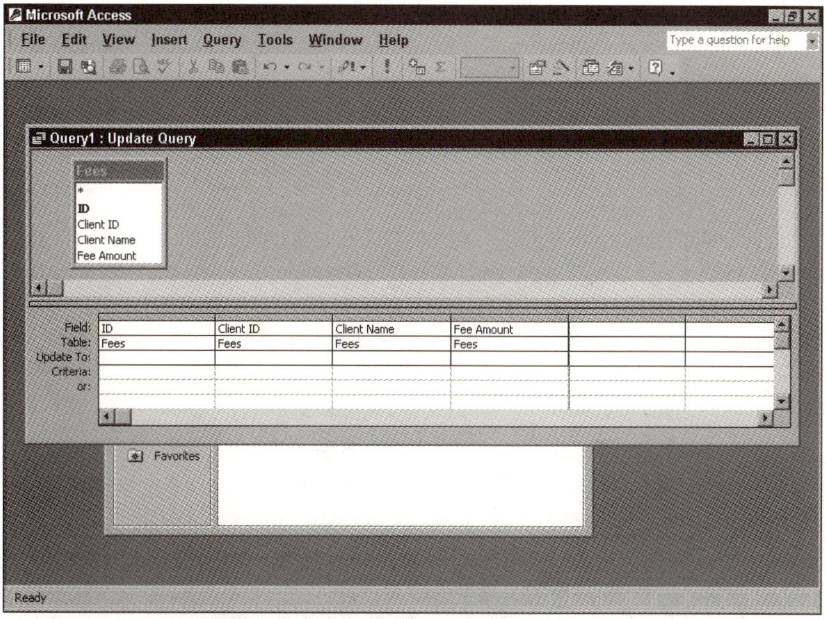

Figure 24-20: The query grid with the Update To row added

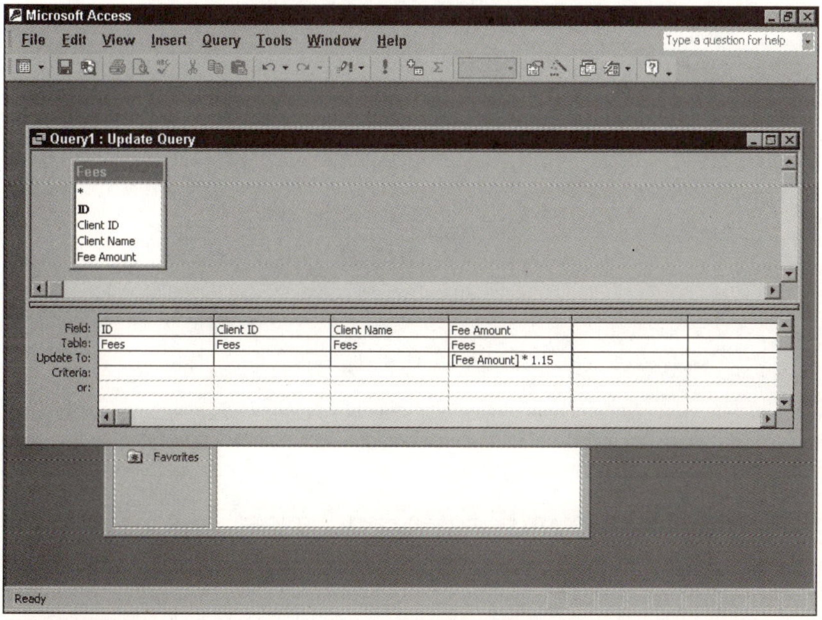

Figure 24-21: The Update To row containing an expression that, when the query runs, will increase the fee amount by 15 percent

Creating and using delete queries

Delete queries delete all records that meet the criteria specified by the query. One common use for delete queries is with operations that archive records; you routinely run a make-table query that copies selected records to another table; then you run a delete query that deletes the previously copied records from the first table. You can create delete queries by performing the following steps:

1. Create the select query that will retrieve the records you want to delete from the table, using the query design techniques outlined previously in "Creating Queries." You can test the query to ensure that it provides the desired results by clicking the Datasheet button in the toolbar in the Query Design window.
2. With the query still open in Design view, choose Query ⇨ Delete Query, or click the arrow beside the Query Type button on the toolbar and choose Delete Query from the menu that opens. After you perform this task, the title of the query changes to *Delete Query*. Also, Access adds a new row to the query, called *Delete*, as shown in Figure 24-22.
3. Run the query by choosing Query ⇨ Run or by clicking the Run button on the toolbar. You see a confirmation dialog box telling you how many records the query will delete.
4. Click OK in the dialog box to run the query and delete the records.

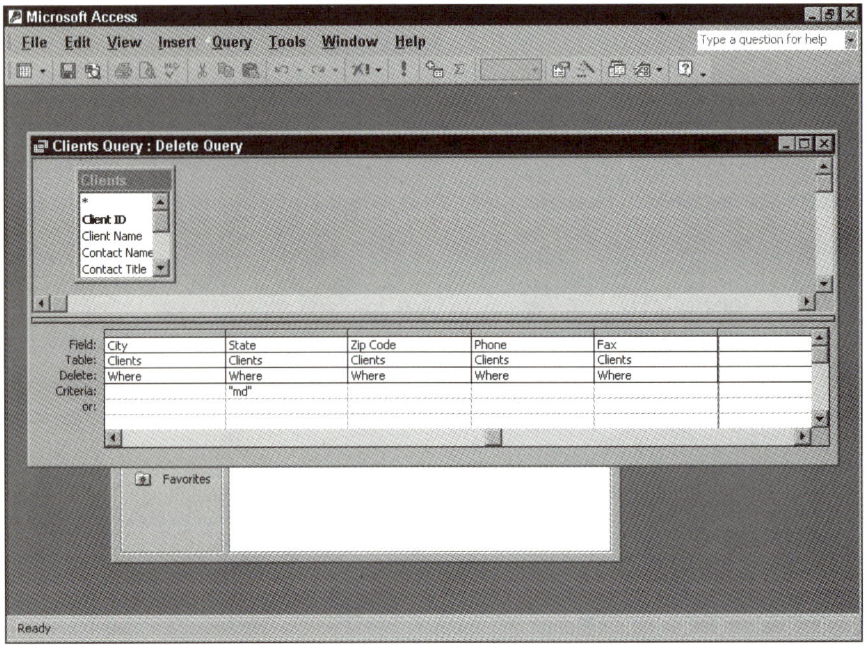

Figure 24-22: The query grid with the Delete row added and with criteria that will delete all records containing "md" in the State field

Troubleshooting problems with action queries

When running action queries, you can run into problems because of various incompatibilities between incoming and existing data or because of record-locking conflicts on a network. If Access runs into a problem when trying to execute an action query, it usually makes you aware of this by displaying some sort of dialog box. (One exception to this is with append queries when a difference in field sizes between a source table and a destination table means that incoming data won't fit in a text field. In such cases, Access simply truncates the incoming data.) Most problems result in the appearance of a dialog box like the one shown in Figure 24-23, and the user can choose Yes (to proceed with as much of the operation as is possible under the circumstances) or No (to cancel the action query). The example shown in this figure is for an append query that has encountered problems.

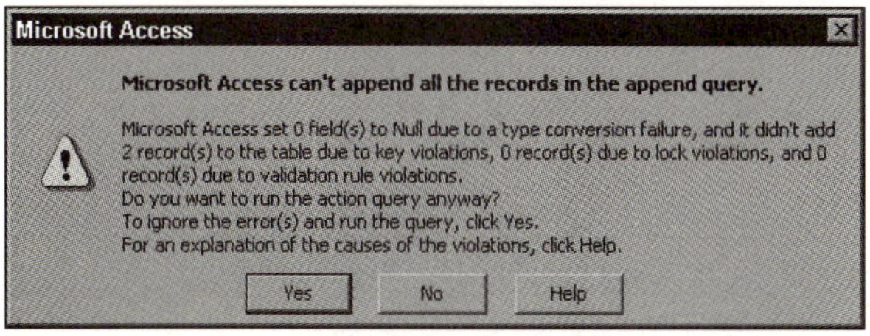

Figure 24-23: A dialog box warning of a problem with an action query

The most common problems with action queries include key violations, data type mismatches, and record-locking conflicts on networks. As Figure 24-23 shows, the dialog box indicates precisely which of these problems halted the operation.

Key violations

Append operations cannot result in changes that would create values identical to existing values in fields that are used as a table's primary key. Update operations also cannot make changes if the changes would result in a primary key field having duplicate values. Access also will not accept any attempt to create *null*, or empty, values in key fields. When an update or append query attempts to create records that violate these guidelines, the result is a *key violation*. You must change the value of the incoming records or in some other manner omit the new records or the changes that are causing the problem.

Data type mismatches

Access won't accept a value if the data types between the fields do not match. For example, if you are performing an append query that attempts to move data from a text field to a number field of the same name, any text that is not composed entirely of numbers does not get appended to the table, and Access inserts null (empty) values in its place.

Locked records

If records are locked by other users on a network, Access will not perform an update or append operation involving the locked records. Note that in this case, the Proceed dialog box option is a dangerous one because if you choose Proceed, Access will perform the update on the unlocked records but will not update the locked ones. You may then have a nightmare figuring out which records were updated and which ones weren't.

Creating Crosstab Queries

In certain types of numeric or financial applications, you may use crosstab queries, which are a specialized form of a select query. They are useful when you need to consolidate numeric or currency data stored in a table in a crosstab-like format. (Crosstabs are typically used to summarize large amounts of data.) For example, Figure 24-24 shows a table containing a set of numeric data of associate hours per case, along with a crosstab query of the data in the table.

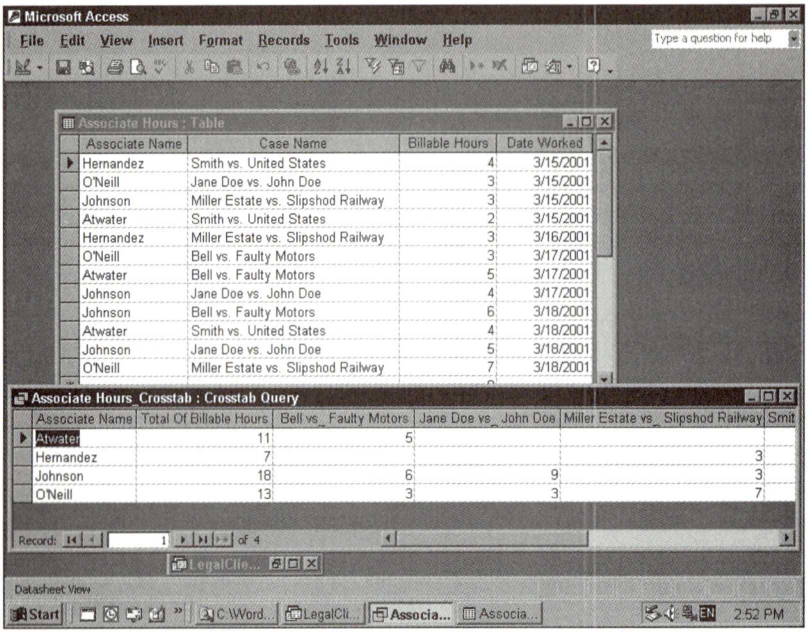

Figure 24-24: The Associate Hours data and the resulting crosstab

You can use one of the Query Wizards to create a crosstab query by performing the following steps:

1. In the Database window, click the Queries tab; then click New.
2. In the New Query dialog box that appears, click Crosstab Query Wizard in the list box of possible query types; then click OK.
3. Next, you see the first Crosstab Query Wizard dialog box, shown in Figure 24-25. This dialog box asks which table or query you want to use as the basis for the crosstab. In the View portion of the dialog box, you can select Tables to show all available tables, Queries to show all available queries, or Both to show both tables and queries. Click the table or query that you want to use; then click Next.

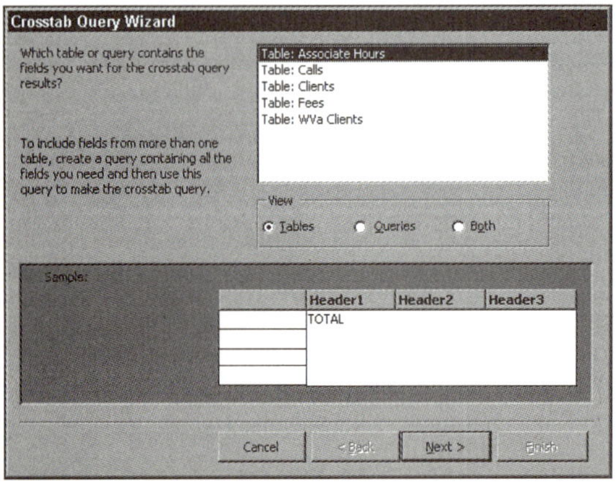

Figure 24-25: The first Crosstab Query Wizard dialog box lets you select the table or query to be used as the basis of the resulting crosstab.

4. The next Crosstab Query Wizard dialog box, shown in Figure 24-26, asks which fields you want to use as row headings in the crosstab. Choose the fields that you want to serve as the row headings and click the right-arrow button to add them to the available fields box; then click Next. You can choose up to three fields, and you should add them in the order you want the data sorted by in the resulting crosstab. For example, if you were using a table with a field for Branch Office and a field for Attorney Name, you could group the values by Branch Office and then by Attorney Name.

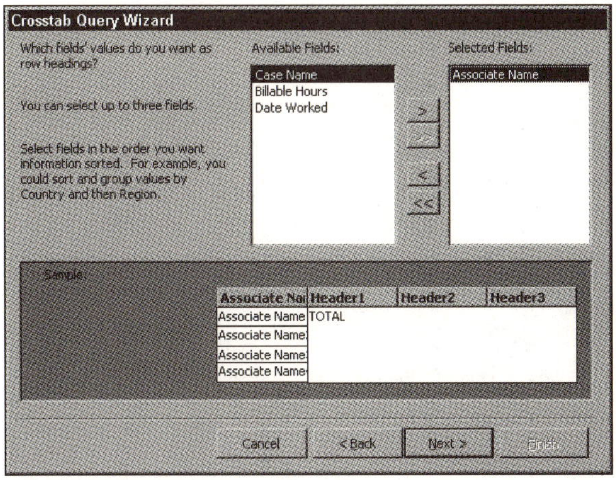

Figure 24-26: The second Crosstab Query Wizard dialog box is used to identify the field or fields that will become row headings in the crosstab.

5. The next Crosstab Query Wizard dialog box, shown in Figure 24-27, asks which fields you want to use as the basis for the column headings. Select the desired field and then click Next. As you make your selection, the Sample portion of the Crosstab Query Wizard dialog boxes displays field names reflecting your choices, as shown in the figure.

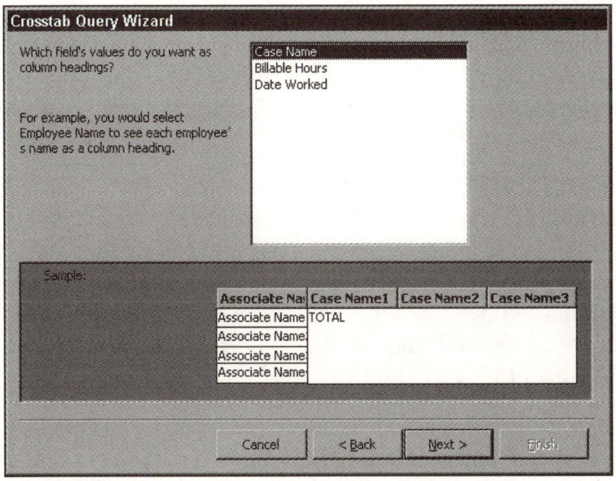

Figure 24-27: The third Crosstab Query Wizard dialog box identifies the fields to be used as column headings in the crosstab.

6. The next Crosstab Query Wizard dialog box, shown in Figure 24-28, asks which fields and what type of calculation you want to use to supply the values that will appear in the crosstab query.

After choosing a field, you can choose from the list of math functions to apply the desired calculation to that field. If you click the Yes, Include Row Sums option, each row of the crosstab will include a summary. Choose the field type and the type of calculation and then click Next.

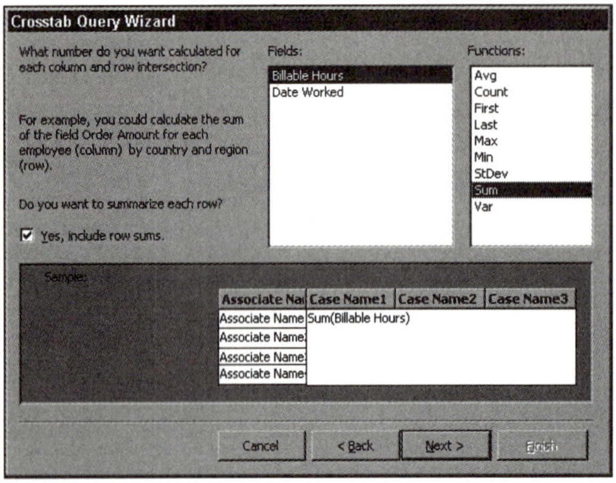

Figure 24-28: The fourth Crosstab Query Wizard dialog box lets you choose the field that will be calculated within the cells of the crosstab, along with the type of calculation.

7. The last dialog box that appears asks you for a name for the query. Enter a name (or accept the default name proposed by Access). Then you can click the View the Query radio button to run the query and display the results of the dynaset, or you can click the Modify the Design radio button to open the query in Design view.

Using Queries in Forms and Reports

When you are accustomed to the techniques of query design, it is helpful to know how you can put queries to work to perform your everyday tasks. You can open queries to view the resulting data and print them directly; you will also often find queries helpful as an underlying data source for your forms and reports. Performing a query and then making use of the results in a form or report is generally the most efficient way to retrieve and display (or print) data. As detailed in Chapters 25 and 26, both forms and reports make use of a Record Source property, which tells Access where the form or report should obtain its underlying data.

When you create a form or a report using a wizard, the wizard automatically sets the Record Source property of the form or report to the table or query you choose by name in the wizard's dialog box. (If you create the form or report manually, it is up to you to set the desired Record Source.) As an example of the Record Source property setting, if you open any report in Design view, choose View ⇨ Properties to reveal the Properties window, and click the Data tab, you see the Record Source property for the report, similar to the example shown in Figure 24-29.

You can click anywhere within the Record Source property and then choose the name of an existing query in the list box. In Figure 24-29, the name of an existing query definition, *Clients Query*, has been selected from the pull-down list. The resulting report, when printed, gets its data from the dynaset produced by the saved query.

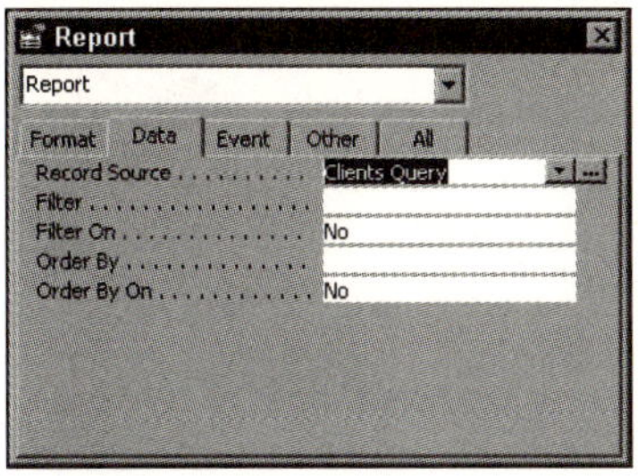

Figure 24-29: The Record Source property for a report

Summary

This chapter has provided a wealth of information about queries, an important feature of Access. In this chapter, you learned the following:

- Access provides two main types of queries: select queries and action queries. A third type, the crosstab query, is a specialized form of select query.
- Using criteria within your queries, you can select records that contain needed data for displaying within forms or for reporting purposes.
- You can use action queries to perform actions such as mass updates or deletions of records.
- There are two ways to establish relationships in Access: at the database level or by creating the relationships as part of the queries.
- You can create crosstab queries to summarize numeric or financial data.
- You can use queries as a data source for your forms and reports by changing the Record Source property of a form or a report to match the name of a query you saved previously.

In the next chapter, you learn how to create and use forms to view and edit your data in Access.

Chapter 25

Working with Forms

In This Chapter

- ♦ Creating a form with the AutoForm feature
- ♦ Creating a form with the Form Wizard
- ♦ Designing forms manually
- ♦ Saving and using the form
- ♦ Using Filter by Form
- ♦ Creating relational forms manually
- ♦ Creating tabbed forms
- ♦ Creating data access pages
- ♦ Working with forms with multiple users

IN THE PREVIOUS CHAPTER, you learned how you can enter data directly into Access tables by typing the data directly into a datasheet (or into a query's dynaset). This can be an easy and straightforward way for you or others to enter data. However, such a direct means of data entry has its disadvantages as well. Users must be familiar with Access to enter data directly into tables or queries; field names may be cryptic in appearance to the user; and few safeguards exist against incorrect data entry. And if the table contains a large number of fields, it may be difficult or impossible to see all the fields without repeated scrolling of the Datasheet window.

To get around these limitations, you can use forms for your data entry and editing. With forms, you have full control over precisely where the fields appear as you design the form. You also can build rules into forms that prevent others from entering incorrect data into your tables. In addition to data entry and editing, you can use forms for printing data (although this is more typically done using reports, as discussed in the next chapter). In this chapter, you'll learn to design and use forms to add data and to view and edit the data stored in your tables. Figure 25-1 shows a typical form.

Access provides a number of ways to create forms. You can create a default form in a matter of seconds, using the AutoForm feature of Access. You also can use a feature known as the *Form Wizard* to quickly create a variety of forms based on a single table or on multiple tables. And if you prefer to maintain full control over the form-creation process, you can design your own forms manually. Often, you can save time when designing forms by combining the last two methods; you can use the Form Wizard to initially create the form and then can make additional changes to the form manually.

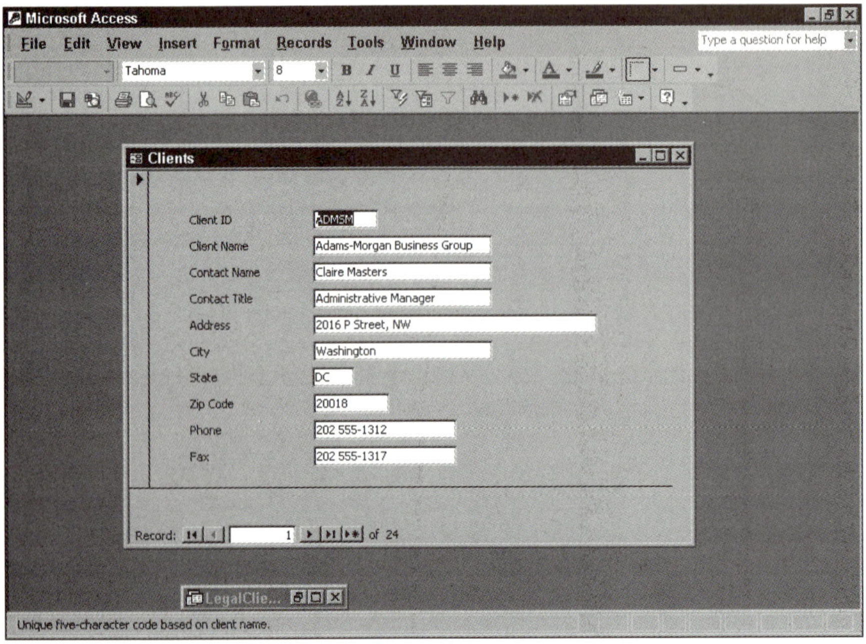

Figure 25-1: You can use Access forms for adding and editing data and for deleting records.

Creating a Form with the AutoForm Feature

If you want to quickly create a default form, the simplest way to do this is to use the AutoForm menu option of the New Object button on the Toolbar. The AutoForm option creates a simple single-column form for whatever table or query is selected in the Database window when you click the button. To create a form using the AutoForm feature, perform these steps:

1. Select the desired table or query to be used as a source of data for the form in the Database window.
2. Click the down arrow to the right of the New Object button in the Toolbar (it's the button with the lightning bolt) and choose AutoForm. In a moment, Access builds a default form for the table or query (refer to Figure 25-1 for an example of such a form).

When you use the AutoForm feature to create a form, you get a form with all the fields aligned at the left side of the form and with the field names used as the default labels for the fields. If the table that you selected is the parent table in a one-to-many relationship and you've already established a relationship between the tables (as outlined in Chapter 23), the AutoForm feature will include a subform for the related table within the design of the form. (If you want to change any of these design aspects of the form, you can easily do so by opening the form in Design view and making changes to the form manually, as detailed later in this chapter.)

Creating a Form with the Form Wizard

When you want a little more control over the end result but still want Access to help you with the overall process, you can use the Form Wizard to assist you in the creation of your forms. Like all wizards in Access, the Form Wizard asks you a series of questions and then produces a finished, ready-to-use object (in this case, a form) based on your answers to the questions. What follows are the overall steps you'll use to create forms with the Form Wizard. The paragraphs that follow these steps describe the steps in greater detail.

1. Click the Forms tab in the Database window.
2. Click New to display the New Form dialog box.
3. At the bottom of the New Form dialog box, select the desired table or query that will supply data to the form.
4. Click Form Wizard in the list portion of the box; then click OK.
5. Follow the directions and answer the appropriate questions that appear in the wizard dialog boxes. In the final dialog box, you can click Open the Form with Data in It and click Finish to begin entering or viewing data in Form view. Alternatively, you can click Modify the Form's Design and click Finish to open the form in Design view if you wish to use manual form design techniques to further modify the design of the form.

Designing forms manually? Let the Form Wizard lend a hand!

In some cases, you may prefer to design your own forms. However, you shouldn't ignore the helpful capabilities of the Form Wizard. You can usually save considerable time and effort by letting the Form Wizard create a form; then you can open that form in Design view and modify the form as desired (using the techniques described in "Designing Forms Manually," later in this chapter).

In a nutshell, that's the process of using the Form Wizard. Now, here is the process in greater detail.

When you click the Forms tab in the Database window and then click New (or if you use the Form option of the New Object button in the Toolbar), the New Form dialog box appears. In the lower portion of this dialog box, you can click the down arrow to open a list box that displays all the available tables and queries in the current database. In the upper portion of the dialog box, a list box contains choices for the type of wizard you want to use. Select Form Wizard from the list and click OK. In a moment, the first dialog box for the Form Wizard appears, as shown in Figure 25-2.

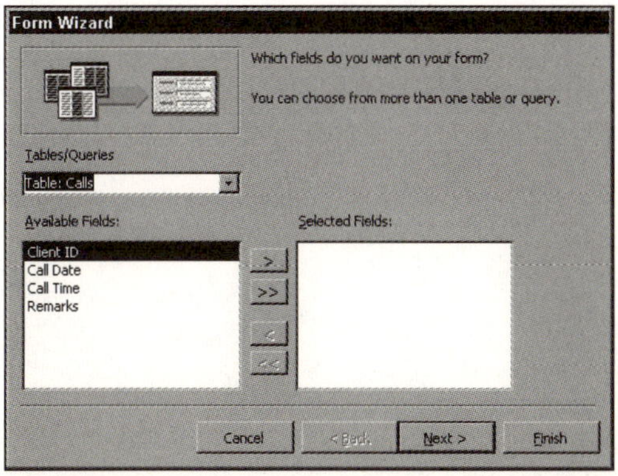

Figure 25-2: Here you select the tables or queries and the accompanying fields to be used within a form.

Choosing the tables and the desired fields

In the initial Form Wizard dialog box, you use the Tables/Queries list box to choose the tables or queries you want to use as the form's data source, and you use the Available Fields box to enter the fields that you want in the form. When you select a table in the Tables/Queries list box, all fields of that table or query appear in the Available Fields list box. You can click a field in this list to select it and click the right arrow button to add the field to the Selected Fields list box, or you can double-click the field in the Available Fields list box to add it to the Selected Fields list box.

Notice that a double-arrow button also appears between the list boxes. Click this button to add all fields in the Available Fields list box to the Selected Fields list box. If you make a mistake and want to remove a field from the Selected Fields list box, click the unwanted field in the Selected Fields list box and click the left arrow button to remove the field from the list. (Clicking the double left arrow button removes all fields from the Selected Fields list box.)

When you want to base the form on more than one table or query and you have added all desired fields for the first table or query, choose another table or query in the Tables/Queries list box and add the desired fields for that table or query. You have the option of using relational queries or using multiple tables or queries for forms that are based on more than one table or query. You can use a relational query, or you can select one table or query and add fields from that table or query and then select another table or query and add fields from that table or query. When you are done adding the desired fields, click Next to proceed.

The dialog box that you now see depends on whether you have chosen fields from a single table or query, or fields from more than one table or query. If you have chosen fields from more than one table or query, you see the dialog box shown in Figure 25-3. Using the options shown in this dialog box, you can decide which table or query you should use to view the data. In effect, you are deciding which table or query will be the *parent* table or query, meaning the table or query with the highest priority, in a form that shows data from more than one table or query. Click the desired table or query in the list box to select it and choose the Form with Subform(s) or Linked Forms option. If you choose the Form with Subform(s) option, Access creates a single form that shows one record at a time from the main table or query and all associated records from the secondary, or *child*, tables or queries. If you choose the Linked Forms option, Access creates two or more forms, with the additional form(s) linked to the first, to display the data from all the tables or queries.

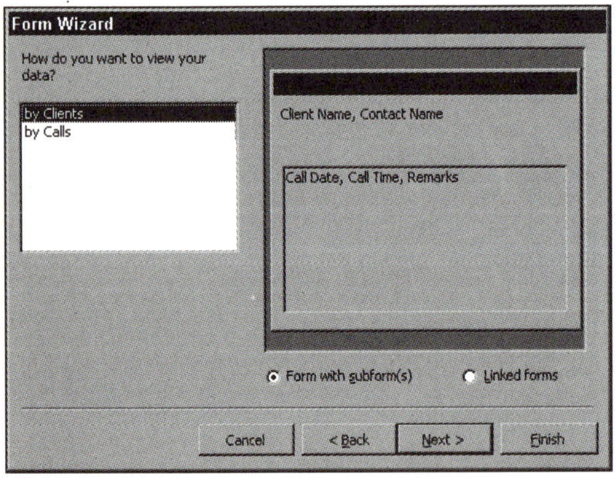

Figure 25-3: The second Form Wizard dialog box (used with multiple tables or queries) lets you determine which table (or query) will serve as the "parent" source of data in a relational form.

If you originally chose fields from only one table or query, you see the Form Wizard dialog box shown in Figure 25-4.

In this dialog box, you are asked to specify a layout for the form. Your choices are Columnar, Tabular, Datasheet, Justified, Pivot Table, and Pivot Chart. The *Columnar* option creates a default form with columnar layout, arranging all fields in a single column on the left side of the form. The *Tabular* option creates a default form with a tabular appearance and with space surrounding each field. The *Datasheet* option creates a default form that has a tabular appearance (similar to that of a datasheet) but with no space around each field. The *Justified* option creates a form with the fields in successive order, widened sufficiently to create a justified right margin. The *Pivot Table* and *Pivot Chart* options let you create forms to view statistical or financial data in the form of pivot tables or pivot charts (see the Excel portion of this book for more details on the use of pivot tables and pivot charts). Choose one of these options in the dialog box and click Next to proceed.

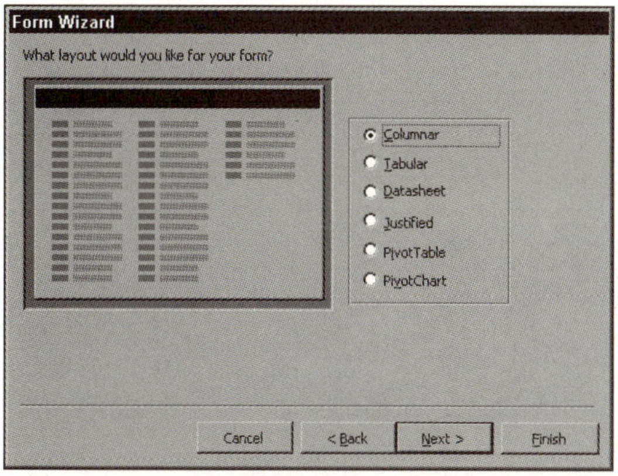

Figure 25-4: The second Form Wizard dialog box (used with a single table or query) lets you choose a desired layout for the form.

The next dialog box presented by the Form Wizard gives you a choice of styles for the form. Access provides ten different styles, or background designs, for forms created with the Form Wizard. Select a style and click Next to proceed.

Even though some of these styles are quite colorful, adding varied designs to a form will increase the time that Access takes to open and display the form. This effect is particularly noticeable on machines running the minimum requirements for Windows.

Completing the design process

The last dialog box that appears asks for a title for the form. If the form is based on more than one table or query, you will also be asked for a title for any subforms that have been created during the process. A default title is provided (which is the same as the primary table or query that the form was based upon), and you can leave this title or change it to any title you want. Additionally, the options in the dialog box let you open the form to view or enter information, or open the form in Design view, where you can make further modifications to the design of the form. After you click Finish, the Form Wizard completes the process of creating the form.

After you have saved the form, it appears in the Database window under the Forms tab, and you can select it and click Open to open the form in Form view, where you can add and edit data. For more details on working with the form, see "Saving and Using the Form," later in this chapter.

Designing Forms Manually

If you prefer the "roll-your-own" method of forms creation, you can design your own forms from scratch, using the manual method of form design. You open a blank form, size the form to the desired width and height, and add the desired design objects, such as text boxes that display the contents of fields, labels, and graphics, to the form. The overall steps behind the manual method of forms creation are as follows:

1. In the Database window, click the Forms tab and then click New.
2. In the New Form dialog box that appears, choose the table or query that should serve as the primary source of data for the form.
3. Leave the Design View option selected in the list and click OK. In a moment, a blank form appears (see Figure 25-5).
4. Using the Toolbox and the Field List, place the desired objects (text boxes, labels, and any other types of controls that are needed) on the form. (If the Toolbox is not visible, you can choose View ⇨ Toolbox to display it; if the Field List is not visible, you can choose View ⇨ Field List to display it.)
5. Choose File ⇨ Save to save the completed form.

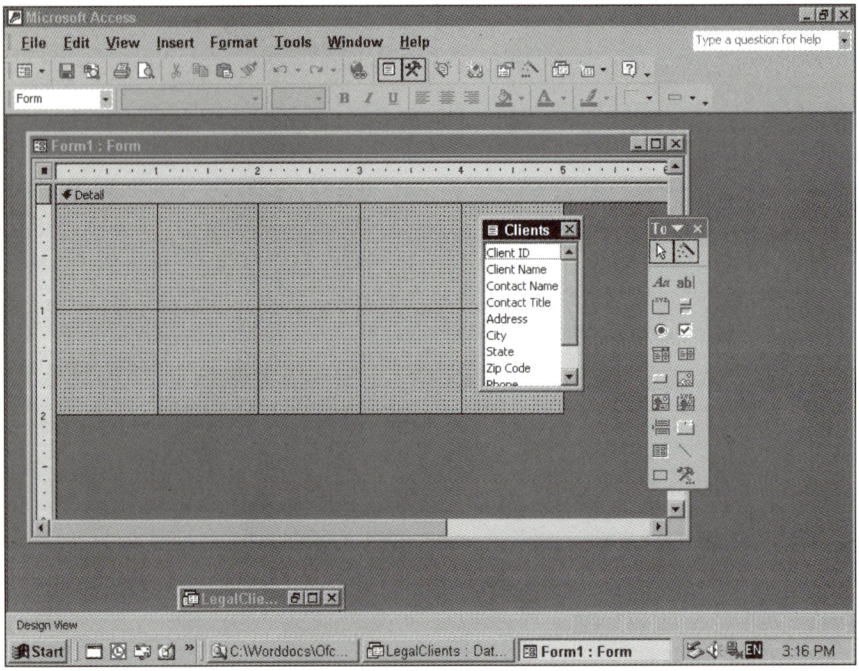

Figure 25-5: A new, blank form in Design view contains just a Detail section, and no fields or labels appear. You must add desired fields, labels, and other controls, using the Toolbox and the Field List.

In addition to manually creating forms from scratch, you also can open existing forms that have been created with the AutoForm feature or with the Form Wizard in Design view. To do so, select the form in the Database window and click Design, or right-click the form in the Database window and choose Design from the menu that appears. Figure 25-6 shows an example of an existing form, created using the Form Wizard, that has been opened in Design view.

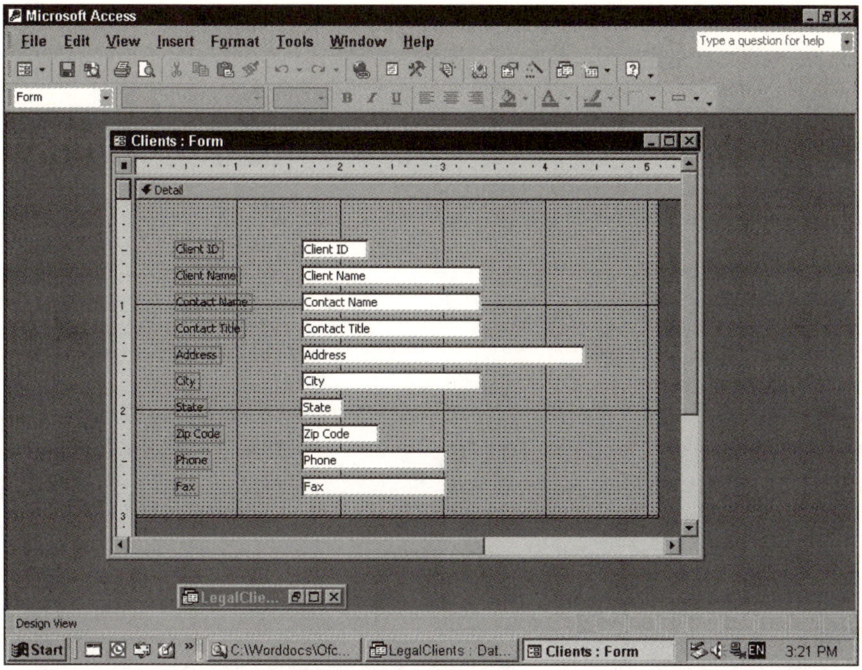

Figure 25-6: An example of an existing form open in Design view. Note the various controls that are used to display the data when the form runs.

Existing forms usually contain text box controls, which are used to display the data contained in the fields of the table or query. Forms also typically contain label controls, which provide the user with feedback about the various objects on the form or about how to use the form. Optionally, forms can contain form headers and form footers.

Adjusting the design surface

When you create a form manually, it initially opens to a default size, as shown previously in Figure 25-5. Rulers appear at the top and left edges of the form, and a grid composed of dots fills the drawing area (unless these options have been turned off with the View ⇨ Ruler or View ⇨ Grid menu options). You can change the size of the form as necessary to accommodate as many fields or other objects as you may need. Use the following steps to change the size of a form:

1. While in Design view, place the pointer on the bottom edge or right edge of the form. The pointer changes to a double-headed arrow.
2. Drag the pointer up or down to change the height of the form, or drag the pointer left or right to change the width of the form. If you want to change both the height and the width of the form at the same time, place the pointer in the lower-right corner of the section until the pointer changes shape to an arrow with four heads; then drag the pointer to adjust the size of the form.

Adding controls to forms

As you design forms, most objects you add to the forms (such as labels, text boxes that display fields) are called *controls*. If you are going to do much work with forms in Design view, you must know how to add controls, move them, and size them as needed. You will find these skills to be useful when designing reports because many of the same techniques used in form design are also used when manually designing reports. In Access, you can add three types of controls to forms (or to reports). They are bound controls, unbound controls, and calculated controls:

- **Bound controls:** These are controls that are connected to a field of the table or query that the form is based upon. In Figure 25-1, the text boxes that display the contents of the fields are bound controls. The most commonly used type of bound control is the text box control. However, other types of bound controls can be used in forms (and reports), such as check boxes, list boxes, toggle buttons, and object frames (which typically display photos stored in OLE fields of a table).
- **Unbound controls:** These are controls that are not connected to any fields of a table or query. In forms created by the Form Wizard, the title that appears in the form header and the labels containing the names of the fields are unbound controls.
- **Calculated controls:** These are controls that display the results of a calculation. The expression used to perform the calculation is typically based on one or more fields of a table.

You add controls to forms using either of two tools: the Field List or the Toolbox. (If the Field List or the Toolbox do not appear when you open a form in Design view, you can display either by choosing View ⇨ Field List or View ⇨ Toolbox from the menus.) Figure 25-7 shows the Field List (on the left) and the Toolbox (on the right).

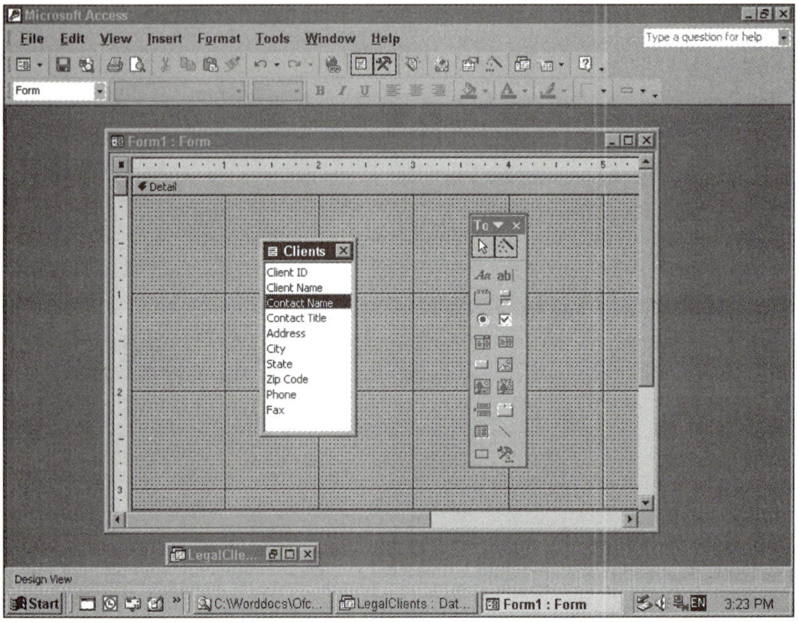

Figure 25-7: The Field List and the Toolbox

When you want to add bound controls to a form, the easiest way to do so is to use the Field List. Assuming that the type of control you want to create is a text box, you just drag the desired field from the Field List to the desired location on the form. When you release the mouse button, a text box bound to the appropriate field appears.

You can add multiple fields to the form as text boxes in a single operation by selecting the first field in the Field List and then pressing the Ctrl key as you select each additional desired field in the list.

When all the needed fields are highlighted, click any selected field and drag the fields onto the form as a group. (Note that if the fields are too close together for your liking, you can easily space them apart by choosing Format ⇨ Vertical Spacing ⇨ Increase from the menus.)

To add other types of controls to a form, you use the assortment of tools shown in the Toolbox. The various controls of the Toolbox and their uses are described in Table 25-1.

To create a label, click the Label tool in the Toolbox. On the form, click where you want to place the label, type the text for the label, and press Enter. (You can change the label's font and size, if desired, by selecting it and then choosing the desired font and font size from the Toolbar.)

The exact steps for creating other types of controls will depend on the type of control, but here are the overall steps you can use:

1. If the Toolbox is not already visible, choose View ⇨ Toolbox to display it.
2. If you don't want to use the Control Wizards to assist in creating the control, click the Control Wizards button in the Toolbox until the button background appears as a lighter shade (not active).
3. Click the desired type of control you want to create in the Toolbox.

Click in the form where you want to place the upper-left corner of the control; then drag the pointer to size the control to the desired size. If the Control Wizards are on and are appropriate to the type of control you are adding, you can follow the directions in the Control Wizard dialog boxes that appear.

Moving, sizing, and deleting controls

As you work with controls, you will often want to move them or change the size of controls. To move a control, first select the control by clicking anywhere within the control. Then move the pointer to any edge of the control where the pointer changes shape to an outstretched palm; drag the control to the desired location.

TIP: You can move a group of controls in one operation by first selecting the controls as a group. To do this, select the first control and then press the Shift key as you select each additional desired control. (Optionally, you can click at the upper-left of one control and drag to the lower-right until a group of controls is enclosed within the dotted line that appears; then release the mouse button.) When all the controls are selected, you can move the pointer to any edge of any selected control where the pointer changes shape to an outstretched palm; then drag the controls as a group to the desired location.

To resize a control, select the control by clicking it. Then move the pointer to any of the control's sizing handles (where the pointer changes shape to a double arrow) and click and drag the control to the desired size. To move a text box control separately from its label, place the pointer over the handle at the upper-left corner of the text box, where the pointer changes to a hand with a pointing finger. Then click and drag the text box to the desired location.

To delete a control that is not wanted, select the control and then press the Delete key.

TIP: Occasionally, you will want to move controls very small distances. You can easily do this by selecting the control and then pressing the Ctrl key while using the arrow keys.

Table 25-1
The Controls of the Toolbox

Tool	*Purpose*
Select Objects	Selects, moves, sizes, or edits objects in the form.
Control Wizards	Turns the Control Wizards on or off.
Label	Adds labels that are convenient for titles, instructions, or descriptive text.
Text Box	Creates text boxes that can display the contents of fields.
Option Group	Adds an option group to the form. Option groups contain check boxes, option buttons, or toggle buttons for a group.
Toggle Button	Adds toggle buttons. This can be used with option groups to select one choice out of many or can be used individually to indicate a yes/no choice.
Option Button	Adds option buttons (also called *radio buttons*). This can be used with option groups to select one choice out of many or can be used individually to indicate a yes/no choice.
Check Box	Adds check boxes. This can be used with option groups to select one choice out of many or can be used individually to indicate a yes/no choice.
Combo Box	Creates combination boxes that let you select one choice from a list of choices or type in a desired value.
List Box	Creates list boxes that let you select one choice from a list of choices.
Command Button	Adds a command button that you can use in the form to carry out commands.
Image	Inserts a frame that displays a static image.
Unbound Object Frame	Inserts a frame that contains an OLE object.
Bound Object Frame	Inserts a frame that contains the contents of an OLE object field.
Page Break	Inserts a page break at a specified location in the form.
Tab	Adds a tabbed form with multiple pages.
Subform/Subreport	Adds an object that contains a subform or a subreport.
Line	Draws lines in a form.
Rectangle	Draws rectangles or squares in a form.
More Controls	Opens a new menu used for adding additional controls (such as Visual Basic VBX controls) to a form.

Changing a control's properties

Controls have properties that affect how the control behaves when the form is used, and you can put these properties to use in designing your forms for ease of use and accurate data entry. To change the properties of a control, first select the control by clicking it. Then choose View ⇨ Properties from the menu, or right-click the control and choose Properties from the shortcut menu, or click the Properties button in the toolbar. When you do this, a Properties window appears for the selected control.

The types of properties that are available will vary, depending on the type of control that you are working with. However, in all cases, you can see a detailed explanation of any particular property by using the help screens. Just click inside the row of the desired property in the Properties window and press F1 to see a help screen that explains how to use the property in question.

To set a property, open the Properties window and click in the property whose value you wish to set. If an arrow appears at the right of the property, you can click it and choose a desired value from the list box that opens. If no arrow appears, you can type the desired setting or expression directly into the property box.

The following list describes some of the more common properties that you will find useful when you work with forms and the controls in those forms:

- **Control Source:** This property tells the control where to obtain the data displayed within the control. When you create text box controls by dragging them from the Field List into the form, this property is defined automatically. You can enter expressions in the Control Source property by typing them in directly or by right-clicking the property and choosing Build from the shortcut menu. Doing so bring ups an Expression Builder that you can use to create an expression.
- **Format:** This property defines any format used to display the data. (The precise types of formats you can use vary, depending on the type of data displayed by the control; for example, with controls that display the contents of number fields, you can use number formats.) You can click the down arrow that appears at the right side of the selected property to open a list box showing the formats available for the type of field with which you are working.
- **Decimal Places:** When working with number or currency fields, you can use this property to display how many decimal places should be used with the numbers displayed. You can choose Auto or enter a value from 0 to 15, indicating the number of decimal places desired. Digits to the left of the decimal appear as specified in the Format property setting, and digits to the right of the decimal appear with the specified number of places.
- **Input Mask:** You can use this property to define an *input mask*, or a format that data must follow when you type data into the control. For example, if you set this property to 000-00-0000, hyphens display in the locations shown, and digits display in the other locations. You can see a list of the symbols you can use for input masks and examples of input masks by placing the insertion point in the property and pressing F1.
- **Default Value:** Use this property to specify a default value for the control. As new records are added to the form, the default value appears in the field used by the control, and users can change it to something else if needed. You also can establish default values during the table design stage, and those default values will always apply, regardless of whether or not you use the form.
- **Validation Rule and Validation Text:** Use these properties to validate data entered into the form. In the Validation Rule property, you enter an expression of your choosing to validate the data. In the Validation Text property, you enter the text you want to display in the status bar if

the data entered into the field does not pass the validation rule. As an example, in a currency field containing salaries, you might enter a validation rule such as *between 15.50 and 21.50*, and in a date field containing hire dates for employees, you could enter a validation rule such as *between #6/1/95# and date()*, which would represent any valid date from June 1, 1995, to the current date according to the computer's clock.

- **Status Bar Text:** This property specifies the text that appears in the status bar as the focus moves into the control. It is a useful property for adding help text for other users of the form, and you can add a string of up to 255 characters.
- **Auto Tab and Enter Key Behavior:** These properties can be used together to determine how Access behaves when a field on the form is filled with characters and how Access responds when a user presses the Enter key while in the field of the form. If the Auto Tab property is set to Yes, a tab is automatically generated (the focus moves to the next field) when the field fills with data. If the Auto Tab property is set to No, the user must press Tab to move the focus to the next field after filling a field with data. The Enter Key Behavior property has two settings: Default and New Line in Field. If the property is set to Default, Access uses the existing setting stored in the Move After Enter option of the Options dialog box. If the property is set to New Line in Field, pressing the Enter key creates a new line in the text box.
- **Visible:** This property determines whether a control is normally visible. For most controls, the property is set to Yes. However, when you want to hide a control and display it under certain circumstances, you can set the property to No and later change the value of the property by using an expression within a macro or by using VBA programming code.
- **Display When:** This property determines when objects or entire sections of a form appear or print. You can set this property to Always, Print Only, or Screen Only. When set to Always, the object appears when you view the form and also when you print the form. Choosing Print Only causes the object to appear when you print the form but hides the object when you view the form in a window. The Screen Only option displays the object when you view the form in a window but omits it when you print the form.
- **Enabled and Locked:** You can use these properties to etermine whether a control can receive the *focus* (that is, a user can move the insertion point into the control) and whether a user can edit the data in the control. Setting the Enabled property to Yes allows the focus to move into the control, and setting it to No prevents the focus from moving into the control. When the Locked property is set to Yes, the property does not permit data to be edited in the control.
- **Tab Stop:** Use the Tab Stop property to determine whether a user will be allowed to move the focus to the control while in Form view. If the property is set to Yes (the default), the focus can be moved to the control. If the property is set to No, a user cannot move the focus to the control.
- **Tab Index:** Use this property to determine he successive tab order for the controls in the form; in other words, you are determining which control gets the focus next as the Tab key is pressed when the form is in use. In this property, you enter a numeric value that ranges from 0 to a value that's one less than the total number of controls on the form. The control with a tab index of 0 is the first control to receive the focus when a form is opened. When Tab is pressed, the focus moves to the control that has a tab index of 1, then to the control with a tab index of 2, and so on. By default, tab index values are assigned according to the order that the controls are initially placed on the form. You can change these values so that the focus "flows" through the form in the order you desire. (Another way to change the tab index values for a form's controls is to open the form in Design view, choose View ⇨ Tab Order, and select the desired tab order in the dialog box that appears.

- **Scroll Bars:** You can use these properties to determine whether a form's horizontal or vertical scroll bars will be visible in Form view. You can choose Horizontal Only, Vertical Only, Both, or Neither.
- **Can Grow and Can Shrink:** These properties are useful for forms that you want to print. They allow the controls to expand and contract as needed to accommodate the data in the control. Setting the Can Grow property to Yes allows the control to increase in size to accommodate the data. Setting the Can Shrink property to Yes allows the control to shrink from its default size when the data in the control does not fill the entire control. When Can Grow is set to Yes, the control grows vertically as needed to accommodate the data. When Can Grow is set to No, the control will not grow beyond its design size, regardless of the amount of data displayed in the control. When Can Shrink is set to Yes, the control can shrink vertically as needed to accommodate the data. When Can Shrink is set to No, the control will not shrink beyond its design size, regardless of the amount of data displayed in the control.
- **Default View and Views Allowed:** You can use these properties to determine how the form initially appears and which views users are allowed to switch to when using the form. Use the Default View property to determine whether the form initially appears as a single form, as a continuous form, or as a datasheet. Use the Views Allowed property to determine which views a user can switch to while using the form. You can choose Form View, Datasheet View, or Both in this property.
- **Caption:** This property is one of the form properties and contains the caption that appears in the form's title bar. You may discover that if you go into the Database window and rename a form you've created with the Form Wizard, the name of the form within the title bar does not change. To change the name shown in the title bar, you need to rename the caption in this property.

Entering expressions for calculated controls

When you add calculated controls, you must enter expressions to display the data you want to appear in the control. You can enter an expression (preceded by an equal symbol) in a text box, and each time a new record is displayed in the form, the expression is re-evaluated. You can enter the expression directly in a text box using these steps:

1. Using the Toolbox, add a text box control to the form.
2. Click inside the text box and type an equal (=) symbol.
3. Type the rest of the needed expression. For example, if the underlying table contained fields named *Bill Rate* and *Hours*, an expression to show the total amount might be as follows:

   ```
   =[Bill Rate] * [Hours]
   ```

4. Click anywhere outside the text box to complete the entry.

Changing a form's background colors

When manually designing forms, you may want to use background colors that are more visually appealing than the default colors. You can easily change a form's background color using the following steps:

1. Right-click any blank space in the form.
2. From the menu that appears, choose Fill/Back Color.
3. Select the desired color from the pop-up menu that appears.

Adding command buttons to Forms

Access provides a Command Button Wizard that helps you add command buttons to forms to perform common tasks such as adding new records, deleting records, or printing the current record displayed in the form. Command buttons can make your forms easier to use, particularly for users who may not be familiar with Access. As an example, Figure 25-8 shows a form containing command buttons used for common database tasks.

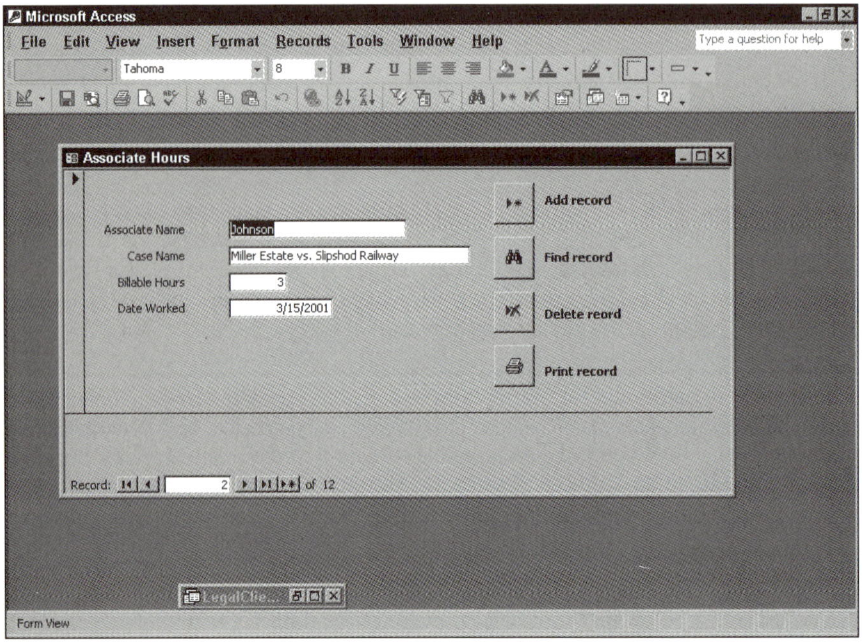

Figure 25-8: Command buttons can be placed on forms to make common database tasks, such as adding and editing records, easier.

You can add a command button to a form with the aid of the Command Button Wizard by using the following steps:

1. In the Toolbox, activate the Control Wizards if they are not already activated (click the Control Wizards button until it appears shaded).
2. In the Toolbox, click the Command Button tool.
3. Click in the form at the location where you want to place the command button.
4. Follow the directions that appear in the Command Button Wizard dialog boxes to finish adding the button.

Table 25-2 shows the types of tasks that can be performed with command buttons added using the Command Button Wizard.

Table 25-2
Command Button Wizard Operations

Available Categories	*When the Button Is Pressed, This Happens:*
Record Navigation	Find Next Find Record Go to First Record Go to Last Record Go to Next Record Go to Previous Record
Record Operations	Add New Record Delete Record Duplicate Record Print Record Save Record Undo Record
Form Operations	Apply Form Filter Close Form Edit Form Filter Open Form Open Page Print Form Print Current Form Refresh Form Data
Report Operations	Mail Report Preview Report Print Report Send Report to File
Application	Quit Application Run Application Run MS Excel Run MS Word Run Notepad
Miscellaneous	Auto Dialer Print Table Run Macro Run Query

TIP: When adding a command button to a form that prints the contents of the form, it is easy to confuse the two options provided by the wizard. In the Form Operations category, you will see Print a Form and Print Current Form. If you choose Print a Form, the resulting button (when clicked) will print a series of forms containing every record in the underlying table or query, which may or may not be what you intended. If you choose Print Current Form, the resulting button (when clicked) will print just the current record that is visible in the form at the time the user clicks the button.

Also, if you plan to print data using forms, you may want to change the background color of the form to white to avoid the use of large amounts of toner or ink in your printer. Generally, printing of data is best accomplished through the use of *reports*, which are the subject of the next chapter.

Adding graphics to forms

You easily can include graphics or pictures in your forms as design elements. Graphics often serve as decorative elements in forms; some of the backgrounds added by the Form Wizard make use of graphic elements. Figure 25-9 shows a form that contains a graphic as a design element.

You can easily insert graphics or pictures from your favorite graphics or photo package (such as Windows Paint or Adobe Photoshop) into your forms as design elements. The easiest method of performing this task is to use the Windows Clipboard, as detailed in the numbered steps that follow. When you paste a graphic from the Clipboard into a form, Access automatically adds an unbound object frame containing the graphic to the form. (You can use these same techniques to paste pictures or graphics into reports.)

Alternatively, you can add an object frame to a form and change its properties or use the Insert ⇨ Object command to add OLE objects containing graphics to the form.

You can copy graphics from other Windows packages into an Access form using the following steps:

1. Open the form in Design view.
2. Start the graphics program in the usual manner and then open the document containing the graphic image that you want to insert into the Access form.
3. Using the Windows selection techniques appropriate for the package you are using, select the portion of the graphic that you want to place in the Access form.
4. Choose Edit ⇨ Copy from your application's menus.
5. Switch back to Access, either with Alt+Tab or by clicking its button in the taskbar.
6. Click any blank area of the form and choose Edit ⇨ Paste. The graphic appears within the form.
7. Using the moving and sizing techniques of Access, place the graphic at the desired location in the form. After you've inserted the graphic, you can manipulate it using the original application by double-clicking the graphic (assuming that the original application supports Windows OLE).

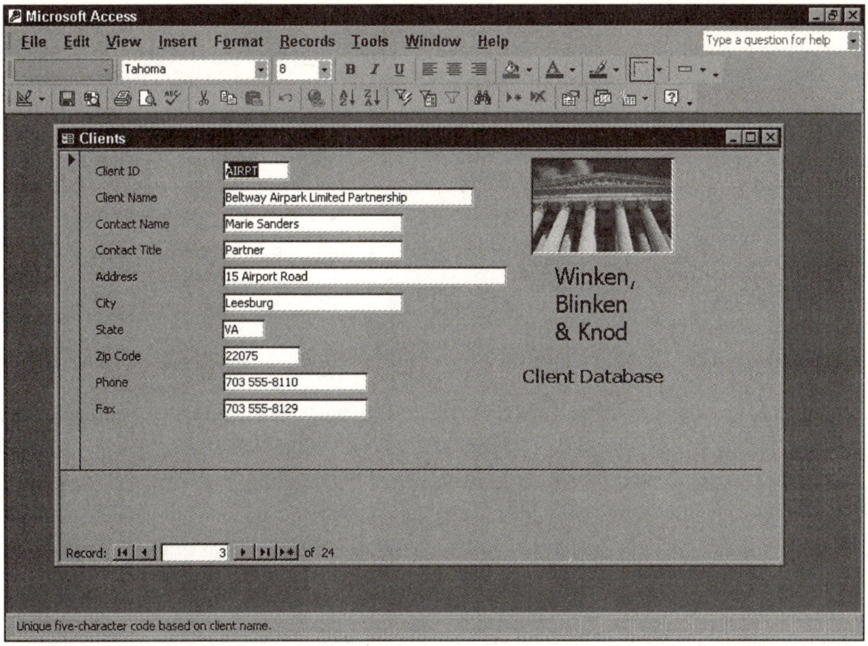

Figure 25-9: Access forms can include graphic images that can be supplied by other Windows software.

Saving and Using the Form

You can save a form with the same techniques you use to save objects elsewhere in Access. Choose File ⇨ Save from the menus, or double-click the form's Close box and answer Yes when asked whether you want to save the changes. If you are saving a form for the first time, Access also asks you for a name for the form. After it's saved, the form appears with all other forms in the Forms tab of the Database window.

To use the form, you can open it by selecting the desired form in the Database window and clicking Open, by double-clicking the form in the Database window, or by right-clicking the form and choosing Open from the shortcut menu that appears. Using any of these methods, the form opens in Form view, and you can view or edit data.

As you add records using a form, many of the techniques that you use are the same as you use for adding data through a table's datasheet. Move to the blank record that exists at the end of any table and enter the data (you can use the navigation buttons at the bottom of the form, or you can choose Edit ⇨ Go To ⇨ New Record from the menus).

When you are editing data, you can use the Tab or Shift+Tab keys to move between fields and use the PgUp and PgDn keys to move between records. You also can use the same search features described in Chapter 23 to find records; click in a field and then click the Find button in the toolbar, or choose Edit ⇨ Find from the menus to display the Find dialog box, which is used to search for data. (For more about the use of the Find dialog box, see the heading "Finding Data" in Chapter 23.)

Using Filter by Form

Access offers a feature known as *Filter by Form* that you can use to limit the data viewed in forms to meet certain criteria. If you've already learned about queries, you can think of Filter by Form as a way to assign a form query-like properties on-the-fly. For example, if you were viewing a table of firm employees in a form, you could use Filter by Form to limit the form so that only associates or only partners are visible in the form. Here are the steps you use to make use of the Filter by Form feature of Access:

1. With the form open in Form view, choose Records ⇨ Filter ⇨ Filter by Form from the menus, or click the Filter by Form button in the toolbar. In a moment, the form reappears with no data in the fields.
2. Type into the appropriate fields of the form criteria that will limit the records. For example, if a form contained a field for Employee Title and you wanted to see only associates, you would type the word *associate* into the Employee Title field. You can enter multiple criteria using the words *AND* or *OR*; for example, entering *associate or partner* in the Employee Title field filters the form to display associates or partners.
3. After you have entered the desired criteria, choose Filter ⇨ Apply Filter Sort, or click the Apply Filter button in the toolbar. The filtered records appear in the form, and the word *filtered* appears at the bottom of the form, informing you that a filter applies to the records you are viewing.

The filter remains in effect until you close the form or remove the filter. To remove the filter, choose Records ⇨ Remove Filter Sort from the menus, or click the Remove Filter button in the toolbar.

TIP: Filters can be saved as part of the form. If you apply a filter to a form and then click the Save button on the toolbar or choose File ⇨ Save, Access saves the filter as part of the form.

Creating Relational Forms Manually

Earlier in the chapter, you learned that you can use the Form Wizard to create *relational* forms, or forms that can be used to view data from more than one table (or query) at a time. Although the Form Wizard provides the easiest way to create relational forms, you also can create relational forms manually. Before doing so, you must create both a main form that contains the data from the parent table and a subform that contains the related data from the child table in the relationship. Figure 25-10 shows an example of a relational form.

If you want to create a relational form manually, you can use the following steps to do this:

1. Open the main form containing the primary, or parent, data in Design view.
2. In the Database window, click the Forms tab to display your stored forms.
3. Drag the form that you want to use as a subform from the Database window onto the main form. When you release the mouse button, a subform control appears in the form, as shown in the lower portion of Figure 25-11.
4. Move the subform control to its desired location within the main form.
5. Right-click the top edge of the subform control and choose Properties. When the Properties window appears, click the Data tab.
6. Examine the Link Master Fields property. If an entry exists, make sure that the entry uses the common field you want to use to link the records displayed within the subform to the record that will appear in the main form. If an entry does not exist, type the field name that should be used to establish the link between the subform and the main form.
7. Choose File ⇨ Save to save the form.

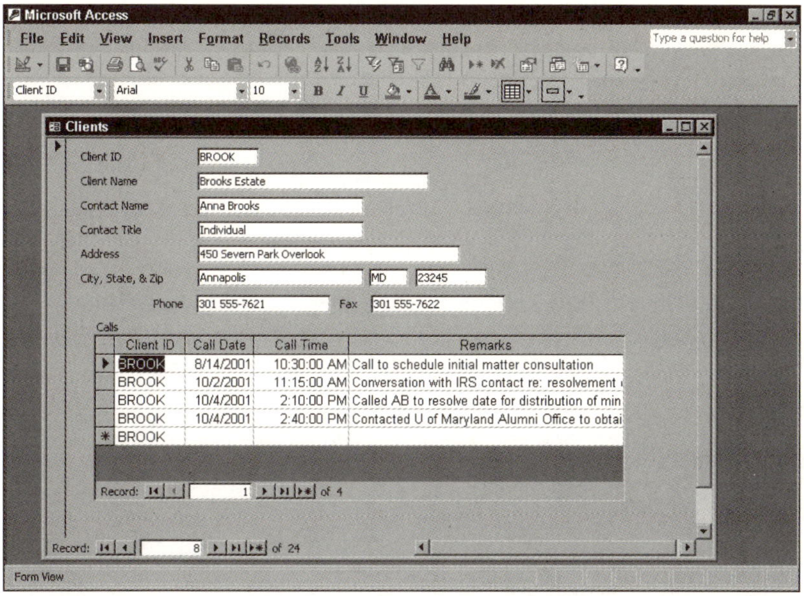

Figure 25-10: A relational form lets you view one record from a parent table and one or more associated records from a related child table.

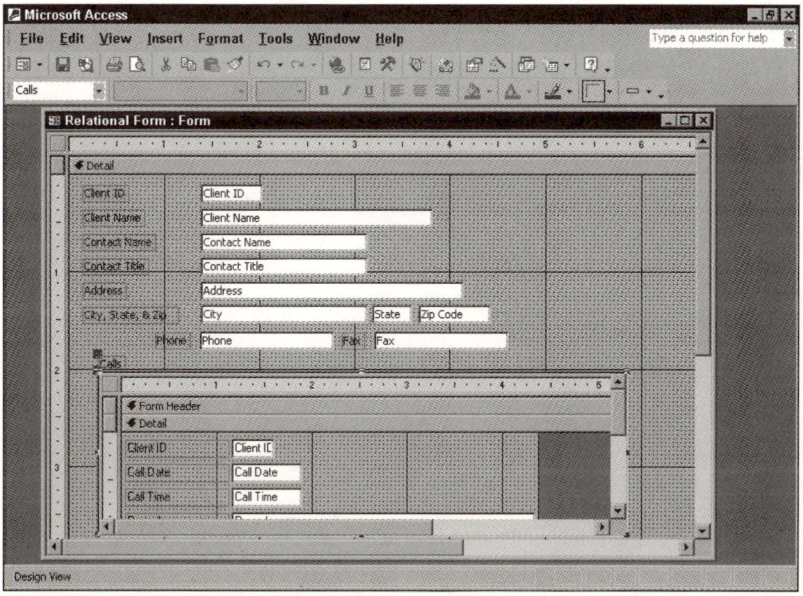

Figure 25-11: A relational form in Design view

Access will automatically establish the proper link needed in Step 6 if you established relationships between the tables being used at the table level as described in Chapter 23. Access will also establish a link if both the main form and the subform use a table that has a matching field (a field with the same field name and field type). If Access cannot establish a link, the Link Master Fields property will be blank, and you will need to fill in the name of the field for the form to operate correctly.

If you design a relational form but don't see the data you want when you switch to Form view, the difficulty may be that Access cannot determine how the underlying data should be used in the form. Assuming that you are using the form to show records from two tables having a *one-to-many* relationship (one record in the parent table being related to many records in the child table), make sure that the main form uses the parent table as its data source and the subform uses the child table as its data source. Keep in mind that the tables you are using to provide data to the main form and the subform must have a common field that serves to establish the relational link between the tables.

Creating Tabbed Forms

One feature of Access that can prove useful when you need to design complex forms containing large amounts of data is its capability to create tabbed forms. Tabbed forms contain multiple tabs, and each tab can contain different objects (such as text boxes, labels, or other controls). Tabbed forms operate in a manner similar to many dialog boxes used by Windows to set various system settings. Figure 25-12 shows an example of a tabbed form.

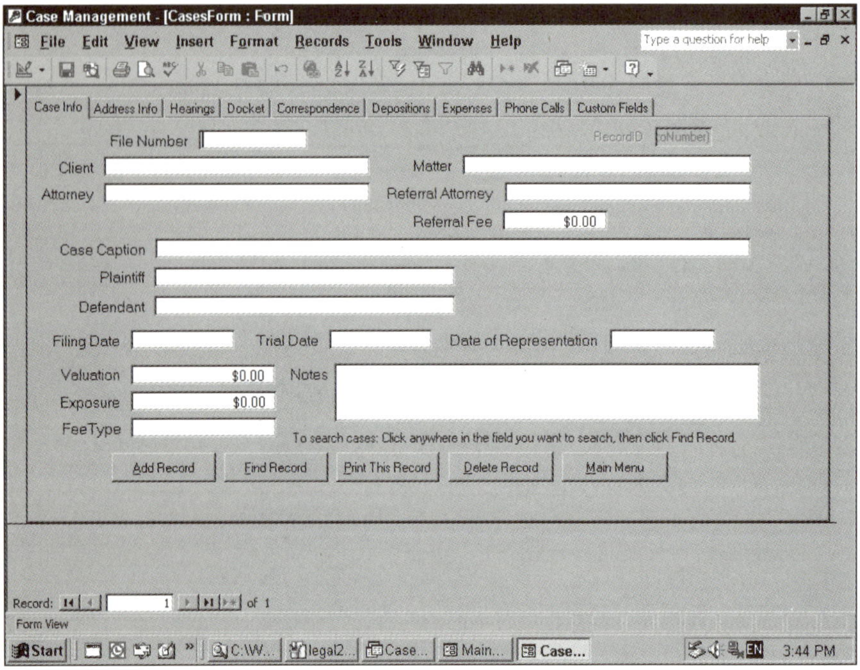

Figure 25-12: Tabbed forms are ideal for tables with large numbers of fields because you can organize the fields into different logical groups and place each group on a separate tab.

Working with tabbed forms is one area in which you must know the basics of manual form design because you cannot create tabbed forms using the Form Wizard. To create a tabbed form, you must use the tab control in the Toolbox. Use the following steps to create a tabbed form:

1. Open a new form in Design view and size the form as desired.
2. In the Toolbox, click the Tab Control tool.
3. In the form, click where you want to place the upper-left corner of the tab control and drag the lower-right corner to size the control as needed. When you release the mouse button, a tab

control containing two tabs appears, as shown in Figure 25-13. (See Step 5 if you need more than two tabs.)

4. To add controls to the tabs, click the desired tab to select it; then add the controls you want to appear on the tab by dragging them from the Field List or using the Toolbox tools.
5. To add more tabs to the tab control, right-click the tab that a new tab should appear to the right of; then choose Insert Page from the shortcut menu that appears, to add the new tab.
6. To change the title of a tab, double-click the tab itself to open a Property window for that tab. Click the Format tab in the Properties window and enter the desired title in the Caption text box.

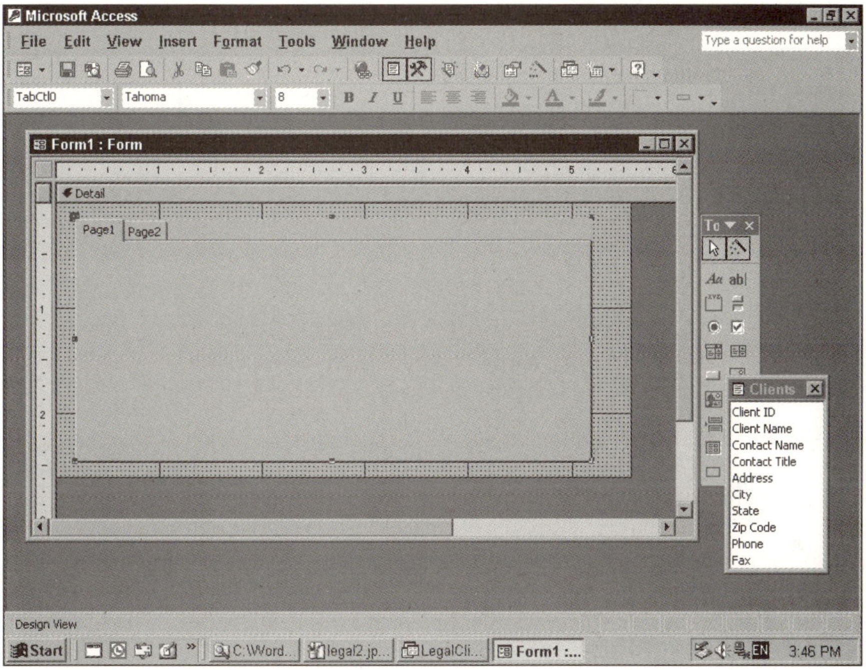

Figure 25-13: A form containing a tab control in Design view

Creating Data Access Pages

You also can use the Form Wizard in Access to create Data access pages. Data access pages resemble forms and, like forms, users can use them to view and edit data. However, the difference between conventional forms and data access pages is that data access pages are saved as HTML files and can be viewed with any Web browser that supports Microsoft's ActiveX technology (which includes versions of Internet Explorer from 5.0 onward). Data access pages are ideal for displaying data on law firm intranets or extranets. You can place the data access page and its supplemental files on your law firm's Web server and store the Access database on a shared network drive. Users throughout the firm can view and edit the data within a Web browser. Figure 25-14 shows a data access page viewed through Internet Explorer.

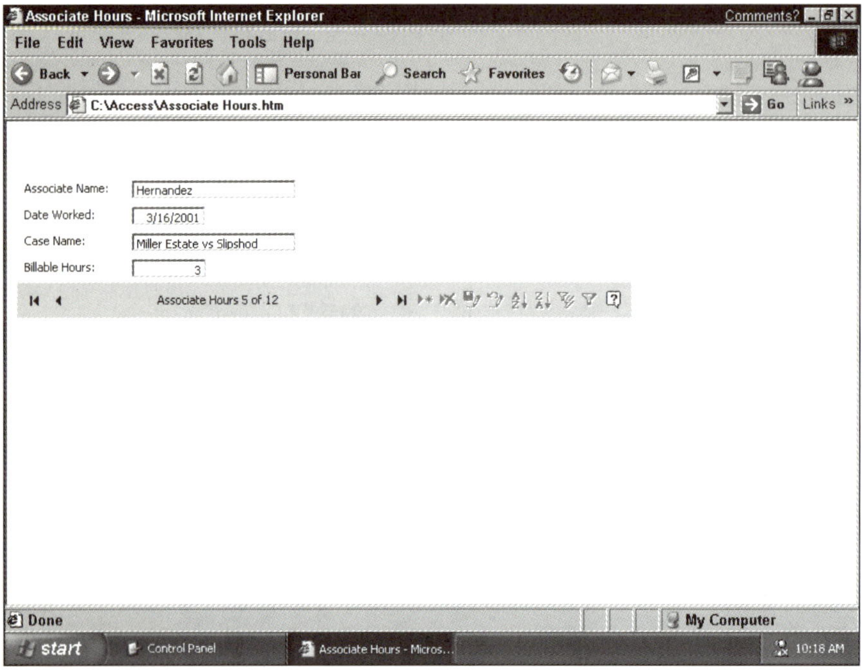

Figure 25-14: A data access page as viewed using Microsoft Internet Explorer

Data access pages are basically HTML forms with the built-in capability to link to the data that is stored within an Access table. (HTML, or *Hypertext Markup Language*, is the language of the World Wide Web, and Web pages are written using HTML.) You can view data access pages using Access or a Web browser such as Internet Explorer. The controls that are placed on a data access page are a special type of Microsoft control known as *ActiveX controls* and are similar in overall capabilities to the controls that you use to design and implement Access forms. The following section details how you can use the Data Access Page Wizard to create data access pages. (You also can design data access pages manually, although that topic is beyond the scope of this book.)

Creating data access pages with the Data Access Page Wizard

To create a data access page with the aid of the Data Access Page Wizard, perform the following steps:

1. In the Database window, click the Pages tab.
2. Double-click Create Data Access Page by Using Wizard. In a moment, the first page of the Data Access Page Wizard appears.
3. In the Tables/Queries list box, select the table or query that is to serve as the source of the data for the data access page.
4. After you select a data source in the Tables/Queries list box, all fields of that table or query appear in the Available Fields list box. You can click a field to select it and then click the right-arrow button to add it to the Selected Fields list box, or you can double-click the field. Or you can click the double-arrow button to add all the fields in the Available Fields list box to the Selected Fields list box. After adding the desired fields, click Next

5. The second page of the Data Access Page Wizard asks whether you want to add any grouping levels to the data access page. If you want to group the records on a field, select the desired field (on the left side of the dialog box) and use the right-arrow key to add it as a grouping level. Note, however, that the addition of grouping to a data access page results in a page that will be read-only when viewed in the Web browser. When you're done with this dialog box, click Next.
6. The third page of the Data Access Page Wizard asks whether you want a sort order for the records shown in the data access page. You can select up to four fields, and you can sort in ascending or descending order. Make any desired selections in this dialog box; then click Next.
7. The final page of the Data Access Page Wizard asks for a title for the page. Using the options shown in this dialog box, you can choose to open the data access page for viewing of the data in Access or open it in the Data Access Page Designer, where you can make additional changes to the design. Make your desired choice in the dialog box and click Finish to complete the data access page.

When the page is completed, an HTML file (with the title that you specified in Step 7 of the wizard and an .htm extension) is created in the default directory. You can copy this file to a location that users on a network can have access to, and the users can open the data access page using their copy of Internet Explorer. The page appears the same to users, whether they are viewing the page through Access or through Internet Explorer. As an example, Figure 25-15 shows the appearance of a data access page when viewed using Access. Figure 25-14, shown earlier, shows the appearance of that same data access page when viewed using Internet Explorer.

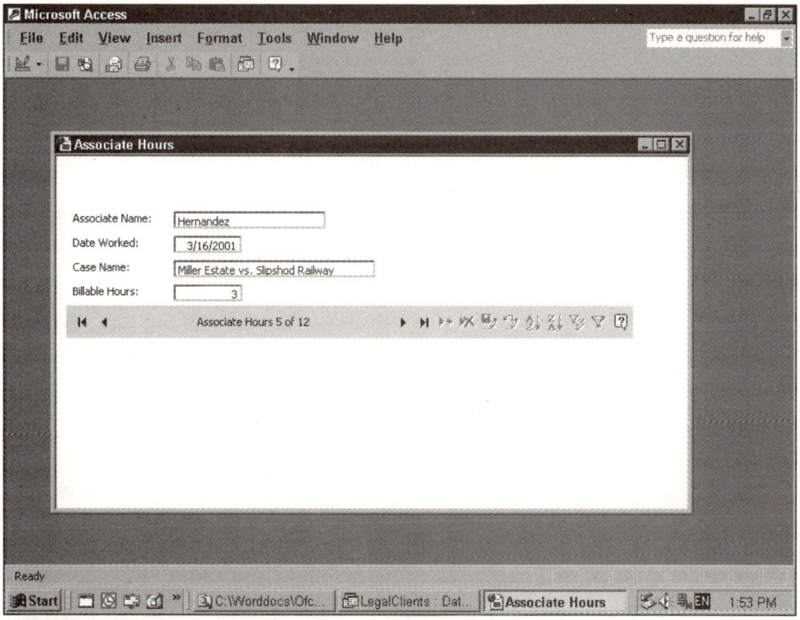

Figure 25-15: A data access page viewed through Access

Publishing a data access page

You typically will share data access pages with others within your law firm or legal department. To do this, you store the data access page, along with its supplemental files, on the Web server where your firm or company intranet is stored. You may need to contact your firm's Webmaster or network administrator to determine the proper location for the storage of these files. You will need to copy the following files to the server:

- The HTML file that contains the data access page
- Any supplemental files, including graphic files, used by the data access page. These will be stored in a subfolder with the same name as the data access page, followed by *_files*.

Additionally, you will need to place the Access database file in a shared directory on your network server if it does not already reside in a shared directory. And if you move the database, you will need to edit the Page Connection property of the data access page so that the data access page can locate the underlying database. To do this, open the data access page in Design view (right-click the data access page in the Database window and choose Design View). Next, right-click the title bar of the data access page and choose Page Connection from the shortcut menu that appears. In the Connection tab of the Data Link Properties dialog box that opens, enter the path and name for the database file. Be sure to use a Universal Naming Convention path (such as \\DCNTServer\intranet\data\staff.mdb), which will allow everyone within your firm to access the data. If you use a local path name (such as c:\intranet\data\staff.mdb), only the computer where the database file is stored will be able to view and edit the data through the data access page.

Working with Forms when You Have Multiple Users

Often (particularly at large law firms that use Access to track thousands of records related to a particular large case), you may have multiple users on a firm network who are adding and editing records in the same table. If you are going to create forms that are used simultaneously by multiple users on a network, you should take the "multiuser" nature of your forms into account during the form design process. Whenever multiple users can edit the same record in a networked environment, conflicts between users can arise.

Here's an example of the problem (which, in the real world, can easily happen with any Access database). The personnel department at a large law firm has a human resources database, running in Access, that tracks personnel data for all of the firm's employees. Employee Sandy Roberts calls John in personnel to change her HMO provider. John brings up Sandy's record in the personnel table by means of a form and begins editing.

Meanwhile, Mary (who works in personnel on the other side of the partition from John) is doing a routine update of employee addresses. She sees in her pile of last week's e-mails that Sandy Roberts sent her an address change last week, so she brings up the record for Sandy Roberts in a form and begins editing the address. Before she can finish these edits, John gets off the phone with Sandy, saves his changes to the record, and heads off to the lunchroom.

Now, when Mary tries to save the changes, she sees this weird Write Conflict dialog box that she's never seen before, as shown in Figure 25-16. Mary knows that John has gone to lunch, and she knows that she and John are the only ones in personnel who make changes to employee records, so she figures that the message must be some kind of system glitch and she clicks Save Record. The result: John's changes are overwritten and disappear into the electronic void. The danger of this kind of conflict between users is a real problem with multiuser databases, and unfortunately, no standard solution to the problem exists. However, Access does provide the settings you will need for dealing with record conflicts in a way that is best for your particular use of a database.

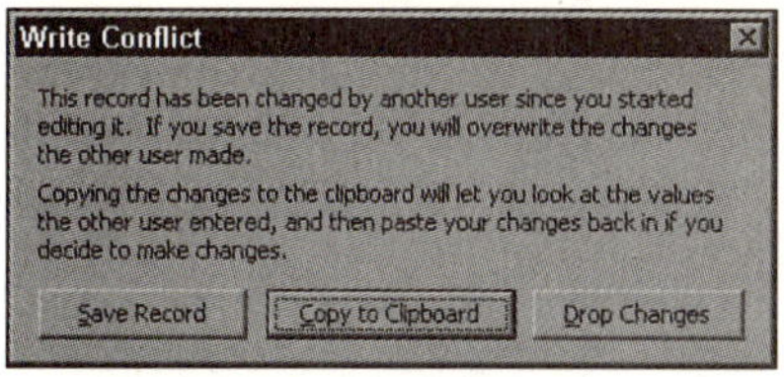

Figure 25-16 : The Write Conflict dialog box

If you use the Form Wizard to create one or more forms, store the database on a shared network drive, and ask a dozen paralegals to begin adding and editing records at the same time, the aforementioned scenario is a real possibility. However, the default setting of forms also affords multiple users with the most flexibility in handling multiuser conflicts (outside the addition of programming code, which is a topic beyond the scope of this book). This is because forms created in Access have a property called *Record Locks* set to No Locks by default. If you open a form in Design view and choose View ⇨ Properties to open the Properties window, the Record Locks property (on the Data tab) offers three choices: No Locks, Edited Record, and All Records.

When a form is set to the default No Locks setting, simultaneous changes are allowed by multiple users. When multiple users edit the same record, the user who saves first "wins." When the other users try to save changes by moving off the record, they see the dialog box shown in Figure 25-16, warning them that the data has been changed while they had the record opened for editing. They can choose to save their changes (overwriting the other users' changes), discard their changes (probably the safest option), or copy their changes to the Clipboard.

If you choose the Edited Record setting, Access locks only the block of data that contains the record being edited. (Depending on the design of the table, this may involve locking one or more nearby records as well; in Access, a *block* contains 2K of data, and that 2K will encompass as many records as can fit.) Other users will not be able to edit any records located in the block containing the locked record until the original user finishes editing the record.

If you choose the All Records setting, the entire table or query used as the form's data source will be locked as soon as a user begins editing in the form. No other users will be able to edit any of the data until the lock is released, which happens when the original user moves to a different record or closes the form. (Other users will be able to view data or print reports based on the data, but they will not be able to make any changes to the data.) Given its restrictive nature, this option makes sense only when you are certain that only one person should ever need to edit the data at a time.

If you are in an environment in which users are few and possible conflicts are rare, you may want to stick with the No Locks setting and train other users exactly how to handle the Write Conflicts dialog box if it ever appears. As long as others understand that they should back out of the record, discard their changes, and then re-open it before making any new changes, things should proceed smoothly. If many users share the records and conflicts are quite common, you may be better off setting the Record Locks property to Edited Record.

Summary

In this chapter, you learned how you can create a variety of forms to use to view and edit your data in Access tables. You learned the following:

- As a time-saver, the Form Wizard offers an automated method of quickly creating a variety of commonly used forms.
- In addition to creating forms with the Form Wizard, you can design forms manually and add controls where needed.
- One of the strengths of Access is the ease with which you can create relational forms that display data from multiple tables.
- You can make use of tabbed forms to display a large number of controls on a single form.
- Filter by Form can be used to analyze data through a form.
- You can use the Data Access Page Wizard to allow others at your firm to view or edit Access data through a Web browser.

The next chapter covers the specifics on creating and using reports to provide printed summaries of your data.

Chapter 26

Working with Reports

In This Chapter

- ♦ Creating a report with the AutoReport feature
- ♦ Creating a report with the Report Wizard
- ♦ Designing reports manually
- ♦ Adding graphics to reports
- ♦ Previewing reports
- ♦ Saving and printing reports
- ♦ Changing a report's data source
- ♦ Adding sorting and grouping to reports
- ♦ Adding page numbers to a report
- ♦ Adding the current date or time to a report
- ♦ Using the IIF function in reports
- ♦ Using summary calculations
- ♦ Creating mailing labels
- ♦ Creating relational reports manually
- ♦ Adding charts to reports

THIS CHAPTER SHOWS YOU HOW to create and use reports, which in many cases represent the end result of all your work in Access. You use reports to produce, on paper, listings of your data in virtually any conceivable format. Access provides reports in a wide variety of formats, with varying levels of detail. You can include graphic elements or photographs stored in a table in your reports. And you can easily create reports formatted as mailing labels to match a variety of popular label sizes.

As with forms, Access provides three overall methods for producing reports. You can use the AutoReport feature of Access to produce a report that is based on a single table or query, in a matter of seconds. Or you can use the Report Wizard to quickly design different types of reports. (Like the Form Wizard, the Report Wizard asks you a series of questions about the design that you prefer and produces a finished result based on your answers to these questions.) Finally, you can design reports manually, maintaining complete control over the design process.

Creating a Report with the AutoReport Feature

If you want to create a report that is based on a single table or query, the simplest way to do this is to use the AutoReport menu option of the New Object button on the toolbar. The AutoReport option creates a simple single-column report for whatever table or query is selected in the Database window when you click the button. To create a report using the AutoReport feature, perform these steps:

1. Select the desired table or query to be used as a source of data for the report in the Database window.
2. Click the down arrow to the right of the New Object button in the toolbar (it's the button with the lightning bolt) and choose AutoReport. In a moment, Access builds a default report for the table or query.

Plan first; create later

When faced with the need to get data from the database onto a printed page, too many Access users leap directly into creating a report, with little or no forethought devoted to the planning process. Some time spent in planning the report can save wasted effort later, especially if the rush to produce the report simply means that you must re-create it later when the managing partner complains that the report isn't what she or he really wanted. Before starting to create a report in Access, it is often a wise idea to lay out the report on paper by creating a hand-drawn sketch. You may want to get the opinions of those who will receive the reports during this "conceptual design" process, to reduce the chances of omitting needed information from the eventual report.

When you have an idea of the overall format your report should take, you should next create and test the queries that will supply the data to the report. (In theory, the report might be based on a table rather than on a query. But in practice, rarely is every single record in a table wanted in a report, so you will probably need queries that sort and select the desired data.)

Finally, with the report's overall design planned and the underlying queries created in Access, you can proceed to create the actual report. You can do this quickly with the assistance of the Report Wizard, or you can manually design the report, placing the desired text boxes, labels, and other design elements at the desired locations within the report.

NOTE: When you use the AutoReport feature to create a report, you get a report with all the fields aligned at the left side of the report, and the field names are used as the default labels for the fields. (If you want to change any of these design aspects of the report, you can easily do so by opening the report in Design view and making changes to the report manually, as detailed later in this chapter.)

Creating a Report with the Report Wizard

When you want a little more control over the end result (or when you need to create a report based on more than one table or query) but you still want Access to help you with the overall process, you can use the Report Wizard to aid in the creation of your reports. Like all wizards in Access, the Report Wizard asks you a series of questions and produces a finished, ready-to-use object (in this case, a report) based on your answers to the questions.

The steps listed below are the overall steps you will use to create reports with the Report Wizard. The paragraphs that follow these steps describe the steps in greater detail.

1. In the Database window, click the Reports tab.
2. Click New to display the New Report dialog box.
3. At the bottom of the New Report dialog box, select the desired table or query that will supply data to the report.
4. Click Report Wizard in the list portion of the box and then click OK.
5. Follow the directions and answer the appropriate questions that appear in the wizard dialog boxes. In the last dialog box that appears, click the Preview the Report option and then click Finish to begin viewing or printing data in Print Preview. Or click Modify the Report's Design and then click Finish to open the report in Design view, where you can make additional changes to the design of the report.

That's the process of using the Report Wizard in a nutshell. Following is the process in greater detail.

When you click the Reports tab in the Database window and then click New, the New Report dialog box appears, as shown in Figure 26-1. (This same dialog box appears if you use the Report option of the New Object button in the toolbar to create a report.)

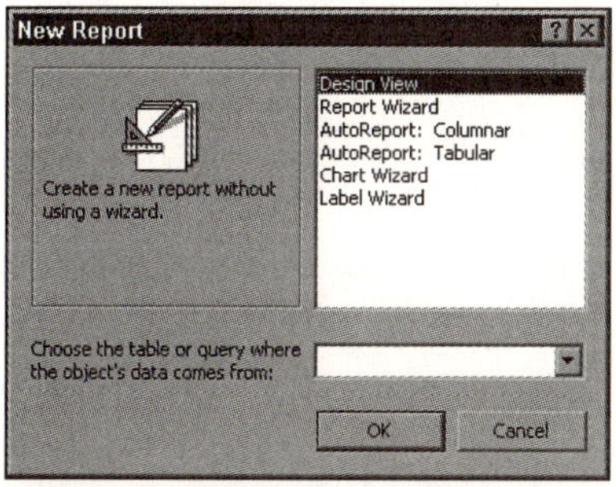

Figure 26-1: The New Report dialog box

In the lower portion of this dialog box, you can click the down arrow to open a list box that displays all the available tables and queries in the current database. In the upper portion of the dialog box, a list box contains choices for the type of wizard you want to use. Select Report Wizard from the list and then click OK. In a moment, the first dialog box for the Report Wizard appears.

At the top of the dialog box is a Tables/Queries list box. As you select a desired table or query from this list, the fields in that table or query appear below in the Available Fields portion of the dialog box. Select any desired field by clicking the field; then click the right-arrow button to add the field to the Selected Fields list within the dialog box. (Alternatively, you can double-click any field in the Available Fields list box to add it to the Selected Fields list box.)

If you want to include all the fields in the table or query in the report, just click the double right-arrow button. If you make a mistake and add a field you don't want in the report, select it in the Selected Fields list box and then click the left-arrow button to remove that field from the list.

If you want to create a *relational report* (a report that is based on more than one table or query), first add all the desired fields from the first table (or query). Then choose another table (or query) in the Tables/Queries list box and add the desired fields for that table or query. After adding all the fields needed by your report, click Next.

The dialog box that appears next depends on whether you have chosen fields from a single table or query or from more than one table or query. If you are using the Report Wizard to create a report based on multiple tables, queries, or both, the next dialog box that you see is the one shown in Figure 26-2. The left side of this dialog box asks you how you want to view the data and provides a list of the tables or queries you have chosen earlier to provide the data to the report. In effect, you are deciding which table (or query) should be the *parent data source*, or the table or query with the highest priority. Make a selection by clicking the desired table or query in the list at the left side of the dialog box; then click Next.

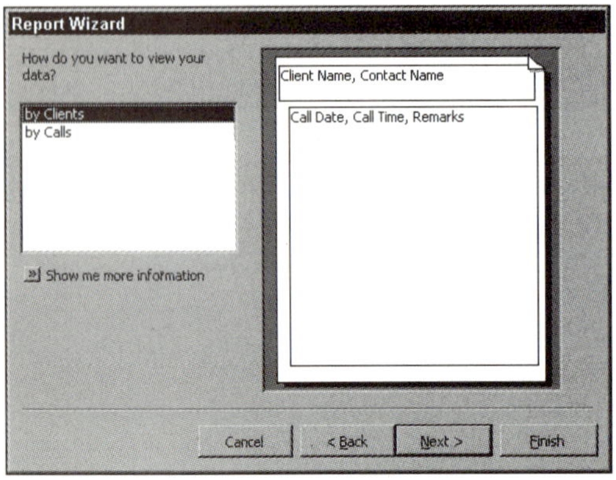

Figure 26-2: The second Report Wizard dialog box (used for multiple tables) lets you determine which table (or query) will serve as the parent source of data in a relational report.

After you make your selection (or if you originally selected fields from only one table or query), you next see the Report Wizard dialog box, shown in Figure 26-3.

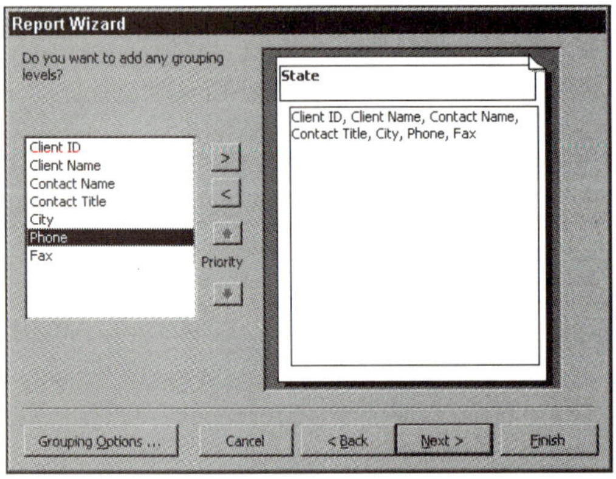

Figure 26-3: The Report Wizard dialog box used for grouping lets you choose a field or fields for grouping records.

You can use the options shown in this dialog box to specify levels of *grouping*, if desired, for the report. To specify grouping levels, select a desired field to base the groups of records on from the list box at the left; then click the right-arrow button to add a group band for that field. (*Group bands* are sections of a report that enable records within the report to be divided into groups.) After choosing any desired grouping, click Next to proceed. Or if you don't want any grouping in the report, you can click Next without selecting any fields in the dialog box. (For more specifics about grouping, see "Adding Sorting and Grouping to Reports," later in this chapter.)

The next dialog box that appears asks you to choose a sort order for the detail records that will appear in the report. You can sort on up to four fields when using the wizards to create a report. When sorting on multiple fields, the first field that you choose has the highest priority in the sort, the second field has the second-highest priority, and so on. Make any desired selections in the dialog box and click Next. (Note that if you need to sort a report on more than four fields, you can manually modify the sorting for the report; see "Adding Sorting and Grouping to Reports," later in this chapter for details.)

The next dialog box to appear asks you to select the desired layout for the report and lets you choose a desired orientation (Portrait or Landscape). You also activate the option that lets Access automatically adjust field widths to fit all fields on a single page. Make your desired selections in the dialog box and then click Next.

The next dialog box to appear lets you choose a report style from a list box. Access offers a number of different report styles, and a representative sample of each style appears in the dialog box as you click each style name. Select the style you want and then click Next to proceed.

The last dialog box that appears asks for a title for the report. A default title is provided (which is the same as the primary table or query that the report was based upon), and you can leave this title or change it to any title you wish.

Additionally, the options in the final dialog box let you open the report in Print Preview mode (where you can see how the report will appear or print the report) or open the report in Design view, where you can make further modifications to the design of the report. After you click Finish, the Report Wizard completes the process of creating the report.

After the report has been saved, it appears in the Database window under the Reports tab. You can select it and click Open to open the report in Print Preview mode, or you can select it and choose File ⇨ Print to print the report. For more details on previewing and printing reports, see "Previewing Reports" or "Saving and Printing Reports," later in this chapter.

Designing Reports Manually

If you prefer the do-it-yourself method for creating reports, Access will certainly not stand in your way. You can design your own reports from scratch using the manual method of report design. With this method, you open a blank report, size the report to the desired width and height, and add the desired design objects, such as text boxes that display the contents of fields, labels, graphics, lines, and so on, to the report. The overall steps behind the manual creation of reports are as follows:

1. Click the Reports tab in the Database window and then click New.
2. In the New Report dialog box that appears, choose the table or query that should serve as the primary source of data for the report.
3. Leave the Design View option selected in the list and click OK. In a moment, a blank report appears (see Figure 26-4).

4. Using the Toolbox and the Field List, place the desired objects (text boxes, labels, and any other types of controls that are needed) on the report. (If the Toolbox is not visible, choose View ⇨ Toolbox from the menus to display it; if the Field List is not visible, choose View ⇨ Field List from the menus to display it.)
5. Specify any desired sorting, grouping, or both within the report.
6. Choose File ⇨ Save from the menus to save the completed report.

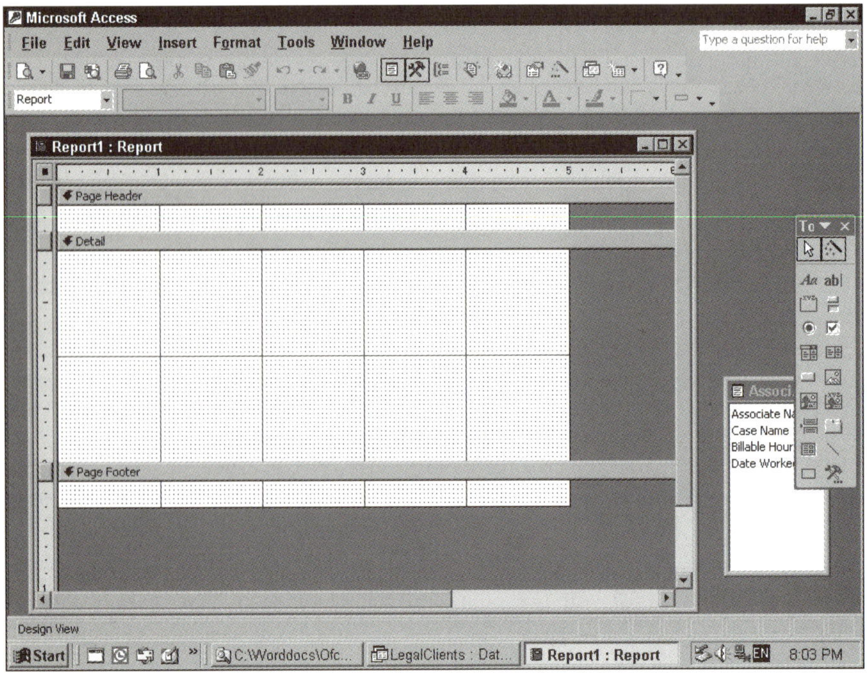

Figure 26-4: A blank report in Design view contains sections for the page header, the page footer, and detail. You can add other sections to the report.

In addition to manually creating reports from scratch, you can open existing reports that have been created with the AutoReport feature or with the Report Wizard in Design view. To do so, select the report in the Database window and click Design, or right-click the report in the Database window and choose Design from the menu that appears. Figure 26-5 shows an example of an existing report, created using the Report Wizard, that has been opened in Design view.

Existing reports will usually contain *text box controls*, which are used to display the data contained in the fields of the table or query. Reports also typically contain *label controls*, which serve to identify fields or act as titles in the report. Optionally, reports can contain report headers and report footers, page headers and page footers, and group headers and group footers, as explained in the paragraphs that follow.

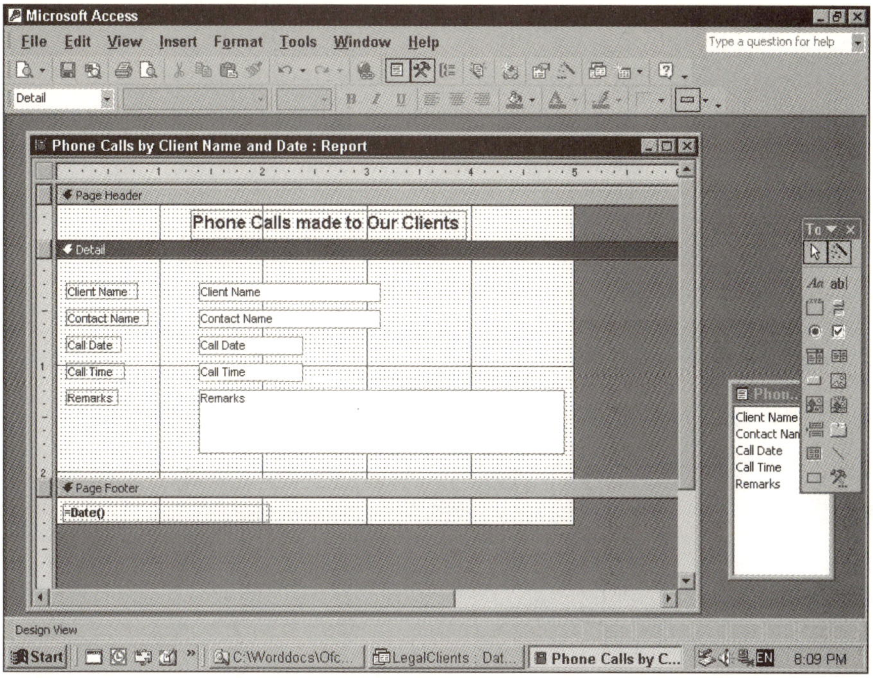

Figure 26-5: An existing report that was opened in Design view

Designing reports manually? Let the Report Wizard lend a hand!

In some cases, you may prefer to design your own reports. However, you shouldn't ignore the helpful capabilities of the Report Wizard. You can usually save considerable time and effort by letting the Report Wizard create a report, and then you can open that report in Design view and make manual changes to the report, using the techniques described in "Designing Reports Manually."

To print the completed report, select it in the Database window and choose File ⇨ Print, or click the Print button on the toolbar. Alternatively, while previewing the report, you can choose File ⇨ Print or click the Print button on the toolbar. For more details about printing, see "Saving and Printing Reports," later in this chapter.

Understanding the report's layout

A report's layout contains a number of different sections called *bands*, which are illustrated in Figure 26-6. Understanding how these bands are used and how they relate to each other is vital in designing effective reports.

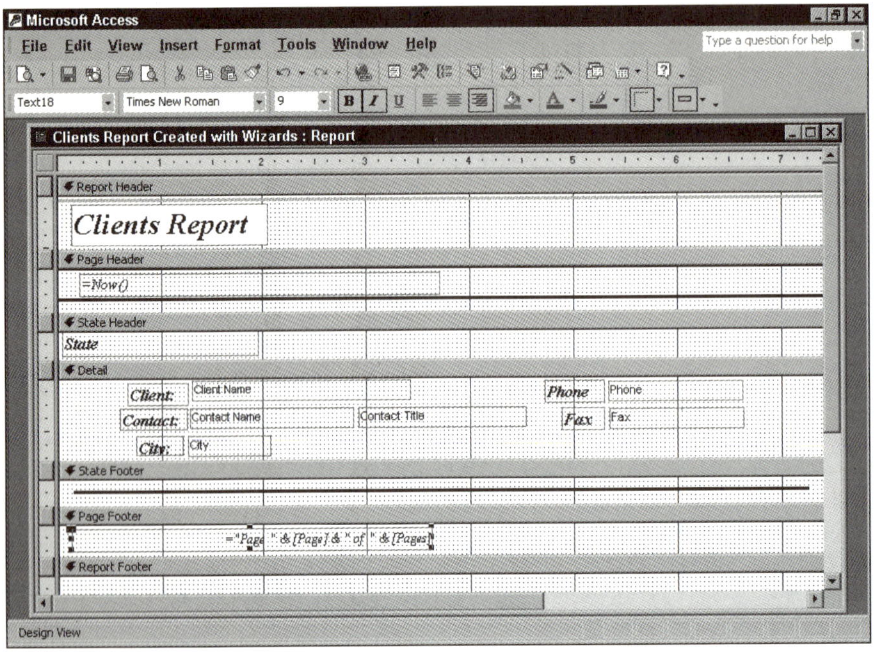

Figure 26-6: The sections of a report

By default, a new report that you create contains a page header band, a page footer band, and a detail band. Optionally, reports can also contain report header bands and report footer bands, and reports can contain group bands.

Report header bands contain information that appears once, at the beginning of the report. (Typically, the title of the report is placed in this area.) *Report footer bands* contain information that appears once, but at the end of the report. (Many financial reports include summary fields that provide numeric or currency totals in the report footer band.) If a report does not contain report header and footer bands, you can add them while in Design view by choosing View ⇨ Report Header/Footer.

Page header bands appear at the top of each page. If the report includes a report header band, the page header band on the first page of the report will appear directly beneath the report header band. With reports that are tabular in nature, the page header band typically contains field names corresponding to the columns of data that will appear underneath. *Page footer bands* appear at the bottom of each page. (Page numbers are usually placed in the page footer band.) If the report includes a report footer band, the page footer band on the last page of the report appears directly above the report footer band. If a report does not contain page header and footer bands, you can add them while in Design view by choosing View ⇨ Page Header/Footer.

The *detail band* contains the actual data that appears in the body of the report. The detail band appears on each page, sandwiched between any page header band and page footer band. Text boxes that contain the contents of the fields from the underlying table or query are typically placed in the detail band.

Group bands, which are optional, appear once for each group of records. When you use group bands, a *group header band* appears above the detail records for the group, and a *group footer band* appears below the detail records for the group. Group bands, when used, typically contain labels or text boxes that serve to identify the group. As an example, if a report contained records of time entries by client and matter, you would probably want to group the records by individual client, and within each client grouping, by matter number.

When Access prepares a report for printing, it begins by printing the contents of the report header band, followed by the contents of the page header band. Then Access prints detail sections until the bottom of the page is reached. Access then prints the contents of the page footer band and sends a page break to the printer to feed the next sheet of paper. Access then prints the contents of the page header band, followed by another detail section, followed by the page footer band and another page break. On the final page of the report, Access follows the same sequence, adding the contents of the report footer band at the end of the report.

The process of printing a report is basically the same when your report includes group bands, with the following exception: Access prints the contents of the group header band before the first record in each group and prints the contents of the group footer band after the last record in each group.

It is important to understand where Access prints each band, because a thorough knowledge of the purpose of each band will ensure that you place the desired controls in the correct bands when designing your reports. For example, if you wanted to place a text title at the top of the first page, you would need to put a label containing the text in the report header band. However, if you wanted that title to appear at the top of every page, you would place the label in the page header band rather than in the report header band.

Working with the design area of a report

When you create a report manually, it initially opens to a default size. Rulers appear at the top and left edges of the report, and a grid composed of dots fills the drawing area (unless these options have been turned off with the View ⇨ Ruler or View ⇨ Grid menu options). You can change the size of the report as necessary to accommodate as many fields or other objects as you may need. Use the following steps to change the size of a report:

1. While in Design view, place the pointer at the top edge of a band or at the right edge of the report. The pointer changes to a double-headed arrow.
2. Drag the pointer up or down to change the height of the band, and drag the pointer left or right to change the width of the report.

Adding controls to reports

As you design reports, most objects you add to the report (such as labels, and text boxes that display fields) are called *controls*. If you are going to do much work with reports in Design view, you must know how to add, move, and size controls as needed. In Access, you can add three types of controls to reports, as follows:

- **Bound controls:** These are controls that are connected to a field of the table or query that the report is based upon. In Figure 26-5, shown previously, the text boxes that display the contents of the fields are bound controls. The most commonly used type of bound control is the text box control. However, other types of bound controls can be used in reports, such as check boxes, list boxes, toggle buttons, and object frames (which typically display photos stored in OLE fields of a table).
- **Unbound controls:** These are controls that are not connected to any fields of a table or query. In reports created by the Report Wizard, the title that appears in the report header and the labels containing the names of the fields are unbound controls.

- **Calculated controls:** These are controls that display the results of a calculation. The expression used to perform the calculation is typically based on one or more fields of a table.

You add controls to reports using either of two tools: the Field List or the Toolbox. (If the Field List or the Toolbox doesn't appear when you open a report in Design view, you can display either by choosing View ⇨ Field List or View ⇨ Toolbox from the menus.) Figure 26-7 shows the Field List (on the left) and the Toolbox (on the right).

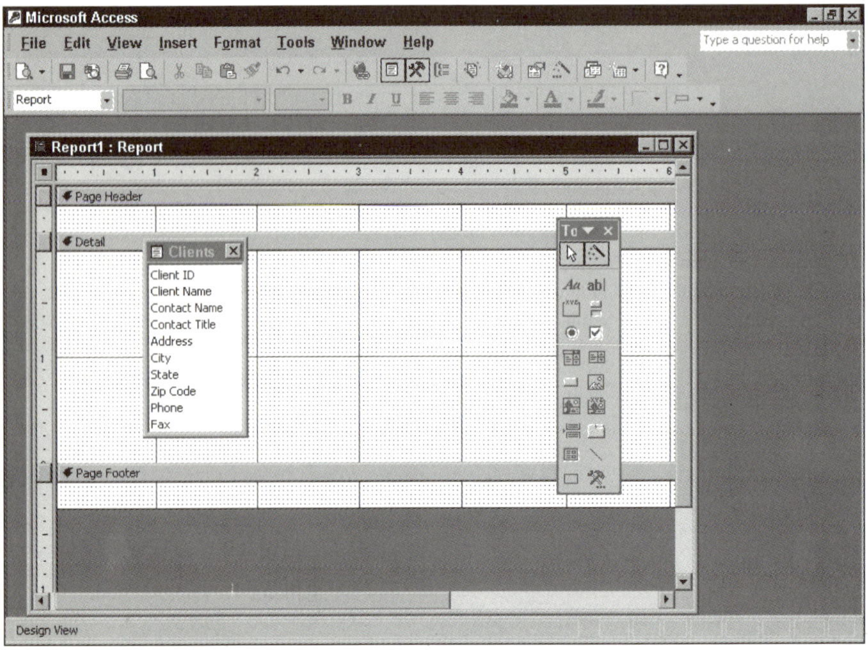

Figure 26-7: The Field List and the Toolbox

When you want to add bound controls to a report, the easiest way to do so is to use the Field List. Assuming that the type of control you want to create is a text box, you just drag the desired field from the Field List to the desired location on the report. When you release the mouse button, a text box bound to the appropriate field appears.

You can add multiple fields to the report as text boxes in a single operation by selecting the first field in the Field List and then holding the Ctrl key as you select each additional desired field in the list. After all the needed fields are highlighted, click any selected field and drag the fields onto the report as a group. (Note that if the fields are too close together for your liking, you can easily space them apart by choosing Format ⇨ Vertical Spacing ⇨ Increase.)

TIP: You easily can add check boxes or option buttons based on Yes/No fields to a report. To do this, first click the Check Box tool or the Option Button tool in the Toolbox. Then drag the desired Yes/No field from the Field List to the desired location on the report. The check box or option button that appears in the report will be based on the corresponding field.

To add other types of controls to a report, you use the assortment of tools shown in the Toolbox. The various controls of the Toolbox and their uses are described in Table 26-1. (Note that because Access uses the same Toolbox for form design and for report design, some controls present in the Toolbox do not actually apply to reports but are used with forms.)

Table 26-1
The Controls of the Toolbox

Tool	***Purpose***
Select Objects	Selects, moves, sizes, or edits objects in the report.
Control Wizards	Turns the Control Wizards on or off.
Label	Adds labels that are convenient for titles, instructions, or descriptive text.
Text Box	Creates text boxes that can display the contents of fields.
Option Group	Adds an option group to the report. Option groups contain check boxes, option buttons, or toggle buttons for a group.
Toggle Button	Adds toggle buttons. Can be used with option groups to indicate one choice out of many or can be used individually to indicate a yes/no choice.
Option Button	Adds option buttons (also called *radio buttons*). Can be used with option groups to indicate one choice out of many or can be used individually to indicate a yes/no choice.
Check Box	Adds check boxes. Can be used with option groups to indicate one choice out of many or can be used individually to indicate a yes/no choice.
Combo Box	Used to create a combination box (combination boxes are used in forms but are not useful in reports).
List Box	Used to create a list box (list boxes are used in forms but are not useful in reports).
Command Button	Adds a command button (command buttons are used in forms but are not useful in reports).
Image	Inserts a frame that displays a static image.
Unbound Object Frame	Inserts a frame that contains an OLE object.
Bound Object Frame	Inserts a frame that contains the contents of an OLE object field.
Page Break	Inserts a page break at a specified location in the report.
Tab Control	Adds a tabbed form (tabbed forms are used in forms but are not useful in reports).
Subform / Subreport	Adds an object that contains a subreport.
Line	Draws lines in a report.
Rectangle	Draws rectangles or squares in a report.
More Controls	Opens a new menu used for adding controls (such as Visual Basic VBX controls) to a report.

To create a label, click the Label tool in the Toolbox. On the report, click where you want to place the label, type the text for the label, and press Enter. (You can change the label's font and size, if desired, by selecting it and then choosing the desired font and font size from the toolbar.)

The exact steps for creating other types of controls will depend on the type of control, but here are the overall steps you can use:

1. If the Toolbox is not already visible, choose View ⇨ Toolbox to display it.
2. If you don't want to use the Control Wizards to assist in creating the control, click the Control Wizards button in the Toolbox until the button is raised (not active).
3. Click the desired type of control you want to create in the Toolbox.
4. Click in the report where you want to place the upper-left corner of the control; then drag the pointer to size the control to the desired size. (Alternatively, you can just click and release the mouse button and you will get a control sized to the default control size.) If the Control Wizards are on and are appropriate to the type of control you are adding, you can follow the directions in the Control Wizard dialog boxes that appear.

TIP: On occasion, you may need to include the name of a law firm in the report header or page header band. And many law firm names include an ampersand character, as in *Winken, Blinken, & Knod.* However, if you create a label control and type a single ampersand (&) character between two names, the character displays or prints as an underscore character in the report. This happens because Access uses the ampersand character as a special character (a hotkey indicator) in form and report design. When you want to include an ampersand character within a label in a form or a report, you must type two ampersands in a row. When the report prints, a single ampersand will be printed in the location where you entered the double ampersand in the label.

Moving, sizing, and deleting controls

As you work with controls, you will often want to move them or change their size. To move a control, first select the control by clicking anywhere within the control. Then move the pointer to any edge of the control where the pointer changes shape to an outstretched palm, and drag the control to the desired location.

TIP: You can move a group of controls in one operation by first selecting the controls as a group. To do this, select the first control and then hold the Shift key as you select each additional desired control. (Alternatively, you can click at the upper-left corner of a group of controls and drag to the lower-right corner of the group of controls.) When all the controls are selected, you can move the pointer to any edge of any selected control where the pointer changes shape to an outstretched palm and drag the controls as a group to the desired location.

To resize a control, select the control by clicking it. Then move the pointer to any of the control's sizing handles (where the pointer changes shape to a double arrow) and click and drag the control to the desired size.

To move a text box control separately from its label, place the pointer over the handle at the upper-left corner of the text box, where the pointer changes to a hand with a pointing finger. Then click and drag the text box to the desired location.

To delete a control that is not wanted, select the control and then press the Del key.

TIP: Occasionally, you will want to move controls very small distances. You can easily do this by selecting the control and then pressing the Ctrl key while using the arrow keys.

Changing a control's properties

Controls have *properties* that affect how the control behaves when the report is used, and you can put these properties to use in designing your reports for the proper printing of data. To change the properties of a control, first select the control by clicking it. Then choose View ⇨ Properties from the menu, or click the Properties button in the toolbar. (Alternatively, you can right-click a control and choose Properties from the menu that appears.) When you do this, a Properties window for the selected control appears. Figure 26-8 shows the Properties window for a text box control, the type of control most commonly used in reports.

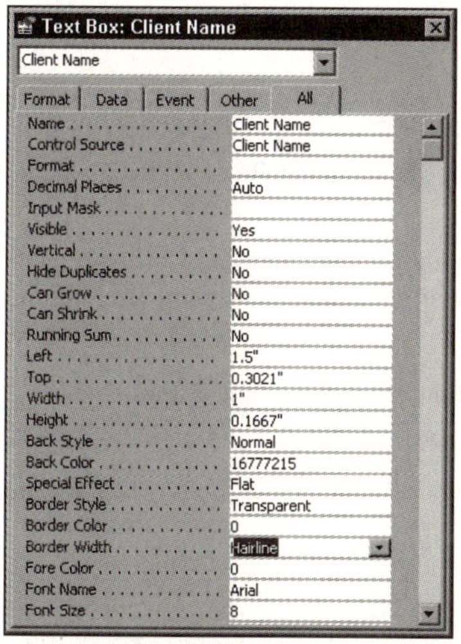

Figure 26-8: The Properties window for a text box control

The types of properties that are available will vary, depending on the type of control that you are working with. However, in all cases, you can see a detailed explanation of any particular property by using the help screens. Just click inside the row of the desired property in the Properties window and press F1 to see a help screen that explains how to use the property in question.

To set a property, first click the desired tab in the Properties window (Format, Data, Event, Other, or All) and then click the name of the property whose value you wish to set. If an arrow appears at the right of the property, you can click it and choose a desired value from the list box that opens. If no arrow appears, you can type the desired setting or expression directly into the property box.

The following list describes some of the more common properties that you will find useful as you add controls to reports:

- **Control Source:** This property tells the control where to obtain the data displayed within the control. When you create text box controls by dragging them from the Field List into the report, the control is created automatically. You can enter expressions in the Control Source property by typing them in directly or by right-clicking the property and choosing Build from the shortcut menu, which brings up an Expression Builder that you can use to create an expression.
- **Format:** This property defines any format used to display the data. (The precise types of formats you can use vary, depending on the type of data displayed by the control; for example, with controls that display the contents of number fields, you can use number formats.) Clicking the down arrow that appears at the right side of the selected property opens a list box showing the formats available for the type of field with which you are working.
- **Decimal Places:** When working with number or currency fields, you can use this property to display how many decimal places should be used with the numbers displayed. You can choose Auto or enter a value from 0 to 15, indicating the number of decimal places desired. Digits to the left of the decimal appear as specified in the Format property setting, whereas digits to the right of the decimal appear with the specified number of places.
- **Input Mask:** You can use this property to define an *input mask*, a format that data must follow as it is displayed or printed. For example, if you set this property to 000-00-0000, hyphens display in the locations shown, and digits display in the other locations. You can see a list of the symbols you can use for input masks, and examples of input masks, by placing the insertion point in the property and pressing F1.
- **Visible:** This property determines whether a control is normally visible or not. For most controls, the property is set to Yes. However, when you want to hide a control and display it under certain circumstances, you can set the property to No and later change the value of the property using VBA programming.
- **Hide Duplicates:** This property determines whether a value displayed or printed in a control within a report should be hidden if the data for a given record is the same as the data for the previous record.
- **Can Grow and Can Shrink:** These properties are useful for reports that will contain large amounts of text. They allow the controls to expand and contract as needed to accommodate the data in the control, as the following table describes.

Property	*Set to Yes*	*Set to No*
Can Grow	Control can increase vertically in size to accommodate the amount of data.	Control will not grow beyond its design size, regardless of the amount of data.
Can Shrink	Control can shrink vertically to a size smaller than its default size when the data in the control does not fill the entire control.	Control will not shrink beyond its design size, regardless of the amount of data displayed in the control.

TIP: One of the more troublesome areas of custom report design is how to handle text boxes that may or may not contain large amounts of text. Memo fields are an excellent example. One row may contain three paragraphs of text in a memo field and the next record may contain five words in the same field. If a text box of one size is allotted for the memo field in a report, some records may not have enough space to display the contents of the memo field, whereas others may waste space. The solution to this problem is to use the Can Grow and Can Shrink properties. Access gives you these options to enable text box controls to grow or shrink vertically, depending on how much text is in the record being displayed or printed. The Can Grow property, when set to Yes, allows the text box control to grow vertically in size to accommodate additional text if the text in the record cannot fit within the confines of the field. The Can Shrink property, when set to Yes, allows the text control to shrink vertically if the text in the record does not fill up the field.

To set either property, click the text box tool to select it, open the Properties sheet for the text box by choosing View ⇨ Properties, and click in either the Can Grow or the Can Shrink property. Set either option to Yes or No as desired.

Entering expressions for calculated controls

When you add calculated controls, you must enter expressions to display the data you want to appear in the control. You can enter an expression (preceded by an equal symbol) in a text box, and each time a new record is displayed in the report, the expression is reevaluated. You can enter the expression directly in a text box using these steps:

1. Using the Toolbox, add a text box control to the report.
2. Clicke inside the text box and type an equal (=) symbol.
3. Type the rest of the needed expression. For example, if the underlying table contained fields named *Bill Rate* and *Hours*, an expression to show the total amount might be as follows:

   ```
   =[Bill Rate] * [Hours]
   ```

4. Click anywhere outside the text box to complete the entry.

Adding Graphics to Reports

On occasion, you may have a need for graphics or pictures in your reports as design elements. Graphics often serve as decorative elements in reports. Figure 26-9 illustrates a report that contains a graphic as a design element.

Technically, you could use the Image tool of the Toolbox to insert an object frame and place the graphic inside that object frame. However, if all you need is a graphic, it is easier to just paste in the graphic from another Windows application. When you paste in a graphic that you copy from another Windows program into a report in Design view, the graphic automatically appears in an unbound object frame, and you can move or size the frame as desired. Use the following steps to paste a graphic into a report as a design element:

1. Open the report in Design view.

2. Switch to the graphics program you are using and open the file containing the desired graphic.
3. Using the selection techniques appropriate for the graphics program you are using, select the desired portion of the graphic image.
4. From the menus, choose Edit ⇨ Copy to copy the graphic to the Windows Clipboard.
5. Use the Windows Taskbar to switch back to Access.
6. Click in the section of the report where you want the graphic to appear; then choose Edit ⇨ Paste.
7. Use the moving and sizing techniques covered earlier in this chapter to size the graphic and place it in the desired location in a report.

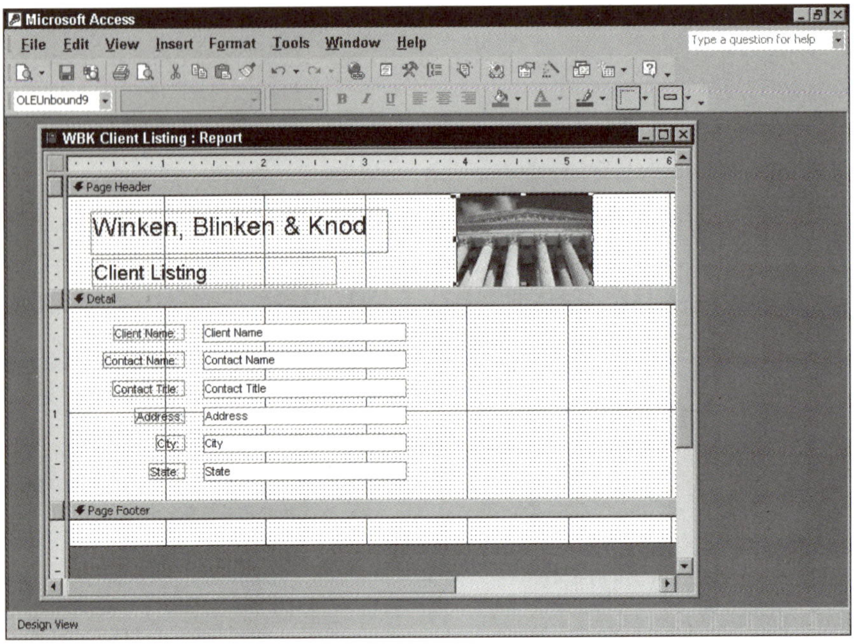

Figure 26-9: In Access, reports can include graphic images that can be supplied by other Windows software.

Previewing Reports

At any time during the design process, you can preview the report to see an on-screen representation of how the report will look when it is printed. To preview a report, choose File ⇨ Print Preview, or click the View button on the toolbar. Using either method, a preview of the report appears in a window.

You can use the scroll bars or the PgUp and PgDn keys to see additional portions of the report while in preview mode. And you can use the arrows at the bottom of the window to view other pages of the report. Use the Zoom button in the toolbar of the preview window to enlarge the image that you are viewing, and use the Close button to close the preview window when you are done previewing the report.

Saving and Printing Reports

You can save a report with the same techniques you use to save objects elsewhere in Access. Choose File ⇨ Save from the menus, or double-click the report's Close box and answer Yes when asked whether you want to save the changes. If you are saving a report for the first time, Access will also ask you for a name for the report. After it's saved, the report appears with all other reports in the Reports tab of the Database window.

To print an existing report, highlight the desired report in the Database window and choose File ⇨ Print, or right-click the desired report in the Database window and choose Print from the shortcut menu that appears. In a moment, the Print dialog box appears. In the dialog box, you can choose a range of pages, the number of copies to be printed, and the printer to use. Make your desired selections in the dialog box and click OK to begin printing.

Alternatively, if you want just one copy of the report sent to the default printer, you can select the desired report in the Database window and then click the Print button on the toolbar to print the report.

Changing a Report's Data Source

When you initially create a report (whether you use the Report Wizard or design the report manually), you indicate the source of the data by choosing a table or query during the report-creation process. That table or query name is saved to the report's record source property so that Access knows where to find the data for the report. Occasionally, you may need to change the record source property for an existing report so that the report uses a different table or query (of course, the table or query must contain all the fields needed by the report). You can change the record source property for a report using the following steps:

1. Open the report in Design view.
2. From the menus, choose Edit ⇨ Select Report (to ensure that the report, and not a control, is selected).
3. If the Properties window is not already visible, choose View ⇨ Properties from the menu to display the window.
4. Click the Data tab in the Properties window.
5. In the Record Source box, choose the desired query or table that should provide the data to the report.
6. Save the report by choosing File ⇨ Save.

Adding Sorting and Grouping to Reports

Most reports are designed with the data sorted in a specific order. You can include a sort order in the design of a report. (If a report is based on a query that includes a sort order and no sort order is specified for the report, the records will appear sorted according to the design of the query. If the report is based on a query and the query and the report specify different sort orders, the reports' sort order overrides that of the query when the report is printed.)

In addition to sorting, you can also group records by sorted categories. Sorting and grouping work hand in hand because when you include a sort order in a report, the records appear in groups based on the fields used for the sort. You control both sorting and grouping in Access reports by means of the Sorting and Grouping dialog box. You can add sorting and, optionally, grouping (the presence of group bands) to a report with the following steps:

1. Open the report in Design view.
2. From the menus, choose View ⇨ Sorting and Grouping or click the Sorting and Grouping button on the toolbar. The Sorting and Grouping dialog box, shown in Figure 26-10, appears.

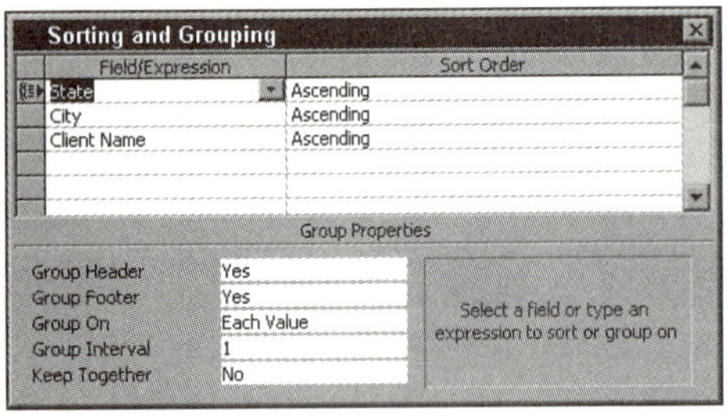

Figure 26-10: The Sorting and Grouping dialog box

3. In the first row of the Field/Expression column, click to open the drop-down list and choose the field with the highest priority for the sort.
4. In successive rows of the Field/Expression column, choose any desired fields for additional levels of sorting.
5. Set the Sort Order column for each field used in the sort to Ascending or Descending, as desired.

Additionally, if you want to include group bands within the report for the sorted fields, perform these steps:

1. In the upper half of the Sorting and Grouping dialog box, click anywhere in the field for which you want to add a group band.
2. In the lower half of the dialog box, set the Group Header option to Yes if you want to include a group header band, and set the Group Footer option to Yes if you want to include a group footer band.

If you decide to include a group header band with your report, you will likely want to include the field that identifies the group within the band. (For example, if a report is grouped by client ID number, it would make sense to include the client ID field in the group header band.) As you make your various selections in the Sorting and Grouping dialog box, remember that you can always visually check the effects of your selections by choosing File ⇨ Print Preview or clicking the View button in the toolbar.

Adding Page Numbers to a Report

You can easily include the current page number in reports that you design manually. (Reports created with the Report Wizard automatically include page numbers in the design of the reports.) You can add a page number to any report with these steps:

1. Open the report in Design view.
2. From the menus, choose Insert ⇨ Page Numbers. The Page Numbers dialog box appears.
3. Choose the desired format, position, and alignment for the page numbers from the options shown in the dialog box.
4. To include page numbering on the first page of the report, click the Show Number on First Page check box.
5. Click OK.

TIP: If for some reason you want to start page numbering of a report with a number other than 1, you will need to use a procedure somewhat different from the one listed above. You must manually add a text box control to the page footer band of the report. (If the report does not have a page footer band, choose View ⇨ Page Header/Footer to add one.) Use the Toolbox to add a textbox control to the band. Then click inside the text box and type the following expression:

=[Page] + starting number - 1

where *starting number - 1* is a value that is one less than the desired starting page number for the report. (Note that the spaces are included here for clarity, but they do not need to be present within the formula; the formula will work with or without the spaces.) For example, if you want the first page of the report to have a page number of 25, enter **=[Page] + 24** into the text box.

Adding the Current Date or Time to a Report

You can also easily add the current date or time to a report that you design manually. Here are the steps needed to do so:

1. Open the report in Design view.
2. From the menus, choose Insert ⇨ Date and Time. The Date and Time dialog box appears (see Figure 26-11).
3. To include a date, check the Include Date option. To include a time, check the Include Time option.
4. Choose the desired date or time format from the available options and then click OK. In a moment, a text box appears in the report, containing the expression needed for the date and/or time.
5. Drag the text box to the desired location in the report.

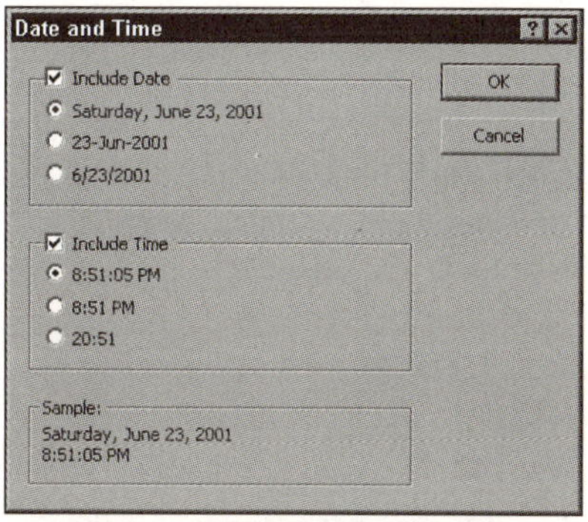

Figure 26-11: The Date and Time dialog box

Using the IIF Function in Reports

Access provides an Immediate IF function, written as `IIF( )`, that can be helpful within reports, as well as in forms. You can use the `IIF( )` function to display one set of data if a condition is true and another set of data if the condition is false. For example, you may need to print the contents of a

Yes/No field as text with a string other than the words "*Yes*" or "*No*." In a table of employees with a Yes/No field called `DentalInsurance`, the records would contain a logical value of –1 indicating a yes entry, or 0 indicating a no entry. You can format a text box to display values of yes/no, on/off, or true/false in the report, but in some cases you may prefer a different text string. In the report, where you wanted to print the value using a custom text string rather than yes/no or true/false values, you could include a text box containing an expression like this one:

```
=IIF([DentalInsurance] = -1, "Insured" , "No insurance")
```

You could place the expression in the Record Source property for the text box control, or you could type it directly into the text box. Using either method, you give the report the capability to print the desired text string depending on the value contained in the Yes/No field.

Using Summary Calculations

You can include summary calculations in your reports by placing expressions that use calculated values in the appropriate footers of the report — the group footer, the page footer, or the report footer. Use the `SUM( )` function to provide a sum total of a numeric value, use the `COUNT( )` function to provide a count of the values, and use the `AVG( )` function to provide an average of the values. For example, if you had a field named `ClientCharges` used to store currency values for the billing costs for every record in the table or query, you might add a text box with the following expression to the page footer of a report:

```
=SUM([ClientCharges])
```

and the result would be a running sum total of the client charges, appearing in the page footer for each page of the report.

As you use these functions, remember that the basis for the calculation depends upon which footer you place the control containing the expression into. For example, if you add the expression to a footer for a group section of the report, the value in the sum reflects all the records within that group. If the control is placed in the page footer, the value reflects all the records printed on that page. And if the value is placed in the report footer, the value reflects all the records in the report.

Creating Mailing Labels

Access provides a Mailing Label Wizard, which helps you create reports formatted as mailing labels. You can create reports to produce labels in a variety of formats, including most popular Avery sizes of labels. Figure 26-12 shows an example of a report designed to produce mailing labels.

Use the following steps to create mailing labels:

1. In the Database window, click the Reports tab and then click New.
2. In the New Report dialog box that appears, choose Label Wizard.
3. In the list box at the bottom of the dialog box, select the table or query that is to provide the data for the mailing labels; then click OK. In a moment, the first Label Wizard dialog box appears.
4. Choose the label manufacturer name, the label size, and the type of label desired, and then click Next.

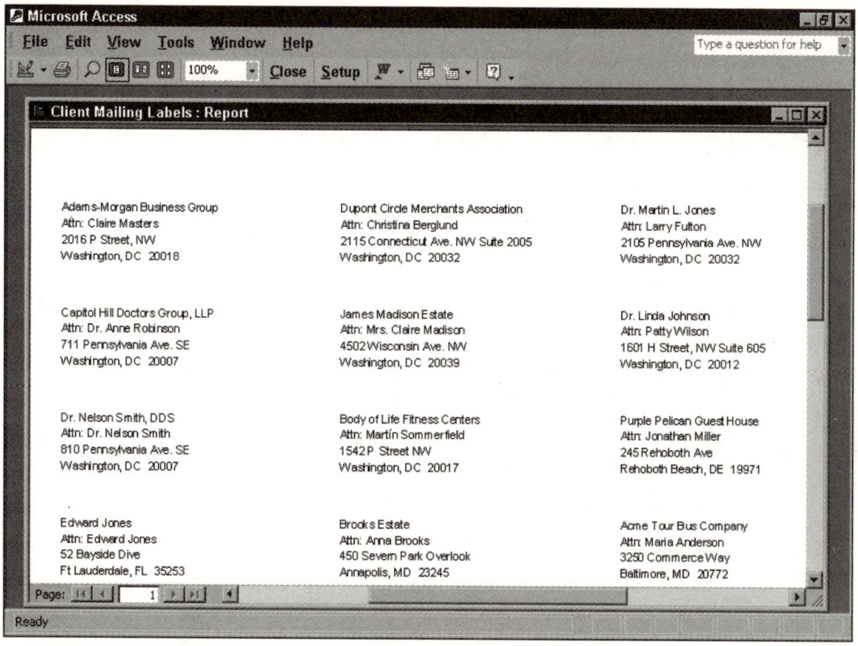

Figure 26-12: A report designed for producing mailing labels

5. In the next Label Wizard dialog box that appears, choose the font and colors desired for the label and then click Next. In a moment, the third Label Wizard dialog box appears, asking which fields should appear on each label.
6. Select the first field that should appear on the first line of the label and then click the > button to place that field in the Prototype Label list box at the right side of the dialog box.
7. To follow the field you just added with any spaces or punctuation, type the spaces or punctuation needed.
8. To add another field to the same line of the label, select that field in the Available Fields list and then click the > button.
9. To add a field to the next line of the label, press Enter, select the field in the Available Fields list, and then click the > button.
10. Repeat Steps 6 through 9 for each successive row of the label. As you create the label, the Prototype Label portion of the dialog box shows how the label will appear.
11. When you have added all necessary fields, click Next. In a moment, the fourth Label Wizard dialog box appears, asking how the labels should be sorted.
12. Select the field to be used as the highest priority for any sort order and then click the > button.
13. If desired, select the next field to be used in any sort order and then click the > button.
14. Repeat Step 13 for each additional field you want to use in the sort order.
15. When done choosing fields for the sort order, click Next. Access will display a final Label Wizard dialog box, asking whether you want to see the labels in preview mode or modify the labels (open the report in Design view). Make your desired selection in the dialog box and click Finish.

After you have completed creating the mailing labels, you can print the labels at any time, as you would print any other report. Do so by selecting the report in the Database window and choosing File ⇨ Print from the menus.

Creating Relational Reports Manually

Earlier in the chapter, you learned that you can use the Report Wizard to create *relational reports*, which are reports that can be used to print data from more than one table (or query) at a time. Although the Report Wizard does an admirable job of creating relational reports, you can also create relational reports manually. Before doing so, you must create both a *main report*, which contains the data from the parent table or query, and a *subreport*, which contains the related data from the "child" table or query in the relationship. Figure 26-13 illustrates an example of a relational report.

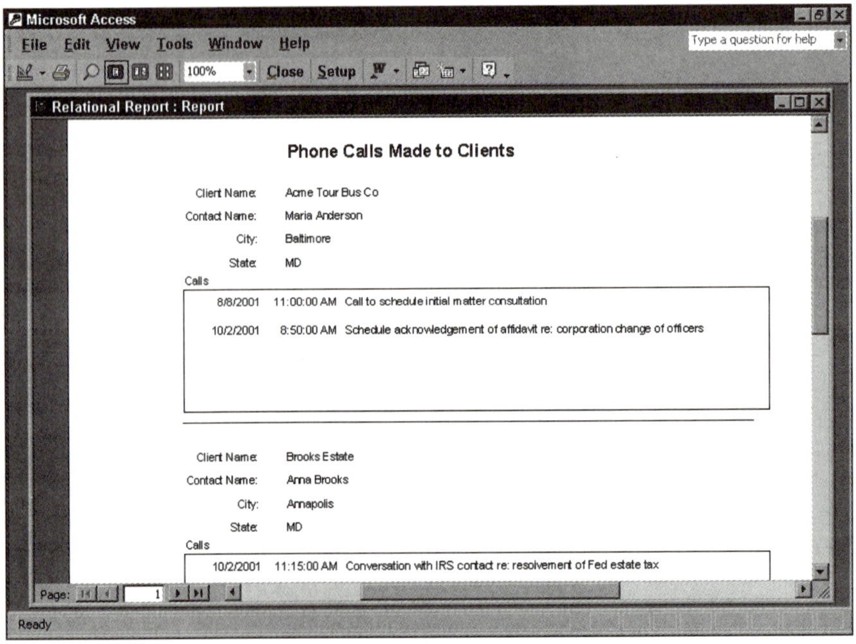

Figure 26-13: An example of a relational report

Adding the subreport to the main report

To create a relational report manually, use the following steps:

1. Open the main report containing the primary, or parent, data in Design view.
2. In the Database window, click the Reports tab to display your stored reports.
3. Drag the report that you want to use as a subreport from the Database window onto the main report. When you release the mouse button, a subreport control appears in the report, as shown in the lower portion of Figure 26-14.
4. Move the subreport control to its desired location within the main report.
5. Right-click the top edge of the subreport control and choose Properties. When the Properties window appears, click the Data tab.

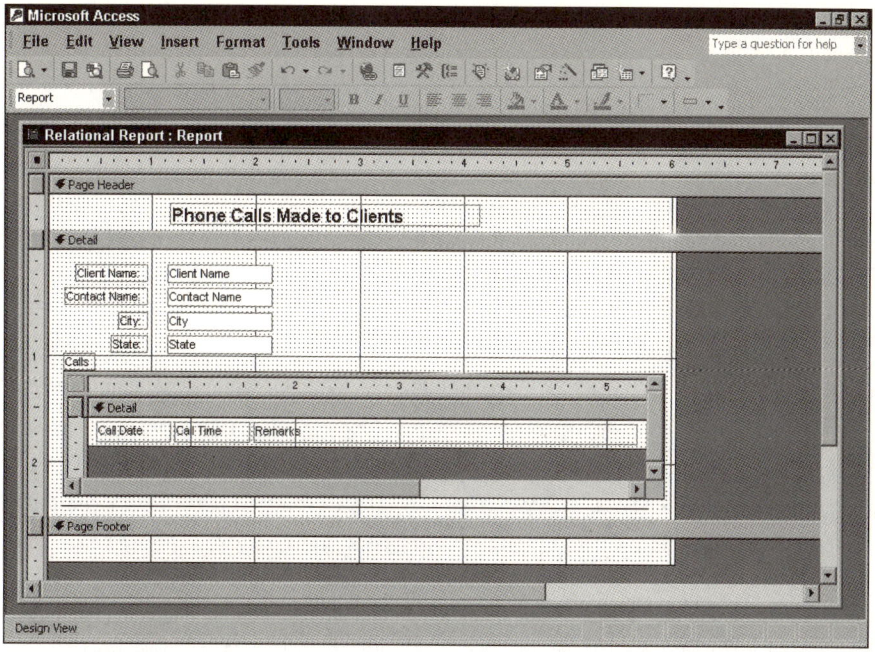

Figure 26-14: The relational report in Design view

6. Examine the Link Master Fields property. If an entry exists, make sure that the entry uses the common field you want to use to link the records displayed within the subreport to the records that will appear in the main report. If an entry does not exist, type the field name that should be used to establish the link between the subreport and the main report.
7. Choose File ⇨ Save to save the report.

Access will automatically establish the proper link needed in Step 6 if you established relationships between the tables being used at the table level, as described in Chapter 23, "About Databases and Tables." Access will also establish a link if both the main report and the subreport use a table or query that has a matching field (a field with the same field name and the same field type). If Access cannot establish a link, the Link Master Fields property will be blank, and you will need to fill in the name of the field for the report to operate correctly.

Solving possible problems with relational reports

If you design a relational report and then, when you switch to Print Preview, you don't see the data you want, the difficulty may be that Access cannot determine how the underlying data should be used in the report. Assuming that you are using the report to show records from two tables having a *one-to-many* relationship (one record in the parent table being related to many records in the child table), make sure that the main report uses the parent table as its data source and the subreport uses the child table as its data source. Keep in mind that the tables you are using to provide data to the main report and the subreport must have a common field that serves to establish the relational link between the tables.

Design tips for relational reports

Keep in mind the size limitations of the subreport. Because you'll want to fit the subreport inside a larger (main) report, you'll need to be efficient with the use of available space. Omit any fields that aren't really needed. You may also be able to use a smaller font for the data in the subreport.

Don't duplicate main form and report controls in the subreport. Controls that are already in the main report generally serve no useful purpose when they appear again in the subreport. Because the subreport repeats the contents of a control for each record, any control that contains the entries from the common (linking) field should be placed in the main report rather than in the subreport.

Avoid page breaks or page numbers in subreports and remove unneeded headers and footers. You usually do not want to insert a forced page break inside a subreport, and you usually do not need headers and footers because the main report typically has its own headers and footers.

Adding Charts to Reports

In Access, charts can be added directly to your reports either manually or with the Chart Wizard. Unless you have unusual design requirements, using the Chart Wizard to create charts is easier than creating charts manually. The steps for creating a chart with the Chart Wizard and the techniques for editing a chart are discussed in the following sections.

Understanding chart terminology

In case you are not already familiar with chart terminology, an explanation of terms that are used in this section is in order. Any chart comprises a series of *markers* that represent the numeric data stored within your table or query. The appearance of the markers varies according to what type of chart you insert into your Access report. In a bar chart, the markers appear as a series of horizontal bars. In a column chart, the markers look like a series of vertical columns. Line charts use markers that look like a series of thin lines. In pie charts, the markers are the wedges of the pie, and doughnut charts use markers that appear as slices of the doughnut.

With the exceptions of pie charts and doughnut charts, all charts have at least two axes: a horizontal axis (also known as the *category axis*) and a vertical axis (also known as the *value axis*). Three-dimensional charts also have a third axis, called the *series axis*.

In addition to the markers aligned along the axes, charts can also contain titles and *legends* that identify the categories that various markers represent. Using the various menu options within Access, you can customize these items in charts that you insert in reports.

Adding charts to reports with the Chart Wizard

You can use the Chart Wizard to create a chart by performing the following steps:

1. Click the Reports button in the Database window; then click New to open the New Report dialog box.
2. In the list box, click Chart Wizard to select it.
3. In the list box at the bottom of the New Report dialog box, choose the table or query that will provide the data for the chart. After you make a selection and click OK, the first Chart Wizard dialog box appears.
4. The dialog box asks which fields contain the data you want to use for the chart. Make the selections and then click Next.
5. The second Chart Wizard dialog box asks what type of chart you want. (The various chart types are described in Table 26-2, later in this chapter.) Select the appropriate chart type by clicking the desired chart icon in the dialog box; then click Next.
6. The third Chart Wizard dialog box asks you to choose how you want to lay out the data in the chart. In this dialog box, you can drag and drop the field buttons at the desired locations on the sample chart to change which field serves as the value axis, which field serves as the category axis, and which field summarizes or groups the data. At any point in this step, you can click the Preview Chart button to see a representative sample of how your chart will appear.
7. If you want to change how the chart summarizes or groups data, double-click any desired number field or date field you've placed in the dialog box. A Summarize dialog box appears. You can choose the summary method that you want to use in your chart and then click OK. After you've finished using the options in the third Chart Wizard dialog box, click Next to proceed.
8. The final Chart Wizard dialog box asks for a title for the chart. The dialog box also provides options for displaying a legend. You can choose to open the report with the chart displayed or with the report in Design view, where you can modify the design of the report. Make the desired selections in the dialog box and then click Finish to produce the report containing your chart.

Editing charts

After your chart appears in an Access report, you may want to alter certain aspects of that chart's appearance. Using the toolbar and menu options of Microsoft Graph, you can change design aspects such as the chart type, the data series used by the chart, and the appearance of the axes and the legends.

CROSS-REFERENCE: Microsoft Graph, the mini-application used to produce charts in Access reports, is also used by Microsoft Word and Microsoft PowerPoint. After you open a document (in Word), a presentation (in PowerPoint), or a report's design (in Access) and double-click a chart to edit it, the chart-related options are identical. You can find a more detailed discussion of the Microsoft Graph options for editing and enhancing the appearance of charts in Chapter 21 of this book, which deals with creating charts in PowerPoint.

To edit a chart, open the report that contains the chart in Design view (click the Reports button in the Database window, click the report to select it and then click the Design button). When the report opens in Design view, double-click anywhere within the chart. In a moment (it may take a long moment because Microsoft Graph must start up behind the scenes), the window containing Microsoft

Graph running within Access appears. Figure 26-15 shows the appearance of a chart, the menu bar, and toolbars after starting Microsoft Graph within Access. The chart in Figure 26-15 is in the process of being edited.

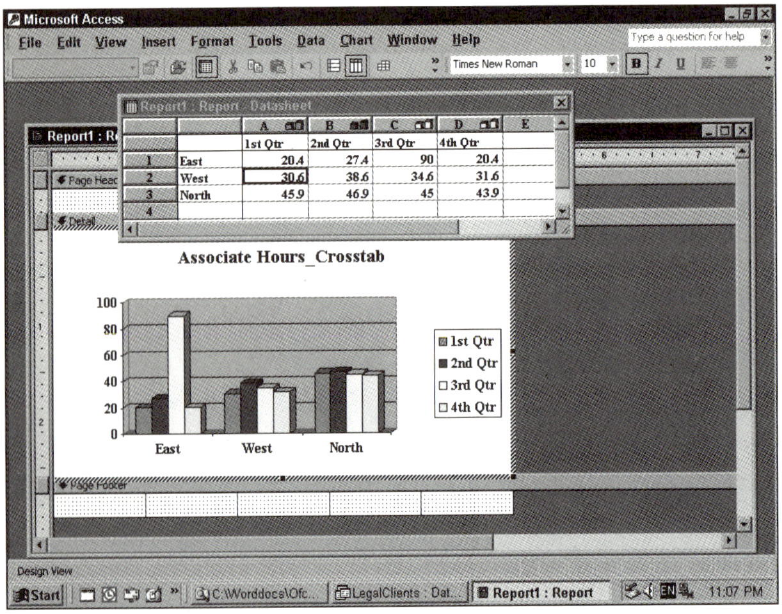

Figure 26-15: The appearance of a chart while it is being edited

You can change the chart type while the chart is in the editing phase described above. To do this, open the Chart menu and choose Chart Type to display the Chart Type dialog box. Here you can select area, bar, column, line, pie, doughnut, radar, scatter, surface, bubble, stock, cone, cylinder, or pyramid, and you can choose a two-dimensional or a three-dimensional chart type in the Chart Sub-Type area of the dialog box. After choosing the desired options, click OK.

You can also add, delete, and change the location of a legend in an existing chart while the chart is in the editing phase. To add a legend to an existing chart, choose Chart ⇨ Chart Options, click the Legend tab, and check the Show Legend check box. To delete an existing legend, click the legend to select the legend and press the Del key. To change the location of the legend, click the legend to select it and choose Format ⇨ Selected Legend; then, in the dialog box that appears, click the Placement tab and choose the desired location (bottom, corner, top, left, or right).

You can also change the size of a chart, change the colors for any data series (the markers that represent a set of data), and change the series or line styles in an axis. To change the size of a chart, click its borders and drag the borders to the desired size. To change the colors used for any data series, double-click the data series and choose a desired color in the Format Data Series dialog box that appears. To change the series or line styles used in an axis, double-click the axis to open the Format Axis dialog box and choose the desired settings. After making the desired changes to the chart, click anywhere outside the chart and save the report. The changes made to the chart will appear in the report when it is previewed or printed.

You can produce several different chart types in Access (see Table 26-2). These chart types are identical to charts that can be produced in Microsoft Word and Microsoft PowerPoint, because Word, PowerPoint, and Access all use the mini-application known as Microsoft Graph to produce charts.

Table 26-2
Available Chart Types

Chart Type	***Description***
Area	Shows the significance of change during a given time period. The top line of the chart totals the individual series, so area charts make it visually apparent how each individual series contributes to the overall picture. Area charts emphasize the magnitude of change as opposed to the rate of change. (If you want to emphasize the rate of change, use line charts instead.)
Bar	Uses horizontal bars to show distinct figures at a specified time. Each horizontal bar in the chart shows a specific amount of change from the base value used in the chart. Bar charts visually emphasize different values, arranged vertically.
Column	Very much like bar charts, using columns to show distinct figures over a time period. The difference is that column charts are oriented horizontally, with the columns running up or down from a base value used in the chart. When you want to show numeric values across a passage of time in the chart, column charts usually work well.
Line	Perfect for showing trends in data over a period of time. Like area charts, line charts show the significance of change, but line charts emphasize the rate instead of the magnitude of change.
Pie	Shows relationships between the pieces of a picture. This also shows the relationship between a piece of the picture and the entire picture. You can use a pie chart to display only one series of data at a time because each piece of a pie chart represents part of a total series. If you have a large number of series to plot, however, you are probably better off with a column chart because a pie crowded with slices is hard to interpret.
Doughnut	Shows relationships between pieces of a picture, as does a pie chart. The difference is that the doughnut chart has a hollow center.
Radar	Shows the changes or frequencies of a data series in relation to a central point and to each other. (Every category has an axis value that radiates from a center point. Lines connect all data in the same series.) Radar charts can be difficult to interpret unless you're accustomed to working with them.
XY Scatter	Shows relationships between different points of data to compare trends across uneven time periods or to show patterns as a set of *x* and *y* coordinates. These charts are commonly used to plot scientific data.
Surface	Shows trends in values across two dimensions in a continuous curve.
Bubble	Compares sets of three values. In appearance, these are similar to scatter charts, with the third value interpreted by the size of the bubbles.
Stock	Also known as *open-hi-lo-close* charts. They are used to display the day-to-day values of stocks, commodities, or other financial market data. Stock charts require series containing four values to plot the four points (open, high, low, and close).
Cylinder	Column charts with the columns appearing as cylindrical shapes.
Cone	Column charts with the columns appearing as cone shapes.
Pyramid	Column charts with the columns appearing as pyramid shapes.

Summary

In this chapter, you learned the techniques needed to create reports for your use in Access, whether you create them with the aid of the Report Wizard or by means of the manual report design process. You learned the following:

- You can create reports quickly with the aid of the Report Wizard.
- If the reports that you create with the Report Wizard don't provide the kind of design flexibility that you need, you must resort to designing reports manually or modifying reports created by the wizards.
- You can add controls where needed and modify their properties to accomplish the desired results.
- You can add other common reporting elements, such as headers, footers, page numbers, and graphics, to reports.
- The data shown or printed in reports can be sorted or grouped as part of a report's design.
- Like a relational form, a relational report contains a record from the "one" side of a one-to-many relationship in the main report and contains all associated records from the "many" side of the relationship in the subreport.
- You can add charts to a report using the Chart Wizard.

Using the techniques learned in this chapter and in the previous three chapters, you can effectively work with the primary objects needed to do everyday work using Access. The next two chapters show how you can make your work with Access more efficient by automating common tasks with macros and by designing complete, custom applications that make Access tasks easier for novice users within a legal environment.

Chapter 27

Working with Macros

In This Chapter

- ♦ Creating a macro
- ♦ Saving a macro
- ♦ Running macros
- ♦ Copying macros
- ♦ Creating macros that run automatically
- ♦ Typical uses for macros
- ♦ Examples of macro usage

THIS CHAPTER DETAILS HOW you can use macros, which can significantly help you accomplish routine tasks in Access at your law firm. As your tasks in Access grow in complexity, you may find yourself working with the same tables, queries, forms, and reports. Macros can help you reduce the tediousness of working with common objects in Access.

In Access, a *macro* is a list of actions specified in advance. These actions are stored in a table-like window called a *macro window*, and the actions appear in the order that you want the macro to carry them out. When you run the macro, Access carries out the specified actions. For example, if on a monthly basis you must run an append query to copy records to an archive table, followed by a delete query to delete the records from the original table, at which point you need to print a report, you can create a macro that performs all these steps in a single operation. After you have created and saved the macro, you can just run the macro each month, and all these steps will occur in order.

Many experienced Access users consider macros to be a simple method of programming in Access. Macros aren't as powerful as the programming language (called *Visual Basic for Applications*, or *VBA*) that is an integral part of Access, but you can use macros to design automated applications ranging from the simple to the moderately complex.

If you are familiar with how macros operate in Microsoft Word and Excel, you should be aware that macros in Access are designed differently than in those products. Although many long-time users of Word and Excel are accustomed to creating macros by turning on a "macro recorder" and then performing operations in the program, you should note that there is no macro recorder in Access. You design macros in Access by choosing the actions that you want to perform from a design grid inside a macro window.

In Access, a macro is nothing more than a list of tasks that Access should perform in an automated manner. Those tasks can include opening or closing forms, running queries, producing reports, exporting data to different file formats, and more. Figure 27-1 shows the design of a macro that, when run, will open a form, maximize that form's window, and move to a new record in the form.

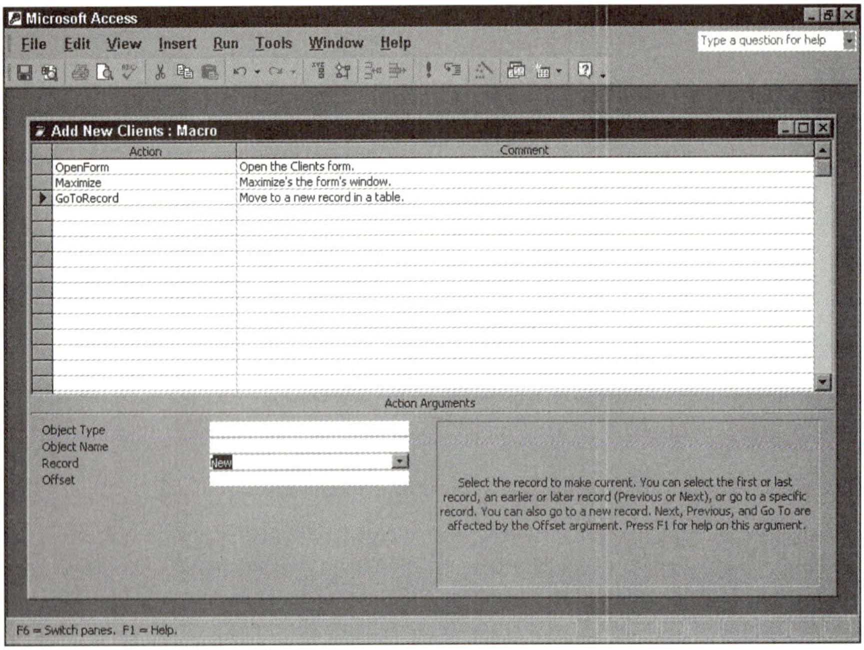

Figure 27-1: An Access macro specifies various actions that are carried out in sequence as the macro runs.

Any macro that you create contains an Action column and a Comment column. In the rows of the Action column, you choose the actions, or tasks, that you want the macro to perform. Comments are optional; in the Comment column, you can type comments that describe your particular macro.

Optionally, macros can also have a *macro name* column and a *condition* column. (These columns do not appear by default but can be turned on, using options of the View menu, while a macro is open in Design view.) The macro name column and the condition column apply to macros that use a more advanced type of design, which is beyond the scope of this book.

After you choose a desired action in the Action column, the bottom half of the macro window contains *action arguments* that apply to the action you've chosen. You can set these action arguments as desired to control precisely how the macro performs your chosen tasks.

Creating a Macro

You create new macros from the Macros tab of the Database window. Use the following steps to create a macro:

1. In the Database window, click the Macros tab.
2. Click New. In a moment, a new macro window opens (see Figure 27-2).
3. Click the drop-down arrow in the first empty row underneath the Action column and choose the type of action that you want the macro to perform.
4. If desired, enter any optional comments in the Comment column.
5. In the Action Arguments portion of the dialog box, specify any action arguments needed for the macro action. (For example, if you choose OpenForm as a macro action, you must specify a form name under Action Arguments.)

6. On successive rows of the macro, repeat Steps 3 through 5 for any additional actions that you want the macro to perform.

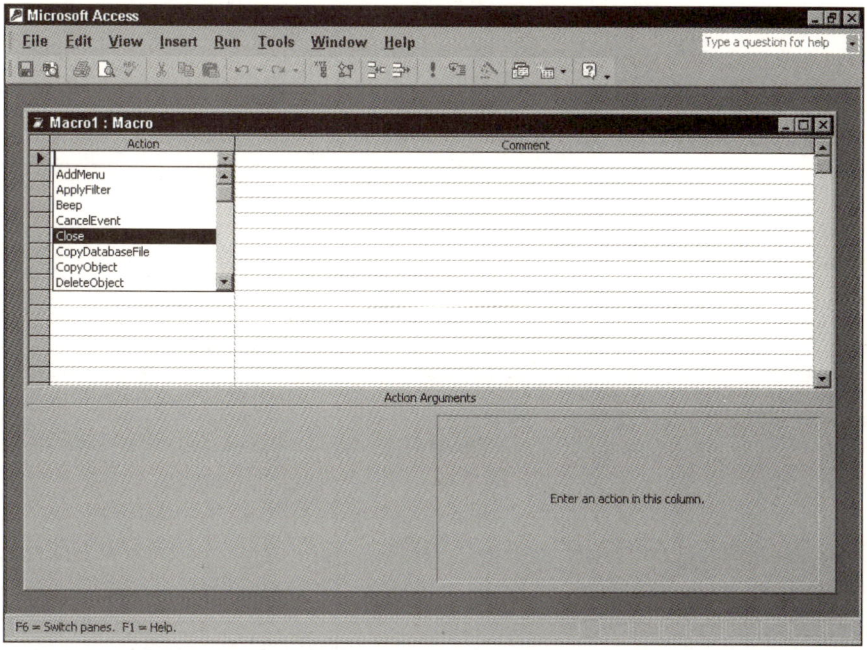

Figure 27-2: A new macro window contains an Action column and a Comment column by default.

As you choose your macro actions, selecting the needed action arguments is important so that the macro action has the desired effect. For example, when you specify an action to open a report, you use the action arguments to identify the report that Access should use and the view in which Access should open it. Table 27-1 details the various macro actions available in Access, along with their purposes and arguments.

As you build the macro, you can insert new actions between existing ones by selecting the row where the new action's row should be added and pressing the Insert key or by choosing Insert ⇨ Rows. You can delete existing actions by selecting the row that contains the action and pressing Delete or by choosing Edit ⇨ Delete Rows. You can move existing rows to new locations in the macros (changing the order of actions performed by the macro) by first selecting the row you want to move and then clicking the row and dragging it to the new desired location.

Table 27-1
Macro Actions, Purposes, and Arguments

Action	***Purpose***	***Arguments***
AddMenu	Adds a drop-down menu to a custom menu bar	Menu Name
ApplyFilter	Applies a filter, a query, or an SQL WHERE clause to a form or report to filter or sort the records	Filter Name, Where Condition
Beep	Sounds a beep using the PC speaker	None
CancelEvent	Cancels the event that caused Access to run the macro containing the action	None
Close	Closes the specified object or the active window when no object is specified	Object Type, Object Name
CopyDatabaseFile	Copies the current database (.MDB) file to a new database	Database File Name, Overwrite Existing File, Disconnect All Users
CopyObject	Copies the selected database object to a different database or to the same database under another name	Destination Database, New Name, Source Object Name, Source Object Type
DeleteObject	Deletes the specified object	Object Name, Object Type
Echo	Determines whether Access updates the screen as the macro executes	Echo On, Status Bar Text
FindNext	Finds the next record that meets criteria specified by the last Find Record action or by the entries in the Find dialog box	None
FindRecord	Finds the first record that meets criteria specified by the Find Record action or by the entries in the Find dialog box	Find What, Where, Match Case, Direction, Search as Formatted
GoToControl	Moves the insertion point to the field or control on the active form, datasheet, or query dynaset	Control Name
GoToPage	Moves the insertion point to the specified page of the active form	Page Number, Right, Down
GoToRecord	Moves the insertion point to the specified record	Object Name, Object Type, Record, Offset
Hourglass	Changes the shape of the mouse pointer to an hourglass as the macro runs	Hourglass On, Hourglass Off
Maximize	Maximizes the active window	None
Minimize	Minimizes the active window	None
MoveSize	Moves or resizes the active window	Right, Down, Width, Height
MsgBox	Displays a message box containing an informational message or a warning	Message, Beep, Type, Title

Action	***Purpose***	***Arguments***
OpenDataAccessPage	Opens a data access page in Browse view or Design view	Data Access Page Name, View
OpenDiagram	Opens a database schema in Design view or Print Preview	Diagram Name
OpenForm	Opens a form in Form view, Design view, Print Preview, or Datasheet view	Form Name, View, Filter Name, Where Condition
OpenFunction	Opens a VBA function in Design view	Function Name, View, Data Module
OpenModule	Opens the specified Visual Basic for Applications module	Module Name, Procedure Name
OpenQuery	Opens a select query in Datasheet view, Design view, or Print Preview	Query Name, View, Data Mode
OpenReport	Opens a report in Design view or Print Preview, or prints a report	Report Name, View, Filter Name, Where Condition
OpenStoredProcedure	Opens a stored procedure in Datasheet view, Design view, or Print Preview	Procedure Name, View, Data Mode
OpenTable	Opens a table in Datasheet view, Design view, or Print Preview	Table Name, View, Data Mode
OpenView	Opens a view in Datasheet view, Design view, or Print Preview	View Name, View, Data Mode
OutputTo	Outputs data to a foreign file	Object Type, Object Name, Output Format, Output File, Auto Start
PrintOut	Prints the active object	Print Range, Page From, Page To, Print Quality, Copies, Collate Copies
Quit	Exits Access	Options
Rename	Renames the selected object	New Name, Object Type, Old Name
RepaintObject	Finishes any pending screen updates for the specified object or for the active object if an object is not specified	Object Type, Object Name
Requery	Updates the data in a specified control by requerying the data source	Control Name
Restore	Restores a maximized or minimized window to its previous size	None
RunApp	Runs a Windows or DOS application	Command Line
RunCode	Runs a Visual Basic procedure	Procedure Name
RunCommand	Executes a menu command	Menu Bar, Menu Name, Command, Subcommand
RunMacro	Runs another macro	Macro Name, Repeat Count, Repeat Expression

Continues

Table 27-1 continued

Action	***Purpose***	***Arguments***
RunSQL	Runs a query using an SQL statement	SQL Statement
Save	Saves the specified object	Object Type, Object Name
SelectObject	Selects the specified object	Object Type, Object Name, In Database Window
SendKeys	Sends keystrokes directly to Access or to an active Windows-based application	Keystrokes, Wait
SendObject	Includes a specified object in an e-mail message	Object Type, Object Name, Output Format, To, Cc, Bcc, Subject, Message Text, Edit Message
SetMenuItem	Sets the state of a menu item	Menu Index, Command Index, Subcommand Index, Flag
SetValue	Sets the value of a field, control, or property	Item, Expression on a form, a datasheet, or a report
SetWarnings	Turns system messages on or off	Warnings On, Warnings Off
ShowAllRecords	Removes applied filters from the active form	None
ShowToolbar	Displays or hides the toolbar	Toolbar Name, Show
StopAllMacros	Halts all macros that are currently executing	None
StopMacro	Halts the current macro	None
TransferDatabase	Imports or exports data between the current database and another Access database	Transfer Type, Database Type, Database Name, Object Type, Source, Destination, Structure Only
TransferSpreadsheet	Imports or exports data between the current database and a spreadsheet file	Transfer Type, Spreadsheet Type, Table Name, File Name, Has Field Names, Range
TransferText	Imports or exports data between the current database and a text file	Transfer Type, Specification Name, Table Name, File Name, Has Field Names

Saving Macros

To save a macro, choose File ⇨ Save, or click the Save button in the toolbar. If you are saving the macro for the first time, Access prompts you for a name for the macro. Enter a desired name in the dialog box and click OK to save the macro to the current database.

Running Macros

In Access, there are a number of different ways to run a macro. One obvious method is to select the macro in the Database window and click Run. Alternatively, you can double-click the macro in the Database window.

You can also run macros by calling them from command buttons that you place on forms. If you open a form in Design view and drag any existing macro from the Database window onto the form, a command button appears. When you switch to Form view and click the button, the macro will run. (See the next chapter for details on how you can create easy-to-use menus for your Access applications using this technique.)

Copying Macros

You can copy macros from one database to another, and you can copy them to new macro names in the same database. This can be a time-saving technique when you need to create a number of macros that perform similar tasks. Instead of creating each macro from scratch, you can create one macro, copy it to different names, and modify thc actions and arguments of the copied macros to fit the desired action. You can copy an existing macro with the following steps:

1. In the Database window, click the macro to select it.
2. Choose Edit ⇨ Copy.
3. If you want to copy the macro to a different database, close the current database, open the database to which you want to copy the macro and click the Macros tab in the Database window.
4. Choose Edit ⇨ Paste.
5. In the dialog box that appears, enter a name for the macro. (If you are copying the macro to the same database as the existing macro, you have to give the copied macro a different name from the original.)

Creating Macros That Run Automatically

You can create and save a macro that runs automatically whenever a database is first opened. To do this, create the macro as described earlier and then save the macro with the name *Autoexec*. Whenever Access initially opens a database, it looks for a macro with the name *Autoexec*. If Access finds a macro by this name, Access runs that macro, performing all the actions stored within the macro.

TIP: You can prevent an Autoexec macro from running by holding down the Shift key as you open the database.

Typical Uses for Macros

How you design your macros depends entirely on what tasks you want to automate. This will vary widely from law firm to law firm. However, here are some common tasks that you can automate using macros:

- Opening and closing a group of forms
- Applying or removing filters or sort orders for forms
- Printing a group of reports
- Running a make-table query to produce a new table and exporting the new table's data to another file format (such as Excel)

- Importing data from another file (such as a delimited-format file uploaded from an accounting system) into an Access table
- Launching another Windows application automatically from within Access

The best way to determine how you can use macros at your particular firm is to experiment with the tasks that you perform using Access on a regular basis.

Examples of Macro Usage

To provide an idea of the kinds of everyday tasks you can automate by means of macros, this portion of the chapter contains descriptions of how you can create macros for specific tasks.

Opening a form to add new records

If you have a group of users who are performing massive amounts of data entry for a major project at your firm, you've probably designed a form that is used for adding records to a table. You could create a macro that would open the form, maximize the form's window, and automatically move to a new, blank record, using these steps:

1. In the Database window, click the Macros tab; then click New.
2. In the Action column of the first row, choose OpenForm.
3. Under Action Arguments at the bottom of the macro window, click in the Form Name box and choose the form that you want to open from the list.
4. Also under Action Arguments, click in the Data Mode box and choose Add. (This tells the macro to open the form in data entry view, allowing only the addition of new records.)
5. Click in the second row of the macro under the Action column and choose Maximize from the list.
6. Save the macro by choosing File ⇨ Save. When asked for a name, supply an appropriate name (such as *Add New Records*, *Add Clients*, or *Add Depositions*).
7. Close the window by clicking the Close button or by pressing Ctrl+F4.

Opening a form to search for a record to edit

You can create a macro that opens a form displaying records in a table, maximizes the form's window, and automatically opens a Find dialog box so that users can search for a record that is to be edited. Here are the steps you can use to create such a macro:

1. In the Database window, click the Macros tab; then click New.
2. In the Action column of the first row, choose OpenForm.
3. Under Action Arguments at the bottom of the macro window, click in the Form Name box and choose the form that you want to open from the list.
4. Click in the second row of the macro under the Action column and choose Maximize from the list.
5. Click in the third row of the macro under the Action column and choose RunCommand from the list.
6. Under Action Arguments at the bottom of the window, click in the Command box and choose Find from the list.

7. Save the macro by choosing File ⇨ Save. When asked for a name, supply an appropriate name (such as *Edit Records*, *Edit a Client*, or *Edit a Deposition*).
8. Close the window by clicking the Close button or by pressing Ctrl+F4.

Creating a macro to print a report

You can easily create a macro that opens a report in Print Preview mode or that sends a report to the printer. Although this may seem to be a trivial use for a macro, such a macro can prove useful for adding command buttons to a menu that novice users can use (as described in the following chapter). Here are the steps that you can use to create such a macro:

1. In the Database window, click the Macros tab; then click New.
2. In the Action column of the first row, choose OpenReport from the list.
3. Under Action Arguments at the bottom of the macro window, click in the Report Name box and choose the desired report from the list.
4. In the View box under Action Arguments, if you want to print the report immediately, choose Print. To open the report in Print Preview mode, choose Print Preview.
5. Save the macro by choosing File ⇨ Save. When asked for a name, supply an appropriate name (such as *Print Clients Report* or *Print Depositions*).
6. Close the window by clicking the Close button or by pressing Ctrl+F4.

Creating a macro to export data to an Excel file

You can create a macro that, when run, exports data from a table or query to an Excel worksheet (or to other spreadsheet formats supported by the export feature of Access, including Lotus 1-2-3). You can use the following steps to create a macro that performs this task:

1. In the Database window, click the Macros tab; then click New.
2. In the Action column of the first row, choose TransferSpreadsheet from the list.
3. Under Action Arguments in the bottom of the macro window, click in the Transfer Type box and choose Export.
4. Click in the Spreadsheet Type box and choose the spreadsheet format that you want use to export the data.
5. Click in the Table Name box and type the name of the table (or query) that contains the data that you want to export as a spreadsheet file.
6. Click in the File Name box and enter a filename (including the path) for the exported file that you want to create.
7. In the Has Field Names box, choose Yes if you want the first row of the resulting spreadsheet to contain the field names from the table or query, or choose No to omit the field names.
8. Save the macro by choosing File ⇨ Save. When asked for a name, supply an appropriate name (such as *Export Client Data* or *Create Excel File*).
9. Close the window by clicking the Close button or by pressing Ctrl+F4.

TIP: If you regularly need to export financial data to a file on disk that gets sent to your accounting department, you can use steps like the ones listed above to automate the process. In the File Name box under Action Arguments, just enter an appropriate path for your floppy disk drive (such as **A:acctrecs.xls**) and remember to insert a blank disk in the drive before running the macro. If others will use the macro, you may want to remind them to insert the disk by adding a MsgBox action in the row of the macro above the TransferSpreadsheet action. Under Action Arguments, you can add the text of an appropriate warning message, such as *please insert formatted disk in drive A, and then strike any key.*

Summary

In this chapter you learned how to create and run Access macros and how you might use them. We covered the following topics:

- How to create and save macros
- Various ways to run a macro
- How to create a macro that runs automatically when a database is initially opened
- Typical uses for Access macros

In the next chapter you will learn how you can combine all of the Access objects discussed so far — tables, queries, forms, reports, and macros — into a complete, ready-to-use system that other users at your firm can use with little or no specialized training in Access.

Chapter 28

Developing Legal Applications Using Access

In This Chapter

- Planning the building blocks of the application
- Creating custom applications
- Using the applications included on the CD-ROM

ALTHOUGH THERE WILL CERTAINLY BE complex applications that require your hiring an outside consultant (or bringing an experienced Access programmer on board), many applications ranging from simple to moderately complex can be created with just a basic knowledge of tables, queries, forms, reports, and macros. You can design your own switchboards to serve as main menus for common tasks that users must perform when using Access. *Switchboards* are nothing more than blank forms with command buttons added. You use the buttons to perform the desired tasks, such as opening other forms for data entry and editing, or printing reports. For example, the Case Management database included on the CD-ROM makes use of a switchboard as a main menu. Figure 28-1 shows the main menu for the Case Management database.

You can use macros (covered in more detail in Chapter, "Working with Macros") to create ready-to-use applications like the one shown in the figure. The advantage of an application like this one is that others can use the application with little or no specific knowledge of Access. When designing a complete application in this fashion, you create a form that serves as a main menu for all the tasks that should be performed by your users. You must also create macros that perform the tasks that should occur when the various buttons of the menu are pressed.

NOTE: The Case Management databbase shown in Figure 28-1 is just one of six ready-to-use, legal-specific databases that are provided on the CD-ROM. See the end of this chapter for additional details regarding these databases.

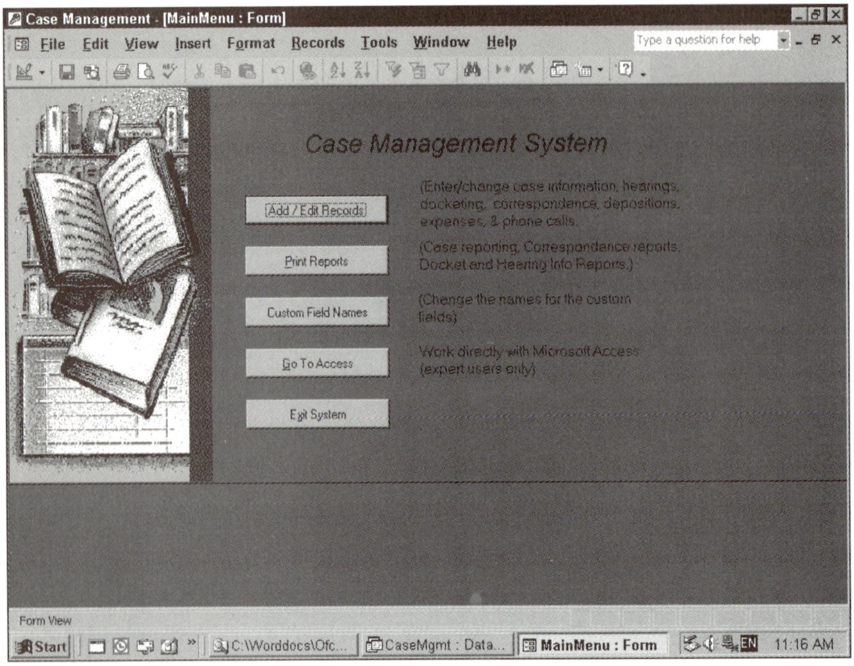

Figure 28-1: The Case Management database allows users with no specific Access training to track case information stored in an Access database.

Planning the Building Blocks of the Application

Before you proceed to "connect the dots" by means of a menu-driven application (as described in the following section), you must first create the underlying building blocks of the application. In Access, these building blocks are your Access objects — the tables, queries, forms, and reports — that you need to perform a given task. For example, a simple database designed to track client names, addresses, and phone numbers might contain the following items:

- A table containing a record for each client, with the client's name, address, and telephone number
- A parameter query that would display all clients located in a particular city
- A form used to add, edit, and delete records in the clients table
- A report, formatted to provide a listing of all clients in the form of a telephone directory
- Another report, formatted to print mailing labels for the clients to support mass mailings of the firm newsletter

You can use the design techniques outlined in Chapters 23–27 to create any of these basic Access objects needed for your particular application. After creating these objects, you can use the process outlined in the next section to create an application that other users (who may have little or no specific Access training) can utilize to accomplish database-related legal tasks.

Creating a Custom Application

If you are starting to create a ready-to-use Access application for others in your office, you should first plan and create all the necessary macros for each of the buttons you want to place on the main menu. When all your tables, queries, forms, and reports exist, you can use the following steps to create a ready-to-use application with a main menu:

1. Create a macro for each button that should appear on the main menu. For example, if you want a button that will open a form for adding and editing records in a table, create a macro that will open the form. If you want another button that prints a report, create a macro that opens that report in Print Preview or sends the report to the printer. (As an example of this technique, Figure 28-2 shows a database containing macros for adding records to a table, editing records, printing a report, and printing labels. For more details regarding macros, see Chapter 27.)

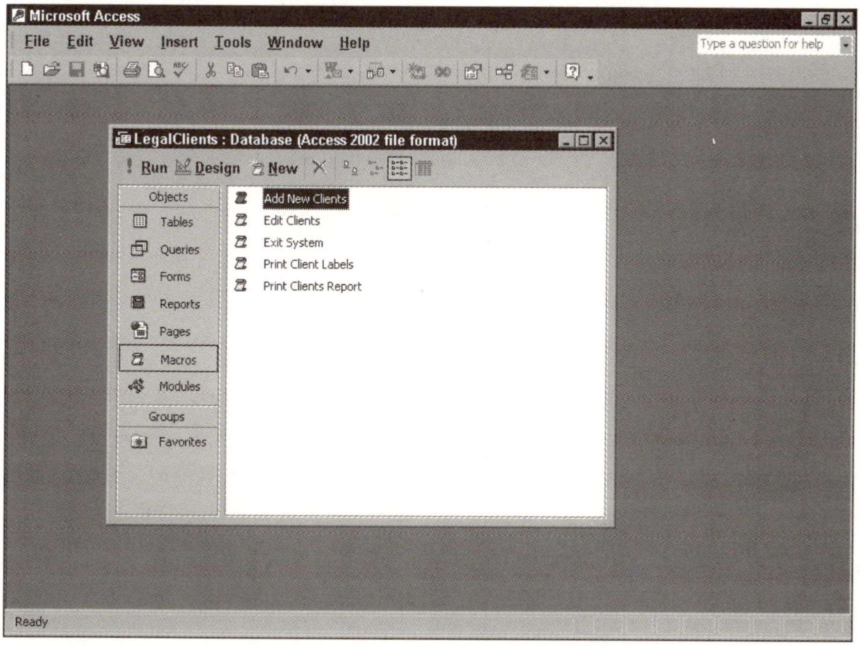

Figure 28-2: A database with macros created for common tasks

2. Create a new, blank form to serve as the main menu. To do so, click the Forms tab in the Database window; then click New. In the New Form dialog box that appears, leave the Choose a Table or Query list box empty, leave Design View selected in the list portion of the dialog box, and click OK to open a blank form in Design view.
3. Size the form as needed to accommodate the desired menu buttons and any labels you plan to add to the menu. (For more details on designing forms, see Chapter 25, "Working with Forms".)
4. Move the Database window so that you can see portions of both the Database window and the form at the same time.
5. In the Database window, click the Macros tab to display your existing macros.
6. Click a desired macro and drag it onto the form. When you release the mouse button, a command button appears that, when pressed by a user, will run the macro (see Figure 28-3).

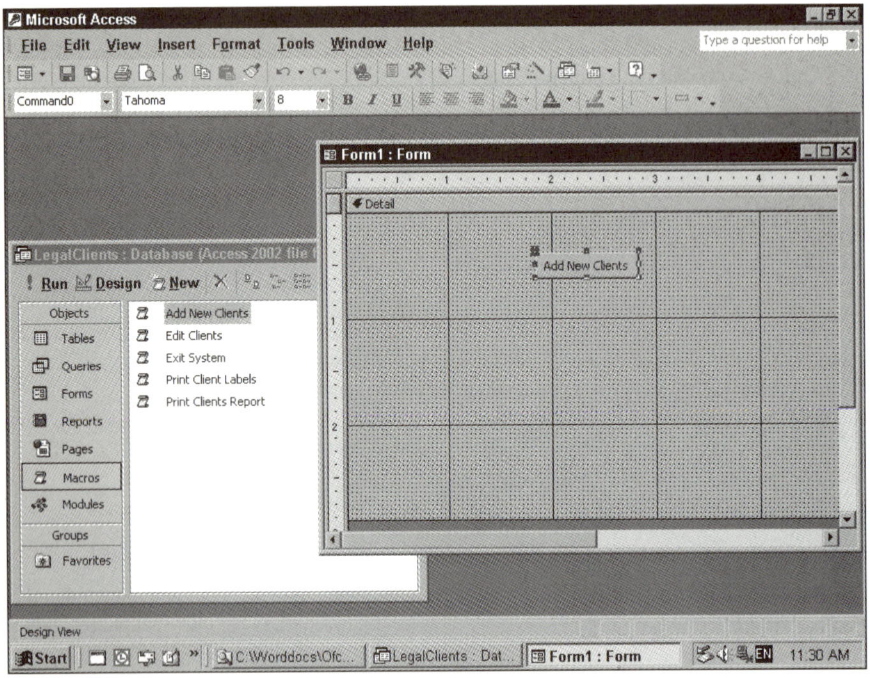

Figure 28-3: Dragging a macro onto a form to create a command button

7. Repeat Step 6 for every button that you want to place on the menu.
8. Use the form design techniques outlined in Chapter 25 to move and size the buttons as needed, and add any desired text labels to the form.
9. Save and close the form. You can give it any name you wish (such as *main menu*).
10. Create a new macro. Set the first action of the macro to OpenForm, and under Action Arguments (in the lower portion of the macro window), set the Form Name argument to the name you gave the form in Step 9.
11. Set the second action of the macro to Maximize.
12. Save the macro. When asked for a name, call the macro *Autoexec*.

When you close the database and it is reopened (by you or by another user), the Autoexec macro loads the menu form and maximizes the form's window. Users can then click the buttons in the form to perform common tasks within the database. If users need to get back to the Database window, they can simply click the Close button in the menu form.

TIP: You can also make use of the Command Button Wizards to add command buttons to forms that perform relatively specialized tasks. See Chapter 25 for more specifics on adding command buttons to forms with the aid of the Command Button Wizards.

Using the Applications on the CD-ROM

This book includes a number of database applications on the accompanying CD-ROM that are designed specifically for use at law firms and within the legal environment. Note that these applications are necessarily more complex than the simple example of an application described in this chapter. Most contain more than one form, and they contain numerous reports, many of which are based on parameter queries. And rather than use macros, the applications on the CD-ROM make extensive use of Visual Basic for Applications, the programming language that is an integral part of Access. The workings of Visual Basic for Applications are beyond the scope of this book. However, you can use the techniques taught in this book to create your own simple applications and to modify the applications provided with this book to suit your own needs. You can add fields to the tables, queries, forms, and reports of the sample applications so that they better suit any unusual needs at your particular law firm.

The CD-ROM contains six ready-to-use database applications that are designed for legal-specific use and which are described in the following six chapters (you'll also find these chapters, labeled Bonus Chapters 1–6, on the CD-ROM). These include the following:

- The Case Management System tracks case-related information, hearings, docket information, correspondence, records of depositions, case expenses, and phone calls related to cases.
- The Litigation Support database tracks litigation-related information, such as the source and type of documents, the type of deponent and deponent name, the parties involved, discovery requests, and notes.
- The Firm Marketing database helps you manage the marketing-related database needs of a small or midsize law firm.
- The Lawyer Recruiting System helps a law firm track numerous statistics for potential new hires for the various associate practice groups.
- The Pleadings Tracker System tracks pleadings for any number of cases, with fields that include the Bates stamp number, the case name and number, the plaintiff and defendant, the name of the court and judge, and comments.
- The CLE Tracker is designed to track Continuing Legal Education (CLE) courses taken and credits attained for attorneys.

Additionally, if you plan on delving into programming in Access, there are a variety of books that can help. Although none of these is geared to the specific needs of the legal profession, each teaches Access programming, and you can apply the skills that you learn to your particular needs. For more in-depth information, you may want to consider *The Microsoft Access 2002 Bible,* by Cary N. Prague and Michael R. Irwin, which can be obtained through your local bookstore or by ordering online at the Hungry Minds Web site (`www.hungryminds.com`).

Summary

In this chapter, you saw how to connect the dots from all the other chapters in this section. You learned the following:

- You can combine all the Access objects detailed in preceding chapters into a complete, working system that can be used by others with little or no specialized training.
- A complete application will require a collection of tables, queries, forms, and reports designed to accomplish a given database task.
- The applications contained on the CD-ROM make use of Visual Basic for Applications, a programming language available within Access that you can learn about from advanced Access books.

The next six chapters describe the six application databases provided on the CD-ROM.

Chapter 29

The Case Management System

In This Chapter

- Using the Case Management system
- Adding hearings, docket info, correspondence, depositions, expenses, and phone calls
- Printing reports
- Using the custom fields
- Exiting the system
- Technical details

The Case Management system tracks case-related information, hearings, docket information, correspondence, records of depositions, case expenses, and phone calls related to cases. The database for the Case Management system is stored in the `Legal-specific databases and files/Access/Databases` folder of the CD-ROM, and the database is named CaseMgmt.mdb. To use the database, copy the file from the CD-ROM to the desired directory on your hard drive or your network drive (**but see the important note that follows**).

NOTE: All files stored on the CD-ROM are read-only (this is the way CD-ROMs are created). Therefore, when you copy a file from the CD-ROM to your hard drive or network drive, the file retains its "read-only" status. You MUST change this status before you can use the database. To change this status after copying the database file, locate the file on your hard drive or network drive using My Computer or Windows Explorer. Right-click the filename or icon and choose Properties from the menu that appears. In the Properties dialog box that opens, click the General tab, remove the check mark from the Read-Only check box, and click OK.

Using the Case Management System

When you load the Case Management system in Access, a main menu appears like the one shown in Figure 29-1.

To add or edit case records, click the Add/Edit Records button. When you do so, a tabbed form appears (see Figure 29-2) which you can use to add new case information, edit existing case information, or add and edit hearings, docket information, correspondence, depositions, expenses, and phone calls for a particular case.

In the fields of the Case Info tab, fill in the information pertaining to each case. To add a new case when done, click the Add Record button at the bottom of the tab and fill in the information for the next case. Figure 29-2 shows the Case Info tab of the system.

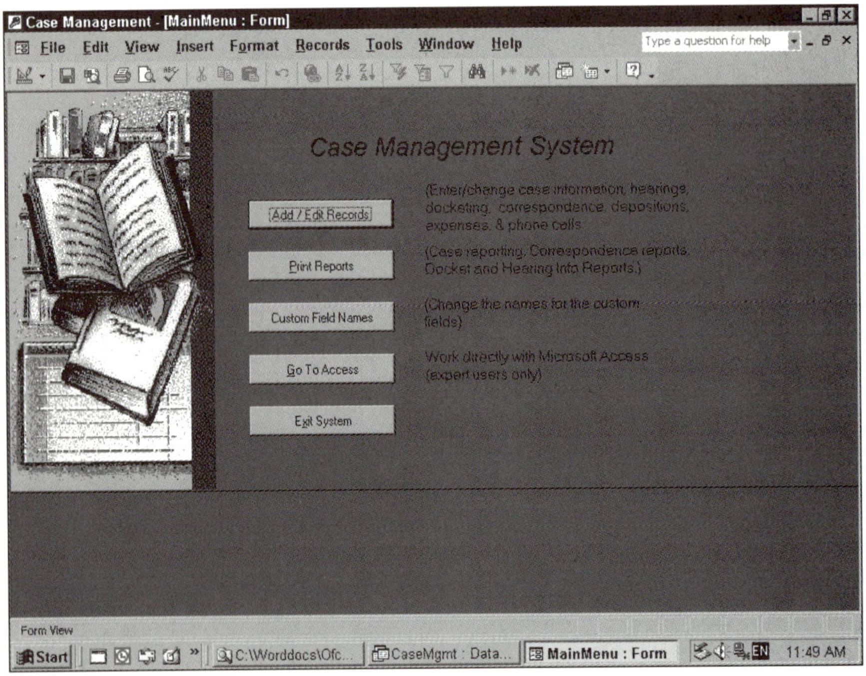

Figure 29-1: The main menu of the Case Management system

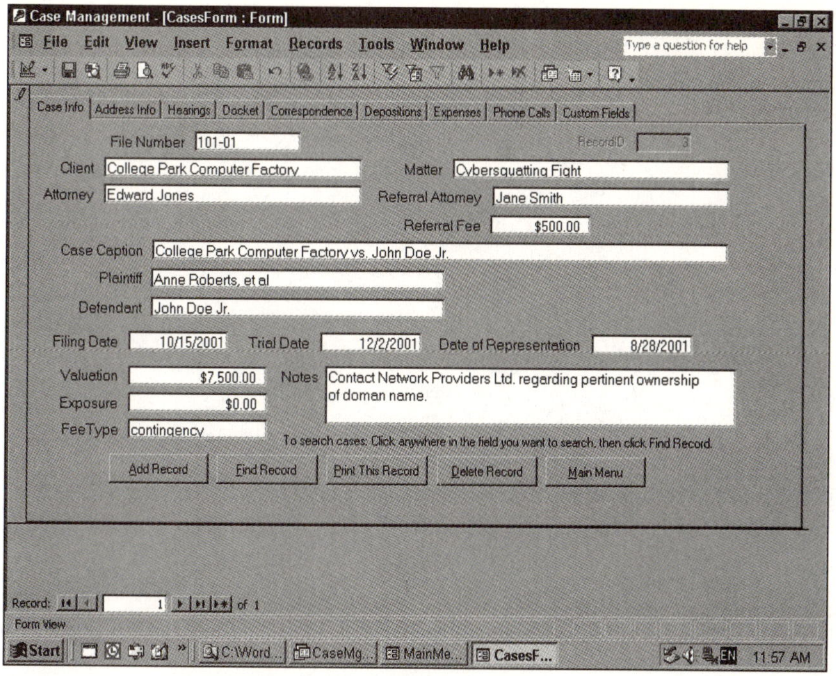

Figure 29-2: The Case Info tab of the Case Management system

To find an existing case, click anywhere within a field that you want to search; then, click the Find Record button. In the Find dialog box that appears, enter the search term and then click Find Next to locate the desired record. If another record exists with that same search term, you can again use the Find Record button and click the Find Next button in the dialog box to locate successive records matching your search term.

To print the case-related information for a single record, locate the desired record and then click the Print This Record button at the bottom of the Case Info tab.

To delete a case from the system, first locate the desired record on the Case Info tab using the Find Record button. When the record appears, click the Delete Record button.

In addition to the information shown on the Case Info tab, you also can enter the company or law firm name, address, phone number, and e-mail address of both the client and the opposing counsel involved in the case. To do this, click the Address Info tab. The Address Info page appears as shown in Figure 29-3, and you can proceed to enter the necessary information.

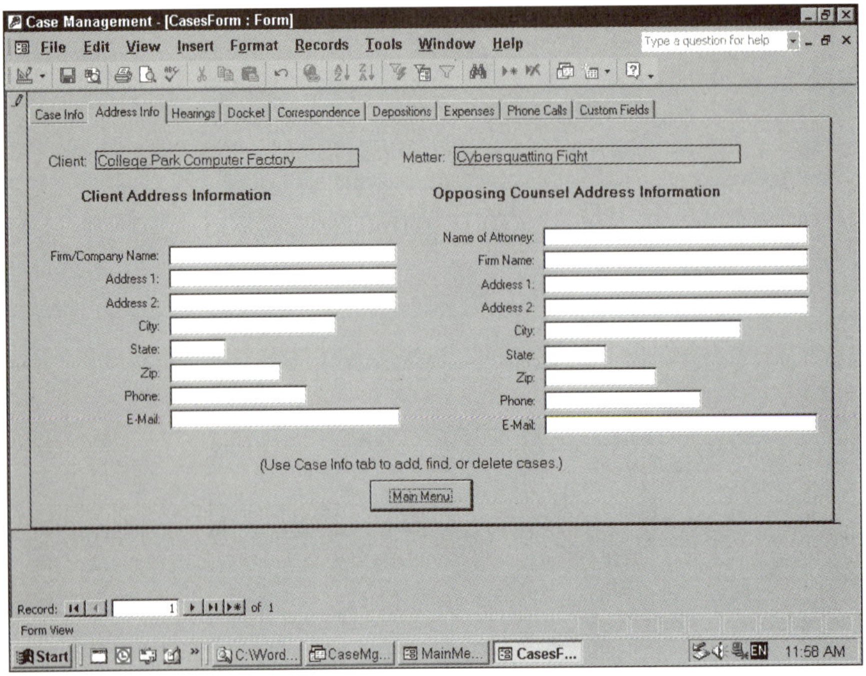

Figure 29-3: The Address Info tab of the Case Management system

Adding Hearings, Docket Info, Correspondence, Depositions, Expenses, and Phone Calls

After you have entered cases, you can add hearings, docket-related information, correspondence, depositions, case expenses, or phone calls related to any given case. To do so, first locate the desired case using the search procedures described earlier. Then click the appropriate tab (hearings, docket, correspondence, depositions, expenses, or phone calls) and enter information in the fields shown. For any given case, you can have multiple records regarding hearings, docket information, correspondence, depositions, case-related expenses, or phone calls. Each respective tab contains an Add button, a Find button, and a Delete button. You can use these to add, search for, or delete respective items under the Hearings, Docket, Correspondence, Depositions, Expenses, or Phone Calls tabs. Figure 29-4 shows the Hearings tab. Figure 29-5 shows the Docket tab of the system, and Figure 29-6 shows the Correspondence tab of the system.

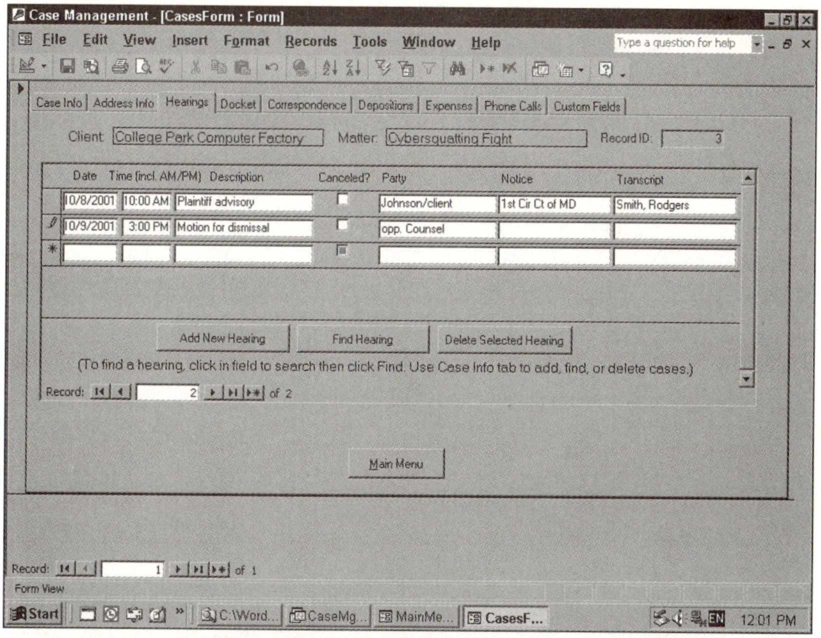

Figure 29-4: The Hearings tab of the Case Management system

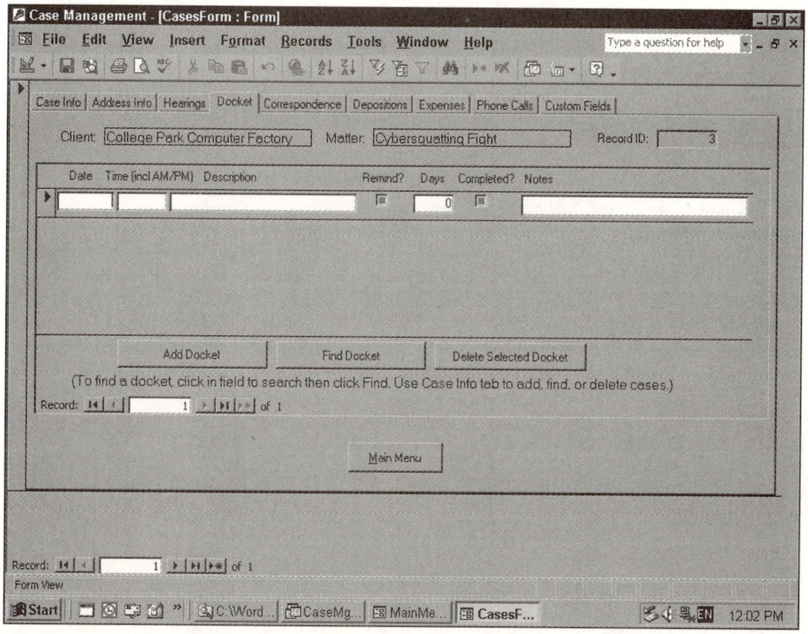

Figure 29-5: The Docket tab of the Case Management system

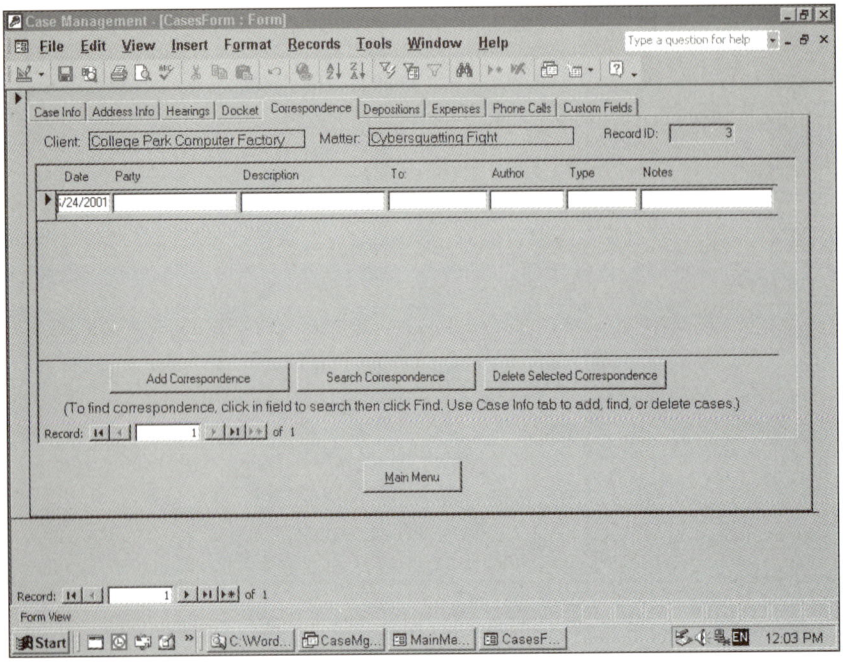

Figure 29-6: The Correspondence tab of the Case Management system

Figure 29-7 shows the Depositions tab of the system. Note that you can print a report containing all depositions related to a particular case by clicking the Print button at the bottom of this form.

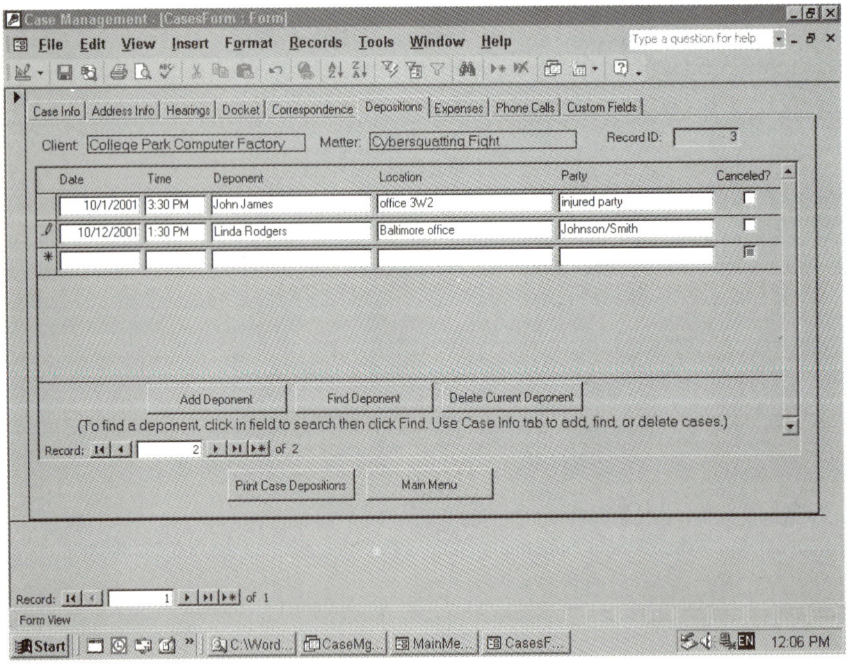

Figure 29-7: The Depositions tab of the Case Management system

Figure 29-8 shows the Expenses tab of the system, and Figure 29-9 shows the Phone Calls tab of the system. Note that you can print expenses or phone calls related to a particular case using the Print buttons at the bottom of these tabs.

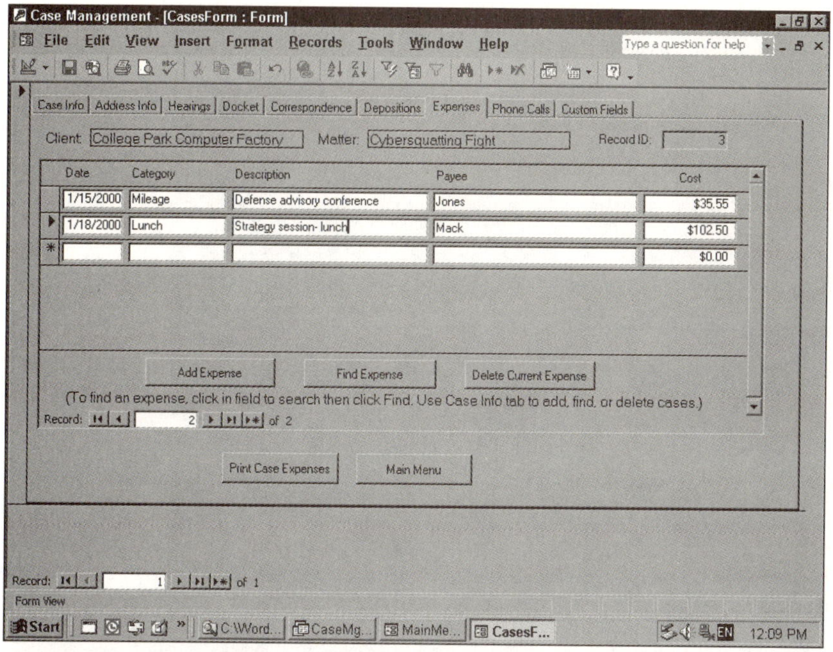

Figure 29-8: The Expenses tab of the Case Management system

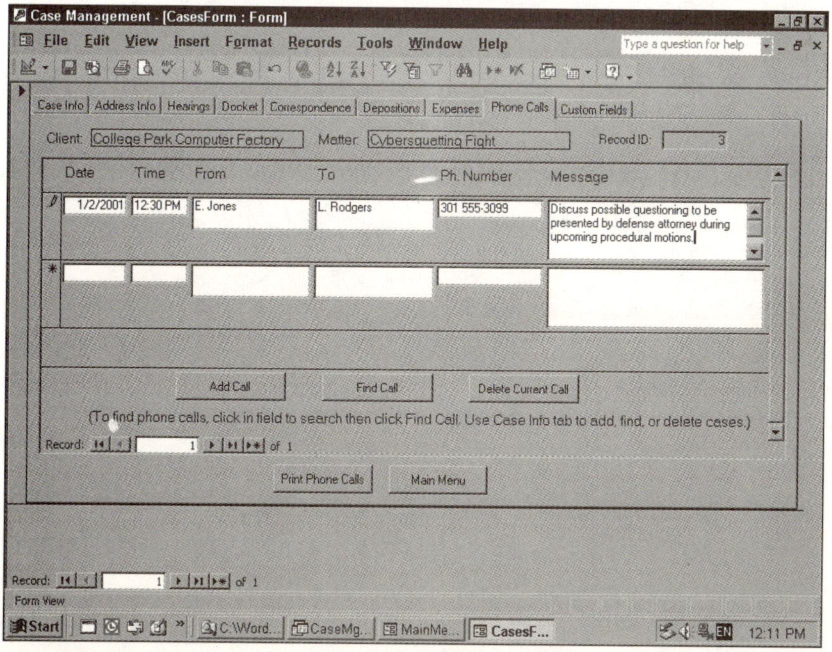

Figure 29-9: The Phone Calls tab of the Case Management system

Printing Reports

To print reports, from the main menu, click the Print Reports button. The Reports Menu, shown in Figure 29-10, will appear.

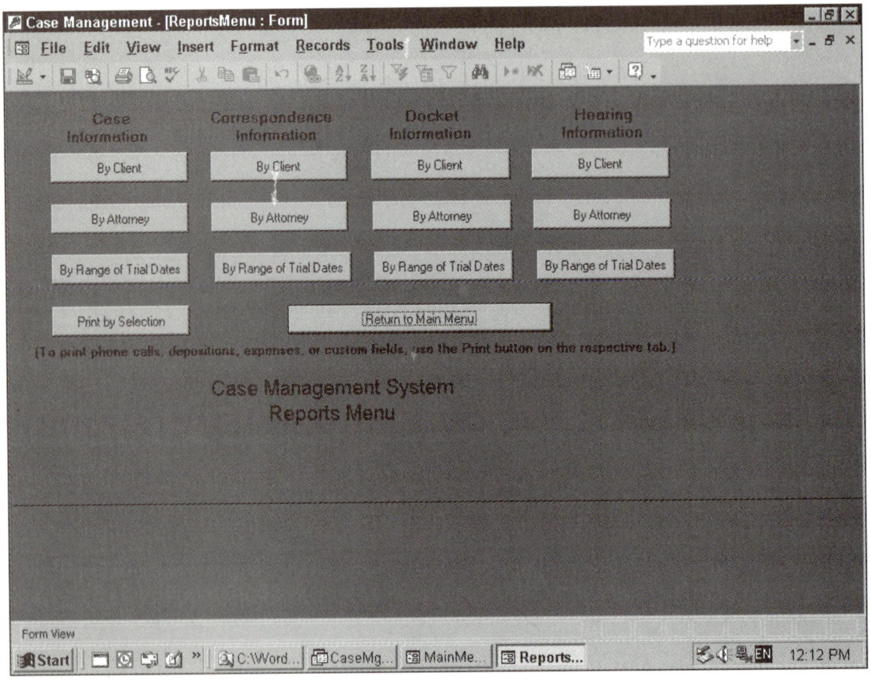

Figure 29-10: The Reports Menu of the Case Management system

From this menu, you can choose from a variety of reports by clicking the desired button. You can print reports containing case information, docket information, hearing information, or correspondence information. (To print the depositions, expenses, or phone calls related to a case, use the Print buttons at the bottom of the respective tabs.) You also can choose to print the reports by client, by attorney, or by a range of trial dates. When you select a report, you are first prompted for any needed information (such as the name of the client or attorney). Respond to any prompts, and the desired report appears in preview mode. You can then click the Print icon in the toolbar to send the report to the default printer.

Additionally, you can choose to print the Case Information report by selection (matching a specific criteria that you enter). If you choose to print this report by selection, another screen appears like the one illustrated in Figure 29-11. You can fill in the matching criteria to select the records to print; then click Print. For example, you could choose to print the Case Information Report by Referral Attorney by entering part or all of the name of the referring attorney in the Referral Attorney box.

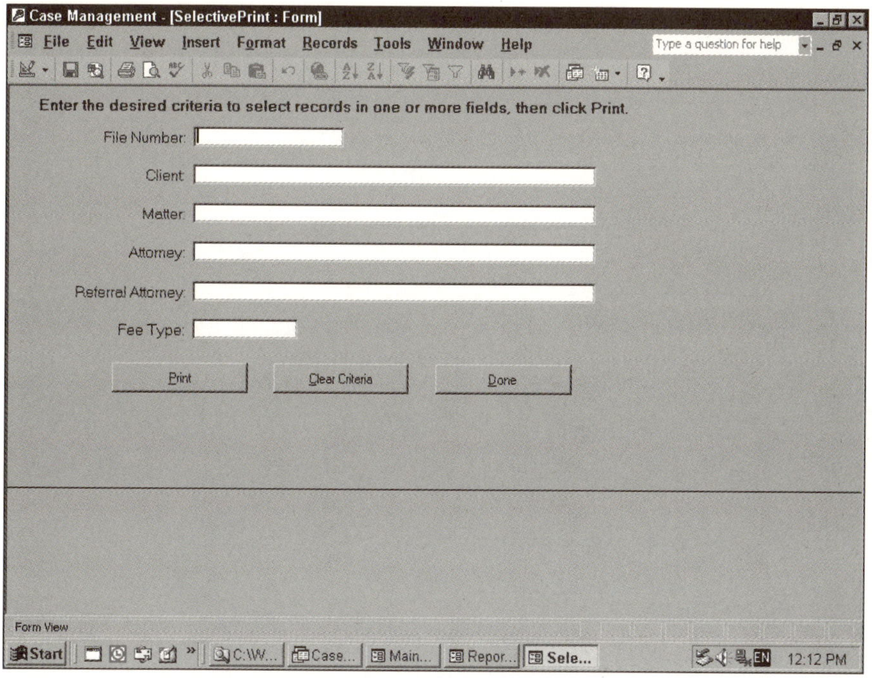

Figure 29-11: The selection screen for printing Case Information by selection

Using the Custom Fields

In addition to the predefined fields for each case, the Case Management system provides two custom text fields, two custom date fields, and two custom currency amount fields that can be used for any purpose. The custom fields are located on the Custom Fields tab of the system, as shown in Figure 29-12. To add information in these fields, first locate the desired case using the search methods described earlier. Then click the Custom Fields tab and enter the desired information.

You can search for any case within the system on the basis of information stored within any of the custom fields. To do this, first click anywhere within the particular custom field that you want to search and then click the Search button at the bottom of the tab. In the Find dialog box that appears, enter the search string in the Find What box. Click the Find Next button to locate the first occurrence of the search term. If additional records containing the search term exist, you can repeatedly click the Find Next button to locate successive occurrences of the search term.

To print a report containing the information stored in the custom fields, first locate the desired case using the search methods described earlier. Then click the Custom Fields Report button at the bottom of the Custom Fields tab. The report will appear in a preview window, and you can click the Print icon to print the report at the default printer.

You can change the names displayed (and printed on reports) for the custom fields by going back to the main menu and clicking the Custom Field Names button. You can then enter new names for any of the custom fields on the next form that appears.

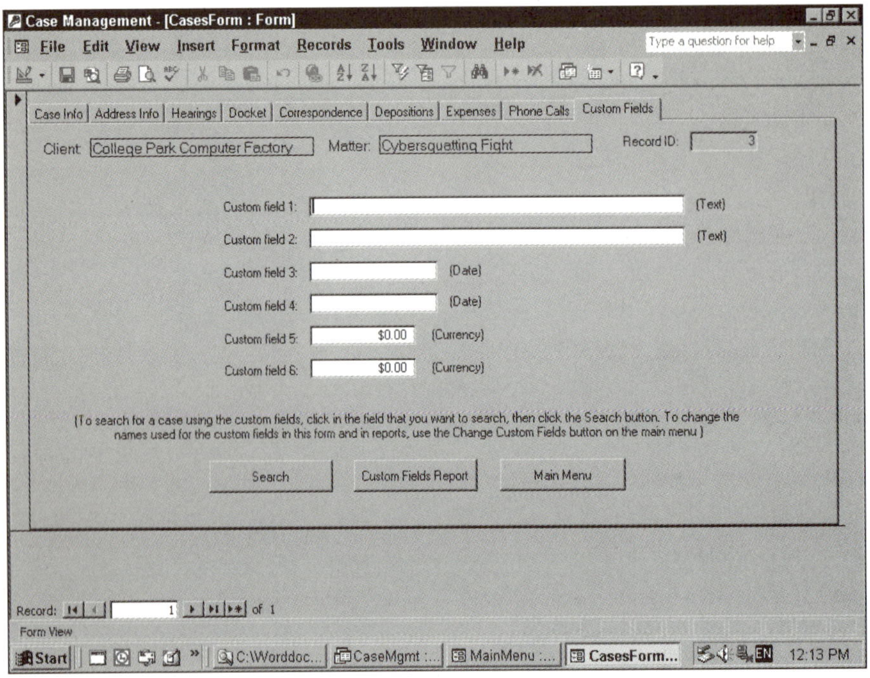

Figure 29-12: The Custom Fields tab

Exiting the System

To exit the system, click the Main Menu or the Return to Main Menu buttons from any other screen to get back to the main menu. Then click Exit System.

Technical Details

This portion of the chapter has been provided for experienced Access gurus and/or in-house programmers or hired consultants working at law firms. The following paragraphs outline the workings behind the application described in this chapter and offer suggestions (where applicable) for custom modifications that individual firms may prefer to see implemented with the databases that they are using.

CAUTION: Note that you should *not* attempt to make changes to the design of objects in the database unless you are intimately familiar with Access. Otherwise, the application may fail to operate properly.

The Case Management system uses one main table (Cases) and six related tables (Correspondence, Docket, Hearings, Expenses, Depositions, and PhoneCalls). The structure of the tables and their relationships is shown in Figure 29-13. One additional table, called Cfields, contains a single record and is used to store the names assigned to the custom fields. On the Custom Fields tab and in reports, the `Dlookup` function is used to retrieve and display the names used for the custom fields.

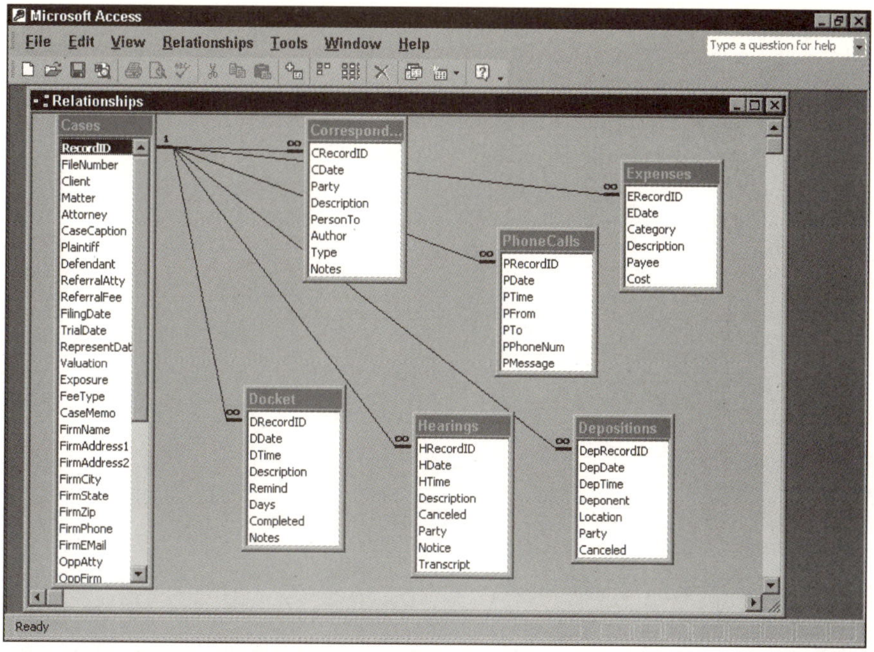

Figure 29-13: The table structures and relationships

The main form used by the system, the CasesForm, contains a tabbed control with nine tabs. The Case Info and Address Info tabs contain controls based on the fields in the Cases table, whereas the remaining tabs contain controls from the other respective tables (Correspondence, Docket, Hearings, Depositions, Expenses, PhoneCalls, and Custm Fields). The Hearings, Docket, Correspondence, Depositions, Expenses, and Phone Calls tabs are each divided into a form/subform arrangement to display the relational data. Hence, when any particular case is visible on the Case Info tab, the related hearings, docket records, correspondence records, depositions, case-related expenses, or phone calls for that particular case appear within the subform.

Report design

With the exception of the Print By Selection option of the Case Information report, all reports are based on select queries, or parameter queries. For example, the ByAttorney report uses the ByAttorney query as its data source, the ByClient report uses the ByClient query as its data source, and so on.

The Case Information and Custom Fields reports are nonrelational because they obtain all needed information from the Cases table. The remaining reports are relational reports and are all based on relational queries.

The Print By Selection option of the Reports menu makes use of VBA code to construct a `WHERE` clause using the search criteria entered in the unbound fields of the SelectivePrint form. The VBA code, which is attached to the Print button's OnClickevent, follows.

```
Private Sub SelPrinter_Click()
    '  Create a WHERE clause using search criteria entered by user and
    '  set RecordSource property of SelectivePrint form.

    Dim MySQL As String, MyCriteria As String, MyRecordSource As String
    Dim ArgCount As Integer

    '  Initialize argument count.
    ArgCount = 0

    '  Initialize SELECT statement.
    MySQL = "SELECT * FROM CASES WHERE "
    MyCriteria = ""

    '  Use values entered in text boxes in form to create
    '  the criteria used for the WHERE clause.
    '  Note that AddToWhere is another subroutine in this module.
    AddToWhere [M_FileNumber], "[FileNumber]", MyCriteria, ArgCount
    AddToWhere [M_Client], "[Client]", MyCriteria, ArgCount
    AddToWhere [M_Matter], "[Matter]", MyCriteria, ArgCount
    AddToWhere [M_Attorney], "[Attorney]", MyCriteria, ArgCount
    AddToWhere [M_RefAttorney], "[ReferralAtty]", MyCriteria, ArgCount
    AddToWhere [M_FeeType], "[FeeType]", MyCriteria, ArgCount

    '  If no criterion specifed, return all records.
    If MyCriteria = "" Then
        MyCriteria = "True"
    End If

    '  Create SELECT statement.
    MyRecordSource = MySQL & MyCriteria
    '  Set RecordSource property of destination object.
    DoCmd.OpenReport "BasicReport", A_PREVIEW, , MyCriteria
End Sub
```

When the user enters criteria into one or more fields in the form and clicks the Print button, the resulting SQL `SELECT` statement is assembled based on the criteria in the unbound controls of the form. The statement is then used as part of the `DoCmd.OpenReport` statement at the end of the routine to launch the report containing the selected records. This code also makes use of a user-defined function named `AddToWhere`. This function's code resides in the same class module and is as follows:

```
Private Sub AddToWhere(FieldValue As Variant, FieldName As String, MyCriteria
As String, ArgCount As Integer)

    '  Create criteria for WHERE clause.
    If FieldValue <> "" Then
        '  Add "and" if other criterion exists.
        If ArgCount > 0 Then
            MyCriteria = MyCriteria & " and "
        End If
```

```
        '  Append criterion to existing criteria.
        '  Enclose FieldValue and asterisk in quotation marks.
        MyCriteria = (MyCriteria & FieldName & " Like " & Chr(39) & Chr(42) &
FieldValue & Chr(42) & Chr(39))

        '  Increase argument count.
        ArgCount = ArgCount + 1
    End If
End Sub
```

The remaining code in the class module is used to clear entries from the text box controls in the SelectivePrint form or to close the form.

Notes about modifications

In general, reports can be modified with no interdependent effects on the rest of the system. New fields can be added to the Cases table and their respective controls added to the Case Info tab of the Cases form, to dependent queries, and to the associated reports. Adding fields to the Hearings, Docket, and Correspondence tabs may be trickier because of the tabular nature of the subform design and the limited amount of real estate available on the form. (Of course, with patience, virtually any modification is possible!) If you need room to add additional fields of your own choosing, you can make use of the Custom Fields tab or consider adding another tab to the tabbed form. Just open the form titled CasesForm in Design view, click the tab *after which* you want to place the new tab, and choose Insert ⇨ Tab Control Page from the menus. To change the name of the new tab that appears, right-click the tab, choose Properties, and type the name you want in the Caption property of the Format tab that appears. Of course, in addition to adding the new tab, you will also need to create your new fields in the Cases table and create any desired reports. You can add command buttons to the new tab to print any new reports that you create; for details on adding command buttons to forms, see "Designing Forms Manually" in the chapter that deals with working with forms in the Access section of the book.

All VBA code in this application is attached to buttons on forms; there is no VBA code stored in any global modules. The main form initially appears because of a Display Form setting in the Tools/Startup dialog box.

Summary

This chapter provided details regarding the Case Management system:

- This system provides a tabbed form that lets you add records pertaining to a particular case. With the various tabs of the main form, you can add case and client address data, hearings, docket information, records of correspondence, depositions, expenses, and phone calls.
- A custom fields tab provides two text fields, two date fields, and two currency fields that can be used for any purpose.
- The Case Management system uses one main table containing the records regarding each case, and six related tables containing associated records of correspondence, docket, hearings, deposition, expense, and phone calls information. A one-to-many relationship exists between the main table and each of the associated tables.

The next chapter details the use of the Litigation Support database, another legal-specific database provided on the CD-ROM.

Chapter 30

The Litigation Support Database

In This Chapter

- ♦ Using the Litigation Support database
- ♦ Printing reports
- ♦ Exiting the system
- ♦ Technical details

THE LITIGATION SUPPORT DATABASE tracks litigation-related information, such as the source and type of documents, type of deponent and deponent name, parties involved, discovery requests, and notes. The Litigation Support database is stored in the folder called `Legal-specific databases and files/Access/Databases` on the CD-ROM, and the database is named LitSupp.mdb. To use the database, copy the file from your CD-ROM to the desired directory on your hard drive or your network drive (but *see the important note that follows*).

NOTE: All files stored on the CD-ROM are read-only (this is the way CD-ROMs are created). Therefore, when you copy a file from the CD-ROM to your hard drive or network drive, the file retains its "read-only" status. You MUST change this status before you can use the database. To change this status after copying the database file, locate the file on your hard drive or network drive using My Computer or Windows Explorer. Right-click the filename or icon; then choose Properties from the menu that appears. In the Properties dialog box that opens, click the General tab, remove the check mark from the Read-Only check box, and click OK.

TIP: Because the default file format used by Access 2002 is the Access 2000 file format, the ready-to-use legal databases on the CD-ROM exist in Access 2000 format. This enables law firms that have a mix of users (some using Access 2002 and others using Access 2000) to share the same databases on a firm network.

Using the Litigation Support Database

When you load the Litigation Support Database in Access, a main menu appears like the one shown in Figure 30-1.

To add or edit records, click the Add/Edit Records button. When you do so, a form appears that you can use to add new records (see Figure 30-2). Fill in the information desired, using the Tab key to move from field to field. In the logical (Yes/No) fields such as Exhibit, Agreed, Admitted, Denied, and Objected, you can enter a check mark by pressing the spacebar while the cursor is in the field, or by clicking the desired field.

To add a new record when done, click the Add Record button at the bottom of the tab and fill in the information for the next record.

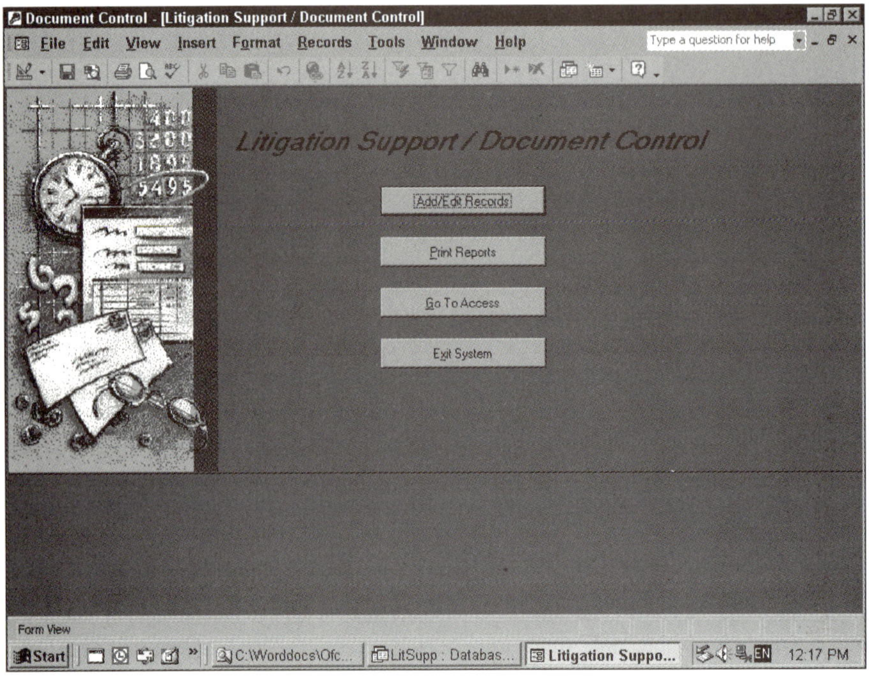

Figure 30-1: The main menu of the Litigation Support database

To find an existing record, click anywhere within a field that you want to search; then click the Search button. In the Find dialog box that appears, enter the search term and then click Find Next to locate the desired record. If another record exists with that same search term, you can again use the Search button and repeatedly click the Find Next button in the dialog box that appears to locate successive records matching your search term.

To delete a record from the system, first locate the record that you want to delete, using the search procedures described above. Then click the Delete Record button.

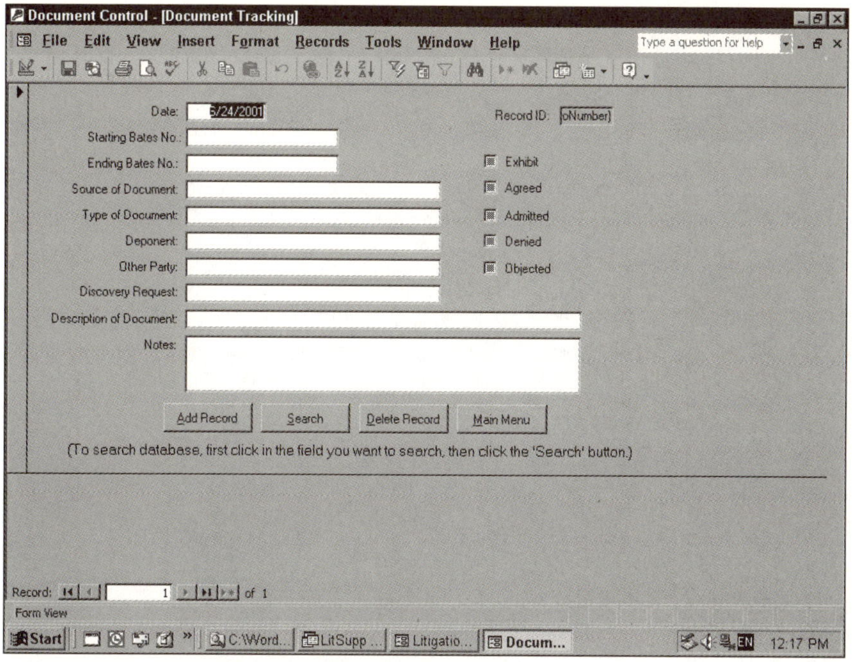

Figure 30-2: The form used to add records to the database

Printing Reports

To print reports, go to the main menu and click the Print Reports button. The Reports Menu, shown in Figure 30-3, will appear.

From this menu, you can print reports based on a range of dates, by bates stamp numbers, by deponent, or by selective query. If you choose By Date Range, you are asked for a starting and ending date, and the resulting report includes all records within that range of dates. If you choose By Bates Stamp Numbers, you are asked for a starting and ending bates stamp number, and the resulting report includes all records within that range of bates stamp numbers. If you choose By Deponent, you are asked for a text string to enter as the desired deponent name, and all appropriate records for that deponent will appear.

After the desired report appears in a preview window, you can click the Print icon on the toolbar to send the report to the default printer.

Additionally, you can choose to print reports By Selective Query (matching criteria that you enter). If you choose to print this report, another screen appears like the one shown in Figure 30-4. Fill in the matching criteria to select the records to print; then click Print. For example, you could choose to print the a report based on a deponent name along with a keyword entered into the Description of Document field, by entering part or all of the deponent name into the Deponent Name field and entering the keyword into the Description of Document field. When the report appears in a preview window, click the Print icon on the toolbar to send the report to the default printer.

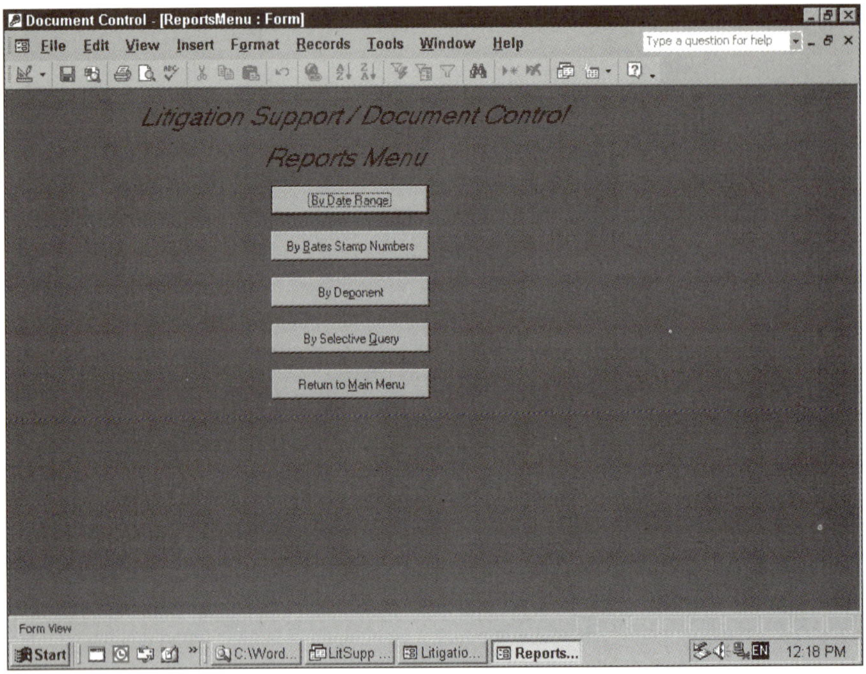

Figure 30-3: The Reports Menu of the Litigation Support database

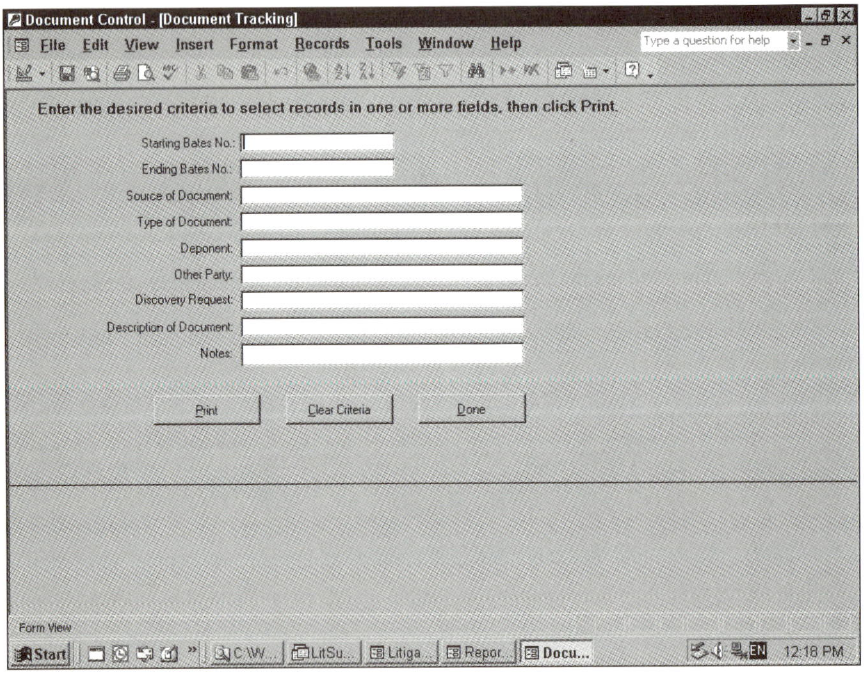

Figure 30-4: The criteria screen used for printing selective reports

Exiting the System

To exit the system, click the Main Menu or the Return to Main Menu buttons from any other form to get back to the main menu. Then, click Exit System.

Technical Details

This portion of the chapter has been provided for experienced Access gurus and/or in-house programmers or hired consultants working at law firms. The following paragraphs outline the workings behind the application described in this chapter and offer suggestions (where applicable) for custom modifications that individual firms may prefer to see implemented with the databases that they are using.

CAUTION: Note that you should *not* attempt to make changes to the design of objects in the database unless you are intimately familiar with Access. Otherwise, the application may fail to operate properly.

The Litigation Support database uses a single table, called Litigate, to contain all the data stored by the system. The table structure is shown in Figure 30-5.

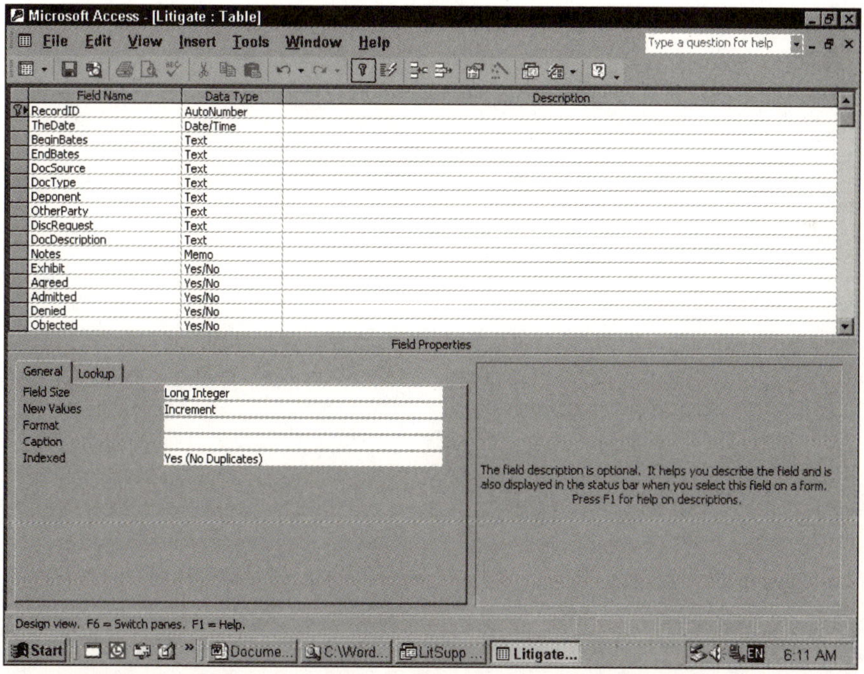

Figure 30-5: The table structure for the Litigate table of the Litigation Support database

The Litigation Support database uses a form as its main menu. This form, appropriately named MainMenu, is named in the Tools/Startup option of the database, so it appears when the database is initially loaded. (This form and all other forms used by the system also have a macro, named MaximizeMe, called from the form's On Activate event. The macro serves to maximize the window of any form as it opens.) The command buttons on the form were created with the aid of the Command Button Wizards, and they use VBA code to open respective forms or to exit from Access (with the exception of the Go To Access button, which runs a macro that displays a dialog box and closes the menu form).

The VBA code attached to the Add/Edit Records button uses a `DoCmd.OpenForm` statement to open the form named DocTracking. This is a basic form with text boxes for the text, date/time, and memo fields and check boxes for the yes/no fields, used to display or edit data in the Litigate table. The respective buttons on this form were all created with the aid of the Command Button Wizards, and they use appropriate VBA code to perform their respective tasks.

Report design

With the exception of the All Records Report and the By Selective Query report, the reports in the Litigation Support database are based on parameter queries. For example, the ByBates report uses the ByBates query as its data source, the ByDeponent report uses the ByDeponent query as its data source, and so on. The AllRecords report is based directly on the Litigate table, because it includes all records (sorting is built into the report's design, via the Sorting and Grouping dialog box).

The By Selective Query option of the Reports menu uses a `DoCmd.OpenForm` statement to open the form named SelectivePrint. The Print button on this form makes use of VBA code to construct a `WHERE` clause, using the search criteria entered in the unbound fields of the form. The VBA code is attached to the Print button's On Click event, and the code looks like this:

```
Private Sub SelPrint_Click()
    '  Create a WHERE clause using search criteria entered by user and
    '  set RecordSource property of SelectivePrint form.

    Dim MySQL As String, MyCriteria As String, MyRecordSource As String
    Dim ArgCount As Integer

    '  Initialize argument count.
    ArgCount = 0

    '  Initialize SELECT statement.
    MySQL = "SELECT * FROM LITIGATE WHERE "
    MyCriteria = ""

    '  Use values entered in text boxes in form to create
    '  the criteria used for the WHERE clause.
    '  Note that AddToWhere is another subroutine in this module.
    AddToWhere [M_BeginBates], "[BeginBates]", MyCriteria, ArgCount
    AddToWhere [M_EndBates], "[EndBates]", MyCriteria, ArgCount
    AddToWhere [M_DocSource], "[DocSource]", MyCriteria, ArgCount
    AddToWhere [M_DocType], "[DocType]", MyCriteria, ArgCount
    AddToWhere [M_Deponent], "[Deponent]", MyCriteria, ArgCount
    AddToWhere [M_OtherParty], "[OtherParty]", MyCriteria, ArgCount
    AddToWhere [M_DiscRequest], "[DiscRequest]", MyCriteria, ArgCount
    AddToWhere [M_DocDescription], "[DocDescription]", MyCriteria, ArgCount
    AddToWhere [M_Notes], "[Notes]", MyCriteria, ArgCount

    '  If no criterion specifed, return all records.
    If MyCriteria = "" Then
```

```
        MyCriteria = "True"
    End If

    '  Create SELECT statement.
    MyRecordSource = MySQL & MyCriteria
    '  Set RecordSource property of destination object.
    DoCmd.OpenReport "AllRecords", A_PREVIEW, , MyCriteria

End Sub
```

When the user enters criteria into one or more fields in the form and clicks the Print button, the resulting SQL `SELECT` statement is assembled based on the criteria in the unbound controls of the form. The statement is then used as part of the `DoCmd.OpenReport` statement at the end of the routine to launch the report containing the selected records. This code also makes use of a user-defined function named `AddToWhere`. This function's code resides in the same class module and is as follows:

```
Private Sub AddToWhere(FieldValue As Variant, FieldName As String, MyCriteria
As String, ArgCount As Integer)

    '  Create criteria for WHERE clause.
    If FieldValue <> "" Then
        '  Add "and" if other criterion exists.
        If ArgCount > 0 Then
            MyCriteria = MyCriteria & " and "
        End If

        '  Append criterion to existing criteria.
        '  Enclose FieldValue and asterisk in quotation marks.
        MyCriteria = (MyCriteria & FieldName & " Like " & Chr(39) & Chr(42) &
FieldValue & Chr(42) & Chr(39))

        '  Increase argument count.
        ArgCount = ArgCount + 1
    End If
End Sub
```

The remaining code in the class module is used to clear entries from the text box controls in the SelectivePrint form, or to close the form.

Notes about modifications

In general, reports can be modified with no interdependent effects on the rest of the system. New fields can be added to the Litigate table and their respective controls added to the DocTracking form and to the queries and reports included with the system. All VBA code in this application is attached to buttons on forms; there is no VBA code stored in any global modules. The main form initially appears due to a Display Form setting in the Tools/Startup dialog box.

Summary

This chapter provided details regarding the Litigation Support database, one of the legal-specific databases provided on the CD-ROM. The chapter covered the following points:

- The Litigation Support database provides a single form to track documents involved in a litigation matter, such as the source and type of documents, type of deponent and deponent name, parties involved, discovery requests, and notes.
- The Reports Menu of the database allows you to print reports based on a range of dates, by bates stamp number, by deponent name, or by a selective query.

The next chapter details the use of the Firm Marketing database, another legal-specific database provided on the CD-ROM.

Chapter 31

The Firm Marketing Database

In This Chapter

- ♦ Using the Firm Marketing database
- ♦ Adding and editing contacts
- ♦ Deleting a contact
- ♦ Registering a contact to receive a mailing
- ♦ Linking an attorney to a contact
- ♦ Viewing associations between contacts and mailings or attorneys
- ♦ Printing reports
- ♦ Removing associations
- ♦ Removing a contact from a mailing list
- ♦ Exiting the system
- ♦ Technical details

IT'S NO SECRET THAT MARKETING is an important task at any law firm. Although large firms typically purchase comprehensive databases designed to handle the needs of a marketing or a practice development group, small to mid-size firms often do not have the luxury of spending hundreds or thousands of dollars on such packages. Fortunately, such firms can use the power of Microsoft Access to manage the mailings of brochures, letters, and other marketing literature to a list of the firm's clients and other contacts.

The Firm Marketing database provided with this book illustrates how you can use Access to manage the marketing-related database needs of a small or midsize law firm. Using the database, you can generate mailing labels or mail-merge files to produce form letters (using a word processor such as Microsoft Word) for specific names from your firm's list of contacts. You can establish and track working relationships between an attorney and a group of contacts. And you can register any number of contacts to receive various mailings.

The Firm Marketing database is stored in the `Legal-specific databases and files/Access/Databases` folder of the CD-ROM, and the database is named Marketing.mdb.To use the database, copy the file from your CD-ROM to the desired directory on your hard drive or your network drive (*but see the important note that follows*).

NOTE: All files stored on the CD-ROM are read-only (this is the way CD-ROMs are created). Therefore, when you copy a file from the CD-ROM to your hard drive or network drive, the file retains its "read-only" status. You MUST change this status before you can use the database. To change this status after copying the database file, locate the file on your hard drive or network drive using My Computer or Windows Explorer. Right-click the filename or icon and then choose Properties from the menu that appears. In the Properties dialog box that opens, click the General tab, remove the check mark from the Read-Only check box, and click OK.

TIP: Because the default file format used by Access 2002 is the Access 2000 file format, the ready-to-use legal databases on the CD-ROM exist in Access 2000 format. This enables law firms that have a mix of users (some using Access 2002 and others using Access 2000) to share the same databases on a firm network.

Using the Firm Marketing Database

When you load the Firm Marketing database in Access, a main menu appears like the one shown in Figure 31-1.

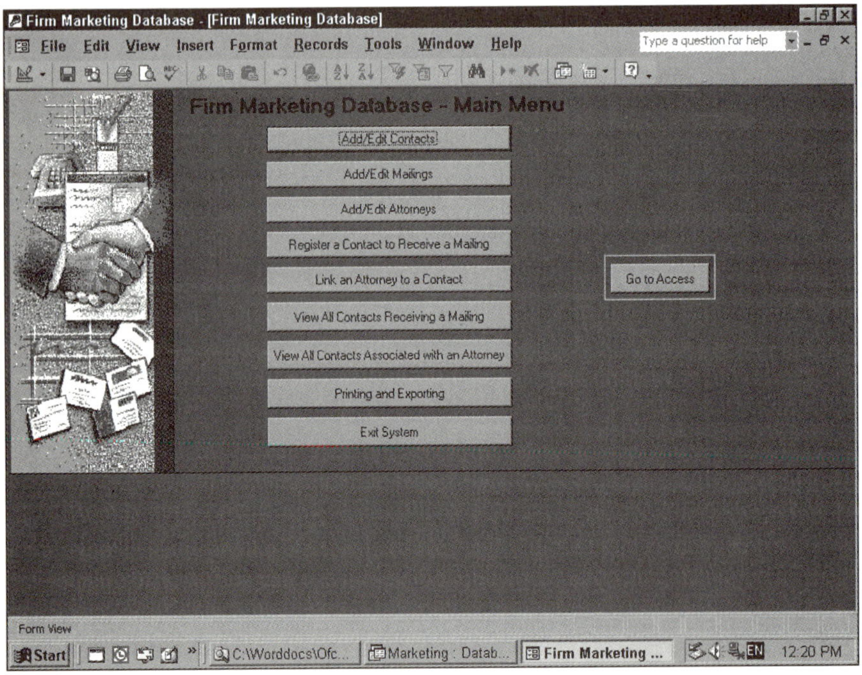

Figure 31-1: The main menu of the Firm Marketing database

Before adding contacts to the system, you should add the names of the attorneys at your firm, and the names of the mailings that are to be sent to the various contacts. To add attorneys, click the Add/Edit Attorneys button on the main menu and then click the Add New Attorney button on the Attorneys form that appears (Figure 31-2). Enter the information shown for each attorney at your firm who will be linked to any of the contacts. You can use this same form to make name or telephone number changes or to delete attorneys who are no longer with the firm.

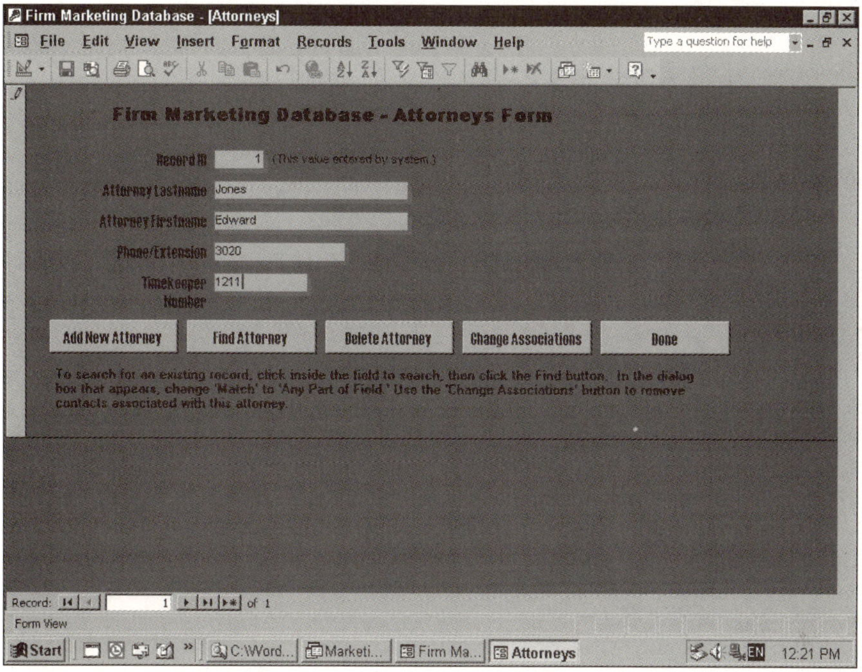

Figure 31-2: The Attorneys form

TIP: If you are an experienced Access user, you can probably save time by appending data into the PartnerSource table of the database from another source (such as from an Excel spreadsheet or from another Access table that has the names and phone extensions of all your firm's attorneys.) Hold down the Shift key while opening the Firm Marketing database so that the main menu does not appear. Under the Tables tab of the database, you will see a table called PartnerSource. You can design and run an append query that adds data from your existing data source into the PartnerSource table. (See the chapter relating to queries in the Access section of the book for specifics on how to design and use append queries.)

After you have entered the attorneys, you will need to enter the names of your mailings. From the main menu, click Add/Edit Mailings to bring up the Mailings form (Figure 31-3). Enter the information shown for each mailing that is to be sent to clients or other contacts from your firm; then click the Done button when you're done to return to the main menu.

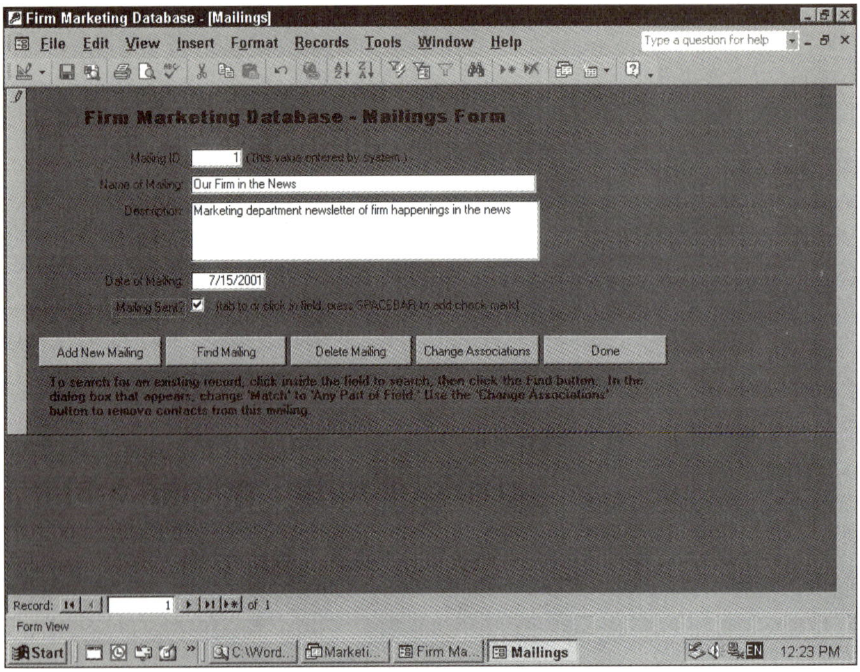

Figure 31-3: The Mailings form

Adding and Editing Contacts

At the main menu, click the Add/Edit Contacts button to bring up the Contacts form, shown in Figure 31-4. From here, you can add new contacts, search for contacts that are stored within the database, or delete an existing contact.

To add a new contact, click the Add New Contact button. The fields will clear and you can proceed to fill in the fields as desired. When done adding the contact, you can click the Add New Contact button again if you want to add successive contacts, or you can click the Done button to return to the main menu.

To find an existing contact (so that you can make changes to the record or delete it), first click in the field you want to search and then click the Find Contact button. In a moment, a Find dialog box appears, like the one shown in Figure 31-5.

In the dialog box, enter the search term in the Find What box and change the Match entry option to Any Part of Field. Click the Find Next button to search for the first occurrence of the term, or use the same button to search for successive occurrences of the term. When you find the desired contact, click Cancel to close the Find dialog box.

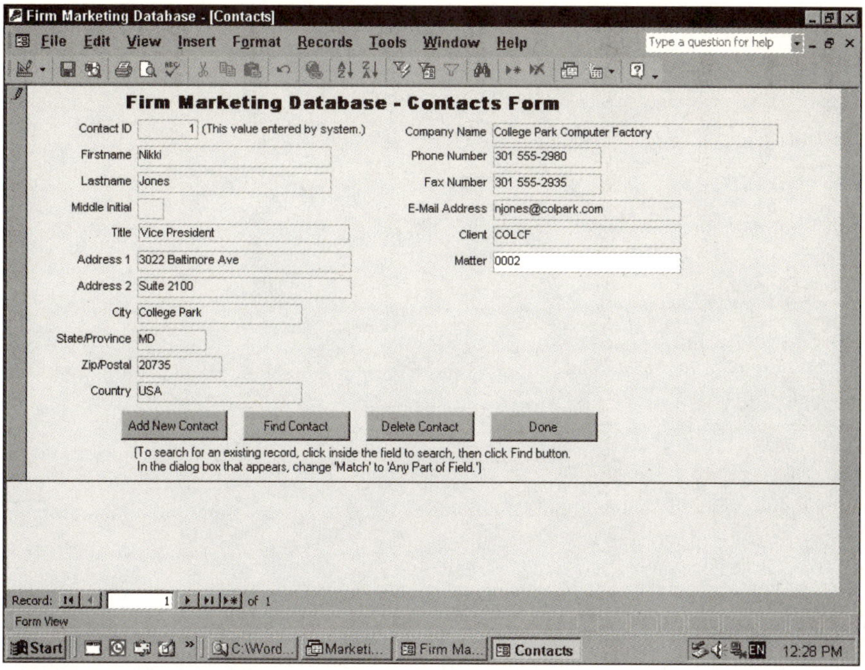

Figure 31-4: The Contacts form

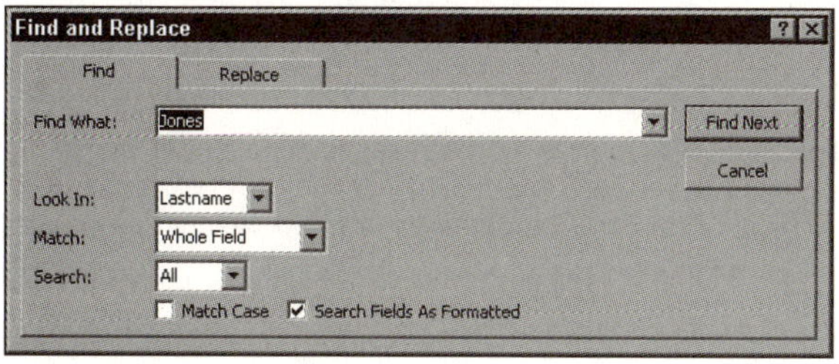

Figure 31-5: The Find dialog box

Deleting a Contact

To delete a contact that is no longer desired, first locate the unwanted contact using the procedure described above. Then click the Delete Contact button in the Contacts form. (When you delete a contact from the database, the contact is automatically removed from any mailings that the contact was previously registered to receive.)

Registering a Contact to Receive a Mailing

After you have entered your firm's contacts and the names of your mailings, you can register any contact to receive one or more mailings. To register a contact to receive a mailing, click the Register a Contact to Receive a Mailing button on the main menu. In a moment, a form appears like the one shown in Figure 31-6.

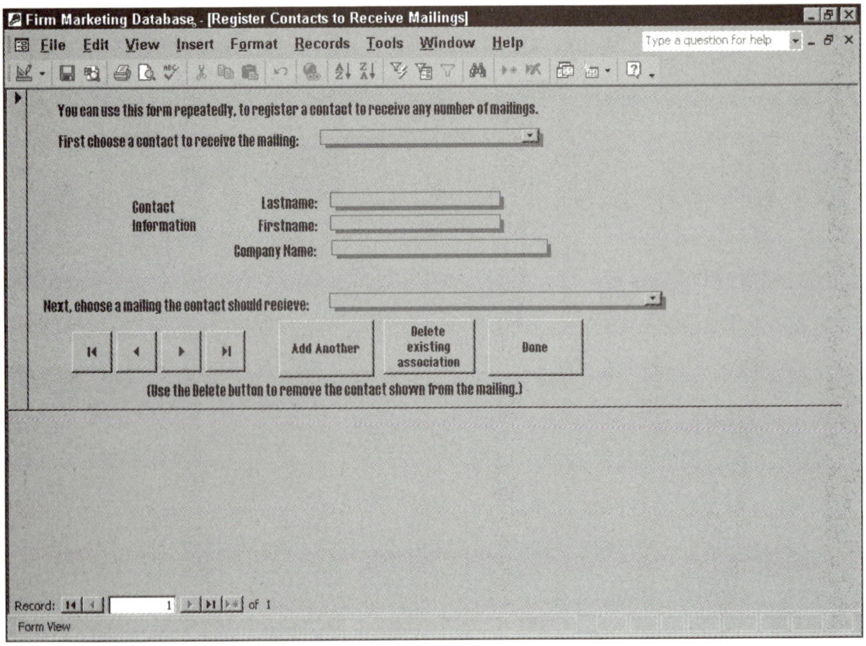

Figure 31-6: The Register a Contact to Receive a Mailing form

First, from the drop-down list at the top of the screen, choose the desired contact that should receive the mailing. Then, from the drop-down list at the bottom of the screen, choose the mailing that the contact should receive. These are all the steps needed to register a contact to receive a mailing.

You can register additional contacts to receive mailings by using the Add Another button at the bottom of the form. The form will clear, and you can repeat the steps for the next contact. You can register any contact to receive any number of mailings. When finished, click the Done button to return to the main menu.

Linking an Attorney to a Contact

You can link attorneys to contacts to enable your firm to track working relationships between your attorneys and clients or other contacts on your firm's contact list. You can link one or more attorneys to any single contact.

To link an attorney to a contact, click Link an Attorney to a Contact on the main menu. In a moment, a form appears like the one shown in Figure 31-7.

First, from the drop-down list at the top of the screen, choose the desired contact that should be linked to an attorney. Then, from the drop-down list at the bottom of the screen, choose the attorney that the contact should be associated with. Finally, from the list box at the bottom of the screen, choose the type of working relationship between the attorney and the contact. These are all the steps needed to link an attorney to a contact.

You can link additional contacts to attorneys by using the Link Another button at the bottom of the form. The form will clear, and you can repeat the steps for the next contact. You can link any contact to any number of attorneys. (Doing so lets you later generate labels or mail-merge files in Word for all the contacts associated with a particular attorney.) When finished, click the Done button to return to the main menu.

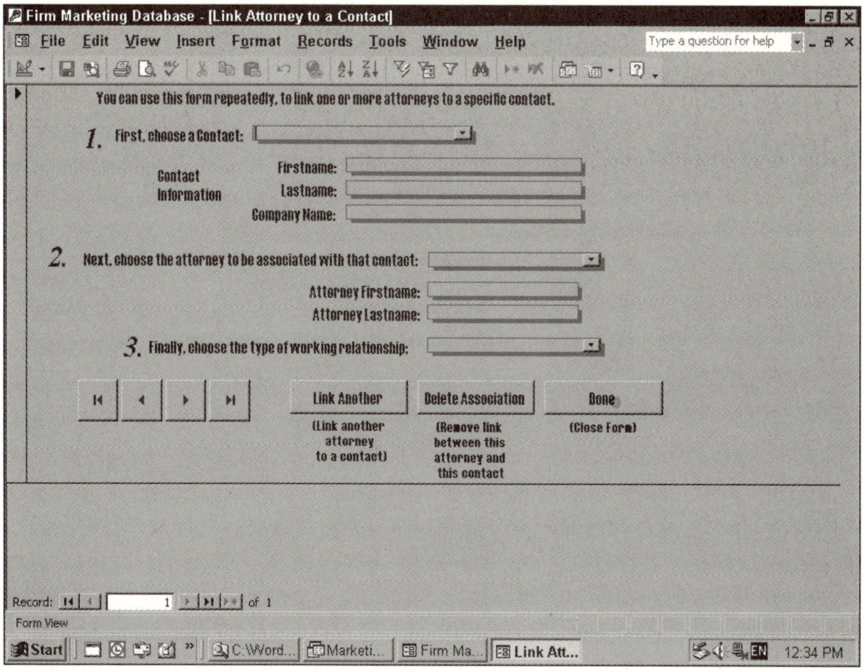

Figure 31-7: The form used to link an attorney to a contact

Viewing Associations Between Contacts and Mailings or Attorneys

At any point, you can see all contacts associated with an attorney and all contacts who are to receive a particular mailing. To see all contacts who are to receive a specific mailing, click the button labeled View All Contacts Receiving a Mailing on the main menu. You will see a prompt asking for the mailing name, as shown in Figure 31-8.

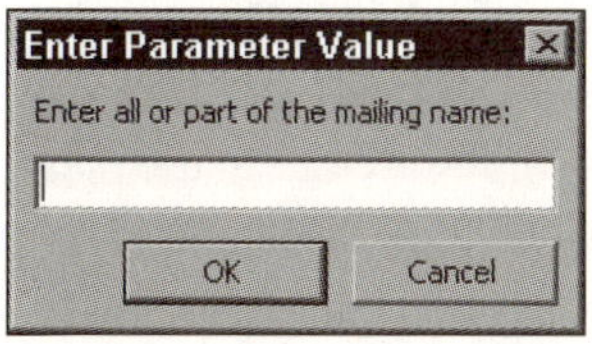

Figure 31-8: The prompt asking for a mailing name

You can enter all or part of the name of the mailing (you need only enter enough characters for Access to find the specific mailing name). After you enter the name of the mailing and click OK, a form like the example shown in Figure 31-9 appears. The upper portion of the form shows the name and description of the mailing and the mailing date, and the lower portion of the form shows all contacts who are registered to receive the mailing. (You can use the scroll bars in the lower portion of the form to view additional fields for the contacts.)

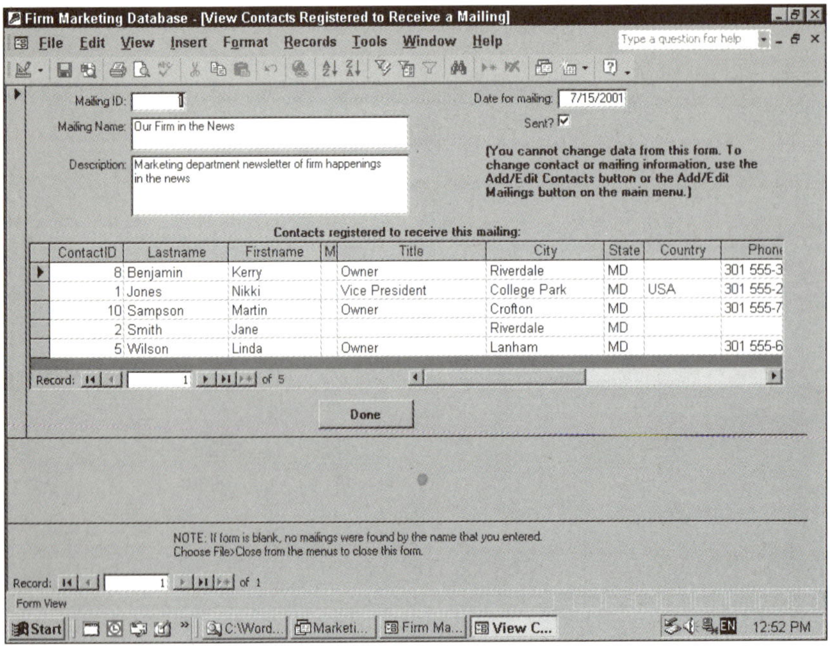

Figure 31-9: The View Contacts Registered to Receive a Mailing form

You *cannot* make changes in this form, but you can see all the contacts registered to receive the mailing. When you're done using this form, click the Done button at the bottom of the form to return to the main menu.

NOTE: To make changes, use the Add/Edit Contacts button or the Add/Edit Mailings button on the main menu.

To see all contacts who have a working relationship with a specific attorney, click the button labeled View All Contacts Associated with an Attorney on the main menu. You will be asked for the last name of the attorney, followed by the first name of the attorney. After you enter the name of the attorney and click OK, a form like the example shown in Figure 31-10 appears. The upper portion of the form shows the attorney name, telephone number, and timekeeper number, and the lower portion of the form shows all contacts that have a working relationship with the attorney. (You can use the scroll bars in the lower portion of the form to view additional fields for the contacts.)

You *cannot* make changes in this form, but you can see all the contacts associated with a specific attorney. When you're done using this form, click the Done button at the bottom of the form to return to the main menu.

NOTE: To make changes, use the Add/Edit Contacts button or the Add/Edit Attorneys button on the main menu.

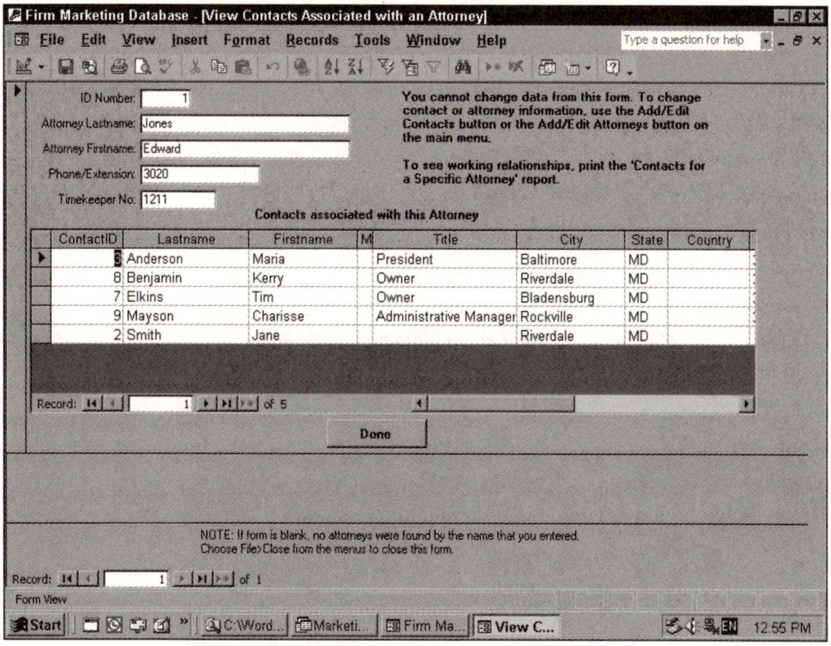

Figure 31-10: The View Contacts Associated with an Attorney form

Printing Reports

The Firm Marketing database provides a variety of reports. In addition to printing reports and mailing labels, you can export selective lists of contacts for use with Microsoft Word (or another word processor) in a mail-merge format. To produce reports, mailing labels, or exported (mail-merge) files, from the main menu, click Printing and Exporting. The Printing and Exporting menu will appear. From this menu, choose Produce Mailing Labels, Produce Reports, or Export Data to a File. The next menu that appears will provide a variety of choices for the type of report you have chosen; Figure 31-11 shows an example of the menu that appears when you select Mailing Labels.

You can choose to print reports, produce mailing labels, or export data for all contacts; for contacts for a specific attorney; for all contacts registered to receive a specific mailing; or by city, state/province, country, or company name of the contact. Choose the desired option from the menu and answer any prompts that appear. (For example, if you select labels for all contacts for a certain attorney, the system will ask for the last and first name of the attorney.) After you answer any prompts, the report appears in preview mode. You can then click the Print icon in the toolbar to begin printing.

TIP: The mailing labels are formatted to use the popular Avery 5160 style of three-across mailing labels. If you are an experienced Access user, you can change the design of the labels (or design and save your own labels) that make use of a different label size.

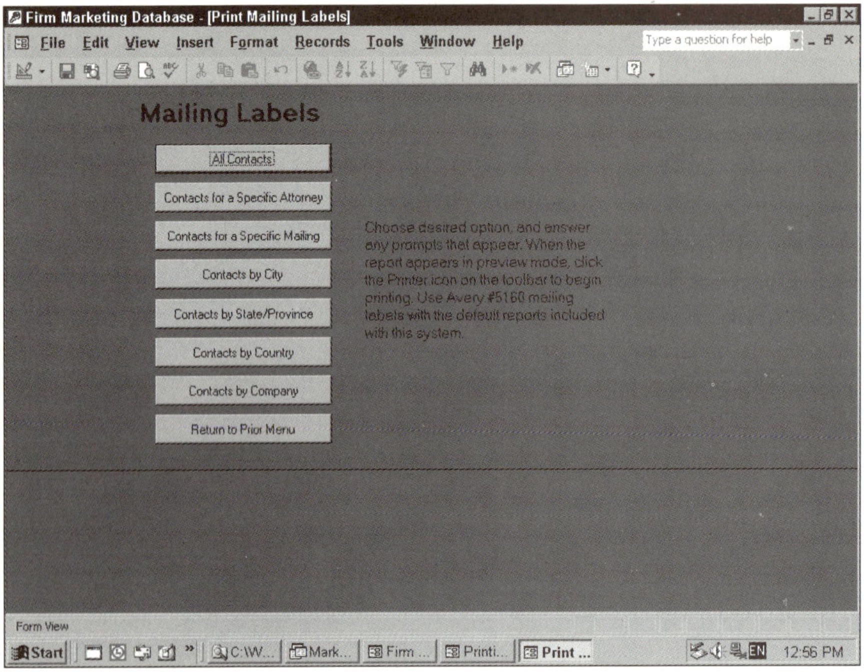

Figure 31-11: The Mailing Labels menu

If you choose to export the data to a file, you will be asked to insert a blank, formatted disk in your A drive. After you answer any prompts that appear, a Word for Windows mail-merge file containing the exported data will be copied to the disk. The file will be assigned a name of `outfile.doc`, and the data will be in ASCII-delimited format, usable with any version of Microsoft Word or with virtually all other popular word processors. Note that if you choose Produce Reports from the Printing and Exporting Menu, the Reports menu that appears contains two additional choices, as shown in Figure 31-12.

The additional choices are Mailings List and Attorney List. Choosing either of these options causes a formatted report containing all your mailings or attorneys to appear in a preview window. You can then click the Print icon in the toolbar to print the list.

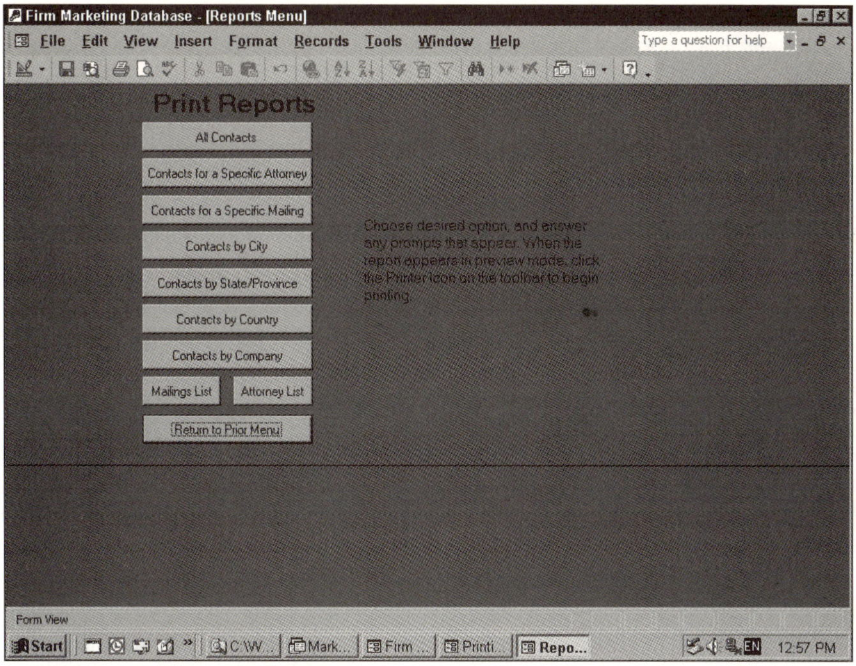

Figure 31-12: The Print Reports menu

Removing Associations

At times, you may want to remove an association between an attorney and a contact, or you may want to remove a particular contact from a mailing list. To remove an association between an attorney and an existing contact, first click Add/Edit Attorneys at the main menu, and locate the desired attorney using the Find Attorney button. After you have located the attorney, click the Change Associations button. The next form that appears will show all contacts that are associated with that attorney. Use the Navigation Buttons at the lower left to display the contact that you want to remove from the attorney's list of contacts; then click the Delete Association button.

NOTE: Clicking the Delete Association button does *not* delete the contact from the firm's list of contacts; it only removes the contact shown from the specific attorney's list of contacts.

When finished, use the Done buttons to close the forms and to return to the main menu.

Removing a Contact from a Mailing List

To remove a particular contact from a mailing list, first click Add/Edit Mailings at the main menu and locate the desired mailing using the Find Mailing button. After you have located the desired mailing, click the Change Associations button. The next form that appears will show all contacts that are registered to receive that mailing. Use the Navigation Buttons at the lower left to display the contact that you want to remove from the mailing list; then click the Delete Association button.

NOTE: This does *not* delete the contact from the firm's list of contacts; it only removes the contact shown from the specific mailing list.

When finished, use the Done buttons to close the forms and to return to the main menu.

Exiting the System

To exit the system, click the Done or the Return to Main Menu button from any other form to get back to the main menu. Then, click Exit System.

Technical Details

This portion of the chapter has been provided for experienced Access gurus and/or in-house programmers or hired consultants working at law firms. The following paragraphs outline the workings behind the application described in this chapter and offer suggestions (where applicable) for custom modifications that individual firms may prefer to see implemented with the databases that they are using.

CAUTION: Note that you should *not* attempt to make changes to the design of objects in the database unless you are intimately familiar with Access. Otherwise, the application may fail to operate properly.

The Firm Marketing database uses one main table (ContactSource), two indirectly related tables (MailingSource and PartnerSource) and two intermediate tables (ContactMailing and ContactPartner). The ContactSource table stores the name, address, telephone numbers, and other information for each contact on the firm's mailing list. The MailingSource table stores the name and description of each mailing, and the PartnerSource table maintains the name, timekeeper number, and telephone number for each attorney who has a working relationship with a contact. An additional table named RelationshipTypes is used as a lookup table for a combo box in the form used to link an attorney to a contact. (Although some tables and other objects in the system were originally created using the name *Partner*, users of the system can store any attorneys in the system, not just partners.)

This application is unique among the sample applications in this book in that it makes use of many-to-many relationships. The MailingSource table has a many-to-many relationship with the ContactSource table. Hence, a single mailing can be sent to any number of contacts, and a single contact can be registered to receive any number of mailings. In similar fashion, the PartnerSource table also has a many-to-many relationship with the ContactSource table. Hence, any single attorney can have a working relationship with any number of contacts, and any single contact can have a working relationship with a number of attorneys.

Access does not directly support the creation of many-to-many relationships between tables. However, the same result can be indirectly achieved by including an intermediate (linking) table between the indirectly related tables. The ContactMailing table provides the many-to-many link between the ContactSource table and the MailingSource table, and the ContactPartner table provides the many-to-many link between the ContactSource table and the PartnerSource table. The ContactPartner table also contains a field titled Relationship. This field is used to store the type of working relationship between the attorney and the contact. The structure of the tables and their relationships is shown in Figure 31-11.

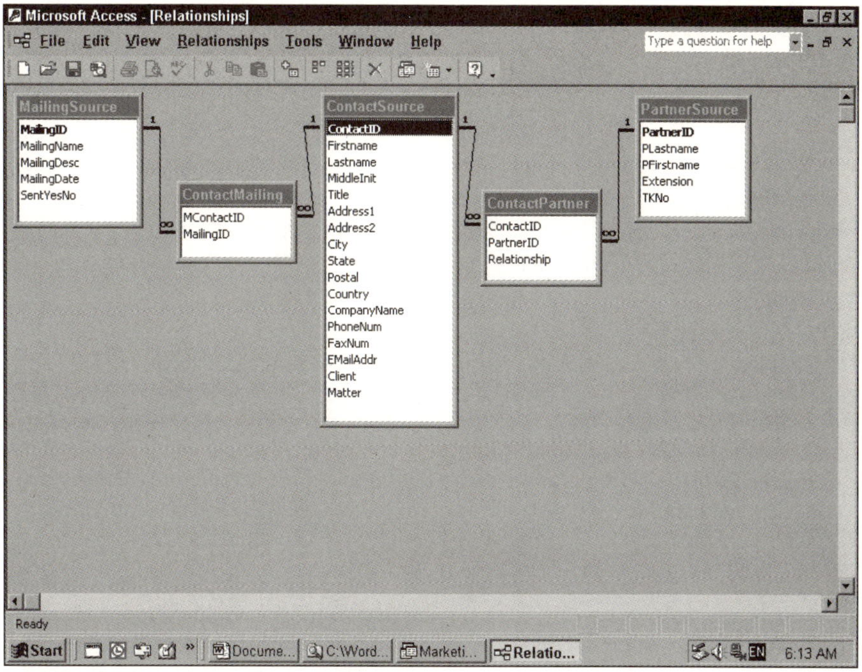

Figure 31-13: The table structures and relationships

Referential integrity has been established at the table level. This allows deletions of a contact, mailing, or attorney to automatically delete associated records in the appropriate intermediate table.

The Firm Marketing database uses a form as its main menu. This form, appropriately named MainMenu, is named in the Tools/Startup option of the database, so it appears when the database is initially loaded. (This form and all other forms used by the system also have a macro, named MaximizeMe, called from the form's `OnOpen` event. The macro serves to maximize the window of any form as it opens.) The command buttons on the forms were created with the aid of the Command Button Wizards and use VBA code to open respective forms or to exit from Access (with the exception of the Go To Access button, which runs a macro that displays a dialog box and closes the menu form).

The system uses a combination of forms for various tasks. The Contacts form is used to add, edit, or delete contacts from the contact mailing list. The Mailings form is used to add, edit, or delete mailings from the list of firm mailings, and the Partners form is used to add, edit, or delete attorneys from the list of firm attorneys. These forms are all nonrelational in nature. They are based on queries that provide the appropriate source data in alphabetical order (sorted in each case by last and then first names).

Two relational read-only forms are provided as part of the system. These are titled ViewMailing and ViewPartner, respectively. Each of these forms contains a subform, appropriately named ViewMailingSubform and ViewPartnerSubform. The relational read-only forms provide users with a fast way to see all contacts registered to receive a mailing, or to see all contacts who have a working relationship with an attorney. Both relational read-only forms draw their source data from parameter queries that prompt the user for the attorney name or the name of the mailing before the appropriate form loads.

Additionally, a relational form is provided to register a contact to receive a mailing, and another is provided to link an attorney to a given contact. These forms are very similar in design and provide partial editing capabilities. These forms are opened to a view that (indirectly) displays all records in the intermediate tables by means of the Register a Contact to Receive a Mailing button or the Link Attorney to a Contact button on the main menu. Additionally, these same forms are used to remove existing associations between contacts and mailings or between contacts and attorneys by means of the Change Associations button on the Mailings form or the Partners form. When either of these buttons is used, VBA code linked to the `OnClick` event of the button applies criteria so that the forms display only those contacts that are appropriate to the displayed mailing or attorney.

Reports

The various reports provided are conventional in design and receive their data by means of select queries or parameter queries. Note that this application does *not* follow the naming convention used in other applications described earlier in this book, in which reports were assigned the same names as the queries that provided the data. In this application, a single query may provide data to a columnar report, to a report formatted as mailing labels, or to a macro used to export data for a mail-merge operation. Hence, the query names imply the type of data provided to the appropriate destination object. For example, the rptContactsByCity report, the lblContactsByCity report, and the ExportCityContacts macro all use the Contacts By City query as a data source.

Note that the rptContactsforAPartner report differs slightly in design from the other columnar reports. This report includes a page header band that contains text boxes displaying or printing the name of the attorney related to the particular contact. Because the report is based on a query that extracts data by attorney name, the resulting report provides all contacts for that attorney. The report also includes the working relationship between the attorney and the contact in the Detail Band, drawn from the Relationship field in the ContactPartner table of the source query's design.

Exporting features

Because legal marketing or practice development groups routinely generate form letters based on all or part of a firm's contact list, the system provides users with the ability to export data. A series of macros each uses the TransferText action to export data to a disk file. You can change the action arguments for these macros if you need to export the data to a specific network drive or to a different file format.

Notes about modifications

In general, reports can be modified with no interdependent effects on the rest of the system. New fields can be added to the ContactSource table and associated queries and reports, and the respective controls added to the Contacts form. New fields can also be added to the MailingSource table or to the PartnerSource table, and to associated queries and reports as well as to the Mailings form or the Attorneys form.

All VBA code in this application is attached to buttons on forms; there is no VBA code stored in any global modules. The main form initially appears because of a Display Form setting in the Tools/Startup dialog box.

The system uses a table named RelationshipTypes as a lookup table. This table supplies the combo box of possible working relationships in the form used to link an attorney to a contact. The table contains a single field with entries of Billing Partner, Co-Counsel, Family/Relative, Former Classmate, Friend/Acquaintance, and Other. You can modify or add additional types of working relationships to this table and your changes will appear in the combo box on the form.

Summary

This chapter provided details regarding the Firm Marketing database, one of the legal-specific databases provided on the CD-ROM. The chapter covered the following points:

- The Firm Marketing database provides a complete system to manage the mailings of brochures, letters, and other literature to a list of firm clients or other contacts.
- The main menu of the system provides access to forms used to add and edit contacts, mailings, or attorneys.
- Any number of contacts can be linked to a particular mailing, and an number of attorneys can be linked to a particular contact.
- Reports and mailing labels can be produced for all contacts, for all contacts related to a particular attorney, for all contacts linked to a specific mailing, or for contacts by city name, state name, country name, or company name.
- Contact data can be exported to an ASCII text file, for use with word processors or other programs.
- The system makes use of a many-to-many relationship between the ContactSource table (which contains data regarding each contact) and the MailingSource and ContactPartner tables (which contain data regarding each mailing and each attorney).

The next chapter details the use of the Lawyer Recruiting database, another legal-specific database provided on the CD-ROM.

Chapter 32

The Lawyer Recruiting System

In This Chapter

- Using the Lawyer Recruiting system
- Adding letters, other education, clerkships, and employment details
- Using the custom fields
- Printing reports
- Using the setup options
- Exiting the system
- Technical details

In any mid-sized or large firm, lawyer recruiting is an intensive yearly process requiring the tracking of numerous statistics for potential new hires for the various associate practice groups. The Lawyer Recruiting system was designed to allow a firm's professional development or recruiting department to use Microsoft Access to manage such information. The database for the Lawyer Recruiting system is stored in the `Legal-specific databases and files/Access/Databases` folder of the CD-ROM, and the database is named Recruiting.mdb. To use the database, copy the file from the CD-ROM to the desired directory on your hard drive or your network drive (*but see the important note that follows*).

NOTE: All files stored on the CD-ROM are read-only (this is the way CD-ROMs are created). Therefore, when you copy a file from the CD-ROM to your hard drive or network drive, the file retains its "read-only" status. You MUST change this status before you can use the database. To change this status after copying the database file, locate the file on your hard drive or network drive using My Computer or Windows Explorer. Right-click the filename or icon, and choose Properties from the menu that appears. In the Properties dialog box that opens, click the General tab, remove the check mark from the Read-Only check box, and click OK.

TIP: Because the default file format used by Access 2002 is the Access 2000 file format, the ready-to-use legal databases on the CD-ROM exist in Access 2000 format. This enables law firms that have a mix of users (some using Access 2002 and others using Access 2000) to share the same databases on a firm network.

Using the Lawyer Recruiting System

When you load the Lawyer Recruiting System in Access, a main menu appears like the one shown in Figure 32-1.

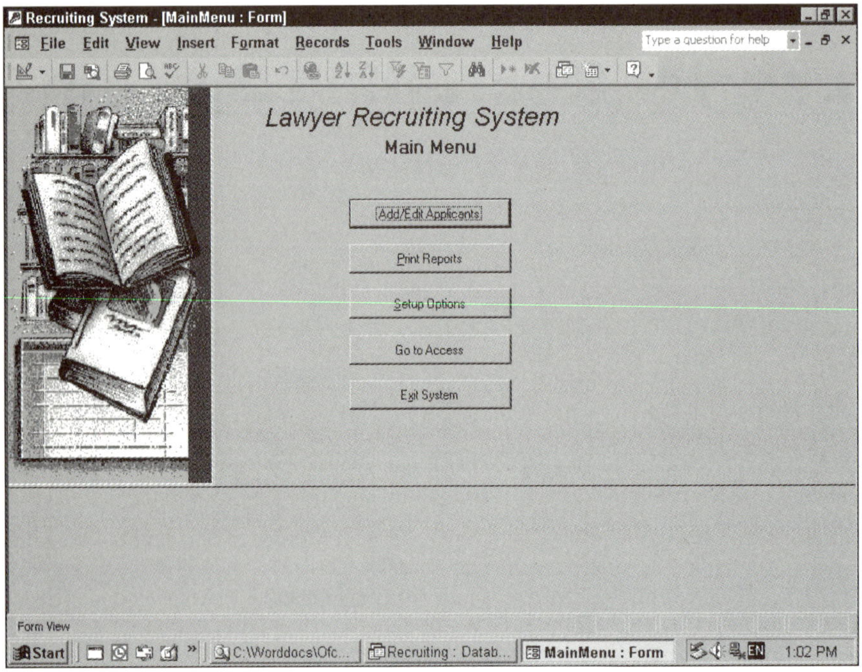

Figure 32-1: The main menu of the Lawyer Recruiting system

To add or edit "applicants" (law students who are potential hires as possible associates), click the Add/Edit Applicants button. When you do so, a tabbed form appears which you can use to add a variety of data related to each applicant. The Primary Info and Secondary Info tabs contain fields for the applicant's name, address, law school and bar, desired practice groups for possible placement at the firm, and comments. Figure 32-2 shows the Primary Info tab of the Lawyer Recruiting system, and Figure 32-3 shows the Secondary Info tab of the Lawyer Recruiting system.

Using the Primary Info and Secondary Info tabs, you can add records for each desired applicant. To add a new applicant when done, click the Add Applicant button at the bottom of the Primary Info tab, and fill in the information for the applicant, using the Primary Info and Secondary Info tabs.

To find an existing applicant, at the Primary Info tab, click in any field you want to search (typically the last name); then click the Find Applicant button. In the Find dialog box that appears, enter the search term and click Find Next to locate the desired record. If another record exists with the same search term, you can use the Find Applicant button in the dialog box to locate successive records matching your search term. Applicants appear in the system in alphabetical order by last name, and where last names are the same, by first name.

You can delete an unwanted applicant by first searching for the applicant using the search techniques just described. When the name of the unwanted applicant is visible on the Primary Info tab, click the Delete applicant button to delete the applicant from the system. When asked for confirmation, click Yes to confirm the deletion of the applicant.

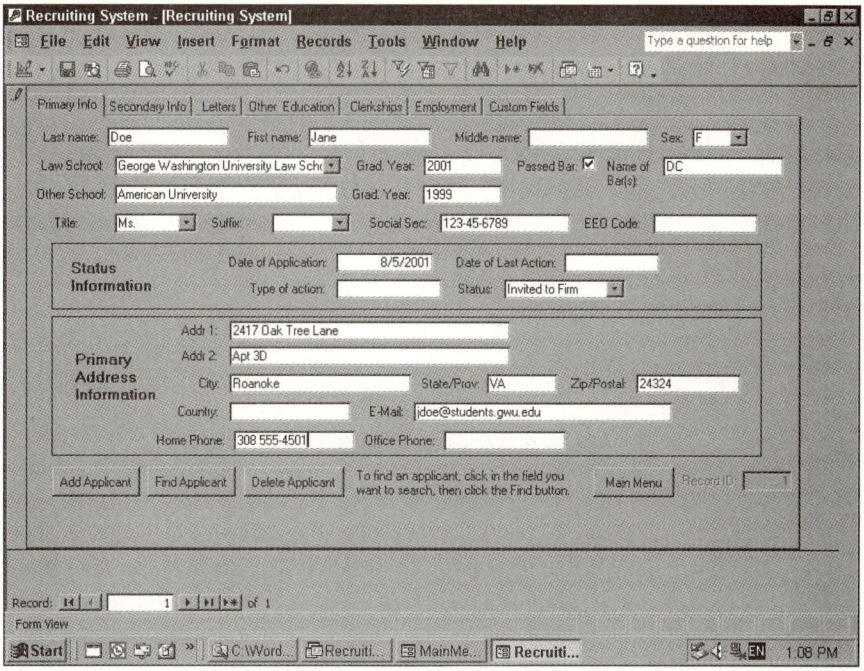

Figure 32-2: The Primary Info tab of the Lawyer Recruiting system

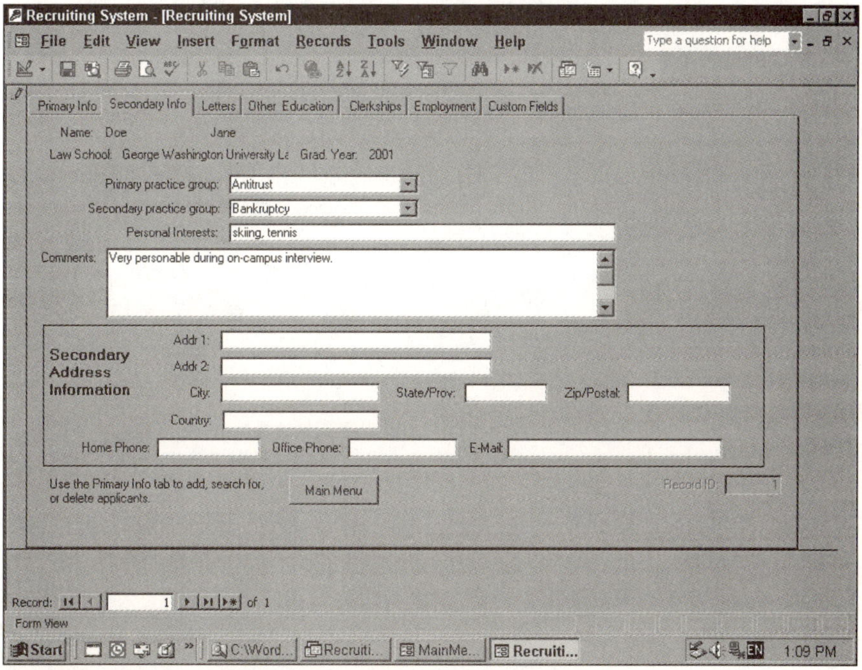

Figure 32-3: The Secondary Info tab of the Lawyer Recruiting system

Adding Letters, Other Education, Clerkships, and Employment Details

For any given applicant, you can add any number of records regarding letters sent to or received from students, education (in addition to the name of the law school recorded on the Primary Info tab), clerkships, and past employment. To do so, *first locate the desired applicant*, using the search procedures described earlier. Then click the appropriate tab (Letters, Other Education, Clerkships, or Employment) and enter the information in the fields shown.

For any given applicant, you can add multiple records regarding letters, education, clerkships, or employment. Each respective tab contains an Add button, a Find button, and a Delete button. You can use these to add, search for, or delete respective items under the Letters, Other Education, Clerkships, or Employment tabs. Figure 32-4 shows the Letters tab and Figure 32-5 shows the Other Education tab.

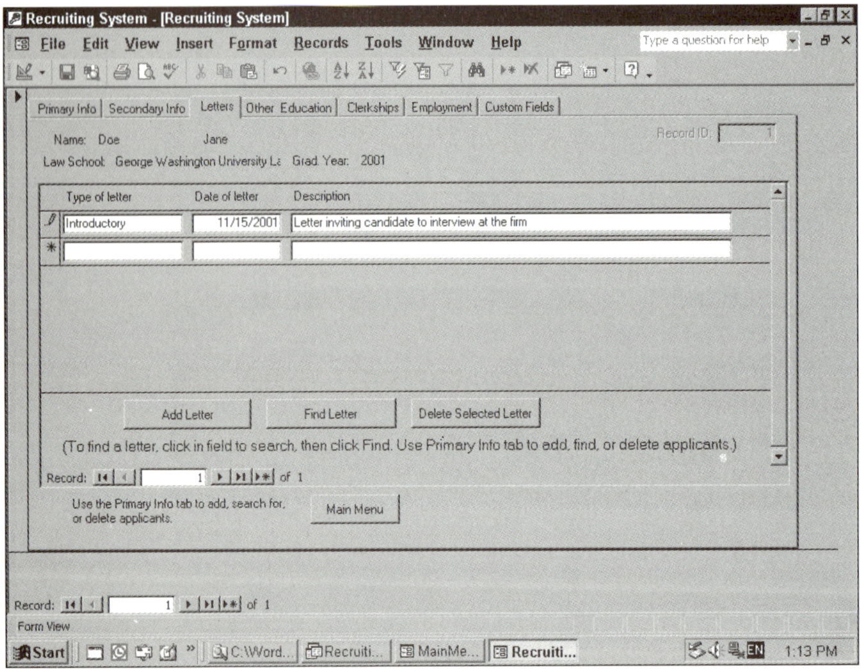

Figure 32-4: The Letters tab of the Lawyer Recruiting system

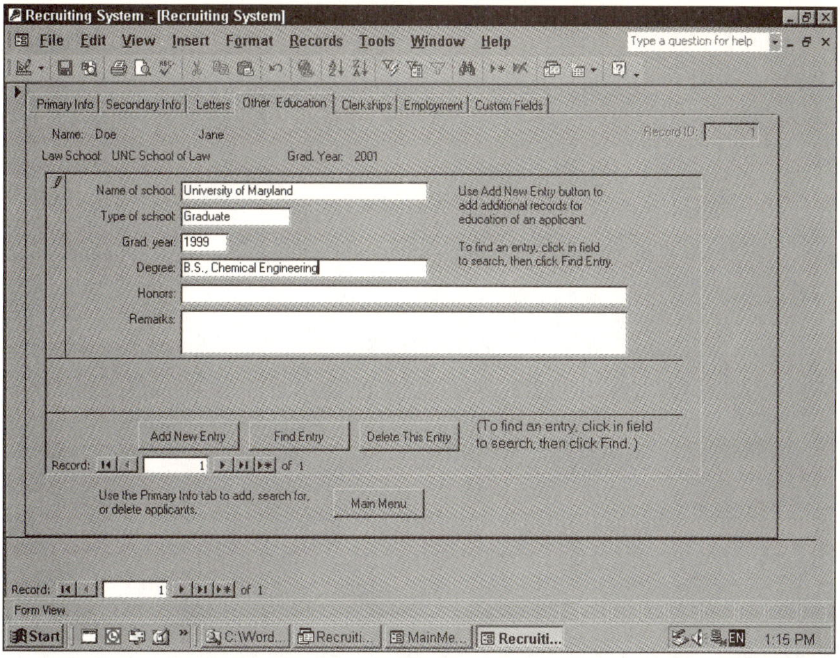

Figure 32-5: The Other Education tab of the Lawyer Recruiting system

Figure 32-6 shows the Clerkships tab and Figure 32-7 shows the Employment tab of the Lawyer Recruiting system.

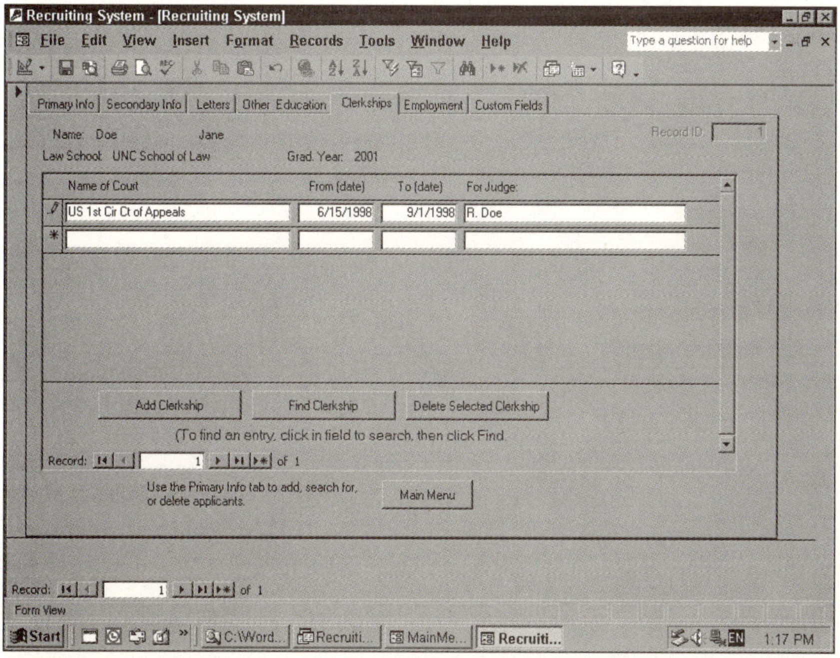

Figure 32-6: The Clerkships tab of the Lawyer Recruiting system

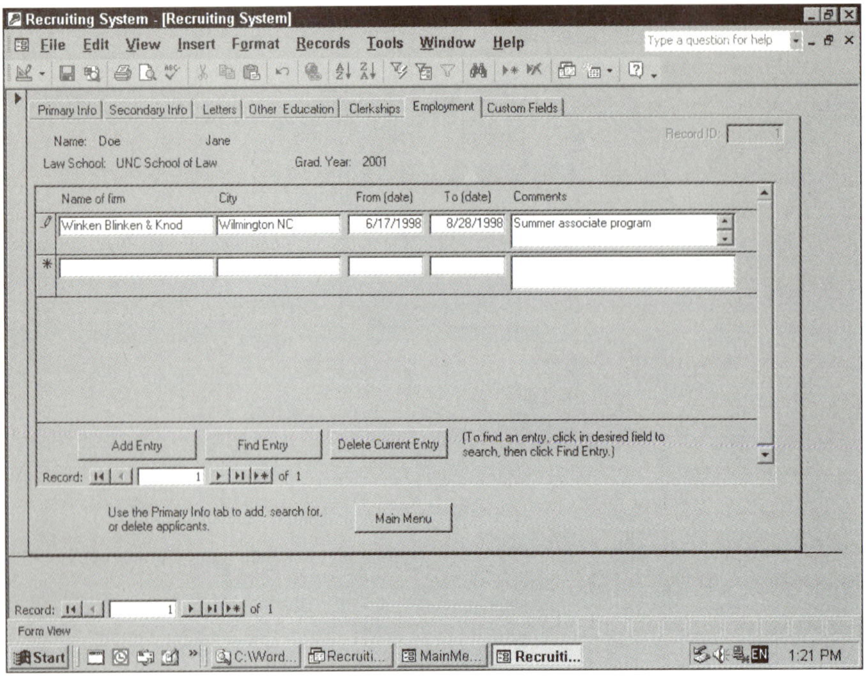

Figure 32-7: The Employment tab of the Lawyer Recruiting system

Using the Custom Fields

In addition to the pre-defined fields for each applicant, the Lawyer Recruiting system also provides two custom text fields and two custom date fields that can be used for any purpose. The custom fields are located on the Custom Fields tab of the system, as shown in Figure 32-8.

You can change the names displayed (and printed on reports) for the custom fields by going back to the Main Menu and clicking the Setup Options button. This causes a Setup Options form to appear. From this form, click the Change Custom Field Names button and you can enter new names for any of the custom fields at the next form that appears.

Printing Reports

To print reports, from the main menu, click the Print Reports button. The Reports menu shown in Figure 32-9 will appear. From this menu, you can choose from a variety of reports by clicking on the desired button. You can print reports containing overall applicant information, letters, education, clerkship, or employment information, or information stored in the custom fields. You can choose to print the reports by applicant name, by year of graduation, by name of the law school, or by status of the applicant. When you select a report, you are first prompted for any needed information (such as the name of the applicant or the year of graduation). Respond to any prompts; the desired report then appears in preview mode. You can then click the Print icon in the toolbar to send the report to the default printer.

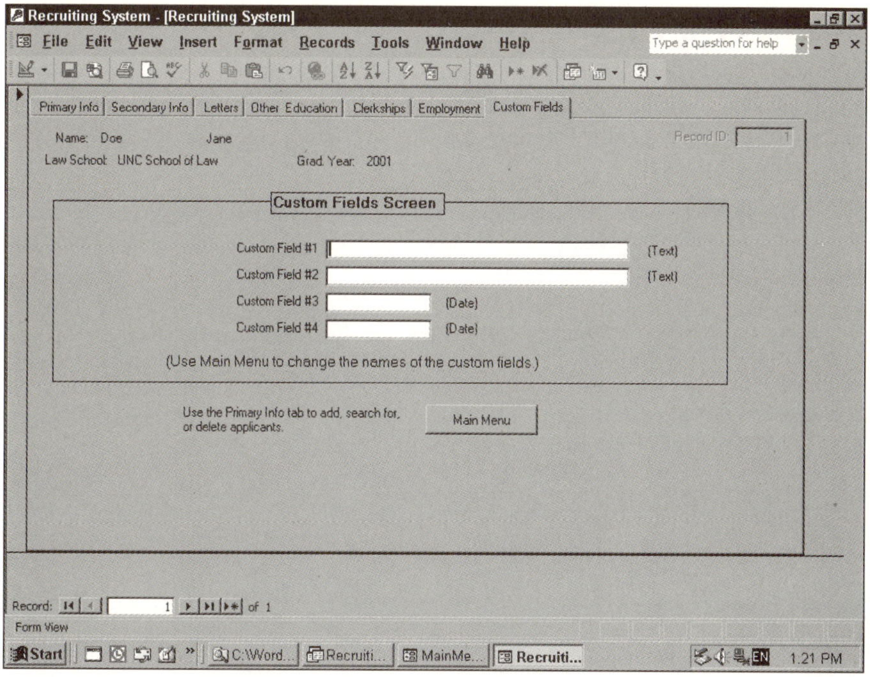

Figure 32-8: The Custom Fields tab

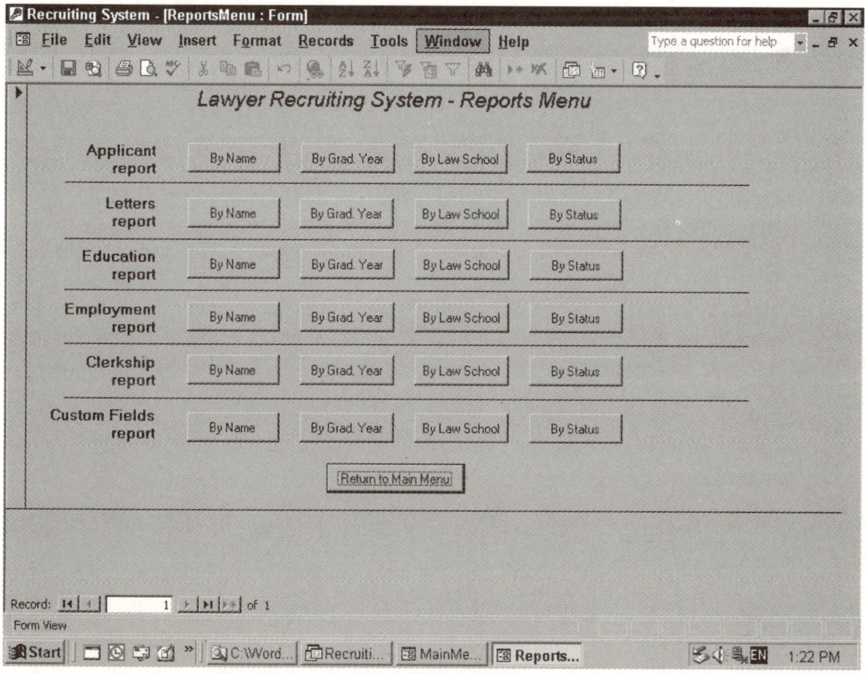

Figure 32-9: The Reports menu of the Lawyer Recruiting system

Using the Setup Options

In addition to changing the names of the custom fields, you can use the choices in the Setup Options menu to add or edit the available practice groups, law school names, and status choices that appear when adding applicants. At the main menu click the Setup Options button to display the Setup Options menu, shown in Figure 32-10.

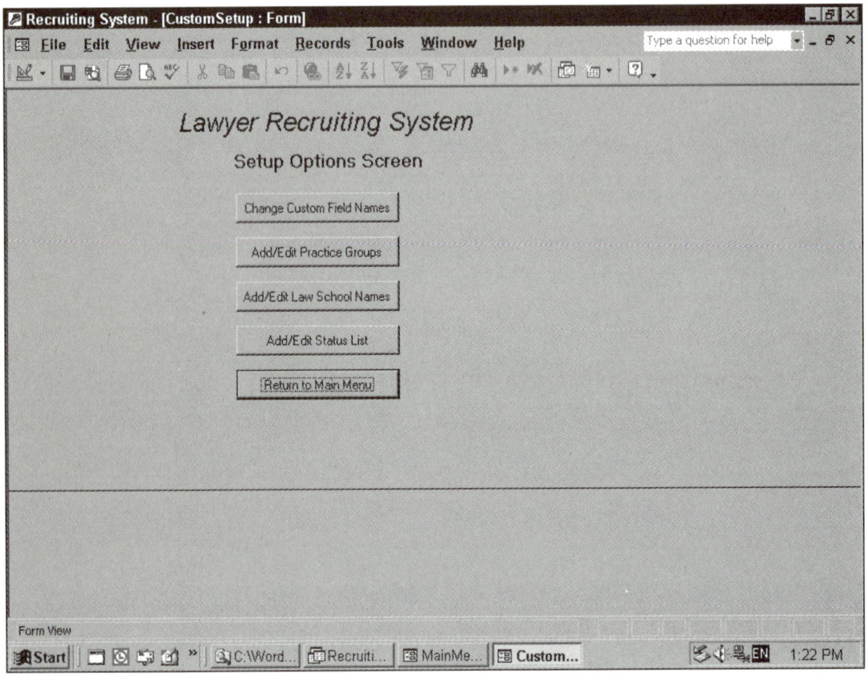

Figure 32-10: The Setup Options menu of the Lawyer Recruiting system

As explained earlier, you can use the Change Custom Field Names button to change the names of the custom fields. You can also use the Add/Edit Practice Groups button to change the practice groups that appear in the drop-down lists of primary and secondary practice groups on the Secondary Info tab. Use the Add/Edit Law School Names button to change the default names of the law schools that appear in the drop-down list of law school names in the Primary Info tab. And use the Add/Edit Status List button to change the default Status options that appear in the drop-down list for the Status field when adding applicants. When any of these buttons is clicked, a tabular form appears where you can add, edit, or delete these options. When done making any of the changes, you can click the Done button at the bottom of any of these forms to return to the Setup Options menu.

Exiting the System

To exit the system, click the Main Menu or the Return to Main Menu buttons from any other form to get back to the main menu. Then, click Exit System.

Technical Details

This portion of the chapter has been provided for experienced Access gurus and/or in-house programmers or hired consultants working at law firms. The following paragraphs outline the workings behind the application described in this chapter, and offer suggestions (where applicable) for custom modifications that individual firms may prefer to see implemented with the databases that they are using.

CAUTION: Note that you should not attempt to make changes to the design of objects in the database unless you are intimately familiar with Access. Otherwise, the application may fail to operate properly.

The Lawyer Recruiting System uses one main table (Applicants) and four related tables (AppLetters, AppSchools, Clerkships, and WorkInfo). The structure of the tables and their relationships are shown in Figure 32-11.

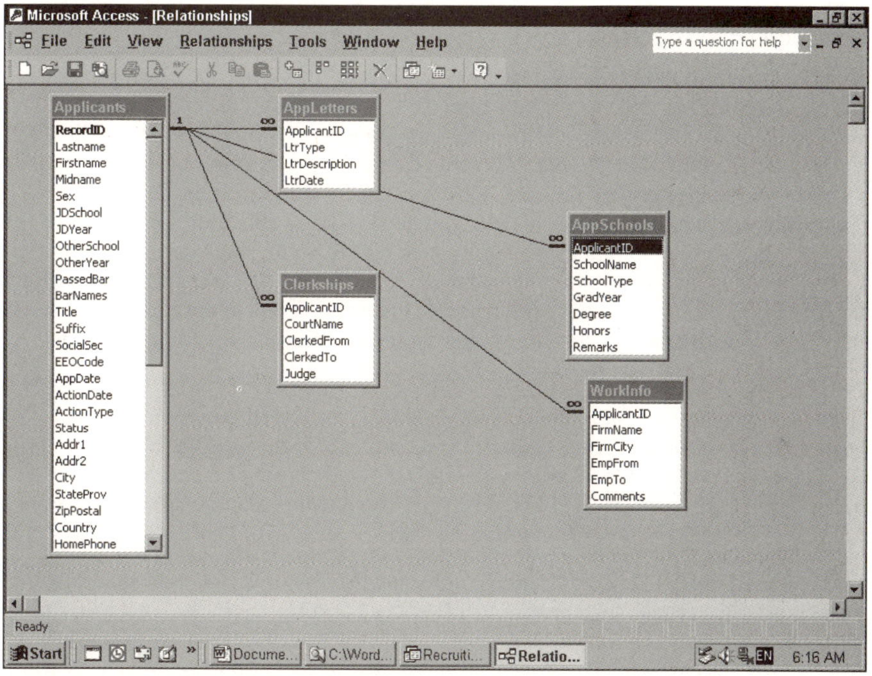

Figure 32-11: The table structures and relationships

One additional table, called Cfields, contains a single record and is used to store the names assigned to the custom fields. On the Custom Fields tab of the main form (and in the Custom Fields report), the `Dlookup` function is used to retrieve the actual entries from the respective fields of the single record and to display those entries as the field names on the Custom Fields tab, or in the report. The Cfields form allows the user access to the record to change the names of the custom fields. Because the form intentionally lacks any provision for adding a new record (with the form's Allow Additions property set to No), the user sees and edits the single record that stores the names for the custom fields.

The main form used by the system, titled MainForm, contains a tabbed control with seven tabs. The Primary Info, Secondary Info, and Custom Fields tabs contain controls based on the fields in the Applicants table, whereas the remaining tabs contain controls from the other respective tables (AppLetters, AppSchools, Clerkships, and WorkInfo). These four remaining tabs are divided into a form/subform arrangement to display the relational data. Hence, when any particular applicant is visible on the Primary Info tab, the related letters, education records, clerkship records or employment records for that particular applicant appear within the subforms of the respective tabs (letters, education, clerkships, or employment).

Report design

All reports are based on select queries, or parameter queries. For example, the By Status report uses the AppsByStatus query as its data source, the By Grad. Year report uses the AppsByYear query as its data source, and so on.

The Applicant and Custom Field reports are nonrelational because they obtain all needed information from the Applicants table. The letters, education, clerkships and employment history reports are relational reports and are all based on relational queries.

Notes about modifications

In general, reports can be modified with no interdependent effects on the rest of the system. New fields can be added to the Applicants table and their respective controls added to the Primary or Secondary Info tab of the MainForm, to dependent queries, and to the associated reports. Adding fields to the letters, education, clerkships, and employment tabs may be trickier because of the tabular nature of the subform design and the limited amount of "real estate" available on the form. (Of course, with patience, virtually any modification is possible!) If you need room to add additional fields of your own choosing, you can consider adding another tab to the tabbed form. Just open the form titled MainForm in Design view, click the tab *after which* you want to place the new tab, and choose Insert ⇨ Tab Control Page from the menus. To change the name of the new tab that appears, right-click the tab, choose Properties, and type the name you want in the Caption property of the Format tab that appears.

Of course, in addition to adding the new tab, you will also need to create your new fields in the Applicants table and create any desired reports. You can add command buttons to the new tab to print any new reports that you create; for details on adding command buttons to forms, see the chapter on working with forms in the Access section of the book. (Alternatively, you can just make use of the Custom Fields feature to store additional information.)

All VBA code in this application is attached to buttons on forms; there is no VBA code stored in any global modules. The main form initially appears due to a Display Form setting in the Tools/Startup dialog box.

Summary

This chapter provided details regarding the Lawyer Recruiting database, one of the legal-specific databases provided on the CD-ROM. The chapter covered the following points:

- The Lawyer Recruiting database allows a mid-sized or large law firm's recruiting department to track information and statistics for potential new hire associates or paralegals.
- The main form used by the system contains tabs for adding and editing name and address information for each applicant, letters sent to or received from law students, education information, clerkship information, and employment information.
- A custom fields tab provides two text fields, two date fields, and two currency fields that can be used for any purpose.
- Reports can be printed containing overall applicant information, letters, education, clerkships, employment, or information stored in the custom fields.

- The Lawyer Recruiting database uses one main table containing the records regarding each applicant, and four related tables containing associated records of letters, education, employment, and clerkship information for an applicant. A one-to-many relationship exists between the main table and each of the associated tables.

The next chapter details the use of the Pleadings Tracking database, another legal-specific database provided on the CD-ROM.

Chapter 33

The Pleadings Tracker System

In This Chapter

- Using the Pleadings Tracker system
- Printing reports
- Exiting the system
- Technical details

THE PLEADINGS TRACKER SYSTEM tracks pleadings for any number of cases, with fields that include Bates stamp number, case name and number, plaintiff and defendant, name of the court and judge, and comments. The database for the Pleadings Tracker system is stored in the `Legal-specific databases and files/Access/Databases` folder of the CD-ROM, and the database is named Pleadings.mdb. To use the database, copy the file from your CD-ROM to the desired directory on your hard drive or your network drive (*but see the important note that follows*).

NOTE: All files stored on the CD-ROM are read-only (this is the way CD-ROMs are created). Therefore, when you copy a file from the CD-ROM to your hard drive or network drive, the file retains its "read-only" status. You MUST change this status before you can use the database. To change this status after copying the database file, locate the file on your hard drive or network drive using My Computer or Windows Explorer. Right-click the filename or icon and choose Properties from the menu that appears. In the Properties dialog box that opens, click the General tab, remove the check mark from the Read-Only check box, and click OK.

TIP: Because the default file format used by Access 2002 is the Access 2000 file format, the ready-to-use legal databases on the CD-ROM exist in Access 2000 format. This enables law firms that have a mix of users (some using Access 2002 and others using Access 2000) to share the same databases on a firm network.

Using the Pleadings Tracker System

When you load the Pleadings Tracker system in Access, a main menu appears like the one shown in Figure 33-1.

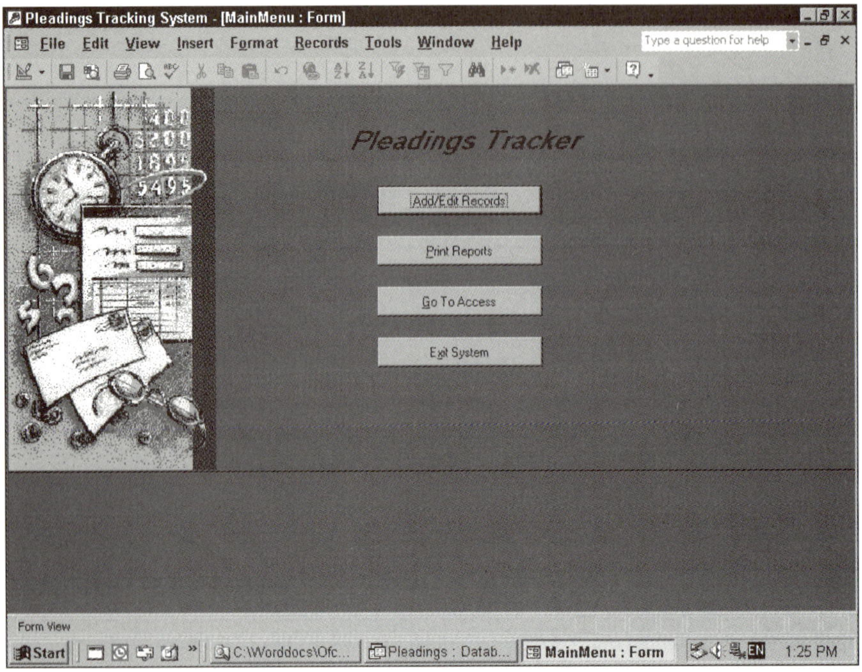

Figure 33-1: The main menu of the Pleadings Tracker system

To add or edit records, click the Add/Edit Records button. When you do so, a Pleadings Tracker form appears that you can use to add new records (see Figure 33-2). Fill in the information desired, using the Tab key to move from field to field. As you complete a record, when you press Tab at the last field, you are automatically moved to another new record.

To add a new record at any time from the Pleadings Tracker form, click the Add Record button at the bottom of the tab and fill in the information for the new record.

To find an existing record, click anywhere within a field that you want to search; then click the Search button. In the Find dialog box that appears, enter the search term and click Find Next to locate the desired record. If another record exists with that same search term, you can again use the Search button and click the Find Next button in the dialog box that appears to locate successive records matching your search term.

To delete a record from the system, first locate the record that you want to delete using the search procedures described above. Then click the Delete Record button.

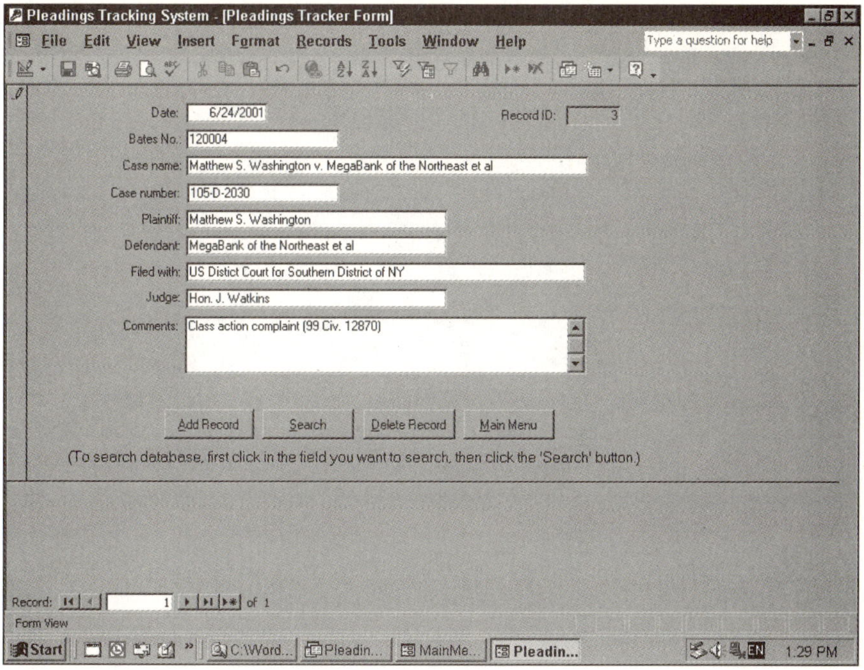

Figure 33-2: The form used to add records to the system

Printing Reports

To print reports, from the main menu, click the Print Reports button. The Reports Menu, shown in Figure 33-3, will appear.

From this menu, you can print reports based on a range of dates, by Bates stamp number, by the name of the case, or by a selective query. If you choose By Date Range, you are asked for a starting and ending date, and the resulting report includes all records within that range of dates. If you choose By Bates Stamp Numbers, you are asked for a Bates stamp number, and the resulting report includes the record containing that Bates stamp number. If you choose By Case Name, you are asked for a text string to enter as the search term, and all appropriate records containing the search string in the Case Name field will appear.

When the desired report appears in a preview window, you can click the Print icon on the toolbar to send the report to the default printer.

Additionally, you can choose to print reports By Selective Query (matching criteria that you enter). If you choose to print this report, another form appears like the one shown in Figure 33-4. You can fill in the matching criteria to select the records to print; then click Print. For example, you could choose to print the report based on all pleadings before a particular judge, and one or more keywords entered into the Comments field. You would do this by entering part or all of the name of the judge into the Judge field, and the keywords into the Comment field, as shown in the figure. You would then click the Print button. When the report appears in a preview window, click the Print icon on the toolbar to send the report to the default printer.

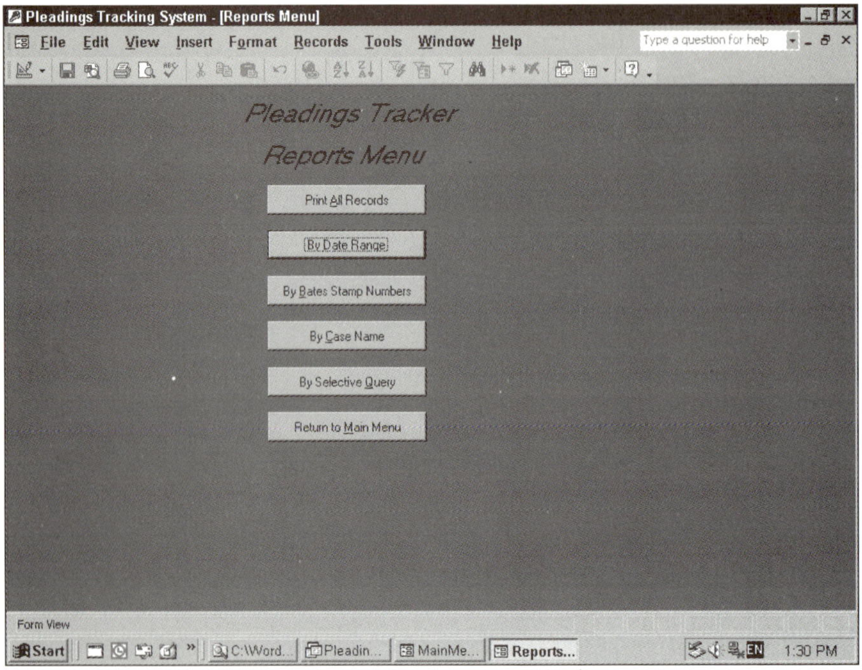

Figure 33-3: The Reports Menu of the Pleadings Tracker system

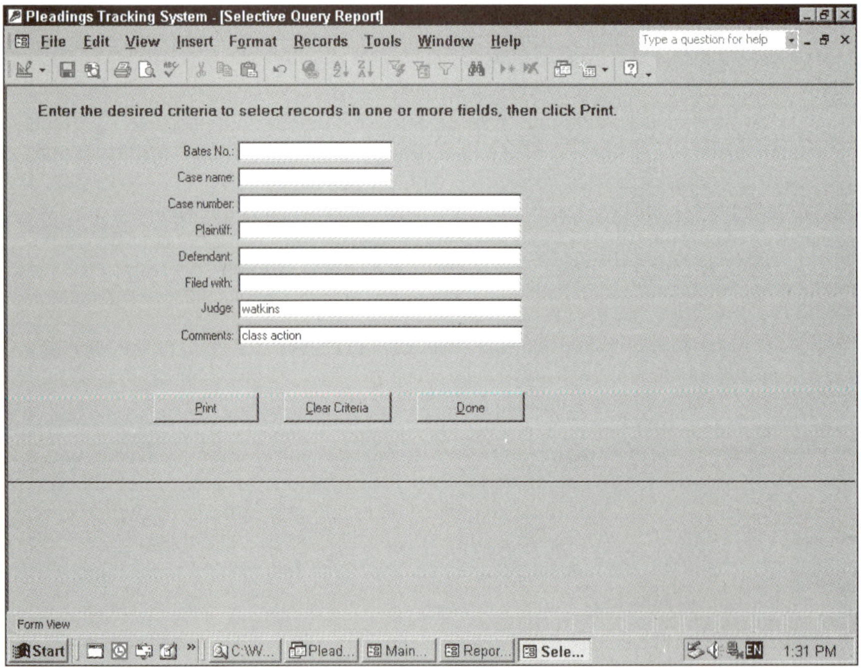

Figure 33-4: The criteria screen used for printing selective reports

Exiting the System

To exit the system, click the Main Menu or the Return to Main Menu buttons from any other form to get back to the main menu. Then, click Exit System.

Technical Details

This portion of the chapter has been provided for experienced Access gurus and/or in-house programmers or hired consultants working at law firms. The following paragraphs outline the workings behind the application described in this chapter and offer suggestions (where applicable) for custom modifications that individual firms may prefer to see implemented with the databases that they are using.

CAUTION: Note that you should *not* attempt to make changes to the design of objects in the database unless you are intimately familiar with Access. Otherwise, the application may fail to operate properly.

The Pleadings Tracker system uses a single table, called Pleadings, to contain all the data stored by the system. The table structure is shown in Figure 33-5.

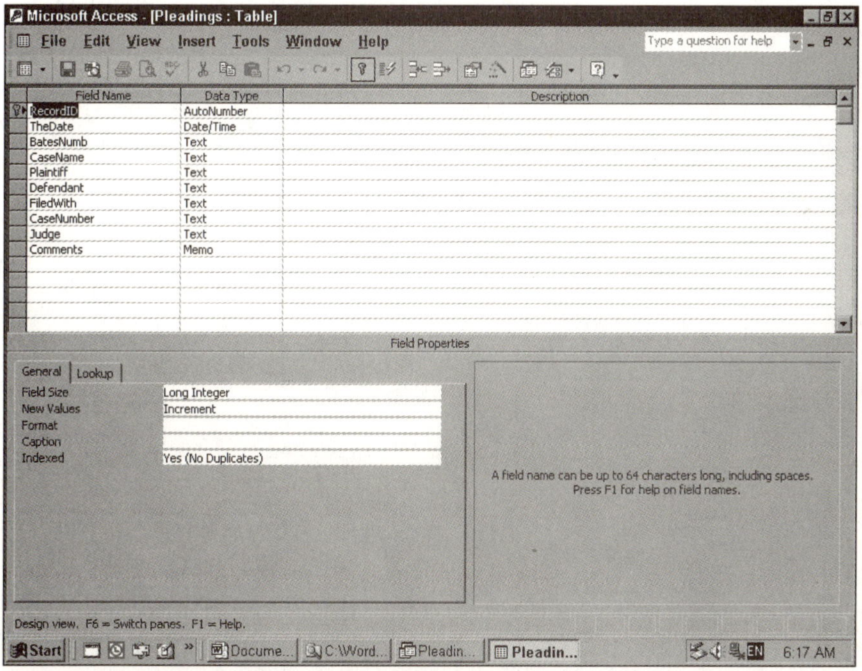

Figure 33-5: The table structure for the Pleadings Tracker system

The Pleadings Tracker system uses a form as its main menu. This form, appropriately named MainMenu, is named in the Tools/Startup option of the database, so it appears when the database is initially loaded. (This form and all other forms used by the system also have a macro, named MaximizeMe, called from the form's `OnActivate` event. The macro serves to maximize the window of any form as it opens.) The command buttons on the form were created with the aid of the Command Button Wizards and use VBA code to open respective forms or to exit from Access (with the exception of the Go To Access button, which runs a macro that displays a dialog box and closes the menu form).

The VBA code attached to the Add/Edit Records button uses a `DoCmd.OpenForm` statement to open the form named Pleadings. This is a basic form with text boxes for the text and date/time fields used to display or edit data in the Pleadings table. The respective buttons on this form were all created with the aid of the Command Button Wizards and use appropriate VBA code to perform their respective tasks.

Report design

With the exception of the AllRecords Report used to print all records and used with the Selective Query screen, the reports in the Pleadings Tracker system are based on parameter queries. For example, the ByBates report uses the ByBates query as its data source; the ByCaseName report uses the ByCaseName query as its data source; and so on. The AllRecords report is used in two ways. When the Print All Records button is clicked, the report is opened and uses the Pleadings table as its data source so that all records appear in the report. Additionally, when the By Selective Query button is clicked, this same report is used, but a `DoCmd.OpenForm` statement opens the form named SelectivePrint. The Print button on this form makes use of VBA code to construct a `WHERE` clause, using the search criteria entered in the unbound fields of the form. The VBA code is attached to the Print button's `OnClick` event, and the code looks like this:

```
Private Sub SelPrint_Click()
    '  Create a WHERE clause using search criteria entered by user and
    '  set RecordSource property of SelectivePrint form.

    Dim MySQL As String, MyCriteria As String, MyRecordSource As String
    Dim ArgCount As Integer

    '  Initialize argument count.
    ArgCount = 0

    '  Initialize SELECT statement.
    MySQL = "SELECT * FROM PLEADINGS WHERE "
    MyCriteria = ""

    '  Use values entered in text boxes in form to create
    '  the criteria used for the WHERE clause.
    '  Note that AddToWhere is another subroutine in this module.
    AddToWhere [M_Bates], "[BatesNumb]", MyCriteria, ArgCount
    AddToWhere [M_CaseName], "[CaseName]", MyCriteria, ArgCount
    AddToWhere [M_CaseNumber], "[CaseNumber]", MyCriteria, ArgCount
    AddToWhere [M_Plaintiff], "[Plaintiff]", MyCriteria, ArgCount
    AddToWhere [M_Defendant], "[Defendant]", MyCriteria, ArgCount
    AddToWhere [M_FiledWith], "[FiledWith]", MyCriteria, ArgCount
    AddToWhere [M_Judge], "[Judge]", MyCriteria, ArgCount
    AddToWhere [M_Comments], "[Comments]", MyCriteria, ArgCountArgCount
    AddToWhere [M_Notes], "[Notes]", MyCriteria, ArgCount

    '  If no criterion specifed, return all records.
```

```
    If MyCriteria = "" Then
        MyCriteria = "True"
    End If

    '  Create SELECT statement.
    MyRecordSource = MySQL & MyCriteria
    '  Set RecordSource property of destination object.
    DoCmd.OpenReport "AllRecords", A_PREVIEW, , MyCriteria

End Sub
```

When the user enters criteria into one or more fields in the form and clicks the Print button, the resulting SQL `SELECT` statement is assembled based on the criteria in the unbound controls of the form. The statement is then used as part of the `DoCmd.OpenReport` statement at the end of the routine to launch the AllRecords report containing the selected records. This code also makes use of a user-defined function named AddToWhere. This function's code resides in the same class module and is as follows:

```
Private Sub AddToWhere(FieldValue As Variant, FieldName As String, MyCriteria
As String, ArgCount As Integer)

    '  Create criteria for WHERE clause.
    If FieldValue <> "" Then
        '  Add "and" if other criterion exists.
        If ArgCount > 0 Then
            MyCriteria = MyCriteria & " and "
        End If

        '  Append criterion to existing criteria.
        '  Enclose FieldValue and asterisk in quotation marks.
        MyCriteria = (MyCriteria & FieldName & " Like " & Chr(39) & Chr(42) &
FieldValue & Chr(42) & Chr(39))

        '  Increase argument count.
        ArgCount = ArgCount + 1
    End If
End Sub
```

The remaining code in the class module is used to clear entries from the text box controls in the SelectivePrint form or to close the form.

Notes about modifications

In general, reports can be modified with no interdependent effects on the rest of the system. New fields can be added to the Pleadings table and their respective controls added to the Pleadings form and to the queries and reports included with the system. All VBA code in this application is attached to buttons on forms; there is no VBA code stored in any global modules. The main form initially appears due to a Display Form setting in the Tools ⇨ Startup dialog box.

Summary

This chapter provided details regarding the Pleadings Tracking database, one of the legal-specific databases provided on the CD-ROM. The chapter covered the following points:

- The Pleadings Tracking database provides a single form to track pleadings for any number of cases, with fields that include bates stamp number, case name and number, plaintiff and defendant, name of the court and judge, and comments..
- The Reports Menu of the database allows you to print reports based on a range of dates, by bates stamp number, by the name of the case, or by a selective query.
- The By Selective Query option of the Reports menu displays a form where you can enter criteria that controls the records which appear in a resulting report.

The next chapter details the use of the CLE Tracker database, another legal-specific database provided on the CD-ROM.

Chapter 34

The CLE Tracker System

In This Chapter

- Using the CLE Tracker
- Adding CLE courses
- Editing CLE records
- Printing reports
- Using the setup options
- Existing the System
- Technical details

THE CLE TRACKER IS DESIGNED to track Continuing Legal Education (CLE) courses for attorneys. The database for the CLE Tracker is stored in the `Legal-specific databases and files/Access/Databases` folder of the CD-ROM, and the database is named CLETracker.mdb. To use the database, copy the file from your CD-ROM to the desired directory on your hard drive or your network drive (*but see the important note that follows*).

NOTE: All files stored on the CD-ROM are read-only (this is the way CD-ROMs are created). Therefore, when you copy a file from the CD-ROM to your hard drive or network drive, the file retains its "read-only" status. You MUST change this status before you can use the database. To change this status after copying the database file, locate the file on your hard drive or network drive using My Computer or Windows Explorer. Right-click the filename or icon and choose Properties from the menu that appears. In the Properties dialog box that opens, click the General tab, remove the check mark from the Read-Only check box, and click OK.

TIP: Because the default file format used by Access 2002 is the Access 2000 file format, the ready-to-use legal databases on the CD-ROM exist in Access 2000 format. This enables law firms that have a mix of users (some using Access 2002 and others using Access 2000) to share the same databases on a firm network.

Using the CLE Tracker

When you load the CLE Tracker in Access, a main menu appears like the one shown in Figure 34-1.

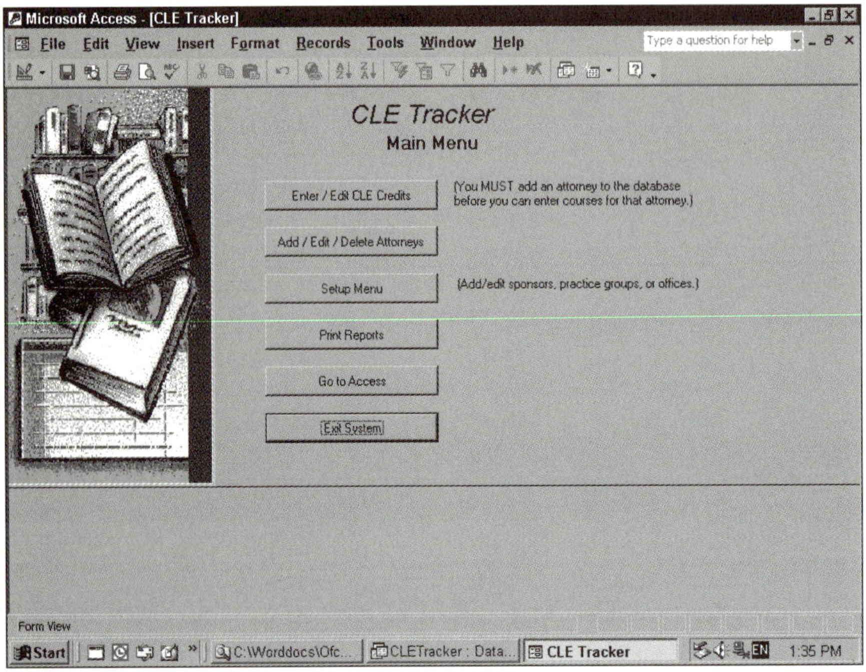

Figure 34-1: The main menu of the CLE Tracker

Before you can add assignments, you must first add the names of the attorneys for whom you want to track CLE courses within the system. To add attorneys, click the Add/Edit Attorneys button on the main menu and enter the desired information in the Attorneys screen that appears (Figure 34-2). When done entering an attorney, click the Add New Attorney button to add another attorney. Enter the information shown for each attorney that you want to track CLE courses for at your firm.

You can use this same screen to make changes or to delete attorneys who are no longer at the firm. First, click in any field you want to search; then click Find Attorney and enter a search string in the dialog box that appears. After the desired attorney is located, you can make the necessary changes or click Delete Attorney to remove that attorney from the system.

TIP: If you are an experienced Access user, you can probably save time by appending data into the Attorneys table of the database from another source (such as from an Excel spreadsheet or from another Access table that contains the names and positions of your firm's attorneys.) Hold down the Shift key while opening the CLE Tracker database so that the main menu does not appear. Under the Tables tab of the database, you will see a table called Attorneys. You can design and run an append query that adds data from your existing data source into the Attorneys table. (See Chapter 24 for details on how to create and use append queries.) If the data at the other source is an exact match in terms of field types (such as last names, first names, and middle initials all stored in character fields), you can also *link* to the existing data, which will save you the effort of having to perform updates to the attorney names in the CLE Tracker database. For details on linking to other data sources, see the section "Using External Data in Access" in Chapter 23.

After you have entered the attorneys into the system, you can use the system to track CLE courses taken by those attorneys.

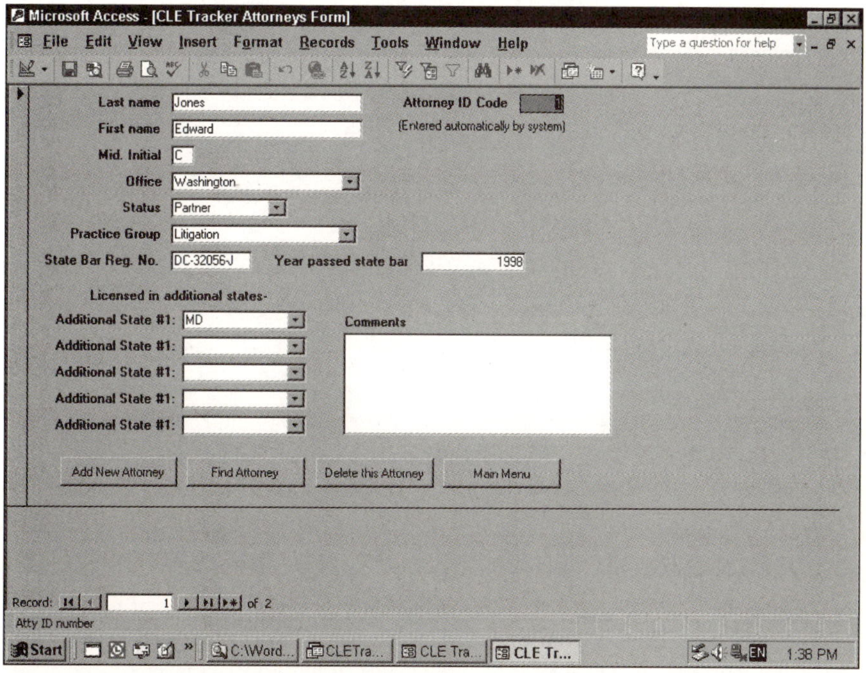

Figure 34-2: The Attorneys screen of the CLE Tracker

Adding CLE Courses

To add a CLE course for a particular attorney, from the main menu, click the Enter/Edit CLE Credits button. In a moment, the CLE Credits screen appears (Figure 34-3).

First, select the appropriate attorney from the Attorney ID drop-down list box at the upper left. (The list box shows the attorney ID code and the attorney's name.) When you make a selection, the attorney's name will appear at the upper right.

After the correct attorney is shown at the top of the screen, enter the desired information pertaining to the CLE course in the fields shown. You can enter the course name, date of the course, course location, course sponsor, the course fee and the actual cost, and the state that the CLE credits will be applied toward. At the bottom of the screen, you can enter the number of CLE credits provided by the course in any of the categories shown (general, ethics, teaching, professional, or substance abuse).

To add another CLE credit for an attorney, click the Add CLE Record button at the bottom of the screen. When the screen clears, choose an attorney by name using the picklist at the top of the screen; then enter the desired information.

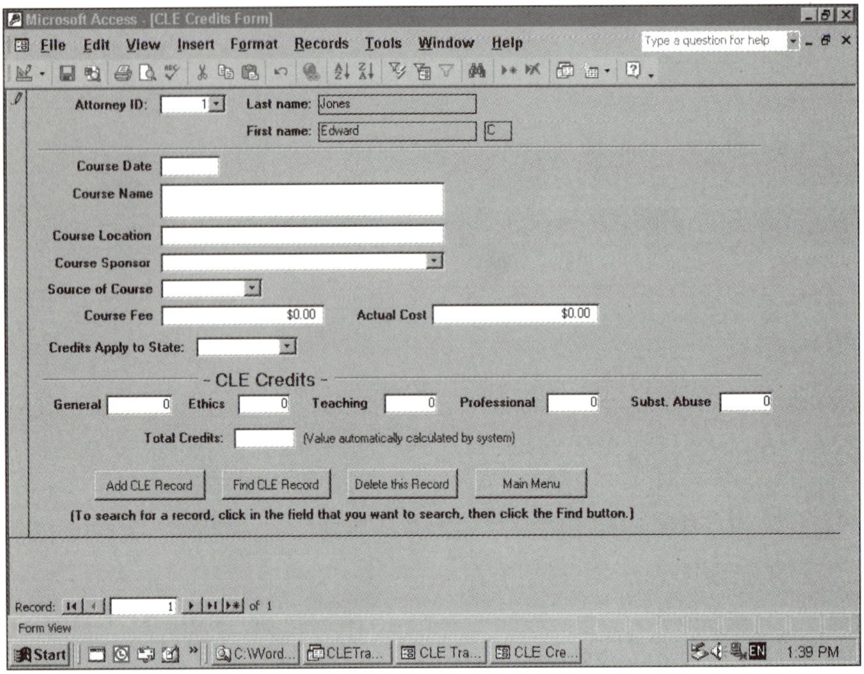

Figure 34-3: The CLE Credits screen

Editing CLE Records

To find an entry (so that you can make changes to the information or delete the record of the CLE course), click in the field that you wish to search and click the Find CLE Record button. A Find and Replace dialog box for that field will appear, like the example shown in Figure 34-4.

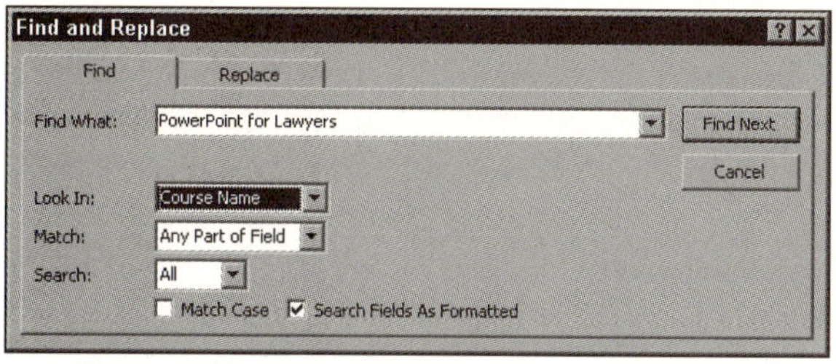

Figure 34-4: The Find and Replace dialog box displayed by the CLE Tracker during a record search

Enter a search term in the Find What portion of the dialog box and then change the Look In option to the name of the field that you wish to search. Set the Match option to Start of Field; then click the Find Next button to find the first occurrence of the search term in the CLE records. If you want to search for additional records containing that same search term, click the Find CLE Record button again and then click Find Next.

After Once the desired record has been located, you can make changes to the existing fields of the entry. Or you can delete the entry if it is no longer needed in the database by clicking the Delete This Record button.

Printing Reports

To print reports, from the main menu, click the Print Reports button. The Reports Menu shown in Figure 34-5 will appear. This menu lets you produce a variety of reports from the CLE Tracker.

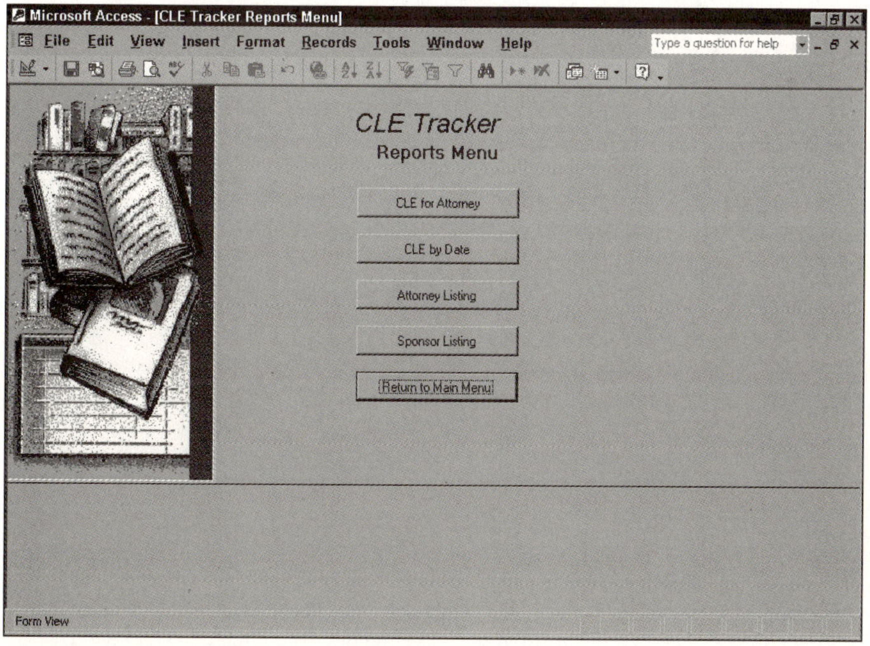

Figure 34-5: The Reports Menu of the CLE Tracker

To print a report showing all CLE courses taken by a specific attorney, click the CLE for Attorney button. You will be asked for a last name and a first name for the desired attorney. Fill in the prompts, and a report showing all CLE course entries for that attorney will appear. You can then click the Print icon in the toolbar to send the report to the default printer.

You also can print a report that lists all the CLE courses taken on a specific date, or between a range of two dates. To do so, click the CLE by Date button. You will be asked for a starting date and an ending date. (To print all courses taken on a certain day, enter the same starting and ending date.) After you respond to the prompts, a report showing all CLE course entries for that range of dates will appear. You can then click the Print icon in the toolbar to send the report to the default printer.

Use the Attorney Listing and Sponsor Listing buttons to print reports that contain listings of all the attorney information, or of the sponsors for courses. Click either button, and a report will appear in preview mode. You can then click the Print icon in the toolbar to send the report to the default printer.

Using the Setup Options

You can use the choices within the Setup Options menu to add or edit the available practice groups, course sponsors, and office names that appear when adding and editing CLE course entries. At the main menu, click the Setup Menu button to display the Setup Options menu, shown in Figure 34-6.

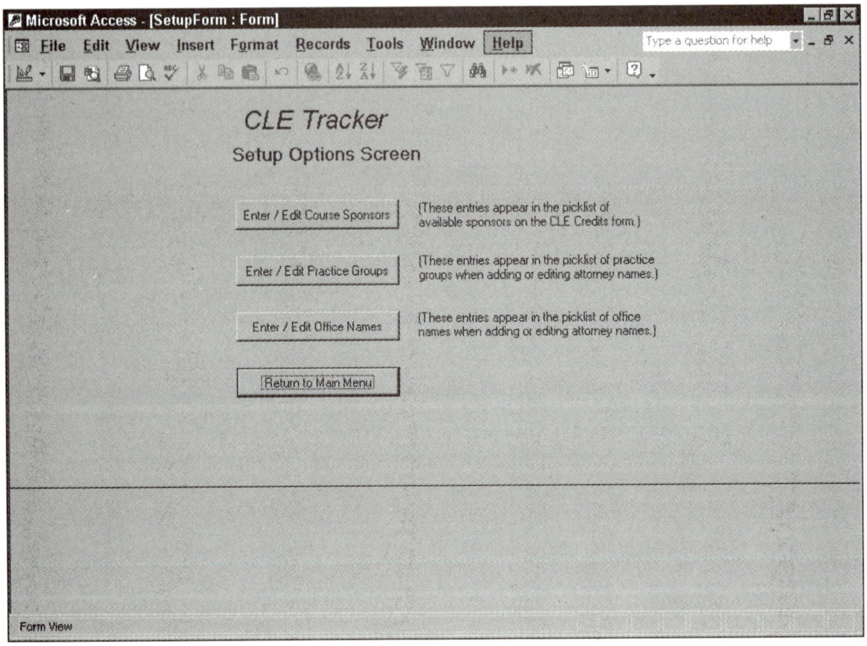

Figure 34-6: The Setup Options menu

You can use the Enter/Edit Practice Groups button to change the practice groups that appear in the drop-down lists of practice groups on the CLE Courses screen. Use the Enter/Edit Course Sponsors button to change the default names of the sponsors that appear in the drop-down list of sponsor names. And use the Enter/Edit Office Names button to change the default office names that appear in the drop-down list for the office names field when adding entries. When any of these buttons are clicked, a form appears where you can add, edit, or delete these options. When done making any of the changes, you can click the Done button at the bottom of any of these forms to return to the Setup Options menu.

Exiting the System

To exit the system, click the Main Menu or the Back to Main Menu buttons from any other form to get back to the main menu. Then, click Exit System.

Technical Details

This portion of the chapter has been provided for experienced Access gurus and/or in-house programmers or hired consultants working at law firms. The following paragraphs outline the workings behind the application described in this chapter and offer suggestions (where applicable) for custom modifications that individual firms may prefer to see implemented with the databases that they are using.

CAUTION: Note that you should *not* attempt to make changes to the design of objects in the database unless you are intimately familiar with Access. Otherwise, the application may fail to operate properly.

The CLE Tracker uses two tables named Attorneys and Courses. The Attorneys table contains a record for each attorney, and the Courses table contains a record for each CLE course. A one-to-many relationship exists between the Attorneys table and the Courses table; hence, for each attorney, there can be one or more related courses. The structure of the tables and their relationship is shown in Figure 34-7.

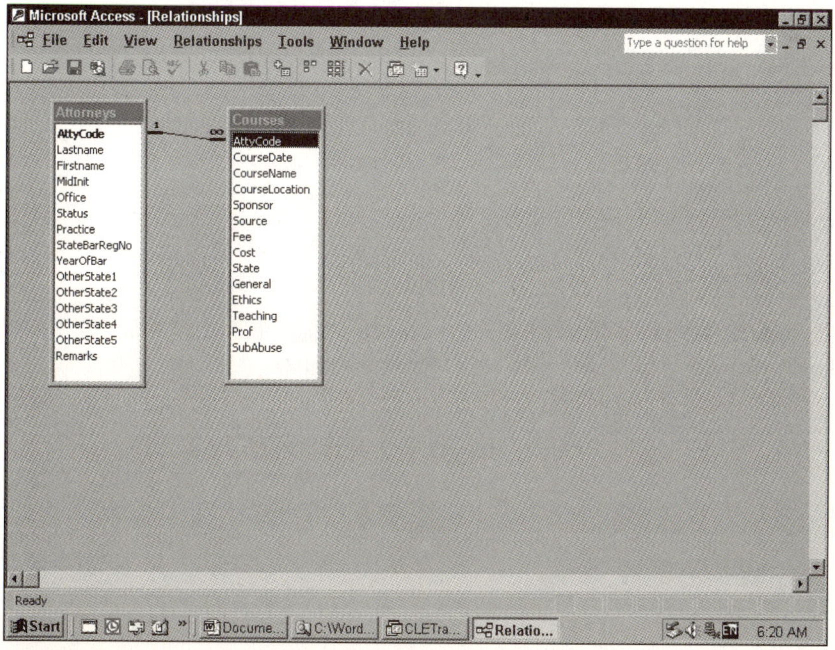

Figure 34-7: The table structures and relationships

In addition to these tables that are used to store the attorney and CLE course information, four additional tables serve as lookup tables for the picklists used in the CLE Courses form. These are as follows: the Offices table (stores the names of the firm's branch offices); the PracticeGroups tables (stores the names of the practice groups); the Sponsors table (stores the names of the sponsors); and the States table (contains the names and the two-letter abbreviations of the states).

The CLE Tracker uses a form as its main menu. This form, appropriately named Main Menu, is named in the Tools/Startup option of the database, so it appears when the database is initially loaded. (This form and all other forms used by the system also have a macro, named MaximizeMe, called from the form's On Activate event. The macro serves to maximize the window of any form as it opens.) The command buttons on the form were created with the aid of the Command Button Wizards and VBA code to open respective forms or to exit from Access (with the exception of the Go To Access button, which runs a macro that displays a dialog box and closes the menu form).

The VBA code attached to the Add/Edit/Delete Attorneys button uses a `DoCmd.OpenForm` statement to open the form named Attorneys. This is a basic form with text boxes to display or edit data in the Attorneys table. The respective buttons on the form were all created with the aid of the Command Button Wizards and use appropriate VBA code to perform their respective tasks.

The VBA code attached to the Enter/Edit CLE Credits button uses a `DoCmd.OpenForm` statement to open the form named Courses. This is a relational form that is based on a relational query named `CoursesFormSource`. The relational query provides all of the fields from the Courses table along with the corresponding attorney name from the Attorneys table.

Report design

The `CLEByDate` and CLEforAttorney reports are based on relational parameter queries. The `CLEByDate` report uses the `CoursesReportByDate` query as its data source, and the CLEforAttorney report uses the `CoursesReportSource` query as its data source.

The Attorneys Report and the Sponsors Report are nonrelational because they obtain all needed information from the Attorneys table and from the Sponsors table, respectively. The other reports used by the system are relational reports and are based on relational queries.

Notes about modifications

In general, reports can be modified with no interdependent effects on the rest of the system. New fields can be added to the Attorneys table, and their respective controls added to the Attorneys form, to the Attorney Form Source query, and to the Attorney report. Fields can also be added to the Courses table, to dependent queries, and to the associated reports. If you add new fields to the Courses table, you may want to include those new fields in the design of all of the relational queries (depending on whether those fields will be added to the dependent reports).

All VBA code in this application is attached to buttons on forms; there is no VBA code stored in any global modules. The main form initially appears due to a Display Form setting in the Tools/Startup dialog box.

Summary

This chapter provided details regarding the CLE Tracker database, one of the legal-specific databases provided on the CD-ROM. The chapter covered the following points:

- The CLE Tracker database tracks Continuing Legal Education (CLE) courses for attorneys.
- The database contains a form for adding and editing attorneys, and a form for adding records of CLE courses taken by a particular attorney.
- You can print reports of all courses taken by a particular attorney, all courses taken within a given date range, all attorneys in the system, or sponsor names of the CLE courses.
- The CLE Tracker uses one table containing a record for each attorney, and one related table containing associated records for each course taken by that attorney. A one-to-many relationship exists between the Attorneys table and the Courses table.

This concludes the Access section of *Office XP for Law Firms*. The next section details how you can use Outlook, Microsoft's e-mail client and personal information manager, within the legal environment.

Part V

Outlook

Chapter 35

Outlook in a Nutshell

In This Chapter

- ♦ Introducing Outlook
- ♦ Reading and sending e-mail
- ♦ Taking a quick look at the calendar
- ♦ Working with contacts
- ♦ Working with multiple profiles
- ♦ Configuring Outlook to use e-mail

OUTLOOK IS THE UNIFIED information-management tool that you can use whether you are a solo practitioner or one member of a large law firm or organization. Outlook combines e-mail, a calendar, contact management, group scheduling, a task list, and a journal into a single package. Outlook can help you to organize your life because it has the capability to track your appointments, meetings, tasks, contacts, and events and to manage your e-mail.

Introducing Outlook

In Outlook, you'll find a unified set of tools for sending, receiving, and managing messages, for keeping your calendar and address book, and for prioritizing the tasks on your to-do list. If much of your everyday work includes dealing with messages, participating in meetings, and handling or delegating tasks, Outlook can help you manage your time effectively. Outlook includes the following primary components:

- ♦ **Inbox:** This is the primary view to your e-mail. From the Inbox, you can read, compose, and send e-mail messages, whether you are in or out of the office. Outlook can send and receive messages by means of network e-mail servers or through an Internet service provider such as MSN (the Microsoft Network). Outlook can be configured to work with nearly all Internet service providers (however, note that "nearly all" does *not* include America Online; a limitation of AOL is its lack of support of outside e-mail standards).
- ♦ **Calendar:** Like its printed counterpart, the Outlook calendar provides a central location for marking date-based events, setting appointments, and scheduling meetings. Unlike its printed counterpart, the Outlook calendar can audibly remind you when you are about to miss a meeting.

- **Contacts:** Here you can store information about people with whom you have working relationships, such as clients, co-counsel, and coworkers. You can keep different address books, you can view and sort contacts in different ways, and you can use the names and addresses stored here in Word documents such as letters, or within other views in Outlook.
- **Tasks:** Here you can create a to-do list that you can use for your business or personal tasks. You can prioritize your to-do items, and if you are using Outlook on a network, you can delegate tasks to others.
- **Journal:** Here you can track the history of activities that you want to record on a time-line basis. You can set the journal to automatically record many activities, such as e-mail messages from certain contacts. Also, you can manually add any activity you wish to your journal.
- **Notes:** These are the electronic equivalent of those yellow sticky notes that are so common in many offices. You can use these to jot quick reminders or notes to yourself.

In addition to these categories, which are clearly visible at the left side of the Outlook window, you can also use the Other category (accessed by clicking the Other Shortcuts button at the lower left) to view files and directories on your hard drive or on your network. From within Outlook, you can copy and delete files and view network directories. Also, Outlook contains a built-in Web browser. If you are connected to the Internet, you can view Web sites from within Outlook.

This chapter provides you with an introductory look at the most commonly used Outlook features. You can learn to navigate within Outlook, read and send messages, view your calendar and create appointments, and add and edit contact information. The other chapters in this section of the book deal with using these features of Outlook in further detail, as well as Outlook features such as the Tasks list, Notes, and Journal.

NOTE: The first part of this chapter assumes that Outlook has already been installed as your e-mail component. If this is not the case, see "Configuring Outlook to Use E-Mail" near the end of this chapter before proceeding.

Starting and exiting Outlook

You launch Outlook from the Windows desktop by clicking Start ⇨ Programs ⇨ Microsoft Outlook or by double-clicking the Outlook icon on your desktop. If a Choose Profile dialog box appears, click OK to accept your default e-mail profile, or choose a desired e-mail profile. After the Outlook program window appears, you can leave Outlook running throughout the day, minimizing the Outlook window or covering it with open windows of other software that you use throughout your workday.

When you are done with Outlook, you can click the Close icon in the upper-right corner of the Outlook window or choose File ⇨ Exit from the menus to exit the program.

Introducing the Outlook window

Because you can use Outlook to perform so many different tasks, it's important to gain a familiarity with the various parts of the Outlook program window. Figure 35-1 shows the Outlook window.

You can think of the Outlook window as providing a view to all the major components of Outlook. The window is divided into three major sections: the Outlook Bar, the Folder List, and the Information Viewer. If you can't see the Outlook Bar or the Folder list, don't panic — just read on. The Folder List is not on by default unless you turned it on during an earlier session with Outlook or the settings were migrated from a previous version of Outlook. The Outlook Bar, located at the far left, contains icons for each of the Outlook folders. Click an icon in the Outlook Bar and the Outlook window changes to reveal that particular aspect of Outlook. For example, you can click the Inbox icon to view and read your e-mail, or you can click the Contacts icon to view the names and addresses stored under Contacts. (Alternatively, you can choose View ⇨ Go To and then choose any of the folders from the submenu that appears: Outlook Today, Inbox, Calendar, Contacts, or Tasks.)

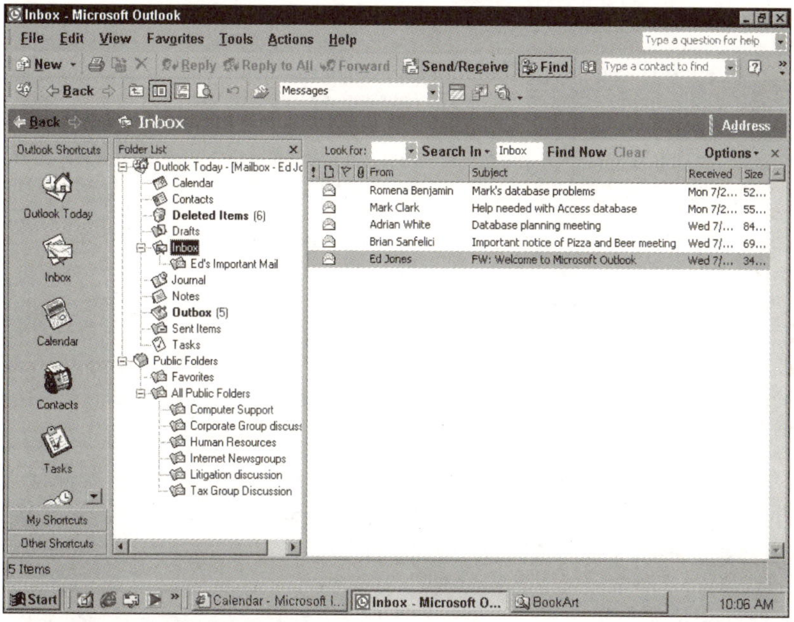

Figure 35-1: The Outlook window

In Outlook, some of the menu options and most of the toolbar icons change, depending on which folder of Outlook is currently open. Keep in mind that you can reveal the purpose of any toolbar button by holding the mouse stationary over the desired button. When you do this, a small window (called a *ToolTip*) appears, describing the purpose of the toolbar button. Also remember that you can choose View ⇨ Toolbars at any time and use the options on the submenu that appears to display or hide the various toolbars in Outlook.

Understanding Outlook folders

Outlook makes use of a *folder-based* metaphor in which various items — such as contacts, tasks, calendar entries, and notes — are stored in a series of folders. You can liken its various working areas to folders stored in a filing cabinet. You access the various folders of Outlook by clicking an appropriate icon in the Outlook Bar, which is at the far left. For example, e-mail messages are stored in the Inbox folder, appointments and events are stored in the Calendar folder, and contact names, addresses, and phone numbers are stored in the Contacts folder. Outlook also stores deleted items and items that are still in draft form, such as unsent letters, in folders.

The Folder List, located immediately to the right of the Outlook Bar, shows all the folders available in Outlook. In Outlook, you can create additional custom folders to store various items, including mail messages, contacts and journal entries, appointments, notes, and tasks. For example, if you are a solo practitioner, you might decide to create additional folders for each client matter and store your mail messages related to a client matter in a particular folder.

The Outlook Bar is visible by default, whereas the Folder List is normally hidden when you start Outlook for the first time. You can display or hide either of these; when you hide them, they remain hidden until you choose to display them again. To display or hide the Outlook Bar, choose View ⇨ Outlook Bar from the menus. To display or hide the Folder List, choose View ⇨ Folder List from the menus.

What's a profile?

If you are using Outlook on a network with multiple users and an e-mail server (such as Microsoft Exchange), you will have at least one Outlook profile. A *profile* is a collection of settings that tells Outlook who you are, where your mail servers are, what the properties of those servers are, and what address book should be used when you create and save new contacts. You may have more than one profile; for example, if you travel with a laptop, you might use one profile when you're connected to the network at the office and another profile when you're on the road. If you work at a large law firm or corporation, the network administrator or computer support person at your firm or organization will create profiles for you based on your use of Outlook and on the type of mail servers used by your organization. Note that unlike versions of Outlook prior to Outlook 2000, Outlook 2002 doesn't require multiple profiles to support different e-mail services. However, it will work with multiple profiles if you've upgraded from a version of Outlook prior to Outlook 2000 and are accustomed to using multiple profiles.

If you are a solo practitioner or a member of a small firm using Outlook with an Internet service provider, the initial setup of Outlook will automatically configure a default profile that works with your Internet service provider. You can add additional mail services to your Outlook profile at any time by choosing Tools ⇨ E-mail Accounts from the menus. (If you have been using Outlook without a mail connection, you will need to configure the program to work with e-mail connectivity.) For more on this topic, see "Configuring Outlook to Use E-Mail" near the end of this chapter.

The Information Viewer typically comprises most of the right half of the Outlook window. (Note that you can resize any of these window sections to occupy more or less of the screen as desired; you resize by holding the mouse pointer over the border until it changes shape to a double-headed arrow and then dragging the border.) In the Information Viewer, you see the actual Outlook items that you are working with, such as your mail messages in the Inbox portion or the names and addresses of contacts in the Contacts portion.

Throughout this section of the book, we use Microsoft's terminology of *panes* to refer to the particular Outlook folders as they are visible in the Information Viewer area; hence, the contacts portion of the Information Viewer may be referred to as the Contacts pane, the notes area as the Notes pane, the journal items area as the Journal pane, and so on.

Using the Preview pane

Optionally, a portion of the Information Viewer area can be dedicated to a Preview pane. The Preview pane is a useful feature of Outlook 2002. When visible, the Preview pane occupies the lower half of the Information Viewer area. In this area, you can view a preview of the item that is currently selected in your Inbox or other Outlook folder. You can alternately show or hide the Preview pane by choosing View ⇨ Preview Pane from the menus. Outlook remembers the last setting of the Preview pane for any particular folder, so if it was visible when you left that folder or shut down Outlook, it will appear when you return to that folder or next start Outlook. Figure 35-2 shows the appearance of the Outlook window when the Preview pane is visible and the Inbox folder has been selected.

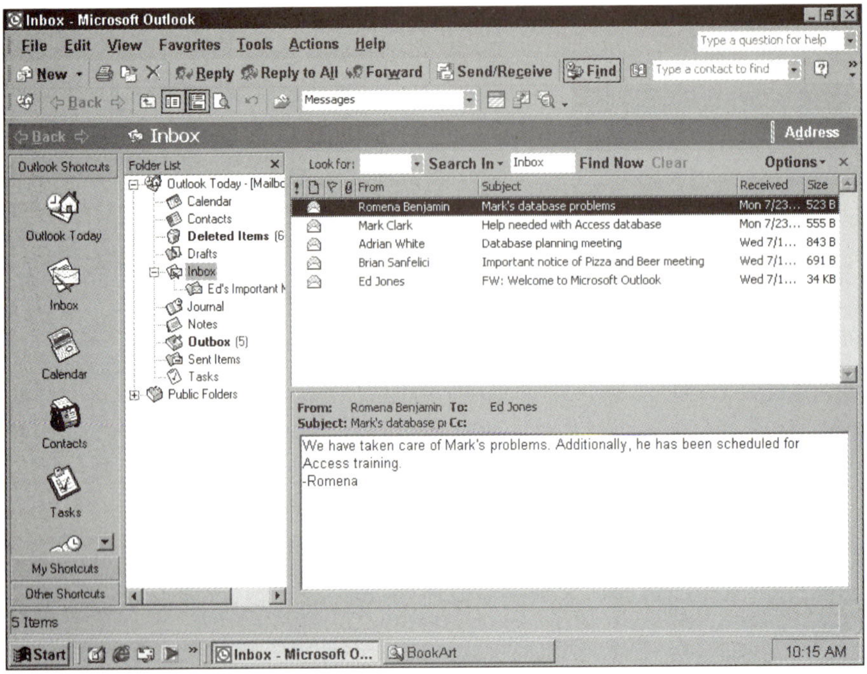

Figure 35-2: The Preview pane of the Outlook window lets you preview selected items.

With views of Outlook that display forms (such as contacts and appointment items), remember that the Preview pane is just that — a way of *previewing* information. You cannot edit items within the Preview pane.

Using Outlook Today

Although an Outlook Today icon appears on the Outlook toolbar, Outlook Today isn't really a type of folder, as are the Inbox, Calendar, Contacts, Tasks, Journal, and Notes. Rather, think of Outlook Today as an at-a-glance view of current activities within Outlook. (If Outlook Today isn't visible, you can click the Outlook Today icon in the Outlook Bar or choose View ⇨ Go To ⇨ Outlook Today to display it.) Figure 35-3 shows the appearance of Outlook Today.

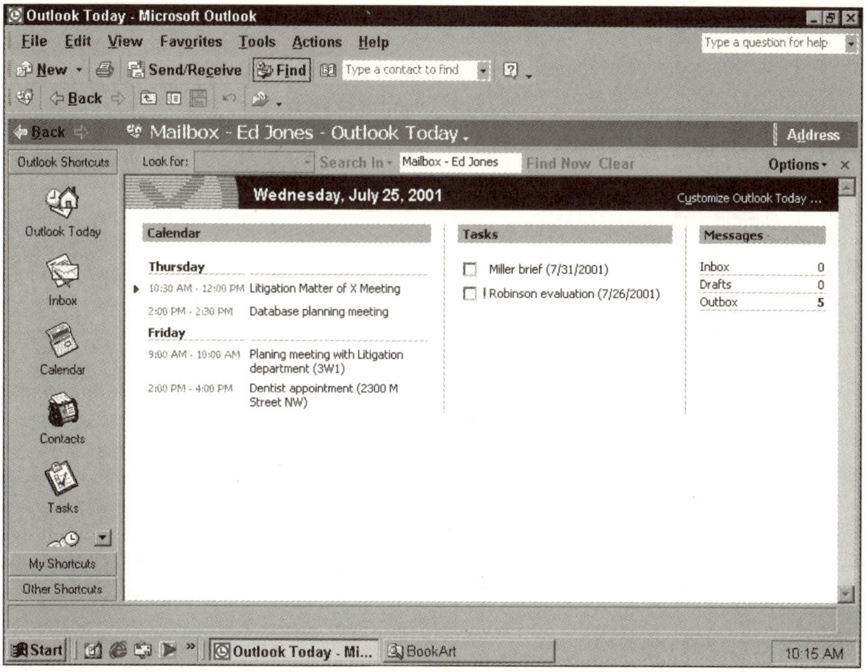

Figure 35-3: You can see your daily activities at a single glance in the Outlook Today view.

Outlook Today normally shows the following information:

- All activities on your calendar for the current day and for the next few days
- Tasks stored in your Task List
- The number of unread messages in your Inbox
- The number of unsent draft messages in your Drafts folder
- The number of unsent messages in your Outbox folder

The page displayed by Outlook Today is a type of Web page, so the items listed within the page are links that you can click to jump to another area. For example, under Messages, you can click Inbox to jump to your Inbox.

Getting help

If you get stuck when using a particular feature of Outlook, you can quickly obtain help by using the Ask a Question box at the right side of the menu bar. Just click in the text box, type a question (such as "How do I send attachments?"), and press Enter. A pop-up menu appears, containing a list of possible topics that are related to your question. You can then click a desired topic to see a help screen containing detailed information in response to your question.

About the no-mail mode of Outlook

When you install and start Outlook for the first time, the second start-up dialog box asks whether you would like to choose an e-mail account. If you choose no, you are selecting Outlook's no-mail mode. In its no-mail mode, you use Outlook as a personal information manager only, with no capability of sending and receiving e-mail. You may prefer this mode of Outlook if you don't intend to use your computer for e-mail or if you are using a different software program for your e-mail.

In the no-mail mode, Outlook makes use of a Personal Folders file, where it saves your calendar, contacts, tasks, journal, and notes on your hard drive. (Outlook also uses the Personal Folders file for storage of Outlook items if your e-mail connectivity takes place entirely through an Internet service provider, and no network Exchange Server.) You can share the information stored in your personal folders file with other Outlook users in the same way that you share other files.

Reading and Sending E-Mail

Using the Inbox, the messaging component of Outlook, you can read, compose, and send e-mail. The next few paragraphs give you the basics, but keep in mind that when it comes to mail, Outlook offers many capabilities worth exploring. For example, you can format messages using a variety of colors and fonts. You can create distribution lists for groups of individuals to whom you regularly send messages. You can address messages based on your personal e-mail lists or based on directories of individuals stored on your firm or organization's mail servers.

CROSS-REFERENCE: See Chapter 36 for details on the further capabilities of Outlook.

Clicking the Inbox icon in the Outlook Bar reveals the Inbox, as shown in Figure 35-4. Note that if you are using an Internet service provider and a modem to send and receive e-mail, you must have Windows Dial-Up Networking already installed to send and receive mail through Outlook. (If you can browse the Internet from a Web browser, you can safely assume that this component is working. For more details, see Windows Help for specifics on installing Dial-Up Networking.) If you are using Outlook on your firm's network, see your computer support person or your network administrator for help in configuring Outlook to work with your firm's e-mail servers.

As Figure 35-4 shows, when you are using the Inbox, your messages are displayed in the Information Viewer portion of the window. If View ⇨ AutoPreview is turned on, each message displays the first three lines of the message text.

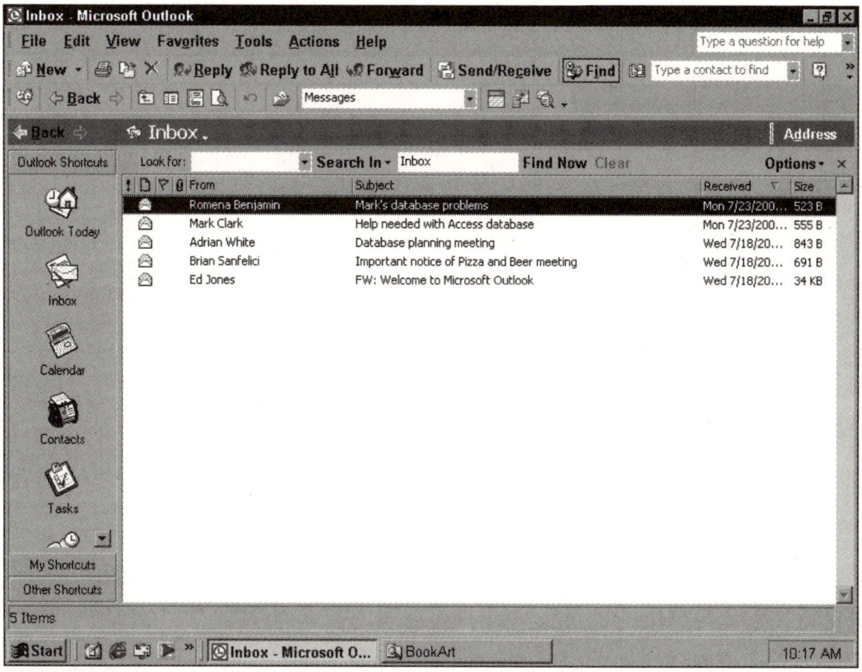

Figure 35-4: Use the Inbox folder of Outlook to view and manage your e-mail.

Reading e-mail

To read a message you've received, just double-click the message in the Inbox. In a moment, the message appears within a message window.

You can reply to the message by clicking the Reply button in the toolbar of the message window and typing a reply in the window that appears. (Use the Reply to All button to reply to the sender, as well as to anyone who was copied on the message.) You can forward the message to another person by clicking the Forward button in the toolbar and filling in the recipient's address in the To box of the message window that appears.

If you have a number of messages in your Inbox to be read, after you open one, you don't need to close the window and open another. You can use the Next button (the one containing the Down arrow) in the toolbar to read the next message in the same window, and you can use the Previous button (the one containing the Up arrow) in the toolbar to read the preceding message.

If you are connected to a network with a mail server, you don't need to do anything specific to retrieve your mail; Outlook displays the mail as it is received from your mail server. However, you can force Outlook to check for new mail by choosing Tools ⇨ Send/Receive ⇨ Send and Receive All (or by pressing the F9 key or clicking the Send/Receive button in the Standard toolbar). If you are retrieving mail from an Internet service provider over a dial-up connection, you can choose Tools ⇨ Send/Receive and then choose your Internet service provider by name from the next menu that appears. Windows Dial-Up Networking will initiate a phone call to your Internet service provider, and Outlook will retrieve your e-mail from that service.

Outlook to go? Well, sort of. . .

Anyone who is out of the office on a regular basis (a description that includes many attorneys) will find the ability to carry Outlook data on a handheld computer to be a valuable asset. The bad news is that Outlook does not directly support synchronization with handheld devices, possibly due in part to the variety of choices in handhelds on the market. However, the good news is that there's no shortage of third-party products to let you easily accomplish this feat. Most handheld devices, such as a Palm III or Palm V, Handspring Visor, Compaq iPAQ, or Sony CLIÉ are supplied with docking cradles that attach to a serial port or USB port on your desktop or laptop computer running Outlook. Using a software package provided by a third-party vendor, you can download and synchronize your Outlook calendar, mail, contacts, tasks, notes, and (depending on the software) journal with your handheld device. One of this book's authors uses one such product — PocketMirror — with a Palm 5x. That's not meant to be an endorsement of any sort; it's simply a statement of firsthand experience regarding the usefulness of such a product. (There's nothing quite like being able to catch up with dozens of e-mail messages while seated on the commuter train.) The following is a list of third-party vendors that provide software tools for synchronizing data between Outlook and a variety of handheld devices:

Companion Link Express: CompanionLink Software (`www.companionlink.com`)

Desktop To Go: DataViz (`www.dataviz.com`)

Intellisync: Puma Technology (`www.pumatech.com`)

PocketMirror: Chapura, Inc. (`www.chapura.com`)

Psi-Sync: Gadec (`www.gadec.com`)

Sending e-mail

To create and send a message, click the New Message button on the toolbar, or choose File ⇨ New ⇨ Mail Message. With either method, a new message opens, as shown in Figure 35-5.

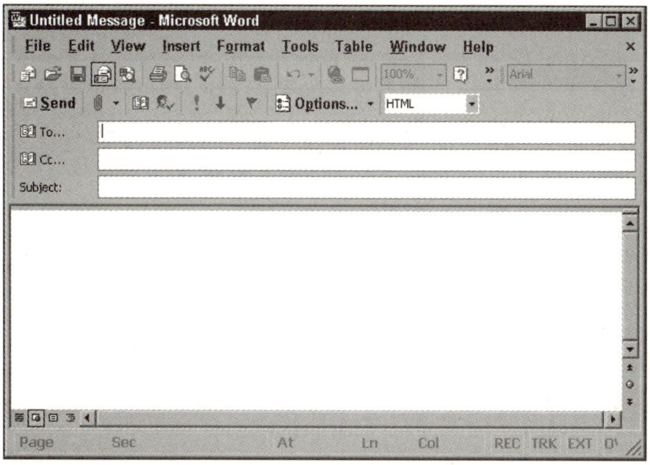

Figure 35-5: A new mail message in a message window

If you know the names of the recipient, you can type them directly into the To box. Recipients who are to have copies can have their names entered in the Cc box. If you don't know the e-mail addresses, you can click the To or the Cc button to reveal a Select Names dialog box (see Figure 35-6).

In the dialog box, you can enter a name or select it from a list you've entered previously. You can use the Show Names From The list box at the upper right to cause the list to display names from within your personal Contacts list or from your firm or organization's mail server if you are on a network. After you locate the desired name in the list, double-click it to move it to the Message Recipients portion of the dialog box. Repeat this step for every person you want to send the message to; then click OK to close the dialog box.

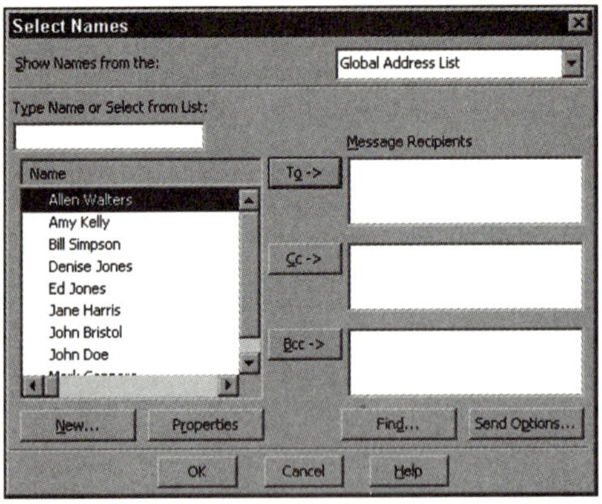

Figure 35-6: The Select Names dialog box

After you've entered the recipients in the To and Cc boxes, you can enter a desired subject in the Subject box and then click in the text box and type the text of your message. You can attach a file to the message by using the Insert ⇨ File command or clicking the paper clip icon on the Standard toolbar (see Chapter 36, "Using Outlook E-Mail," for details). After completing the message, click the Send button on the toolbar of the Message window (or choose File ⇨ Send) to send the message. Outlook automatically closes the Message window after you send the message.

If you are on a network configured with Microsoft Exchange Server, the message is sent automatically. If you are using an Internet service provider and a dial-up connection, Outlook places the message in your Outbox folder, along with any other messages that are waiting to be sent. When you are ready to send messages, you can choose Tools ⇨ Send/Receive or use the Send/Receive button on the Standard toolbar and then choose your Internet service provider by name from the next menu that appears. Windows Dial-Up Networking will initiate a phone call to your Internet service provider, and Outlook will send your e-mail using your Internet account.

Deleting e-mail

To delete messages you've already read, just select the unwanted message in the Inbox and press the Delete key. You can select a group of messages for deletion by selecting the first message and then holding down the Ctrl key as you select each additional message. You also can select a contiguous group of messages by selecting the first message in the group, holding the Shift key down, and selecting the last message in the group. When the group of unwanted messages is selected, press the Delete key.

CROSS-REFERENCE: Additional ways to manage your mail are detailed in Chapter 36.

TIP: If you are on a network with Microsoft Exchange Server and you are going to be out of the office for a given period, you can automatically send replies to people who send you e-mail, advising them of that fact. Choose Tools ⇨ Out of Office Assistant, turn on the I Am Currently out of the Office' option in the dialog box that appears, enter a message you want sent automatically in the first text box, and click OK. For more details on this feature, see "Using the Out of Office Assistant" in Chapter 36.

A Quick Look at the Calendar

The Calendar feature of Outlook can provide an efficient way of tracking and planning your daily schedule. Click the Calendar icon in the Outlook Bar or choose View ⇨ Go To ⇨ Calendar to display the Calendar within Outlook. Figure 35-7 shows the Calendar displayed by the week.

As you view the Calendar, you can view the days and navigate within the Calendar in many ways. You can view the Calendar by day, by workweek, by full week, or by month. To change the view, click the Day, Work Week, Week, or Month button in the toolbar, or select Day, Work Week, Week, or Month from the View menu. In any view, the easiest way to jump to a specific date is to click that date, either in the main portion of the Calendar or in the monthly calendar that appears at the upper right when you are viewing by the day, workweek, or full week.

If you are viewing the Calendar by the week or month, you can use the arrow keys to move between different days. (If you're viewing the Calendar by the day or workweek, the Up and Down arrow keys move you between hours of the day, and the Left and Right arrow keys move you between days.) While viewing the day, workweek, or full week, you can also click any day shown in the small monthly calendar (at the upper right) to jump directly to that day, and you can jump to any date by choosing View ⇨ Go To ⇨ Go to Date. This command opens a Go To Date dialog box, in which you can enter the desired date to go to in any acceptable date format, such as American (mm/dd/yy or mm-dd-yy) or European (dd/mm/yy or dd-mm-yy).

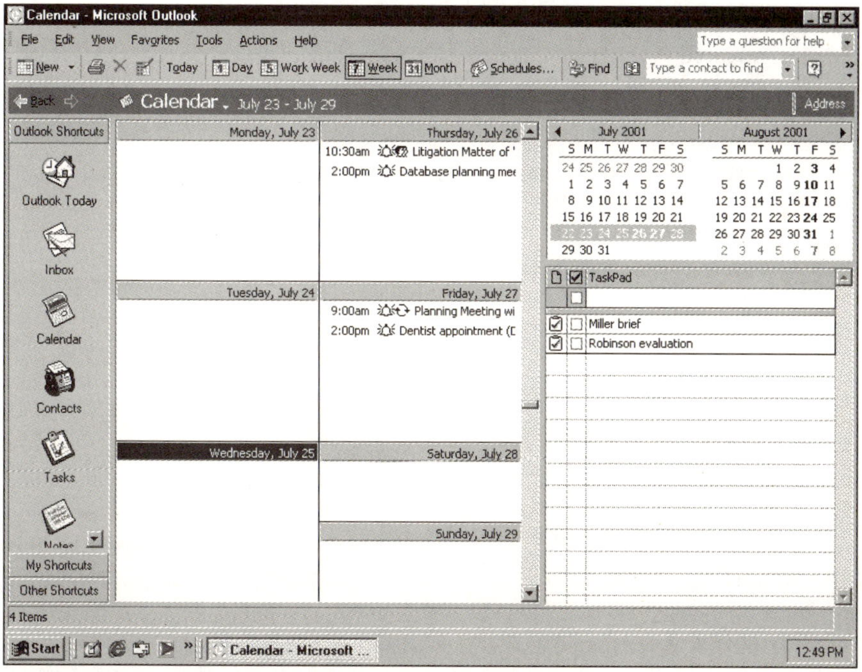

Figure 35-7: The Calendar folder of Outlook provides a calendar that you can use to schedule your daily appointments and events.

You can add appointments to your Outlook calendar to remind yourself of important meetings, events, or time-related tasks you must perform. You can even set reminders to remind you ahead of time, and the reminders will cause a message box to be displayed on your screen in advance of the appointment, along with the sounding of an audible tone (assuming that your volume is turned up in the Windows Control Panel). To set an appointment, use these steps:

1. Open the Calendar and locate the desired day in the Calendar. (Note that if you are viewing the Calendar by the week and you are at the wrong week, one way to move around is to use the PgUp and PgDn keys to move forward or backward a week at a time.)
2. Double-click the desired day (or, if you are viewing by the day, double-click at the desired starting hour for the appointment). When you do this, a new window appears with the Appointment tab selected, as shown in Figure 35-8.
3. Enter a subject for your appointment in the Subject box; also add a location if desired in the Location box.
4. If you want the appointment to be a recurring appointment, click the Recurrence button in the Standard toolbar and fill in the Recurrence options in the dialog box that appears.
5. If you are entering an all-day event, turn on the All day event check box.
6. If desired, change the start and end times.
7. If you want a reminder of the appointment, turn on the Reminder check box and choose the delay time between the appearance of the reminder and the appointment. Click the Sound button if you want to hear a reminder tone.

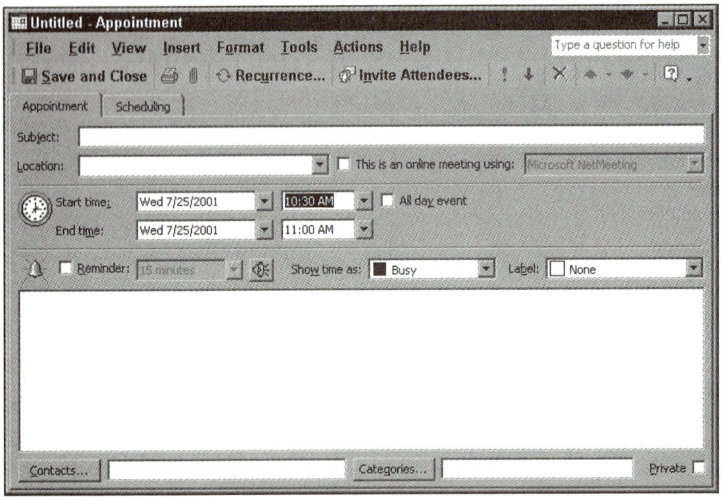

Figure 35-8: A new appointment in an Appointment window

8. Make any desired selection in the Show Time As list box. You can choose Free, Tentative, Busy, or Out of Office. (On a network, checking an option in this box enables others to view your schedule; see Chapter 38, "Scheduling Your Time and Tasks in Outlook," for details.)
9. Enter any desired comments describing the appointment or event in the lower portion of the window.
10. Click Save and Close to save the appointment or event.

TIP: You can easily print your calendar to have a handy printed version of your upcoming schedule. When you use the toolbar's Print icon or the File ⇨ Print command, the Calendar prints using the view that you are currently using in Outlook. Hence, if you wanted a calendar for a particular week, you would go to that week and display it, using the Week view. After you have the display set as desired, click the Print icon on the toolbar, or choose File ⇨ Print to print your calendar.

CROSS-REFERENCE: Remember that this discussion of the Calendar only scratches the surface in terms of features. You can create appointments based on incoming e-mail by dragging the e-mail from the Inbox to the Calendar icon in the Outlook Bar. If you are using Outlook as your e-mail client, you can schedule meetings with others who have e-mail addresses. These topics and more are covered in detail in Chapter 38.

Working with Contacts

You can use the Contacts feature of Outlook to display all your business or personal contacts. Clicking the Contacts icon in the Outlook Bar reveals the Outlook window with the Contacts pane visible.

You can display your contacts using a number of different views: as address cards, as more detailed address cards, as a phone list, by categories, by companies, or by location. You choose the desired view by selecting it from the Current View list box in the toolbar or by clicking View ⇨ Current View and then selecting the desired view from the submenu that appears.

Adding a contact

To create a new contact, click the New Contact button in the toolbar. (You can also choose File ⇨ New ⇨ Contact, but clicking the button is easier.) When you do this, a new Contact window appears.

You can enter the desired information into the fields of the window. In the Full Name box, you enter the person's name, using the format of first name followed by a middle initial (if desired) and then last name. (Outlook automatically discerns where the first name ends and the last name begins when it sorts your data.) The remaining fields are self-explanatory; you can fill in the company name (if any) and the address and phone numbers. Outlook even includes fields for e-mail and Web page addresses. Note that with all the phone numbers, you can click any of the down arrows and change the category. For example, you can change a phone number's category from Business to Car or from Home 1 to Home 2.

In the Comments portion in the lower half of the dialog box, you can enter any comments to help you remember what's important about this contact. Also, you can use the Categories button (at the bottom of the window) to bring up a list box of categories you can choose to add to the field to the right of the button. (This feature proves helpful if you want to be able to view your contacts by category.) When you're done entering the contact information, click the Save and Close button in the toolbar to save the contact and close the window.

Opening and editing a contact

You can open any contact for viewing or editing by double-clicking that contact or by clicking it with the mouse or highlighting it with the Shift+arrow keys and pressing Enter. Using either method, the contact appears in a Contact window like that shown in Figure 35-9.

You can edit any of the desired fields; when you click the Save and Close button in the toolbar, the changes will be saved.

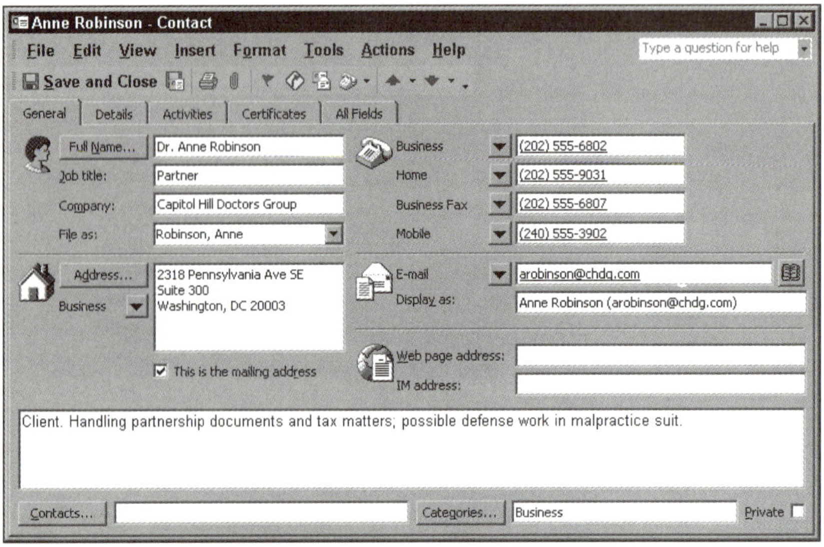

Figure 35-9: An existing contact shown in the Contact window

Deleting a contact

To delete a contact, right-click the unwanted contact in the Contacts pane and choose Delete. Alternatively, you can click the header of the contact to select it. Then, press the Delete key or click the Delete button in the toolbar. Keep in mind that you can remove a number of contacts simultaneously by selecting all the unwanted contacts (press the Ctrl key as you click the header of each contact). With all the unwanted contacts selected, press the Delete key.

Printing a list of contacts

You can print a list of your contacts by making the Contacts pane visible and clicking the Print icon in the toolbar or by choosing File ⇨ Print from the menu bar. Keep in mind that your contacts will print in a format that's similar to the view you are currently using to see your contacts. In other words, if you have Phone List selected as the current view, your contacts will print as a phone list. If you have Address Card selected as the current view, your contacts will print as address cards. You can get an idea of what the printout in any view will look like by choosing File ⇨ Print Preview from the menu bar.

Working with Multiple Profiles

The e-mail account and the Outlook personal information file that are created as parts of the initial setup of Outlook are part of the current Outlook profile. When you start Outlook for the first time and step through the initial dialog boxes, a default profile is created for you automatically. However, at some law firms or organizations, you may prefer to use more than one profile. For example, if your organization is using a mix of Outlook 2002 and older versions of Outlook, you may have multiple e-mail accounts, and each account can make use of a different profile. (If all users are on Outlook 2002, this approach can still be used, but it isn't really necessary because Outlook 2002 can be configured for multiple e-mail accounts within the same profile. For details, see Chapter 36.)

You might have two or more individuals using Outlook on the same computer. If each individual wants his or her own set of folders, you need a separate profile for each individual.

Mail profiles are stored outside Outlook; they are actually part of the Windows operating system. You can create additional profiles using the following steps:

1. In the Windows Control Panel (to get to it, choose Start ⇨ Settings ⇨ Control Panel), double-click the Mail icon.
2. Click the Show Profiles button in the Mail Setup dialog box that appears.
3. Click the Add button in the Mail dialog box (see Figure 35-10) and enter a name of your choosing for the new profile when asked.
4. Define your desired e-mail account using the E-mail Accounts dialog boxes that appear (see Step 6 in the following section for additional details).
5. When you have finished creating the new profile, you will be returned to the Mail dialog box. Select Prompt for a Profile to Be Used and then click OK. This will let you choose a desired profile from a list of multiple profiles each time that you start Outlook.

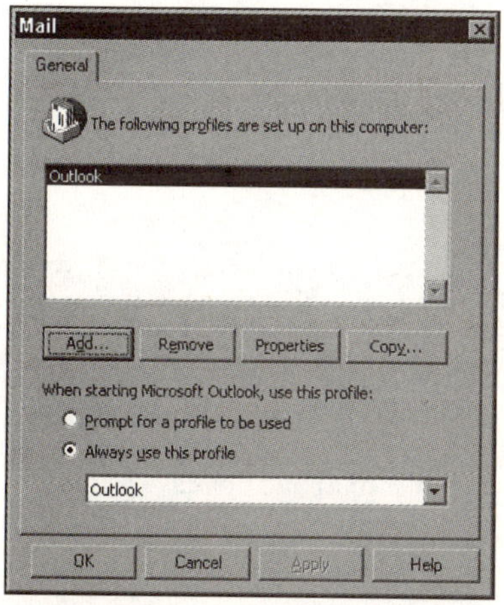

Figure 35-10: The Mail dialog box can be used to add profiles for use with Outlook.

Configuring Outlook to Use E-Mail

If you have just installed Outlook on your system, or if you have been using Outlook in its no-mail mode and you now wish to add e-mail connectivity, you need to configure your e-mail connection. (If you have been using Outlook in no-mail mode and want to add e-mail connectivity at this time, start Outlook, choose Tools ⇨ E-mail Accounts from the menus, and proceed to Step 4 of the steps that follow.)

When Outlook starts for the first time, you see a series of dialog boxes requesting the information needed to configure Outlook to send and receive your e-mail messages. The exact sequence of dialog boxes that you see will vary, depending on whether you have a previous version of Outlook installed on your computer or are using another e-mail program, such as Microsoft Schedule+. If you installed Outlook on a computer that had no previous version of Outlook (with the exception of Microsoft Outlook Express), you will see the Outlook Startup dialog box. Perform the steps that follow.

1. Click Next. You see an E-Mail Accounts dialog box that asks whether you want to configure Outlook to operate with e-mail.
2. Click Yes and then click Next. You will see the E-mail Upgrade Options dialog box. You can use this dialog box to import the mail messages, addresses, and other settings from an existing e-mail program on your computer. (Outlook can import e-mail messages and settings from Netscape Mail, Qualcomm Eudora, and Outlook Express.)
3. Turn on the Upgrade From option and select the program in the list if you want to import your settings from your old e-mail program. Turn on the Do Not Upgrade option if you do not want to import your settings from your old e-mail program.
4. Click Next in the dialog box. If you import settings from an existing e-mail program, Outlook uses those settings for the remainder of this process and displays a final dialog box. You can click Finish in that dialog box to complete the setup process.
5. If you do not import settings from an existing e-mail program, or if you are adding e-mail connectivity when you have been using no-mail mode, you see the E-mail Accounts Server Type dialog box. Here, you can choose to configure an e-mail account using the Exchange Server, another e-mail server, or an Internet service provider. Choose the appropriate account type and click Next. If you are unsure as to which type is appropriate for your e-mail provider, refer to the documentation provided by your Internet service provider, or ask the network administrator who maintains your e-mail server.
6. The next dialog box that you see will vary, depending on the type of e-mail service that you selected in the preceding dialog box. Figure 35-11 shows the dialog box that appears if you use a POP3 account, the most common type of nonproprietary protocol used for receiving Internet e-mail. Fill in the required information as provided from your Internet service provider or your network administrator; then click the Next button.

Outlook uses the settings you enter in the dialog box to configure your e-mail and displays a final dialog box. You can click Finish in that dialog box to complete the setup process.

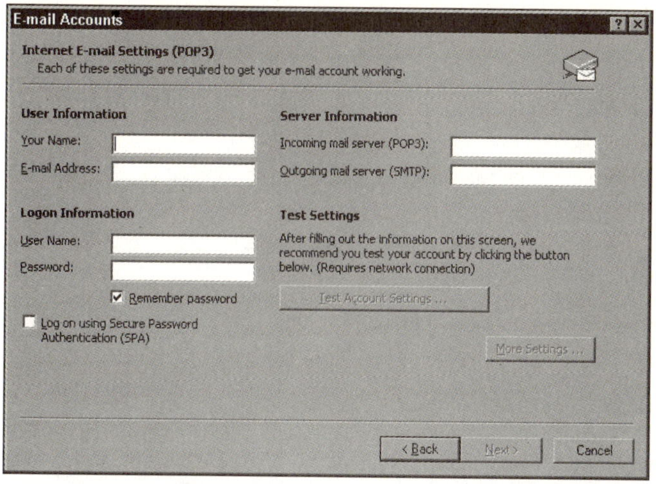

Figure 35-11: The E-mail Accounts dialog box used to configure Outlook to work with a POP3 account

Choosing an E-Mail Methodology at Small Firms

Deciding how to install Outlook to support e-mail is easy if you are a solo practitioner or part of a very small firm (perhaps two or three attorneys). In such cases, you are likely to use an Internet service provider that supports Outlook, such as AT&T WorldNet, EarthLink, or your local cable TV or phone service provider. (As of this writing, America Online does *not* support the use of Microsoft Outlook as an e-mail client.) You fill in the settings provided by your Internet service provider in the setup dialog boxes that appear when you start Outlook for the first time (or choose Tools ⇨ E-mail Accounts from the Outlook menus to set up an account matching the settings of your Internet service provider), and you're in business.

Setting up Outlook for e-mail connectivity at a large firm or organization also tends to be a simple matter because someone with a high degree of technical skills (such as your network administrator or a consultant hired by your firm to set up the Exchange Server) has already configured Outlook to work with your network. In these cases, you simply "go with the flow" of what has been dictated by the powers that be, and you call your computer support department's help desk if things aren't working properly. It's at small firms of perhaps one to two dozen employees where the choice gets difficult. In such situations, both approaches — using modems and an Internet service provider or using dedicated network mail servers such as Microsoft Exchange — have their advantages and disadvantages. Outlook configured to operate with an Internet service provider has the advantages of simplicity and relatively low cost. The disadvantages are that each user requires a modem and access to a phone line, or you must set up a small network with a shared modem (not easy for the nontechnically minded).

If your small office needs internal e-mail but no Internet access, or if you can get by with Internet access at one or two stations, your best bet may be to use Exchange Server under Microsoft's Small Business licensing (talk to your computer consultant or Microsoft representative for details). You can have a consultant set up Exchange Server on a Windows NT/2000 server (which you may already have for storing your firm documents), and you can install modems and phone lines at the locations that require Internet access. If most people in your office require access to internal e-mail and to the Internet (or if you expect your firm or organization to quickly grow in size beyond the dozen or so people who may be working there presently), it's probably best to bite the bullet in terms of cost and to pay a consultant to set up a dedicated Exchange Server on your network, along with a shared connection to the Internet. Using a server-based system allows you to share a single connection to the Internet among multiple users, an approach that will probably save money in the long run.

Summary

This chapter covered the basics of Outlook and how to configure it for use at your particular law firm or organization. We discussed the following:

- Outlook uses a folder-based metaphor, where all items (such as contacts, e-mail messages, tasks, and journal entries) are stored in a series of folders.
- Using the Inbox folder, you can read and send e-mail (assuming that you have configured Outlook to work with an e-mail service).
- The Calendar folder provides a calendar you can use to keep track of events, such as appointments and meetings.
- The Contacts folder lets you store names, addresses, and phone numbers of your various business and personal contacts.

In the next chapter, you learn more detailed aspects involving the use of e-mail within Outlook.

Chapter 36

Using Outlook E-Mail

In This Chapter

- ♦ Receiving and reading e-mail
- ♦ Composing and sending e-mail
- ♦ Searching for messages in your inbox
- ♦ Deleting e-mail
- ♦ Moving e-mail to a folder
- ♦ Organizing your mailbox
- ♦ Using the Out of Office Assistant
- ♦ Using the Address Book
- ♦ Subscribing to and participating in legal newsgroups
- ♦ Creating and using distribution lists
- ♦ Adding an additional e-mail account
- ♦ Using the mailbox cleanup feature

OUTLOOK DOES A NUMBER OF THINGS well, but it is best known for its e-mail capabilities. Assuming that you have set up one or more e-mail accounts to be used with Outlook, you can use Outlook to send, receive, and organize your e-mail.

Outlook makes use of four folders to manage your e-mail messages: the Inbox folder, the Outbox folder, the Drafts folder, and the Sent Items folder.

Received messages are stored in the Inbox folder. As you compose a message, Outlook stores it in the Drafts folder until you send it. When you send a message, Outlook temporarily puts it in the Outbox folder until you send it to your mail server. (With some mail servers, such as Microsoft Exchange Server on a firm's internal network, this process is virtually instantaneous.) After you send the message, Outlook stores a copy of the message in your Sent Items folder.

TIP: For information on setting up Outlook to use an e-mail service for the first time, see Chapter 35.

Receiving and Reading E-Mail

If your computer is connected to a network that uses an internal mail server, the server will automatically deliver new mail to Outlook on a regular basis. If you are using a mail service through your Internet service provider, you can use these steps to retrieve your mail:

1. In the Outlook Bar, click the Inbox icon to display the Inbox folder.
2. Click the Send/Receive button in the Standard toolbar (or choose Tools ⇨ Send/Receive and choose your Internet service provider by name from the next menu to appear).

   Outlook connects to your mail server and downloads your messages. (At the same time, any outgoing messages that are residing in the Outbox folder will be sent.)

Unread messages appear in your Inbox with a small icon of an unopened envelope at the left side of the Inbox, as shown in Figure 36-1. (Unread messages also appear in bold type, in contrast to read messages, as shown in the figure.)

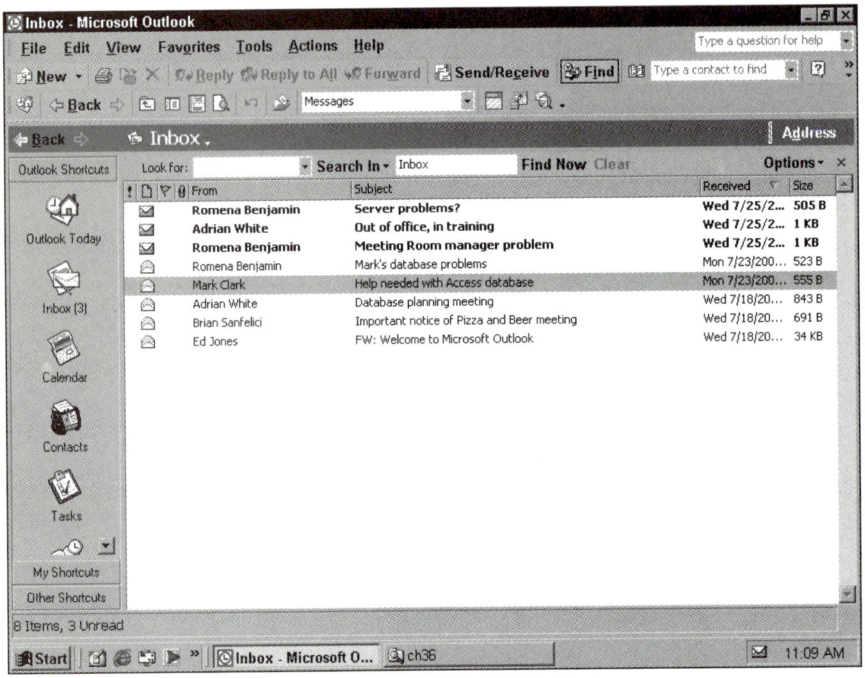

Figure 36-1: A group of unopened messages in the Inbox

You can open and read a message by double-clicking the message or by selecting the message in the Inbox and pressing Enter. You also can right-click on the message in the list and choose Open, or you can select the desired message and then choose File ⇨ Open ⇨ Selected Items. With either step, the message opens inside a Message window similarly to the example shown in Figure 36-2.

After a message is opened in a Message window, you can use the buttons in the toolbar of the Message window to perform common message-related tasks. Click the Reply button to reply to the sender of the message, or click the Reply To All button to reply to the sender and to all recipients of the original message. Use the Forward button to forward the message to another recipient; when you click this button, To and CC fields are added to the message, and you can specify a recipient's address to forward the message to.

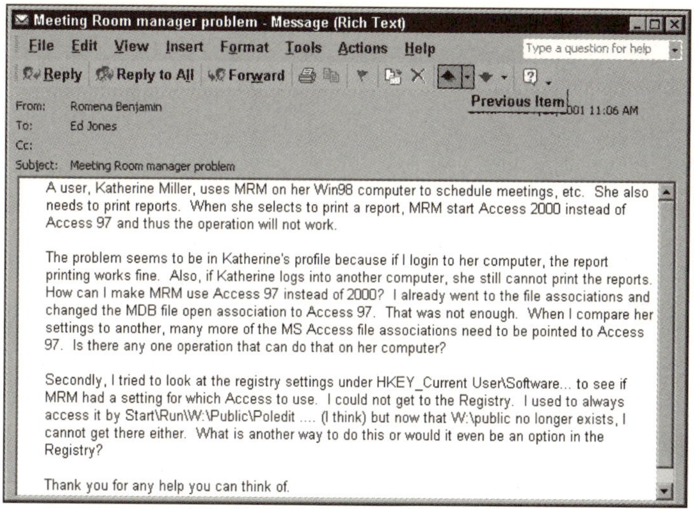

Figure 36-2: A message displayed within a Message window

Printing or deleting messages

Click the Print icon in the toolbar to print the message, or click the Delete icon in the toolbar to delete the message. You can also move the message to a folder of your choosing; for details on how to do this, see "Creating Folders and Moving Mail to a Folder," later in this chapter.

Working with attachments

When a message includes an attachment, a small paper clip icon appears to the left of the message in the Inbox. After you open a message containing an attachment, an icon representing the type of attachment appears inside the Message window, as shown in the example in Figure 36-3.

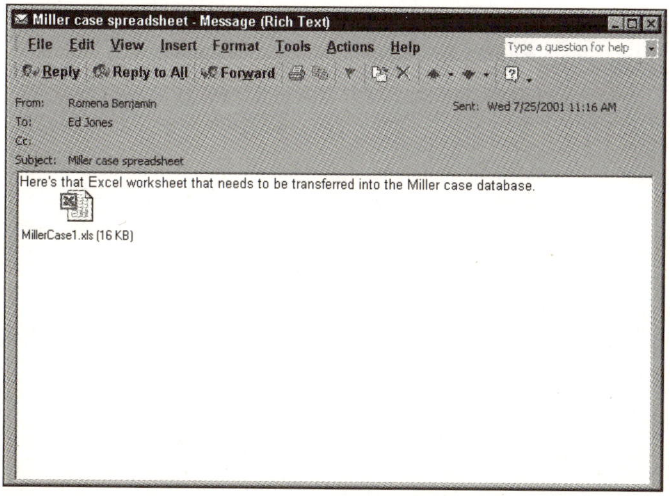

Figure 36-3: A message containing an Excel spreadsheet as an attachment

You can double-click the attachment to open it inside the type of program originally used to create the attachment (for example, if you double-click an attachment that is a Word document, Word launches and displays the attachment within a document window).

Alternatively, to save the attachment to a disk file, you can right-click the icon of the attachment, choose Save As, and enter a path and filename in the dialog box that appears.

CAUTION: When it comes to attachments, you should exercise extreme care if you receive an attachment you are not expecting. Many destructive viruses make use of attachments inside Outlook messages to spread their malicious effects. Even when the message appears to come from someone you know, you can't be sure because some viruses use a recipient's Address Book entries to spread further. If in doubt, checking with the sender (by phone) as to whether an attachment was sent intentionally would be prudent.

Composing and Sending E-Mail

You can send an e-mail message to any recipient who has an e-mail address, whether that person is listed in your Address Book or in your list of contacts. (Of course, you also can just enter the recipient's e-mail address in the To field.)

Composing a new e-mail message

To create and send a new message, use the following steps:

1. In the Outlook Bar, click the Inbox icon.
2. Click the New button in the Standard toolbar. In a moment, a new Message window appears (see Figure 36-4).

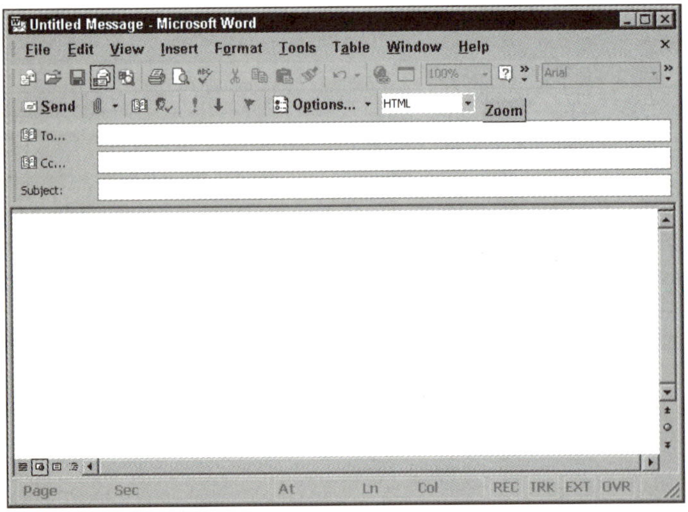

Figure 36-4: A new Message window used to compose new mail

If you know the names of the recipients, you can type them directly into the To box. Recipients who are to have copies can have their names entered in the Cc box. If you don't know the e-mail addresses, you can click the To or the Cc button to display the Select Names dialog box (see Figure 36-5).

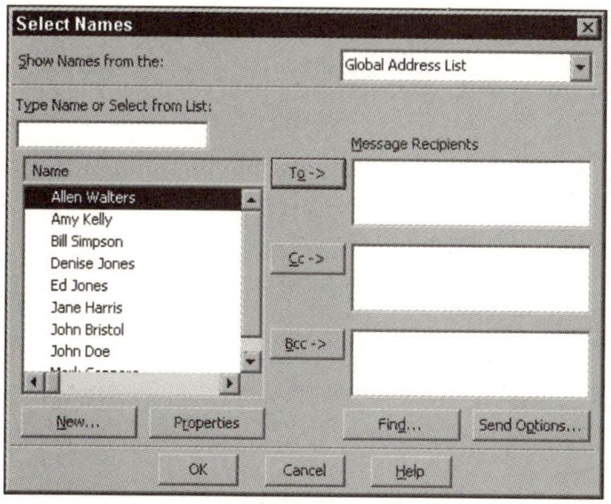

Figure 36-5: The Select Names dialog box

In the dialog box, you can enter a name or select it from a list you've entered previously. You can use the Show Names From The list box at the upper right to cause the list to display names from within your personal Contacts list or from your firm or organization's mail server if you are on a network. When you locate the desired name in the list, double-click it to move it to the Message Recipients portion of the dialog box. Repeat this step for every person you want to send the message to, and click OK to close the dialog box.

After you enter the recipients in the To and Cc boxes, you can enter a desired subject in the Subject box; then click the text box and type the text of your message. After completing the message, click the Send button on the toolbar (or choose File ⇨ Send) to send the message. Outlook automatically closes the mail window after you send the message.

TIP: If you want to send a message to multiple recipients and you want to preserve the anonymity of each recipient, use the BCC (Blind Carbon Copy) button in the Select Names dialog box. Recipients who are placed in the BCC text box receive messages without the e-mail addresses of the other recipients appearing in the message header. You can leave the To box blank or enter your own e-mail address in the To box as a means of verifying that your message was sent.

Adding attachments

In the legal environment, many messages that you send may need attachments included. For example, you may want to send an e-mail message to a client, and you may need to attach a Word document to the e-mail for review by the client. To add an attachment, create the message using the steps outlined previously. Then, before sending the message, choose Insert ⇨ File (or click the Insert File button on the toolbar — the button resembling a paperclip) to display the Insert File dialog box (see Figure 36-6).

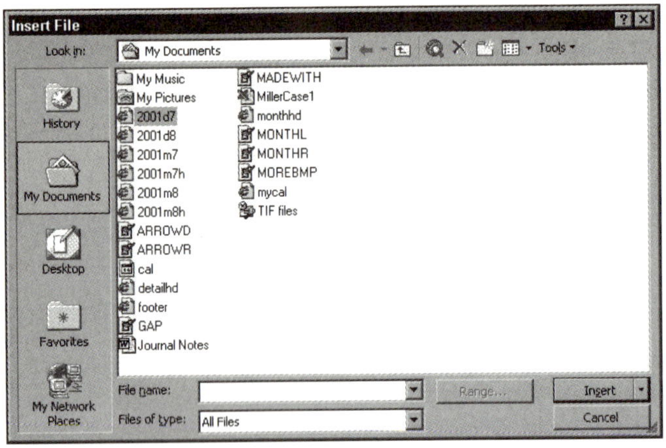

Figure 36-6: The Insert File dialog box

In the dialog box, navigate to the desired file, select it, and click Insert to insert a file as an attachment. Repeat the use of the Insert ⇨ File command to insert additional files as attachments to the same message. (You also can hold down the Ctrl key and click multiple files to select more than one file as an attachment.)

TIP: You can also insert an attachment by dragging a file from another window (such as My Computer or Windows Explorer) and dropping it into the text box of the Message window.

NOTE: Outlook lets you insert multiple files into a single message as attachments. However, if you are sending the message over the Internet, you should check with the recipient to be sure that his or her mail provider supports the use of multiple attachments. Most but not all Internet service providers support multiple attachments.

Replying to an e-mail

To reply to a message you've received, open the message and click the Reply button, or right-click the message in the Inbox and choose Reply from the menu that appears. With either method, the original message appears within a reply window. The window contains the text of the original message and the sender's address in the To field.

You can add the text of your reply above the original message and then click Send in the toolbar to send the reply.

Forwarding an e-mail

To send a received message on to someone else, open the message and click the Forward button. Or you can right-click the message in the Inbox and choose Forward from the menu that appears. With either method, the original message appears within a Forward window. The window contains the text of the original message and a blank To field.

Enter the name of the recipient in the To box (or click the To button and choose a name in the Select Names dialog box that appears). Add any desired new text above the original message and then click Send in the toolbar to forward the message.

Formatting text

By default, Outlook uses Microsoft Word as its e-mail editor. Hence, the formatting power of Word is at your disposal when you compose mail messages. How these messages will appear to the recipient, of course, depends on the software used by the recipient to view your messages. If the recipient is also using Outlook, any formatting that you send will come across in the received message. If the recipient is using an Internet-based e-mail package that supports minimal formatting, the recipient may not see the formatting.

When you compose a new message, Outlook uses one of three possible e-mail formats — plain text, rich text, or HTML — to create the message. (By default, Outlook uses HTML, but you can select plain text or rich text by choosing Tools ⇨ Options and selecting the desired message format in the Mail Format tab of the dialog box that appears. Also, note that if you select plain text, many of the formatting options described here will be grayed out in the menus and therefore unavailable.) When you reply to a message or forward a message, Outlook uses the format of the original message. If the message is sent using rich text or HTML formats, the formatting you choose will be received intact by the recipient. Most e-mail clients in use at large firms and organizations (including Novell GroupWise and Lotus Notes) recognize rich text or HTML formatting. If you send a message containing formatting to a person who has an e-mail client that does not recognize the formatting, the message appears as plain text.

You can use either of two methods to format your text. You can choose a font, font size, or style in the Formatting toolbar and then type your text, or you can select text you've already typed and then use the Formatting toolbar to apply formatting to the text. (If the Formatting toolbar isn't visible when you compose a message, choose View ⇨ Toolbars ⇨ Formatting from the menus within the New Message window to display the toolbar.)

Use these steps to format text within a message:

1. If you want the formatting to apply to a selection, select the desired text.
2. To change fonts, open the Font drop-down list in the Formatting toolbar and select the desired font.
3. To change the font size, open the Font Size drop-down list in the toolbar and select the desired size, or type the size value directly into the box. (If you just want to make the font slightly larger or smaller, you can use the Increase Font Size and Decrease Font Size buttons on the toolbar.)
4. To add a desired style (such as underlining, bold, or italic), click the appropriate toolbar button.
5. To change the color used for the text, click the Color button and choose a color from the Color palette that appears.
6. Choose a desired alignment by clicking the Align Left, the Center, or the Align Right toolbar button.
7. Add or remove text indents as desired by clicking the Increase Indent or the Decrease Indent button in the toolbar. (Each button adds or removes a one-half inch indent each time you click the button.)

TIP: If you apply a formatting change and you don't care for the change, remember that you can undo it by choosing Edit ⇨ Undo from the menus (or by pressing Ctrl+Z).

Checking your spelling

Outlook includes the spell-checking capability that is built in to all Microsoft Office products. To check the spelling in a message that you are composing, choose Tools ⇨ Spelling and Grammar, or press F7. Outlook checks the spelling in the message. If it finds what it thinks is a misspelled word, you'll see the Spelling and Grammar dialog box.

When Outlook finds a misspelling, it tries to provide a number of options for a correct spelling of the word in the Suggestions list box. In the Not in Dictionary text box, you can enter the correct spelling, or you can click one of the suggested spellings in the Suggestions list box. You can then click the Change button to make the change and to proceed to the next misspelling (if any exist).

The Ignore Once button lets you leave a word as is, and the Cancel button stops the entire spell checking operation at that point. Clicking Ignore All tells Outlook to ignore all suspected misspellings of the same term; Change All tells Outlook to change all misspellings to the entry that you type or accept in the Suggestions box. The Add to Dictionary button lets you add a word to the selected custom dictionary, which is named Custom.DIC by default.

CROSS-REFERENCE: For details on creating and changing custom dictionaries, see Chapter 6 of this book.

Use the Options button to display a Spelling Options dialog box, where you can change options used by the spelling checker. You can choose whether to ignore words in all uppercase, whether to ignore words containing numbers, whether to always check spelling before sending a message, whether to ignore the original message within a reply or a forwarded message, and which language dictionary to use.

Changing the importance or sensitivity level of a message

By default, messages are sent with an importance level of Normal. You can change this, as desired, for any message that you are in the process of composing. To do so, with the Message window open, open the Options menu on the toolbar to display the Message Options dialog box for the message.

In the Importance drop-down list, click the down arrow to choose a desired importance level (Low, Normal, or High), and in the Sensitivity drop-down list, click the down arrow to choose a desired level (Normal, Personal, Private, or Confidential). You can also request a Delivery receipt or a Read receipt, by checking the appropriate check boxes. When you're done choosing your settings in the dialog box, click OK and then finish composing and sending your message. When the recipient opens the message, the header bar shows the level of sensitivity. Also, messages marked with an Importance level of High are displayed in the recipient's Inbox with an exclamation mark to the left of the message.

Flagging a message

You can draw attention to a message you are sending by flagging the message. The flagged message appears in the recipient's Inbox with a small icon of a flag to the left of the From header. You can also set a reminder to cause the flagged message to display a reminder to the recipient on a chosen date. (These features assume that the recipient is also using a version of Outlook 97 or later.)

Here are the steps you can use to flag a message:

1. With the message you are composing open in a Message window, click the Message Flag button in the Standard toolbar to display the Flag for Follow Up dialog box (see Figure 36-7).
2. In the drop-down Flag To list box, choose a type of flag you want to use.
3. If you don't want to include a reminder date with the flag, leave the Due By list box set to None. If you want to include a calendar date, open the drop-down list under Due By to display a calendar; then select a desired date in that calendar. After you select a date, it appears in the Due By box.
4. Click OK. The chosen flag appears in the header area of the Message window.

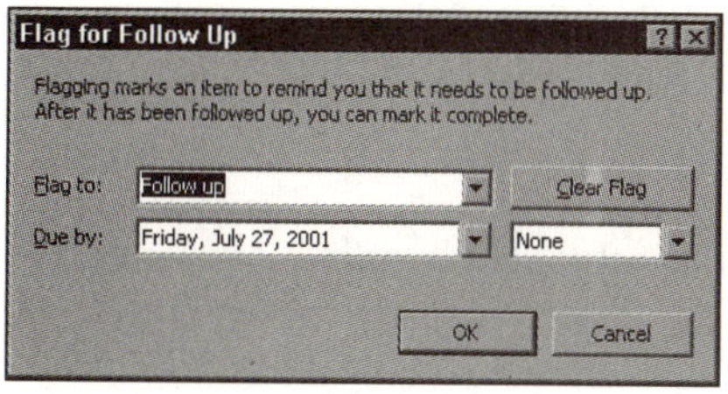

Figure 36-7: The Flag for Follow Up dialog box

When the message appears in the recipient's Inbox, the flag appears to the left of the From column, indicating the presence of a flagged message. Also, if you set a reminder, the recipient will see a message box referring to the flagged message on the date of the reminder if the message remains in the Inbox. Note that if the recipient moves the message to another folder or deletes the message, the reminder will not appear.

Searching for Messages in Your Inbox

When you have been using Outlook for any length of time, your Inbox can become crowded with dozens or even hundreds of old messages. If you need to find a previously received message weeks or months after you have read it, you need a fast, efficient way to search for that message. Fortunately, Outlook provides you with a search feature that makes quick work of finding old messages. To find a message, choose Tools ⇨ Find (or press Ctrl+E). A Look For text box appears above the Inbox.

Type the search text into the Look For box and then click Find Now. Outlook searches all the text in each message in your Inbox and displays all messages with any text that matches your search term. When you're done, click the X in the upper-right corner of the Find area to close that portion of the window.

You can also perform a more selective type of search using the Advanced Find feature. To do so, choose Tools ⇨ Advanced Find or press Ctrl+Shift+F. The Advanced Find dialog box appears.

Here you can search for words in the subject field only or in both the subject field and message body. You can search based on an entry in the From or the To field, and you can search based on a time that a message was sent, received, created, modified, or due. Additional options on the More Choices and Advanced tabs of this dialog box let you refine your search in other specific ways, such as by category (if you make use of the categorizing feature), by importance level, or even by the size of the message. Fill in any desired options in the dialog box and click Find Now to search for messages matching your chosen criteria.

Deleting Mail

As your Inbox fills with mail, you'll likely need to delete items that are no longer necessary. You can do this in a number of ways:

- You can select any unwanted item in the Inbox and press the Delete key or click the Delete button in the toolbar.
- To delete a contiguous group of messages, select the first message, hold down the Shift key, and select the last message to highlight the group. Then press the Delete key or click the Delete button in the toolbar.
- To delete a noncontiguous group of messages, select the first message and then hold down the Ctrl key as you select each additional message. When all the desired messages are selected, press the Delete key or click the Delete button in the toolbar.

Mail that you delete isn't permanently removed; rather, Outlook moves the deleted mail out of your Inbox and places it into your Deleted Items folder. This "holding tank" serves as a safety precaution, enabling you to recover deleted items by opening the Deleted Items folder, selecting any message, choosing Edit ⇨ Cut, moving to the Inbox, and choosing Edit ⇨ Paste to recover the message. If you are sure that you want to erase the deleted items (and recover disk space), choose Tools ⇨ Empty "Deleted Items" Folder from the menus.

Creating New Folders and Moving Mail to a Folder

At times, you may not want to delete mail, but you may not want it to clutter your Inbox, either. For example, you may want to keep all mail from a certain client or all mail related to a certain case in a separate location, where you can easily refer to that mail when needed. You can create custom folders dedicated to certain purposes, and you can move mail to those folders.

First, to create a new folder, make the Inbox visible and then choose File ⇨ Folder ⇨ New Folder (or press Ctrl+Shift+E). Doing so opens the Create New Folder dialog box (see Figure 36-8).

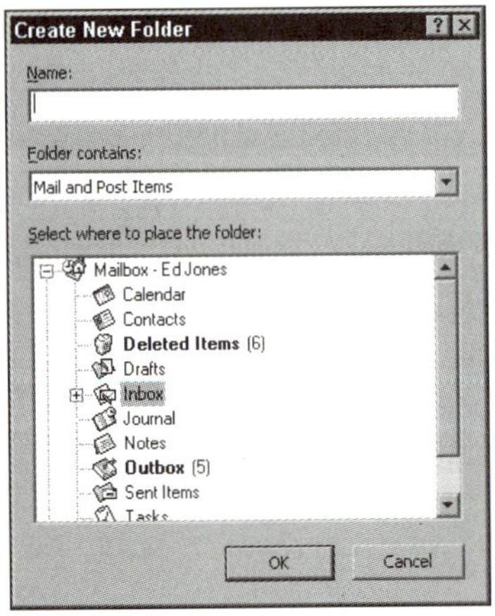

Figure 36-8: The Create New Folder dialog box

Make sure that the Folder Contains list box is set to Mail and Post Items, give the folder a name in the Name box, and click OK to create the folder. The new folder appears in the Folder List, underneath your Inbox. When the folder exists, you can move mail into the folder as desired.

To move mail to a folder, select one or more items to be moved in the Inbox. Then right-click the selection and choose Move to Folder from the shortcut menu that appears. In the Move Items dialog box that opens, select the folder where you want to move the items, and click OK.

Organizing Your Mailbox

You can organize your mailbox in a number of ways. One way is to create additional folders and categorize your mail by moving selected messages into those folders. (The steps for doing this are covered in the preceding section.) Another way to organize your mail is to use the handy Organize feature built in to Outlook. With this feature, you can organize your messages by folders, by colors, or by views.

To open the Organizer panel, make the Inbox folder visible and then click the Organize toolbar button, or choose Tools ⇨ Organize from the menu bar. The Organizer panel appears directly above your Inbox, as shown in Figure 36-9.

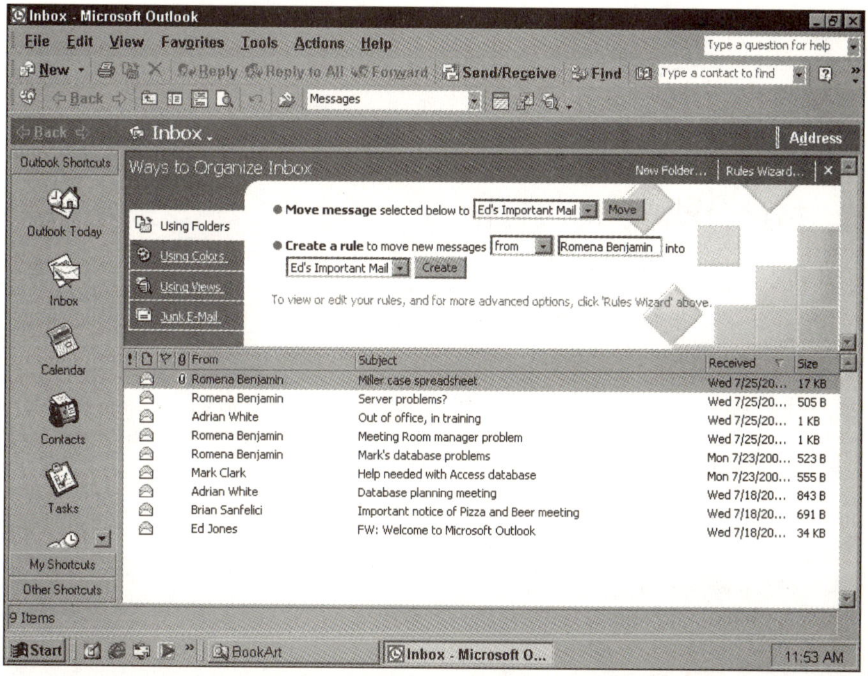

Figure 36-9: The Organizer panel helps you organize your mail in a variety of ways.

You can use the Organizer panel to move a selected message to a particular folder by selecting the message in the Inbox, selecting the desired folder beside Move Message Selected Below To, and clicking the Move button.

Another way to move messages is to create a *rule*, which gives Outlook a command to perform this task automatically. To create a rule to have Outlook move all messages from a particular sender into a given folder, select an existing message from that sender in the Inbox (or enter the sender in the box beside Create a Rule to Move New Messages From). Then select the desired folder in the list box under Create a Rule to Move New Messages From, and click the Create button. Figure 36-9 shows a rule being created that tells Outlook to move all new messages from Romena Benjamin into a folder called *Ed's Important Mail*.

You can also use colors to organize your mail. Select a message from a given sender in the Inbox and click Using Colors in the Organizer panel. You see options to make all messages from that sender appear in a particular color. For example, you might want all messages received from your law firm's managing partner to show up in red. The Using Views option in the Organizer panel changes how your messages appear in the Inbox. You can select messages from one of the following: messages with AutoPreview (which makes the first three lines of text appear with each message); last seven days; flagged for next seven days; by conversation topic; by sender; unread messages; sent to; or message timeline.

Finally, the Junk E-Mail option in the Organizer panel lets you apply a particular color to junk mail and to adult content mail. (Note that Outlook uses built-in filters to determine mail that may be classified as junk mail or adult content, but these filters may not be fully accurate.)

To close the Organizer panel when you're done with it, click the X in the upper-right corner of the panel.

TIP: You can quickly remove old messages from your mailbox by using the Mailbox Cleanup feature of Outlook 2002. Choose Tools ⇨ Mailbox Cleanup to display the dialog box used by this feature. For additional details, see "Using the Mailbox Cleanup feature" at the end of this chapter.

Using the Out of Office Assistant

When you know that you are going to be away from the office for any length of time — such as for a planned day off, a trip to another branch office, a court case, or a vacation — you can set the Out of Office Assistant to automatically send replies to anyone who sends you an e-mail, telling them that you are out of the office. (For this feature to work, you must be connected to a Microsoft Exchange Server on a network; obviously, if you are using a standalone machine with a dial-up connection to the Internet, you can't use this feature when no one is around to turn on the computer and connect to the Internet.) To automatically reply to others when you plan to be away from the office, simply perform these steps just before leaving your office:

1. Choose Tools ⇨ Out of Office Assistant to display the Out of Office Assistant dialog box (see Figure 36-10).

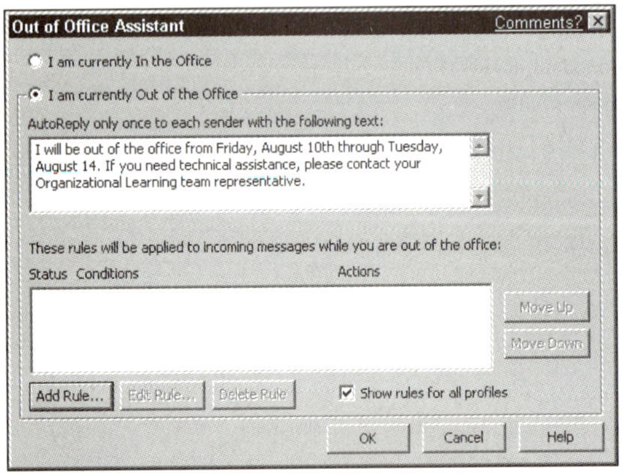

Figure 36-10: The Out of Office Assistant dialog box lets you quickly define automatic replies that are sent to others who send you mail when you are away from the office.

2. Click the I Am Currently Out of the Office option.
3. In the space beneath AutoReply Only Once to Each Sender with the Following Text, type the text of your desired reply and click OK.

You can now shut down Outlook and leave the office; the information used to reply to incoming messages is stored on the Exchange Server. While you are gone, all your incoming messages will be stored in your Inbox on the server. When you return to the office and restart Outlook, you will see a dialog box reminding you that the Out of Office Assistant is currently on and asking whether you would like to turn it off. To do so, click Yes.

Using the Address Book

The Address Book used by Outlook is actually a combination of address books provided by Outlook, Microsoft Exchange Server, or Internet directory services, depending on how your copy of Outlook is configured. You use the Address Book to look up and select names and corresponding e-mail addresses when you address messages. When you type a name into the To, the CC, or the BCC box, Outlook checks whether the name that you typed matches a name contained in the Address Book. If it finds a match, the corresponding mail address is used to send the message. If Outlook doesn't find a match, it prompts you for further information by displaying the Check Names dialog box. At any time, you can view the Address Book by choosing Tools ⇨ Address Book from the menus.

Several types of address books can be shown in the Address Book dialog box:

- **Global Address List:** The Global Address List exists if you are on a network that is using Microsoft Exchange Server as its mail server. Exchange Server contains all network user and distribution list e-mail addresses within your firm or organization. The Exchange Server Administrator creates and updates this address book. The Global Address List may also contain public folder e-mail addresses.
- **Internet Directory Services:** Internet Directory Services are used to find e-mail addresses that are not in a local address book or a firmwide directory such as the Global Address List. You need an Internet connection to view this type of address book, unless the Internet directory is already part of your firm or organization's network.
- **Outlook Address Book:** The Outlook Address Book is created automatically by Outlook. It contains the e-mail addresses for all contacts in your Contacts folder (see the following chapter for details on creating and editing contacts). As the next chapter shows, you use the Contacts folder to store all types of information about your contacts, such as e-mail addresses, telephone and fax numbers, street addresses, and Web page addresses. When you update an e-mail address in a contact, the Outlook Address Book is updated automatically.
- **Personal Address Book:** A Personal Address Book can be used to store group lists that you use regularly, such as the members of your favorite golf foursome or everyone on your bowling team. E-mail addresses of your personal contacts can be stored in your Contacts folder (the recommended location) or in the Exchange Personal Address Book, if your Exchange administrator has your system configured to allow Personal Address Books to be stored on the Exchange Server.

When you click the To button within a new Message window to display the Select Names dialog box, you gain access to any and all names and addresses stored in your own Contacts list, in a Personal Address List that you've created or in the Global Address List (if your network is using Exchange Server).

You can view additional details about any entry in the Address Book by double-clicking any name in the Address Book. A Properties window appears, containing the person's name, address type, and type of network used to connect with the person.

You can send a message to anyone listed in the Address Book by selecting the name in the list and choosing File ⇨ New Message in the Address Book window.

Subscribing to and Participating in Legal Newsgroups

Many attorneys and paralegals find *Internet newsgroups* to be a valuable resource. You can use Outlook to participate in Internet newsgroups that have a legal slant (or any other newsgroups, for that matter). Outlook makes use of the Outlook Newsreader (which is actually a component of Internet Explorer) when providing access to Internet newsgroups. You need to have Internet Explorer installed on your computer (it is normally installed along with Outlook, if it isn't already on your computer as part of the Windows operating system), and you need to have a connection to the Internet.

Gaining access to a newsgroup

Assuming that you already have Internet Explorer and an Internet connection, use the following steps to gain access to Internet newsgroups:

1. In Outlook, choose View ⇨ Go To ⇨ News to display the Outlook Newsreader.
2. Choose Tools ⇨ Accounts and click the News tab in the dialog box that appears. Depending on your setup of Outlook and your mail provider, you may see a wizard asking you for a name, an e-mail address, and the name of the news server to which you want to subscribe. After entering such information (if prompted), the Outlook Newsreader displays a list of your news accounts, similar to the example shown in Figure 36-11.

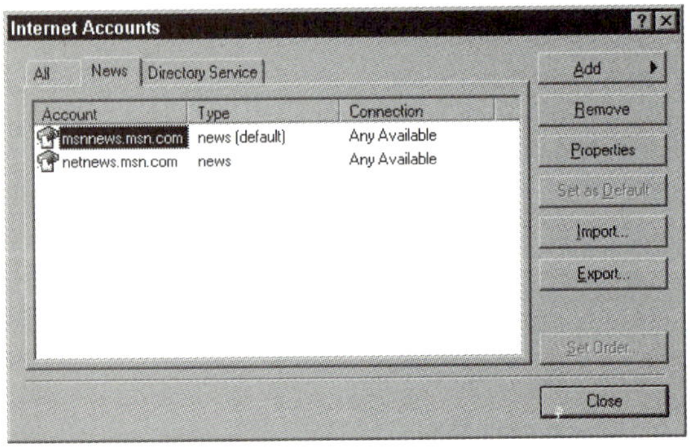

Figure 36-11: A list of available news accounts shown in the Outlook Newsreader

3. Click the Add button and choose News from the pop-up submenu to display the first dialog box of the Internet Connection Wizard.
4. In the Display Name box, type a name that you want your messages to post under when you post to newsgroups. Then click Next to display the second dialog box of the Internet Connection Wizard.
5. Other individuals can reply to your newsgroup messages by posting to the newsgroup or sending you e-mail. Enter the e-mail address you want people to use to reply to your postings if they

choose to send e-mail, and click Next to display the third dialog box of the Internet Connection Wizard.

6. In this dialog box, enter the name of the news server you want to use in the News (NNTP Server) box. If you are using a private news server that requires you to log on with a user name and password, check the box next to My News Server Requires Me to Log On, click Next, and enter a logon name and password in the dialog box that appears. Click Next to display the final dialog box of the wizard.

The final dialog box of the wizard simply advises you that you have completed the process of adding a newsgroup. Click Finish in this dialog box to return to the Internet Accounts dialog box that lists your news servers, and click Close in that dialog box to return to the Outlook Newsreader.

Subscribing to a newsgroup

After you gain access to a particular newsgroup, you set up *subscriptions* to that group. Use the following steps to do so:

1. In Outlook, choose View ⇨ Go To ⇨ News to display the Outlook Newsreader.
2. In the Folders pane at the left, select the news server that provides the newsgroups to which you want to subscribe. If you have never accessed this news server, you will see a dialog box stating that you are not subscribed to any newsgroups and asking whether you would like to see a list of newsgroups. Click Yes and Outlook will download a list of available newsgroups. (With a dial-up connection to the Internet, this downloading may take a few moments.) Eventually, you will see a list of available newsgroup subscriptions, similar to the example shown in Figure 36-12.

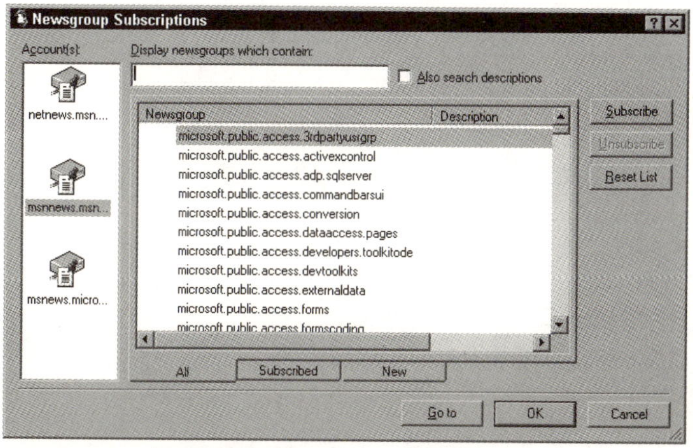

Figure 36-12: A list of available newsgroup subscriptions from the Microsoft Public newsgroup news server

3. Scroll down the list until you locate the newsgroup to which you want to subscribe. (You can narrow the available selection by entering a search term in the Display Newsgroups Which Contain text box.) Select the desired newsgroup in the list and click the Subscribe button. After subscribing to your desired newsgroups, click OK to close the dialog box.

TIP: If you work within the computer-support area of a law firm or legal organization, you may find the LawNet-SIG-Microsoft newsgroup to be well worth your time. This newsgroup consists of an independent network of legal automation professionals and is maintained by LawNet, Inc. For details on joining the newsgroup, go to `www.peertopeer.org` and click the Special Interest Groups link.

Participating in a newsgroup

After you've subscribed to one or more newsgroups, those newsgroups appear in the Folders pane on the left side of the Outlook Newsreader. Remember, you can launch the Outlook Newsreader at any time by choosing View ⇨ Go To ⇨ News from the Outlook menus.

To access any newsgroup, select it in the Folders pane. (If you are using a dial-up connection and are not online, Windows Dial-Up Networking displays a dialog box prompting you to connect to the Internet by means of your particular Internet service provider.) After a short delay, you will see a list of message headers in the upper-right pane. You can select any message header to view the message in the lower-right pane, similar to the example shown in Figure 36-13.

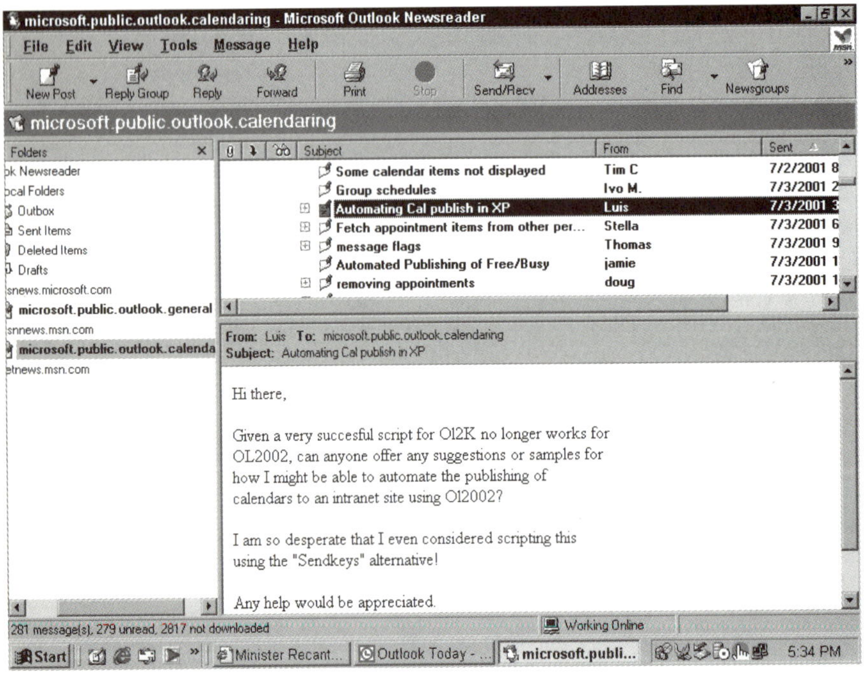

Figure 36-13: A message from a newsgroup viewed in the Outlook Newsreader

After you select a message, you can use any of the toolbar buttons in the Outlook Newsreader to participate in the newsgroup. You can use the buttons for the following purposes:

- **New Post:** Create a new message that you want to post to the newsgroup.
- **Reply Group:** Post a reply to a selected message that will be available to all participants in the newsgroup.

- **Reply:** Send your reply to the selected message as an e-mail to the member of the newsgroup who posted the original message.
- **Forward:** Forward a selected message as an e-mail to another individual.
- **Print:** Print the selected message.
- **Stop:** Stop sending and receiving messages.
- **Send/Receive:** Send messages in your Outbox waiting to be sent, and receive messages awaiting delivery to you from the newsgroup.
- **Address:** Display a dialog box showing your contacts' e-mail addresses in Outlook.
- **Find:** Search for a message in the newsgroup.
- **Newsgroups:** Display the Newsgroup Subscriptions dialog box (refer to Figure 36-12), in which you can subscribe to another list provided by a news server.

The overall topic of setting up and maintaining subscriptions to Internet newsgroups can get more involved than this book can possibly cover. If you want more detailed information, you may want to refer to a book dedicated to the use of Internet Explorer, such as Hungry Minds' *Internet Explorer 5.5 for Windows For Dummies,* by Doug Lowe. Also useful would be *Outlook 2002 For Dummies,* by Bill Dyszel.

Creating and Using Distribution Lists

After you've saved a number of contacts in your Contacts folder (or if you already have a list of names and e-mail addresses stored on a network mail server), you can create and use distribution lists based on these contacts or addresses. A *distribution list* is any prearranged group of mail recipients to whom you regularly send an e-mail message.

NOTE: If you are upgrading to Outlook 2002 from Outlook 97 or Outlook 98 and you've used distribution lists before, you should examine the following steps. Outlook 2002 (and Outlook 2000) use a different procedure for creating distribution lists than earlier versions of Outlook.

Creating a distribution list

Here are the steps you can use to create a distribution list:

1. With the Contacts pane visible in the Outlook window, choose Actions ⇨ New Distribution List (or press Ctrl+Shift+L). The Distribution List window appears.
2. Click the Select Members button to display the Select Members dialog box (see Figure 36-14).
3. In the Select Members dialog box, double-click each desired name or click a name and click Members to add the name to your distribution list. (If you are using Outlook on a network with a mail server, you can use the Show Names From The list box at the upper-right to alternate between your own contacts and the Global Address List stored on the server.) When done adding names using the Select Members dialog box, click OK.

TIP: If you have a large number of contacts, you may want to use the Find button in the Select Members dialog box to search for a contact name, rather than rely on the scroll bar.

---

4. If you want to add a name that's not in your Contacts list or on a network mail server address list, click the Add New button in the Distribution List window. This displays the Add New Member dialog box (see Figure 36-15).

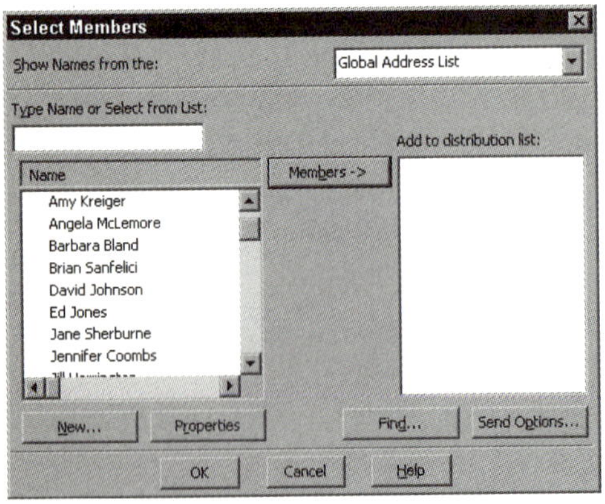

Figure 36-14: The Select Members dialog box lets you add names from your Contacts list (or from an address book on a network mail server) to a distribution list.

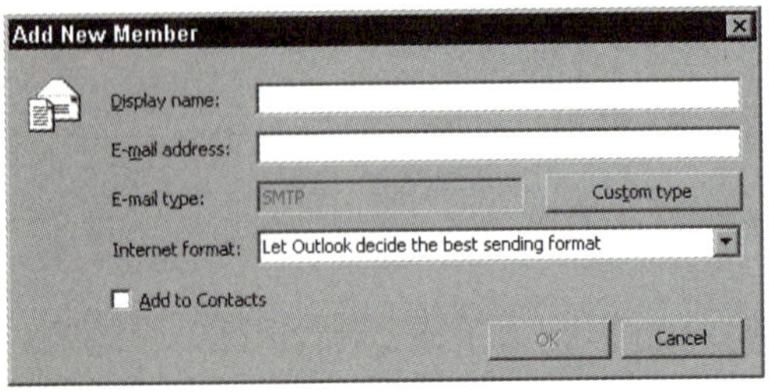

Figure 36-15: The Add New Member dialog box lets you add distribution list members that do not exist in your list of contacts (or in any address list stored on a network mail server).

5. Enter a name and e-mail address in the Display Name and E-mail Address boxes. If desired, use the Internet Format list box to choose plain text or rich text format for messages sent to this member of the distribution list. (If you don't make a choice, Outlook makes its best guess based on the type of e-mail address.) Check the Add to Contacts check box if you want to add the member to your existing list of contacts, and click OK.

6. Use the Name box in the Distribution List window to give your distribution list a name.

7. Click the Categories button (at the lower left) and assign one or more categories by checking any desired boxes in the Categories dialog box that appears.

8. If you want to keep the distribution list private from others on a network, check the Private check box at the lower right.

9. Choose Save and Close in the Standard toolbar of the Distribution List window to save the distribution list to your Contacts folder.

Using a distribution list

After you create a distribution list, it appears in your Contacts folder under the name that you assigned to the list. You can address a single message to everyone on the list by opening a new

Message window, clicking the To button, choosing Contacts in the Show Names list box of the Select Names dialog box, and selecting your list in the Name box.

TIP: If you want to keep the e-mail addresses of all the members of your distribution list private (from one another) when sending the message, add the distribution list to the BCC field of the message, rather than to the To field of the message.

To modify a distribution list, locate the distribution list in your Contacts folder and open it to display the Distribution List window. You can make the desired changes and then click Save and Close to save the changes.

To delete a distribution list that is no longer needed, right-click it in your Contacts folder and choose Delete from the shortcut menu that appears.

Adding E-Mail Accounts

Prior versions of Outlook require multiple profiles to utilize different mail services. For example, if you use Outlook 97 or Outlook 2000 on a network with Exchange Server and your network also provides Internet access, you can't use the same Outlook profile to access a Web-based e-mail account (such as Microsoft Hotmail). Outlook 2002 overcomes this limitation by providing support for multiple mail accounts using a single Outlook profile. To add an additional mail account to your existing Outlook profile, use the following steps:

1. Choose Tools ⇨ E-mail Accounts to display the E-mail Accounts dialog box.
2. Click Add a New E-mail Account and then click Next to display the E-mail Accounts Server Type dialog box.
3. In this dialog box, choose the type of mail server that you want to add. (If you want to add a Web-based e-mail service such as Microsoft Hotmail or Yahoo! Mail, choose HTTP in the dialog box.) Then click Next.
4. The next dialog box that appears will vary, depending on your choice in the preceding dialog box. In all cases, you will be asked for information appropriate to your new mail service. Enter the information requested by the dialog box, such as the server name or location, your name, e-mail address, user name, and password, if requested. Then click Next.
5. In the final dialog box, which acknowledges that you have successfully set up an additional e-mail account, click Finish.

After you add an additional e-mail account to Outlook, the new account appears as an icon in the Outlook Bar, and an Inbox for the account is visible in the Folder List. Figure 36-16 shows an example of Outlook that has been configured for two e-mail accounts — one from an Exchange Server on an internal network and the other from a Web-based e-mail account, using Microsoft Hotmail. Note that the Outlook Bar contains two Inbox icons — one at the top, which corresponds to the Exchange Server on the network, and another beneath the first, which corresponds to the Web-based Hotmail account.

When you have multiple e-mail accounts set up in Outlook and you address a new message, by default Outlook uses the account that was set up during Outlook installation to send the message. If you are replying to a message, Outlook normally uses the account to which the message was originally sent. You can change these defaults by choosing the desired account to send any message from the Accounts menu that appears in the toolbar of the Message window. For example, the new message in Figure 36-16 shows the options available to the Outlook user described in Figure 36-17.

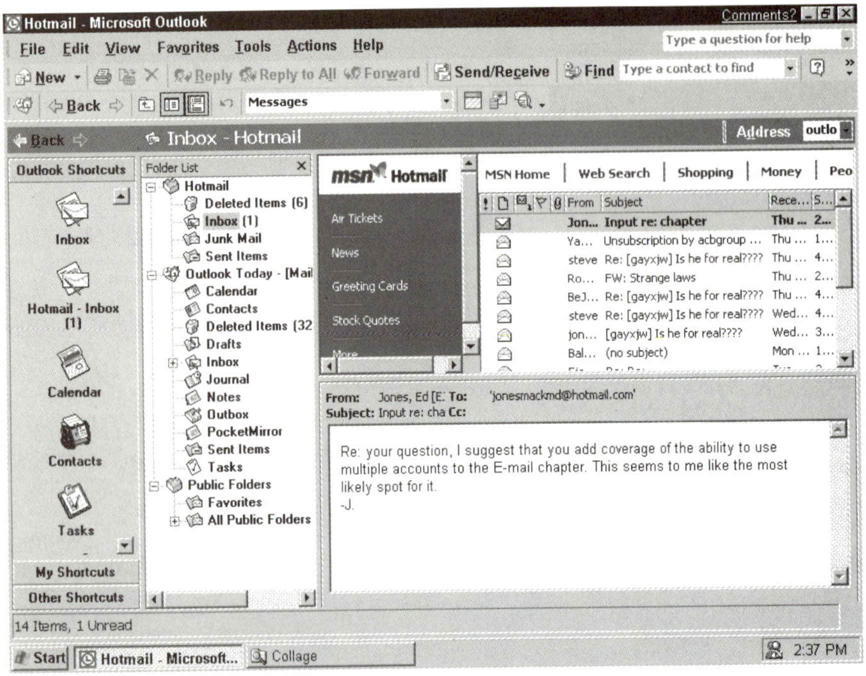

Figure 36-16: Outlook configured to support two e-mail accounts

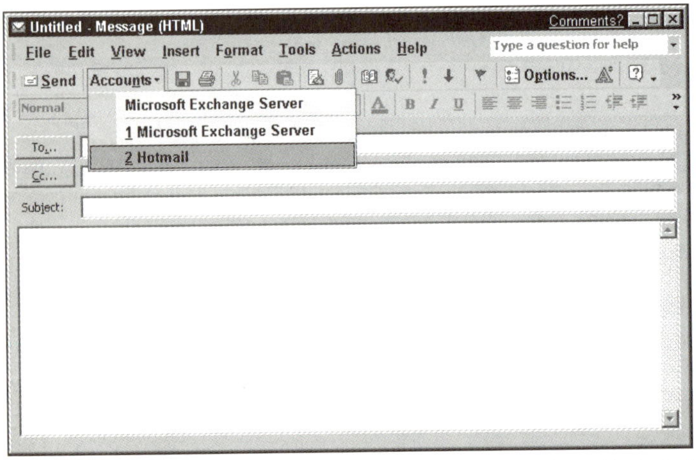

Figure 36-17: When you have more than one e-mail account configured in Outlook, the Accounts menu of the Message window can be used to select an e-mail account that should be used to send a message.

Using the Mailbox Cleanup Feature

As time goes by, your mailbox is likely to fill with messages that you have no need to save. You can manually delete old messages, but there is a faster way to keep your mailbox at a reasonable size. Outlook 2002 has a new feature, the Mailbox Cleanup feature, which automatically deletes old messages or messages over a certain size (in terms of disk space). To use the Mailbox Cleanup feature, choose Tools ⇨ Mailbox Cleanup to display the Mailbox Cleanup dialog box.

You can display a dialog box that shows the size of your mailbox in terms of disk space by clicking the Click Here button near the top of the dialog box. You can use the AutoArchive button to automatically move items older than a set number of days (the default being 90 days) to the archive file on your hard drive, thus freeing up space on your network's mail server. And you can click the Empty button to quickly empty your Deleted Items folder.

Summary

This chapter has covered the variety of ways in which you can use e-mail messaging features of Outlook. In this chapter, you learned the following:

- You can use the Inbox folder in Outlook to read, compose, and manage your e-mail.
- You can attach files, such as Word documents or Excel worksheets, to e-mail messages that you send from within Outlook.
- You can format the text of an e-mail message in a variety of ways.
- You can change the importance level or the sensitivity level of a message, to draw the sender's attention to the message.
- You can create folders in Outlook and store your mail in those folders.
- You can use the Outlook Newsreader to join and participate in newsgroups on the Internet.
- You can create distribution lists to easily send the same message to a group of recipients.

The next chapter details how you can manage your personal and business contacts using Outlook.

Chapter 37

Working with Outlook Contacts

In This Chapter

- ♦ Creating a contact
- ♦ Editing or deleting contacts
- ♦ Finding contacts
- ♦ Viewing your contacts
- ♦ Printing your contacts
- ♦ Communicating with a contact
- ♦ Importing contacts from other software

IN ANY LEGAL ENVIRONMENT, YOUR contacts are a vital part of your workflow process. During the course of a typical day, you may need to call a co-worker to schedule a meeting, talk to an attorney or a paralegal about a citation needed for a motion being prepared, find the fax number of an out-of-town law firm for a referral, or look up the mailing address of your daughter living on campus at the state university. All these individuals are contacts of one kind or another. Your contacts are the people and businesses with whom you need to communicate. Outlook provides a Contacts folder, through which you can manage your list of contacts.

In Outlook, a *contact* is an individual or organization stored in your Contacts folder as a single entry consisting of a name, an address, a phone number, an e-mail address, and other related information. When you click the Contacts icon in the Outlook Bar, the Contacts pane appears in the Information Viewer area of the Outlook window, as shown in Figure 37-1.

After you store your contacts in Outlook, you can use the information elsewhere within Outlook for a variety of purposes. For example, you can send an e-mail message to a contact, schedule a meeting with one or more contacts, create a letter in Microsoft Word containing the name and address of a contact, create a journal entry based on a phone conversation with a contact, and so on.

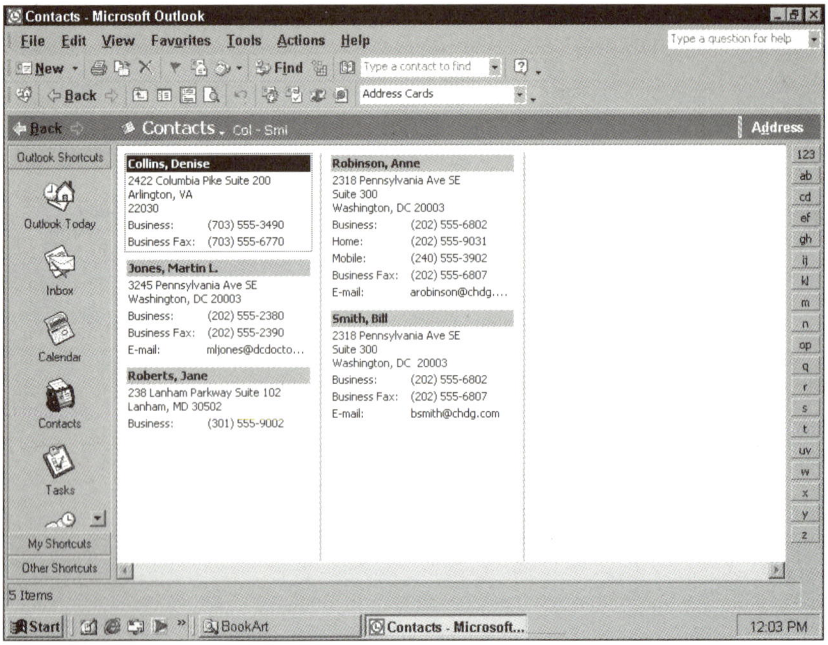

Figure 37-1: Contacts viewed within Outlook

Creating a Contact

You can create new contacts in Outlook by performing the following steps:

1. Click the Contacts icon in the Outlook Bar.
2. Click the New Contact button on the Standard toolbar, or choose Actions ⇨ New Contact from the menus, or press Ctrl+N. A new Contact window appears, with the General tab displayed, as shown in Figure 37-2.

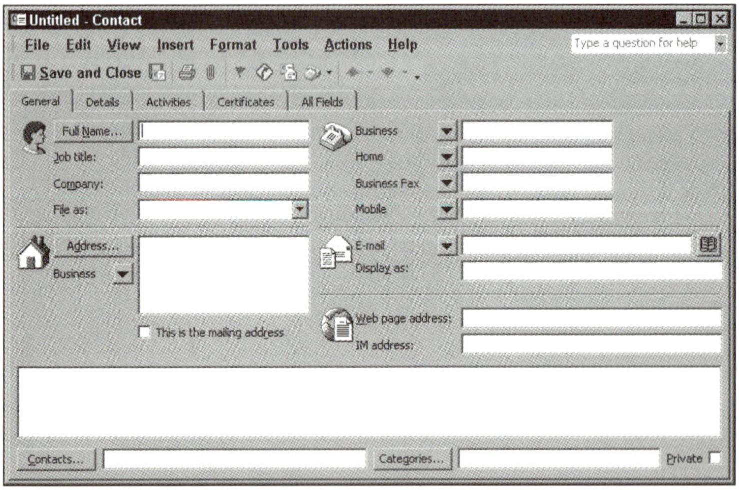

Figure 37-2: The General tab of the Contact window enables you to add general information about a contact.

3. In the Full Name text box, you can enter the contact's name, in the order of first name followed by last name. Alternatively, click the Full Name button to display the Check Full Name dialog box (see Figure 37-3). In that dialog box, you can enter the first, middle, and last names, the contact title, and any desired suffix. Click OK when done to close this dialog box and return to the Contact window.

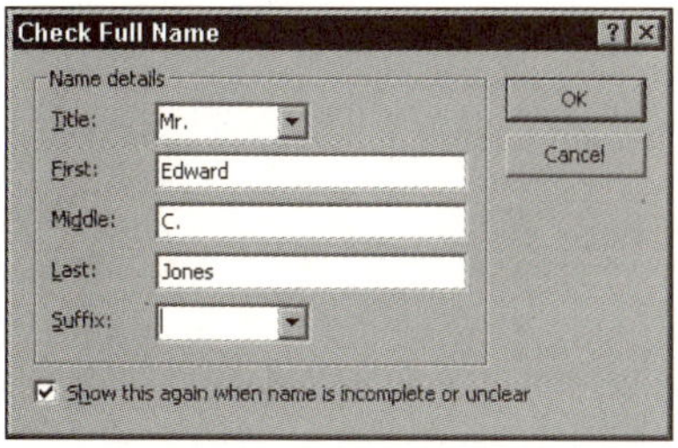

Figure 37-3: The Check Full Name dialog box lets you enter a title, the first, middle, and last names, and a suffix.

4. Enter any desired information in the Job Title and Company fields.
5. In the File As drop-down list, choose a method that you prefer to use to file the contact. You can select last name first, first name first, or the name of the company if you made an entry in the Company box. For most users of Outlook, the default choice of last name first works best.
6. In the Address box, enter an address and use the drop-down arrow to indicate whether the address applies as the contact's business address, home address, or other. (Alternatively, click the Address button to open a dialog box in which you can enter the street address, city, state or province, and postal code separately.) You can enter up to three addresses for a contact by using the drop-down arrow to select a different category (Business, Home, or Other) and then entering another address.
7. Using the Phone drop-down lists, choose the type of phone number and enter the number in the corresponding fields. You can enter up to four different phone numbers, and the drop-down lists let you choose from up to nineteen types, including business, home, business fax, home fax, mobile, pager, car, company, and other.
8. Enter one or more e-mail addresses in the E-mail address box. (You can enter up to three e-mail addresses by choosing E-mail, E-mail 2, or E-mail 3 in the drop-down list and entering the address.)

NOTE: When you enter multiple e-mail addresses for a contact, Outlook uses the first e-mail address as the default in the Message window when you create new mail based on that contact. You can double-click the contact's name in the To field of the Message window and then choose an alternative name from the properties dialog box that appears.

9. In the Web Page Address box, you can enter the Web page address for the contact or the contact's organization.
10. Use the Comment box near the bottom of the window to enter any desired description or other necessary comments about the contact.
11. If you have Internet connectivity, you can use the IM Address box to enter an Instant Messaging Internet address.

12. If desired, click the Categories button and select one or more categories for the contact from the Categories dialog box that appears (see Figure 37-4). This option can prove useful if you later want to view your contacts by category.

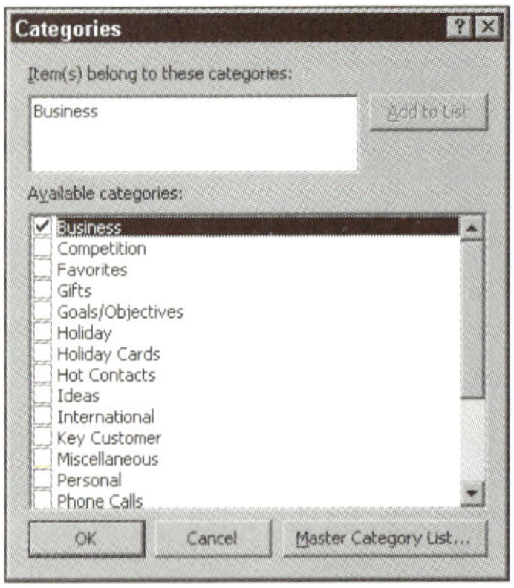

Figure 37-4: The Categories dialog box

13. If desired, use the Details tab (see Figure 37-5) to enter additional details, such as a contact's nickname, a spouse's name, a birthday, or an anniversary.
14. Click the Save and Close button if you don't need to add another contact, or choose File ⇨ Save and New if you want to save the contact and add another contact.

TIP: If you want to add another contact located at the same company address, choose Actions ⇨ New Contact from Same Company from the menus of the New Contact window. A new contact window will appear, with the same company name and address as the preceding contact.

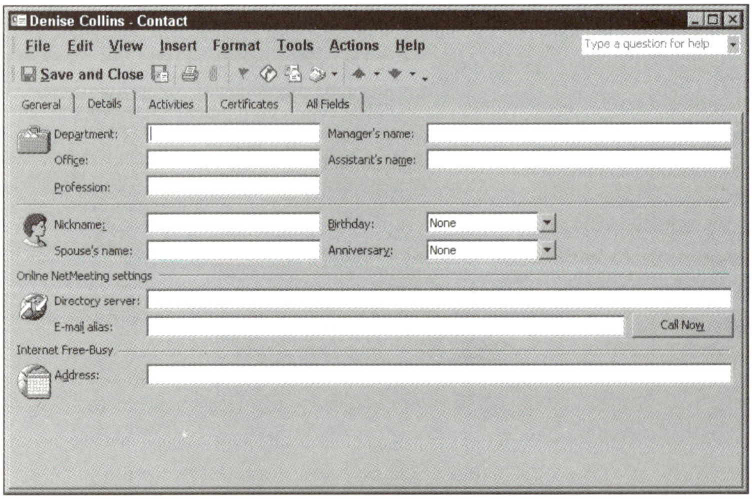

Figure 37-5: The Details tab of the Contact dialog box

Editing or Deleting Contacts

You can open any contact for viewing or editing by double-clicking that contact or by highlighting it with the mouse or the cursor keys and pressing Enter. Using either method, the contact appears in a Contact window. You can edit any of the desired fields; when you click the Save and Close button in the toolbar, Outlook saves the changes.

To delete a contact, first click the header of the contact to select it. Then press the Delete key or click the Delete button in the toolbar. Keep in mind that you can remove a number of contacts simultaneously by selecting all the unwanted contacts (hold down the Ctrl key as you click the header of each contact). You also can select a contiguous group of contacts by selecting the first contact, holding down the Shift key, and selecting the last contact in the group. With all the unwanted contacts selected, press the Delete key or click the Delete button in the toolbar.

Finding Contacts

When your contacts list becomes large (and trust us, we've seen some attorneys with more than a thousand contacts stored in Outlook), you will need a way to search for a given contact. You can easily do so using the Find a Contact box in the toolbar. With the Contacts folder visible, click the Find toolbar button or choose Tools ⇨ Find (or press Ctrl+E) to display the Find a Contact box within the toolbar. In the Find a Contact box, type all or part of the name of the desired contact. You can enter a partial name, a first name or last name, an e-mail address, or a company name. Press Enter after typing an entry, and the Contacts folder will display all records found that match your search. You can click the Clear link in the upper-right portion of the Contacts folder to restore your view of all your contacts.

Viewing Your Contacts

By default, Outlook displays your contacts using the Address Cards view, unless you've changed the view previously while using Outlook. (Refer back to Figure 37-1 to see the Address Cards view.) You can also view your contacts using the Detailed Address Cards view. This view is similar to the Address Cards view but shows more details for each contact. Choose View ⇨ Current View and then choose Detailed Address Cards from the submenu that appears to display this view. Figure 37-6 shows an example of the Detailed Address Cards view.

Alternatively, you can choose to view your contacts in the form of a phone listing. To do this, choose View ⇨ Current View and then choose Phone List from the submenu that appears. Figure 37-7 shows an example of contacts displayed as a phone list.

Keep in mind that the view you use to display your contacts also determines how they will appear when printed.

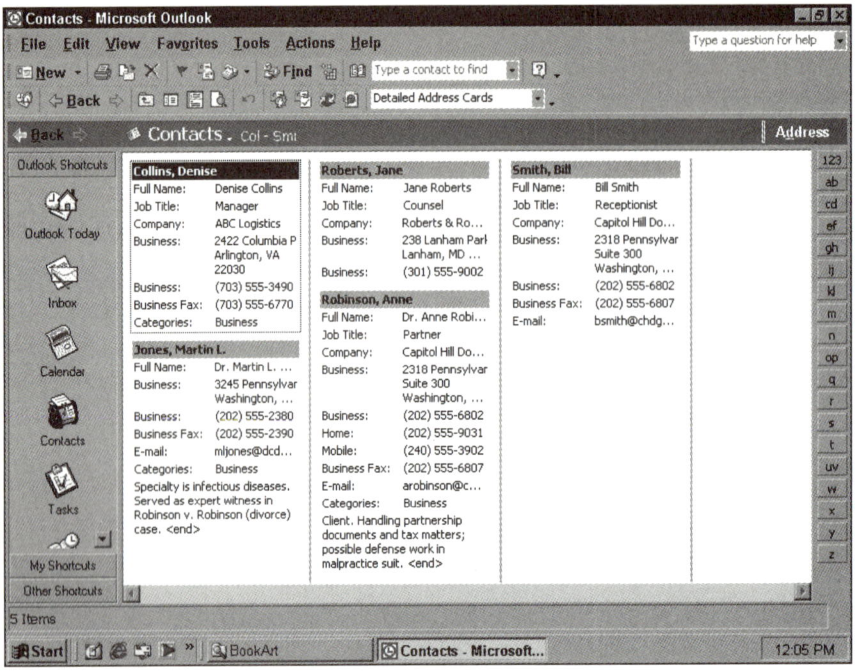

Figure 37-6: Contacts shown using the Detailed Address Cards view

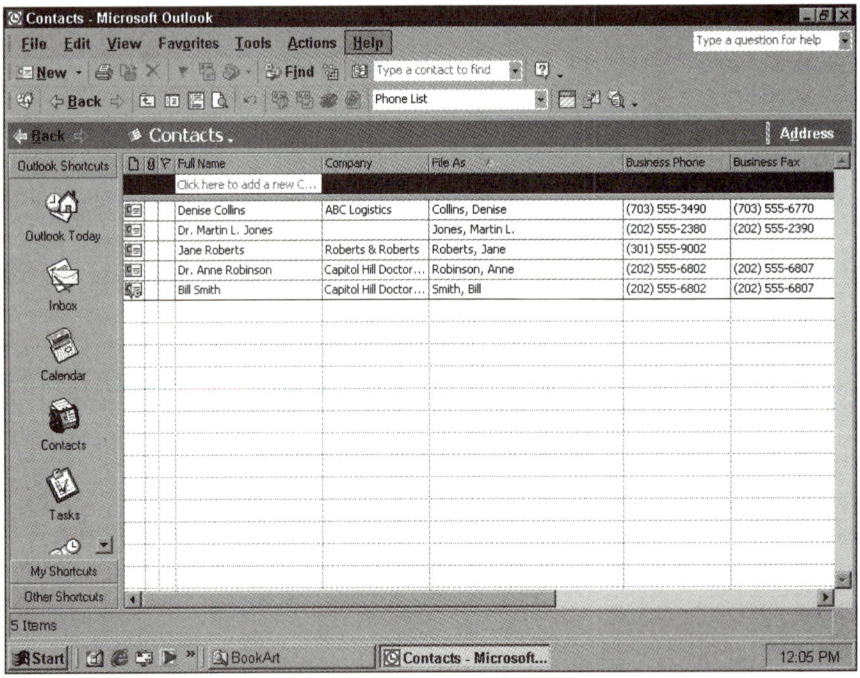

Figure 37-7: Contacts displayed as a phone list

> **Where are my contacts stored?**
>
> The answer to that question depends on your setup of Outlook. If you are using Outlook in a standalone mode, with e-mail connectivity provided by your Internet service provider, your contacts are stored on your hard drive. If you are using a network with Exchange Server as your mail server, your contacts are stored on the Exchange Server. (If you travel with a laptop that's connected to your network when you're at the office, you can download contacts to your laptop for offline use by choosing Tools ⇨ Send/Receive ⇨ Download Address Book. Any changes are synchronized with the Exchange Server when you are back in the office.)

Printing Your Contacts

To provide a useful printed directory of your contacts, you can print the contacts using any of the three views described in the preceding section. The printout will resemble the view that you see on the screen. To print your contacts, use View ⇨ Current View to select the desired view (Address Cards, Detailed Address Cards, or Phone List) and then choose File ⇨ Print, click the Print icon in the toolbar, or press Ctrl+P. Before printing, you can use the File ⇨ Print Preview command to see an on-screen representation of the way your contacts will be printed. Choose File ⇨ Print Preview. If you want to enlarge the image to full size, use the Zoom button that appears in the preview window. Figure 37-8 shows an example of contacts shown in a preview window.

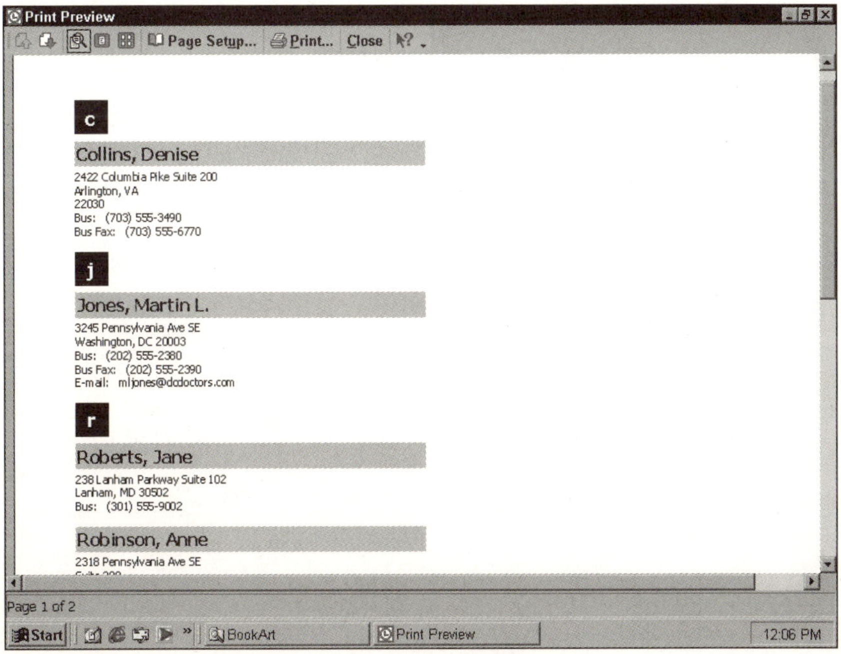

Figure 37-8: Contacts displayed using the Print Preview command

Communicating with a Contact

One of the more powerful aspects of Outlook's type of contact management is the capability it gives you, assuming that you are using Outlook as your e-mail client, to communicate with contacts in a number of ways. You can schedule meetings with contacts, send an e-mail to a contact, assign a task to a contact, or write a letter using the name and address of a contact. You can use Outlook this way whether you are a solo practitioner using Outlook with your Internet service provider or you serve as one member of a multinational law firm with hundreds of Outlook users.

NOTE: To send e-mail, schedule meetings, or assign tasks to contacts, you must have Outlook e-mail connectivity configured. You cannot perform these tasks if you are using Outlook in its no-mail configuration.

Sending e-mail to a contact

To send e-mail to a contact, right-click the desired contact in the Contacts folder and choose New Message to Contact from the shortcut menu. A new Message window appears, with the e-mail address of the contact automatically placed in the To field. Fill in a desired subject in the Subject field, type your message into the Message box, click Insert ⇨ File if you want to add any attachments, and click Send.

CROSS-REFERENCE: For more specifics on sending mail, see Chapter 36.

Scheduling an appointment with a contact

You can create an appointment with a contact and automatically store that appointment in your Outlook Calendar. To create an appointment with a contact, right-click the desired contact in the Contacts folder and choose New Appointment with Contact from the shortcut menu. An Appointment window appears, and you can fill in the subject, location, date and time, and other information about the appointment. When you're done, click Save and Close in the Appointment window to store the appointment in your Outlook Calendar.

Scheduling a meeting with a contact

The process of scheduling meetings is similar to that of scheduling appointments; however, you must have e-mail capability to schedule meetings, and the contact must have a valid e-mail address. To schedule a meeting, right-click the desired contact in the Contacts folder and choose New Meeting Request to Contact from the shortcut menu. A new Meeting window appears, in which you can fill in the subject, location, date and time, and other information about the meeting. When done, click Save and Close in the Meeting window to store the appointment in your Outlook Calendar.

CROSS-REFERENCE: For more specifics on creating appointments, scheduling meetings, and assigning tasks, see Chapter 38. For more specifics on creating journal entries, see Chapter 39.

Assigning a task to a contact

You can use Outlook to delegate tasks to contacts. Because contacts are notified of tasks via e-mail, you must be using Outlook as your e-mail client to delegate tasks. To assign a task to a contact, right-click the desired contact in the Contacts folder and choose New Task for a Contact from the shortcut menu. In the Task window that appears, enter a desired subject, a due date, the status, and any other needed information; then click Send.

Creating a journal entry based on a contact

You can create a new journal entry in your Outlook Journal based on the name of an existing contact. To do this, right-click the desired contact in the Contacts folder and choose New Journal Entry for a Contact from the shortcut menu. A Journal Entry window appears, and you can fill in the subject, location, date and time, and other information about the journal entry. When done, click Save and Close in the Journal Entry window to store the journal entry in your Outlook Journal.

Writing a letter to a contact

You can use a Letter Wizard built in to Outlook to create a letter addressed to the name and address of a particular contact (assuming that you are using Microsoft Word as your word processor). To send a letter to a contact, select the desired contact in the Contacts folder and then choose Actions ⇨ New Letter to Contact. In a moment, a document window opens in Microsoft Word and the first dialog box of the Letter Wizard appears. Follow the directions in the dialog boxes of the wizard to insert the contact name, the address, and optional greeting, closing, and signature lines into the letter.

Dialing a contact's phone number

If your computer has a modem attached, you can dial the phone number of a contact. To dial a contact, select the desired contact in the Contacts folder, choose Actions ⇨ Call Contact, and then choose the desired phone number from the submenu that appears. Alternatively, you can click the Autodialer button on the Standard toolbar and choose the desired phone number from the drop-down list, or you can right-click the contact and choose Call Contact from the shortcut menu that appears. From the next menu, choose New Call. The New Call dialog box appears, as shown in Figure 37-9.

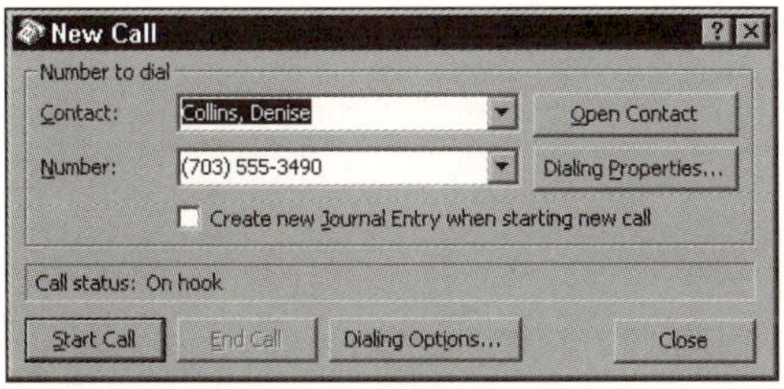

Figure 37-9: The New Call dialog box

Click the Start Call button to dial the phone using your modem. You can then pick up your phone and click the Talk button in the Call Status dialog box that appears. When you click the Talk button, the modem disengages, and you can carry on your conversation with your contact.

Importing Contacts from Other Software

If you are moving to Outlook from another personal information manager, chances are that you can import your existing list of contacts from your older program. Outlook can import data from a variety of programs, including ACT! (versions 2.0, 3.*x*, and 4.0), ECCO (versions 2.0, 3.0, and 4.0), and Lotus Organizer (versions 4.*x*, 5.*x*, and 97). You can also import contacts stored in Access databases, dBASE database files, FoxPro database files, and Excel worksheet files; from Microsoft Schedule+ versions 1.0 and 7.0; or as comma-delimited or tab-delimited text files. Outlook provides an import/export wizard that steps you through the process of importing information from other software packages. Use these steps to start the Import and Export Wizard:

1. From the menus, choose File ⇨ Import and Export. The first Import and Export Wizard dialog box appears (see Figure 37-10).

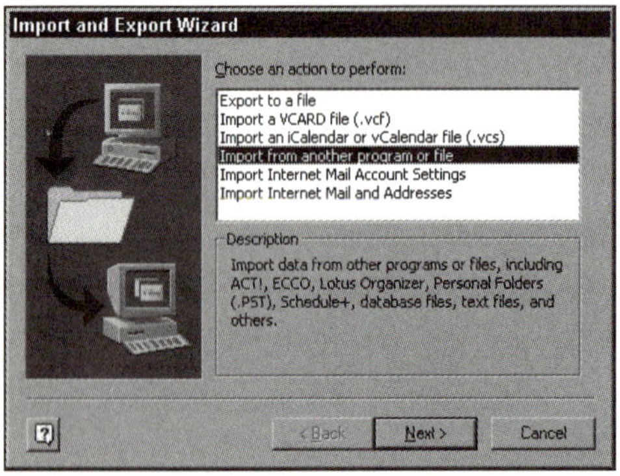

Figure 37-10: The first Import and Export dialog box

2. In the list, click Import from Another Program or File and then click Next.
3. In the next dialog box that appears, choose a file type from which to import; then click Next.
4. Depending on your choice, you may see a dialog box asking you to install a required translator. If so, click Yes and insert your Office CD if prompted.

The remaining dialog boxes that you see will depend on the type of file you are importing. In all cases, you will see a file dialog box that asks you to locate the file you want to use to import the data. Select the file in this dialog box, click Next, and follow the directions in the remaining dialog boxes.

Summary

In this chapter, you learned various ways to create and manage your contacts within Outlook. You learned the following:

- You can create contacts, with name and address information, e-mail addresses, and other information from each contact.
- You can view or print your contacts in the form of address cards, detailed address cards, or a phone listing.
- You can send e-mail messages to contacts, schedule appointments with contacts, schedule meetings with contacts, assign tasks to contacts, or create a journal entry based on a contact.
- You can use a letter wizard to write a letter in Word, using a contact's name and address.
- You can import contacts from a variety of other personal information managers and data files, including Act!, ECCO, Lotus Organizer, Microsoft Access, FoxPro, dBASE, and Schedule+.

In the next chapter, you can learn ways to manage your time and tasks, using the features of Outlook.

Chapter 38

Scheduling Your Time and Tasks in Outlook

In This Chapter

- Navigating within the calendar
- Working with appointments and events
- Printing your calendar
- Scheduling meetings and inviting attendees
- Publishing your free/busy information
- Working with tasks

OUTLOOK'S TIME-RELATED AND task-management–related features can serve as useful aids for anyone working in the field of law, as well as for law students. You can use your Outlook Calendar to schedule appointments, manage your to-do list, and remind you of court dates, appointments with clients, and meetings with co-workers. If you are using Outlook as your e-mail client, you can schedule meetings and invite others to those meetings. You can create and track tasks and delegate tasks to others. You can publish your free/busy times from your calendar, and you can view the free/busy times of your co-workers' calendars as you schedule meetings. All these topics are explored in this chapter.

Navigating within the Calendar

The Outlook Calendar can provide a valuable view of your workday, week, or month. You can schedule, move, and cancel appointments and use the Calendar to keep up with your daily tasks.

To open the Calendar, click the Calendar icon in the Folder bar, or choose View ⇨ Go To ⇨ Calendar. Figure 38-1 shows the Outlook Calendar. This particular view of the Calendar is by day; other available views (by week, by workweek, or by month) are detailed shortly.

You can navigate through the Calendar in a variety of ways:

- You can use the scroll bar at the right edge of the Schedule pane to locate and view the time of an appointment.
- When viewing the Calendar by the week or month, you can use the arrow keys to move between different days. (When viewing the Calendar by the day or workweek, the up and down arrow keys move you between hours of the day; the left and right arrow keys move you between days.)
- In the Monthly calendar pane, you can click on a particular date and then choose View ⇨ Day to show that date in the Schedule pane.

- You can use the left and right arrows at the top of the Monthly Calendar pane to move forward or backward a month at a time.
- To quickly jump to a given date, you can right-click in the Schedule pane, choose Go To Date and enter a date in the dialog box that appears .
- If you are at a different date from the current day, you can quickly return to today's date by clicking the Today button in the Standard toolbar.

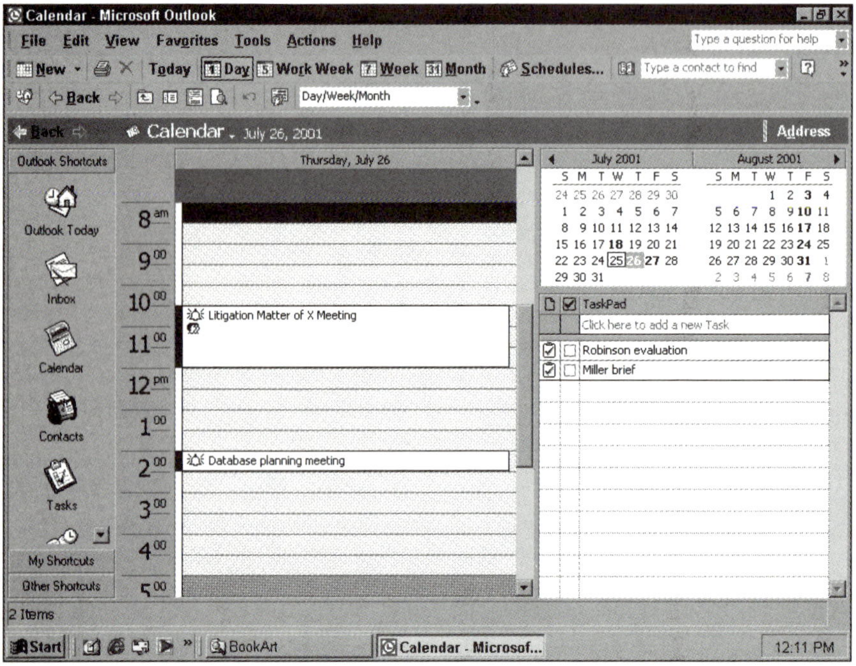

Figure 38-1: A Day view of the Calendar in Outlook

Outlook provides four types of date-based views within the Calendar: by day, by workweek, by week, and by month. You can select a desired view by clicking the corresponding button in the Standard toolbar or by choosing your desired view from the View menu. Figure 38-1 shows the Calendar view by day. The Work Week view of the Calendar is shown in Figure 38-2.

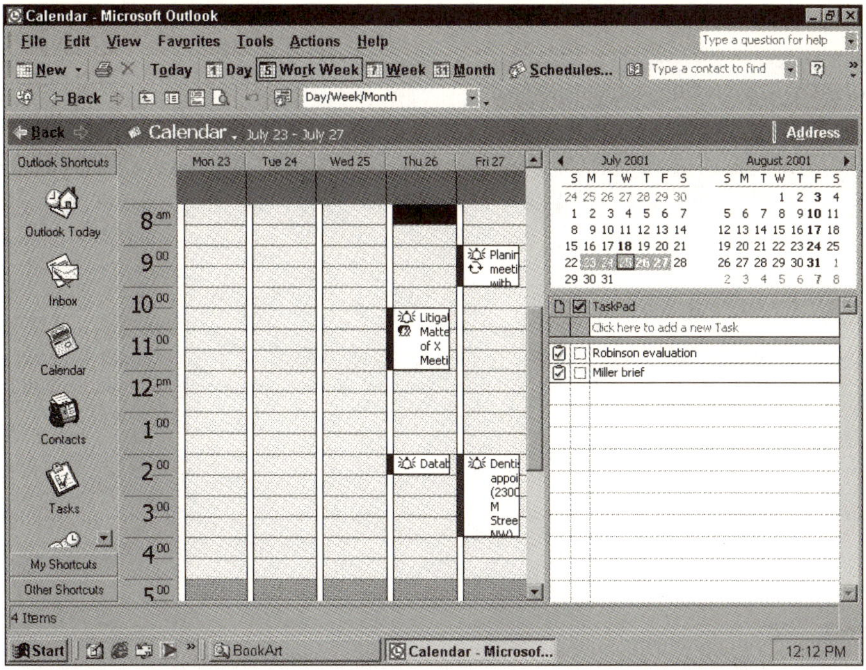

Figure 38-2: The Work Week view of the Calendar in Outlook displays a traditional workweek in the Schedule pane.

The Week view of the Calendar shows all the days of the week in the Schedule pane (see Figure 38-3) and the Month view displays an entire month in the Schedule pane (see Figure 38-4).

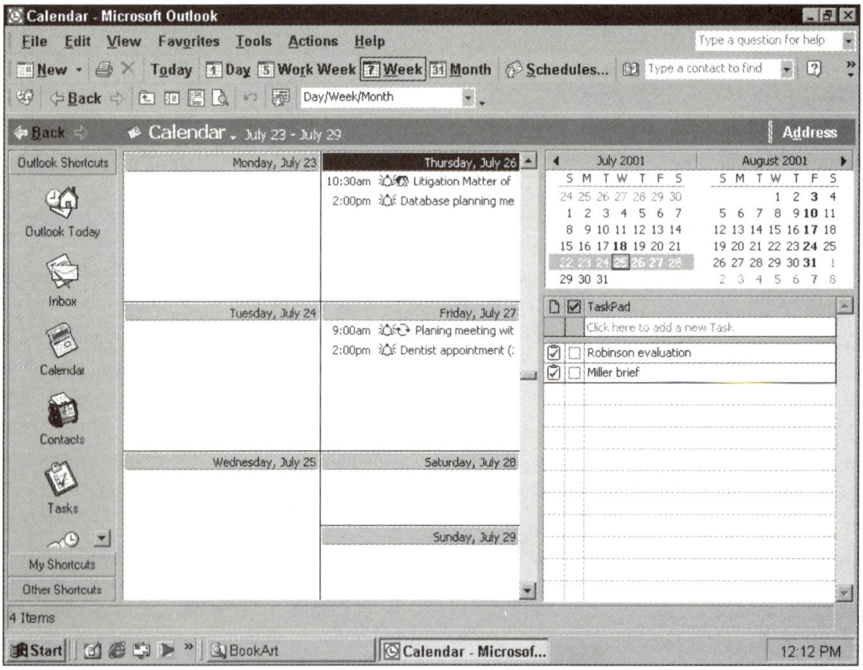

Figure 38-3: The Week view of the Calendar in Outlook displays an entire week in the Schedule pane.

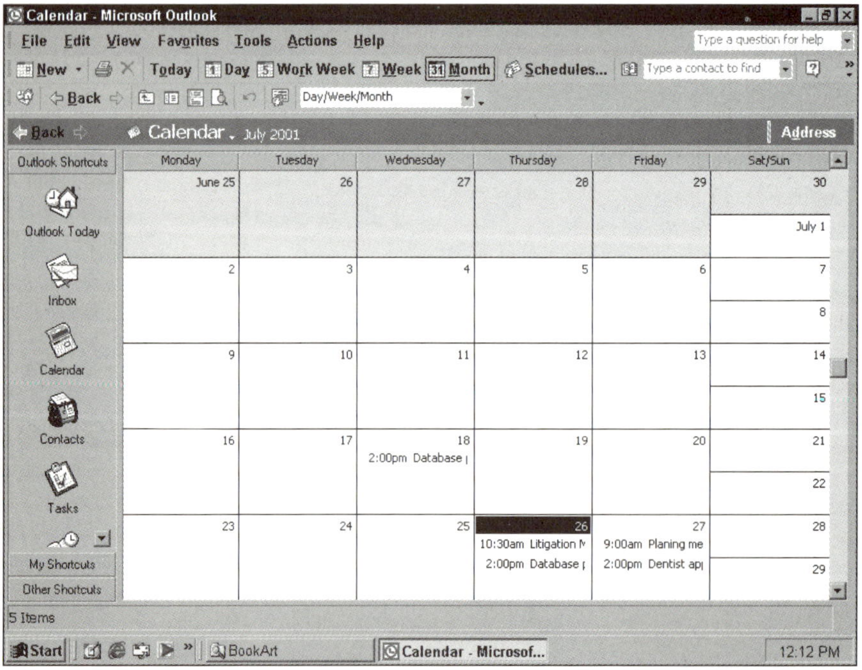

Figure 38-4: The Month view of the Calendar in Outlook displays an entire month in the Schedule pane.

TIP: If your workweek differs from the traditional "Monday through Friday, 8 a.m. to 5 p.m." variety, you can change how Outlook displays the workweek. To select the days and times of your workweek, choose Tools ⇨ Options, click the Preferences tab, click Calendar Options, and use the check boxes and the Start Time and End Time boxes shown in the Calendar Work Week portion of the dialog box that appears.

Working with Appointments and Events

You can add appointments or events to your Outlook calendar to remind yourself of important meetings, events, or time-related tasks you must perform. You can even set audible and visual reminders to have Outlook inform you ahead of time. These reminders will cause Outlook to display a message box on your screen, optionally accompanied by a sound, in advance of the appointment.

While you're working with appointments and events, note the difference between the two. They appear very similar in Outlook, and both are entered using the same Appointment window. The only difference between the two is that *appointments* have a specific time attached to them, whereas *events* occur on a certain day but are not linked to a particular time. A scheduled meeting with co-workers at 2 p.m. on January 9 or a visit with your dentist at 3 p.m. on Friday would be considered *appointments* in your Outlook Calendar. By comparison, your birthday, an anniversary, or a holiday would be considered *events*.

Creating an appointment or event

You can create an appointment or event within your Outlook Calendar by using the following steps:

1. Locate the desired day in the Calendar. (Note that if you are viewing the Calendar by the week and you are at the wrong week, one way to move around is to use the PgUp and PgDn keys to move forward or backward a week at a time.)
2. In the Schedule pane, double-click the desired day (or, if you are viewing by the day, double-click at the desired starting hour for the appointment). When you do this, a new Appointment window appears, with the Appointment tab selected (see Figure 38-5).

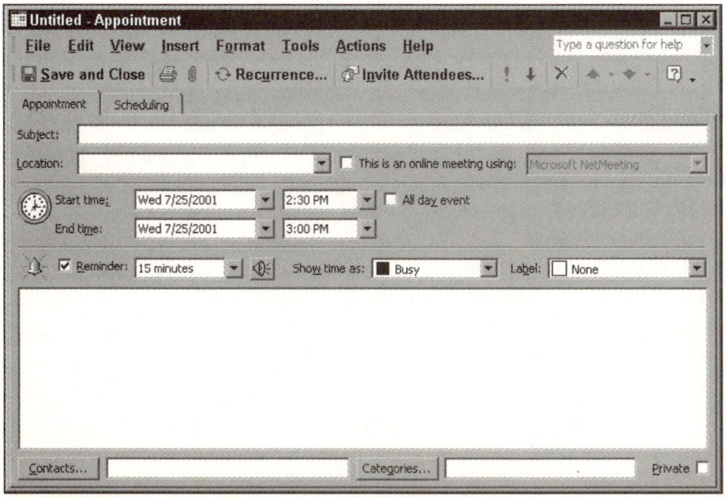

Figure 38-5: A new appointment in an Appointment window

3. Enter a subject for your appointment or event in the Subject box and a location in the Location box.
4. If you are entering an all-day event, click the All Day Event check box.
5. If desired, change the Start Time and End Time using the drop-down arrows to the right to show a list of other times.
6. If you want a reminder of the appointment or event, click the Reminder check box and choose the delay time between the appearance of the reminder and the appointment or event.
7. Make any desired selection in the Show Time As list box. You can choose Free, Tentative, Busy, or Out of Office. (On a network, this selection enables others to view your schedule when planning meetings, as detailed later in this chapter.)
8. Enter any desired comments describing the appointment or event in the text box that occupies most of the lower half of the dialog box.
9. If you want the appointment or event to be private, click the Private check box at the lower right. This feature hides the details of the appointment or event from any shared group calendar viewed by others on a network. (Others will be able to see your out-of-office or busy selections for a block of time, but they will not be able to see details as to *why* you are not available.)
10. Click Save and Close to save the appointment or event and to close the dialog box.

NOTE: If you set a reminder and Outlook is not running when the time for that reminder passes, you will not be notified. However, the next time that you launch Outlook, a dialog box for the reminder will appear, even if the date and time of the reminder are already past.

Creating a recurring appointment

You can create *recurring appointments*, which are appointments that occur repeatedly on a regular basis. For example, if you meet with the senior partner of your particular practice group in a large law firm every Friday at 10 a.m., you might want to create a recurring appointment to receive regular reminders.

You create a recurring appointment using the same overall steps as those for a one-time appointment (see the preceding section). After you choose the desired date and time in the new Appointment window, click the Recurrence button in the Standard toolbar of the window to display the Appointment Recurrence dialog box, shown in Figure 38-6.

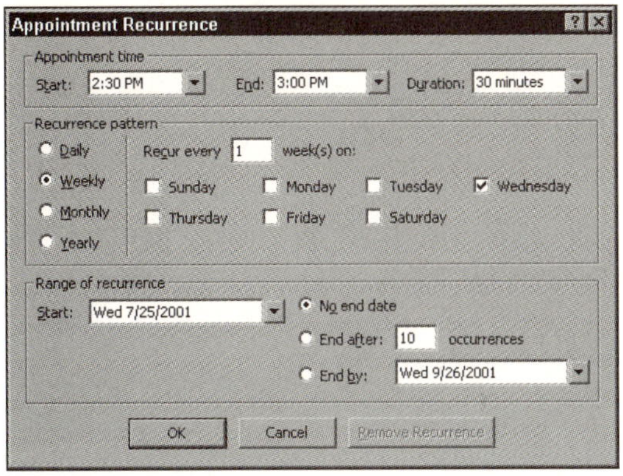

Figure 38-6: The Appointment Recurrence dialog box lets you schedule recurrences of a particular appointment.

In the Recurrence Pattern portion of the dialog box, select whether you want the appointment to repeat on a daily, weekly, monthly, or yearly basis, and define the desired interval for the recurrence. In the Range of Recurrence portion of the dialog box, specify when you want the repeating appointments to cease. You can choose indefinitely (No End Date), or you can end the recurrences after a specific number of repetitions or after a specific date in the future.

When you finish setting your options for the recurring nature of the appointment, click OK. Outlook returns you to the Appointment window, where you can continue entering information for the appointment.

Opening an existing appointment or event

To open an appointment or an event, right-click it in your Calendar and choose Open, or double-click it in your Calendar. Alternatively, you can select the entry by clicking it and then choosing File ⇨ Open ⇨ Selected Items.

Creating appointments by dragging e-mail messages

If you are using Outlook as your e-mail client, you may find Outlook's capability to create appointments based on incoming mail messages extremely useful. (For specifics on managing your e-mail, see Chapter 36.) You can create appointments based on mail messages using these steps:

1. At the Inbox, click and drag the desired message onto the Calendar icon in the Outlook Bar (at the far left of the Outlook window). When you do this, a new Appointment window opens, with the subject of the message entered in the Subject box and the text of the message entered in the Comments window of the message.
2. If desired, enter a location in the Location box.
3. Enter your desired dates and starting and ending times for the appointment.
4. Choose any additional options desired and then click Save and Close.

Scheduling calendar time by dragging tasks

Outlook lets you schedule time in your calendar for tasks that you previously entered in the Tasks portion of Outlook. (For specifics on creating tasks, see "Working with Tasks," later in this chapter.) You can create appointments based on existing tasks with these steps:

1. In the Tasks pane, click and drag the desired task onto the Calendar icon in the Outlook Bar (at the far left of the Outlook window). When you do this, a new appointment window opens with the Subject, Due Date, and Status of the task already entered in the Comments window of the message.
2. Enter the location in the Location box.
3. Enter your desired dates and starting and ending times for the appointment.
4. Choose any additional options desired and click Save and Close.

Moving and deleting calendar items

You can move appointments around in the Calendar (which is far easier than deleting and re-entering them), and you can delete unneeded appointments. One way to move an appointment is to use these steps:

1. In the Calendar, place the mouse pointer at the left side of the appointment you want to move.
2. When the pointer takes the shape of a cross with arrows on each end, click the appointment.
3. Choose Edit ⇨ Cut from the menus.
4. In the Schedule pane of the Calendar, click the new date and time for the appointment.
5. Choose Edit ⇨ Paste.

Another way to move an item to a different date or time is to open the item, change the dates and times within the window, and click Save and Close.

To delete any appointment, right-click the item in your Calendar and choose Delete from the shortcut menu, or select the unwanted appointment by clicking it and then pressing the Delete key, or choose Edit ⇨ Delete. Also, note that you can delete multiple Calendar entries by holding down the Ctrl key, clicking the unwanted items, and then pressing the Delete key.

Adding holidays to your calendar

You can automatically add holidays to your calendar that match the holidays for most nations and major cultures of the world. Outlook contains holidays for more than 70 nations and cultures, and you can add the holidays for one or more nations or cultures to your Calendar by using these steps:

1. Choose Tools ⇨ Options and make sure that the Preferences tab shows in the dialog box that appears.
2. Click the Calendar Options button to display a Calendar Options dialog box.
3. Click the Add Holidays button to display the Add Holidays to Calendar dialog box (see Figure 38-7).
4. Click the check boxes for any countries or cultures for which you want to add holidays. Click OK and then click OK twice more to close the Calendar Options and Options dialog boxes.

You are not limited to a single choice when adding holidays to the Outlook Calendar. For example, a resident of Puerto Rico can add holidays for both the United States and Puerto Rico to the Outlook Calendar by clicking the check boxes for these in the Add Holidays to Calendar dialog box.

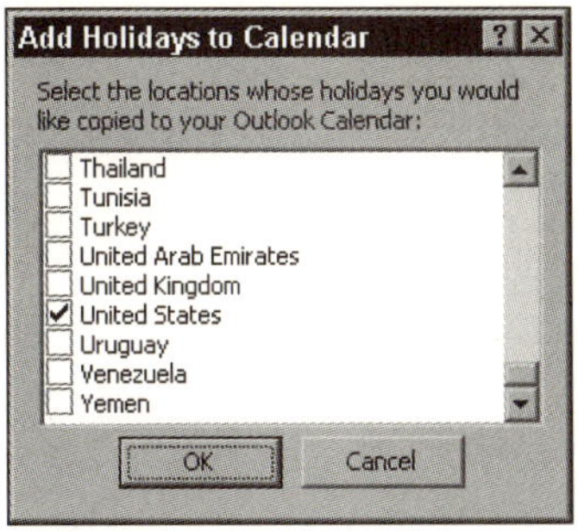

Figure 38-7: The Add Holidays to Calendar dialog box lets you add holidays for a nation or a particular culture to your Outlook Calendar.

Printing Your Calendar

You can easily print your calendar to have a handy printed version of your upcoming schedule, events, appointments, and various tasks. Use the Print icon on the toolbar or simply choose File ⇨ Print, and the Calendar prints, using the view that you are currently using in Outlook. Hence, if you wanted a calendar for a particular week, you would go to that week and display it using the Week view. (Alternatively, you can choose the Print Style from the Print dialog box, allowing you to choose the view you want from there.)

TIP: Click File ⇨ Print Preview if you want to see how your printed calendar will appear in a given view before you print it.

You also can print your Calendar using a specific format with the File ⇨ Page Setup command. Choose File ⇨ Page Setup and then choose a desired view of the Calendar from the submenu that appears. You can select Daily Style, Weekly Style, Monthly Style, Tri-Fold Style, Calendar Details Style, or Memo Style. When you make a selection from the submenu, a dialog box appropriate to your selection appears; Figure 38-8 shows the dialog box that appears when you choose Weekly Style. Use the options on the three tabs of the dialog box to select how you want your Calendar items printed, and click Print in the dialog box to begin printing, using the style and options that you selected.

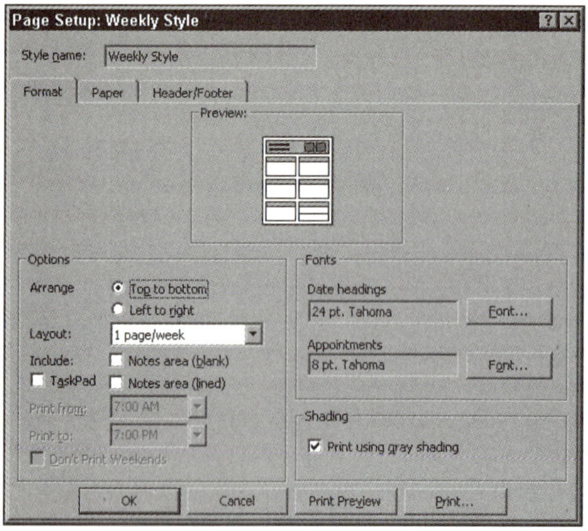

Figure 38-8: The Page Setup dialog box lets you control how your Calendar will be printed.

Scheduling Meetings and Inviting Attendees

The Calendar includes a Meeting Planner feature, a real time saver when you work with others on a network. You can quickly set up meetings, check the free time of others who are using Outlook to manage their calendars, and send meeting reminders via e-mail. If you're on a network, use these steps to plan a meeting:

1. In the Calendar, select the desired day of the meeting.
2. Click the Plan a Meeting icon in the toolbar, or choose Actions ⇨ Plan a Meeting. In a moment, the Plan a Meeting dialog box appears (see Figure 38-9).
3. Click Add Others and choose Add from Address Book to open the Select Attendees and Resources dialog box (see Figure 38-10).

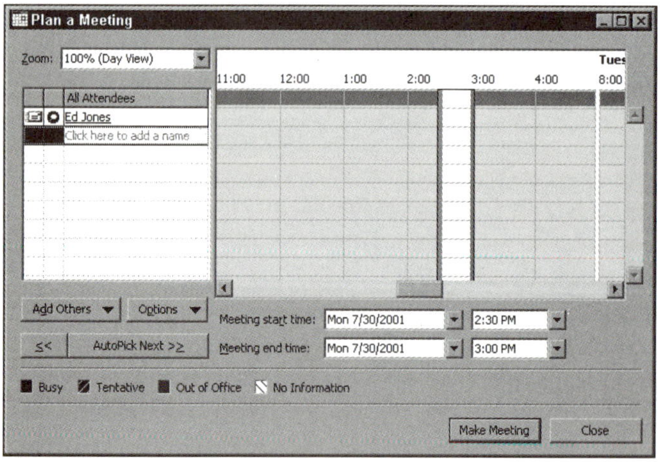

Figure 38-9: The Plan a Meeting dialog box is used to schedule meetings and invite others them.

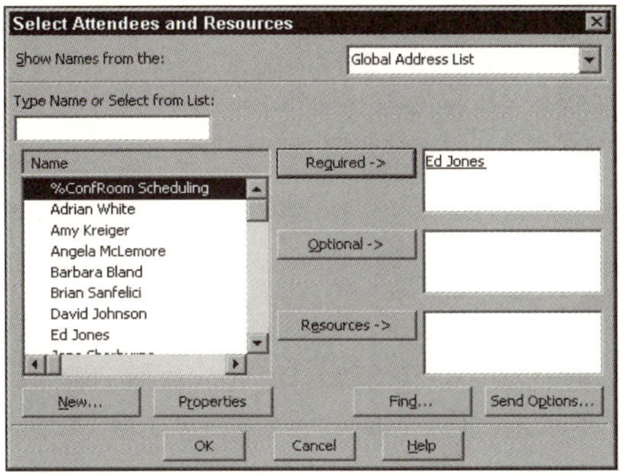

Figure 38-10: The Select Attendees and Resources dialog box lets you select the attendees for a particular meeting.

4. In the Show Names From The list box at the upper-right corner of the dialog box, choose the desired contact list or e-mail server containing the names of the people you want to invite. When you do this, the names appear in the Name list box at the left.
5. Click each desired name to select it; then click Required (if the person's attendance is mandatory) or Optional (if the person's attendance is optional). When you're done selecting the names, click OK. If the people you selected are also using Outlook on your network, you will see their busy and free times in the scheduling portion of the Plan a Meeting dialog box (the upper portion of the box).
6. Choose a desired starting and ending time for the meeting. You can use the list boxes near the bottom of the dialog box to do this, or you can drag the colored vertical bars in the scheduling portion of the dialog box. If your workgroup is using Outlook on a network and the people you've invited have conflicting amounts of free and busy time, you can click the AutoPick Next>> button, and Outlook will choose a time to accommodate the highest available number of attendees.
7. Click Make Meeting to close the Plan a Meeting dialog box. When you do this, a new Meeting message window appears, with the attendees' e-mail addresses automatically entered in the To box, as shown in Figure 38-11.
8. Enter a subject for the meeting in the Subject box and enter a location for the meeting in the Location box.
9. Enter any desired comments in the Comment window near the bottom of the dialog box.
10. Click Send to send the invitations to your meeting via e-mail.

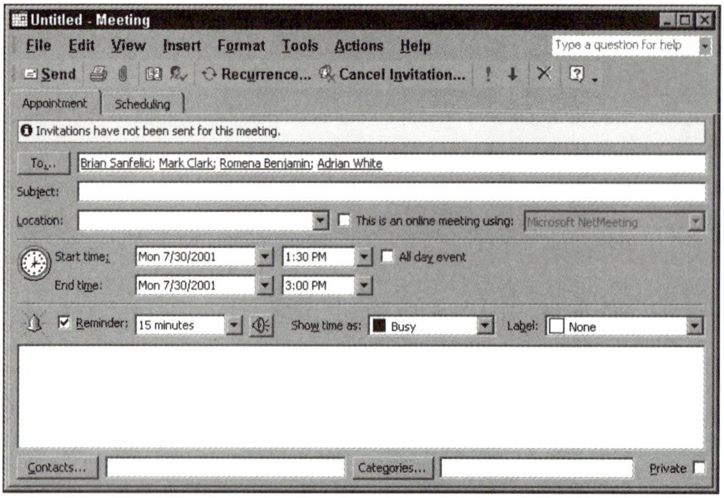

Figure 38-11: The new Meeting message window containing attendees' e-mail addresses

Changing a meeting attendee's status

You can manually change the status information for an attendee who has not yet responded to your meeting request. For example, if someone calls you by phone to decline your meeting invitation, you can change that attendee's Response status to Declined. If the person is a Required Attendee and you decide to have the meeting anyway, you can change that person's Attendance status to Optional Attendee. Use these steps to change the status of a meeting attendee:

1. Find the meeting in your Calendar and double-click it to open the meeting.
2. Click the Scheduling tab.
3. For the person whose status you want to change, click in the column to the left of the person's name and then choose the desired status from the pop-up menu that appears.

Canceling a meeting

When you need to cancel a meeting that you have scheduled, you can easily do so. To cancel a meeting, find the meeting in your Calendar and double-click it to open the meeting. Next, click Actions ⇨ Cancel Meeting. The attendees are automatically notified of the cancellation of the meeting via e-mail, and (assuming that they are using any version of Outlook from Outlook 97 onward) the event is automatically removed from their calendars.

Publishing Your Free/Busy Information

You can publish your free/busy information from your Outlook Calendar for others to view. If you are on a network using an Exchange Server, this is done automatically, although you may want to change how often updated information is made available to others on the network. If you are not using Exchange Server but you are on a network with others, you can publish the information to a page of your internal intranet (assuming that you are given rights to create and store files in a directory in which pages of the intranet will be stored). If you are using Outlook with an Internet service provider, you can publish the information to an Internet Web site as an HTML page.

By default, Outlook publishes your free/busy information to the Exchange Server every 15 minutes, and it publishes two months' worth of information. You can change these defaults as desired. To change the defaults or to publish information to an intranet or Internet Web site, use the following steps:

1. Choose Tools ⇨ Options and make sure that the Preferences tab shows in the dialog box that appears.
2. Click the Calendar Options button to display a Calendar Options dialog box.
3. Click the Free/Busy Options button to display the Free/Busy Options dialog box, shown in Figure 38-12.

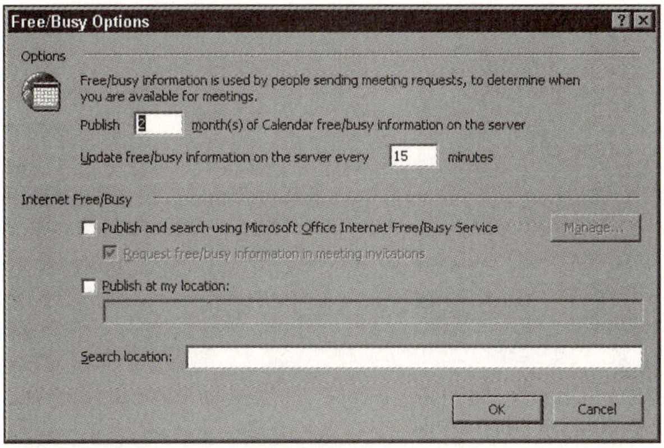

Figure 38-12: The Free/Busy Options dialog box

4. Enter the number of months for which you want to publish the free/busy time in the Publish…Month(s) of Calendar Free/Busy Information on the Server box.
5. If you want to publish your free/busy information on an intranet at your location, click the Publish at My Location check box and enter the UNC (Universal Naming Convention) address for the directory where the information should be stored. If you are not sure what to enter here, contact your firm or organization's intranet Webmaster for assistance.
6. If you want to publish your free/busy information at an Internet Web site, click the Publish and Search Using Microsoft Office Internet Free/Busy Service check box. Click the Manage button and then follow the directions in the Internet Connection Wizard dialog boxes that appear.

Another simple way to publish your Calendar information on an intranet or Internet Web site is to view the Calendar pane in Outlook and choose File ⇨ Save as Web Page from the menus. In the dialog box that appears, choose a starting and ending date, check the Include Appointment Details box if you want to include appointment data, specify a location for the resulting HTML file in the File Name box, and click Save. You can then upload the resulting HTML file to your Web server. When displayed in a Web browser, the file resembles the example shown in Figure 38-13. If you use this method, remember that you need to repeat this step each time that you want to provide an updated view of your calendar on the Web site.

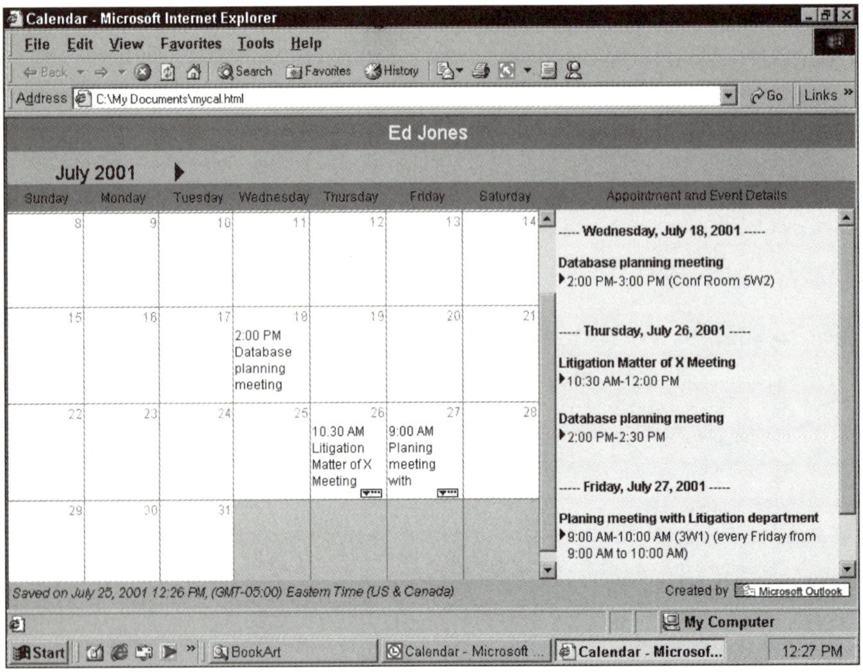

Figure 38-13: A calendar saved as a Web page and viewed using Internet Explorer

Creating Group Schedules in Outlook

A new feature added to Outlook 2002 is the built-in capability to combine the calendars of a number of people into a group schedule. Using a group schedule, you can see the combined schedules of a group of people at a single glance. You can have multiple group schedules, with each showing a different group of people. For example, one group schedule might show the calendars for all attorneys and paralegals in a firm's litigation practice group, and another might show all attorneys and paralegals in the firm's tax and finance practice group.

Group schedules make setting up meetings among individuals in a workgroup easier. In addition to inviting co-workers to meetings, you can also schedule resources (such as conference rooms). To schedule resources such as conference rooms using Outlook, the resource must be assigned its own mailbox on the Exchange Server, and resource scheduling for the resource must be enabled (talk to your Exchange Server Administrator for details). A group schedule contains free/busy information for each member of a group unless the individual member has marked a calendar item as private. To create a group schedule, use the following steps:

1. Click the Calendar icon in the Outlook Bar.
2. Click Schedules on the Standard toolbar or choose Actions ⇨ View Group Schedules to display the Group Schedules dialog box (see Figure 38-14).

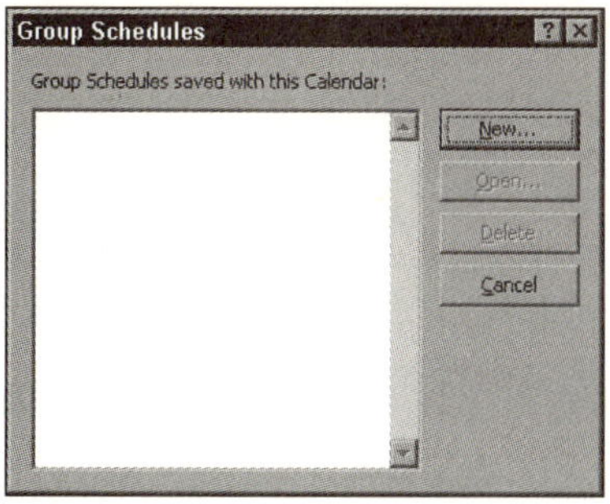

Figure 38-14: The Group Schedules dialog box is used to create new group schedules, open existing group schedules, and delete group schedules from your Calendar view.

3. In the dialog box, click New.
4. Type a name for the group schedule in the dialog box that appears and click OK. A group schedule dialog box for the new group appears, as shown in Figure 38-15.

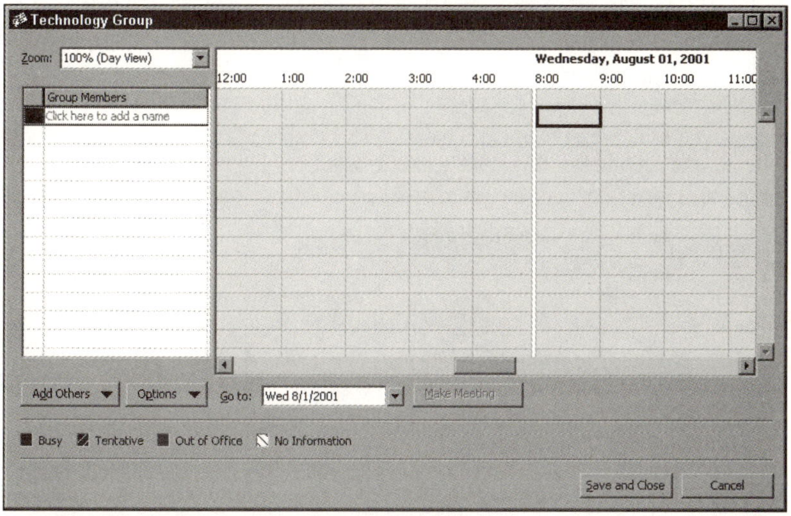

Figure 38-15: A new, blank, group schedule for a group

5. At the lower-left corner of the dialog box, click Add Others and then choose Add from Address Book from the submenu that appears.
6. Select the desired names for the group from the Select Members dialog box (see Figure 38-16), using the To button in the center of the dialog box to add the names to the list at the right.

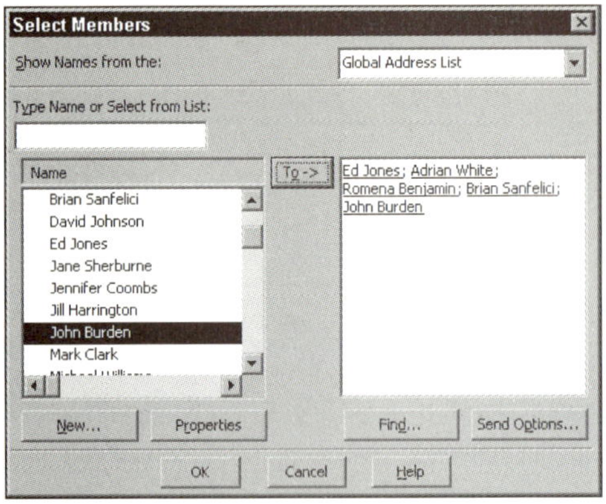

Figure 38-16: The Select Members dialog box lets you choose new members to be added to a group schedule.

7. When you finish adding members to the group, click OK to close the Select Members dialog box.

After a group schedule exists, you can view it at any time. While in any Calendar view, click the Schedules button on the toolbar, select the group schedule that you want to view in the Group Schedules dialog box that appears, and click Open. You can delete the group schedule from your view of Outlook at any time by using the Delete button in this same dialog box. Figure 38-17 shows an example of the free/busy time for a group of employees, displayed within a group schedule.

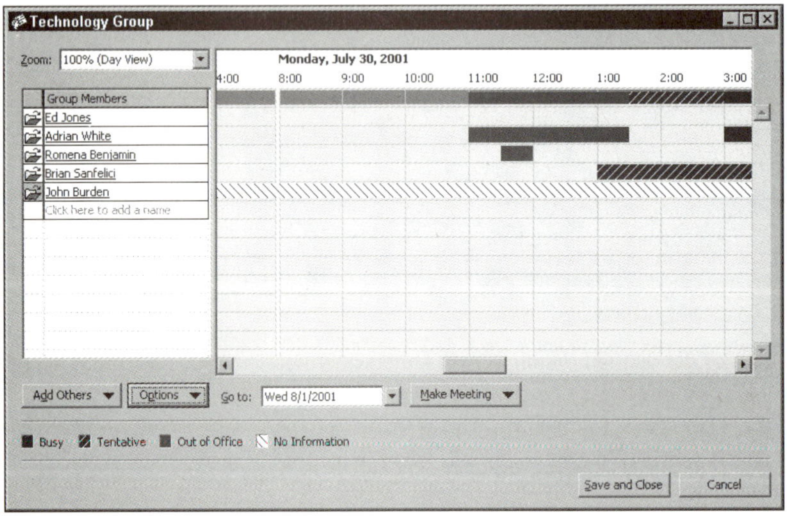

Figure 38-17: A group schedule shows the free-busy time for employees.

Group schedules make scheduling meetings with all members of the group easy. To do so, open the group schedule, click and drag across a block of available time within the schedule, and then click the Make Meeting button at the bottom. Choose New Meeting with All from the submenu that appears. A new Meeting window opens, with the names of the group members automatically entered in the To box and with the starting and ending times filled in according to the block of time you chose in the group schedule window. Enter a subject, a location, and any desired comments for the meeting and click Send.

With group schedules that require resources such as conference rooms, the availability of the resources may change on a regular basis. Your view of the free/busy times for the group is accurate at the time you open the schedule in a window but may not be later. To refresh the free/busy data shown on the group schedule, click Options at the bottom of the dialog box and choose Refresh Free/Busy from the submenu that appears.

Working with Tasks

The Tasks component of Outlook lets you organize and keep track of your business and personal tasks. *Tasks* are activities that you plan to perform at some future time but *not necessarily on a specific date*. This is what makes them differ from appointments and events, which are scheduled around a specific day (or days) of the year. Tasks may need to begin by a certain date and often must be completed by a certain date, but they usually don't need to occur on a certain date. When you're due in court for a trial on Monday at 10 a.m., that's an appointment. When the firm's managing partner tells you, "I'd like to have a draft of that filing on my desk by next Friday," that's a task.

As you work, you can get a visual idea of the progress you've made on your tasks. You also can set reminder messages for tasks to have Outlook remind you of the tasks at a certain date and time. You can create multiple categories for different projects, and you can group your tasks by the various categories. You can even assign tasks to others who are using Outlook on your network. Clicking the Tasks icon in the Outlook Bar reveals the Tasks pane of Outlook, as shown in Figure 38-18.

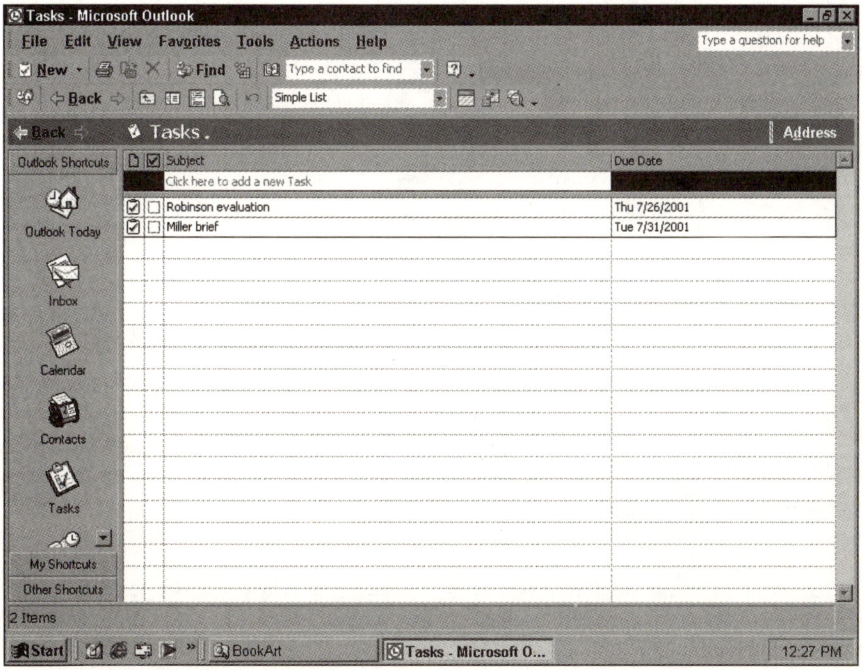

Figure 38-18: The Outlook window, with the Tasks pane visible

TIP: In the Tasks pane of Outlook, you see a list of your tasks. One important point to note is that this is not the only place in Outlook where you can view your tasks. Because tasks you perform are, by nature, time-related, Outlook also provides an easy way to see them in the Task Pad that is a part of the Calendar. Whenever you are viewing the Calendar by day, workweek, or week, the Task Pad appears at the right side of the window. Figure 38-1, shown at the start of this chapter, shows the Calendar view of Outlook. In that figure, the Task Pad is visible in the lower-right portion of the Outlook window.

If you prefer to view your tasks from the Calendar portion of Outlook, keep in mind that the Task Pad does not appear if you are viewing the Calendar by month. You should also note that when you start Outlook for the first time, the Calendar shows your tasks for the current day only. To make all the tasks appear in the Calendar, choose View ⇨ TaskPad View and select All Tasks from the submenu that appears.

Creating a task

To create a new task from the Tasks portion of Outlook, while viewing the Tasks pane, click the New button in the toolbar or choose File ⇨ New ⇨ Task. Alternatively, from the Task Pad of the Calendar, double-click at the left of the area that reads Click Here to Add a New Task. With either method, a new Task window appears, like the one shown in Figure 38-19.

In the Subject box, enter a subject for the task. If the task has a due date, click the down arrow to the right of the Due Date field to open a calendar in which you can choose the desired due date. You can click Start Date and use the same technique to enter a starting date for the task, if desired.

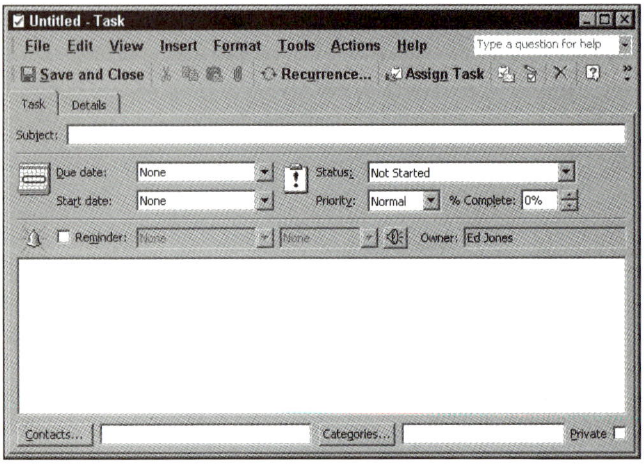

Figure 38-19: The Task window for a new task

You can use the remaining options in the dialog box to enter a status, a priority, and a percentage completed for the task. You can click the Reminder check box and choose a date and time in the entry boxes to the right of the Reminder check box, causing Outlook to display a visible reminder for the task when the chosen time passes. In the Comments text box (which occupies most of the lower half of the window), you can enter any desired comments for the task. You can click the Categories button (at the lower center) to bring up a list box of categories from which you can choose to add to the field to the right of the button. (This proves helpful if you later want to view your tasks by category.)

You can enter details concerning a task on the Details tab of the Task window. If you click the Details tab, you see the options shown in Figure 38-20.

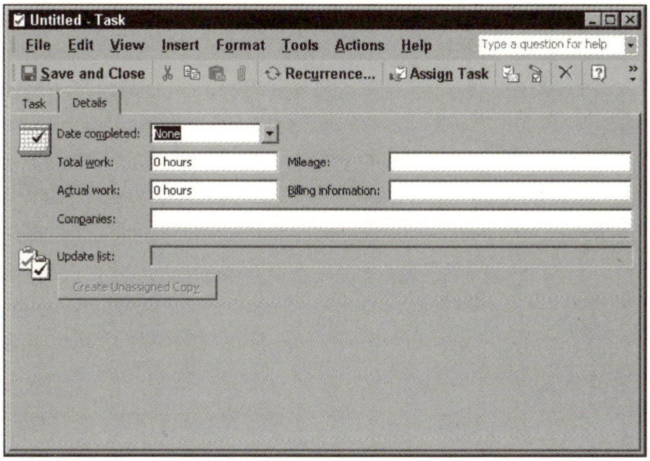

Figure 38-20: The Details tab of the Task window

You can enter time-based amounts for actual work and total work, such as 30 minutes, 5 hours, 3 days, or 2 months, in the Total Work and Actual Work boxes. You can also enter mileage, billing information, and the names of companies that may be related to the task in the respective boxes. When you're done creating the task and entering your information, click Save and Close in the Task window.

Creating tasks based on e-mail messages

You can create a task based on an e-mail message by opening the Inbox and dragging the desired message onto the Tasks icon in the Outlook Bar. Doing so opens the Task window, with the subject of the message entered in the Subject box and the text of the message in the Comments box of the Task window. You can then make any desired changes to the options in the window. Click Save and Close to save the changes.

Opening and editing tasks

You can open tasks from the Tasks pane of Outlook or from the Calendar. To open a task, find the desired task in the Tasks pane or in the Task Pad of the Calendar and double-click it. When you double-click a task, it appears in a Task window (refer to Figure 38-19).

While the task is open in the Task window, you can edit any of the entries for the tasks. These include the subject, due date, start date, status, priority, and percentage of the task that's been completed. Make the desired entries in the window and then click Save and Close to save any changes.

Marking a task as complete

When you want to mark a task as complete but retain it in your Tasks list, just click the empty check box in the Completed column (the second box from the left) in the Tasks pane or in the Task Pad portion of the Calendar. You can also change a task that was previously marked as completed back to uncompleted by clicking the checked box in the Completed column.

Deleting a task

To delete a task, select the task in the Task pane or in the Task Pad of the Calendar. Then press Delete or click the Delete button in the toolbar. Note that if you assign a task to someone else on a network and you then delete it, the task is deleted from your task list only. It is not removed from the task list of the person who received the task.

Assigning tasks to others

You can create and assign tasks to others by sending the other person a task request. (The person who receives the request can then accept it, decline it, or assign it to someone else.) Use these steps to create and assign a new task to another person:

1. Choose File ⇨ New ⇨ Task Request from the menus (or press Ctrl+Shift+U).
2. In the To. . . box, enter the name of the person you want to assign the task to, or click the To. . . button and choose a name from the list.
3. Enter a name for the task in the Subject box.
4. Choose the due date and remaining status options desired.
5. If you want to keep an updated copy of the task in your task list, click the Keep an Updated Copy of This Task on My Task List check box. If you want to receive a status report by return e-mail when the task is complete, click the Send Me a Status Report When This Task Is Complete check box.

To assign an existing task to another individual, right-click the existing task in the Tasks pane or in the Task Pad of the Calendar and choose Assign Task from the shortcut menu that appears. When the existing task opens, enter the name of the person you want to assign the task to in the To… box, fill in or change any other desired information in the window, and click Send.

Changing the task options

You can change the various default options that affect the appearance and behavior of tasks in Outlook. These options include the colors used to display completed and overdue tasks, information regarding tasks you assign to others, and whether reminders are included by default. You change these options using the Task Options dialog box, which you can display using the following steps:

1. Choose Tools ⇨ Options from the menus.
2. Make sure that the Preferences tab shows in the dialog box that appears.
3. Click the Task Options button to display the Task Options dialog box (see Figure 38-21).

By default, the Task Pad shows incomplete tasks that are not overdue in black, overdue tasks in red, and completed tasks in gray. You can change the colors used to display overdue and completed tasks (other types of tasks are always shown in black). To change the colors for overdue or completed tasks, click the down arrow next to the applicable list box and choose the desired colors.

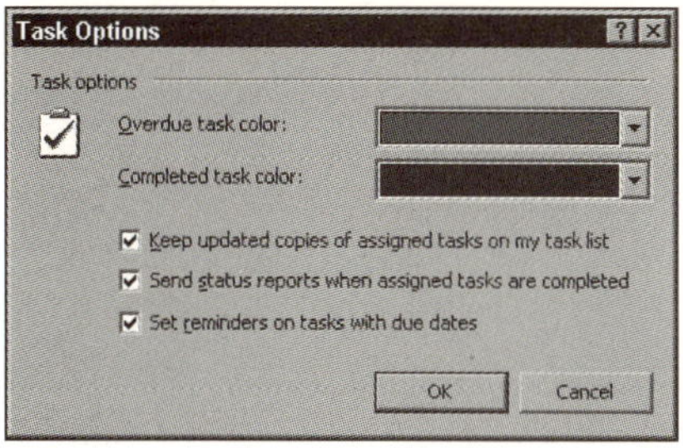

Figure 38-21: You can use the Task Options dialog box to change the colors for overdue and completed tasks.

Use the check boxes shown in the dialog box to determine the remaining Task Options settings. You can choose among the following: whether to keep updated copies of tasks that you assign to others on your tasks list, whether you should receive status reports when assigned tasks are completed, and whether reminders should be set for tasks with due dates.

When done setting the various options, click OK to close the Task Options dialog box and click OK again to close the Options dialog box.

Summary

In this chapter, you learned how you to use Outlook to perform a variety of tasks related to time management. You learned the following:

- You can use the Outlook Calendar to provide a view of your workday, workweek, week, or month, and you can print your calendar entries in a variety of formats.
- You can store appointments or events in your Calendar and create reminders of those appointments and events.
- If you are using Outlook as your e-mail client, you can schedule meetings and invite attendees to your meetings.
- You can use the group schedules feature of Outlook 2002 to create group schedules that display the free/busy times for a group of individuals, and you can use these group schedules to easily schedule meetings with members of the group.
- You can keep track of your tasks using Outlook.

The next chapter discusses the use of the Outlook Journal, the Notes feature of Outlook, and the capability of Outlook to be used as a Web browser.

Chapter 39

Using the Outlook Journal, Notes, and Web Browser

In This Chapter

- ♦ Using the Journal
- ♦ Tracking billable time with the Journal
- ♦ Using Notes
- ♦ Browsing the Web in Outlook

THIS CHAPTER DETAILS THE USE of the Outlook Journal, the Notes feature of Outlook, and the capability of Outlook to be used as a Web browser. Using the Journal, you can create a running record of your work, including your activities, tasks, phone conversations, faxes, e-mail messages, and the like. You also can keep a record of documents or files that you create in Office applications such as Word, Excel, PowerPoint, and Access. The Notes feature of Outlook lets you create notes to jot down any information you would normally put on a sticky note. If you have an Internet connection, you can browse Web sites directly from the Outlook window.

Using the Journal

The Journal component of Outlook is precisely what its name implies: an electronic version of a journal that can record the variety of activities in your business day. The Journal tracks all your activities on a timeline so that you can easily obtain a visual representation of where you are spending your time. You can record many activities automatically, and you can make manual entries into the Journal. Figure 39-1 shows the Outlook window that appears after the Journal icon is clicked in the Outlook Bar.

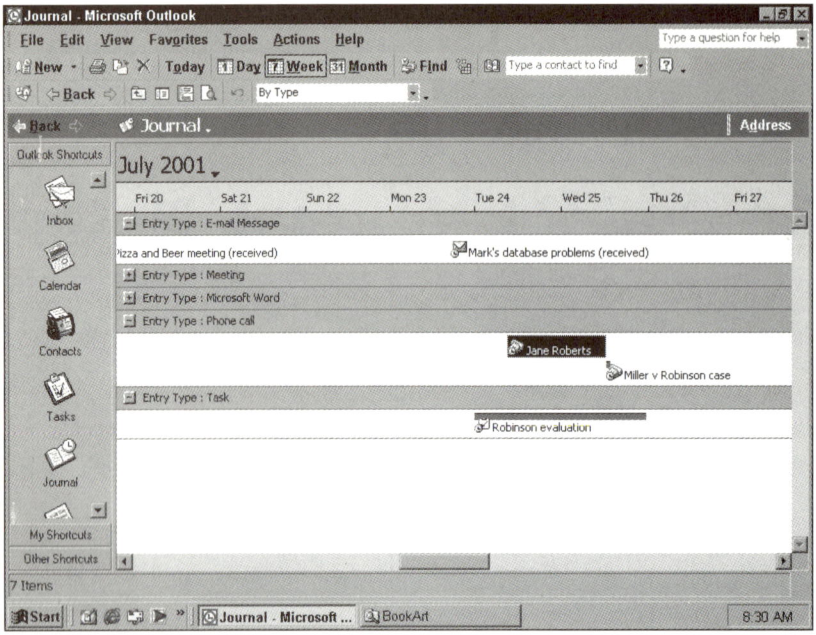

Figure 39-1: In the Outlook window, the timeline appears at the top of the Information Viewer area in the Journal.

As with its paper-based counterpart, most of what you do with the Journal is to record activities and view them. The Journal lets you set options to automatically record Office documents that you create and revise, so that you have a timeline record of when you worked with what documents. This feature goes beyond just proving to the managing partner or your supervisor that you've been working: Because Office documents recorded in the Journal serve as shortcuts, you can use the Journal as a handy way to open documents. For example, if you want to open a Word document that you worked on last Thursday, but can't remember where you saved it, you can find the record of the document in the Journal and can then click it to launch Word and open the document. The Journal also can automatically keep a record of all e-mail sent to and received from a specific person. Although Outlook appointments aren't recorded automatically, you can easily add manual Journal entries of appointments by simply clicking and dragging the appointments to the Journal icon in the Outlook Bar. .

Opening, viewing, and jumping to Journal entries

The Journal displays the entries in groups called *Entry Types*. When you start the Journal for the first time, all the Entry Types (visible in the Information Viewer portion of the Outlook window) are closed. You can open any Entry Type by clicking the small icon with the plus or minus symbol to the left of the words *Entry Type*. A plus symbol indicates that the group is closed; a minus symbol indicates that it's open. Refer back to Figure 39-1, which shows the groups for e-mail messages, phone calls, and tasks as open and the groups for meetings and Microsoft Word documents as closed. To open any Journal entry, right-click the item and choose Open from the shortcut menu that appears. Alternatively, you can select the item in the Journal and choose File ⇨ Open ⇨ Selected Items (or just press Ctrl+O).

All Outlook items and Office documents that you see in any open groups are hotlinks, which is one of the Journal's most notable and useful features. You can double-click any icon to open that Journal entry and go directly to that Outlook entry or Office document. For example, if you have a record of an e-mail stored in the Journal under a certain date, you can double-click that e-mail in the Journal to jump directly to a message window containing that e-mail. If you are automatically recording all your edits to Word documents, you can double-click any document shown in the Journal's timeline to jump to that document within Word. .

Recording Journal entries automatically

To use the Journal most effectively, you may want to take advantage of its capability to record entries automatically. The Journal can keep track of your activities behind the scenes as you perform your daily work. To automatically record entries in the Journal, choose Tools ⇨ Options from the menus and click the Journal Options button on the Preferences tab of the dialog box that appears. When you click the button, the Journal Options dialog box appears (see Figure 39-2).

CAUTION: If you are at a law firm that uses a document management software program to index, track, and manage documents (such as Imanage, PC Docs, or Worldox), you should *not* enable automatic recording for Word (or for any other Office application whose files are tracked by your document management software). The automatic recording of documents in the Journal may interfere with the operation of your document management software.

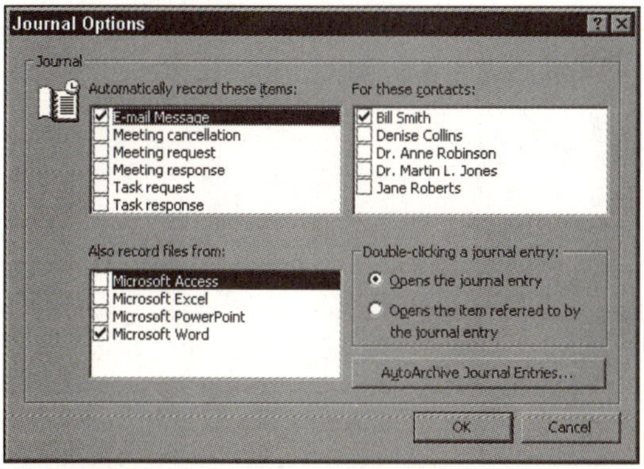

Figure 39-2: The Journal Options dialog box

In the upper half of the dialog box, you can choose the Outlook items that you want to have recorded for any person in your Contacts list. At the left side, click the check boxes for the items you want recorded. (You can enable e-mail messages, meeting cancellations, meeting requests, meeting responses, task requests, and task responses.) At the right side, click the check boxes beside the contacts you want events recorded for. .

CROSS-REFERENCE: For details on adding individuals to your Contacts list, see Chapter 37.

In the lower half of the dialog box, you can choose any or all Office files for which you want Journal entries recorded, including those of Access, Excel, Word, and PowerPoint.

At the lower right, you need to choose whether double-clicking a Journal entry opens the entry or opens the actual item that the entry refers to. After you make all the desired selections in the dialog box, click OK.

TIP: When you add a new contact to your Contacts list (covered in Chapter 37), you can easily set items you want automatically recorded for that contact by selecting the Automatically Record Journal Entries for This Contact check box on the Journal tab of the contact.

NOTE: Turning on Outlook's automatic recording of items in the Journal results in an Outlook data file that rapidly grows in size and can therefore slow Outlook's performance. If you decide to enable automatic recording, you should do so only for items that you truly need to have recorded in the Journal.

Recording Journal entries manually

For those Outlook appointments and items that can't be recorded automatically, the Journal provides the capability to manually add entries. You can manually add an Outlook item to the Journal by dragging the item onto the Journal icon in the Outlook Bar. When you do this, a new Journal Entry window appears for the item (see Figure 39-3). Enter any desired options for the Journal entry and then click Save and Close to save the entry. .

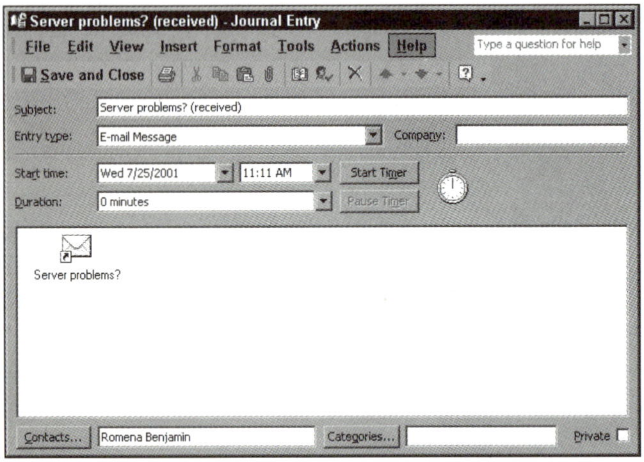

Figure 39-3: The new Journal Entry window that was manually created by dragging an item (in this case, a mail message) onto the Journal icon in the Outlook Bar

If you want to add an entry to the Journal that's not based on any Outlook or Office item (such as a phone call from Mom), you can do so by using these steps:

1. With the Journal open, click the New button in the toolbar, or choose Actions ⇨ New Journal Entry (or press Ctrl+N). In a moment, a blank Journal Entry window appears.
2. Enter any desired options for the Journal entry; then click Save and Close to save the entry. .

Moving and deleting Journal entries

You can move items to different locations along the timeline in the Journal. First, open the Journal entry (right-click the item in the Journal and choose Open from the shortcut menu). In the Journal Entry window that appears, enter the new start date and time; then click Save and Close.

To delete any Journal entry, click the entry to select it. Then press Delete, or click the Delete icon in the toolbar, or choose Edit ⇨ Delete from the menus.

Printing Journal entries

Journal entries must be printed individually. To print an entry, select the desired entry in the Journal. Click the Print icon on the Standard toolbar, or choose File ⇨ Print from the menus. (You can use File ⇨ Print Preview to see how the Journal entry will appear when printed.) .

Tracking Billable Time with the Journal

For any law firm, one very helpful use of the Journal is to time meetings with clients, phone calls to clients (or on behalf of a particular client), or other client-related activities. You can record such activities in the Journal and later print a record of the activities to be used as a reference when you (or an assistant) are entering information in your time-and-billing software.

When performing client work, meeting with clients, or making client phone calls, create a new Journal entry for the event. With the Journal pane visible within Outlook, click the New button (or type Ctrl+N, or choose Actions ⇨ New Journal Entry). Then enter the client code or client name in the Subject box, choose an appropriate entry (such as Meeting or Phone Call) in the Entry Type box, and click the Start Timer button. Figure 39-4 shows an example of this type of Journal usage.

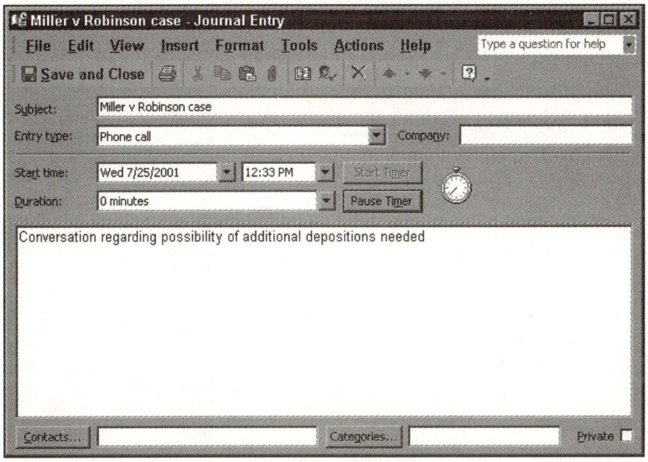

Figure 39-4: A Journal entry used to track billable time

As your client-related assignment progresses, you can enter comments in the Comments box of the window and use the Pause timer and Start Timer buttons to keep a running record of your billable time. You can minimize the window and work with other Windows applications while the timer continues to run in the background. When you complete the assignment, click Save and Close in the Journal Entry window. The total time is reflected in the Duration box of the Journal Entry window.

TIP: As soon as you save and close the Journal entry, right-click it in the Journal pane, choose Print from the shortcut menu that appears, and place the printed copy in that "billable hours" stack of items that is probably somewhere on your desk. If you get in the habit of doing this, you'll find it much easier to go back at the end of a given day or week and accurately calculate your billable time.

If you have a modem attached to your computer, you can also dial a contact's phone number and begin a new Journal entry at the same time. To do so, select the desired contact in your Contacts folder and click the Dial button (which looks like a telephone) in the toolbar, or you can choose Actions ⇨ Call Contact. Then choose New Call and, in the New Call dialog box that appears, click the Create New Journal Entry When Starting New Call check box.

Using Notes

Notes are the electronic equivalent of those popular sticky paper notes used in many offices. Figure 39-5 shows an example of the use of notes. You'll find notes handy for ideas, questions, details of phone conversations, assorted bits of information, and any other item you might put on a paper note. You can minimize the Outlook window and leave notes open and on the screen as you work with other Windows applications. (Pressing Alt+Tab brings the notes into view. Windows considers each open note to be a separate running application.)

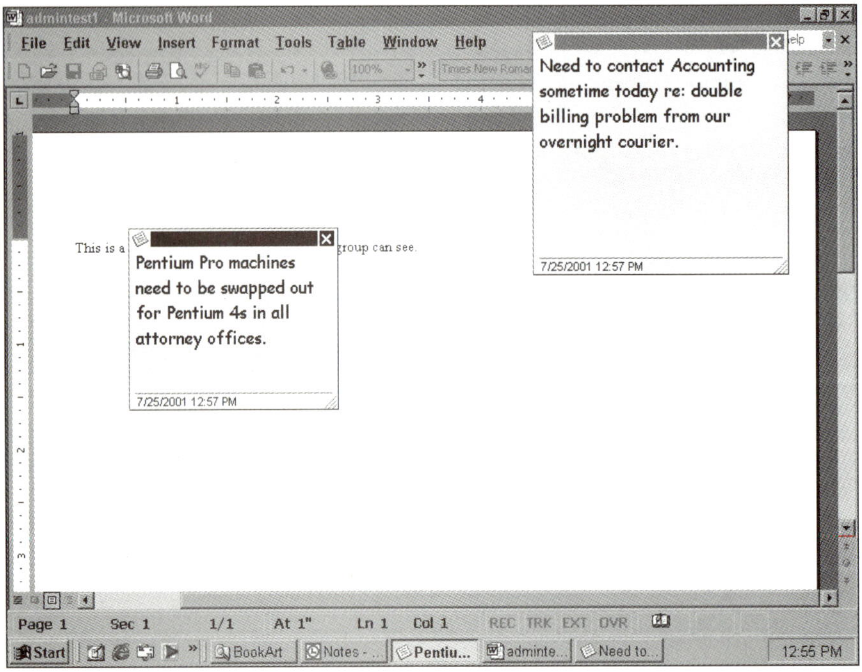

Figure 39-5: Outlook notes in other Office and Windows applications

Creating notes

To create a note from anywhere in Outlook, press Ctrl+Shift+N. Alternatively, you can choose File ⇨ New ⇨ Note or click the down arrow to the right of the New button in the toolbar and choose Note.

The note appears with the cursor flashing within it, and you can type the text of the note. To close the note, click the X icon at the upper-right corner of the note.

Although notes may appear small on the screen, you are not limited in the amount of text that you can enter in your notes. If you fill a note with text, the existing text scrolls as you continue to enter text.

If an existing note is already open on the screen, you can easily create a new note by clicking the icon at the upper-left corner of the note and choosing New Note from the shortcut menu that appears.

Opening existing notes

To open an existing note, click the Notes icon in the Outlook Bar (this displays all your notes). Then double-click the desired note to open it. You can resize the note, if desired, by dragging the lower-right corner of the note.

Categorizing notes

You can place your notes into various categories, which proves helpful when you want to view the notes by category (see "Viewing notes" later in this section). To categorize a note, right-click the note in the Notes pane and choose Categories from the shortcut menu that appears. In the Categories dialog box that appears, click the check box for a desired category and click OK.

Deleting notes

To delete an existing note, right-click the note in the Notes pane of Outlook and choose Delete from the shortcut menu that appears. Alternatively, you can click the Notes icon in the Outlook Bar. Click the desired note to select it; then press the Delete key, or click the Delete icon on the toolbar.

You also can delete notes that are open. To do so, click the note icon at the upper-left corner of the note. Then choose Delete from the shortcut menu that appears.

Viewing notes

You can view your notes in the Notes pane of Outlook in a number of ways. By default, notes are displayed as icons. You can change the way that notes appear in the Notes pane by selecting a desired view (Large Icons, Small Icons, or List) in the Standard toolbar when the Notes pane is visible in Outlook. While the Notes pane is visible, you also can right-click in any blank area of the toolbar and choose Advanced, which displays a list box in the toolbar area. In the list box, you can choose Icons, Notes List (which displays the title or first line of the note, along with the successive line of text from the note), Last Seven Days, By Category, or By Color. Choosing Define Views from the list displays a dialog box in which you can choose various custom options for displaying your notes. If you display more than one note at a time on your screen, you can use the Alt+Tab key to move between notes (and between your other open Windows applications).

Printing notes

You can print the text of your notes. First, open the note, using any of the techniques described in the previous "Opening existing notes" section. Then click the icon in the upper-left corner of the note and choose Print from the shortcut menu that appears. Select the desired options in the Print dialog box that opens and click OK to begin printing.

Saving notes as text

Normally, you don't have to do anything special to save notes. They are saved automatically, along with all the other entries that you make in Outlook. But if you want to save the text contained in a note to a text file, you can do so. Open the note, using the steps described in the previous "Opening existing notes" section. Then click the icon in the upper-left corner of the note and choose Save As from the shortcut menu that appears. In the Save As dialog box that opens, choose a file format (RTF for rich text format or Text Only for plain ASCII text), enter a filename, and click Save.

Setting your notes options

From any view within Outlook, you can change the default color, size, and font used by your notes. Choose Tools ⇨ Options and, in the Preferences tab of the dialog box that appears, click the Note Options button to display the Note Options dialog box (see Figure 39-6).

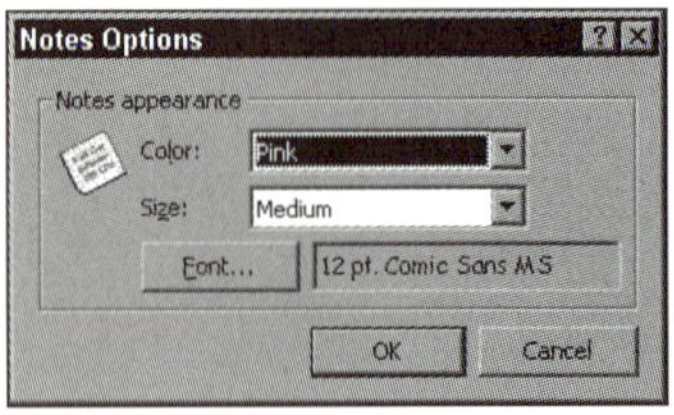

Figure 39-6: The Note Options dialog box

Use the Color list box to change the color of your notes (your choices are blue, green, pink, yellow, and white). In the Size list box, you can select small, medium, or large for the size of your notes. You can click the Font button to display a Font dialog box, where you can choose a desired font, font style, and font size.

Browsing the Web in Outlook

If you have a connection to the Internet, you can browse Web sites from directly within the Outlook window. To view a Web site, display the Address bar by double-clicking or by dragging the Address label at the right side of the Folder header (see Figure 39-7).

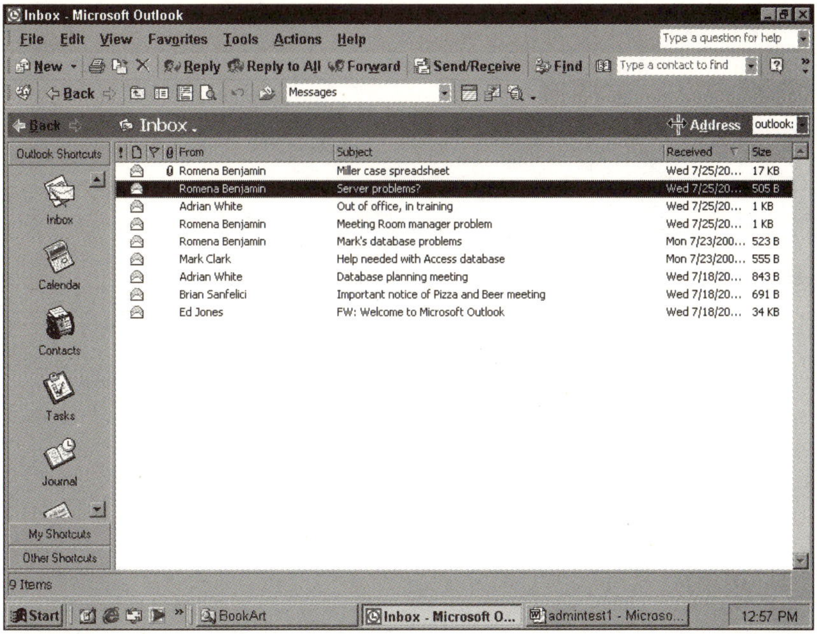

Figure 39-7: The Address label of the Folder header can be expanded to reveal an Address text box.

When you drag the Address label to the left, a text box appears to the right of the Address label, like this:

You can type your Web address into the text box and press Enter, or you can click the Go button at the right of the text box to go to the Web site. The site appears within the Outlook window, similar to the example shown in Figure 39-8.

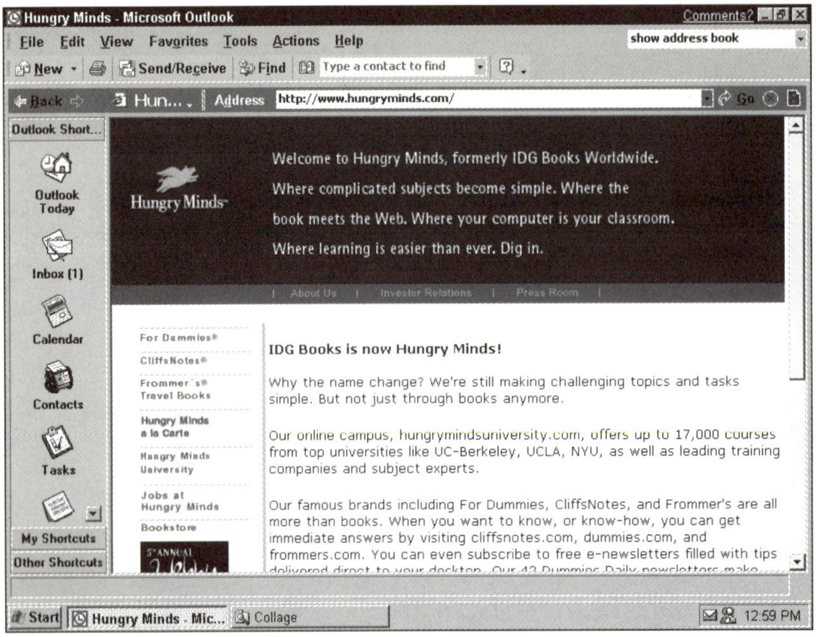

Figure 39-8: A Web page displayed within Outlook

You also can open the Favorites menu in Outlook to access your Internet Explorer favorites. You can select any of your favorites from the menu to open the corresponding Web page within Outlook.

Summary

In this chapter, you learned to use the Journal, Notes, and Web Browser features of Outlook. The chapter covered the following topics:

- You can use the Journal to record activities along a timeline.
- You can create manual entries in the Journal or set Outlook to automatically record certain types of activities.
- You can use the Start Timer and Pause Timer buttons to track billable time for any kind of client activity.
- The Notes feature in Outlook provides you with the electronic equivalent of paper sticky notes. You can create an unlimited number of notes, categorize them, view them in different ways and in other Office XP applications, and print their contents.
- You can browse Web sites from directly within the Outlook window by entering a Web address in a text box that appears to the right of the Address label in the Folder header.

In the next chapter, you learn how to work with files and folders within Outlook.

Chapter 40

Working with Folders and Files in Outlook

In This Chapter

- Viewing the folder list
- Working with folders
- Working with public folders
- Managing files from Outlook

AS CHAPTER 35 MENTIONS, OUTLOOK makes use of a design that stores your various Outlook items — messages, contacts, tasks, journal entries, and so on — in folders. These aren't folders of the type that you're accustomed to using on your hard drive or network drive. Rather, they can be likened to a specialized type of container designed to store Outlook items. These folders reside on your hard drive if you are using Outlook in a standalone mode. If you use Outlook on a network with Exchange Server, most of the folders actually exist in a space on the server that is assigned to your mailbox name under Exchange. That space is known as the *Exchange Store*.

The folders that are supplied with the default installation of Outlook are designed to handle your typical information-management tasks, but you can do more by customizing your use of these folders. You can create your own folders to better organize your various Outlook items. Also, you can use Outlook to perform basic file-management tasks (the kinds of tasks you might otherwise perform using Windows Explorer or My Computer). This chapter examines these topics at length.

Viewing the Folder List

When you click a particular icon in the Outlook Bar, Outlook opens the folder appropriate to that icon and displays the contents of the folder in the Information Viewer area of the Outlook window. For example, when you click the Contacts icon in the Outlook Bar, Outlook opens the Contacts folder and displays your list of contacts. You also can see the contents of any folder by choosing View ⇨ Folder List and then clicking a desired folder in the Folder List. Figure 40-1 shows the Folder List, just to the right of the Outlook Bar.

If you (or someone else) have not added any custom folders of your own design, you will see the following standard folders in the Folder List as a part of Outlook:

- Calendar
- Contacts
- Deleted Items

- Drafts
- Inbox
- Journal
- Notes
- Outbox
- Sent Items
- Tasks

If you are using Outlook on a network with Exchange Server, you will also see a folder titled Public Folders. Depending on how your network has been configured, you will probably see additional subfolders underneath the Public Folder.

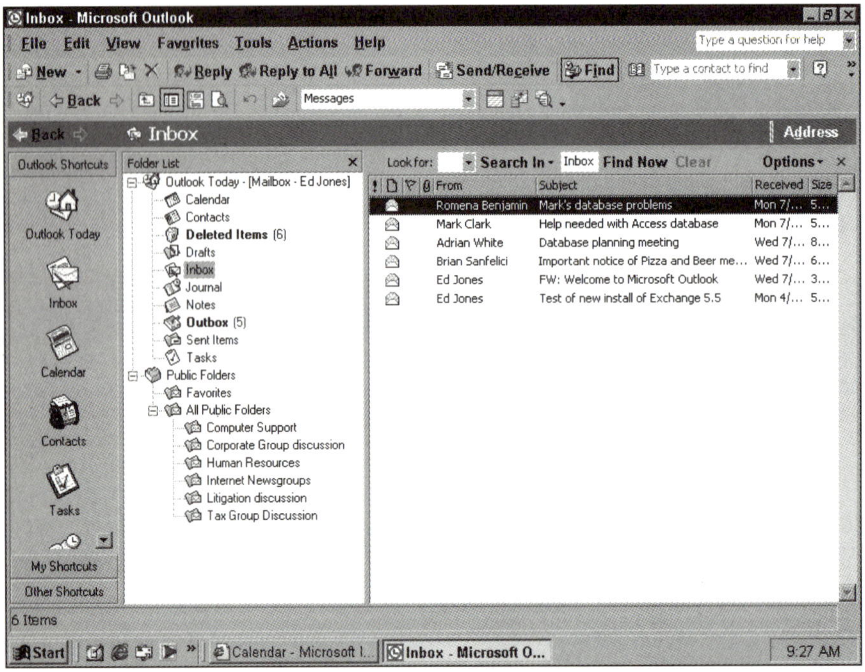

Figure 40-1: The Folder List appears at the right of the Outlook Bar and shows all your Outlook folders.

Working with Folders

When the Folder List is visible in the Outlook window, you can right-click any folder to display a shortcut menu with various options that prove useful when you're working with folders. (If you right-click one of Outlook's standard folders, some of the menu options are dimmed and therefore unavailable. For example, you cannot delete any of the standard folders supplied with Outlook, nor can you delete the Public Folder on an Exchange Server.) Figure 40-2 shows the shortcut menu that appears when you right-click a folder in the Folder List. The paragraphs that follow examine these menu options in greater detail.

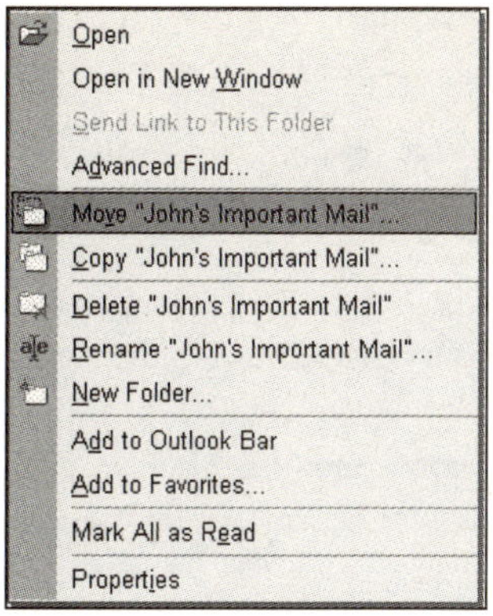

Figure 40-2: You can use the shortcut menu that appears when you right-click a folder in the Folder List to perform various actions associated with that folder.

Opening a folder

You can use the Open command of the shortcut menu to open a particular folder, but it's easier just to click the desired folder in the Folder List.

More useful is the Open in New Window command of the shortcut menu. This option is helpful when you want to have more than one Outlook window visible on the screen simultaneously to refer to different types of information (such as your contacts and your Inbox). This menu option also is handy when you want to open two folder windows so that you can move an item from one folder to another (see "Copying and moving items between folders").

Creating a new folder

When you have a large number of Outlook items, you can aid your organization of those items substantially by creating additional folders in which to store your items. For example, you could have one folder for client contacts, another for law-firm related contacts, and still another for personal contacts. You could have a folder for current mail and additional folders for mail that is older than a certain date. You can easily create additional folders within Outlook. A new folder that you create can visually reside at any of these levels in the Folder List:

- At the same level as the standard Outlook folders
- As a subfolder underneath one of the standard Outlook folders
- As a subfolder underneath a folder you previously created that resides at the same level as the standard Outlook folders
- As a subfolder underneath a subfolder

To create a new folder, do one of the following:

- If you want the folder to be at the same level as the standard Outlook folders, right-click your Outlook Today - Personal Folders file or, if you're using Outlook on a network with Exchange Server, right-click your Exchange mailbox name at the top of the Folder List. Then choose New Folder from the shortcut menu that appears.
- If you want the folder to be a subfolder under an existing folder, right-click the existing folder under which you want to create the new folder. Then choose New Folder from the shortcut menu that appears.

With either step, you now see the Create New Folder dialog box, shown in Figure 40-3. Use the steps that follow to define the new folder:

1. In the Name box, enter a name for the folder. (You can duplicate names, but *not* at the same level; in other words, the name must be different from the name of every folder that exists at the same level as the new folder.)
2. In the Folder Contains list box, choose the type of item that will be stored in the folder. In Outlook, a folder can contain only one type of item (with the exception of the Mail folder, which can contain mail and post items).
3. In the Select Where to Place the Folder portion of the dialog box, choose the folder below which the new folder should appear; then click OK to create the folder.

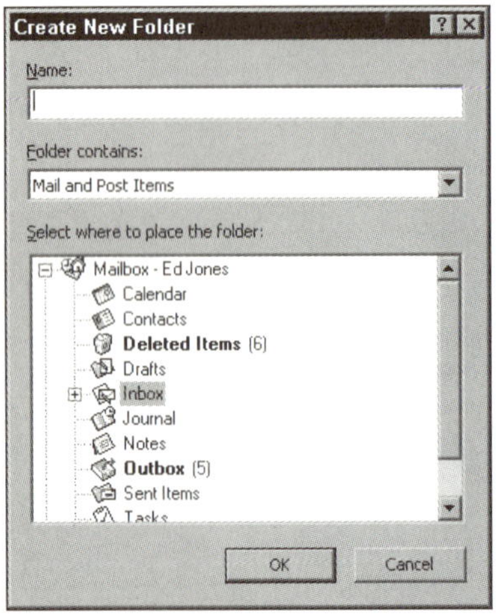

Figure 40-3: The Create New Folder dialog box is used to name a new folder, define the type of Outlook items it will contain, and specify a location for the new folder.

Copying and moving items between folders

After creating your new custom folders, you need to know how to copy and move existing items from other folders to those folders. Although you easily can copy or move items from one Outlook folder to another, remember that a folder can store only a specific type of Outlook item. If you copy or move an Outlook item from one folder to another folder of the same type — such as from the Outlook Contacts folder to a folder you've created to store contact items — the item type remains the same. But if you copy or move an item from one type of folder to another type of folder, Outlook changes the item type to match the destination folder. For example, if you move a mail message from your Inbox into a custom folder that you created to store tasks, Outlook changes the message to a task.

You can copy an item from one folder to another by selecting the item, choosing Edit ⇨ Copy, and then selecting the destination folder and choosing Edit ⇨ Paste. Or use the keyboard shortcuts: Ctrl+C for Copy and Ctrl+V for Paste. Either method leaves the original item in the original folder while placing a copy of the item in the new folder.

To completely remove an item from one folder and place it in another, open the source folder in the Folder List and drag the item from the Information Viewer area to the destination folder. You also can use the Edit ⇨ Cut and Edit ⇨ Paste commands or the keyboard shortcuts Ctrl+X for Cut and Ctrl+V for Paste.

Copying and moving folders

You can copy or move any folder (along with the contents of the folder) to another location in the Folder List. Note that you can copy or move only the folders that you have created; you cannot copy or move any of the standard Outlook folders.

To copy or move a folder, right-click the desired folder within the Folder List and choose either Copy or Move from the shortcut menu to open the applicable dialog box. Figure 40-4 shows the Move Folder dialog box.

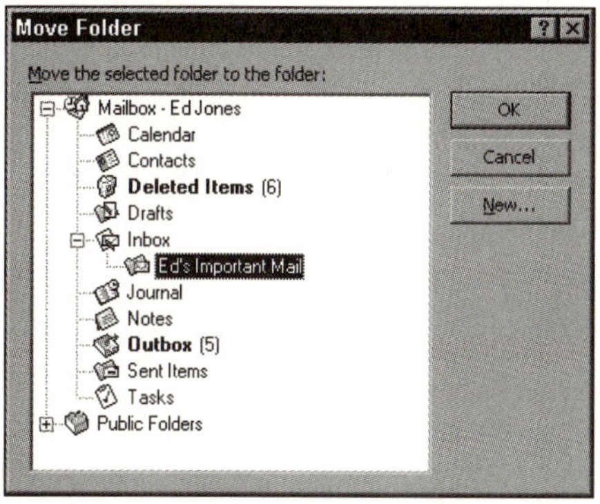

Figure 40-4: Use the Move Folder dialog box to move a folder to another location within the Folder List.

In the Folder List within the dialog box, choose a folder beneath where you want the moved or copied folder to appear and then click OK to move or copy the folder.

TIP: You also can move a custom folder by dragging the folder to a new location within the Folder List.

Deleting a folder

You can delete any folder that you have created. To delete a folder, right-click the folder in the Folder List and choose Delete from the shortcut menu. Outlook displays a warning dialog box asking you to confirm the deletion of the folder and any contents within the folder. When you click Yes in the dialog box, the folder is deleted.

Renaming a folder

To rename a folder that you have created, right-click the folder in the Folder List and choose Rename from the shortcut menu. When you do so, the insertion pointer appears within the folder name in the Folder List, and you can edit the contents. After you make your changes and press Enter, the new name is applied to the folder.

Adding an icon for a folder to the Outlook Bar

By default, the Outlook Shortcuts and My Shortcuts groups within the Outlook Bar contain the standard icons that are a part of Outlook. If you create your own custom folders and use them often, you may want to add shortcuts for your folders to the Outlook Bar. You can easily create an icon for a custom folder in the Outlook Bar by performing the following steps:

1. In the Outlook Bar, select the group where you want to place the icon (such as Outlook Shortcuts or My Shortcuts).
2. In the Folder List, right-click the folder for which you want to create the shortcut.
3. From the shortcut menu that appears, choose Add to Outlook Bar.

Working with Public Folders

If you use Outlook on a network with Exchange Server, you likely also have the use of public folders at your disposal. Public folders, as their name implies, are Outlook folders that can be used by large groups of individuals within a firm or organization. (Actually, the term *public* isn't technically accurate in most cases because firms and organizations typically restrict the use of public folders to internal employees. However, it is technically possible to design a public folder that can be accessed from a Web site, making such a public folder truly *public*.) Some examples of using public folders within the legal environment include the following:

- Providing storage folders for files related to a particular client matter
- Providing a bulletin-board type of discussion for individual practice groups within a large law firm
- Making human resource materials available to the support staff
- Providing postings of personal items for sale by employees of the firm

Public folders are created under the top-level public folder in the Exchange Store. The Exchange Administrator at your firm or organization will control the permissions for public folders, and you may need to check with the Exchange Administrator or with the computer support staff to determine whether you have the permissions needed to create public folders. After you speak to the appropriate computer mavens at your firm or organization, you can create a public folder using the following steps:

1. Choose View ⇨ Folder List to display the Folder List.
2. In the list, expand the Public Folders by clicking the plus symbol to the left of Public Folders; then expand All Public Folders by clicking the plus symbol to the left of All Public Folders.
3. Right-click All Public Folders (make sure that you right-click All Public Folders and *not* Public Folders); then choose New Folder from the shortcut menu that appears. The Create New Folder dialog box (refer back to Figure 40-3) appears.
4. In the Name box, enter a name for the public folder.
5. In the Folder Contains list box, choose the type of item that will be stored in the folder. (If you are setting up a public folder for others to place messages in, or to use as a sort of bulletin board, leave the list box set to the default of Mail and Post Items.)
6. If you want the folder to exist as a subfolder beneath an existing public folder, select the folder below which the new folder should appear.
7. Click OK to create the new public folder.

After the public folder exists, you can make use of it just as you would use any Outlook folder. With public folders, the difference is that others in your organization can also make use of the public folder. Everyone who has been granted access to public folders on the Exchange Server can see your public folder within the All Public Folders list.

About public folder permissions

By default, only two individuals have full rights to do anything within a public folder: the "owner" or person who created it (that's you) and the Exchange Administrator. Others have varying rights, and the Exchange Administrator can modify these rights. By default, anyone who has access rights to the Exchange Server public folders can read items and can submit items or files to your public folder. As the owner, you can create, read, modify, and delete any items or files in the folder, and you can create subfolders under your public folder. You also can delete the public folder, along with all its contents.

Technically, as the owner of the folder, you also can set different permissions that control the rights others have in using your public folder. You set permissions by right-clicking your public folder, clicking Properties in the shortcut menu that opens, clicking the Permissions tab in the dialog box that appears, and choosing the permissions options. However, the subject of permissions of public folders on an Exchange Server is a complex one that is beyond the scope of this book. If you feel a need to modify the default permissions given to a public folder, it is best to have a discussion with your Exchange Administrator. She or he can come up with an appropriate strategy that provides the best mix of availability and security for the particular task that you have in mind.

Managing Files from Outlook

In terms of file management, you can use Outlook as a substitute for Windows Explorer or My Computer. Without leaving Outlook, you can browse files located on your computer's disk drives or on a network attached to your computer. (While you're viewing files, you can quickly open, copy, print, or delete them.) You can even perform searches to find files you are looking for.

To view or open files on your computer or on the network, click the Other Shortcuts button in the Outlook Bar and then click My Computer in the Outlook Bar. When you do this, Outlook displays your computer's resources, as shown in Figure 40-5.

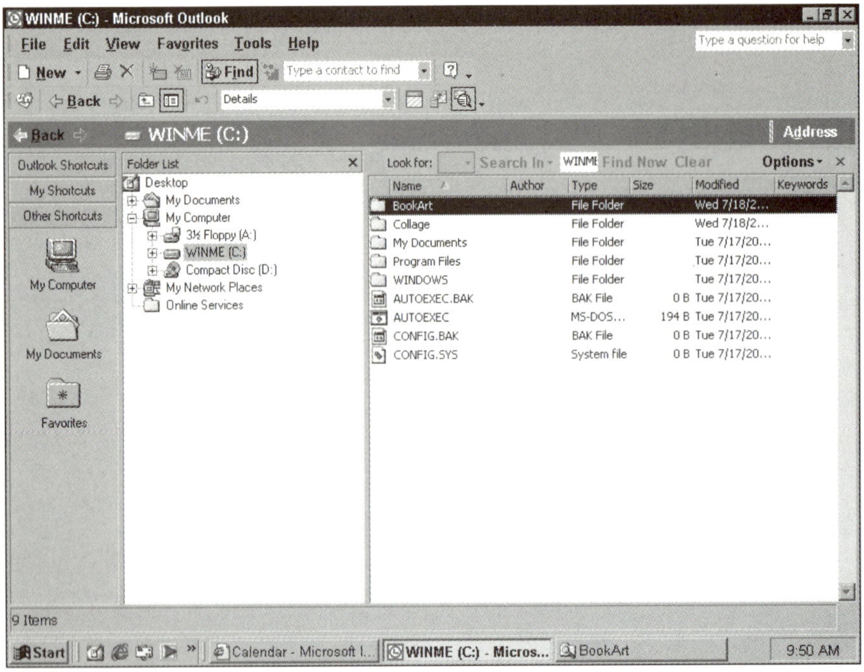

Figure 40-5: Files and folders viewed within Outlook

You can view your files in different ways: as icons, by file details (as shown in Figure 40-5), by author, by file type, along a timeline, or with only folders and program files visible. To change the way Outlook displays your files, choose View ⇨ Current View and then select the desired type of view from the next menu that appears.

Working with files

You can open files from Outlook by using the following steps:

1. Click the Other icon in the Outlook Bar.
2. Click My Computer in the Outlook Bar.
3. Find the desired drive and double-click it.
4. If the desired file is in a folder, double-click the folder.
5. Double-click the file you want to open. The file will open in the appropriate Windows application.

When a file is visible in Outlook, you can perform a number of common tasks by right-clicking the file and choosing a desired option from the shortcut menu that appears. Figure 40-6 shows the shortcut menu that appears when you right-click a file in Outlook.

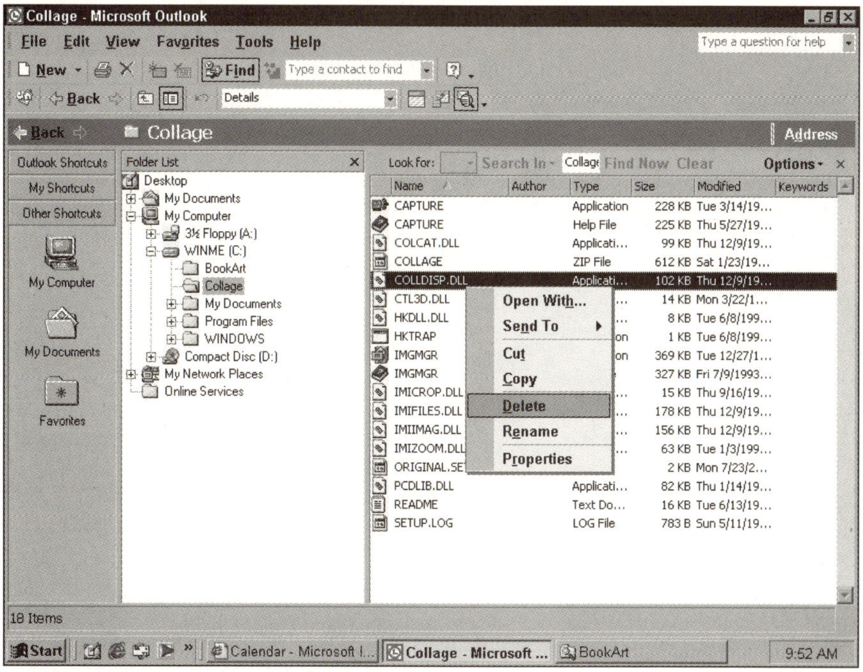

Figure 40-6: The shortcut menu for files in Outlook

The menu offers the most commonly used options of Open With, to open the file using an appropriate Windows application; Rename, to change the name of the file; and Delete, to delete the file. In addition to these options, you can also choose Send To, to copy the file to a diskette or to send it to an e-mail recipient on the network. Finally, the Properties option opens a dialog box that displays the properties for the file.

Finding files in Outlook

For those times when you are working in Outlook and you suddenly need to locate a file, there is no need to close Outlook and go to Windows Explorer or My Computer. You can use the Find window of Outlook to search for files. And you don't need to be viewing files to do this; you can search for files from any view of Outlook. Here's how to find files from Outlook:

1. From any view in Outlook, choose Tools ⇨ Advanced Find (or press Ctrl+Shift+F) to open the Advanced Find window.
2. In the Look For list box, choose Files. The Advanced Find window now looks like the screen shown in Figure 40-7.
3. If the folder you want to search does not appear in the In box (or if you want to search more than one folder), click Browse to select the desired folder or folders. In the Select Folders dialog box that appears, use the plus symbols to expand drives or folders as needed, click the check boxes beside the folders you want to search, clear the check boxes beside the folders you don't want to search, and click OK.
4. If desired, enter a filename or a search pattern to look for in the Named box of the Files tab and choose any other desired options in the Advanced Find window.

5. Click Find Now. When the search is complete, the Advanced Find window expands to show all files located in the lower portion of the window.

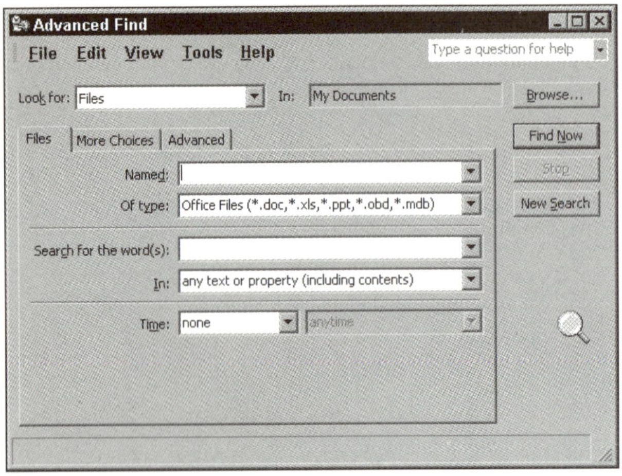

Figure 40-7: The Advanced Find window used for searching for files

---

TIP: If you want to save the search so that you can use the same search at a later time, choose File ⇨ Save Search from the menus of the Advanced Find dialog box and then enter a name for the search in the dialog box that appears. To later run the saved search, choose Tools ⇨ Advanced Find; then choose File ⇨ Open Search in the Advanced Find window and double-click the search you want to use.

Summary

This chapter has provided details on the use of folders and files within Outlook. Folders can serve as valuable organizational aids in managing your various Outlook items. This chapter covered the following:

- You can create custom folders within Outlook to store various Outlook items.
- You can copy and move items between folders.
- You can add shortcuts for your custom folders to the Outlook Bar.
- If you are using Outlook on a network with Exchange Server, you can create public folders that can be used by large groups at your firm or organization.
- You can perform file management tasks within Outlook.

In the next chapter, you learn how to create custom forms that can be used by other Outlook users within a legal environment.

Chapter 41

Creating Legal Forms in Outlook

In This Chapter

- Using custom forms: Why bother?
- Six forms at your beck and call
- Deciding which form to use
- Creating a custom form in Outlook: An example
- Saving a form
- Publishing a form
- Using a custom form
- Showing, hiding, and renaming pages
- Introducing VB script programming

THIS CHAPTER EXAMINES THE concept of *custom forms* in Outlook and how such forms can be used at law firms and within the legal environment. With Outlook custom forms, you are not restricted to the default forms that Outlook provides. You can utilize Outlook's capability to modify and save custom versions of the default forms to construct forms that meet your precise needs and requirements.

Custom Forms: Why Bother?

Outlook is a combination of e-mail client and PIM, or personal information manager. The default forms that are a part of Outlook are well designed to meet the personal information needs of general business computer users. The problem is, law firms and legal environments aren't "general" businesses. As our readers are well aware, the business of law has its own unique demands. To complicate matters, different law firms do things differently.

Outlook addresses the need for flexibility by providing a complete development environment with a variety of tools that can be used to create custom forms. This built-in flexibility means that you are not restricted to the fields in the standard forms that are supplied with Outlook. Figure 41-1 shows just one example of a custom form in Outlook.

Here's a list of just some of the types of tasks you can accomplish with custom forms in Outlook:

- Create Outlook forms to duplicate your new business memo, client/matter information form, or library research request form.
- Design an e-mail message form with additional customized fields, and upon sending, automatically route that form to a particular person or distribution list.
- Produce custom reports using programming code that combines Outlook data with Microsoft Word documents.

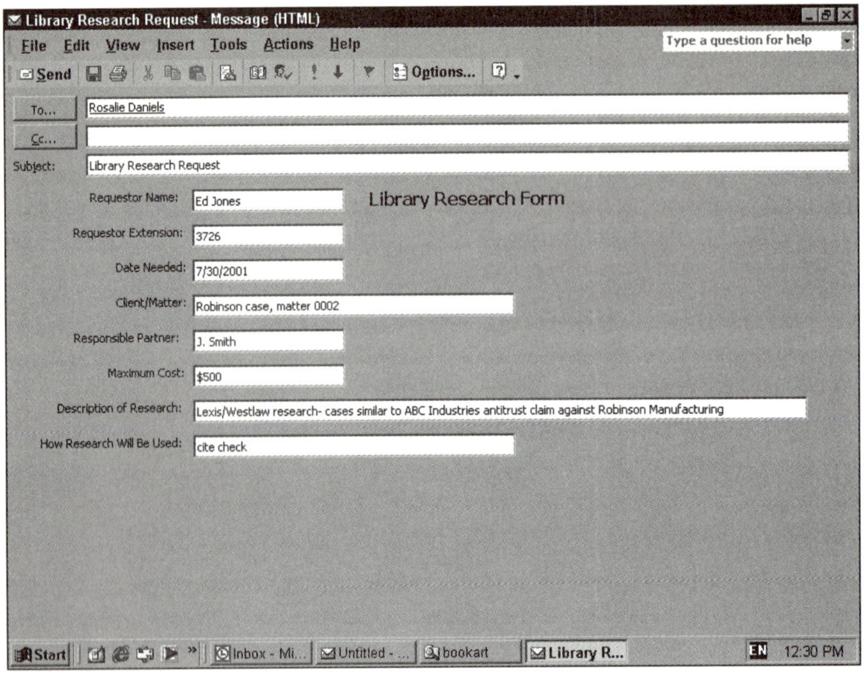

Figure 41-1: A custom form in Outlook

Six Forms at Your Beck and Call

As a custom development environment, Outlook differs from Word, Excel, and Access in one important respect. With Word, Excel, and Access, it is possible to create a custom form from scratch, beginning with a completely blank form. You can add fields to the form and use that form to store information in a Word document, an Excel worksheet, or a table of an Access database. Outlook is different because creating a custom form based on a completely blank form is not possible. Instead, every custom form in Outlook must be based on one of six forms provided with the program. We've purposely listed these in nonalphabetical order — they appear here instead in the order in which they are most likely to be used as custom forms within the legal environment. Before you begin to design a custom form, you must choose a default form upon which you will base the custom form.

To open a form in Design view, click Tools ⇨ Form ⇨ Design a Form from the menus and select one of the default forms in the dialog box that appears. In Design view, you can create and add custom fields to various parts of the form; you also can change the appearance of the form in ways to suit your needs.

CAUTION: In Outlook, you can modify forms and save changes to the default forms that are used by the installation of Outlook on your computer. Typically, you don't want to do this unless you are sure that a desired change to a form should be incorporated into every future use of that form. In most cases, you open a default form in Design view, make changes to the form, and save it *under a different name* to your Personal Forms Library or to the Organizational Forms Library on an Exchange Server. How to do this is detailed later in the chapter.

The Outlook forms that you can customize include the following:

- **The Message form:** This is the most-used Outlook form because it appears whenever you send or read an e-mail message. Many law firms and corporate legal departments use customized versions of Message forms to handle specialized communications such as new business memo forms, associate evaluation review forms, or vacation leave request forms.
- **The Post form:** This form is similar in design to the Message form. Instead of being used to send information to a recipient, the Post form is used to post a message to a specific folder. At many law firms, custom versions of the Post form are used to post information to various folders on an Exchange Server. Examples include forms designed for posting discussion threads related to a particular practice group and forms designed for posting information about personal items for sale by the firm's employees. The default page of the Post form can be modified, as can the optional pages labeled *(P.2)* through *(P.6)*.
- **The Contact form:** Many law firms modify the standard Contact form provided by Outlook to include custom fields for a client name (or client ID code) and matter name or matter ID code. As with the Message form, you can modify the default page of the Contact form, as well as the pages labeled *(P.2)* through *(P.6)*. However, you cannot modify the Details page of the Contacts form.
- **The Appointment form:** The Appointment form stores information about appointments and events. You cannot modify the default page of the Appointment form, nor can you modify the Scheduling page used to indicate when people are available to attend meetings (see Chapter 38 for specifics about scheduling appointments and meetings). You can modify any of the pages labeled *(P.2)* through *(P.6)* of the form, adding custom fields as needed.
- **The Task form:** This form is used to record details of tasks. You cannot modify the standard built-in pages of the Task form (the Task page or the Details page). You can modify any of the pages labeled *(P.2)* through *(P.6)* of the form, adding custom fields as needed.
- **The Journal Entry form:** The Journal Entry form contains one default page, called *General*. You cannot modify the General page, but you can modify any of the pages labeled *(P.2)* through *(P.6)* of the form, adding custom fields as needed.

All Outlook forms contain a series of tabs, although users of the default Message form see only one tab. Each tab reveals a page; if you click the tab while in Design view, the page appears. Pages whose names appear in parenthesis are hidden when a user opens the form, although you can change this aspect for all the optional pages indicated by the tabs labeled *(P.2)* through *(P.6)*.

The All Fields, Properties, and Actions pages are common to all Outlook forms. The All Fields page shows the default fields that are available for use in a form. A *field* is a single fact that is related to a category, such as a Subject (in a Message form), a Company Name (in a Contacts form), or a Start Time (in an Appointment form). In addition to the default fields that exist with forms, you can create your own custom fields, which can be used on the form. This is key to the flexibility offered by the use of custom forms with Outlook. Custom fields can store a variety of types of data, including text, numbers, currency amounts, and date/time values.

The Properties page contains various options that let you control overall settings for the form, such as the icon it displays within Outlook, a description and contact name for the custom form, a version number of your choosing, and an optional category and subcategory of the form.

The Actions page of a form can be used to determine actions that take place when a user performs a certain action, such as replying to a message or posting a reply to a folder.

One important point to note is that with the Message form, you can modify the default, or initial, page of the form. This is not true of all Outlook forms, as you will see in the sections that follow. Only the Message form, the Post form, and the Contact form allow you to modify the default page of the form. The other forms only allow changes on the optional (custom) pages that are labeled *(P.2)* through *(P.6)*. However, you can hide the default pages and use the same fields on a custom page.

CAUTION: If you customize the first page of a Contact form, users of Outlook 97 won't be able to open it. Only Outlook 98 or later versions support the use of custom contact forms with changes made to the default page.

In addition to the six forms described thus far, two forms listed as <Hidden> appear in the Design Form dialog box when you choose Tools ⇨ Form ⇨ Design a Form. These hidden forms are Meeting Request and Task Request. The Meeting Request form is a variation of the Appointment form and is used by Outlook when you schedule meetings. The Task Request form is a variation of the Task form and is used by Outlook when you assign a task to another individual.

Deciding Which Form to Use

Because any custom Outlook form must be based on one of the six forms described, before you begin to design a custom form, you must decide which existing form to use as a starting point. The best way to do this is to think about what you want your custom form to accomplish. You may also find it helpful to open each form in Design view, examine the All Fields page, and see which form already contains most of the fields needed by your custom form. In some cases, your decision will be based on particular features that are included as part of a standard form. For example, if your custom form involves posting messages to a folder, you'll want to use the Post form. If your custom form involves sending messages to various members of your firm or organization, you'll likely make use of the Message form. If your custom form needs a timer with Start and Stop buttons, you will need to use the Journal Entry form.

Creating a Custom Form in Outlook: An Example

To get an idea of the possibilities offered by Outlook form development and the overall process required, this section details the steps needed to create a custom form. The example presented here results in creating the Library Research Request form (refer to Figure 41-1). An attorney or paralegal at a law firm can use the Library Research Request form to send a detailed research request to the firm's librarian or library research staff.

Starting the design of a custom form

First, click Tools ⇨ Form ⇨ Design a Form to display the Design Form dialog box (see Figure 41-2).

The Library Research Request Form will be used to send a custom message to the firm's librarian, so basing the design on a Message form is an appropriate choice. Select Message in the dialog box and click Open. An Outlook Message form appears in Design view (see Figure 41-3). Maximize the form so that you have adequate room to work while designing the custom form.

If your screen looks very different from your typical view of Outlook, don't panic. There's a lot going on here, and this book can't cover all the nuances in complete detail — in fact, entire books have been written on the subject of custom applications development within Outlook. Through the example in this section, we hope to give you an idea of what is possible with custom forms in Outlook and perhaps provide an incentive for learning more.

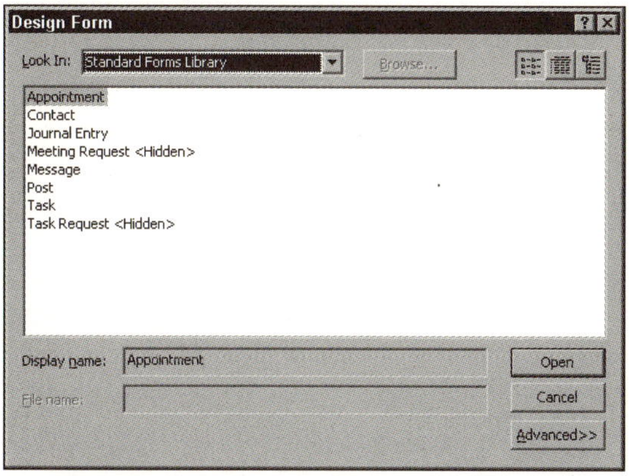

Figure 41-2: The Design Form dialog box lets you choose the type of form on which to base your custom form.

In Design view, you see the basis of the Outlook form. You also see pages indicated by the series of blank tabs mentioned in the preceding section, which are labeled *(P.2)* through *(P.6)*, *All Fields*, *Properties*, and *Actions*. Also visible is the Field Chooser (see Figure 41-3), which lets you add custom fields to an Outlook form (covered in "Creating custom fields for the form" later in this section).

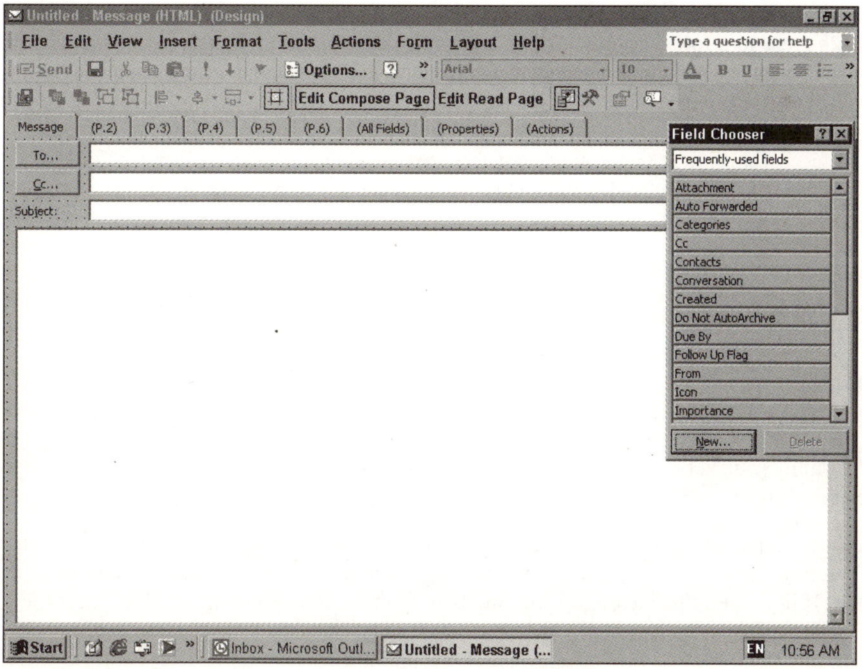

Figure 41-3: The Message form, visible in Design view in an Outlook window

Another resource that you'll use often in designing custom forms is the Control Toolbox. The Control Toolbox doesn't appear by default, but you can display it at any time. Choose Form ⇨ Control Toolbox from the menus to make the Control Toolbox appear (see Figure 41-4). Drag the Control Toolbox to the right of the window so that you have room to work on custom fields that you will later add to the form.

Figure 41-4: The Control Toolbox is used to add a variety of controls, such as text labels, text boxes, check boxes, and buttons, to a custom form.

Currently, the form contains a To button and a corresponding To text box, a Cc button and corresponding Cc text box, a Subject text label and a corresponding Subject text box, and a large text box for the message of the e-mail. Each of the text boxes in the default Message form are actually linked to standard fields that are displayed within the Field Chooser. For example, the To text box is linked to the To field in Outlook, the Cc text box is linked to the Cc field, the Subject text box is linked to the Subject field, and the Message text box (that large box where you type the text of an e-mail) is linked to the Message field.

With custom forms, you often need fields that are not a standard part of Outlook. For example, the Library Research Request form needs fields for the requestor name and telephone extension, the date needed (for the research), the client and matter, a description of the research, a description of how the research will be used, and a maximum cost for the research. Because none of these fields exists in Outlook, you need to create them. You also need to add controls on the form that let users enter information into your custom fields. No matter what the use, creating any custom form in Outlook involves the following series of steps. (This is just an overview here; we go through them in more detail after the next paragraph.)

1. Choose a form to base your custom form upon and open that form in Design view.
2. Add and modify controls, either to the default page or to one of the custom pages.
3. Create any needed custom fields and link these to controls on the form where needed.
4. Test the form.
5. Save the form design as an Outlook template.
6. Publish the form to your Personal Forms Library or to the Organizational Forms Library on the Exchange Server.

The exercise that follows illustrates these steps and builds the custom Library Research Request form in the process. You may already have the Message form open on your screen in Design view from the start of this section. If not, open the Message form and follow these steps to continue designing the custom form:

1. Click anywhere inside the Message box (the large text box that occupies most of the Message form) to select the box; then press the Delete key.

2. Right-click inside the To text box (the box that you would normally use to enter an e-mail address) and choose Properties from the shortcut menu that appears.
3. In the Properties dialog box that opens, click the Value tab.
4. Click the Set the Initial of Value of This Field To check box, click in the text box beneath, and enter the e-mail name of your firm librarian. Figure 41-5 shows an example of this setting. When the form runs, the librarian's e-mail address is filled in automatically.

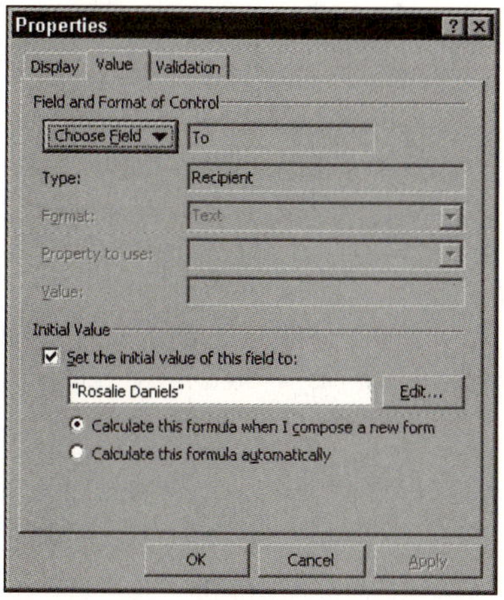

Figure 41-5: A default value entered into the Initial Value area of the Properties dialog box for a field causes that value to automatically appear when the form is used.

5. Click OK in the Properties dialog box to store the setting.
6. Right-click in the Subject text box on the form. Choose Properties again from the shortcut menu.
7. Click the Value tab, turn on the Set the Initial Value of This Field To check box, and enter the text **Library Research Request** in the box beneath. Then click OK.

Creating custom fields for the form

Now you are ready to create custom fields that will be used by the form. The Field Chooser should still be visible on your screen; if it isn't, choose Form ⇨ Field Chooser to display it. Then perform these steps to define the custom fields needed for the form:

1. Click New at the bottom of the Field Chooser, to display the New Field dialog box.
2. Under Name, enter **Requestor Name**. Leave the Type and Format list boxes set to their defaults of Text and click OK. Note that at the top of the Field Chooser, User-Defined Fields in the Inbox now appears in the drop-down list. This indicates that the Field Chooser is now displaying custom fields that you create.
3. Click New in the Field Chooser. In the New Field dialog box, under Name, enter **Requestor Extension**. Leave the Type and Format list boxes set to their defaults of Text and click OK.
4. Click New in the Field Chooser. In the New Field dialog box, under Name, enter **Date Needed**. Change the Type list box to Date/Time and change the Format list box to the month/day/year format that appears in the list box. Then click OK.
5. Click New in the Field Chooser. In the New Field dialog box, under Name, enter **Client/Matter**. Leave the Type and Format list boxes set to their defaults of Text and click OK.

6. Click New in the Field Chooser. In the New Field dialog box, under Name, enter **Responsible Partner**. Leave the Type and Format list boxes set to their defaults of Text and click OK.
7. Click New in the Field Chooser. In the New Field dialog box, under Name, enter **Maximum Cost**. Change the Type list box to Currency and choose the second available format in the Format list box (the one without the cents). Then click OK.
8. Click New in the Field Chooser. In the New Field dialog box, under Name, enter **Description of Research**. Leave the Type and Format list boxes set to their defaults of Text and click OK.
9. Click New in the Field Chooser. In the New Field dialog box, under Name, enter **How Research Will Be Used**. Leave the Type and Format list boxes set to their defaults of Text and click OK.
10. Choose Form ⇨ Control Toolbox to display the Control Toolbox (if it isn't already visible).
11. Drag the Field Chooser and the Control Toolbox to the right side of the screen (if you haven't done so already) so that you can place your new controls and work with their appearance.

Adding custom fields to the form

At this point, you are ready to add your custom fields to the form. You can easily do this by dragging custom fields from the Field Chooser onto the form. Perform the following steps:

1. Drag the Requestor Name field from the Field Chooser onto the form and drop it onto a blank area of the form beneath the Subject field. No matter where in the blank area you drop the field, it appears directly beneath the Subject field.
2. Move the mouse pointer over the Requestor Name field until it changes to the shape of a four-headed arrow. Drag it slightly down and to the right to leave space between the existing Subject field and the new field. Leave at least one inch between the left edge of the form and the start of the label for the field.
3. Drag the Requestor Extension field from the Field Chooser onto the form and drop it beneath the Requestor Name field.
4. Move the mouse pointer over the Requestor Extension field until it changes to the shape of a four-headed arrow. Drag it slightly down and to the right, roughly aligning it horizontally with the Requestor Name field and leaving a small amount of space vertically between the Requestor Name field and the new field.
5. Drag the Date Needed field from the Field Chooser onto the form and drop it beneath the Requestor Extension field.
6. Move the mouse pointer over the Date Needed field until it changes to the shape of a four-headed arrow. Drag it slightly down and to the right to leave space between the existing Requestor Extension field and the new field. (If the fields don't appear perfectly aligned, don't worry; you will address this aspect of the form shortly.)
7. Drag the Client/Matter field from the Field Chooser onto the form and drop it beneath the Date Needed field.
8. Move the mouse pointer over the Client/Matter field until it changes to the shape of a four-headed arrow. Drag it slightly down and to the right to leave space between the existing Date Needed field and the new field.
9. Drag the Responsible Partner field from the Field Chooser onto the form and drop it beneath the Client/Matter field.

10. Move the mouse pointer over the Responsible Partner field until it changes to the shape of a four-headed arrow. Drag it slightly down and to the right to leave space between the existing Client/Matter field and the new field.
11. Drag the Maximum Cost field from the Field Chooser onto the form and drop it beneath the Responsible Partner field.
12. Move the mouse pointer over the Maximum Cost field until it changes to the shape of a four-headed arrow. Drag it slightly down and to the right to leave space between the existing Responsible Partner field and the new field.
13. Drag the Description of Research field from the Field Chooser onto the form and drop it beneath the Maximum Cost field.
14. Move the mouse pointer over the Description of Research field until it changes to the shape of a four-headed arrow. Drag it slightly down and to the right to leave space between the existing Maximum Cost field and the new field.
15. Drag the How Research Will Be Used field from the Field Chooser onto the form and drop it beneath the Description of Research field.
16. Move the mouse pointer over the How Research Will Be Used field until it changes to the shape of a four-headed arrow. Drag it slightly down and to the right to leave space between the existing Description of Research field and the new field.

Earlier in the chapter, you learned that the overall process of custom form design in Outlook includes the step of creating any needed custom fields and linking the custom fields to controls on the form where needed. By dragging controls from the Field Chooser onto a form, you perform both these steps in a single action. Whenever you drag a field from the Field Chooser onto a form, Outlook creates a new control for the field, and it binds or *links* that control to the new field. The other common way to create a control for a field is to click an appropriate control on the Control Toolbox and drag in the form to create the new control. If you use this method, you must then link the desired field to the control (it doesn't happen automatically). You do so by right-clicking the new control and clicking the Choose Field button on the Value tab of the Properties dialog box that appears.

NOTE: Although Outlook may appear to support an unlimited number of custom fields, in practice it has a limit. You can place somewhere between 250 and 400 custom fields on a form before encountering a warning message in Outlook indicating that no more space is left in the portion of memory that Outlook allocates to custom fields. (The exact number varies, depending on the type of fields that you add to a form and the amount of data stored in each field.)

Cleaning up the design of the form

At this point, your form should resemble the example shown in Figure 41-6. Unless you have been extremely careful in placing the fields, the text boxes may appear slightly disorganized because it can initially be difficult to place custom fields in an aligned fashion. Don't be too concerned: The Form Design view provides an easy way to align the fields.

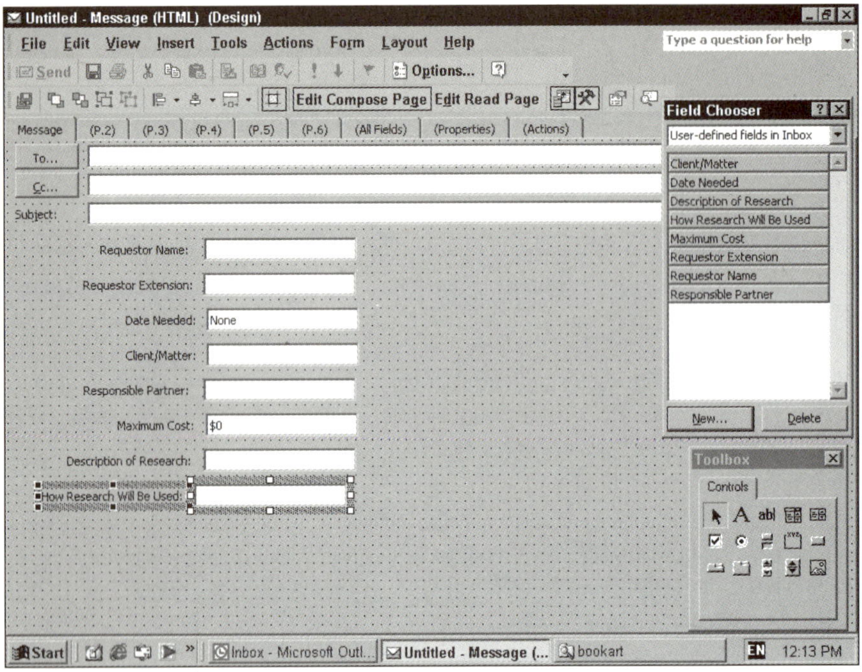

Figure 41-6: The appearance of a custom form after placing the custom fields

Perform these steps to improve the design of the custom form:

1. Click just below and to the right of the text box for the last custom field (How Research Will Be Used) and drag upward to a point just above the text box for the first custom field (Requestor Name). Before releasing the mouse button, make sure that the visible dotted line surrounds part or all of the text boxes for the fields, as shown in Figure 41-7.
2. If desired, you can click each field label (such as the words *Requestor Name* or *Description of Research*) to select the label, move the mouse pointer near the label until it changes shape to a four-headed arrow, and drag the label closer to the corresponding field. This is a typical step in custom form design, making the form appear attractive to the people in your firm or organization who will use the form.
3. Click the text box for the Description of Research field to select it. Move the mouse pointer near the right edge of the field until it changes shape to a double-headed arrow; then drag the field to expand its size to nearly the full width of the form.
4. Using the same technique as described in Step 5, expand the width of the Client/Matter and How Research Will Be Used fields until the fields are roughly half as wide as the form.
5. Click the Label tool in the Control Toolbox (it's the one with a large letter *A*) and click and drag slightly to the right of the Requestor Name field until the dotted rectangle that appears measures roughly three inches wide and one-half inch high. When you release the mouse, a Label control containing the word *Label* followed by a number (such as *Label9*) appears.
6. With the dotted line surrounding all the text boxes for the new fields, release the mouse button. All the text boxes now appear *selected*, surrounded by small white or black squares.
7. From the menus, choose Layout ⇨ Align ⇨ Left. The text boxes automatically align, similar to the example shown in Figure 41-8.

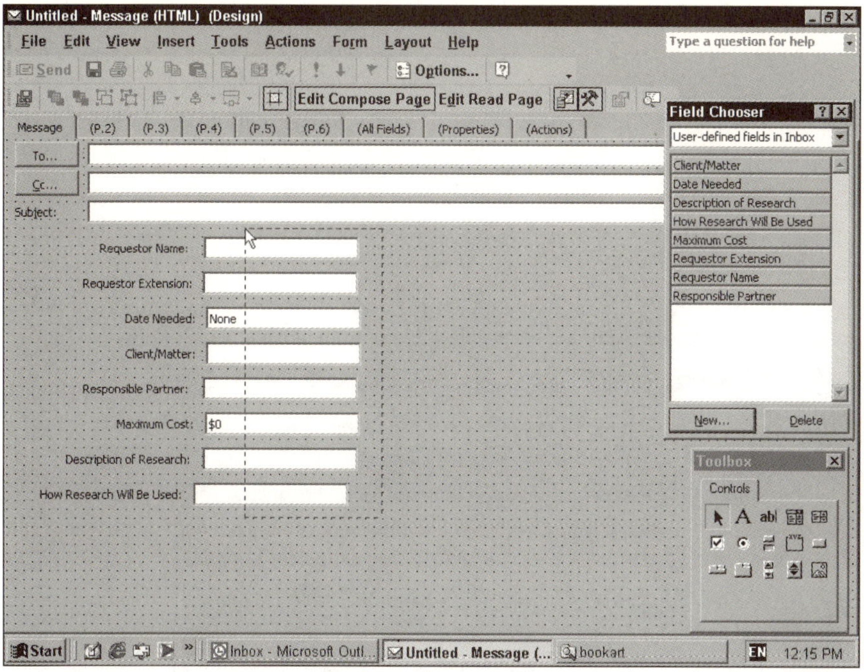

Figure 41-7: The dotted line used to select a group of text boxes

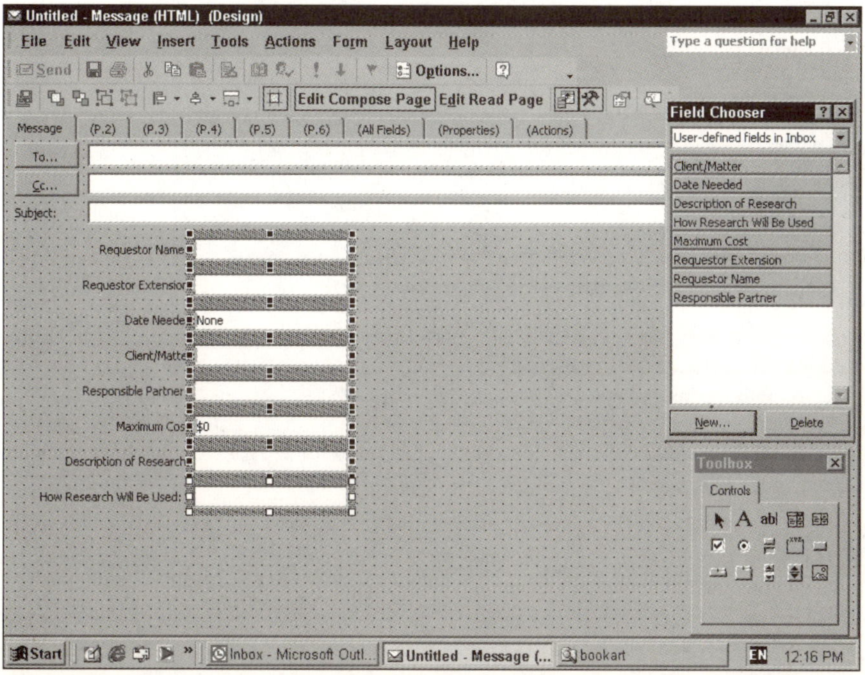

Figure 41-8: Text boxes in a custom form after alignment

8. Click inside the label control until the insertion pointer appears beside the word *Label9*; then use the backspace key to erase the existing text. Type the words **Library Research Request Form** and click anywhere outside the label.
9. Right-click the words in the label and choose Properties from the shortcut menu that appears.
10. On the Display tab of the Properties dialog box that opens, click Font to display a Font dialog box.
11. Change the Font Size to 12; under Font Style, choose Bold. Click OK twice to close the Font dialog box and the Properties dialog box.

At this point, you can close the Field Chooser and the Control Toolbox by clicking the X symbol in the upper-left corner of each. Your form should resemble the example shown in Figure 41-9.

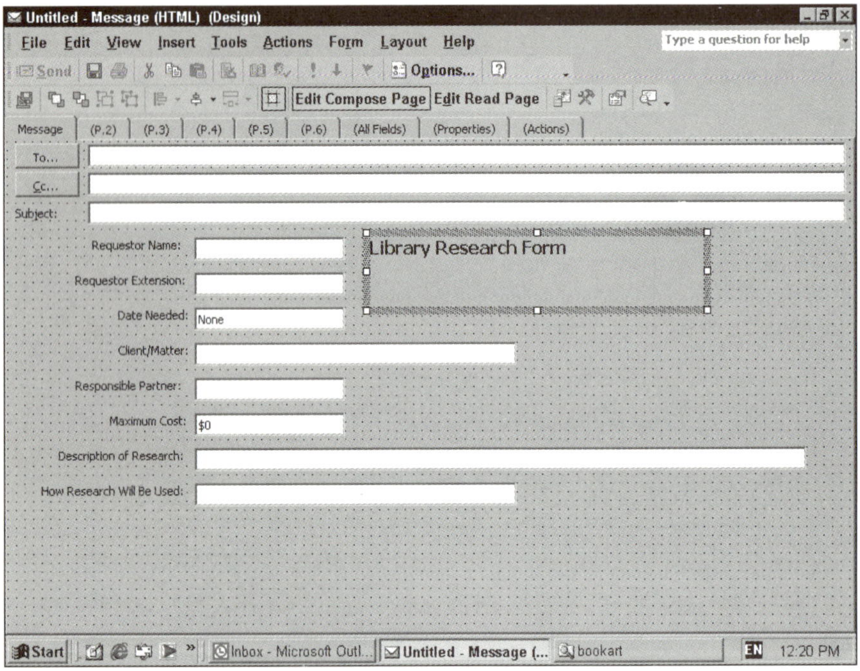

Figure 41-9: The completed Library Research Request form in Design view

One more simple but important step is needed to make your form operational. Open the Form menu and choose Separate Read Layout. A dialog box appears, warning you that any changes you have made to the read layouts will be lost. Click Yes to accept this option. By turning off this option (which is on by default), you force Outlook to use the same form for both data entry and viewing by the recipient. In some cases, design advantages exist to creating forms with separate compose layouts and read layouts, but these are too complex a subject for this brief introduction to custom form design.

Testing the form

Testing your custom form is much easier than designing the form. Open the Form menu and choose Run This Form. The form appears as it would if opened by a user in Outlook (see Figure 41-10).

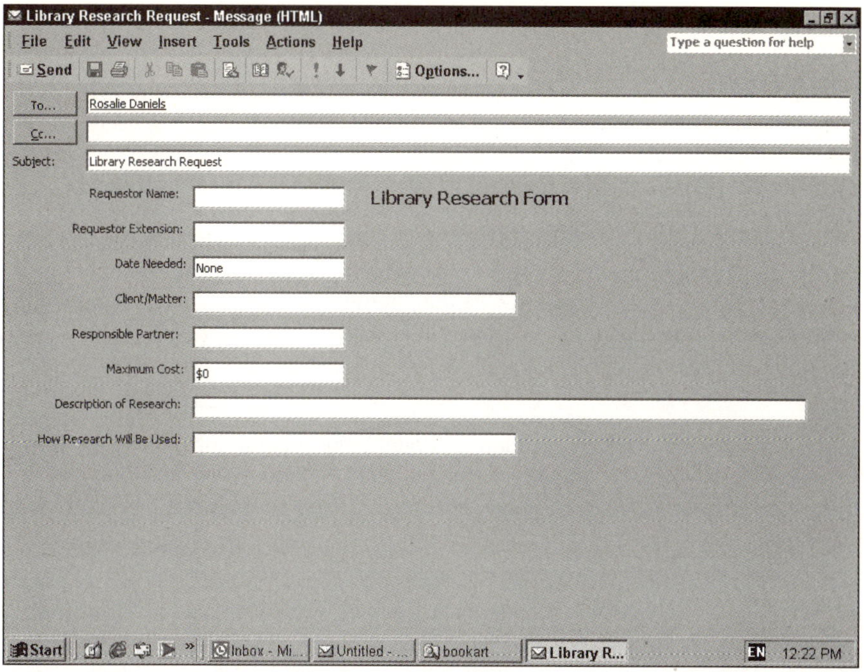

Figure 41-10: The completed Library Research Request form as it appears when the form is run

You can fill in the fields (you might want to replace the librarian's name in the To field with your own name to avoid bombarding your firm librarian with e-mail as you are testing the form). Also, entering your own name lets you see the results of the form posted back to your own Outlook mailbox.

Fill in the fields with sample data and click Send. The design of the form reappears in Design view, and when your network mail server next distributes your mail, the form appears in your Inbox as a message. (If, when you open the form in your Inbox, you see only an empty Message box and none of the custom fields you created, you omitted the last step prior to this subheading. See the paragraph immediately before the "Testing the form" subheading and perform the steps outlined in that paragraph.)

Saving a Form

After a custom form is complete, you need to save your work. Actually, with forms of any complexity, you probably want to save the form regularly as you are designing it. During the development process, you can save a custom form as an Outlook template (*.OFT) file in any folder as long as you remember where you placed it. However, we recommend that you save the form to

\Program Files\Microsoft Office\Templates

on the drive where your copy of Microsoft office is installed. This folder corresponds to your Personal Forms Library location when you choose Tools ⇨ Form ⇨ Choose Form, making it easy to find the form later in case you want to make additional changes.

Choose File ⇨ Save As to display a Save As dialog box. Navigate to a desired folder (such as C:\Program Files\Microsoft Office\Templates), give the template a name of your choosing in the File Name box, and click Save to save the form design.

Don't close the form's Design view window yet, however. One last step remains, which is…

Publishing a Form

Assuming that you (or others) will want to use the custom form on a regular basis, you need to perform one final step. You need to *publish* the form to a location where you or others can readily find the form for regular use. You can publish the form to your Personal Forms Library (if it is exclusively for your own use), or you can publish it to the Organizational Forms Library on the Exchange Server if it is for use by others at your law firm or organization. (You need permissions from your Exchange Server Administrator to publish the form to the Organizational Forms Library. Talk to your Exchange Server Administrator about obtaining permissions, or you can e-mail the OFT file you saved previously to the Administrator, who can install it in the Organizational Forms Library.)

NOTE: Technically, you can publish a form to any Outlook folder, such as your Inbox folder or Contacts folder. However, we recommend that you publish forms to your Personal Forms Library or to an Organizational Forms Library on your network's Exchange Server. Doing so makes it easier to locate a form when you want to use it.

To publish the form, have the form open in Design view and choose Tools ⇨ Forms ⇨ Publish Form As. The Publish Form As dialog box opens. In the Look In list box at the top of the dialog box, choose Personal Forms Library if you want to restrict the form to your personal use, or choose Organizational Forms Library if you have been given rights to this folder on the Exchange Server and you want to publish the form for firmwide use.

In the Form Name box, type a name for the form. In the Display Name box, type a name that you want the form to be listed as in the dialog box that appears when others choose a custom form. (The names can be the same name, if desired.) Finally, click Publish.

If you are publishing the form for the first time, Outlook displays a dialog box recommending that the Save Form Definition with Item check box on the Properties tab of the form be selected. Click Yes to select this option and publish the form.

After the form is saved and published, you can close the form's Design view window.

Using a Custom Form

To use a custom form in Outlook, from any view choose Tools ⇨ Forms ⇨ Choose Form. In the Choose Form dialog box that appears, choose Personal Forms Library or Organizational Forms Library, depending on where you published the form. Select the form in the list box and click Open. Outlook loads and displays the custom form on your machine.

Showing, Hiding, and Renaming Pages

The example described in this chapter makes use of the default page of the Message form, and desired modifications are made to that default page. In many cases, you can't modify the default page of a form. (As noted earlier, the default pages for the Appointment form, Task form, and Journal Entry form cannot be modified.) In some cases, you may have more custom fields than will fit on a default page, even when it can be modified. For such cases, you need to know how to use one or more of the optional pages labeled *(P.2)* through *(P.6)*.

You can place custom fields that you create using the Field Chooser and tools you create using the Control Toolbox onto any of the optional pages of a form, and you can hide or show any of these pages. (By default, all the optional pages of a form are blank and are hidden when a user runs the form.)

To rename a page, have the form open in Design view and click the tab for the desired page to make that page active. Choose Form ⇨ Rename Page from the menus, enter a new name that you want to appear on the tab in the Rename Page dialog box that appears, and click OK.

To hide or show a page, choose Form ⇨ Display This Page. The command functions as a toggle, so choosing it repeatedly alternately hides or shows the page. You can easily tell when a page will be hidden. If the name of the page in the tab appears within parentheses while in Design view, that page will be hidden when the form runs.

TIP: The default pages of custom forms can be hidden with the Form ⇨ Display This Page command. This capability of Outlook form design can prove useful in cases in which the form's default page is not customizable and you want to use most but not all of the default fields on a form's default page. For example, you might want to create a custom form based on the Task form, but you might not want a Due Date or Status field in the form. Because the default page of the Task form cannot be modified, you could drag all the default fields already provided on the Task page from the Field Chooser onto an optional page of the form, omitting the Due Date and Status fields. You could then use the Form ⇨ Display This Page command to hide the default Task page and to show your optional page.

An Introductory Look at VB Script Programming

As if the capability to provide custom forms isn't enough, Outlook even offers a complete *application development environment*, or a platform upon which sophisticated custom applications can be constructed. In different areas, Outlook provides access to both VB Script (Visual Basic Script) and VBA (Visual Basic for Applications). These are programming languages loosely based around Microsoft's Visual Basic programming environment and can be used to perform an unlimited number of custom tasks within Outlook. (If you did not install the Visual Basic programming features as part of Office, you may be prompted to install the Office XP CD before using the features described next.)

As a quick and simple example, perhaps you've created the Library Research Request form using the steps outlined earlier in the chapter, and you would like one simple modification. You decide that it would be nice if the form would warn users to check with a firm partner before sending in requests for research totaling more than $500.00. This is the kind of modification that can easily be performed using VB Script code as part of the custom form. Use the following steps if you want to see how this can be accomplished:

1. Open the Library Research Request form in Design view (choose Tools ⇨ Form ⇨ Design a Form and look in the location where you published the form earlier).
2. Choose Form ⇨ View Code from the menus. A Script Editor window opens, which is where you can write VB Script programming code to perform various tasks as someone uses your custom form.
3. In the menus within the Script Editor window, choose Script ⇨ Event Handler. An Insert Event Handler dialog box opens (see Figure 41-11).

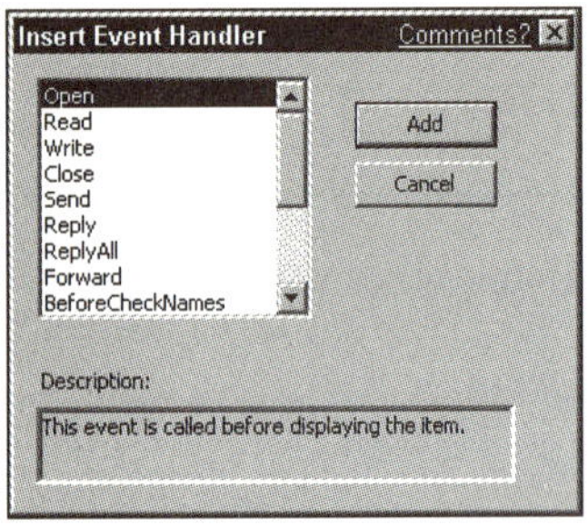

Figure 41-11: The Insert Event Handler dialog box

4. Select Close in the list within the dialog box and click Add. You now see the following VB Script program code added to your Script Editor window, with the insertion pointer flashing between the two new lines of program code:

```
Function Item_Close()

End Function
```

5. Type the following line of program code between the new lines, exactly as shown here:

```
MsgBox "Call for Partner approval on all research over $500.00."
```

6. Don't forget the double quotation marks on both sides of the text string. Then choose File ⇨ Close (or press Alt+F4) to close the Script Editor window.
7. Choose File ⇨ Save As and save the Outlook Template file to the same folder that you saved your work to earlier in the chapter.
8. Choose Form ⇨ Run This Form to test the form with the added VB Script code.

Try filling in sample data in the form and then click Send. Before the form closes, you see a dialog box created by the VB Script program code that you added to the form (see Figure 41-12). Click OK, and Outlook sends the custom form.

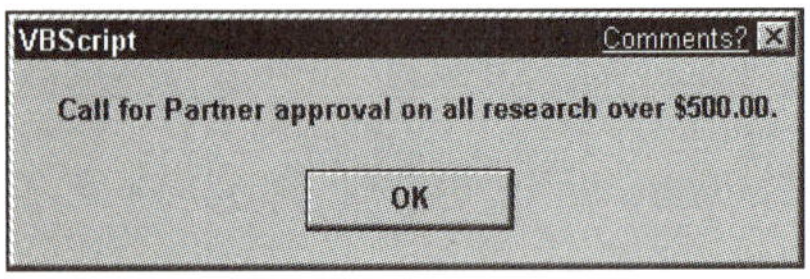

Figure 41-12: A dialog box that appears as a result of programming using VB Script

This was admittedly an extremely simple example of what is possible with programming in Outlook; this example is designed to provide a "get your toes wet" type of introduction. This is *not* a book on Outlook programming, so we won't attempt to do justice to that subject here. However, you should be aware of the fact that powerful custom applications are possible if you choose to learn programming (or choose to turn an experienced Visual Basic programmer loose with Outlook as a development platform).

Just a Beginning...

This chapter has intentionally just scratched the surface of what you can do with custom form design in Outlook. The CD-ROM included with this book also contains examples of custom Outlook forms designed for use in the legal environment, stored as template (.OFT) files. You may want to load and open these forms in Design view to get an idea of what is possible with custom form design in Outlook. To make any of the forms accessible, copy the corresponding .OFT file from the CD-ROM to your \Program Files\Microsoft Office\Templates folder on the hard drive where Office is installed. The form will then appear in the dialog box when you choose Tools ⇨ Form ⇨ Choose Form and select the Personal Forms Library. After you copy the file, you also can choose Tools ⇨ Form ⇨ Design a Form, open a form that you've copied onto your machine, and make any desired changes. You can then save and publish that form to your Personal Forms Library or to the Organizational Forms Library on an Exchange Server.

Summary

This chapter has detailed the use of Outlook to create custom forms that can be used by other Outlook users in a legal environment. In the chapter, you learned the following:

- Using Outlook, you can create custom forms based on one of six standard Outlook forms.
- Before starting the process of creating a custom form, you should decide which of the standard Outlook forms will work best as the basis for your custom form.
- Using the Field Chooser and the Control Toolbox, you can add custom fields and additional controls to pages of an Outlook form.
- You can save forms as Outlook Template (.OFT) files so that you can make future changes to the form, and you can publish forms to your Personal Forms Library, to an Outlook folder, or to the Organizational Forms Library on an Exchange Server,

This chapter completes the coverage of Outlook. The next part of the book provides tips and techniques for using the Office applications with your law firm's intranet or Internet Web site.

Part VI

Office XP and the Law Firm Intranet

Chapter 42

Word, Excel, PowerPoint, and the Law Firm Intranet

In This Chapter

- The Internet and the Web
- Understanding intranets
- Working with HTML
- Saving Word documents as Web pages
- Saving Excel workbooks as Web pages
- Saving PowerPoint presentations as Web pages

ALONG WITH ITS COMPANION chapter that follows, this chapter provides information that you can use in producing content for the law firm intranet. Intranets are virtually a standard at large firms and have come into increasing use by mid-size firms and even by many moderately small firms (those numbering a dozen or so attorneys). The main applications of the Microsoft Office suite — Word, Excel, PowerPoint, and Access— provide easy-to-use and flexible techniques for creating Web pages for use on an intranet. (The same Web pages can also be used on an Internet Web site of a law firm or an organization.)

Because intranets and the Internet are different concepts to many readers, a few explanations of terms may be in order. (If you're intimately familiar with the Internet, intranets and the World Wide Web, you may want to skip this section and the next and dive right into specifics for creating Web pages for your intranet or Internet site using Word, Excel, or PowerPoint.)

The Internet and the World Wide Web

Working with computers on a daily basis, you are likely to be quite familiar with the Internet as an information resource. But even if you are an extensive user of the Internet, the quick summary that follows will serve to establish a definition of terms that are used throughout this chapter and the next.

The *Internet*, of course, is the global collection of computers, linked by means of telephone and microwave lines and generally accessible to the public by means of various connections in offices and homes. The Internet grew out of a research project in the 1970s, which originally linked university and government computers in the United States. Since its inception, the Internet has grown to encompass millions of computers spread throughout hundreds of nations. Any computer user with an Internet connection (either by means of a phone line, cable modem, or direct hookup) can connect to the Internet and gain access to the volumes of information located there.

One major component of the Internet is the World Wide Web. There are other parts of the Internet, but the Web is the most well-known part. The *Web* is that part of the Internet that makes use of graphical software known as *Web browsers* and of files stored primarily in HTML, or HyperText Markup Language format. The computers on the Internet that store the HTML files are also known as *Web servers*. When computers connect to the Internet to retrieve this data, they use Web browser software, which converts the incoming information (encoded in HTML) to graphical pages displayed as a combination of text, graphics, and, in some cases, audio and video. Commonly used Web browsers include Microsoft Internet Explorer and Netscape Navigator.

Web browsers use a number of different methods for communicating with Web servers on the Internet. All these various methods are known as *protocols*. The most commonly used protocol is the Hypertext Transfer Protocol (HTTP). It was originally designed to facilitate the transfer of documents stored in the Hypertext Markup Language (HTML) format, but it has evolved over the years to support an assortment of graphics, audio, video, and other types of content. HTTP is the most widely used but is not the only protocol to move information across the Internet. Additional protocols include File Transfer Protocol (FTP), Telnet, and Gopher.

Each server on the Internet has a unique address, commonly known as the *Internet address* (and less commonly known by the official name of *URL*, or *Uniform Resource Locator*). When you establish an Internet connection, open a Web browser, and enter an Internet address such as `http://www.supremecourtus.gov`, you are entering the address for the Web server that provides the home page for the United States Supreme Court. Most URLs are entered using this syntax:

Protocol://Web-server-address/path

In the preceding syntax, *protocol* identifies the Internet protocol used to establish a connection to the server (commonly `http://`), *Web-server-address* identifies the domain name of the Internet server, and *path* specifies the file or page on that Web server. As an example, the URL to the home page of Microsoft Office is

`http://www.microsoft.com/office`

Understanding Intranets

Many Internet- and intranet-related uses of Word, Excel, and PowerPoint involve making documents, worksheets, and presentations available on *intranets*. An intranet is a private network of computers that is available only to the members of a specific organization, such as a law firm. Intranets are constructed for and managed by the individual organization and provide a way for groups of users to gain important access to information that is relevant to the business groups within the organization. Intranets make use of World Wide Web technology — Web servers, network connections, and Web browser software — to allow members of the organization to share information.

Because intranets provide a cost-effective means for sharing information among knowledge workers at a law firm, they offer tremendous potential. They're relatively easy to deploy and very easy to use. And the secret of the usefulness of any intranet — its content — can be maintained by nontechnical people using tools such as Microsoft Office. (This ease of use frees your firm's technical staff to concentrate on tasks that are more cost-effective for their skills.) Some common uses for the law firm intranet include

- Firmwide announcements
- Listings of billing histories

- Firm newsletters
- Client matter lists
- Discussion groups
- Links to legal research sites
- Practice group resource pages
- Personnel address and phone directories
- Tickler calendars
- Work-in-progress reports
- Frequently asked questions regarding software used by the firm

Intranets are very popular with mid-size to large law firms because intranets let partners, associates, and employees of the firm share work-related information in a confidential manner. Many law firms routinely use intranets to allow employees and attorneys to better communicate with outside clients and with each other. Intranets are commonly used to exchange files, to provide access to client or employee data, and to allow collaboration or workflow sharing between members of a law firm. Figure 42-1 shows an example of the main page of a law firm intranet. Although the example is a figment of the authors' imagination, the layout and structure of the example are typical of many law firms that have chosen to implement an intranet.

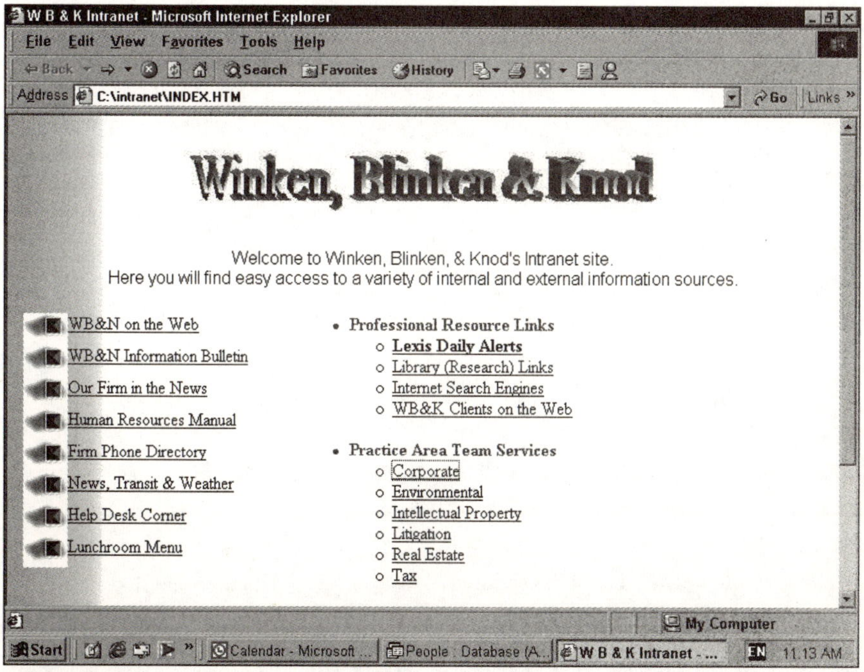

Figure 42-1: The main page of a law firm intranet

Extranets, that "other" net...

Although intranets have become firmly established at many law firms, another type of net is gaining in popularity within law firms and corporate legal departments: the *extranet*. As the Latin roots of the name imply, extranets are aimed at specific outsiders, as opposed to workers within a law firm or organization. Extranets provide private access to a secure number of outsiders (typically, the clients of the firm or the co-counsel). Because extranets (like intranets) are based on Internet technologies, you can use the same techniques as are outlined in this chapter and the next to produce content for extranets. And because extranets also consist of Web pages stored on Web servers, clients and co-counsel need nothing more specialized than a Web browser and an Internet connection to make use of your extranet. The difference between an extranet and an ordinary firm Web site is that extranets provide restricted access to a select group of individuals, normally through some sort of logon and password process. Common uses for a law firm extranet include secure client or co-counsel collaboration with attorneys, providing clients with the ability to view documents relevant to their particular case, and offering online billing summaries and access to deposition transcripts, forms, and model documents.

In an era when clients are expecting more in terms of customer service from law firms, extranets provide a cost-effective means of offering clients value-added services. At the same time, extranets (when implemented with effective planning) can help pay their own costs by saving in terms of other expenses. Your firm can reduce the costs of phone calls, photocopying, and the sending of documents (often via expensive overnight courier services) by making information available on a secured extranet.

Even very small firms can provide clients with the value-added services that an extranet provides, without bearing the expense of a Web server and protective firewall; they can do this by using an outside service provider. If you are setting up an extranet for a very small firm or you are a solo practitioner, you can opt for one of the legal-oriented extranet providers, such as West WorkSpace from Westlaw (`www.westlaw.com`) and TrialNet (`www.trialnet.com`). Or if you or someone on your staff has a moderate level of design skills, you can opt for a general business provider such as Microsoft's bCentral (`www.bcentral.com/services`). For example, it's possible to construct an extranet hosted on bCentral based around Microsoft SharePoint Team Services. You could design the site using Microsoft FrontPage and pay a service fee of around $50 monthly (at the time of this writing), and you would be limited to 20 users of your extranet. Whatever approach you use, keep in mind that extranets are seen and used primarily by your clients as opposed to your co-workers, so there is little room for flaws. You must ensure that your extranet operates smoothly and that content stays updated to meet your clients' needs.

Working with HTML: An Overview

HTML, or Hypertext Markup Language, is the language used for publishing information to the World Wide Web and to intranets that use Web technology. HTML is a text-based language that makes use of special codes called *tags*. These tags are included in the text of the HTML documents and provide instructions to the Web browser software that determine how the data appears when it is viewed by the end user. The HTML tags are commands that appear between the less than (`<`) and greater than (`>`) symbols. Many HTML tags have beginning and ending versions, and the text is contained between the beginning and ending tags. The beginning and ending tags use the same command, but the ending tag includes an extra forward slash symbol (`/`). As an example, a valid statement used within the HTML language might contain the words *bolded text* in bold type, by making use of the following tags:

```
This sentence includes <B>bolded text</B> along with words that are not
bolded.
```

In a Web browser, the sentence would appear as follows:

> This sentence includes **bolded text** along with words that are not bolded.

A minimal document would include a starting `<HTML>` tag and an ending `</HTML>` tag and within these tags, a starting `<BODY>` tag and an ending `</BODY>` tag. All information that could appear in the body of the document (as displayed within the Web browser) could be placed between the `<BODY>` and `</BODY>` tags. Additionally, there are dozens of other tags that can be used within HTML documents to specify attributes such as centering and other text formatting, the use of text and background colors, the placement of graphic images, and the addition of hyperlinks and audio, to name a few. As a very simple example of the use of HTML, the following listing contains data that has been exported from an Access query into an HTML file, and the file has been edited using Windows Notepad in preparation for posting to a law firm's intranet site.

```
<HTML>
<HEAD>
<TITLE>W B & K Phone Listing</TITLE>
</HEAD>
<BODY>
<BODY BGCOLOR = SILVER>
<P>
<BLOCKQUOTE>
<B>Winken, Blinken, & Knod Client Phone Listing</B>
<P>
```

```
<TABLE BORDER>
<CAPTION><B>Client Phone Numbers</B></CAPTION>
<TR><TD>Chi, Laurie</TD><TD>St Thomas</TD><TD>340 555-5601</TD></TR>
<TR><TD>Drew, James</TD><TD>Atlanta</TD><TD>308 555-7923</TD></TR>
<TR><TD>Epstein, Tony</TD><TD>Toronto</TD><TD>416 555-2391</TD></TR>
<TR><TD>Green, Greg</TD><TD>Bel Air</TD><TD>213 555-4343</TD></TR>
<TR><TD>Harris, Scott</TD><TD>Tiburon</TD><TD>304 555-3437</TD></TR>
<TR><TD>Jones, Jarel</TD><TD>Carmel</TD><TD>305 555-1267</TD></TR>
<TR><TD>Moore, Harry</TD><TD>Vancouver</TD><TD>604 555-3532</TD></TR>
<TR><TD>Manzick, Dave</TD><TD>Seattle</TD><TD>206 555-0934</TD></TR>
<TR><TD>Ortiz, Manuel</TD><TD>Tuscon</TD><TD>802 555-3672</TD></TR>
<TR><TD>Rogers, Lisa</TD><TD>Sanford</TD><TD>415 555-1293</TD></TR>
</TABLE>
</BLOCKQUOTE>
<P>
<HR>
<P><A HREF="index.html">Return to WB&K Intranet Home Page</A>
</BODY>
</HTML>
```

Figure 42-2 shows how a Web browser would display the preceding HTML file.

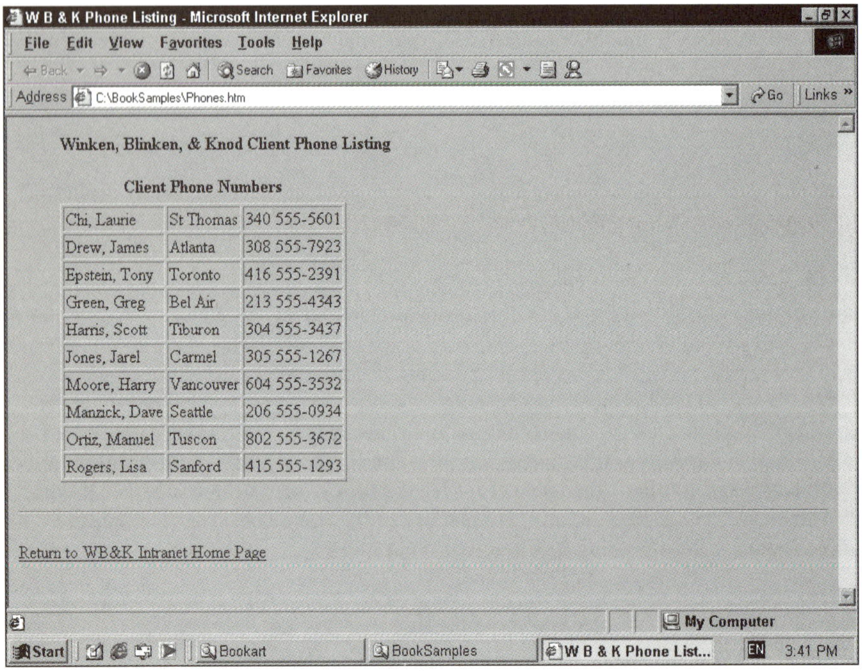

Figure 42-2: The resulting display of the HTML code when viewed through a browser

As mentioned earlier, Word, Excel, and PowerPoint are each capable of creating Web pages, which consist of one or more files in HTML format. You can also edit the HTML files produced by any of the Office programs, using any editor that can save files in plain text format. Additionally, numerous tools on the market automate the creation of HTML files and professional-looking Web pages, such as Microsoft's own FrontPage, which is supplied with some versions of Office.

Although you don't need to know all the nuts and bolts of HTML coding to work with Word, Excel, PowerPoint, Access, and your intranet or Internet Web site, it's a good idea to at least be familiar with some minimal basics of HTML coding and with the concept of saving your data in HTML file format. In order to publish documents or data on your intranet or on the Internet, you'll need to save that data as Web pages and upload it to your Web server. If you are dealing with a law firm or organization intranet, your Webmaster can tell you how to upload the HTML files you produce to your firm or organization's Web server. If you are managing a Web site on the Internet or on an intranet, you already know how to do this. Much of the rest of this chapter deals with getting Word, Excel, or PowerPoint data ready for uploading to your server. (The following chapter covers the same topic for Microsoft Access.)

TIP: When you are using Word, Excel, or PowerPoint, you can at any time get an idea of how a document, worksheet, or presentation published as a Web page will appear. Choose File ⇨ Web Page Preview while the document, worksheet, or presentation is open. Your default Web browser will launch, and the Web page that would be produced by saving the file as a Web page will appear within the browser window.

Saving Word Documents as Web Pages

Word provides significant support for saving documents as Web pages. In fact, because the HTML file format is one of Word's available standard file formats, Word provides round-trip editing support for HTML. *Round-trip editing* means that you can save your Word documents as HTML files and later open the HTML files in Word and save them back to a Word document file format. You can do this with almost no loss of formatting. Figure 42-3 shows a Word document that has been saved as a Web page, viewed in a Web browser.

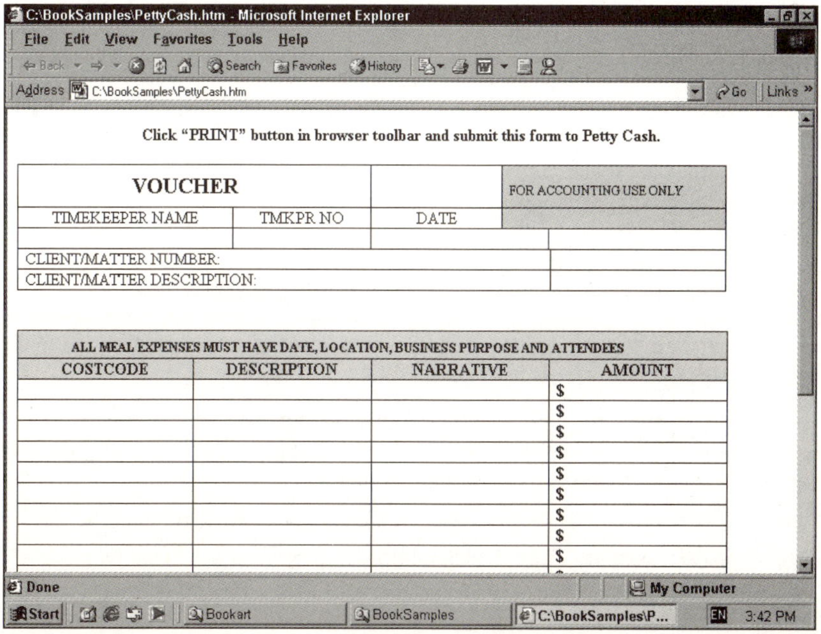

Figure 42-3: An example of a Word document viewed in a Web browser after being saved as a Web page

Word provides you with three options for creating Web pages for your firm intranet or for an Internet Web site. You can save a Word document as a Web page, you can use a Web page template to create a new Web page, or you can use the Web Page Wizard to create an entire Web site. All three options are detailed in the paragraphs that follow.

Using the Save as Web Page command

Probably the fastest way to get your existing Word documents ready for copying to your intranet or Internet Web site is to use the Save as Web Page command of the File menu. To save an existing document as a Web page, open the desired document and choose File ⇨ Save as Web Page. The Save As dialog box appears, with Web Page chosen in the Save as Type list box (see Figure 42-4).

By default, Word will use the first line of text in your document as a title that appears in the Title bar of the Web browser when the page is displayed. You can change this if desired. Click the Change Title button in the Save As dialog box and enter a title for the Web page in the dialog box that appears.

Enter a name for the Web page in the File Name box and click Save if you want to accept the defaults for the Web page (see the next paragraph for more on these options). Word will create the resulting HTML file and save it with an extension of .HTM to the named directory. If the page contains any graphics or supporting files, Word will create a subdirectory containing the graphic images or supporting files. When you upload the HTML file to your Web server, you must include the subdirectory.

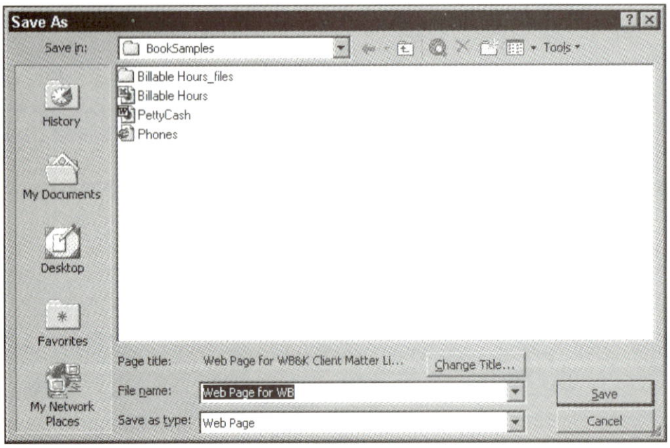

Figure 42-4: You can use the Save As dialog box to save an existing document as a Web page.

Word offers several HTML formats in the Save As dialog box when you choose File ⇨ Save as Web Page. In the Save as Type list box, you can choose any of the following:

- **Web Page (*.htm, *.html):** This is the default choice. With this option, the document is saved as an HTML file, and graphics and other supporting data are saved in separate files. This option offers the best support for round-trip editing of Word documents.
- **Web Archive (*.mhtm, *.mhtml):** This option saves all elements — the document, the graphics, and any other supporting files — in a single Web archive file. This option also supports round-trip editing of Word documents.

- **Web Page, Filtered (*.htm, *.html):** This option saves only essential HTML information. It produces a smaller file that is easier to edit with other programs, but it does not provide support for round-trip editing without a significant loss of Word formatting.

After you've saved your document as a Web page, you can publish it on your intranet or Internet Web site by copying the HTML files and any supporting files or folders to your Web server. Contact your firm's Webmaster or your Web hosting service for details on how to do this.

Using a Web page template

You can also create and save a Web page based on one of a number of Web page templates that are provided with Word. To do so, choose File ⇨ New and click General Templates in the New Document task pane. In the Templates dialog box that opens, click the Web Pages tab to display the available Web page templates (see Figure 42-5).

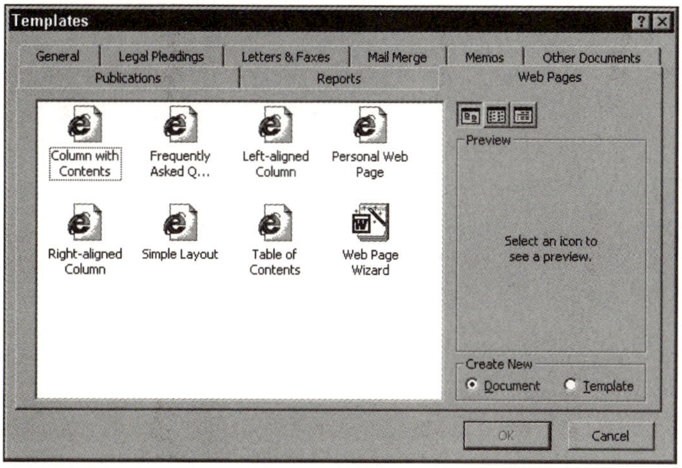

Figure 42-5: The Web Pages tab of the Templates dialog box shows the available Web page templates supplied by Word.

The available templates include Column with Contents, Frequently Asked Questions, Left-Aligned Column, Personal Web Page, Right-Aligned Column, Simple Layout, and Table of Contents.

Select a desired template in the dialog box and click OK. Word will open a new document, formatted as a Web page according to the chosen template. You can modify the document as needed and save it under a desired filename. When you save the document, it will be saved as a Web page, using Word's default HTML file format.

Using the Web Page Wizard

You can also create a series of Web pages — in effect, an entire Web site — using the Web Page Wizard feature of Word. The Web Page Wizard can create a complete Web site, with a series of pages that are linked to other pages in the site based on options you choose when you run the wizard.

To use the Web Page Wizard, choose File ⇨ New and click Web Page Wizard in the New Document task pane. In a moment, the first dialog box of the Web Page Wizard appears. You can follow the directions that appear in the various dialog boxes of the wizard to create your Web site. The options presented by the dialog boxes will let you enter a title, choose a directory where the pages will be stored, determine a method of navigation for the site, add pages to the site, and select a visual theme for the site.

When you click Finish in the final dialog box of the wizard, Word will create and display a series of Web page templates that you can modify by adding your own desired text. You can navigate between the various pages of the Web site while in design mode in Word by holding the Ctrl key while clicking a link for an appropriate page.

When done making the desired changes to each page of the Web site, click Save in the Standard toolbar and exit from Word. (If you are prompted as to whether you want to save changes to additional pages, click Yes.) A main page (named *default.htm*) and a series of supporting pages and subdirectories will exist in the directory that you specified as a Save location in the wizard dialog boxes. You can copy these files and folders to your Web server, using the procedures applicable to your server.

Saving Excel Workbooks as Web Pages

You can use Web publishing features that are built in to Excel to make Excel worksheets and charts available on your intranet or on an Internet Web site. Figure 42-6 shows an example of an Excel worksheet that has been saved as a Web page, viewed in a Web browser.

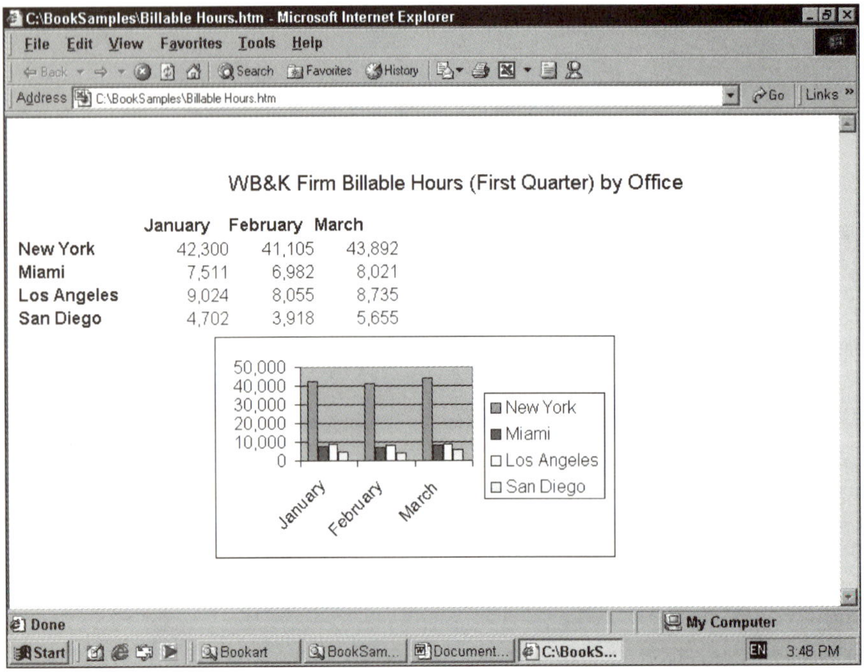

Figure 42-6: An example of an Excel worksheet viewed in a Web browser after being saved as a Web page

To save an Excel worksheet as a Web page, use these steps:

1. Open the workbook containing the desired data in Excel and display the desired tab of the workbook.
2. From the menus, choose File ⇨ Save as Web Page. The Save As dialog box opens, with the Save as Type list set to Web Page (see Figure 42-7).

3. Navigate to a desired directory and enter a name for the HTML file in the File Name box.
4. If you just want the selected sheet saved as an HTML file, click the Selection: Sheet option. To save all the sheets contained in the workbook, click the Entire Workbook option. (If you select the Entire Workbook option, each sheet gets saved as a separate HTML file.)
5. Click Save. Excel will create the resulting HTML file and save it with an extension of .HTM to the named directory. If the page contains any graphics or supporting files, Excel will create a subdirectory containing the graphic images or supporting files. When you upload the HTML file to your Web server, you must include the subdirectory.

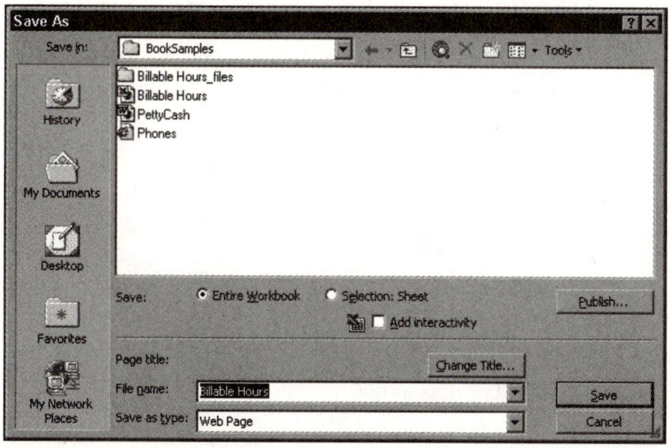

Figure 42-7: The Save As dialog box displayed by Excel can be used to save a worksheet or workbook as a Web page or to publish an interactive version of the workbook.

The preceding steps create static HTML files that you can upload to your Web server; hence, the information that appears on the Web page is based on the data stored in your Excel workbook at the time you created the HTML files. Note that you can also *publish* interactive versions of Excel worksheets to a Web server on your network; you do so by checking the Add Interactivity check box and clicking the Publish button in the Save As dialog box, shown in Figure 42-4. (There are some important limitations to this, as explained in the Note following this paragraph.) When you choose this option, another dialog box will appear, asking you to choose the items in the workbook you want to publish and to select the type of interactivity to publish. (The available types will depend on what you are publishing; for worksheets, you can select Spreadsheet functionality, and for charts and pivot tables, you can select Chart functionality.)

NOTE: When you publish interactive worksheets, others who work with your Excel data on a Web site must be using Microsoft Internet Explorer 4.1 or higher, and they must have an existing license of Microsoft Excel or Microsoft Office installed on the computer.

Saving PowerPoint Presentations as Web Pages

You can provide viewers of your intranet or Internet site with access to PowerPoint presentations by saving your presentation as a Web page. When you save a presentation as a Web page and upload the resulting files to your Web server, the presentation automatically includes the following:

- A navigation frame at the left, which lets users click links to view the individual slides

- A slide frame at the right, where each slide appears
- A control (at the bottom left) to show or hide the outline of the presentation
- Previous Slide and Next Slide navigation buttons (at the bottom center)
- A control (at the bottom right) to expand the view to a full-screen slide show

Figure 42-8 shows an example of a PowerPoint presentation that has been saved as a Web page, viewed in a Web browser.

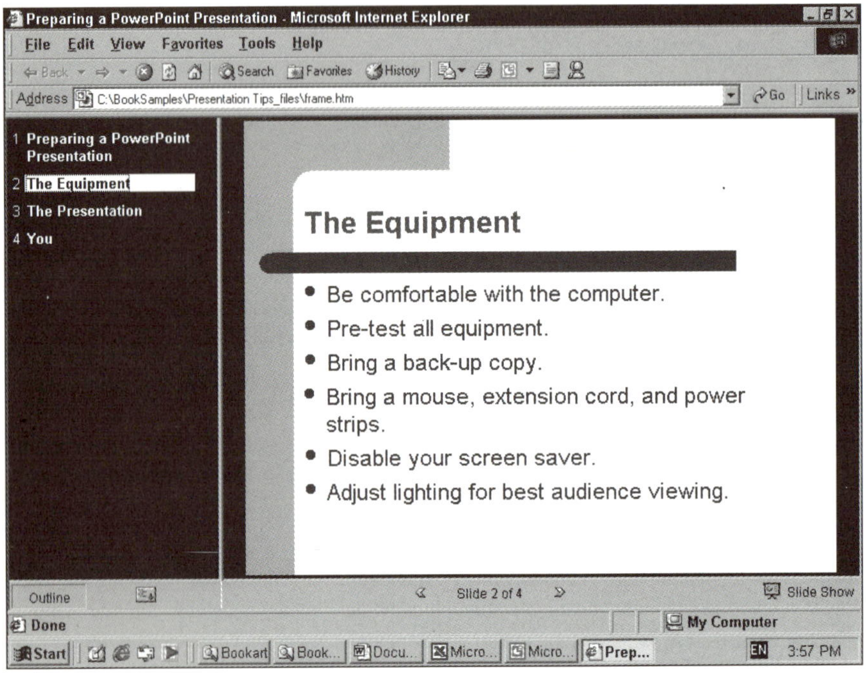

Figure 42-8: A PowerPoint presentation viewed in a Web browser after being saved as a Web page

You can use the Save as Web Page command in PowerPoint to save an entire presentation as a series of HTML files, and a Webmaster can then upload those HTML files to an intranet or Internet site. You can use the following steps to save a PowerPoint presentation as HTML files for publication on the Web:

1. Open the presentation that you want to save as a series of Web pages.
2. Choose File ⇨ Save as Web Page. The Save As dialog box will appear, with the Save as Type list box automatically set to Web Page.
3. Navigate to the desired folder where the main HTML file and all associated files should be saved; enter a name for the file in the File Name text box.
4. Click Change Title and enter a title in the dialog box that appears, if you want to change the page title that is visible in the browser when the presentation is viewed on the Web. Then click Save.

PowerPoint creates a series of HTML files and saves them, along with all necessary graphics and animations, in the specified folder. You can then upload these files to the Web server that hosts your intranet or Internet Web site.

When you save a PowerPoint presentation as a Web page, it is optimized for display using Microsoft Internet Explorer (versions 4.0 and above). You should note that some features — particularly the use of animations (including slide transitions), music, and video — may not be supported in older browsers or in non-Microsoft browsers.

Summary

In this chapter, you learned how to use features of Word, Excel, and PowerPoint to produce content that can be used on a law firm intranet or on an Internet Web site. The chapter covered the following points:

- Intranets use established Internet technologies, such as Web servers, Web browsers, and HTML pages, to share information among members of a law firm or organization.
- In Word, Excel, and PowerPoint, you can use the File ⇨ Save as Web Page command to save documents, workbooks, and presentations as Web pages, which are collections of one or more HTML files.
- In Word, you can use one of seven available templates to create Web pages having a prearranged layout.
- You can use the Web Page Wizard in Word to create a complete Web site, with multiple pages and links between the pages.

The chapter that follows details how you can produce Web content based on various database objects, using Microsoft Access.

Chapter 43

Access and the Law Firm Intranet

In This Chapter

- Access and the Web
- About intranets
- Importing and linking HTML data
- Saving Access data as HTML files
- Using macros to export data to HTML
- Using hyperlinks in tables
- Using hyperlinks in forms and reports

IN THE SPACE OF A DECADE, THE Internet has moved from a means of communication for the "techie" crowd to a global resource for information. Millions of computer users are connected to the World Wide Web, and Web sites are routinely plastered on billboards and included with virtually every form of commercial advertising. When you work within a law firm, chances are that your clients — whether corporations, organizations, government agencies, or private individuals — are routinely connecting to and utilizing the Internet. This chapter shows how you can use Access to retrieve or publish information for use on your law firm intranet or Internet Web site to support the needs of co-workers within the firm or clients and the public who access a firm's Internet site.

NOTE: This chapter assumes a basic working knowledge of the Internet and a familiarity with terms such as *Web browsers*, *Web servers*, and *HTML* (Hypertext Markup Language). If these terms are unfamiliar, refer to Chapter 42.

Access and the Web

As far as features go, a major claim to fame of Microsoft Office is the availability of so many options for working with the Internet and an intranet. Access is no slouch in this area; you can easily create Web page files based on tables, queries, and forms, and you can produce reports in HTML format, ready for inclusion on your Web pages. Figure 43-1 shows data in an Access table, published as a Web page on an intranet and viewed using Microsoft Internet Explorer, a popular Web browser.

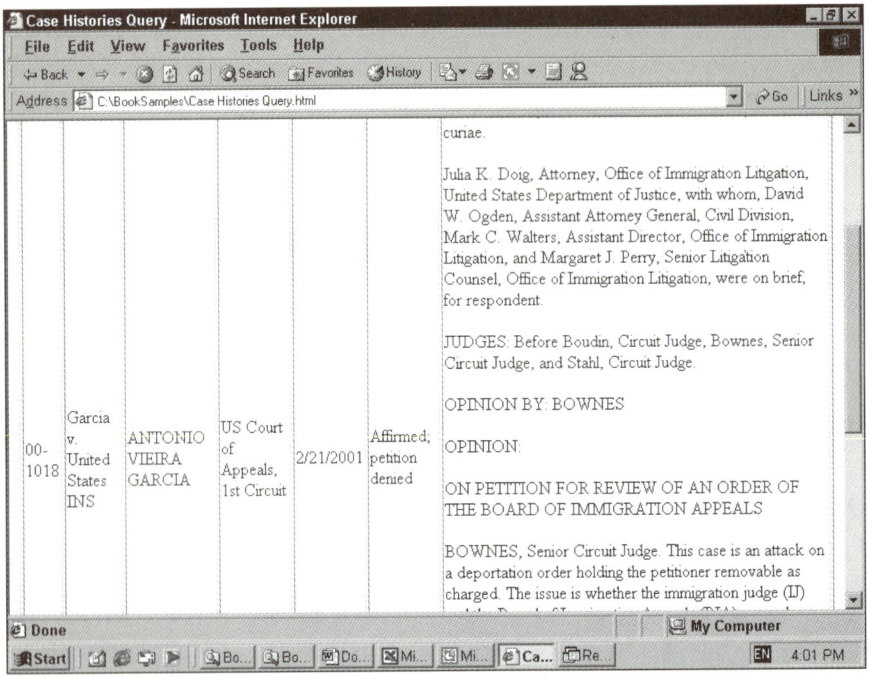

Figure 43-1: An Access table published as a Web page

Using Access, you can perform a number of intranet- and Internet-related tasks. If you need to retrieve or publish data on a law firm intranet or on an Internet Web site, Access is a powerful tool for accomplishing such tasks. You can include *hyperlinks* as fields in the design of a table. As data is entered in the table, Web site addresses can be stored in the hyperlink fields. You can place these same fields in forms and reports, and when users of the database click the fields in a form, they can jump directly to the Web pages on an intranet or on the Internet. You can save table data in HTML format, the publishing lingua of the World Wide Web. And you can produce reports for publishing to Web sites. Each of these topics is covered in further detail throughout this chapter.

About Intranets

Many Internet- and intranet-related uses of Access involve making data stored in an Access database available on *intranets.* An intranet is a private network of computers that is available only to the members of a specific organization, such as a law firm. Intranets are constructed for and managed by the individual organization and provide a way for groups of users to gain important access to information that is relevant to the business groups within the organization. Intranets make use of World Wide Web technology — Web servers, network connections, and Web browser software — to allow members of the organization to share information.

Intranets are very popular with mid-size to large law firms because they let partners, associates, and employees of the firm share work-related information in a confidential manner. Many law firms routinely use intranets to allow employees and attorneys to better communicate with outside clients and with each other. Intranets are commonly used to exchange files, provide access to client or employee data, and allow collaboration or "workflow-sharing" between members of a law firm.

As mentioned earlier, you can use Access to create files in HTML format that are based on tables, queries, forms (in datasheet view) or reports. You can also edit the HTML files that Access exports, using any editor capable of saving files in plain text format. Additionally, numerous tools are on the market that automate the creation of HTML files and professional-looking Web pages, such as Microsoft's own FrontPage. (You could combine HTML files created by Access with the files produced by such other tools to provide detailed Web pages containing Access data for your intranet or Internet site.)

Although you need not be a seasoned HTML expert to work with Access and the Web, it often helps to be minimally familiar with the basics of HTML coding and with the concept of saving your data in HTML file format. In order to publish Access data on the Internet or on an intranet, you'll need to save that data in HTML format and then transfer (or *upload*) that data to your Web server. If you are dealing with a law firm or organization intranet, your Webmaster can provide details as to how you can upload the HTML files that Access produces to your company's Web server. If you are managing a Web site on the Internet or on an intranet, you already know how to do this; much of the rest of this chapter will deal with getting that Access data ready for uploading to your server.

Importing and Linking HTML Data

You can use existing HTML data stored in files or posted at Web sites as a data source in an Access database. You can import data that is stored on the Web, or you can link to the data. The data that you import or link to must exist in tabular (row-and-column) format. Also, note that HTML files or Web sites that you link to (as opposed to importing) are read-only in nature; you cannot make changes to the data. When you import or link to HTML data, Access copies the data into a local file that it creates on the hard drive, and it then parses the information to create an equivalent table containing the data. Use these steps to import or link to HTML data from within Access:

1. Choose File ⇨ Get External Data; then choose Import or Link Tables.
2. In the Files of Type list box in the Import or Link dialog box that appears, choose HTML Documents. Figure 43-2 shows the Import dialog box.
3. Use the Look In box to navigate to the location of the HTML file, or type a URL representing a valid Web site (this URL can start with either *http:* or *ftp:*). Or in the Look In box, click FTP Locations and choose a previously defined FTP site.
4. Click Import (if in the Import dialog box) or Link (if in the Link dialog box) to start the Import HTML Wizard or the Link HTML Wizard.
5. The first dialog box of the Import HTML Wizard (if you chose Import) or Link HTML Wizard (if you chose Link) appears. Indicate whether the first row of the HTML table contains names to be used as column headings in the Access table; then click Next.
6. If you chose Import, the next dialog box of the wizard asks whether you want to store the data in a new table or an existing table. Make the desired selection and click Next. (If you chose Link, this dialog box is skipped and the dialog box described in Step 7 appears.)
7. The next dialog box that appears asks whether you wish to specify any desired field names and data types for the new table. If you are linking rather than importing, the Indexed option of the dialog box will be dimmed and unavailable. Make your desired selections in this dialog box; then click Next.
8. If you are importing the data into a new table, the fourth dialog box to appear asks whether you want to include a primary key for the new table. Make your desired selection in this dialog box; then click Next. (If you are linking to the data, this dialog box is skipped and the dialog box described in Step 9 appears.)

9. In the last dialog box to appear, enter a name for the table and click Finish. The imported or linked table appears in the Database window.

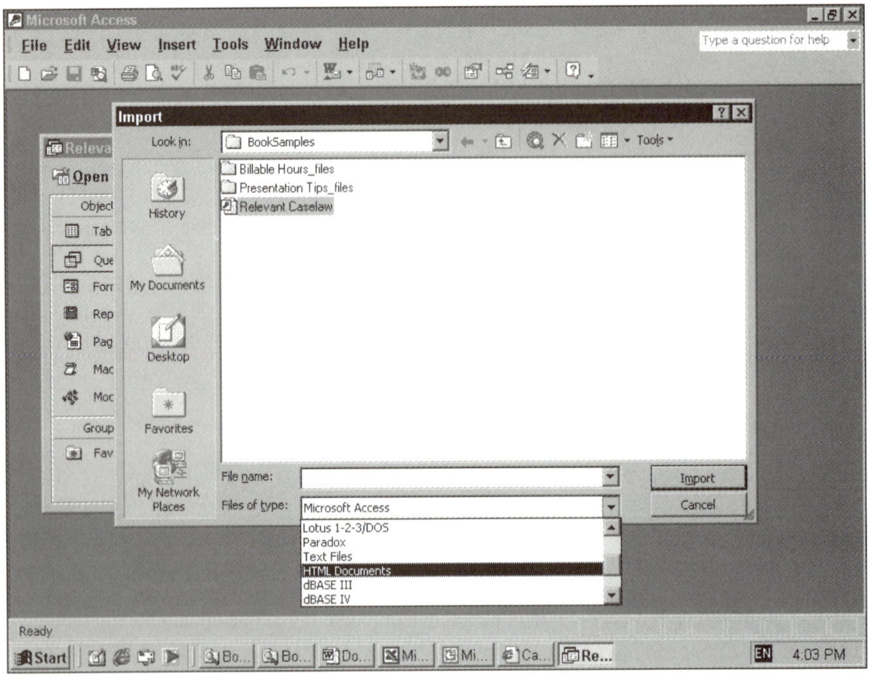

Figure 43-2: The Import dialog box

Obviously, the HTML data that you import or link to must be tabular data. Access follows certain rules when it parses or interprets the incoming HTML file. Access uses the HTML <TABLE> tags and the associated HTML tags to determine the beginning and end of a table of data and where the columns of data start and end. The <TABLE> tag marks the beginning of the data, and the </TABLE> tag marks the end of the data. The <TR> tag is interpreted by Access to indicate the start of a new row in the table, and the </TR> tag is used to indicate the end of a row. The <TD> tag is interpreted by Access as the start of a column of data, and the </TD> tag is interpreted as the end of the column. The <TR> tag isn't necessarily required to designate a new row; if a <TD> tag follows a </TR> tag, Access assumes the start of a new row. Also, if a </TABLE> tag is not preceded by </TR> tag, Access assumes the end of the row, as well as the end of the table.

Note that if any of the cells of the HTML table contain embedded graphics referenced with the <IMG SRC> tag and the tag includes any text, Access imports the text, but it does *not* import the referenced graphic.

If you are going to be working with Access data and HTML files for downloading or uploading to an intranet or to the Internet and you are not already familiar with the meaning of these HTML tags, you should spend time with a book on the basics of HTML, the lingua franca of the World Wide Web. Some good choices are *HTML 4 For Dummies,* by Ed Tittel, Natanya Pitts, and Chelsea Valentine, or *HTML 4 For Dummies Quick Reference,* 2nd Edition, by Deborah S. Ray and Eric J. Ray, both published by Hungry Minds, Inc.

Saving Access Data as HTML Files

You can produce HTML files from within Access for use on the Internet or on an intranet by exporting the files to HTML format. You can save any of the basic Access objects — tables, queries, forms, or reports — as HTML files. With HTML files that you create with the File ⇨ Export command or with the Export command from a shortcut menu, the HTML file is based on what the data looks like at the instant the HTML file is created.

To save a table, query, form (in datasheet view), or report as an HTML file that can then be uploaded to the Internet or to an intranet, use the following steps:

1. In the Database window, right-click the desired table, query, form, or report.
2. From the shortcut menu that appears, choose Export. An Export dialog box appears, similar to the example shown in Figure 43-3.

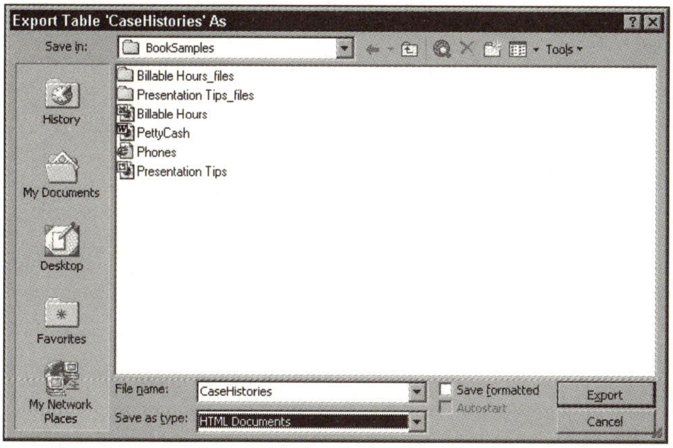

Figure 43-3: The Export dialog box

3. In the Save as Type list box, change the file format to HTML Documents.
4. If you want to apply formatting to the file that causes the resulting HTML document to appear in a grid format, check the Save Formatted check box.
5. If you want to see the resulting HTML document in your browser, check the Autostart checkbox. (If the Save Formatted check box is not checked, this check box will be dimmed.)
6. Specify a filename and a location for the HTML file; then click Export.
7. If an HTML Output Options dialog box appears, specify whether you want Access to use an existing HTML template to format the resulting HTML document; then click OK. (If you don't want to use any template, leave the entry blank and click OK.)

When you save a table, query, or form as an HTML document, the result is a simple tabular document based on the existing layout of the table or query, or in the case of forms, the appearance of the form in datasheet view. (The result of saving a report as an HTML document is discussed after tables, queries, and forms.) Any Order By or Filter property settings of a form or report are applied to the resulting HTML data. Also, if the export is based on a parameter query, Access first prompts you for the parameters of the query before performing the export.

Static HTML versus dynamic HTML

When saving data using the File ⇨ Export command, you save it in what is known as *static HTML*. With static HTML files, the data is unchanging. The HTML file is based on what the data looks like at the instant that you create the HTML file. In Access, it is also possible to export data as *dynamic HTML* files. With dynamic HTML files, the data presented by the HTML file is reflective of the data that is stored in the tables at any given time. Each time the Web browser displays a dynamic page, the display represents the current contents of the underlying table.

Although this description alone sounds deceptively simple, note that there's a major catch when it comes to the dynamic display of data. Any combination of hardware and a Web browser can support the display of static HTML files, and the process of producing such files using Access is relatively simple. But the use of dynamic HTML files involves a familiarity with the use of a Web server that supports Microsoft Access Server Pages or HTC/IDC–compatible files. These are subjects that demand a high level of technical involvement and are beyond the scope of this book. If you desire information about using Access to produce dynamic HTML files, consult an advanced Access text, such as *The Microsoft Access 2002 Bible,* by Cary N. Prague and Michael R. Irwin (published by Hungry Minds Inc.).

How Access stores tables, queries, and forms as HTML

With tables, queries, and forms, the resulting HTML document is provided as a single HTML file. (With large underlying tables or queries, this may mean a lot of scrolling in the Web browser to view all the data.) The HTML document will approximate, as closely as possible, the overall formatting and margins of the table or query or of the form as it appears in datasheet view. Values from most fields (with the exception of OLE Object fields and Hyperlink fields) are formatted the way they appear in the datasheet, and any Format or Input Mask properties of the fields are reflected in the data that appears in the HTML document. OLE Object fields are not exported, and fields that use the Text and Memo field types are output with the strings left-aligned; all other field types are output with the strings right-aligned.

Hyperlink field types are output as hyperlinks in the resulting HTML document, using the `<A HREF>` tags. If the hyperlink stored in the field of the table does not include a subaddress, Access outputs the hyperlink as follows:

```
<A HREF="address">displaytext</A>
```

If the hyperlink includes a subaddress, Access outputs the hyperlink as follows:

```
<A HREF="address#subaddress">displaytext</A>
```

If the hyperlink does not include any display text, Access outputs the hyperlink as follows:

```
<A HREF="address">address</A>
```

Access produces the *address*, *subaddress*, and *displaytext* values by parsing (separating) the values that are stored in the hyperlink field of the table.

If you want to change the margins in the resulting HTML document, you will need to choose File ⇨ Print, click the Setup button in the dialog box that appears for the table, query, or form, and change the margin settings before producing the HTML document. Figure 43-4 shows an example of a query saved as an HTML document when viewed through a Web browser. (Tables saved as HTML files take on a similar appearance.) Figure 43-5 shows a form saved as an HTML document and viewed through a Web browser.

Figure 43-6 shows an example of the resulting HTML code behind a table that is produced by the conversion process. Assuming that you are familiar with the use of HTML, you can open the resulting file in a text editor (such as Windows Notepad) and make any desired changes to the HTML coding to produce a document that is displayed on your firm intranet or on the Internet with your own custom touches. (Many Web page editing programs, such as Microsoft FrontPage, also let you take an HTML file produced with Access and add other effects, such as headings or colors, to the page.)

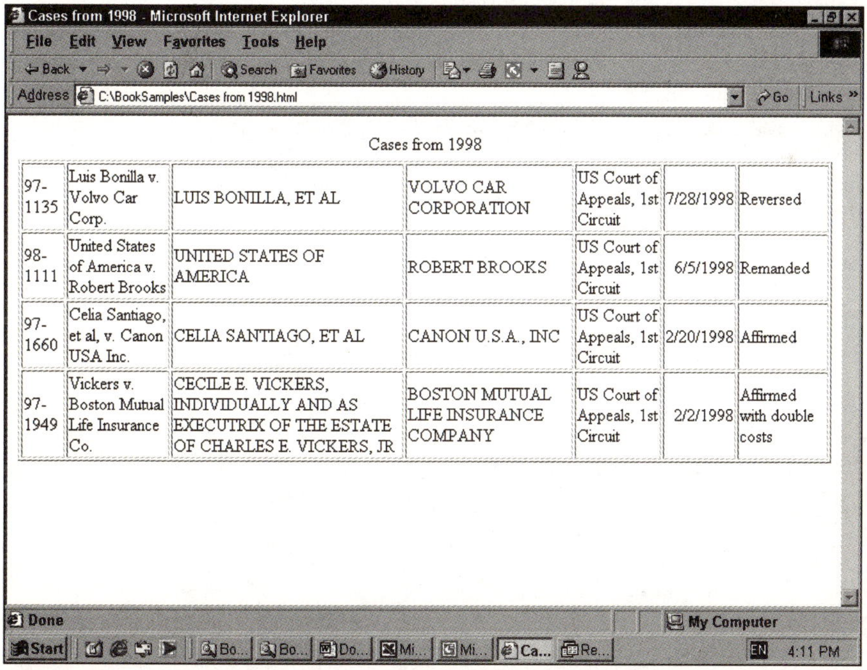

Cases from 1998

97-1135	Luis Bonilla v. Volvo Car Corp.	LUIS BONILLA, ET AL	VOLVO CAR CORPORATION	US Court of Appeals, 1st Circuit	7/28/1998	Reversed
98-1111	United States of America v. Robert Brooks	UNITED STATES OF AMERICA	ROBERT BROOKS	US Court of Appeals, 1st Circuit	6/5/1998	Remanded
97-1660	Celia Santiago, et al, v. Canon USA Inc.	CELIA SANTIAGO, ET AL	CANON U.S.A., INC	US Court of Appeals, 1st Circuit	2/20/1998	Affirmed
97-1949	Vickers v. Boston Mutual Life Insurance Co.	CECILE E. VICKERS, INDIVIDUALLY AND AS EXECUTRIX OF THE ESTATE OF CHARLES E. VICKERS, JR	BOSTON MUTUAL LIFE INSURANCE COMPANY	US Court of Appeals, 1st Circuit	2/2/1998	Affirmed with double costs

Figure 43-4: A query saved as an HTML document and viewed by a browser

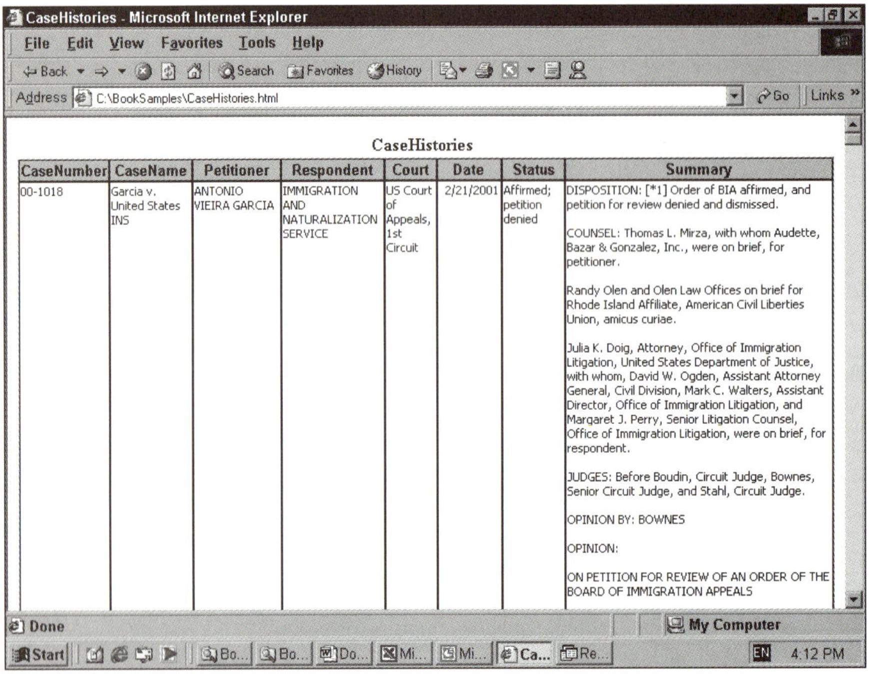

Figure 43-5: A form saved as an HTML document and viewed by a browser

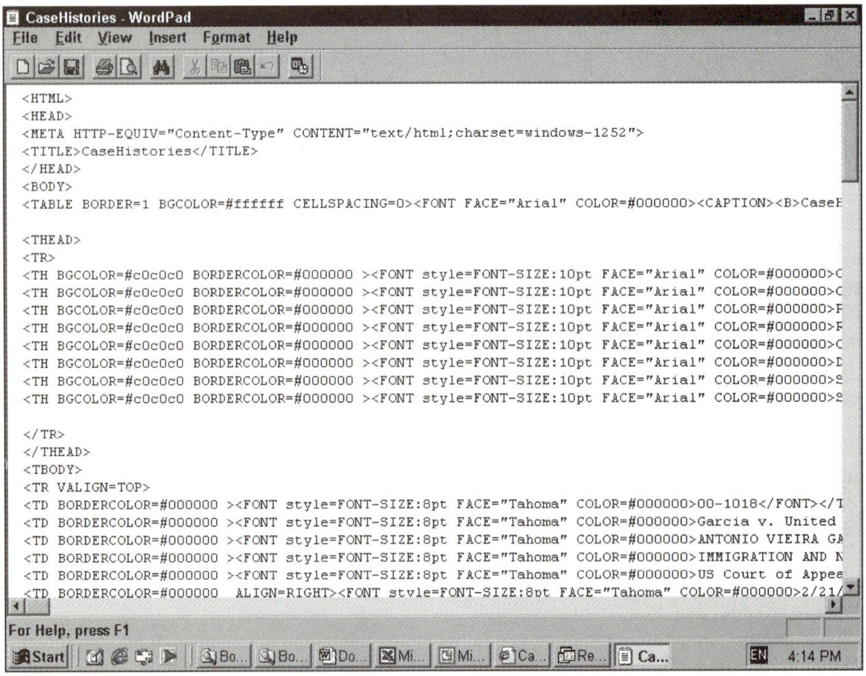

Figure 43-6: The resulting HTML code behind a table saved as an HTML document

How Access saves reports as HTML

Reports that you save as HTML documents are formatted differently than are tables, queries, and forms. With reports, as much of the report's actual formatting as possible is carried over to the resulting HTML documents. Also, the process of saving as HTML produces a separate HTML file for each page of the report. To name each resulting HTML file, Access uses the report name and appends *Page#* to the end of each page after the first page. Hence, if you save a report named *RptClients* as an HTML document and the report (when formatted for printing) is four pages long, Access names the resulting files *RptClients.htm, RptClients_Page2.htm, RptClients_Page3.htm, and RptClients_Page4.htm*. At the bottom of each HTML document, Access also adds navigation links that let the users jump to the first page, the preceding page, the next page, or the last page in a series of HTML documents produced from a report.

As an example of this conversion, Figure 43-7 shows an existing report in Page Preview in Access. Figure 43-8 shows a page of that report after it has been saved as an HTML document, when viewed in a Web browser.

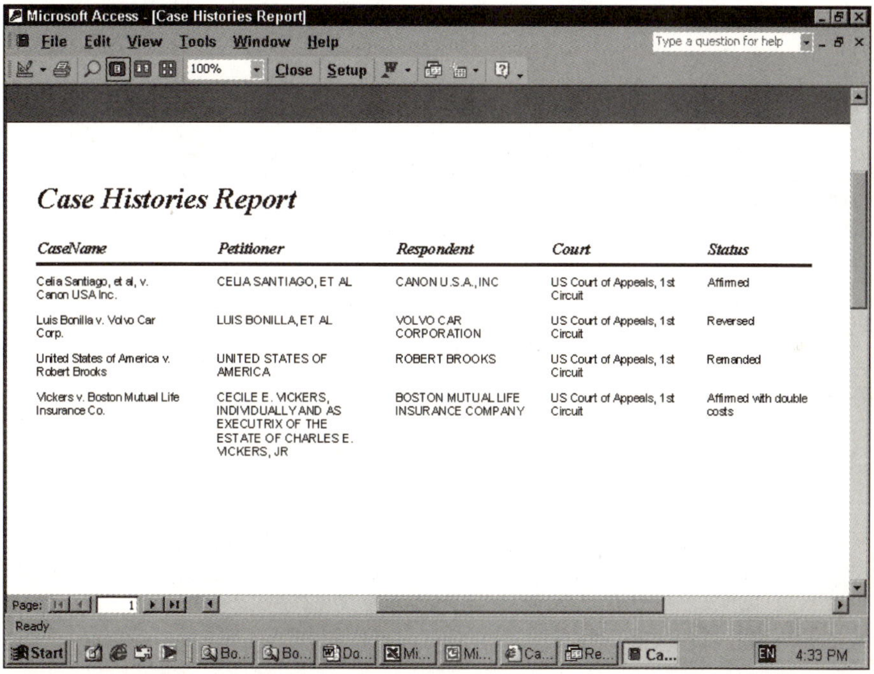

Figure 43-7: An existing report saved in Page Preview

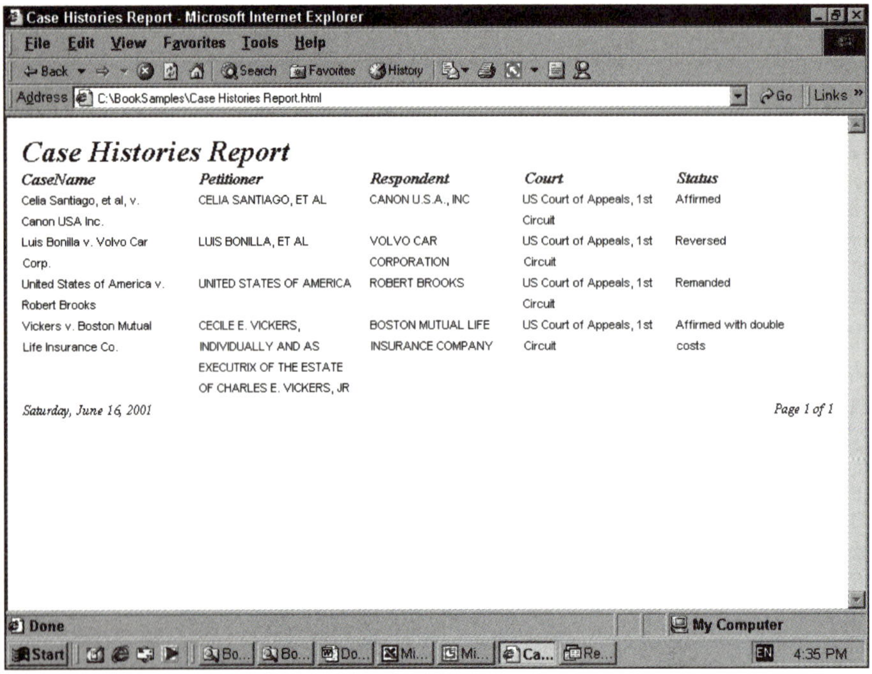

Case Histories Report

CaseName	*Petitioner*	*Respondent*	*Court*	*Status*
Celia Santiago, et al, v. Canon USA Inc.	CELIA SANTIAGO, ET AL	CANON U.S.A., INC	US Court of Appeals, 1st Circuit	Affirmed
Luis Bonilla v. Volvo Car Corp.	LUIS BONILLA, ET AL	VOLVO CAR CORPORATION	US Court of Appeals, 1st Circuit	Reversed
United States of America v. Robert Brooks	UNITED STATES OF AMERICA	ROBERT BROOKS	US Court of Appeals, 1st Circuit	Remanded
Vickers v. Boston Mutual Life Insurance Co.	CECILE E. VICKERS, INDIVIDUALLY AND AS EXECUTRIX OF THE ESTATE OF CHARLES E. VICKERS, JR	BOSTON MUTUAL LIFE INSURANCE COMPANY	US Court of Appeals, 1st Circuit	Affirmed with double costs

Saturday, June 16, 2001 *Page 1 of 1*

Figure 43-8: The existing report saved as an HTML document and viewed in a browser

As the figures show, you can use the powerful report-formatting capabilities provided by the report design surfaces in Access to design complex reports and output those reports as HTML documents for inclusion on a Web site with much of the formatting intact.

Using Macros to Export Data to HTML

If you need to regularly produce HTML files for your law firm or organization's intranet based on data stored in Access tables, you can automate the process by using macros. (See Chapter 27, "Working with Macros," for specifics on creating and running Access macros.)

To create a macro that exports a table or a query to an HTML file, open a new macro and set the Action to Transfer Text. Under Action Arguments, set the Transfer Type argument to Export HTML. In the Table Name box, enter the name of the table or query that is to be used as the data source for the HTML file. And under File Name, enter the full path and filename for the HTML file. The remaining arguments in the macro can be left blank when you are exporting table or query data to an HTML file. As an example of the required macro settings, Figure 43-9 shows the design of a macro that, when executed, will produce an HTML file based on an existing query in the database.

TIP: As Chapter 28 details, you can create a command button on a form that runs a macro by dragging the existing macro from the Database window to a form that is open in Design view. This can be a useful technique for providing a simple method for administrative personnel to create HTML files for your firm intranet.

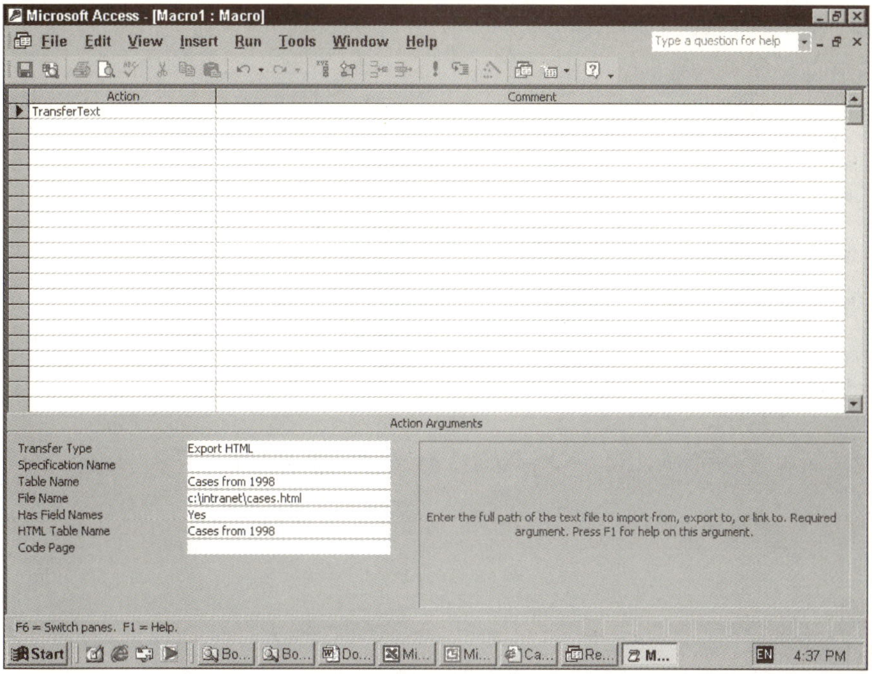

Figure 43-9: A macro design for exporting an existing query to an HTML file

Access and XML support

A new standard known as *XML*, for *Extensible Markup Language*, is gaining in popularity as of this writing. XML is used to describe and deliver data on the Internet and on intranets, just as HTML is the accepted language for creating and displaying Web pages. Access 2002 is the first version of Access to provide built-in support for producing XML files based on Access database objects.

You can export Access tables, queries, forms, and reports as XML documents. You do so by selecting a table, query, form, or report in the Database window, choosing File ⇨ Export from the menus, and choosing XML documents in the Save as Type list of the Export dialog box. Access provides various options that let you choose whether to export XML data, an XML schema file, or an Extensible Stylesheet Language (XSL) presentation file. The overall topic of XML and its use is beyond the scope of this book, but you can find more details about Access support for XML by typing **XML** into the Ask a Question help text box in Access.

Using Hyperlinks in Tables

As mentioned in Chapter 23, "About Databases and Tables," when you create tables in Access, you define your fields with an appropriate data type. In Access, one of the available data types is the hyperlink. Hyperlink fields are designed to store Internet addresses or locations to jump to in other documents. Access recognizes the format of Web addresses and automatically translates the text you type in the hyperlink field into valid Internet addresses. Hyperlink fields make it easy for persons using your Access database to jump to the Web sites stored in the fields as addresses. Of course, these users must have an Internet connection to reach the Web.

When you begin the process of creating a new table, you see the Table Design window, as detailed in Chapter 23. After entering a name for the field in the Field Name column, click the arrow to the right of the Data Type column and choose Hyperlink from the list of data types, as shown in Figure 43-10. You can then continue the design process outlined in Chapter 23 and save the table's structure in the usual manner.

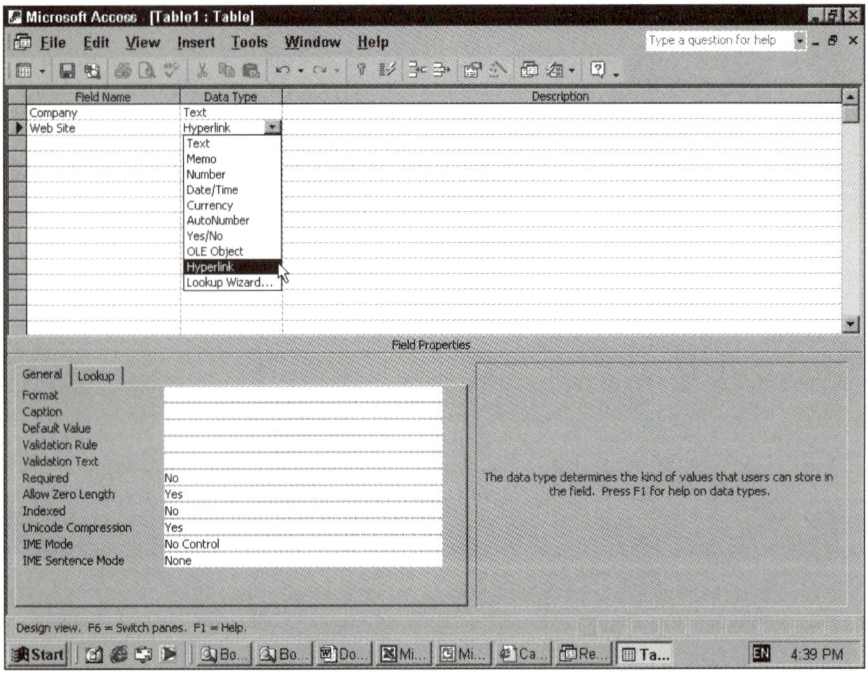

Figure 43-10: Choosing a hyperlink field type during a table's design

After the table exists, you can enter Web addresses in the same manner as you enter other textual data in an Access field: by typing it directly into the field of a table's datasheet or into the field of a form that's based on the table. You can also place the insertion pointer in the field and then click the Insert Hyperlink button on the Standard toolbar to open an Insert Hyperlink dialog box, where you can type the path for the link into the Address text box. Using the Insert Hyperlink dialog box, you can also browse to a file location to add a hyperlink to that file.

If you want to edit the entry stored in the hyperlink field, you can't just click in the field and retype it, because clicking in a field with an existing entry takes you to the link. Instead, right-click the entry and choose Hyperlink ⇨ Edit Hyperlink from the shortcut menus. An Edit Hyperlink dialog box appears, and you can change the entry. (In appearance, the Edit Hyperlink dialog box is identical to the Insert Hyperlink dialog box, with the exception of the caption shown in the title bar.)

Using Hyperlinks in Forms and Reports

You can use the same design techniques detailed in Chapters 25 and 26 to add hyperlink fields to the design of forms and reports. You can add a hyperlink field to a form or a report by performing the following steps:

1. Open the desired form or report in Design view.
2. If the Field List is not visible, choose View ⇨ Field List to display it.
3. Drag the desired hyperlink field from the Field List to the desired location in the form or report.

When you view the form, the contents of the hyperlink field change as you move between records, to reflect the addresses stored in the field for each record in the underlying table. With reports, the addresses stored in each record print in the reports like all other data.

Although hyperlinks are commonly used to store Web addresses, you can also use them to jump to files created using other Office applications. For example, you can use hyperlinks to jump to an Excel worksheet, a Word document, or a PowerPoint presentation. Click in the hyperlink field of the table (or in the control on the form that is bound to the hyperlink field) at the appropriate record and then click the Insert Hyperlink button in the toolbar. In the dialog box that appears, click the Browse for File button at the top of the dialog box to locate the file that you want to link to. In the Link to File dialog box that appears, locate the desired file that you want to link to and click OK. Then, click OK in the Insert Hyperlink dialog box to complete the link.

When the person using the database views the table (or form that's based on the table) and clicks the hyperlink, the appropriate Office application launches (if it isn't already running) and the linked document appears.

Summary

This chapter covered the details behind sharing your Access data with Internet/intranet users. One of the primary uses of the law firm intranet is to make database information readily available to people within the law firm, and Access serves as a powerful tool for accomplishing that goal. Points covered in this chapter included the following:

- You can import or link to tabular data that is stored on a Web page on the Internet or on a corporate intranet.
- You can export from Access tables, queries, forms, or reports to static or dynamic HTML files, for use on an intranet or for posting to an Internet Web site.
- You can use macros to automate the process of exporting Access data to HTML files.
- The hyperlink field type can be used as a part of a table's design, and data stored in hyperlink fields can be used as the basis for jumps to hyperlinks from bound controls on forms.
- Users can use hyperlinks to jump to pages on the Internet or an intranet or to other Office documents.

This concludes the “Office XP and the Law Firm Intranet” portion of this book. In the appendixes that follow, you will find a research guide to legal software and legal research providers, specifics on using the speech recognition feature of Office XP, and instructions for using the CD-ROM, along with a listing of the CD-ROM’s contents.

Appendix A

Resource Guide: Legal Software and Research Providers

THIS APPENDIX PROVIDES A LISTING of brief descriptions, contact phone numbers, e-mail addresses, and/or Web site locations of popular legal-specific software packages, as well as listings of dial-up or Internet-based providers of legal research services.

Case Management

This category includes software designed to track, organize, and search various aspects of cases. Some packages listed in this category contain features that appear in other categories, such as document management and document assembly.

AbacusLaw (Abacus Data Systems -- Comprehensive legal case management organizer and database includes calendaring, tracking of client and case information, conflict-of-interest checking, contacts management, tickler system, and document assembly. Offers time and billing links to Timeslips (time and billing software), Palm PDA synchronization, and HotDocs (document assembly software).

Phone: (800) 726-3339
E-mail: `sales@abacuslaw.com`
Web: `www.abacuslaw.com`

Amicus Attorney (Gavel & Gown Software) -- Case management package includes scheduling, contact tracking, phone call tracking, recording of to-do lists, tracking of billable time, messages/e-mail tracking, conflict checking, and more. E-mail integration with Microsoft Outlook, device integration with wireless PDAs such as Blackberry and Palm VII, and direct synchronization capabilities with any Palm OS–based PDA.

Phone: (800) 472-2289 or (416) 977-6633
E-mail: `info@amicusattorney.com`
Web: `www.amicusattorney.com`

Case Master (Software Technology, Inc.) -- Case calendaring/scheduling, case management, conflict checking, document assembly integration using Microsoft Word and HotDocs, document history tracking, and statute of limitations tracking. Integrates with TABS III time and billing software and with Microsoft Outlook; includes synchronization software for Palm OS–based PDAs.

Phone: (402) 423-1440
E-mail: `sales@stilegal.com`
Web: `www.stilegal.com`

CaseTrack for Windows (Economic Analysis Group, Ltd.) -- Matter management software designed for use by corporate legal departments at large firms and corporations provides separate modules for tracking matters, docket/calendar, timekeeping, invoicing, and budget. Includes enhanced search features, ad hoc query builder, and extensive reporting capabilities. Supports task-based billing and electronic invoicing; interfaces with law firm time-and-billing systems.

Phone: (202) 367-2950
E-mail: info@eagltd.com
Web: www.case-track.com

Law Manager (Elite Information Systems) -- Case and matter management for law firms, government agencies, and corporate legal departments. Provides calendar/docketing, records and conflict management, document management, time and expense tracking, E-invoicing, and auditing.

Phone: (323) 642-5000
E-mail: eramirez@elite.com
Web: www.eliteis.com

LegalEdge Law Firm Suite (LegalEdge Software) -- Complete matter-management software designed for law firms, corporate legal departments, and government agencies. Includes calendaring/docketing, contact and case management, conflict checking, time and costs tracking, and document assembly. Integrates with many word processing, e-mail, time and billing, and document management systems.

Phone: (610) 975-5888
E-mail: info@legaledge.com
Web: www.legaledge.com

Vision (CompuLaw) -- Full-featured calendar/docket software for Windows 9X, Windows NT, and Windows 2000. Graphical on-screen calendars. Tracks court holidays by venue and court rule sets by jurisdictions. Understands complex court rules, secondary formulas, and many branching options. Allows for virtually unlimited submatters for any client/matter. Wide area network and client/server versions are available.

Phone: (800) 444-0020
E-mail: info@compulaw.com
Web: www.compulaw.com

Client Relationship/Contact Management

Software listed within this category is used to manage a list of clients at a law firm or organization (and in many cases, to better utilize the relationships between clients or contacts and members of the firm).

Aptus (Scout Solutions) -- Web browser–based client relationship management system, scalable from small offices to firms or organizations with thousands of users. Designed to manage knowledge about contacts both inside and outside a firm and to show the relationships between members of a firm and its contacts, to further overall business objectives. Built-in reporting and mail merge via Microsoft Word are supported, and fields are highly customizable.

Phone: (240) 631-8080
E-mail: shall@scoutsolutions.com
Web: www.scoutsolutions.com

ContactEase and MarketEase (Cole Valley Software) -- Contact management and marketing management software for workgroups and for enterprise-based law firms and organizations. Tracks client, prospect, and referral information; tracks events; links to mailing lists (by assignee); analyzes by attorney, practice group, referral source; and more. ContactEase offers firmwide sharing of contacts. MarketEase for Workgroups supports 1–10 users; MarketEase Enterprise supports multiple users throughout a large firm or organization.

Phone: (415) 552-7900
E-mail: `sales@colevalley.com`
Web: `www.colevalley.com`

Elite CRM (Elite Information Systems) -- Client relationship management system is an integrated system providing firmwide contact management with individual personalized phone lists on each desktop, direct link to word processing software for customized mailings, e-mail link to generate electronic mailings, relationship tracking, list tracking, and seminar/event management.

Phone: (323) 642-5000
E-mail: `eramirez@elite.com`
Web: `www.eliteis.com`

GoldMine (Frontrange Solutions) -- Client contact management designed for workgroups manages potential client and existing client information. Automates marketing procedures and synchronizes with Palm-based or Windows CE–based PDAs.

Phone: (800) 654-3526
E-mail: `sales@frontrange.com`
Web: `www.frontrange.com/goldmine/`

H4 (Hubbard One) -- Enterprisewide software family of products designed to facilitate knowledge management. Allows a large law firm or corporate legal department to merge the knowledge of the enterprise into a single system that powers intranets, extranets, Web sites, and wireless devices.

Phone: (312) 939-5000
E-mail: `cmathy@hubbardone.com`
Web: `www.hubbardone.com`

Interaction (Interface Software) -- Relationship management software manages contact and relationship tracking for mid-size to large law firms. Centralizes a firm's collective knowledge about clients and contacts, making that knowledge available to multiple authorized users. Integrates with various SQL servers, including Microsoft SQL Server, and aggregates and manages intelligence about people, companies, relationships, experience, and expertise.

Phone: (630) 572-1400
E-mail: `info@interfacesoftware.com`
Web: `www.interfacesoftware.com`

Combination Software

Software and Web-based service providers within this category provide a combination of features that would individually fall under other categories, such as docketing/scheduling, time and billing, and case management.

JDUSA Law Desk (JurisDictionUSA, Inc.) -- Internet-based provider of calendaring and case management, document management and document storage, time and billing, back-office accounting, secure e-mail, legal research, and custom forms.

Phone: (888) 593-9600
E-mail: `info@jdusa.net`
Web: `www.jurisdictionusa.net`

Law.com -- Comprehensive legal Internet site and provider of legal application solutions. Manage your practice with Web-based and desktop applications, track breaking developments in the law, research issues and cases, attend online continuing legal education seminars, explore nationwide job openings in the legal industry, and more.

Phone: (800) 628-1160
Web: `www.law.com`

Legal Files Case Management Groupware (Legal Files Software, Inc.) -- Case and office management software that includes timekeeping, litigation support and document management and assembly features, integrated calendars, ticklers, contact management, and reporting. Links to Microsoft Outlook and Microsoft Word; also links to Timeslips, Peachtree, QuickBooks, and TABS III (accounting software).

Phone: (800) 500-0537
E-mail: `info@legalfiles.com`
Web: `www.legalfiles.com`

PerfectLaw Front Office Suite (Perfect Law Software) -- Integrated suite of legal applications for time tracking, time and billing, case management, contact management, docketing/scheduling, document assembly, conflict checking, and e-mail integration. Integrates with PerfectLaw Back Office Suite for billing, accounts payable and accounts receivable, and general ledger. Offers contacts synchronization with Microsoft Outlook and Palm OS–based PDAs.

Phone: (800) 749-6200
Web: `www.perfectlaw.com`

ProLaw (Provolution Corp.) -- Combines with Microsoft's Small Business Server to manage front office/back office tasks and offer extranet support. Provides case management, contact/relationship management, document management, time and billing, and records management. Integrates with Microsoft Outlook and Novell GroupWise for e-mail and with Elite or CMS Open for back-office billing functions. Also integrates with PC Docs, iManage, and Worldox document management systems.

Phone: (800) 977-6529
E-mail: `info@prolaw.com`
Web: `www.prolaw.com`

Time Matters (Data.TXT Corporation) -- Practice management software in personal, professional, and enterprise editions is scalable for all sizes of law firms and provides calendaring and task management, ticklers, client relations management, document management, time and billing, and communications management. Offers synchronization with Palm OS–based and Windows CE–based PDAs.

Phone: (800) 328-2898
E-mail: `sales@timematters.com`
Web: `www.timematters.com`

VisualONE (ASA Legal Systems) -- VisualONE is an integrated software system designed for mid-size firms that combines relationship management, docket/scheduling, marketing projects, mailing list management, case management, conflicts avoidance, and CLE tracking in a single package.

Phone: (800) 341-4012
E-mail: `legalinfo@asaint.com`
Web: `www.asalegal.com`

Document Assembly

Document assembly software operates in combination with a word processor — such as Microsoft Word — to assemble commonly used documents (such as legal forms) based on a user's responses to a series of questions.

HotDocs (Capsoft Development) -- HotDocs is a software tool that lets you create reusable interactive templates using Microsoft Word (or other popular Windows word processors) that can be used to assemble detailed customized documents. Using HotDocs, you can transform a Word document into an interactive template by replacing changeable text with HotDocs variables. When you later want to generate the document, you use the HotDocs template to assemble a custom version of the document. Also available separately (from LexisNexis) are HotDocs forms for a variety of uses, including Federal court forms, bankruptcy forms, U.S. Social Security disability-related forms, and UCC (Uniform Commercial Code) forms.

Phone: (800) 500-3627
Web: `www.capsoft.com`

Document Conversion/Document Templates

This category includes document conversion tools and conversion vendors and suppliers of document templates. These are commonly used by law firms and legal departments when converting documents from a non-Microsoft format (such as Corel's Word Perfect) to Microsoft Word. As Chapter 2, "Understanding Word's Interface," details, Word is capable of opening Word Perfect documents, and saving documents in Word Perfect format. However, the demanding needs presented by complex legal documents often tax the capabilities of the program when it comes to converting documents, and many law firms and legal departments find add-on programs (outside Microsoft Office) or services to be useful in dealing with document conversions and in the creation of custom templates.

DocXchange (Microsystems, Inc.) -- DocXchange converts Word Perfect (Windows and DOS) documents to Microsoft Word format and also migrates documents created in earlier versions of Word to Word 2000/Word 2002 file formats. Sophisticated conversion technology lets you incorporate Word-specific characteristics, such as templates and styles.

DocXtools provides a variety of tools that aid users in the final cleanup of complex converted documents. The tools handle problems with paragraph numbering, styles, formatting and structural problems, and preparation of documents for use with redliners such as CompareRite.

The company (Microsystems) also provides large-scale conversion services for law firms or departments faced with the task of converting large numbers of Word Perfect (or other format) documents to Microsoft Word file formats, with support for a firm's document management system.

Phone: (630) 261-0111
E-mail: `info@microsystems.com`
Web: `www.microsystems.com`

Legal MacPac (The Legal MacPac) -- Legal MacPac is a sophisticated, comprehensive package of customized legal document templates, macros, styles, numbering schemes, and databases that reduces the document creation and formatting process into a few simple steps. Legal MacPac includes document features for creating, editing, and managing legal documents and features available globally, such as legal numbering, legal symbols, and integration.

Phone: (415) 252-8842
E-mail: `lsackett@legalmacpac.com`
Web: `www.macpac.com`

Document Management

Document management systems are used by law firms to store, index, and search large numbers of files (typically word processing documents) created by Microsoft Office applications or by other popular Windows software. Document management systems can be used to search thousands of documents for all documents matching a specific client/matter ID or for all documents containing specific keywords that are stored in an index of the document management system. Most (but not all) implementations of document management require the use of a SQL server, such as Microsoft SQL Server.

CyberDOCS, PowerDOCS, and DOCS Open (Hummingbird, Ltd.) -- CyberDOCS is a Web-enabled document management system providing full document-management functionality via a Web browser. PowerDOCS is a three-tiered Windows-based document management system with extensive search-and-retrieval capabilities, document check in/check out, version controls, audit trails, and storage management. DOCS Open is a client/server–based document management system enabling users to store, locate, and manage information across a wide range of platforms and networks.

Phone: (877) 359-4866
E-mail: `getinfo@hummingbird.com`
Web: `www.hummingbird.com`

iManage WorkDocs (iManage) -- WorkDocs provides secure Web-based document management functionality via the Internet, intranets, and extranets. Capture, store, and search for information stored under multiple formats, including documents, faxes, forms, e-mail, voice mail, records, and multimedia. Create a centrally accessed repository for managing documents, and offer controlled access to the repository via intranets and extranets, using standard Web browsers.

Phone: (877) 4iManage
Web: `www.imanage.com/legal/`

Worldox 2000 and Worldox Web (World Software Corp.) -- Worldox 2000 and Worldox Web are document management solutions with powerful search capabilities, compatible with Microsoft Office, Corel Word Perfect, and other popular Windows programs. Worldox can be used by law firms varying in size from small to large and does not require the use of a SQL server. Worldox Web offers access to documents via a Web browser–based interface. Integrates with Time Matters, Case Master, and Amicus Attorney V.

Phone: (800) 962-6360
E-mail: sales@worldox.com
Web: www.worldox.com

Legal Research Resources

Sources of legal research provide access (typically via a private dial-up connection or via the Internet) to case law and case statutes, case histories, government regulations, public records, and other similar information.

Aspire.Net (Union Square Technology Group, LLC) **--** Aspire.Net is a Web-based service provider offering managed services for law firms and corporate legal departments. Aspire.Net offers client extranet and collaborative work sharing, database services, document management, desktop applications and editing tools, messaging, time entry, and more.

Phone: (212) 253-3535
E-mail: info@aspire.net
Web: www.aspire.net

CourtLink (CourtLink Corporation) **--** CourtLink is an online platform for retrieving court records and filing legal documents. It provides online access to current cases, federal and state court records, e-mail alerts regarding case activity, case tracking, online filing, processing, and serving of legal documents to courts and case parties.

Phone: (800) 774-7317
E-mail: sales@courtlink.com
Web: www.courtlink.com

BNA (The Bureau of National Affairs, Inc.) **--** BNA is a leading publisher of print and electronic news, analysis, and reference products, providing coverage of legal and regulatory developments. BNA provides reporting on developments in health care, business, labor relations, law, economics, taxation, environmental protection, safety, and other public policy and regulatory issues.

Phone: (800) 372-1033
E-mail: customercare@bna.com
Web: www.bna.com

FindLaw.com (FindLaw Corp.) **--** FindLaw is a popular Web portal and search engine focused on law and government. It provides access to a comprehensive online library of legal resources for use by legal professionals, consumers, and small businesses. Features include Web search utilities, cases and codes, legal news, and community-oriented tools, such as a secure document management utility, mailing lists, message boards, and free e-mail.

Phone: (650) 210-1900
Web: www.findlaw.com

LawCommerce.com (LawCommerce.com, Inc.) **--** Online marketplace for the legal profession, featuring more than one million products and services. Links to legal research, forms, and agreements, training and CLE resources, practice areas, news and information, technology center, and more.

Phone: (415) 771-5900
E-mail: `customerservice@lawcommerce.com`
Web: `www.lawcommerce.com`

Lawyers.com (Martindale-Hubbell Division of LexisNexis Group) -- Free attorney referral service aimed at individuals and small businesses. Provided by Martindale-Hubbell, the site offers lawyer referral, legal news, message boards, and legal resources.

Phone: (800) 526-4902
E-mail: `info@martindale.com`
Web: `www.lawyers.com`

LexisNexis (LexisNexis Group) -- Legal research, corporate research, and knowledge management databases for firms of all sizes, corporations, and government agencies. Searchable access to more than three billion documents from thousands of services. Available via the Internet, on CD-ROM, and via private dial-up connection.

Phone: (800) 227-4908
E-mail: `newsales@lexisnexis.com`
Web: `www.lexis.com`

LexisONE.com (LexisNexis Group) -- Internet-based source of legal research, legal news, legal forms, practice management, and professional development for solo practitioners and small law firms. Includes client development and marketing tools and access to other Lexis-Nexis services, including LexisNexis Bookstore and Shepard's Citations.

Phone: (800) 227-4908
E-mail: `lexisone@lexisnexis.com`
Web: `www.lexisone.com`

Lois Law Library (Aspen Publishers) -- Internet-based law library for U.S. federal and state jurisdictions, containing case law, statutes, court rules, jury instructions, opinions of attorneys general, and more.

Phone: (800) 364-2512
E-mail: `info@loislaw.com`
Web: `www.loislaw.com`

Martindale-Hubbell Law Directory (LexisNexis Group) -- The accepted guide to information about attorneys and law firms throughout the world contains nearly one million lawyer and law firm listings and is organized by city, state, and country, with cross-listings by area of law practice. Available in printed form, on CD-ROM, online via LexisNexis, and on the Internet.

Phone: (800) 526-4902
E-mail: `info@martindale.com`
Web: `www.martindale.com`

Matthew Bender (Matthew Bender & Co. Division of LexisNexis Group) -- Matthew Bender is a major publisher of analytical legal research for specific practice areas such as antitrust, banking, bankruptcy, business, estate planning, employment, environment, government, family law, health care, immigration, intellectual property, real estate, and tax law. The information is available in printed form, on CD-ROM, online via LexisNexis, and on the Internet. (Subscribers to Shepard's Citations can access legal research from the Matthew Bender databases directly.)

Phone: (800) 833-9844
E-mail: `newsales@lexisnexis.com`
Web: `www.bender.com`

Shepard's Citations (LexisNexis Group) -- Shepard's is a major publisher of legal research with an emphasis on citations. The Shepard's database contains nearly 150 million citing references from more than seven million cases, plus references to nonlegal citations, including patents, trademarks, and copyrights.

Phone: (800) 899-6000
E-mail: `newsales@lexisnexis.com`
Web: `www.lexisnexis.com/shepards/`

Trademark.com (Information Holdings, Inc.) -- Trademark.com is an online searchable trademark database with complete access to federal and state databases. The site also provides access to a collection of common law files and a searchable Internet domain name with registrant (ownership) database.

E-mail: `sales@trademark.com`
Web: `www.trademark.com`

Versuslaw (Versuslaw, Inc.) -- Online legal research site containing searchable appellate decisions from state and federal courts, searchable federal code and regulations, 20,000 U.S. legal forms, and online CLE courses.

Phone: (425) 250-0142
E-mail: `service@versuslaw.com`
Web: `www.versuslaw.com`

Westlaw (West Group) -- Online comprehensive source of legal research for firms of all sizes, with access to more than 15,000 legal databases from an array of jurisdictions and practice areas. Fully searchable information includes federal and state court cases and statutes, federal regulations, public records, securities law information, and domestic and international business news.

Phone: (800) 328-4880 (billing and account inquiries), 800-WESTLAW (technical support)
E-mail: `info@westlaw.com`
Web: `www.westlaw.com`

Legal-Specific Database Software

This category includes database software designed to handle specific legal needs at a law firm or within a corporate legal department.

CaseMap (CaseSoft) -- Case knowledge manager for trial research and trial preparation organizes facts, individuals, and issues regarding a specific case. Supports the creation of visual aids for use with deposition and trial preparation and lets you study case chronology using a graphical timeline.

Phone: (904) 273-5000
E-mail: `info@casesoft.com`
Web: `www.casesoft.com/casemap.htm`

Concordance (Dataflight Software, Inc.) -- Concordance is a popular full-text database management system for litigation support. It supports depositions, document productions, e-mail repositories, importing of Adobe Acrobat files, and integration with LiveNote for transcript management. Images, audio, Web links, and movies can also be hyperlinked. The data can be stored locally, on a LAN, at remote locations through a wide area network, on the Internet, or on CD-ROM.

Phone: (310) 471-3414
E-mail: `sales@dataflight.com`
Web: `www.dataflight.com`

Summation (Summation Legal Technologies, Inc.) -- Litigation-support database software in a variety of packages (including Summation Blaze and Summation iBlaze) offers document management and transcript searching and indexing tools within a single integrated application. A new interface mimics the familiar Windows Explorer, and a "chain of evidence" function allows users to create links between full-text documents and other evidence. Support from various products for Internet/intranet/extranet access to document searches.

Phone: (800) 735-7866
E-mail: `sales@summation.com`
Web: `www.summation.com`

Time and Billing

Software programs and online service providers in this category handle both time and expense tracking and client billing for law firms and legal organizations.

Carpe Diem (Sage U.S. Holdings, Inc.) -- Time and expense tracking software designed to capture time for multiple timekeepers at mid-size to large firms and interface with a variety of back-office accounting systems. Supports validated lists of clients, matters, projects, and activities and exports to all popular billing and cost accounting systems.

Phone: (800) 477-6763
E-mail: `cdsales@sageus.com`
Web: `www.carpediemets.com`

Elite Enterprise Professional Billing System (Elite Information Systems) -- Comprehensive time and billing application that includes cost collection, trust accounting, budgeting, profitability, performance analysis, and inquiry systems. Accommodates unique pricing arrangements and task-based billing and is scalable for firms from 10 to thousands of timekeepers.

Phone: (323) 642-5000
E-mail: `eramirez@elite.com`
Web: `www.eliteis.com`

Juris (Juris, Inc.) -- Comprehensive time and billing package provides both front-end functionality (capturing of time and expense tasks by individual timekeepers) and back-end functionality, including billing, accounts payable, accounts receivable/check writing, trust accounting, bank reconciliation, general ledger and financial reporting, and conflict search capabilities.

Phone: (615) 377-3740
E-mail: `info@juris.com`
Web: `www.juris.com/public/default.asp`

PC Law, PC Law Pro, ePCLaw (Alumni Computer Group, Inc.) -- PC Law and PC Law Pro are time and billing/accounting software packages designed for law firm use. The software features time tracking, client summary drill-down, bank and trust reporting, conflict checking, and contact management. PC Law is designed for firms with 1–10 timekeepers, whereas PC Law Pro is designed for firms with 10–200 timekeepers. ePCLaw provides Web-based time entry and reporting that works in conjunction with a PC Law installation at an office.

Phone: (800) 387-9785
E-mail: `sales@pclaw.com`
Web: `www.pclaw.com`

TABS III (Software Technology, Inc.) -- Comprehensive time and billing for small and medium-size law firms. Records and organizes daily time charges, advances, expenses, and payments. Tracks work-in-progress and offers prebill tracking, accounts receivable reporting, client ledger, and attorney profitability reporting. Integrates with other STI systems, including Case Master (case management), general ledger, and accounts payable systems.

Phone: (402) 423-1440
E-mail: `sales@stilegal.com`
Web: `www.stilegal.com`

Timeslips (Sage U.S. Holdings, Inc.) -- Complete time and billing packages support a range of firm sizes from solo practitioners to large firms, using one of three variations (Timeslips Express, Timeslips Standard Edition, and Timeslips Enterprise). Features included in all versions, including Timeslips Express (aimed at solo practitioners and small firms), include time and expense tracking with stopwatch timer; setup wizard; simple, flat-fee, and adjustment bill arrangements; customizable bill formats; and unlimited timekeeper capacity. Timeslips Standard Edition (aimed at mid-size forms) adds contingency and percentage-based billing, custom client fields, trust accounts, budgeting, and practice management reporting. Timeslips Enterprise (aimed at large firms) includes all features of Express and Standard editions, plus client/server–based architecture, extended budgeting, fee allocation, and audit trails. TimeReporter option allows time and expense entry using Palm OS–based PDAs.

Phone: (800) 285-0999
E-mail: `tssupport@timeslips.com`
Web: `www.timeslips.com`

Visual Pyramid (ASA Legal Systems) -- Visual Pyramid is a fully integrated time, billing, and accounting system designed for mid-size law firms. Visual Pyramid includes extensive client/matter inquiry screens, attorney remote time entry, comprehensive reporting, flexible bill format options, and rate schedules. The system provides the ability to track client, matter, and attorney profitability.

Phone: (800) 341-4012
E-mail: `legalinfo@asaint.com`
Web: `www.asalegal.com`

Appendix B

Using Speech Recognition with Office XP

In This Appendix

- Introducing speech recognition
- Training and using speech recognition
- Adding custom words to the speech dictionary
- Adding and changing speech recognition users

A MAJOR NEW CAPABILITY OF OFFICE XP applications that is particularly useful to the legal community is *speech recognition*. Speech recognition offers to turn into reality that long-hoped-for, science-fiction promise of being able to dictate text to a computer and have that computer understand your spoken word. The hope has been for the computer (and software) to accurately understand and translate speech, freeing us from the drudgery of the keyboard. The slow development of the science of speech recognition has been closely monitored by many within the legal profession, particularly attorneys. Because so much of any attorney's time involves getting legal thoughts composed into stored and printable documents, any automation that can make this task significantly easier would be welcome. Anything that greatly increases attorney efficiency makes an attorney's highly billable time ever more valuable to the client. And, let us never forget, client satisfaction is what makes it possible for all of us employed in any aspect of this profession to get paid for what we do!

Speech Recognition: Ready for Prime Time?

So, can you finally trash your legal pads (despised by many since the days of Torts 101 during first-year law school) and move to a world of dictating your effortless legal prose directly into a word processor's screen? At the time of this writing, the realistic answer is *not so fast, counselor*. Probably not today, and perhaps not completely within the next decade, given the demands that speech recognition places on the limits of current science in terms of both hardware and software engineering. In the real world, the accuracy of speech recognition isn't sufficiently high for most users to let computer keyboards begin gathering dust in favor of microphones and headsets. But, depending on how poor a typist you may be (or on what physical limitations, such as the dreaded carpal tunnel syndrome, you may face), speech recognition capability may prove to be worth investigating. Because the technology is built in to the software suite that you are currently using, there's little to lose, other than the time spent learning to use the feature and training the computer to better understand your speech patterns.

Make sure that your hardware is up to the task

If you hope to make effective use of the speech recognition technology that's built in to Office XP, you may avoid unnecessary disappointment by first ensuring that your hardware is up to the task. Because a relatively efficient and modern computer is needed to run Office XP, you might think that this alone would be sufficient. Unfortunately, the demands of speech recognition add yet another layer of need to realistic hardware requirements in order to obtain what many would consider to be satisfactory results. According to Microsoft, the minimum requirements for running the Office XP suite are 200 mHz, IBM-compatible, equipped with 64MB of RAM if using Windows 98 or Windows ME or 96MB of RAM if using Windows NT, Windows 2000, or Windows XP. We've tried the speech recognition feature with Microsoft Word on a machine meeting this minimal level of hardware, as well as on machines meeting higher hardware standards. In our opinion, the minimal hardware level specified is simply not enough if you want to be happy with the speech recognition features of Office. From a software engineering standpoint, there's a great deal of effort going on behind the scenes with successful (or even minimally satisfactory) use of speech recognition. On hardware that meets the minimum specifications for Office XP, you're likely to see the recognition (and appearance on the screen) of your spoken words lag noticeably behind the words themselves. (This often leads to annoying breaks in your train of thought.) Your best bet is a computer with a processor compatible to the Intel Pentium III or Pentium IV or better (and *not* the lower-priced Celeron processor) with a processor speed of at least 400 mHz and a *minimum* of 128MB of RAM (256MB would be better). Also, don't settle for the minimal-quality microphone that may be supplied with your computer (or that may sell for roughly $9.95 U.S. at the local computer store). In our experience, a good-quality microphone can work wonders in improving the quality of your recognized speech. With hardware, this is truly one of those areas in which the old adage "You get what you pay for" still rings painfully true.

Speech Recognition: Before You Get Started

Before you put the speech recognition features of Office XP to use, you'll want to take a few initial steps to ensure maximum accuracy, efficiency, and satisfaction with a technology that is admittedly still in its infancy. (See the sidebar, "Make sure that your hardware is up to the task," if you haven't done so already.) Make sure that your microphone is connected to the correct input jack on your computer and that your microphone's on/off switch, if it has one, is turned on. If you use a combined headset/microphone combination (which we strongly recommend because such designs tend to keep the microphone correctly positioned in relation to the speaker's lips), ensure that the headphone plug is also connected to your computer's sound hardware. Finally, turn on the speech recognition feature by choosing Tools ⇨ Speech within Word (or in any Office XP application). After you turn on the feature, you can use it in any of the Office XP applications.

TIP: If you choose the Speech option from the Tools menu and are asked to insert the Office CD, you haven't installed the speech recognition feature. Rerun Office Setup, choose the Run from My Computer option for the Speech feature, select Alternative User Input, and then select Office Shared Features.

Training Speech Recognition

As a developing technology, the speech recognition that is built in to Office XP cannot automatically deal with the vast range of human speech. After all, even the powerful human brain can have trouble dealing with a deep southern (U.S.) accent if it is accustomed to hearing a New England dictation pattern. You must *train* the speech recognition feature of Office to understand your typical speech patterns. Office provides two wizards to help accomplish this task.

TIP: If speech recognition is already in use by another user of your computer, see the heading "Adding and Changing Speech Recognition Users," near the end of this appendix, for instructions on how you can add a profile and launch a training session for your own use of the speech recognition feature.

First, to ensure that your microphone is positioned properly and operating correctly, Office runs the Microphone Wizard when you initially try to use speech recognition (see Figure B-1).

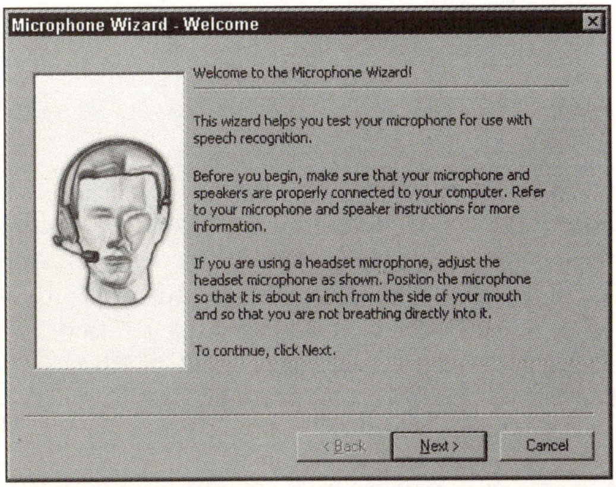

Figure B-1: The introductory dialog box of the Microphone Wizard

This dialog box simply reminds you to take the steps mentioned previously: Make sure that your microphone (and headset or speakers) is properly connected. The dialog box also provides tips on the best positioning of a headset/microphone combination. As the dialog box notes, the microphone should be positioned roughly an inch away from the side of your mouth for optimal results. After reading the dialog box and applying the tips noted, click Next and follow the instructions in the remaining Microphone Wizard dialog boxes to ensure that your microphone is operating correctly. The remaining steps of the Microphone Wizard will test and adjust the sensitivity of your microphone and help you to position the microphone for best results.

As part of the second (and somewhat more time-consuming) step of the process, you must use the Speech Recognition Training Wizard to train Office to recognize your particular speech patterns. This process automatically begins after you've completed the Microphone Wizard. The training process begins when Office displays the first Speech Recognition Training Wizard dialog box.

Before proceeding with the training process, you should ensure that the room where you are located is a quiet one. Also, be prepared to spend roughly ten to fifteen minutes of time reading selected paragraphs of text that will be displayed on the screen during the training process. When you are ready to proceed with the training session, click Next and follow the directions that appear in the successive wizard dialog boxes.

During the training process, you should speak naturally, using your normal tone of voice. However, if you naturally tend to speak at a rapid pace, you may want to try to slow down somewhat and concentrate on using clearer-than-normal dictation when training and when using the speech recognition feature of Office.

TIP: Although the introductory training session is mandatory (as is indicated by the initial dialog boxes presented by the wizard), additional training sessions are purely optional. However, to improve the accuracy of your speech recognition, you should run at least one or two additional training sessions. To run additional training sessions at any time, just click the Tools button on the Language Bar, choose Training from the drop-down menu that appears, and follow the directions in the successive dialog boxes.

When the initial training process is complete, Office automatically launches Internet Explorer to play a short video that presents a tutorial on the use of the speech recognition features of Office. (Your computer may need to download and install a Flash plug-in to display the video.)

Using Speech Recognition

After you've finished training the speech recognition feature to recognize your voice, the Speech Recognition Language Bar appears in any Office application when you turn on the speech recognition feature. (You can turn on speech recognition by choosing Tools ⇨ Speech from the menus within any Office application.) Figure B-2 shows the appearance of the Language Bar within Microsoft Word. In the figure, the Language Bar is at the top of the screen and the Tools menu has been opened from within the Language Bar. (Note that although the Language Bar menus are the same in all Office applications, the available menu choices that appear when you open a menu from the Language Bar may vary, depending on which Office application you are using.)

You can move the Language Bar to any location on the screen. To do so, move the mouse pointer over the left border of the Language Bar until it changes shape to a double-headed arrow; then drag the Language Bar to the desired position on the screen. You can also hide the Language Bar by clicking the Minimize button at the right side of the Language Bar. If you do so, the Language Bar appears as an icon on the Windows taskbar. You can then redisplay the Language Bar at any time by clicking the icon and then clicking Show the Language Bar in the pop-up menu that appears within the taskbar.

Because the Language Bar is used by all the major Office applications, if you display it within one application (such as Word) and then launch another Office application (such as Excel), the Language Bar will remain displayed within the other application.

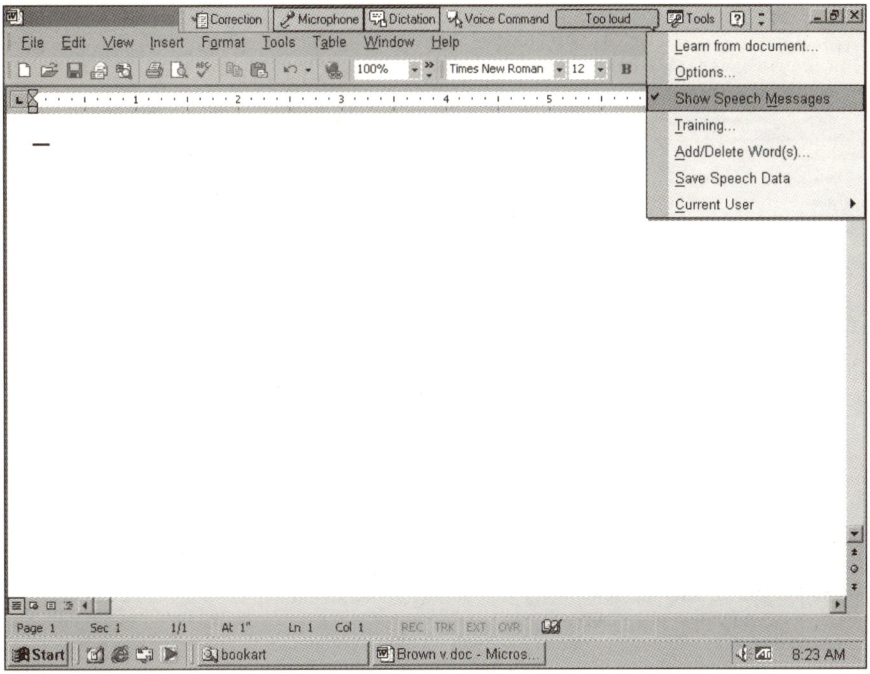

Figure B-2: The Language Bar provides menu options that are related to the speech recognition features of Microsoft Office.

Using speech recognition in dictation mode

You can use the speech recognition feature in one of two modes. One is *dictation mode*, which lets you dictate text that is to appear within an Office document (such as a Word document or an Outlook e-mail). The other is *voice command mode*, which lets you select Office menu options and commands by means of the speech recognition feature.

To use speech recognition in its dictation mode, click the Dictation button in the Language Bar. The dictation mode is turned on, and your spoken words appear at the insertion pointer position as you speak. For example, in a Word document, you can place the insertion pointer at the desired position within the document, click the Dictation button on the Language Bar, and begin speaking.

If the speech recognition feature incorrectly interprets a spoken phrase, you can easily make corrections. Right-click any recently dictated word to display a shortcut menu containing a list of available alternatives at the top of the menu (see Figure B-3).

If the correct word appears in the list of alternatives, select it from the menu. If you don't see the correct word, click More in the menu to display a submenu containing additional alternatives. If you still don't see an acceptable word, you can choose Delete from the menu and try dictating the word again (or simply use the keyboard to manually type the word).

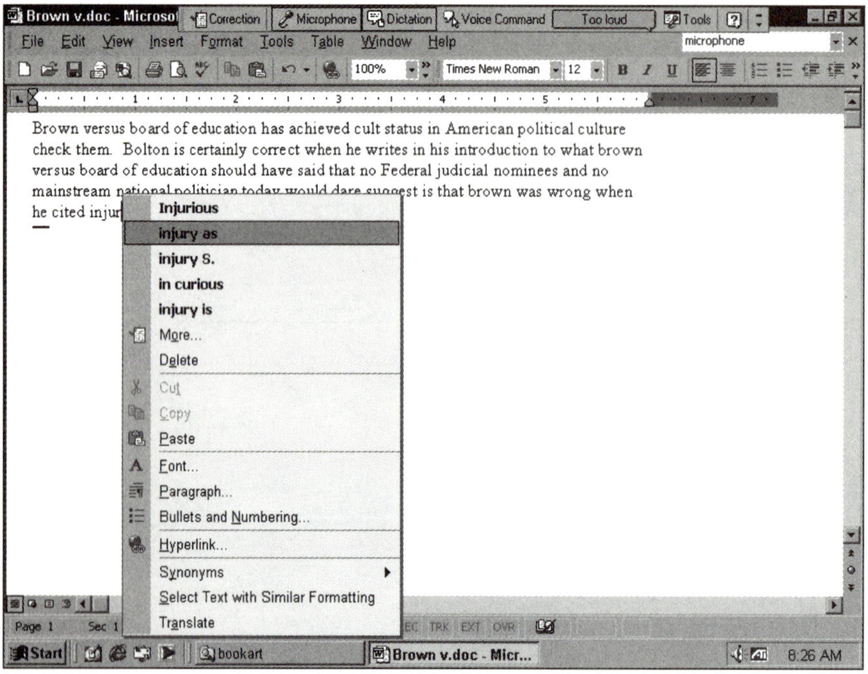

Figure B-3: You can use a shortcut menu to correct an incorrect word added by the speech recognition feature while in dictation mode.

Adding punctuation while dictating

For punctuation, there is no need to resort to the use of the keyboard. You can add punctuation while in dictation mode by speaking any of the phrases shown in Table B-1.

NOTE: When you use dictation mode, by default, part of the speech recognition process involves recording your spoken words to your hard drive. The information is saved in audible form so that you (or your secretary or office assistant) can later right-click any spoken word while editing and choose More from the shortcut menu that appears to replay the spoken word through your headset or speakers. If Embed Linguistic Data is turned on in the Save tab of Word's Tools ⇨ Options dialog box, and if the Save Speech Data option is enabled in the Tools menu of the Language Bar, Word saves the spoken data as part of the Word document. (As you might imagine, this can greatly increase the size of your Word document files.) On the other hand, you can turn off one or both of these options. If both options are turned off, Word does not save any audible information. If you turn off the Save Speech Data option but leave the Embed Linguistic Data option turned on, Word discards the recorded audible information as soon as you close the document.

Table B-1 - Spoken Phrases Used to Add Punctuation

To insert this symbol or character...	***Say this...***
&	Ampersand
*	Asterisk
@	At sign
\	Backslash
}	Close brace
]	Close bracket
)	Close paren
:	Colon
,	Comma
=	Equals
!	Exclamation point
>	Greater than
-	Hyphen
<	Less than
(new line symbol)	New line
(new paragraph symbol)	New paragraph
{	Open brace
[	Open bracket
(	Open paren
%	Percent sign
.	Period
+	Plus sign
#	Pound sign
?	Question mark
“	Quote
]	Right bracket
;	Semicolon
‘	Single quote
/	Slash
(tab character)	Tab
~	Tilde

Note that two punctuation characters, the open parenthesis and the close parenthesis, can easily be confused by the speech recognition feature of Office if you say the complete word *parenthesis*. What you are likely to see if you speak this word is a parenthesis immediately followed by the words *this is*.

Using speech recognition in voice command mode

The *voice command* mode of the speech recognition feature of Office lets you use dictation to issue basic Office menu commands. For example, you can save a file, print a document, insert a row or column into an Excel worksheet, or insert a new slide into a PowerPoint presentation. To use the voice command mode, click the Voice Command button in the Language Bar. You can then just speak the name of the desired menu command. For example, first speak the menu name, such as *File* or *Format*, and then say the name of the menu command, such as *Open* or *Paragraph*. You can print the current page of a Word document by clicking the Voice Command button in the Language Bar and saying *File print current page OK*. Saying these words chooses the Print command from the File menu, turns on the Current Page option in the Print dialog box that appears, and selects the OK button.

You can also select a toolbar button while using the voice command mode. To do so, first make sure that the desired toolbar is visible. Then say the button name — the name that appears as a ToolTip if you hold the mouse pointer stationary over the toolbar button.

Adding Custom Words to the Speech Dictionary

Although the speech dictionary built in to the software contains a broad range of words, you may specialize in an area that requires an array of unusual terms. For example, if you deal with a large number of medical malpractice cases, your dictation may contain a number of medical terms that Office doesn't recognize by default. At any time, you can add words to the speech dictionary used by Office to process your dictation.

To add words, open the Tools menu on the Language Bar and choose Add/Delete Words. The Add/Delete Word(s) dialog box appears (see Figure B-4).

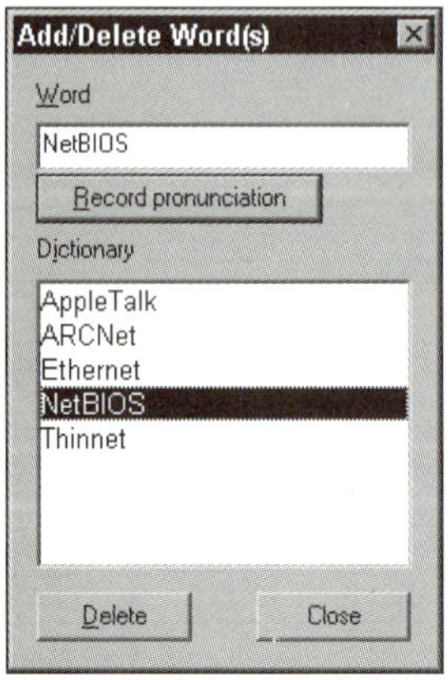

Figure B-4: You use the Add/Delete Word(s) dialog box to add (or delete) words used by a custom dictionary during the speech recognition process.

First, type the word that you want to add in the Word text box. Then, click the Record Pronunciation button and speak the word. The word will appear within the Dictionary list box. (If the word does not appear, Office was unable to record a sufficiently precise sound pattern, and you may have to repeat the word.) You can repeat this step for as many unusual words or terms that you would like Office to recognize during your dictation. (You can also remove words from the dictionary at any time by highlighting the unwanted word in the Dictionary list and clicking the Delete button.) When done with the dialog box, click Close.

Adding and Changing Speech Recognition Users

With systems that are shared among more than one regular user, each user must individually train the computer to recognize his or her speech patterns if that user wishes to make use of the speech recognition feature within Office. In Office, you can have multiple *profiles,* one for each user of the speech recognition feature. To change a profile (or add a profile for another user), open the Tools menu on the Language Bar and choose Options to display the Speech Properties dialog box (see Figure B-5).

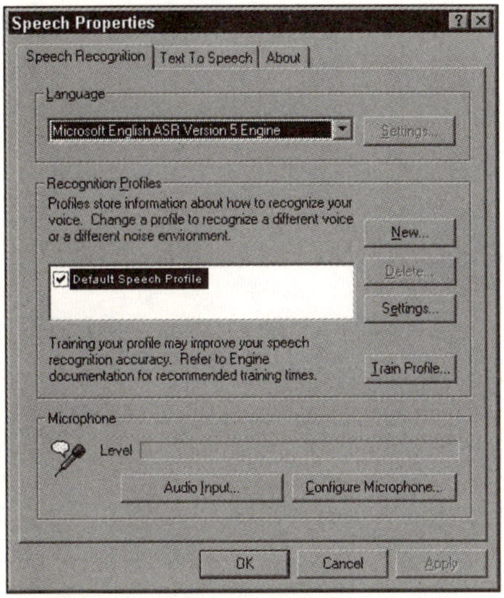

Figure B-5: You use the Speech Properties dialog box to add another profile for a different user.

To create a new speech recognition profile, click the New button on the Speech Recognition tab of the dialog box. Doing so starts the Profile Wizard. This wizard asks for a name used to identify the new user; then it runs the Microphone Wizard, followed by the Voice Training Wizard. The first profile created by the speech recognition feature is always named *Default Speech Profile*, but you can assign additional profiles using any names that you prefer.

When a new profile exists, different users can switch between the available stored profiles by opening the Tools menu on the Language Bar and choosing Current User. From the submenu that appears, choose the name of the profile that matches the desired user.

Summary

This appendix has provided the tips and techniques to make use of the speech recognition feature present in the Office XP applications. Remember that dictation of Word documents is not the only possible use for speech recognition — you use it, both for dictation and for voice commands, in all the other Office applications, such as Excel, PowerPoint, Access, and Outlook.

Appendix C

What's on the CD-ROM

THIS APPENDIX PROVIDES YOU with information on the contents of the CD that accompanies this book. For the latest and greatest information, please refer to the ReadMe file located at the root of the CD. Here is what you will find:

- System requirements
- Using the CD
- What's on the CD
- Troubleshooting

System Requirements

Make sure that your computer meets the minimum system requirements listed in this section. If your computer doesn't match up to most of these requirements, you may have a problem using the contents of the CD.

For Windows 9*x*, Windows 2000, Windows NT4 (with SP 4 or later), Windows Me, or Windows XP:

- PC with a Pentium processor running at 120 Mhz or faster.
- At least 32MB of total RAM. For best performance, we recommend at least 64MB.
- A CD-ROM drive.

Using the CD with Windows

To install the items from the CD to your hard drive, follow these steps:

1. Insert the CD into your computer's CD-ROM drive.
2. A window will appear with the following options: Install, Explore, eBook, Links, and Exit:
   - **Install:** Gives you the option to install the supplied software and/or the author-created samples on the CD-ROM
   - **Explore:** Allows you to view the contents of the CD-ROM in its directory structure
   - **eBook:** Allows you to view an electronic version of the book
   - **Exit:** Closes the autorun window

If you do not have autorun enabled or if the autorun window does not appear, follow these steps to access the CD:

1. Click Start ⇨ Run.

2. In the dialog box that appears, type ***d*:\setup.exe**, where *d* is the letter of your CD-ROM drive. This will bring up the autorun window described above.
3. Choose the Install, Explore, eBook, or Exit option from the menu. (See Step 2 in the preceding list for a description of these options.)

What's on the CD

The following sections provide a summary of the software and other materials you'll find on the CD.

Author-created and contributed materials

All author-created material from the book, including code listings and samples, is on the CD as follows.

Access database applications

These six ready-to-use databases (Case Management, Litigation Support, Firm Marketing, Lawyer Recruiting, Pleadings Tracking, and CLE Tracker) are located in the following folder: `Legal-specific databases and files/Access/Databases`. A Readme file with instructions for converting the files from read-only to fully functional files are in the `Legal-specific databases and files/Access/Databases/Readme` folder.

Bonus Access chapters

Bonus Chapters 1–6 (which appear in the Access section of the book as well) supply specific instructions for using the sample Access database applications provided on the CD. Find these chapters in `Legal-specific databases and files/Access/Bonus chapters`.

Word templates

You can find three ready-to-use Word templates in the following folder: `Legal-specific databases and files/Word`. These templates are as follows: the sample pleading template, which uses formats and numbering styles commonly seen in legal briefs filed in a variety of courts and contains outline numbering styles and styles for the body of the document; the sample memo template, which includes a table for the memo header to make it easy to address to multiple recipients and a style for the body of the memo; and the Security Agreement template, which includes styles to produce document and outline numbering formats commonly seen in legal agreements. This template also includes a table of contents that can be easily modified.

Outlook custom forms

The forms included here are the Associates Project Evaluation form, a Receptionist Visitor Notification form, and a Law Student Interview Evaluation form. Use the Readme file for instructions on installing these forms in your Outlook program. The forms are in the folder `Legal-specific databases and files/Outlook custom forms` and the Readme file is in the folder `Legal-specific databases and files/Outlook Readme`.

Excel legal worksheets

These three worksheets were contributed by attorneys and include one for Section 1031 calculations for taxpayers, one example of a typical allocation of charges, and one example that shows capital gains and losses for a partnership. Find these worksheets in the following folder: `Legal-specific databases and files/Excel`.

Applications

The following applications are on the CD.

HotDocs

HotDocs is a document assembly tool that's in use by numerous law firms. It lets you create reusable interactive templates based on your own Word documents. You can use HotDocs to reduce the amount of time spent generating repetitive legal documents such as contracts and court forms.

DeltaView

Workshare® DeltaView® is a document comparison program that compares one version of a document against another, producing a third document showing the differences. DeltaView integrates with existing document management systems and also offers e-mail integration. One option that DeltaView offers is the ability to view simultaneously the original and revised documents, showing the changes on-screen while providing useful navigational features. DeltaView also allows comparison between WordPerfect and Word documents. The enclosed CD contains a seven-day evaluation copy of the software. After seven days, you can call Workshare Sales at 888-404-4246 to extend this evaluation period to thirty days.

Acrobat Reader

Freeware. The full version of the Adobe Acrobat Reader is included on the CD-ROM, which enables you to view and print PDF (Portable Document Format) files. For more information, visit Adobe at `www.adobe.com/products/acrobat/readstep.html`.

Shareware programs are fully functional, trial versions of copyrighted programs. If you like particular programs, register with their authors for a nominal fee and receive licenses, enhanced versions, and technical support. *Freeware programs* are copyrighted games, applications, and utilities that are free for personal use. Unlike shareware, these programs do not require a fee or provide technical support. *GNU software* is governed by its own license, which is included inside the folder of the GNU product. See the GNU license for more details.

Trial, demo, or evaluation versions are usually limited either by time or functionality (such as being unable to save projects). Some trial versions are very sensitive to system date changes. If you alter your computer's date, the programs will "time out" and will no longer be functional.

eBook version of *Office XP for Law Firms*

The complete text of this book is on the CD in Adobe's Portable Document Format (PDF). You can read and search through the file with the Adobe Acrobat Reader (also included on the CD).

Troubleshooting

If you have difficulty installing or using any of the materials on the companion CD, try the following solutions:

- **Turn off any anti-virus software that you may have running.** Installers sometimes mimic virus activity and can make your computer incorrectly believe that it is being infected by a virus. (Be sure to turn the anti-virus software back on later.)
- **Close all running programs.** The more programs you have running, the less memory you have available to other programs. Installers also typically update files and programs; if you keep other programs running, installation may not work properly.

♦ **Reference the ReadMe:** Please refer to the ReadMe file located at the root of the CD-ROM for the latest product information at the time of publication.

If you still have trouble with the CD, please call the Hungry Minds Customer Care phone number: (800) 762-2974. Outside the United States, call 1 (317) 572-3994. You can also contact Hungry Minds Customer Service by e-mail at `techsupdum@hungryminds.com`. Hungry Minds will provide technical support only for installation and other general quality-control items; for technical support on the applications themselves, consult the program's vendor or author.

Index

3

A

B

C

D

F

K

L

M

N

O

P

Q

S

X

Y

Z

Hungry Minds, Inc.
End-User License Agreement

READ THIS. You should carefully read these terms and conditions before opening the software packet(s) included with this book ("Book"). This is a license agreement ("Agreement") between you and Hungry Minds, Inc. ("HMI"). By opening the accompanying software packet(s), you acknowledge that you have read and accept the following terms and conditions. If you do not agree and do not want to be bound by such terms and conditions, promptly return the Book and the unopened software packet(s) to the place you obtained them for a full refund.

1. **License Grant.** HMI grants to you (either an individual or entity) a nonexclusive license to use one copy of the enclosed software program(s) (collectively, the "Software") solely for your own personal or business purposes on a single computer (whether a standard computer or a workstation component of a multi-user network). The Software is in use on a computer when it is loaded into temporary memory (RAM) or installed into permanent memory (hard disk, CD-ROM, or other storage device). HMI reserves all rights not expressly granted herein.

2. **Ownership.** HMI is the owner of all right, title, and interest, including copyright, in and to the compilation of the Software recorded on the disk(s) or CD-ROM ("Software Media"). Copyright to the individual programs recorded on the Software Media is owned by the author or other authorized copyright owner of each program. Ownership of the Software and all proprietary rights relating thereto remain with HMI and its licensers.

3. **Restrictions On Use and Transfer.**

   (a) You may only (i) make one copy of the Software for backup or archival purposes, or (ii) transfer the Software to a single hard disk, provided that you keep the original for backup or archival purposes. You may not (i) rent or lease the Software, (ii) copy or reproduce the Software through a LAN or other network system or through any computer subscriber system or bulletin-board system, or (iii) modify, adapt, or create derivative works based on the Software.

(b) You may not reverse engineer, decompile, or disassemble the Software. You may transfer the Software and user documentation on a permanent basis, provided that the transferee agrees to accept the terms and conditions of this Agreement and you retain no copies. If the Software is an update or has been updated, any transfer must include the most recent update and all prior versions.

4. **Restrictions on Use of Individual Programs.** You must follow the individual requirements and restrictions detailed for each individual program in What's on the CD-ROM appendix of this Book. These limitations are also contained in the individual license agreements recorded on the Software Media. These limitations may include a requirement that after using the program for a specified period of time, the user must pay a registration fee or discontinue use. By opening the Software packet(s), you will be agreeing to abide by the licenses and restrictions for these individual programs that are detailed in the What's on the CD-ROM appendix and on the Software Media. None of the material on this Software Media or listed in this Book may ever be redistributed, in original or modified form, for commercial purposes.

5. **Limited Warranty.**

(a) HMI warrants that the Software and Software Media are free from defects in materials and workmanship under normal use for a period of sixty (60) days from the date of purchase of this Book. If HMI receives notification within the warranty period of defects in materials or workmanship, HMI will replace the defective Software Media.

(b) **HMI AND THE AUTHOR OF THE BOOK DISCLAIM ALL OTHER WARRANTIES, EXPRESS OR IMPLIED, INCLUDING WITHOUT LIMITATION IMPLIED WARRANTIES OF MERCHANTABILITY AND FITNESS FOR A PARTICULAR PURPOSE, WITH RESPECT TO THE SOFTWARE, THE PROGRAMS, THE SOURCE CODE CONTAINED THEREIN, AND/OR THE TECHNIQUES DESCRIBED IN THIS BOOK. HMI DOES NOT WARRANT THAT THE FUNCTIONS CONTAINED IN THE SOFTWARE WILL MEET YOUR REQUIREMENTS OR THAT THE OPERATION OF THE SOFTWARE WILL BE ERROR FREE.**

(c) This limited warranty gives you specific legal rights, and you may have other rights that vary from jurisdiction to jurisdiction.

6. **Remedies.**

(a) HMI's entire liability and your exclusive remedy for defects in materials and workmanship shall be limited to replacement of the Software Media, which may be returned to HMI with a copy of your receipt at the following address: Software Media Fulfillment Department, Attn.: Office XP for Law Firms, Hungry Minds, Inc., 10475 Crosspoint Blvd., Indianapolis, IN 46256, or call 1-800-762-2974. Please allow four to six weeks for delivery. This Limited Warranty is void if failure of the Software Media has resulted from accident, abuse, or misapplication. Any replacement Software Media will be warranted for the remainder of the original warranty period or thirty (30) days, whichever is longer.

(b) In no event shall HMI or the author be liable for any damages whatsoever (including without limitation damages for loss of business profits, business interruption, loss of business information, or any other pecuniary loss) arising from the use of or inability to use the Book or the Software, even if HMI has been advised of the possibility of such damages.

(c) Because some jurisdictions do not allow the exclusion or limitation of liability for consequential or incidental damages, the above limitation or exclusion may not apply to you.

7. **U.S. Government Restricted Rights.** Use, duplication, or disclosure of the Software for or on behalf of the United States of America, its agencies and/or instrumentalities (the "U.S. Government") is subject to restrictions as stated in paragraph (c)(1)(ii) of the Rights in Technical Data and Computer Software clause of DFARS 252.227-7013, or subparagraphs (c) (1) and (2) of the Commercial Computer Software - Restricted Rights clause at FAR 52.227-19, and in similar clauses in the NASA FAR supplement, as applicable.

8. **General.** This Agreement constitutes the entire understanding of the parties and revokes and supersedes all prior agreements, oral or written, between them and may not be modified or amended except in a writing signed by both parties hereto that specifically refers to this Agreement. This Agreement shall take precedence over any other documents that may be in conflict herewith. If any one or more provisions contained in this Agreement are held by any court or tribunal to be invalid, illegal, or otherwise unenforceable, each and every other provision shall remain in full force and effect.